July 12–16, 2014
Vancouver, BC, Canada

Association for
Computing Machinery

Advancing Computing as a Science & Profession

GECCO'14

Companion Publication of the 2014 Genetic and Evolutionary Computation Conference

Sponsored by:

ACM SIGEVO

Association for
Computing Machinery

Advancing Computing as a Science & Profession

The Association for Computing Machinery
2 Penn Plaza, Suite 701
New York, New York 10121-0701

Notice to Past Authors of ACM-Published Articles
ACM intends to create a complete electronic archive of all articles and/or other material previously published by ACM. If you have written a work that has been previously published by ACM in any journal or conference proceedings prior to 1978, or any SIG Newsletter at any time, and you do NOT want this work to appear in the ACM Digital Library, please inform permissions@acm.org, stating the title of the work, the author(s), and where and when published.

ISBN: 978-1-4503-3276-7 (Digital)

ISBN: 978-1-4503-3269-9 (Print)

Additional copies may be ordered prepaid from:

ACM Order Department
PO Box 30777
New York, NY 10087-0777, USA

Phone: 1-800-342-6626 (USA and Canada)
+1-212-626-0500 (Global)
Fax: +1-212-944-1318
E-mail: acmhelp@acm.org
Hours of Operation: 8:30 am – 4:30 pm ET

Printed in the USA

Welcome

On behalf of the Organizing Committee, I would like to welcome you to Vancouver for the 2014 Genetic and Evolutionary Computation Conference (GECCO 2014). This year's GECCO is comprised of 20 tracks, including the new Artificial Immune Systems and Hot Off the Press (HOP) tracks. The latter offers authors of outstanding research recently published in journals and other conferences the opportunity to present their work to the GECCO community. Under the guidance of Editor-in-Chief Christian Igel, the Track Chairs and Program Committee have selected 180 out of the 544 submissions received in all tracks (excluding HOP) for oral presentation as full papers, resulting in an acceptance rate of 33%. Close to 100 short papers will be presented in the poster session.

Highlights of the conference include keynote talks by Yoshua Bengio on "Deep Learning and Cultural Evolution", and by Dario Floreano on "Bridging Natural and Artificial Evolution", as well as an invited talk by Sumit Gulwani in the Genetic Programming track. Altogether 32 tutorials cover topics ranging from broad and introductory to specialized and at the frontier of current research. GECCO also hosts fifteen workshops, including several new ones as well as at least one that predates GECCO itself. Further high points include the 11th Annual "Humies" Awards for Human-Competitive Results, which are again generously supported by John Koza, and five competitions, ranging from Art, Design, and Creativity to the Industrial Challenge. Finally, Evolutionary Computation in Practice continues to be an important and integral part of GECCO.

I would like to thank the entire Organizing Committee for their work and dedication over the past year. Thanks also go to the Track Chairs and the Program Committee for their careful reviewing of the large number of submissions received. Finally, thanks are due to Roxane Rose and Cara Candler from *Executive Events*, who have been in charge of logistical aspects and registration, Lisa Tolles and her team at *Sheridan Communications* for the production of the proceedings, Mark Montague and his team at *Linklings* for their conference management tool and support of the reviewing process, and Gerardo Valencia for artwork and website management.

I wish you all a productive and enjoyable conference.

Dirk Arnold
General Chair

A Word from the Chair of SIGEVO

Welcome to the Proceedings of GECCO 2014, the sixteenth GECCO, the "recombination" of the 23rd International Conference on Genetic Algorithms (ICGA) and the 19th Genetic Programming Conference (GP). This year, Dirk Arnold was General Chair of GECCO 2014 acting with great diligence and care. Christian Igel, the Editor-in-Chief of GECCO-2014 has done an excellent job at coordinating the reviewing process and leading the effort to select papers for publication. The results of the effort of them and their team are presented here.

GECCO is the premiere venue for presenting papers in the area of Genetic and Evolutionary Computation worldwide. The quality of papers submitted to GECCO is very high, and GECCO has a rigorous paper selection process. This means that the best and most important work in Evolutionary Computation and on related topics is presented at GECCO. Our conference is consistently ranked at the top of Evolutionary Computation conferences, exceeding in citation counts well known journals and other venues.

If you were not able to attend GECCO 2014 in person, the Proceedings are in the ACM Digital Library; they are globally accessible and readily found, which benefits both readers and authors.

ACM SIGEVO

Members of ACM SIGEVO, sponsor of GECCO, continue to draw major benefits from joining ACM. First is a discount at SIGEVO sponsored conferences, at GECCO as much as $100 per registrant. Members have, for a fee, access to the ACM Digital Library, a large and continuously growing resource for research in computing. Another key benefit is the outstanding newsletter *SIGEVOlution* produced by Pier Luca Lanzi and his excellent editorial board. If you are accessing these proceedings and are not a member of SIGEVO, please consider joining (for the low price of $25/year for non-students, and $10/year for student members). This will help us a lot in promoting our community.

Involvement in ACM SIGEVO

SIGEVO became a Special Interest Group (SIG) of the ACM in 2005. ACM considers its SIGs as the lifeblood of the organization. We are governed by bylaws available on the SIGEVO web pages. There, you also find a list of members of the 18-member Executive Committee.

Since 2011, I serve as chair of SIGEVO, together with a team of officers: Una-May O'Reilly (Vice-Chair), Marc Schoenauer (Secretary), and Franz Rothlauf (Treasurer). The Executive, its Officers and I are dedicated to continuously improve our organization. If you have any suggestions how to make GECCO or SIGEVO better, please let us know.

Wolfgang Banzhaf
SIGEVO Chair

Table of Contents

Track: Artificial Life, Robotics, and Evolvable Hardware Posters

Track: Biological and Biomedical Applications Posters

Track: Digital Entertainment Technologies and Arts Posters

Track: Estimation of Distribution Algorithms Posters

Track: Evolution Strategies and Evolutionary Programming Posters

Track: Evolutionary Combinatorial Optimization & Metaheuristics Posters

Track: Evolutionary Machine Learning Posters

Track: Evolutionary Multiobjective Optimization Posters

Track: Generative and Developmental Systems Posters

Track: Genetic Algorithms Posters

Track: Genetic Programming Posters

Track: Integrative Genetic and Evolutionary Computation Posters

Track: Parallel Evolutionary Systems Posters

Track: Real World Applications Posters

Track: Search Based Software Engineering Posters

Track: Self-* Search Posters

Track: Theory Posters

Introductory Tutorials

Advanced Tutorials

Specialized Tutorials

17th Annual International Workshop on Learning Classifier Systems

Eighth Annual Workshop on Evolutionary Computation and Multi-Agent Systems and Simulation

Student Workshop

Workshop: Visualisation Methods in Genetic and Evolutionary Computation

Workshop: Evolutionary Computation Software Systems

Workshop: Evolutionary Synthesis of Dynamical Systems

Workshop: Green and Efficient Energy Applications of Genetic and Evolutionary Computation

Workshop on Problem Understanding and Real-World Optimisation

Workshop on Genetic and Evolutionary Computation in Defense, Security and Risk Management

Workshop: Evolutionary Computation for Big Data and Big Learning

Workshop: Medical Applications of Genetic & Evolutionary Computation

Workshop: Symbolic Regression and Modelling

4th Workshop on Evolutionary Computation for the Automated Design of Algorithms

Workshop on Metaheuristic Design Patterns

Late Breaking Abstracts

Women@GECCO 2014

Organizers

General Chair:	Dirk V. Arnold, *Dalhousie University*
Editor-in-Chief:	Christian Igel, *University of Copenhagen*
Publicity Chair:	Christian Gagné, *Université Laval*
Local Chair:	Elena Popovici, *Icosystem Corporation*
Students Chair:	Petr Pošík, *Czech Technical University*
Tutorials Chair:	Mengjie Zhang, *Victoria University of Wellington*
Workshops Chair:	Per Kristian Lehre, *University of Nottingham*
Competitions Chair:	Amy K. Hoover, *University of Central Florida*
Late Breaking Abstracts Chair:	Dirk Sudholt, *University of Sheffield*
Evolutionary Computation in Practice Chairs:	Thomas Bartz-Beielstein, *Cologne University of Applied Sciences* Anna I. Esparcia-Alcázar, *S2 Grupo* Jörn Mehnen, *Cranfield University*
Business Committee:	Jürgen Branke, *University of Warwick* Darrell Whitley, *Colorado State University*

Track Chairs

Anne Auger, *INRIA Saclay*

Jaume Bacardit, *Newcastle University*

Dimo Brockhoff, *INRIA Lille*

Stefano Cagnoni, *Università degli Studi di Parma*

Kalyanmoy Deb, *Michigan State University*

Benjamin Doerr, *École Polytechnique de Paris*

James Foster, *University of Idaho*

Tobias Glasmachers, *Ruhr-Universität Bochum*

Emma Hart, *Edinburgh Napier University*

Malcolm I. Heywood, *Dalhousie University*

Hitoshi Iba, *University of Tokyo*

Christian Jacob, *University of Calgary*

Thomas Jansen, *Aberystwyth University*

Yaochu Jin, *University of Surrey*

Marouane Kessentini, *University of Michigan*

Joshua D. Knowles, *University of Manchester*

William B. Langdon, *University College London*

Pedro Larrañaga, *Technical University of Madrid*

Sean Luke, *George Mason University*

Gabriel Luque, *Universidad de Málaga*

John A. W. McCall, *Robert Gordon University Aberdeen*

Marco A. Montes de Oca, *University of Delaware*

Alison Motsinger-Reif, *North Carolina State University*

Yew Soon Ong, *Nanyang Technological University*

Michael Palmer, *Stanford University*

Konstantinos E. Parsopoulos, *University of Ioanninia*

Günther Raidl, *Vienna University of Technology*

Sebastian Risi, *IT University of Copenhagen*

Guenther Ruhe, *University of Calgary*

Tom Schaul, *New York University*

Thomas Schmickl, *Karl-Franzens-Universität Graz*

Bernhard Sendhoff, *Honda Research Institute Europe*

Kenneth O. Stanley, *University of Central Florida*

Thomas Stützle, *Université Libre de Bruxelles*

Dirk Thierens, *Universiteit Utrecht*

Julian Togelius, *IT University of Copenhagen*

Carsten Witt, *Technical University of Denmark*

Christine Zarges, *University of Birmingham*

Program Committee

Abbass, Hussein, *University of New South Wales*
Abdelbar, Ashraf, *Brandon University*
Abraham, Ajith, *Machine Intelligence Research Labs*
Acampora, Giovanni, *Nottingham Trent University*
Adamatzky, Andrew, *University of the West of England*
Adami, Chris, *Michigan State University*
Affenzeller, Michael, *University of Applied Sciences Upper Austria*
Aguirre, Hernan, *Shinshu University*
Ahn, Chang Wook, *Sungkyunkwan University*
Ahrens, Barry, *Nova Southeastern University*
Aickelin, Uwe, *University of Nottingham*
Akimoto, Youhei, *Shinshu University*
Alba, Enrique, *Universidad de Málaga*
Alden, Kieran, *University of York*
Aler, Ricardo, *Universidad Carlos III de Madrid*
Alfaro-Cid, Eva, *Universidad Politécnica de Valencia*
Allmendinger, Richard, *University College London*
Alshahwan, Nadia, *University College London*
Amoretti, Michele, *Università degli Studi di Parma*
Amos, Ng, *University of Skövde*
Andrews, Paul, *University of York*
Antoniol, Giuliano, *École Polytechnique de Montréal*
Arcuri, Andrea, *Simula Research Laboratory*
Arias Montaño, Alfredo, *CINVESTAV-IPN*
Arita, Takaya, *Nagoya University*
Arredondo, Antonio D. Masegosa, *Universidad de Granada*
Arvin, Farshad, *University of Lincoln*
Avigad, Gideon, *Braude College of Engineering*
Aydin, Nizamettin, *Yildiz Technical University*
Azad, Raja Muhammad Atif, *University of Limerick*
Babovic, Vladan, *National University Singapore*
Bader-El-Den, Mohamed, *University of Essex*
Bai, Ruibin, *University of Nottingham Ningbo*
Ballester, Pedro J., *European Bioinformatics Institute*
Bandyopadhyay, Sanghamitra, *Indian Statistical Institute*
Bankovic, Zorana, *IMDEA Software Institute*
Banzhaf, Wolfgang, *Memorial University of Newfoundland*
Barbosa, Helio J. C., *National Laboratory for Scientific Computation, Brazil*
Bardenet, Remi, *University of Oxford*
Barros, Marcio, *Universidade Federal do Estado do Rio de Janeiro*
Bartz-Beielstein, Thomas, *Cologne University of Applied Sciences*
Basgalupp, Marcio, *Universidade Federal de São Paulo*
Bassett, Jeffrey K., *George Mason University*
Basseur, Matthieu, *Université d'Angers*
Bastos Filho, Carmelo J. A., *University of Pernambuco*
Batista, Lucas, *Universidade Federal de Minas Gerais*
Beal, Jacob, *BBN Technologies*
Bechikh, Slim, *University of Michigan–Dearborn*
Bennell, Julia, *University of Southampton*
Bentley, Peter J., *University College London*
Bergstra, James, *University of Waterloo*
Bernardino, Heder, *Universidade Federal de Juiz de Fora*
Bernt, Matthias, *University of Leipzig*
Berry, Rod, *University of Technology, Sydney*
Bersano, Tom, *Google Inc.*
Besada-Portas, Eva, *Universidad Complutense de Madrid*
Beyer, Hans-Georg, *Vorarlberg University of Applied Sciences*
Bezerra, Leonardo, *Université Libre de Bruxelles*
Bhanu, Bir, *University of California at Riverside*
Biazzini, Marco, *INRIA Rennes*
Bielza, Concha, *Universidad Politécnica de Madrid*
Biesinger, Benjamin, *Technische Universität Wien*
Birattari, Mauro, *Université Libre de Bruxelles*
Blackwell, Tim, *Goldsmiths, University of London*
Blekas, Konstantinos, *University of Ioannina*
Blesa, Maria J., *Universitat Politècnica de Catalunya*
Blum, Christian, *University of the Basque Country*
Bollegala, Danushka, *University of Tokyo*
Bongard, Josh, *University of Vermont*
Booker, Lashon, *The MITRE Corporation*
Bosman, Peter A.N., *Centrum Wiskunde & Informatica*
Boudjeloud, Lydia, *Université de Lorraine*
Boumaza, Amine, *Université de Lorraine*
Bouvry, Pascal, *University of Luxembourg*
Bown, Ollie, *University of Sydney*
Brabazon, Anthony, *University College Dublin*
Branke, Jürgen, *University of Warwick*
Bredeche, Nicolas, *Université Pierre et Marie Curie*
Breen, David E., *Drexel University*
Bringmann, Karl, *Max Planck Institut für Informatik*
Browne, Will N., *Victoria University of Wellington*
Brownlee, Alexander E. I., *University of Stirling*
Buarque, Fernando, *University of Pernambuco*
Bui, Lam Thu, *Le Quy Don Technical University*
Bui, Thang, *Penn State*
Bull, Larry, *University of the West of England*
Bullinaria, John A., *University of Birmingham*
Burelli, Paolo, *Aalborg University*
Burjorjee, Keki Mehernosh, *Brandeis University*
Burke, Edmund, *University of Stirling*
Butz, Martin V., *University of Tübingen*
Buzdalov, Maxim, *Saint-Petersburg National Research University of Information Technologies, Mechanics & Optics*
Buzdalova, Arina, *Saint-Petersburg National Research University of Information Technologies, Mechamics & Optics*
Cagnina, Leticia, *Universidad Nacional de San Luis*
Cairns, David, *University of Stirling*
Campelo, Felipe, *Universidade Federal de Minas Gerais*
Campo, Alexandre, *Université Libre de Bruxelles*
Cangelosi, Angelo, *University of Plymouth*
Capodieci, Nicola, *University of Modena and Reggio Emilia*
Carvalho, Andre, *Universidade de São Paulo*

Castelli, Mauro, *Universidade Nova de Lisboa*
Castellini, Alberto, *University of Verona*
Ceschia, Sara, *University of Udine*
Chakraborty, Uday, *University of Missouri*
Chang, Pei-Chann, *Yuan Ze University*
Chelly, Zeineb, *University of Tunis*
Chen, Ying-ping, *National Chiao Tung University*
Chen, Tianshi, *Chinese Academy of Sciences*
Cheong, Yun-Gyung, *IT University of Copenhagen*
Chiarandini, Marco, *University of Southern Denmark*
Chicano, Francisco, *Universidad de Málaga*
Chiong, Raymond, *University of Newcastle*
Chipperfield, Andrew J., *University of Southampton*
Chong, Siang Yew, *University of Nottingham*
Christensen, Anders, *University Institute of Lisbon*
Christensen, David Johan, *Technical University of Denmark*
Chu, Dominique, *University of Kent*
Chuang, Chung-Yao, *Carnegie Mellon University*
Clark, John, *University of York*
Clerc, Maurice
Clune, Jeff, *University of Wyoming*
Coelho, Leandro, *Pontifícia Universidade Católica do Paranà*
Coello Coello, Carlos A., *CINVESTAV-IPN*
Cohen, Myra, *University of Nebraska–Lincoln*
Colby, Mitch K., *Oregon State University*
Colmenar, J. Manuel, *Universidad Complutense de Madrid*
Colton, Simon, *Imperial College London*
Congdon, Clare Bates, *University of Southern Maine*
Connelly, Brian, *University of Washington*
Cook, Michael, *University of London*
Cordon, Oscar, *European Centre for Soft Computing*
Corns, Steven M., *Missouri University of Science and Technology*
Correia, Luís, *Universidade de Lisboa*
Costa, Lino António, *Universidade do Minho*
Costa, Ernesto, *University of Coimbra*
Cotta, Carlos, *Universidad de Málaga*
Cowling, Peter, *University of York*
Craenen, Bart G.W., *Brunel University*
Cui, Wei, *University College Dublin*
Cummins, Ronan, *University of Greenwich*
Cussat-Blanc, Sylvain, *University of Toulouse*
D'Ambrosio, David B., *University of Central Florida*
Dahal, Keshav, *University of the West of Scotland*
Dahlskog, Steve, *Malmö University*
Dahlstedt, Palle, *University of Gothenburg*
Dang, Duc-Cuong, *University of Nottingham*
Darabos, Christian, *Dartmouth College*
Das, Swagatam, *Indian Statistical Institute*
Datta, Dilip, *Tezpur University*
Datta, Rituparna, *Indian Institute of Technology Kanpur*
David, Cornforth, *University of Newcastle*
De Causmaecker, Patrick, *KU Leuven*
De Jong, Kenneth, *George Mason University*
de la Fraga, Luis Gerardo, *CINVESTAV-IPN*
de la Ossa, Luis, *University of Castilla–La Mancha*
Deakin, Anthony, *University of Liverpool*
Della Cioppa, Antonio, *University of Salerno*
Delong, Andrew, *University of Toronto*
Derbel, Bilel, *INRIA Lille*
Dhaenens, Clarisse, *INRIA Lille, CNRS*
Di Caro, Gianni, *IDSIA*
Di Gaspero, Luca, *University of Udine*
Di Penta, Massimiliano, *University of Sannio*
Diaconescu, Ada, *Télécom ParisTech*
Ding, Yongsheng, *Donghua University*
Dinh, Huy, *University of Tokyo*
Dinneen, Michael J., *University of Auckland*
Dittrich, Peter, *Friedrich-Schiller-Universität Jena*
Divina, Federico, *Pablo de Olavide University*
Doerr, Carola, *Université Pierre et Marie Curie, CNRS*
Doncieux, Stéphane, *Université Pierre et Marie Curie*
Dorin, Alan, *Monash University*
Dorronsoro, Bernabe, *Université Lille Nord de France*
Dozal, León, *Centro de Investigación Científica y de Educación Superior de Ensenada*
Drugan, Madalina, *Vrije Universiteit Brussel*
Drugowitsch, Jan, *Université de Genève*
Dubois-Lacoste, Jérémie, *Université Libre de Bruxelles*
Ebner, Marc, *Ernst-Moritz-Universität Greifswald*
El-Abd, Mohammed, *American University of Kuwait*
Emmerich, Michael T. M., *Universiteit Leiden*
Engelbrecht, Andries P., *University of Pretoria*
Epitropakis, Michael, *University of Stirling*
Eremeev, Anton V., *Sobolev Institute of Mathematics, Omsk*
Esponda, Fernando, *Instituto Tecnológico Autónomo de México*
Evelyne, Lutton, *INRIA Saclay*
Everson, Richard, *University of Exeter*
Fan, Patrick, *Virginia Tech*
Farooq, Muddassar, *Institute of Space Technology, Pakistan*
Feldt, Robert, *Chalmers University of Technology*
Fenet, Serge, *Université Lyon 1*
Ferariu, Lavinia, *"Gheorghe Asachi" Technical University of Iaşi*
Fernandez, Jose David, *Universidad de Málaga*
Fernández de Vega, Francisco, *Universidad de Extremadura*
Festa, Paola, *Universitá degli Studi di Napoli*
Fialho, Álvaro, *GE Global Research*
Fieldsend, Jonathan Edward, *University of Exeter*
Figueredo, Grazziela, *University of Nottingham*
Filipic, Bogdan, *Jožef Stefan Institute*
Finck, Steffen, *Vorarlberg University of Applied Sciences*
Fink, Andreas, *Helmut Schmidt University Hamburg*
Fischer, Asja, *Ruhr-Universität Bochum*
Fleming, Peter, *University of Sheffield*
Folino, Gianluigi, *Institute of High Performance Computing and Networking, Italy*
Fraser, Gordon, *University of Sheffield*
Freisleben, Bernd, *Universität Marburg*

Freitas, Alex A., *University of Kent*
Friedrich, Tobias, *Friedrich-Schiller-Universität Jena*
Frowd, Charlie, *University of Winchester*
Gagliolo, Matteo, *Vrije Universiteit Brussel*
Gagné, Christian, *Université Laval*
Gallagher, Marcus R., *University of Queensland*
Galvan, Edgar, *Trinity College Dublin*
Galway, Leo, *University of Ulster*
Gambardella, Luca Maria, *IDSIA*
Gamez, Jose A., *Universidad de Castilla–La Mancha*
Gandibleux, Xavier, *Université de Nantes*
Gandomi, Amir Hossein, *University of Akron*
Gao, Yang, *Nanjing University*
Garcia-Nieto, Jose, *Universidad de Málaga*
Garcia-Piquer, Alvaro, *Institute of Space Sciences, Mexico*
García-Martínez, Carlos, *Universidad de Córdoba*
García-Sánchez, Pablo, *Universidad de Granada*
Garnier, Simon, *New Jersey Institute of Technology*
Garousi, Vahid, *University of Calgary*
Garrett, Deon, *Icelandic Institute for Intelligent Machines*
Gaspar-Cunha, Antonio, *Universidade do Minho*
Geem, Zong Woo, *Gachon University*
Gelareh, Shahin, *Université d'Artois*
Gershenson, Carlos, *Universidad Nacional Autonoma de México*
Gervasi, Osvaldo, *University of Perugia*
Giacobini, Mario, *University of Torino*
Giagkiozis, Ioannis, *University of Sheffield*
Giavitto, Jean-Louis, *Institut de Recherche et Coordination Acoustique/Musique, France, CNRS*
Gießen, Christian, *Christian-Albrechts-Universität zu Kiel*
Giraldez Rojo, Raul, *Pablo de Olavide University*
Giustolisi, Orazio, *Technical University of Bari*
Goeffon, Adrien, *Université d'Angers*
Goh, Chi-Keong, *Rolls-Royce*
Goldbarg, Marco César, *Universidade Federal do Rio Grande do Norte*
Goldman, Brian W., *Michigan State University*
Gomez-Pulido, Juan A., *Universidad de Extremadura*
Gong, Wenyin, *China University of Geosciences*
Goodman, Erik D., *Michigan State University*
Grasemann, Uli, *University of Texas, Austin*
Greenfield, Gary, *University of Richmond*
Greensmith, Julie, *University of Nottingham*
Greiner, David, *Universidad de Las Palmas de Gran Canaria*
Grewal, Gary William, *University of Guelph*
Gross, Roderich, *University of Sheffield*
Grouchy, Paul, *University of Toronto*
Gu, Feng, *Kingston University London*
Guerreiro, Andreia P., *University of Coimbra*
Guinand, Frederic, *Université du Havre*
Gutjahr, Walter J., *University of Vienna*
Hagelbäck, Johan, *Blekinge Tekniska Högskola*
Hamann, Heiko, *University of Paderborn*
Hamel, Lutz, *University of Rhode Island*
Hamzeh, Ali, *Shiraz University*
Hanafi, Said, *University of Valenciennes*
Handa, Hisashi, *Kindai University*
Handl, Julia, *University of Manchester*
Hansen, Nikolaus, *IRIA Saclay*
Hao, Jin-Kao, *Université d'Angers*
Harman, Mark, *University College London*
Harvey, Inman, *University of Sussex*
Hasegawa, Yoshihiko, *University of Tokyo*
Hasle, Geir, *SINTEF ICT*
Hastings, Erin, *University of Central Florida*
Hauert, Sabine, *Massachusetts Institute of Technology*
Hauschild, Mark W., *University of Missouri–St. Louis*
He, Jun, *Aberystwyth University*
Heckendorn, Robert, *University of Idaho*
Heidrich-Meisner, Verena, *Christian-Albrechts-Universität zu Kiel*
Helbig, Marde, *Council for Scientific and Industrial Research, South Africa*
Hendtlass, Tim, *Swinburne University of Technology*
Hereford, James, *Murray State University*
Hernandez, Daniel Eduardo, *Centro de Investigación Científica y de Educación Superior de Ensenada*
Hernández-Aguirre, Arturo, *Centre for Research in Mathematics, Mexico*
Hernández-Díaz, Alfredo G., *Pablo de Olavide University*
Hidalgo, J. Ignacio, *Universidad Complutense de Madrid*
Hingston, Philip, *Edith Cowan University*
Holdener, Ekaterina, *Exegy, Inc.*
Holladay, Kenneth, *Southwest Research Institute*
Holmes, John H., *University of Pennsylvania*
Hoover, Amy K., *University of Central Florida*
Hornby, Gregory S., *University of California at Santa Cruz*
Howard, Gerard, *Commonwealth Scientific and Industrial Research Organisation*
Hsiao, Michael S., *Virginia Tech*
Hu, Bin, *Technische Universität Wien*
Hu, Jianjun, *University of South Carolina*
Husbands, Phil, *Sussex University*
Hutter, Frank, *University of Freiburg*
Iclănzan, David Andrei, *Sapientia Hungaryan University of Transylvania*
Iida, Fumiya, *ETH Zürich*
Ikegami, Takashi, *University of Tokyo*
Inführ, Johannes, *Technische Universität Wien*
Iori, Manuel, *University of Modena and Reggio Emilia*
Ishibuchi, Hisao, *Osaka Prefecture University*
Istvan, Juhos, *University of Szeged*
Jackson, David, *University of Liverpool*
Jakob, Wilfried, *Karlsruhe Institute of Technology*
Janikow, Cezary Z., *University of Missouri–St. Louis*
Jayadeva, *Indian Institute of Technology Delhi*
Jiang, Siwei, *Nanyang Technological University*
Johannsen, Daniel, *SAP Innovation Center*
Johansson, Ulf, *University of Boråas*

Johnson, Colin Graeme, *University of Kent*
Jones, Ben, *University of Birmingham*
Joshi, Ayush, *University of Birmingham*
Jourdan, Laetitia, *INRIA Lille*
Joó, András, *Sapientia University*
Juarez, Reyes, *Universidad Autónoma de Baja California*
Julstrom, Bryant Arthur, *St. Cloud State University*
Kaban, Ata, *University of Birmingham*
Kaboudan, Mak, *University of Redlands*
Kampouridis, Michael, *University of Kent*
Karsai, Istvan, *East Tennessee State University*
Karthik, Sindhya, *University of Jyväskylä*
Kattan, Ahmed, *Umm Al-Qura University*
Kendall, Graham, *University of Nottingham*
Khaled Ahsan Talukder, A. K. M., *George Mason University*
Khan, Gul Muhammad, *University of Engineering & Technology Peshawar*
Khare, Vineet, *Amazon Development Centre, India*
Kirshenbaum, Evan, *HP Labs*
Kisi, Ozgur, *Canik Basari University*
Klamroth, Kathrin, *University of Wuppertal*
Klazar, Ronald, *University of Pretoria*
Knust, Sigrid, *University of Osnabrück*
Köppen, Mario, *Kyushu Institute of Technology*
Komosinski, Maciej, *Poznan University of Technology*
Kontis, Lysimachos, *University of Ioannina*
Korb, Oliver, *Cambridge Crystallographic Data Centre*
Kordon, Arthur K., *Dow Chemical*
Kotsireas, Ilias, *Wilfrid Laurier University*
Kötzing, Timo, *Max Planck Institut für Informatik*
Kovacic, Miha, *University Of Nova Gorica*
Kramer, Oliver, *University of Oldenburg*
Kratica, Jozef, *Serbian Academy of Sciences and Arts*
Krause, Oswin, *University of Copenhagen*
Krawiec, Krzysztof, *Poznan University of Technology*
Kritzinger, Stefanie, *Johannes Kepler Universität Linz*
Kronberger, Gabriel, *University of Applied Sciences Upper Austria*
Kubalik, Jiri, *Czech Technical University in Prague*
Künnemann, Marvin, *Max Planck Institut für Informatik*
Lamont, Gary Byron, *U.S. Air Force Institute of Technology*
Lampinen, Jouni, *University of Vaasa*
Landa-Silva, Dario, *University of Nottingham*
Langer, Philip, *Technische Universität Wien*
Lanzi, Pier Luca, *Politecnico di Milano*
Lara, Adriana, *CINVESTAV-IPN*
LaTorre, Antonio, *Universidad Politécnica de Madrid*
Lau, Henry, *University of Hong Kong*
Lau, Hoong-Chuin, *Singapore Management University*
Legrand, Pierrick, *Université Bordeaux*
Leguizamon, Guillermo, *Universidad Nacional de San Luis*
Lehre, Per Kristian, *University of Nottingham*
Leibnitz, Kenji, *National Institute of Information and Communications Technology, Japan*
Lengler, Johannes, *ETH Zürich*
Leo, Cazenille, *Université Paris Diderot*
Leon, Coromoto, *Universidad de La Laguna*
Leung, Kwong Sak, *Chinese University of Hong Kong*
Lewis, Peter R., *Aston University*
Lewis, Matthew, *Ohio State University*
Li, Ke, *City University of Hong Kong*
Li, Xianneng, *Waseda University*
Li, Bin, *University of Science and Technology of China*
Liang, Feng, *Nanyang Technological University*
Liang, Yiwen, *Wuhan University*
Liao, Tianjun, *Université Libre de Bruxelles*
Liapis, Antonios, *IT University of Copenhagen*
Lichodzijewski, Peter, *Dalhousie University*
Liefooghe, Arnaud, *Université Lille Nord de France*
Limmer, Steffen, *University of Erlangen-Nuremberg*
Ling, Ping, *Jiangsu Normal University*
Lioret, Alain, *Université de Vicennes à Saint-Denis*
Lipinski, Piotr, *University of Wroclaw*
Lissovoi, Andrei, *Technical University of Denmark*
Liu, Bo, *Chinese Academy of Sciences*
Lobo, Daniel, *Tufts University*
Lobo, Fernando G., *University of Algarve*
Loiacono, Daniele, *Politecnico di Milano*
Lones, Michael, *Heriot-Watt University*
López-Ibáñez, Manuel, *Université Libre de Bruxelles*
López-Jaimes, Antonio, *CINVESTAV-IPN*
Loshchilov, Ilya, *École Polytechnique Fédérale de Lausanne*
Louis, Sushil, *University of Nevada*
Lozano, Manuel, *Universidad de Granada*
Lozano, Jose A., *University of the Basque Country*
Lucas, Simon, *University of Essex*
Lukasiewycz, Martin, *TUM CREATE, Singapore*
Luna, Francisco, *Universidad de Extremadura*
Luna, J. M., *Universidad de Córdoba*
Luo, Wenjian, *University of Science and Technology of China*
Lust, Thibaut, *Université Pierre et Marie Curie*
Mabu, Shingo, *Yamaguchi University*
Machado, Penousal, *University of Coimbra*
Macia, Nuria, *Universitat Ramon Llull*
Madureira, Ana Maria, *Polytechnic Institute of Porto*
Majercik, Stephen, *Bowdoin College*
Malago, Luigi, *Università degli Studi di Milano–Bicocca*
Malo, Pekka, *Aalto University*
Mambrini, Andrea, *University of Birmingham*
Mancoridis, Spiros, *Drexel University*
Manderick, Bernard, *Vrije Universiteit Brussel*
Mandziuk, Jacek, *Warsaw University of Technology*
Manzoni, Luca, *Université Nice Sophia Antipolis*
Marchiori, Elena, *Radboud University Nijmegen*
Marinakis, Yannis, *Technical University of Crete*
Maringer, Dietmar, *University of Basel*
Marks II, Robert, *Baylor University*
Marmion, Marie-Eleonore, *Université Lille Nord de France*
Martin, Andrew, *University College London*
Martinez, Hector P., *IT University of Copenhagen*

Martinez, Ivette C., *Universidad Simon Bolivar*
Mascia, Franco, *Université Libre de Bruxelles*
Maslov, Igor V., *EvoCo Inc.*
Matsui, Shouichi, *Central Research Institute of Electric Power Industry, Japan*
Mauri, Giancarlo, *Università degli Studi di Milano–Bicocca*
Mayer, Helmut A., *University of Salzburg*
McDermott, James, *University College Dublin*
McEwan, Chris, *Microsoft Research*
McIntyre, Andrew Ryan, *Dalhousie University*
McKay, Bob, *Seoul National University*
McMinn, Phil, *University of Sheffield*
McPhee, Nicholas Freitag, *University of Minnesota, Morris*
Meignan, David, *University of Osnabrück*
Melab, Nouredine, *Université Lille Nord de France*
Melkozerov, Alexander, *Tomsk State University of Control Systems and Radioelectronics*
Mendes, Rui, *Universidade do Minho*
Mendiburu, Alexander, *University of the Basque Country*
Menzel, Stefan, *Honda Research Institute Europe*
Merelo-Guervós, Juan-Julián, *Universidad de Granada*
Mesejo Santiago, Pablo, *Université d'Auvergne*
Meyer, Bernd, *Monash University*
Meyer-Nieberg, Silja, *Universität der Bundeswehr, München*
Mezura-Montes, Efrén, *Universidad Veracruzana*
Miconi, Thomas, *The Neurosciences Institute*
Middendorf, Martin, *University of Leipzig*
Miettinen, Kaisa, *University of Jyväskylä*
Miikkulainen, Risto, *University of Texas, Austin*
Miklic, Damjan, *University of Zagreb*
Miller, Julian, *University of York*
Minai, Ali, *University of Cincinnati*
Minku, Leandro, *University of Birmingham*
Miramontes Hercog, Luis, *Self-Organizing Solutions*
Misir, Mustafa, *Singapore Management University*
Mitchell, George, *CCKF Ltd.*
Mjolsness, Eric, *University of California at Irvine*
Moen, Hans Jonas Fossum, *Norwegian Defence Research Establishment*
Mohan, Chilukuri K., *Syracuse University*
Montanier, Jean-Marc, *Norwegian University of Science and Technology*
Montemanni, Roberto, *IDSIA*
Moore, Jason, *Dartmouth College*
Mora, Antonio, *Universidad de Granada*
Moraglio, Alberto, *University of Birmingham*
Moses, Melanie, *University of New Mexico*
Möslinger, Christoph, *Karl-Franzens-Universität Graz*
Mostaghim, Sanaz, *Karlsruhe Institute of Technology*
Mouret, Jean-Baptiste, *Université Pierre et Marie Curie, CNRS*
Muelas, Santiago, *Universidad Politécnica de Madrid*
Müller, Christian Lorenz, *New York University*
Mumford, Christine Lesley, *Cardiff University*
Musliu, Nysret, *Technische Universität Wien*
Nagata, Yuichi, *Tokyo Institute of Technology*
Nakib, Amir, *Laboratoire LISSI*
Narukawa, Kaname, *Honda Research Institute Europe*
Nashed, Youssef, *Università degli Studi di Parma*
Naujoks, Boris, *Cologne University of Applied Sciences*
Nebro, Antonio, *Universidad de Málaga*
Neirotti, Juan, *Aston University*
Nejati, Shiva, *University of Luxembourg*
Neri, Ferrante, *University of Jyväskylä*
Neumann, Frank, *University of Adelaide*
Nguyen, Huy, *Misfit Wearables*
Nguyen Xuan, Hoai, *Hanoi University*
Nicolau, Miguel, *University College Dublin*
Nievola, Julio Cesar, *Pontifícia Universidade Católica do Paraná*
Nobile, Marco, *Universitàdegli Studi di Milano–Bicocca*
Nojima, Yusuke, *Osaka Prefecture University*
Noman, Nasimul, *University of Newcastle*
Ó Cinnéide, Mel, *National University of Ireland, Dublin*
O'Neill, Michael, *University College Dublin*
O'Riordan, Colm, *National University of Ireland, Galway*
Ochoa, Gabriela, *University of Stirling*
Ofria, Charles, *Michigan State University*
Oh, Choong Kun, *U.S. Naval Research Laboratory*
Okabe, Tatsuya, *Honda R&D Co., Ltd.*
Olhofer, Markus, *Honda Research Institute Europe*
Oliveira, Pedro N. F. P., *Universidade do Minho*
Oliveto, Pietro S., *University of Sheffield*
Oliwa, Tomasz, *University of Georgia*
Olmo, Juan Luis, *Universidad de Córdoba*
Ombuki-Berman, Beatrice, *Brock University*
Omran, Mohammed, *Gulf University for Science & Technology*
Ono, Isao, *Tokyo Institute of Technology*
Ortega, Julio, *Universidad de Granada*
Ouni, Ali, *Université de Montréal*
Özcan, Ender, *University of Nottingham*
Palafox, Leon, *University of Tokyo*
Pang, Wei, *University of Aberdeen*
Parque, Victor, *Toyota Technological Institute*
Pasquier, Philippe, *Simon Fraser University*
Pedro, Castillo, *Universidad de Granada*
Pellegrini, Paola, *Université Libre de Bruxelles*
Pereira, Francisco Baptista, *Instituto Superior de Engenharia de Coimbra*
Perez Caceres, Leslie, *Université Libre de Bruxelles*
Peña, Jose-Maria, *Universidad Polytécnica de Madrid*
Phelps, Steve, *University of Essex*
Philippides, Andrew, *University of Sussex*
Pibernat, Hugo, *King Games Inc.*
Polani, Daniel, *University of Hertfordshire*
Poles, Silvia, *EnginSoft*
Poloczek, Jendrik, *University of Oldenburg*
Pop, Petrica, *North University of Baia Mare*
Popovici, Elena, *Icosystem Corp.*
Porumbel, Daniel, *Université Lille Nord de France*

Pošík, Petr, *Czech Technical University in Prague*
Potter, Walter, *University of Georgia*
Poulding, Simon, *University of York*
Prandtstetter, Matthias, *Austrian Institute of Technology*
Prestwich, Steve, *University College Cork*
Preuss, Mike, *Technische Universität Dortmund*
Price, Kenneth
Puchinger, Jakob, *Austrian Institute of Technology*
Puente, Cesar, *Universidad Autónoma de San Luis Potosi*
Puerta, Jose Miguel, *Universidad de Castilla–La Mancha*
Punch, William F., *Michigan State University*
Purshouse, Robin, *University of Sheffield*
Qin, Kai, *RMIT University*
Randall, Marcus Christian, *Bond University*
Ranjithan, Ranji S., *North Carolina State University*
Rasheed, Khaled, *University of Georgia*
Ray, Tom, *University of Oklahoma*
Ray, Tapabrata, *University of New South Wales*
Read, Mark, *University of Sydney*
Reed, Patrick M., *Cornell University*
Reif, David, *U.S. Environmental Protection Agency*
Rhee, Phill Kyu, *Inha University*
Rhyd, Lewis, *Cardiff University*
Riff, Maria Cristina, *Universidad Técnica Federico Santa Maria*
Robert, Wille, *University of Bremen*
Robilliard, Denis, *Université Lille Nord de France*
Rohlfshagen, Philipp, *SolveIT Software*
Roper, Marc, *University of Strathclyde*
Ross, Brian J., *Brock University*
Ross, Peter, *Edinburgh Napier University*
Rothlauf, Franz, *Universität Mainz*
Rowe, Jonathan, *University of Birmingham*
Rudolph, Günter, *Technische Universität Dortmund*
Ruhul, Sarker, *University of New South Wales*
Ruiz, Ruben, *Universidad Polytécnica de Valencia*
Runkler, Thomas, *Siemens AG*
Ryan, Conor, *University of Limerick*
Sagarna, Ramon, *University of the Basque Country*
Sahin, Erol, *Middle East Technical University*
Sahraoui, Houari, *Université de Montréal*
Salem, Ziad, *Karl-Franzens-Universität Graz*
Sanchez, Luciano, *Universidad de Oviedo*
Santana, Roberto, *University of the Basque Country*
Santibáñez Koref, Iván, *Technische Universität Berlin*
Sarro, Federica, *University College London*
Sato, Hiroyuki, *University of Electro-Communications*
Sato, Yuji, *Hosei University*
Sawada, Hideyuki, *Kagawa University*
Schillaci, Massimiliano, *Dora S.p.A.*
Schoenauer, Marc, *INRIA Saclay*
Schütze, Oliver, *CINVESTAV-IPN*
Scully, Peter, *Aberystwyth University*
Segura, Carlos, *Universidad de La Laguna*
Sekanina, Lukas, *Brno University of Technology*
Semet, Yann, *Thales*
Sen, Sandip, *University of Tulsa*
Seppi, Kevin, *Brigham Young University*
Serpell, Martin, *University of the West of England*
Sevaux, Marc, *Université de Bretagne-Sud*
Shaheen, Fatima, *Loughborough University*
Shaker, Noor, *IT University of Copenhagen*
Shakya, Siddhartha, *British Telecom*
Shapiro, Jonathan Lee, *University of Manchester*
Shengxiang, Yang, *De Montfort University*
Shihab, Emad, *Rochester Institute of Technology*
Shukla, Pradyumn Kumar, *Karlsruhe Institute of Technology*
Siarry, Patrick, *Université Paris–Est Créteil*
Silva, Fernando, *Universidade de Lisboa*
Sim, Kevin, *Edinburgh Napier University*
Simões, Anabela, *Polytechnic Institute of Coimbra*
Sinha, Ankur, *Aalto University*
Sipper, Moshe, *Ben-Gurion University*
Skurikhin, Alexei N., *Los Alamos National Laboratory*
Smith, Jim, *University of the West of England*
Smith, Stephen L., *University of York*
Smith, Alice, *Auburn University*
Smyth, Tamara, *University of California at San Diego*
Snoek, Jasper, *Harvard University*
Solnon, Christine, *Institut National des Sciences Appliquées de Lyon*
Song, Andy, *RMIT University*
Sossa, Humberto, *Instituto Politécnico Nacional, México*
Souza, Jerffeson, *State University of Ceara*
Spector, Lee, *Hampshire College*
Spicher, Antoine, *Université Paris–Est Créteil*
Squillero, Giovanni, *Politecnico di Torino*
Standish, Russell, *High Performance Coders*
Stepney, Susan, *University of York*
Stibor, Thomas, *GSI Helmholtz Centre for Heavy Ion Research*
Stich, Sebastian, *ETH Zürich*
Stonedahl, Forrest, *Northwestern University*
Stouch, Daniel W., *Charles River Analytics*
Straccia, Umberto, *Istituto di Scienza e Tecnologie dell'Informazione*
Stracquadanio, Giovanni, *Johns Hopkins University*
Stradner, Jürgen, *Karl-Franzens-Universität Graz*
Sudholt, Dirk, *University of Sheffield*
Sun, Xiao-yan, *China University of Mining and Technology*
Sun, Yi, *Google Inc.*
Sun, Chaoli, *Taiyuan University of Science and Technology*
Sutton, Andrew Michael, *Friedrich-Schiller-Universität Jena*
Suzuki, Reiji, *Nagoya University*
Swan, Jerry, *University of Stirling*
Takadama, Keiki, *University of Electro-Communications*
Talbi, El-Ghazali, *INRIA Lille*
Tan, Ying, *Peking University*
Tanaka, Kiyoshi, *Shinshu University*
Tanev, Ivan, *Doshisha University*
Tang, Ke, *University of Science and Technology of China*
Tarantino, Ernesto, *Institute of High Performance Computing*

and Networking, Italy
Tauritz, Daniel R., *Missouri University of Science and Technology*
Tavares, Jorge, *Microsoft*
Tavares, Roberto, *Universidade Federal de São Carlos*
Taylor, Tim, *Goldsmiths, University of London*
Terashima Marín, Hugo, *Tecnológico de Monterrey*
Tettamanzi, Andrea G. B., *Université Nice Sophia Antipolis*
Teuscher, Christof, *Portland State University*
Textor, Johannes, *Universiteit Utrecht*
Teytaud, Fabien, *Université Lille Nord de France*
Teytaud, Olivier, *INRIA Saclay*
Thawonmas, Ruck, *Ritsumeikan University*
Thiele, Lothar, *ETH Zürich*
Thompson, Tommy, *University of Derby*
Timmis, Jonathan, *University of York*
Ting, Chuan-Kang, *National Chung Cheng University*
Tino, Peter, *University of Birmingham*
Tiwari, Santosh, *General Motors Company*
Tiwari, Ashutosh, *Cranfield University*
Tomassini, Marco, *Université de Lausanne*
Tonda, Alberto Paolo, *Institut National de la Recherche Agronomique, France*
Topchy, Alexander, *Nielsen Media Research*
Torres-Jimenez, Jose, *CINVESTAV-IPN*
Torresen, Jim, *University of Oslo*
Trefzer, Martin, *University of York*
Trianni, Vito, *Institute of Cognitive Sciences and Technologies, Italy*
Trujillo, Leonardo, *Instituto Tecnológico de Tijuana*
Tsang, Edward, *University of Essex*
Tuci, Elio, *Aberystwyth University*
Tufte, Gunnar, *Norwegian University of Science and Technology*
Tušar, Tea, *Jožef Stefan Institute*
Tutum, Cem Celal, *Michigan State University*
Twycross, Jamie, *University of Nottingham*
U, Man Chon, *University of Georgia*
Ugolotti, Roberto, *Università degli Studi di Parma*
Urbanowicz, Ryan, *Dartmouth College*
Urquhart, Neil, *Edinburgh Napier University*
Vašíček, Zdeněk, *Brno University Of Technology*
Van den Herik, H. Jaap, *Tilburg University*
Vanneschi, Leonardo, *Universidade Nova de Lisboa*
Vatolkin, Igor, *Technische Universität Dortmund*
Ventura, Sebastian, *Universidad de Córdoba*
Verel, Sebastien, *Université du Littoral Côte d'Opale*
Vergilio, Silvia, *Federal University of Paraná*
Viana, Ana, *Polytechnic Institute of Porto*
Vladislavleva, Ekaterina, *Evolved Analytics Europe*
Von Zuben, Fernando J., *Universidade Estadual de Campinas*
Vrahatis, Michael N., *University of Patras*
Wagner, Tobias, *Technische Universität Dortmund*
Waldock, Antony, *BAE Systems*
Walsh, Paul, *Cork Institute of Technology*
Wang, Yong, *Central South University*
Wang, Ziyu, *University of British Columbia*
Wanka, Rolf, *University of Erlangen-Nuremberg*
Weimer, Westley, *University of Virginia*
Weise, Thomas, *University of Science and Technology of China*
Werfel, Justin, *Harvard University*
Wessing, Simon, *Technische Universität Dortmund*
Whigham, Peter Alexander, *University of Otago*
White, David, *University of Glasgow*
Wilkerson, Josh, *Missouri University of Science and Technology*
Wilson, Garnett, *Afinin Labs Inc.*
Wilson, Stewart W., *Prediction Dynamics*
Wimmer, Manuel, *Technische Universität Wien*
Wineberg, Mark, *University of Guelph*
Winkler, Stephan, *University Of Applied Sciences Upper Austria*
Wong, M. L. Dennis, *Swinburne University of Technology*
Woodward, John R., *University of Stirling*
Wright, Alden H., *University of Montana*
Wrobel, Borys, *Adam Mickiewicz University*
Wu, Zheng Yi, *Bentley Systems*
Wu, Annie S., *University of Central Florida*
Xie, Huayang, *Oracle New Zealand*
Yamada, Takeshi, *NTT Communication Science Labs*
Yamamoto, Lidia, *Université de Strasbourg*
Yannakakis, Georgios, *IT University of Copenhagen*
Yeh, Wei-Chang, *National Tsing Hua University*
Yoo, Shin, *University College London*
Yu, Tina, *Memorial University of Newfoundland*
Yu, Tian-Li, *National Taiwan University*
Yu, Yang, *Nanjing University*
Zafra, Amelia, *Universidad de Córdoba*
Zahadat, Payam, *Karl-Franzens-Universität Graz*
Zaharie, Daniela, *West University of Timisoara*
Zambetta, Fabio, *RMIT University*
Zapf, Michael, *Georg Simon Ohm University of Applied Sciences Nuremberg*
Zapotecas Martínez, Saúl, *CINVESTAV-IPN*
Zell, Andreas, *Universität Tübingen*
Zexuan, Zhu, *Shenzhen University*
Zhang, Mengjie, *Victoria University of Wellington*
Zhang, Fu, *Mathworks*
Zhang, Yuanyuan, *University College London*
Zhang, Byoung-Tak, *Seoul National University*
Zhong, Yanfei, *Wuhan University*
Zhou, Aimin, *East China Normal University*

Best Paper Nominations

Track: Generative and Developmental Systems

Track: Genetic Algorithms

Track: Genetic Programming

Track: Parallel Evolutionary Systems

Track: Real World Applications

Track: Search Based Software Engineering

Track: Theory

Student Workshop Chairs' Welcome

It is our great pleasure to welcome you to the GECCO'14 Student Workshop!

The goal of the Student Workshop, organized as a joined event for graduate and undergraduate students, is to assist the students with their research in the field of Evolutionary Computation.

Exceeding our expectations in both the number and quality of submitted papers, 14 peer-reviewed papers have finally been accepted for presentation at the workshop. They cover a wide range of subjects in evolutionary computation, presenting advances in theory as well as applications, e.g. robotics and the travelling salesman problem. The topics include particle swarm algorithms as well as flood evolution, reinforcement learning, parallelism, niching, and parameter tuning, and many more, all yielding interesting contributions to the field.

During the workshop, the students will receive useful feedback on the quality of their work and presentation style. This will be assured by a question and answer period after each talk led by a mentor panel of established researchers. The students are encouraged to use this opportunity to get highly qualified feedback not only on the presented subject but also on future research directions. As it was good practice in the last years, the best contributions will receive a small award sponsored by GECCO.

In addition, the contributing students are invited to present their work as a poster at the GECCO'14 Poster Session – an excellent opportunity to network with industrial and academic members of the community.

We hope that the variety of covered topics will catch the attention of a wide range of GECCO'14 attendees, who will learn about fresh research ideas and meet young researchers with related interests. Other students are encouraged to attend the workshop to learn from the work of their colleagues and broaden their (scientific) horizons.

We would like to thank the GECCO'14 General Chair, Dirk Arnold, for his assistance throughout the process of organizing the workshop. We would also like to express our gratitude to the distinguished members of the mentor panel and to the authors of submitted papers, all contributing to the success of this workshop.

Tea Tušar
Student Workshop Chair
Jožef Stefan Institute, Slovenia

Boris Naujoks
Student Workshop Chair
Cologne University of Applied Sciences, Germany

GECCO'14 Student Workshop Organization

General Chairs: Tea Tušar
Boris Naujoks

Mentor Panel: Anna I. Esparcia-Alcázar *(S2 Grupo, Spain)*
Jürgen Branke *(University of Warwick, UK)*
Tobias Glasmachers *(Ruhr-Universität Bochum, Germany)*

Program Committee: Matej Črepinšek *(University of Maribor, Slovenia)*
Erik Dovgan *(Jožef Stefan Institute, Slovenia)*
Oliver Flasch *(Cologne University of Applied Science, Germany)*
Martina Friese *(Cologne University of Applied Science, Germany)*
Patrick Koch *(Cologne University of Applied Science, Germany)*
Barbara Koroušić Seljak *(Jožef Stefan Institute, Slovenia)*
Marjan Mernik *(University of Maribor, Slovenia)*
Boris Naujoks *(Cologne University of Applied Science, Germany)*
Gregor Papa *(Jožef Stefan Institute, Slovenia)*
Tea Tušar *(Jožef Stefan Institute, Slovenia)*
Vida Vukašinović *(Jožef Stefan Institute, Slovenia)*

Effects of Personality Decay on Collective Movements

Jeremy Acre
Dept. of Mathematics
Southern Nazarene University
Bethany, OK, USA
jeacre@mail.snu.edu

Nicholas Zoller
Dept. of Mathematics
Southern Nazarene University
Bethany, OK, USA
nzoller@snu.edu

Brent E. Eskridge
Dept. of Computer Science
and Network Engineering
Southern Nazarene University
Bethany, OK, USA
beskridge@snu.edu

ABSTRACT

In natural systems, many animals organize into groups without a designated leader and still perform complex collective behaviors. Although individuals in the group may be considered equal, all the individuals differ in the traits each of them possess. Of particular interest is the idea of an individual's personality as it often plays a role in determining which individuals lead collective behaviors. Personality is, in part, developed and maintained by an individual's experiences. However, neither an individual, nor its environment remains unchanged. Therefore, there is a need for an individual to continue to gain new experiences to ensure that its information about itself and its environment are current. Since observations have shown that the effects of experience on personality can decay over time, we investigate the effects of this decay on the emergence of leaders and followers and the resulting success of a group's collective movement attempts. Results show that personality decay has a negative effect on the overall success of the group in collective movements as it prevents the emergence of distinct personalities, a necessary requirement for individuals to assume distinct leader and follower roles.

Categories and Subject Descriptors

I.2.11 [**Artificial Intelligence**]: Distributed Artificial Intelligence—*coherence and coordination,multiagent systems*

Keywords

collective movement, coordination, leadership, adaptation

1. INTRODUCTION

There are many examples in the natural world where animals form large groups and engage in collective behavior. While there is not a consistent leader in many situations, there are leaders for each individual movement. An individual's personality has been shown to be a factor in determining which individuals will be leaders and which will be followers. Bold individuals are generally leaders, while shy individuals are generally followers [6]. However, personalities are not fixed and are known to sometimes change in response to positive and negative experiences [3]. Furthermore, the effects of experience on personality decay over time and are eventually lost. In this work, we investigate the effects of such personality decay on the emergence of leaders and followers in a collective movement. Results show that the rapid decay of personalities to an initial value, regardless of the type of decay, prevents the emergence of distinct personality types, and, therefore, the emergence of distinct leaders and followers.

GECCO'14, July 12–16, Vancouver, BC, Canada.

http://dx.doi.org/10.1145/2598394.2605678.

2. METHODS

The simulations used for this work used a modified version of a collective movement model developed through observations of collective movement attempts in a group of white-faced capuchin monkeys [4, 10]. Its generality was later verified in observations of sheep [11]. Despite being a collective movement model, actual movement through an environment is not a part of the model. Rather, the focus of the model is on the decision-making process that precedes a movement. Examples of such situations are found in nature where individuals exhibit notifying behaviors indicating a preferred direction of movement during a predeparture period [12].

2.1 Collective Movement Model

The collective movement model uses three rules to govern the decision-making process involved in starting collective movements [4, 10]. The first rule assumes that all individuals within the group can initiate a collective movement attempt with a constant rate of $1/\tau_o$.

The second rule describes the rate at which followers join the collective movement attempt and is calculated by $1/\tau_r$. The time constant τ_r for the following rate is calculated using the following:

$$\tau_r = \alpha_f + \beta_f \frac{N-r}{r} \tag{1}$$

where α_f and β_f are constants determined through direct observation, N is the number of individuals in the group, and r is the number of individuals following the initiator. As the number of individuals following the initiator increases, the rate at which individuals join the movement also increases.

Not all initiation attempts are successful as initiators often cancel and return to the group. The third rule calculates this cancellation rate using the following:

$$C_r = \frac{\alpha_c}{1 + (r/\gamma_c)^{\varepsilon_c}} \tag{2}$$

where α_c, γ_c, and ε_c are constants determined through direct observation, and r is the number of individuals following the initiator. Simulations of the model include the implicit assumption that a successful collective movement requires all of the members of the group to participate, since there is a non-zero probability of canceling even if all but one member participates. While this is not necessarily the case in nature, cohesive collective movements are the primary focus of this work and, as such, incomplete movements are considered failures.

2.2 Integrating Personality

To investigate the effects of altering the rate at which individuals initiate, follow an initiator, and cancel a movement, Gautrais added an individual-specific constant, referred to as a "k factor," to the rate calculations of the collective movement model [4]. Initiation attempts were now calculated at the constant rate of k/τ_o, and the following and canceling rate calculations were modified as follows:

$$\tau_r = \frac{1}{k}\left(\alpha_f + \beta_f \frac{N-r}{r}\right) \tag{3}$$

$$C_r = k\left(\frac{\alpha_c}{1 + (r/\gamma_c)^{\varepsilon_c}}\right) \tag{4}$$

where the variables are defined as before. Since this k factor can either increase or decrease the three decision-making rates, it was an ideal means of incorporating the effects of personality into the model.

Three important points were considered in integrating personality with the collective movement model. First, personality has been observed in natural systems to affect the events used in this model in different ways. For example, a bold personality should result in a higher initiation rate and lower following and canceling rates, while a shy personality should result in a lower initiation rate and higher following and canceling rates [5]. Second, the magnitude with which a shy personality affects the model should be the same as a bold personality so as not to bias the model towards one personality over another. Since k had a non-inclusive lower limit of zero, the non-inclusive upper limit of two was chosen to ensure balance. In the simulations described below, personalities were limited to the range [0.1 : 0.9] to ensure these limits were satisfied. Lastly, although neither the original model, nor the observations on which the model was based, discussed the personality of the individual animals involved, it was assumed that the observed group members could be classified as having either bold or shy personalities. However, since the personalities of the observed individuals were unknown, all individuals were assumed to have had a default moderate personality ($p_i = 0.5$), which produced the same results as the original model. To accentuate the effects of even minor differences in personality in values close to a moderate personality and minimize the effects of differences in extreme personalities, a personality p was converted to a corresponding k value using the following sigmoid function:

$$k = 2\left(1 + e^{\frac{0.5-p'}{10}}\right)^{-1} \tag{5}$$

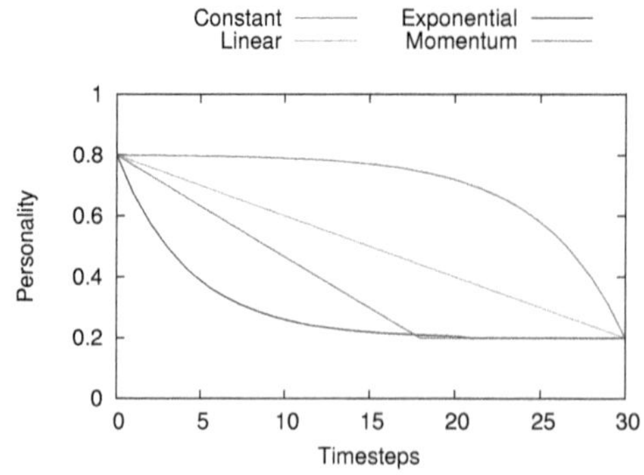

Figure 1: The four different personality decay equations evaluated are shown for a bold personality value ($p = 0.8$) that decays to the initial, shy personality value ($p = 0.2$).

where p' is p for initiating decisions and is $1-p$ for canceling and following decisions.

The initiator's personality was updated after every collective movement initiation attempt using the following standard update (or learning) rule [1, 7, 13]:

$$p_{t+1} = p_t(1-\lambda) + \lambda r \tag{6}$$

where p_t was the initiator's personality for the current movement, p_{t+1} was the personality after the movement, λ was the rate at which updates changed the personality, and r was the reinforcement value used to update the personality. When λ was low, personality was primarily determined through long-term historical success and changes were minor. When λ was high, personality was primarily determined through short-term success, and changes from one attempt to the next were significant. For the simulations described in this work, a low value of lambda was chosen ($\lambda = 0.02$) to emphasize long-term initiation success. For successful initiations, the reinforcement was $r = 1$, while it was $r = 0$ for unsuccessful initiations.

2.3 Personality Decay

Personalities were decayed using four different decay equations. They were:

1. Constant decay:

$$p_{t+1} = \begin{cases} p_l - \Delta t d_t & \text{if } p > p_i, \\ p_l + \Delta t d_t & \text{if } p < p_i. \end{cases} \tag{7}$$

2. Linear decay:

$$p_{t+1} = p_l + \Delta t \frac{p_i - p_l}{d_t} \tag{8}$$

3. Exponential decay:

$$p_{t+1} = (p_l - p_i)\left(e^{(\Delta t - d_t)/5}\right) + p_i \tag{9}$$

4. Momentum decay:

$$p_{t+1} = (p_l - p_i)\left(1 - e^{(\Delta t - d_t)/5}\right) + p_i \tag{10}$$

where p_{t+1} was the decayed personality for the next simulation, p_l was the personality after the last initiation attempt,

p_i was the initial personality, d_t was the treatment's decay time, and Δt was the number of simulations since the individual's last initiation attempt. The first two decay equations model simple decay approaches, while the exponential decay equation is more biologically relevant. Although the momentum decay is not biologically based, a preliminary analysis of the other three decay equations indicated the need for an approach that initially yielded minimal decay, but still allowed for decay within a reasonable amount of time. Figure 1 illustrates the differences between each of these decay equations.

Since the group size affects the number of initiations an individual may make, different decay times ranging from $10 \times N$ to $2000 \times N$ were evaluated where N was the size of the group. Although many of these decay times were either too short or too long, their use allowed for a better analysis of the difference between the decay equations.

2.4 Numerical Implementation

Numerical simulations of the collective movement model were implemented in Java using a customized version[1] of the original algorithm [4]. The time of each event was calculated as a random number drawn from an exponential distribution using the appropriate rate. As such, the simulations used continuous time events, and not discrete time.

The original model was only evaluated with a group size of 10, but other work has shown that the success of collective movement initiations increases as the group size is increased, with most success differences present in group sizes of 50 or less and diminishing effects beyond a group size of 100 [2]. As such, evaluating different group sizes presents an opportunity to evaluate the effects of personality with different group dynamics. To evaluate the impact of the initial personality value, treatments were performed using the following personality values for all individuals within a group: shy ($p_v = 0.2$), moderate ($p_v = 0.5$), and bold ($p_v = 0.8$). Within each treatment, group sizes from 20 to 50 were used. Fifty evaluations were performed for each group size, each with a different random seed. A single evaluation consisted of $2,000 \times N$ simulations, where N was the group size. Each simulation constituted a single attempt at a collective movement and ended in either success (all individuals participating in the movement) or the initiator canceling. Individual personality values were reset at the beginning of each evaluation and persisted from one simulation to the next. The model parameters used were the same as those used in the original model [4, 10].

The R `changepoint` package was used to analyze trends in personality values of successive attempts in an evaluation [8]. This software package allowed for the identification of shifts in the mean personality value for a particular individual. In our simulations, these shifts, referred to as changepoints, represented a potential personality transition. Since personalities were not constant and the analysis produced a linear approximation of a portion of a personality value time series, we defined a personality to be bold if a segment of the personality had a mean value greater than or equal to 0.85. The high threshold was needed to differentiate truly bold individuals from individuals with an initial personality of 0.8 that had not yet had an opportunity to gain experience.

[1]Simulation source code and data analysis scripts are available for download from `https://github.com/snucsne/bio-inspired-leadership`.

3. RESULTS & ANALYSIS

Figure 2 shows the mean initiation success percentages for each decay rate equation and group size combination for a decay time of $t = 100 \times N$. Simulations using the linear and momentum decay rates had significantly higher leadership success than simulations using the constant and exponential decay rates. Previous work using baseline simulations without personality had leadership success percentages ranging from 30% to 50% and simulations with personality that did not decay had success percentages ranging from 60% to 85%. When these previous results are compared to the results of simulations with personality decay, it is evident that simulations using the exponential decay rate performed only marginally better than the baseline simulations, indicating that personality decay has a negative impact on leadership success, namely due to its role in inhibiting the emergence of distinct personalities.

For decay times shorter than $t = 100 \times N$, the constant and exponential decay equations resulted in success percentages that were marginally better than the default model implementation without personality. Simulations using the linear rate equation had higher success, but simulations using the momentum decay equation performed statistically significantly better. Even with a decay time of $t = 10 \times N$, simulations using the momentum decay equation had higher success than non-personality simulations.

For decay times longer than $t = 100 \times N$, all decay equations had higher leadership success. Since simulations using the momentum decay equation already had high success, the effects were less pronounced. Simulations using the other decay equations, however, exhibited marked improvements in leadership success. Despite this improvement, simulations using personality decay performed worse than simulations using personality, but no personality decay.

4. DISCUSSION

The addition of personality decay to the collective movement model was far more destructive than originally anticipated. Given the biologically inspired nature of the exponential decay equation, it was anticipated that it would provide the best performance. However, its performance, along with the performance of simulations using the constant and linear decay equations, was so poor that the momentum decay equation was developed.

A closer analysis of the results indicates that the primary reason for the loss in leadership success after the addition of personality decay is that personalities decayed too rapidly to maintain distinct personality types, and, therefore, distinct roles of leader and follower within the group. There were too few opportunities for individuals to gain recent experience and minimize the effects of personality decay.

Although the results presented here indicate that personality decay is destructive to the success of collective movements, it may still prove to be a useful concept as it has been observed in natural systems and provides an opportunity for the group to quickly adapt to environmental changes. There are a number of approaches using evolutionary computation that could be used to continue this line of investigation. One line of investigation would be to use genetic programming to evolve alternative decay equations that allow for the emergence of distinct personality types. Another approach would be to use grammatical evolution to evolve a ruleset to adapt personalities both with and without current experiences [9].

5. ACKNOWLEDGMENTS

This material is based upon work supported by the National Science Foundation under Grant No. BCS-1124837. Some of the computing for this project was performed at the OU Supercomputing Center for Education & Research (OSCER) at the University of Oklahoma.

6. REFERENCES

[1] C. Bernstein, A. Kacelnik, and J. Krebs. Individual decisions and the distribution of predators in a patchy environment. *The Journal of Animal Ecology*, 57(3):1007–1026, 1988.

[2] B. E. Eskridge. Effects of local communication and topology on collective movement initiation. In *International Conference on the Simulation and Synthesis of Living Things*, volume 13, pages 155–162, 2012.

[3] A. Flack, B. Pettit, R. Freeman, T. Guilford, and D. Biro. What are leaders made of? the role of individual experience in determining leader–follower relations in homing pigeons. *Animal Behaviour*, 83(3):703–709, 2012.

[4] J. Gautrais. The hidden variables of leadership. *Behavioural Processes*, 84(3):664–667, 2010.

[5] J. L. Harcourt, T. Z. Ang, G. Sweetman, R. A. Johnstone, and A. Manica. Social feedback and the emergence of leaders and followers. *Current Biology*, 19(3):248–252, 2009.

[6] R. Johnstone and A. Manica. Evolution of personality differences in leadership. *Proceedings of the National Academy of Sciences*, 108(20):8373–8378, 2011.

[7] E. Katsnelson, U. Motro, M. Feldman, and A. Lotem. Evolution of learned strategy choice in a frequency-dependent game. *Proceedings of the Royal Society B: Biological Sciences*, 279(1731):1176–1184, 2012.

[8] R. Killick and I. Eckley. *changepoint: An R package for changepoint analysis*, 2013. R package version 1.1.

[9] M. O'Neill and C. Ryan. *Grammatical Evolution: Evolutionary Automatic Programming in an Arbitrary Language*. Kluwer Academic Publishers, Norwell, MA, USA, 2003.

[10] O. Petit, J. Gautrais, J.-B. Leca, G. Theraulaz, and J.-L. Deneubourg. Collective decision-making in white-faced capuchin monkeys. *Proceedings of the Royal Society B: Biological Sciences*, 276(1672):3495–3503, 2009.

[11] M.-H. Pillot, J. Gautrais, P. Arrufat, I. D. Couzin, R. Bon, and J.-L. Deneubourg. Scalable rules for coherent group motion in a gregarious vertebrate. *PLoS ONE*, 6(1):e14487, 01 2011.

[12] L. Pyritz, A. King, C. Sueur, and C. Fichtel. Reaching a consensus: Terminology and concepts used in coordination and decision-making research. *International Journal of Primatology*, 32(6):1268–1278, 2011.

[13] R. S. Sutton and A. G. Barto. *Reinforcement Learning: An Introduction*. MIT Press, 1998.

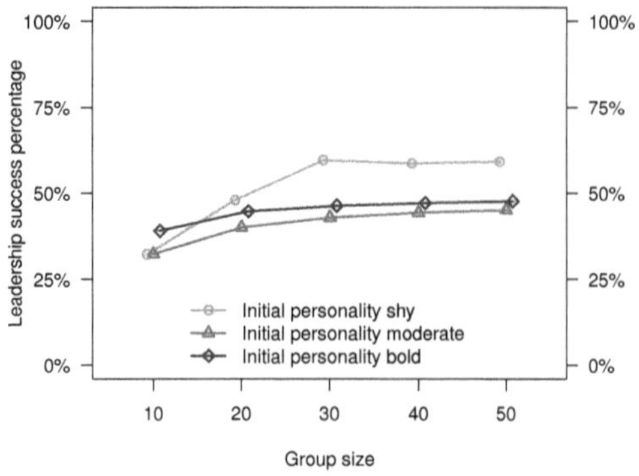

(a) Constant Decay

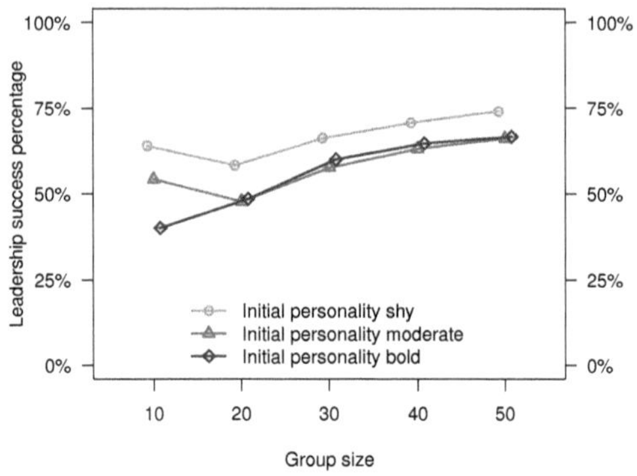

(b) Linear Decay

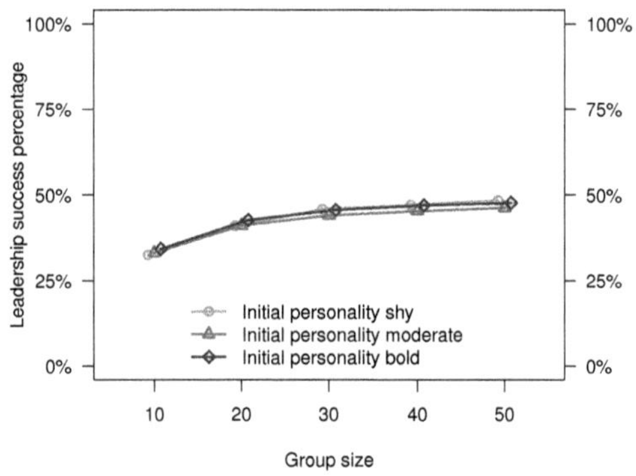

(c) Exponential Decay

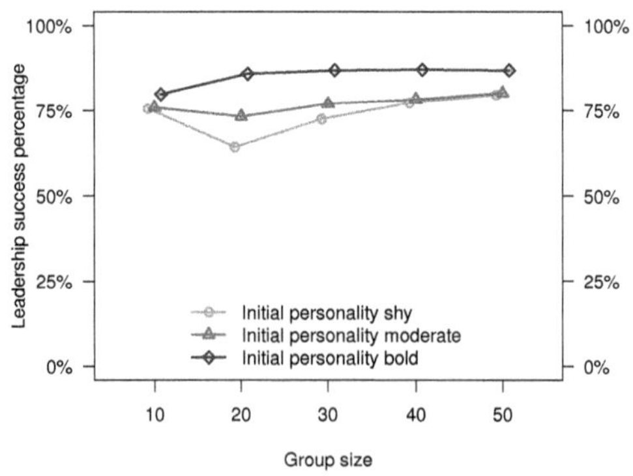

(d) Momentum Decay

Figure 2: The mean initiation success percentages for each decay rate equation and group size combination are shown for a decay time of $t = 100 \times N$.

An Efficient Fitness-based Stagnation Detection Method for Particle Swarm Optimization

Hazem Radwan Ahmed
School of Computing, Queen's University
25 Union Street, Kingston, Ontario,
Canada K7L 3N6.
hazem@cs.queensu.ca

ABSTRACT
Stagnation is a prevalent issue in many heuristic search algorithms, such as Particle Swarm Optimization (PSO). PSO stagnation occurs when the rate of position changes (or velocities) that attract particles to the global best position approaches zero, potentially leading the swarm to being trapped in a local optimum, especially for deceptive multimodal optimization problems. This paper proposes a novel fitness-based stagnation detection method that effectively and efficiently restarts the search process to escape potential local optima. The main idea of the proposed method is to make use of the already calculated fitness values of swarm particles, instead of their pairwise distance values, to predict an imminent stagnation situation. That is, the proposed fitness-based method does not require any computational overhead of repeatedly calculating pairwise distances between all particles at each iteration. The proposed fitness-based method substantially outperforms the commonly used distance-based method when tested on several classical and advanced (shifted/rotated) benchmark optimization functions in three ways: 1) The optimization performance is significantly better performing (using Wilcoxon rank-sum test). 2) The optimization performance is considerably faster (up to three times). 3) The proposed fitness-based method is less dependent on the problem search space, compared with the distance-based method.

Categories and Subject Descriptors
I.2.8 [**Artificial Intelligence**]: Problem Solving, Control Methods, and Search—*Heuristic methods*

Keywords
multi-start particle swarm optimization; fitness-based stagnation detection; search diversification; speedup technique.

GECCO'14, July 12–16, 2014, Vancouver, BC, Canada..

ACM 978-1-4503-2881-4/14/07…$15.00.
http://dx.doi.org/10.1145/2598394.2605669

1. INTRODUCTION
Drawing inspiration from the sociological behavior associated with bird flocking, Particle Swarm Optimization (PSO) has had growing scientific attention in many diverse domains [16] since its inception in 1995 [10]. While PSO algorithms showed efficient, robust and fast-convergence behavior on several optimization problems, they suffered from a number of key issues, such as swarm explosion and swarm stagnation. The early versions of PSO suffered from the swarm explosion issue [4], in which particle velocities indefinitely grow, causing divergence of swarm particles for some values of the inertia and learning coefficients. Among early attempts to address this issue was the 'velocity clamping' strategy, which limits the velocity magnitude to a maximum velocity threshold. This strategy avoids increasing particle velocities indefinitely and prevents particles from taking extremely large shifts from their current position, realistically simulating the incremental change of human learning [9].

A better strategy to address the swarm explosion issue is the use of a 'constriction coefficient', which was first proposed by Clerc in 1999 [2]. Then shortly after, in 2000, Eberhart and Shi [6] analyzed the convergence behavior of PSO and suggested the popular settings of the constriction and learning coefficients (i.e., χ= 0.729 and c_1=c_2=2.05), which ensures that the particle velocities will shrink over time, rather than indefinitely growing to infinity. While the Constriction Coefficient PSO (CC-PSO) guarantees convergence to a stable point, there is no guarantee that this point is a quality point in the search space. Thus, Van der Berg, in 2002 [18], introduced the Guaranteed Convergent PSO (GC-PSO) to address this issue. Nonetheless, the effectiveness of the GC-PSO was only remarkable on unimodal optimization problems, rather than complex multimodal problems.

Among earlier attempts to better handle multimodal problems was the Species-based PSO (SPSO), proposed by Li in 2004 [11]. Although SPSO worked fairly well on multimodal function optimization using sub-swarm (or species), it was challenging to define the best species radius, especially for multimodal problems with little (or no) prior knowledge about their search space. A number of years later, Van den Bergh provided a formal convergence proof for PSO [19], and argued that the use of a multi-start strategy can potentially convert the PSO algorithm from a local to global optimizer, even on complex multi-modal optimization problems.

This paper is organized as follows: Section 2 provides a brief background on different stagnation detection methods used in the literature to restart PSO. Section 3 describes the proposed fitness-based stagnation detection method for PSO. Section 4 discusses the experimental results and observations. The last section concludes the study and suggests possible future work.

2. BACKGROUND

2.1 Stagnation Detection Methods

PSO stagnation, or premature convergence, issue occurs when the private experiences of the particles (or, their individual best positions) do not change relative to the swarm social experience (or, the global best position) for a number of iterations [3]. This critical issue vanishes the rate of position changes (or velocities) that attract particles to the global best position prematurely, making the swarm prone to being trapped into local optima, especially for deceptive multimodal optimization problems.

Different stagnation detection methods have been studied in the literature [21] to restart the search process of PSO, such as Maximum Swarm Radius, Cluster Analysis and Objective Function Slope [17]. The Maximum Swarm Radius method restarts the swarm when the most-distant particle from the global best particle reaches a predefined minimum distance, while the Cluster Analysis method restarts the swarm when the majority of swarm particles (e.g., >60%) reaches a predefined minimum distance from the global best particle. Both the Maximum Swarm Radius and Cluster Analysis are distance-based stagnation detection methods that check how close the particles are to the global best particle. The third method, Objective Function Slope, detects stagnation and restarts the swarm when the change rate in the objective function remains negligible for a predefined number of iterations. It has been claimed that distance-based methods outperform the Objective Function Slope method [7]; thus, the Maximum Swarm Radius method was adopted in Regrouping PSO [7], as well as in a number of other more recent studies [14; 23]. The main disadvantages, however, of the distance-based methods is that they are computationally expensive and dependent on the range of the search space [15].

On the contrary, the proposed stagnation detection method restarts particle positions and resets their velocity and memory using a criterion that is not based on the relative distances between particles and the global best particle to the problem search range (as in the Maximum Swarm Radius and Cluster Analysis methods), nor based on the change rate in the objective function (as in the Objective Function Slope method). Instead, the proposed method is based on the swarm-wide performance on the objective function with relative to the global best performance. That is why the proposed fitness-based method is more efficient and less dependent on the search range, compared with the commonly used distance-based methods for stagnation detection.

3. METHODOLOGY

The proposed stagnation detection method uses a more efficient fitness-based criterion to effectively trigger what we called the "Agile Restart" mechanism, as needed. In general, agility is the ability to change the body's position rapidly and efficiently as required, which is basically what the proposed "Agile Restart" attempts to accomplish when particles are trapped in a local optimum. The proposed method uses a Performance-based Stagnation Indicator (PSI) based on Average Swarm Fitness to define a potential stagnation situation to be imminent when the fitness of the global best particle becomes almost the same as the average fitness of the entire swarm, as shown in (1). The proposed fitness-based criterion has a computational advantage over the distance-based criterion of $O(nk)$ for a swarm of n particles in k number of iterations, since it makes use of the already calculated fitness values of swarm particles to trigger the restart mechanism, instead of calculating their pairwise distances at each iteration. Interestingly, the efficiency of the proposed criterion does not come at the cost of the solution quality. The proposed PSI criterion showed competitive results when compared with the distance-based Maximum Swarm Radius criterion, on several classical and advanced benchmark optimization functions.

$$f(P_g) \geq \psi * Average\,(f(P_i)) \quad (1)$$

Where: f is the objective (minimization) function, $f(P_i)$ is the corresponding fitness vector of particles' historically best positions, $f(P_g)$ is the fitness value of the global best particle position, and ψ is the *PSI threshold*, which is a positive percentage value defined by the user to adaptively control the restart mechanism. In particular, unlike some methods that reset the PSO algorithm every fixed K number of iterations [20], the proposed method does not trigger the restart mechanism according to some artificially fixed cycles of equal length; it is rather dynamically triggered (as needed) according to the '*run-time*' behaviour of the search process. The smaller the value of ψ, the more frequent the restart mechanism will be triggered. Thus, PSI value clearly affects the algorithm sensitivity to triggering the restart mechanism. It was empirically found that this approach works well when the PSI threshold is set between 90% for low-dimensional problems and 70% for high-dimensional problems. The reason why higher-dimensional problems generally require lower PSI threshold is because of the fact that the chance of stagnation situation usually increases as the problem dimensionality increases. It is perhaps worth mentioning that the proposed stagnation detection method was successfully applied to a real-life computational biology problem in our recent work [1].

4. RESULTS AND DISCUSSION

The proposed fitness-based stagnation detection method is tested on a set of 8 classical and advanced (shifted/rotated) benchmark optimization functions, and compared with the commonly used distance-based stagnation detection method on the same set of general optimization benchmarks. This set is sufficient to include various classes of optimization problems with different regularity, modality, separability and dimensionality [7; 22], such as Ackley, Griewank, Quadric, Rastrigin, Rosenbrock and Spherical functions [7], each at 3 to 30 dimensions. A function is called unimodal if it only has one global optimum with no local optima, whereas a function is called multimodal if it has more than one local optimum, besides at least one global optimum. A function of variables is called separable if it can be rewritten as a sum of functions of only a single variable [8].

Three performance evaluation metrics are considered in this experiment: 1) the achieved solution quality or the algorithm's effectiveness, 2) the search effort or the number of function evaluations required to reach the solution, and 3) the algorithm's efficiency, represented as the CPU time needed to reach the solution. It is worth emphasizing here that the goal of this experiment is not to compare two different Multi-Start PSOs (MPSOs) but to compare the effect of using the popular distance-based stagnation detection method with the proposed fitness-based method on any MPSO model. In this paper, an MPSO model based on the Constriction Coefficient PSO (CC-PSO) [4] was used for all of the comparisons. The performance was recorded over 50 independent runs (with different random seeds) per benchmark with a maximum of 800,000 function evaluations per run, using a swarm size of 20 and Clerc's constriction model with $\chi = 0.729$ and $c_1 = c_2 = 2.05$.

The first comparison metric that we considered in this experiment is the solution quality, or algorithm's effectiveness. We, therefore, performed the Wilcoxon rank-sum test [5], using Matlab statistical toolbox, to validate if (and when) the proposed fitness-based stagnation detection methods is significantly better performing (i.e., P-Value < 0.05, h=1 and Z-Score > 0) [13] than the commonly used distance-based stagnation detection method over the 50 conducted independent runs. Table 1 confirms that the proposed fitness-based method is indeed significantly better performing than the distance-based method, except for a few highlighted values in bold and red color (i.e., when Z-Score < 0 and P-Value < 0.05).

In particular, as shown in Table 1, the proposed fitness-based stagnation detection methods outperformed the distance-based method on most tested benchmark functions at lower dimensionality (n=3 and n=10), except for the Shifted Rosenbrock and Rotated Rastrigin functions. Nonetheless, while the proposed method achieved better performance (Z>0) in the classical Griewank function, the improved performance in this particular case (at n=10) is not, but almost, significantly validated at 95% confidence level (P = 0.0672). Concerning higher-dimensional problems (at n=30), the proposed method showed significantly better performance on unimodal functions, such as Quadric and Spherical functions. As for multimodal functions at higher dimensions (i.e., n=30), the proposed method showed overall better performance on Ackley and Shifted Rosenbrock, and showed significantly better performance on the Rotated Rastrigin benchmark.

The second comparison metric is the search effort or the number of function evaluations required to find the optimal solutions. The termination criterion of the search process is considered the sooner of reaching a maximum of 800,000 function evaluations per run, or reaching a 64-bit, double-precision value of zero, which is the global optimum on all tested benchmarks (except for the Shifted Rosenbrock function with a global optimum of 390). In our experiments, the proposed fitness-based method generally exhibited same or less search effort on most tested functions at different dimensionality. In particular, the proposed method remarkably exhibited less search effort on most tested benchmarks with n = 3 and 10, and fairly less search effort on Griewank and Classical Rastrigin with n =30. On the other hand, the commonly used distance-based method never achieved a better (i.e., fewer) number of function evaluations compared with the proposed fitness-based method (except for the low-dimensional Quadric function at n=3).

The third comparison metric is the algorithm's efficiency, represented as the CPU time needed to reach the solution (in seconds). All experiments were executed on a 2.20 GHz, 64-bit Core-i7 processor with 8 GB RAM. As shown in Figure 1, the CPU time is remarkably improved on the first 6 tested classical benchmarks at different dimensions. The improvement is generally stronger, however, in low-dimensional problems as opposed to high dimensional problems. The time improvement is particularly impressive for the Rastrigin, Quadric and Spherical functions. The average improvement on the first 6 classical benchmarks with low dimensionality (n = 3) is about 308%, which means PSO with Agile Restart is about 3 times faster than PSO with Distance-based Restart. It is also about 203% faster for n = 10 and 121% faster for n=30, on average.

As for the advanced (shifted/rotated) benchmarks [12; 24], we observed a slight time improvement, but not as substantial as the time improvement for the 6 tested classical benchmarks, as shown in Figure 1. The aggregated average time improvement on all 8 tested benchmarks became 238%, 159%, and 117% for n = 3, 10 and 30, respectively. This considerable CPU time improvement was expected, as discussed earlier, due to the fact that the proposed fitness-based method does not require the time consuming process of calculating pairwise distances between all particles and the global best. Instead, the stagnation is detected using the Average Swarm Fitness criterion, making use of the already calculated fitness values for each particle. Replacing distance-based criterion with the proposed fitness-based criterion can, therefore, be used to increase the computation speed for any Multi-Start PSO algorithm (MPSO) that uses Maximum Swarm Radius, such as RegPSO [7], which showed rather slow performance when recently applied to data clustering [15].

Table 1. Wilcoxon Rank-Sum Significance Test Results

Dimensions	*n = 3*		*n = 10*		*n = 30*	
Significance	P	Z (h)	P	Z (h)	P	Z (h)
Ackley	3.31E-20	9.21 (1)	4.73E-20	9.17 (1)	3.03E-01	1.03 (0)
Griewank	6.64E-04	3.40 (1)	6.72E-02	1.83 (0)	5.14E-09	-5.84 (1)
Quadric	1.69E-18	8.78 (1)	5.26E-19	8.91 (1)	7.07E-18	8.61 (1)
Rastrigin	1.85E-13	7.36 (1)	3.31E-20	9.21 (1)	1.33E-03	-3.21 (1)
Rosenbrock	2.75E-18	8.72 (1)	2.37E-06	4.72 (1)	7.49E-01	-0.32 (0)
Spherical	2.06E-17	8.49 (1)	3.31E-20	9.21 (1)	7.07E-18	8.61 (1)
Rotated Rastrigin	8.40E-01	0.20 (0)	5.06E-01	-0.67 (0)	1.58E-09	6.04 (1)
Shifted Rosenbrock	1.05E-06	-4.88 (1)	1.74E-15	-7.96 (1)	2.16E-01	1.24 (0)

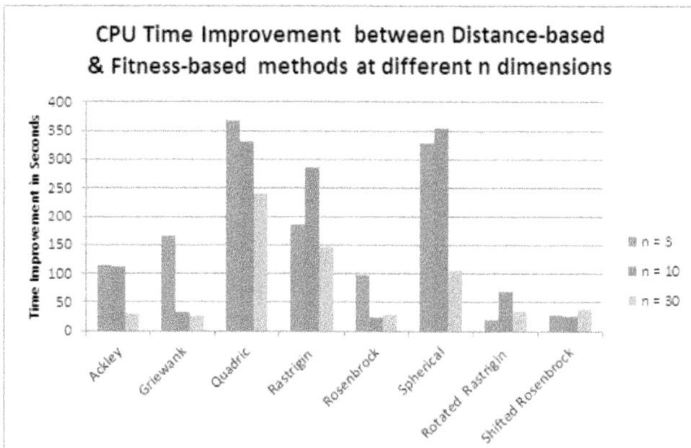

Figure 1. The run-time improvement between the proposed fitness-based (Agile) restart and the popular distance-based restart is up to three times better, on average.

5. CONCLUSIONS

This paper addresses the popular premature convergence issue of PSO by restarting particle positions and resetting their velocities and memories when an imminent stagnation situation is detected, using a novel stagnation detection method. The proposed stagnation detection method uses a more efficient fitness-based criterion to effectively trigger what we called the "Agile Restart" mechanism, as needed, by collectively incorporating the fitness performances of the swarm relative to the objective function, and comparing the Average Swarm Fitness with the global best fitness. The proposed fitness-based criterion has a computational advantage over the distance-based criterion of $O(nk)$ for a swarm of n particles in k number of iterations. This is because it makes use of the already calculated fitness values of each particle to trigger the restart mechanism without the overhead of calculating all pairwise distances between particles and the global best at each iteration.

Interestingly, the efficiency of the proposed fitness-based criterion did not come at the cost of the solution quality. The proposed stagnation detection method demonstrated superior solution quality (compared with the commonly used distance-based method) on most tested optimization benchmarks, verifying not only a significantly better, but also a remarkably more efficient performance. The significance of the performance comparison results over 50 independent runs was validated by the Wilcoxon rank-sum test at 95% confidence level.

The performance comparison between the distance-based method and the fitness-based stagnation detection methods was conducted at low-to-moderate dimensionality that ranges from 3 to 30, on a test set of 8 general optimization benchmarks. It is therefore planned for our future work to carry out further verification simulations on a more comprehensive set of benchmarks at even higher dimensions (i.e., greater than 30).

6. REFERENCES

[1] Ahmed, H.R. and Glasgow, J.I., 2014. An Improved Multi-Start Particle Swarm-based Algorithm for Protein Structure Comparison. In *Proceedings of the 2014 Genetic and Evolutionary Computation Conference (GECCO 2014)* (Vancouver, Canada 2014).

[2] Clerc, M., 1999. The swarm and the queen: towards a deterministic and adaptive particle swarm optimization. In *Evolutionary Computation, 1999. CEC 99. Proceedings of the 1999 Congress on* IEEE, Washington, DC.

[3] Clerc, M., 2006. Stagnation analysis in particle swarm optimisation or what happens when nothing happens. *HAL : hal-00122031, version 1.*

[4] Clerc, M. and Kennedy, J., 2002. The particle swarm-explosion, stability, and convergence in a multidimensional complex space. *Evolutionary Computation, IEEE Transactions on 6*, 1, 58-73.

[5] Derrac, J., García, S., Molina, D., and Herrera, F., 2011. A practical tutorial on the use of nonparametric statistical tests as a methodology for comparing evolutionary and swarm intelligence algorithms. *Swarm and Evolutionary Computation 1*, 1, 3-18.

[6] Eberhart, R.C. and Shi, Y., 2000. Comparing inertia weights and constriction factors in particle swarm optimization. In *Evolutionary Computation, 2000. Proceedings of the 2000 Congress on* IEEE, La Jolla, CA, 84-88.

[7] Evers, G.I. and Ben Ghalia, M., 2009. Regrouping particle swarm optimization: a new global optimization algorithm with improved performance consistency across benchmarks. In *Systems, Man and Cybernetics, 2009. SMC 2009. IEEE International Conference on* IEEE, 3901-3908.

[8] Hadley, G., 1964. *Nonlinear and Dynamic Programming*. Addison-Wesley.

[9] Kennedy, J., 1997. The particle swarm: social adaptation of knowledge. In *Evolutionary Computation, 1997., IEEE International Conference on* IEEE, 303-308.

[10] Kennedy, J. and Eberhart, R., 1995. Particle swarm optimization. In *Neural Networks, 1995. Proceedings., IEEE International Conference on* IEEE, 1942-1948.

[11] Li, X., 2004. Adaptively choosing neighbourhood bests using species in a particle swarm optimizer for multimodal function optimization. In *GECCO 2004* Springer, 105-116.

[12] Liang, J., Qu, B., Suganthan, P., and Hernández-Díaz, A.G., 2013. Problem Definitions and Evaluation Criteria for the CEC 2013 Special Session on Real-Parameter Optimization. *Technical Report, Computational Intelligence Laboratory, Zhengzhou University.*

[13] Lu, H. and Chen, X., 2011. A new particle swarm optimization with a dynamic inertia weight for solving constrained optimization problems. *Information Technology Journal 10*, 8, 1536-1544.

[14] Mitchell, Y., Ardi, H., and Hung, N., 2011. Optimization of head movement recognition using augmented radial basis function neural network. In *the IEEE conf. on Engineering in Medicine and Biology Society*, Boston, MA, 2776-2779.

[15] Moulton, B., Yuwono, M., Nguyen, H., and Su, S., 2012. Method for increasing the computation speed of an unsupervised learning approach for data clustering. In *CEC 2012* IEEE, Brisbane, Australia.

[16] Poli, R., 2007. An analysis of publications on particle swarm optimization applications. *Technical Report, Department of Computer Science, University of Essex, UK.*

[17] Van Den Bergh, F., 2002. An analysis of particle swarm optimizers. PhD Thesis, Department of Computer Science, University of Pretoria, South Africa.

[18] Van Den Bergh, F. and Engelbrecht, A., 2002. A new locally convergent particle swarm optimizer. In *Proceedings of the IEEE Conf on systems, man, and cybernetics*, 96-101.

[19] Van Den Bergh, F. and Engelbrecht, A.P., 2010. A convergence proof for the particle swarm optimiser. *Fundamenta Informaticae 105*, 4, 341-374.

[20] Vargas, Y.N. and Chen, S., 2010. Particle swarm optimization with resets–improving the balance between exploration and exploitation. In *Advances in Soft Computing* Springer, 371-381.

[21] Worasucheep, C., 2008. A particle swarm optimization with stagnation detection and dispersion. In *Evolutionary Computation, CEC 2008.* IEEE, 424-429.

[22] Yang, X.S., 2010. Appendix A: Test Problems in Optimization. In *Engineering Optimization* John Wiley & Sons, 261-266.

[23] Yuwono, M., Su, S., and Moulton, B., 2011. Fall detection using a Gaussian distribution of clustered knowledge, augmented radial basis neural-network, and multilayer perceptron. In *Broadband and Biomedical Communications (IB2Com), 6th International Conference on* IEEE, 145-150.

[24] Zhan, Z.-H., Zhang, J., Li, Y., and Shi, Y.-H., 2011. Orthogonal learning particle swarm optimization. *Evolutionary Computation, IEEE Trans on 15*, 6, 832-847.

Selecting Evolutionary Operators using Reinforcement Learning: Initial Explorations

Arina Buzdalova
ITMO University
49 Kronverkskiy prosp.
Saint-Petersburg, Russia
abuzdalova@gmail.com

Vladislav Kononov
ITMO University
49 Kronverkskiy prosp.
Saint-Petersburg, Russia
kononov@rain.ifmo.ru

Maxim Buzdalov
ITMO University
49 Kronverkskiy prosp.
Saint-Petersburg, Russia
mbuzdalov@gmail.com

ABSTRACT

In evolutionary optimization, it is important to use efficient evolutionary operators, such as mutation and crossover. But it is often difficult to decide, which operator should be used when solving a specific optimization problem. So an automatic approach is needed. We propose an adaptive method of selecting evolutionary operators, which takes a set of possible operators as input and learns what operators are efficient for the considered problem. One evolutionary algorithm run should be enough for both learning and obtaining suitable performance. The proposed EA+RL(O) method is based on reinforcement learning. We test it by solving H-IFF and Travelling Salesman optimization problems. The obtained results show that the proposed method significantly outperforms random selection, since it manages to select efficient evolutionary operators and ignore inefficient ones.

Categories and Subject Descriptors

I.2.6 [**Artificial Intelligence**]: Learning

General Terms

Algorithms, Experimentation

Keywords

evolutionary algorithms; parameter control

1. INTRODUCTION

Evolutionary operators such as mutation and crossover are used to generate offsprings. Operators influence the performance of an algorithm a lot [8]. Choosing the best operator manually is resource and time consuming, so automation is needed. There are different techniques of adjusting evolutionary algorithms [4], including methods for adjusting and modifying of operators, but there is no the most efficient one. Therefore, a new method of adjusting evolutionary algorithm by choosing evolutionary operators is of interest.

GECCO'14, July 12–16, 2014, Vancouver, BC, Canada.

ACM 978-1-4503-2881-4/14/07 ...$15.00.
http://dx.doi.org/10.1145/2598394.2605681.

Reinforcement learning is usually used to adjust some numerical parameters of evolutionary algorithms, such as mutation rate or population size [3, 9, 11]. To the best of our knowledge, there is only one method of selecting operators with reinforcement learning [10]. One of the most important differences between the method we propose and this one is that we apply the selected operator to the whole population, while in the method described in [10] an operator is chosen separately for each individual. We also applied simpler definitions of states and reward, which are needed for reinforcement learning.

In our previous works, we proposed the EA+RL method of extra fitness function selection based on reinforcement learning [2]. The method was shown to be efficient, both empirically (for a number of problems, including a real-world application [1]) and theoretically (for a model OneMax problem [2]). Thus in this paper we propose a method of evolutionary operators selection based on our previous ideas, which seems to be promising.

2. METHOD DESCRIPTION

It is assumed that there is a finite set of evolutionary operators consisting of mutation and crossover operators. It is unknown which operators are the most efficient ones, this information should be learned by the reinforcement learning agent (an efficient operator allows to optimize the fitness function in a less number of generations). The agent chooses an operator and the next population of the evolutionary algorithm is generated. Then an *immediate* numerical *reward*, as well as some representation of the algorithm *state*, are returned to the agent. The agent updates its estimations with the new values and the process repeats.

The scheme of the described method is shown in Fig. 1. The proposed method is similar to the previously proposed EA+RL, but here an evolutionary operator is selected instead of an extra fitness function. Thus let us call the newly proposed method EA+RL(O), where "O" stands for "operator".

The reward is calculated as the difference of the best individual fitness in a two consequent generations of the evolutionary algorithm. We used different states definitions for different problems, they are described later in the corresponding sections.

In reinforcement learning algorithms, the agent learns to perform such actions, that maximize the total reward, which is proportional to the sum of all immediate rewards [5, 13]. So in the proposed method the operators that maximize the fitness function should be selected eventually. In other

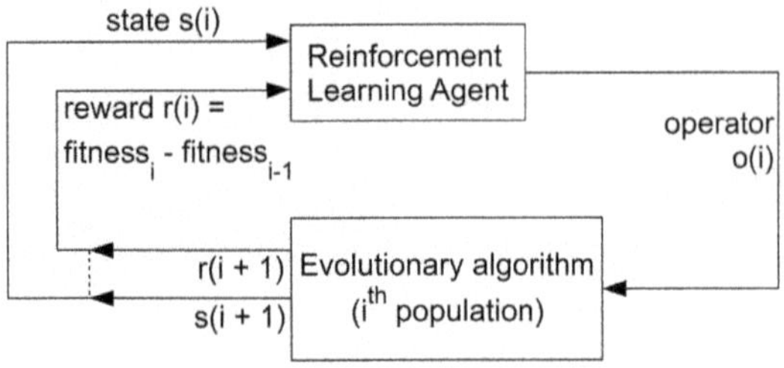

Figure 1: Scheme of the proposed EA+RL(O) method

words, the most efficient operators should be selected, since the goal of an evolutionary algorithm is the fitness function optimization.

3. EXPERIMENT 1: H-IFF OPTIMIZATION PROBLEM

In this section the first problem solved using the proposed method is described. It is a model problem called Hierarchical-if-and-only-if function (H-IFF), which is often used to test genetic algorithms [6, 14].

3.1 Problem Description

Consider the H-IFF optimization problem. The search space consists of bit strings of a fixed length l. The function takes a bit string $B = b_1b_2 \dots b_l$ as an argument and interprets it as a binary tree of string blocks. The root of the tree is the input string itself, and the siblings are the left (B_L) and the right (B_R) halves of their parental blocks. The fitness function f is a sum of lengths of those blocks that consist of equally valued bits. Its recursive formula is given below. Notice that there are two possible optima in this problem. One optimum is a string of 0-bits and another is a string of 1-bits.

$$f(B) = \begin{cases} 1 & \text{if } |B| = 1, \text{ else} \\ |B| + f(B_L) + f(B_R) & \text{if } \forall i\{b_i = 0\} \text{ or } \forall i\{b_i = 1\} \\ f(B_L) + f(B_R) & \text{otherwise} \end{cases}$$

3.2 State definition

Consider a string block $B_{\max}$ that consists of equal valued bits (all zeros or all ones) and has the maximal length among all other such blocks in the current population. The state of the evolutionary algorithm used in the reinforcement learning algorithm is calculated as $\log_2 B_{\max}$.

3.3 Evolutionary Operators

The following operators are used in the evolutionary algorithm optimizing H-IFF:

- inversion mutation: a one random bit of an individual is inverted;
- tail inversion mutation: all the bits after a random position in an individual are inverted;
- obstructive mutation: an individual is replaced with the 010101…01 string;
- two-point crossover: a segment of a random length is chosen at random, then the corresponding bits of parents are swapped;
- hybrid crossover: each bit of the first parent are replaced with the corresponding bit of the second parent with some probability (we used probability of 0.5).

Applying the *obstructive* mutation operator decreases the fitness function. This operator is included in the set of operators in order to demonstrate that the proposed EA+RL(O) method is able to ignore inefficient operators. The inversion mutation is expected to be less powerful than the tail inversion one, because the former inverts just one bit. Thus it should be checked that EA+RL(O) selects inversion mutation less frequently.

3.4 Experiment Description

During the experiment, the EA+RL(O) algorithm was run 101 times with the obstructive operator included, as well as with the obstructive operator excluded for the same number of times. An evolutionary algorithm with a random operator selection was also run for 101 times in order to compare it with the proposed method. The length of an individual was 64 bits, hence the maximal possible fitness value was 448. In each run, the evolutionary algorithm was stopped when the maximal possible fitness value was reached. There were 100 individuals in a generation. The probability of applying an operator was 100% in all cases. To perform a crossover, the tournament selection of one tour was used, the probability of selecting the fitter individual was 90%. The Q-learning algorithm with softmax and ε-greedy ($\varepsilon = 0.1$) exploration strategies [13] was used as the reinforcement learning algorithm.

3.5 Experiment Results

The average number of generations needed to obtain the maximal possible value of H-IFF function using considered algorithms is shown in Table 1. One can conclude, that using EA+RL(O) allows to maximize H-IFF in less number of generations than a random strategy does. According to the one-way ANOVA test we have performed [12], p-value for the EA+RL(O) and random selection was less than 5×10^{-4}, so they are statistically distinguishable.

It is also important to notice that EA+RL(O) successfully handles the obstructive operator case. The number of generations needed to optimize H-IFF in the presence of the obstructive operator is comparable to the number of generations needed when there is no obstructive operator.

Table 1: Average number of generations needed to obtain the maximal possible H-IFF value

Algorithm	Generations in average	Deviation
Without the obstructive operator		
EA+RL(O), softmax	801.8	298.1
EA+RL(O), ε-greedy	850.0	292.4
Random operator selection	1295.7	454.7
With the obstructive operator		
EA+RL(O), softmax	863.8	277.1
EA+RL(O), ε-greedy	890.6	308.0
Random operator selection	1654.2	478.8

In Fig. 2 the number of times when the operator was selected is shown for each operator. As expected, EA+RL(O) selects the obstructive operator for the least number of times.

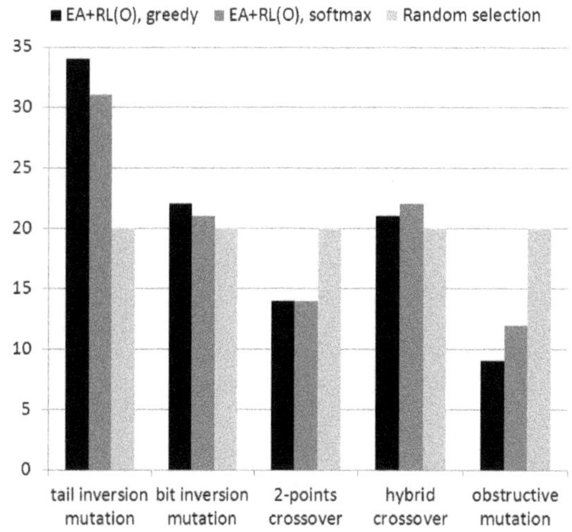

Figure 2: Number of times each operator was selected, %

It also selects the tail inversion mutation more often than the less powerful inversion mutation. Random selection chooses each operator equiprobably, which leads to worse performance of the evolutionary algorithm.

4. EXPERIMENT 2: TRAVELLING SALESMAN PROBLEM

Consider another optimization problem. Let us test the proposed EA+RL(O) method by solving the Travelling Salesman Problem (TSP), which is NP-hard [7]. We consider it as a problem of finding a Hamiltonian cycle with minimal weight in a fully connected weighted graph. Therefore this is a minimization problem.

4.1 State Definition

The state used in the reinforcement learning algorithm is represented as a vector of values, those are listed below.

- Population number interval. Numbers of generations are split in four intervals: $[0 \dots 400)$, $[400 \dots 1600)$, $[1600 \dots 3200)$, $[3200 \dots 6400)$ and the number of a current interval is put in the first position of the vector.
- Fitness function interval. The fitness of the best individual in the current population is divided by the fitness of the best individual in the initial population. This value can belong to a one of the following intervals: $[0, 0.2)$, $[0.2, 0.5)$, $[0.5, 0.8)$, $[0.8, 1]$. The number of the corresponding interval is put in the second position of the vector.

Notice that, if we replace the numerical values mentioned above with parameters, this state is problem-independent, thus can be used for solving any problem with EA+RL(O) method. Concept of this state is close to the one proposed in [10].

4.2 Evolutionary operators

In our approach, an individual is a correct permutation of vertices. All the considered operators preserve the correctness. The operators are as follows:

- inversion mutation: the order of vertices is inverted starting from a randomly chosen position;
- shuffle mutation: vertices are shuffled starting from a randomly chosen position;
- swapping mutation: two randomly chosen vertices are swapped;
- one-point match crossover with repair [7];
- two-point match crossover with repair [7].

4.3 Experiment Description

Five fully connected graphs of 80 vertices with edge weights from 0 to 100 were randomly generated. Then both an evolutionary algorithm with random operator selection and EA+RL(O) were run on these graphs for 100 times each. The algorithms were stopped after 6400 generations were evolved. There were 100 individuals in a generation. The probability of applying an operator was 100% in all cases. To perform a crossover, the tournament selection of one tour was used, the probability of selecting the fitter individual was 90%. As the reinforcement learning algorithm, the Q-learning algorithm with softmax and ε-greedy ($\varepsilon = 0.1$) exploration strategies was used [13].

4.4 Experiment Results

In Table 2 the best fitness in the final generation averaged over all the algorithm runs is shown. It can be seen that EA+RL(O) outperforms the evolutionary algorithm with random selection of operators. According to the one-way ANOVA test we performed [12], p-value for the EA+RL(O) and random selection is less than 5×10^{-4}, so they are statistically distinguishable.

Table 2: Average best fitness of TSP obtained in the final generation

Algorithm	Best fitness in average	Deviation
EA+RL(O), ε-greedy	1304.2	73.9
EA+RL(O), softmax	1323.9	69.8
Random operator selection	1436.0	68.4

In Fig. 3 the number of times when the operator was selected is shown for each operator. It can be assumed that the proposed EA+RL(O) algorithm selects the efficient operators more often than less efficient ones, since it outperforms random selection. Random selection chooses each operator equiprobably, which leads to worse performance of the evolutionary algorithm.

In Fig. 4 fitness optimization until the 9600 generations limit is shown. One can conclude that EA+RL(O) outperforms random selection during almost all optimization process.

5. CONCLUSION

A new EA+RL(O) method of adaptive selection between evolutionary operators using reinforcement learning is proposed. The method is aimed to enhance the performance of an evolutionary algorithm by selecting efficient operators from a set of ones. EA+RL(O) is based on the previously

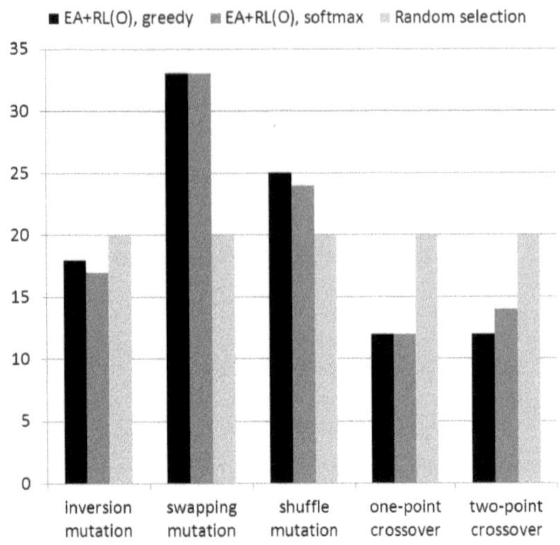

Figure 3: Number of times each operator was selected, %

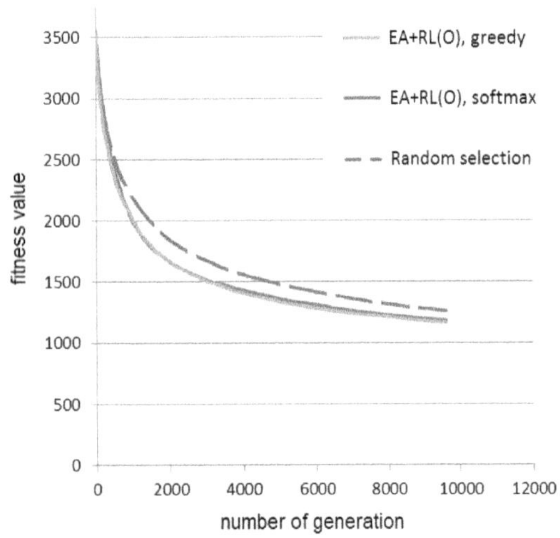

Figure 4: TSP fitness minimization

proposed EA+RL method used for selection between fitness functions. The proposed method was tested on two optimization problems. In both cases, it significantly outperformed random selection. Future work includes testing the proposed method on a wider range of problems, as well as obtaining its runtime analysis. It is also important to compare it with some other methods of evolutionary algorithms adjusting.

6. ACKNOWLEDGMENTS

This work was partially financially supported by the Government of Russian Federation, Grant 074-U01.

7. REFERENCES

[1] M. Buzdalov, A. Buzdalova, and I. Petrova. Generation of Tests for Programming Challenge Tasks Using Multi-Objective Optimization. In C. Blum and E. Alba, editors, *GECCO (Companion)*, pages 1655–1658. ACM, 2013.

[2] M. Buzdalov, A. Buzdalova, and A. Shalyto. A First Step towards the Runtime Analysis of Evolutionary Algorithm Adjusted with Reinforcement Learning. In *Proceedings of the International Conference on Machine Learning and Applications*, volume 1, pages 203–208. IEEE Computer Society, 2013.

[3] A. E. Eiben, M. Horvath, W. Kowalczyk, and M. C. Schut. Reinforcement learning for online control of evolutionary algorithms. In *Proceedings of the 4th international conference on Engineering self-organising systems ESOA'06*, pages 151–160. Springer-Verlag, Berlin, Heidelberg, 2006.

[4] A. E. Eiben, Z. Michalewicz, M. Schoenauer, and J. E. Smith. Parameter control in evolutionary algorithms. In *Parameter Setting in Evolutionary Algorithms*, pages 19–46. 2007.

[5] L. P. Kaelbling, M. L. Littman, and A. W. Moore. Reinforcement Learning: A Survey. *Journal of Artificial Intelligence Research*, 4:237–285, 1996.

[6] J. D. Knowles, R. A. Watson, and D. Corne. Reducing local optima in single-objective problems by multi-objectivization. In *Proceedings of the First International Conference on Evolutionary Multi-Criterion Optimization*, EMO '01, pages 269–283, London, UK, 2001. Springer-Verlag.

[7] P. Larrañaga, C. M. H. Kuijpers, R. H. Murga, I. Inza, and S. Dizdarevic. Genetic algorithms for the travelling salesman problem: A review of representations and operators. *Artif. Intell. Rev.*, 13(2):129–170, Apr. 1999.

[8] M. Mitchell. *An Introduction to Genetic Algorithms*. MIT Press, Cambridge, MA, 1996.

[9] S. Müller, N. N. Schraudolph, and P. D. Koumoutsakos. Step size adaptation in evolution strategies using reinforcement learning. In *Proceedings of the Congress on Evolutionary Computation*, pages 151–156. IEEE, 2002.

[10] J. E. Pettinger and R. M. Everson. Controlling genetic algorithms with reinforcement learning. In *Proceedings of the Genetic and Evolutionary Computation Conference*, GECCO '02, page 692, San Francisco, CA, USA, 2002. Morgan Kaufmann Publishers Inc.

[11] Y. Sakurai, K. Takada, T. Kawabe, and S. Tsuruta. A method to control parameters of evolutionary algorithms by using reinforcement learning. In *Signal-Image Technology and Internet-Based Systems (SITIS), 2010 Sixth International Conference on*, pages 74–79, 2010.

[12] D. S. Soper. Analysis of variance (anova) calculator - one-way anova from summary data [software], 2014.

[13] R. S. Sutton and A. G. Barto. *Reinforcement Learning: An Introduction*. MIT Press, Cambridge, MA, USA, 1998.

[14] R. A. Watson and J. B. Pollack. Analysis of recombinative algorithms on a hierarchical building-block problem. in foundations of genetic algorithms. *Foundations of Genetic Algorithms (FOGA)*, 2000.

Improving the Quality of Supervised Finite-State Machine Construction Using Real-Valued Variables

Igor Buzhinsky, Daniil Chivilikhin, Vladimir Ulyantsev, Fedor Tsarev
ITMO University
Computer Technologies Laboratory
Saint Petersburg, Russia
{buzhinsky, chivdan, ulyantsev, tsarev}@rain.ifmo.ru

ABSTRACT

The use of finite-state machines (FSMs) is a reliable choice for control system design since they can be formally verified. In this paper a problem of constructing FSMs with real-valued input and control parameters is considered. It is supposed that a set of human-created behavior examples, or tests, is available. One of the earlier approaches for solving the problem suggested using genetic algorithms together with a transition labeling algorithm. This paper improves this approach via the use of real-valued variables which are calculated using the FSM's input data. FSMs with real-valued variables are represented as systems of linear controllers. The new approach allows to synthesize FSMs of better quality than it was possible earlier.

Categories and Subject Descriptors

I.2.2 [**Artificial Intelligence**]: Automatic Programming—*Program synthesis*

Keywords

Finite-State Machine; Finite-State Machine Construction; Ant Colony Optimization

1. INTRODUCTION

In this paper we deal with the problem of test-based finite-state machine (FSM) [10] construction for controlling objects in complex environments. The use of behavior examples, or tests, is reasonable when it is difficult to formalize the desired system behavior. Finite-state machines are widely used in the development of reactive systems [8,9] and can be easily verified using the *Model Checking* [6] approach, which allows to check whether some temporal properties are satisfied for them. The ease of FSM verification, which is the main advantage of their application, contributes to their ability to be the components of reliable software. FSMs can also be used as models of existing software systems [16].

GECCO'14, July 12–16, 2014, Vancouver, BC, Canada.
Copyright 2014 ACM 978-1-4503-2881-4/14/07 ...$15.00.
http://dx.doi.org/10.1145/2598394.2605679.

Manual FSM construction is usually hard. For example, the optimal FSM for the Artificial Ant problem [11] was found only using automated FSM synthesis [15] with genetic algorithms [11]. Genetic algorithms and other search optimization techniques require a fitness function, a measure of the solution quality, to be defined. There are two approaches for FSM fitness function definition. One approach, which often leads to huge time requirements, is to model FSM execution in a simulated environment [14]. In [2], another approach, which suggested using a computationally cheap test-based fitness function, was applied for searching FSMs capable of controlling an aircraft model. FSMs in [2] were equipped with real-valued output actions which were assigned automatically given the transition function of an FSM. This approach is model-free and thus is applicable for various controlled objects.

Model-based approaches are also known for similar problems. One of such approaches [1], which does not use FSMs and is mostly based on machine learning techniques, was developed for the autonomous helicopter control and suggested finding a hidden trajectory which is implicitly encoded in tests. Another approach [13] allows to create correct-by-design finite-state controllers.

In this paper the approach suggested in [2] is improved. The same controlled object as in [2], an aircraft model, is used. This paper suggests a way to construct FSMs with better correspondence to tests, which remains computationally inexpensive and model-free. A key feature of the proposed method is the use of so-called real-valued variables as inputs for FSMs.

In section 2 we formally describe the problem being solved. Section 3 describes the FSM construction method used in this paper. Finally, in section 4 the experimental evaluation of the method is presented.

2. PROBLEM STATEMENT

An FSM is a sextuple $(S, s_0, E, A, \delta, \lambda)$ where S is a finite set of states, $s_0 \in S$ is a start state, E is a set of input events, A is a set of output actions, $\delta : S \times E \to S$ is a transition function, and λ is an output function ($\lambda : S \times E \to A$ for Mealy machines and $\lambda : S \to A$ for Moore machines). An FSM execution is a sequence of cycles: on each cycle the FSM receives an input event, generates an output action according to λ and changes its active state according to δ. In this paper the cycles are equally spaced in time with an interval of 0.1 seconds. The way how FSMs deal with real-valued inputs and outputs will be explained later.

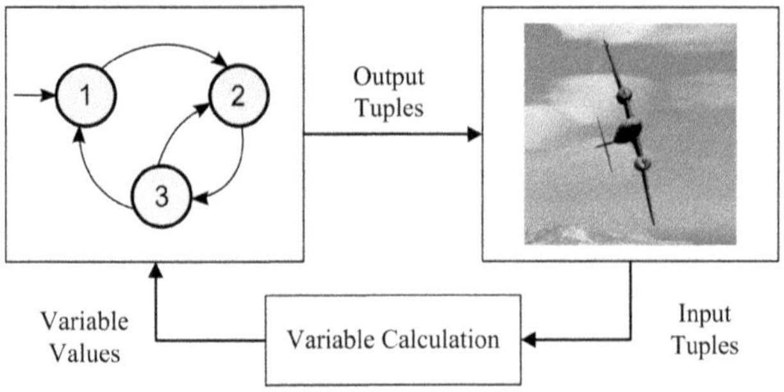

Figure 1: Aircraft control procedure

Consider a finite set of tests which describe the proper behavior of the controlled object. Informally, a test consists of the input data describing the object's state at different timestamps and the output data which shows how the object should be controlled. Tests are obtained from a human expert. The problem is to construct an FSM with a behavior close to the one recorded in the tests.

From now on, we will focus on the unmanned aircraft control problem. The *FlightGear* flight simulator (`http://www.flightgear.org/`) is used for test recording and FSM execution. The input part of the tests consists of flight parameters: altitude, airspeed, etc. The output part is formed by aircraft control device (elevator, ailerons, etc.) positions characterized by real values, which will be referred to as control parameters.

2.1 Control Procedure

An *input tuple* is a sequence of P real numbers $(i_1, ..., i_P)$. Applied to the problem under consideration, each number corresponds to one of the flight parameters of the unmanned aircraft. The controlled object also has C control parameters. They are of two types: discrete (e.g. starter position), which have finite domains, and continuous, or real-valued ones (e.g. rudder position). For instance, the rudder position from the leftmost to the rightmost can be described by values from $[-1, 1]$. From now on, we will assume that all control parameters are continuous.

An *output tuple* $(o_1, ..., o_C)$ is a snapshot of all C control parameters at some timestamp. As the control parameters are bounded, for each parameter i and for each output tuple o there exist $c_i^{\min}$ and $c_i^{\max}$ such that $c_i^{\min} \le o_i \le c_i^{\max}$.

At the beginning of each cycle the FSM receives an input tuple. After that, *variable* values are calculated. Variables are functions of input tuples and their history. For instance, a variable can transform the aircraft's altitude to its derivative or to its square, or it can just return the altitude untransformed. A specific class of variables, predicates, have Boolean domain. The statement "altitude is decreasing" is an example of a predicate. Variable values determine the FSM's output actions on the current cycle and its new state. The scheme of the control procedure is shown in Fig. 1.

2.2 Tests

Tests describe tasks (e.g. aerobatic figures) an unmanned aircraft is desired to perform. Denote the length of the i-th test in a test set ($1 \le i \le N$, where N is the number of tests) as $\text{len}[i]$. It is equal to the number of timestamps recorded in a test. The difference between the recorded timestamps is equal to the cycle length (0.1 s). Test i is formed by two sequences. The input sequence, $\text{in}[i]$, consists of input tuples $\text{in}[i, t]$, where t ($1 \le t \le \text{len}[i]$) is the time in cycles. The output sequence, $\text{out}[i]$, consists of output tuples $\text{out}[i, t]$.

3. PROPOSED APPROACH

In this section the proposed improvement of the method [2] is described. The general scheme of the used approach does not differ significantly from the one from [2]: FSM search is based on metaheuristics, and the individuals are FSMs with undefined output functions, or *skeletons*. The output function is derived automatically for each individual.

The main novelty of the proposed approach involves representing FSMs as systems of linear controllers. The fitness function was also modified to simplify the search of visually simpler FSMs with clearly distinct states. Instead of a genetic algorithm applied in [2], we use an ant colony optimization (ACO) [7] algorithm suggested in [5]. It has some benefits in computational effort on the considered problem [3] and does not require to define a crossover operator.

3.1 FSM Representation

The previous approach [2] for the problem considered in this paper only allowed to construct FSMs which used predicates, or Boolean variables, for output action generation. This led to the impossibility of inferring smooth control laws. The presence of the issue has been tested experimentally: the aircraft model under control of such FSMs was unable to perform a 180° turn in the horizontal plane.

We use a new method of FSM representation which involves both predicates and real-valued variables. Predicates are only used as transition conditions. Consider a set of predicates $p_1, ..., p_m$. In each state only several of them are *significant*: for each state $s \in S$ and a combination of significant predicate values in s, a transition is defined. To encode such data in individuals, a Boolean mask defining which predicates are significant, and a transition table are stored for each state (assume that $|S|$ is fixed during optimization). This *reduced table* approach was suggested in [14].

Oppositely, real-valued variables are only used for output generation. For each control parameter j consider a set of real-valued variables $v_{j,1}, ..., v_{j,n_j}$. Each state $s \in S$ defines a controller for each control parameter, which uses the corresponding variable values as inputs. The controllers were chosen to be linear to make the automatic derivation of the output function simple. Assume u_j is the j-th control parameter value and s is the current state, then on each cycle the change of u_j is calculated according to the formula:

$$\Delta u_j = \sum_{i=1}^{n_j} r_{s,i,j} v_{j,i}. \tag{1}$$

Real-valued variables, as well as predicates, are to be defined before the optimization, but the numbers $r_{s,i,j}$ are chosen automatically. Firstly, some of the variables are actually not used in some states (for each control parameter a significance mask for real-valued variables is also stored), so the corresponding $r_{s,i,j}$ are equal to zero. The use of significance masks for both types of variables makes the proposed FSM representation scalable for large values of m and $n_1, ..., n_C$. The remaining coefficients are set to maximize the fitness function for a given skeleton.

An example of a transition diagram of a three-state FSM (in case of a single control parameter u) is shown in Fig. 2.

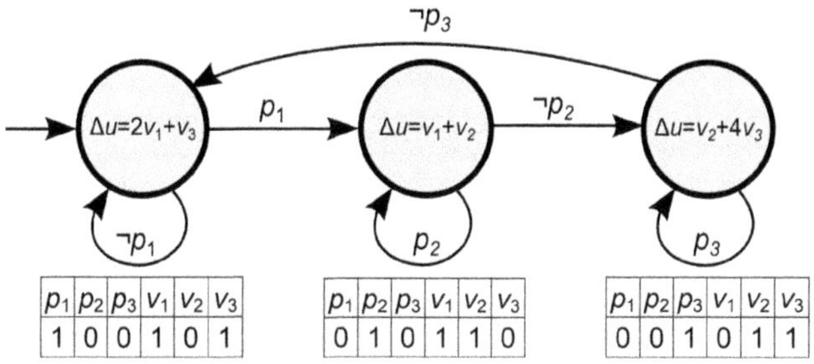

Figure 2: A transition diagram of an FSM

3.2 Fitness Function

Assume ans$[i]$ is the output tuple sequence generated by a fixed FSM in response to in$[i]$. To measure FSM behavior quality on a single test, the following distance between the output sequences is considered:

$$\rho\left(\text{ans}[i], \text{out}[i]\right) = \sqrt{\frac{1}{\text{len}[i]} \sum_{t=1}^{\text{len}[i]} \frac{1}{C} \sum_{j=1}^{C} \left(\frac{\text{ans}[i,t]_j - \text{out}[i,t]_j}{c_j^{\max} - c_j^{\min}} \right)^2}$$

Another measure we found to be essential is the number of times an FSM changes its state during the execution on tests. When this number is large, it is usually difficult to assign intuitive meanings to different states. The values $\max(\tau_i - |S| + 1, 0)$, where τ_i is the number of state changes on test i, can serve as additional penalties. The described distances and penalties for different tests can be combined:

$$P_\rho = \sqrt{\frac{1}{N} \sum_{i=1}^{N} \rho^2(\text{ans}[i], \text{out}[i])},$$

$$P_\tau = \sqrt{\frac{1}{N} \sum_{i=1}^{N} (\max(\tau_i - |S| + 1, 0))^2}.$$

Finally, the fitness function f is defined in the following way:

$$f = 1 - P_\rho - K \cdot P_\tau,$$

where K is a small number (we used $K = 0.00015$). A fitness function similar to f, but which did not include the transition penalties P_τ, was used in [2].

A so-called transition labeling algorithm was used in [2] to automatically derive the output functions of FSMs to maximize the fitness function. A similar approach was developed for the presented FSM representation. We omit the math, which partly repeats the one from [2], and only present the result: the problem of maximizing f is reduced to solving C systems of linear equations. To compute a single system's matrix, $O\left(M_j^2 \sum_{i=1}^{N} \text{len}[i]\right)$ time is required, where M_j is the number of non-zero values $r_{s,i,j}$ (for a fixed j). Then each system can be solved in $O(M_j^3)$ time. The linearity of the resulting systems comes from the linearity of (1).

4. EXPERIMENTAL EVALUATION

The experiments, which were performed to evaluate the proposed FSM representation, included running FSM construction with two FSM representations (the one from [2] and the proposed one) and measuring the solution quality in *FlightGear*. This evaluation is an extended version of the one presented in [4]. To perform the evaluation, three test sets were recorded in *FlightGear*. They included a loop (33 tests), a barrel roll (28 tests) and a banked 180° turn in the horizontal plane (19 tests). Fig. 3 shows several examples of paths performed by the aircraft during test recording.

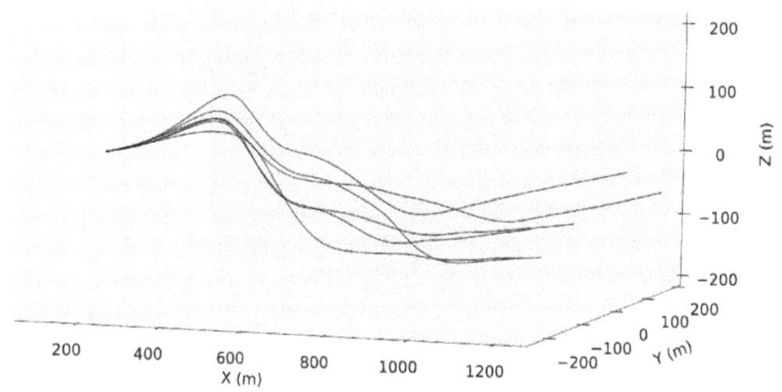

Figure 3: Several aircraft paths from the barrel roll test set

Table 1: Parameter values tuned with *irace*

FSM representation	N_{ants}	N_{mut}	n_{stag}	p_{new}
Proposed in this paper	5	13	55	0.1428
Previous one	2	29	8	0.2471

The penalties P_τ were disabled ($K = 0$) while constructing FSMs with the previous representation to make f similar to the one from [2]. For each test set a predicate set was chosen for the previous FSM representation, and both predicate and variable sets were chosen for the proposed representation. The variable choice process was iterative: if the method did not yield an FSM with proper quality (measured in simulation), the variable set was adjusted. We failed to come up with a good predicate set to construct an FSM performing the 180° turn with the previous representation, which led to poor simulation results for this case.

For each of three test sets, for $|S| = 3, 4, 5$ and for each FSM representation 50 ACO executions were performed. Pheromone-based edge selection was changed to uniformly random, as pheromone did not influence the algorithm's performance in a measurable way. The number of ants N_{ants} and other pheromone non-related parameters N_{mut}, n_{stag}, p_{new} (see [5]) were tuned with the *irace* [12] package (1000 ACO runs were performed for each representation, see Table 1 for the tuned values). The termination criterion was stagnation during 5000 fitness evaluations. In Table 2 (columns 3–5) the median fitness values reached on different problem instances are shown. The table shows that the use of the proposed FSM representation slightly improves the fitness value on the loop and barrel roll test sets, and retains the fitness value nearly the same on the turn test set. The time required for a single ACO run often did not exceed 10 minutes on a personal computer with a quad-core *Intel Core i7–2670QM* 2.2GHz processor. These performance results are close to the ones from [3].

The constructed FSMs were also examined in computer simulation. Two quality criteria measured the average pitch and roll deviations from the values recorded in the tests. The pitch criterion value was equal to the average distance $|\alpha_{i,t}^{\text{test}} - \alpha_{j,t}^{\text{run}}|$ between the pitch angles at timestamps t of the i-th test ($\alpha_{i,t}^{\text{test}}$) and of the j-th FSM execution in simulation

Table 2: **FSM quality metric values on different problem instances**

$\|S\|$	FSM Representation	Median fitness values			Median roll errors (°)			Median pitch errors (°)		
		Loop	Barrel roll	Turn	Loop	Barrel roll	Turn	Loop	Barrel roll	Turn
3	Proposed in this paper	0.9856	0.9854	0.9892	1.71	16.52	4.80	17.21	3.20	1.95
	Previous one	0.9812	0.9832	0.9894	6.37	18.56	50.29	20.54	4.44	7.58
4	Proposed in this paper	0.9866	0.9863	0.9898	2.41	15.35	4.10	23.04	2.51	1.42
	Previous one	0.9836	0.9856	0.9901	6.32	21.86	57.04	22.11	4.08	6.79
5	Proposed in this paper	0.9873	0.9868	0.9901	3.21	14.74	4.07	25.27	2.43	1.36
	Previous one	0.9842	0.9858	0.9902	9.54	22.99	45.83	24.44	4.68	7.83

($\alpha_{j,t}^{\text{run}}$), where $i = 1..N, t = 1..\text{len}[i]$ and $j = 1..10$. A similar criterion was used for the roll angle. For each problem instance, 50 FSMs with the best fitness values (each FSM from a separate run) were examined in simulation. Table 2 (columns 6–11) shows the median quality criteria values for the described FSM groups. It implies that the quality values are generally better for the suggested FSM representation.

Rather high pitch and roll error values for the 180° turn performed by FSMs with the previous representation signify their poor quality. None of such FSMs were able to perform the turn from the beginning to the end. The situation is different for the suggested FSM representation.

A video record of the Gloster Meteor jet fighter performing the turn is available at `http://youtu.be/n9q5FmCYs6M`.

5. CONCLUSION

An earlier developed method [2] of supervised finite-state machine construction has been improved. The improvement allows to synthesize FSMs which use real-valued variables to form output actions. The benefits of the suggested approach were shown on three test sets for the unmanned aircraft control problem. The use of the modified method improves the quality of generated solutions. The failure of the original method on one of the test sets is no longer the case for the new FSM representation.

6. ACKNOWLEDGEMENTS

This work was financially supported by the Government of Russian Federation, Grant 074-U01, and by RFBR, research project No. 14-07-31244 mol_a.

7. REFERENCES

[1] P. Abbeel, A. Coates, and A. Ng. Autonomous helicopter aerobatics through apprenticeship learning. *The International Journal of Robotics Research*, 29(13):1608–1639, 2010.

[2] A. Alexandrov, A. Sergushichev, S. Kazakov, and F. Tsarev. Genetic algorithm for induction of finite automata with continuous and discrete output actions. In *Proceedings of the 13th annual conference companion on Genetic and evolutionary computation (GECCO '11)*, pages 775–778. ACM, 2011.

[3] I. Buzhinsky, V. Ulyantsev, and A. Shalyto. Test-based induction of finite-state machines with continuous output actions. In *Proceedings of the 7th IFAC Conference on Manufacturing Modelling, Management, and Control (MIM '13)*, pages 1049–1054. IFAC, 2013.

[4] I. Buzhinsky, V. Ulyantsev, F. Tsarev, and A. Shalyto. Search-based construction of finite-state machines with real-valued actions: New representation model. In *Genetic and Evolutionary Computation Conference (GECCO '13) Companion*, pages 199–200. ACM, 2013.

[5] D. Chivilikhin and V. Ulyantsev. Muacosm – a new mutation-based ant colony optimization algorithm for learning finite-state machines. In *Proceedings of the Genetic and Evolutionary Computation Conference (GECCO '13)*, pages 511–518. ACM, 2013.

[6] E. Clarke, O. Grumberg, and D. Peled. *Model checking*. MIT press, 1999.

[7] M. Dorigo and T. Stutzle. *Ant Colony Optimization*. MIT Press, US, 2004.

[8] D. Harel and A. Pnueli. On the development of reactive systems. *Logic and Models of Concurrent Systems*, pages 477–498, 1985.

[9] D. Harel and M. Politi. *Modeling Reactive Systems with Statechart. The Statemate Approach*. McGraw-Hill, NY, 1998.

[10] J. Hopcroft, R. Motwani, and J. Ullman. *Introduction To Automata Theory, Languages, and Computation (3rd Edition)*. Prentice Hall, 2006.

[11] J. Koza. *Genetic programming: on the programming of computers by natural selection*. MIT Press, Cambridge, MA, USA, 1992.

[12] M. López-Ibáñez, J. Dubois-Lacoste, T. Stützle, and M. Birattari. The irace package, iterated race for automatic algorithm configuration. Technical Report TR/IRIDIA/2011-004, IRIDIA, Université libre de Bruxelles, Belgium, 2011.

[13] M. Mazo, A. Davitian, and P. Tabuada. Pessoa: A tool for embedded control software synthesis. *Lecture Notes in Computer Science*, 6174:566–569, 2010.

[14] N. Polikarpova, V. Tochilin, and A. Shalyto. Method of reduced tables for generation of automata with a large number of input variables based on genetic programming. *Journal of Computer and Systems Sciences International*, 49(2):265–282, 2010.

[15] F. Tsarev and A. Shalyto. Use of genetic programming for finite-state machine generation in the smart ant problem. In *Proceedings of the IV International Scientic-Practical Conference "Integrated Models and Soft Computing in Artificial Intelligence"*, pages 590–597, 2007.

[16] N. Walkinshaw, R. Taylor, and J. Derrick. Inferring extended finite state machine models from software executions. In *Proceedings of the 20th Working Conference on Reverse Engineering (WCRE '13)*, pages 301–310. IEEE Computer Society Press, 2013.

Multi-core GE : Automatic Evolution of CPU Based Multi-core Parallel Programs

Gopinath Chennupati
BDS Group
CSIS Department
University of Limerick, Ireland
gopinath.chennupati@ul.ie

R. Muhammad Atif Azad
BDS Group
CSIS Department
University of Limerick, Ireland
atif.azad@ul.ie

Conor Ryan
BDS Group
CSIS Department
University of Limerick, Ireland
conor.ryan@ul.ie

ABSTRACT

We describe the utilization of on-chip multiple CPU architectures to automatically evolve parallel computer programs. These programs have the capability of exploiting the computational efficiency of the modern multi-core machines.

This is significantly different from other parallel EC approaches because not only do we produce individuals that, in their *final form*, can exploit parallel architectures, we can also exploit the same parallel architecture during evolution to reduce evolution time.

We use Grammatical Evolution along with OpenMP specific grammars to produce natively parallel code, and demonstrate that not only do we enjoy the benefit of final individuals that can run in parallel, but that our system scales effectively with the number of cores.

Categories and Subject Descriptors

I.2.8 [**Artificial Intelligence**]: Problem Solving, Control Methods, and Search - Heuristic methods

Keywords

Grammatical Evolution; Multi-cores; Parallel Programming; Symbolic Regression; OpenMP.

1. INTRODUCTION

Real-world applications of evolutionary algorithms (EA) vary dramatically in terms of the computation power required. Depending on the specific problem, techniques varying from caching up to parallel evaluation of both individuals and testcases can be used to reduce computation time.

While there have been some instances where EAs were used to convert existing sequential code to functionally identical parallel code [12], as well as concurrent code [14], there has been no work that produces code that natively exploits multi-core architectures.

It is a well known factor that the execution time limits the emergence of Evolutionary Computation (EC) techniques into the traditional machine learning domain when experimented on large datasets. In fact it is a major concern for any prediction system, for example, if a weather prediction system consumes more than a day or two to produce predictions for the next days then, it is pointless to use that predictor.

The primary reason behind this high computational cost is that the stochastic nature of the EC techniques requires a number of candidate evaluations to produce an optimal solution of certain quality. Genetic Programming (GP) [6] and Grammatical Evolution (GE) [11] are such EAs that require optimization in their computational effort spent on the evaluation of the candidate solutions.

There have been a number of attempts from machine code generation to the usage of parallel computational resources that address this issue. Graphics Processing Units (GPUs) attracted a lot of attention from the EC community with their high computational capabilities through light weighted cores. One such work related to GP is [10] that tried to reduce the evaluation time while it also questions the high performance speedups reported in the other GPU based EC implementations. Another attempt in [4] tried to reduce the execution time through the termination of the runs that produce low quality solutions.

However, recent desktops and PCs are made of multiple cores that have better compute capabilities to improve the speedup at a reasonable cost. These multi-core processors are equipped with a shared memory configuration that can be accessed by all the cores which in turn helps to achieve efficient parallelization. Little work has been done on exploiting the compute capabilities of these architectures. However, utilizing the power of the multi-cores can optimize the execution time significantly.

This paper proposes to automatically evolve parallel computer programs that have the ability to exploit the compute capabilities of the modern CPU based multi-core architectures. We use OpenMP thread based programming practices along with GE grammars for the automatic evolution of these parallel programs. This approach is assessed on two standard bench mark problems: 6-multiplexer and a sextic polynomial regression.

2. BACKGROUND

GE is an evolutionary algorithm that can evolve computer programs in an arbitrary language through a linear genome representation and the rules of the BNF grammars. Each individual in the GE population is a variable length binary string and, typically, the genome is divided into 8 bit *codons*,

GECCO'14, July 12–16, 2014, Vancouver, BC, Canada.
Copyright 2014 ACM 978-1-4503-2881-4/14/07 ...$15.00.
http://dx.doi.org/10.1145/2598394.2605670.

which are used to select the possible rules of the grammar. GE *mapping* is a crucial component of its evolutionary cycle which is responsible for producing code in any programming language, and is an extra step which does not occur in GP.

2.1 Phenotype Evaluation

A general consensus in the EC community is that an EA's fitness evaluation is the most computationally expensive task. Particularly in GE, experimental observations presented in [3] confirm this statement (with 66% of total execution time) while GE mapping (with 33% of total execution time) is the next computationally expensive task. GE is unique in its fitness evaluation as it is calculated through the evaluation of phenotype whereas all the remaining genetic operations (such as crossover, mutation) are performed on the genotype. This separation between the solution and the search space has been made possible with the help of the Context Free Grammars (CFGs) and the GE specific *mapping* process as explained here.

GE *mapping* process converts a genotype into phenotype, a computer program in a user specified language. GE first decodes a variable length binary string to a string of eight bit integers term known as *codons*. These codons are then used to pick rules from a CFG with this function:

Rule = (Codon Integer Value) % (# rules for this non-terminal)

Most often (not always), the fitness of the phenotype is evaluated using a complier, an *evaluator* in GE. It evaluates the evolved computer program serially over all the fitness cases. One drawback with the current GE system is that it can only use the compute capabilities of only one core that leaves the remaining cores of a multi-core machine idle. In this paper we focus only on optimizing the execution time of GE phenotype evaluations that can make use of the computational power of these modern machines.

2.2 Related Work

Most of the EC approaches (GA, GP) are inherently parallel or contain the design that is suitable for explicit parallelization. The explicit parallelization approaches can largely be classified as *population parallel* and *data parallel* as shown in [8]. The former deals with a population of individuals with different sets of configurations that exploit the power of multiple computers, while the latter deals with simultaneous data computations. Cantú-Paz [2] contemplated different parallelization configurations in GAs whereas [8] (Chapter 10) listed out different approaches that can accelerate GP. However, recently graphics processing units (GPUs) emerged as highly parallel computing resources. Robilliard et al. [10] tried to exploit the power of G80 GPUs in paralleling GP fitness evaluations. Chitty [5] demonstrated a population parallel approach that fully exploits the power of CPU based multi-cores on a new implementation of GP.

Along these EC approaches, also the design of GE is "embarrassingly parallel" that takes advantage from the separation offered through its mapping. The first parallelization attempt on GE was made in [13] with an island model that was implemented in python programming language. It optimized the total execution time when tested on a 17 node cluster with each node containing the Intel Pentium IV Dual Core processor. Osmera et al. [7] proposed a two level population parallel approach with GE in the first level and Differential Evolution in the next level in a hierarchical master-slave configuration, where the slaves port their best candidate solutions to the master. They tested it on a group of 6 computers networked together with one master and five slaves with two populations (female, male) on each one.

Recently, for the first time [9] reported promising acceleration in the execution time by the entire GE algorithm on GPU cores. Although the proposed approach optimized the execution time, they also have reported a serious limitation on the use of GPU memory that would decelerate the speed of execution as the population size scales up.

Parallel GE implementations are relatively few in number due to the need to access specialized parallel hardware such as GPUs. However, modern CPU vendors (Intel i7) are offering desktop computers with multiple cores with each core having the power of a standard single core processor. The computational power of these architectures has been little explored leaving a lot of scope for us to investigate. Despite the parallelization investigations in the literature, to the best of our knowledge for the first time we propose to exploit the compute capabilities of multi-core architectures through an automatic evolution of parallel programs through grammars. In fact the automatic evolution of parallel programs frees us from the shackles of maintenance costs of parallelization that parallel programming researchers often face.

```
<start> ::= <omp_pragmas><for_loop><data>
  <evolved_expr>
<omp_pragmas> ::= #pragma omp parallel
  shared(Evolved, chunk) private(i) {
  #pragma omp for schedule (dynamic,chunk)
<for_loop> ::= for(i=0; i<FITNESS_CASES;
  i=i+1) {
<data> ::= xvals[i]; yvals[i];
<evolved_expr> ::= temp= <expr>;<assign>
<expr> ::= mymul(<expr>, <expr>) |
  mysub(<expr>, <expr>) |
  myadd(<expr>, <expr>) |
  pdiv(<expr>, <expr>) |
  if_cond(<expr>, <expr>, <expr>, <expr>)
  | (<expr>) | sin(<expr>) | cos(<expr>)
  | tan(<expr>) | exp(<expr>) | xvals[i]
  | yvals[i] | 1.000 | <const> | -<const>
<const> ::= 0.<digit><digit><digit>
<digit> ::= 0 | 1 | 2 | 3 | 4 | 5 | 6 |
  7 | 8 | 9
<assign> ::= if(temp < 0) { Evolved[i] = 0;
  } else { Evolved[i] = 1; } }
```

Figure 1: Design of multi-core grammars

3. MULTI-CORE GE

Each core of a multi-core machine is a single unique CPU. Utilizing the compute capabilities of these cores is relatively a simple process in comparison with the GPU cores. Creating different threads on each core enables us to exploit the power of these cores. Thus, under any operating system environment, calling OpenMP enabled C/C++ function creates user requested number of threads. OpenMP offers parallel programming *pragmas* that can execute independent threads on cores.

We use these OpenMP *pragmas* to automatically evolve parallel programs that are compatible with multi-core CPU shared memory architectures. Figure 1 presents the grammars that are used in the automatic evolution of parallel programs. For these preliminary investigations, the evolved programs follow a *data parallel* approach so that at any given period of time only one phenotype is evaluated across multiple fitness cases in parallel.

In this approach, load balancing is a serious concern that was caused by thread scheduling. OpenMP improves this inefficiency with the help of a few thread scheduling options, *dynamic scheduling* is the best option among them. It dynamically assigns t iterations of the remaining iterations to the threads that are idle, finding the optimal t can be hard some times. That means the available data is divided into chunks of size t and allocates each chunk dynamically to the threads immediately upon completion of their execution.

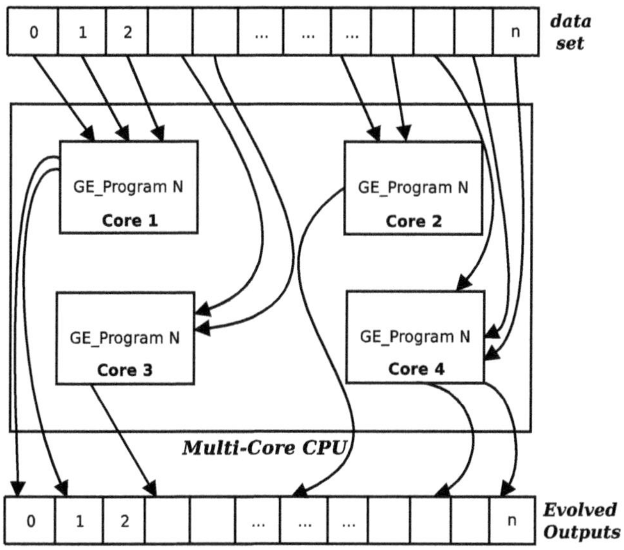

Figure 2: Parallel evaluation scheme of the evolved GE program on a multi-core CPU.

Figure 2 shows the phenotype evaluation scheme across multiple cores of a modern CPU. The main characteristic of this approach is, a **single** GE program is executed across all the cores with a different set of fitness cases, thus making the execution single instruction multiple data (SIMD). That is fitness cases are processed in parallel across all the cores. For example on a 4 core machine, every core evaluates $1/4^{th}$ of the fitness cases (this may vary due to dynamic scheduling) ideally and must report an evaluation speedup factor of 4.

In this scheme some threads finish their execution early while the others fall behind so that we end up with an issue of thread synchronization in calculating the final fitness value. In such instances the OpenMP *parallel reduction* is applied on squared error (regression problems), the number of hits (classification problems) in a separate function. Since both the operations involve summation that can be generalized as the sum of n numbers for which the time complexity is $O(n^2)$. With the reduction operation the complexity has been reduced to $O(nlogn)$. In reduction there is a chance for the occurrence of *race* condition when the evolved class values are compared with that of the target (*if (evolved[i] == target[i])*) where the evolved class in thread 1 might race to check the equivalence with thread 2 of the target class. In order to prevent this an OpenMP *critical section* was used where only one thread can execute at any given time in that region.

4. EXPERIMENTS

In order to test the proposed approach the experiments were carried out on a cluster node with an Intel (R) Xeon (R) CPU E7-4820 with a processor speed of 2 GHz. It contains 16 cores each of which are enabled by hyper threading with an ability to run 2 independent threads per core and 18 Mb of L3 cache memory was shared among all the cores. The experimental parameters were set as follows. The population was initialized randomly with the maximum depth set to 25, while the minimum depth was 15. It is interesting to see the performance of the proposed approach with various population sizes and a variable number of CPU cores. Hence, the population sizes were kept at $25, 50, 100, 200, 400$ while the number of CPU cores were at $2, 4, 8, 16$. One point crossover with a probability 0.9, point mutation with a probability 0.01 were used. We used steady state GA where the best individuals replace the worst in the population. GNU GCC evaluator is used for phenotype evaluations. A total of 30 runs were conducted with a generation count of 50.

4.1 Results

We evaluate the performance of our approach on two standard benchmark problems: 6-multiplexer and, sextic polynomial regression ($x^6 - 2x^4 + x^2$). The first benchmark contains 64 training points with 2 address bits (A0-A1), 4 data bits (D0-D4) and the second benchmark is a regression problem that also has 64 training points in the range [-1.5,+1.5]. A complete description of the serial implementation of the grammars can be found in [1]. We focus on our goal of optimizing the phenotype evaluation time and report those results, despite the fact that there is no significant difference in the serial and the parallel (proposed) version of the solutions. The total execution time results were measured using the OpenMP platform independent timer utility function.

Table 1 demonstrates the performance of multi-core GE. The average evaluation time of fitness evaluation results of the evolved parallel programs with varying number of CPU cores is shown over 30 runs on both the bench mark problems. On 6-multiplexer problem, with 2 cores there is no significant difference in the average evaluation time whereas for the remaining cores $(4, 8, 16)$ it was reduced significantly recording better speedups. For sextic symbolic regression, incrementing the cores to 2 has in fact increased the average evaluation time as it a well known OpenMP pattern. Except that, for the remaining configurations significant reductions were observed. Overall, the performance of the multi-core parallel programs reported promising results in the fitness evaluations.

5. CONCLUSION AND FUTURE WORK

In this paper we presented a new method to exploit the power of modern multi-core machines through an automatic evolution of parallel programs that can reduce the risk of maintaining the parallel programming. Modern multi-cores are more suitable for multiple instruction multiple data (MIMD) style of execution, whereas the proposed approach follows SIMD, following multi-core adaptable style of execution might

Table 1: **Average evaluation time (in secs) results (average [standard deviation]) of multi-core GE over 30 runs on 6-multiplexer and sextic regression problems.**

Problem	Pop Size	Cores				
		1	2	4	8	16
6-multiplexer	25	88.49 [11.86]	92.78 [6.01]	41.54 [6.45]	22.01 [6.82]	12.6 [6.41]
	50	226.29 [24.65]	173.26 [12.31]	123.65 [16.52]	46.56 [10.47]	30.13 [15.23]
	100	347.13 [25.40]	335.84 [27.32]	177.11 [24.81]	69.56 [21.92]	44.16 [21.95]
	200	703.21 [35.42]	698.76 [19.14]	285.86 [12.61]	185.54 [17.32]	86.28 [17.92]
	400	1399.54 [15.95]	1428.75 [28.42]	897.14 [23.36]	392.03 [26.70]	169.85 [33.51]
sextic regression	25	107.96 [17.71]	152.07 [25.44]	36.86 [20.60]	17.27 [21.06]	10.77 [20.88]
	50	217.69 [26.52]	279.65 [21.68]	82.86 [26.63]	35.03 [33.14]	22.62 [32.94]
	100	482.91 [34.37]	601.77 [33.43]	183.88 [24.82]	80.28 [29.78]	55.54 [29.32]
	200	847.17 [26.14]	1361.33 [37.93]	498.85 [22.50]	168.64 [20.41]	118.35 [17.01]
	400	1748.67 [33.87]	3757.92 [27.34]	1030.70 [16.24]	405.21 [18.41]	261.86 [18.93]

report much better performance with optimal efficiency. Recall that we evaluated the final fitness of the phenotype in synchronous fashion using a *critical* section where some threads wait for the others to finish their execution. Although we observed improvement in the speedups this synchronous execution makes the cores to sit idle as a result CPU time is underutilized. Asynchronous phenotype evaluation is one of the recommended directions to investigate.

It is interesting to see the length of the genotypes as it is clear from the presented grammars that the size of the grammars is larger than the serial version for the respective problems. There is a chance to get longer individuals that are being evaluated in less time. It is also possible to investigate by incrementing the size of the fitness cases, using a generational strategy as opposed to the used steady state replacement procedure that which might pose different challenges with an increased breeding time.

Experimenting with highly decomposable problems such as quick sort, vertex colouring and the ones that also involve task level parallelism is another interesting research direction.

6. REFERENCES

[1] R. M. A. Azad and C. Ryan. An examination of simultaneous evolution of grammars and solutions. In T. Yu, R. Riolo, and B. Worzel, editors, *Genetic Programming Theory and Practice III*, volume 9, pages 141–158. Springer, US, 2006.

[2] E. Cantú-Paz. A survey of parallel genetic algorithms. *Calculateurs paralleles, reseaux et systems repartis*, 10(2):141–171, 1998.

[3] G. Chennupati, C. Ryan, and R. M. A. Azad. An empirical analysis through the time complexity of GE problems. In R. Matousek, editor, *19th International Conference on Soft Computing, MENDEL'13*, pages 37–44, Brno, Czech Republic, Jun, 26-28 2013.

[4] G. Chennupati, C. Ryan, and R. M. A. Azad. Predict the performance of an evolutionary algorithm run. In *the Genetic and Evolutionary Computation Conference*, GECCO '14, Vancouver, BC, Canada, Jul, 12–16 2014, to appear.

[5] D. M. Chitty. Fast parallel genetic programming: multi-core cpu versus many-core gpu. *Soft Computing*, 16(10):1795–1814, 2012.

[6] J. R. Koza. *Genetic Programming: On the Programming of Computers by Means of Natural Selection*. MIT Press, Cambridge, MA, USA, 1992.

[7] P. Osmera, O. Popelka, and P. Pivonka. Two level parallel grammatical evolution. In *IEEE World Congress on Computational Intelligence, IEEE Congress on Evolutionary Computation, CEC 2008*, pages 2473–2480, June 2008.

[8] R. Poli, W. B. Langdon, and N. F. McPhee. *A Field Guide to Genetic Programming*. Lulu Enterprises, UK Ltd, 2008.

[9] P. Pospichal, E. Murphy, M. O'Neill, J. Schwarz, and J. Jaros. Acceleration of grammatical evolution using graphics processing units. In *Proceeding of Genetic and Evolutionary Computation Conference*, GECCO '11, pages 431–438. ACM, 2011.

[10] D. Robilliard, V. Marion, and C. Fonlupt. High performance genetic programming on GPU. In *Proceedings of the Bio-inspired algorithms for distributed systems*, pages 85–94. ACM, 2009.

[11] C. Ryan, J. J. Collins, and M. O'Neill. Grammatical evolution: Evolving programs for an arbitrary language. In W. Banzhaf, R. Poli, M. Schoenauer, and T. C. Fogarty, editors, *Proceedings of the First European Workshop on Genetic Programming*, volume 1391 of *LNCS*, pages 83–95. Springer, 1998.

[12] C. Ryan and P. Walsh. The evolution of provable parallel programs. In J. R. Koza, K. Deb, M. Dorigo, D. B. Fogel, M. Garzon, H. Iba, and R. L. Riolo, editors, *Genetic Programming 1997: Proceedings of the Second Annual Conference*, pages 295–302, Stanford University, CA, USA, 1997. Morgan Kaufmann.

[13] M. Stallard. A parallel approach to grammatical evolution in python, 2006.

[14] A. Trenaman. Concurrent genetic programming, tartarus and dancing agents. volume 1598 of *LNCS*, pages 270–282. Springer, 1999.

Parameter Tuning in Quantum-Inspired Evolutionary Algorithms for Partitioning Complex Networks

Shikha Gupta
Department of Computer Science
University of Delhi
New Delhi, India
shikha.gupta.cs.du@gmail.com

Naveen Kumar
Department of Computer Science
University of Delhi
New Delhi, India
nk.cs.du@gmail.com

ABSTRACT

We propose a numeric variant of quantum-inspired evolutionary algorithm (QIEA) where gene in the quantum chromosome is a superposition of k qubits, thus allowing the genes of the classical chromosome to take numeric values. We also present a modified form of real observation QIEA. Both these techniques are applied to the problem of partitioning a complex network. The algorithm parameters are tuned using an evolutionary bilevel search optimization technique.

Keywords

Genetic Algorithm; Complex Network; Community detection; Quantum-inspired evolutionary algorithm; Modularity; NMI; Evolutionary bilevel Optimization

1. INTRODUCTION

Quantum-inspired evolutionary algorithms (QIEAs) are evolutionary algorithms (EAs) using the quantum computing concepts like quantum bits (qubits), superposition, and unitary transformations of quantum states. A QIEA works with quantum population comprising of chromosomes. Each chromosome is represented as a string of qubits with the advantage that it can represent a linear superposition of states in search space probabilistically. The original QIEA, first implemented by Han and Kim [3], involves measuring the quantum population to generate a classical population followed by an update operation that involves application of quantum gate as variation operator. Survey of extensions and applications of the QIEA [12] categorizes QIEA that are characterized by the qubit representation, measurement process and quantum gates into binary observation QIEA (*bQIEA*), and real observation QIEA (*rQIEA*) based on the type of data assumed in the classical chromosome. Both these variants allow one qubit per gene. In this paper, we propose a numeric variant (*numQIEAm*) that allows the genes of the classical chromosome to take numeric values. Here, every gene in the quantum chromosome is superposition of k qubits. This formulation is useful for combinatorial optimization problems where the data type of a gene in the classical chromosome is numeric. We also present a modified form of *rQIEA* (*rQIEAm*). Both the techniques are applied to the problem of partitioning complex networks. The problem is modeled as an evolutionary bilevel optimization problem for parameter tuning [2]. In the rest of the paper, section 2 describes the proposed strategies, section 3 details the experimentation conducted and is followed by concluding remarks.

GECCO'14, July 12–16, 2014, Vancouver, BC, Canada.

ACM 978-1-4503-2881-4/14/07 ...$15.00.
http://dx.doi.org/10.1145/2598394.2605672 .

2. QIEA

The smallest unit of information stored in two-state quantum system is called a qubit which may be in "1" state, "0 "state, or in any superposition of "1" and "0" states. The state of a qubit can be represented as $|\Psi >= a\ |0> +b\ |1>$, where a and b are complex numbers specifying the probability amplitudes of the corresponding states. $|a|^2$ and $|b|^2$ denote the probabilities that the qubit may be found in states 0 and 1 respectively. The condition $|a|^2 + |b|^2 = 1$ guarantees normalization. Thus, a qubit is defined using a pair of complex numbers (a, b), represented by the vector $[a, b]^T$. The proposed numeric observation QIEA algorithm with mutation (*numQIEAm*) and the modified real observation QIEA algorithm with mutation (*rQIEAm*), both follow the general steps of the algorithm *QIEAm*. The specific details for the proposed strategies are elaborated in further sections.

Procedure QIEAm: QIEA with quantum mutation operator

Input: Graph $G = (V, E)$
Output: Best solution B
  $t \leftarrow 0$
  initialize quantum population $Q(t)$
  determine $P(t)$ by measuring $Q(t)$ (Measure function)
  repair $P(t)$
  evaluate $P(t)$, that is, compute fitness function (network modularity) for each chromosome
  store the best solution (that gives a positive gain in network modularity) among $P(t)$ in B
  while not termination condition **do**
    $t \leftarrow t+1$
    determine $P(t)$ by measuring $Q(t-1)$
    evaluate $P(t)$
    for all chromosome in $Q(t)$ and $P(t)$ **do**
      mutate and repair the chromosome
      modify $Q(t)$ using quantum gates (update operation)
      update B with the best solution among $P(t-1)$ and $P(t)$
    end for
  end while

2.1 Binary Observation QIEA

In a binary observation QIEA (*bQIEA*), a chromosome encoding binary representation of the solution uses a representation based on qubits. Thus, n qubits may be used to represent a *quantum chromosome* of size n as follows,

$$q = \left[\begin{array}{c|c|c|c} a_1 & a_2 & \ldots & a_n \\ b_1 & b_2 & \ldots & b_n \end{array} \right] \quad (1)$$

Here, the states are in superposition and can be represented as,

$$|\Psi>= a_1a_2\ldots a_n|00\ldots0> + a_1a_2\ldots a_{n-1}b_n|00\ldots01> + a_1a_2\ldots a_{n-2}b_{n-1}a_n|00\ldots010> + \ldots + b_1b_2\ldots b_n|11\ldots1>$$

For example, consider the following 3-qubit chromosome with three pairs of amplitudes,

$$q = \left[\begin{array}{c|c|c} \frac{1}{\sqrt{2}} & \frac{\sqrt{3}}{2} & \frac{-1}{\sqrt{2}} \\ \frac{1}{\sqrt{2}} & \frac{1}{2} & \frac{1}{\sqrt{2}} \end{array} \right]$$

Here, the states can be represented as,

$$|\Psi>= \frac{-\sqrt{3}}{4}|000> + \frac{\sqrt{3}}{4}|001> - \frac{1}{4}|010> + \frac{1}{4}|011> - \frac{\sqrt{3}}{4}|100> + \frac{\sqrt{3}}{4}|101> - \frac{1}{4}|110> + \frac{1}{4}|111>$$

This implies that states $|000>$, $|001>$, $|010>$, $|011>$, $|100>$, $|101>$, $|110>$, and $|111>$ occur with probabilities 3/16, 3/16, 1/16, 1/16, 3/16, 3/16, 1/16, and 1/16 respectively.

A system of n-qubits can represent 2^n states at the same time but each qubit collapses to a single state 0 or 1 when measured, resulting in a classical binary chromosome. Considering n=12, a 12-qubit chromosome
$a_1|0> + b_1|1>, a_2|0> + b_2|1>, \ldots, a_{12}|0> + b_{12}|1>$
when measured may yield a binary chromosome such as,

0	1	1	1	0	0	1	1	0	1	1	0

For the ith qubit in the chromosome, given by probability amplitudes $[a_i, b_i]^T$, a random number r in the range [0, 1] is generated. If $r < |a|^2$, then the corresponding classical bit is set to 0 else to 1. In the context of community detection, the values 0 and 1 in the above chromosome may be interpreted as a community IDs associated with the corresponding nodes. Thus, the above chromosome may be interpreted as,

Node no.	1	2	3	4	5	6	7	8	9	10	11	12
Community ID	0	1	1	1	0	0	1	1	0	1	1	0

That is, nodes 1, 5, 6, 9, and 12 belong to the community 0 while nodes 2, 3, 4, 7, 8, 10, and 11 belong to the community 1.

2.2 Numeric Observation QIEA

The proposed *numQIEAm* algorithm (m for mutation) according to terminology given by Zhang [12], follows the basic steps of the algorithm *QIEAm*. In a numeric observation QIEA (*numQIEAm*), the genes of the classical chromosome take numeric values and genes in the quantum chromosome are each a superposition of k qubits. This allows $nc = 2^k$ possible states for every gene. This formulation is suitable for problems like that of discovering communities in complex networks where each gene in the classical chromosome may take discrete values representing the partition number of the corresponding node. We assume that the partition number values lie in the known range $[1, nc]$, nc being the estimated number of communities, input by the user during algorithm initialization, with a maximum value n, number of nodes in the network. The *quantum chromosome* of size n may be represented with n (k-qubits) as,

$$q = \left[\begin{array}{c|c|c|c} g_1 & g_2 & \ldots & g_n \end{array} \right] \quad (2)$$

The ith gene may be represented as,

$$g_i = \left[\begin{array}{c|c|c|c} a_1 & a_2 & \ldots & a_k \\ b_1 & b_2 & \ldots & b_k \end{array} \right]$$

For example, consider the following 2-qubit gene with two pairs of amplitudes,

$$g = \left[\begin{array}{c|c} \frac{1}{\sqrt{2}} & \frac{\sqrt{3}}{2} \\ \frac{1}{\sqrt{2}} & \frac{1}{2} \end{array} \right]$$

Here, the states of a gene are in superposition and can be represented as, $|\Psi_g>= \frac{\sqrt{3}}{2\sqrt{2}}|00> + \frac{1}{2\sqrt{2}}|01> + \frac{\sqrt{3}}{2\sqrt{2}}|10> + \frac{1}{2\sqrt{2}}|11>$. This implies that states $|00>$, $|01>$, $|10>$, and $|11>$ occur with probabilities 3/8, 1/8, 3/8, and 1/8 respectively. Renaming the states as 0_d, 1_d, 2_d, 3_d, we can interpret this gene as having 4 possible quantum states, thus allowing a maximum of 4 communities in the network. In general, we can represent the probability amplitudes for state $|\Psi_{g_i}>$ of the k-qubit i^{th} gene g_i as $|\Psi_{g_i}> = [t_{i_1}, t_{i_2}, \ldots, t_{i_{nc}}]^T$. A system of n (k-qubits) can represent $(2^k)^n$ states at the same time and each gene will collapse to a single state between 0 and $nc - 1 = 2^k - 1$ when measured, resulting in a numeric chromosome. For example, a 12 (2-qubit) chromosome represented as, $|\Psi_{g_1}>, |\Psi_{g_2}>, \ldots, |\Psi_{g_{12}}>$, further expanded as,
$t_{1_1}|0_d> + t_{1_2}|1_d> + t_{1_3}|2_d> + t_{1_4}|4_d>$, $t_{2_1}|0_d> + t_{2_2}|1_d> + t_{2_3}|2_d> + t_{2_4}|3_d>$, $\ldots$, $t_{12_1}|0_d> + t_{12_2}|1_d> + t_{12_3}|2_d> + t_{12_4}|3_d>$
when measured may yield a numeric chromosome such as,

3_d	2_d	1_d	1_d	0_d	1_d	1_d	3_d	2_d	1_d	3_d	0_d

In the context of community detection, the values 0_d, 1_d, 2_d, and 3_d in the above chromosome may be interpreted as community IDs. That is, nodes 5 and 12 belong to the community 0_d, nodes 3, 4, 6, 7, and 10 belong to community 1_d, nodes 2 and 9 belong to community 2_d, and nodes 1, 8, and 11 belong to the community 3_d.

2.2.1 *Quantum Population Initialization*

For a quantum chromosome, as given in (2), every k-qubits gene is initialized as:
$1/\sqrt{nc}\,|0_d> + 1/\sqrt{nc}\,|1_d> + \ldots + 1/\sqrt{nc}\,|(nc-1)_d>$, where $nc = 2^k$.

2.2.2 *Measure Function*

For the ith gene in the quantum chromosome, given by probability amplitudes $[t_{i_1}, t_{i_2}, \ldots, t_{i_{nc}}]^T$, a random number r in the range [0, 1] is generated. If $r < \sum_{l=j}^{nc} |t_{i_l}|^2$, $j = nc, \ldots, 1$, then the corresponding classical bit is set to j. Thus, a gene in the classical chromosome takes a value in the range $[1, nc]$.

2.2.3 *Mutation*

A classical chromosome is selected for mutation with a probability of *mutRate*, an algorithm parameter. For every gene in the selected chromosome, a random number r in the range [0, 1] is generated. If $r < 1/n$, the ith gene is selected for mutation [7]. The selected gene with value x is mutated to value $x' = \lfloor (nc - 1)\, r \rfloor$. For the ith gene in the corresponding quantum chromosome, the x'-th and x-th amplitudes are interchanged. The chromosome is then repaired, that is, new community ID is assigned to all the neighbors of the node and their corresponding quantum genes are also mutated. The mutation is accepted if the mutated gene in $P(t)$ increases the network modularity.

2.2.4 *Repair Function*

Tasgin and Bingol (2006) [9] repaired the generated classical chromosome to improve the convergence of the algorithm. A chromosome is randomly picked for repair with probability α and a

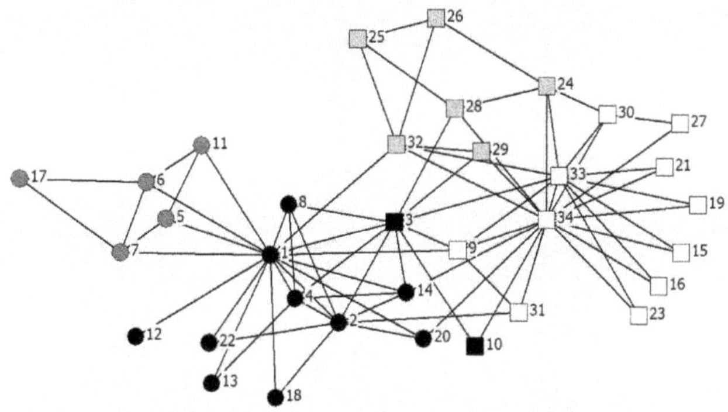

Figure 1: Partitioning structure for Zachary karate club network (NMI=1). Vertex color represents the division into four communities. Vertex shape represents the principle division into two communities

node v is randomly picked with probability β. The community ID of v is then assigned to all of its neighbors in the chromosome. α and β are algorithm parameters.

2.2.5 Update Function

As given by Han and Kim (2000) [3], qubits in $Q(t)$ are updated by applying quantum rotation gate,

$$U(\Delta\theta_i) = \begin{pmatrix} cos(\Delta\theta_i) & -sin(\Delta\theta_i) \\ sin(\Delta\theta_i) & cos(\Delta\theta_i) \end{pmatrix} \quad (3)$$

where, $\Delta\theta_i$ (Table 2), $i = 1,2,\ldots,n$ is the rotation angle of the qubit q_i, towards the fitter state. x_i is the ith gene of the classical chromosome corresponding to the ith quantum gene being mutated. B_i is the ith bit of the best solution (B) achieved so far. Let the x_i^{th} and B_i^{th} probability amplitudes in the quantum gene be t_{x_i} and t_{B_i} respectively. Then the updated probability amplitudes are calculated as $[t'_{x_i}, t'_{B_i}]^T = U(\Delta\theta_i)\,[t_{x_i}, t_{B_i}]^T$. The magnitude of $\Delta\theta_i$ has an effect on the speed of convergence, but for very large values, the solutions may diverge or converge prematurely to a local optimum.

2.3 Modified rQIEA

The proposed modified *rQIEA* algorithm, called as *rQIEAm* (m for mutation) according to terminology given by Zhang [12], follows the basic steps of the algorithm *QIEAm*.The quantum population in *rQIEAm* is similar to that in *bQIEA*. But the classical population for the two differ in that *rQIEA* allows genes to take real values. Following is the description of modified functions:

Quantum Population Initialization: For the quantum population $Q(t) = \{q_1^t, q_2^t, \ldots, q_{pop}^t\}$, q_i^t (1) is initialized as $a_i^t = 1/\sqrt{2}$, $b_i^t = 1/\sqrt{2}$, $i = 1, \ldots, n$. *pop* being the population size.

Measure: Measure function is modified to suit the problem of community detection. For the ith qubit in the chromosome, given by probability amplitudes $[a_i, b_i]^T$, a random number r in the range [0, 1] is generated. If $r > 0.5$, then the corresponding classical bit is set to $\lfloor (n-1)\,|b|^2 \rfloor$ else to $\lfloor (n-1)\,|a|^2 \rfloor$, n being the chromosome size. Thus, a gene in the classical chromosome takes a value in the range [1, n], denoting the community ID of the corresponding node.

Mutation: A chromosome is selected for mutation with a probability of *mutRate*, an algorithm parameter. The ith gene is selected for mutation with probability $1/n$ [7]. The ith gene with value x is then mutated to value $n - x$. The ith qubit in the corresponding quantum chromosome, given by probability amplitudes $[a_i, b_i]^T$, is mutated to probability amplitudes of $[b_i, a_i]$. The new community ID of the ith gene in the classical chromosome is then propagated to all the neighbors of the node and their corresponding quantum genes are also mutated. The mutation is accepted if the mutated gene in $P(t)$ increases the network modularity.

Table 1: Lookup table for quantum rotation gate, applied to i^{th} qubit. Values for θ_1, θ_2 are given in Table 2

x_i	B_i	$f(x) \geq f(B)$	$\Delta\theta_i$
0	0	false	0
0	0	true	θ_2
0	1	false	θ_1
0	1	true	θ_2
1	0	false	$-\theta_1$
1	0	true	$-\theta_2$
1	1	false	0
1	1	true	θ_2

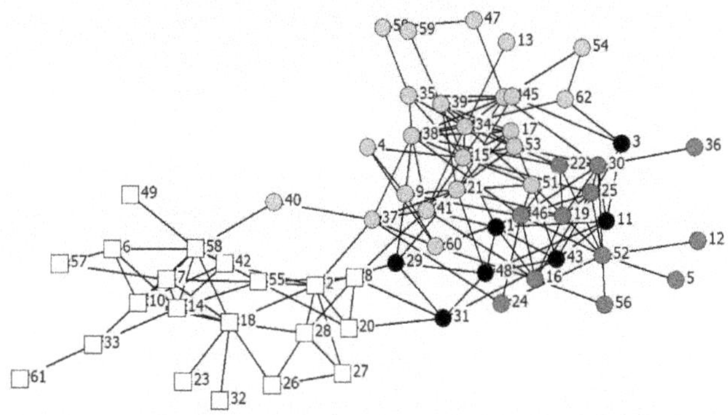

Figure 2: Partitioning structure for Dolphins social network (NMI=1). Vertex color represents the division into four communities. Vertex shape represents the division into two communities

3. EXPERIMENTAL RESULTS

We make use of MATLAB implementation of NSGA-II as in [8]. The algorithms use the catastrophe operation to avoid premature convergence [10]. We have experimented on two most popular benchmark real-world social networks: Zachary Karate Club Network (Figure 1) [11] and Dolphins Network (Figure 2) [5].

3.1 Partition Similarity Metric

Normalized Mutual Information (NMI) is a popular measure of partition similarity between a pair of partitions [1]. Given a known partitions P_1 (for benchmark datasets) and found partition P_2 (found by proposed algorithm), let $N = (N_{ij})$ be the confusion matrix where the rows and columns correspond to the community structure in P_1 and P_2 respectively and N_{ij} is the number of nodes in the community i that appear in the community j. Then normalized mutual information NMI(P_1, P_2) is defined as:

$$NMI(P_1, P_2) = \frac{-2\sum_{i=1}^{c_1}\sum_{j=1}^{c_2} N_{ij}\,log(\frac{N_{ij}\,n}{N_{i.}\,N_{.j}})}{\sum_{i=1}^{c_1} N_{i.}\,log(\frac{N_{i.}}{n}) + \sum_{j=1}^{c_2} N_{.j}\,log(\frac{N_{.j}}{n})} \quad (4)$$

where c_1 and c_2 are the number of communities in P_1 and P_2 respectively and n is the number of nodes in the network. NMI values range between 0 and 1, 1 when P_1 and P_2 are exactly same.

Table 2: Parameter Tuning- NC and NC_l give the number of communities in found and known partitions, Q and Q_l give the modularity of found and known partitions, Misclass. Nodes: Nodes in the known partition that are misclassified in the found partition.

Dataset	Algorithm	Q_l	NC_l	Parameter Solution					Q	NMI	NC	Misclass. Nodes
				θ_1	θ_2	α	β	mutRate				
Zachary	numQIEAm $k = 2$	.4188	4	.061	.0047	.36	.11	.36	**.4198**	.9233	4	10
				.0074	.0038	.52	.13	.13	**.4188**	1.0	4	none
				.083	.0045	.13	.46	.63	**.4188**	1.0	4	none
	rQIEAm	.4188	4	.034	0	.51	.25	.78	**.3975**	.825	4	12
		.36	2	.054	.0002	.062	.3	.6	**.36**	1	2	none
				.055	.0047	.43	.37	.025	**.36**	1	2	none
				.035	.0038	.77	.2	.31	**.36**	1	2	none
				.034	0	.51	.25	.079	**.36**	1	2	none
Dolphins	numQIEAm $k = 3$	.5191	4	.033	.0036	.36	.21	.8	**.5268**	.7830	4	4,9,40, 54,60,62
				.51	.005	.31	.22	.033	**.5191**	1.0	4	none
				.0074	.0038	.52	.13	.13	**.5191**	1.0	4	none
	rQIEAm	.5191	4	.028	.0027	.49	.41	.23	**.5106**	.7473	4	3,4,9,21, 40,51,63
				.073	.0026	.6	.49	.91	**.5147**	.7731	4	4,9,21,37 ,40,51,60
				.03	.0028	.53	.4	.19	**.506**	.8643	6	13, 36, 40, 51
				.072	.0026	.59	.49	.11	**.5064**	.8615	6	13, 40, 51, 61

3.2 Parameter Tuning

In evolutionary optimization, bilevel programming problems are those in which an upper level solution is feasible only if it is one of the optimum of a lower level optimization problem. The efficiency of the algorithms proposed in this paper depend on the algorithm parameters. The parameter tuning is an essential task that can be posed as lower level optimization task in a bilevel optimization framework. Community detection problem is then the upper level optimization task and requires searching among the solutions obtained from the lower level task to find an optimal solution corresponding to one or more different (higher level) objectives [2]. Thus, we model our task as an evolutionary bilevel optimization problem where the lower level task tunes the algorithm parameters- θ_1, θ_2, α, β, *mutRate* by using NSGA-II for multi-objective optimization of network modularity and Normalized Mutual Information (NMI) [1]. A good set of parameters will not only maximize modularity but also maximize NMI for benchmark datasets. The results obtained are shown in Table 2.

4. CONCLUSION AND FUTURE WORK

The paper presents novel variants of quantum-inspired genetic algorithms and applies the techniques to the problem of detecting communities in complex networks. The algorithms do not require any decoding step at the end to realize the communities from the solution chromosomes. Experiments on real life benchmark networks show that the methods are able to successfully reveal community structure with high modularity. We plan to study the scalability of approach in future. The proposed QIEA variants may also be tested on other combinatorial optimization problems. We also intend to explore a parallel implementation with a view to reduce the computation time as the quantum-inspired algorithms lend themselves naturally to parallel computation.

5. ACKNOWLEDGEMENTS

The work is supported by University of Delhi research grant no. DRCH/R&D/2013-14/4155.

6. REFERENCES

[1] L. Danon, A. Diaz-Guilera, J. Duch, and A. Arenas. Comparing community structure identification. *Journal of Statistical Mechanics: Theory and Experiment*, 2005(09):P09008, 2005.

[2] K. Deb and A. Sinha. Solving bilevel multi-objective optimization problems using evolutionary algorithms. In *Evolutionary Multi-Criterion Optimization*, pages 110–124. Springer, 2009.

[3] K.-H. Han and J.-H. Kim. Genetic quantum algorithm and its application to combinatorial optimization problem. In *Evolutionary Computation, 2000. Proceedings of the 2000 Congress on*, volume 2, pages 1354–1360. IEEE, 2000.

[4] E. A. Leicht and M. E. Newman. Community structure in directed networks. *Physical review letters*, 100(11):118703, 2008.

[5] D. Lusseau. The emergent properties of a dolphin social network. *Proceedings of the Royal Society of London. Series B: Biological Sciences*, 270(Suppl 2):S186–S188, 2003.

[6] M. E. J. Newman and M. Girvan. Finding and evaluating community structure in networks. *Physical Review*, E 69(026113), 2004.

[7] G. Ochoa. *Error thresholds and optimal mutation rates in genetic algorithms*. PhD thesis, 2000.

[8] A. Seshadri. Nsga - ii: A multi-objective optimization algorithm, July 2009.

[9] M. Tasgin and H. Bingol. Community detection in complex networks using genetic algorithm. In *ECCS '06: Proc. of the European Conference on Complex Systems*, Apr. 2006.

[10] L. Wang, H. Wu, F. Tang, and D.-Z. Zheng. A hybrid quantum-inspired genetic algorithm for flow shop scheduling. In *Advances in Intelligent Computing*, pages 636–644. Springer, 2005.

[11] W. W. Zachary. An information flow model for conflict and fission in small groups. *Journal of anthropological research*, pages 452–473, 1977.

[12] G. Zhang. Quantum-inspired evolutionary algorithms: a survey and empirical study. *Journal of Heuristics*, 17(3):303–351, 2011.

Developing Morphological Computation in Tensegrity Robots for Controllable Actuation

Mark Khazanov
Union College
807 Union St.
Schenectady, NY
khazanom@union.edu

Julian Jocque
Union College
807 Union St.
Schenectady, NY
jocquej@union.edu

John Rieffel
Union College
807 Union St.
Schenectady, NY
rieffelj@union.edu

ABSTRACT

Conventionally control can be achieved by attempting to simplify complex dynamics. The field of morphological computation explores how mechanical complexity can be advantageous. In this paper we demonstrate morphological computation in tensegrity robots. We present a novel approach to tensegrity actuation and explore the capabilities of our self-evolving system. Methods of finding desirable gaits through both hand selection and evolution are described and the effectiveness of the system is demonstrated by our robot's ability to pursue a moving target. We conclude with a discussion of a bootstrapped system with the potential of significantly reducing evolution time and need for user presence.

Categories and Subject Descriptors

I.2.9 [**Robotics**]: Propelling Mechanisms

Keywords

Morphological Computation; Tensegrity; Hill Climber; Bootstrapping

1. INTRODUCTION

Due to the ability of the natural world to deal with high levels of dynamic complexity, there has been resurgence in the implementation of natural systems in robotic design. The field of morphological computation [4] can allow for a decrease in the cost of control, allowing for individual components to react to each other instead of a central processor [7] [6] and allow for neural pathways that are interconnected to devote resources to higher level tasks. This can be seen in biological systems such as the tendinous network of the human hand [9].

Tensegrities, structures composed of rods for compression and strings for tension, are difficult to control by conventional means due to high levels of dynamic coupling. The majority of the development of locomotion in tensegrity robotics has been done through varying the resting lengths of springs [5]. Unfortunately, this approach leads to slow locomotion.

Much like tensegrities, many natural systems are inherently dynamic, involving a large number of degrees of freedom. These properties of living systems are accompanied by tight dynamic coupling between components [8] that are conventionally avoided in engineering. More predictable, kinematic systems, are easier to understand and implement.

What is then interesting to consider is how dynamically complex biological systems are able to attain controllability. Our exploration of tensegrity locomotion attempts to explain how controllability can be achieved through more dynamic methods. Through the use of a simple tensegrity structure, actuated with vibrational motors, and a mounted camera used as a sensing environment, we are able to achieve controllability allowing for the tensegrity to chase a moving target in real time. We begin the paper with a description of the design of our robot. We continue on to demonstrate the abilities of the evolved gaits, and conclude with a discussion of a bootstrapped system, which is able to evolve gaits without the need for the presence of a user.

GECCO'14, July 12–16, 2014, Vancouver, BC, Canada.

http://dx.doi.org/10.1145/2598394.2605680 .

2. FROM STRUCTURE TO ROBOT

Tensegrity structures can be found in various architectural foundations ranging from towers to camping tents. Tensegrities are also present in the biological realm, integrated into the structure of cellular cytoskeletons [10] and proteins [2].

While conventional approaches to tensegrity locomotion deal with dampening the dynamic complexity of the system, an emerging method of movement is actuation through vibration [3] [1]. Our approach exploits the dynamic movements of the tensegrity, vibrating the structure to produce locomotion. With the use of three vibrational motors attached to struts, we were able to gain locomotive control of the system. The struts were connected with springs and the completed robot is shown in Figure 1. With the ability of our tensegrity to achieve locomotion we demonstrate a novel way of exploiting dynamic complexity as an advantage in the actuation of our robot.

2.1 Design

Our tensegrity, VALTR (Vibrationally Actuated Locomotive Tensegrity Robot), is a 6-bar structure that is powered by vibration alone. 3 pager motors attached to 3 distinct struts of the robot are activated through the use of 2 Pololu microcontrollers attached to a 3V power source. Different oscillation frequencies were achieved by sending a

Figure 1: Tensegrities consist of rigid elements (struts) connected with tensile elements (springs). Their shape is obtained through the interplay of these forces. Above is the fully constructed tensegrity robot with vibrational motors attached.

voltage value to the motors, allowing it to turn with varying speeds. Thin wires were connected to the motors, allowing the tensegrity to move with as little resistance as possible.

The struts were made from 6.35 mm graphite composite tubes that were cut to a length of 9.4 cm. The motors used were Precision Microdrives vibration motors, Model 312-107, which operate between 100 and 260 Hz. These motors were mounted to the flat outer surface of the graphite rods. Selection of springs was given the most consideration, as they would have the greatest affect on VALTR's morphology. The basic strategy in string selection was to try and produce the smallest number of natural frequencies. This was due to the assumption that small natural frequencies would lead to large displacement amplitudes, possibly allowing for the tensegrity to achieve rolling. With these considerations spring were chosen with a constant of 0.209 N/cm.

3. EVALUATION

The robots design was crafted specifically for the maximization of resonance. We proceed by quantifying the results of VALTR's vibrational motion. We explain how the system was evolved, and demonstrate our robots advanced capacity for controllability.

3.1 Setup

The robot was placed on a 91x61 cm table with a removable cork-board sheet as the surface. The specific board was used to provide enough friction for the tensegrity to move freely, but also allow for its base to grasp against the surface. Wooden borders surrounded the testing environment to guard the tensegrity from falling during trials. Thin wires were used to prevent the robot from being tethered by its connections and preventing its ability move with its greatest possible range.

A USB camera was mounted above the testing arena. Below we describe how the camera was used in the process of evaluation and how evolution of motion was achieved through the use of still images of the tensegrity. We then proceed to describe how the evolved motion and the mounted camera worked in tandem to create a system where our tensegrity could autonomously chase a moving target.

Figure 2: The process of measuring fitness by taking the difference between start and end positions is displayed.

3.2 Discovering Motion

3.2.1 Evolution of Physical Systems

While a virtual evolution of gaits may seem more practical, there are many problems associated with this approach. The dynamic complexity of the tensegrity does not allow for an accurate virtual representation of its dynamics. Attempting to implement virtually evolved gaits to the physical system does not provide similar results to evolving the gaits within the physical world. Embodied evolution allows us to address this issue [11], eliminating the problem of a reality gap.

3.2.2 Hand Selected Gaits

Our first process of selecting gaits was done through trial and error. By varying the voltages passed to the motors we were able to change the motion of the tensegrity. An "interactive" feature was implemented where voltage could be changed manually while the tensegrity was active, and the system would respond in real time. Two gaits were selected as "turning" gaits as they were most effective in rotating the tensegrity clockwise and counterclockwise.

3.2.3 Evolution by Hill Climber

A Hill Climber algorithm was used for the evolution of a forward propagating gate. Consisting of 10 individuals, a population was first chosen at random with the top half best-fit individuals continuing on to the next generation. Each individual (genotype) consisted of 3 loci, one for each motor voltage. Each genotype's loci were chosen randomly for the first population and were either mutated or re-evaluated for every successive generation.

With the use of a mounted camera we were able to take pictures of the tensegrity before and after a trial run. Images taken were first converted to black and white and then overlapped. The average difference in white pixels (the space the tensegrity occupied) was calculated and was used in the evaluation of the specific individual of the population 2.

By choosing individuals of the population that were able to travel the furthest distance within the allotted 7 seconds, a new population was then created with children of the survivors of the previous population slightly mutated. The new population was reassessed and new individuals were chosen to continue on to produce offspring. Figure 3 shows 25 generations of a 10 member population evolving over time.

The data shows an increase in maximum fitness over the first 25 generation. After the maximum is achieved, fur-

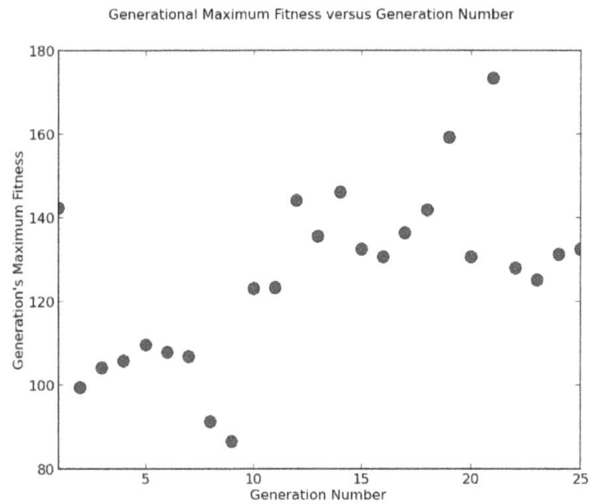

Figure 3: 25 generations of the hill climber evolution are shown. Individuals were assessed based on distance traveled and top performers continued onto the next population.

ther evaluations of the similar frequencies prove to be less successful.

The largest difficulty faced during evolution was the constant need for a manual reset of the system. After each trial the tensegrity would need to be physically moved to its initial location. Other than the repositioning of the robot there was no other necessity for a user. Naturally, this prompted a desire for an automated process in the resetting of the tensegrity. At first an omnidirectional treadmill was considered. When this proved impractical the feasibility of a mechanical arm was put into question. The solution to repositioning was found in the capabilities of the tensegrity itself, using its newly developed ability to navigate.

3.2.4 Navigation

By attaining gaits that were able to produce clockwise, counterclockwise, and forward locomotion in the tensegrity we were able to steer the tensegrity towards a destination. Using left and right arrow keys we were able to turn the tensegrity and press forward when we desired for forward motion towards a target. Once the controllability of the tensegrity had reached this level we proceeded to create a completely autonomous system.

The first step in our automation process was the development of a tracking system. By placing colored markers at three points of the tensegrities upper surface we were able to include a directional property in our system. The different colors were detected and an angle was calculated between the measured angle of the forward vector of the tensegrity and the vector from the center of our robot to the target. Figure 4 shows the tensegrity placed into an environment with a yellow ball acting as the target.

By implementing the state machine shown in Figure 5 our robot was able to track a moving target. VALTR would first calculate the angle between his forward vector and the target. If the angle was below -30 degrees or above 30 degrees, our state machine would either choose to turn clockwise or counterclockwise. Only when in the 60 degree range between -30 and 30 would the robot locomote forward towards the target. When the tensegrity was switching from one movement to another it would stop momentarily so that its components could settle. Once the tensegrity was less than a specified distance away from the target the process would conclude.

Figure 4: Our tensegrity robot with colored markers used for tracking and navigation. The yellow ball is used as movable target, which the tensegrity is able to pursue.

3.2.5 Semi-Autonomous Evolution

With a system that is autonomous, we began to incorporate this feature into the evolution of our robot. Instead of having a user place the tensegrity back to its initial location after each evaluation of an individual, the tensegrity was able to reposition itself autonomously. This significantly reduced the need for user interference. The problem of tangled wires still remained, but no manual repositioning of the robot was necessary during the evolution process.

Our next step to completely eliminate the necessity for user interference is the development of a wireless system. Work currently being done includes a wireless implementation of the tensegrity robot.

3.2.6 A Bootstrapped Implementation

The autonomous navigation of our system spurred the idea for a bootstrapped evolutionary process. While the bootstrapped design has not been fully completed it assumes that when we find better forward propagating gaits we will be able to implement them in the navigational frequencies that return our robot to its original position. In this way the process of evolution will decrease in time because the forward propagation gait will improve, repositioning the robot at a faster and faster rate. The problem with this implementation is that "forward" gaits are currently non-directional. They are achieved by finding gaits that produce the furthest distance traveled and then the forward vector is accommodated for through hardcoding. Currently, we are redeveloping the system to include directional vectors that accompany the distance and speed of our current evaluation process.

4. CONCLUSIONS

Tensegrities have begun to grow in popularity in the field of soft robotics. Their morphology allows for an incredibly versatile range of motion and malleability. While tensegri-

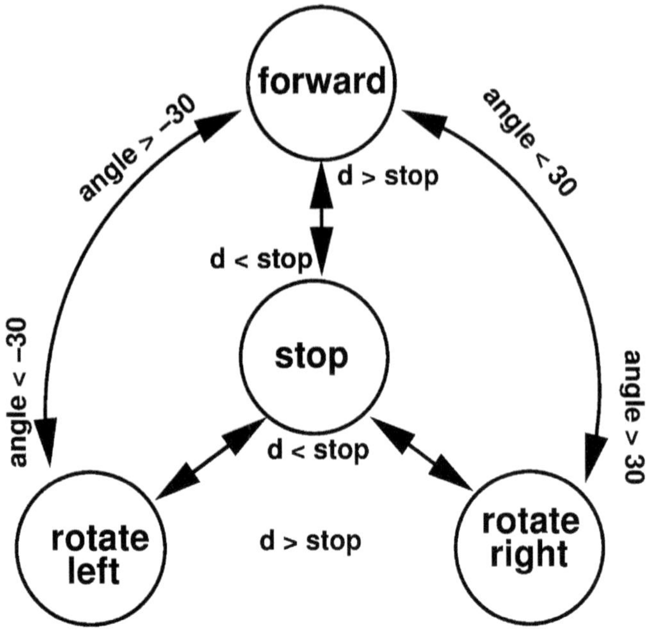

Figure 5: Above is a state machine implemented in the navigation process. Depending on the distance from the target and the angle between the robots forward vector and the vector which points in the direction of the target, the robot is able to change its gaits to either turn clockwise, counterclockwise, or propagate forward.

ties have been most commonly actuated through processes that suppress the resonance of the structures, our approach was to exploit their dynamic complexity, actuating the tensegrity through vibration only. This exploitation of mechanical complexity allows us to further implement morphological computation, in which a greater dynamic coupling can decrease the cost of control. Through the implementation of a tracking system and evolved gaits for directional propagation, our robot is able to achieve robust and agile controllability accompanied by impressive speeds.

Our ability to control the robot has not only led to the creation of an autonomously navigable system, but also an autonomous evolution process. By combining controllable locomotion with the self-positioning provided by the tracking system, our robot is able to perform evaluations and reposition itself without the need for human interference. With a bootstrapped evolution process we will be able to implement the gaits of the most fit individuals directly into our navigational abilities and repositioning speeds. We believe this bootstrapped evolution system to be the first of its kind implemented in physical robotics. Given the vast applications of tensegrity robotics ranging from biomedical devices to search-and-rescue operations, our hope is that this autonomous self-improving evolution system can both advance the locomotive abilities of tensegrity robotics as well as the evolutionary process of dynamically complex systems. In this way we can push the boundaries of technology, our understanding of living systems, and our interaction with the natural world.

5. ACKNOWLEDGMENTS

The authors would like to thank Steve Stangle for assisting in this research as part of an undergraduate practica for Union College. We would also like to thank William Keat of the Mechanical Engineering department of Union College for his extensive work on the mechanical design of the tensegrities used. Funding for undergraduate summer research by authors Mark Khazanov and Julian Jocque was provided through the generosity of the Union College Summer Research Fellowship Program. Materials were paid in part by Union College Internal Education Fund (IEF) grants as well as Student Research Grants (SRG) to the authors.

6. REFERENCES

[1] V. Bohm and K. Zimmermann. Vibration-driven mobile robots based on single actuated tensegrity structures. In *Robotics and Automation (ICRA), 2013 IEEE International Conference on*, pages 5475–5480. IEEE, 2013.

[2] D. E. Ingber. The architecture of life. *Scientific American*, 278(1):48–57, 1998.

[3] M. Khazanov, B. Humphreys, W. Keat, and J. Rieffel. Exploiting dynamical complexity in a physical tensegrity robot to achieve locomotion. In *Advances in Artificial Life, ECAL*, volume 12, pages 965–972, 2013.

[4] C. Paul. Morphological computation: A basis for the analysis of morphology and control requirements. *Robotics and Autonomous Systems*, 54(8):619–630, 2006.

[5] C. Paul, F. J. Valero-Cuevas, and H. Lipson. Design and control of tensegrity robots for locomotion. *Robotics, IEEE Transactions on*, 22(5):944–957, 2006.

[6] R. Pfeifer and J. Bongard. *How the body shapes the way we think: a new view of intelligence.* MIT press, 2007.

[7] R. Pfeifer, M. Lungarella, and F. Iida. Self-organization, embodiment, and biologically inspired robotics. *science*, 318(5853):1088–1093, 2007.

[8] B. A. Trimmer. New challenges in biorobotics: Incorporating soft tissue into control systems. *Applied Bionics and Biomechanics*, 5(3):119–126, 2008.

[9] F. J. Valero-Cuevas, J.-W. Yi, D. Brown, R. V. McNamara, C. Paul, and H. Lipson. The tendon network of the fingers performs anatomical computation at a macroscopic scale. *Biomedical Engineering, IEEE Transactions on*, 54(6):1161–1166, 2007.

[10] N. Wang, K. Naruse, D. Stamenović, J. J. Fredberg, S. M. Mijailovich, I. M. Tolić-Nørrelykke, T. Polte, R. Mannix, and D. E. Ingber. Mechanical behavior in living cells consistent with the tensegrity model. *Proceedings of the National Academy of Sciences*, 98(14):7765–7770, 2001.

[11] R. A. Watson, S. G. Ficici, and J. B. Pollack. Embodied evolution: Distributing an evolutionary algorithm in a population of robots. *Robotics and Autonomous Systems*, 39(1):1–18, 2002.

A Reference Points-based Evolutionary Algorithm for Many-objective Optimization

Yiping Liu
School of Information and Electrical Engineering, China University of Mining and Technology, Xuzhou, China
lyp.cumt@gmail.com

Dunwei Gong
School of Information and Electrical Engineering, China University of Mining and Technology, Xuzhou, China
dwgong@vip.163.com

Xiaoyan Sun
School of Information and Electrical Engineering, China University of Mining and Technology, Xuzhou, China
xysun78@126.com

Yong Zhang
School of Information and Electrical Engineering, China University of Mining and Technology, Xuzhou, China
yongzh401@126.com

ABSTRACT
Many-objective optimization problems are common in real-world applications, few evolutionary optimization methods, however, are suitable for them up to date due to their difficulties. We proposed a reference points-based evolutionary algorithm (RPEA) to solve many-objective optimization problems in this study. In RPEA, a series of reference points with good performances in convergence and distribution are generated according to the current population to guide the evolution. Furthermore, superior individuals are selected based on the assessment of each individual by calculating the distances between the reference points and the individual in the objective space. The algorithm was applied to four benchmark optimization problems and compared with NSGA-II and HypE. The results experimentally demonstrate that the algorithm is strengthened in obtaining Pareto optimal set with high performances.

Categories and Subject Descriptors
I.2.8 [**Computing Methodologies**]: Artificial Intelligence – *Problem Solving, Control Methods, and Search*

Keywords
Evolutionary Optimization; many-objective optimization; reference point; distance

1. INTRODUCTION
Various optimization problems with multiple objectives commonly exist in real-world applications. Their common characteristics are that they contain more than one objective and there exist some conflicts among these objectives, indicating that there is no solution which is optimal for all objectives. They are termed as multi-objective optimization problems (MOP). Problems with more than three objectives are defined as many-objective optimization problems (MaOP). Without loss of generality, the MOP considered in this study is formulated as follows:

GECCO'14, July 12–16, 2014, Vancouver, BC, Canada.

http://dx.doi.org/10.1145/2598394.2605674

$$\min \boldsymbol{f}(\boldsymbol{x}) = \left(f_1(\boldsymbol{x}), f_2(\boldsymbol{x}), \ldots, f_M(\boldsymbol{x})\right)$$
$$s.t. \boldsymbol{x} \in S \subset \boldsymbol{R}^n \quad (1)$$

Where $\boldsymbol{x}$ represents an n-dimensional decision variable in space S. $f_m(\boldsymbol{x}), m = 1,2,\ldots,M$ is the m-th objective to be minimized, and M is the number of objectives. When M>3, this problem is a MaOP.

Classical multi-objective evolutionary algorithms (MOEA), e.g., nondominated sorting genetic algorithm II (NSGA-II) [1], have been successfully applied to a large number of MOPs. But these Pareto-based algorithms noticeably deteriorate their search ability when solving MaOPs. One major reason is that the proportion of nondominated solutions in a population rises rapidly with the number of objectives. This makes the Pareto-based selection fail to distinguish individuals. Hence, seeking for new methods to effectively solve MaOPs is of considerable necessity.

Reference points have been employed to guide the evolution in many situations. On account of the assessment of individuals by the distances between reference points and them, the selection pressure of superior individuals will not lose in many-objective optimization. Since existing reference points-based approaches usually adopt only one reference point to search solutions in objective sub-spaces of interest to the decision maker, intuitively, adopting a series of uniformly distributed reference points to obtain the whole Pareto front has the potential in solving MaOPs. Furthermore, the true Pareto front of a practical optimization problem is usually unknown, and continuously generating appropriate reference points for the problem is advantageous to achieve the solution set with perfect performance.

In view this, RPEA was proposed in this study. During the evolution, a series of reference points with good performances in convergence and distribution are adaptively generated according to the current population. Then, based on the assessment of each individual by calculating the distances between the reference points and the individual, superior individuals are selected in the environment selection process.

This study has the following contributions: (1) presenting an approach to generating reference points which are adaptive to optimization problems; (2) proposing a method of selecting superior individuals based on the distances between reference points and individuals; (3) validating the superiority of the proposed algorithm by optimizing four classical benchmark MaOPs.

The remainder of this paper is organized as follows. Section 2 reviews the related work. The proposed approach, RPEA, is presented in Section 3. Section 4 is the applications of RPEA in several benchmark MaOPs and the comparative experiments. Finally, Section 5 concludes this paper and offers suggestions on possible opportunities for future research.

2. RELATED WORK

2.1 Reference Points-based Evolutionary Optimization

Existing reference points-based approaches usually adopt only one reference point to represent the decision maker's ideal solution. Wierzbicki [2] suggested a reference point approach in which the goal is to achieve a Pareto optimal solution closest to a supplied reference point of aspiration level based on solving an achievement scalarize problem. Deb et al. [3] adopted a predator-prey approach to find a preferred set of solutions near the reference point in parallel. Mohammadi et al. [4] combined decomposition strategies with reference point approaches to search for preferred regions.

Up to date, there is little research on achieving the whole Pareto optimal solution set by employing multiple reference points. Figueira et al. [5] generated reference points by estimating the bounds of the Pareto front and searched solutions near each reference point in parallel. Deb et al. [6] adopted a family of well-distributed direction vectors to generate reference points, which makes a difference to the distribution of the solution set. Wang et al. [7] proposed a co-evolution method to simultaneously optimize solutions and reference points, but the fitness value of an individual is also calculated by the traditional Pareto dominance.

In the approach proposed in this study, reference points are suitable for different problems by continuously generating reference points based on the current population; the selection pressure in many-objective optimization is improved by calculating the distances between these reference points and individuals.

3. PROPOSED METHOD

The general ideas of RPEA are as follows. First, a series of reference points with good performances in convergence and distribution are generated according to the current population. Then, each individual in the current population and the temporary population generated by the former is assessed by calculating the distances between the reference points and the individual, and the new population is formed by selecting superior individuals.

3.1 Generation of Reference Point

In this section, the concept of reference point was first presented; a method of generating reference points with good performances in convergence and distribution was then proposed.

3.1.1 Concept of Reference Point

Loosely, the reference point is a point in the objective space that guides the evolution. There are two types of reference points, i.e., ideal point and nadir point.

For a point in the objective space, if its value(s) is (are) not inferior to that (those) of a part of the known solutions, it is termed as a local ideal point. For instance, when solving the problem represented as formula (1) with a MOEA, $\boldsymbol{r}^l=(r_1^l,r_2^l,\dots,r_M^l)$ is a local ideal point, when

$$r_m^l=\min_{x\in P_l} f_m(\boldsymbol{x})+e_m, m=1,2,\dots,M \tag{2}$$

where P_l is a subset of the current (t-th generation) population $P(t)$. $e_m=0 \text{or} -\varepsilon$, and ε is an arbitrarily small positive. In particular, the local ideal point

$$\boldsymbol{r}^l=(f_1(\boldsymbol{x}),\dots,f_m(\boldsymbol{x})-\varepsilon,\dots,f_M(\boldsymbol{x})) \tag{3}$$

must be superior to solution $\boldsymbol{x}$.

For a point in the objective space, if its value(s) is (are) not inferior to that (those) of all the known solutions, it is termed as a global ideal point. If

$$r_m^g=\min_{x\in Pg} f_m(\boldsymbol{x})+e_m, m=1,2,\dots,M \tag{4}$$

where P_g is equal to $P(t)$, $\boldsymbol{r}^g=(r_1^g,r_2^g,\dots,r_M^g)$ is a global ideal point.

Similarly, a local nadir point and a global nadir point can also be defined. It is worth nothing that a local ideal point can become a local nadir point, and vice versa. A reference point may be a local ideal point for some solutions; however, it may be a local nadir point for other more optimal solutions, and vice versa.

3.1.2 Generation of Reference Points

If only one (local) ideal point is adopted to guide the evolution, it is difficult to obtain the whole Pareto front of a problem. But adopting a series of local ideal points instead, the whole Pareto front can be easily obtained.

While solving a problem with a MOEA, it is easy to seek for a new solution superior to the known solution in one objective. Nonetheless, it is hard to seek for a superior solution in several objectives. Therefore, a local ideal point superior in only one objective is beneficial to select solutions with good performance, and a local ideal point superior to only one solution is also helpful, compared to that superior to several solutions. To this end, formula (3) was adopted to generate reference points in this study.

The population size is supposed to be N_p. From formula (3), there exist MN_p possible reference points with better performance in convergence than the current population. However, they may not have good performance in distribution. On account of this, a method with low computation complexity for generating well diversified reference points was proposed in this section. The detailed procedure is described in algorithm1.

Algorithm1. Generation of reference points

1: $R_\Sigma(t)=\varnothing$

2: **for** $m=1,2,\dots,M$ **do**

3: Sort the individuals in $P(t)$ based on the crowding distances [1] in the m-th dimensional objective space, and select $\lceil \alpha N_p \rceil \left(\frac{N_r}{MN_p}\le\alpha\le 1\right)$ well-distributed individuals. Let $e_m=-\varepsilon$, according to formula (3), generate reference points based on the selected individuals, and form set $R_m(t)$;

4: $R_\Sigma(t)=R_\Sigma(t)\cup R_m(t)$

5: **end for**

6: Select N_r reference points from $R_\Sigma(t)$ based on the crowding distances in the M-dimensional objective space, and form set $R_s(t)$

When $\alpha=\frac{N_r}{MN_p}$, the aforementioned method has the lowest computation complexity, represented as $O(MN_p\log N_p)$. In such scenarios, the reference points are well-distributed, and the computation complexity is substantially reduced.

3.2 Selection of Individuals

In this section, the method of selecting superior individuals was given based on the assessment of each individual by calculating the distances between the reference points and it.

In [3], a superior individual is regarded as the one close to the reference point. It is appropriate when the reference point is a local ideal point. However, for other more optimal individuals, the reference point could be a nadir point, and the closer these individuals are to the reference point, the worse performance they have. Therefore, when a reference point is employed to select individuals, it should be judged whether it is a local nadir point or not. A new method of assessing individuals was proposed in this section, which is described as follows.

The temporary population generated by the current population $P(t)$ is denoted as $Q(t)$, and the population constituted by $P(t)$ and $Q(t)$ is denoted as $P'(t)$. The p-th individual in $P'(t)$ is denoted as $\boldsymbol{x}_p, p=1,2,\ldots,|P'|$, where $|P'|$ represents the number of individuals in $P'(t)$. The q-th reference point in $R_s(t)$ is denoted as $\boldsymbol{r}_q, q=1,2,\ldots,N_r$. Then the distance between $\boldsymbol{x}_p$ and $\boldsymbol{r}_q$ can be formulated as

$$d(\boldsymbol{x}_p,\boldsymbol{r}_q)=\theta\sqrt{\sum_{m=1}^{M}\left(r_{qm}-f_m(\boldsymbol{x}_p)\right)^2} \quad (5)$$

where

$$\theta=\begin{cases}-1, \forall m=1,2,\ldots,M, f_m(\boldsymbol{x}_p)\le r_{qm} \\ 1, \quad \text{other conditions}\end{cases} \quad (6)$$

Formulas (5) and (6) tell that, if $\boldsymbol{r}_q$ is a local nadir point with respect to $\boldsymbol{x}_p$, $d(\boldsymbol{x}_p,\boldsymbol{r}_q)$ represents the opposite Euclidean distance between them; otherwise, $d(\boldsymbol{x}_p,\boldsymbol{r}_q)$ represents the Euclidean distance between them. For $\boldsymbol{r}_q$, the individual with good performance can be obtained by seeking for the one with the smallest $d(\boldsymbol{x}_p,\boldsymbol{r}_q), p=1,2,\ldots,|P'|$.

The method of selecting individuals is showed in algorithm2.

Algorithm2. Selection of individuals

1: $P(t+1)=\varnothing$

2: For $\forall \boldsymbol{x}_p \in P'(t), p=1,2,\ldots,|P'|$ and $\forall \boldsymbol{r}_q \in R_s(t), q=1,2,\ldots,N_r$, calculate $d(\boldsymbol{x}_p,\boldsymbol{r}_q)$ according to formula (5), and form set $D=\{d(\boldsymbol{x}_p,\boldsymbol{r}_q) \mid p=1,2,\ldots,|P'|, q=1,2,\ldots,N_r\}$

3: **for** $i=1,2,\ldots,N_p$ **do**

4: Seek for the individual with the smallest $d(\boldsymbol{x}_{p_{\min}},\boldsymbol{r}_{q_{\min}})$ in D

5: $P(t+1)=P(t+1)\cup\{\boldsymbol{x}_{p_{\min}}\}$

6: Delete $d(\boldsymbol{x}_p,\boldsymbol{r}_{q_{\min}}), p=1,2,\ldots,|P'|$ and $d(\boldsymbol{x}_{p_{\min}},\boldsymbol{r}_q), q=1,2,\ldots,N_r$ from D

5: **end for**

As can be observed from the aforementioned analysis, the new population generated in this way has better performances in convergence and distribution than the old. As a result, the Pareto optimal set of the problem can be obtained along with the population's evolution.

3.3 Steps of Proposed Algorithm

Combining Section 3.1 with Section 3.2, the steps of RPEA are described as follows:

Algorithm3. RPEA

1: Set the values of the control parameters, let $t=0$, and initialize the population $P(t)$

2: **while** the termination criterion is not met **do**

3: According to algorithm1, generate a series of reference points, denoted as $R_s(t)$, based on $P(t)$

4: Perform genetic operators on $P(t)$ so as to generate a temporary population $Q(t)$ with the same size as $P(t)$, and let $P'(t)=P(t)\cup Q(t)$

5: According to algorithm2, form $P(t+1)$ by selecting N_p individuals from $P'(t)$, based on $R_s(t)$

6: $t=t+1$

7: **end**

8: Output the optimal solutions

4. EXPERIMENTS

In this section, the performances of RPEA were investigated by comparing it with the other two state-of-the-art MOEAs, NSGA-II [1] and HypE [8]. NSGA-II is a very popular MOEA which adopts the traditional Pareto domination to select individuals. HypE is an indicator-based algorithm which employs a Monte Carlo simulation to approximate the exact hypervolume value, and enables the hypervolume-based search to be easily applied to many-objective optimization. These three methods were applied to solve the following four benchmark optimization problems, i.e., DTLZ1, DTLZ2, DTLZ3, and DTLZ5 [9], and metric IGD [10] were adopted to compare them.

4.1 Parameter Settings

The following parameter settings were adopted by all these methods. The population size was 100 and the size of tournament selection was chosen as 2. The operators for crossover and mutation were simulated binary crossover and polynomial mutation with distribution indexes 20 and 10. The crossover and mutation probabilities were 1.0 and $1/n$, repectively. The termination criterion was that the number of evaluations reaches to the predefined one. For DTLZ1 and DTLZ3, it was set 100 000, and for DTLZ2 and DTLZ5, 30 000.

In RPEA, a large value of α can improve the distribution of reference points, but the time consumption could be very high. A large value of ε is beneficial to improve the efficiency of the evolution, while a small value of ε can diversify the solution set. Basing on our previous experiments, it was appropriate to set α and ε as 0.5 and 0.01, respectively. In HypE, the number of sampling points to estimate hypervolume was set 10 000.

Each algorithm run 30 times on each optimization problem, and the mean values and variances of IGD were calculated. In addition, Mann-Whitney U distribution test was employed to determine whether the metrics obtained by one algorithm has significant differences with those obtained by the other. Finally, the null hypothesis was rejected at a significant level of 0.05.

4.2 Results and Analysis

Table 1 shows metric IGD obtained by different methods, where 'obj' represents the number of objectives contained in an optimization problem, the boldface data are the best among these methods, and those labeled by '†' mean data significantly different from RPEA's.

Table 1. Metric IGD of different methods

Problem	Obj	NSGA-II	HypE	RPEA
DTLZ1	6	4.784E+1 (2.5E+1)†	1.616E+0 (1.0E+0)†	**3.321E-1 (9.4E-2)**
	9	5.652E+1 (4.2E+1)†	1.777E+0 (8.4E-1)†	**5.719E-1 (2.9E-1)**
	12	7.818E+1 (5.0E+1)†	2.522E+0 (9.7E-1)†	**1.363E+0 (7.1E-1)**
DTLZ2	6	1.722E+0 (1.9E-1)†	5.340E-1 (5.4E-2)†	**3.176E-1 (1.3E-2)**
	9	2.071E+0 (1.4E-1)†	6.967E-1 (4.2E-2)†	**5.461E-1 (1.7E-2)**
	12	2.139E+0 (2.0E-1)†	8.508E-1 (6.0E-2)†	**6.964E-1 (3.1E-2)**
DTLZ3	6	1.207E+2 (5.7E+1)†	**3.259E+0 (3.0E+0)**	3.312E+0 (2.1E+0)
	9	1.343E+2 (7.3E+1)†	**3.439E+0 (2.4E+0)†**	4.953E+0 (2.2E+0)
	12	1.405E+2 (8.6E+1)†	**3.874E+0 (1.8E+0)†**	6.874E+0 (2.9E+0)
DTLZ5	6	1.461E-1 (3.2E-2)†	1.565E-1 (7.4E-2)†	**1.043E-1 (4.5E-2)**
	9	4.711E-1 (3.0E-1)†	1.980E-1 (7.7E-2)†	**1.495E-1 (4.3E-2)**
	12	9.118E-1 (2.6E-1)†	2.096E-1 (9.9E-2)†	**1.774E-1 (5.1E-2)**

Based on table 1, (1) when tackling DTLZ1, DTLZ2, and DTLZ5, RPEA has a significantly smaller value of IGD than the other two, therefore has the best performances in convergence and distribution, which validates that the proposed method is very competitive in solving MaOPs; (2) when tackling DTLZ3, RPEA is significantly superior to NSGA-II, but inferior to HypE. The possible reason is that the objective functions have a large range and the individuals close to the boundary have poor performances. By using the reference points generated by these individuals, new superior individuals can hardly be selected in such limited areas. As a result, the population is difficult to evolve. This drawback could potentially be overcome by introducing a new approach to updating the individuals close to the boundary, which will be investigated in future work.

5. CONCLUSIONS

This paper exploited the potential of the reference points in handling MaOPs. The proposed method, RPEA, can mainly be characterized as: (1) adaptively generating a series of reference points with good convergence and distribution based on the evolution of a population; (2) greatly increasing the selection pressure toward the true Pareto front by calculating the distances between the reference points and the individuals in the environment selection process.

The propose method was applied to four benchmark MaOPs, and compared with the other two method to evaluate its performance. The results reveal that RPEA is very competitive to the others in terms of seeking for a solution set with good approximation and distribution in many-objective optimization. The results show that RPEA can achieve a good tradeoff among the convergence and the diversity under a proper setting.

It is worth mentioning that RPEA has been applied only to optimization problems with numerical objectives. Its effectiveness in other optimization problems, especially in engineering optimization, should further be confirmed. In addition, RPEA adopts a key parameter, ε, which will affect its performance. If appropriate methods are employed to adaptively adjust the value of ε during the evolution, the performance of RPEA will further be improved, which is also our further research work.

6. ACKNOWLEDGMENTS

This work was jointly supported by the National Science Foundation of China with granted number 61375067, 61105063, and 61075061.

7. REFERENCES

[1] Deb, K., Pratap, A., Agarwal, A. and Meyarivan, T. 2002. A fast and elitist multiobjective genetic algorithm: NSGA-II. *IEEE Transactions on Evolutionary Computation*, 6(2), 182-197.

[2] Wierzbicki, A. P. 1980. The use of reference objectives in multiobjective optimization. *Multiple Criteria Decision Making Theory and Application*. Springer-Verlag, Berlin, 468-486.

[3] Deb, K. and Sundar, J. 2006. Reference point based multi-objective optimization using evolutionary algorithms. In *Proceedings of the 8th Annual Conference on Genetic and Evolutionary Computation*, (Seattle, WA, USA, 2006), ACM, 635-642.

[4] Mohammadi, A., Omidvar. M. N. and Li, X. 2012. Reference point based multi-objective optimization through decomposition. In *Proceedings of the Congress of Evolutionary Computation*, (Brisbane, QLD, 2012), IEEE, 1150-1157.

[5] Figueira, J. R., Liefooghe, A., Talbi, E. G. and Wierzbicki, A. P. 2010. A parallel multiple reference point approach for multi-objective optimization. *European Journal of Operational Research*, 205(2), 390-400.

[6] Deb, K. and Jain, H. 2013. An evolutionary many-objective optimization algorithm using reference-point based non-dominated sorting approach, part I: solving problems with box constraints. *IEEE Transactions on Evolutionary Computation*, 99, 1.

[7] Wang, R., Purshouse, R. C. and Fleming, P. J. 2012. Preference-based solution selection algorithm for evolutionary multiobjective optimization. *IEEE Transactions on Evolutionary Computation*, 16(1), 20-34.

[8] Bader, J. and Zitzler, E. 2011. HypE: an algorithm for fast hypervolume-based many-objective optimization. *Evolutionary Computation*, 19(1), 45-76.

[9] Deb, K., Thiele, L., Laumanns, M. and Zitzler, E. 2002. Scalable test problems for evolutionary multiobjective optimization. In *Proceedings of the 2002 IEEE Congress on Evolutionary Computation*, (Hawaii, US, 2002), IEEE Computational Intelligence Society, 825-830.

[10] Zhang, Q. F., Zhou, A. M., Zhao, S. Z., Suganthan, P. N., Liu, W. D. and Tiwari, S. 2008. *Multiobjective Optimization Test Instances for the CEC 2009 Special Session and Competition*. Technical Report. University of Essex, Colchester, UK and Nanyang Technological University, Singapore.

Particles Types in a Swarm: Searching for Efficiency

Łukasz Rokita
Cardinal Stefan Wyszyński University
Faculty of Mathematics and Natural Sciences
Wóycickiego 1/3, 01-938 Warsaw, Poland
lukasz.rokita@op.pl

Przemysław Ogrodowski
Cardinal Stefan Wyszyński University
Faculty of Mathematics and Natural Sciences
Wóycickiego 1/3, 01-938 Warsaw, Poland
przemek.ogrodowski@gmail.com

ABSTRACT

This research is devoted analysis of convergence in particle swarm where each of the particles can represent different dynamic behaviour in search space.

Categories and Subject Descriptors

I.2.8 [**Artificial Intelligence**]: Problem Solving, Control Methods, and Search

Keywords

Particle Swarm Optimization; Convergence Analysis; Discrete-Time Dynamic Systems

1. INTRODUCTION

Particle swarm is one of heuristic optimization approaches being a subject of great interest. This is a population-based method proposed by Kennedy and Eberhart in 1995 [2] where members of population, called particles, represent a sample of solutions of a given problem. A set of all possible solutions, called search space, is a subject of exploration by the algorithm. With use of the population, the algorithm samples the space. During this process the particles exchange information with each other like, for example, a swarm of bees or school of fishes. This way they coordinate their movement through the space searching for more promising regions. The quality of the points in the search space is defined by the evaluation function. The swarm is searching for the best point in the space, that is, for the optimum (maximum or minimum) of the evaluation function. Thus, the swarm can be called a heuristic optimization algorithm.

A simple scheme of the particle swarm optimization algorithm is given in Algorhitm 1. A particle $\mathbf{y}_i$ represents the best solution found by the i-th particle (called particle attractor), and a particle $\mathbf{y}^*$ – the best solution found by the swarm (called swarm attractor).

Numerous implementations are based on the particle parameters values presented by Clerc and Kennedy [1]. This method of balancing global and local searches known as *constriction* defines the particle speed equation as follows:

$$v_j^{t+1} = w[v_j^t + c_1 \cdot r_1^t \cdot (y_j^t - x_j^t) + c_2 \cdot r_2^t \cdot (y_j^{*t} - x_j^t)]\,, \quad (1)$$

where:
v_j^t — particle's velocity,
x_j^t — particle's location,
y_j^t — the best solution the particle $\mathbf{x}^t$ has found so far,
y_j^{*t} — the best value obtained so far by any particle in the neighborhood of $\mathbf{x}^t$.
r_1, r_2 — random values: $U(0,1)$
$c_1 = c_2 = c$ as proposed by Clerc and Kennedy [1]

The value of w is derived from the existing constants in the velocity update equation:

$$w = \frac{2 \cdot \kappa}{|2 - \varphi - \sqrt{\varphi^2 - 4\varphi}|} \quad \text{where } \varphi = c_1 + c_2 \quad (2)$$

The factor κ controls balance between exploration and exploitation:

1. $\kappa \approx 0$: fast convergence, local exploitation,
2. $\kappa \approx 1$: slow convergence, high degree of exploration.

For $w > 4$ and $\kappa \in [0, 1]$ the swarm convergence would be quick and guaranteed. So, using the constant $\varphi = 4.1$ to ensure convergence, Clerc and Kennedy proposed the values $c = 2.05$ and $w = 0.729843788$.

In our paper we study features of particles defined with different values of parameters c and w and propose a new, nonuniform configuration of particle parameters in the swarm. Presented results of experimental tests show that for some classes of problems this configuration is more efficient, that is, less computational cost is needed to find points located in a very close boundary of the global optimum.

Algorithm 1 the particle swarm optimization

```
Create and initialize the swarm: x_1, ..., x_N
repeat
  for i = 1 to N do
    if f(x_i) > f(y_i) then
      y_i = x_i
    end if
    if f(y_i) > f(y*) then
      y* = y_i
    end if
  end for
  update location and velocity of all the particles
until stop condition is satisfied
```


GECCO'14, July 12–16, 2014, Vancouver, BC, Canada.

http://dx.doi.org/10.1145/2598394.2605682.

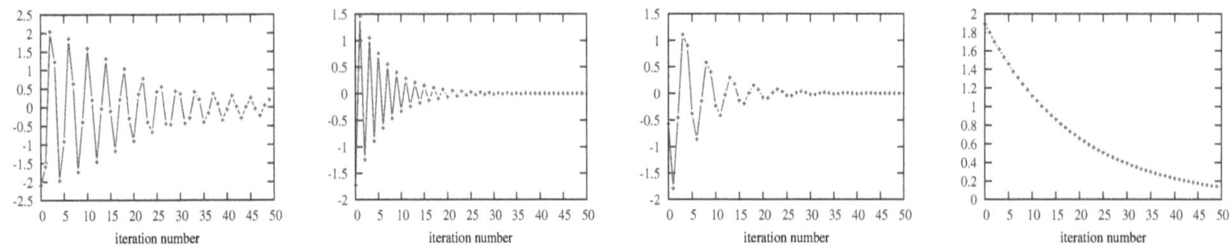

Figure 1: Convergence of particles of type: A, B, C, and D (from left to right).

2. THE SELECTED MODEL OF PARTICLE MOVEMENT

In our research a model of particle movement proposed in [1, 4] is investigated:

$$\mathbf{y}^{t+1} = A\mathbf{y}^t + Bp \tag{3}$$

where:

$$A = \begin{bmatrix} 1-c & w \\ -c & w \end{bmatrix} \quad \mathbf{y}^k = \begin{bmatrix} x^k \\ v^k \end{bmatrix} \quad B = \begin{bmatrix} c \\ c \end{bmatrix} \tag{4}$$

The model is equivalent of the model proposed by Shi and Eberhart [3] with the inertia weight factor. In [1, 4] authors convert the equations into the form applied in the theory of linear, discrete-time dynamic systems. This way particles with different movement characteristics can be identified easily, that is convergent particles, or particles with harmonic oscillatory behaviour or with zigzagging behaviour.

3. PARTICLE BEHAVIOR TYPES

Four types of particles are considered in our research. Their characteristics are depicted in Figure 1.

The safe configuration proposed in [1] represents uniform swarm which consists of particles of the same type. In our research we give careful consideration to the swarms assembled of some numbers of representatives for all the four types.

The most efficient configurations of particle types within a swarm are searched experimentally. The results of experiments for three types of test cases are presented in the next section.

4. BENCHMARKS

Three test-cases are selected for the research:

- a unimodal function defined with a formula same as 1-dimensional Gaussian probability density function:

$$f(x) = 1/(\sqrt{2\pi\sigma^2})\exp(\frac{(x-\mu)^2}{2\sigma^2}) \tag{5}$$

  with a mean μ and a standard deviation σ,

- a multimodal function build of two neighbouring hills (two Gaussian p.d.f.),

- the Ackley function:

$$f(\mathbf{x}) = -20\exp\left(-0.2\sqrt{\frac{1}{n}\sum_{i=1}^{n} x_i^2}\right) - \exp\left(\frac{1}{n}\sum_{i=1}^{n}\cos(2\pi x_i)\right) + 20 + e \tag{6}$$

5. METHODOLOGY OF EXPERIMENTAL RESEARCH

5.1 Test-cases and evaluation measures

Two groups of experiments were performed:

1. with uni- and duo-modal function in one-dimensional search space,
2. with the Ackley function in two and five-dimensional search space.

For the evaluation of the results: for selected test-case and for a series of 100 executions of particle swarm optimization algorithm the mean values of numbers of execution of evaluation function to converge. The convergence is defined as finding a solution located in euclidean distance not greater than 10^{-3} from the optimum. The maximum number of iterations to converge is set to 1000. In the case of exceeding this limit the result is set to the upper boundary, that is, 1000.

5.2 Tested swarm configurations

A single swarm might consist of four types of particles, identified as A,B,C, and D.

In the first group of experiments the swarms consisted of: 1, 2, 3, and 5 particles of any type. For swarms of size 1 and 2 all the possible sets of particles were tested. In the remaining two just the selected configurations were applied. All the cases, that is, 1, 2, 3, and 5 particles, were also tested with swarms consisting of standard particles, that is, having the parameters of velocity formula defined as advised in [1]. It is worth noting that the behaviour of the standard particles is of type A, however, the proposed configuration of particles of type A has slightly different values of parameters.

In the second group of experiments the swarm configurations originated from the output of a genetic algorithm (GA). First, GA searched for the most promising sets of particles where the chromosome represented the entire single swarm of a given size. The chromosomes sizes: from 1 to 20 with step 1 for 2-dimensional search space and from 30 to 50 with step 5 and also for a size of 100 for 5-dimensional search space. The value of a chromosome is defined as the mean value of numbers of iterations to converge for a series of 100 executions. The population consisted of 100 chromosomes. Every time, a single GA execution consisted of 15 iterations. For each of the chromosome sizes GA was executed 20 times for 5D search space and 50 times for 2D.

Then the obtained best chromosomes, that is, the best configurations of swarms were subject of more detailed analysis. For each of the test-cases from the series of 20 (for 5D)

Table 1: Convergence for single particles of the four types and two types of fitness landscape

landscape\type	A	B	C	D
Unimodal	**23.84**	39.88	24.91	67.47
Duomodal	**24.37**	37.12	31.72	80.33

Table 2: Convergence for swarms of size two and unimodal fitness landscape

type\type	A	B	C	D
A	**257.0**	566.46	501.34	598.7
B		1808.32	1201.46	1728.88
C			514.04	1116.72
D				1291.42

or 50 (for 2D) outputs (that is, the best chromosomes in the final population) the best among them was selected. For the obtained chromosome the number of particles for each of the four types is counted. The histogram with the counted numbers is the final result of experiment for a given swarm size.

6. RESULTS OF EXPERIMENTS

6.1 First group of experiments

Experiments from the first group are presented in Tables 1, 2, 3, 4 and 5.

Tables 1, 2 and 3 show the convergence for swarms consisting of one and two particles. Particles of type A give the best convergence, however, for the duo-modal landscape and two particle-swarm the winner configuration are ex aequo AA and AC. Dominance of A type which is the same type as proposed in [1] is evident.

For the swarms of size 3 and 5 and the unimodal landscape the highest convergence can be obtained with mix of A, C and D type, however, the second best results is without C, which means that the role of C particle is very similar to A. This can be observed also in Table 3 where the winning configuration also contains particle of type C. For the remaining cases (see Table 4) the common observation is that A particles should be the majority of a swarm, but for better results a small fraction of C particles should appear. For the swarm of size 5 in both cases there is also a particle of type B.

Table 5 shows the convergence of the swarms of size 1, 2, 3 and 5 which are build of standard particles. The standard swarm convergence is worse for all the cases except from the swarm of size 5 where the convergence of standard swarm significantly outperforms nonuniform swarms.

Table 3: Convergence for swarms of size two and duomodal fitness landscape

type\type	A	B	C	D
A	636.52	908.12	**635.0**	740.16
B		1927.12	1411.52	1871.36
C			1012.56	1277.78
D				1658.94

Table 5: Convergence for four swarm sizes with standard particles

landscape\size	1	2	3	5
Unimodal	43.49	639.3	342.69	**166.25**
Duomodal	**42.49**	927.72	821.61	439.1

Table 6: Configurations of swarms: numbers of particles of a given type for the types A, B, C, and D for different swarm sizes in 2-dimensional search space

size\type	A	B	C	D	convergence
2	2	0	0	0	1325
3	3	0	0	0	916.5
4	3	0	1	0	510.8
5	3	0	1	1	526,5
6	0	0	6	0	243
7	2	0	5	0	233.8
8	2	0	6	0	264.0
9	6	1	2	0	248.4
10	4	0	6	0	268.0
11	3	2	5	1	288.2
12	3	1	7	1	254.4
13	6	1	4	2	257.4
14	4	1	7	2	312.2
15	3	2	9	1	285.0
16	5	2	8	1	286.4
17	6	1	8	2	294.1
18	4	5	9	0	306.0
19	4	3	11	1	321.1
20	5	5	10	0	300.0

6.2 Second group of experiments

Experiments from the second group with the Ackley function are presented in Tables 6, 7 and 8.

Table 6 shows the best configurations and convergence levels for swarms of size from two to 20 found by GA for the Ackley function defined in 2-dimensional search space. One can see, that there is a significant rise of the number of A particles as the swarm size grows. The proportion between the types of particles for the very small swarm sizes shows the dominance of particle A. For larger swarm sizes the number of particles A remains constant whereas the number of particles C grows. In both cases the numbers of particles B and D stay low.

Table 7 shows the best swarm configurations and convergence levels obtained as previously but for the 5-dimensional search space and swarm sizes from 20 to 50 with step 5. As in the case of two-dimensional search space the numbers of particles A and C are higher than the numbers of particles B and D.

The results for the final part of experiments is presented in Table 8. Based on the observation obtained so far, the structure of swarms applied in these experiments was: 3 parts of particles A and 2 parts of particles C and with no particles B and D regardless of the search space dimensionality (briefly 3A2C-swarm). In particular, for the swarm of size 20 there are 12 A particles and 8 C particles, and for the swarm of size 50 there are 30 A particles and 20 C particles and so on. The obtained number is a mean of numbers of evaluation function executions in 100 runs of particle swarm

Table 4: **Convergence for 10 best swarms of size 3 and 5 for uni- and duomodal fitness landscape**

	three particles		five particles	
rank\landscape	Unimodal	Duomodal	Unimodal	Duomodal
The best – 1	354.42- ACD	365.88 - AAC	504.75 - AAABC	560.65 - AAABC
2	357.12 - AAD	527.43 - AAB	506.05 - ABCCD	575.55 - ABBCC
3	362.07 - CCC	547.23 - ACD	507.3 - AABCD	590.08 - AACCD
4	416.79 - AAA	548.85 - ACC	508.15 - AAACD	597.7 - AAAAC
5	432.27 - ABB	597.6 - ABC	509.95 - AAADD	617.7 - ACCCD
6	432.93 - ABD	668.94 - AAD	515.3 - AAAAB	642.7 - AABBC
7	456.15 - CCD	734.64 - AAA	515.6 - ACCCD	643.7 - AAACD
8	480.45 - ADD	824.91 - ABD	517.2 - AADDD	646.15 - AABCD
9	511.83 - BCC	837.18 - BCC	526.8 - ACCCC	696.15 - ACCCC
10	789.99 - BCD	873.78 - CCD	528.65 - AAAAD	704.35 - AAACC

Table 8: No. of evaluation function executions of swarms (mean value, the std. deviation and Student's t-test value) with the best configurations compared with the convergence of standard swarms

	two dimensional search space			five dimensional search space		
size\conf.	3A2C	Std	t-test	3A2C	Std	t-test
20	701.36 ±38.86	818.66 ±273.26	6,68246E-07	13280.24±821.02	12545.98 ±847.16	0.20790
25	825.625 ±47.2	937.725 ±70.469	5,80947E-32	12829.225±1213.75	11982.325 ±1121.55	0.06603
30	967.53 ±285.3	1087.56 ±46.77	4,92E-05	13103.73±1223.04	11758.74 ±1120.89	0.00759
35	1049.265 ±55.615	1235.885 ±58.205	0,000369	13486.48±1503.88	12071.29 ±1484.91	0.37055
40	1172.8 ±52.84	1371.12 ±72.36	2,24579E-36	13498.92±1639.56	12519.36 ±1819.28	0.21277
45	1270.8 ±57.105	1511.955 ±62.46	9,66967E-49	13962.69±1877.04	13026.96 ±2008.755	0.08600
50	1375.35 ±57.05	1651.1 ±69.4	6,22448E-48	14622.35±2063.2	13228.50 ±1874.05	0.01534

Table 7: Configurations of swarms: numbers of particles of a given type for the types A, B, C, and D for different swarm sizes in 5-dimensional search space

size\type	A	B	C	D	convergence
20	5	5	9	1	11326.0
25	8	3	9	5	21159.0
30	7	5	9	9	11787.0
35	11	6	10	8	9943.5
40	13	3	17	7	5460.0
45	14	10	15	6	8347.5
50	15	5	17	13	6855.0

optimization algorithm until solution is located in euclidean distance not greater than 10^{-3} from the optimum. This is compared with the same mean for the uniform swarm consisting only of standard particles. In addition there is also standard deviation for the given mean.

For the two-dimensional search space in every case the 3A2C-swarm outperforms the uniform one.

For the five-dimensional search space mean values for the uniform swarm has a slight advantage over the values for the 3A2C-swarm. However, due to large values of standard deviations we decided to do additional statistical tests. Student's t-test for the compared convergence means revealed lack of statistical difference for 5 out of 7 swarm sizes selected for experiments. Therefore, assuming normal distribution of the results we may say that for 5-dimensional search space the two swarm types offer similar efficiency of the algorithm.

7. CONCLUSIONS

This paper demonstrates the performance of nonuniform swarms, consisting of 4 types of particles, compared to uniform consisting only of standard particles.

We tested nonuniform swarms configurations in order to find the fastest converging one. Aforementioned experiments show clearly that nonuniform swarms can be optimized to perform similar or even better than uniform swarms consisting solely of particles proposed in [1].

Additional research can be conducted to test other values for parameters w and c as well as other swarms' compositions in order to improve convergence.

8. REFERENCES

[1] M. Clerc and J. Kennedy. The particle swarm-explosion, stability, and convergence in a multidimensional complex space. *IEEE Transactions on Evolutionary Computation*, 6(1):58–73, 2002.

[2] J. Kennedy and R. C. Eberhart. Particle swarm optimization. In *Proc. of the IEEE Int. Conf. on Neural Networks*, pages 1942–1948, Piscataway, NJ, 1995. IEEE Service Center.

[3] Y. Shi and R. C. Eberhart. A modified particle swarm optimizer. In *Proceedings of the IEEE Congress on Evolutionary Computation 1998*, pages 69–73. IEEE Press, 1998.

[4] I. C. Trelea. The particle swarm optimization algorithm: convergence analysis and parameter selection. *Information Processing Letters*, 85(6):317 – 325, 2003.

Flood Evolution: Changing the Evolutionary Substrate from a Path of Stepping Stones to a Field of Rocks

David Shorten
University of Cape Town
Private Bag X3
Rondebosch 7701
dshorten@cs.uct.ac.za

Geoff Nitschke
University of Cape Town
Private Bag X3
Rondebosch 7701
gnitschke@cs.uct.ac.za

ABSTRACT

We present ongoing research that is an extension of novelty search, flood evolution. This technique aims to improve evolutionary algorithms by presenting them with large sets of problems, as opposed to individual ones. If the older approach of incremental evolution were analogous to moving over a path of stepping stones, then this approach is similar to navigating a rocky field. The method is discussed and preliminary results are presented.

Categories and Subject Descriptors

I.2.6 [**Artificial Intelligence**]: Learning

General Terms

Algorithms

Keywords

Novelty Search

1. INTRODUCTION

This is a position paper detailing a current research topic and results of a case study are discussed. This topic is *flood evolution*, an extension to *novelty search*.

Assume one is trying to navigate across a field, from point A to point B, by only setting foot on rocks. If one is traveling along a path of stepping stones, one's journey will be terminated if the gap between any two stones is too large to be crossed. However, if one is moving across a field strewn with rocks and boulders, then in the instance that one reaches a rock from which no unvisited rocks are within the range of a single jump, one can backtrack and attempt to find an alternate route to the desired point.

There exists very little knowledge concerning what determines the difficulty, from the perspective of evolution, of jumping from one stone to another. This paper argues that, given this, it is beneficial for *Evolutionary Algorithms* (EAs) to be presented with a large field of stones through which they can determine their own path.

GECCO'14, July 12–16, 2014, Vancouver, BC, Canada.

ACM 978-1-4503-2881-4/14/07$15.00.
http://dx.doi.org/10.1145/2598394.2605675.

It is necessary to point out that the usage of the stepping stone metaphor in this paper is subtly different to that in important related literature (eg: [4, 10]). In that context it is referring to an intermediate phenotype which allows for the evolution of a more complicated one. However, here it is referring to the act of providing an incentive towards the development of such a phenotype. Although intermediate phenotypes can emerge for reasons other than selective pressure [13], rewarding a phenotype requires a definition of it. Thus, the reward of a phenotype and the phenotype itself are two inextricably linked concepts. It is for this reason that it is justifiable to use the stepping stone metaphor in this different, but closely related, context. However, to avoid confusion, this concept shall be referred to as a *stepping stone incentive* for the rest of this paper.

2. THE GRAPH OF PROBLEMS

A good way of making the field of rocks metaphor more precise is to employ the mathematical abstraction of a graph. A stepping stone incentive can be viewed as a synonym for a problem which is presented to an EA. *Flood evolution* presents EAs with sets of problems. A set of problems, Π, can be represented as a graph $G = (E, V)$. Each problem $P \in \Pi$ can have an associated node $p \in V$. Given $P, Q \in \Pi$ and their corresponding nodes $p, q \in V$, then the edge $(p, q) \in E$ can be defined as existing if and only if, for a given a population of solutions γ, which contains a solution to P, it is easy to evolve a solution to Q using γ as the initial population. This definition of an edge is analogous to an evolutionary jump between stones. It is, however, imprecise, due to the stochastic nature of EAs [5].

A given graph representing a set of problems may have connected subgraphs. Assume one wants a solution to the problem B. Assume also that one has a set of problems Π and that $B \in \Pi$. Further assume that Π is constructed such that it is feasible to randomly instantiate a population of solutions γ such that γ contains a solution to a problem in Π. This problem can be labeled A, and in the graph representation of Π, the nodes representing A and B can be labeled a and b, respectively. If a and b are part of the same connected subgraph then one could apply an evolutionary algorithm which continuously attempts to jump from all solved problems to all others. This algorithm is guaranteed to find the solution to b and is an application of flood fill [8]. This approach shall be referred to as *flood evolution*.

It is intuitively likely that, the larger a given problem set, the more edges each node in the associated graph will have. Moreover, increasing the size of the problem set should increase the probability that a randomly instantiated population solves a problem within it. From this it follows that increasing the size of a problem set increases the chance that a randomly instantiated population will be able to evolve a solution to a desired problem within it.

It is necessary to clarify what exactly is meant by two different problems. In this context, two problems are considered different unless they are identical in every way. So, for instance, two pole balancing problems [7] would be considered different if they had slightly different initial conditions.

3. BACKGROUND

Current theories in Biology state that the evolution of complicated features requires many incremental stepping stones [4, 3]. Moreover, the evidence for this viewpoint is overwhelming [12]. Although we have some understanding of the stepping stones which led to complicated life on Earth, our knowledge of them is sparse [18, 2].

There exists much exploration of the use of sequential, linear, stepping stone incentives in the EA literature [6, 15, 16, 17, 20]. This approach has often been termed *incremental evolution*. It has been shown that this approach allows certain EAs to solve problems which they would have otherwise been unable to.

The ideas presented here are largely inspired by the *novelty search* of Lehman and Stanley [10]. The authors view the work described in this paper as an extension of the ideas contained therein. In this paradigm the authors replace the more traditional fitness function, which rewards solutions based on how close they are to a single goal, with one which rewards solutions based on how novel they are. The consequence of this is that there is an evolutionary incentive for solving many problems closely related to the target problem.

Novelty search has been demonstrated to be a powerful method [10, 11, 14]. This paper proposes that a reason for this success is that it is closer to the rocky field metaphor. More specifically, it has two key differences from the older approach of incremental evolution:

1. There is a larger variety of intermediate problems.
2. The path through these intermediate problems is unspecified; evolution is allowed to figure out its own path.

The authors interpret the success of novelty search as evidence towards the plausibility of flood evolution being a useful technique.

Similar ideas to what is being proposed here have been explored within the framework of *artificial life*. Lenski et al [12] ran simulations which rewarded genomic programs for executing one of nine logical operations. The reward received for executing them was proportional to the complexity of the operation. They were able to demonstrate that the evolution of complex operations requires simpler operations as intermediate goals. Arthur and Polak demonstrated a similar result with regards to the evolution of technology [1]. These results are interpreted as further evidence for the utility of providing evolution with a non-linear substrate of incentives.

4. FLOOD EVOLUTION

Similar to novelty search, flood evolution is an augmenting technique which can be applied to a given evolutionary algorithm.

At the start of evolution, a population of candidate solutions must be initialized. At the same time, a set of problems must also be instantiated (see section 5 for further discussion). Each individual candidate solution is always evaluated on all the problems in the in the problem set. A solution receives fitness for each problem which it solves. However, in order to provide an incentive for unsolved problems in the set to be solved, fitness sharing is implemented. In the present preliminary experiments, a solution receives fitness β/n^2, where β is a constant and n is the number of solutions which solve that particular problem. A solution's total fitness is the sum of all the fitness it receives from all the problems which it solves. The manner in which the authors foresee this strategy running is displayed in figure 1. These predictions are already partially confirmed (see section 6).

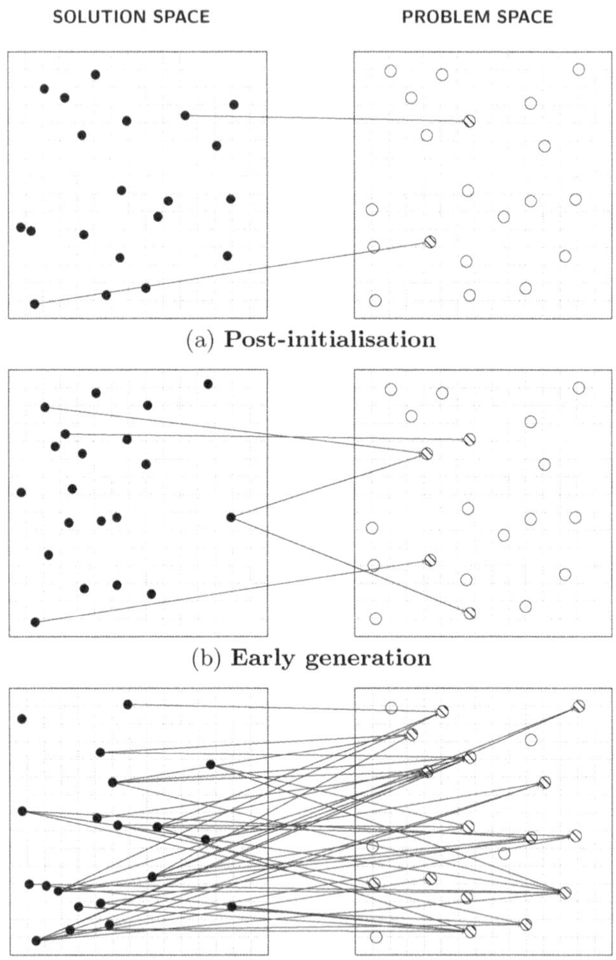

(a) **Post-initialisation**

(b) **Early generation**

(c) **Late generation**

Figure 1: The change in state of a hypothetical but representative evolutionary run over a problem space. The squares in the left column represent the solution space squashed into two dimensions. Similarly, the right squares represent the problem space. Nodes which are filled represent points in the solution space. Nodes which are empty represent unsolved points in the problem space and nodes with hatching represent solved points. An edge from a solution node to a problem node signifies that the solution solves the problem.

5. PROBLEM SETS

In order to implement flood evolution, it is necessary to have a method by which very large sets of problems can be easily instatiated. This paper proposes two case studies, the second of which is already partially implemented. Both use *Artificial Neural Networks* (ANNs) as their solutions. As such, this research falls under the umbrella of *Neuro-Evolution* (NE). A question which these case studies intend to address is the effect of having mixed problem sets which contain multiple problem types.

5.1 Maze-Solving

Maze solving is already an established testing environment for NE algorithms [10]. Furthermore, there exists freely-available software which implements NE over a maze-solving environment[1]. There also exist many algorithms for automatically constructing mazes [19]. This means that the construction of a problem field which consists of many mazes should be an easy task.

5.2 Polynomial-Interval-Finding

A polynomial-interval-finding problem set, Π, will have three variables constant across it. These are the scaling factor, s (see below), the numbers of inputs and outputs, m and n respectively, which all solution ANNs will have and the number of iterations t which each ANN will be evaluated over. Each $P \in \Pi$ is specified by a set of inputs H, a set of coefficients C, a set of exponents E as well as an interval on the real number line, described by a lower bound l and an upper bound u. The notation $P = (H, C, E, l, u)$ could be used. Necessary specifications are imposed on the sizes of H, C and E. More specifically, $|H| = tm$ and $|C| = |E| = tn$. An ANN is evaluated on a problem as follows. The first m inputs from H are supplied to the ANN, that is, the ANN receives the input vector $\langle h_1, h_2, \ldots, h_m \rangle$ where $h_a \in H$, $1 \geq a \leq mt$. The ANN will then produce the output vector $\langle o_1, o_2, \ldots, o_n \rangle$. In the next iteration the input vector will be $\langle h_{m+1}, h_{m+2}, \ldots, h_{2m} \rangle$ and the output vector will be $\langle o_{n+1}, o_{n+2}, \ldots, o_{2n} \rangle$. This continues until, in the tth iteration, the input vector is $\langle h_{(t-1)m+1}, h_{(t-1)m+2}, \ldots, h_{tm} \rangle$ and, similarly, the output vector is $\langle o_{(t-1)n+1}, o_{(t-1)n+2}, \ldots, o_{tn} \rangle$. A result r can then be calculated as specified in equation (1).

$$r = \sum_{i=1}^{tn} c_i \left(s o_i\right)^{e_i} \qquad (1)$$

The problem is considered solved if $u < r < l$.

The motivation for this case study is that it is easy to implement and testing an ANN on it uses comparatively little computational resources.

6. SAMPLE RUN

An implementation of the polynomial-interval-finding problem set was made and incorporated into Joel Lehman's *Novelty Search C++* [1] as described in [9]. A few things to note regarding this incorporation:

1. The implementation of fitness search [10], as opposed to novelty search, was used.
2. The parameter values used for the rtNEAT implementation included in this package were the default ones.

[1]`http://eplex.cs.ucf.edu/software/NoveltySearchC++.zip`

Table 1: Parameters used in creation of the polynomial-interval-finding problem set

set size	1000
l (lower bound)	uniform random numbers in range [-100, 100]
u (upper bound)	$l + 2.0$
t (iterations)	10
n (number inputs)	11
m (number outputs)	2
s (scaling factor)	10
I (input set)	uniform random numbers in range [0, 1]
C (coefficients set)	uniform random numbers in range [-10, 10]
E (exponents set)	random numbers from set {0, 1, 2, 3, 4}

This was with the exception of the population size, which was increased from 250 to 1000.

3. All solutions were evaluated on all problems each generation.
4. In the original version of the package, each generation, one solution was added and one removed from the population. This number was changed to 100.
5. The parameters pertaining to the problem set are shown in table 1. These parameters were used as preliminary experiments showed that they allowed for the near complete solution of the set within a relatively small amount of wall time.

The implementation was run for 640 generations. Figure 2 displays two measures of the change in state of the algorithm during these generations. A number of interesting features can be observed. The first is that, despite the fact that the total number of problems solved did start to plateau around generation 300, progress was still being made right until the end of the 640 generations (figure 2(a)). Before generation 500, the largest number of problems solved in any generation was 978. The number of problems solved in generation 640 was 989. The second interesting feature is that *general* solutions were being found (figure 2(b)). In later generations, on average, solutions were solving more than four problems each. From generation 287 until the end of the run, there was at least one solution which was solving 15 or more problems.

The authors are aware that it is not possible to draw solid conclusions from a single run. These are, however, early, preliminary results and a more rigorous analysis is presently underway. Furthermore, other experimental runs produced similar results.

7. FUTURE RESEARCH

At present, a more detailed and rigorous analysis of the performance of flood evolution on polynomial-interval-finding problems is underway. An important goal is to establish whether flood evolution can solve problems which other NE techniques are unable to solve. We also intend to implement and test maze-solving problem sets. Another avenue of exploration which the authors are considering exploring is the coevolution of the problem set. Problems could be represented by genotypes and rewarded for producing more complicated individuals in the solution population.

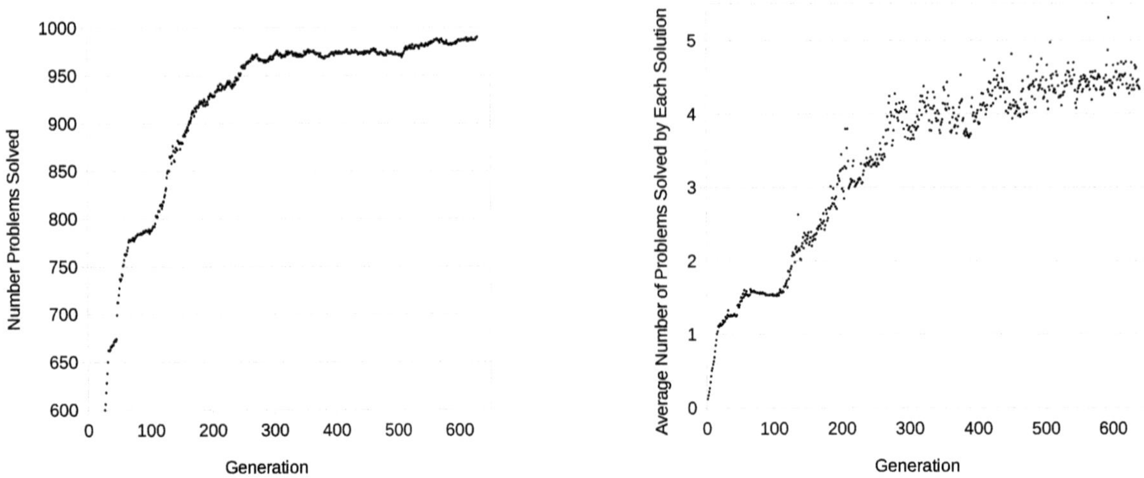

(a) **Saturation of the problem space** (b) **Generality of solutions**

Figure 2: Graphs showing the interaction between the problem and solution spaces during a run of flood evolution.

8. CONCLUSIONS

It is concluded that flood evolution is a promising area of research which has the potential to improve the power of NE algorithms as well as aid our understanding of the underlying mechanisms of evolution.

9. REFERENCES

[1] W. B. Arthur and W. Polak. The evolution of technology within a simple computer model. *Complexity*, 11(5):23–31, 2006.

[2] J. W. O. Ballard and M. C. Whitlock. The incomplete natural history of mitochondria. *Molecular ecology*, 13(4):729–744, 2004.

[3] C. Darwin and W. F. Bynum. *The origin of species by means of natural selection: or, the preservation of favored races in the struggle for life.* AL Burt, 2009.

[4] R. Dawkins. *The selfish gene.* Oxford university press, 2006.

[5] A. E. Eiben and J. E. Smith. *Introduction to evolutionary computing.* springer, 2003.

[6] F. Gomez and R. Miikkulainen. Incremental evolution of complex general behavior. *Adaptive Behavior*, 5(3-4):317–342, 1997.

[7] F. J. Gomez and R. Miikkulainen. Solving non-markovian control tasks with neuroevolution. In *IJCAI*, volume 99, pages 1356–1361, 1999.

[8] C. Y. Lee. An algorithm for path connections and its applications. *Electronic Computers, IRE Transactions on*, (3):346–365, 1961.

[9] J. Lehman and K. O. Stanley. Exploiting open-endedness to solve problems through the search for novelty. In *Proceedings of the Eleventh International Conference on Artificial Life (ALIFE XI)*, Cambridge, MA, 2008. MIT Press.

[10] J. Lehman and K. O. Stanley. Abandoning objectives: Evolution through the search for novelty alone. *Evolutionary computation*, 19(2):189–223, 2011.

[11] J. Lehman and K. O. Stanley. Evolving a diversity of virtual creatures through novelty search and local competition. In *Proceedings of the 13th annual conference on Genetic and evolutionary computation*, pages 211–218. ACM, 2011.

[12] R. E. Lenski, C. Ofria, R. T. Pennock, and C. Adami. The evolutionary origin of complex features. *Nature*, 423(6936):139–144, 2003.

[13] M. Lynch. The frailty of adaptive hypotheses for the origins of organismal complexity. *Proceedings of the National Academy of Sciences*, 104(suppl 1):8597–8604, 2007.

[14] S. Risi, C. E. Hughes, and K. O. Stanley. Evolving plastic neural networks with novelty search. *Adaptive Behavior*, 18(6):470–491, 2010.

[15] N. Saravanan and D. B. Fogel. Evolving neural control systems. *IEEE Intelligent Systems*, 10(3):23–27, 1995.

[16] A. P. Wieland. Evolving controls for unstable systems. In *Connectionist models: proceedings of the 1990 summer school*, pages 91–102, 1990.

[17] A. P. Wieland. Evolving neural network controllers for unstable systems. In *Neural Networks, 1991., IJCNN-91-Seattle International Joint Conference on*, volume 2, pages 667–673. IEEE, 1991.

[18] J. J. Wiens. Missing data, incomplete taxa, and phylogenetic accuracy. *Systematic Biology*, 52(4):528–538, 2003.

[19] J. Xu and C. S. Kaplan. Image-guided maze construction. In *ACM Transactions on Graphics (TOG)*, volume 26, page 29. ACM, 2007.

[20] C. H. Yong and R. Miikkulainen. Coevolution of role-based cooperation in multiagent systems. *Autonomous Mental Development, IEEE Transactions on*, 1(3):170–186, 2009.

Consensus Costs and Conflict in Robot Swarms

Timothy Solum
Dept. of Computer Science and Network Engineering
Southern Nazarene University
Bethany, OK, USA
tsolum@mail.snu.edu

Brent E. Eskridge
Dept. of Computer Science and Network Engineering
Southern Nazarene University
Bethany, OK, USA
beskridge@snu.edu

Ingo Schlupp
Dept. of Biology
University of Oklahoma
Norman, OK, USA
schlupp@ou.edu

ABSTRACT

It is commonly observed that aggregation in nature provides significant benefits to the group members. However, to reach a consensus individual preferences are frequently lost. Conflict is generally avoided because of the negative influence it could have on the success of collective movements. However, it could be used to balance consensus costs with individual preferences. Using a biologically-based collective movement model, this work investigates the possibility of conflict in a group movement allowing for differing individual goals to be accomplished, while still maintaining group cohesion much of the time. Individuals focus on their own needs, which may include the protection of being a part of a group or the desire to move away from the group and towards its preferred destination. Results show that by allowing conflict in group decision-making, consensus costs were balanced with individual preferences in such a way that group level success still occurred, while significantly improving the success of differing goals.

Categories and Subject Descriptors

I.2.11 [**Artificial Intelligence**]: Distributed Artificial Intelligence—*coherence and coordination,multiagent systems*

Keywords

conflict of interest, collective movement, swarm robotics, coordination

1. INTRODUCTION

Group living provides significant benefits in nature, ranging from increased protection from predators to increased foraging success [13]. The flocking of birds [6], schooling of fish [5], and mass herds of migrating wildebeests [2] are just some of the examples of large-scale aggregation and coordination that have been observed and studied in nature. The same is true in artificial systems, such as robot swarms where robustness, flexibility, and scalability are beneficial [11]. To maintain these benefits, collective decision-making and the associated coordination are necessary [8].

Collective behavior is usually viewed as a benefit for those involved, but what if the cost of the consensus was greater than that of the individuals' preferences? Conflict, however, is commonly treated as an inhibitor of collective behavior. One of the most common effects of conflict on collective behavior is to increase the time taken to complete the group's goal, sometimes to the point of even causing the group to fail to complete their goal. This work uses a biologically-based model to explore the positive effects of conflict on collective movements. Results show that conflict can increase individual goal completion percentage while still allowing for group cohesion, with a small average time difference to complete the first consensus goal.

2. METHODS

The simulations used for this work were performed using a modified version of a collective movement model developed through observations of collective movement attempts in a group of white-faced capuchin monkeys [4, 9]. The model was later confirmed in observations of sheep [10]. To integrate conflict and spatial movement into the model, significant modifications were required, including converting the model from the usage of continuous time to discrete time.

2.1 Collective Movement Model

The collective movement model uses three rules to govern the decision-making process involved in starting collective movements [4, 9]. The first rule assumes that all individuals within the group are identical and can initiate a collective movement attempt with a rate of $1/\tau_o$.

The second rule describes the rate at which followers join the collective movement attempt and is calculated by $1/\tau_r$. The time constant τ_r for the following rate is calculated using the following:

$$\tau_r = \alpha_f + \beta_f \frac{N-r}{r} \tag{1}$$

where α_f and β_f are constants determined through direct observation, N is the number of individuals in the group, and r is the number of individuals following the initiator. As the number of individuals following the initiator increases, the rate at which individuals join the movement also increases.

Not all initiation attempts are successful as initiators often cancel and return to the group. The third rule calculates this

GECCO'14, July 12–16, Vancouver, BC, Canada.

http://dx.doi.org/10.1145/2598394.2605683.

cancellation rate using the following:

$$C_r = \frac{\alpha_c}{1 + (r/\gamma_c)^{\varepsilon_c}} \tag{2}$$

where α_c, γ_c, and ε_c are constants determined through direct observation, and r is the number of individuals following the initiator.

2.2 Integrating Conflict

To investigate the effects of altering the rate at which individuals initiate, follow an initiator, and cancel a movement, Gautrais added an individual-specific constant, referred to as a "k factor," to the rate calculations of the collective movement model [4]. Initiation attempts were now calculated at the constant rate of k/τ_o, and the following and canceling rate calculations were modified as follows:

$$\tau_r = \frac{1}{k}\left(\alpha_f + \beta_f \frac{N-r}{r}\right) \tag{3}$$

$$C_r = k\left(\frac{\alpha_c}{1 + (r/\gamma_c)^{\varepsilon_c}}\right) \tag{4}$$

where the variables are the same as before. Since this k factor can either increase or decrease the three decision-making rates, it was an ideal means with which the effects of conflict could be incorporated into the model.

Like other work involving conflicts of interest [1], conflict was introduced into the group by giving individuals different preferred goal destinations. To maximize the costs associated with conflict, equal numbers of individuals were given different goals, thus ensuring that the group as a whole would encounter high levels of conflict, regardless of the current initiator's destination. However, unlike other work on conflict, individuals were considered homogeneous, other than their different preferred destinations, and did not posses an individual "degree of assertiveness." This decision was made for two reasons. First, it minimized the number of confounding variables in the system, thus simplifying the analysis of results. Second, it was consistent with other work in the area of robot swarms in which swarm members are assumed to be identical [11].

The conflict value c_i for individual i in following a potential leader was calculated using the angle θ between the leader's observed direction of movement $\vec{v_l}$ and the direction $\vec{d}$ to the individual's preferred destination from the leader's current position as follows:

$$c_i = \frac{|\theta|}{\pi} \tag{5}$$

with θ having a range of $[-\pi, \pi]$ and calculated using the dot product of the vectors $\vec{v_l}$ and $\vec{d}$. If a potential leader was not moving, θ was defined to be π, resulting in maximum conflict. Although neither the original model, nor the observations on which the model was based, discussed conflicts of interest for the individual animals involved, we assumed that the observed individuals encountered moderate conflict. Therefore, the integration of conflict incorporated the concept of moderate conflict ($c_i = 0.5$) which produced the same results as the original model. Also, the magnitude with which low conflict affected the model was designed to be the same as high conflict so as not to bias the model towards one conflict value over another. As a result, the conflict value c_i was then used to calculate k, as follows:

$$k = 2c_i \tag{6}$$

where the variables were the same as before. Since k had a non-inclusive lower limit of zero, the non-inclusive upper limit of two was chosen to ensure balance. In the simulations described below, conflict was limited to the range $[0.1 : 0.9]$ to ensure these limits were satisfied.

2.3 Conversion to Discrete Time

The collective movement model originally used continuous time events. However, such an approach was not practical for simulating spatial movement with discrete time requirements. As a result, significant modifications were made to the implemented algorithm to use discrete time.

First, instead of using the individual decision rates to generate decision times from an exponential distribution, the decision rates were used to calculate the probability of the decision being made at a given time step. This was straightforward since the inverse of the decision rate is the instantaneous probability.

Second, because it was possible that an individual could make a new decision at every time step, a "do nothing" decision was added to the decision-making process. This allowed the individual to continue executing a decision it had previously made (e.g., following a leader or continue initiating). However, there were situations in which a decision to "do nothing" was not valid. For example, if a leader canceled its movement or instead decided to follow another leader, a follower was required to make a new decision to either follow a new leader or initiate its own movement. With this restriction, an agent would not be forced to follow a leader in the decision to join the group.

2.4 Numerical Implementation

Numerical simulations of the collective movement model were implemented in Java[1] using the original algorithm as a starting point [4]. However, as noted above, the algorithm was converted to use discrete time events, instead of the continuous time events in the original.

The original model only used a group size of 10, but other work has shown that the success of collective movement initiations increases as the group size is increased, with most differences present in group sizes of 50 or less [3]. As such, evaluating different group sizes presents an opportunity to evaluate the effects of conflict with different group dynamics. For each evaluation environment, 2,000 simulations, each with a different random seed, were performed using group sizes from 10 to 50. Each simulation constituted a single attempt for individuals to move to their preferred destination and had a maximum of 20,000 time steps. Unlike the original model, multiple initiators were allowed at any given time step and a cancellation was not classified as an immediate failure. The model parameters used were the same as those used in the original model [4, 9].

The results that follow were from a simulation environment that was used to evaluate the effect of conflict on consensus costs when the group began a movement with moderate initial conflict. In this environment, two destinations were located at an equivalent distance from where the group began. These destinations were separated by a $74°$ angle. Since there was no bias in the simulations towards one destination over another, the analysis of the simulations took

[1]Simulation source code and data analysis scripts are available for download from `https://github.com/snucsne/bio-inspired-leadership`.

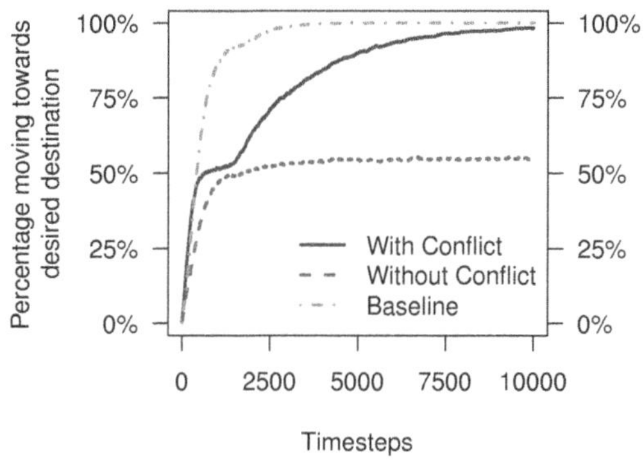

(a) $N = 10$

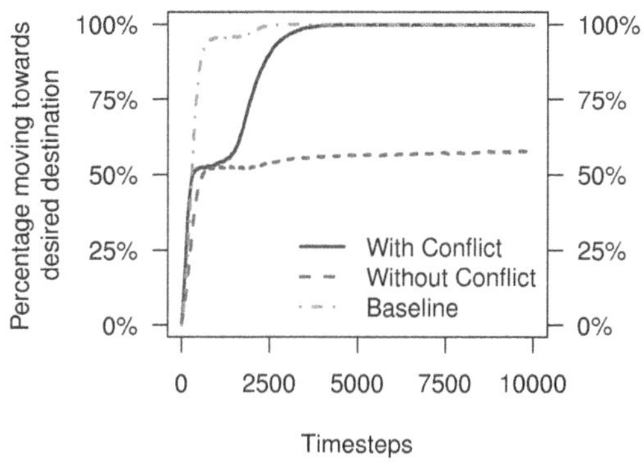

(b) $N = 50$

Figure 1: The percentage of the total number of agents moving towards their preferred destination are shown for groups of size $N = 10$ and $N = 50$.

Group Size	Conflict With	Conflict Without
10	9.9 ±0.3	5.6 ±1.1
20	19.9 ±0.2	11.7 ±2.6
30	29.9 ±0.2	17.8 ±4.1
40	39.9 ±0.7	24.3 ±5.8
50	49.9 ±0.3	30.5 ±7.1

Table 1: The mean number of agents that arrived at their preferred destination in each simulation are shown (mean ± std. deviation). All results for simulations with conflict are statistically significantly larger ($p << 0.0001$).

into account that the identity of the destinations was not important. Simulation results were organized into first and second destination categories, as determined by the median times in which the destinations were reached in a given simulation. Individuals evaluated in this environment initially experienced moderate conflict in deciding to follow a leader moving towards the non-preferred destination.

3. RESULTS & ANALYSIS

Three treatments were used to determine the effects of conflict on consensus decision-making: a) individuals preferred one of two destinations and conflict was used; b) two destinations were used, but not conflict; and c) a baseline

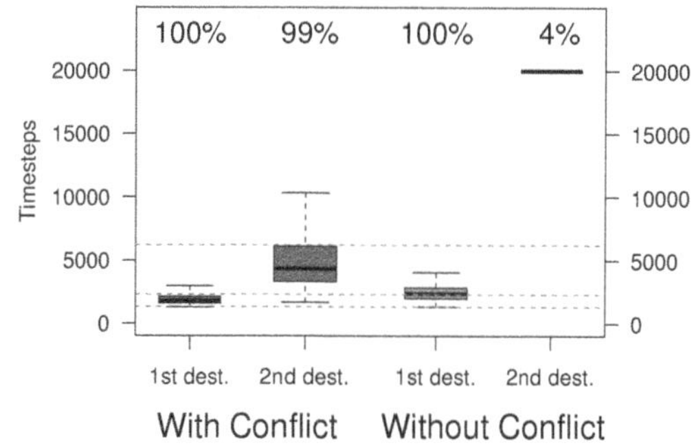

(a) $N = 10$

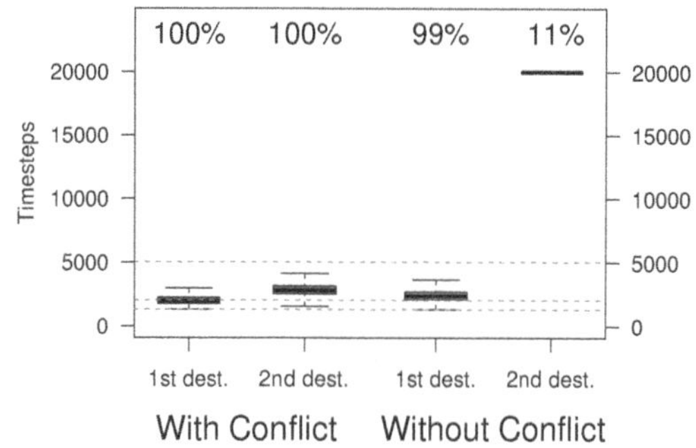

(b) $N = 50$

Figure 2: The median number of timesteps and the interquartile range needed for agents to reach their preferred destination are shown for groups of size $N = 10$ and $N = 50$. Percentages indicate the fraction of agents that reached a particular, preferred destination. Horizontal dashed lines represent the minimum, mean, and maximum times for baseline simulations. Times for agents not reaching their preferred destination were truncated at the maximum number of timesteps.

treatment in which all individuals preferred the same destination and conflict was not used. Two metrics were used to measure the effects of conflict on collective movements. The mean percentage of individuals that reached their preferred destination was used to determine the consensus costs incurred by individuals in the swarm. This was done by comparing the results from the treatments with conflict and without conflict to observe the difference in percentage of agents moving towards their preferred destination. The second metric that was the mean time taken for individuals to reach their preferred destination. To properly use this metric, times for agents that failed to reach their goal were truncated at the maximum number of timesteps.

Figure 1 shows the mean percentage of individuals moving towards their preferred destination during a simulation for each treatment. Simulations in the baseline treatment, as expected, had on average more individuals moving towards their goal at every time step (see Figure 2a and Figure 2b). By 10,000 time steps, simulations using conflict had comparable percentages to the baseline simulations, while simulations without conflict had approximately only 50% of the individuals moving towards their preferred destination. Increasing the group size from 10 to 50 resulted in fewer timesteps before the simulations with conflict had comparable percentages to the baseline system. However, the larger group size only had minor effects on the simulation without conflict.

Table 1 lists the mean number of individuals that arrived at their preferred destination by the end of the simulation. When conflict was used, nearly 99% of the individuals that preferred the second goal were able to reach their goal for groups 10, and the 100% of individuals were able to reach their goal for groups of 50. Without conflict, the percentage that reached the second destination ranged from 4% for groups of 10 to 11% for groups 50 (see Figure 2).

4. DISCUSSION

In simulations without conflict, an agent that had a preferred destination that was different than that of the consensus was highly unlikely to be able to reach its goal. By integrating conflict, these agents were able to reach their goal destination with only minor increases to the time for the group to reach the first goal destination.

The median time required for agents to reach their preferred destination decreased as the size of the group was increased. Figure 2 illustrates this and shows the interquartile range of these times for groups of 10 and 50. This was consistent with baseline simulations in which increasing the group size decreased the mean time for agents to reach their preferred destinations.

These simulations made the assumption that consensus costs were too high and thus, individual goals must be fulfilled. There are times in which cohesion of a group is more important than individual preferences. For example, group cohesion is essential to the hunting success of a group of lions, regardless of individual goals. In this case, larger groups complicate this cohesion. On the other hand, larger fish shoals are a more effective defense against predation than smaller groups. Cohesion also reduces the negative effects of incorrect information on the success of the group. In an environment where consensus is not the primary objective of the swarm, conflict could provide a balance between consensus costs and individual preference.

5. CONCLUSIONS AND FUTURE WORK

This work has two significant contributions. First, these results show that the simple addition of conflict can balance consensus costs with individual preferences in a manner that still allows group level success, while significantly improving individual success. Second, these results show that the consensus costs in swarms with differing preferences can be significant if cohesion is enforced, even to the point where individuals are unable to meet their goals.

This work is part of a larger research project on collective decision-making. In the future, we plan to implement a more comprehensive concept of a "level of dissatisfaction" in place of the simplified conflict model used here. This would include situations such as too many individuals in a group, a dependence on resources, and the notion of time. Evolutionary approaches would be particularly effective in combining the various components. One particularly interesting approach would be to use grammatical evolution to evolve decision rules for determining conflict [7]. Furthermore, the current model is not very tunable. We plan on transitioning to an alternative model [12] that allows for more customization of the decision rates, particularly for tasks other than collective movements. Evolutionary approaches would again be particularly effective in finding the appropriate parameters for each task.

6. ACKNOWLEDGMENTS

This material is based upon work supported by the National Science Foundation under Grant No. BCS-1124837. Some of the computing for this project was performed at the OU Supercomputing Center for Education & Research (OSCER) at the University of Oklahoma.

7. REFERENCES

[1] L. Conradt and T. J. Roper. Conflicts of interest and the evolution of decision sharing. *Philosophical Transactions of the Royal Society B: Biological Sciences*, 364(1518):807–819, 2009.

[2] I. D. Couzin and J. Krause. Self-organization and collective behavior in vertebrates. *Advances in the Study of Behavior*, 32:1–75, 2003.

[3] B. E. Eskridge. Effects of local communication and topology on collective movement initiation. In *International Conference on the Simulation and Synthesis of Living Things*, volume 13, pages 155–162, 2012.

[4] J. Gautrais. The hidden variables of leadership. *Behavioural Processes*, 84(3):664–667, 2010.

[5] C. Hemelrijk and H. Hildenbrandt. Self-organized shape and frontal density of fish schools. *Ethology*, 114(3):245–254, 2008.

[6] M. Nagy, Z. Ákos, D. Biro, and T. Vicsek. Hierarchical group dynamics in pigeon flocks. *Nature*, 464(7290):890–893, 2010.

[7] M. O'Neill and C. Ryan. *Grammatical Evolution: Evolutionary Automatic Programming in an Arbitrary Language*. Kluwer Academic Publishers, Norwell, MA, USA, 2003.

[8] O. Petit and R. Bon. Decision-making processes: The case of collective movements. *Behavioural Processes*, 64(3):635–647, 2010.

[9] O. Petit, J. Gautrais, J.-B. Leca, G. Theraulaz, and J.-L. Deneubourg. Collective decision-making in white-faced capuchin monkeys. *Proceedings of the Royal Society B: Biological Sciences*, 276(1672):3495–3503, 2009.

[10] M.-H. Pillot, J. Gautrais, P. Arrufat, I. D. Couzin, R. Bon, and J.-L. Deneubourg. Scalable rules for coherent group motion in a gregarious vertebrate. *PLoS ONE*, 6(1):e14487, 01 2011.

[11] E. Şahin. Swarm robotics: From sources of inspiration to domains of application. In *Swarm robotics*, volume 3342 of *Lecture Notes in Computer Science*, pages 10–20. Springer, 2005.

[12] C. Sueur and J. Deneubourg. Self-organization in primates: Understanding the rules underlying collective movements. *International Journal of Primatology*, 32(6):1413–1432, 2011.

[13] C. Sueur and O. Petit. Shared or unshared consensus decision in macaques? *Behavioural Processes*, 78(1):84–92, 2008.

A Case Based Approach for an Intelligent Route Optimization Technology

Masaki Suzuki, Takaaki Motomura, Taro Matsumaru and Setsuo Tsuruta
School of Information Environment
Tokyo Denki University
2-1200 Muzai Gakuendai
Inzai, Chiba, 270-1382, Japan
+81 476 46 8493
13jkm15@ms.dendai.ac.jp

Rainer Knauf
Faculty of Computer Science and Automation
Ilmenau University of Technology
PO Box 10 05 65
98684 Ilmenau, Germany
+49 3677 69 1445
rainer.knauf@tu-ilmenau.de

Yoshitaka Sakurai
School of Interdisciplinary Mathematical Sciences
Meiji University
4-21-1 Nakano Nakano-ku
Tokyo, 164-8525, JAPAN
+81 3-5343-8307
sakuraiy@meiji.ac.jp

ABSTRACT
The paper introduces a Case Based Approximation method to solve large scale Traveling Salesman Problems in a short time with a low error rate. It is useful for domains with most solutions being similar to solutions that have been created. Thus, a solution can be derived by (1) selecting a most similar TSP from a library of former TSP solutions, (2) removing the locations that are not part of the current TSP and (3) adding the missing locations of the current TSP by mutation, namely Nearest Insertion (NI). This way of creating solutions by Case Based Reasoning (CBR) avoids the computational costs to create new solutions from scratch.

Categories and Subject Descriptors
D.2.6 [**Evolution Support Environment**]: Evolutionary Computation – *Genetic Algorithms, Case Based Reasoning, fitness, diversity*

General Terms
Algorithms

Keywords
Traveling Salesman Problems (TSP), Genetic Algorithm (GA), Heuristics, Case Based reasoning (CBR), Knowledge Maintenance

1. INTRODUCTION
The efficiency of product distribution in Japan is low compared to other industrialized countries. This inefficiency also causes social problems and economical losses. Namely, we are facing the necessity of urgently reducing the volume of car exhaust gases to meet environmental requirements as well as curtailing transport expenses in Japan. Thus, it should be optimized.

A round delivery comprises more than several tens or hundreds of different locations. The optimization of a delivery route can be modeled as a large-scale of Traveling Salesman Problem (TSP).

GECCO'14, July 12–16, 2014, Vancouver, BC, Canada.

The TSP is a combinatorial problem that causes computational explosion due to the *n!* order of combinations for an *n*-city TSP. Thus, to practically obtain an efficient delivery route of such a distribution system, a near optimal solving method of TSP is indispensable. Moreover, the practical use of such a solving method on an actual site needs human confirmation (which is difficult to formulate) of the solution, since social and human conditions are involved. Human users should verify the practicability of a solution. Users sometimes need to adjust manually or select an alternative solution to meet miscellaneous technical and social side conditions. Therefore, the TSP solving methods are required to ensure a response time necessary for the above human interaction. Moreover, it is necessary to use comparatively simple strategies (heuristics) that users and human specialists can optimize the delivery schedule.

Interestingly, solutions generated by domain experts may have 2-3% of deviation from the mathematical optimal solution, but they never generate worse solutions, which may cause practical problems. On the other hand, conventional approximate methods for solving the TSP [13][7][3] may generate even mathematically optimal solutions in particular cases but cannot ensure that the amount of errors is below 2-3%.

Simple strategies to create a delivery schedule are repeated methods such as stepwise inserting new delivery locations near the roughly imaged delivery route until the route includes all delivery locations, and modifying the traveling order of the delivery locations in order to decrease the total traveling distance. This is a method called "Nearest Insertion" (NI). Another strategy is repeating exchanges of combinations of routes in the delivery schedule. This is a method called "2-opt".

Complex strategies such as the Lin-Kernighan (LK) [8] method or Karp's partitioning [6] are not considered as practical methods from the above-mentioned viewpoint. This is because these methods are not familiar to field experts though theoretically their way of modification matched to deliverer's convenience.

In our former work, we proposed some types of Genetic Algorithms (GAs) [9]. These GA incorporated simple heuristics aiming at interactive real-time response as well as avoiding significant errors for any kinds of delivery location patterns.

A simple GA incorporating 2-opt type heuristics tends to fall into a local optima with certain delivery location patterns though it performs well for others. Therefore, we proposed a multi-outer-world GA (Mow-GA) [10], which overcomes some 2-opt type GA's drawbacks by cascading NI type GA to 2-opt type GA.

However, the Mow-GA has also some defects. It starts NI type GA from the first generation without inheriting the information of the elite individuals generated in the 2-opt type GA. It cannot have enough performance for large scale problems within about 3 seconds. Moreover, the complementary effects caused by combination of such heuristics did not work [10].

As an improved version of the Mow-GA, Multi-inner-world Genetic Algorithm (Miw-GA) was proposed [11]. It improved the search efficiency through complementary effects that supplement the weak points mutually by processing two types of heuristics (2-opt and NI) in each generation.

To simplify the searching processes, the searching operator of our GA was limited to the mutation to improve individuals. The Miw-GA can obtain high accurate solutions for various kinds of delivery location patterns within interactive response time. However, when the number of cities in TSP became more than 200, the average error rate from the optimal solution exceeded 4% in some cases.

Therefore, we proposed a so called Backtrack and Restart GA (BR-GA) [12], which maintains a population's diversity by conducting random restart and fostering new children. It achieves below 3% error rate for less than 1000 cities TSPs within 3 seconds.

Even the world's fastest exact algorithms called Concorde [1] needs 10- 100 seconds to solve the same size of TSPs. As to approximation algorithms, LKH [8][4] can solve below 1000 cities TSPs within about 3 seconds. This marks the world's top level accuracy and speed in solving TSPs by implementing an effective branch & cut in the search process.

Our BR-GA can also solve below 2000 cities TSPs within 10 seconds. However, LKH is an improved version of the fairly complex method called LK. This is not easy for application domain engineers to understand and to modify a solution depending on field social conditions, and to practically use.

An exact solution or too much accuracy is not valuable since 2-3% error is not recognizable for field users. Moreover, complex methods have problems in flexibility. Application field engineers have difficulties in modifying the method to derive solutions suitable for the deliverer's convenience.

However, in practice, new TSPs distinguish from formerly solved ones very slightly. The changes in the locations to visit are less than 10 – 30 % and about 5 % in average.

Here, we introduce an alternative method to solve TSPs by Case Based Reasoning (CBR) [5]. In CBR, former solutions of a problem are collected in a case base (CB) and new problems are solved by (1) retrieving the most appropriate case from the CB, (2) mutating its solution towards a solution of the actual TSP, (3) validating or revising the solution, and (4), if applicable, adding the created solution to the CB.

This paper is organized as follows. In the next section, the delivery route optimization problem and its technical problems are described. Section three introduces our method for solving the problem. In section four, experiments to validate this method are shown and section six concludes the paper.

2. DELIVERY ROUTE OPTIMIZATION

A delivery network is represented by a weighted complete graph $G = (V, E, W)$. V is a node set. A node $v_i \in V$ $(i = 1, \dots, n)$ represents a location (address) for delivery. $N=|V|$ is the number of nodes. $E \subseteq V \times V$ is a set of edges. An edge e_{ij} represents a route from v_i to v_j. W is an edge weight set. An edge weight d_{ij} represents a distance (or the costs to go) from v_i to v_j. Here, we presume $d_{ij} = d_{ji}$. The problem to find the minimal-length Hamilton path in such a graph $G = (V, E, W)$ is called Traveling Salesman Problem (TSP).

Delivery zones that are covered by one vehicle are different according to the region. Delivery locations are comparatively overcrowded in the urban area, whereas scattered in the rural area. Therefore, the number of locations for delivery differs - over several tens or hundreds up to 2000 or so - depending on the region and period of time.

It is necessary to compose and optimize a new delivery route for each round delivery since delivery locations change frequently. Though human or social factors should be considered, this is a problem to search the shortest path or route, modeled as a famous "Traveling Salesman Problem (TSP)".

The computer support by nearly optimal solving methods is quite useful even though the method is an approximation algorithm. This reduces the burden and time loss of workers as well as costs and car exhaust gases in distribution networks.

3. PROPOSED TECHNIQUE

CBR is a usual problem solving method in fields, were creating a new solution to a problem from scratch is expensive and solutions to similar problems are available: justice, architecture, and even bigger programming projects are partially done in such a way.

CBR holds a CB with pairs *[problem, solution]* of formerly solved problems and consists of the steps (1) case retrieval, (2) case reuse, (3) case revision, and (4) case retaining.

In the case retrieval step, a case of the CB needs to be identified, which is "most similar" to the present case. An appropriate ways to define "similarity" for our application and not losing the attention to fitness issues at the same time needs to be found.

In the reuse step, the solution of the retrieved case needs to be adapted to the needs of the current problem.

The revision step aims at validating the adapted solution in the real world application and revising it according to the results of the real world application. In some application fields, there are good reasons to omit or just simulate this step, namely (1) in case the application in the real world bags risks according security or safety of people or other important goods, but also (2) in case the reuse technology already includes a check, whether or not a potential change can improve the solution.

The retain step a crucial issue. The question, whether or not a new case should be included as a new case into the CB, may be easy to answer in most application fields. Also, adding new cases without considering the removal of (other) cases (1) "blows up" the CB and (2) bags the risk to "sponsor" old solutions that are outperformed by more recent solutions.

3.1 Case Retrieval

If a new problem has to be solved, a "most similar" TSP needs to be retrieved from the CB. Here, we define similarity as the fraction of locations (cities) in the actual TSP, which are also in TSP of the CB. For example, if we have to solve a TSP with the scale 200 and 180 out of these 200 cities are in a TSP solution of the CB, its similarity is 180 / 200 = 0.9. If there are several solutions with the same highest degree of similarity, the fittest one will be defined as "most similar".

However, a less similar TSP solution may be appropriate, too, in case its fitness is better than the fitness of the most similar one. There might be a TSP in the CB, which even covers all locations (cities) of the current TSC, i.e. with a similarity of 1, but the scale of this "very similar" TSP is 10 times bigger and thus, it is not a good candidate to derive a solution for the actual TSP from it.

Therefore, we consider fitness, too. We retrieve the case with the next lower degree of similarity (respective the fittest one among them, if there are several ones) and look, whether this case has a higher fitness than the most similar case.

We define the fitness gain of a TSP solution s_1 with the fitness f_1 related to a solution s_2 with a fitness f_2 as $(1 - f_2/ f_1)$. For example, if the most similar solution s_1 has a fitness of $f_1 = 100$ (units of length for the complete distance of the tour) and the solution with the next better degree of similarity s_2 has a fitness of $f_2 = 80$, the fitness gain of s_2, related to solution s_1 is $(1 - 80/100) = 0.2$.

Also, we define the similarity loss of a TSP solution s_1 with a similarity sim_1 to the actual TSP, related to the solution s_2 with the next lower degree of similarity to the actual TSP of sim_2 as $(sim_1 - sim_2)$. For example, if the most similar solution s_1 has a similarity of 0.9 to the actual TSP and the solution with the 2nd highest similarity s_2 has a similarity of 0.8 to the actual TSP, the similarity loss is 0.1.

In our case retrieval strategy, we continue considering the next similar TSPs (to the currently considered one in the CB) as long as the fitness gain is higher than the similarity loss. When we come to a point, at which the next similar solution has a higher similarity loss then fitness gain (or even has a negative fitness gain), we refuse the next similar solution and retrieve the currently considered solution.

3.2 Case Reuse and Revision

After retrieving a solution from the CB, the redundant places (locations that are not in the current TSP) are removed from it.

After removal, the deficient locations (locations of the actual TSP, which are not in the TSP retrieved from the CB) are added by the Nearest Insertion (NI) technique. This technique finds the position of a new location to insert, at which the increment of the complete tour length is minimal.

Since this reuse method already includes optimization issues by finding the optimal place for each inserted location, there is no explicit revision of this result in our CBR application here.

3.3 Case Retaining and CB Maintenance

First, we determined a reasonable number of TSP solutions in the CB. This number should be related to the scale n of the largest TSP to be solved. By some experiments we found that

(1) in CBs with less than n/2 TSP solutions there is not much hope to retrieve an appropriate case,

(2) in CBs with around n TSP solutions we always found an appropriate case in a reasonable time of 50 – 100 ms, which is negligible, compared to the permitted solution time 3 s, and

(3) in CBs 2n cases and more the search time for an appropriate case is not acceptable any more (9 s, in some cases).

There are two important CB maintenance issues, namely (1) it should contain the fittest individuals (shortest TSP tours), but also (2) diversity, i.e. individuals, which are not too similar to each other to ensure not to fall into local optima.

We are still in the process to collect cases for the CB. Therefore, we currently add all solutions created by our technique to the CB.

Later, we have to come up with a concept for CB maintenance, which ensures that the size of the CB (and thus, the computational costs for finding a most similar case in it) stays limited and the cases in the CB are "useful" in terms of fitness and diversity.

4. EXPERIMENTS AND RESULTS

We compared the proposed method with our former one, namely BR-GA. The comparison experiments were done by solving two TSPLIB problems.

The experiments were conducted under the following computation environment. Namely, the CPU is an AMD Athlon 64 X2 3800+ 2GHz processor. It is almost the same performance as Athlon 64 3200+ 2GHz, because of its execution performance on the single core mode with 1 GB memory.

The programs were written in C language, compiled by Microsoft Visual C++ .NET 2003 ver. 7.1.3091 with the /02 option (directing the execution speed preference), and executed on Windows XP Professional.

Table 1 shows the error rates of our former approach BR-GA and the method proposed here for 2 instances of large scale TSP benchmarks, namely u1432+30 and rl1889+30.

By error rate, we define the percentage of the TSP solution's total distance being longer that the optimal solution, which we also computed – of course with much more computation cost – for this evaluation purpose. These results are pretty convincing that deriving new TSP solutions from a good former solution of a similar TSP, is a good idea. The error rate is about 10 times better that it was with our former approach.

Table 1. Experimental results

TSP	Worst error rate after 3 seconds runtime	
	BR-GA	proposed method
u1432+30	5.92	0.68
rl1889+30	10.26	0.88

The search of the most similar case in the CB took between 50 and 100 ms.

The performance regarding computational complexity (run time) is theoretically that of *n/5* of BR-GA, since a maximum of 20 % of a solution is created, the rest of the solution is just adopted from its "parent", a former TSP solution.

5. SUMMARY AND OUTLOOK

We introduced a Case Based approximation method to solve up to 2000 cities TSP problems in a required maximal response time of 3 seconds with a required maximum error rate of 3 %.

This method is based on the insight, that most solutions are very similar to solutions that have been created. Thus, in many cases a solution can be derived from former solutions (1) selecting a most similar TSP from a library of former TSP solutions, (2) removing the locations that are not part of the current TSP and (3) adding the missing locations of the current TSP by mutation, namely Nearest Insertion (NI).

This way of creating solutions by Case Based Reasoning (CBR) avoids the computational costs to create new solutions from scratch.

In our former work, we tried to keep diversity in terms of solutions and defined common subsequences of TSP solutions by a pattern set. We feel, for creating new solutions that are required to be different enough from a current population's majority, this is a good idea, but for case base maintenance the computational costs are very high. Therefore, we shifted from the idea of considering diversity of solutions towards the idea of promoting diversity of problems, for which a CB provides a solution. For the solutions, we now here consider fitness as a more important point then diversity.

The evaluation of this new method revealed remarkable results according the error rate of the derived solutions within a run time that is just 20% of the time to create a new solution from scratch plus 50-100 ms for searching the most similar case in the library of former TSP solutions.

For future work, we aim at reaching the following objectives.

For adapting a former solution toward an actual one, we extend the simple NI method towards a multiple NI in parallel. After that, we extend it by also including edges assembly crossover (EAX). This way, new TSP can adopt useful properties (fitness, being divers from others in the population) from two parents and utilize the best of each parent. We hope to stay within the required limit of computational costs by these extensions and think about using parallel computation to still meet this requirement.

Our maintenance technique for the CB is still rudimentary, because we are still suffering from haven too few. We think about extending it concept that ensures a well-balanced trade-off between fitness and diversity within the TSP solutions of the case base.

Moreover, we investigate ways to extend the class of TPS problems towards practical requirements from field experts, who like to include one-way traffic (asymmetric TSPs), road conditions (instead of just considering the distance as fitness), and other issues to make the system more practicable.

6. ACKNOWLEDGMENTS

This work was sponsored by KAK ENHI (23500288) and the Research Institute for Science and Technology of Tokyo Denki University

7. REFERENCES

[1] http://www.math.uwaterloo.ca/tsp/concorde/index.html.

[2] *Proc. IEEE Symp. Computational Intelligence in Scheduling (SCIS 07)*, IEEE Press, 57-64.

[3] Gutin, G., Punnen, A. P. 2007. *The Traveling Salesman Problem and its Variations*, Springer, NY, USA.

[4] Helsgaun, K. 2009. General k-opt submoves for the Lin–Kernighan TSP heuristic. *Mathematical Programming Computation*, 1, 119-163.

[5] Huellermeier, E. 2007. *Case-Based Approximate Reasoning*. Springer, Berlin.

[6] Karp, R. M., 1977. "robabilistic analysis of partitioning algorithms for the traveling-salesman problem in the plane. *Math. Oper. Res.*, 2, 3, 209–224.

[7] Ken, H., Kokolo, I., Jun, S., Isao, O., and Shigenobu, K. 2006. Hybridization of Genetic Algorithm with Local Search in Multiobjective Function Optimization : Recommendation of GA then LS. *Transactions of the Japanese Society for Artificial Intelligence*, 21, 482-492.

[8] Lin, S., Kernighan, B. W. 1973. An Effective Heuristic Algorithm for the Traveling-Salesman Problem. Operations Research 21 (2), 498–516.

[9] Nguyen, H. D., Yoshihara, I., Yamamori, K., Yasunaga, M. 2007. Implementation of an Effective Hybrid GA for Large-Scale Traveling Salesman Problems. *IEEE Transactions on Systems, Man and Cybernetics*, Part B, 37, 1, 92-99.

[10] Sakurai, Y., Onoyama, T., Kubota, S., Nakamura, Y., Tsuruta, S. 2006. A Multiworld Intelligent Genetic Algorithm to Interactively Optimize Largescale TSP. *Proc. of the 2006 IEEE International Conference on Information Reuse and Integration (IEEE IRI2006)*, 248-255.

[11] Sakurai, Y., Onoyama, T., Kubota, S., Tsuruta, S. 2008. A Multi-inner-world Genetic Algorithm to Optimize Delivery Problem with Interactive-time. *Proc. of 4th IEEE Conf. on Automation Science and Engineering (CASE 2008)*, 583-590.

[12] Sakurai, Y., Takada, K., Tsukamoto, N., Onoyama, T., Knauf, R. 2011. A Simple Optimization Method based on Backtrack and GA for Delivery Schedule. *Proc. of the IEEE Congress on Evolutionary Computation 2011 (CEC 2011)*, 2790-2797.

[13] Yamamoto, Y., and Kubo, M. 1997. *Invitation to Traveling Salesman Problem.* Asakura Syoten, Tokyo.

A Niching Cumulative Genetic Algorithm with Evaluated Probability for Multimodal Optimization

Hongjun Yang, Yixu Song, Lihua Wang, Peifa Jia
State Key Laboratory on Intelligent Technology and Systems
Tsinghua National Laboratory for Information Science and Technology
Department of Computer Science and Technology, Tsinghua University, Beijing 100084, P.R. China
yanghj_72@126.com, songyixu@163.com
jinziye@sina.com.cn, dcsjpf@mail.tsinghua.edu.cn

ABSTRACT
Multi-modal problems with multiple local/global optima are ubiquitous in real-world application. Many multi-modal optimization algorithms have been developed to search as many local/global optima as possible. However, to locate and maintain many optima simultaneously, both the search quality and efficiency of these algorithms may be influenced. Here, we propose a new niching genetic algorithm that attempts to improve both the search quality and efficiency. To the end, we incorporate two mechanisms into the algorithm: cumulative population technique and an evaluated probability of new individuals. The first mechanism is designed to keep the found solutions by storing all known information, whilst the second is responsible for exploiting unexplored space effectively by guiding the exploration process. The proposed approach is compared with five different niche genetic algorithms on six well known multimodal functions of different characteristics. Empirical results indicate that the proposed approach outperforms other algorithms. It not only increases the probability of finding both global and local optima, but also reduces the average number of function evaluations.

Categories and Subject Descriptors
G.1.6 [**Numerical Analysis**]: Optimization; I.2.8 [**Artificial Intelligence**]: Problem Solving, Control Methods and Search

General Terms
Algorithms

Keywords
Niching Genetic Algorithms; Fitness Evaluation; Multimodal Optimization; Cumulative population; Evaluated Probability

1. INTRODUCTION
The problems of interest in scientific and engineering field are or can be advantageously formulated as optimization problems. Due to physical (and/or cost) constraints, these problems may contain several high quality global or local solutions which have to be identified and the most appropriate solution should be chosen [1]. These problems are known as multimodal optimization problems.

GECCO'14, July 12–16, 2014, Vancouver, BC, Canada.

http://dx.doi.org/10.1145/2598394.2605677.

Many Evolutionary Algorithms(EAs) introducing niching technique [2-5] have recently been proposed and attempt to solve the multimodal optimization problem. Niching technique can maintain diversity of population and converge in parallel to multiple solutions by restrictive reproduction. Various niching techniques were proposed in the past few decades, such as crowding [6, 7], fitness sharing [8, 9], clearing [10], clustering [11], Multi-Niche Crowding [12], etc.

However, these niching algorithms need take more computing efforts to locate and maintain many optima. Therefore, many algorithm [4, 13] incorporating local search technique, known as memetic algorithms, greatly improve the ability of evolutionary algorithms to accurately locate optimal solutions. But, these approaches usually need a large number of fitness evaluations to find high quality solutions, which might not always be an effective approach especially for problem with very expensive function evaluation. To reduce the number of fitness evaluation, M. Hall [14] proposed that new individual should be evaluated according to its cumulative local information. But, it needs to set a distance threshold which can depends on prior knowledge about optimization problem. Improper setting may make the algorithm get into the repeated check.

Motivated by these observations, a new niching genetic algorithm is developed to improve the search quality and efficiency. It introduces two mechanisms: cumulative population technique and an evaluated probability of new individual. The first mechanism can keep the found solutions by storing all known information, whilst the second is responsible for exploiting unexplored space effectively.

The remainder of the paper is organized as follows. Some related works are briefly described in Section 2. Implementing details of the proposed algorithm is presented in Section 3. In section 4, we evaluate the proposed algorithm and discuss its outcomes based on experiment results. The paper ends in section 5 with a brief discussion.

2. RELATED WORK
2.1 Crowding
Crowding was proposed by De Jong to preserve population diversity and prevent premature convergence. Crowding is applied in the replacement step of GAs in order to decide which individuals and their offspring will remain in the population according to a similarity metric which is based on the number of matching alleles. Depending on the replacement strategies, crowding approach is classified as Deterministic crowing [6] and Probabilistic crowding [7]. Deterministic Crowding selects the fittest individual in the replacement step. Probabilistic Crowding

selects the surviving individual based on a probabilistic formula that takes fitness into account.

The Multi-Niche Crowding, propose by Cede [12], differs from the above crowding approaches by implementing the crowding concept in the selection rules and replacement rules. In crowding selection, each individual in the population has the same chance for mating in every generation. First, an individual is selected for mating sequentially or randomly. Secondly, other individual is selected from a group of individuals of size , picked at random from the population. The other individual chosen must be the one who is the most "similar" to the first individual. In the replacement rules, MNC uses a replacement policy called worst among the most similar. Its goal is to pick replacement individual which is the worst in similar individuals to offspring. Its disadvantage need also set some parameters by prior knowledge.

2.2 Fitness Sharing

Fitness sharing, proposed by Goldberg and Richardson, alter the fitness of each individual according to its neighboring individuals. It is based on the penalization of the areas of the searching space with more solutions within the population. The detail can be found in [8]. Fitness sharing maintains the diversity of population by adjusting the fitness of the individuals according to sharing function. The shortcoming of this approach is that sharing function and the niche radius, which are related to optimization problem, need be set firstly. Clearing proposed by Petro ski [10] is a special fitness sharing method. By comparing all individuals in the niche radius and setting the capacity of each niche, several best individuals survive and the others are all cleared. Dynamic niche sharing also belongs to fitness sharing method in [9]. It identifies niche by niche radius and the number of peaks to identify. At the same time, the disadvantage of clearing and dynamic niche sharing is similar to that of fitness sharing.

2.3 Dynamic Niche Clustering

Dynamic niche clustering [11] proposed by Gan and Warwick combines clustering and fitness sharing. For each generation, a clustering operation is executed with a dynamically updated cluster number. Next, fitness sharing is implemented with the niche radius provided by clustering. But it is not an easy task to calculate the cluster number, which will affect the quantity and quality of identified optimal solutions greatly.

3. Niching Cumulative Genetic Algorithm with Evaluated Probability (EPNCGA)

Based on niching genetic algorithms(NGAs), the EPNCGA use cumulative population and evaluated probability to implement multimodal function optimization. We know that all information may help us solve the problem, the cumulative population can prevent the loss of useful information or redundant fitness evaluation by storing all evaluated information; on the other hand, we can also determine if new individual is evaluated by evaluated probability to reduce the number of fitness function evaluation. The algorithmic flow of the proposed algorithm can be depicted in Algorithm 1. After the initial population is created, every individual is evaluated by special problem. Next, the proposed niche identification method (NIM) is implemented to find all interesting area of peak. Selection, crossover, and mutation are then performed. Finally, evaluated probability of new individual is calculated to determine if new individual from crossover and mutation is evaluated and add to population. The evolutionary process is repeated until the stopping criterion is satisfied. The detail steps are described in the algorithm 1.

Algorithm 1. Algorithmic Flow of EPNCGA

1.	*pop*=GenerateInitialPopulation(*pop_size*);
2.	Evaluate(*pop*);
3.	while the stopping criterion not met do
3.1	*niches*=NIM(*pop*);
3.2	*crossoveroffspring* = Select(*niches*,*pop*) ;
3.3	Crossover(*crossoveroffspring*);
3.4	Evaluate_and_Add(*crossoveroffspring*);
3.5	repeat 3.2-3.4 until add *Nc* individuals
3.6	*mutationoffspring*=randselect(*pop*);
3.7	Mutate(*mutationoffspring*);
3.8	Evaluate_and_Add(*mutationoffspring*);
3.9	repeat 3.6-3.8 until add *Nm* individuals
3.10	end while

3.1 Niche Identification Method

Niching technique is an effective approach which can locate and maintain many solutions. A niche can be defined as a subspace in the search space which includes a global or local optima. Therefore, accurate identification of niches is the key to improving the accuracy and efficiency of these solutions. Standard fitness sharing requires a unified sharing radius, but it doesn't suit for the multimodal problems where niches have different shape and range. Dynamic niche cluster methods [11] can determine clusters of different size, but two further parameters need be set firstly. Lin et al. [15] proposed a niche identification method which can determine the center location and radius of each of existing niches based on fitness topographical information of individuals. It also set one parameter by prior knowledge. Hill-climbing function [13] was used to identify niche, but it need to evaluate the positions between two individuals. By modifying the method proposed by [15], a new niche identification method is proposed.

Empirically, if two closer niches A and B satisfy the following condition, we should merge these two niches. This condition expresses that all individuals of niche B far away from x_A than x_B.

Condition 1: $f(x_A)>f(x_B)$ and $\forall\, x \in B,\ d(x_A, x_B)\leq d(x_A, x)$

Here, for convenience, x_N denotes the optimum individual in a niche N, which also is referred as niche center; $d(x, y)$ denote the Euler distance between two individuals x and y; $f(x)$ denotes the fitness of the individual x .

Using condition 1, the complete niche identification procedure can then be defined as follows.

1. The individual x with the highest fitness in the population is selected as the center x_C of the first niche C (C=1), and this individual is then marked.

2. Calculate the distances between x_C and all other individuals, and construct an individual's sequence $(x^1, x^2, x^3 ...)$ such that $d(x^1, x_C)\leq d(x^2, x_C)\leq d(x^3, x_C)\leq ...)$.

3. Sequentially check the fitness $f(x^i)$ and $f(x^{i+1})$of the adjacent two individuals $x^i$and x^{i+1} until $f(x^{i+1}) > f(x^i)$. Mark all individuals $x^1, x^2, x^3 ..., x^i$ in niche C.

4. The individual with the highest fitness in all unmarked individuals is selected as the center of new niche C (C=C+1) and repeat process 2) and 3) until all individuals are marked.

5) Check all niches the algorithm will merge two closer niches which satisfy condition 1.

3.2 Evaluated probability of new individual

Each new individual should help improve the accuracy of solutions or maintain diversity of population. Empirically, if the density of evaluated individuals in one niche meets the normal distribution rather than uniform distribution, or, the density nearby niching center is higher, search quality and efficiency of the algorithm may be greatly improved. Inspired by these, we design an evaluated probability function of new individual.

Suppose optimization problem meets continuity, new individual's feature is similar to the nearest. At n generation, we can calculate evaluated probability $p(x, y, n, N)$ of new individual x by the nearest y in niche N. $p(x, y, n, N)$ relates the distance $d(x, y)$ and the fitness difference f between y with x_N.

$$p(x,y,n,N)=\begin{cases}\frac{1}{2}+[\frac{\alpha(n)d(x,y)-f}{1-f}]^{-7}/2, & \alpha(n)d(x,x_n)\geq f \\ \frac{1}{2}-[\frac{f-\alpha(n)d(x,y)}{f}]^{-7}/2, & \textit{otherwise}\end{cases} \tag{1}$$

Here, the difference f can be denoted as $f=\frac{f(x_N)-f(x_n)}{f(x_N)-f_{\min}}$, $f_{\min}$ is the minimum fitness in niche N, $\alpha(n)=\varphi(1/\rho)$ is increasing function, ρ denotes the average density of individuals in the search space .

The complete evaluating procedure can be defined as follows.

1. Finding the nearest individual y and niche N by x ;
2. Calculating f and $p(x,y,n,N)$ by formula(1);
3. Generating a random number r between 0 and 1;
4. If $r \leq p(x,y,n,N)$, then x is evaluated and inserted to population.

3.3 Selection, Crossover and Mutation

To make sure that the algorithm can locate and maintain many optima simultaneously, we use fitness-proportionate selection to select a niche according to the average space of each individual in niche. Then, Tournament selection operator is applied to the current niche to generate two offspring. Next, random single point crossover operator is used. The mutation operator may maintain the diversity of population and prevent the genetic algorithm from premature convergence. The algorithm adopts random selection operator to select a offspring and random mutation operator to generate a new individual.

4. Performance Evaluation

4.1 Experiment Setting and Measures

4.1.1 Benchmark Function

To assess the performance of the proposed approach, we compare its result with those obtained by five other NGAs, Clearing (CPGA)[10], Dynamic Niche Sharing(DNSGA) [9], Deterministic Crowding(DCGA) [6], Multi-niche Crowding (MNCGA) [12] and CMNGA [14]. We adopted 6 multimodal benchmark functions, namely F4, F5, F6, F7, F8 and F9 from [16]. They have different characteristics, such as multiple even and uneven niche, multiple equal and unequal maxima. Their detail can be found in [16].

4.1.2 Evaluation Measures

We use peak ratio (PR) and peak accuracy (PA) measure [17] to judge convergence speed and the ability to locate and maintain all fitness function peaks. The details can be found in [17].

$$PR=\frac{\textit{Number of the found peaks}}{\textit{Total number of peaks}} \tag{2}$$

$$PA=\sum_{i=1}^{N_{peaks}}|f(x_i)-f(peak_i)| \tag{3}$$

4.1.3 Parameter Setting

N_p denotes the population size; p_c denotes the probability of crossover; p_m denotes the probability of mutation; g_{max} denotes the max number of generations. In DNSGA and CPGA, σ_{sh} denotes a niche radius. N_{peak} denotes the number of peak in DNSGA; N_{kappa} denotes the capacity of niche in CPGA; C_s denotes the crowding selection size, C_f denotes Crowding factor, and S denotes the crowding factor group size in MNCGA; N_i denotes initial the population size, N_e denotes the max number of evaluation, N_c denotes the number of crossover, and N_m denotes the number of mutation in CMNGA and EPNCGA; N_{crowd} denotes the crowding selection size, and N_{min} denotes the number of the nearest neighbors in CMNGA. The following is Parameter Setting.

Table 1. Parameter Setting

Method	Parameter	F4	F5	F6	F7	F8	F9
CPGA DNSGA DCGA MNCGA	N_p	50	50	50	50	100	100
	p_c	0.9	0.9	0.9	0.9	0.9	0.9
	p_m	0.01	0.01	0.01	0.01	0.01	0.01
	g_{max}	500	500	500	500	1000	1200
CPGA	σ_{sh}	0.2	0.2	0.2	0.2	2	0.5
	N_{peak}	6	6	6	6	8	10
DNSGA	σ_{sh}	0.2	0.2	0.2	0.2	2	0.5
	N_{kappa}	9	9	9	9	10	12
MNCGA	C_s	15	15	15	15	25	30
	C_f	3	3	3	3	3	4
	S	15	15	15	15	25	30
CMNGA EPNCGA	N_i	30	30	30	30	50	50
	N_e	600	600	600	600	1500	1500
	N_c	5	5	5	5	8	8
	N_m	10	10	10	10	20	20
CMNGA	N_{crowd}	10	10	10	10	10	10
	N_{min}	5	5	5	5	8	8

4.2 Experiment result

Convergence speed of the algorithm is determined by the number of fitness evaluations that the algorithm requires to locate all optima, within a fixed accuracy level ε . We evaluate their performance in two accuracy level, $\varepsilon \in \{1E-2, 1E-3\}$. Table 2 shows the average performance of the algorithm (mean) and its standard deviation(std). we can clearly observe that the proposed approach produces faster convergence speed in the majority of benchmark functions. Though all approach almost can locate all peaks within 1500 fitness evaluations in the accuracy level $\varepsilon = 1E-2$, the EPNCGA and CMNGA show remarkable performance. They can locate and maintain all peaks within 550, but EPNCGA performs better in the majority of the functions. These data illustrate the EPNCGA improve the search efficiency by evaluated probability. Figure 1 presents the value of PR and PA during the run of each approaches(mean of 100 independent runs) for 2D function F8. Again, the EPNCGA exhibits better performance with respect to locating the peaks and fine-tuning the solutions found. Within 200 fitness evaluations, the EPNCGA can locate all peaks and has the best peak accuracy. This figure also illustrates that the EPNCGA can improve both the search quality and efficiency. Figure 2 shows contour plots of 2D function F9 and the positions of all individuals evaluated by the EPNCGA. The number of individuals is 600. The red symbol △ denotes the position of peak and the black point denotes evaluated individual.

Figure 2 presents the distribution of individuals. The more individuals concentrate on the area nearby peaks, the fewer are on the area far away from peaks. Also, the distribution of individuals is similar to the normal distribution. Overall, the EPNCGA can identify and maintain most peaks in the multimodal function.

Table 2. Convergence speed in two accuracy level

Method	Accuracy level	F4		F5		F6		F7		F8		F9	
		Mean	Std	Mean	Std	Mean	Std	Mean	Std	Mean	Std	Mean	Std
EPNCGA	1E-2	62	16	72	40	64	18	66	20	64	18	547	276
	1E-3	142	36	204	102	139	28	208	85	139	28	1240	8
CMNGA	1E-2	70	30	70	21	80	61	80	76	80	61	485	190
	1E-3	195	98	221	92	180	88	254	150	180	88	1199	287
DNSGA	1E-2	167	85	189	120	180	119	299	284	181	120	*	*
	1E-3	772	290	13352	7099	754	351	15860	5160	754	351	*	*
CPGA	1E-2	348	456	1002	1533	296	336	1047	1664	296	336	*	*
	1E-3	1754	1407	16284	4708	1864	1222	17173	3353	1864	1222	*	*
DCGA	1E-2	1923	2358	703	2775	1152	3877	3142	6832	1152	3877	*	*
	1E-3	8955	4371	17611	6311	8893	8192	18232	5456	8893	8192	*	*
MNCGA	1E-2	691	1824	927	2153	1021	2533	523	845	1021	2533	*	*
	1E-3	3357	2534	14263	8582	7393	8467	15673	7553	7393	8467	*	*

*:the algorithm only finds part of all optima.

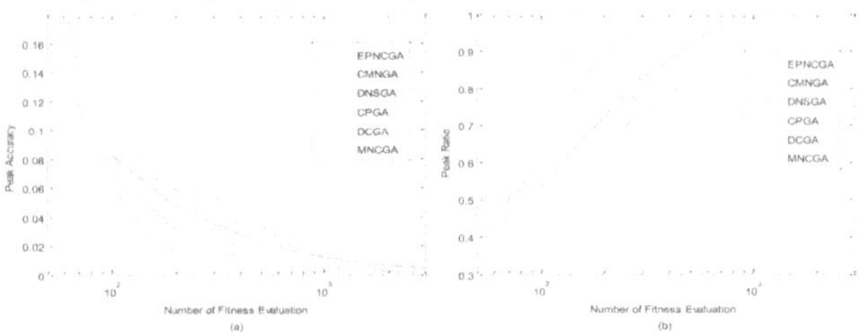

Figure 1. Peak Accuracy and Peak Radio of F8 function

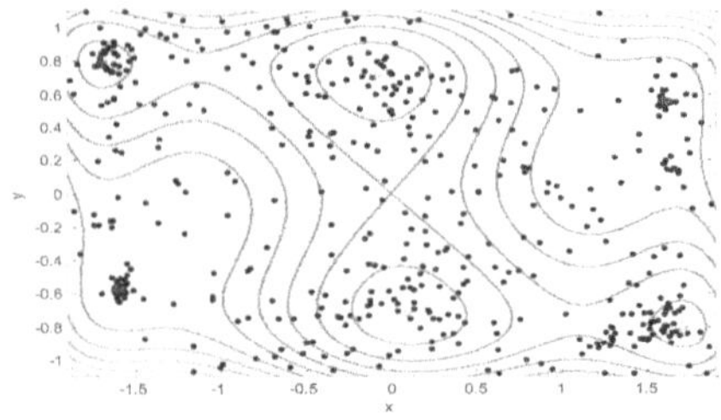

Figure 2. Contour Plot of F9 by EPNCGA

5. CONCLUSION

Multi-modal optimization algorithms need locate and maintain many optima simultaneously, so both the search quality and efficiency of these algorithms may be influenced. Here, we attempt to overcome these influence by introducing two mechanisms into the algorithm: cumulative population technique and an evaluated probability of new individuals. The first mechanism is designed to keep the found solutions by storing all known information, whilst the second is responsible for exploiting unexplored space effectively by guiding the exploration process. Comparing experimental results with 5 different NGAs on 6 well known multimodal functions of different characteristics, show that the proposed approach outperforms other algorithms. Among most benchmark functions, the proposed approach not only increases the probability of finding both global and local optima, but also reduces the average number of function evaluations.

In the future, we will apply the proposed algorithm to study the higher dimensions and the expensive multimodal problem.

6. ACKNOWLEDGMENTS

This work is supported by National Key Technology R&D Program of China under Grant 2013BAI01B01.

7. REFERENCES

[1] M.G. Epitropakis, et al., Multimodal optimization using niching differential evolution with index-based neighborhoods, in *2012 IEEE Congress on Evolutionary Computation. CEC 2012*, pages 1-8, 2012.

[2] M.G. Epitropakis, et al., A dynamic archive niching differential evolution algorithm for multimodal optimization, in *2013 IEEE Congress on Evolutionary Computation (CEC)*, pages 79-86, 2013.

[3] E. Cuevas and M. González, An optimization algorithm for multimodal functions inspired by collective animal behavior, *Soft Computing*, 17(3), pages 489-502, 2013.

[4] B.Y. Qu, et al., Niching particle swarm optimization with local search for multi-modal optimization, *Inform Sciences*, 197, pages 131-143, 2012.

[5] M. Li, et al., A hybrid niching PSO enhanced with recombination-replacement crowding strategy for multimodal function optimization, *Applied Soft Computing*, 12(3), pages 975-987, 2012.

[6] R. Manner, et al., Crowding and Preselection Revisited, *Parallel Problem Solving from Nature*, pages 27-36: North-Holland, 1992.

[7] O.J. Mengshoel and D.E. Goldberg, The Crowding Approach to Niching in Genetic Algorithms, *Evolutionary Computation*, 16(3), pages 315-354, 2008.

[8] B. Sareni and L. Krahenbuhl, Fitness Sharing and Niching Methods Revisited, *IEEE transactions on Evolutionary Computation*, 2(3), pages 97-106, 1998.

[9] B.L. Miller and M.J. Shaw, Genetic algorithms with dynamic niche sharing for multimodal function optimization, in *Proceedings of IEEE International Conference on Evolutionary Computation* , pages 786-791, 1996.

[10] A. Petrowski, A clearing procedure as a niching method for genetic algorithms, in *Proceedings of IEEE International Conference on Evolutionary Computation*, pages 798-803, 1996.

[11] J. Gan and K. Warwick, A Genetic Algorithm with Dynamic Niche Clustering for Multimodal Function Optimisation, *Artificial Neural Nets and Genetic Algorithms*, Springer Vienna, pages 248-255, 1999.

[12] W. Cedeño, et al., Multi-niche crowding in genetic algorithms and its application to the assembly of DNA restriction-fragments, *Evolutionary Computation*, 2, pages 321-345, 1995.

[13] J.E. Vitela and O. Castaños, A sequential niching memetic algorithm for continuous multimodal function optimization, *Appl Math Comput*, 218(17), pages 8242-8259, 2012.

[14] M. Hall, A Cumulative Multi-Niching Genetic Algorithm for Multimodal Function Optimization, *International Journal of Advanced Research in Artificial Intelligence*, 1(9), 2012.

[15] C. Lin and W. Wu, Niche identification techniques in multimodal genetic search with sharing scheme. *Advances in Engineering Software*, 33, pages 779-791, 2002.

[16] S. Das, et al., Real-parameter evolutionary multimodal optimization — A survey of the state-of-the-art, *Swarm and Evolutionary Computation*, 1(2), pages 71-88, 2011.

[17] R. Thomsen, Multimodal optimization using crowding-based differential evolution, in *Congress on Evolutionary Computation CEC2004*, pages 1382-1389, 2004.

A Quantitative Analysis of the Simplification Genetic Operator

Haoxi Zhan
Hampshire College
Amherst, MA, 01002
hz12@hampshire.edu

ABSTRACT

The simplification function was introduced to PushGP as a tool to reduce the sizes of evolved programs in final reports. While previous work suggests that simplification could reduce the sizes significantly, nothing has been done to study its impacts on the evolution of Push programs. In this paper, we show the impact of simplification as a genetic operator. By conducting test runs on the U.S. change problem, we show that using simplification operator with PushGP, lexicase selection and ULTRA could increase the possibility to find solutions in the short term while it might remove some useful genetic materials for the long term.

Categories and Subject Descriptors

I.2.2 [**Automatic Programming**]: Program modification

General Terms

Experimentation

Keywords

Genetic Programming; Genetic Operator; Push; Clojush; Simplification

1. INTRODUCTION

Programs produced by genetic programming systems are often filled with unused instructions. Some of them are useless while the others might provide some useful genetic materials for future generations. These redundant instructions increase the sizes of programs and make them complex. Not only might they prevent the genes from evolving, they slow down the evolutionary processes significantly.

Simplification was introduced to counteract the negative impacts of the redundancy. Usually, the simplification function is applied after the evolution to remove such instructions. A recent study has shown that the simplification function in PushGP could reduce the sizes of programs significantly[3]. However, simplifying programs after the evolution could only improve the readability of the final programs in the reports. In order to reduce the program sizes and to speed up the evolution, we need to apply simplification during the evolution. Although this approach has been studied in the past[6], its impact on PushGP is still unknown.

GECCO'14, July 12–16, 2014, Vancouver, BC, Canada.

ACM 978-1-4503-2881-4/14/07 ...$15.00.
http://dx.doi.org/10.1145/2598394.2605684.

Push is a stack-based programming language which is especially designed for evolutionary computation[1, 5]. In Push, there's a stack for each data type. The instructions take their inputs from relative stacks and then push the outputs to the specific stacks. If the input stack is empty when an instruction is being executed, the instruction will be "no-op"ed and it will do nothing. Thus, the only requirement on syntax is the balance of parenthesis, which could be easily fixed. As a result, we are able to do arbitrary modifications to Push programs without worrying about syntax.

PushGP is a Genetic Programming system based on Push. While mutation, crossover and tournament selection are still available, a few new methods has been developed in PushGP recently. Lexicase selection is a new selection method based on multiple fitness cases[2]. When selecting parents, all fitness cases will be randomly sorted. Individuals who performed the best in the first case will survive and join the competetion of the next case until there's only one candidate or one case. ULTRA, which stands for "Uniform Linear Transformation with Repair and Alternation", is a new genetic operator which travels the linearized parents, produces children and then repairs them[4].

In this paper, we analyze the impact of the simplification genetic operator on evolution which is based on PushGP, lexicase selection and ULTRA. By dividing the evolution into several phases, we examine the performances in each phase. Then we compare the success rates, program sizes, running times and fitness values with and without simplification.

2. METHODS

2.1 The Problem

The problem we chose in this research is the U.S. change problem. The input is a specific amount of money in the integer stack and the evolved programs are supposed to return the minimum number of U.S. coins to make a change.

2.2 Fitness Evaluation

For each individual generated during the evolution, a fitness test is performed. Due to the employment of lexicase selection[2], the fitness evaluations are based on 150 different test cases. In each test case, an error value is calculated and then stored in the error vector. The error vector is defined as:

$$\text{Vec}[\epsilon] = (\epsilon_1, \epsilon_2, \cdots, \epsilon_{150})$$

If a program fails to produce a number in test case n, an error score of 1000 is assigned. Thus, $\epsilon_n = 1000$. Otherwise, the error value is the difference between the solution and the output:

$$\epsilon_n = |\text{solution} - \text{output}|$$

2.3 Simplification

The simplification operator we used in this study is based on hill climbing algorithm. For each simplification step, it removes a pair of parenthesis or several instructions. There's a 20% probability to remove a pair of parenthesis while the probability to remove instructions is 80%. The maximum number of instructions to remove is 2. After each step, a fitness evaluation will be performed. Only if the new program's error vector is exactly the same as the error vector of the original program, the new program will be kept.

2.4 Parameters

To test the impacts of the simplification operator, we conducted 2 experiments on U.S. Change problem. In order to guarantee moderate success rates, the parameters we used is based on our previous experiments. Experiment NO-SIMP was solely based on ULTRA and lexicase selection. In experiment SIMP-1, there's a 10% probability to use the simplification operator while the probability of ULTRA was 90%. After several tests, we decided to use only 1 simplification step as it's already enough to counteract the code growth.

To ensure the fairness, we made the total number of fitness evaluations equal. As the use of simplification will increase the number of fitness tests per individual, the population size of SIMP-1 was reduced to 1818. The calculation of the moderate population size is based on probability.

$$1001 \times s + 1000 \times s \times 0.1 = 2000 \times 1001 \Rightarrow s \approx 1818$$

Notice that due to the existence of the initial generation, fitness tests will be performed to a total of 1001 generations.

The details of our parameters are listed in Table 1.

Table 1: The parameters we used for our experiments

Experiment	NO-SIMP	SIMP-1
Basic parameters		
Number of Runs	100	100
Max Generations	1000	1000
Population Size	2000	1818
Max Size	500	500
Selection	lexicase	lexicase
Genetic Operators		
ULTRA Probability	1	0.9
Simplification Probability	0	0.1
Simplification Step	N/A	1
Instruction Remove Limit	N/A	2

3. RESULTS AND DISCUSSIONS

We conducted 100 runs for each experiment. Table 2 presents the general performances of our experiments. Notice that the average sizes in the table are based on the program sizes of each run's last generation.

Table 2: general performances

Runs	NO-SIMP	SIMP-1
Success Rate	82%	75%
Average Sizes	338.2	31.13
Average Time(h)	15.305	3.238
Average Generations	548.63	541.78

The average size of NO-SIMP runs is 338.2 whereas SIMP-1 runs have an average size of only 31.3. The huge difference in average program size indicates that the simplification genetic operator successfully controlled the code growth. As expected, the introduction of simplification significantly reduced the running time. However, 82 runs succeeded in the NO-SIMP experiment while only 75 SIMP-1 runs succeeded ($p = .067$). The success rate of SIMP-1 runs is 7% lower than the one of NO-SIMP runs. Surprisingly, while SIMP-1 runs have a lower success rate, their average number of generations is still lower. This implies that successful SIMP-1 runs might tend to find the solution faster. Hence we divided the evolution process into several phases and analyzed the performances of each phase.

3.1 Performance by phase

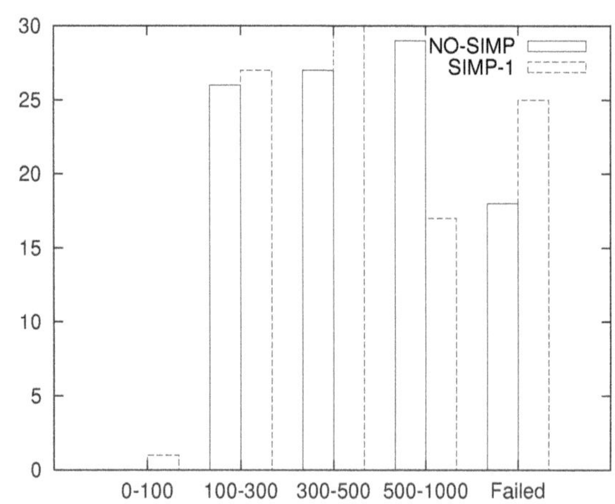

Figure 1: Performances by phases

As shown in Figure 1, SIMP-1 runs tend to find the solution faster. In the first 500 generations, 58% of SIMP-1 runs succeeded while only 53% of NO-SIMP runs found the solution. Among those who didn't terminate in the first 500 generations, 61.7% NO-SIMP runs returned the correct program in 1000 generations while only 40.5% SIMP-1 runs succeeded. The detailed success rates by phase are presented in Table 3. For each phase, the precentages reveal how many runs that didn't terminate before the phase succeeded in that specific phase.

Table 3: Success rates by phase

Phase	NO-SIMP	SIMP-1
0-100	0%	1%
100-300	26%	27.3%
300-500	36.5%	41.7%
500-1000	61.7%	40.5%

3.2 Average size by generation

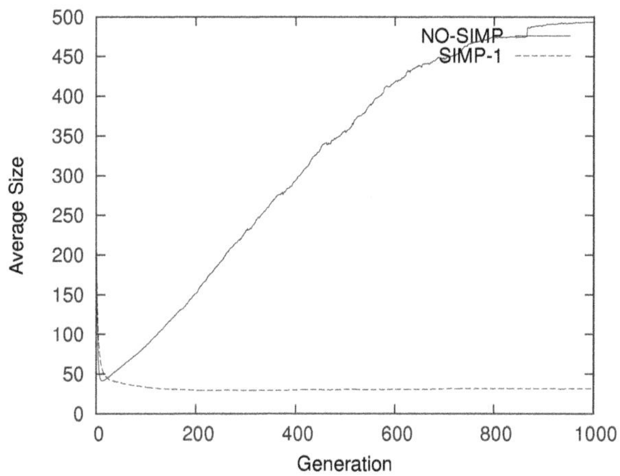

Figure 2: Average size by generation

Figure 2 presents the average program size by generation. As all initial programs were generated by the same function, both NO-SIMP runs and SIMP-1 runs started at around 250. Both experiments reveal a dramatic drop after the beginning of the evolution. Then the average size of NO-SIMP runs started to rise steadily, nearly reaching the maximum program size 500 in the last 100 generations. Meanwhile, the average size of SIMP-1 runs leveled off since the 200th generation.

3.3 Median error by generation

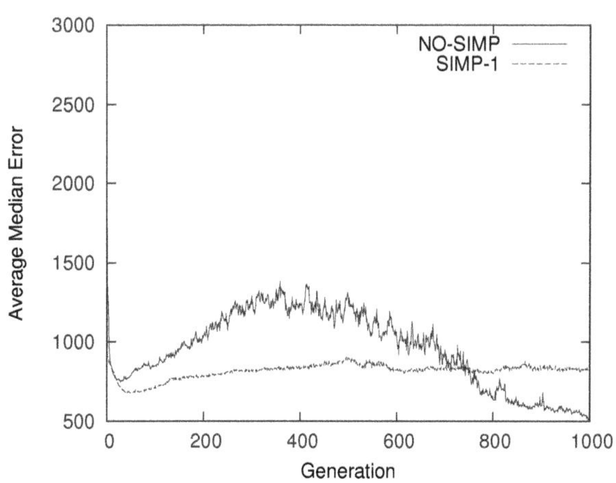

Figure 3: Median error by generation

Because average error is easily influenced by extreme individuals, median error is considered to be a better representation of the whole population's fitness. As shown in Figure 3, after a rapid decrease at the beginning, the median error of NO-SIMP runs grew steadily until the 400th generation. Then it gradually dropped. Finally it reached a low level at the end of the evolution. The change of SIMP-1 runs' median error is slightly different. It kept growing slowly for the remaining generations.

The information provided by Table 3 and Figure 3 is consistent. For instance, during the generation 300-500, NO-SIMP runs had a slightly higher median error. Meanwhile, it also has a lower success rate in that phase.

3.4 Best fitness by generation

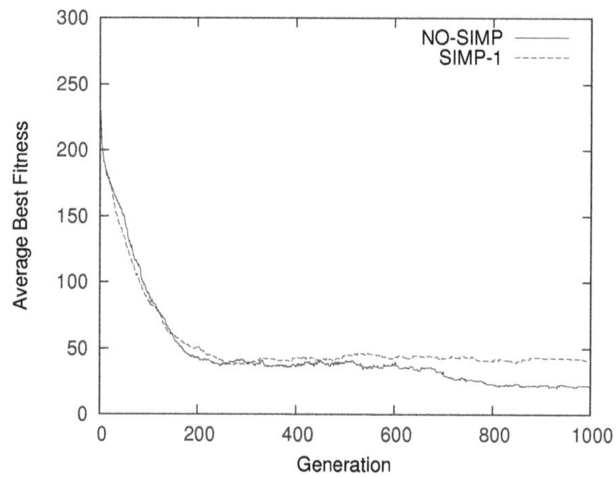

Figure 4: Best fitness by generation

While the median error represents the fitness of the whole population, the best fitness, which is shown in Figure 4, represents the elite group of each generation. Notice that as our fitness scores are represented by error values, the lower the value is, the better the program performs. For both the experiments, the best fitness dropped immediately after the beginning of evolution. Then SIMP-1 runs maintained a stable best fitness value, whereas for NO-SIMP runs the decrease continued. An unpaired t-test shows that $p = .084$ for the difference in best fitness.

Interestingly, SIMP-1 runs experienced no improvements on both median error and best fitness since the 200th generation. This implies that the evolution of the programs was kept stagnant due to the employment of simplification.

3.5 Number of unique programs by generation

One conjecture we had about the previous fact is that the diversity of programs is reduced by simplification. However, the number of unique programs, which is shown in Figure 5, disproved it. SIMP-1 runs show a fall in number of unique programs within the first 400 generations, followed by stable sizes around 1700. For NO-SIMP runs, most programs in the populations were unique in the first 400 generations. Then more and more duplicated programs were produced. In the last generation, only a bit more than 1300 programs were unique.

One possible reason for the rapid decrease experienced by NO-SIMPs runs is that the alternation of programs was limited by the size. When the parents had difficulty producing

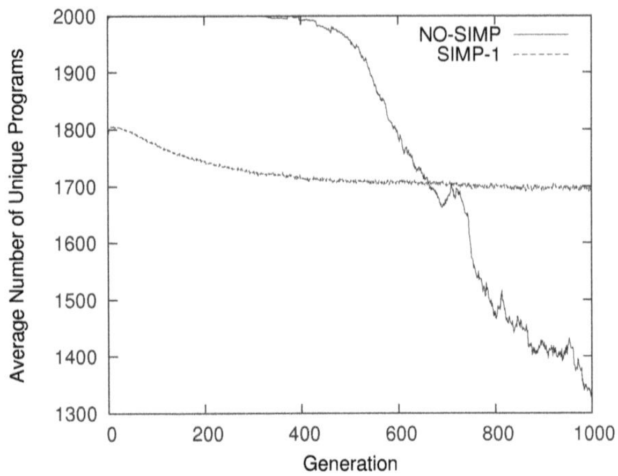

Figure 5: Number of unique programs by generation

children without exceeding the maximum size limit, one parent will be directly copied to the next generation. On the other hand, it's also possible that the population was gradually approaching the solution. This conjecture is supported by the data on median error and best fitness.

4. CONCLUSIONS, CONJECTURES AND FUTURE WORK

In this research we studied the impact of the simplification genetic operator in a PushGP environment with lexicase selection and ULTRA operator. The phase-based analysis revealed that the introduction of simplification operator will benefit the evolution in short term while it's harmful for the long run. By analyzing the data on median error and best fitness, we showed that in the runs with simplification, the evolution was actually almost stagnant. Then we used the diagram of the number of unique programs to prove that stagnancy was not caused by the lost of diversity.

Although we've got some interesting results, there are still many unknowns. Here we list the two major open problems: (1) How do the runs with simplification achieve a higher success rate in the short term? (2) Why is the simplification operator harmful in the long run?

Based on our data and analyzes, we have several conjectures on these problems. For problem 1, we conjecture that there are two reasons. Firstly, as the program sizes are successfully controlled by the simplification operator, the combinatorial search space is much smaller. Thus, the possibility to find a solution by luck is higher. Secondly, it's possible that the majority of the unused instructions will only be turned into useful ones in the long run. Thus, by simplifying the programs, most short-term-useless instructions are removed. For problem 2, we conjecture that many useful genetic materials are removed by simplification. While the populations of NO-SIMP runs are evolving towards the right direction, the evolution in runs with simplification relies more on randomness due to the lack of genetic materials.

In the future, we plan to develop a tracking system which is able to track the behavior of each individual in the population and conduct more experiments for a deeper research.

5. ACKNOWLEDGMENTS

We thank Lee Spector and Thomas Helmuth for creating Clojush, which is the PushGP implementation used in this research. We also appreciate Josiah Erikson for maintaining the Hampshire College Cluster Computing Facility. This research is based upon work supported by National Science Foundation under Grant No. 1017817 and 1129319. Any opinions, findings, and conclusions or recommendations expressed in this publication are those of the authors and do not necessarily reflect the views of the National Science Foundation.

6. REFERENCES

[1] L. Spector. Autoconstructive evolution: Push, pushgp, and pushpop. In L. Spector, E. Goodman, A. Wu, W. Langdon, H.-M. Voigt, M. Gen, S. Sen, M. Dorigo, S. Pezeshk, M. Garzon, and E. Burke, editors, *Proceedings of the Genetic and Evolutionary Computation Conference, GECCO-2001*, pages 137–146, San Francisco, CA, USA, July 2001. Morgan Kaufmann.

[2] L. Spector. Assessment of problem modality by differential performance of lexicase selection in genetic programming: a preliminary report. In K. McClymont and E. Keedwell, editors, *1st workshop on Understanding Problems (GECCO-UP)*, pages 401–408, Philadelphia, Pennsylvania, USA, July 2012. ACM.

[3] L. Spector and T. Helmuth. Effective simplification of evolved push programs using a simple, stochastic hill-climber. In *Proceeding of the sixteenth annual conference companion on Genetic and evolutionary computation conference companion.*

[4] L. Spector and T. Helmuth. Uniform linear transformation with repair and alternation in genetic programming. In R. Riolo, J. H. Moore, and M. Kotanchek, editors, *Genetic Programming Theory and Practice XI.*

[5] L. Spector, J. Klein, and M. Keijzer. The push3 execution stack and the evolution of control. In H.-G. Beyer, U.-M. O'Reilly, D. V. Arnold, W. Banzhaf, C. Blum, E. W. Bonabeau, E. Cantu-Paz, D. Dasgupta, K. Deb, J. A. Foster, E. D. de Jong, H. Lipson, X. Llora, S. Mancoridis, M. Pelikan, G. R. Raidl, T. Soule, A. M. Tyrrell, J.-P. Watson, and E. Zitzler, editors, *Proceedings of the Genetic and Evolutionary Computation Conference (GECCO-2005)*, volume 2, pages 1689–1696, Washington DC, USA, June 2005. ACM Press.

[6] M. Zhang, P. Wong, and D. Qian. Online program simplification in genetic programming. In T.-D. Wang, X. Li, S.-H. Chen, X. Wang, H. A. Abbass, H. Iba, G. Chen, and X. Yao, editors, *Simulated Evolution and Learning, Proceedings 6th International Conference, SEAL 2006*, pages 592–600. Springer, October 2006.

Visualisation in Genetic and Evolutionary Computation (VizGEC'14) Chairs' Message

As work on visualisation in the evolutionary computation field continues to grow, we are pleased to be organising the fifth GECCO workshop on visualisation in genetic and evolutionary computation (VizGEC 2014).

Following a call for papers, three papers were accepted for presentation at the workshop. The papers cover a diverse range of topics, and we are particularly pleased to note that one of them builds on a discussion that took place at last year's workshop. Topics include visualising stability within an evolutionary algorithm, the visualisation of trade-offs in many-objective optimisation, and finally a method for visualising empirical attainment function differences. In addition to the presentation of papers, we are inviting demonstrations of tools that are used by people engaged in evolutionary computation research. We hope that by presenting a range of different tools and techniques we will encourage a discussion on visualisation methods that people find useful, as well as how the current state-of-the-art can be extended, with the development of new techniques and the application of existing methods to new problems, to fulfill researcher's visualisation needs.

We hope that the workshop will appeal to a wide range of GECCO attendees, from those with experience of developing novel visualisation methods, to those who simply use them as a tool to illustrate their work. We also intend that the workshop will provide an attractive opportunity for those with visualisation problems to find opportunities to engage with the visualisation community and identify potential collaborations.

The organisation of VizGEC 2014 has been made possible with invaluable assistance from the GECCO organising committee. We would particularly like to thank the GECCO 2014 Workshops Chair, Per Kristian Lehre, for providing helpful comments and advice throughout the process of organising the workshop.

We look forward to welcoming you to VizGEC 2014.

David Walker
VizGEC 2014 Chair
University of Exeter, UK

Richard Everson
VizGEC 2014 Chair
University of Exeter, UK

Jonathan Fieldsend
VizGEC 2014 Chair
University of Exeter, UK

EA Stability Visualization: Perturbations, Metrics and Performance

Matthew J. Craven
SoCM, University of Plymouth
Drakes Circus, Plymouth
PL4 8AA, UK
matthew.craven@plymouth.ac.uk

Henri C. Jimbo
RISE, Waseda University
3-4-1 Okhubo, Shinjuku-Ku
Tokyo 165-8555, Japan
jimbo_maths@yahoo.com

ABSTRACT

It is well-known that Evolutionary Algorithms (EAs) are sensitive to changes in their control parameters, and it is generally agreed that too large a change may turn the EA from being successful to unsuccessful. This work reports on an experimental hybrid visualization scheme for the determination of EA stability according to perturbation of EA parameters. The scheme gives a visual representation of local neighborhoods of the parameter space according to a choice of two perturbation metrics, relating perturbations to EA performance as a variant of Kolmogorov distance. Through visualization and analysis of twelve thousand case study EA runs, we illustrate that we are able to distinguish between EA stability and instability depending upon perturbation and performance metrics. Finally we use what we have learnt in the case study to provide a methodology for more general EAs.

Categories and Subject Descriptors

D.2.8 [**Software Engineering**]: Metrics—*complexity measures, performance measures*; G.1.6 [**Optimization**]; I.4.10 [**Image Representation**]: *multidimensional*

General Terms

Algorithms, Experimentation, Performance

Keywords

Evolutionary Algorithm; performance; perturbation; stability; visualization

1. INTRODUCTION

Visualization exists to communicate data in a form understandable (by, or pleasing to) the eye, enabling the understanding of that data in such a way that the user is able to strike conclusions or make decisions which would be more difficult to make by other methods of communication. It is well-known that visualization has many applications, including assisting the understanding of Evolutionary Algorithm (EA) output, runs and states (which are all referred to as *data*). EA data in practice tends to be vast and multidimensional [13].

There are common techniques for static visualization of EA data in at most four dimensions, such as contour maps or heat maps, but for dimension numbers beyond four the problem becomes difficult. One school of thought is in favor of dimensionality reduction through statistical techniques. For example, linear techniques such as Principal Component Analysis (PCA) or Canonical Correlation Analysis, or nonlinear techniques such as Kernel PCA or Local Linear Embedding may be used (see [15] for a comparative review of the above techniques). Alternatively, just part of the information may be presented through a simple projection. Another school of thought favors judicious presentation of statistics or consequences of the data. The popular taxonomy of this type of visualization is due to [12], which considers that the course and state of the EA may be separately visualized.

Past work on visualization focussed mainly on summarizing the EA course and state, where parameters and other EA settings were assumed to be constants. In particular, there seems to be an absence of work on visualizing what happens to an EA when its parameters are changed, at random or otherwise. The common EA paradigm of sensitivity to parameter change is well known [4], it being generally agreed that "bad" values of control parameters may render the EA ineffective. Hence for effective EA performance it is intuitively useful to find some way of measuring long-term EA behavior given this sensitivity. Broadly this is referred to as measuring EA stability. In this work we report on a preliminary study concerning EA stability visualization.

There are various kinds of stability which may be measured, such as Lyapunov stability or Input-Output stability for dynamical systems [14] which have well-known mathematical treatments. However, there is a paucity of work dealing with stability of EAs (for example, [9]) in general, and via visualization in particular. We seek to characterize the long-run stability of EAs under perturbation of their control parameters by using a parametric visualization, giving some examples of the visualization in action on twelve thousand runs of a case study EA from previous work [3]. Specifically, we shall answer the following question:

> If the control parameters are changed from a "standard" set then how does the EA performance change, visually speaking?

GECCO'14, July 12–16, 2014, Vancouver, BC, Canada.

http://dx.doi.org/10.1145/2598394.2610549.

Our visualization scheme provides information to determine whether a given EA is stable under change of control parameters and, in particular, a boundary where the phase transition between stability and instability occurs. This is not always a simple transition, however, because "bad" parameter values may not be located on or close to a clear boundary (that is, such values may occur in unexpected locations in parameter space).

This paper is organized as follows. In Section 2, we review relevant work in EA visualization before specializing context and preparing our case study in Section 3. In Section 4 we give further details of the visualization and some results, before concluding the work in Section 5.

2. PREVIOUS WORK IN EA VISUALIZATION

In this section we review relevant work in EA visualization. There are generally two separate well-known methods of processing visualizations: online and offline. Online visualization refers to visualization while the EA is running and is more immediate. It may be useful in order to track the behavior of runs, leading to possible conclusions before the end of a run. Offline visualization is based on a summary of EA run information, or statistics collected after completion of the run. Some popular visualization works are as follows.

The work of [12] gives many examples of online EA visualization and also details GEATbx, a GA toolbox for MATLAB. Another work is that of [7], where in their visualization package EAVis the authors used a so-called evolution map that "holds various information about the evolution of a whole system over the time". The map is comprised of lines (representing mutations), boxes (inversion) and circles (crossover) positioned at random. The work of [6] introduced GAVEL, an offline Java package that assists in reverse tracking GA runs in order to uncover the lineage of good solutions. This enables generation of displays such as "number of chromosomes in the ancestry tree per generation" and "origin of genes in final solution".

The work of [2] exemplified the popular EA visualization tool Gonzo which enables the generation of most common visualizations (fitness-time graphs, basic search space visualization, schema highlighting). Other visualizations of this type have been performed, most notably those of [8] for GraphDice which visualized EA solution space and [10] for high-dimension fitness landscape analysis. The work of [8] was later built upon, combining stochastic optimization with GraphDice to produce EvoGraphDice [1]. EvoGraphDice combines dimensions in an evolutionarily learned manner, with user input, to facilitate dimensionality reduction.

In the work of [16], the authors visualized "mutually non-dominating solutions" coming from a large number of dimensions in the Multi-Objective Evolutionary Algorithm context. Parameter space and objective space were visualized with the help of heatmaps and the RadViz mechanism. Their visualization was in the form of an n-vertex polygon, each vertex corresponding to an objective of the problem at hand. Finally, the work of [11] also considered visualizations of clusters of EA outputs. The authors attempted to measure solution sensitivity in an EA through a variation of standard deviation, but control parameters were not considered.

The above visualizations aim to tell the user more about the processes of the EA in an attempt to understand results. Distinct to the above works, we shall treat the EA as a black box and thus will not consider the visualization of process or objectives. We simply wish to determine EA performance stability, through visualization, under control parameter perturbation. Our visualization is presented as a "fusion" of parameter and performance metrics, and was borne out of an investigative approach to the mathematical aspects of EA stability. We wish to use the visualization to analyze the parameter space landscape, uncovering not only whether a particular EA is stable or not but also at what magnitude of parameter perturbation the EA makes a transition from stability to instability.

3. CASE STUDY AND EA SETUP

In this section we consider the EA presented in [3] with the intention of using it as a case study. The mentioned work details an EA to solve a cryptographic problem in groups. We shall not present a treatment of the mathematical problem here, but do direct the interested reader to the above work for further details. The EA has input of a pair of n-ary strings, output a choice of a pair of n-ary strings or "no solution reached" and is set according to the values of its control parameters. Each string represents a word in a particular group, G. To solve the problem, an exact solution is required. If the problem is not solved within s generations then the EA terminates.

Starting with a population size of q (in this work we take $q = 200$) these parameters control the numbers of individuals produced from the following operations (in this order): crossover, mutation (of which there are three types), selection and random immigration. This yields a six-dimensional parameter space, $S = \left\{(p_i)_{i=1}^{6} : \sum p_i = q, p_i \geq 0\right\}$, although for EAs with $n \geq 6$ parameters our resulting visualization may, of course, be generalized. Below we summarize the main notations, which are described in more depth in the article [5], first covering the parameter space and the metrics over it and, second, the EA performance measure.

3.1 Parameter Space

We may represent a parameter set as an ordered vector $\underline{p} = (p_1, p_2, \ldots, p_6) \in S$. For example, the parameter vector $\underline{p} = (22, 40, 21, 54, 39, 24)$ denotes that, out of each population, twenty-two individuals were produced from the previous population by crossover, forty by the first type of mutation, and so on. Given a parameter vector $\underline{p}$ (the *base vector*) for which the EA achieves a given level of performance we may define a perturbation in two ways. First we may define the vector $\underline{p}'$ that is produced from $\underline{p}$. As we assume the population size is constant, the sum of the vector $\underline{p}'$ will be preserved. Second, we may define the perturbation itself as $\underline{\varepsilon} = (\varepsilon_1, \varepsilon_2, \ldots, \varepsilon_6)$ such that $\underline{p} + \underline{\varepsilon} = \underline{p}'$ by elementwise addition. It is easy to observe that $\sum_{i=1}^{6} \varepsilon_i = 0$. We now may define metrics over S. Two examples of such metrics producing non-negative integer outputs are the l_1- and l_∞-norms over S. As perturbation metrics, these may be written as

$$d_1(\underline{\varepsilon}) = \sum_{i=1}^{6} |\varepsilon_i|, \tag{1}$$

$$d_\infty(\underline{\varepsilon}) = \max_{i=1,\ldots,6} |\varepsilon|. \tag{2}$$

We naturally define the parameter vector $b-$neighborhoods

$$N_{1,b}(\underline{p}) = \{\underline{p}' \in S : \underline{p} + \underline{\varepsilon} = \underline{p}', d_1(\varepsilon) \leq b\} \quad (3)$$

$$N_{\infty,b}(\underline{p}) = \{\underline{p}' \in S : \underline{p} + \underline{\varepsilon} = \underline{p}', d_\infty(\varepsilon) \leq b\} \quad (4)$$

to denote the set of all parameter vectors up to and including a distance of b from the given base parameter vector $\underline{p}$ and metric. These neighborhoods will be our search spaces.

3.2 EA Performance Metric

There are several well-known performance metrics for EA runs, depending upon the structure of the problem at hand. For example, we may wish to find the average objective value, a solution within a specified tolerance of the optimum or a solution achieving a given objective value. In our work we take the EA performance to be the *generation count*, which is simply the number of required generations to find an exact solution to a given problem instance. From the generation count, we define the EA performance metric as an analogue of Kolmogorov distance

$$d_K(\underline{p}, \underline{p}') = (E_r(\underline{p}) - E_r(\underline{p}'))^2, \quad (5)$$

where $\underline{p}' \in N_{\bullet,b}(\underline{p})$ is a parameter vector chosen from the b-neighborhood of $\underline{p}$. The mean generation count from r independent trials of the EA with the given parameter vector is denoted $E_r(\cdot)$ [4], with r the *resolution*. Given a bound $b > 1$ and a parameter vector $\underline{p}$, it is clear that the sizes of the above neighborhoods become large relatively quickly. For instance, for $b = 30$ we have $|N_{1,30}(\underline{p})| = 1894007$ and $|N_{\infty,30}(\underline{p})| = 844596302$, making sampling of whole neighborhoods inefficient and thus justifying the sampling strategy used in Section 4.1.

3.3 Setup

We used a short instance (instance (I1) of [3]), fixed for all experiments. This particular instance was used for efficiency purposes, as each figure in this paper is comprised of $1000r$ EA runs. To provide a comparison, we used two base parameter vectors for our experiments (more details are given in Section 4.2). In the next section we detail the visualization of EA performance and give experimental results.

4. VISUALIZATION AND RESULTS

In this section we first give details of the parameter space projection and describe the two distinct types of visualization that will be performed using that projection. We follow this with results of the EA runs, contrasted by parameter base vector and including visual EA stability analysis.

4.1 Explanation of Visualization

In [5] we introduced a mathematical approach to EA stability determination, and in this work, focus upon the visualization and evaluation of it. The codes to produce the visualization are implemented in MATLAB. As the means of evaluation of the visualization we introduce a visual notion of EA stability, judging stability by sight rather than by statistical methods. Our visualization is one of the EA performance landscape rather than of the solution space or objective functions, and is achieved through a projection

$$\pi : G^2 \times S \to \mathbb{R}^+ \times C, \quad (6)$$

where S is the parameter space, G^2 is the direct product of two copies of the group G (each containing one word of the instance) and C is the color space. The color space in MATLAB is a collection of 64 colors mapped to values in the range 0,1,. . .,63. We elected to use the standard heatmap, with small values in the range mapped to blue colors and large values to red colors.

We take the codomain of the projection π to be a section of EA output. From this we term our visualization to be one of *parameter-output space*. The visualization is with respect to distance of perturbation (rather than the perturbation itself, which would not be representable) and size of performance effect, combined in a 2-D representation. The first factor of the codomain of π is associated to the distance from the origin of the plot. We have the two choices of either mapping $d_\bullet(\varepsilon)$ or mapping $d_K(\underline{p}, \underline{p}')$ onto $\mathbb{R}^+$. In the former case its image is restricted to the set of all positive integers. The second factor of the codomain of π, the color space, has the alternate metric mapped to it. In other words, we have two types of visualization, where each given parameter vector is represented by a colored dot.

Type 1: The distance of the dot from the center represents the size of perturbation under the parameter metric d_1 or d_∞. The Kolmogorov distance is represented by a color.

Type 2: The distance of the dot from the center represents the scaled Kolmogorov distance, and the color represents the size of perturbation with respect to the given parameter metric.

On the visualization there are concentric circles provided for ease of visualization and for convenience (the circles are not intended to convey a sense of location in the neighborhood). The samples depicted in each visualization are produced by repeated EA trials with the sampling being uniformly at random, without replacement, in the neighborhood. We fixed the sample size to $N = 1000$ output distance measurements (and so $1000r$ EA runs per visualization). To produce each diagram we fixed a base parameter vector $\underline{p}$ and a perturbation bound b and then sampled $N - 1$ parameter vectors $\{\underline{p}_i\}_{i=1}^{N-1}$ in the neighborhood $N_{\bullet,b}(\underline{p})$. As above, we may use either metric such that the metric is fixed throughout the runs that produce the visualization. The value of the Kolmogorov (output) metric $d_K(\underline{p}, \underline{p}_i)$ was then calculated via performing EA runs as described.

4.2 Results of Runs

The following two subsections give examples of visualizations under both the l_1 and l_∞ metrics, comparing the type 1 and type 2 outputs under an example of a, so-called, efficient parameter base vector and an inefficient parameter base vector. Both vectors were chosen by experimentation on account of encouraging distinct EA performance in terms of mean generation count and the standard deviation (see subsections 4.2.1 and 4.2.2). In all figures we chose the bound $b = 50$ and resolution $r = 3$, omitting other plots for smaller bounds and smaller resolutions. We shall observe that changing the base parameter vector affects the output produced, and by extension, the visualization.

4.2.1 An Efficient Parameter Base Vector

The "efficient" parameter vector was chosen to be $\underline{p} = (5, 33, 4, 128, 30, 0)$, giving a mean generation count over ten independent EA runs of 179 for the instance, and for which an EA termination constant of $s = 1500$ was used. This was chosen as the EA performance was relatively consistent; over ten runs the standard deviation was 51.8 generations [5].

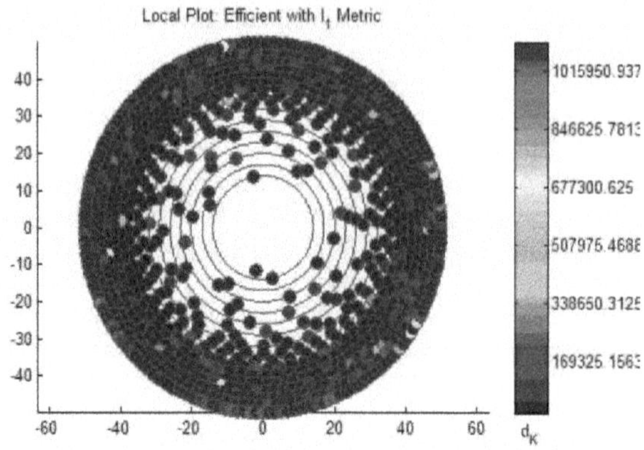

(a) EA performance differences under the l_1 metric as the radius.

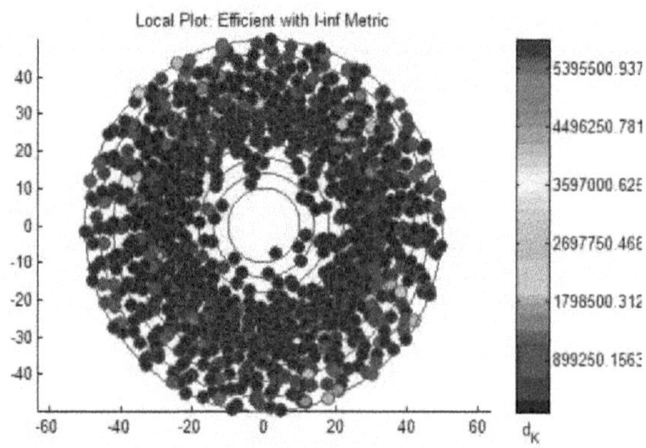

(b) EA performance differences under the l_∞ metric as the radius.

Figure 1: Typical type 1 plots for an efficient parameter vector, showing colored EA performance differences under the l_1 metric and l_∞ metric. Each plot uses a distinct set of EA runs.

Fig. 1 presents two type 1 plots. In this figure we observe that the smaller perturbations encourage only small performance differences (blue colors) in the EA when compared to the base performance using parameter vector $\underline{p}$. As the perturbation size (radius) increases, other colors begin to appear. This is more noticeable on the l_∞ metric plot (Fig. 1(b)). The different clustering behaviors between Figs 1(a) and 1(b) correspond to the distinct definitions of the l_1 and l_∞ metrics. For example, if we take the parameter vector $\underline{p}' = (5, 23, 7, 135, 25, 5)$ we see that $\underline{\varepsilon} = \underline{p}' - \underline{p} = (0, -10, 3, 7, -5, 5)$, and so $d_1(\underline{\varepsilon}) = 30$ while $d_\infty(\underline{\varepsilon}) = 10$. We may see this difference as greater information loss under the l_∞ than the l_1 metric. That is, under the l_∞ metric the dots have a closer clustering behavior towards the center of the plot, as a large value of the l_1 metric is likely to be much smaller under the l_∞ metric.

For the l_1 metric (Fig. 1(a)) we notice that non-blue dots begin to appear at around radius 30-40. Correspondingly on the l_∞ metric (Fig. 1(b)), non-blue dots appear to occur appreciably earlier, at around radius 20. This shows that outside the given bounds for each metric the EA begins to exhibit instability (with respect to the base parameter vector). Thus the visualization shows where the zone of EA stability ends, something difficult to predict from repeated EA runs alone. We include only the resolution $r = 3$ but note that, for $r = 1$, fewer dots are in the blue range (that is, there is more performance variation, which should be expected). This indicates that as r increases the EA performance is less variable under perturbation of the base parameter vector $\underline{p}$. Examples of type 2 plots are given in Fig. 2.

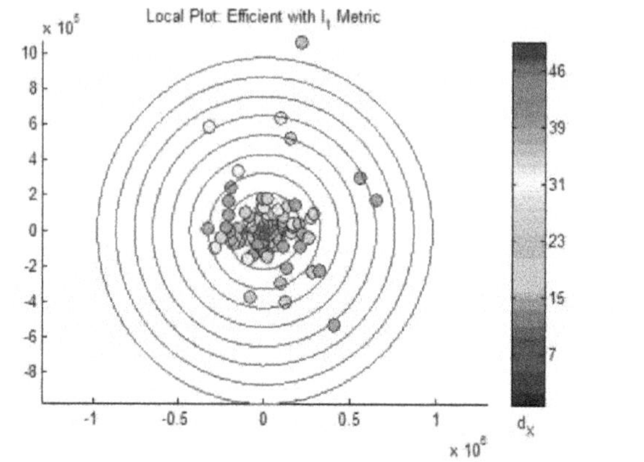

(a) EA performance differences under the l_1 metric as the color.

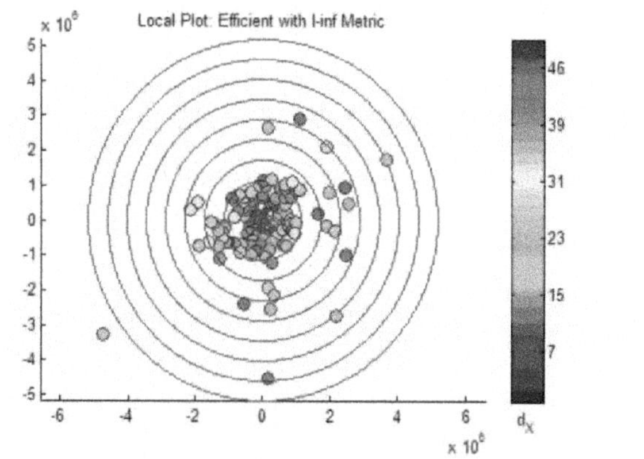

(b) EA performance differences under the l_∞ metric as the color.

Figure 2: Typical type 2 plots for the same sets of runs as Fig. 1 under an efficient parameter vector. Now, the radius denotes a performance measure rather than perturbation size (denoted by color).

The type 2 visualization displays a much more intuitive picture of stability. The values given on the axes may be ignored (we clearly do not have negative output distance d_K) on the grounds of it being purely a diagrammatic representation. In Fig. 2 there is clear clustering behavior around the center for each metric, which is expected and this result is in accordance with those of Fig. 1. The majority of the dots are within the circle denoting a Kolmogorov distance of approximately 5×10^5. However, for the l_∞ metric (Fig. 2(b)) there seems to be a greater variety of colors within that clustering, showing that there is a smaller correlation between performance and perturbation size with that metric. There is a wider spread of the dots, the majority of which are within a Kolmogorov distance of approximately 3.2×10^6, approximately one order of magnitude larger than the spread with the l_1 metric. Next we consider visualizations of the EA with an inefficient parameter vector.

4.2.2 An Inefficient Parameter Base Vector

Our second base vector was $\underline{p}' = (22, 40, 21, 54, 39, 24)$, giving a mean generation count of 1060 over ten independent EA runs. This was chosen because the EA performance was rather variable: the standard deviation over those runs was 480.9 generations. Because of the relatively high standard deviation we increased the termination constant to $s = 3000$.

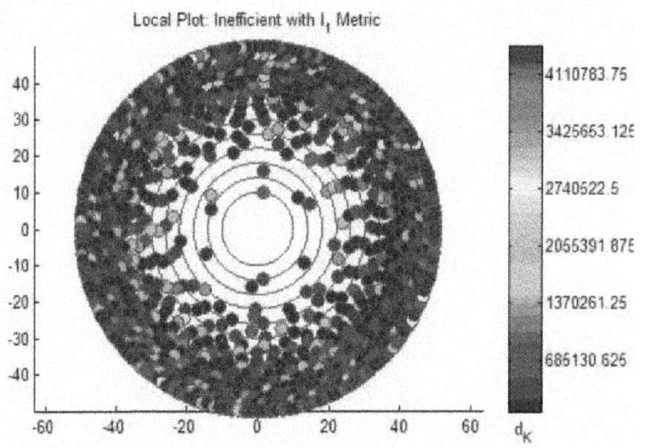

(a) EA performance differences under the l_1 metric as the radius.

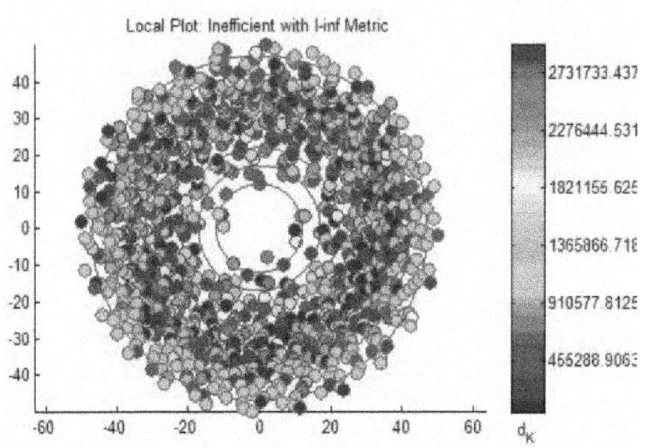

(b) EA performance differences under the l_∞ metric as the radius.

Figure 3: Type 1 plots for an inefficient parameter vector. The upper subfigure shows the distribution under the l_1 metric, and the lower the l_∞ metric.

In Fig. 3, it is clear there is far wider variation in EA performance for both parameter metrics than in Fig. 1. For the l_1 metric (Fig. 3(a)) there are already many more lighter colors compared to Fig. 1(a), which had an efficient base parameter vector. There is still a reasonable radius of stability, although this does not seem to be clear (due to the color variation even within a small radius). However, for the l_∞ metric (Fig. 3(b)) the effect is starkly apparent. There seems to be a small zone of stability (for example, to radius 10 at most) but this contains many perturbations that produce large changes in EA performance (light blue colors). There are also a preponderance of red colors and thus large EA performance differences. As the radius increases, large changes in EA performance become apparent. Hence the radius of stability is smaller than that of an efficient base parameter vector, if such a radius exists at all.

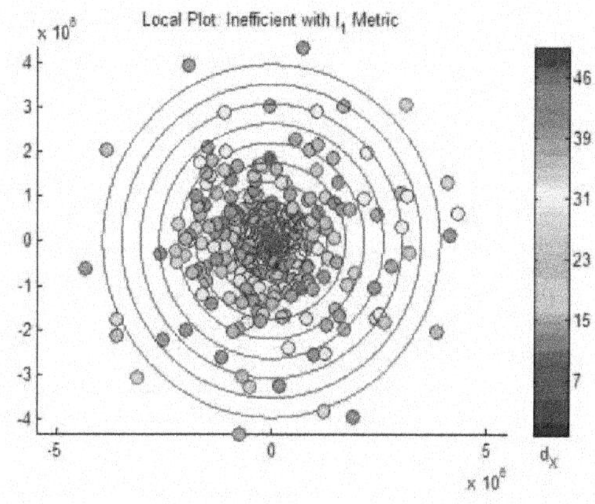

(a) EA performance differences under the l_1 metric as the color.

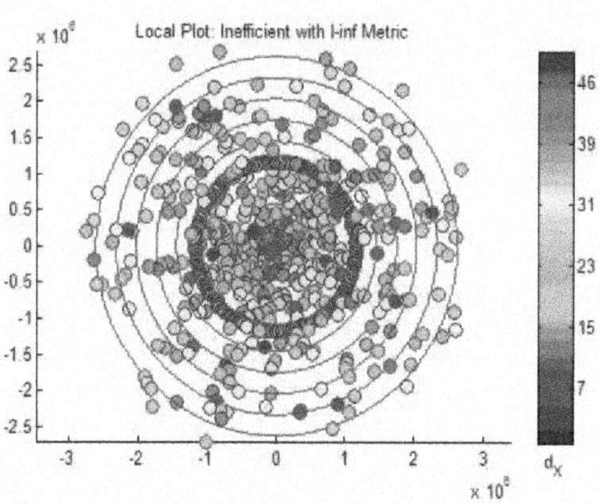

(b) EA performance differences under the l_∞ metric as the color.

Figure 4: Type 2 plots for an inefficient parameter vector, corresponding to the type 1 plots of Fig. 3.

Fig. 4 displays type 2 plots for an inefficient parameter vector. Compared to Fig. 2, on each subfigure there is a much wider spread of dots (as the EA performance differs more). An intuitive conclusion from this figure is that an inefficient parameter vector is likely to induce a type of less controllable randomness in the EA. This is supported by the counterpart plots of Fig 4, where this increased randomness is illustrated by a large variety of colors.

For the l_1 metric plot of Fig. 4(a), even the outer circle denoting a Kolmogorov distance of approximately 4×10^6 has a large number of dots on or outside it. As we should expect in the l_∞ metric case (Fig. 4(b)), the visualization seemingly has no central clustering with respect to Kolmogorov distance, a conclusion also supported by its counterpart Fig. 3(b). In the next section we summarize our findings and conclude the work.

5. CONCLUSIONS

In this work we presented a novel experimental visualization of EAs under control parameter perturbation, using a case study of a published EA in cryptography. The visualization was a hybrid, representing a combination of projections of two metrics. The first metric was on the parameter space and the second was an EA performance metric based upon Kolmogorov distance. This enabled us to achieve a more substantial picture of EA stability than would be possible by basic statistical methods.

Our visualization captures the radius of stability under a typical efficient parameter vector and also the step change which occurs when the parameter vector is changed to an inefficient one. We observed when running the EA repeatedly with an efficient parameter vector that there was a clear radius of stability. This is given by type 1 plots where we have a preponderance of dark blue colors and by type 2 plots where there was an identifiable radius with the majority of dots inside it. This was certainly true for the l_1 metric, albeit the conclusion was weaker for the l_∞ metric. Contrary to the above findings are the conclusions for when an inefficient parameter vector is used. In this case there does not seem to exist such a clear radius of stability for type 1 visualizations under the l_1 metric. For the l_∞ metric there is no identifiable radius of stability. These conclusions are reinforced by the type 2 visualizations of Fig. 4. This provides a positive evaluation of the visualization; that is, we may distinguish between EA stability and instability depending upon perturbation and performance metrics.

We may thus answer the question posed in the introduction as follows. If the standard set of control parameters is efficient then there is a clear bound on EA performance change (in terms of the defined output metric) given by an identifiable radius of stability with little variation outside this radius. This is illustrated by both type 1 and type 2 visualizations. If the standard set of control parameters is inefficient then there often does not exist a clear bound on EA performance change. The key part of our visualization is that we may visualize why exactly this does not occur and also the performance distribution with respect to perturbation size. This performance distribution assists in the identification of parameter vectors which encourage atypical EA behavior and are worth investigating further. This further investigation may entail approximating the objective landscape and runtime analysis calculations. It may also assist as a method of nonlinear stochastic parameter optimization, with the identification of "sweet spots" (and the converse!) in the parameter distribution.

Turning to generalized EAs, our visualization may be easily generalized. If we have a general EA with parameter vector $\underline{p} = (p_1, p_2, \ldots, p_n)$ for $n > 1$ then the metrics we used for the case study are still suitable. Our treatment makes the assumption that the sum of a parameter vector is constant, using that assumption in the definition of the neighborhoods. As the visualization is created through projection of only part of the EA output, it may offer an insight into parameter spaces of arbitrary finite dimension.

Our visualization has the feature that there is no information loss. The visualization is created from a log file generated by the repeated EA runs, which contains the pertinent information. Thus the original information may be recovered. The advantage of our offline visualization is that it may be customized to any number of EA runs. However, the visualization also has the clear disadvantage that conclusions are difficult to reach until the end of a set of runs. This gives several sources of further work which we intend to pursue:

1. We wish to extend the visualization to an online visualization in order to enable further human intervention after a comparatively small number of runs. The update speed of visualization would depend upon the instance and resolution chosen.

2. This paper chronicles just two of the possible parameter metrics that may be used. It is also clear that the chosen parameter space metric dramatically affects the visualization. Hence we should like to attempt other parameter and performance metrics in an integrated approach.

3. Finally, we intend to pursue research in other types of visualization, including those giving some indication of the "direction" of the perturbation in the parameter space.

Due to time constraints other EA instances were not considered, but the visualizations (and the conclusions on EA stability therein) are not expected to radically change. From experience [4], the majority of runs under our setup are on the same performance spectrum of parameters (from which we have chosen two parameter vectors at opposite ends of the spectrum and so have presented two opposing visualizations). Overall, then, we have shown an interesting and novel visualization which proposes some interesting and potentially fruitful directions for EA performance analysis and research.

Acknowledgements

We thank the University of Plymouth and RISE, Waseda University for their generous research support during preparation of this paper. We also thank the anonymous referees for their helpful comments.

6. REFERENCES

[1] W. Cancino, N. Boukhelifa, A. Bezerianos, and E. Lutton. Evolutionary visual exploration: Experimental analysis of algorithm behaviour. In *VizGEC '13 (Proc. GECCO'13)*, pages 1373–1380. ACM, 2013.

[2] T. D. Collins. Applying software visualization technology to support the use of evolutionary algorithms. *J. Visual Lang. and Comp.*, 14:123–150, 2003.

[3] M. J. Craven. An evolutionary algorithm for the solution of two-variable word equations in partially commutative groups. *Studies in Comp. Intel.*, 153:3–19, 2008.

[4] M. J. Craven and H. C. Jimbo. A kolmogorov-type stability measure for evolutionary algorithms. In *"EvoCOP 2011" (P. Merz and J. -K. Hao, eds.), LNCS 6622*, pages 26–37. Springer, 2011.

[5] M. J. Craven and H. C. Jimbo. Stability of evolutionary optimization algorithms: Comparison and visualization of perturbation metrics. *Submitted to Proc. NACA2013*, 2014.

[6] E. Hart and P. Ross. GAVEL - a new tool for genetic algorithm visualization. *IEEE Trans. Evol. Comp*, 5(4):335–348, 2005.

[7] A. Kerren and T. Egger. EAVis: A visualization tool for evolutionary algorithms. In *"Proc. VL/HCC 2005"*, pages 299–301. IEEE, 2005.

[8] E. Lutton and J. D. Fekete. Visual analytics and experimental analysis of evolutionary algorithms. *INRIA Rapport de Recherche*, 7605, 2011.

[9] J. Ombach. Stability of evolutionary algorithms. *J. Math. Analysis and Appl.*, 342:326–333, 2008.

[10] B. Østman and C. Adami. Predicting evolution and visualizing high-dimensional fitness landscapes. *arXiv:1302.2906v2*, 2013.

[11] I. Packham and I. Parmee. Data analysis and visualisation of cluster-orientted genetic algorithm output. In *Proc. IEEE Intl. Conf. on Info. Visualization*, pages 173–178. IEEE, 2000.

[12] H. Pohlheim. Visualization of evolutionary algorithms - set of standard techniques and multidimensional visualization. In *Proc. GECCO'99*, pages 533–540. ACM, 1999.

[13] G. Romero, J. J. Merelo, P. A. Castillo, J. G. Castellano, and M. G. Arenas. Genetic algorithm visualization using self-organizing maps [sect. 2 and 3]. In *"PPSN VII" (J. J. Merelo Guervós et al., eds.), LNCS 2439*, pages 442–451. Springer, 2002.

[14] E. D. Sontag and Y. Wang. Notions of input to output stability. *Systems & Control Letters*, 38:236–248, 1999.

[15] L. J. van der Maaten, E. O. Postma, and H. J. van den Herik. Dimensionality reduction: A comparative review. *Journal of Machine Learning Research*, 10(1-41):66–71, 2009.

[16] D. J. Walker, R. M. Everson, and J. E. Fieldsend. Visualizing mutually nondominating solution sets in many-objective optimization. *IEEE Trans. Evol. Comp.*, 17(2):165–184, 2013.

On the Visualization of Trade-offs and Reducibility in Many-Objective Optimization

Alan R. R. Freitas
Department of Computer Science
Universidade Federal de Ouro Preto
Ouro Preto, Brazil
alandefreitas@iceb.ufop.br

Rodrigo C. P. Silva
Department of Electrical and Computer Engineering
McGill University
Montreal, QC
Canada
rodrigo.silva@mail.mcgill.ca

Frederico G. Guimarães
Department of Electrical Engineering
Universidade Federal de Minas Gerais
Belo Horizonte, Brazil
fredericoguimaraes@ufmg.br

ABSTRACT

This paper proposes a technique of Aggregation Trees to visualize the results of high-dimensional multiobjective optimization problems, or many-objective problems. The high-dimensionality makes it difficult to represent the relation between objectives and solutions. Most approaches in the literature are based on the representation of solutions in lower dimensions. The technique of Aggregation Trees proposed here is based on iterative aggregation of objectives which are represented in a tree. Besides, the location of conflict is also calculated and represented on the tree. Thus, the tree can represent which objectives and groups of objectives are harmonic the most, what sort of conflict is present between groups of objectives, and which aggregations would be more interesting in order to reduce the problem dimension.

Categories and Subject Descriptors

G.1.6 [**Optimization**]: Stochastic programming; H.3 [**Information Storage and Retrieval**]: Information Search and Retrieval

Keywords

Aggregation Trees, Multiobjective Optimization, Many-Objective Optimization, Visualization, Objective Reduction

1. INTRODUCTION

Multiobjective optimization is a very important tool to solve real-world problems. As the number of objectives grow in those problems, we reach the field of Many-objective Problems (Section 2). Visualizing the relation between objectives in those problems becomes more difficult as most solutions become incomparable in relation to Pareto dominance.

In this paper, we propose a method of Aggregation Trees (Section 3) to represent the relation between objectives according to their reducibility in a way that we can represent the relation between groups of objectives for a problem.

Thus, Aggregation Trees can be used to easily visualize the results of Many-objective problems, group objectives according to their reducibility, show the amount of conflict and harmony between objectives. The technique is based on an objective reduction algorithm.

Also, in the context of many-objective optimization, the trees provide the decision maker with information on where it could be convenient to restrict the preference area for the next optimization round.

We then show results for some test problems (Section 6) and conclude our paper with discussions about the method and suggestions concerning possible future work (Section 7).

GECCO'14, July 12–16, 2014, Vancouver, BC, Canada.

http://dx.doi.org/10.1145/2598394.2610550.

2. VISUALIZATION IN MANY-OBJECTIVE OPTIMIZATION

A multiobjective optimization problem can be mathematically defined as:

$$\min(f_1(x), f_2(x), \ldots, f_k(x)),\ x \in \mathcal{F} \tag{1}$$

where $f_i(x)$ is the i-th objective function to be minimized. Each function $f_i(x)$ maps the optimization variables of a candidate solution x to an objective value represented in one dimension of the objective space. The set of all combinations of possible values for optimization variables defines the search space:

$$\mathcal{S} = \{x = \{(x_1, v_1), \ldots, (x_n, v_n)\} : v_i \in \mathcal{D}_i\} \tag{2}$$

where each variable x_i assumes the value v_i in its respective domain $\mathcal{D}_i$.

If the problem has constraints, those constraint functions define the feasible set of solutions:

$$\mathcal{F} = \{x \in \mathcal{S} : g_k(s) \leq 0, k = 1, \ldots, r\} \tag{3}$$

Thus, solving the optimization problem defined in Equation 1 means to find the set of solutions which are Pareto-optimal, that is, solutions that cannot be improved in any of the objectives without implying in a worse result for another objective. In mathematical terms, a feasible solution $x^1 \in \mathcal{F}$ dominates another solution $x^2 \in \mathcal{F}$ if the conditions below are attained:

$$f_i(x^1) \leq f_i(x^2) \qquad \text{for all i} \in \{1, 2, 3, \ldots, \text{k}\} \tag{4}$$

$$f_j(x^1) < f_j(x^2) \quad \text{for at least one j} \in \{1, 2, 3, \ldots, \text{k}\} \tag{5}$$

With a Pareto-based fitness assignment scheme, Evolutionary Algorithms have been the most common strategy to tackle Multiobjective Problems [7]. Those strategies usually permit diversity control [3], real-time interaction with the decision maker [34], and are elitist [8, 17].

However, the difficulty of the problem grows exponentially with the number of objectives and problems with more than three objectives have been called Many-objective Problems [15]. Besides the memory cost of representing a multidimensional Pareto-front, the convergence of Evolutionary Algorithms is compromised because Pareto-based ranking does not work as a good discriminator of solutions in those problems [16] as most solutions are non-dominated. Even when we have a reasonable solution, the visualization of those solutions in the objective space is also a difficult problem for the Decision Maker.

Palliative solutions for those problems are (i) considering more relaxed dominance relations to facilitate discrimination [3], (ii) modifying fitness measures [10, 2], (iii) optimizing scalarized single-objective functions [33], and (iv) dimensionality reduction through identification of redundant objectives [13].

Still in the category of objective reduction, the main approaches are (i) finding a minimum objective subset within a given error and according to a dominance relation[5, 6], (ii) Principal Component Analysis (PCA) or PCA techniques adapted to handle non-linear relations between objectives [27, 28], (iii) unsupervised feature selection [20], (iv) focusing on the corners among non-dominated solutions [29], and (v) mathematical formulation and aggregation of the most harmonic objectives [13].

The results for problems with 2 or 3 dimensions can be easily represented in 2 or 3 axis as in Figure 1. In that Figure, we have the quality of many solutions, each represented by a point. The non-dominated solutions are the ones marked with a number 1 in the first front and all the other solutions are worse than at least one solution in the first front. In most cases, the dominated solutions are not shown in the graph in order to make the information clearer.

For visualizing non-dominated results in many-objective optimization, the most common approach is parallel coordinates, as represented in Figure 2 for 7 objectives. In this graph, each line represents the quality of a solution and the objective values are normalized. When there are many lines crossing between 2 adjacent objectives, that means there is conflict between those objectives. Problems with this representation method are that (i) we can only see conflict between adjacent objectives; (ii) the representation can become very confusing when the number of solutions or objectives increase.

Other approaches for visualization of solution quality in many-objective optimization are (i) trying to map the values on lower dimensions with minimum loss of information [22, 18], (ii) cloud visualization [11], (iii) self-organizing maps (SOM) [23, 35], (iv) Interactive Decision Maps [21], (v) a Hyper-space Diagonal Counting method [1], (vi) level diagrams [4], and prosections [30].

In more recent approaches, Kurasova et al. [19] propose an approach based on neural gas clustering and multidimensional scaling dimension reduction to project the solution onto a plane, where the points are marked with their distance to the ideal point.

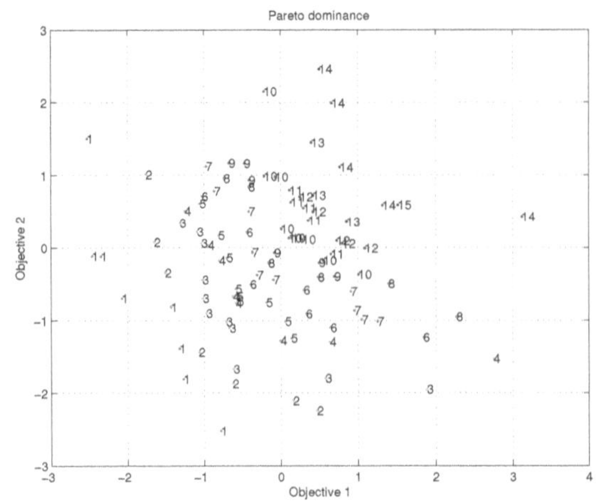

Figure 1: Results for a 2-dimensional problem

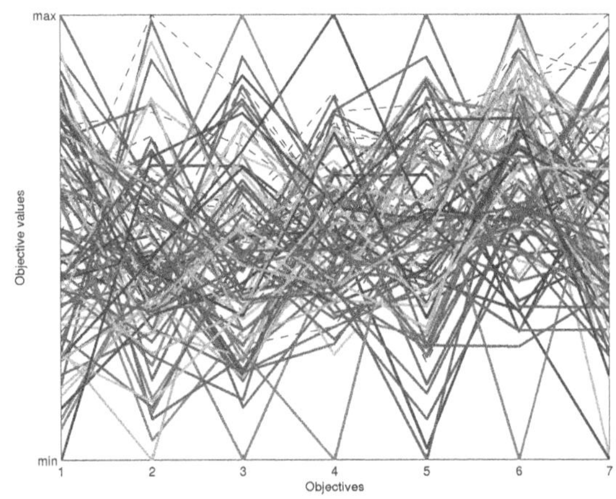

Figure 2: Representing the quality of solution for Many-objective Problems

Walker et al. [31] did an extensive review on methods for Pareto-visualization and presented their own methods. They use spectral seriation to rearrange the solutions and objectives plotted on a heatmap. They also present two methods to visualize solutions in a plane: one that maps a set to the interior of a polygon on a plane, and another that uses a measure of dominance distance between solutions to yield visualizations in two dimensions.

Fieldsend and Everson [12] propose a method to visualize Pareto relationships in two-dimensional scatterplots. They attempt to create a two-dimensional projection with minimal loss of dominance information. In their plot, points represent solutions and connecting lines represent dominance relations.

In this context, we need visualization methods in which we can visualize the relation between objectives and groups of objectives with minimum loss of information. Besides, it is important to give relevant information to the decision maker so that they can choose how to best restrict the preference area until they get to a single solution.

3. AGGREGATION TREES

The Aggregation Trees presented on this paper are based on a specific objective reduction algorithm [13] that measures harmony between objectives. The more harmonious two objectives are the higher is their reducibility [24, 25].

In order to exemplify the utility of the proposed Harmony Trees, consider the set of solutions represented in the Parallel Coordinates of Figure 3. Objectives 1, 2, 4, 6, 8, 10, and 12 have the same values for all solutions and therefore are in complete harmony.

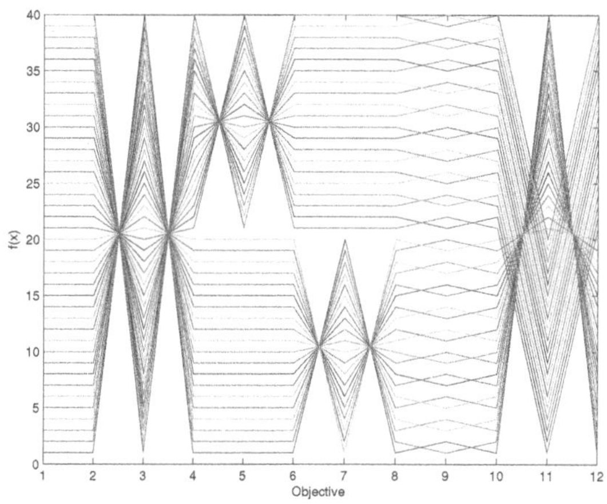

Figure 3: A set of solutions with many sorts of conflict

The Aggregation Tree in Figure 4 represents the relation between those objectives and their reducibility in the structure of a tree. The child nodes represent objectives and parents represent aggregations of those objectives. The percentages on parent nodes represent the conflict between its two children.

Parents represent a compound objective formed by the aggregation of the child objectives and renormalization of the values. Below every parent node, we have the children that are aggregated in that node and the conflict between its two direct children. For example, the node $f_{11} + f_3 -$ 25% represents a compound objective with the aggregation of objectives f_{11} and f_3 through summation. Those two objectives have 25% of non-parametric conflict, which can be used as a measure of the loss of information implied by this aggregation on the representation of the Pareto front. Other parent nodes represent higher order compound objectives formed in a similar way but their value of conflict represent only their direct children.

By visualizing objectives in the Aggregation Tree, it is easy to see the relation between the objectives and in case the decision maker wants to make compound objectives to reduce their preference area, the nodes give information on which would be the best ones to group. Instead of only showing the conflict between every two objectives, the tree also shows the conflict between groups of objectives that could be put together.

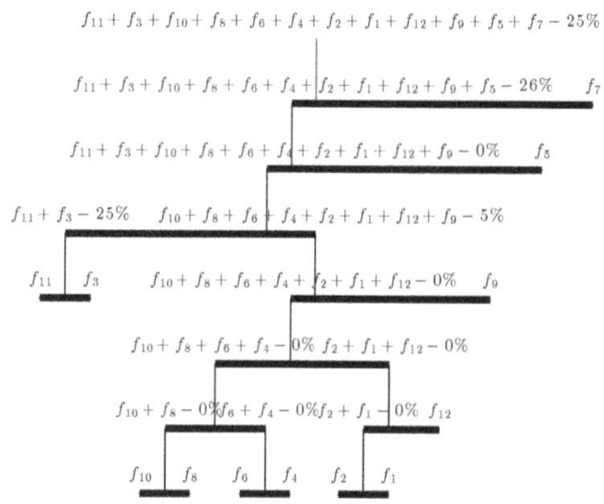

Figure 4: Aggregation Tree on the set of solutions from Figure 3

The order of aggregation of the objectives is according the their harmony and distant leaf nodes in the tree are objectives with little harmony. Thus, if we perform a depth-first search on the child nodes of the tree, we can have a recommendation of a convenient way to choose good adjacent objectives in parallel coordinates, such as the one in Figure 5, where it is easier to see the relation between the objectives as the most harmonious objectives are grouped together.

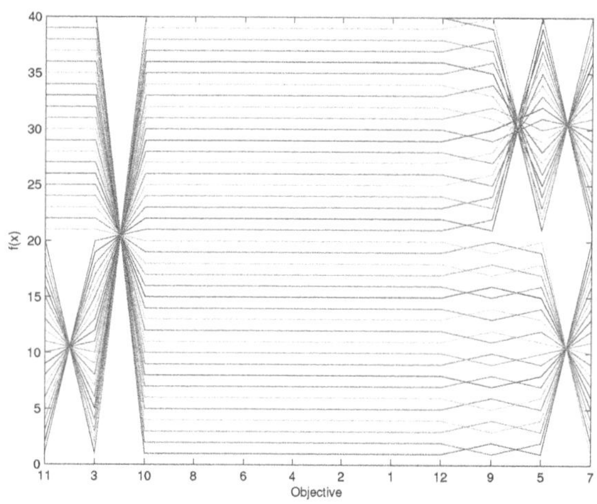

Figure 5: Parallel coordinates with the objectives ordered by the tree.

Thus, an Aggregation Tree can help decision makers visualize redundancy, conflict, and harmony between objectives and groups of objectives. The source code in MATLAB for all those algorithms is available from `http://www.alandefreitas.com/`.

4. OBJECTIVE AGGREGATION

Figure 3 represented many kinds of conflict and harmony among many objectives in parallel coordinate graphs. When good values for one objective imply bad values for another objective, there is conflict between these objectives [25, 14]. When improvement in one objective leads to improvement in another objective, there is harmony between these objectives.

Harmonious objectives can be perceived in parallel coordinates by non-crossing lines. This relation makes it related to the possibility of reducing the number of objectives without losing information in the Pareto front. According to those definitions, we use a non-parametric metric of harmony [13] to measure which pair of objectives should be aggregated next and represented on the tree.

The non-parametric measure H_{ab} of harmony between objectives f_a and f_b is defined in Equation 6. $\mathbf{X}_{ij}$ is the value of the solution i on the objective j and $\mathbf{R}_{ij}$ is the rank of $\mathbf{X}_{ij}$ within $\mathbf{X}_{.j}$. Thus, $\mathbf{X'}_{ij}$ represents the values of $\mathbf{X}_{ij}$ normalized according to $\mathbf{R}_{ij}$. C_{ab} is the non-parametric conflict between the objectives f_a and f_b. This measure is equivalent to Spearman's footrule between the ranks in objectives f_a and f_b. $c_{\min} = 0$ is the minimum value possible of conflict between two objectives. $c_{\max}$ is the maximum value of conflict for two objectives, being n the existing number of points.

$$\begin{aligned} \mathbf{X'}_{ij} &= \mathbf{R}_{ij} \\ C_{ab} &= \sum_i |\mathbf{X'}_{ia} - \mathbf{X'}_{ib}| \\ c_{\max} &= \sum_{i=1}^{n} |2i - n - 1| \\ H_{ab} &= 1 - \frac{C_{ab}}{c_{\max}} \end{aligned} \tag{6}$$

This measure of harmony is insensitive to any previous non-disruptive normalization of the values, that is, insensitive to any normalization that does not alter the order or the values in the set of solutions. That means that the objectives can use different units. In fact, the measure reflects how much the lines would be crossing between objectives f_a and f_b on parallel coordinates. When we divide C_{ab} by $c_{\max}$ to get our measure of harmony, we guarantee that all harmony values range from 0 to 1.

As mentioned before, the most harmonious two objectives are the better candidates they are to be grouped into a new compound objective and this fact is conveniently used by the Aggregation Trees to represent the relationship between objectives.

5. THE PSEUDOCODE

The construction of a tree is an iterative process in which we aggregate two objectives at each iteration. In order to aggregate two objectives, we calculate the harmony between every pair of objectives. The process is described in Algorithm 1.

A more detailed description is as follows:

- Line 1: structure of the tree is initialized with a root node as the parent of all objectives.

Data: Set $\mathbf{X}$ of Points in the Objective Space
Result: Harmony Tree t

1 Initializes tree t with a root node and all objectives as children;
2 **while** *there are still objectives to be grouped* **do**
3     $\mathbf{X'} \leftarrow$ reduce($\mathbf{X}$);
4     $\mathbf{X'} \leftarrow$ normalize($\mathbf{X'}$);
5     $\mathbf{H} \leftarrow$ harmony_matrix($\mathbf{X'}$);
6     $a, b \leftarrow$ leaf or compound objectives of $\mathbf{X'}$ with the most harmony;
7     $c \leftarrow$ conflict($\mathbf{X'}, a, b$);
8   t receives a new node nn;
9   nn receives a and b as children;
10   nn keeps the values (c);
11   a and b are grouped. Next iteration has one objective less;
12 **end**
13 Plot the Harmony Tree t;
14 *order* $\leftarrow$ leaf nodes of t in the order as they appear in t;
15 Plot the objective values in parallel coordinates considering *order*;

Algorithm 1: Constructing an Aggregation Tree

- Line 2: the iterative loop begins. At each iteration, the two most harmonious objectives will be aggregated into a new parent node.
- Line 3: a new version of the objective values is created for the iteration of the loop. That new version considers all the aggregations done so far. Those aggregations are performed by ranking the objective values and summing them. This summation can lead to values that can go from 1 to $2n$ because the rank values of two objectives are being considered in the summation.
- Line 4: this new version of $\mathbf{X'}$ is normalized once more on the aggregated objectives to find the ranking values $\mathbf{R}_{ij}$ from 1 to n.
- Lines 5-6: the pair of objectives with the most harmony is calculated.
- Line 7: the conflict between the two most harmonious objectives is calculated.
- Line 8: a new node is included in the tree as a child of the root node.
- Line 9: this new node receives the nodes that were representing the most harmonious objectives so far.
- Line 10: the value of conflict for the most harmonious objectives is also kept by this new node. The root node has now one objective less and a new iteration of algorithm begins in line 3.
- Line 13: we plot the resulting tree.

Briefly, the reduction algorithm aggregates the two most harmonic objectives at each iteration until there is only one objective left. The tree represents all the aggregations until we form the single objective that represents the simple summation of all objective values and the values of conflict are represented. The order of the elements in the tree suggests an order for the absolute objective values to be plotted on parallel coordinates.

Being n the number of solutions and m the number of objectives, the normalization of the results is $O(mn \log n)$ at the first iteration and $O(n \log n)$ at other iterations. Calculating the harmony matrix has cost $O(nm^2)$. Thus, being m also the number of iterations, the final cost of the algorithm is $O(\max(m^3 n, mn \log n))$. If we use a comparison-based sorting algorithm $O(n)$, we have a total cost $O(m^3 n)$ at all cases.

6. RESULTS ON TEST PROBLEMS

In order to show how the tree can represent the trade-offs involved in the results of the optimization of many objectives, we use the algorithm PICEA-g [32] to optimize solutions for the test problem DTLZ2 [9].

This test function is useful to investigate the scalability of MOEAs in the context of many-objectives. The function is optimized for 20 objectives during 600 generations with 100 individuals each. Figure 6 shows the solutions in the objective space. In order to facilitate visualization, the solutions clustered with a PSA algorithm [26] into 7 clusters and solutions in the same clusters have the same colors.

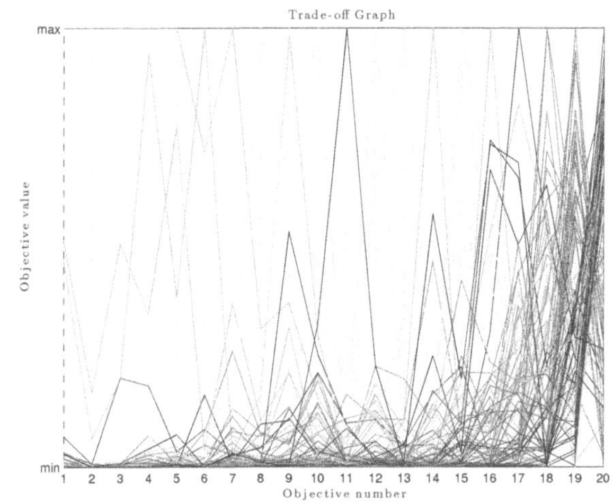

Figure 6: DTLZ2 - Parallel Coordinates

As expected, it is difficult to notice the exact relation between the objectives. Thus, we analyse the relation between objectives and show the resulting tree in Figure 7. The two most harmonious objectives are f_2 and f_3, with only 18.172% of non-parametric conflict.

According to the tree and the harmony values, the next consecutive aggregations involve objectives f_1, f_4, f_{11}, f_{10}, respectively. As we know that the aggregations with lowest conflict happen first, we can find all the aggregations between the objectives until we have only one objective, which would be the normalized summation of all objective values, represented by the root node.

By looking at intermediate parent nodes, we can also notice the relation between groups of objectives. This relation can be transferred back to parallel coordinates to give us the representation of absolute objective values for all the objectives. However, the position of leaf nodes in the tree can suggest their position in parallel coordinates in such a way that harmonious objectives are put together and the contrast between conflicting groups is made clear. Figure 8 shows this rearranged representation of the solutions. The solutions were also clustered by a PSA algorithm.

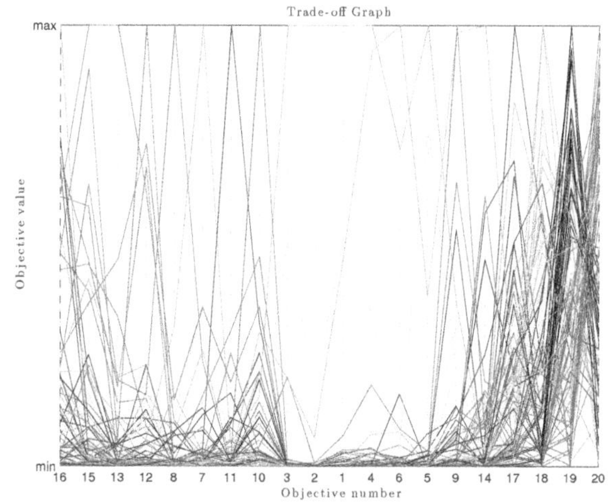

Figure 8: DTLZ2 - Rearranged Parallel Coordinates

In the rearranged graph it is easier to perceive the difference between groups recognized by the tree. Firstly, we have a group with objectives 3, 2, 1, 4, 6, and 5 in the middle of graph. Those are the most harmonious objectives according to the tree. By looking at their objective values, most solutions are very close to their minimum at each of the objectives.

To the left and to the right of this middle group, there are two conflicting groups separated by the tree. Solutions with high values for the objectives on the left tend to have low values for objectives on the right and vice-versa. Thus, the combination of the tree with parallel coordinates can give a better global understanding of the relation between objectives and their values.

Due to space limitation, the results for all other DTLZ test problems are available from `www.alandefreitas.com`.

7. DISCUSSION AND FUTURE WORK

In this paper we presented the Aggregation Trees. The tree is a method for visualization of many-objective solutions. Nodes represent aggregations of objectives which are iteratively detected according to their harmony so the relation between groups of relevant objectives can be analysed.

Non-parametric measures of conflict and harmony are used to build the tree. Therefore, the tree does not depend on any implicit relation between the objectives to infer their reducibility. Each node has also the value of conflict involved in the last aggregation. This is useful for the decision maker as they can understand the cost involved in each of those reductions.

If the decision maker wants to reduce their preference area to focus on a more specific set of solutions, the way in which the tree represents iterative aggregations can show which aggregation should happen first.

The trees can also include dominated solutions in the analysis. That makes the measure of harmony detect if objec-

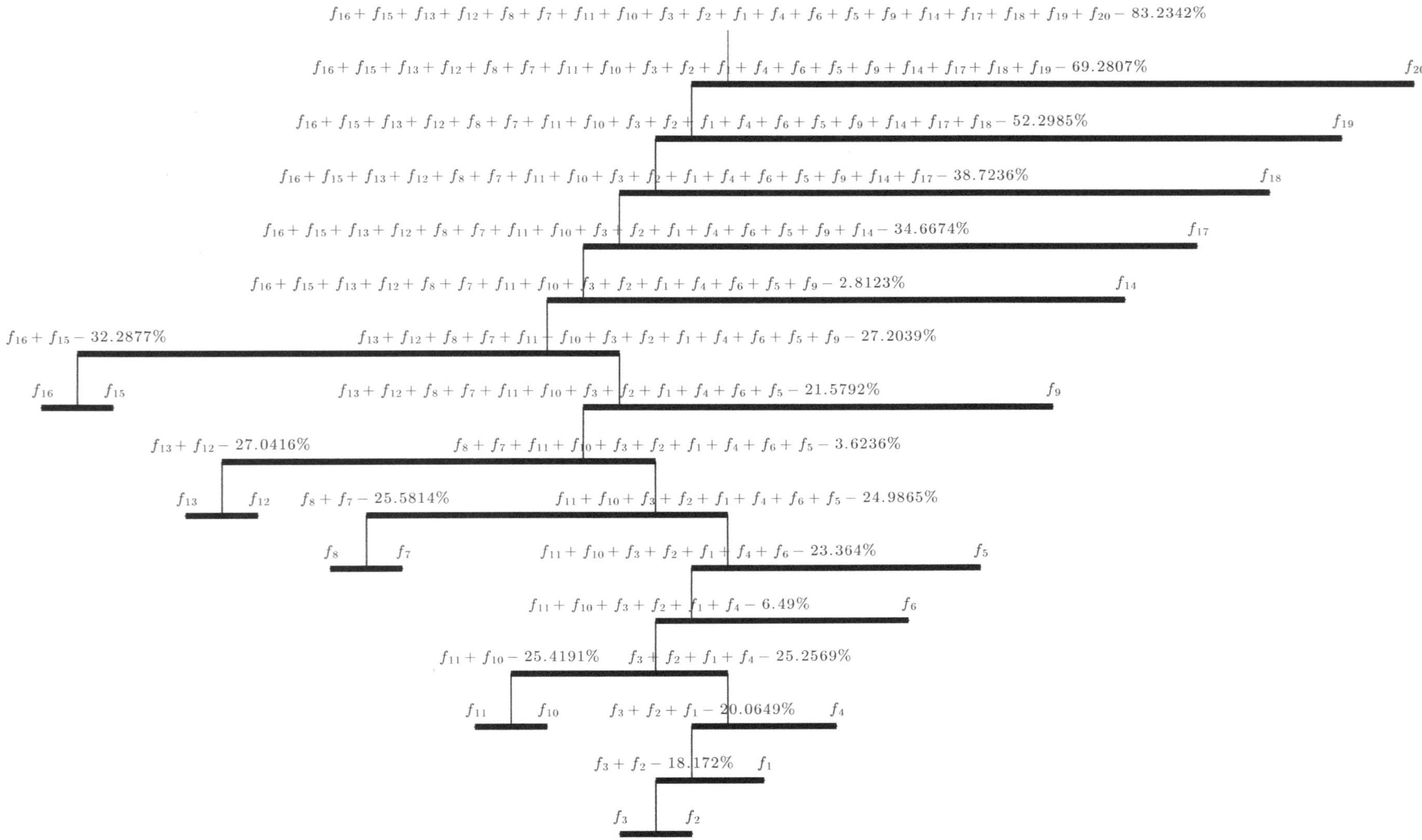

Figure 7: DTLZ2 - Aggregation Tree

tives are correlated even for non-optimal solutions. However, if the number of objectives is very high, most solutions will tend to be non-dominated.

As future work, it is possible to study the effect of other objective reduction techniques in the formation of the tree.

Acknowledgements

This work has been supported by the Brazilian agencies CAPES, CNPq, and FAPEMIG. We would also like the thank the support from the Federal University of Ouro Preto (UFOP) and the Federal University of Minas Gerais (UFMG).

8. REFERENCES

[1] G. Agrawal, C. Bloebaum, and K. Lewis. *Intuitive Design Selection using Visualized n-Dimensional Pareto Frontier*. American Institute of Aeronautics and Astronautics, 2014/01/16 2005.

[2] A. Auger, J. Bader, D. Brockhoff, and E. Zitzler. Hypervolume-based multiobjective optimization: Theoretical foundations and practical implications. *Theoretical Computer Science*, 425:75–103, 2012.

[3] L. Batista, F. Campelo, F. Guimarães, and J. Ramírez. Pareto cone ε-dominance: improving convergence and diversity in multiobjective evolutionary algorithms. In *Evolutionary Multi-Criterion Optimization*, pages 76–90. Springer, 2011.

[4] X. Blasco, J. Herrero, J. Sanchis, and M. Martínez. A new graphical visualization of n-dimensional pareto front for decision-making in multiobjective optimization. *Information Sciences*, 178(20):3908 – 3924, 2008. <ce:title>Special Issue on Industrial Applications of Neural Networks</ce:title> <xocs:full-name>10th Engineering Applications of Neural Networks 2007</xocs:full-name>.

[5] D. Brockhoff and E. Zitzler. Are all objectives necessary? on dimensionality reduction in evolutionary multiobjective optimization. *Parallel Problem Solving from Nature-PPSN IX*, pages 533–542, 2006.

[6] D. Brockhoff and E. Zitzler. Dimensionality reduction in multiobjective optimization: The minimum objective subset problem. *Operations Research Proceedings 2006*, pages 423–429, 2007.

[7] C. Coello, G. Lamont, and D. Veldhuizen. *Evolutionary Algorithms for Solving Multi-Objective Problems*. Genetic and evolutionary computation series. Springer, 2007.

[8] K. Deb, S. Agrawal, A. Pratap, and T. Meyarivan. A fast elitist non-dominated sorting genetic algorithm for multi-objective optimization: Nsga-ii. *Lecture notes in computer science*, 1917:849–858, 2000.

[9] K. Deb, L. Thiele, M. Laumanns, and E. Zitzler. Scalable test problems for evolutionary multiobjective optimization. In A. Abraham, L. Jain, and R. Goldberg, editors, *Evolutionary Multiobjective Optimization*, Advanced Information and Knowledge Processing, pages 105–145. Springer London, 2005.

[10] N. Drechsler, R. Drechsler, and B. Becker. Multi-objective optimisation based on relation favour. In *Evolutionary Multi-Criterion Optimization*, pages 154–166. Springer, 2001.

[11] J. Eddy and K. E. Lewis. Visualization of multidimensional design and optimization data using cloud visualization. In *ASME 2002 Design Engineering Technical Conferences and Computers and Information in Engineering Conference*. ASME, 2002.

[12] J. Fieldsend and R. Everson. Visualising high-dimensional pareto relationships in two-dimensional scatterplots. In R. Purshouse, P. Fleming, C. Fonseca, S. Greco, and J. Shaw, editors, *Evolutionary Multi-Criterion Optimization*, volume 7811 of *Lecture Notes in Computer Science*, pages 558–572. Springer Berlin Heidelberg, 2013.

[13] A. R. Freitas, P. J. Fleming, and F. G. Guimaraes. A non-parametric harmony-based objective reduction method for many-objective optimization. In *Systems, Man, and Cybernetics (SMC), 2013 IEEE International Conference on*, pages 651–656, 2013.

[14] I. Giagkiozis, R. Purshouse, and P. Fleming. Generalized decomposition and cross entropy methods for many-objective optimization. 2012.

[15] H. Ishibuchi, N. Tsukamoto, and Y. Nojima. Evolutionary many-objective optimization: A short review. In *Evolutionary Computation, 2008. CEC 2008.(IEEE World Congress on Computational Intelligence). IEEE Congress on*, pages 2419–2426. IEEE, 2008.

[16] V. Khare, X. Yao, and K. Deb. Performance scaling of multi-objective evolutionary algorithms. In *Evolutionary Multi-Criterion Optimization*, pages 72–72. Springer, 2003.

[17] J. Knowles and D. Corne. Approximating the nondominated front using the pareto archived evolution strategy. *Evolutionary computation*, 8(2):149–172, 2000.

[18] M. Koppen and K. Yoshida. Visualization of pareto-sets in evolutionary multi-objective optimization. In *Hybrid Intelligent Systems, 2007. HIS 2007. 7th International Conference on*, pages 156–161. IEEE, 2007.

[19] O. Kurasova, T. Petkus, and E. Filatovas. Visualization of pareto front points when solving multi-objective optimization problems. *Information Technology And Control*, 42(4):353–361, 2013.

[20] A. López Jaimes, C. A. Coello Coello, and D. Chakraborty. Objective reduction using a feature selection technique. In *Proceedings of the 10th annual conference on Genetic and evolutionary computation*, GECCO '08, pages 673–680, New York, NY, USA, 2008. ACM.

[21] A. Lotov. Approximation and visualization of pareto frontier in the framework of classical approach to multi-objective optimization. In J. Branke, K. Deb, K. Miettinen, and R. E. Steuer, editors, *Practical Approaches to Multi-Objective Optimization*, number 04461 in Dagstuhl Seminar Proceedings, Dagstuhl, Germany, 2005. Internationales Begegnungs- und Forschungszentrum für Informatik (IBFI), Schloss Dagstuhl, Germany.

[22] C. A. Mattson and A. Messac. Concept selection using s-pareto frontiers. *AIAA Journal*, 41(6):1190–1198, 2014/01/16 2003.

[23] S. Obayashi and D. Sasaki. Visualization and data mining of pareto solutions using self-organizing map. In *Evolutionary multi-criterion optimization*, pages 71–71. Springer, 2003.

[24] R. Purshouse and P. Fleming. Conflict, harmony, and independence: Relationships in evolutionary multi-criterion optimisation. In C. Fonseca, P. Fleming, E. Zitzler, L. Thiele, and K. Deb, editors, *Evolutionary Multi-Criterion Optimization*, volume 2632 of *Lecture Notes in Computer Science*, pages 16–30. Springer Berlin Heidelberg, 2003.

[25] R. Purshouse and P. Fleming. On the evolutionary optimization of many conflicting objectives. *Evolutionary Computation, IEEE Transactions on*, 11(6):770–784, 2007.

[26] S. Salomon, C. Domínguez-Medina, G. Avigad, A. Freitas, A. Goldvard, O. Schütze, and H. Trautmann. Psa based multi objective evolutionary algorithms. In O. Schuetze, C. A. Coello Coello, A.-A. Tantar, E. Tantar, P. Bouvry, P. D. Moral, and P. Legrand, editors, *EVOLVE - A Bridge between Probability, Set Oriented Numerics, and Evolutionary Computation III*, volume 500 of *Studies in Computational Intelligence*, pages 233–259. Springer International Publishing, 2014.

[27] D. Saxena and K. Deb. Non-linear dimensionality reduction procedures for certain large-dimensional multi-objective optimization problems: Employing correntropy and a novel maximum variance unfolding. In *Evolutionary Multi-Criterion Optimization*, pages 772–787. Springer, 2007.

[28] D. Saxena, J. Duro, A. Tiwari, K. Deb, and Q. Zhang. Objective reduction in many-objective optimization: Linear and nonlinear algorithms. *Evolutionary Computation, IEEE Transactions on*, 17(1):77–99, 2013.

[29] H. Singh, A. Isaacs, and T. Ray. A pareto corner search evolutionary algorithm and dimensionality reduction in many-objective optimization problems. *Evolutionary Computation, IEEE Transactions on*, 15(4):539–556, 2011.

[30] T. Tušar and B. Filipič. Visualizing 4d approximation sets of multiobjective optimizers with prosections. In *Proceedings of the 13th Annual Conference on Genetic and Evolutionary Computation*, GECCO '11, pages 737–744, New York, NY, USA, 2011. ACM.

[31] D. Walker, R. Everson, and J. Fieldsend. Visualizing mutually nondominating solution sets in many-objective optimization. *Evolutionary Computation, IEEE Transactions on*, 17(2):165–184, 2013.

[32] R. Wang, R. Purshouse, and P. Fleming. Local preference-inspired co-evolutionary algorithms. In *Proceedings of the fourteenth international conference on Genetic and evolutionary computation conference*, pages 513–520. ACM, 2012.

[33] U. Wickramasinghe and X. Li. Using a distance metric to guide pso algorithms for many-objective optimization. In *Proceedings of the 11th Annual conference on Genetic and evolutionary computation*, pages 667–674. ACM, 2009.

[34] J. Xiong, Y. Chen, K. Yang, Q. Zhao, and L. Xing. A hybrid multiobjective genetic algorithm for robust resource-constrained project scheduling with stochastic durations. *Mathematical Problems in Engineering*, 2012, 2012.

[35] M. Yoshimi, T. Kuhara, K. Nishimoto, M. Miki, and T. Hiroyasu. Visualization of pareto solutions by spherical self-organizing map and it's acceleration on a gpu. *Journal of Software Engineering and Applications*, 5(3), 2012.

Initial Experiments in Visualization of Empirical Attainment Function Differences using Maximum Intensity Projection

Tea Tušar
Department of Intelligent Systems
Jožef Stefan Institute, and
Jožef Stefan International Postgraduate School
Jamova cesta 39
SI-1000 Ljubljana, Slovenia
tea.tusar@ijs.si

Bogdan Filipič
Department of Intelligent Systems
Jožef Stefan Institute, and
Jožef Stefan International Postgraduate School
Jamova cesta 39
SI-1000 Ljubljana, Slovenia
bogdan.filipic@ijs.si

ABSTRACT

In multiobjective optimization, the Empirical Attainment Function (EAF) can be used to determine which areas of the objective space are attained by an optimization algorithm. If two algorithms are to be compared, differences in EAF values show which areas of the objective space are more often attained by one of the algorithms. While the visualization of EAF values and differences is rather straightforward in 2D, the 3D case presents a great challenge as we need to visualize a large number of 3D cuboids. This paper presents a method for computing the cuboids with constant EAF values and reports on initial experiments using Maximum Intensity Projection, a very-well known volume rendering technique used in medicine.

Categories and Subject Descriptors

G.1.6 [**Numerical Analysis**]: Optimization

General Terms

Algorithms

Keywords

Multiobjective optimization, Empirical attainment function, Visualization, Maximum intensity projection

1. INTRODUCTION

Real-world optimization problems often consist of two, three or even more conflicting objectives that cannot be simply aggregated into a single value. Therefore, the optimization algorithms used for solving these problems offer a set of trade-off solutions, where no solution from the set is better than any other in all objectives. This is called an *approximation set*. If the algorithm is stochastic, as is the case with evolutionary multiobjective algorithms generally used for such problems [1], it returns a different approximation set in every run.

Whether constructing a new optimization algorithm or improving an existing one, researchers need tools to assist them in the comparison between algorithms. While the performance of algorithms can be (and most often is) measured using different performance metrics, visualization of their approximation sets can give important insight into the properties of the algorithms (or the problem at hand) and inspire ideas for further improvement. In two- and three-objective optimization, the easiest way to visualize an approximation set is by simply plotting each solution it contains[1]. Such plots can also be used to visually compare two or more approximation sets, for example, each from a different optimization algorithm. However, there is a limitation to this technique—if an optimization algorithm is run multiple times and the resulting approximation sets are to be visualized simultaneously, the produced output can become too cluttered and loose its interpretation potential.

This difficulty can be overcome with the use of the Empirical Attainment Function (EAF), which assigns to each vector in the objective space a value signifying how often the vector was attained by the given approximation sets [3]. In the 2D case, the performance of an algorithm represented by several approximation sets can be visualized by plotting rectangles of different colors (or gray shades) representing different EAF values. Similarly, two algorithms can be compared by showing differences in these values [4, 6]. Such plots are very informative, providing an easy to understand visualization of the areas of the objective space where one algorithm outperforms the other one (and vice versa).

In the 3D case, however, visualization of EAF values and differences is less trivial. The attained areas are not rectangles, but cuboids, or rather, unions of cuboids, which need to be computed first. If the approximation sets of one algorithm consistently outperform the approximation sets of another algorithm, the positive EAF differences between the two algorithms look similar to a 3D 'cloud' of cuboids where the cuboids with the highest values lie in the center of the cloud, surrounded by cuboids with gradually decreasing values. Direct volume rendering of such clouds would show only the outer cuboids that correspond to smaller differences be-

[1]Approximation sets of higher dimensions that require more sophisticated methods to be visualized will not be discussed in this paper. The interested reader is referred to [7] for a comprehensive review of such methods.

GECCO'14, July 12–16, 2014, Vancouver, BC, Canada.
Copyright is held by the owner/author(s). Publication rights licensed to ACM.
ACM 978-1-4503-2881-4/14/07 ...$15.00.
http://dx.doi.org/10.1145/2598394.2610548.

tween the algorithms and are thus less interesting than the inner cuboids. This paper tackles the task of visualizing clouds of cuboids so that the cuboids with highest values have precedence over those with lower values. In previous work, we have sliced through the clouds of EAF values and differences under different angles and visualized the slices obtained in this way [6]. Here, we limit ourselves to the visualization of EAF differences using the Maximum Intensity Projection (MIP) method [8], which gives us a kind of 'X-ray' visualization of the cloud, where the cuboids with highest EAF differences are best seen. The analogy with X-rays is not coincidental as MIP is mostly used in medical imaging [5]. The MIP visualization nicely complements the slices, and taken together, the visualizations give a good idea of the 3D cloud of cuboids.

The next section provides some background on the relations used in multiobjective optimization, the EAF and the MIP method. Section 3 is devoted to solving a subproblem in the visualization of EAF differences—the computation of the attained area, which in turn requires finding the *opposite* of an approximation set. Section 4 demonstrates how MIP can be used for visualizing EAF differences. Finally, Section 5 concludes the paper with ideas for future work.

2. BACKGROUND

2.1 Relations in Multiobjective Optimization

The multiobjective optimization problem consists of finding the optimum of a function

$$\boldsymbol{f}\colon X \to F$$
$$\boldsymbol{f}\colon (x_1, \ldots, x_n) \mapsto (f_1(x_1, \ldots, x_n), \ldots, f_m(x_1, \ldots, x_n)),$$

where X is an n-dimensional decision space, and F is an m-dimensional objective space ($m \geq 2$). Each solution $\boldsymbol{x} \in X$ is called a decision vector, while the corresponding element $\boldsymbol{z} = \boldsymbol{f}(\boldsymbol{x}) \in F$ is an objective vector. Without loss of generality we assume that $F \subseteq \mathbb{R}^m$ and all objectives $f_i\colon X \to \mathbb{R}$ are to be minimized.

As this paper deals with visualization in the objective space, which can be viewed rather independently from the decision space, the following definitions are confined to the objective space.

Definition 1 (Weak Pareto dominance of vectors). The objective vector $\boldsymbol{z}^{\mathrm{A}} = (z_1^{\mathrm{A}}, \ldots, z_m^{\mathrm{A}})$ *weakly dominates* the objective vector $\boldsymbol{z}^{\mathrm{B}} = (z_1^{\mathrm{B}}, \ldots, z_m^{\mathrm{B}})$, i.e. $\boldsymbol{z}^{\mathrm{A}} \preceq \boldsymbol{z}^{\mathrm{B}}$, if

$$z_i^{\mathrm{A}} \leq z_i^{\mathrm{B}} \text{ for } \forall i \in \{1, \ldots, m\}.$$

Definition 2 (Strict Pareto dominance of vectors). The objective vector $\boldsymbol{z}^{\mathrm{A}} = (z_1^{\mathrm{A}}, \ldots, z_m^{\mathrm{A}})$ *strictly dominates* the objective vector $\boldsymbol{z}^{\mathrm{B}} = (z_1^{\mathrm{B}}, \ldots, z_m^{\mathrm{B}})$, i.e. $\boldsymbol{z}^{\mathrm{A}} \prec\prec \boldsymbol{z}^{\mathrm{B}}$, if

$$z_i^{\mathrm{A}} < z_i^{\mathrm{B}} \text{ for } \forall i \in \{1, \ldots, m\}.$$

Definition 3 (Incomparability of vectors). The objective vectors $\boldsymbol{z}^{\mathrm{A}} = (z_1^{\mathrm{A}}, \ldots, z_m^{\mathrm{A}})$ and $\boldsymbol{z}^{\mathrm{B}} = (z_1^{\mathrm{B}}, \ldots, z_m^{\mathrm{B}})$ are *incomparable*, i.e. $\boldsymbol{z}^{\mathrm{A}} \parallel \boldsymbol{z}^{\mathrm{B}}$, if

$$\boldsymbol{z}^{\mathrm{A}} \npreceq \boldsymbol{z}^{\mathrm{B}} \text{ and } \boldsymbol{z}^{\mathrm{B}} \npreceq \boldsymbol{z}^{\mathrm{A}}.$$

Definition 4 (Approximation set). A set of objective vectors $Z \subseteq F$ is called an *approximation set* if $\boldsymbol{z}^{\mathrm{A}} \parallel \boldsymbol{z}^{\mathrm{B}}$ for any two objective vectors $\boldsymbol{z}^{\mathrm{A}}, \boldsymbol{z}^{\mathrm{B}} \in Z$.

Definition 5 (Weak Pareto dominance of approximation sets). The approximation set Z^{A} *weakly dominates* the approximation set Z^{B}, i.e. $Z^{\mathrm{A}} \preceq Z^{\mathrm{B}}$, if every $\boldsymbol{z}^{\mathrm{B}} \in Z^{\mathrm{B}}$ is weakly dominated by at least one $\boldsymbol{z}^{\mathrm{A}} \in Z^{\mathrm{A}}$.

2.2 Empirical Attainment Function

The attainment function is based on the multiobjective concept of goal-attainment [3]: an objective vector is *attained* when it is weakly dominated by the approximation set returned by an optimization algorithm. If the algorithm is run r times, each objective vector can be attained between 0 and r times. The *empirical attainment function* of the objective vector $\boldsymbol{z}$ gives the frequency of attaining $\boldsymbol{z}$ by the approximation sets $Z_1, \ldots, Z_r$:

$$\alpha_r(\boldsymbol{z}) = \frac{1}{r} \sum_{i=1}^{r} \boldsymbol{I}\left(Z_i \preceq \{\boldsymbol{z}\}\right),$$

where $\boldsymbol{I}$ is the indicator function, defined as

$$\boldsymbol{I}(b) = \begin{cases} 1 & \text{if } b \text{ is true,} \\ 0 & \text{otherwise,} \end{cases}$$

and $\preceq$ is the weak Pareto dominance relation between sets.

Every vector in the objective space is thus assigned an EAF value from the interval $[0, 1]$. Of course, in practice the EAF cannot be computed for every objective vector, but only the boundaries of the regions of the objective space with a constant EAF value are of interest. They are called k *%-attainment surfaces* (also *summary attainment surfaces*) and consist of the tightest objective vectors that have been attained in at least k % of the runs. The attainment surfaces are well-defined by a finite set of objective vectors that we call *attainment anchors*[2]. Attainment anchors include other vectors beside the vectors from the approximation sets. Fonseca et al. [2] provided efficient algorithms for computing attainment anchors and their EAF values for the 2D and 3D cases.

Consider the example shown in Figure 1, where three approximation sets contain four objective vectors each (denoted with circles). The lines represent three attainment surfaces that partition the objective space into areas with distinct EAF values. The attainment anchors define these surfaces and are shown with circles and dots (the dots are those that are not present in the approximation sets).

Now imagine that two algorithms, A and B, are run r times each. This yields two sets of approximation sets. The algorithms can be compared by computing their EAF values α_r^{A} and α_r^{B} separately. However, there exists a straightforward way to directly compare the algorithms by joining their approximation sets [4]. First, the overall attainment surfaces for the $2r$ approximation sets need to be computed. Then, for each attainment anchor $\boldsymbol{z}$, the *difference in EAF values* can be calculated by counting the number of times each of the algorithms managed to attain that anchor and subtracting the two numbers:

$$\delta^{\mathrm{A-B}}(\boldsymbol{z}) = r\alpha_r^{\mathrm{A}}(\boldsymbol{z}) - r\alpha_r^{\mathrm{B}}(\boldsymbol{z}).$$

Defined in this way, the differences can adopt values from $\{-r, \ldots, 0, \ldots, r\}$. Positive EAF differences denote areas in

[2]These vectors are called *output points* in the context of the EAF computation [2], where the *input points* represent the objective vectors from the approximation sets.

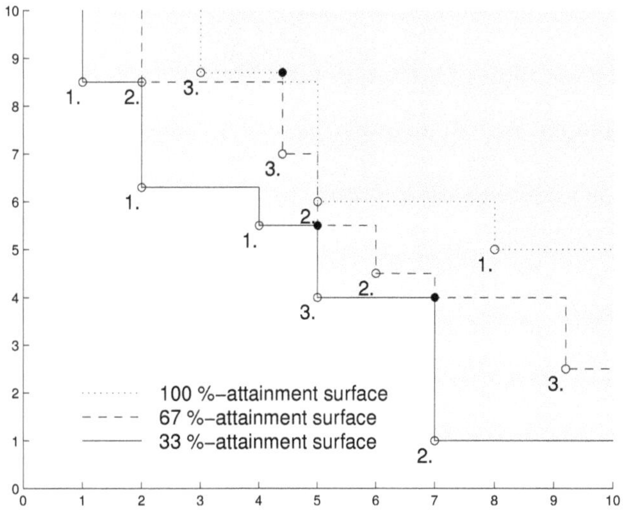

Figure 1: Attainment surfaces for three approximation sets. The circles labels denote the different approximation sets. All circles and dots represent the attainment anchors.

the objective space where the algorithm A outperforms the algorithm B, while negative EAF differences denote areas in the objective space where the algorithm B outperforms the algorithm A. Naturally, where the differences are zero, both algorithms attain the area equally well.

In order to visualize the EAF differences, the attained areas need to be computed. As presented later, this is easier to do in 2D, where these areas are unions of rectangles, than in 3D, where the areas are unions of cuboids, and require the computation of a opposite of an approximation set. Additional practical difficulties in visualizing EAF differences arise from the high number of attainment anchors l. As proven in [2], in the 2D case, $l \in \Theta(ra)$, while in the 3D case, $l \in O(r^2a)$, where r is the number of approximation sets (runs) and a the total number of objective vectors contained in the approximation sets. In Section 4 we will see on an example how these bounds on the number of attainment anchors translate to actual figures.

2.3 Maximum Intensity Projection

Maximum intensity projection (MIP) is a volume rendering method for spatial data represented by voxels, i.e. values in a 3D grid. The method inspects voxels in direction of parallel rays traced from the viewpoint to the projection plane, and takes the maximum value encountered in the voxels along a ray as the projection value for the ray (see the schematic presentation in Figure 2).

The method, originally called maximum activity projection (MAP) [8], was proposed for 3D image rendering in nuclear medicine and tested in tomographic studies. It was later accepted not only in medical imaging, but in scientific data visualization in general.

The advantages of MIP are its simplicity and efficiency, and the ability of achieving high contrast, which arises from the fact that maximum voxel values are projected. On the other hand, as a limitation, the resulting projections lack the sense of depth of the original data. Moreover, the viewer cannot distinguish between left or right and front and back.

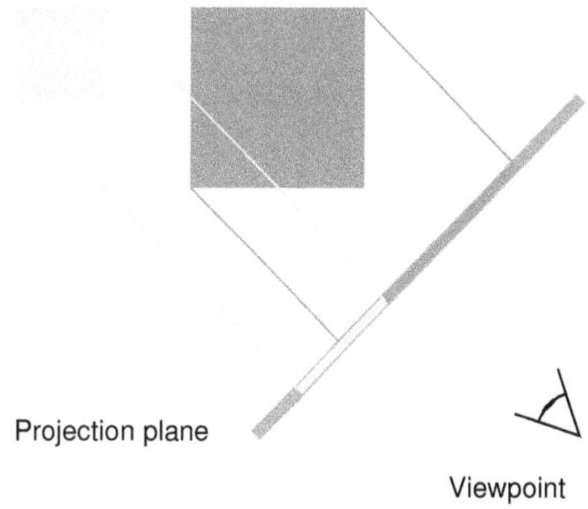

Figure 2: Schematic presentation of MIP.

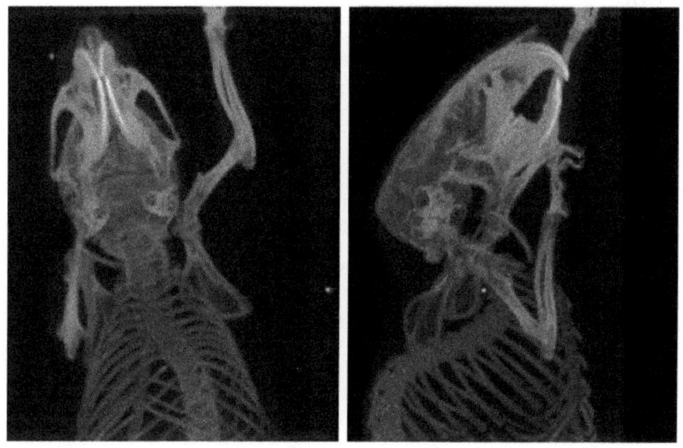

Figure 3: CT of a mouse visualized using MIP at two different viewpoints, ©Christian Lackas.

As an improvement, animations are usually provided, consisting of a sequence of MIP renderings at slightly different viewpoints, which results in the illusion of rotation (see an example of visualization using MIP at two different viewpoints in Figure 3).

3. COMPUTING THE ATTAINED AREA

Before tackling the visualization of EAF differences, let us focus on the problem of computing the areas attained by the anchors, which are unions of rectangles in 2D, and unions of cuboids in 3D. Consider two consecutive attainment surfaces Z_1 and Z_2. Each rectangle (or cuboid) between the two attainment surfaces is defined by exactly two vectors—one attainment anchor from Z_1 and a dominated vector from Z_2. We call these 'dominated vectors' the *opposite* of the set of anchors.

3.1 Opposite of an Approximation Set

The opposite O of an approximation set Z depends only on Z and two reference vectors $\boldsymbol{r}^1$ and $\boldsymbol{r}^2$ denoting the boundaries of the observed objective space ($\{\boldsymbol{r}^1\} \preceq Z \preceq \{\boldsymbol{r}^2\}$). The attainment surface of the approximation set Z divides the observed objective space in two areas—vectors in the first area are not attained by Z, while vectors in the second area are attained by Z. The opposite O is the set of vectors that would yield the same attainment surface, i.e.

Algorithm 1: Computing the opposite of a 2D approximation set.

Input: Approximation set Z and reference vectors $\boldsymbol{r}^1$ and $\boldsymbol{r}^2$ such that $\{\boldsymbol{r}^1\} \preceq Z \preceq \{\boldsymbol{r}^2\}$
Output: The opposite O

Sort the vectors from Z in ascending order of the first objective to obtain $Z = \{\boldsymbol{z}^1, \ldots, \boldsymbol{z}^k\}$;
$O \leftarrow \{\}$;
if $z_1^1 \neq r_1^1$ **then**
  | $O \leftarrow \{(z_1^1, r_2^2)\}$;
end
for $i \leftarrow 2$ **to** k **do**
  | $O \leftarrow O \cup \{(z_1^i, z_2^{i-1})\}$;
end
if $z_2^k \neq r_2^2$ **then**
  | $O \leftarrow O \cup \{(r_1^2, z_2^k)\}$;
end

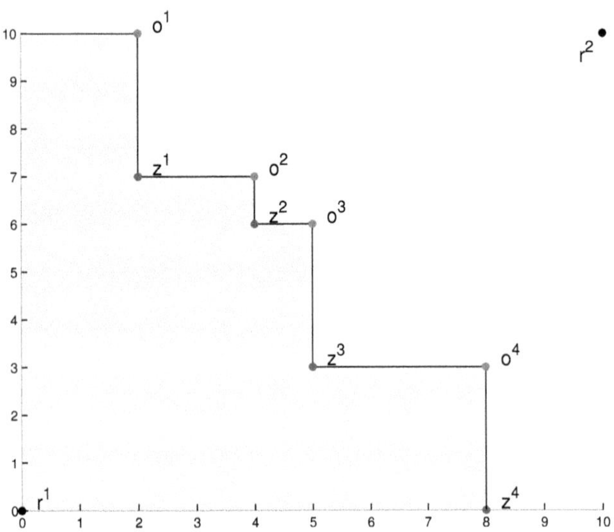

Figure 4: Example of a 2D approximation set $Z = \{\boldsymbol{z}^1, \ldots, \boldsymbol{z}^4\}$ and its opposite $O = \{\boldsymbol{o}^1, \ldots, \boldsymbol{o}^4\}$ with regard to reference vectors $\boldsymbol{r}^1$ and $\boldsymbol{r}^2$.

divide the observed objective space in exactly the same areas, if the minimization problem would be transformed into a maximization problem.

In 2D, computing the opposite of an approximation set Z given two reference vectors $\boldsymbol{r}^1$ and $\boldsymbol{r}^2$ is very simple (see Algorithm 1 and Figure 4 for an example). First, the vectors in the approximation set Z are sorted with regard to their values in the first objective. Then for each vector $\boldsymbol{z}^i \in Z$, a vector $\boldsymbol{o}^i$ in the opposite O is created by 'raising' $\boldsymbol{z}^i$ to match the second objective value of its predecessor $\boldsymbol{z}^{i-1}$. The first vector has no predecessor, therefore it is raised to the level of the second reference vector $\boldsymbol{r}^2$. In addition, the last vector of the opposite is created by combining the first objective value of the $\boldsymbol{r}^2$ and the second objective value of the last vector from Z. The first and last vectors are retained in the opposite only if they are strictly dominated by the first reference vector $\boldsymbol{r}^1$ (this is the reason why there is no $\boldsymbol{o}^5 = (10, 0)$ in the example from Figure 4).

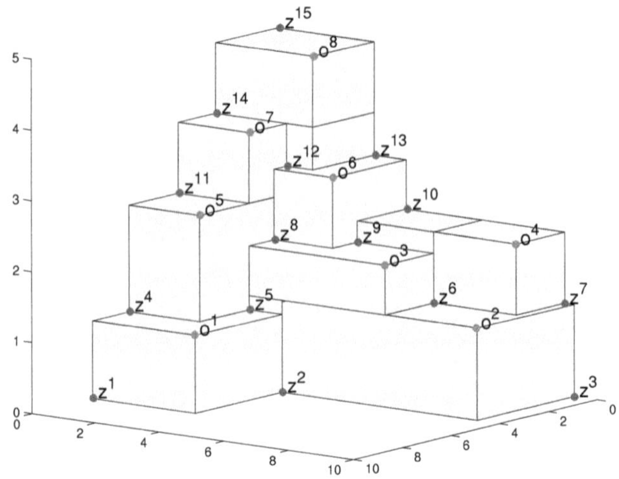

Figure 5: Example of a 3D approximation set $Z = \{\boldsymbol{z}^1, \ldots, \boldsymbol{z}^{15}\}$ and its opposite $O = \{\boldsymbol{o}^1, \ldots, \boldsymbol{o}^8\}$ with regard to reference vectors $\boldsymbol{r}^1 = (0, 0, 0)$ and $\boldsymbol{r}^2 = (10, 10, 5)$ (not pictured).

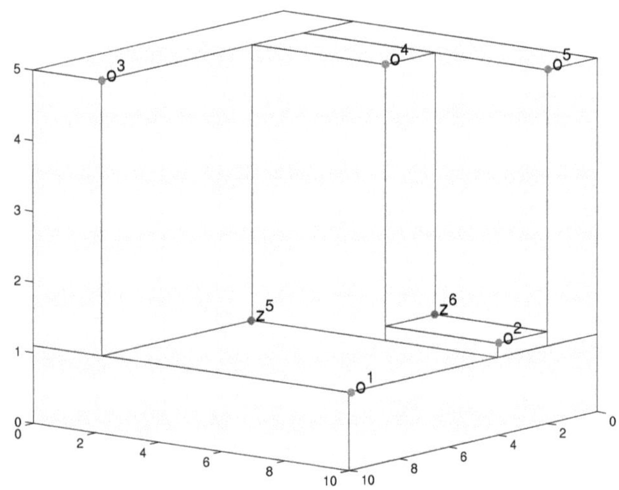

Figure 6: An intermediate step in the construction of the opposite of set Z from Figure 5 showing the opposite for the set $\{\boldsymbol{z}^5, \boldsymbol{z}^6\}$.

While finding the opposite of a 3D approximation set is more demanding, there exists an elegant way to do it. We will explain it with the help of Figures 5, 6 and 7. Again, we know the approximation set Z and two reference vectors $\boldsymbol{r}^1$ and $\boldsymbol{r}^2$. The desired outcome is shown in Figure 5. It can be constructed gradually, by taking into consideration one vector from Z at a time. Note that the vectors from Z do not need to be sorted.

Imagine a single cuboid defined by the reference vectors $\boldsymbol{r}^1$ and $\boldsymbol{r}^2$. The only vector in the opposite at this point is $\boldsymbol{r}^2$. Every time a vector from Z is 'cut into' the existing cuboid, new vectors are added into the opposite. Assume we have already performed this step for vectors $\boldsymbol{z}^5$ and $\boldsymbol{z}^6$ (see Figure 6) and vector $\boldsymbol{z}^9$ is next in line (see Figure 7). First, we delete from the opposite all vectors that are strictly dominated by the current vector $\boldsymbol{z}$ (this means that in our

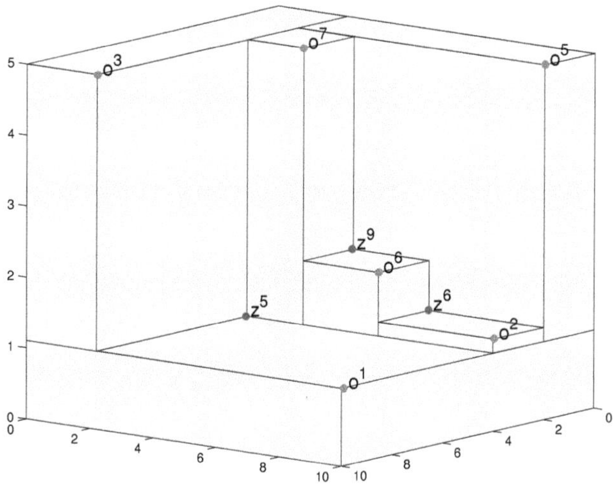

Figure 7: An intermediate step in the construction of the opposite of set Z from Figure 5 showing the opposite for the set $\{z^5, z^6, z^9\}$.

Algorithm 2: Computing the opposite of a 3D approximation set.

Input: Approximation set Z and reference vectors r^1 and r^2 such that $\{r^1\} \preceq Z \preceq \{r^2\}$
Output: The opposite O

$O \leftarrow \{r^2\}$;
foreach $z \in Z$ **do**
  $O' \leftarrow \{o \in O; z \prec\prec o\}$;
  $O \leftarrow O - O'$;
  foreach $o \in O'$ **do**
    $o^{n_1} \leftarrow (z_1, o_2, o_3)$;
    $o^{n_2} \leftarrow (o_1, z_2, o_3)$;
    $o^{n_3} \leftarrow (o_1, o_2, z_3)$;
    for $i \leftarrow 1$ **to** 3 **do**
      if $\neg$ coplanar(o^{n_i}, r^1) $\wedge$ $\neg$ collinear(o^{n_i}, O) **then**
        $O \leftarrow O \cup \{o^{n_i}\}$;
      end
    end
  end
end

Algorithm 3: Computing the attained areas between two attainment surfaces.

Input: Attainment surfaces Z_1 and Z_2, for which $Z_1 \preceq Z_2$, and reference vector r^2
Output: The set of attained areas A

$r^1 \leftarrow$ component-min(Z_1);
$O \leftarrow$ opposite(Z_1, r^1, r^2);
foreach $z \in Z_1$ **do**
  $O' \leftarrow \{o \in O; z \prec\prec o\}$;
  foreach $o \in O'$ **do**
    $A \leftarrow A \cup$ new-area(z, o, value(z));
  end
end

---

example we delete vector o^4, but not o^5). Next, for every deleted vector o we create three new vectors in the following way:

$$o^{n1} = (z_1, o_2, o_3)$$
$$o^{n2} = (o_1, z_2, o_3)$$
$$o^{n3} = (o_1, o_2, z_3)$$

Finally, each of these vectors is added to the opposite if it is not coplanar with r^1 and not collinear with any of the vectors from the current opposite. In our example, we add to the opposite vectors o^6 and o^7, but not $o^8 = (2, 6.5, 5)$ (not pictured in the figure) as it is collinear with o^5. When these steps have been taken for every vector from Z, the resulting set O represents the opposite of Z. See also Algorithm 2 for the algorithmic notation of the described procedure.

Note that the same idea of cutting into the objective space could also be used for the 2D case. However, Algorithm 1 is so simple that there is no need to look for an alternative.

3.2 From Opposites to Areas

Let us return to the example of two consecutive attainment surfaces Z_1 and Z_2. If the opposite O of Z_2 is known, it is rather straightforward to compute the attained areas between Z_1 and Z_2 and can be done in a uniform way for both the 2D and 3D case (see Algorithm 3). For every attainment anchor $z \in Z_1$ and every vector $o \in O$ that is strictly dominated by z, an area enclosed by these two vectors is added to the set of attained areas.

In addition, each area can be associated with a value—either the EAF value of the difference between EAF values of the attainment anchor z. While some areas might overlap, this is not a problem since all overlapping areas have the same value (if they did not have the same value, another anchor vector would have already split the area).

The Algorithm 3 computes the attained areas between two consecutive attainment surfaces. In order to compute the areas for the whole objective space, we need to iterate the algorithm over all consecutive pairs of attainment surfaces.

4. VISUALIZING EAF DIFFERENCES USING MAXIMUM INTENSITY PROJECTION

The procedure for visualizing EAF differences between two sets of approximation sets consists of the following steps:

1. Combine all approximation sets and calculate the EAF values and the differences in those values.

2. Compute the cuboids between all pairs of attainment surfaces.

3. Plot separately the cuboids with positive and negative EAF differences using MIP.

Let us assume we wish to plot the cuboids using a standard plotting tool able to visualize 3D data. Usually, the 3D rendering tools do not allow for cuboids with larger EAF differences to cover those with smaller EAF differences, as is the principle of MIP, but visualize the cuboids in a sequence that maintains some notion of depth (cuboids near the viewpoint are shown in front of the cuboids further away). Therefore, MIP can be performed only after the viewpoint has been set and the cuboids are plotted onto 2D. Now we can choose to

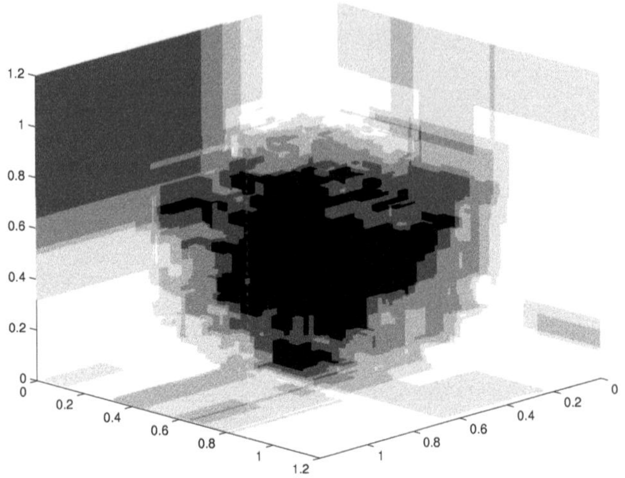

Figure 8: Areas in the objective space where the linear approximation sets outperform the spherical ones as shown by MIP (darker areas denote larger differences).

visualize them in a predefined order from the smallest to the largest EAF difference. If plotted in this way, cuboids with larger EAF differences cover those with smaller differences, effectively achieving the MIP visualization of the cloud of cuboids.

Now, let us demonstrate the visualization of EAF differences by means of MIP on an example. The attainment surfaces used in this example are not the product of optimization algorithms, but rather benchmark approximation sets with known properties used for visualization purposes [7].

The first set consists of five linear approximation sets with a uniform distribution of vectors that satisfy the constraint

$$\sum_{i=1}^{3} z_i = c_{\mathrm{L}}.$$

In order to simulate the behavior of a stochastic algorithm, the values of c_{L} for different sets follow the normal distribution with mean 1 and variance 0.05. The second set contains five spherical approximation sets with a non-uniform distribution of vectors where only few vectors are located in the middle of the approximation set, while most of them are near its corners. The vectors from the spherical approximation sets satisfy the constraint

$$\sum_{i=1}^{3} z_i^2 = c_{\mathrm{S}}^2,$$

where the values of c_{S} for each of the five sets follow the normal distribution with mean 0.75 and variance 0.05. Each individual approximation set contains 100 objective vectors.

The values of c_{L} and c_{S} were chosen so that the sets are always intertwined—in one region, the linear approximation sets dominate the spherical ones, while in others, the spherical sets dominate the linear ones. This means that there will be visible differences in EAF values for the two sets of approximation sets.

Figure 8 shows the areas of the objective space where the linear approximation sets outperform the spherical ones.

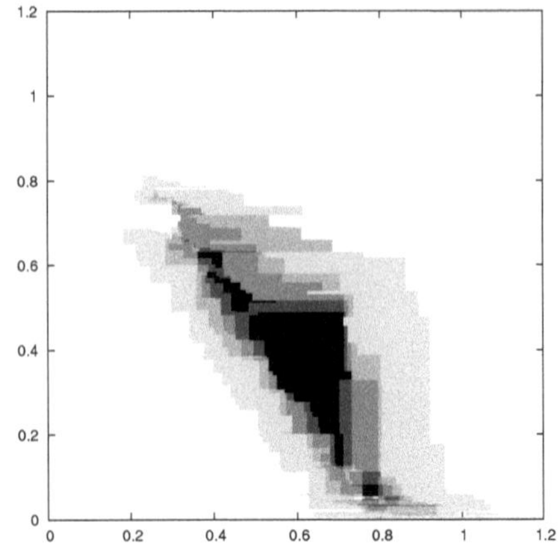

Figure 9: The intersection between the cuboids showing outperformance of the linear approximation sets with the plane crossing the origin and cutting the xy plane at the angle of $45°$.

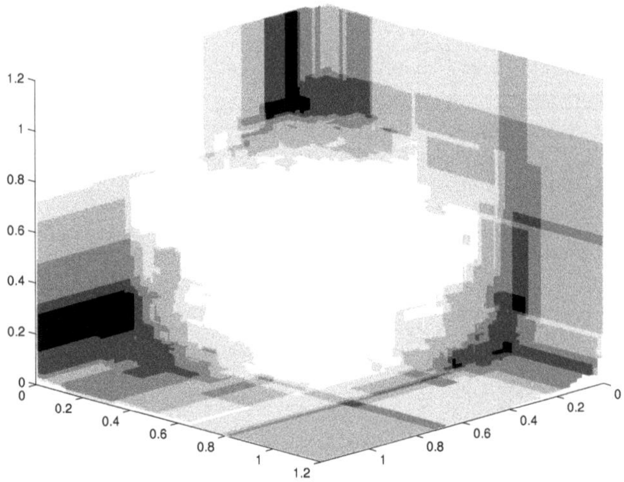

Figure 10: Areas in the objective space where the spherical approximation sets outperform the linear ones as shown by MIP (darker areas denote larger differences).

Here the cloud of cuboids is nicely visualized. We can see that the largest values are in its center, surrounded by decreasing values. Nevertheless, this MIP visualization shares the same disadvantages as MIP visualizations in medicine—because we can see through the cloud of cuboids, we loose the sense of depth. While it is inevitable to lose some information when projecting 3D structures onto 2D, this can be amended by combining two visualization techniques—MIP and slicing through the cloud, which visualizes the intersection between the cuboids and the cutting plane (see [6] for details and the example of such a cut in Figure 9). Now we can see that the cloud is not round at its side closest to the origin, but flat as the best approximation sets in that area of the objective space are the linear ones.

Similarly, we can use MIP to visualize the areas of the objective space where the spherical approximation sets outperform the linear ones (see Figure 10). As it could be expected,

Table 1: The number of attainment anchors and cuboids depending on the number of approximation sets.

No. of sets	No. of all vectors	No. of attainment anchors	No. of cuboids with $\delta^{L-S} \neq 0$	No. of cuboids with $\delta^{L-S} > 0$	No. of cuboids with $\delta^{L-S} < 0$
10	1 000	8 093	22 577	14 470	8 107
20	2 000	49 044	91 088	58 392	32 696

we can see that the spherical sets dominate the linear ones only near the corners of the objective space.

Finally, a note on the complexity of such visualizations. In our example we have used two sets of five approximation sets, each containing 100 objective vectors. In addition, we have performed the same experiments on two sets with ten approximation sets, again containing 100 objective vectors each. Table 1 collects the number of objective vectors, attainment anchors and cuboids in each experiment. As we can see, the number of attainment anchors significantly increases with the growing number of approximation sets (as already mentioned in Subsection 2.2). What these numbers mean in practice is that it is very difficult to visualize all areas with non-zero EAF differences when dealing with ten or more runs per algorithm since this entails visualizing approximately 50 000 cuboids. As we are usually interested mainly in the areas where the differences between algorithms are large (or even statistically significant), one possibility is to remove the cuboids with smaller EAF differences before visualization with MIP, thus decreasing their number.

The Algorithm 3 constructing the cuboids allows them to overlap. As we can see from Table 1, this happens very often (there are between two and three cuboids per attainment anchor). It might be interesting to explore if posing a restriction on overlapping would bring better results in terms of faster rendering of the cuboids. While non-overlapping cuboids would be smaller (and therefore easier to visualize), they might increase in number, which makes it hard to predict if such a procedure would be advantageous.

5. CONCLUSION

We have tackled the visualization of 3D EAF differences between two optimization algorithms, which consists of two subproblems. In order to show the EAF differences, the objective space needs to be first divided into cuboids with constant differences. Second, to compute these cuboids, the opposites of all attainment anchors must be found. We have presented algorithms to solve these subproblems and shown some preliminary results of the visualization with MIP on two sets of benchmark approximation sets.

In the future, we intend to provide more combined MIP and slicing visualization examples, including those from real-world optimization problems. Also, the algorithms presented in this paper could probably be further improved, for example, by storing the already computed relations between objective vectors. Additionally, it might be interesting to explore a completely different approach where the objective space would not contain exact cuboids, but would be discretized into voxels with values approximating the EAF differences in the covered area. While any discretization would surely yield only an approximation of the true cloud of cuboids, it could provide better efficiency. Moreover, existing MIP rendering software could then be used to visualize the voxels (including interactive rotations).

6. ACKNOWLEDGMENTS

The work presented in this paper was carried out as part of research program P2-0209 and research projects L2-3651 and J2-4120, all funded by the Slovenian Research Agency.

The first author wishes to acknowledge Richard Everson and Manuel López-Ibáñez for discussing some ideas presented in this paper at GECCO'13.

7. REFERENCES

[1] K. Deb. *Multi-Objective Optimization Using Evolutionary Algorithms.* John Wiley & Sons, Chichester, UK, 2001.

[2] C. M. Fonseca, A. P. Guerreiro, M. López-Ibáñez, and L. Paquete. On the computation of the empirical attainment function. In *Proceedings of the 6th International Conference on Evolutionary Multi-Criterion Optimization, EMO 2011*, volume 6576 of *Lecture Notes in Computer Science*, pages 106–120, 2011.

[3] V. D. Grunert da Fonseca, C. M. Fonseca, and A. O. Hall. Inferential performance assessment of stochastic optimisers and the attainment function. In *Proceedings of the First International Conference on Evolutionary Multi-Criterion Optimization, EMO 2001*, volume 1993 of *Lecture Notes in Computer Science*, pages 213–225, 2001.

[4] M. López-Ibáñez, L. Paquete, and T. Stützle. Exploratory analysis of stochastic local search algorithms in biobjective optimization. In T. Bartz-Beielstein, M. Chiarandini, L. Paquete, and M. Preuss, editors, *Experimental Methods for the Analysis of Optimization Algorithms*, pages 209–222. Springer, 2010.

[5] S. Schreiner and R. L. Galloway. A fast maximum-intensity projection algorithm for generating magnetic resonance angiograms. *IEEE Transactions on Medical Imaging*, 12(1):50–57, March 1993.

[6] T. Tušar and B. Filipič. An approach to visualizing the 3D empirical attainment function. In *Proceedings of the 15th Annual Conference Companion on Genetic and Evolutionary Computation*, GECCO '13 Companion, pages 1367–1372, 2013.

[7] T. Tušar and B. Filipič. Visualization of Pareto front approximations in evolutionary multiobjective optimization: A critical review and the prosection method. *IEEE Transactions on Evolutionary Computation*, 2014. In press.

[8] J. W. Wallis, T. R. Miller, C. A. Lerner, and E. C. Kleerup. Three-dimensional display in nuclear medicine. *IEEE Transactions on Medical Imaging*, 8(4):297–230, December 1989.

Evolutionary Computation Software Systems (EvoSoft'14) Chairs' Welcome

It is our great pleasure to welcome you to the GECCO Workshop on Evolutionary Computation Software Systems (EvoSoft).

The evolution of so many different metaheuristic optimization algorithms results from the fact that no single method can outperform all others for all possible problems. As postulated in the No Free Lunch Theorem, a general-purpose and universal optimization strategy is impossible. The only way how one strategy can outperform another is to be more specialized to the structure of the tackled problem. Consequently it always takes qualified algorithm experts to select and tune a metaheuristic algorithm for a specific application.

Choosing an appropriate method for a certain problem is not trivial, as problem characteristics may change remarkably for different instances and the performance of a metaheuristic may vary considerably for different parameter settings. Therefore the choice of a well suited method and according parameter values is a crucial aspect when applying metaheuristics.

Because of these issues it is not advisable to implement only one specific metaheuristic algorithm for a specific problem, as it cannot be determined in advance whether the chosen method is suitable for the tackled problem or not. Thus soundly engineered, reusable, flexible, user-friendly and interoperable software systems are required which offer a broad spectrum of different metaheuristic algorithms and support researchers in adapting and comparing these methods for different problems in order to bridge the gap between theoretical research and practical applications.

However, the development of such systems is both, time consuming and complex. Surprisingly the chance to join forces in the development of evolutionary computation software systems is not yet seized sufficiently within the evolutionary computation research community. Instead of reusing existing software and continuing their work on the shoulders of others, many researchers implement individual and highly specialized applications. Often these systems are not even publically released which hinders comparability and replicability of research results.

The EvoSoft Workshop should highlight the importance of software engineering and software quality in the domain of evolutionary computation and should enable researchers to exchange their ideas on how to develop and apply generic and reusable software systems. It should provide a common platform to present open and freely available frameworks, to discuss novel approaches in their development, to identify cooperation potentials and synergies between research groups, and to define common standards.

Many thanks go to the authors, reviewers, and Program Committee members whose efforts make this workshop possible in the first place. We genuinely hope that you enjoy the EvoSoft Workshop and that it will boost joint efforts in the development of evolutionary computation software systems.

Stefan Wagner
EvoSoft'14 General Chair
University of Applied Sciences
Upper Austria, Austria

Michael Affenzeller
EvoSoft'14 General Chair
University of Applied Sciences
Upper Austria, Austria

GECCO'14 Evolutionary Computation Software Systems (EvoSoft) Organization

General Chairs: Stefan Wagner *(University of Applied Sciences Upper Austria, Austria)*
Michael Affenzeller *(University of Applied Sciences Upper Austria, Austria)*

Program Chair: Stefan Wagner *(University of Applied Sciences Upper Austria, Austria)*

Program Committee: Gabriel Kronberger *(University of Applied Sciences Upper Austria, Austria)*
Francesco Longo *(University of Calabria, Italy)*
José Antonio Parejo Maestre *(University of Sevilla, Spain)*
Stephan Winkler *(University of Applied Sciences Upper Austria, Austria)*

Additional reviewers: Andreas Beham
Johannes Karder
Michael Kommenda
Erik Pitzer
Andreas Scheibenpflug

Scripting and Framework Integration in Heuristic Optimization Environments

Andreas Beham, Johannes Karder, Gabriel Kronberger,
Stefan Wagner, Michael Kommenda, Andreas Scheibenpflug

University of Applied Sciences Upper Austria
Heuristic and Evolutionary Algorithms Laboratory
Softwarepark 11, 4232 Hagenberg, Austria
(abeham, jkarder, gkronber, swagner, mkommend, ascheibe)@heuristiclab.com

Johannes Kepler University Linz
Institute for Formal Models and Verification
Altenberger Straße 69, 4040 Linz, Austria
(andreas.beham, michael.kommenda)@students.jku.at

ABSTRACT

Rapid prototyping and testing of new ideas has been a major argument for evolutionary computation frameworks. These frameworks facilitate the application of evolutionary computation and allow experimenting with new and modified algorithms and problems by building on existing, well tested code. However, one could argue, that despite the many frameworks of the metaheuristics community, software packages such as MATLAB, GNU Octave, Scilab, or RStudio are quite popular. These software packages however are associated more closely with numerical analysis rather than evolutionary computation. In contrast to typical evolutionary computation frameworks which provide standard implementations of algorithms and problems, these popular frameworks provide a direct programming environment for the user and several helpful functions and mathematical operations. The user does not need to use traditional development tools such as a compiler or linker, but can implement, execute, and visualize his ideas directly within the environment. HeuristicLab has become a popular environment for heuristic optimization over the years, but has not been recognized as a programming environment so far. In this article we will describe new scripting capabilities created in HeuristicLab and give information on technical details of the implementation. Additionally, we show how the programming interface can be used to integrate further metaheuristic optimization frameworks in HeuristicLab.

Categories and Subject Descriptors

I.2.5 [**Artificial Intelligence**]: Programming Languages and Software

General Terms

Algorithms, Experimentation

GECCO'14, July 12–16, 2014, Vancouver, BC, Canada.

ACM 978-1-4503-2881-4/14/07 ...$15.00.
http://dx.doi.org/10.1145/2598394.2605690.

Keywords

HeuristicLab; Evolutionary Computation Frameworks; Metaheuristic Optimization Frameworks; Scripting

1. INTRODUCTION

The behavior and performance of metaheuristic optimization methods is often influenced by small details. To avoid confusion such methods are often shared with the community as a concrete implementation, for example in a given programming language. Because of the requirement to compare new algorithms with existing ones and an explosion of different metaheuristic algorithms, metaheuristic optimization (MOP) frameworks have emerged that contain implementations of such methods [9]. But while frameworks aim to provide mostly a well-designed API, software environments go one step further and define not only extension points for concrete applications, but provide a run-time environment in which the user can prototype and test new ideas.

HeuristicLab[1] has evolved over the years as an environment for heuristic optimization and became a popular tool for researchers and practitioners [10, 11]. Extensibility is a strong requirement of such an environment so that tools and methods to answer new research questions can be implemented. The benefit of the API and the reuse of existing methods, analysis and visualizations often outweighs the integration effort and can compensate for disadvantages such as a steeper learning curve [8]. Software environments attempt to mitigate the use of traditional development environments, i.e. IDE, compiler and linker. In HeuristicLab tasks such as algorithm prototyping, running and analyzing experiments can be performed in the run-time environment. Still, often when finding answers to new research questions, it is required to use traditional development tools to extend the functionality.

The ability to write and execute code while running HeuristicLab has been present since the release of version 3.3.0, but was restricted to operators that were executed inside an algorithm. Starting from HeuristicLab 3.3.10 programming directly within the environment has been significantly improved. This allows to prototype and test new ideas faster, especially for those users that are familiar with programming languages and the Microsoft .NET Framework. Additionally, tasks such as advanced experiment cre-

[1] `http://dev.heuristiclab.com`

ation could be more complex than what is already featured in the environment. Sometimes such advanced tasks can be integrated into the UI easily, but sometimes the additions would make the UI complex and confusing. With the addition of a scripting interface the user is able to implement a customized experiment generator that handles more complex requirements. Users are able to quickly write new algorithms for existing problems and reuse existing visualization and analysis features. An additional option that arises and which is further looked at in this paper concerns the integration of further MOP frameworks in HeuristicLab. Features, algorithms, and problems available in other frameworks are valuable and we aim to make these available within the HeuristicLab optimization environment.

1.1 Related Work

To the best of the authors' knowledge the integration of different MOP frameworks and direct reuse of algorithms and problems has not yet been described before. There have been some attempts at a generic and open data exchange between problem specific and algorithm specific parts. For instance, in the PISA project[2] an exchange was realized using text files, in GenOpt[3] a file-based exchange was realized to interconnect optimization and simulation, and also in HeuristicLab protocol-based data exchange has been implemented to communicate with external evaluation processes [1]. However, data exchange is only one aspect of interconnection. The ability to execute code written in other MOP frameworks requires an integration at the programming language level. Fortunately, a lot of progress has been made here by at least two projects that we aim to introduce and evaluate their usefulness in the context of bringing together different MOP frameworks. However, first we want to describe the scripting capabilities and how we allow writing and executing code within the running HeuristicLab application.

2. SCRIPTING IN HEURISTICLAB

A script in HeuristicLab can be created similar to how a problem or an algorithm would be created. Once a script is created three aspects of the script are presented in the GUI as can be seen in Figure 1:

- Script code
- Store for variables
- Console output log

Different scripts do not share these elements, so each script has access to its own console and variable store. The user can however use drag and drop to copy or link variables in the variables store from one script to another. Thus, different scripts can be created and applied to the same data. Unlike running algorithms in a typical MOP framework all variables remain present after the script has finished executing. These variables might then be stored together with the script code.

The language that is available for scripting as of version 3.3.10 is C#, which is natural for those familiar with the HeuristicLab API. Furthermore, a script type based on the Python programming language, which is popular among scientists, is under development and will be part of a future release. It is certainly desirable to include more script types with further languages, however the limitation is that all of these languages need to be compiled to or interpreted in the Microsoft Intermediate Language (MSIL) of the .NET Framework. We take a look at some options in Section 3.

C#-based Scripting

The class diagram that supports creating C# scripts is shown in Figure 2. The code is dynamically compiled to a class which derives from *CSharpScriptBase*. When the script is to be run, an object is instantiated, the variable store is passed to the instance, wrapped inside *Variables* and the *Main()* method of the *CSharpScript* is called.

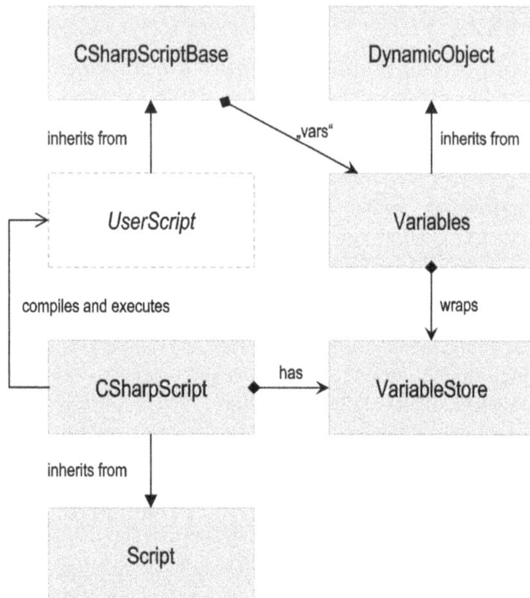

Figure 2: Two main classes provide scripting support: *Script* is the "design-time" class that contains the code, its subclass *CSharpScript* additionally contains the *VariableStore*, while *CSharpScriptBase* is the "run-time" class from which the compiled script derives.

Script Code

The code in a HeuristicLab script is presented as a simple string object. This object is updated through a code editor window that is based on SharpDevelop 3[4]. The editor features syntax highlighting and code completion for C# which are very valuable functions when developing scripts.

When the script is run it is compiled through the use of the *Microsoft.CSharp.CSharpCodeProvider* and further classes in the *System.CodeDom* namespace. Compile errors will be listed in a separate tab together with line and column number, and the compile error message. The script is executed in a separate thread which can be aborted in the case the user wants to prematurely terminate the script. When the user presses the stop button, the common language runtime

[2]`http://www.tik.ee.ethz.ch/sop/pisa/`

[3]`http://simulationresearch.lbl.gov/GO/`

[4]`http://www.icsharpcode.net/opensource/sd/`

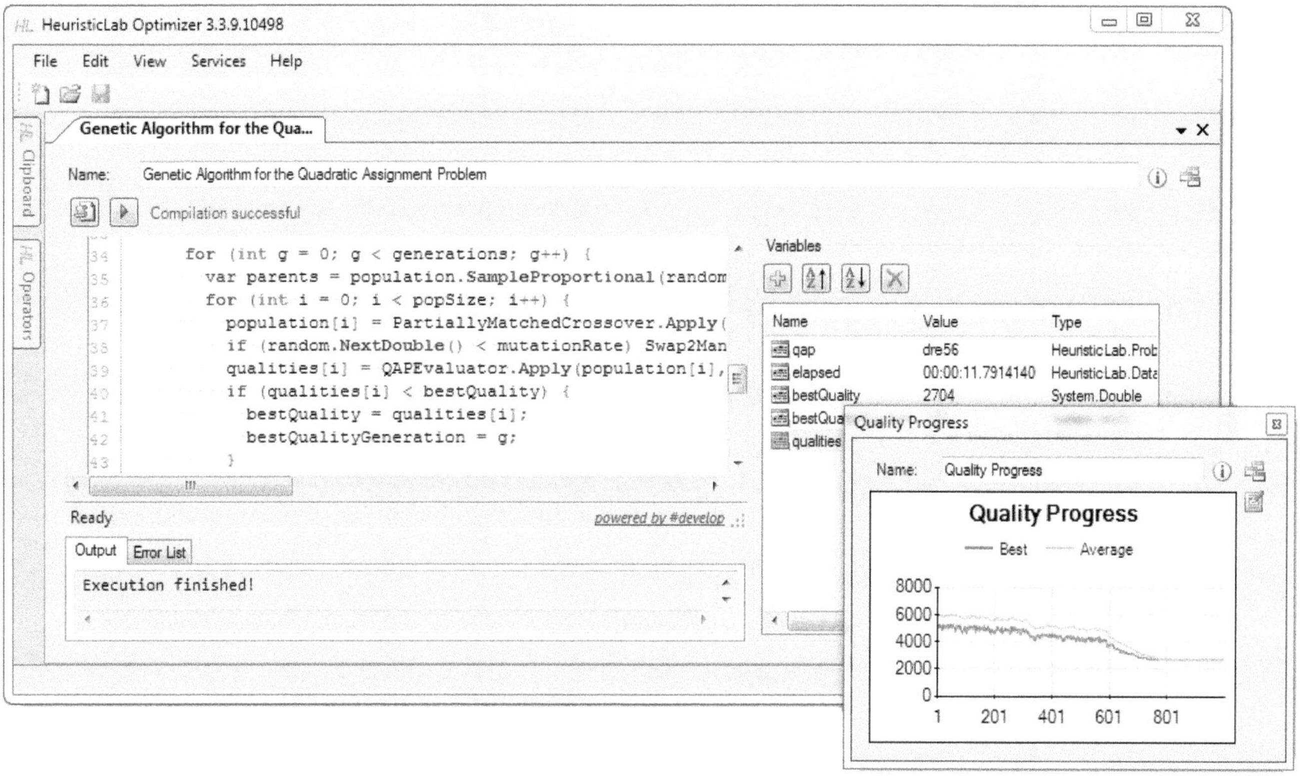

Figure 1: Screenshot of a C# script that executes a genetic algorithm on an instance of the quadratic assignment problem. The quality progress chart is shown in a separate window in the lower right.

throws a *ThreadAbortException*. Scripts can catch this exception in critical parts of the script in order to terminate gracefully, but care should be taken in order to terminate quickly. There is no method to force a thread to abort, a hanging thread can therefore only be stopped if the whole environment is restarted.

Variable Store

The variable store makes use of the dynamic language runtime (DLR) introduced in the Microsoft .NET Framework 4.0. This greatly facilitates access to variables as they can be defined by simply assigning a value to a name. In the background the variable store will create a new or overwrite an existing entry in a dictionary. The variable store can be accessed in scripts through the field *vars*. For instance, if the user writes `vars.x = 1`, a new variable x will be created in the store or if it already exists the value of x will be overwritten. The store displays the value of each variable as returned by the *ToString()* method.

Each variable has to have a unique name and a certain value. The value can be anything from primitive types such as int, double, DateTime, etc. to complex types such as DataTable or problem instances. Since basically any .NET object can be added as a variable, a problem with the serialization mechanism emerges. Any item in HeuristicLab and many .NET items can be written to a file, however instances of e.g. a Thread class cannot be serialized. Thus the variable store will indicate if it contains types which may not be serialized by an error icon next to the variable.

The variable store allows drag and drop behavior, so that an item in HeuristicLab can be dragged onto the variable store. The user could thus configure a problem instance in the GUI, drag it into the variable store and execute the script. When using drag and drop the user is given the option to name that variable, otherwise a default name is chosen.

If there is a default view for an item present in the variable store, that variable can be double clicked and the respective view for the value will open. Any changes made in that view will be applied to the variable's value. Items for which there is no view, ie. int, double, etc. cannot be changed in the GUI. However HeuristicLab has wrappers for these types such as IntValue or DoubleValue which may be viewed and edited [11].

Console Output

Scripts that need to output information to a console can write to the Console property. Although this property doesn't have the same functionality as the corresponding *System.Console*, it shares the write methods. We wanted to make it very similar so that existing pieces of code that should be run inside HeuristicLab can be quickly adapted. The console however does not feature input, therefore it is not possible to write interactive scripts.

Python-based Scripting

The *Python Script* in HeuristicLab is very similar to the C# script described above in that the variable store and the classes for handling console output are reused. The only difference is that the code is not compiled using .NET's CodeDom features, but executed with the help of the Iron-

Python[5] project. When the script is executed a *PyEngine* is instantiated. All HeuristicLab plugins are loaded into the engine and a *PyScope* is created which contains the variable store as variable *vars*. Thus, the access to the variable store is completely identical to the C# script. The user writes code which writes to or reads from *vars* or with the help of local variables that do not leave the PyScope. Console output redirection is achieved by adding an event handler to the engine's output *PyConsoleStream*. This raises another event of the *PythonScript* class to which the *PythonScriptView* listens. Python support via IronPython is added to HeuristicLab through a plugin which makes this feature generally available within the environment. The integration need not be performed for each script separately.

```
from System import *
from System.Linq import *
from HeuristicLab.Encodings.PermutationEncoding import *
from HeuristicLab.Problems.QuadraticAssignment import *
from HeuristicLab.Random import *

if not vars.Contains("qap"):
  print "qap is not defined!"

# Variables
N = vars.qap.Weights.Rows
w = vars.qap.Weights
d = vars.qap.Distances
popSize = 100
maxGen = 10000
mutRate = 0.05
rng = MersenneTwister()
start = DateTime.UtcNow
bestQuality = Double.MaxValue
bestQualityGeneration = 0
bestSolution = None

# Population Initialization
pop = [Permutation(PermutationTypes.Absolute, N, rng)] * popSize
qual = []
for i in range(0, popSize):
  qual.append(QAPEvaluator.Apply(pop[i], w, d))
  if qual[i] < bestQuality:
    bestQuality = qual[i]
    bestSolution = pop[i]

# Main Loop
for g in range(0, maxGen):
  par = Enumerable.ToArray(RandomEnumerable.SampleProportional(
    pop, rng, 2 * popSize, qual, True, True))
  for i in range(0, popSize):
    pop[i] = PartiallyMatchedCrossover.Apply(
      rng, par[i*2], par[i*2+1])
    if rng.NextDouble() < mutRate:
      Swap2Manipulator.Apply(rng, pop[i])
    qual[i] = QAPEvaluator.Apply(pop[i], w, d)
    if qual[i] < bestQuality:
      bestQuality = qual[i]
      bestQualityGeneration = g
      bestSolution = pop[i]

# Display Results
vars.elapsed = DateTime.UtcNow - start
vars.bestQuality = bestQuality
vars.bestQualityGeneration = bestQualityGeneration
vars.bestSolution = bestSolution
```

Figure 3: Genetic algorithm sample that solves a quadratic assignment problem written in Python and using the .NET and HeuristicLab API.

[5]http://ironpython.net/

3. FRAMEWORK REVIEW AND INTEGRATION

In a well-received survey on evolutionary computation frameworks ten different MOP frameworks are compared [8]. A large number of features are being analyzed in that study and an extensive comparison is being performed. Apart from the differences between frameworks, it is also obvious that many frameworks share features and algorithms are implemented many times anew. It is certainly understandable that an algorithm that is adapted to the peculiarities of a certain framework is easier to use and can make use of all the features, but at the same time we have to raise the question if it would not be possible to reuse features of one framework in another. We think that a promising future direction, at least for the HeuristicLab environment, would be the integration of different frameworks and to provide a development environment in which it is possible to run and experiment with algorithms of various frameworks. In this section we want to review and evaluate two frameworks, namely the Python-based DEAP[5] framework and the Java-based jMetal[4] framework. Both frameworks are licensed under the LGPL enabling an integration in HeuristicLab which is licensed under GPLv3.

Benefits of Framework Integration

The integration of frameworks is especially helpful when considering the need for comparison of different methods with each other. Methods that are implemented in a certain framework will have to be reimplemented in another framework for comparison purposes. Often this process takes a lot of time and is subject to certain coding standards enforced by the framework. This creates a barrier for comparing against a range of alternatives. Often the experimenting API and statistical evaluation of the results differs from framework to framework which makes it an arduous task to compare methods of different frameworks. There have been attempts at unifying parameterization of experiments [3], however this approach requires that the individual frameworks agree to a common description. So far, it has been difficult to enforce a standard in this context. In contrast, if the algorithms can be started and their results can be queried from a single framework, then the experiment analysis can also be unified in that framework. For instance, in HeuristicLab, each run of an optimization algorithm is stored in a *Run* object that contains dictionaries for the parameters and the results. It is possible to script the execution of an algorithm from a different framework, but generate and then compare those Run objects as results. Additionally, if the script produces the set of experiments that are calculated, this script can be shared together with the publication and the results can be reproduced by a reviewer.

DEAP

DEAP[6] 1.0.0, which was released in February 2014, is a relatively young framework developed at the Computer Vision and Systems Laboratory (CVSL) in the Faculty of Science and Engineering at Laval University, Québec, Canada. The first tag in the source tree dates back to 2010. It is implemented in Python which makes it attractive for prototyping new ideas as the IPython shell also provides a run-time environment. DEAP includes several algorithms such as genetic

[6]http://code.google.com/p/deap/

algorithms with arbitrary representations, genetic programming, evolution strategies, multi-objective algorithms such as NSGA-II[2] and SPEA2[12], co-evolution approaches, and many others.

jMetal

The jMetal 4.5 framework[7], which was releaed in January 2014, is implemented by Antonio J. Nebro and Juan J. Durillo from the Universidad Málaga. The framework is a bit more mature in that developments already started in 2004. It is a framework written in Java and which is especially targeted for solving multi-objective optimization problems. It includes a very large range of multi-objective algorithms which include NSGA-II variants, SPEA2, PAES[6], AbYSS[7], and many other algorithms. There are also a number of multi-objective problems implemented with and without constraints that are often used in testing as well as multi-objective quality indicators such as hypervolume metric, spread and generational distance. jMetal also features single-objective algorithms and problems such as genetic algorithms, evolution strategies, and many more.

We think that these, as well as many other frameworks are well suited for conducting research as they are created and maintained by researchers with a high visibility in the field of evolutionary computation. We think that new developments can be sparked in an attempt to bring these frameworks together. That is, we aim to provide the possibility to use the API of other metaheuristic frameworks from within the HeuristicLab optimization environment.

A major problem that we have to overcome in this goal is to cross the "language barrier". As described in [8], HeuristicLab is the only framework that is based on the .NET Framework. From the other considered frameworks in their study three are written in C++ and six frameworks are written in Java. This means that we cannot directly reference other frameworks and include them in a HeuristicLab plugin. However, a number of projects exist which make it easier to integrate different languages.

Dynamic Language Runtime

Microsoft laid the foundation for the integration of dynamically typed languages with the .NET Framework 4.0 and the inclusion of the dynamic language runtime (DLR). The DLR and the included hosting infrastructure is the base of the IronPython project. IronPython is an implementation of Python 2.7 for the .NET framework. IronPython was initially started and developed at Microsoft, but has been released to the public and is maintained by volunteers. The developments for IronPython 3 have started only recently. IronPython is available under the Apache 2.0 license which is compatible to the GPLv3 license.

Integration of the DEAP framework can be achieved by creating a transport plugin for the IronPython assemblies as well as the Microsoft.Scripting and Microsoft.Dynamic assemblies. When creating a python script the path to DEAP and the path to the IronPython *Libs* directory have to be added to the list of search paths before importing DEAP modules and running DEAP examples. Of course it is also possible to use the PythonEngine in a C# script to execute Python code. Data exchange between the Python code and the C# part can be achieved through the *PyScope* object which represents the global scope of the Python script and which can be read after executing the *PyEngine*.

We also encountered some problems in using these projects to integrate different frameworks. Using the famous Python libraries NumPy[8] and SciPy[9] in IronPython is rather experimental. We encountered several problems when trying to run DEAP algorithms that depend on NumPy using a .NET port of NumPy.

.NET Java Virtual Machine

A further project that is of high interest for our goals is the IKVM[10] project which is an implementation of Java for the .NET Framework. IKVM provides the ability to convert Java class and jar files to .NET assemblies. These assemblies then reference a port of OpenJDK to the .NET Framework which provides the Java API. IKVM allows both .NET developers to use Java classes and Java developers to use .NET classes. However, Java developers that seek to link against .NET assemblies first have to create stub classes against which Java can compile against. IKVM however does not provide a Java compiler, so e.g. Oracle's Java SDK has to be used. IKVM is public software that is free to use and free to modify. OpenJDK is licensed under GPL and LGPL.

Integration of jMetal could be achieved using IKVM. First we created a .NET assembly using the ikvm compiler *ikvmc*. We excluded classes with external references and which were not necessary for programming against the framework such as the NUnit tests. Then we created a transport plugin for the IKVM and OpenJDK assemblies and also for the generated jMetal assembly. This plugin is available as an add-on[11] to the HeuristicLab development trunk and may be part of a future release. It shall be noted that this enables users only to program against the API of jMetal. The algorithms in jMetal are not available as HeuristicLab algorithms so far. This would require a much deeper integration which is beyond the scope of this article.

C and C++

The integration of C code is generally possible in C# by using platform invoke (PInvoke). Methods of C DLLs can be called by defining those methods in C# as *extern* and attributing them with *DLLImport*. This requires that the method signature given in C# is the same as in the DLL. However, PInvoke cannot be used to marshal native C++ classes and also the use of PInvoke is not without dangers. We have experienced, that an exception inside a native function cannot be catched in managed code and the whole environment crashes immediately and without error notification.

To make native C++ code available within HeuristicLab one would need to write a managed C++ wrapper class for all the native classes. The managed C++ DLL could then be referenced in a C# project, i.e. a HeuristicLab plugin. Another option would be to create *extern "C"* wrapper functions for creating and destroying objects and all of its public methods. An excellent article is available on codeproject[12]. Of course this is much more effort than the approaches stated

[7] `http://jmetal.sourceforge.net/`

[8] `http://www.numpy.org/`

[9] `http://www.scipy.org/`

[10] `http://www.ikvm.net/`

[11] `http://dev.heuristiclab.com/trac/hl/core/browser/branches/jMetal`

[12] `http://www.codeproject.com/Articles/18032/How-to-Marshal-a-C-Class`

```
ManualResetEvent mutex = new ManualResetEvent(false);

public override void Main() {
  var ga = new GeneticAlgorithm();
  ga.MaximumGenerations.Value = 50;
  ga.PopulationSize.Value = 10;
  ga.Problem = new TravelingSalesmanProblem();

  var experiment = new Experiment();
  for (int i = 0; i < 5; i++) {
    experiment.Optimizers.Add(new BatchRun() {
    Optimizer = (IOptimizer)ga.Clone(),
    Repetitions = 10 });
    ga.PopulationSize.Value *= 2;
  }

  experiment.ExecutionStateChanged += OnStateChanged;
  experiment.Start();
  mutex.WaitOne();
  MainFormManager.MainForm.ShowContent(experiment);
  MainFormManager.MainForm.ShowContent(experiment.Runs,
    typeof(RunCollectionTableView));
}

private void OnStateChanged(object sender, EventArgs e) {
  if (((IExecutable)sender).ExecutionState
    == ExecutionState.Stopped) mutex.Set();
}
```

Figure 4: Part of a script that shows GUI automation capabilities. It runs an experiment and displays the relevant results in a bubble chart.

above as the wrappers would need to be written for each framework anew.

Framework Design for Integration

In experimenting and evaluating the interplay of different frameworks we already noticed a few design decisions that make it difficult for frameworks to interoperate. In this section we want to state two specific points that are worth considering. The discussion may seem shallow, but an in-depth examination would require an article of its own. The aim here is to spark a discussion on framework design from the point of view of reuse in other frameworks.

Custom Data Types

The use of custom data types on the one hand eases manipulation in one framework, but is a stumbling block for the integration. Data has to be converted from one data type to the other which requires lengthy pieces of code and challenges run-time performance. In jMetal 4.5 the *Solution* class is a data type that links various parts of the framework such as the *Problem*, *SolutionType*, and *Variable* class. This class is often used in public interfaces of operators. Therefore in an integrated approach one would have to provide an additional implementation of, e.g. the problem, as extensions to jMetal objects. The public interfaces cannot be used unless the solution is reconstructed. In DEAP 1.0.0 there is a creator for dynamically creating classes which many algorithms use to create a class *Individual*. This individual is then the expected contract of many operators also impeding data reuse. In HeuristicLab there are also objects, but often they wrap a single simple datatype such as the *RealVector* or *DoubleMatrix*. Additionally, there are static methods in many places which provide a very simple API. In Figure 3 it can be seen that the problem variable *qap* only encapsulates the weights and distance matrices, but does not contain any logic. Proportional selection is implemented for 'IEnumerable' which is the base of arrays, lists, dictionaries, etc. However, there are also parts in HeuristicLab that still need to be improved. Historically, the objects in HeuristicLab have been designed around the operator paradigm. Some of these operators provide a static interface as well as an interface to the operator execution API, others lack a static API and therefore cannot be used as easily in a script. Recommendation: Create APIs that use the most basic data types available. Compose objects into classes, but decompose them before handing them to relevant functions. This enables better reuse of those functions in other frameworks.

Composition of Algorithms

Additionally, when integrating frameworks, extension by composition is probably the more promising approach than by inheritance. If a framework provides only an algorithm which implements most of the code in a single method it is difficult to inject code from other frameworks and alter or analyze the behavior. The more algorithms can be composed of modular parts of the framework, the more possibilities for combining parts from different frameworks. In DEAP 1.0.0 the algorithms are mostly combinations of simpler operations. The operations are implemented as methods and some of them provide more or less functionality. The methods are linked into operations through a toolbox which combines the method reference and several parameters into a partial function. In contrast in jMetal 4.5 and HeuristicLab 3.3.9 there is an *Algorithm* class that is used for representing algorithms. While the algorithms in jMetal are rather monolithic, the algorithms in HeuristicLab again are composed of smaller operators and can be adapted by modifying the operator graph. Still, it would currently be difficult to integrate a crossover of another framework into a HeuristicLab algorithm. In jMetal, most of the code is grouped within an *execute()* method which is not optimal with respect to code reuse. Recommendation: Use inheritance or sub-classing only when necessary. Instead of deep inheritance hierarchies it would be better to create a shallow layer of full-featured classes that can be extended through composition.

4. EXAMPLES

Not only can scripts be used to perform small tasks or prototype entire algorithms, scripts can also be used to open views and show them to the user. Figure 4 shows a script which creates a new experiment, runs it and displays the results in a table view.

Other kind of automated tasks, which do not require to use the MainForm API could be to load a set of files from a directory, perform some calculation and save that file again. This could be useful if a certain value should be calculated in a run, e.g. the parameter of exponential growth or decay in the quality progress chart. If the quality chart is contained within the run, but this value was not calculated, a script could be used to calculate it later on.

Figure 3 shows an example of a genetic algorithm written in Python that uses the HeuristicLab API to be applied to the quadratic assignment problem (QAP). The code calls static methods which perform the necessary operations for a genetic algorithm: selection, crossover, mutation, and evaluation. We also compared the run-time difference between the Python script and a C# script implementation of that

Table 1: **Time measured in seconds to run a genetic algorithm with 10,000 generations and a population size of 100 on different QAP instances.**

Problem Size	C# Script	Python Script	Difference
19	4.65	6.51	+40.0%
25	6.92	8.80	+27.2%
36	13.08	14.97	+14.4%
50	24.16	26.45	+9.5%
100	95.12	97.39	+2.4%
150	208.89	211.58	+1.3%

algorithm. The algorithm in Figure 3 was used in the given configuration and applied to problems of different sizes. It can be seen in Table 2 that the Python engine is a little bit slower, but as the problem dimension increases the difference vanishes. All performance tests in this article were conducted on an Intel Core i7 with 2.6 Ghz, the run-times are given in seconds and averaged over 10 executions.

Figure 5 shows an example of using the SPEA2 algorithm defined in the jMetal framework to solve a multi-objective test function problem. The algorithm is executed inside a C# script which will create a new run object after every execution. Again it is interesting to evaluate the performance when that algorithm is executed inside HeuristicLab, when it is executed using IKVM's Java Virtual Machine (JVM) and when using Oracle's JVM. We modified the algorithm given in Figure 5 and measured the time before *settings.configure()* and after *algorithm.execute()*.

Table 2 shows the results of this performance test. Interestingly, a fast way to execute the jMetal SPEA2 algorithm on the ZDT1 multi-objective test function is using the jMetal plugin in HeuristicLab and running it with a C# script. Using Oracle's JVM (version 1.7.0u55 and 1.8.0u5) is comparable to using the IKVM.NET virtual machine (version 7.2.4630.5).

Table 2: Time measured in seconds to execute the SPEA2 algorithm implementation in jMetal 4.5 on the ZDT1 problem using a maximum of 50,000 evaluated solutions.

PopSize	HeuristicLab	IKVM	JVM 1.7	JVM 1.8
100	6.20	6.82	6.67	6.55
500	8.66	9.32	9.34	9.25
1000	13.36	14.16	14.41	14.26

5. CONCLUSIONS

We have described the integration of scripting in HeuristicLab and have evaluated possibilities of integrating metaheuristic optimization frameworks in the HeuristicLab optimization environment which may be a highly interesting path for future development. The reuse of algorithms of different frameworks is still an experimental task which may raise many questions regarding a suitable design of those frameworks. Each framework itself is certainly a well-rounded package, but there is a big potential in combining the strengths of these frameworks in one environment. We have evaluated two frameworks that allow interoperation of C# with Python and Java so that algorithms implemented in these languages can be reused in HeuristicLab. We have further made two performance comparisons, which on the one hand show that for higher dimensional problems the performance difference between C# and Python becomes irrelevant and on the other hand show that compiling the jMetal library with IKVM.NET and running algorithms from a C# script in HeuristicLab is not a slow solution at all. This would make it a feasible option to do performance and results comparison in a common framework.

```
using System;
using System.Linq;
using HeuristicLab.Analysis;
using HeuristicLab.Common;
using jmetal.core;
using jmetal.experiments.settings;
using jmetal.qualityIndicator.fastHypervolume;

public class UserScript
  : HeuristicLab.Scripting.UserScriptBase {
  public override void Main() {
    var settings = new SPEA2_Settings("ZDT1");
    settings.maxEvaluations_ = 50000;
    settings.populationSize_ = 200;
    settings.crossoverProbability_ = 0.8;
    settings.mutationProbability_ = 0.1;
    var algorithm = settings.configure();
    var numObj = algorithm.getProblem().getNumberOfObjectives();
    var solutionSet = algorithm.execute();

    var solutionIterator = solutionSet.iterator();
    var front = new ScatterPlot();
    var row = new ScatterPlotDataRow();
    front.Rows.Add(row);

    while (solutionIterator.hasNext()) {
      var solution = (Solution)solutionIterator.next();
      var objectives = Enumerable.Range(0, numObj)
        .Select(x => solution.getObjective(x)).ToArray();
      row.Points.Add(
        new Point2D<double>(objectives[0], objectives[1]));
      Console.WriteLine(string.Join("; ", objectives));
    }
    vars.front = front;
    vars.HV = new FastHypervolume()
      .computeHypervolume(solutionSet);
  }
}
```

Figure 5: SPEA2 that solves the ZDT1 problem using both the jMetal and HeuristicLab API.

6. ACKNOWLEDGMENTS

The work described in this paper was done partly within the Josef Ressel Centre for Heuristic Optimization (*Heureka!*) sponsored by the Austrian Research Promotion Agency (FFG).

7. REFERENCES

[1] A. Beham, E. Pitzer, S. Wagner, M. Affenzeller, K. Altendorfer, T. Felberbauer, and M. Bäck. Integration of flexible interfaces in optimization software frameworks for simulation-based optimization. In *Companion Publication of the 2012 Genetic and Evolutionary Computation Conference, GECCO'12 Companion*, pages 125–132, Philadelphia, PA, USA, July 2012.

[2] K. Deb, A. Pratap, S. Agarwal, and T. Meyarivan. A fast and elitist multiobjective genetic algorithm: NSGA-II. *Evolutionary Computation, IEEE Transactions on*, 6(2):182–197, 2002.

[3] F. Dobslaw. Input: The intelligent parameter utilization tool. In *Companion Publication of the 2012 Genetic and Evolutionary Computation Conference, GECCO'12 Companion*, pages 149–156, Philadelphia, PA, USA, July 2012.

[4] J. J. Durillo and A. J. Nebro. jMetal: A java framework for multi-objective optimization. *Advances in Engineering Software*, 42:760–771, 2011.

[5] F.-A. Fortin, F.-M. De Rainville, M.-A. Gardner, M. Parizeau, and C. Gagné. DEAP: Evolutionary algorithms made easy. *Journal of Machine Learning Research*, 13:2171–2175, jul 2012.

[6] J. Knowles and D. Corne. The pareto archived evolution strategy: A new baseline algorithm for pareto multiobjective optimisation. In *Evolutionary Computation, 1999. CEC 99. Proceedings of the 1999 Congress on*, volume 1. IEEE, 1999.

[7] A. J. Nebro, F. Luna, E. Alba, B. Dorronsoro, J. J. Durillo, and A. Beham. Abyss: Adapting scatter search to multiobjective optimization. *Evolutionary Computation, IEEE Transactions on*, 12(4):439–457, 2008.

[8] J. A. Parejo, A. Ruiz-Cortés, S. Lozano, and P. Fernandez. Metaheuristic optimization frameworks: a survey and benchmarking. *Soft Computing*, 16(3):527–561, 2012.

[9] S. Voß and D. L. Woodruff. *Optimization software class libraries*. Springer, 2002.

[10] S. Wagner. *Heuristic Optimization Software Systems - Modeling of Heuristic Optimization Algorithms in the HeuristicLab Software Environment*. PhD thesis, Johannes Kepler University, Linz, Austria, 2009.

[11] S. Wagner, G. Kronberger, A. Beham, M. Kommenda, A. Scheibenpflug, E. Pitzer, S. Vonolfen, M. Kofler, S. Winkler, V. Dorfer, and M. Affenzeller. *Advanced Methods and Applications in Computational Intelligence*, volume 6 of *Topics in Intelligent Engineering and Informatics*, chapter Architecture and Design of the HeuristicLab Optimization Environment, pages 197–261. Springer, 2014.

[12] E. Zitzler, M. Laumanns, and L. Thiele. SPEA2: Improving the Strength Pareto Evolutionary Algorithm for Multiobjective Optimization. In K. Giannakoglou et al., editors, *Evolutionary Methods for Design, Optimisation and Control with Application to Industrial Problems (EUROGEN 2001)*, pages 95–100. International Center for Numerical Methods in Engineering (CIMNE), 2002.

Working with OpenCL to Speed Up a Genetic Programming Financial Forecasting Algorithm: Initial Results

James Brookhouse
School of Computing
University of Kent
Canterbury, UK
jb733@kent.ac.uk

Fernando E. B. Otero
School of Computing
University of Kent
Chatham Maritime, UK
F.E.B.Otero@kent.ac.uk

Michael Kampouridis
School of Computing
University of Kent
Chatham Maritime, UK
M.Kampouridis@kent.ac.uk

ABSTRACT

The genetic programming tool EDDIE has been shown to be a successful financial forecasting tool, however it has suffered from an increase in execution time as new features have been added. Speed is an important aspect in financial problems, especially in the field of algorithmic trading, where a delay in taking a decision could cost millions. To offset this performance loss, EDDIE has been modified to take advantage of multi-core CPUs and dedicated GPUs. This has been achieved by modifying the candidate solution evaluation to use an OpenCL kernel, allowing the parallel evaluation of solutions. Our computational results have shown improvements in the running time of EDDIE when the evaluation was delegated to the OpenCL kernel running on a multi-core CPU, with speed ups up to 21 times faster than the original EDDIE algorithm. While most previous works in the literature reported significantly improvements in performance when running an OpenCL kernel on a GPU device, we did not observe this in our results. Further investigation revealed that memory copying overheads and branching code in the kernel are potentially causes of the (under-)performance of the OpenCL kernel when running on the GPU device.

Categories and Subject Descriptors

I.2.8 [**Artificial Intelligence**]: Problem Solving, Control Methods, and Search—*Heuristic methods*

General Terms

Algorithms

Keywords

Genetic Programming, OpenCL, financial forecasting, GPU

1. INTRODUCTION

EDDIE is a Genetic Programming algorithm that makes predictions about potential opportunities in the stock market. Recently additional features have been added to EDDIE, which significantly further improved its predictive performance. However, these features also led to a greatly increased execution time [13, 11], making the algorithm impractical to run in big scale experiments.

Speed can be an important aspect in financial trading. For example, in the field of algorithmic trading, the trading orders take place electronically, by using pre-programmed trading strategies. Therefore, slow algorithms can have devastating effects on a traders' profitability, as other, faster, algorithms might place an important order first, and thus attract all financial gain.

Our aim in this paper to develop an EDDIE implementation that can take advantage of multi-core CPUs and GPUs providing EDDIE with a substantial performance increase. A number of routes could be taken to improve the execution time of EDDIE. GPUs have already been used to perform general purpose computing. Additionally, they have also been successfully used in the area of evolutionary algorithms. A number of different architectures exist for GPGPU including NVIDIA's CUDA and OpenCL. OpenCL has an advantage of working over a number of platforms including both CPUs and GPUs. For the purposes of this work, OpenCL was chosen, as it provides a platform agnostic view through a hardware abstraction, allowing programs to be developed that can run on different hardware with minimal changes.

The paper is structured in the following way: Section II will present the genetic programming tool EDDIE including a brief history. Section III will summarise relevant works that have been carried out in the field of GPUs. Section IV provides a description of the OpenCL implementation added to EDDIE. Finally in sections V and VI we will present our results and conclusions.

2. EDDIE

2.1 Description of the Algorithm

EDDIE is a Genetic Programming (GP) [14, 18] financial forecasting algorithm, which learns and extracts knowledge from a set of data. The question EDDIE tries to answer is 'will the price increase within the n following days by $r\%$?' The user first feeds the system with a set of past data; EDDIE then uses this data and through a GP process, it creates and evolves Genetic Decision Trees (GDTs), which make recommendations of buy (1) or not-to-buy (0).

The set of data used is composed of three parts: (i) daily closing price of a stock, (ii) a number of attributes, and (iii) signals. Stocks' daily closing prices can be obtained online on websites such as `http://finance.yahoo.com` and also from financial statistics databases like *Datastream*.[1] The attributes are indicators commonly

[1] Available at: `http://thomsonreuters.com/datastream-professional/`

GECCO'14, July 12–16, 2014, Vancouver, BC, Canada.

ACM 978-1-4503-2881-4/14/07 ...$15.00.
http://dx.doi.org/10.1145/2598394.2605689.

<Tree> ::= `If-Then-Else` <Condition> <Tree> <Tree> | Decision
<Condition> ::= <Condition> `AND` <Condition> |
<Condition> `OR` <Condition> |
`NOT` <Condition> |
<VarConstructor> <RelationOperation> Threshold
<VarConstructor> ::= MA period | TBR period | FLR period | Vol period
| M period | MMA period
<RelationOperation> ::= ">" | "<" | "="
Terminals:
MA, TBR, FLR, Vol, Mom, MomMA are function symbols
Period is an integer within a parameterized range, [MinP, MaxP]
Decision is an integer, Positive or Negative implemented
Threshold is a real number

Figure 1: The Backus Normal Form of EDDIE

used in technical analysis [6]; which indicators to use depends on the user and his belief of their relevance to the prediction. The technical indicators that are used in this work are: Moving Average (MA), Trade Break Out (TBR), Filter (FLR), Volatility (Vol), Momentum (M), and Momentum Moving Average (MMA).[2]

The signals are calculated by looking ahead of the closing price for a time horizon of n days, trying to detect if there is an increase of the price by $r\%$ [20]. In other words, the GP is trying to use some of the above indicators to forecast whether the daily closing price is going to increase by $r\%$ within the following n days.

After feeding the data to the system, EDDIE creates and evolves a population of GDTs. Figure 1 presents the Backus Normal Form (BNF) [4] (grammar) of EDDIE. As we can see, the root of the tree is an `If-Then-Else` statement. The first branch is either a boolean (testing whether a technical indicator is greater than/less than/equal to a value), or a logic operator (`AND`, `OR`, `NOT`), which can hold multiple boolean conditions. The `Then` and `Else` branches can be a new GDT, or a decision, to BUY or NOT-BUY (denoted by `1` and `0`, respectively).

A sample GDT of EDDIE is presented in Figure 2. As we can see, if the *2 days MMA* is greater than *127.994* and the *17 days M* is less than *152.158*, then the user is advised to not-buy; otherwise, the user is advised to buy.

Depending on the classification of the predictions, we can have four cases: True Positive (TP), False Positive (FP), True Negative (TN), and False Negative (FN). As a result, we can use the metrics presented in Equations 1, 2 and 3:

Rate of Correctness

$$RC = \frac{TP + TN}{TP + TN + FP + FN} \tag{1}$$

Rate of Missing Chances

$$RMC = \frac{FN}{FN + TP} \tag{2}$$

Rate of Failure

$$RF = \frac{FP}{FP + TP} \tag{3}$$

[2]We use these indicators because they have been proved to be quite useful in developing GDTs in previous works like [16], [1] and [3]. Of course, there is no reason not to use other information like fundamentals or limit order book. However, the aim of this work is not to find the ultimate indicators for financial forecasting.

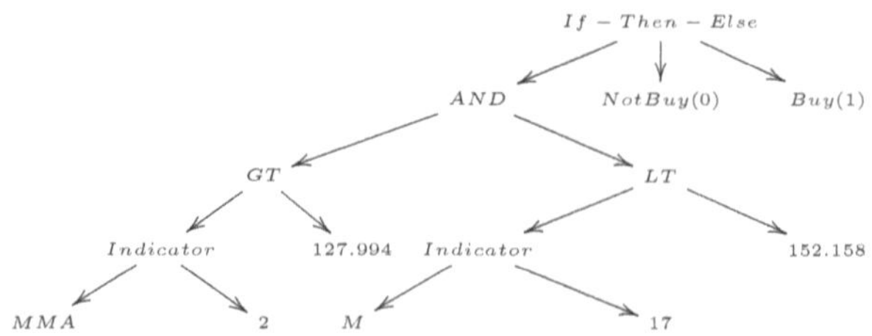

Figure 2: A sample EDDIE Tree generated by executing EDDIE, when it is executed the first branch of the If-Then-Else statement, if it evaluates true then the first branch is taken and it then follows that a false evaluation will take the second branch.

The above metrics combined give the following fitness function, presented in Equation 4:

$$ff = w_1 * RC - w_2 * RMC - w_3 * RF \tag{4}$$

where w_1, w_2 and w_3 are the weights for RC, RMC and RF respectively. These weights are given in order to reflect the preferences of investors. For instance, a conservative investor would want to avoid failure; thus a higher weight for RF should be used.

2.2 Brief History

EDDIE was originally created from a horse prediction algorithm, which was then adapted to predict the stock markets [20]. One of the latest EDDIE versions is EDDIE 8. This version is the one presented in the previous section. The advantage of this version is that the algorithm is not constrained to pre-specified periods, as is usually the case in industry.[3] As a consequence, it is up to the GP and the evolutionary process to look for the optimal periods values from the period range provided. For instance, if this range is 2 to 65 days, then EDDIE can create Moving Averages with any of these periods, e.g., 20 days MA, 25 days MA, and so on.

However, while the above approach returned positive predictive results [13, 12], it also dramatically increased the search space of EDDIE. This then led the algorithm to occasionally miss good solutions, due to ineffective search. To address this issue, local search algorithms were applied to the period leaf nodes of the trees, by means of hyper-heuristic frameworks [10, 11]. These frameworks used a number of different hill climbers and mutators at every generation, and made marginal changes to the period leaf nodes of the trees of the population. As a result, the search became more effective, as more exploitation was taking place.

While the fitness of the trees produced by EDDIE further increased thanks to the hyper-heuristics, the execution time also increased dramatically. Initial EDDIE 8 versions would have average single run times of around 3 minutes. With the introduction of hyper-heuristics, however, this increased to 12 minutes per run [11].

[3]In the literature, the users of similar algorithms pre-specify certain periods that they consider useful. For instance, *20 days* MA, and *50 days* MA. The indicators (e.g., MA) together with their respective period (e.g., 20) are treated by the GP as a single leaf node. Thus, the numbers 20 and 50 cannot change during the evolutionary process. In our previous work [13, 12], we questioned this approach, because nobody can guarantee that, for instance, a 20 days MA is better than a 25 days MA. To address this issue, we created EDDIE, which is able to search in the space of technical indicators and their periods.

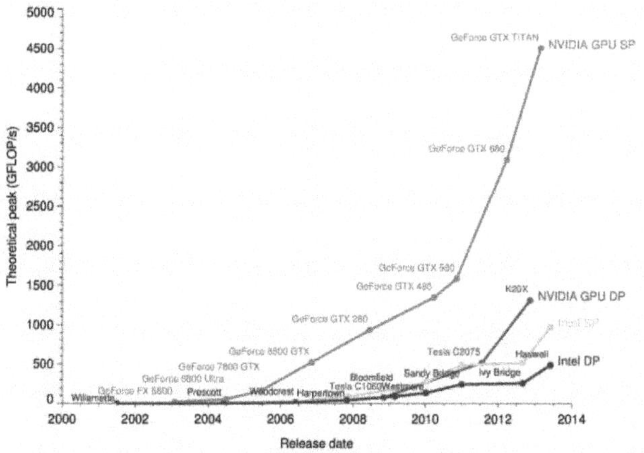

Figure 3: Comparison of NVIDIA graphics cards and Intel x86 CPUs in single and double precision floating point operations. Figure is reproduced from: http://hemprasad.wordpress.com/2013/07/18/cpu-vs-gpu-performance/.

As we can observe, the addition of the hyper heuristic framework slowed EDDIE down significantly. This was because of the increased number of fitness evaluations that were taking place. Effectively, every time a marginal change would take place in a leaf node of a tree, the fitness would have to be re-calculated and compared to the old one. Since this was taking place multiple times per generation (in addition to the typical GP fitness evaluations) the execution time was affected, slowing down the algorithm. This thus led us to consider ways of parallelising the process, especially since the additional computational times were due to the same process (i.e., fitness evaluation) happening multiple times.

3. RELATED WORK

The performance of GPUs has massively increased in recent years. Floating point performance of GPUs is now an order of magnitude higher than those found in high-end CPUs. Figure 3 shows that while CPU performance has increased over the last 10 years to 150 GFlops/second, GPUs now operate at over 4000 GFlops/second, illustrating how powerful GPUs have become when compared to CPUs.

This performance has been utilised in many computational intelligence applications, including neural networks and ant colony optimisation algorithms [15]. Delevacq et al [5] created a solution that used GPUs to speed up an ant colony optimisation algorithm. This was accomplished by deploying parallel ants in two separate modes: one where each ant has its own stream processor; the second gives each ant a block (group of stream processors). The first strategy has the advantage of allowing a huge number of ants to be evaluated at the same time. The second strategy allows the evaluation of each ant to take advantage of parallelism in finding the optimum path. Speed ups of between 5 and 15 times are observed, with a greater improvement seen when using the second strategy [5].

Moving on to parallelism in genetic programming application, Langdon [15] describes a method of using stacks and RPN (Reverse Polish Notation) to create a stack based SIMD (Single Instruction, Multiple Data) interpreter, which will leave the results on the top of the stack at the end. This method does require the tree to be stored in an appropriate format or converted to one [15].

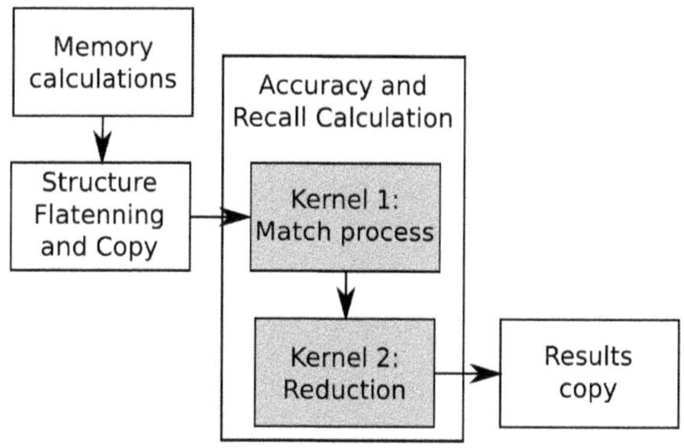

Figure 4: The process involves flattening and copying data from host to GPU, then the evaluation can be performed. The second kernel is required to reduce the amount of data returned from the kernel. Finally the data is copied back to the host platform. Figure is reproduced from [7].

An alternative approach to an interpretor is to compile each tree, since historically interpreter based platforms in computer science are regarded to be slower than compiled solutions. This is due to the benefits gained when the compiled code is run many times. However, as the programs created by a Genetic Programming tool are only evaluated a few times, interpreted based methods are usually faster due to compilation overhead [15].

Franco et al. [7] have implemented a GPU based fitness evaluation for the BioHEL evolutionary learning system. The implementation uses the CUDA platform with a two stage kernel solution. Figure 4 shows the stages of the fitness evaluation [7]. First, memory requirements are calculated to ensure all data will fit on the GPU or if multiple evaluations are required. The structure is then flattened to become compatible with GPUs. Flattening is the process of converting data structures from a many dimensional structure such as a tree or 2+ dimensional array into a one dimensional array. This is important as GPUs will only accept one dimensional arrays as kernel arguments. The data is then copied on to the GPU, where two kernels are executed: the first is to calculate the fitness function; the second is to reduce the amount of data that is read back from the GPU. The results are then read back to the host platform.

Franco et al. [7] achieved very large speed ups in their implementation, with a maximum speed up of 52.4x when compared to the original speed ups. This was achieved when the testing data was between 25,000 and 50,000. It is hypothesized that for values lower than 25,000, the serial method can keep all of the data in its fast cache, while the peak in performance and drop off over 50,000 may be due to the transfer of larger amounts of data.

It was also found that experiments that contained more decisions were slowed down compared to those that were linear. This is to be expected as the SIMD architecture of GPUs is heavily penalised by divergent code, where many threads may be idling when the other branches are being evaluated [7].

Data transfer times are a key overhead that occurs when attempting to use GPUs. This has also been discussed by Franco et al. [7], who executed an additional kernel that would reduce the data that was sent back to the host device. This is a known issue and as such, NVIDIA have released plans for reduction algorithms that have a higher bandwidth than the PCI Express bus, allowing a more efficient kernel to be utilised [8].

While early attempts to use GPUs mainly used NVIDIA's CUDA platform, successful implementations using the OpenCL platform do exist. Augusto and Barbosa achieved this with GPOCL [2]. The implementation was built from scratch with the intention to use OpenCL. This enabled the authors to implement a linear prefix stack based structure which is inherently suitable to evaluation using OpenCL. This allows the flattening stage seen in [7] to be avoided; instead, an interpretor-based kernel could then be used to evaluate the genetic programming programs. GPOCL achieved impressive results, where a 12-core Intel Xeon can evaluate 1.590 Billion GPop/s while a Nvidia GTX-285 achieved 10.75 billion GPop/s, representing a speed up of over 5 times.

Augusto and Barbosa [2] investigated optimisation techniques that can be applied to OpenCL programs. These include various memory optimisations, such as the use of constant memory where the GPU can detect and optimise multiple reads to the same memory location. Local memory usage is very fast and can be shared across all process elements. GPOCL caches genetic programming programs prior to execution and performs a reduction inside the local memory before copying the result back to global memory. Native function usage can also increase performance. OpenCL provides a number of mathematical functions in three flavours, IEEE-754 float, IEEE-754 half float and native. While the native functions can violate the IEEE standard, they do provide increased performance [2].

The previous literature identifies the fitness calculation performed by genetic programming algorithms as the most computationally expensive. This operation requires many calculations on different data independently,. For the reasons listed above a parallel approach becomes obvious. For these reasons it is the first part that is normally implemented on a GPU [15].

Pusniakowski and Bednarczyk [19] proposed an implementation that executes the entire genetic algorithm on the GPU using the OpenCL platform. The algorithm has been split into a number of different kernels, which are then called in the appropriate order. The first kernel called will create the initial population. As has been discussed earlier, the fitness function will be calculated in a second kernel. This kernel uses private memory so it can take advantage of the increased performance of this fast memory.

One difference between this implementation than those discussed previously is the parallelism of the genetic operations. The authors implemented two algorithms: the roulette wheel which is a fitness weighted method; and tournament selection, which takes n individuals (where n is equal to two or greater) and uses the fitness to determine the winner. While both implementations were effective and gave reasonable gains, it was found that the roulette wheel operation was much less efficient, taking considerably longer to produce very fit populations.

4. OPENCL IMPLEMENTATION

Previous work identifies that the biggest gains are found when using an OpenCL or CUDA platform to calculate the fitness function, since many solutions' fitnesses can be calculated in parallel. Given that EDDIE calls the fitness function many times, an straightforward OpenCL-enabled implementation will simply replace these multiple calls by a singe call to the OpenCL kernel.

The OpenCL enhancement in EDDIE can be split into a sequence of steps: the first is the process of flattening of trees from an object-orientated tree to a flatter GPU friendly structure; the second step is the OpenCL environment preparation; and the third is the fitness evaluation (kernel) that needs to be queued ready for execution on the OpenCL device. The OpenCL kernel can then be executed before the results are read back from the OpenCL device and analysed to produce a fitness for each tree.

4.1 Tree Flattening Into Byte Arrays

Before trees can be executed on the OpenCL device, they need to be prepared into a data structure that can be used in an OpenCL environment. OpenCL can only use a limited set of data structures as inputs due to its ability to run on a number of different hardware architectures. The flattening process must be quick to ensure that the speed improvements gained by executing the fitness function on the device are not wasted at this stage.

The Java API provides a `ByteBuffer` data structure in the `java.nio` package [17]. This data structure allows the construction of arrays containing multiple data types, as longer primitives are split into bytes and their bit representations are then written to the array. This also allows the programmer to retrieve the values stored in the array as long as they know the underlying data structure. The advantage of a byte buffer is the decreased size of the flattened data structure. This decreases the overall memory size required to store the GP population, which in turn decreases the time taken to transfer the population to the OpenCL device.

The tree-based structure used by EDDIE can be split into nodes, which are based around a boolean test. The test takes two arguments, an indicator and a constant. The result of this test will then determine the next action to be taken. In the array structure this will involve jumping to a new location (a new index in the array) in the `ByteBuffer`. Jump can either be positive, when the test evaluates to true, and negative, when the test evaluates to false.

The general node layout is shown in Table 1. All jumps in the byte array are absolute jumps expressed in the number of bytes since the beginning of the array. Figure 5 shows an example EDDIE tree and the corresponding nodes stored in the byte array (each line of the table in Figure 5 corresponds to a node). The total size of the array for this tree is 48 bytes (4 times the size of a single node), where the size using a float array would have been 96 bytes. Therefore, the trees produced using a byte array are half the size of the float array. Another advantage of using a byte array is that integer constants do not have to be converted to floats and then back again to integers in the OpenCL kernel.

4.1.1 NOT operator

An interesting problem found when flattening trees was the NOT operator. The first idea to deal with this involved flipping the positive / negative jumps of the associated operators. This 'jump flipping' ensured that a true test evaluation resolves to the false branch while a false evaluation will jump to the positive branch, mimicking the flip created by a NOT operator. While this worked for most cases, it produced incorrect trees in cases involving nested NOT operators.

A solution was finally found when NOTs were 'pushed' down the tree until they reached a comparison function. If an AND or OR function is encountered, the rules of logical equivalence found in Equations 5 and 6 allow the NOT operator to be pushed through the function descending down the tree further. This solution successfully works for all trees that contain the NOT operator.

$$\neg(A \vee B) = \neg A \wedge \neg B \tag{5}$$

$$\neg(A \wedge B) = \neg A \vee \neg B \tag{6}$$

When the tree reaches a comparison operator they are changed from 'Less Than' to 'Greater Than or Equal To'; 'Greater Than'

Table 1: The general node structure along with brief description of each element used to convert trees into byte arrays. Each node takes a total of 12 bytes.

Type	Name	Description
short	- Indicator	Which Indicator to use
byte	- Period	Period of the chosen indicator
byte	- Operator	What Operation to perform
float	- Comparison	Comparison value for the operator
short	- Positive Jump	Where to go if operator evaluates true
short	- Negative Jump	Where to go if operator evaluates false
Total Size - 12 Bytes		

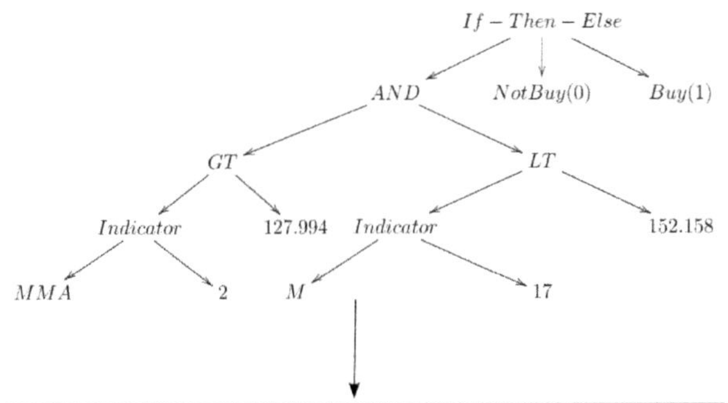

Indicator	Period	Operator	Comparison	+ive Jump	-ive Jump
MMA	2	Greater Than	127.994	12	36
M	17	Less Than	152.158	24	36
Not Buy (0)	-	-	-	-	-
Buy (1)	-	-	-	-	-

Figure 5: The representation of an EDDIE tree as nodes using the structure presented in Table 1.

becomes 'Less Than or Equal To.' Finally the third test 'Equal To' becomes 'Not Equal To.'; thus completing the NOT chain.

4.2 JOCL

Java OpenCL (JOCL) [9] is an open-source project which provides OpenCL bindings for Java. Since EDDIE was originally written in Java, the use of JOCL avoids the requirement to pass program parameters to a native program, which would require the use of either the Java Native Interface (JNI) or the Java Native Access (JNA). Therefore, to implement the OpenCL-enabled fitness evaluation in EDDIE we used the JOCL library - this extended EDDIE version is called EDDIE-JOCL.

There are two parts that makes up the OpenCL/JOCL implementation of any application: the host program and a kernel.

The host program creates the OpenCL device and deals with the scheduling and execution of kernel instances. It provides the bridge between the two architectures. The general process requires the selection and initialisation of an OpenCL device. Once an OpenCL device has been created you can then specify the data that is to be sent across and queue work items to be processed. After execution, data can then be retrieved from the OpenCL device.

The OpenCL kernel contains the code that will be executed on an OpenCL enabled device (CPU or GPU device). It generally consists of the internals of a *for loop*, which has been unravelled so that it can be executed in parallel. Each work unit on the OpenCL device has its own `id` which can be obtained with the following snippet of code:

```
int gid = get_global_id(0);
```

This allows each work unit to identify which bit of data it should be using in its execution. In EDDIE, this parameter is used to identify which day of the training or test data we want to evaluate.

Inside EDDIE's kernel, we have a struct that is overlaid onto the incoming tree to convert the bytes back into their original types. The struct displayed below corresponds to the OpenCL version of the same node structure in Table 1:

```
// node structure used to flatten
// the trees in EDDIE-JOCL
struct node {
    short indicator;
    char period;
    char operator;
    float comparison;
    short pos_jump;
    short neg_jump;
};
```

First the kernel places this node struct over the start of the byte array received by the kernel. It then evaluates the node and decides whether it should move to the position specified by positive jump or negative jump. The node is then repositioned and then the new node is evaluated. This process is shown in the following code:

```
// we will now decide whether we
// will true jump or false jump
int pos = eval(ind,
               node->operator,
               node->comparison);

if (pos == 0) {
    ptree = &tree[node->neg_jump];
} else if (pos == 1) {
    ptree = &tree[node->pos_jump];
} else { // catch evaluation error
    // insert error code
    fitnessValue[gid] = -1;
    return;
}

// move the position of the node
node = ptree;
```

The test is evaluated and then the code decides whether to use the positive or negative jump. We then reassign the void pointer `ptree` before then assigning its address as the next node to evaluate.[4]

This process will then continue until a BUY or NOT BUY node is reached. If malformed trees are introduced to the system, a potentially dangerous situation could occur where the OpenCL kernel could loop indefinitely. While a maximum iteration could be applied to the loop this would reduce performance as this comparison will have to be checked every loop. In this implementation no protection is provided against malformed trees, apart from the correctness of the tree flattening process, which ensure that maximum performance can be extracted from the OpenCL device.

[4]The complete OpenCL kernel used by EDDIE-JOCL can be found at `#pre-print version#`.

Table 2: The parameter values of EDDIE used in the experiments.

Experiment Parameter	Value
Stock names:	Aggreko – FTSE 100 stock GSK – FTSE 100 stock Lloyds – FTSE 100 stock
Maximum initial depth:	6
Maximum depth:	8
Primitive probability in Grow method:	0.6
Terminal node crossover bias:	0.1
Hill Climbing probability:	0.001
No of generations:	51
Population size:	*variable*
Tournament size:	2
Crossover probability:	0.9
Reproduction probability:	0.1
Mutation probability:	0.01
Elitism percentage:	0.01
[w1, w2, w3]:	[0.6, 0.1, 0.3]
Training Days:	1000
Testing Days:	300

Table 3: Summary of the experiments concerning the execution time in seconds (*average time* [*standard error*]).

Stock	Pop.	EDDIE	EDDIE-JOCL	
			CPU	GPU
Aggreko	50	84.1 [20.5]	4.0 [0.4]	109.7 [12.5]
	250	447.3 [84.2]	22.3 [1.9]	574.4 [52.9]
	500	885.3 [119.9]	47.3 [2.8]	1170.5 [102.9]
	750	1406.8 [186.5]	71.3 [3.1]	1743.9 [131.5]
	1000	1597.3 [201.1]	95.2 [6.1]	2474.4 [168.0]
GSK	50	81.7 [23.9]	4.5 [0.5]	95.8 [12.6]
	250	422.7 [91.4]	19.8 [3.7]	563.2 [60.7]
	500	1005.7 [145.1]	41.9 [3.0]	1208.3 [167.5]
	750	1498.3 [198.0]	73.0 [4.2]	1807.6 [143.8]
	1000	1617.0 [267.2]	98.2 [6.0]	2398.6 [232.8]
Lloyds	50	77.1 [18.3]	3.7 [0.5]	94.2 [11.3]
	250	457.7 [79.1]	23.1 [2.6]	611.4 [65.5]
	500	809.4 [124.0]	44.1 [3.0]	1386.1 [208.8]
	750	1451.6 [203.6]	84.8 [3.6]	1761.2 [173.8]
	1000	1603.0 [278.1]	103.3 [6.0]	2397.4 [221.4]

5. RESULTS

We evaluated the performance of the improved EDDIE-JOCL implementation against the original EDDIE, running on both the CPU and GPU. All performance tests were run on the following hardware:

CPU - Intel Core i7-3770K

RAM - 8GB DDR3

GPU - AMD 7970 (Tahiti XT)

OS - Ubuntu 12.10 x86-64

The parameter values of EDDIE used in the computational experiments are shown in Table 2. The only parameter that is changed during the experiments is the population size. To test the scalability of the improved EDDIE-JOCL, we used population sizes {50, 250, 500, 750, 1000}. We also tested both the CPU and GPU devices. While there are less work units—less parallel fitness evaluations by consequence—when using the CPU, there is no memory copy overhead, since both the host and OpenCL processes are using the main memory. By using the GPU, we can significantly increase the number of work units, but we also introduce a memory copy overhead to copy the data from the main memory to the GPU memory.

The computation results are summarised in Table 3 and presented graphically in Figure 6. Overall, large speeds up were obtained by the EDDIE-JOCL when running in the CPU—average speed up of 19 times across all 5 population sizes, with the maximum speed up seen being 21 times the original EDDIE implementation. It is also interesting to note that the execution times do not vary significantly across different datasets (stock data)—the nature of the data (daily closing prices) and the problem are the same.

As can be seen, the execution time of EDDIE-JOCL using the GPU was considerably slower than the CPU. This was unexpected as the large number of stream processors available in the GPU should have given it a significant advantage—the more work units, the more parallel fitness evaluations. To explore the reason behind this occurrence, the fitness evaluation times of both GPU and CPU execution were recorded. Figure 7 shows the time taken for each EDDIE variation to evaluate a single tree. A single run with a population size of 50 trees was used across all three versions and the same seed was also used to ensure that the same trees were evaluated every time. The trees were then sorted by length and the average times for each tree length was calculated. The slowest version is EDDIE-JOCL when running on the GPU, with a time approximately 30% slower than EDDIE; the faster is EDDIE-JOCL running on the CPU is over 6 times faster than EDDIE.

The evaluation times confirmed the previous results: EDDIE-JOCL running on the GPU is the slowest of all three versions. To further investigate what was causing the difference between the two EDDIE-JOCL versions, both the evaluation and kernel times were recorded for EDDIE-JOCL. These times are shown in Figures 8 and 9, respectively. They compare the average time taken to evaluate one tree including all overheads, such as OpenCL set-up times, memory transfer times when sending and receiving data from and to the OpenCL device. The kernel time corresponds to the time to execute the kernel. The difference between the two time measures corresponds to the overheads created by JOCL and the OpenCL environment.

It can be seen that when running on the CPU, the kernel time accounts for a large proportion of the total evaluation time, since there is no memory copy overhead. This is not the case on the GPU, where the kernel time corresponds to very small proportion of the total evaluation and the OpenCL overheads dominate.

5.1 Discussion

5.1.1 CPU speed ups

EDDIE-JOCL running on the CPU showed large speed ups between 21 and 16 times, depending on the population size, and an average of 19 over the five population sizes. This speed up is very significant as only four cores and eight threads are available to EDDIE-JOCL. If the both evaluation methods on EDDIE and EDDIE-JOCL were equally as efficient, then a maximum speed up of eight times would be expected. There must be another reason for the extra efficiency and we hypothesise that this extra efficiency is due to the change from an object orientated paradigm to a procedural paradigm.

The original evaluator found in EDDIE uses the `eval` method

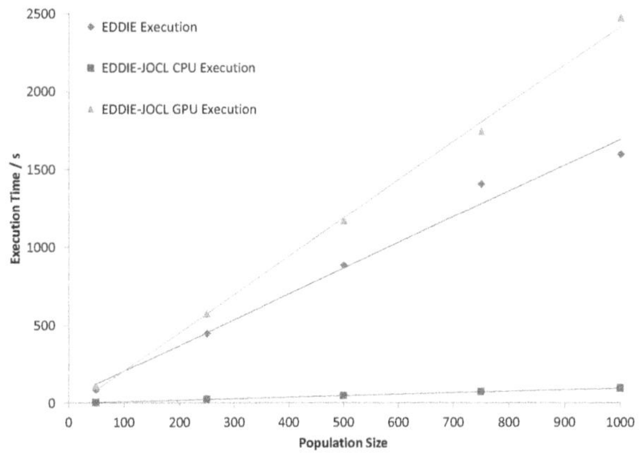

Figure 6: Execution times at five different population sizes for EDDIE and EDDIE-JOCL. Large speed ups are achieved when EDDIE-JOCL is using the CPU device—the maximum speed increase of 21 times over EDDIE was achieved at a population size 1000.

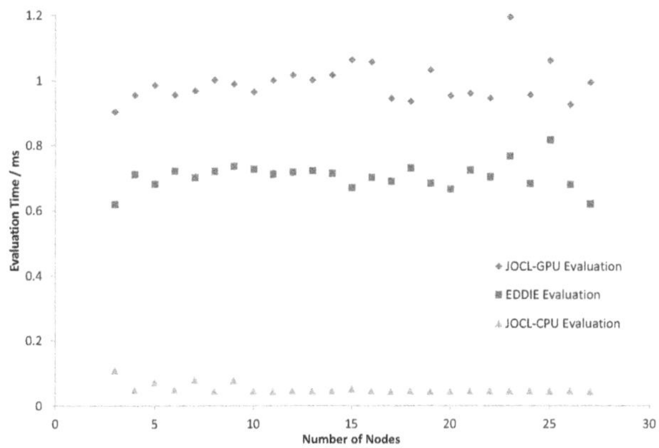

Figure 7: Evaluation times according to the number of nodes in the trees of the original EDDIE algorithm compared with EDDIE-JOCL running on both the CPU and GPU.

found inside every function that makes up a tree, following a object orientated paradigm. Therefore, to evaluate a tree, there is a need to traverse an object structure, which may incur method overheads when the program wants to move to the next object. In the EDDIE-JOCL implementation the trees are stored as arrays and the time to traverse an array is much faster than traversing an object structure

5.1.2 GPU (under-)performance

Despite the performance increases found when EDDIE-JOCL was run on the CPU, EDDIE-JOCL when running on the GPU proved to be slower than EDDIE, as can be seen in Figure 7. This was surprising as the highly parallel nature of the GPU architecture should have lent itself to speeding up the fitness function of EDDIE.

This result suggests that the losses are occurring as a result of OpenCL overheads. When running on the CPU, memory transfer overheads are not relevant as no memory copies are necessary—both host and OpenCL processes are using the main memory. But when running on the GPU, a memory copy does have to take place. This is confirmed by Figures 8 and 9, where the kernel times for

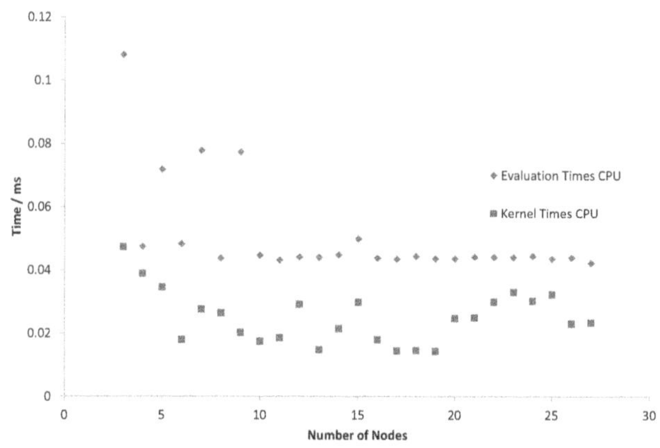

Figure 8: Evaluation and kernel times according to the number of nodes in the trees for EDDIE-JOCL when running on the CPU.

the CPU (Figure 8) are much closer to the total evaluation time. On the other hand, Figure 9 shows that the kernel times on the GPU are less than a tenth of the total evaluation time. The two configurations share the same code, so the only differences between the two is the memory transfer times, which seem to be very expensive in our case.

Looking only at the kernel times, the average kernel time on the CPU are 0.025ms whilst on the GPU they are 0.089ms. These differences could have a number of possible reasons. First, the cores contained on the CPU are much more complex than those found on the GPU. This, combined with the higher clock rate (1050Mhz on the GPU compared with 3500MHz on the CPU), allows the CPU to execute more instructions in the same time period. Secondly, the training data only contained 1000 samples, a small data size could cause some of the GPU stream processors (work units) to be under utilised.

Thirdly, the CPU does not subscribe to the SIMD (Single Instruction, Multiple Data) architecture, so is not penalised by branching code. In EDDIE, this occurs when the test results in each node evaluate differently for different elements in the testing data. On the CPU this is not a problem and all cores execute separately. However on the GPU, both positive and negative jumps on the node have to be evaluated sequentially and the stream processors waste cycles as they evaluate branches that are of no relevance to their calculation—the stream processors in the GPU must execute the same line of code. This was also noticed by Franco et al. in their implementation [7].

5.1.3 Possible improvements

The implementation discussed here could be further improved by changing the way the trees are dispatched to the OpenCL kernel. All the trees could be dispatched in one go. This is likely to decrease the transfer time as a single large block transfer would be quicker than many small transfers.

Once all the trees are on the OpenCL device there are two possible routes that could be taken to calculate the fitness function: the first is to let each stream processor calculate the entire fitness function of a single tree; the second is to parallelise both the trees and fitness function evaluation. This would require more logic in the kernel, as each instance would have to know which tree to evaluate along with the specific data that is to be used.

Finally a large amount of data is returned by the kernel, as the

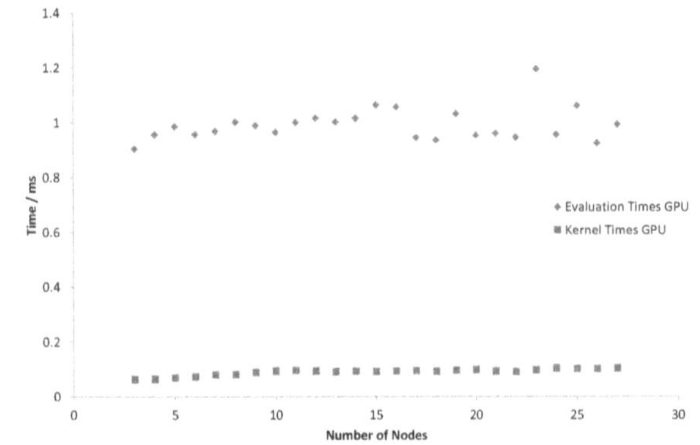

Figure 9: Evaluation and kernel times according to the number of nodes in the trees for EDDIE-JOCL when running on the GPU.

final fitness calculation is still calculated by EDDIE. A second kernel could be created to reduce this data into a single fitness value for each tree, which would then be returned, reducing the amount of memory that needs to be copied back.

6. CONCLUSION

In this paper we presented an extension to the financial forecasting algorithm EDDIE, called EDDIE-JOCL. As explained, speed is a very important aspect for financial forecasting algorithms, and can lead to significant increases in investors' profitability. Our goal thus in this paper was to improve EDDIE's computational performance by using an OpenCL kernel to evaluate candidate solutions. This allowed the parallel evaluation of solutions, both using multi-core CPUs and GPUs, by implementing the fitness function as an OpenCL kernel—following the assumption that the fitness evaluation is usually the expensive process in the GP run. EDDIE-JOCL achieved a maximum speed up of 21 times and an average of 19 times over the original EDDIE, when the OpenCL kernel was run in a multi-core CPU. Differently than previous results in the literature, running the kernel on a GPU device did not resulted in improvements over the CPU results. We identified the memory copy overheads from the main memory to the GPU memory and branching code (code that executes different instructions based on the input data) as potential causes of the somewhat unexpected (under-) performance of the GPU. As an overall observation, it seems that it is not guaranteed that by using GPUs, a performance increase will be achieved—specific refactorings to the code might be needed to fully use the potential of GPUs.

We have identified future improvements to better use the GPU resources and optimise memory copy overheads, which have the potential to lead to further performance gains. This include the copying of all candidate solutions (trees) in one operation, a more complex kernel that parallelises the evaluation of multiple trees and fitness cases and the use of a second kernel to compute the final fitness value of solutions.

7. REFERENCES

[1] F. Allen and R. Karjalainen. Using genetic algorithms to find technical trading rules. *Journal of Financial Economics*, 51:245–271, 1999.

[2] D. A. Augusto and H. J. Barbosa. Accelerated parallel genetic programming tree evaluation with OpenCL. *Journal of Parallel and Distributed Computing*, 73(1):86–100, 2013.

[3] M. Austin, G. Bates, M. Dempster, V. Leemans, and S. Williams. Adaptive systems for foreign exchange trading. *Quantitative Finance*, 4(4):37–45, 2004.

[4] J. Backus. The syntax and semantics of the proposed international algebraic language of Zurich. In *International Conference on Information Processing*, pages 125–132. UNESCO, 1959.

[5] A. Delévacq, P. Delisle, M. Gravel, and M. Krajecki. Parallel ant colony optimization on graphics processing units. *Journal of Parallel and Distributed Computing*, 73(1):52–61, 2013.

[6] R. Edwards and J. Magee. *Technical Analysis of Stock Trends*. Taylor & Francis, 1992.

[7] M. A. Franco, N. Krasnogor, and J. Bacardit. Speeding up the evaluation of evolutionary learning systems using GPGPUs. In *Proceedings of the 12th annual conference on Genetic and evolutionary computation*, pages 1039–1046. ACM, 2010.

[8] M. Harris. Optimizing parallel reduction in CUDA.

[9] M. Hutter. JOCL API documentation.

[10] M. Kampouridis. An initial investigation of choice function hyper-heuristics for the problem of financial forecasting. In *Evolutionary Computation (CEC), 2013 IEEE Congress on*, pages 2406–2413, 2013.

[11] M. Kampouridis, A. Alsheddy, and E. Tsang. On the investigation of hyper-heuristics on a financial forecasting problem. *Annals of Mathematics and Artificial Intelligence*, 2012. Accepted for Publication.

[12] M. Kampouridis and E. Tsang. EDDIE for investment opportunities forecasting: extending the search space of the GP. In *Evolutionary Computation (CEC), 2010 IEEE Congress on*, pages 1–8. IEEE, 2010.

[13] M. Kampouridis and E. Tsang. Investment Opportunities Forecasting: Extending the Grammar of a GP-based Tool. *International Journal of Computational Intelligence Systems*, 5(3):530–541, 2012.

[14] J. Koza. *Genetic Programming: On the programming of computers by means of natural selection*. Cambridge, MA: MIT Press, 1992.

[15] W. B. Langdon. Graphics processing units and genetic programming: an overview. *Soft Computing*, 15(8):1657–1669, 2011.

[16] S. Martinez-Jaramillo. *Artificial Financial Markets: An agent-based Approach to Reproduce Stylized Facts and to study the Red Queen Effect*. PhD thesis, CFFEA, University of Essex, 2007.

[17] Oracle. java.nio.bytebuffer API.

[18] R. Poli, W. Langdon, and N. McPhee. *A Field Guide to Genetic Programming*. Lulu.com, 2008.

[19] T. Puźniakowski and M. A. Bednarczyk. Towards an OpenCL implementation of genetic algorithms on gpus. pages 190–203, 2012.

[20] H. Wang and A. S. Weigend. Data mining for financial decision making. *Decision support systems*, 37(4):457–460, 2004.

Distributed Optimization on Super Computers: Case Study on Software Architecture Optimization Framework

Ramin Etemaadi
Leiden Institute of Advanced Computer Science
Faculty of Science, Leiden University
Leiden, the Netherlands
etemaadi@liacs.nl

Michel R.V. Chaudron
Dept. of Computer Science and Engineering
Chalmers University of Technology
Gothenburg, Sweden
chaudron@chalmers.se

ABSTRACT

Nowadays advanced software systems need to satisfy large number of quality attributes at the same time. It is a very complex optimization problem which software architects must address. Evolutionary algorithms can help architects to find optimal solutions which meet these conflicting quality attributes. However, these metaheuristic approaches in multiobjective problems especially for high dimensions mostly take so long time to be executed. One of the best solutions to speed up this process is distributing execution of evolutionary algorithm on multiple nodes of a super computer or on the cloud.

This paper presents the results of distributed execution of evolutionary algorithm for multiobjective optimization of software architecture. We report implementation of two different ways for distributed execution of evolutionary algorithm: (1) Actor-based approach, (2) MapReduce approach. The case study in this experiment is an industrial software system which is derived from a real world automotive embedded system.

The results of this computationally-intensive experiment on a super computer give us 81.27% parallelization efficiency for distribution among 5 nodes.

Categories and Subject Descriptors

D.2.7 [**Software Engineering**]: Distribution, Maintenance, and Enhancement; D.2.11 [**Software Engineering**]: Software Architectures; D.2.2 [**Software Engineering**]: Design Tools and Techniques

Keywords

Distributed Execution; MapReduce Paradigm; Actor-based Distribution; Metaheuristic Optimization; Evolutionary Multiobjective Optimization Algorithms (EMOA); Software Architecture Design Optimization; Component-Based Software Engineering (CBSE)

GECCO'14, July 12–16, 2014, Vancouver, BC, Canada.
Copyright 2014 ACM 978-1-4503-2881-4/14/07 ...$15.00.
http://dx.doi.org/10.1145/2598394.2605686.

1. INTRODUCTION

The architecture has deep impact on non-functional properties of a system such as performance, safety, reliability, security, energy consumption and cost. Due to the complexity of today's software systems, designing a system which meets all its quality requirements becomes increasingly complex. Hence, system architects have to employ optimization techniques to be able to explore more design possibilities and to find optimal architectural solutions. Metaheuristic approaches frame the challenge of designing architectures as an optimization problem and iteratively try to improve a candidate solution with regard to the given quality attributes. Evolutionary Algorithms (EA), as a well-known metaheuristic approach, is a common optimization technique for solving system architectural problems. However, evolutionary algorithms are generally slow especially when evaluation function is computationally-intensive and slow. It takes so long for an evolutionary algorithm to find near optimal solutions, therefore techniques are needed to speed up this process. Distributing the optimization process is one of the best solutions to achieve this goal.

This paper shows the results of distributed execution of evolutionary algorithm for multiobjective optimization of software architecture. For distributed execution of evolutionary algorithm, we have implemented two approaches: (1) Actor-based approach, (2) MapReduce approach. To execute our distributed implementation on a super computer, we have used DAS-4 (The Distributed ASCI Supercomputer 4) [16] to setup a computationally-intensive experiment. Our distributed implementation have been applied to a case study derived from a real world automotive system.

The paper is organized as following: Firstly, Section 2 describes our optimization framework, and its detailed modeling, optimization and evaluation parts. Then, Section 3 discusses our two proposed approaches for distributed execution. We have applied our approach on a case study, which is described in Section 4. Finally, the paper concludes in Section 5.

2. AQOSA FRAMEWORK

In this section, we present the AQOSA framework which our new degrees of freedom is implemented on. First, we start with general process of AQOSA framework in Section 2.1. Section 2.2 describes AQOSA modeling. Section 2.3 describes the optimization process in detail. Then, the evaluator evaluates each architecture for various quality attributes. Section 2.4 describes the used evaluation techniques.

2.1 Process

AQOSA is a framework which uses genetic algorithm optimization approach for automated software architecture design. The framework supports analysis and optimization of multiple quality attributes including response time, processor utilization, bus utilization, safety and cost. Figure 1 shows the architecture of the AQOSA framework. It uses an architectural Intermediate Representation (IR) model for describing the architectural design problem. The tool takes the following as input: i) an initial functional part of the system (i.e. components that provide the needed functionality and their interactions with other components), ii) a set of typical usage scenarios (includes trigger to create workloads), iii) an objective function (implying which architecture properties should be optimized), iv) a repository that contains a set of specifications of hardware and software components.

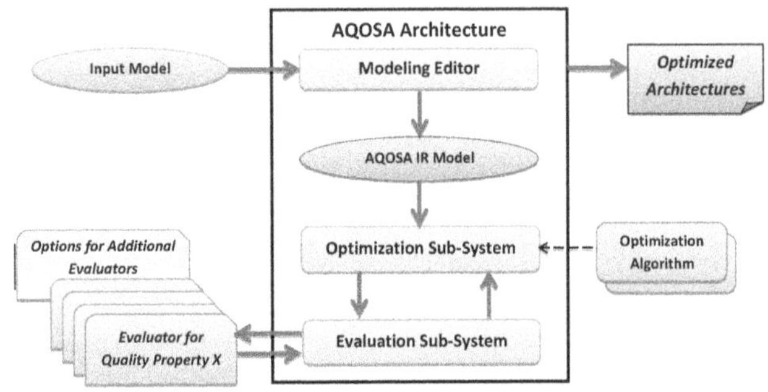

Figure 1: AQOSA overall architecture.

Then, AQOSA iterates through the following steps:

1. Generate a new set of candidate architecture solutions: To this end, AQOSA uses a representation of the architecture where it knows which are the degrees of freedom in the design and how to generate alternative architecture instances.
2. Evaluate the new set of candidate architecture solutions for multiple quality properties: This works by generating analysis models from the architecture model using model transformations and then analyzing these models.
3. Select a set of (so far) Pareto-optimal solutions.
4. Iterate to step 1 until some stopping criterion holds. This can be a maximum number of generations or a criterion on the objective function.

2.2 Architecture Modeling

Because AQOSA is designed to optimize architectures in a wide range of domains, it aims to be independent from specific modeling languages. Hence, it uses its own internal architecture representation, AQOSA intermediate representation (AQOSA-IR). AQOSA architecture modeling is based on an Eclipse EMF [5] model. AQOSA-IR model integrates multiple quality modeling perspectives (such as performance, safety, etc.) for the architectural level optimization purpose.

AQOSA-IR consists of four major parts: Assembly, Scenarios, Repository and Objectives.

- Assembly: It includes software components and their assembly for delivering system functionalities. Every component provides some services, and interaction between different components are defined by flows and actions within flows.
- Scenarios: It defines expected scenarios for the system. So, the architect can define best-case, worse-case or normal-case for the system. It stores real-time constrains of the system such as expected completion time and deadline.
- Repository: It stores various possible choices for processors, buses and component implementations. Based on this repository, the AQOSA framework is able to change assigned processor for each node, or assigned bus instance for each bus line, etc. It contains required specifications of each possible hardware or software.
- Objectives: It defines the objectives which the framework optimizes.

A sample of AQOSA-IR model is presented in [8].

2.3 Architecture Optimization

The AQOSA optimizer tries to optimize software architecture with respect to potentially contradicting quality attributes based on evolutionary algorithms. In general, various global optimization techniques have been used in handling complex engineering problems. Younis et al. [18] compared variety of optimization methods and revealed the pros and cons of these global optimization methods. For AQOSA framework, we have chosen Genetic Algorithms (GA) for optimization method.

In the following, first we describe compatible evolutionary algorithms with AQOSA framework. After that, we discuss implemented degrees of freedom for our architecture optimizer. And then, we detail how we represent software architecture in the form of a genotype. This shows how we would be able to generate various architectures.

2.3.1 *Evolutionary Algorithms*

Because of conflicts between different quality attributes in the software architecture, AQOSA uses Evolutionary Multi-Objective Algorithms (EMOA) to improve the architecture. It has been implemented based on the Opt4J optimization framework [14]. The system designer can choose one of the following GA algorithms for his design problem:

- NSGA-II (non-dominated sorting based multi-objective evolutionary algorithm): It is one of the most widely used EMOA techniques and has been proposed by Deb [4].
- SPEA2 (an improved version of Strength Pareto Evolutionary Algorithm): It has been suggested by Zitzler and Thiele [19], and it is also widely used.
- SMS-EMOA (S-Metric Selection Evolutionary Multi-Objective Algorithm): It has been proposed by Emmerich, Beume and Naujoks [6]. It is a representative of the class of hypervolume-based EMOA, which recently gained popularity in the EMOA field.

A comparison of EMOA algorithms for software architecture domain is discussed in our earlier work [13].

2.3.2 *Degrees of Freedom*

When an architect finalizes an architectural design for a system, generally there are still some ways in which the solution can be varied without changing the functionality. We call them *Degrees of Freedom*(DoF). The component-based paradigm that underlies our approach, allows us to recompose components in different topologies and wrappers. However, we only consider variations of architectural designs that do not modify the interfaces used in the architecture in order to guarantee that our optimization process does not change the functionality of the system.

In the following, we describe the degrees of freedom supported by AQOSA framework:

Number of hardware nodes .
If an architectural model contains `n` software components, then these can be deployed on a number of hardware nodes, ranging between a minimum of `1` and a maximum of `K·n` hardware nodes (for some natural number `K > 0`), because the number of nodes in an architecture is finite. Adding more hardware nodes may provide more processing capacity and therefore give better performance. Vice versa, removing hardware nodes may reduce the total cost of the system.

Number of connections between hardware nodes .
If `n` hardware nodes are chosen for the deployment of components, then the maximum number of connections between hardware nodes can be calculated by $Max_c(n) = \frac{n(n-1)}{2}$. This maximum represents a case that all of the nodes are connected 1-by-1 together by a dedicated connection. As a minimum we can assume a single central bus which connects all of the nodes. This DoF has significant impact on performance and cost of the system.

Network topology.
By definition, network topology is the layout of interconnections between hardware nodes. Figure 2 shows some possible topologies for connecting a network with 4 nodes. Even with the same number of nodes and the same number of connections, network topologies might be different. The impact and importance of this DoF is discussed in authors' previous work [7]. Obviously, not all possible topologies are valid and therefore AQOSA performs a validation process before evaluation.

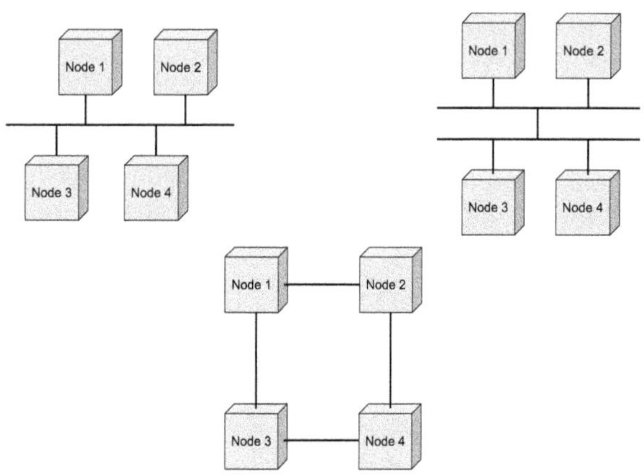

Figure 2: Three possible topologies for a 4-node network.

Software on hardware allocation .
Given a hardware network topology, allocation of software components on hardware nodes is another degree of freedom. This degree of freedom also has large effect on the processors utilization and performance of the whole system.

Software components replacement .
Different components (e.g. developed by different vendors) that implement the same functionality are considered different architectural alternatives. Our assumption is that one component can replace another if and only if they implement the same functionality. If not, the replacement violates the system functionality which is not accepted.

Processors replacement .
This degree of freedom entails that each hardware node can be replaced by another hardware node (processor) in the repository. These processors may be different in processing clock rate, energy consumption, failure probability range, and cost. It has large effect on all quality attributes.

Buses replacement .
This degree of freedom is similar to the hardware components replacement, but is aimed at replacement of buses. They may be different in communication bandwidth, communication delay, failure probability range, and cost as well.

2.3.3 *Architecture Genotype*

Inspired by the biological concept of genotypes, in genetic programming and evolutionary algorithms, the genotype is the genetic representation of an *individual* which in this case is an architecture design. AQOSA framework used a genotype which consists of a set of 5 genomes.

The deployment genome encodes that each software component is deployed on which hardware node. The framework calculates the number of nodes based on deployment of software components and then stores it in the nodes genome. The nodes genome encodes which hardware specification is chosen for each node in the system. The specification for each hardware node includes processing clock rate, range of failure probability, and cost. The communication genome, like the nodes genome, encodes which hardware specification is chosen for each communication line. Their specification includes bandwidth, transmit delay, and cost. Topology is represented by two Boolean matrices which we call it connection genomes. These matrices show the connections between buses to nodes and amongst buses themselves. Each cell in the matrix can have value True or False, where True means this particular node and particular line are connected (or that these particular lines are connected).

Genotype Validation.
Evolutionary algorithms in AQOSA can apply various genetic operators such as *Copy*, *Mutate* or *Crossover* to the genotype. However there is no guarantee that valid architectures will be generated as offspring. Therefore, it is necessary to validate the offspring. In this process the optimizer performs sanity checks for each genotype in the generated offspring. For example, if the model defines that *component3* should communicate with *component5* and then the generated offspring deploys *component3* on *node2* and *component5* on *node4*, this process should check whether there are any communication paths between *node2* and *node4*.

2.4 Architecture Evaluation

The AQOSA evaluation sub-system gets an evaluation model (e.g. Queuing Networks and Fault Tree) which is transformed from a combination of the AQOSA IR and a genotype (which is described in Section 2.3.3) for a particular quality attribute (e.g. Response Time or Safety). It feeds evaluation models to each evaluator and returns the results to the optimization sub-system.

It should be pointed out that our framework is aimed at optimizing architectures. So, from optimization point of view, the framework is targeted for supporting relative comparisons between architectural solutions. For this purpose, AQOSA uses analysis tools for particular quality attributes as plug-ins. We assume that these analysis tools are developed and validated by domain experts. However, to examine the accuracy of AQOSA evaluation implementation, we have compared our tool results with results reported in relevant publications. In case of performance attributes, our QN implementation can achieve the same results as the results published in [17]. In case of FTA, we compared our results with the results published in [10].

In the following, we describe the supported quality attributes by the AQOSA framework.

Response Time.

Response time refers to a time interval during which the response to an event must be executed. The time interval defines a response window given by a starting time and an ending time. These can either be specified as absolute times (time of day, for example) or offsets from an event which occurred at some specified time [2]. The ending time is also known as a deadline. AQOSA measures response time for each event in the system as offsets from the request time, and then scores them based on predefined deadlines. More technically, within the QN simulation process, it generates scenario events as the queuing network inputs and records the response time of outputs for the events.

Processor Utilization.

Processor utilization is the percentage of time which a resource is busy. AQOSA measures this percentage for each processor in the architecture separately. To do so, it translates the architecture to the queuing network. After the simulation of the network, this quality attribute will be retrieved from the network statistics. Regarding the final measure for this metric, AQOSA can be configured to return either average, minimum, or maximum of processors utilizations in the network.

Bus Utilization.

Like processor utilization, bus utilization is the percentage of bandwidth that a bus uses. Similar to above, AQOSA measures this metric for each bus in the architecture separately. Again, this metric can be configured to return either average, minimum or maximum of buses utilizations.

System Safety.

Förster [11] claims: *"Software does not fail randomly but will invariably fail again in the same way under the same conditions. While for mass-produced hardware parts it is possible to assign a failure probability, for software a similar assumption does not seem entirely realistic".* Accepting this hypothesis, we assume for each component that the output fails if either the input fails or the hosting hardware crashes. So, AQOSA analyzes the corresponding fault tree for each system output and calculates the failure probability of each output based on its fault tree dependability on various inputs and related hardware nodes.

System Cost.

The cost quality attribute is important from a market point of view. Fortunately, it is easily calculated by adding the cost of used software components, hardware nodes, and communication lines.

3. PARALLEL EXECUTION

In the following, we discuss two approaches for parallel execution of evolutionary algorithms which we implemented in our framework:

3.1 Actor-based Distribution (Akka Framework [1])

The Actor Model provides a higher level of abstraction for writing concurrent and distributed systems. It alleviates the developer from having to deal with explicit locking and thread management, making it easier to write correct concurrent and parallel systems. Actors were defined by Carl Hewitt [12] but have been popularized by the Erlang language.

Akka is a framework which helps developers in writing correct concurrent, fault-tolerant and scalable applications. Akka by using the Actor Model raises the abstraction level and provides a better platform to build correct concurrent and scalable applications. Actors also provide the abstraction for transparent distribution and the basis for truly scalable and fault-tolerant applications.

Actors give developers:

1. simple and high-level abstractions for concurrency and parallelism,
2. asynchronous, non-blocking and highly performant event-driven programming model,
3. very lightweight event-driven processes.

Fault tolerance through supervisor hierarchies with "let-it-crash" semantics. Excellent for writing highly fault-tolerant systems that never stop, systems that self-heal. Supervisor hierarchies can span over multiple JVMs to provide truly fault-tolerant systems.

3.2 MapReduce Paradigm (Hadoop Framework [15])

MapReduce was firstly introduced by Dean et al. in [3]. MapReduce is a programming model designed for processing large volumes of data in parallel by dividing the work into a set of independent tasks. MapReduce programs are written in a particular style influenced by functional programming constructs, specifically idioms for processing lists of data. This requires dividing the workload across a large number of machines. This model would not scale to large clusters if the components were allowed to share data arbitrarily. The communication overhead required to keep the data on the nodes synchronized at all times would prevent the system from performing reliably or efficiently at large scale. Users

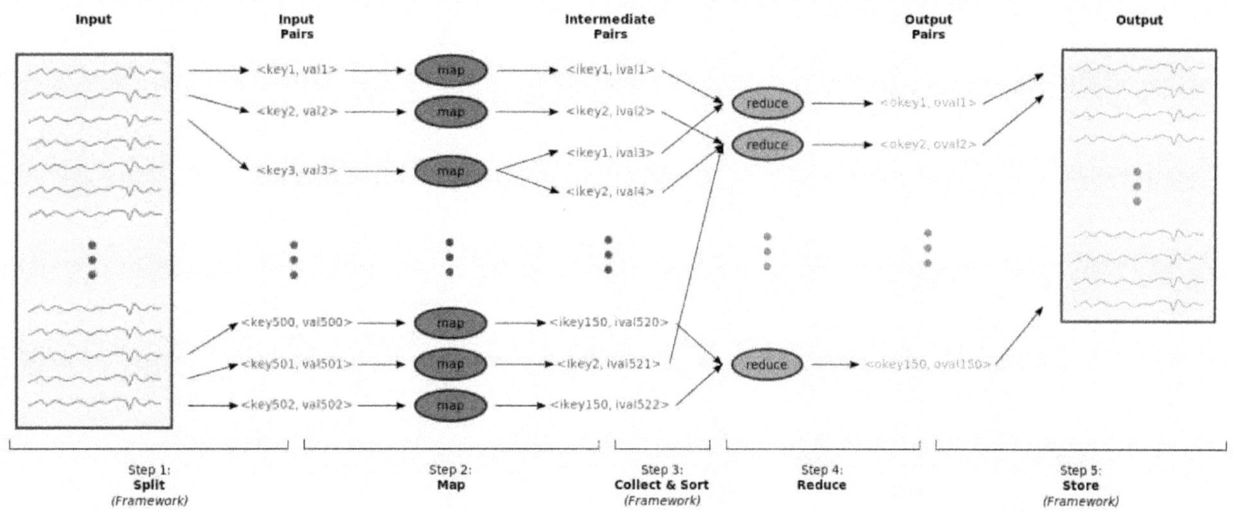

Figure 3: A visualization of Map and Reduce processes.

specify a map function that processes a key/value pair to generate a set of intermediate key/value pairs, and a reduce function that merges all intermediate values associated with the same intermediate key. Programs written in this functional style are automatically parallelized and executed on a large cluster of commodity machines.

The Apache Hadoop software library is a framework that implemented MapReduce programming model. This framework allows for the distributed processing of large data sets across clusters of computers using MapReduce paradigm. Conceptually, MapReduce programs transform lists of input data elements into lists of output data elements. A MapReduce program will do this twice, using two different list processing idioms: *map*, and *reduce*. The Hadoop MapReduce framework takes these concepts and uses them to process large volumes of information. Figure 3 shows a visualization of this process.

Mapping List.

The first phase of a MapReduce program is called mapping. A list of data elements are provided, one at a time, to a function called the Mapper, which transforms each element individually to an output data element. As an example of the utility of map: Suppose you had a function toUpper(str) which returns an uppercase version of the input string. You could use this function with map to turn a list of strings into a list of uppercase strings. Note that we are not modifying the input string, we are returning a new string that will form part of a new output list.

Reducing List.

Reducing lets you aggregate values together. A reducer function receives an iterator of input values from an input list. It then combines these values together, returning a single output value. Reducing is often used to produce "summary" data, turning a large volume of data into a smaller summary of itself. For example, "+" can be used as a reducing function, to return the sum of a list of input values.

4. CASE STUDY

4.1 Implemented Actor-based Distribution

Figure 4 depicts scheme of our implemented Akka actors. We used 5 nodes, 1 master node and 4 worker nodes. On each worker node, Akka framework was set to be initialized which run 4 actors on ports 2551, 2552, 2553 and 2554 respectively. Therefore, 16 actors in total were set to be initialized. They were responsible for evaluating an individual based on requested software quality attributes, such as response time, processor utilization, bus utilization, safety and cost. On the master node, Akka framework was set to start an actor called 'Evaluator Balancer' (as depicted in Figure 4). This actor is responsible for distributing evaluation jobs to other 16 worker actors. It used a round-robin balancing for the for distribution of assigned jobs. AQOSA framework also started on master node and it was calling balancer actor whenever it wanted to evaluate an individual.

This experiment has been run on DAS-4 [16] super computer that every node is a powerful computer with a 8-core (each core runs 2.67GHz and 12MB cache) processor and 48GB memory.

4.2 Automotive Subsystem

To examine the efficiency of actor-based distributed implementation of our software architecture optimization framework, we applied it to a real case study from automotive industry. The case study was conducted at Saab Automobile AB and has been reported in the previous authors' work [9]. The system represents the Saab 9-5 Instrument Cluster Module ECU (Electronic Control Unit, a node in a network) and the surrounding sub-systems. It consists of 18 components as depicted in Figure 5. The Instrument Cluster Module is responsible for 8 concurrent user functions. Hence, for providing these functionalities, it should be able to response 6 sporadic tasks and 4 periodic tasks concurrently. Details of these tasks have been reported in [9] and [8].

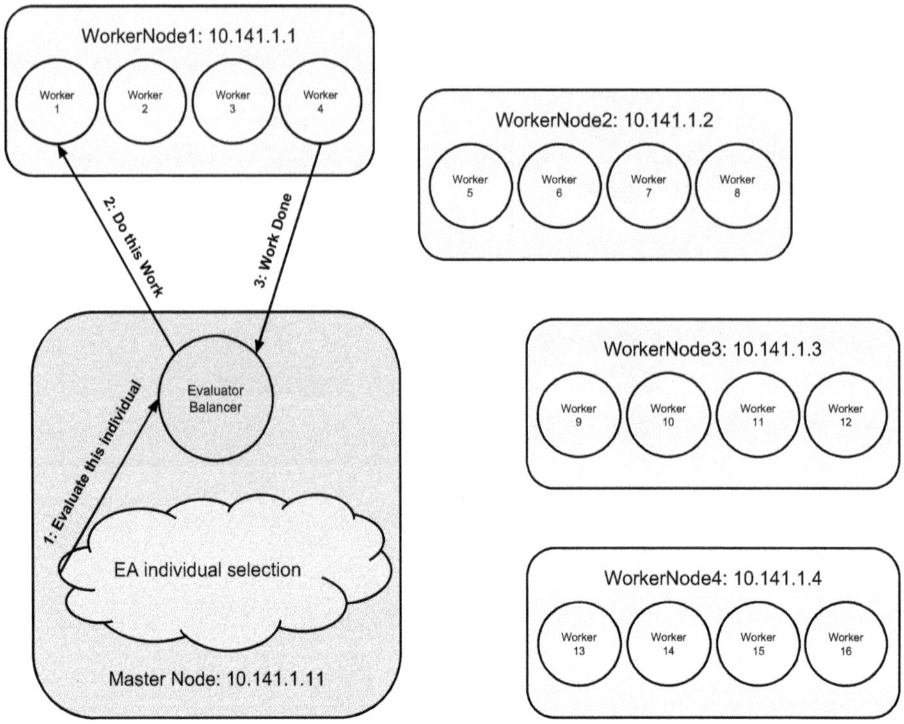

Figure 4: AQOSA implementation of actor-based distribution scheme.

For generating new architectural solutions, the repository of hardware components contains these elements:

- 28 Processors: ranging over 14 various processing speeds from 66MHz to 500MHz; Each has two levels of failure rate. A processor is more expensive if it has less chance of failure and vice versa.
- 4 Buses: with bandwidths of 10, 33, 125, and 500 kbps, and latencies of 50, 16, 8, and 2 ms. A bus is more expensive if it supports higher bandwidth.

As an estimate of the size of the design space in this case study, consider the following reasoning: Assume we omit architecture topology changing and fix an architecture with six processors and three bus lines for their interconnections (exactly like the current realization in the industry). For these constraints there are $28^6 \cdot 4^3$ different possibilities, which is more than 30 billion architectures. When also considering variations in the architecture topologies, this number would be even considerably higher.

After defining the above hardware options, AQOSA was run 30 times based on NSGA-II algorithm with these adopted parameter settings: initial population size(α) = 256, parent population size (μ) = 64, number of offspring(λ) = 64, archive size = 32, number of generations = 60, crossover rate set to 0.95, and all quality attributes are aimed to be minimized.

4.3 Results

Table 1 shows the execution times (in milliseconds) of 30 runs of the experiment. The first column is the execution number. The second column is the execution times of actor-based distributed implementation. As described in Section 4.1, it was distributed on 1 master node and 4 worker nodes. The third column shows the execution times of running the same design problem on single node.

In parallel computing speedup parameter has been defined by the following formula:

$$S_p = \frac{T_1}{T_p}. \tag{1}$$

where p is the number of processors, T_1 is the execution time of the sequential algorithm, and T_p is the execution time of the parallel algorithm with p processors. Therefore, in our experiment speedup for the average of 30 times run is equal to:

$$S_5 = \frac{684,116}{168,353} = 4.0635 \tag{2}$$

Moreover, efficiency of parallel algorithm has been defined by this formula:

$$E_p = \frac{S_p}{p} = \frac{T_1}{pT_p}. \tag{3}$$

This means when running an algorithm with linear speedup, doubling the number of processors doubles the speed. However, this case is ideal situation and it is considered ideal scalability.

To calculate the efficiency of our implemented actor-based distributed algorithm, we apply the aforementioned formula, and therefore:

$$E_5 = \frac{S_5}{5} = \frac{4.0635}{5} = 0.8127 \tag{4}$$

In other words, our implemented actor-based distributed algorithm in case of this experiment on a real-world case study shows 81.27% efficiency which is acceptable metric.

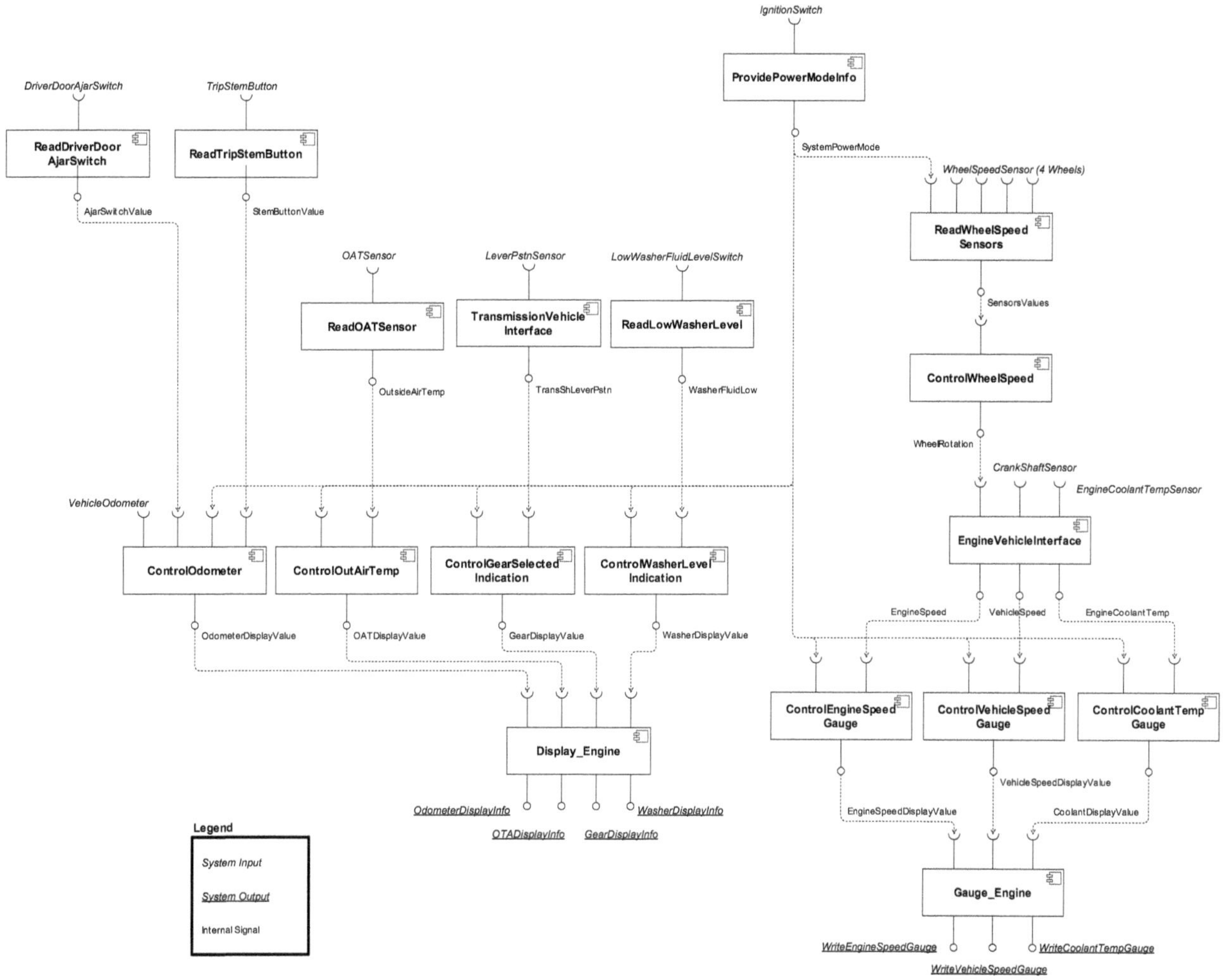

Figure 5: Component diagram of Automotive Instrument Cluster system.

4.4 Actor-based vs. MapReduce Approach

To compare two different distribution approaches which are described in Section 3, we set another experiment to run both approaches for the same case study. The case study is the same real-world automotive system which is already discussed in previous section.

In this experiment, we employed cluster of 16 nodes from DAS-4. 8 nodes for running actor-based distribution and 8 nodes for running MapReduce distribution. In this experiment, every node had a dual Intel® Xeon® Processor E5-2620 (15M Cache, 2.00 GHz) as processor and 64GB of memory. Both implementations only distribute the task for evaluation of an individual solution.

We started both implementations at the same time. The results show by the time 30 executions were completed using actor-based approach, MapReduce program managed to finish only 10 executions. Therefore, we can conclude that actor-based approach is faster for evolutionary algorithms, at least for this case study.

One explanation for this behaviour can be the number of nodes in the cluster. MapReduce approach probably needs large-size cluster of nodes to achieve its performance. Unfortunately, we did not have access to Hadoop cluster larger than 8 nodes to test this hypothesis.

5. CONCLUSION

In this paper we presented the results of a software architecture optimization experiment which calculates the efficiency of parallel execution for evolutionary algorithm. We defined this experiment based on a real world case study and we applied it for a software architecture optimization problem with five objectives. We showed that parallel execution of evolutionary algorithm for software architecture optimization can improve execution time significantly with acceptable efficiency in multiobjective optimization context.

The results showed that for cases in which evaluation process is significant compare to updating Pareto front (selection process), efficiency of parallelization is considerable. However, for cases in which evaluation process is fast, parallelization would not help considerably. Comparing actor-based distribution and MapReduce distribution, in our case study, shows that actor-based distribution performs faster.

As the future work, it is interesting to extend the parallelization of execution to the selection process of evolutionary algorithm as well. In this way, in addition to evaluation process, selection algorithm would also execute in parallel which helps efficiency of parallelization even more. This should be implemented separately for each selection algorithm (such as NSGA-II, SPEA2, etc).

Run #	Distributed (1 Master-Node + 4 Worker-Nodes)	Single-Node
1	168,346	685,668
2	163,278	691,741
3	171,185	687,933
4	191,425	678,725
5	173,486	683,875
6	212,667	697,605
7	185,926	681,893
8	169,970	689,065
9	135,545	695,583
10	162,341	687,381
11	176,953	693,289
12	164,833	689,954
13	153,570	681,492
14	184,530	692,063
15	148,388	655,434
16	169,537	669,622
17	166,597	686,289
18	212,164	676,475
19	158,257	676,324
20	163,089	684,778
21	170,300	677,652
22	138,852	684,308
23	169,592	691,148
24	155,911	671,799
25	166,818	692,061
26	182,757	680,180
27	143,056	689,571
28	161,778	690,718
29	158,040	681,744
30	171,396	679,107
Average	168,353	684,116

Table 1: Execution time (in ms) of 30 runs of experiment

6. ACKNOWLEDGMENTS

This work has been supported by the Netherlands national project OMECA (Optimization of Modular Embedded Computer-vision Architectures).

This research has been executed on Dutch super computer DAS-4 (The Distributed ASCI Supercomputer 4). DAS-4 is a six-cluster wide-area distributed system designed by the Advanced School for Computing and Imaging (ASCI).

7. REFERENCES

[1] Akka Framework: an open-source toolkit and runtime simplifying the construction of concurrent and distributed applications on the JVM. http://akka.io/.

[2] M. Barbacci, M. H. Klein, T. A. Longstaff, and C. B. Weinstock. Quality Attributes. Technical Report CMU/SEI-95-TR-021, Carnegie Mellon, 1995.

[3] J. Dean and S. Ghemawat. Mapreduce: Simplified data processing on large clusters. In *OSDI*, pages 137–150. USENIX Association, 2004.

[4] K. Deb, S. Agrawal, A. Pratap, and T. Meyarivan. A fast and elitist multiobjective genetic algorithm: Nsga-ii. *IEEE Transactions on Evolutionary Computation*, 6(2):182–197, 2002.

[5] Eclipse Modeling Framework (EMF). http://www.eclipse.org/modeling/emf/.

[6] M. Emmerich, N. Beume, and B. Naujoks. An EMO Algorithm Using the Hypervolume Measure as Selection Criterion. In C. A. C. Coello, A. H. Aguirre, and E. Zitzler, editors, *EMO*, volume 3410 of *LNCS*, pages 62–76. Springer, 2005.

[7] R. Etemaadi and M. R. V. Chaudron. Varying topology of component-based system architectures using metaheuristic optimization. In V. Cortellessa, H. Muccini, and O. Demirörs, editors, *EUROMICRO-SEAA*, pages 63–70. IEEE Computer Society, 2012.

[8] R. Etemaadi, K. Lind, R. Heldal, and M. R. V. Chaudron. Details of an automotive sub-system: Saab instrument cluster module. *CoRR*, abs/1306.0555, 2013.

[9] R. Etemaadi, K. Lind, R. Heldal, and M. R. V. Chaudron. Quality-driven optimization of system architecture: Industrial case study on an automotive sub-system. *Journal of Systems and Software*, 86(10):2559–2573, 2013.

[10] M. Förster and D. Schneider. Flexible, Any-Time Fault Tree Analysis with Component Logic Models. In *ISSRE*, pages 51–60. IEEE Computer Society, 2010.

[11] M. Förster and M. Trapp. Fault Tree Analysis of Software-Controlled Component Systems Based on Second-Order Probabilities. In *ISSRE*, pages 146–154. IEEE Computer Society, 2009.

[12] C. Hewitt, P. Bishop, and R. Steiger. A universal modular actor formalism for artificial intelligence. In N. J. Nilsson, editor, *IJCAI*, pages 235–245. William Kaufmann, 1973.

[13] R. Li, R. Etemaadi, M. T. M. Emmerich, and M. R. V. Chaudron. An Evolutionary Multiobjective Optimization Approach to Component-Based Software Architecture Design. In *IEEE CEC*, pages 432–439. IEEE, 2011.

[14] M. Lukasiewycz, M. Glaß, F. Reimann, and J. Teich. Opt4J: a modular framework for meta-heuristic optimization. In N. Krasnogor and P. L. Lanzi, editors, *GECCO*, pages 1723–1730. ACM, 2011.

[15] The Apache™ Hadoop® project. http://hadoop.apache.org/.

[16] The Distributed ASCI Supercomputer 4. http://www.cs.vu.nl/das4/.

[17] E. Wandeler, L. Thiele, M. Verhoef, and P. Lieverse. System architecture evaluation using modular performance analysis: a case study. *International Journal on Software Tools for Technology Transfer (STTT)*, 8(6):649–667, 2006.

[18] A. Younis and Z. Dong. Trends, features, and tests of common and recently introduced global optimization methods. *Engineering Optimization*, 42(8):691–718, 2010.

[19] E. Zitzler, M. Laumanns, and L. Thiele. SPEA2: Improving the Strength Pareto Evolutionary Algorithm for Multiobjective Optimization. Technical report, ETH Zurich, 2002.

HYPERION^2
A toolkit for {meta-, hyper-} heuristic research

Alexander E.I. Brownlee
Division of Computer Science
and Mathematics
University of Stirling
Stirling, UK
sbr@cs.stir.ac.uk

Jerry Swan
Division of Computer Science
and Mathematics
University of Stirling
Stirling, UK
jsw@cs.stir.ac.uk

Ender Özcan
School of Computer Science
University of Nottingham
Nottingham, UK
ender.ozcan@nottingham.ac.uk

Andrew J. Parkes
School of Computer Science
University of Nottingham
Nottingham, UK
andrew.parkes@nottingham.ac.uk

ABSTRACT

In order for appropriate meta-heuristics to be chosen and tuned for specific problems, it is critical that we better understand the problems themselves and how algorithms solve them. This is particularly important as we seek to automate the process of choosing and tuning algorithms and their operators via hyper-heuristics. If meta-heuristics are viewed as sampling algorithms, they can be classified by the trajectory taken through the search space. We term this trajectory a *trace*. In this paper, we present HYPERION^2, a Java^{TM} framework for meta- and hyper- heuristics which allows the analysis of the trace taken by an algorithm and its constituent components through the search space. Built with the principles of interoperability, generality and efficiency, we intend that this framework will be a useful aid to scientific research in this domain.

Categories and Subject Descriptors

I.2.8 [**Artificial Intelligence**]: Problem Solving, Control Methods, and Search—*Heuristic methods*; D.1.5 [**Object-oriented Programming**]

Keywords

Metaheuristics, Hyper-heuristics, analysis, experimental framework, search space

1. INTRODUCTION

Metaheuristics and related methods are reaching maturity as a research domain. An extensive literature covers a large number of approaches, from broad algorithm paradigms to individual operators, and over the past couple of decades metaheuristics have increasingly gained acceptance for application to real-world problems in industry [1]. However, in many respects there is still something of an art in terms of finding the right algorithm for the right problem. Much research still focuses on developing tweaks to existing algorithms and operators to suit new application domains, treating the search process itself as a black box and focussing on metrics such as convergence speed and solution quality in empirical comparisons. Approaches to automating the processes of algorithm selection and tuning have been made, notably hyper-heuristics, which operate in the space of heuristics [2]. However, for such approaches to be effective, it remains critical that we better understand the nature of problems themselves and how algorithms solve them. The ultimate goal is to classify search algorithms and problems [3] so it becomes possible to match a problem with an appropriate algorithm [4].

If metaheuristics are viewed as sampling algorithms [5], they can be classified by the trajectory (which we term a *trace*) that they take through the search space. Understanding the influence of operators on the trace produced by a search will provide essential information for algorithm designers (human or otherwise). Whitebox information about traces (e.g. which bit was flipped, knowing the lineage of individuals in a population) allows the search process to proceed in a more informed manner [6], and can be seen as the principled incorporation of (both problem and solution) domain information in a manner than has proved to be effective (e.g. as evidenced by the tabu search metaheuristic [7]). It is claimed that machine learning approaches are needed to move beyond the 'persistent operator tweaking' that plagues metaheuristic design [8, 9, 10] and options for learning are clearly facilitated by the availability of such trace information. In particular, the incorporation of traces is vital for the creation of an 'interoperable universal signature' for metaheuristics, something which is clearly necessary for automatic hybridization. Further, detailed trace information can be used to generate a proxy for fitness in genetic programming and hyper-heuristics, where traces model algorithm behaviour [10, 11].

GECCO'14, July 12–16, 2014, Vancouver, BC, Canada.

ACM 978-1-4503-2881-4/14/07 ...$15.00.
http://dx.doi.org/10.1145/2598394.2605687.

It is in this context that we propose HYPERION^2, a Java^{TM} framework to aid scientific research, allowing sound analysis of meta- and hyper- heuristics by providing a general approach for describing the trace taken by an algorithm and its constituent components through the search space.

HYPERION^2 is a research toolkit for non-global optimization that aims to maximize expressive power whilst maintaining ease-of-use. Based on [12], it has evolved through several incarnations and attempts to incorporate the best elements of solution-domain frameworks such as [13], [14] and most notably [15].

The specific design goals of HYPERION^2 include:

1. Promoting interoperability via component interfaces. These interfaces are type-parameterized by solution-state representation and objective-value (the latter allowing for multi-objective formulations).
2. Allow rapid prototyping of meta- and hyper- heuristics, with the potential to use the same source code in either case.
3. Provide generic templates for a variety of local search and evolutionary computation algorithms, allowing popular variants to be readily constructed from pre-existing components.
4. Facilitate the construction of novel meta- and hyper-heuristics by hybridization (via interface interoperability) or extension (subtype polymorphism).
5. 'Only pay for what you use' — a design philosophy that attempts to ensure that generality doesn't necessarily imply inefficiency.

In this paper we present an overview of the framework's core interfaces, discuss the key concepts and give some implementation examples including the well-known 'onemax' problem [16], random search and steepest-ascent hillclimbing.

2. RELATED WORK

There are many existing frameworks for construction and analysis of metaheuristics: [17] cites several current examples. The HeuristicLab framework [18] also implements a generic approach to algorithm construction. Two popular frameworks, ECJ [19] and EpochX [20] offer event driven approaches to analyse the progress of evolution, but none offers the level of control, genericity or level of granularity that are present in HYPERION^2.

Besides HYPERION^2 and the original HYPERION, HY-FLEX [21] and hMod [22] are (to the authors' knowledge) the only other existing frameworks for hyper-heuristics. Hy-Flex is concerned with building reusable elements for common problem domains, and recent work [23, 24] has seen the development of additional tools for generating hyper-heuristics in HY-FLEX.

CluPaTra [25, 26] and FloTra [27] are approaches which make use of trajectories in parameter tuning.

3. CORE INTERFACES

The basic interoperability mechanism in HYPERION^2 follows from the observation that a heuristic (equivalently meta- or hyper- heuristic hereafter) is essentially defined by its solution trajectory (*trace*) in the state-space graph. A heuristic h_S over some solution-state representation of type S (e.g. S might be a bitstring, permutation, vector of reals, graph etc) is recursively defined as a function:

$$h_S : Traces_S \rightarrow Traces_S$$

where $Traces_S = (h_S, S)^*$

i.e. a Trace is a list of zero or more (heuristic, solution-state) pairs, with each pair representing a single transition in the state-space.

The implied semantics are that a heuristic h_S takes a trace as input and returns a (possibly extended) trace. Primitive heuristics (such as a bit-flip) extend the trace by a single move, metaheuristics have the potential to extend it by multiple moves. The explicit provision of the input trace means that history-sensitive metaheuristics (e.g. tabu-search, EDA approaches and adaptive variants of simulated annealing) can be implemented with a minimum of additional effort. In addition, the inclusion of previously-applied heuristics in the trace information means that domain-specific information (e.g. knowledge of algebraic relationships between heuristics) can be used to inform metaheuristics in a domain-neutral fashion.

As shown in Listing 1, the corresponding JAVA API is rather more straightforward than the above definition might suggest. Trace<S> is essentially a list of Move<S>, the latter being the pairing of a heuristic with the target state which results from the application of that heuristic, as described above. The additional Random parameter supplied to the apply method of Heuristic allows for the provision of a better random number generator than JAVA's builtin 48-bit linear-congruential implementation, this being essential for fair sampling of large state-spaces.

Other elementary components of the framework are given in Listing 2. ValueFn<S,Value> defines the evaluation function for a state, where Value is a generic type than can include multiobjective representations, with Acceptance and IsFinished defining the interfaces for acceptance and termination criteria respectively.

Another key concept in HYPERION^2 is that of LOCALITY, representing the ubiquitous concept of local search neighbourhood. The HYPERION^2 locality concept is factored into three - ITERABLELOCALITY, GENERATIVELOCALITY and RANDOMACCESSLOCALITY. ITERABLELOCALITY defines some neighborhood of a state, successive elements of which are accessed via the *Iterator* design pattern [28]. GENERATIVELOCALITY provides for the creation of randomly-generated neighbors and RANDOMACCESSLOCALITY allows a neighbor to be accessed via an integer index in O(1) time. The rationale for factoring out these concepts is to reduce the implementation burden for custom neighborhoods. There is explicit support within HYPERION^2 for bit-flip and permutation-swap neighborhoods.

HYPERION^2 also supports compile-time checking for minimization or maximization, through the 'curiously recurring template pattern' [29]. This means that any algorithm implementation can be entirely independent of whether a problem is minimization or maximization. More importantly, this will trap 'wrong direction' mixing of maximization and minimization at compile-time. Listing 3 gives the general implementation of this.

```
public interface Heuristic<S>
{
        public Option< Move< BitString > > apply( Trace< BitString > inputTrace, Random rng )
        public Trace<S> iterate( Trace<S> inputTrace, Random rng );
}

public final class Move<S>
{
        public Heuristic<S> getHeuristic() { /* ... */ }
        public S getTargetState() { /* ... */ }

        // Other details omitted ...
}

public final class Trace<S>
{
        public int length() { /* ... */ }
        public Move<S> getMove( int index ) { /* ... */ }

        // Other details omitted ...
}
```

Listing 1: Hyperion^2 Heuristic interface and associated classes.

```
public interface ValueFn<S,Value>
{
        public Value apply( S state );
}

public interface Acceptance<S>
{
        public Probability apply( Trace<S> trace, Move<S> suggestedMove, double temperature );
}

public interface IsFinished<S>
{
        public boolean apply( Trace<S> trace, long numIterations );
}
```

Listing 2: Core Hyperion^2 interfaces.

```
public interface DirectedValue< Derived >
extends Comparable< Derived > {}

public final class Max< Value extends Comparable< Value > >
implements DirectedValue< Max< Value > > {
	private final Value value;

	public Max( Value value ) {
		this.value = value;
	}

	@Override
	public int compareTo( Max< Value > other ) {
		return value.compareTo( other.value );
	}

	// Other details omitted ...
}

public final class Min< Value extends Comparable< Value > >
implements DirectedValue< Min< Value > > {
	private final Value value;

	public Min( Value value ) {
		this.value = value;
	}

	@Override
	public int compareTo( Min< Value > other ) {
		return -value.compareTo( other.value );
	}

	// Other details omitted ...
}
```

Listing 3: Compile-time checking of min vs max functions using CRTP

```
final class OnemaxValueFn
extends ValueFn<BitString, Double> {
	@Override
	public boolean isMinimizing() { return false; }

	@Override
	public Double apply( final BitString x ) {
		return x.cardinality() / (double)x.length();
	}
}

final class UniformMutation
implements Heuristic<BitString> {
	@Override
	public Option< Move<BitString>> apply( Trace<BitString> t, Random random ) {
		final int bitToFlip = random.nextInt( t.getLastState().length() );
		Heuristic<BitString> h = new BitFlip( bitToFlip );
		return h.apply( t, random );
	}
}

final class OnemaxSolutionFound
implements IsFinished<BitString> {
	@Override
	public boolean apply( Trace<BitString> t, long iteration ) {
		return t.getLastState().cardinality() == t.getLastState().length();
	}
}
```

Listing 4: Concrete subclasses for the onemax problem.

```
public static void runRandomSearch( BitString initialState, Comparator< BitString > compareStates, Random random ) {
        IsFinished< BitString > isFinished = new OnemaxSolutionFound();
        RandomAccessLocality< BitString > locality = new BitFlipLocality( random );

        Acceptance< BitString >acceptance = new AllMoves< BitString >();
        Metaheuristic< BitString > meta = new RandomSearch< BitString >( locality, acceptance, isFinished );

        Trace< BitString > result = meta.iterate( Trace.cons( initialState ), random );

        BitString bestState = result.bestState( compareStates );
        System.out.println( "best:" + bestState );
}
```

Listing 5: Invoking a Random-search metaheuristic.

```
public static void runSteepestAscent( BitString initialState, Comparator<BitString> compareStates, Random random ) {
        RandomAccessLocality< BitString > locality = new BitFlipLocality( random );

        Metaheuristic< BitString > meta = new SteepestAscent< BitString >( locality, compareStates );

        Trace< BitString > result = meta.iterate( Trace.cons( initialState ), random );

        BitString bestState = result.bestState( compareStates );
        System.out.println( "best:" + bestState );
}
```

Listing 6: Invoking a Steepest-ascent metaheuristic.

4. METAHEURISTIC TEMPLATES

A number of local search algorithms are currently provided as an illustration of how to implement and/or customize metaheuristics. These include random search; iterated perturbation; iterated local search; various flavours of tabu search and a simple simulated annealing variant.

As a concrete example, Listings 4-6 give client code for the well-known 'onemax' problem, chosen for its simplicity so that problem-specifics do not obfuscate the details of how metaheuristics are configured. Listing 4 show how the evaluation function and a uniform mutation heuristic are defined. Listings 5 and 6 demonstrate the configuration of random search and steepest-ascent hillclimbing respectively. Although these two listings contain some domain-specific details in order to provide a concrete example, it will hopefully be clear that it is entirely possible to write these kind of templates in a solution-independent manner. As is typical of JAVA, the listings are rather syntactically-verbose, but since many of the interfaces being subclassed consist of a single method, much simplification of client code will be possible when support for lambdas/closures is added in JAVA 8.

5. TRACES

One option available to the algorithm designer is the *level of granularity* at which traces are described. This is of particular importance because, at a hyper-heuristic level, we can consider metaheuristics to be operators [12, 30]. We may therefore wish to compress all the activity of a metaheuristic to a single operator, either to save memory or to explicitly denote it for purposes of subsequent metaheuristic choice (for example, determination of equivalent and inverse operator pairs at a given level of algorithm operation). In the general case of stochastic operators, the designer may elect to have the trace represent either the generalised stochastic operation or else the specific concrete change made to the underlying solution representation.

To illustrate this, we give an example traces for the application of Iterative Local Search on a 5-bit onemax problem. If we elect to record concrete changes, we obtain output of the following form:

$$
\begin{aligned}
&([01000])\\
\rightarrow&(BitFlip(0), [11000])\\
\rightarrow&(BitFlip(3), [11010])\\
\rightarrow&(BitFlip(4), [11011])\\
\rightarrow&(BitFlip(2), [11111])
\end{aligned}
$$

where (BitFlip(i) is a mutation applied to a specific variable i.

If the user elects for more coarse-grained information, then the output might appear as follows:

$$
\begin{aligned}
&([01000]),\\
\rightarrow&(UniformMutation@a1e6661, [11000])\\
\rightarrow&(UniformMutation@a1e6661, [11010])\\
\rightarrow&(UniformMutation@a1e6661, [11011])\\
\rightarrow&(UniformMutation@a1e6661, [11111])
\end{aligned}
$$

where UniformMutation@a1e6661 is simply the generic uniform mutation operator with no record of the specific bit changed.

It is implicit in the nature of multi-level search methodologies such as hyper-heuristics that it should be possible to make decisions based on operator application at different heirarchical scales, and the mechanism we provide here makes this an explicit part of the API.

6. CONCLUSION AND FUTURE WORK

In this paper, we have presented HYPERION^2, a framework to support scientific research in meta- and hyper- heuristics, with a particular focus on mapping the traces taken through the search space by algorithms and their components.

The framework promotes interoperability via component interfaces and is generic enough that meta- and hyper- heuristics can reuse the same source code. Generic templates for a variety of local search algorithms are already implemented, and novel meta- and hyper- heuristics may be constructed by hybridization or extension. The framework follows an 'only pay for what you use' design philosophy, for more efficient concrete implementations and rapid prototyping.

We have described the framework's core interfaces, and given some implementation examples. We have also provided a concrete example of a trace output by the framework. HYPERION^2 is in continuing development, with several remaining priorities.

The original HYPERION [12] implementation additionally provided generic templates for Ant-Cycle System, Evolutionary Strategies and Genetic Algorithms. In order to align these with the trace-based extensions of HYPERION^2, it will be necessary to introduce some form of 'multi-trace' support (i.e. each member of the population having its own trace). Furthermore, this would allow extension to multi-objective problems, with each member of a Pareto front having a corresponding trace. Given the 'only pay for what you use' design criterion, it remains to be discussed how best to achieve this. One option is to use a shared workspace in the manner of [30] as the repository for multi-traces, with their presence being at the option of the client-programmer.

7. REFERENCES

[1] E. K. Burke, G. Kendall, Search methodologies, Springer, 2005.

[2] E. K. Burke, M. Hyde, G. Kendall, G. Ochoa, E. Özcan, J. R. Woodward, A classification of hyper-heuristic approaches, in: M. Gendreau, J.-Y. Potvin (Eds.), Handbook of Metaheuristics, Vol. 146 of International Series in Operations Research and Management Science, Springer US, 2010, pp. 449–468.

[3] J. R. Woodward, J. Swan, Why classifying search algorithms is essential, in: Progress in Informatics and Computing (PIC), 2010 IEEE International Conference on, Vol. 1, IEEE, 2010, pp. 285–289.

[4] P. Ross, S. Schulenburg, J. G. Marín-Blázquez, E. Hart, Hyper-heuristics: Learning to combine simple heuristics in bin-packing problems, in: Proceedings of the Genetic and Evolutionary Computation Conference 2002, Morgan Kaufmann Publishers Inc., San Francisco, CA, USA, 2002, pp. 942–948.

[5] S. Luke, Essentials of Metaheuristics, 2nd Edition, Lulu, 2013, available for free at http://cs.gmu.edu/~sean/book/metaheuristics/.

[6] A. J. Parkes, Combined Blackbox and AlgebRaic Architecture (CBRA), in: Proc. of PATAT 2010 (extended abstract), 2010, pp. 535–538.

[7] F. Glover, Tabu Search - Part I, INFORMS Journal on Computing 1 (3) (1989) 190–206.

[8] J. R. Woodward, J. Swan, The automatic generation of mutation operators for genetic algorithms, in: Proceedings of the 14th Genetic and Evolutionary Computation Conference Companion, GECCO Companion '12, ACM, New York, NY, USA, 2012, pp. 67–74. doi:10.1145/2330784.2330796.

[9] J. R. Woodward, J. Swan, Automatically designing selection heuristics, in: Proceedings of the 13th Conference Companion on Genetic and Evolutionary Computation, GECCO '11, ACM, New York, NY, USA, 2011, pp. 583–590. doi:10.1145/2001858.2002052.

[10] K. Krawiec, J. Swan, Pattern-guided genetic programming, in: Proceeding of the 15th Genetic and Evolutionary Computation Conference, GECCO '13, ACM, New York, NY, USA, 2013, pp. 949–956. doi:10.1145/2463372.2463496.

[11] K. Krawiec, J. Swan, Guiding evolutionary learning by searching for regularities in behavioral trajectories: A case for representation agnosticism, in: 2013 AAAI Fall Symposium Series, 2013, pp. 41–46.

[12] J. Swan, E. Özcan, G. Kendall, Hyperion: a recursive hyper-heuristic framework, in: Proceedings of the 5th international conference on Learning and Intelligent Optimization, LION'05, Springer-Verlag, Berlin, Heidelberg, 2011, pp. 616–630.

[13] C. Voudouris, R. Dorne, D. Lesaint, A. Liret, iOpt: A Software Toolkit for Heuristic Search Methods, in: T. Walsh (Ed.), Principles and Practice of Constraint Programming CP 2001, Vol. 2239 of Lecture Notes in Computer Science, Springer Berlin / Heidelberg, 2001, pp. 716–729.

[14] L. D. Gaspero, A. Schaerf, Easylocal++: An Object-oriented Framework for the flexible design of Local-Search Algorithms, Softw., Pract. Exper. 33 (8) (2003) 733–765.

[15] A. Fink, S. Voß, Hotframe: A heuristic optimization framework, in: S. Voß, D. Woodruff (Eds.), Optimization Software Class Libraries, OR/CS Interfaces Series, Kluwer Academic Publishers, Boston, 2002, pp. 81–154.

[16] M. Mitchell, An Introduction to Genetic Algorithms, The MIT Press, 1998.

[17] J. A. Parejo, A. Ruiz-Cortés, S. Lozano, P. Fernandez, Metaheuristic optimization frameworks: a survey and benchmarking, Soft Computing 16 (3) (2012) 527–561.

[18] S. Wagner, G. Kronberger, A. Beham, M. Kommenda, A. Scheibenpflug, E. Pitzer, S. Vonolfen, M. Kofler, S. Winkler, V. Dorfer, M. Affenzeller, Advanced Methods and Applications in Computational Intelligence, Vol. 6 of Topics in Intelligent Engineering and Informatics, Springer, 2014, Ch. Architecture and Design of the HeuristicLab Optimization Environment, pp. 197–261.
URL `http://link.springer.com/chapter/10.1007/978-3-319-01436-4_10`

[19] S. Luke, L. Panait, G. Balan, S. Paus, Z. Skolicki, E. Popovici, S. K, J. Harrison, J. Bassett, R. Hubley, A. Chircop, H. W. Compton J, S. Donnelly, B. Jamil, J. O'Beirne, ECJ: A Java based evolutionary computation research system (2009).
URL `http://cs.gmu.edu/~eclab/projects/ecj/`

[20] F. Otero, T. Castle, C. Johnson, EpochX: Genetic programming in java with statistics and event monitoring, in: Proceedings of the 14th genetic and

evolutionary computation conference companion, ACM, 2012, pp. 93–100.

[21] E. K. Burke, T. Curtois, M. Hyde, G. Kendall, G. Ochoa, S. Petrovic, J. A. Vazquez-Rodriguez, HyFlex: A Flexible Framework for the Design and Analysis of Hyper-heuristics, in: Multidisciplinary International Scheduling Conference (MISTA 2009), Dublin, Ireland, Dublin, Ireland, 2009, pp. 790–797. URL http://www.asap.cs.nott.ac.uk/publications/pdf/MISTA09HyFlex.pdf

[22] E. Urra, D. Cabrera-Paniagua, C. Cubillos, Towards an object-oriented pattern proposal for heuristic structures of diverse abstraction levels, in: Workshop on Agents and Collaborative Systems (WACS), School of Computer Engineering, Catholic University of Temuco, 2013. URL jcc2013.inf.uct.cl

[23] A. Elyasaf, M. Sipper, HH-evolver: a system for domain-specific, hyper-heuristic evolution, in: Proceeding of the 15th conference companion on Genetic and evolutionary computation conference companion, ACM, 2013, pp. 1285–1292.

[24] H. K. Cora, H. T. Uyar, A. Ş. Etaner-Uyar, HH-DSL: a domain specific language for selection hyper-heuristics, in: Proceeding of the 15th Genetic and evolutionary computation conference companion, ACM, 2013, pp. 1317–1324.

[25] Lindawati, H. Lau, D. Lo, Instance-based parameter tuning via search trajectory similarity clustering, in: C. Coello (Ed.), Learning and Intelligent Optimization, Vol. 6683 of Lecture Notes in Computer Science, Springer Berlin Heidelberg, 2011, pp. 131–145. doi:10.1007/978-3-642-25566-3_10.

[26] Lindawati, H. Lau, F. Zhu, Instance-specific parameter tuning via constraint-based clustering, in: Proc. of the 1st Int. Workshop on COmbining COnstraint solving with MIning and LEarning(CoCoMile' 12), joint with ECAI, Montpellier, France, 2012.

[27] L. Lindawati, F. ZHU, H. C. LAU, FloTra: Flower-shape trajectory mining for instance-specific parameter tuning, 10th edition of the Metaheuristics International Conference (MIC 2013), 2013.

[28] E. Gamma, R. Helm, R. E. Johnson, J. M. Vlissides, Design patterns: Abstraction and reuse of object-oriented design, in: ECOOP '93: Proceedings of the 7th European Conference on Object-Oriented Programming, Springer-Verlag, London, UK, 1993, pp. 406–431.

[29] J. O. Coplien, Curiously recurring template patterns, C++ Rep. 7 (2) (1995) 24–27. URL http://dl.acm.org/citation.cfm?id=229227.229229

[30] J. Swan, J. Woodward, E. Özcan, G. Kendall, E. Burke, Searching the hyper-heuristic design space, Cognitive Computation 6 (1) (2014) 66–73.

A Scalable Symbolic Expression Tree Interpreter for the HeuristicLab Optimization Framework

Simone Cirillo
cirillo@almontcapital.com

Stefan Lloyd
lloyd@almontcapital.com

Almont Capital LLC
12800 Hillcrest Road
Dallas, Texas 75230

ABSTRACT

In this paper we describe a novel implementation of the Interpreter class for the metaheuristic optimization framework HeuristicLab, comparing it with the three existing interpreters provided with the framework. The Interpreter class is an internal software component utilized by HeuristicLab for the evaluation of the symbolic expression trees on which its Genetic Programming (GP) implementation relies. The proposed implementation is based on the creation and compilation of a .NET Expression Tree. We also analyze the Interpreters' performance, evaluating the algorithm execution times on GP Symbolic Regression problems for different run settings. Our implementation results to be the fastest on all evaluations, with comparatively better performance the larger the run population size, dataset length and tree size are, increasing HeuristicLab's computational efficiency for large problem setups.

Categories and Subject Descriptors

D.3.4 [**Programming Languages**]: Processors—*Interpreters*; D.2.8 [**Software Engineering**]: Metrics—*Performance measures*; D.2.11 [**Software Engineering**]: Software Architectures—*Domain-specific architectures*; I.2.2 [**Artificial Intelligence**]: Automatic Programming—*Program synthesis*

Keywords

Genetic Programming; HeuristicLab; Interpreter; .NET Expression Trees; Performance

1. INTRODUCTION

HeuristicLab is an open-source metaheuristic optimization framework developed and maintained by the Heuristic and Evolutionary Algorithms Laboratory of the Upper Austria University of Applied Sciences [14, 13]. HeuristicLab supports a variety of heuristic optimization techniques, among which Genetic Programming. Algorithms are implemented using an Operator Graph: a series of loosely-coupled `Operator` objects executed in sequence exposing values and other objects to each other, representing the successive steps in the algorithm workflow as well as the solution analysis process.

Thanks to an entirely modular, plugin-based architecture, HeuristicLab decouples the heuristic algorithm from the problem to be solved, provided the two are compatible. Examples of supported problems are, as of version 3.3.9, Symbolic Regression, Symbolic Classification, Artificial Ant, Traveling Salesman, and Vehicle Routing. HeuristicLab is open-source, and developers are encouraged to write their own plugins for use-cases not supported out of the box.

HeuristicLab supports communication to and from other software [7]; one of the intended uses for this feature is the optimization of simulation-based problems for which the simulation environment is external, as described by Beham et al. [2, 3]; in these documented implementations HeuristicLab was used to optimize simulation parameters and settings. This contrasts with algorithms evolving agents or models acting in a simulation environment, as with Genetic Programming. External evaluation, additionally, is not a feasible approach when the simulation software cannot be interfaced to other programs, or where doing so would be structurally inconvenient and computationally costly, or finally where the optimization algorithm requires inputs representing simulation state variables.

Considering there are no clear guidelines or previous examples regarding the implementation of such a scenario and that HeuristicLab provides all the necessary source files and tools, encouraging the development of additional functionality, our final goal is the development of a series of HeuristicLab plugins implementing a general framework for the internal evaluation of Genetic Programming solutions for simulation-based problems, providing a clear execution flow and domain-specific abstractions and features.

In order to make HeuristicLab capable of running Genetic Programming simulation-based evaluations internally, several components of its execution flow have to be reworked.

1.1 GP Interpreters

The Genetic Programming (GP) implementation present in HeuristicLab is tree-based, an approach popularized by Koza [8]. In tree-based GP individuals consist of expression trees: data structures used to represent and evaluate mathematical (algebraic, boolean) expressions. In an expression tree leaf nodes contain operands, while internal nodes contain the operators. To evaluate the expression, the repre-

GECCO'14, July 12–16, 2014, Vancouver, BC, Canada.

ACM 978-1-4503-2881-4/14/07 ...$15.00.
http://dx.doi.org/10.1145/2598394.2605692.

sentation tree has to be traversed. In HeuristicLab, this functionality is implemented by the `Interpreter` class [7].

HeuristicLab provides three alternative implementations of the `Interpreter` class, they implement a common interface and they are therefore interchangeable to other `Operator` objects requiring their functionality; however their internal structure and logic are substantially different.

The `Interpreter`'s public method returns, as its output, the raw numerical values resulting from the evaluation of the individual on the dataset; these are then passed on to the `Evaluator` operator, where the fitness score is computed. This is an acceptable solution for regression and classification problems, both of which are prominent HeuristicLab use-cases, however it is not optimal for simulation problems.

Therefore, as the first step towards the implementation of a HeuristicLab plugin framework able to evolve symbolic Genetic Programming solutions for simulation problems, in this work we will describe an `Interpreter` with a modified public interface as well as a novel internal implementation and we will compare its performance against the `Interpreter` implementations provided together with HeuristicLab.

In Section 2 we will review the three `Interpreter` implementations provided with HeuristicLab and identify their weaknesses on the prospective use on simulation problems. In Section 3 we will describe our novel `Interpreter` implementation. In Section 4 we will evaluate the `Interpreters`' performance in terms of run execution times. In Section 5 we will draw conclusions and outline future steps.

2. GP INTERPRETERS IN HEURISTICLAB

HeuristicLab, as of version 3.3.9, provides three different `Interpreter` implementations able to process GP trees encoding mathematical expressions: `SymbolicDataAnalysisExpressionTreeInterpreter`, `SymbolicDataAnalysisExpressionTreeILEmittingInterpreter`, and `SymbolicDataAnalysisExpressionTreeLinearInterpreter`; these can be interchangeably used in the Symbolic Regression, Symbolic Classification, Time Series Evaluation and Trading problem templates.

The three symbolic tree interpreters all implement the `ISymbolicDataAnalysisExpressionTreeInterpreter` interface, exposing the `IEnumerable<double> GetSymbolicExpressionTreeValues(ISymbolicExpressionTree tree, Dataset dataset, IEnumerable<int> rows)` method; from the method's signature, it is evident how the `Interpreter` objects are not only performing tree interpretation and evaluation, but they are also responsible for computing and returning the output values given a dataset.

For the sake of completeness, we mention that HeuristicLab also features other `Interpreter` classes; these are however specific to the type of optimization problem they are used for and do not evaluate mathematical expressions, therefore we will briefly describe them in Section 2.5 but we will not be analyzing their performance.

2.1 Common Logic

Part of the three `Interpreter`'s internal workflow is common. In computing, an interpreter can be defined as a program that implements a virtual machine using a programming language as its own assembly language. As such, the three HeuristicLab interpreters all start by traversing the expression tree, parsing it into a linear, one-dimensional array of `Instruction` objects. `Instruction` is a data structure comprising an `OpCode` that specifies an operation and appropriate operands (data, number of arguments, addressing), as described by Kommenda et al. [7]. After the `Instruction[]` corresponding to the program has been generated, it is iterated a second time to specify the jump locations for flow control instructions, if any. Finally, it is iterated a third time to finalize input variable referencing: `Instruction` objects referring to variables are assigned, as their data field, the entire set of values for that variable contained in the problem `Dataset`.

`Instruction` objects therefore represent assembly-level instructions for the virtual machine the HeuristicLab GP individuals run on. The `Instruction[]` is produced and then processed differently for the three `Interpreter` implementations.

2.2 SymbolicDataAnalysis-ExpressionTreeInterpreter

Here to create the `Instruction[]` the tree is traversed in pre-order fashion, then the list is passed to the `Evaluate (Dataset dataset, ref int row, InterpreterState state)` method. `Evaluate` is recursive, calling itself on the following `Instruction` number of arguments times. Therefore its operations are analogous to a post-order evaluation of the original expression tree. `InterpreterState` is a class containing the `Instruction[]` and a simple call-stack implementation; this allows `SymbolicDataAnalysisExpressionTreeInterpreter` to support GP individuals featuring Automatically Defined Functions (ADFs).

`Evaluate` is called at the root level, and therefore the entire `Instruction[]` list is interpreted, once per evaluated row. This results in computational overhead proportional to the number of evaluated rows length, `SymbolicDataAnalysisExpressionTreeInterpreter` is therefore best suited for the evaluation of short datasets.

Throughout the rest of this paper this interpreter will be referred to as `Standard`.

2.3 SymbolicDataAnalysisExpressionTree-ILEmittingInterpreter

`SymbolicDataAnalysisExpressionTreeILEmittingInterpreter`, from here on referred to as `IL`, strictly speaking, is an interpreter only partially. The class, before performing evaluation, first traverses the tree in pre-order, like `Standard`; however later it performs a recursive post-order parsing of the `Instruction[]`, translating it directly into Common Intermediate Language (CIL) instructions, making use of the `Reflection.Emit` capabilities of .NET.

CIL is is the lowest-level human-readable language defined by the Common Language Infrastructure specification and used by the .NET Framework; CIL is an object-oriented assembly language, and it is entirely stack-based [5].

Once all the CIL instructions for the program have been obtained, the .NET Just-In-Time compiler is called, returning an executable handle for the function in the form of a `delegate` method with input signature matching the `Dataset` variables. Therefore, `IL` is a compiler: it produces an executable function implementing the operations encoded in the original expression tree.

Successively, to evaluate the function, the delegate is invoked once per row to obtain the output values. In terms of computational overhead this approach results in an initial one for every GP individual, due to the invocation of the .NET compiler; however, as there is no re-interpretation or re-compilation for every row, such overhead is completely independent from the number of rows to be evaluated. For this reason `IL` is much more suited for the evaluation of longer datasets than `Standard`, the creators state 10,000 rows as the point where this interpreter starts performing better [7]. Currently, `IL` does not support ADFs.

2.4 SymbolicDataAnalysisExpressionTreeLinearInterpreter

`SymbolicDataAnalysisExpressionTreeLinearInterpreter`, from now `Linear`, is a refinement of `Standard`: they share the general concept as well as the interpreted approach. However, in this implementation `Instruction` is extended to `LinearInstruction`, adding a `value` and a `childIndex` field.

The initial tree traversal is here performed breadth-first, therefore the obtained `LinearInstruction[]` is in different order than with the other two interpreters. `childindex` is initialized to contain the instruction number for the first argument to the instruction while the others, given the traversal, will be found in the adjacent successive positions; `value` will be used at evaluation time to store partial results.

This implementation results in behavior analogous to that of a linear register machine: the `value` fields of `LinearInstruction` act as the linear registers. At evaluation time, the `LinearInstruction[]` is iterated starting from the bottom. This resolves the `value` fields in a leaves-to-root direction, ensuring by design that the value of arguments to a `LinearInstruction` have already been computed when the instruction is executed.

As a consequence of this, the `Evaluate(Dataset dataset, int row, LinearInstruction[] code)` method of this interpreter is recursion-free and executes the `LinearInstruction[]` entirely linearly. Therefore, the computational overhead due to row-by-row interpretation is substantially reduced compared to `Standard`. Currently, `Linear` does not support ADFs.

It is worth specifying that even though the individual evaluation is performed using a linear machine abstraction, the type of Genetic Programming in use is still Tree Genetic Programming, as opposed to Linear Genetic Programming (LGP) [1, 4]. That is because the GP Selection, Crossover and Mutation operators still act on the original tree representations.

2.5 Problem Specific Interpreters

In addition to the three interpreters described so far, HeuristicLab relies on this architectural pattern for other types of optimization problems as well. Examples of these are `Lawnmower.Interpreter` and `ArtificialAnt.AntInterpreter`. The interpreters for such other problems are, however, far less generic and generalizable. These do not compute mathematical expressions nor they output a list of numerical values: they operate instead on tree structures featuring problem-specific types of nodes and directly output an action to be performed in response to the inputs.

2.6 Limitations

As mentioned in Section 2, the symbolic expression interpreters' `GetSymbolicExpressionTreeValues(ISymbolicExpressionTree tree, Dataset dataset, IEnumerable <int> rows)` method returns the raw output numerical values resulting from the evaluation of the GP individual on the dataset; the `Evaluator` computing the fitness score assumes this behavior, as specified by the `ISymbolicExpressionTreeInterpreter` interface. Therefore, in order to comply to this specification, for a simulation-based evaluation the running of the simulation would have to be implemented within the `Interpreter`, providing the `Evaluator` with the values required to compute the individual's fitness.

For the Santa Fe Trail problem implementation [9], the `ArtificialAnt.Interpreter` mentioned in Section 2.5 is realized exactly in such a way: `ArtificialAnt.Interpreter` does not implement the `ISymbolicExpressionTree` interface but does instead expose a `Run()` method inside which the ant world simulation takes place, once `Run()` completes execution the fitness score is retrieved. The design works well if the simulation to be run is relatively simple, with few evaluation and performance measures. If the simulation problem or the evaluations and analyses to be performed are more complex instead, such design choice becomes constraining and intensive from a developmental and computational point of view:

- HeuristicLab does not provide a structured class and interface framework to generalize tree interpretation and simulation running within an `Interpreter`, so for every problem type `Interpreter`, `Evaluator`, and `Analyzer` classes would have to be written ad-hoc, in addition to the code for the simulation logic itself.

- Interpreting a symbolic expression and evaluating its fitness are two distinct and separate tasks, implementing them inside the same logical object implicitly promotes the emergence of unnecessary dependencies and greatly reduces the maintainability and reusability of the code base.

- Another drawback is the computational impact of having an interpreted approach, even if partial, as opposed to a compiled one: for very large population and dataset sizes, as it is common with simulation problems, the once-per-row overhead of interpreted GP individuals becomes dominant with respect to the initial, once-per-individual, overhead of compiled individuals; resulting in substantially longer execution times for algorithm runs.

- Finally, in the case GP individuals are not only to have access to external, provided inputs, but to simulation state variables depending on their own actions on previous datapoints as well, it follows that it is impossible to obtain these internal state values without running the simulation itself, which is also what ultimately produces the fitness score, de facto coinciding with the intended functionality of `Evaluator`.

Given that the architecture of HeuristicLab strongly relies on interface and inheritance mechanisms to provide as much generalization as possible, we think that a framework of classes providing the necessary abstractions enabling HeuristicLab to internally run GP encoding mathematical expressions on simulation problems fits well with HeuristicLab's vision and purpose, as it would add a very general and useful problem type to its capabilities.

To achieve such goal, partial reimplementation of **Interpreters**, **Evaluators**, and **Analyzers** is required. We will begin from the **Interpreter** class because it is the first one to be employed in HeuristicLab's execution workflow.

3. .NETEXPRESSIONINTERPRETER

3.1 Design Overview

As stated in Section 2.6, our goal is to have compiled GP individuals as well as separating interpretation/compilation from evaluation, therefore our interpreter does not implement the `ISymbolicDataAnalysisExpressionTreeInterpreter` interface and the `GetSymbolicExpressionTreeValues` method described in Section 2.

Our interpreter instead is designed to interface with its `Evaluator` via the `Func<int, double[][], double[], double> GetCompiledFunction(ISymbolicExpressionTree tree)` method. In C#, `Func` is an anonymous, generic function type [11]; the `GetCompiledFunction` method therefore outputs an executable function with `int`, `double[][]`, and `double[]` arguments and with `double` return value.

It will be then the `Evaluator` to be responsible for evaluating the individual on the problem data, running the simulation.

3.2 .NET Expressions

.NET Expression Trees are data structures used to represent, construct, compile and run code itself [10]. In an Expression Tree, nodes are constituted by `Expression` objects. `Expression` objects can be used to represent many code constructs including constant values, variables, mathematical operations, method calls, control flow statements, scope blocks, etc... [12].

`Expression` trees can be constructed programmatically by combining single `Expression` objects, passing them as constructor parameters to others, resulting in a tree structure. Finally, an `Expression` tree can be converted into a lambda expression, specifying one or more `ParameterExpression` as its argument(s), and then compiled into an executable delegate which, invoked, executes the function encoded by the original tree.

The code in Listing 1 shows a simple example of this process for an expression tree representing the sum of two elements of an array.

.NET Expression Trees allow the conversion of a tree data structure into executable code. Given how closely this behavior matches with the concept of Tree GP, we chose to rely on .NET Expression Trees for the implementation of our `Interpreter` class: `DotNETExpressionInterpreter`.

Compared with emitting CIL instructions and then calling the compiler on them, as in the case of `IL`, the use of `Expression` trees entails a slightly larger initial computational overhead: in the former case assembly instructions are already specified so the compiler is invoked directly, while in the latter the `Expression` tree has to first be parsed into CIL and compiled subsequently. However, the use of `Expression` trees give several advantages over explicit CIL emission:

```
ParameterExpression inputs =
    Expression.Parameter
      (typeof(double[]), "inputs");

BinaryExpression i1 =
    Expression.ArrayIndex
      (inputs, Expression.Constant(0));

BinaryExpression i2 =
    Expression.ArrayIndex
      (inputs, Expression.Constant(1));

BinaryExpression sum =
    Expression.Add(i1, i2);

Expression<Func<double[], double>> lambda =
  Expression.Lambda<Func<double[], double>>
      (sum, new ParameterExpression[] {inputs});

Func<double[], double> method = lambda.Compile();

double[] values = {1, 2};

method(values);
```

Listing 1: Construction, parameterization, compilation and invocation of a .NET Expression Tree implementing the sum of two numbers

- The `Interpreter`'s own code is much more readable and understandable
- Expressions can be visualized and printed in linear, parenthesized, infix form via their `ToString()` method, therefore the correctness of the tree building process can be easily verified
- Considering how `Expression` objects can represent arbitrary method calls, it is in principle possible to rely on such technique to support ADFs
- Relieving the developer from directly writing CIL instructions makes it easier to implement functionality for tree nodes representing more elaborate instructions

3.3 Workflow

1. Our `DotNETExpressionInterpreter` has a pre-processing step, shown in Listing 2, executing only when the `Dataset` object for the problem setup is modified. Here the names of the `Dataset` variables are mapped to `ParameterExpression` objects containing their column index, later allowing to build the `Expression` tree using parameterized input arguments whose value will only be specified when the already compiled tree is evaluated.

2. `DotNETExpressionInterpreter` parses the HeuristicLab `SymbolicExpressionTree` recursively, in post-order; each recursive call on a node returns the compound `Expression` representing that node's subtree including itself. No additional tree traversal is needed to produce the final `Expression` tree, as the input variables have been mapped in pre-processing.

   The code in Listing 3 shows parts of the tree parsing logic exemplifying the processing for different types of nodes.

```
...

private Dictionary<string, Expression> paramVarMap;
private Dictionary<string, Expression> inputsVarMap;

...

private void UpdateInputsMap(IEnumerable<string> vars)
{

  paramVarMap = new Dictionary<string, Expression>();
  inputsVarMap = new Dictionary<string, Expression>();

  ParameterExpression varParam =
      Expression.Parameter
          (typeof(double[][]), "variables");

  ParameterExpression rowIndexParam =
      Expression.Parameter
          (typeof(int), "rowIndex");

  paramVarMap.Add("variables", varParam);
  paramVarMap.Add("rowIndex", rowIndexParam);

  List<string> varNames = vars.ToList();
  for (int i = 0; i < vars.Count(); i++)
      inputsVarMap.Add
          (varNames[i], Expression.Constant(i));

}
```

Listing 2: `DotNETExpressionInterpreter` pre-processing stage. Dataset variable names are mapped to `ParameterExpression` objects, later enabling the compiled `Expression` tree to be evaluated on arbitrary inputs

3. The tree, as described earlier, is then wrapped into a `LambdaExpression`.

4. The .NET compiler is invoked on the `LambdaExpression`.

5. `DotNETExpressionInterpreter` outputs a compiled `Func<int, double[][], double[], double>`, mapped to a `double CompiledFunction(int rowindex, double[][] data, double[] states)` for better typed access.

   `double[][] data` is the entire problem dataset in matrix form (HeuristicLab's `Dataset` was modified to provide such accessor), `int rowindex` represents the row to be evaluated in the call, `double[] states` is the input vector representing the internal simulation state variables for the problem.

6. At Evaluation time a compatible `Evaluator` will be responsible for running the simulation, making use of the now compiled individual.

4. PERFORMANCE ANALYSIS

In order to comparatively evaluate the performance of the three interpreters described in Section 2 as well as `DotNETExpressionInterpreter` (`.NET`), we wrapped the latter in logic implementing the `ISymbolicDataAnalysisExpressionTreeInterpreter` interface, enabling it to run on HeuristicLab's problem templates without the need for developing additional code.

```
private Expression RecursiveParser
    (ISymbolicExpressionTreeNode node)
{
    ISymbol s = node.Symbol;
    Expression expr = null;

    if (s is Addition)
    {
      Expression left =
          RecursiveParser(node.GetSubtree(0));
      Expression right =
          RecursiveParser(node.GetSubtree(1));
      expr = Expression.Add(left, right);
    }
    ...
    else if (s is Sine)
    {
      Expression sub =
          RecursiveParser(node.GetSubtree(0));
      expr = Expression.Call
          (null, typeof(Math).GetMethod("Sin"), sub);
    }
    ...
    else if (s is Variable)
    {
      VariableTreeNode vn = node as VariableTreeNode;
      Expression ve = Expression.ArrayIndex
          (Expression.ArrayIndex
              (paramVarMap["variables"],
               paramVarMap["rowIndex"]),
          inputsVarMap[vn.VariableName]);

      if (vn.Weight != 1)
      {
        Expression we = Expression.Constant(vn.Weight);
        expr = Expression.Multiply(ve, we);
      }
      else
        expr = ve;
    }

   return expr;
}
```

Listing 3: `DotNETExpressionInterpreter` parsing logic for tree nodes representing a binary operator (`Addition`), a unary operator (`Sine`), and a terminal node (`Variable`)

The fraction of the total GP algorithm run time taken up by tree interpretation and evaluation is proportional to the number of dataset rows, while the execution time for other algorithm steps such as tree creation, selection, crossover, mutation, etc... is not dependant on it. In the case of HeuristicLab Kommenda et al. note that tree interpretation and evaluation dominate the total runtime for datasets exceeding 1,000 rows [7]. Since we will be analyzing cases with no less than 5,000 dataset rows, such considerations allow us to approximate the evaluation of the interpreters' performance to the simple measuring of the total algorithm execution time.

All the presented evaluations were performed on an Intel Core i7-2600K machine set at a frequency of 3.8 GHz with 16GB of RAM.

4.1 Population Size

The performance of all four interpreters was tested by running the Genetic Programming - Symbolic Regression problem template on the Real World Benchmark Problems - Tower dataset, both provided with HeuristicLab.

Common settings for the runs are 20 calculated generations, a dataset length of 5,000, a parallelization setting of

Population	Interpreter			
	Standard	Linear	IL	.NET
1,000	34.2 (1.2)	20.2 (1.3)	20.3 (1.2)	19.6 (0.8)
2,000	79.8 (0.6)	43.7 (0.4)	43.9 (0.5)	42.4 (0.6)
5,000	253.1 (0.4)	125.2 (0.5)	128.3 (0.5)	121.3 (0.1)
10,000	421.5 (0.4)	225.1 (0.2)	233.5 (0.7)	221.3 (0.7)

Table 1: Average (s) and relative standard deviation (%) values of the algorithm run times for different population sizes

Dataset Length	Interpreter		
	Linear	IL	.NET
5,000	103.4 (2.7)	103.0 (0.2)	99.1 (0.5)
10,000	166.9 (1.0)	144.7 (0.3)	136.7 (0.5)
15,000	234.3 (0.4)	192.4 (0.4)	176.4 (0.5)

Table 2: Average (s) and relative standard deviation (%) values of the algorithm run times for different dataset lengths

4, probabilistic tree creator with maximum tree size 150, and a fixed, constant seed value to ensure the interpreters evaluate the very same expression trees. For each of the four interpreters we performed 5 runs for each of the following population sizes: 1,000, 2,000, 5,000, 10,000. Table 1 shows the average and relative standard deviation of the obtained execution times.

Confirming the observation by Kommenda et al. in [7], for such dataset lengths the run times increase linearly with respect to the total number of tree evaluations performed, this results to be true regardless of the interpreter.

It is evident how `Standard` is consistently the slowest by a considerable margin: on average `Standard` times are 1.8 longer. The overhead with respect to the others also appears to be increasing with growing population sizes. This first evaluation demonstrates how the `Standard` interpreter is not suited for large population runs and therefore we will not be evaluating it further.

`.NET` is the best performing across all population sizes, even if by a small margin compared to `IL` and `Linear`.

4.2 Dataset Length

The Tower dataset used previously only provides 5,000 datapoints, so to investigate the relation between dataset length and execution times we used the Bike Sharing dataset [6]. We evaluated the `Linear`, `IL`, and `.NET` interpreters on the on the first 5,000, 10,000, and 15,000 rows of the dataset, performing 3 runs per setting. Population size is set at 5,000; other settings are the the same as the ones in Section 4.1. The results for this evaluation are reported in Table 2.

Kommenda et al. mention 10,000 as the number of dataset rows where the use of `IL` is recommended over `Standard` and `Linear` [7]; on our results such threshold appears to be at a lower row count: at 10,000 rows `Linear` is already 15% slower than `IL`.

The values clearly show how `Linear` goes from having a comparable performance to `IL` and `.NET` for 5,000 datapoints (4% slower than `.NET`, 0.4% than `IL`), to being considerably worse at 15,000 (33% slower than `.NET`, 22% slower than `IL`). This growing gap is explained by the inherent per-datapoint overhead of having an individual interpreted, as opposed to compiled; therefore, `Linear` too would not be a good choice for large population, long dataset runs.

Tree Length	Interpreter		
	Linear	IL	.NET
100	76.9 (0.2)	81.1 (0.3)	77.5 (0.7)
150	159.3 (1.1)	157.8 (0.3)	148.5 (0.3)
200	435.3 (0.3)	386.1 (0.4)	341.7 (0.3)

Table 3: Average and relative standard deviation (%) of the algorithm run times for different tree sizes

To explain the increasing performance difference between `IL` and `.NET` on this test: a 3% difference for 5,000 rows and a 9% one for 15,000, one possibility could be the way the variables are accessed at evaluation time. `.NET`'s input is a two-dimensional array; while `IL` partially relies on a list, bound to have a slight performance overhead over the former when accessing elements.

4.3 Tree Length

Another factor affecting interpreter performance is length of the symbolic trees; we analyzed the execution times of `Linear`, `IL` and `.NET` changing only the maximum allowed tree size: 100, 150, 200. This evaluation was performed on the 5,000 rows Tower dataset, with a population size of 5,000. In order to magnify the effect of tree length on performance for this run we utilized the full tree creator rather than the probabilistic one. Table 3 displays the results.

`Linear` exhibits a behavior analogous to the one it has in the evaluation on different dataset lengths described in Section 4.2: it goes from having a very slight, sub-second, performance advantage for length 100, to a very slight overhead at 150, to lastly obtaining significantly slower times than the other two for tree length 200. The increasingly worse performance is still because of a per-datapoint overhead, this time due to longer, deeper, trees requiring more time to be parsed rather than having more rows to evaluate.

`.NET` results to be the best performer on this evaluation as well, the performance gains with respect to both `Linear` and `IL` positively correlate with tree size.

The growing difference between `IL` and `.NET` could be explained by the fact that for the former the starting `SymbolicExpressionTree` is parsed three times to arrive to its compiled form; in the case of the latter instead it is explicitly parsed once in the interpreter and another time by the compiler, for a total of two. Furthermore, considering that in `IL` the logic for CIL translation was coded manually, another possibility could be the presence of suboptimalities in the generated CIL instructions, leading to an increasing overhead over a compiler-optimized CIL the more instructions, and correspondingly tree nodes, there are.

5. CONCLUSION

The high sensitivity of `Standard` to population size and of `Linear` to dataset length demonstrate how a compiled execution of GP individuals is crucial to have usable performance in large population, long dataset scenarios.

Considering how our `DotNETExpressionInterpreter` performs better than `IL` in all three performed evaluations and furthermore that the difference in performance is also proportional to increasing population size, dataset length, and tree length, we consider our implementation a success.

The shown good performance scaling is not only of key importance in the prospected context of simulation-based problem GP evaluations within HeuristicLab; but it can also be useful in large population, long dataset setup for more conventional problem types such as symbolic regression and symbolic classification.

An issue not addressed in this work that could still pose a challenge for GP runs entailing a very large number of evaluations is that dynamically emitted code, as both `IL` and `.NET` do, is not removed by the .NET Garbage Collector; potentially leading to system memory exhaustion before the optimization process is complete. Therefore, further examination of this phenomenon is required to assess its quantitative impact.

The following steps for the implementation of the entire simulation-problem framework consist in the establishing of common Interfaces and reimplementation of Evaluators and Analyzers.

6. REFERENCES

[1] W. Banzhaf, P. Nordin, R. E. Keller, and F. D. Francone. *Genetic programming: an introduction*, volume 1. Morgan Kaufmann San Francisco, 1998.

[2] A. Beham et al. Simulation optimization with HeuristicLab, 2008.

[3] A. Beham, M. Kofler, S. Wagner, and M. Affenzeller. Coupling simulation with HeuristicLab to solve facility layout problems. In *Winter Simulation Conference*, WSC '09, pages 2205–2217. Winter Simulation Conference, 2009.

[4] M. F. Brameier and W. Banzhaf. *Linear genetic programming*. Springer, 2007.

[5] ECMA. *Common Language Infrastructure (CLI) Partitions I to VI*, chapter Partition III: CIL Instruction Set, pages 290–432. ECMA International, 6th edition, June 2012.

[6] H. Fanaee-T. Uci machine learning repository: Bike sharing dataset data set. `https://archive.ics.uci.edu/ml/datasets/Bike+Sharing+Dataset`, March 2014.

[7] M. Kommenda, G. Kronberger, S. Wagner, S. Winkler, and M. Affenzeller. On the architecture and implementation of tree-based genetic programming in HeuristicLab. In *Proceedings of the fourteenth international conference on genetic and evolutionary computation conference companion*, pages 101–108. ACM, 2012.

[8] J. R. Koza. *Genetic Programming: vol. 1, On the programming of computers by means of natural selection*, volume 1. MIT press, 1992.

[9] J. R. Koza. *Genetic Programming: vol. 1, On the programming of computers by means of natural selection*, volume 1, pages 147–155. MIT press, 1992.

[10] MSDN. Expression Trees (C# and Visual Basic). `http://msdn.microsoft.com/en-us/library/bb397951.aspx`, March 2014.

[11] MSDN. Func(T1, T2, T3, TResult) Delegate. `http://http://msdn.microsoft.com/en-us/library/bb549430%28v=vs.110%29.aspx`, March 2014.

[12] MSDN. System.Linq.Expressions Namespace. `http://msdn.microsoft.com/en-us/library/system.linq.expressions.aspx`, March 2014.

[13] S. Wagner and M. Affenzeller. HeuristicLab: A generic and extensible optimization environment. In *Adaptive and Natural Computing Algorithms*, pages 538–541. Springer, 2005.

[14] S. Wagner, G. Kronberger, A. Beham, M. Kommenda, A. Scheibenpflug, E. Pitzer, S. Vonolfen, M. Kofler, S. Winkler, V. Dorfer, and M. Affenzeller. *Advanced Methods and Applications in Computational Intelligence*, volume 6 of *Topics in Intelligent Engineering and Informatics*, chapter Architecture and Design of the HeuristicLab Optimization Environment, pages 197–261. Springer, 2014.

A Genetic Programming Problem Definition Language Code Generator for the EpochX Framework

Claris Leroux
INSA Rouen
Haute-Normandie
France
claris.leroux@insa-rouen.fr

Fernando E. B. Otero
School of Computing
University of Kent
Chatham Maritime, UK
F.E.B.Otero@kent.ac.uk

Colin G. Johnson
School of Computing
University of Kent
Canterbury, UK
C.G.Johnson@kent.ac.uk

ABSTRACT

There are many different genetic programming (GP) frameworks that can be used to implement algorithms to solve a particular optimization problem. In order to use a framework, users need to become familiar with a large numbers of source code before actually implementing the algorithm, adding a learning overhead. In some cases, this can prevent users from trying out different frameworks. This paper discusses the implementation of a code generator in the EpochX framework to facilitate the implementation of GP algorithms. The code generator is based on the GP definition language (GPDL), which is a framework-independent language that can be used to specify GP problems.

Categories and Subject Descriptors

I.2.8 [**Artificial Intelligence**]: Problem Solving, Control Methods, and Search—*Heuristic methods*

General Terms

Algorithms

Keywords

EpochX, genetic programming, GPDL, code generator

1. INTRODUCTION

EpochX [6] is an open source genetic programming (GP) framework, which provides three flavours of GP representations: strongly-typed tree GP (STGP) [1, 3], context-free grammar GP (CFG-GP) [9], and grammatical evolution (GE) [5]. The framework has a modular and flexible architecture that allows the customization of almost every aspect of a GP algorithm and, at the same time, it provides default implementations of popular procedures (e.g., roulette/tournament selection, grow/full/ramped half-and-half tree initialisation). It also provides an event-based framework to track the progress of the algorithm, allowing users to register listeners that receive notifications about its lifecycle (e.g., at the start/end of a generation, when a particular genetic operator is used). The information provided by the events can also be used to generate elaborated output, such as GUI interfaces [7], without requiring any extra implementation in the GP algorithm.

While EpochX structure is clear and the framework provide base classes to help the definition/implementation of new algorithms, a user has to become familiar with their purposes and uses. For new users, coming from a different framework, there might not be much similarities that can reduce the effort of implementing an algorithm in EpochX. Kronberger et al. [2] identified that implementing GP algorithms using specific frameworks involves writing a lot of code that is not directly related to the problem specification, but required to fit the problem implementation into the framework. The Genetic Programming Problem Definition Language (GPDL), proposed in [2], is designed as alternative to specify GP problems with the aim of reducing the effort of implementing GP algorithms. This paper presents a code generator for the EpochX framework that takes a GPDL problem definition to generate the required source code to run the GP problem in the EpochX framework. The motivation is to reduce the effort of writing GP algorithms using EpochX, since most of the framework-specific details are automatically generated by the code generator and the user only needs to focus on the GPDL problem description.

The remainder of the paper is structured as follows. Section 2 presents an overview of the genetic programming problem definition language, which is the language used to specify the GP problem to the code generator. Section 3 presents the details of the code generator. Section 4 presents a complete example of a GP problem definition written in GPDL for the EpochX framework. Finally, Section 5 concludes the paper and presents future research directions.

2. GPDL

The Genetic Programming Problem Definition Language (GPDL) was proposed by Kronberger et al. [2] as a framework-independent language to specify GP problems. One of the main motivations of the GPDL proposal was to reduce the effort of using a GP framework to implement new GP algorithms. As discussed by Kronberger et al., the implementation of a GP algorithm requires a lot of boilerplate code, which most of the time is very repetitive—e.g., in object-oriented GP frameworks, the definition of a new non-terminal (function) involves the sub-classing of a base

GECCO'14, July 12–16, 2014, Vancouver, BC, Canada.

ACM 978-1-4503-2881-4/14/07 ...$15.00.
http://dx.doi.org/10.1145/2598394.2605691.

non-terminal class, in combination to adding package imports and other specific language requirements. On top of this, the user of the GP framework has to become familiar with a large amount of framework-specific source code—since frameworks generally have a very different API and can be implemented in different programming languages—instead of focusing only on the problem definition.

A problem definition written in GPDL allows the user to specify all details of the GP problem in a single file, including the definition of the syntax (e.g., terminal and non-terminal symbols, grammar rules) and the semantics (e.g., non-terminal behaviour, fitness function). The main sections in a GPDL problem definitions are:

- `PROBLEM <name>`: Begins the problem definition and it is followed by the name of the problem;
- `CODE`: Allows the inclusion of additional source code—e.g., variable declarations;
- `INIT`: Allows the inclusion of additional source code that is run only once at the beginning of the execution;
- `NONTERMINALS`: Contains the definition of non-terminal symbols, including its name, parameters and semantic action (behaviour);
- `TERMINALS`: Contains the definition of terminal symbols, including its name, semantic action and constraints (e.g., values range);
- `RULES`: Grammar rules of the problem, using the terminals and non-terminals defined previously;
- `MAXIMIZE` or `MINIMIZE`: The objective (fitness) function to be either maximized or minimized.

While the GPDL is independent of the framework and programming language, a problem definition specified using the GPDL will eventually be dependent on the specific framework and programming language, as can be seen in Section 4. This is due to the fact that the GPDL allows and requires the specification of the semantics (behaviour) and other source code fragments in the target programming language, and therefore, the problem definition will have non-standard code. This arguably can be seen as a weakness of the GPDL, but it does not take the usefulness of having problem definitions in GPDL. It is much easier and quicker to convert the framework-specific problem definition to be used in a different framework than to re-write the whole source code.

3. IMPLEMENTING GPDL SUPPORT IN EPOCHX

The first requirement in order to support GPDL in a GP framework is to create a GPDL compiler. The compiler is created using the Coco/R compiler generator [4]. Coco/R takes the GPDL syntax definition[1] as an input, which is an attribute grammar (ATG) file describing the lexical and syntactical structure of the language as well as its semantic actions for the target framework, and produces a scanner and

[1]A generic GPDL attribute grammar syntax definition is available at http://dev.heuristiclab.com/GPDL, which can be used as a starting point to create the GPDL definition for the target framework.

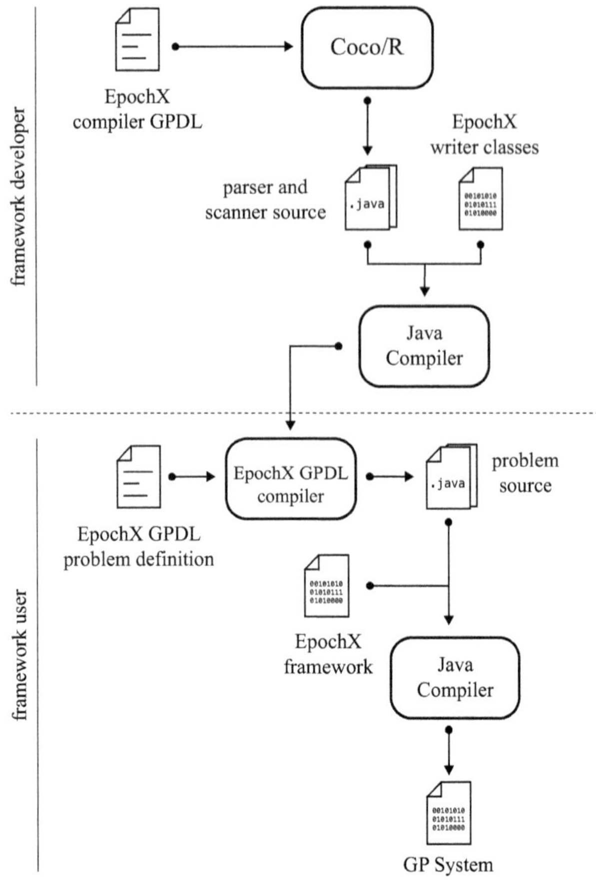

Figure 1: Diagrams showing the steps involved in generating a GPDL compiler (framework developer tasks) and in generating a specific GP system implementation from a GPDL problem description (framework user tasks). Note that the GPDL compiler generation only needs to be done once—it has to be repeated in case the GPDL compiler definition changes.

parser for the GPDL language. The scanner is responsible for reading tokens from the input buffer. The parser is responsible for processing the tokens and generating the source code (implementation) of the problem definition, according to the grammar definition and semantic actions. This process is illustrated in Figure 1. It should be noted that the scanner and parser generation only need to be performed once and it should be repeated in case of a new GPDL specification.

The scanner and parser created by Coco/R—together with auxiliary file writers discussed in subsection 3.1—are used to create the GPDL compiler for the EpochX framework, which can take a GPDL problem definition file and generate the framework-specific classes required to run the problem. As we mentioned before, while the GPDL language is independent of the target framework, the semantic actions are framework-dependent. EpochX support different representations—context-free grammar (CFG-GP) and grammatical evolution (GE)—and therefore, the same GPDL problem definition file can be reused to generate the source code for these representations. Given the modular architecture of EpochX, there is no need to use a different GPDL definition nor generate different scanner and parser. Depending on the representation chosen, EpochX GPDL parser uses the corresponding representation-specific file writers—these are detailed in subsection 3.1.4.

While EpochX also supports tree-based GP, we have not included support for the tree representation in the GPDL compiler. This is due to the fact that grammar-based representations are a straightforward fit for the GPDL, since the problem definition in GPDL uses grammar rules to define the individual structure. This prevents the problem of not being able to express the rules specified in the grammar or having to employ constraints to the grammar rules—e.g., the GPDL reference implementation in HeuristicLab [8] for tree representation requires that all alternatives in the grammar must contain a single symbol only [2].

3.1 Architecture

3.1.1 Project Manager

The project manager is the most important class in the code generator. It links the parser generated by Coco/R with all other classes involved in generating the problem source code. The current version of EpochX code generator creates an Eclipse[2] project with all required directories and configuration files, as well as the source files.

The main functionality of the project manager is to handle the writing queue, which is created during the parsing of the GPDL problem definition:

```
private ArrayList<WritingInfo> writingQueue;
```

The queue contains the list of files to be generated, including the path of the files and their content. To support multiple representations—CFG-GP or GE in the current implementation—the writers are chosen according to the representation being used.

3.1.2 File Writers

The writer classes are responsible for creating and writing the content of the source files based on the GPDL problem definition. By using separate writers for each section of the GPDL file, it is easy to provide alternative implementations depending on the representation—e.g., while CFG-GP and GE share the same grammar writer, their fitness writer is different given that the individual representation is different.

The different writers and their purpose are:

- `MainWriter`: generates the main class, which provides the facility to run the problem and to set the default parameters. This is a representation-dependent writer;
- `GrammarWriter`: generates the grammar described in the `RULES` section of the GPDL file and sends it to the MainWriter once it is ready;
- `FitnessWriter`: generates the file corresponding to the fitness function, which also contains the code in the `INIT` section of the GPDL file. This is a representation-dependent writer;
- `SymbolWriter`: is a template to define grammar symbols. It contains the information needed for both non-terminal and terminal symbols (i.e., name of the symbol, information concerning its output, list of grammar productions);
- `NonTerminalWriter`: extends the `SymbolWriter` class. It builds the part of the grammar corresponding to each non-terminal symbol and sends it to the GrammarWriter. This writer also produces the source files representing the non-terminal symbols;
- `TerminalWriter`: extends the `SymbolWriter` class. It builds the part of the grammar corresponding to each terminal symbol and sends it to the GrammarWriter. This writer also produces the source files representing the terminal symbols.

It should be noted that the GPDL syntax allows the use of out/ref parameters in symbols of the grammar, which are not supported by Java. To overcome this limitation, `NonTerminalWriter` and `TerminalWriter` use return statements to implement the behaviour of out parameters. There are two uses of out parameters: (i) in the definition of a grammar symbol (left side of the '='); (ii) in the definition of productions (right side of the '='). This is illustrated in the following example:

```
NOT<<Context context, out boolean b>> =
   EXPR<<context, out b>>              SEM<<b = !b;>>
.
```

In the first case (definition of a grammar symbol), the out parameter is used to specify the return type of the method generated to evaluate the symbol. It is also used to define a local variable, which is returned at the end of the method:

```
public Boolean evaluate(Context context) {
   Boolean b;

   // semantic actions

   return b;
}
```

In the second case (definition of productions), the out parameter is used to specify the variable that holds the return value of evaluation of the symbols of the production. In the example above, the use of `out b` specifies that the return of the evaluation of `EXPR` should be stored in the variable `b`:

```
b = (Boolean) get(0).evaluate(context);
```

The method call `get(0)` returns the first symbol of the production (the `EXPR` symbol). Note that at this point the variable `b` already exists, since it is the same variable name as the one in the symbol definition. The complete `NOT` evaluate implementation, including the semantic action, would be:

```
public Boolean evaluate(Context context) {
   Boolean b;

   b = (Boolean) get(0).evaluate(context);
   b = !b;

   return b;
}
```

[2] http://www.eclipse.org/

This example shows two limitations of the current implementation of both `NonTerminalWriter` and `TerminalWriter`. Firstly, it is only possible to specify a single out parameter, since only a single value can be returned. While this can be seen as a limitation, nodes usually evaluate to a single value in most GP systems and therefore, might not present a problem. If there is the need to return multiple values, due to the use of multiple out parameters, the use of struct-like data types could be explored.

Secondly, all symbol implementations follow the contract of the interface `Function`, which specifies the method:

```
public abstract Object evaluate(Context context);
```

Therefore, only the `Context` object can be used as an argument in grammar symbols. This is due to a design decision of re-using the existing EpochX classes to represent the nodes in GP trees. The `Context` class represents the evaluation context as a hash map-like structure, storing pairs of key-value objects, and terminal nodes can query the values of the input variables. Using a fixed interface to evaluate nodes, it is possible to simplify the code of the writers, since the method call to evaluate different symbols is uniform. This does not limit the values that can be passed to symbols—multiple key-value pairs can be set in the same context.

3.1.3 Error detection

In addition to the syntax checker provided by the parser, we incorporated additional error checking of the input file. This allows the compiler to check whether the the GPDL problem definition is well-constructed and complies with the requirements of the EpochX framework.

We can distinguish three different types of errors:

- *Grammar definition errors*: when the grammar rules defined in the `RULES` section of the GPDL file is not valid (e.g., it contains duplicated symbols, not declared symbol). Note that a grammar can be syntactically correct and, at the same time, it can represent a malformed grammar;
- *GPDL error*: when the file does not comply with one of the constraints of GPDL. This type of error is originated by the parser;
- *EpochX not compatible file*: when the file does not comply with one of the constraints specific to EpochX (e.g., a symbol can only have one out parameter, an evaluation function must appear in the `MAXIMIZE` or `MINIMIZE` section).

All errors defined above are reported to the parser as semantic errors and detailed with an appropriate error message. The actual position (line and column numbers) is then added by the parser and the message is printed. Since all errors are reported to the parser, we have a global number of both syntactic and semantic errors. At the end of the parsing process of the GPDL file, if the number of errors detected by the parser is zero, the EpochX source code of the problem definition will be generated.

3.1.4 Representation-specific compiler

Since EpochX supports the generation of both CFG-GP and GE representations from the same GPDL problem definition, there are two different compilers—one for each representation. At the same time, both compilers share the same parser and most of the file writers, taking advantage of the modular architecture of EpochX. The parser generated by Coco/R is not tied to use a specific file writer, but it uses a reference to the file writer. Therefore, a compiler can set the value of the file writer to be used before invoking the parser.

For example, the CFG-GP and GE use a different `FitnessWriter`. The `ProjectManager` class defines a constant to reference the fitness writer:

```
public static ConfigKey<FitnessWriter> FITNESS_WRITER =
  new ConfigKey<FitnessWriter>();
```

The parser can use this reference to retrieve the fitness writer to be used, without requiring a specific one to be hard-coded:

```
Config.getInstance().get(ProjectManager.FITNESS_WRITER)
```

Each compiler can then set its corresponding fitness writer before invoking the parser:

```
// sets the GE fitness writer
Config.getInstance().set(ProjectManager.FITNESS_WRITER,
  new FitnessWriterGE());
```

Given that both CFG-GP and GE are grammar-based representation, there is no need to provide specific writers for the grammar, symbols, non-terminals and terminals. The only other representation-specific writer is the `MainWriter`, which is responsible to write the file that contains the default parameters values as well as to set the genetic operators.

One advantage of being able to generate the code to different GP representations from the same GPDL problem definition is that a user can easily compare the results using different GP representations, while just having to write a single GPDL file. There is no need to manually write representation-specific classes, significantly reducing (or in some cases even eliminating) the effort of experimenting with alternative representations.

4. EXAMPLE OF AN EPOCHX GPDL PROBLEM DEFINITION

The following listing presents a GPDL problem definition for the N-Multiplexer problem compatible with EpochX. The start of the file contains the problem name:

```
PROBLEM Multiplexer
```

The `CODE` section specifies the number of variables dynamically, which will be used to define the terminal symbols of the problem. The size of the Multiplexer problem is specified by the `address` variable, which correspond to the number of address inputs available:

```
CODE<<
  import org.epochx.gpdl.tools.Tools;

  private int address = 3;
  private int size = (int)Math.pow(2,address) + address;
  private boolean[][] data =
    new boolean[(int) Math.pow(2,size)][];

  public String[] variables = Tools.getVariables(
    new Tools.Variable[] {
      new Tools.Variable("a", address),
      new Tools.Variable("d", size - address)});
>>
```

The data array representing the fitness cases is initialised once at the beginning of the run:

```
INIT<<
  import java.math.BigInteger;

  for (int i = 0; i < data.length; i++) {
    data[i] = new boolean[size];
    int mask = BigInteger.ONE.shiftLeft(size - 1)
      .intValue();

    for (int j = 0; j < data[i].length; j++) {
      data[i][j] = (i & (new BigInteger(
        String.valueOf(mask)).shiftRight(j).intValue()))
          > 0;
    }
  }
>>
```

Each non-terminal symbol is then declared:

```
NONTERMINALS
  PROGRAM<<Context context, out boolean b>>.
  EXPR<<Context context, out boolean b>>.
  AND<<Context context, out boolean b>>.
  OR<<Context context, out boolean b>>.
  IF<<Context context, out boolean b>>.
  NOT<<Context context, out boolean b>>.
```

The terminals are defined using the names from the `variables` using the GPDL constraints facility:

```
TERMINALS
  VAR<<Context context, out String value>>
    CONSTRAINTS
    value IN SET <<variables>> .
```

The productions of the previously declared non-terminal symbols are now defined in the `RULES` section, which represents the grammar. Note that the semantic action of each non-terminal is also defined here, following the GPDL syntax:

```
RULES

  PROGRAM<<Context context, out boolean b>> =
    EXPR<<out b>>
  .

  EXPR<<Context context, out boolean b>> =
                               LOCAL<<String value;>>
    AND<<context, out b>>
    | OR<<context, out b>>
    | IF<<context, out b>>
    | NOT<<context, out b>>
    | VAR<<context, out value>>
            SEM<<b = (boolean) context.get(value);>>
  .

  AND<<Context context, out boolean b>> =
                              LOCAL<<boolean b1,b2;>>
    EXPR<<context, out b1>> EXPR<<context, out b2>>
                                  SEM<<b=b1 && b2;>>
  .

  OR<<Context context, out boolean b>> =
                              LOCAL<<boolean b1,b2;>>
    EXPR<<context, out b1>> EXPR<<context, out b2>>
                                  SEM<<b=b1 || b2;>>
  .

  NOT<<Context context, out boolean b>> =
    EXPR<<context, out b>>                  SEM<<b=!b;>>
  .

  IF<<Context context, out boolean b>> =
                                 LOCAL<<boolean test;>>
    EXPR<<context, out test>>         SEM<<if (test){>>
    EXPR<<context, out b>>              SEM<<} else {>>
    EXPR<<context, out b>>                     SEM<<}>>
  .
```

Finally, the last part of the problem definition specifies the fitness function. EpochX requires that fitness functions have the same method signature:

```
public double evaluate(Function executable,
                       Context context)
```

The first argument is the program (expression) represented by the current individual being evaluated; the second argument is the evaluation context object. While we could have omitted the requirement of having to specify the method signature, we decided to keep it to make explicit the objects available for the fitness function.

Note `Context` object is used to set the input values of the current fitness to the variables—these values can be looked up using variable name. At the end of the file, `END` section closes problem the definition:

```
MINIMIZE<<
  public double evaluate(Function executable,
                         Context context) {
    int correct=0;

    for (int i=0; i<data.length ; i++) {
      int expected = 0;
      int index = data[i].length - 1;

      for (int j = index; j >= 0; j--) {
        if (j < address) {
          context.set("a" + ((address - 1) - j),
                      data[i][j]);

          if (data[i][j]) {
            expected += Math.pow(2, (address - 1) - j);
          }
        } else {
          context.set("r" + (index - j), data[i][j]);
        }
      }

      boolean result = (boolean) executable
        .evaluate(context);

      if (data[i][index - expected] == result) {
        correct++;
      }
    }

    return data.length - correct;
  }
>>

END Multiplexer.
```

5. CONCLUSION

In this paper we presented a GPDL code generator for the EpochX framework using a GPDL-enabled compiler based on a parser generated by Coco/R. The aim of the compiler is to generate the source code of the corresponding GP system structured as an Eclipse project, given a GPDL problem definition. We discussed the steps involved in the compiler generation, which only need to be performed once and they should be repeated in case of a new GPDL syntax specification. We identified an interesting advantage of using GPDL as a problem definition: it allows a user to write a single problem definition to generate the corresponding source code for different representations (e.g., CFG-GP and GE in the current implementation), facilitating the experimentation of different representations.

There are several improvements that can be made to the current implementation. At the moment, the default parameters (e.g., population size, genetic operators probabilities) are not specified in the GPDL problem definition, nor are the selection of genetic operators. We are currently exploring alternatives to relax the requirement that all symbols implement the interface `Function`, to omit the fitness function signature from the GPDL problem definition and we are also investigating the implementation of the tree-based GP compiler. The current version of the compiler generates the source code and places them in a Eclipse project structure. Nothing prevents the EpochX compiler to call the Java compiler immediately after the generation of the files to start the execution of the algorithm, as it occurs in the HeuristicLab reference implementation [2]—this is something that can also be explored. The requirement of having language-specific code and text in the problem definition file is not ideal. This could be improved by providing a GPDL editor, which could include an inline syntax analyser. Another possibility is to separate the textual definitions and the language-specific code in different files, facilitating the reuse of the GPDL definition across different frameworks.

EpochX is available for download, including source code and documentation at: `http://www.epochx.org/`

6. ACKNOWLEDGEMENTS

Claris Leroux thanks the ERASMUS *Student Mobility for Placements*, the *Conseil Général de Haute Normandie* and the *Ministère de l'Éducation Nationale (Aide à la Mobilité Internationale)* for their scholarships.

7. REFERENCES

[1] J. R. Koza. *Genetic Programming: On the Programming of Computers by Means of Natural Selection.* MIT Press, 1992.

[2] G. Kronberger, M. Kommenda, S. Wagner, and H. Dobler. Gpdl: A framework-independent problem definition language for grammar-guided genetic programming. In *GECCO'13 Companion*, pages 1333–1340. ACM, 2013.

[3] D. J. Montana. Strongly typed genetic programming. *Evolutionary Computation*, 3(2):199–230, 1995.

[4] H. Mössenböck. A generator for fast compiler front-ends. In *Report 127, Dept. Informatik, 28 pages.* ETH Zürich, 1990.

[5] M. O'Neill and C. Ryan. Grammatical evolution. *IEEE Transactions on Evolutionary Computation*, 5(4):349–358, Aug. 2001.

[6] F. Otero, T. Castle, and C. G. Johnson. Epochx: Genetic programming in java with statistics and event monitoring. In *GECCO'12 Companion*, Philadelphia, PA, USA, July 2012.

[7] L. Vaseux, F. Otero, T. Castle, and C. G. Johnson. Event-based graphical monitoring in the epochx genetic programming framework. In *GECCO'13 Companion*, Amsterdam, The Netherlands, July 2013.

[8] S. Wagner. *Heuristic Optimization Software Systems – Modeling of Heuristic Optimization Algorithms in the HeuristicLab Software Environment.* PhD thesis, Institute for Formal Models and Verification, Johannes Kepler University Linz, Austria, 2009.

[9] P. Whigham. Grammatically-based genetic programming. In *Proceedings of the Workshop on Genetic Programming: From Theory to Real-World Applications*, pages 33–41, 1995.

NodEO, a Multi-Paradigm Distributed Evolutionary Algorithm Platform in JavaScript

Juan-Julián Merelo, Pedro Castillo, Antonio Mora
GeNeura, ETSIIT + CITIC, U. Granada
jmerelo,pedro,amorag@geneura.ugr.es

Anna Esparcia-Alcázar
S2 Grupo
aesparcia@s2grupo.es

Víctor Rivas-Santos
Universidad de Jaén
vrivas@ujaen.es

ABSTRACT

After existing for more than fifteen years, JavaScript has finally risen as a popular language for implementing all kind of applications, from server-based to rich internet applications. The fact that it is implemented in the browser and in server-side tools makes it interesting for designing evolutionary algorithm frameworks that encompass both tiers, but besides, they allow a change in paradigm that goes beyond the canonical evolutionary algorithm. In this paper we will experiment with different architectures, client-server and peer to peer to assess which ones offer most advantages in terms of performance, scalability and ease of use for the computer scientist. All implementations have been released as open source, and besides showing that the concept of working with evolutionary algorithms in JavaScript can be done efficiently, we prove that a master-slave parallel architecture offers the best combination of time and algorithmic improvements in a parallel evolutionary algorithm that leverages JavaScript implementation features.

Categories and Subject Descriptors

H.4 [**Information Systems Applications**]: Miscellaneous; D.2.8 [**Software Engineering**]: Metrics—*complexity measures, performance measures*

Keywords

JavaScript; `node.js`; parallel evolutionary algorithms; asynchronous evolution; implementation issues

1. INTRODUCTION

JavaScript (JS from now on) was introduced in 1998 as a browser-embedded language by Netscape [6]; it was quickly adopted, in several versions, by the rest of the existing browsers (Internet Explorer, Opera and the offspring of Netscape, Mozilla and then Firefox). It later became a standard by the European Association for Standardizing Information and Communication Systems in 1999 [5]. Despite this standard it was for a long time considered just a language for the browser, and in fact most books on JS start by telling you how to embed your scripts in the HTML code of a web page.

Even as such embedded language, JavaScript is an interpreted language that uses classes and objects, functions as first-rate types, and which is dynamic and weakly typed-checked (a variable can change its type during its lifetime, but whatever type it has needs to be explicitly coerced to other type in some contexts, but not in all). These features make it an ideal language for quick prototyping and productive programming.

However, the graduation of JS to a full-fledged language did not start to arrive until the first years of this century with the introduction of standalone interpreters such as SpiderMonkey or Rhino [17], but it was not until Google's introduction of the V8[20] interpreter and its adoption by the `node.js` JavaScript virtual machine that it started to become what it is now, one of the most (or arguably the most) popular development languages [18]. At the same time, it is the only language of which it can be said that it is truly ubiquitous; every Internet-connected device has at least one interpreter [4] (often as a browser), but you can find it also as the language of choice of the Gnome user-interface in Linux, CouchDB object database, and in many Platform-as-a-service (PaaS) products such as Heroku, Nodejitsu or Openshift. It can also be easily installed in IaaS (Infrastructure-as-a-Service) products, such as Windows Azure or Amazon. That makes it the right choice for parasitic-style or volunteer computing platforms such as Crowdprocess[1].

The fact that there are interpreters embedded in browsers and in server-side services makes it the only language in which you can develop both the client and server tier of a client-server application (and, for that matter, any other tier in between).

What we propose in this paper is to measure different ways of implementing distributed evolutionary algorithms using JS. It has already been proved that implementation matters [16], and it does so, since the evolutionary framework must be translated to a particular language in a way that goes with its grain and not in the way that is more easily translated from C or Java, but also because it offers new ways of implementing evolutionary algorithms. In many cases, the environments where JS excels, such as the browser, for instance, might need proper support in the shape of evolutionary algorithms; finally, creating distributed evolutionary

[1]https://crowdprocess.com

GECCO'14, July 12–16, 2014, Vancouver, BC, Canada.

ACM 978-1-4503-2881-4/14/07 ...$15.00.
http://dx.doi.org/10.1145/2598394.2605688.

algorithms is easy using JS; so easy, in fact, that there are so many ways of doing it, and mixing and matching them (WebSockets, Ajax and REST, just to name a few) that it becomes necessary to give an initial idea of how to make them useful for evolutionary algorithms and what is the performance we should expect.

The experiments proposed in this paper have been released under an open source license and are available at `https://github.com/JJ/nodeo`. They offer a glimpse into the different possibilities of programming using JS, but at the same time show the kind of performance we should expect from them and what it wins from parallel operation. In doing so, our intention is to prove that the translation of the usual distributed evolutionary paradigm into this new language is valid, but also which option offers the best performance in terms of scalability and number of evaluations needed to reach the solution.

The rest of the paper is organized as follows: next we describe the state of the art in new and uncanny implementations of evolutionary algorithms, and a description of the past implementations using different JS interpreters. The algorithm that has been adapted to JS is described next along with the experimental setup in Section 3; finally results are presented in Section 4 and its implications discussed in the last section of the paper.

2. STATE OF THE ART

Evolutionary algorithms have always been targeted by new programming languages, with implementations cutting across paradigms and computing platforms; the relatively new language Clojure (which is 17th in the RedMonks ranking), for instance, has been used to implement the PushGP system (which uses its own language, Push) [8]; Ruby (7th in the ranking) was used as the backoffice for a JavaScript evolutionary algorithm in the AGAJAJ system [13] but it actually implements an evolutionary algorithm within a testing framework called RuTeG [12] using this language. In fact, this use has not been limited to new and paradigm-heavy languages; Langdon used the venerable `awk` to handle populations of millions of regular expressions in [11] and claims:

> Although this may seem complex, gawk (Unix' free interpreted pattern scanning and processing language) can handle populations of a million motifs.

This, in fact, proves that in many cases using new tools outside the mainstream programming languages can lead to new insights on the algorithm (in this case, the use of populations much bigger than is usual in evolutionary algorithms) and, of course, faster and more efficient solutions of the problem at hand.

However, JavaScript has not been the subject of extensive experimentation until now. The first mention of JS in relation with evolutionary algorithms was in 1996, when Smith and Sugihara [21] used it for creating the user interface of a browser-based evolutionary building system, that was, in fact, based in Java. It was not much later, in 1998, when a single-browser evolutionary algorithm for evolving the layout of a web newspaper was published [19]. In this case an outstanding feature of JS, the fact that it is embedded in the browser, was used to evolve the document object model in a native way; it could not have been done in any other way since the intention was that a personalized page was generated by every user and rendered using the user's own computing power, without needing to overload the server with the generation of pages for thousands of users. In this sense it also pointed out to the *unwitting* [9] use of resources, which was taken full advantage later on for the generation of L-System (a grammar for describing fractal objects) in a distributed way [10] once again, and in the same way that has been mentioned before, a proof of choosing the right language for the evolutionary algorithm outside the mainstream languages.

The distributed capabilities of JS were discovered later on with the realization of the possibilities of Ajax for distributing information mediated by a server. This was implemented in different ways, [14, 9, 13]. These initial experiments mainly revealed that the usual ways of distributing evolutionary algorithms (farming out evaluation or using synchronous islands) were not suitable to an ephemeral client that could enter into a particular experiment at any time. It was clear also that new paradigms, based on using *pools* of resources and dealing with them asymmetrically could also be better suited to this environment that symmetric algorithms with uniform distribution of their population. Several systems have recently been tested with this premise [24, 15]. Although most of them use JavaScript, those that do not use it (like EvoSpace, [24]) reach conclusions that can be applied to JS-based evolutionary algorithms as well.

The current state of the art shows that JS can, indeed, be used in a cloud computing environment, but that an assessment of its performance in different situations, frameworks and methodologies might be in order. This is what we will carry out in this paper via different implementations mainly done in the asynchronous JS interpreter `node.js`; what this asynchrony means will be explained next.

3. AN EVOLUTIONARY ALGORITHM IN NODE.JS

`node.js` (which, from now on, we will simply call Node) is a JS interpreter based on the V8 virtual machine created by Google. It is designed to use asynchronous input/output by default, including an event model that makes event-driven programming extremely easy [23]. Since it is essentially a JS interpreter, sequential and synchronous programs are possible and, due to the speed of the underlying JS virtual machine, have a high performance, but the best way of using it is by taking advantage of the asynchronous I/O features that make it different from other JS interpreters such as SpiderMonkey or Rhino and, in fact, closer to the event-driven programming that is usual in browsers.

From the point of view of distributed evolutionary algorithms, which will have to perform input/output operations to interact with the rest of the islands, this implies that this pattern

```
generate_population();
do {
  single_generation();
  if (time_to_migrate()) {
    migrate_out();
    migrate_in();
  }
} until evolution_end();
```

will not work as expected. The main problem is that all input/output operations will create events in the implicit event loop, which will generate callbacks once the request has been completed. The code shown above will work, but will *never* have time to process the events and thus migrations, either in or out, will never take place, or rather, inbound requests will be made but not processed and outbound requests will actually be made, but if the client on the other side works in the same way, it will never be processed. So, instead of this sequential loop, a loop intended to run for many iterations must be done this way in Node [22]:

```
generate_population();
do_evolution();

function do_evolution(){
  single_generation();
  if (time_to_migrate()) {
    migrate_out();
    migrate_in();
  }
  if ( !evolution_end() ) {
    do_after_callbacks( do_evolution );
  }
}
```

This is not only a way of writing the programs using different patterns, it is also a different way of understanding the algorithm sequence. Please note that `do_after_callbacks` receives a function *pointer*, not a function call; so it is not a recursive call, but actually the definition of a callback. In a synchronous framework, the first pseudo-code should be expected to behave in this way:

```
Generation 1
Generation 2
...
Generation 20
Migration-out
Migration-in
```

However, what we will find in an evolutionary algorithm programmed in Node as above will be something like

```
Generation 1
Generation 2
...
Generation 20
Request-Migration-out
Request-Migration-in
...
Generation 22
Migration-in taking place
...
Generation 27
Migration-out taking place
```

Asynchronous programming not only means that events will be happening at an undetermined time in the future, but also that they might take place out of sequence; in fact the sequence might very well be

```
Migration-in 2 taking place
...
Migration-out 0 taking place
...
Migration-in 1 taking place
```

When designing an evolutionary library that can be used in the browser *and* in Node, one of the main things that must be taken into account is that longish computational stretches must be divided into more *atomic* chunks so that input-output events can happen between them; however, this concerns mainly the design of library *clients*, not the library itself. Thus, an open source library for Node, which is introduced in this paper, has been released so that it can be used with the Node package manager just by issuing `npm install nodeo`.

The library has been intended mainly as a proof of concept, including the bare minimum to run an evolutionary algorithm: a single mutation and crossover operators, tournament selection and a few test functions, including the Trap function (explained below), that has been selected for making the experiments in this paper.

4. TESTING DISTRIBUTED EVOLUTIONARY ARCHITECTURES

The experiments in the paper have been designed so that different distributed architectures can be tested. All programs have been written in Node, although in principle clients for the browser could also be easily added. Using them, however, would not add much to the conclusions (although, in the future, it would certainly add to the utility of the framework described here). The applications that use the library consider the standard released library plus two Node modules, one designed for creating REST clients called *Restler* and other for REST servers called *express.js*.

The function chosen for doing all the experiments is a classical deceptive function called Trap [1]. This assigns different values to blocks of bits depending on its number of ones. For each block, it assigns the maximum to a block with equal bits and another local maximum to the flipped version of that one. The rest of the values follow this formula

$$T(x) = \begin{cases} a * (z - x)/z & \text{if } x <= z \\ b * (x - z)/(l - z) & \text{if } x > z \end{cases}$$

where x is the number of ones in the block, l is the length of the block, and a and b are two constants that meet the condition $a < b$. In this experiment we will use $z = 3, a = 1, b = 2$ which are the usual in other papers such as [7]. This guarantees the problem is challenging enough for a wide variety of problem sizes. We will consider 30, 40 or 50 blocks, which offer increasing difficulty for evolutionary algorithms.

Initially, we will try to find out what is the right population size for each problem size by doubling its length until we found one in which 100% of the experiments are successful. The base population will be 128 individuals, and we will use the baseline evolutionary algorithm in the library with all the default parameters. This evolutionary algorithm is a generational method with individuals kept as *elite*, 2 tournament for selection, bit-flip mutation, and 2-point crossover. These parameters will be kept constant (except for the population) for all experiments. If the solution is not found after 2 million evaluations, the program stops.

Experiments are repeated 30 times and take place in a Linux Ubuntu 13.10 box with

```
Linux penny 3.8.0-35-generic #50-Ubuntu SMP
```

and a *AMD Phenom(tm) II X6 1090T Processor* with six cores. All experiments will take place in this single computer, with different *nodes* in the experiment being different processes running simultaneously. This was made to make sure that the computing power was homogeneous and to make these results reproducible. In fact, all code and data used to run the programs and also produced by them is available to the public under an open source license; additionally, Ansible configuration for a virtual machine that runs the code has also been published to make easier the reproduction of the results. The version of Node used is 0.10.24.

The results of the experiments to size the population are shown in Figure 1, which shows that 512, 1024 and 2048 are the right size to find the solution to the 4-trap problem of sizes 30, 40 and 50.

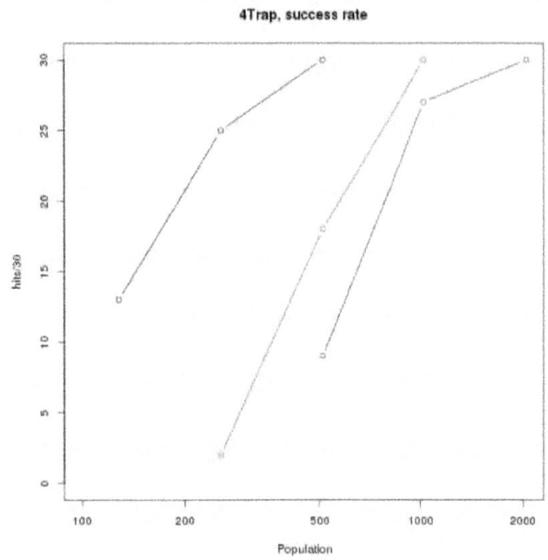

Figure 1: Number of successful runs out of 30; a run is considered successful if the target string (all ones) is found. The leftmost line corresponds to 30 blocks, the one in the middle to 40 and the last one to 50.

The time needed to reach the solution follows a pattern that is similar to the success rate, as shown in Figure 2, which plots the average time needed to find the solution in successful runs. These graphs have two purposes: first, to show the time needed to find the solution in Node, which is around 10 seconds for any of the problems, slightly more for the problem with 50 traps. This time is well in line with other script-based languages and show that JavaScript can be competitive, time wise, with other languages. As a side comment, time decreases with population since the presence of a higher initial diversity is key for a successful initial exploitation, as opposed to an exploration regime that is needed to find the solution with smaller sizes. We will also have to take into account this fact when doing the parallel version of these algorithms, which we will show in the next section.

It should be noted that the number of lines needed to implement this problem is quite small and of the order of a few hundred. This fact, along with the performance obtained when solving this problem, shows that JS and the library used in this paper can be a contender in the arena of evolutionary computation frameworks. We have also tested differ-

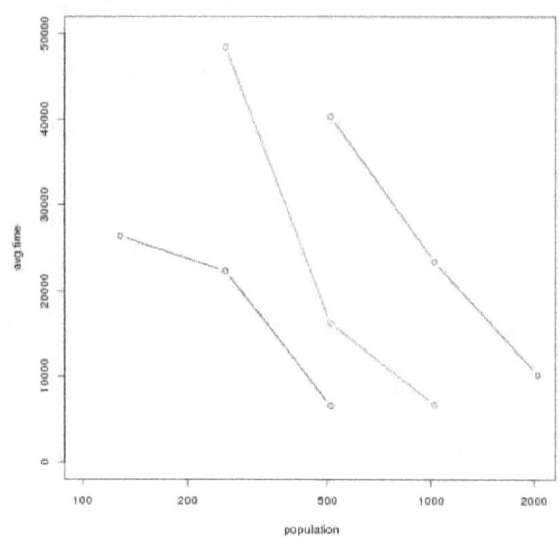

Figure 2: Average time, in milliseconds, for successful runs. The leftmost line corresponds to 30 blocks, the one in the middle to 40 and the last one in the right to 50.

ent JS virtual machines to see if there is a difference between implementations. The fact that it is done in JavaScript allows to easily transform Node code into one that can be run in the browser by just using a tool called `browserify`; the resulting code is, in fact, the same, with the main difference being the way it is called and the fact that it has to be done from a web page. There are also slight differences in the way the loop is done, or rather not done: it has got to stop from time to time to avoid blocking the browser. Even so, benchmark results shown in Figure 3 show that performance of all virtual machines is essentially the same, with a statistical significant difference only between Firefox and Chromium, not between Node and the other two implementations. However, the true worth of `node.js` will be shown in the next section by extending this basic algorithm for parallel execution.

The easiest way of creating a distributed application using Node is adding a RESTful interface to it using `express.js`; in fact, RESTful interfaces are quite efficient and have been tested already in distributed EC experiments [3], finding that they add a small overhead to communications and, besides, can be accessed from a variety of languages, from `node.js` itself to JQuery (a JavaScript library) in the browser. This gives us room for growth, but for the time being we are interested only in showing that a few lines of code can be used to convert a single-process evolutionary algorithm into a distributed evolutionary one.

We will test two different regimes here:

- *P2P*: in it, every *node* (which we will call process from now on, since they are implemented as such and to avoid confusion with `node.js`, the JS interpreter) communicates with the rest.
- *pool-based* communication of one client with other is only done through the server, with each program acting independently and knowing only about this server.

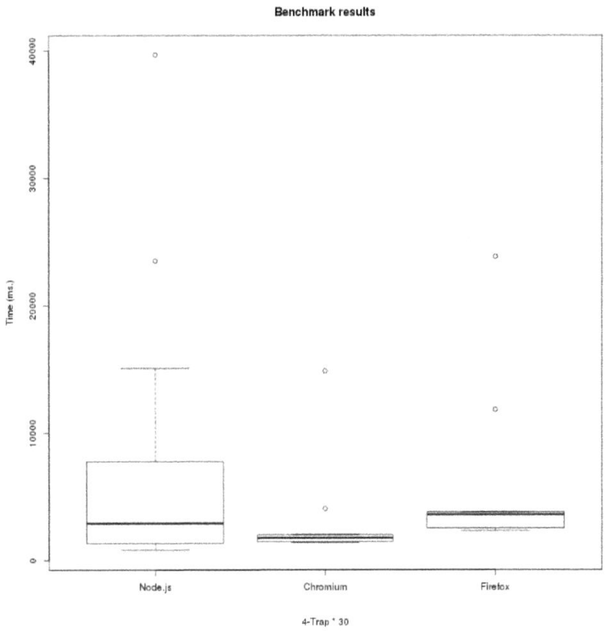

Figure 3: Benchmark comparing running time for `node.js` and two browsers. Node version is 0.10.29, Firefox 26.0 and Chromium 31.0.1650.63, all of them running on Ubuntu 13.10. The first benchmark has been repeated 30 times, and the others 10 times. All results run the same benchmark, with the node version using the same data as that plotted in Figure 2; the benchmark uses 4-trap with 30 blocks and population = 512.

These two implementations will be described in detail in the next two sections, after which we will present and compare the result of the experiments using them.

4.1 P2P implementation

Every program uses `express.js` for implementing a response to GET requests made by other processes. After a number of generations which is configurable, a process makes a request to another process that is selected randomly from the list of processes that are running the same algorithm. Every process runs in its own port; these are assigned sequentially starting by 3000; 4 processes, for instance, will use ports 3000 to 3003.

The queried peer returns the best chromosome in its pool. As pointed out in Section 3, the chromosome is incorporated in a later moment to the pool if the program does not finish before. The new chromosome substitutes the last one in the pool, as it is usual. This is the case too for the other regime.

We call this implementation P2P, because every process is a client (requesting individuals from other processes) and a server (serving those requests). By default, all clients are stored at the same time (except for negligible delays) using a shell script.

Every process is run independently, which accounts for a high load of the machine, approximately 1 per process. Even so, the operating system is able to accommodate 16 processes without experimenting major delays in the rest of the applications (such as music reproducer or the browser) running on the server.

4.2 Pool-based implementation

In this case, processes act only as clients, making GET and PUT requests to a single server. This server runs in a public port (by default, 5000) and handles all requests using `express.js` integrated web server. Since this server is asynchronous it is theoretically able to serve a good amount of simultaneous requests. However, this number is not infinite, as we will see later on. The client always PUTs the best chromosome.

The server provides a random chromosome when requested and when it receives a PUT request it stores this in a hash, in such a way that if the same chromosome is PUT twice it will be stored only once in the server. This is mainly done for efficiency purposes, but also to increase diversity.

The client processes, after a fixed amount of generations, do a PUT and then a GET. As explained in Section 3, this does not guarantee that they will be served in the same order so error-handling provisions are in place in case the server has no chromosomes stored (at the beginning of the simulation) or any other error (like a flooding of the request buffer).

The server is started before the clients, which start all at the same time (but see above). When all client processes have finished, the server is killed so that no results are kept from one run to the next.

4.3 Experiments and results

First we will test if the approach is valid and if by dividing the population in several processes we obtain any kind of improvement. The machine is the same as above and except for some errors all experiments have been repeated 30 times to achieve statistical significance. In many cases, the *generational gap*, that is, the number of generations before migration takes place, has been changed to 10 or 20 if it was considered necessary; the point of the experiment is, anyways, to see how the division of the population influences the performance.

The success rate is shown in Figure 4 for the 10 and 20 generation gap. The results are practically the same, and, in fact, very similar to the success rate we would obtain with a single process; a parallel division, in fact, does not seem to bring a improved success rate even if the total population is the same as the one that obtained 100% success in a single *deme*. The fact that a small variation in the generation gap does not affect the time-to-success (when it is achieved) is also reflected in Figure 5, which also shows the time in the single-process version that was presented in Section 3. It is interesting to see that time improves 5-fold for population = 256 (while the number of processes has only been multiplied by two and success rate is roughly constant) and roughly in the same proportion for population = 128, with the number of processes multiplied by 4. However, it is interesting to note that a increase in the number of nodes from 256 to 128 does not decrease running time and might even increase it.

In fact, an additional experiment with 2 processes, g = 20 and population=512 confirms what we have just seen above: success rate remains 100% but average time needed to find the solution decreases 3 times, to 1746 ms. from 6588.0. This superlinear increase, which has been found in many other experiments, might be due to the asynchronous

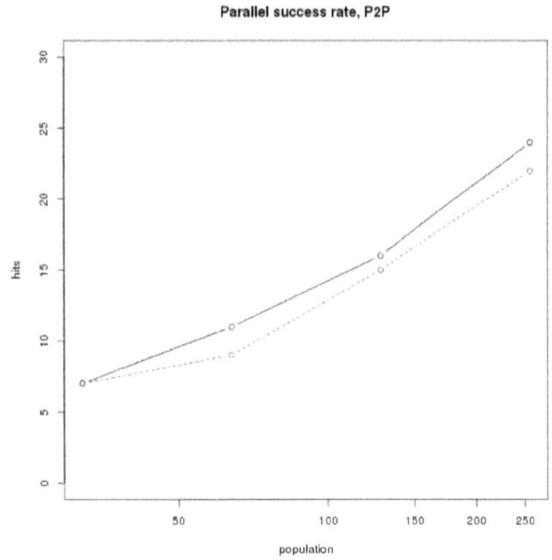

Figure 4: Number of successful runs out of 30. Black, solid line corresponds to migration after 20 generations, light-colored, dashed corresponds to migration after 10 generations.

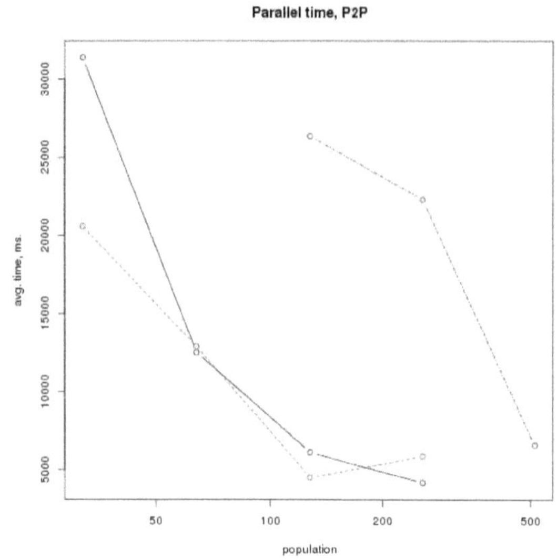

Figure 5: Average time, in milliseconds, for successful runs. Black, solid line corresponds to g (generation gap) $= 10$, light, dashed to $g = 20$, and, for the sake of comparison, the baseline single-node time is included.

nature of Node, which might, in turn, increase diversity, but in any case it proves that, in this P2P regime, adding a single process might bring great improvements in terms of time, even in a single machine. However, designing an experiment that proves this is outside the scope of this paper and. What we can conclude from this set of experiments is that a single machine is able to support a good amount of processes running in parallel, and that adding at least one process can increase speed significantly without too much effort (a few lines of code) from the programming point of view.

However, this programming effort can be used in a different direction, and that is what we have attempted with the pool architecture, with clients all working against a single server. In principle we wanted to test the same architecture with the same generational gap, that is, total population for all nodes equal to 512, with this population divided among processes. However, since all the requests are done to a single process its event queue saturates very fast which led us to increase the generational gap with the number of processes; even so, it brings errors which crash the clients in some cases.

In general and from the point of view of the operating system load, no great change is observed with the addition of one process (n client processes + server) to the pool; if there is any time difference, it should not be attributed to increased OS load or, for that matter, for the small changes in the application architecture done. Even if the P2P applications do a single request (a GET) and this one performs two (first a PUT and then a GET), it probably cancels out with the fact that the P2P processes must also *respond* to requests from time to time. In fact, what we observe in the comparison of both types of architectures in Figure 6 is that there is a difference for the smallest number of processes and the biggest number of processes but they go in different directions, so it is difficult to say if, in general, there is any difference (there is none for $p = 64, 128$) and what is its origin.

But a more dramatic change of scenario is shown in Figure 7, which shows that the success rate increases drastically, although decreasingly so with the increasing population; this is only to be expected since, in fact, success rate increased with the population in the P2P architecture. This makes, from the algorithmic point of view, a better alternative of this pool-based architecture. Since, time-wise, there is no big difference, we have to conclude that, in general and despite server-overload errors, using a pool-based architecture for asynchronous parallel evolutionary algorithms is a better option than either a single-population architecture or a peer-based architecture.

This conclusion is reached on top of the fact that JavaScript, its implementation in `node.js`, and the simple library we are presenting in this paper, are valid platforms for performing distributed computation experiments, since they allow to create rapid prototypes to concentrate on system architecture and the solution of problems via evolutionary algorithms. In an environment with no constraints to choose a particular programming language, JavaScript will probably be slower than Java or C++, although its speed is on par (and may beat) other scripting languages. However, in an environment such as a multi-tier architecture that includes rich internet applications (with an UI written in JavaScript in the browser) or even mobile applications (which can easily be created in JavaScript via, for instance, the PhoneGap framework or simply HTML5 in any browser) JavaScript can offer an excellent performance and even algorithmic advantages in parallel evolutionary algorithms, as we have proved in this paper.

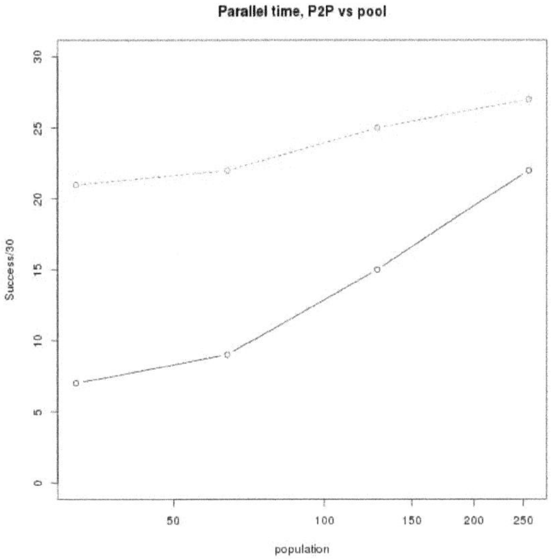

Figure 6: Average time, in milliseconds, for successful runs. Black, solid represents the previously mentioned P2P architecture, while the light, dashed line represents the pool-based, single-server architecture.

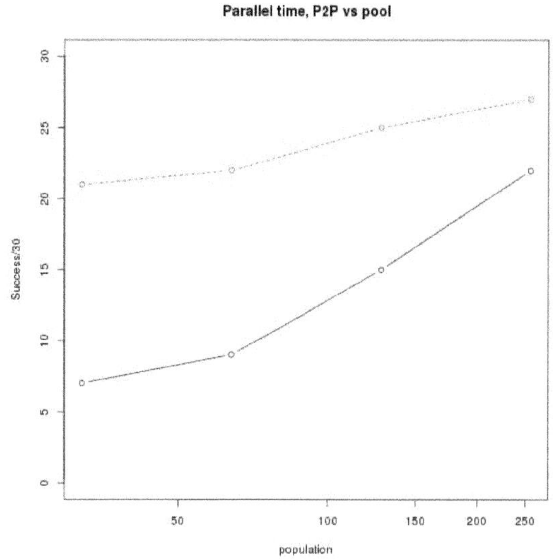

Figure 7: Number of successful runs out of 30. Black, solid line corresponds to the P2P architecture, light-colored, dashed corresponds to the single-server architecture (pool).

5. CONCLUSIONS

In this paper we set to prove the worth of a `node.js`-based distributed evolutionary algorithm. `node.js` is a emerging platform which is receiving a lot of interest in the open source and enterprise arena, but not so much in the scientific community so our intention was to introduce it to the evolutionary computation (EC) community by proving its value as a platform for EC experiments. A basic EC library has been created and released, so it is available to the researches. The library can be expanded and, being open source, can be adapted and suited to the needs of any particular user; due to the expansion of the JavaScript and `node.js` community, it should be increasingly easy to find people interested and skilled enough to work in evolutionary algorithms using JavaScript and `node.js`, and, from the other end, it could get the `node.js` community interested in our area, which might prove the source of interesting problems that can be dealt with from the point of view of metaheuristics.

The main challenge of this paper was to create evolutionary algorithms program that took advantage of the asynchronous nature of `node.js` and the easiness with which asynchronous communication is done using it. To that end, two implementations of a parallel system (that can be easily distributed by changing the configuration files of the clients to reflect the URLs used), one in which evolutionary islands form a *star* topology and are aware and communicate with all other processes, and another in which each client must be aware only of the server it uses to deposit and pick up individuals that are deposited by other clients. These two alternatives offer different advantages from the raw and algorithmic performance point of view: while the P2P setup is able to achieve great improvements by reaching solution in a portion of the time, the server-based setup not only offers improvements of the same order, but also is able to improve the success rate over the P2P and single-server architecture. This despite the disadvantage of the server not being able to process all requests in some occasions.

Why this happens is, however, a different matter. The P2P system always deposits the best individual in the current generation and retrieves also the best from its peer. This might not be the best alternative, as shown in papers such as [2]. However, the peer it takes the chromosome from *is* random, so that might not be the problem. It would be interesting, however, to use other strategies to retrieve individuals from other processes to check what is exactly the reason for this lack of performance. On the other hand, the pool-based system retrieves a random individual from the pool, but this individual has been, in some past moment, the best since they only deposit the best, so the probably increase in diversity afforded by using a random individual from the server might not be the reason; in fact, this was chosen since retrieving the best would probably get the same individual the client had just deposited and checking for that might lead to increasing complexity that we pointedly tried to avoid.

In any case, it is quite clear that the use of this platform and the degrees of liberty in its design open a whole world of possibilities testing uniform vs. heterogeneous settings in nodes. We have been using a single population size, generation gap and tournament size, in general. Using dissimilar and even random values might increase diversity and thus increase the success rate; heterogeneity could come from parameter settings or from different machines being used. Besides, the P2P and pool-based options are not mutually exclusive, since in fact the program used in the P2P setup can be used as a server by adding to it the capability to respond to PUT petitions. Working with different servers and distributing clients might offer a way out of the server overload problem but, at the same time, opens many more possibilities.

We should emphasize too that this research has been carried out in an open science fashion by publishing, as soon as they are produced, all results on a public server whose address is withheld at this point in the evaluation on the paper. We have made sure that these results are fully reproducible by not only releasing the source code, but also all configuration files (in JSON) and data obtained during the experiments, as well as a configuration script in Ansible for the setup of a virtual or real machine.

6. ACKNOWLEDGMENTS

This paper has been developed thanks to the support of the projects CANUBE (CEI2013-P-14), ANYSELF (TIN2011-28627-C04-02) and Muses (`http://musesproject.eu`).

7. REFERENCES

[1] D. H. Ackley. *A connectionist machine for genetic hillclimbing*. Kluwer Academic Publishers, Norwell, MA, USA, 1987.

[2] L. Araujo and J. J. Merelo Guervos. Multikulti algorithm: Using genotypic differences in adaptive distributed evolutionary algorithm migration policies. In *Evolutionary Computation, 2009. CEC '09. IEEE Congress on*, pages 2858–2865, May 2009.

[3] P. A. Castillo, J. L. Bernier, M. García-Arenas, J.-J. Merelo-Guervós, and P. García-Sánchez. SOAP vs REST: Comparing a master-slave GA implementation. *CoRR*, abs/1105.4978, 2011.

[4] D. Crockford. JavaScript: The world's most misunderstood programming language. www.crockford.com, 2001.

[5] ECMA. 262: ECMAScript Language Specification, 1999.

[6] D. Flanagan. *JavaScript*. O'Reilly, 1998.

[7] D. González Lombraña, J. L. J. Laredo, F. Fernández de Vega, and J. J. Merelo Guervós. Characterizing fault-tolerance of genetic algorithms in desktop grid systems. In *Evolutionary Computation in Combinatorial Optimization*, pages 131–142. Springer, 2010.

[8] T. Helmuth and L. Spector. Evolving a digital multiplier with the PushGP genetic programming system. In *Proceeding of the fifteenth annual conference companion on Genetic and evolutionary computation conference companion*, pages 1627–1634. ACM, 2013.

[9] J. Klein and L. Spector. Unwitting distributed genetic programming via asynchronous JavaScript and XML. In *Proceedings of the 9th annual conference on Genetic and evolutionary computation*, pages 1628–1635. ACM, 2007.

[10] W. Langdon. Global Distributed Evolution of L-Systems Fractals. In *Genetic Programming: 7th European Conference, EuroGP 2004, Coimbra, Portugal, April 5-7, 2004, Proceedings*, volume 7, pages 349–358. Springer, 2004.

[11] W. B. Langdon and A. P. Harrison. Evolving DNA motifs to predict GeneChip probe performance. *Algorithms for Molecular Biology*, 4(1):6, 2009.

[12] S. Mairhofer, R. Feldt, and R. Torkar. Search-based software testing and test data generation for a dynamic programming language. In *Proceedings of the 13th annual conference on Genetic and evolutionary computation*, pages 1859–1866. ACM, 2011.

[13] J. J. Merelo, P. Castillo, J. Laredo, A. Mora, and A. Prieto. Asynchronous distributed genetic algorithms with JavaScript and JSON. In *WCCI 2008 Proceedings*, pages 1372–1379. IEEE Press, 2008.

[14] J. J. Merelo, A. M. García, J. L. J. Laredo, J. Lupión, and F. Tricas. Browser-based distributed evolutionary computation: performance and scaling behavior. In *GECCO '07: Proceedings of the 2007 GECCO conference companion on Genetic and evolutionary computation*, pages 2851–2858, New York, NY, USA, 2007. ACM Press.

[15] J. J. Merelo-Guervos, A. Mora, J. Cruz, A. Esparcia-Alcazar, and C. Cotta. Scaling in distributed evolutionary algorithms with persistent population. In *Evolutionary Computation (CEC), 2012 IEEE Congress on*, pages 1 –8, june 2012.

[16] J.-J. Merelo-Guervós, G. Romero, M. García-Arenas, P. A. Castillo, A.-M. Mora, and J.-L. Jiménez-Laredo. Implementation matters: Programming best practices for evolutionary algorithms. In J. Cabestany, I. Rojas, and G. J. Caparrós, editors, *IWANN (2)*, volume 6692 of *Lecture Notes in Computer Science*, pages 333–340. Springer, 2011.

[17] T. Mikkonen and A. Taivalsaari. Using JavaScript as a real programming language. Technical report, Sun Microsystems, Inc., 2007.

[18] S. O'Grady. The RedMonk Programming Language Rankings: January 2014. Tecosystems blog, January 2014.

[19] J. G. Peñalver and J.-J. Merelo-Guervós. Optimizing web page layout using an annealed genetic algorithm as client-side script. In *Proceedings PPSN, Parallel Problem Solving from Nature V*, number 1967 in Lecture Notes in Computer Science, pages 1018–1027. Springer-Verlag, 1998. `http://www.springerlink.com/link.asp?id=2gqqar9cv3et5nlg`.

[20] G. Richards, S. Lebresne, B. Burg, and J. Vitek. An analysis of the dynamic behavior of JavaScript programs. *ACM Sigplan Notices*, 45(6):1–12, 2010.

[21] J. Smith and K. Sugihara. GA toolkit on the Web. In *Proceedings of the First Online Workshop on Soft Computing*, page 12, 1996.

[22] P. Teixeira. Asynchronous Iteration Patterns In Node.js, 2011. `http://metaduck.com/01-asynchronous-iteration-patterns.html`.

[23] S. Tilkov and S. Vinoski. Node.js: Using javascript to build high-performance network programs. *Internet Computing, IEEE*, 14(6):80–83, Nov 2010.

[24] M. G. Valdez, L. Trujillo, F. F. de Vega, J. J. M. Guervós, and G. Olague. Evospace: A distributed evolutionary platform based on the tuple space model. In A. I. Esparcia-Alcázar, editor, *EvoApplications*, volume 7835 of *Lecture Notes in Computer Science*, pages 499–508. Springer, 2013.

A Probabilistic Pareto Local Search based on Historical Success Counting for Multiobjective Optimization

Xinye Cai,Xin Cheng
Computer Science and Technology
Nanjing University of Aeronautics and Astronautics
Nanjing,Jiangsu, P. R. China
xinye@nuaa.edu.cn

Zhun Fan
Department of Electrical Engineering
Shantou University
Shantou, Guangdong, P. R. China
zfan@stu.edu.cn

ABSTRACT

In this paper, we propose a multiobjective probabilistic Pareto local search to address combinatorial optimization problems (COPs). The probability is determined by the success counts of local search offspring entering an external domination archive and this probabilistic information is used to further guide the selection of promising solutions for Pareto local search. In addition, simulated annealing is integrated in this framework as the local refinement process. This multiobjective probabilistic Pareto local search algorithm (MOPPLS), is tested on two famous COPs and compared with some well-known multiobjective evolutionary algorithms. Experimental results suggest that MOPPLS outperforms other compared algorithms.

Categories and Subject Descriptors

D.2.0 [**Computing Methodologies, Artificial Intelligence**]: Problem Solving, Control Methods, and Search—*Heuristic methods*

Keywords

Multiobjective Optimization; Probabilistic; Parteo local search; Aggregation

1. INTRODUCTION

Combinatorial optimization problems(COPs) have been extensively studied by scientists for many years because of their wide application in real life. EAs is a class of stochastic search techniques that have already been successfully applied to a wide range of optimization problems. Originally, EAs draw the inspiration from evolution and mimic genetic operations such as crossover and mutation to sample, learn and adapt from a population of candidate solutions. However, it takes them relatively long time to locate the exact local optimum within the region of convergence when facing complex optimization problems [9]. Genetic local searches [14], also referred to in the literature as Memetic algorithms(MAs), Baldwinian EAs, Lamarckian EAs and cultural algorithms, are extensions of EAs with the introduction of individual learning as a separate process of local refinement for accelerating search.

In addition, many real-world combinatorial optimization problems also involve several conflicting objectives to be simultaneously optimized. Along with it, many local search techniques in single objective heuristics such as variable neighborhood search [11], guided local search [1], simulated annealing [15] and ant colony optimization [6] have been generalized to solve multiobjective COPs. Different from single objective optimization problem where a single optimal solution exists, a multiobjective optimization problem usually has a set of non-dominated solutions, which represent the trade-off between the multiple objectives. Over the past two decades, two different fitness assignment schemes for mutliobjective local search have been frequently used [10,17], as follows.

- *Parteo local search(domination)* [12,13]: It is considered as a natural extension of single objective local search methods. It explores some or all of the neighbors of a set of mutually non-dominated solutions to find new non-dominated solutions for updating at each generation. The replacement of non-dominated solutions is based on the concept of Pareto dominance.
- *Aggregation(decomposition)* [16]: A multiobjective optimization problem(MOP) is transformed into a single objective optimization problem by linearly or nonlinearly aggregating all the objectives into a single objective. Under mild conditions, an optimal solution to this single objective problem is Pareto-optimal to the MOP. Thus, a single objective local search method can be used for finding a set of Pareto optimal solutions by solving a set of such single objective problems with different weights.

Motivated by [10], we propose an multiobjective probabilistic Pareto local search based on aggregation in this paper. In this paper, we propose a multiobjective probabilistic Pareto local search to address combinatorial optimization problems (COPs). The probability is determined by the success counts of local search offspring entering an external archive and this probabilistic information is used to further guide the selection of promising solutions for Pareto local search.

GECCO'14, July 12–16, 2014, Vancouver, BC, Canada.
Copyright 2014 ACM 978-1-4503-2881-4/14/07 ...$15.00.
http://dx.doi.org/10.1145/2598394.2610011.

The main contributions of this paper are as follows.

- A probabilistic Pareto local search framework is proposed and the simulated annealing is integrated as the local search metaheuristic, to tackle multiobjective COPs.

- The proposed approach was tested on multiobjective software next release problem(MONPR) and multiobjective traveling salesman problem(MOTSP) on synthetic test instances and real test instances mined from bug repository [20]. For the real test instances of MONRP, our proposed multiobjective approaches are compared with the state-of-the-art single objective approaches as well as well-known MOEAs. The results show our approach outperforms all the other approaches in comparison.

The rest of this paper is organized as follows. Since this paper focuses on addressing multiobjective optimization problems, Section 2 revisits basic concepts of multiobjective optimization(MOP). The following Section 3 is mainly dedicated to the detailed description of our proposed multiobjective probabilistic Pareto local search framework. Section 4 introduces two representative benchmark multiobjective COPs, that are multiobjective traveling salesman problem (MOTSP) and multiobjective next release problem (MONRP). Experimental studies and discussions are detailed in Section 5. The final conclusions of this paper is made in Section 6.

2. MOP AND MOEAS

Since this paper focuses on addressing multiobjective optimization, this section contributes to the introduction of multiobjective optimization problems and multiobjective evolutionary algorithms. In the multiobjective optimization problem(MOP), two or more usually conflicting objectives are required to be optimized simultaneously. A MOP can be defined as:

Given a problem involving $\boldsymbol{n}$ decision variables $x_1, x_2, \ldots, x_n$ in a search space $\boldsymbol{X} \subset \Re^n$, we assume, without loss of generality, $\boldsymbol{m}$ objectives $f_1(\cdot), \ldots, f_m(\cdot)$ in *objective function space* $\boldsymbol{Y} \subset \Re^m$, are to be minimized.

Minimize $\mathbf{f}(\vec{x}) = ((f_1(x_1, x_2, \ldots, x_n)), \ldots, f_m(x_1, x_2, \ldots, x_n))$

The vector function is a mapping $\boldsymbol{f}\colon \boldsymbol{X} \to \boldsymbol{Y}$.

In MOP, it is usually not possible to find a single solution which is optimal for all the objectives. Instead, many good solutions may exist. These solutions are always "trade-offs" or good compromises among the objectives. Since the conventional concept of optimality does not hold, a concept of Pareto optimality is adopted. The Pareto optimality concept, which was first proposed by Edgeworth and Pareto [18], is formally defined as follows [3]:

Let $\vec{x}$,$\vec{y}$ be two vectors of decision variables in MOP. $\vec{x}$ is considered to dominate $\vec{y}$(written as $\vec{x} \prec \vec{y}$) iff they satisfy the conditions:

$$\begin{array}{l} \vec{x}, \vec{y} \in \mathbf{X}, \forall i \in 1, \ldots, m | f_i(\vec{x}) \leq f_i(\vec{y}) \\ \vec{x}, \vec{y} \in \mathbf{X}, \exists j \in 1, \ldots, m | f_j(\vec{x}) < f_j(\vec{y}) \end{array} \quad (1)$$

On the contrary, a decision vector $\vec{x}$ is considered to be a non-dominated solution iff there is no other solution that satisfies eq.(1). The set of all non-dominated solutions forms a *Pareto optimal set*:

The projection of the Pareto optimal set $\boldsymbol{P}$ in the $\boldsymbol{m}$ dimensional objective function space $\boldsymbol{Y}$ is called *Pareto front*, $\boldsymbol{F}$.

$$\boldsymbol{F} = \{(f_1(\vec{x}), f_2(\vec{x}), \ldots, f_m(\vec{x})) | \vec{x} \in \boldsymbol{P}\} \quad (2)$$

3. THE PROPOSED ALGORITHM

3.1 The Framework

For convenience, the proposed approach is named as multiobjective probabilistic Pareto local search (MOPPLS). MOPPLS decomposes the MOP into N single objective optimization subproblems. For simplicity, the weight sum approach is adopted in this paper, it requires N weight vectors:

$$\lambda^j = (\lambda_1^j, \ldots, \lambda_m^j) \;\; j = 1, \ldots, N. \quad (3)$$

where $\lambda^j \in R_+^m$ and $\sum_{i=1}^m \lambda_i^j = 1$, m is the number of objectives. The k-th subproblem is:

$$\begin{array}{ll} \text{minimize} & g_k^{ws}(x) = \sum_{i=1}^m \lambda_i^j f_i(x) \\ \text{subject to} & x \in \Omega \end{array} \quad (4)$$

For each $k = 1, \ldots, N$, set $B(k)$ contains the indexes of the T closest weight vectors to λ^k in terms of the Euclidean distance. If $i \in B(k)$, then subproblem i is defined as a neighbor of subproblem k. At each generation, the proposed framework maintains several populations as follows. 1) Decomposition population $P = \{x^1, \ldots, x^N\}$, where x^k is the best solution found so far for subproblem k. 2) Domination population A, which contains N solutions selected by using the non-dominated sorting selection and crowding distance methods proposed in [3, 4]. 3) L, which contains the solutions generated by local search and Y, which contains the solutions generated by global search.

The pseudocode of the framework is presented in **Algorithm 1**. It works as follows:

More detailed descriptions of Steps 1-4 are given as follows:

3.2 Initialization

A multiobjective optimization problem is originally decomposed into a number of subproblems based on **eq. 3** . A multiobjecitve COP is decomposed into corresponding N subproblems, when N uniformly distributed weight vectors $\boldsymbol{\lambda}^1, \ldots, \boldsymbol{\lambda}^N$ are generated. Meanwhile, a population P, each solution of which is the best solution found for each subproblem, is randomly generated and assigned to the external archive A, which is used to store diverse non-dominated solutions. The whole process of initialization is shown in Step 1 of **Algorithm 1**.

3.3 Local Search

The whole process of local search is shown in Step 2 of **Algorithm 1**. In this step, local search(SA in our case) is applied to the decomposition population P. Furthermore, we consider individual subset of the population that should undergo the refinement process, which is termed the issue of *the frequency of refinement and individual subset selection* in [19]. In this paper, we propose the adaptive mechanism to adaptively select individuals for local search in Step 2a. We also use two common strategies selecting solutions for local search as the baseline for comparisons. The total two

Algorithm 1:MOPLS

Input:

1. Multiobjective COPs;
2. a stopping criterion;
3. N: the number of subproblems; the population size of P and A;
4. a uniform spread of N weight vectors: $\boldsymbol{\lambda}^1, \dots, \boldsymbol{\lambda}^N$;
5. the size of the neighborhood of each subproblem, denoted as T;

Output: A set of non-dominated solutions A;

Step 1: Initialization:

a) Decompose the original multiobjective COP into N subproblems associated with $\boldsymbol{\lambda}^1, \dots, \boldsymbol{\lambda}^N$.

b) Generate an initial population $P = \{x^1, \dots, x^N\}$ randomly.

c) Assign $A = P$.

d) Compute the Euclidean distance between any two weight vectors and obtain T closest weight vectors to each weight vector. For each $i = 1, \dots, N$, set $B(i) = \{i_1, \dots, i_T\}$, where $\lambda^{i_1}, \dots, \lambda^{i_T}$ are the T closest weight vectors to λ^i.

Step 2:Probabilistic Local search

a) Select N solutions from P.

b) Perform local search to the selected solutions to generate $N * J$ solutions.

Step 3: Global search

For each i $\in P$, do:

a) Randomly select two indexes k and l from $B(i)$.

b) Apply one point crossover and bit-wise mutation operators to x_k and x_l to generate y_i for subproblem i.

Step 4: Population update

/* Use Y to update decomposition population P*/

a) For each i $\in P$, do:

b) If y_i is generated from subproblem i, for each index $k \in B(i)$, if $g^{ws}(y_i|\lambda^k) \le g^{ws}(x_k|\lambda^k)$, then set $x_k = y_i$.

/* Use L to update decomposition population */

c) Set $j = 1$.

d) If L_j is generated from subproblem i, for each index $k \in B(i)$, if $g^{ws}(L_j|\lambda^k) \le g^{ws}(x_k|\lambda^k)$, then set $x_k = L_j$.

e) Set $j \to j+1$. If $j \le J * N$, go back to Step 4d.

/* Use Y and L to update domination population A*/

f) Merge Y with A and new solution set L in Local search;to obtain $Z = A \cup Y \cup L$; sort the merged population Z with fast non-dominated sorting and crowding distance approach of NSGA-II [4] and the best N solutions form the new A.

Step 5: Termination

a) If stopping criteria are satisfied, terminate the algorithm and output A. Otherwise, go to **Step 2**.

---

strategies of the selections of individuals for local search are as follows.

1) *Global search:* For each generation, all the solutions in the decomposition population P are selected to undergo local refinement. The proposed approach that used this selection strategy for local search is called MOPLS in our paper.

2) *Probabilistic Pareto local search algorithm:* In this paper, we proposed an adaptive solution selection for local search based on the learning of domination archive. The domination archive contains very valuable global convergence and diversity information after applying Pareto dominance and diversity maintenance mechanism. Such valuable information can be used to guide the selection of solutions in the decomposition population for local search. In this paper, we adopt non-dominated sorting and crowding distance method in NSGA-II. More detailed description of this mechanism is as follows.

Step 1 Initialization: Initialize P and A.

Step 2 Local Search: Perform local search to P or A and generate a set of new solutions L.

Step 3 Global Search: Perform global search to generate a set of N solutions Y from P.

Step 4 Population Update: Use Y and L to update P and A.

Step 5 Stopping Condition: If a preset stopping condition is met, output A. Otherwise, go to Step 2.

Multiple new solutions are generated by the local search procedure. A new solution is called successful if it enters A. Note that whether or not a new solution enters A is determined by Pareto dominance sorting and crowding distance method proposed in [3,4]. Thus the number of successful solutions generated through local search procedures of a subproblem records the global convergence and diversity information of this subproblem, which can be used to guide the selection of subproblems for local search. We count $ds_{i,g}$ as the number of successful solutions through the local search of the ith subproblem at generation g. The total successful solutions within a certain fixed number of pervious generations, defined as the learning generations(LGs), is used to calculate the probability for each subproblem to be selected for local search as follows.

At each generation $G > LGs - 1$, the probability of choosing the ith$(i = 1, 2, \dots, N)$ subproblem is calculated by

$$prob_{i,G} = \frac{D_{i,G}}{\sum_{i=1}^{N} D_{i,G}} \tag{5}$$

where

$$D_{i,G} = \frac{\sum_{g=G-LGs}^{G-1} ds_{i,g}}{\sum_{g=G-LGs}^{G-1} total_{i,g}} + \epsilon, (i = 1, 2, \dots, N; G > LGs) \tag{6}$$

$D_{i,G}$ represents the proportion of successful solutions through the local search of the ith subproblem within the previous LGs. $ds_{i,g}$ is the number of non-dominated solutions through the local search of the ith subproblem and $total_{i,g}$ is the total number of non-dominated solutions through the local search of all subproblems within the previous LGs. A small constant value $\epsilon = 0.002$ is used to avoid the possible zero selection probabilities. We also normalize $D_{i,G}$ in order to make the summation of $D_{i,G}$ for all subproblems into 1.

A Roulette Wheel Selection is applied to select a subproblem based on the probabilities calculated by eq. 5. The selected subproblem(solution) undergoes local search metaheuristics. Each solution generates J solutions after applying local search. By repeating this procedure N times, a population L with $N * J$ solutions is generated by the local search procedure. To distinguish with our proposed MOPPLS, the algorithm that uses the ordinary Pareto local search is named as multiobjective Pareto local search (MOPLS).

3.4 Global Search

The whole process of the global search is presented in Step 3 of **Algorithm 1**. For the ith subproblem, two parents are selected from its T neighboring subproblems, as shown in Step 3a. In the following Step 3b, a simple one point crossover and a bit-wise mutation operators are applied to the parents to generate an offspring y_i. By repeating this procedure(Step 3a - 3b) N times, an offspring population $Y = \{y_1, \ldots, y_N\}$ is generated.

3.5 Population Update

In Step 4, the newly generated offspring population Y is used to update both P and A. For each solution y_j in Y, suppose it was generated from subproblem i. Step 4b considers all the neighbors of the i-th subproblem, it replaces all neighbors x_k with y_j if y_j performs better than x_k with regard to the k-th subproblem. The update of domination archive is presented in Step 4d. The offspring population Y is merged with A, and population L is produced from the local search in Step 2 of **Algorithm 1**, then the combined population Z(the combinations of Y, A and L) is sorted by the fast non-dominated sorting method and the crowding distance procedure. The best N solutions are kept for A.

4. BENCHMARK PROBLEMS

In this paper, we consider two NP-hard multiobjective COPs: the multiobjective software next release problem(an instance of knapsack problem) and the multiobjective traveling salesman problem. These combinatorial optimization problems have been widely used on testing the performance of various MOEAs [2,7,21].

4.1 The Single and Biobjective Next Release Problem

Assumes that an software system is associated with several *customers* whose requirements need to be considered in the next release. The set S of the customers is denoted by $s_i(1 \leq i \leq m))$. The set R of all the *requirements* that need to be considered is denoted by $r_j(1 \leq j \leq n))$.

Implementation of each requirement need to be allocated with certain number of resources, A cost vector C is represented by $c_j(1 \leq j \leq n))$, where c_i indicates that cost of the requirement $r_i \in R$. A request $q_{ij} \in Q$ represent whether a customer s_i request a requirement r_i, q_{ij}=1 denotes that s_i requests r_i or q_{ij}=0 denotes not. Moreover, we assume that customers can gain different profits, when their requests are satisfied. We represent these profits as W=$w_i(1 \leq i \leq m))$, where w_i denotes the profit when the requests of customer s_i are satisfied in the next release.

The goal of the *Single objective NRP* is to find an optimal solution $X^\star$, to maximize $Profit(X) = \sum_{(i,1)\in X} w_i$ gained by customers, which is the sum of profits gained by the selected customers, subject to $Cost(X) \leq b$, where b is a predefined budget constraint and $cost(X) = \sum_{r_k \in R(X)} c_k$, where $R(X) = \bigcup_{(i,1)\in X, q_{ij}=1} \{r_j\}$ is the requirements for X. Similarly, For *the multiobjective NRP*, The total profit for a solution X is defined by $W(X) = \sum_{(i,1)\in X} s_i$,which is the sum of profits gained by the selected customers. The required $Cost$ for implementing the requirements of a solution X is $Cost(X) = \sum_{r_k \in R(X)} c_k$, where $R(X) = \bigcup_{(i,1)\in X, q_{ij}=1}$ $\{r_j\}$ is the requirements for X.

4.2 The Multiobjective Traveling Salesman Problems

The Traveling Salesman Problem (TSP) can be modeled as a graph G(V,E), where V ={1, . . . , n}is the set of vertices (cities) and E=$\{e_{i,j}\}_{n\times n}$ is the set of edges (connections between cities). The task is to find a Hamiltonian cycle of minimal length, which visits each vertex exactly once. In the case of the multiobjective TSP (MOTSP), each edge $e_{i,j}$ is associated with multiple values such as cost, length, traveling time, etc. Each of them corresponds to one criterion. Mathematically, the MOTSP can be formulated as:

$$minimize \quad f_i(\pi) = \sum_{j=1}^{n-1} c^{(i)}_{\pi(j),\pi(j+1)} + c^{(i)}_{\pi(1),\pi(n)} \qquad i = 1, ..., m \tag{7}$$

where $\pi = (\pi(1), ..., \pi(n))$ is a permutation of cities and $c^{(i)}_{s,t}$ is the cost of the edge between city s and city t regarding criterion i.

5. EXPERIMENTAL STUDIES AND DISCUSSIONS

In this section, we conduct experiments on both MONRP and MOTSP to validate our proposed MOPPLS. Both synthetic and real test instances are used and the introduction of them is included in this section, followed by the experimental setups.

5.1 Test Instances and Experimental Setups

For both MONRP and MOTSP, randomly generated synthetic test instances were used. For MONRP, four sets of test instances were generated with various number of requirements and customers. Similarly, MOTSP test instances of different size were generated. For convenience, the test instances of MONRP and MOTSP are named in the following manners. For example, a 30-customers-and-300-requirements MONRP test instance is denoted as(*cust*30 *req*300). A 500-city MOTSP is denoted as (*tsp*-*c*500). For those real NRP test instances were mined from bug repositories of two open source software projects, namely, Eclipse [5] and Gnome [8]. For convenience, test instances are denoted as nrp-e and nrp-g, respectively, in this paper.

The parameter settings of the compared algorithms for MONRP and MOTSP as follows: the population size of all approaches is set to 200 for MONRP and 100 for MOTSP. The number of neighbors in our proposed MOPLS is set to 10 for them. We set sensitivity of parameter J, which is set to 5 in our experiments. For simulated annealing as the local search meta-heuristic, its initial temperature(Te) is 100 and scheduling factor(α) is set to 0.99. In addition, the number of function evaluations for MONRP is set to 300,000 and all the real test instances. In MOTSP, the number of function evaluation is set to 600,000.

5.2 The Comparison of Various Algorithms

In this section, we conduct experiments to compare multiobjective Pareto local search(MOPLS) and probabilistic Pareto local search(MOPPLS) with other classical multiobjective optimization approaches. Fig. 1 shows the performances of five algorithms in terms of hypervolume values during the whole evolutionary process on two MONRP instances(both synthetic and real NRP Instances) and two MOTSP instances. These five approaches include MOPLS,

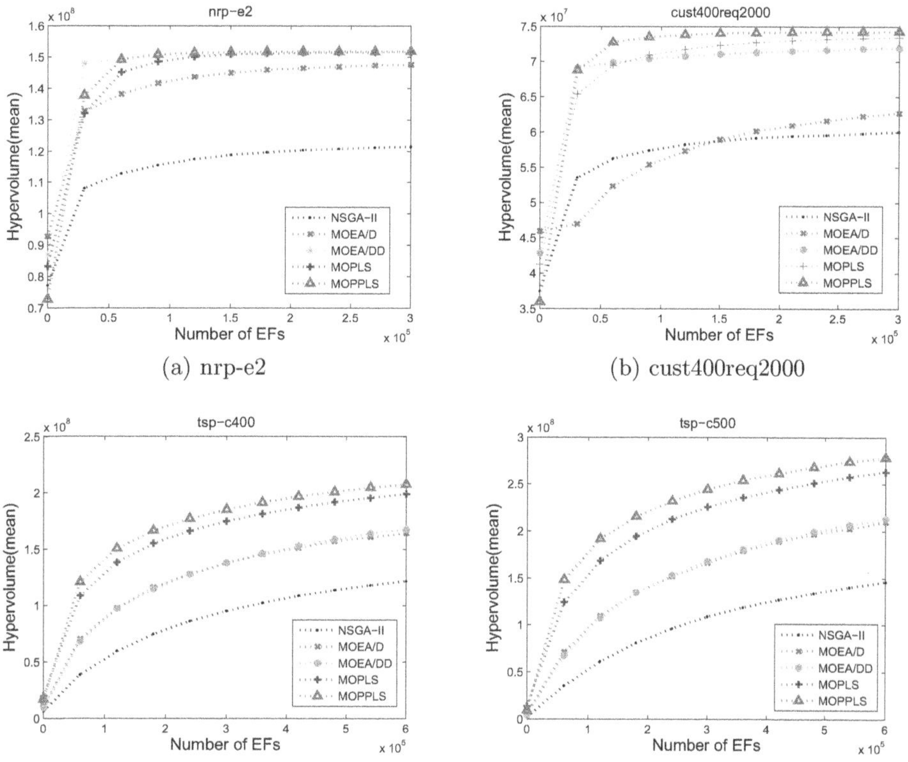

(a) nrp-e2

(b) cust400req2000

(c) tsp-c400

(d) tsp-c500

Figure 1: Convergence graphs in terms of I_H obtained by various algorithms on MONRP and MOTSP

MOPPLS, NSGA-II, MOEA/D and MOEA/DD. NSGAII and MOEA/D are well-known domination and decomposition based approach, respectively. MOEA/DD represents the proposed MOPPLS when no probabilistic Pareto local search is applied or MOPLS when no Pareto local search is applied. The convergence plots in Fig. 1 show that MOPPLS outperforms all other compared algorithms. To validate the results statistically, we use Table 1 to illustrate the mean and standard deviation of hypervolume(I_H), obtained by the five algorithms on MONRP instances and MOSTP instances. It can be observed in the Table 1 that the proposed MOPLS outperforms NSGA-II, MOEA/D and MOEA/DD in terms of hypervolume metric, on all test instances, and MOPPLS further outperforms MOPLS. In other words, MOPPLS always has the best performance compared with other approaches in all test instances.

Table 1: Mean and standard deviation of I_H obtained by various algorithms on MONRP and MOTSP

——		NSGAII	MOEA/D	MOEA/DD	*MOPLS*	*MOPPLS*
cust200req1000	mean	1.6518e+07	1.7793e+07	1.8665e+07	1.8732e+07	**1.8743e+07**
	std	1.9904e+05	1.0193e+05	3.7785e+04	2.5803e+04	1.4609e+04
cust300req1500	mean	3.1568e+07	2.6528e+07	3.5676e+07	3.6332e+07	**3.7184e+07**
	std	4.3181e+05	4.0284e+06	3.4274e+05	6.3052e+05	4.2604e+05
cust400req2000	mean	6.0050e+07	6.2748e+07	7.1928e+07	7.3481e+07	**7.4301e+07**
	std	8.7525e+05	1.1012e+06	5.1543e+05	5.2123e+05	2.2610e+05
cust500req2500	mean	7.6671e+07	7.6933e+07	9.6964e+07	1.0136e+08	**1.0239e+08**
	std	1.4111e+06	2.5817e+06	1.0428e+06	4.3044e+05	2.9678e+05
nrp-e1	mean	1.1617e+08	1.4268e+08	1.4619e+08	1.4635e+08	**1.4655e+08**
	std	1.2917e+06	6.6765e+05	1.8761e+05	1.6063e+05	7.4332e+04
nrp-e2	mean	1.2142e+08	1.4758e+08	1.5142e+08	1.5158e+08	**1.5178e+08**
	std	1.3331e+06	8.2047e+06	1.8171e+05	1.3569e+05	6.8453e+04
nrp-g1	mean	9.4570e+07	1.1548e+08	1.1737e+08	1.1746e+08	**1.1749e+08**
	std	1.1625e+06	4.0086e+05	6.2844e+04	3.1842e+04	1.6110e+04
nrp-g2	mean	7.3694e+07	8.7304e+07	8.7821e+07	8.7826e+07	**8.7829e+07**
	std	7.3188e+05	5.5541e+04	2.0288e+04	1.5200e+04	1.6525e+04
tsp-c300	mean	7.8647e+07	1.0028e+08	1.0172e+08	1.1757e+08	**1.2200e+08**
	std	1.0299e+06	1.0677e+06	1.4351e+06	1.2675e+06	1.5036e+06
tsp-c400	mean	1.2177e+08	1.6419e+08	1.6759e+08	1.9890e+08	**2.0758e+08**
	std	2.2033e+06	4.1758e+06	1.9895e+06	1.8527e+06	2.3867e+06
tsp-c500	mean	1.4621e+08	2.1001e+08	2.1324e+08	2.6294e+08	**2.7813e+08**
	std	2.8420e+06	2.7892e+06	3.6784e+06	3.5585e+06	2.8940e+06
tsp-c600	mean	3.0337e+08	4.4358e+08	4.4479e+08	5.3350e+08	**5.5480e+08**
	std	5.7284e+06	5.9462e+06	5.0039e+06	3.8984e+06	3.7734e+06

6. CONCLUSION

In this paper, we propose a multiobjective probabilistic Pareto local search to address combinatorial optimization problems (COPs). The probability is determined by the success counts of local search offspring entering an external domination archive and this probabilistic information is used to further guide the selection of promising solutions for Pareto local search. In addition, simulated annealing is integrated in this framework as the local refinement process. This multiobjective probabilistic Pareto local search algorithm (MOPPLS), is tested on two famous COPs and compared with some well-known multiobjective evolutionary algorithms. Experimental results suggest that MOPPLS outperforms other compared algorithms.

7. REFERENCES

[1] A. Alsheddy and E. Tsang. Guided pareto local search based frameworks for biobjective optimization. *n IEEE Congress on Evolutionary Computation (CEC)*, pages 1–8, 2010.

[2] X. Cai, O. Wei, and Z. Huang. Evolutonary approches for multi-objective next release problem. *Computing and Informatics*, (4):847–875, 2012.

[3] K. Deb. *Multi-Objective Optimization Using Evolutionary Algorithms*. John Wiley & Sons, Inc., New York, NY, USA, 2001.

[4] K. Deb, A. Pratap, S. Agarwal, and T. Meyarivan. A Fast and Elitist Multiobjective Genetic Algorithm: NSGA–II. *IEEE Transactions on Evolutionary Computation*, 6(2):182–197, April 2002.

[5] Eclipse. http://www.eclipse.org/, July 2011.

[6] C. García-Martínez, O. Cordón, and F. Herrera. A taxonomy and an empirical analysis of multiple objective ant colony optimization algorithms for the bi-criteria TSP. *European Journal of Operational Research*, 180(1):116–148, July 2007.

[7] A. Gaspar-Cunha. A Multi-Objective Evolutionary Algorithm for Solving Traveling Salesman Problems: Application to the Design of Polymer Extruders. In B. Ribeiro, R. F. Albrecht, A. Dobnikar, D. W. Pearson, and N. C. Steele, editors, *Adaptive and Natural Computing Algorithms*, pages 189–193, Coimbra, Portugal, March 2005. Springer.

[8] Gnome. http://www.gnome.org/, July 2011.

[9] D. C. Grosan and A. Abraham. Hybrid evolutionary algorithms: Methodologies, architectures, and reviews. In *Hybrid Evolutionary Algorithms*. Springer, Berlin, Germany, 2007.

[10] L. Ke, Q. Zhang, and R. Battiti. A simple yet efficient multiobjective combinatorial optimization method using decompostion and Pareto local search. *IEEE Trans on Cybernetics*, accepted, 2014.

[11] Y.-C. Liang and M.-H. Lo. Multi-objective redundancy allocation optimization using a variable neighborhood search algorithm. *J. Heuristics*, 16(3):511–535, 2010.

[12] T. Lust and A. Jaszkiewicz. Speed-up techniques for solving large-scale biobjective tsp. *Computers & OR*, 37(3):521–533, 2010.

[13] T. Lust and J. Teghem. Two-phase pareto local search for the biobjective traveling salesman problem. *Journal of Heuristics*, 16(3):475–510, 2010.

[14] Q. H. Nguyen, Y.-S. Ong, and M.-H. Lim. A probabilistic memetic framework. *IEEE Trans. Evolutionary Computation*, 13(3):604–623, 2009.

[15] U. M. S. Saha and K. Deb. A simulated annealing-based multiobjective optimization algorithm: Amosa. *IEEE Transactions on Evolutionary Computation*, 12(3):269–283, 2008.

[16] V. A. Shim, K. C. Tan, and C. Y. Cheong. A hybrid estimation of distribution algorithm with decomposition for solving the multiobjective multiple traveling salesman problem. *IEEE Transactions on Systems, Man, and Cybernetics, Part C*, 42(5):682–691, 2012.

[17] K. Sindhya, K. Miettinen, and K. Deb. A hybrid framework for evolutionary multi-objective optimization. *IEEE Trans. Evolutionary Computation*, 17(4):495–511, 2013.

[18] W. Stadler. A survey of multicriteria optimization or the vector maximum problem, part i: 1776ĺc1960. *Journal of Optimization Theory and Applications*, 29(1):1–52, 1979.

[19] D. Sudholt. Local search in evolutionary algorithms: The impact of the local search frequency. In *17th International Symposium on Algorithms and Computation(ISAAC)*, 2006.

[20] J. Xuan, H. Jiang, Z. Ren, and Z. Luo. Solving the large scale next release problem with a backbone-based multilevel algorithm. *IEEE Trans. Software Eng.*, 38(5):1195–1212, 2012.

[21] Y. Zhang, M. Harman, and S. A. Mansouri. The Multi-Objective Next Release Problem. In D. Thierens, editor, *2007 Genetic and Evolutionary Computation Conference (GECCO'2007)*, volume 1, pages 1129–1136, London, UK, July 2007. ACM Press.

Evolutionary Synthesis of Dynamical Systems – The Past, Current, and Future

Zhun Fan
Department of Electronic Engineering
Shantou University, Guangdong, P.R. China
zfan@stu.edu.cn

Xinye Cai
College of Computer Science and Technology, Nanjing University of Aeronautics and Astronautics, Jiangsu, P.R. China
xinye@nuaa.edu.cn

Wenji Li
Department of Electronic Engineering
Shantou University, Guangdong, P.R. China
wenji_li@126.com

Huibiao Lin
Department of Electronic Engineering
Shantou University, Guangdong, P.R. China
13hblin@stu.edu.cn

Shuxiang Xie
Department of Electronic Engineering
Shantou University, Guangdong, P.R. China
12sxxie1@stu.edu.cn

Sheng Wang
Department of Electronic Engineering
Shantou University, Guangdong, P.R. China
12cwang2@stu.edu.cn

ABSTRACT

When Electronic Design Automation (EDA) has achieved great success both in academy and industry, design automation for mechanical systems seems to be lagged behind. One underlying reason for this is that the coupling of subsystems of mechanical systems is very strong, whereas this coupling for digital electronic system is usually much weaker. Or in other words, the modularity of electronic systems, especially digital electronic systems is much stronger. On the other hand, the mechatronic systems are becoming more and more modularized, which makes them more amenable to be designed automatically, just as digital electronic systems do. In this sense, Mechatronic Design Automation (MDA) is very likely to become the next wave after EDA both in academy and industry. In this paper, we give a survey of the topic of evolutionary synthesis of dynamical systems in general, and wish to shed some light on the future development of this subject.

Categories and Subject Descriptors

B.6.3 [Design Aids]: Automatic Synthesis.

General Terms

Design

Keywords

Automated synthesis, design automation, mechatronic systems

GECCO'14, July 12–16, 2014, Vancouver, BC, Canada.
Copyright © 2014 ACM 978-1-4503-2662-9/14/07…$15.00.
http://dx.doi.org/10.1145/2598394.2610009

1. INTRODUCTION

Mechatronic systems are intrinsically multi-domain physical systems, with possible addition of controllers (both continuous and logic ones). MDA research therefore entails automated concurrent design of both controllers and plant of multi-domain physics. Up to now, there is still no panacea in the research community to automate the optimal design of such a complicated system. The traditional single-discipline sequential-retrospective design model does not only incur long design cycles with frequent modifications, but also cannot guarantee the global optimum of the designed system. It is therefore every relevant and important to study a theory of design automation for general dynamical systems so that innovative designs can be generated automatically to help the designers to improve design efficiency. Moreover, adopting MDA can help the industry to design more innovative products, which will otherwise be difficult, if not impossible to be designed by human designers.

2. STATE-OF-ART OF THE RESEARCH

Design automation of mechatronic systems has not been reported widely in literature. However, design automation of electronic systems has received broad interests from the research community and extensive research results have been reported, especially in the area of design automation of digital electronic systems. Although design automation of electronic systems is focused on one single physical domain, many methods it utilizes can be borrowed in design automation of mechatronic systems. In the following sections, we will discuss related research in the following sequence: design automation of electronic systems -> design automation of MEMS -> design automation of mechatronic systems.

2.1 Design Automation of Electronic Systems (or Electronic Design Automation, EDA)

A lot of research has been conducted in design automation of electronic systems, especially in digital electronic systems.

Because digital electronic systems have very strong modularity, thus are very amenable for automated design. As a result, design automation of digital electronic systems has achieved great success in both academy and industry, and given birth to a huge industry called Electronic Design Automation (EDA) [1]. Compared with the design automaton of digital electronic systems, design automation of analog electronic systems is much more difficult. This is mainly due to two reasons: firstly, analog electronic systems have much stronger couplings between modules, or in other words, their modularity is much weaker than digital electronic systems. In addition, it is more complex to evaluate the performance of the analog electronic systems than that of the digital electronic systems, because more considerations of the design objectives and design constraints have to be taken into account.

Evolutionary algorithms are a class of methods used for automated design of analog electronic systems. Grimbleby [2] proposed using genetic algorithm to automatically design analog electric circuits. Lohn and Colombano [3] used parallel genetic algorithm and successfully designed analog filter and analog amplifier in an automatic manner. Koza et. al. [4] was the first to apply genetic programming in automated design of analog electric circuits. Using a systematic methodology, Koza et. al. have achieved successful results in designing eight different types of analog electrical circuits automatically, which demonstrates that genetic programming has strong capability of concurrent topology exploration and parameter optimization, and serves as a method that can be generalized well in design automaton of various analogy electrical systems. Alpaydin et. al. [5] applied a method that combines evolutionary strategy and simulated annealing to improve the efficiency of automated design, and utilized neuron-fuzzy model to address the issue of parameter uncertainty in manufacturing process. Compared with Koza's work in [4], this work is more emphasized on manufacturability of the circuits automatically designed. In addition, the design method was verified using the circuits manufactured in real world. However, the limitation of the method is that it can only optimize parameters of an electrical system with fixed topology, but lacks the ability to explore the open-ended design space automatically. Zhang et.al. [6] applied genetic algorithm to design power electronic systems automatically. Moreover, an adaptive search mechanism that can be used to coordinate the search in the controller space and the plant space is applied in his approach. The limitation of the approach is also that it can only optimize parameters of an electrical system with fixed topology. Mattiussi and Floreano [7] proposed a novel genetic encoding method inspired by gene regulatory network that enables evolutionary algorithm to achieve automatic design of dynamical systems such as analog electric circuits, neural networks etc. Compared with Koza's method [4], this method utilizes less computing resources, and the encoding does not need to cope with difficult tree structure. Overall, it is a promising approach that deserves further investigation.

Other representative works in this line include: Xie and Xiao [8] has conducted research of automated design of operational amplifier using genetic algorithm. Zhu and Li [9] proposed a concurrent recursive decomposition method that turns the evolutionary design process of the objective electrical systems into concurrent evolutionary design processes of multiple subsystems. It is reported that this method can improve the design efficiency and success rate of automated design of the objective electrical system. All these works in automated design of electrical systems provide significance and inspiration to the research of automated design of mechatronic systems, and dynamical systems in general.

2.2 Design Automation of Micro-Electro-Mechanical Systems (MEMS)

A special type of mechatronic systems – micromechatronic systems or micro-electro-mechanical systems (MEMS) has similar or the same substrate in their manufacture as microelectronic systems. Automated design of MEMS can be considered as an intermediate stage between automated design of electronic systems and automated design of mechanical systems. There have been significant progresses in the automated design of MEMS. For example, Fedder and Jing [10] proposed hierarchical design method. Based on this, Mukherjee and Fedder [11] applied hierarchical design method in automated design of MEMS. But their methods cannot simultaneously design and optimize the topology and parameters of MEMS. Kamalian [12] suggested an interactive evolutionary algorithm that can integrate human's design knowledge and subjective evaluation of the design candidates. The interactive evolutionary algorithm was used to automate the designing of both the topology and parameters of MEMS. Zhang [13] further develops the work of Kamalian in [12], and proposed a hybrid interactive evolutionary algorithm. The algorithm integrates a multi-objective evolutionary algorithm and a local optimization algorithm, which can more flexibly help designers to actively find superior design patterns and then optimize their parameters. In the previous work of the author, a hierarchical automated design framework for MEMS has also been proposed, which combines the capability of genetic programming for system level topology exploration and parameter optimization, and genetic algorithm for device level parameter optimization [14]. In [15], the author also proposed an automated robust design method for MEMS based on improved differential evolution.

2.3 Design Automation of Mechatronic Systems (or Mechatronic Design Automation, MDA)

The most distinguished difference of automated design of mechatronic systems and automated design of electronic systems is that mechatronic systems are intrinsically multi-physics systems with possible integration of controllers [16]. Charkrabarti [17-19] gives a framework of automated synthesis of mechanical systems. This framework can automatically provide a series of conceptual designs that satisfy the functional requirements of the system, without further investigation of the dynamical behaviors of the designed systems. Campbell [20] [21] studies and develops a framework of automated conceptual design of mechatronic systems based on Agent, which can adapt to dynamically changing design environment. The limitation of the framework is also that it lacks detailed analysis of the dynamical behaviors of the designed systems.

Bond graph is a modeling language that can be used to depict uniformly the multi-domain physics as well as the continuous controller, capable of detailed analysis of the dynamical behaviors of the designed systems [22][23]. Bond graph has been widely applied in modeling and analysis of a large variety of real world physical dynamical systems, such as hybrid electric car [24] and smart building [25] etc. Tay et.al. have automatically generated mechatronic designs that satisfy predefined specifications using bond graph as the unified modeling language of mechatronic systems, and genetic algorithm as the search tool in the design space [26]. Seo and the author [27] proposed a framework of automated design of mechatronic systems which combines bond graph as the modeling tool for the multi-domain physics and genetic programming as the search tool for exploration in the design space. The author has made successful designs for electrical circuits and mechatronic systems [28] [29]. Li et.al. also utilized this framework for automated design of a class of analog electrical circuit [30] [31]. Because the efficiency of the search algorithm can be a key for the success of the automated design method, improving the efficiency of the search algorithm is very critical. Hu et.al. proposed a hierarchical fair competition model [32] that can significantly improve the search efficiency of evolutionary algorithms. Oduguwa [33] put forward an intelligent design framework that integrates the exploration in the qualitative space and the search in the quantitative space. This framework can well incorporate human knowledge and judgment, and substantially improves the practicality of the design method.

In previous work, it is rarely reported on how to concurrently design both the controller and the plant of a mechatronic system. Lipson [34] once reported a famous result in Nature, in which he used evolutionary computation to generate the first computer-generated robot system with automatically synthesized neuron controller and plant morphology. The author used bond graph as the representation for both continuous controller and plant of mechatronic systems and automatically designed the plant and the controller of a vehicle suspension system using co-evolutionary algorithm [35] [36]. The author further developed the method so that it can incorporate discrete events and logic controller in the automated design framework. The results are reported in automated designing of a three-tank system [37] and a DC-DC converter [38].

3. FURTHER DEVELOPMENT OF THE RESEARCH

The general research field of the evolutionary synthesis of dynamical systems is going to undergo major progresses with the further developments in the following research directions:

3.1 Multi-objective (or even many-objective) Evolutionary Algorithms

In real world design applications, the designers usually consider not just one single design objective, but more often than not have to consider multiple conflicting design objectives at the same time. As a result, multi-objective evolutionary algorithms (MOEA) gradually become a must in the research of evolutionary synthesis of dynamical systems. When design objectives to be considered simultaneously are more than three, many-objective evolutionary computation is the choice of tool to tackle the automated design problem. Typical MOEAs include NSGA-II [39] and MOEA/D [40]. How to integrate mechanisms of these methods into genetic programming is worthwhile to be investigated in-depth in the future, since genetic programming is very useful to evolve both topology and parameters, and thus a very important tool in evolutionary synthesis of dynamical systems. How to endow genetic programming with multi-objective, and even many-objective search capability is of a critical significance to future development of the general area of evolutionary synthesis of dynamical systems.

3.2 Constrained Optimization Approaches

Real world design applications almost always have to face many design constraints. As a result, EAs, including MOEAs, have to search landscapes with both feasible and infeasible regions. How to handle infeasible solutions in the evolutionary search process becomes a critical issue because this can to a large extent influence the performance of the search algorithm. Deb's constraint handling approach is widely used [41], which is however not necessarily the best choice in all types of applications. Stochastic ranking method [42], for example is found to be more effective among other choices.

3.3 Integrating Data Mining Approaches into Evolutionary Algorithms

A large volume of data is generated in the evolutionary design process. However, most of the data is discarded during the evolutionary process in conventional EAs, without further processing and data mining. As a result, a lot of knowledge is discarded with the data without a chance to be discovered. Researchers have realized that integrating data mining approaches into evolutionary algorithms can not only improve the algorithm performance, but also help discover hidden knowledge in the designing process, thus leading to possible innovations in designs [43].

4. CONCLUSIONS

With the previous success of EDA, and the emerging significance of mechatronic products in the industry (plus upcoming popularity of service robots in our everyday life), there is good reason to believe that MDA, and in general, design automation of dynamical systems will face a bright future and receive increasing attention in the research community. This paper gives a preliminary survey of this research area, attempting to give it a relatively thorough review of the previous research and a momentum to future development.

5. ACKNOWLEDGMENTS

This work is supported by National Natural Science Foundation of China (Grant No. 61175073, 51375287 and 61332002).

6. REFERENCES

[1] Laung-Terng Wang, Yao-Wen Chang, and Kwang-Ting (Tim) Cheng, eds., (2009), *Electronic Design Automation: Synthesis, Verification and Test (Systems on Silicon)*, Morgan Kaufmann, ISBN: 978-0-1237-4364-0, 934 pp.

[2] J. B. Grimbleby, (1995), "Automatic analogue network synthesis using genetic algorithms", in *Proc. 1st Int. Conf. Genetic Algorithms in Engineering Systems: Innovations and Applications* (GALESIA), pp. 53–58.

[3] Lohn, J. D. and Colombano, S. P. (1999), "A circuit representation technique for automated circuit design". *IEEE Transactions on Evolutionary Computation*, **3**(3), 205–219.

[4] Koza, J. R., Bennett, F. H., Andre, D., Keane, M. A. and Dunlap, F. (1997), "Automated synthesis of analog electrical circuits by means of genetic programming". *IEEE Trans. Evolutionary Computation*, **1**(2), 109–128.

[5] Guner Alpaydin, Sina Balkir, and Gunhan Dundar, (2003), "An Evolutionary Approach to Automatic Synthesis of High Performance Analog Integrated Circuits", *IEEE Transactions on Evolutionary Computation*, vol. 7, no. 3, pp. 240 – 252.

[6] J. Zhang, Chung, W.-L. Lo, Hui, and Wu, (2001), "Implementation of a decoupled optimization technique for design of switching regulators using genetic algorithms", *IEEE Transactions on Power Electronics*, vol. 16, no. 6, pp. 752–763.

[7] Claudio Mattiussi and Dario Floreano, (2007), "Analog Genetic Encoding for the Evolution of Circuits and Networks", *IEEE Transactions on Evolutionary Computation*, vol. 11, no. 5, pp. 596-607.

[8] G. Xie, H. Xiao, "Modeling and Automated Design of Operational Amplifier Based on Evolutionary Algorithm" (in Chinese), *Journal of Electronic Measurement and Instrument*, 23(1), 99-95, 2009.

[9] J. Zhu, Y. Li, "Automated Circuit Design Methodology Using Decomposition Evolution" (in Chinese), *Computer Systems and Applications*, 19(8), 52-56, 2010.

[10] G. K. Fedder, and Q. Jing, (1999), "A Hierarchical Circuit-Level Design Methodology for Microelectromechanical Systems", *IEEE Transactions on Circuits and Systems II (TCAS)*, vol. 46, no. 10, pp. 1309-1315.

[11] Tamal Mukherjee, Gary K. Fedder, (1999), "Hierarchical Mixed-Domain Circuit Simulation, Synthesis and Extraction Methodology for MEMS", *Journal of VLSI Signal Processing* (21), pp, 233-249.

[12] R. Kamalian, (2004),"Evolutionary Synthesis of MEMS Devices", PhD thesis,Department of Mechanical Engineering, University of California at Berkeley, CA.

[13] Y. Zhang, (2004), "MEMS Design Synthesis Based on Hybrid Evolutionary Computation", PhD thesis, Department of Mechanical Engineering, University of California at Berkeley, CAZ.

[14] Fan, J. Liu, T. Sørensen, P. Wang, (2009), "Improved Differential Evolution Based on Stochastic Ranking for Robust Layout Synthesis of MEMS Components", *IEEE Transactions on Industrial Electronics* vol: 56, issue: 4,pages: 937-948, 2009.

[15] Z. Fan, J. Wang, S. Achiche, E. Goodman, and R. Rosenberg, (2008), "Structured synthesis of MEMS using evolutionary approaches," *Applied Soft Computing*, vol. 8, no. 1, pp. 579–589.

[16] Youcef-Toumi, K. (1996), "Modeling, design, and control integration: a necessary step in mechatronics". *IEEE/ASME Trans. Mechatronics*, **1**(1), 29–38.

[17] Chakrabarti, T.P. Bligh, (1994), "An Approach to Functional Synthesis of Solutions in Mechanical Conceptual Design. Part I: Introduction and Knowledge Representation," *Research in Engineering Design*, vol. 6, pp.127-141.

[18] Chakrabarti, T.P. Bligh, (1996a), "An Approach to Functional Synthesis of Solutions in Mechanical Conceptual Design. Part II: Kind Synthesis," *Research in Engineering Design*, vol. 8, pp.52-62.

[19] Chakrabarti, T.P. Bligh, (1996b), "An Approach to Functional Synthesis of Solutions in Mechanical Conceptual Design. Part III: Spatial Configuration," *Research in Engineering Design*, vol. 8, pp.116-124.

[20] M. I. Campbell, J. Cagan and K. Kotovsky, (1999), "A-Design: An Agent-Based Approach to Conceptual Design in a Dyanmic Environment," *Research in Engineering Design*, vol. 11, pp.172-192.

[21] M. Campbell, (2000), "The A-Design invention machine: a means of automating and investigating conceptual design". PhD thesis, Department of Mechanical Engineering, Carnegie Mellon University.

[22] D. C. Karnopp, D. L. Margolis, R. C. Rosenberg, (2000), *System Dynamics, A Unified Approach, 3rd Ed.,* John Wiley & Sons.

[23] Zhong Jue, Coupling Design Theory and Methods for Complex Mechatronic Systems (in Chinese), Beijing: Mechanical Industry Press, 2007.

[24] Mariano Filippa, Chunting Mi, John Shen, and Randy C. Stevenson, (2005), "Modeling of a Hybrid Electric Vehicle Powertain Test Cell Using Bond Graphs", *IEEE Transactions on Vehicular Technology*, vol. 54, no. 3, pp. 837-845.

[25] B. Yu, A.H.C. van Paassen, (2004), "Simulink and bond graph modeling of an air-conditioned room", *Simulation Modeling Practice and Theory* 12 61-76.

[26] Tay, E., Flowers, W. and Barrus, J. (1998), "Automated generation and analysis of dynamic system designs". *Research in Engineering Design*, **10**(1), 15–29.

[27] K. Seo, Z. Fan, J. Hu, E. Goodman, R. Rosenberg, (2003), "Toward an Automated Design Method for Multi-Domain Dynamic Systems Using Bond Graph and Genetic Programming," *Mechatronics*, 13 (8-9), pp: 851-885.

[28] Z. Fan, J. Wang, and E. Goodman, (2004), "Exploring open-ended design space of mechatronic systems," *International Journal of Advanced Robotic Systems*, vol. 1, pp. 295–302.

[29] Z. Fan, K. Seo, J. Hu, E. D. Goodman, and R. C. Rosenberg, (2004), "A novel evolutionary engineering design approach for mixed-domain systems," *Engineering Optimization*, vol. 36, no. 2, pp. 127 – 147.

[30] S. Li, J. Hu, Q. Xie, H. Zhang, "Automated Design of Mechatronic Systems Based on Genetic Programming and Bond Graphs" (in Chinese), Journal of System Simulation, 14(11), 1513-1516, 2002.

[31] S. Li, J. Wang, J. Qiang, "Automated Synthesis of Analog Circuit Based on Multi-Modified Site Embryo Bond Graph" (in Chinese), Application Research of Computers, 26(2), 2009.

[32] J. Hu, E. Goodman, K. Seo, Z. Fan, and R. Rosenberg, (2005),"The hierarchical fair competition (HFC) framework for sustainable evolutionary algorithms," *Evolutionary Computation*, vol. 13, no. 2, pp. 241–277.

[33] V. Oduguwa, R. Roy, D. Farrugia, (2007), "Development of a Soft Computing-Based Framework for Engineering Design

Optimisation with Quantitative and Qualitative Search Spaces", *Applied Soft Computing*, 7, pp. 166 – 188.

[34] H. Lipson, J. B. Pollack, (2000), "Automated design and manufacture of artificial lifeforms". *Nature*, 2000; 406: 974-978.

[35] J. Wang, Z. Fan, J. P. Terpenny, and E. D. Goodman, (2004), "Knowledge Interaction with Genetic Programming in Mechatronic Systems Design Using Bond graph," *IEEE Transactions on Systems, Man and Cybernetics, Part C:Applications and Reviews, Special Issue on Knowledge Extraction and Incorporation in Evolutionary Computation* Vol. 35(2), pp. 172-182.

[36] J. Wang, Z. Fan, J. P. Terpenny, and E. D. Goodman, (2008), "Cooperative body-brain coevolutionary synthesis of mechatronic systems." *Artificial Intelligence for Engineering Design, Analysis and Manufacturing (AIEDAM)*, vol. 22, no. 3, pp. 219–234.

[37] Jean F. Dupuis, Zhun Fan, Erik Goodman, "Evolutionary Design of Hybrid Controller for Mechatronic Systems", accepted and published online by *International Journal of System Science*, 2013.

[38] Jean F. Dupuis, Zhun Fan, Erik Goodman, "Evolutionary Design of Both Topologies and Parameters of a Hybrid Dynamical System", *IEEE Trans. Evolutionary Computation* 16(3): 391-405 (2012).

[39] K. Deb, A. Pratap, S. Agarwal, T. Meyarivan, "A fast and elitist multiobjective genetic algorithm: NSGA-II", *IEEE Trans. Evolutionary Computation*, 6(2): 182-197 (2002)

[40] Q. Zhang, H. Li, "MOEA/D: A Multiobjective Evolutionary Algorithm Based on Decomposition", *IEEE Trans. Evolutionary Computation,* 11(6): 712-731 (2007)

[41] K. Deb, "An Efficient Constraint Handling Method for Genetic Algorithms", *Computer Methods in Applied Mechanics and Engineering*, 186(2-4): 311-338 (2000)

[42] Z. Fan, J. Liu, T. Sørensen, P. Wang, "Improved Differential Evolution Based on Stochastic Ranking for Robust Layout Synthesis of MEMS Components", *IEEE Transactions on Industrial Electronics,* 56(4): 937-948 (2009)

[43] K. Deb, "Unveiling Innovative Design Principles by Means of Multiple Conflicting Objectives", *Engineering Optimization*, 35(5): 445-470 (2003)

Design Optimization of MEMS Using Constrained Multi-Objective Evolutionary Algorithm

Wenji Li
Department of Electronic Engineering
Shantou University, Guangdong, P.R. China
wenji_li@126.com

Zhun Fan
Department of Electronic Engineering
Shantou University, Guangdong, P.R. China
zfan@stu.edu.cn

Xinye Cai
College of Computer Science and Technology, Nanjing University of Aeronautics and Astronautics, Jiangsu, P.R. China
xinye@nuaa.edu.cn

Huibiao Lin
Department of Electronic Engineering
Shantou University, Guangdong, P.R. China
13hblin@stu.edu.cn

Shuxiang Xie
Department of Electronic Engineering
Shantou University, Guangdong, P.R. China
12sxxie1@stu.edu.cn

Sheng Wang
Department of Electronic Engineering
Shantou University, Guangdong, P.R. China
12cwang2@stu.edu.cn

ABSTRACT

MEMS layout optimization is a typical multi-objective constrained optimization problem. This paper proposes an improved MOEA called cMOEA/D to solve this problem. The cMOEA/D is based on MOEA/D but also uses the frequency of individual update of sub-problems to locate the promising sub-problems. By dynamically allocating computing resources to more promising sub-problems, we can effectively improve the performance of the algorithm to find more non-dominated solutions in MEMS layout optimization. In addition, we compared two mechanisms of constraint handling, Stochastic Ranking (SR) and Constraint-domination principle (CDP). The experimental results show that CDP works better than SR and the proposed algorithm outperforms the state-of-art algorithms such as NSGA-II and MOEA/D, in terms of convergence and diversity.

Categories and Subject Descriptors

G.1.6 [**Optimization**]: Constrained optimization

General Terms

Algorithms

Keywords

Multi-objective constrained optimization; MEMS layout design

1. INTRODUCTION

Multi-objective evolutionary algorithms have been successfully applied in a large variety of optimization problems in both science and engineering, where multiple and conflicting design objectives exist [1] [2]. Without loss of generality, a multi-objective constrained optimization problem with n design variables, and m design objectives can be defined as follows:

$$\begin{cases} \min \quad F(x) = (f_1(x), f_2(x), \ldots, f_m(x)); \\ \quad \text{s.t.} \quad g_i(x) \geq 0, \quad i = 1,2,\ldots,q \\ \qquad\quad h_j(x) = 0, \quad j = 1,2,\ldots p \end{cases} \tag{1}$$

Where $x = (x_1, x_2, \ldots, x_n) \subset R^n$ is n-dimensional design variables, $F(x) = (f_1(x), f_2(x), \ldots, f_m(x)) \subset R^m$ is m-dimensional objective vector. $g_i(x) \geq 0$ define q inequality constraints, $h_j(x) = 0$ defines p equality constraints.

NSGA-II [3] and MOEA/D [4] are the two typical multi-objective evolutionary algorithms. They represent the two categories of fitness assignment methods, namely fitness assignment based on domination relationship, and fitness assignment using aggregation function based on decomposition. In fitness assignment based on domination relationship, the fitness is decided by non-dominated sorting and crowding distance. Representative algorithms using this type of fitness assignment method include MOGA [5], PAES-II [6], SPEA-II [7] and NSGA-II [3]. In fitness assignment based on decomposition, comparison and sorting of individuals are made via aggregation function with weights allocated specifically to all individuals. Different weight vectors associated with the aggregation function lead to different directions towards the Pareto front. To obtain as many solutions as possible in the entire Pareto front, the weight vector may be adjusted during the evolutionary search process. Typical algorithms of this category include IMMOGLS [8], UGA [9], cMOGA [10], MOGLS [11], and MOEA/D [4].

In multi-objective constrained optimization, traditional constraint handling method is adopting penalty function to penalize the constraint violation. However, it is then necessary to find proper penalty factor to balance objective function and penalty function, which is usually difficult and application-dependent in practice. Stochastic Ranking (SR) [12] and Constraint-domination principle (CDP) [13] are two very promising penalty function methods that can well balance the objective function and penalty function without using a penalty factor. Because both SR and CDP do not

GECCO'14, July 12–16, 2014, Vancouver, BC, Canada.

http://dx.doi.org/10.1145/2598394.2610010

use penalty factor, so there is no need for the user to have prior knowledge about the relative importance of the objective optimization and constraint satisfaction. In SR, usually a small proportion of infeasible solutions are compared with their objective values, while in CDP, all solutions are compared only by their constraint violation levels.

The remainder of the paper is organized as follows: Section 2 explains the framework of the proposed algorithm, Section 3 introduces the MEMS layout optimization problem, Section 4 gives the experimental results of the MEMS layout optimization problem, and Section 5 concludes the paper.

2. THE ALGORITHM

Like other variants of MOEA/D [4], the algorithm proposed in this paper, namely cMOEA/D decomposes a multi-objective constrained optimization problem into N single objective constrained optimization sub-problems. In addition, the cMOEA/D identifies the promising sub-problems using the statistic information of frequency of updating their neighboring solutions, and allocates more computational resources to the promising sub-problems accordingly. In particular, the probability of the sub-problems to be selected is calculated as follows:

$$p_{i,G} = \frac{N_{i,G}}{\sum_{i=1}^{n} N_{i,G}} \quad (2)$$

$$N_{i,G} = \frac{\sum_{g=G-SG}^{G-1} n_{i,g}}{\sum_{g=G-SG}^{G-1} total_g} + \varepsilon \quad (3)$$

Where $n_{i,g}$ represents the number of solutions the i-th sub-problem replaces its neighbors in the g-th generation, $total_g$ represents the total number of solutions that all the sub-problems of the g-th generation replace their neighbors, G is the current generation, and SG is the number of generations counted in the calculation of the statistics. ε is a small constant used to avoid zero in the denominator. In this paper, ε is set to 0.002. In order to ensure the integrity of cMOEA/D, we give all the pseudo-code which may have a lot in common with MOEA/D.

At each generation, cMOEA/D uses a decomposition method named Tchebycheff to maintain:

1. a population of N points $x^1,\ldots x^N$,where x^i is the current solution to the ith subproblem;

2. $F^1,\ldots,F^N$ and $V^1,\ldots,V^N$, where F^i is the F-value of x^i, V^i is the degree of constraint violation of individual x^i.

3. $Z=(z_1,\ldots,z_m)$, where z_i is the best value found so far for objective f_i.

4. an external population (EP) , which is used to store feasible non-dominated solutions found during the search.

5. a matrix $n_{i,g}$, where $n_{i,g}$ is used as a container to store the number of subproblem updated by each subproblem in every generation.

The pseudo-code of CMOEA-D is given in Algorithm 1:

Algorithm1. Pseudo-code of cMOEA/D

1: generate a weight vector λ^i, $i=1,2,\ldots,N$ uniformly

2: generate an initial population $P=\{x^i, i=1,\ldots,N\}$

3: Calculate the T closest weight vectors for each weight vector, set $B(i)=\{\lambda^{i_1},\ldots\lambda^{i_T}\}$ where $\lambda^{i_1},\ldots\lambda^{i_T}$ are the T closest weight vectors to the weight vector λ^i

4: Evaluate x^i, $F(x^i)=(f_1(x^i),f_2(x^i),\ldots,f_m(x^i))$, $V(x^i)=\sum_{j=1}^{p}|\min(g_j(x^i),0)|$, $i=1,2,\ldots,N$. $V(x^i)$ denotes the degree of constraint violation of individual x^i.

5: Initialize $Z=(z_1,\ldots,z_m)$ by setting $z_i=\min\{f_i(x^1),f_i(x^2),\ldots,f_i(x^N)\}$;

6: Set gen = 1;

7: **while** stopping criterion is not satisfied **do**

8: **for** i = 1 to N do

9: select subproblem according to (2), generate an offspring y according to Algorithm2

10: Evaluate y, $F(y)=(f_1(y),f_2(y),\ldots,f_m(y))$, $V(y)=\sum_{j=1}^{p}|\min(g_j(y),0)|$;

11: update Z , for each $j=1,\ldots,m$, if $z_i > f_i(y)$, then set $z_i = f_i(y)$

12: update neighboring solutions according to Algorithm3;

13: set $n_{i,g}$ according to Algorithm3

13: **end for**

14: **end while**

Algorithm 2. Pseudo-code of generate offspring

1: randomly generate a number named rand from (0, 1);

2: **if** rand $<\delta$

3: $P=B(i)$

4: **else**

5: $P=\{1,\ldots N\}$;

6: **end if**

7: Set $r_1=i$ and randomly select two indexes r_2 and r_3 from P, and then generate an offspring Solution y' from x^{r_1}, x^{r_2} and x^{r_3} by a DE operator;

8: Perform a mutation operator on y' with probability p_m to produce a new solution y

9: Repair y ;

Algorithm 3. Pseudo-code of update scheme.

1: update neighboring solutions x^j , $j \in P$ of an offspring y as follows:
2: Set $c = 0$
3: **if** $c = n_r$ or P is empty then
4: set $n_{i,g} = C$ then break;
5: **else**
6: Randomly pick an index j from P;
7: randomly generate a number named r from (0, 1)
8: **if** $(V(y) = V(x^j) = 0)$ or $(r < p_f)$ **then**
9: **if** $g^{te}(y|\lambda^j, Z) \le g^{te}(x^j|\lambda^j, Z)$ **then**
10: $x^j = y, F(x^j) = F(y), V(x^j) = V(y)$ and $c = c+1$
11: **end if**
12: **else**
13: **if** $V(y) < V(x^j)$ **then**
14: $x^j = y, F(x^j) = F(y), V(x^j) = V(y)$ and $c = c+1$
15: **end if**
16: **end if**
17: Remove j from P and go to step3;
18: **end if**

3. MEMS MODEL

3.1 Introduction to the MEMS Model

A case study in the area of MEMS design (taken from [14] [15] [16] [17]) was carried out to verify the effectiveness of the above design optimization methodology following a MOEA/D computational approach. The design problem is a comb-drive micro-resonator (see the layout in Fig. 1), with fourteen mixed-type design variables ($L_b, w_b, L_t, w_t, L_{sy}, w_{sy}, L_{sa}, w_{sa}, w_{cy}, L_c, w_c, x_0, V, N_c$), and twenty four design constraints, both linear and nonlinear. More detailed description of the design problem in terms of analytical equations is given below.

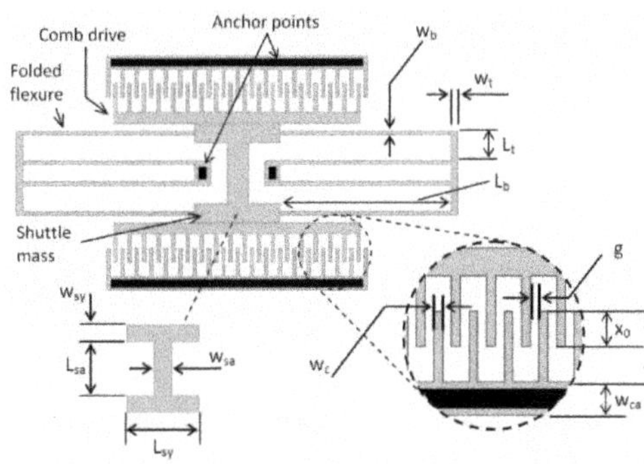

Figure 1. MEMS model (adapted from [14]).

L_b and w_b are the length and the width of the flexure beam (respectively), L_t and w_t are the length and the width of the truss beam (respectively), L_{sy} and w_{sy} are the length and the width of the shuttle yoke (respectively), L_{sa} and w_{sa} are the length and the width of the shuttle axle (respectively), w_{cy} is the width of the comb yoke, L_c and w_c are the length and the width of the comb fingers (respectively), x_0 is the comb finger overlap, V is the voltage amplitude, and N_c is the number of rotor comb fingers. The equations which are necessary to build the parametric layout are given as follows, Eqns. 4-18,

$$L_1 = (N_c - 1)(w_c + 2g) + N_c.w_c \quad (4)$$

$$L_2 = L_1 + 2(g + w_c) \quad (5)$$

$$A_s = w_{sa}.L_{sa} + 2w_{sy}.L_{sy} \quad (6)$$

$$A_b = 4(2L_b.w_b + (L_t + w_a / 2).w_t + (w_a.w_{ba}) / 2) \quad (7)$$

$$A_c = 2(L_1.w_{cy} + N_c.w_c.L_c) \quad (8)$$

$$A_t = 2(w_{ca}.L_2 + (N_c + 1).w_c.L_c) \quad (9)$$

$$B_x = \mu((A_s + 0.5A_t + 0.5A_b).(1/d + 1/\gamma) + (A_c / g)) \quad (10)$$

$$\alpha = (w_t / w_b)^3 \quad (11)$$

$$K_x = 2(E.t.w_b^3 / L_b^3).(L_t^2 + 14\alpha.L_t.L_b + 36\alpha^2 L_b^2) / (4L_t^2 + 41\alpha.L_t.L_b + 36\alpha^2 L_b^2) \quad (12)$$

$$K_y = 2(E.t.w_b^3 / L_b^3).(8L_t^2 + 8\alpha.L_t.L_b + \alpha^2 L_b^2) / (4L_t^2 + 10\alpha.L_t.L_b + 5\alpha^2 L_b^2) \quad (13)$$

$$K_{ey} = 2\varepsilon_0.N_c.V^2.x_0.t / g^3 \quad (14)$$

$$m_x = \rho(A_s + 0.25A_t + (12/35)A_b).t \quad (15)$$

$$Q = (m_x.K_x / B_x^2)^{1/2} \quad (16)$$

$$F_{ex} = 1.12\varepsilon_0.N_c.(t/g).V^2 \quad (17)$$

$$x_{disp} = Q.F_{ex} / K_x \quad (18)$$

where L_1 and L_2 are the lengths of the lower and the upper comb yokes, A_s , A_b , A_c , A_t are the layout areas of the shuttle yokes, the flexure beams, the comb finger sidewalls and the truss beams, respectively, B_x is the damping coefficient, K_x and K_y are the folded flexure spring constants, F_{ex} is the lateral component of the external electrostatic force generated by the comb drives, m_x is the effective masses, Q is the quality factor and x_{disp} is the displacement amplitude. Further details about these analytical equations and derivations of them are given in [16] [17].

3.2 Design Criteria

Several design constrains must be defined to constrain the layout synthesis of the micro resonator. There are 24 linear and nonlinear constraints defined as given in the following Eqns. 19-31.

$$g_{1,2}(x) = 0 < L_2 \le 700(\mu\ m) \quad (19)$$

$$g_{3,4}(x) = 0 < L_{sy} + 2L_b + 2w_t \le 700(\mu\ m) \quad (20)$$

$$g_{5,6}(x) = 0 < 2(w_{ca} + 2L_c - x_0 + w_{cy}) + L_{sa} + 2w_{sy} \le 700(\mu\ m) \quad (21)$$

$$g_{7,8}(x) = 4 < L_c - (x_0 + x_{disp}) \le 200(\mu\ m) \quad (22)$$

$$g_{9,10}(x) = 4 < x_0 - x_{disp} \le 200(\mu\ m) \quad (23)$$

$$g_{11}(x) = (L_t + w_a / 2) \le (L_{sa}/2 + w_{sy} + x_{disp})(\mu\ m) \quad (24)$$

$$g_{12}(x) = (L_{sa}/2 + x_{disp}) \le L_t + w_a / 2 - w_b(\mu\ m) \quad (25)$$

$$g_{13,14}(x) = 2 < L_{sy} / 2 - w_{ba} - w_{sa} / 2 \le 200(\mu\ m) \quad (26)$$

$$g_{15,16}(x) = 2 < x_{disp} \le 100(\mu\ m) \quad (27)$$

$$g_{17,18}(x) = 5 < Q \le 10^5 \quad (28)$$

$$g_{19,20}(x) = 0 < x_{disp} / L_b \le 0.1 \quad (29)$$

$$g_{21,22}(x) = 0 < K_{ey} / K_y \le 1/3 \quad (30)$$

$$g_{23,24}(x) = 4 < L_{sa} / 2 - x_{disp} - w_a / 2 \le 200(\mu\ m) \quad (31)$$

In this section, the multi-objective optimization problem (MOP), briefly described in the previous section that is related to the layout synthesis of MEMS components with respect to dynamic response (i.e. voltage) and the size of the device, is formulated. Optimum design parameters, i.e. geometrical features of the flexure beams, comb drives and the shuttle mass, are investigated to simultaneously minimize the power consumption or in other words the voltage and the area of the problem is given below,

$$\text{Minmize} f_1(\mathrm{x}) : V$$

$$\text{Minmize} f_2(\mathrm{x}) : A_{total} = (A_s + A_t + A_b + A_c) \tag{32}$$

$$\text{subject to: } g_i(\mathrm{x}), \text{for } i = 1, 2, \ldots, 24$$

$$\mathrm{x} = \{L_b, w_b, L_t, w_t, L_{sy}, w_{sy}, L_{sa}, w_{sa}, w_{cy}, L_c, w_c, x_0, V, N_c\}$$

$$\mathrm{x}_{\min} = \{2, 2, 2, 2, 2, 10, 2, 10, 10, 8, 2, 4, 0, 3\};$$

$$\mathrm{x}_{\max} = \{400, 20, 400, 20, 400, 400, 400, 400, 400, 400, 20, 400, 50, 50\}$$

Where $g_i(\mathrm{x})$ are the constraints given in the previous section and x is the vector of design variables. The autonomous optimization methodology to solve this nonlinear constrained optimization problem is given in the following sections.

4. EXPERIMENTAL STUDIES AND DISCUSSIONS

4.1 Experimental Settings

In order to evaluate the performance of CMOEA/D, experimental results on MEMS layout optimization problem are compared with those obtained by two state-of-the-art algorithms NSGA-II and MOEA/D. Ten independent runs with the three algorithms are made, and the following parameters are used:

The parameter settings of the compared algorithms are listed in Table 1 as follows. The population size for NSGA-II, MOEA/D and cMOEA/D is 200, crossover probability is 1.0, probability parameter *pf* = 0, mutation probability is 1/14 and maximum generation is 500.

Table 1. The parameter setting of NSGA-II, MOEA/D and cMOEA/D

	Population size	Crossover rates	Mutation rates	Maximum Generatio n
NSGA-II	200	1.0	1/14	500
MOEA/D	200	1.0	1/14	500
cMOEA/D	200	1.0	1/14	500

For cMOEA/D and MOEA/D, neighbor size *T*=20, neighbor selection probability $\delta = 0.9$, $n_r = 10$

For cMOEA/D, *SG*=5.

4.2 Performance Metric

Performance of a multi-objective evolutionary algorithm can be evaluated in two aspects – convergence and distribution. Convergence describes the closeness of the obtained Pareto front to the true Pareto front. Distribution on the other hand depicts how the solutions in the obtained Pareto are distributed. For the MEMS layout optimization problem, because we do not know the true Pareto front in advance, we select two metrics – Coverage (C) [18] and Hypervolume (HV) [18]. Detailed definitions of them are as follows:

Coverage Metric

C can manifest domination relationship between two approximate Pareto fronts. Assume that A and B are two Pareto fronts obtained with two different multi-objective evolutionary algorithms, C can be defined as:

$$C(A, B) = \frac{\left|\{u \in B \mid \exists v \in A : v \succeq u\}\right|}{|B|} \tag{33}$$

Here, $|B|$ represents the number of items (solutions) in *B*. $v \succeq u$ means v dominates u or v equals u .Normally $C(A,B) \neq 1 - C(B,A)$. $C(A,B) = 1$ means that all solutions in B are dominated by some solutions from *A*. On the other hand, $C(A,B) = 0$ indicates that no individual in *B* is dominated by any solution from *A*. When $C(A,B) > C(B,A)$, *A* is considered superior to *B*.

Hypervolume (*HV*) Metric

HV simultaneously considers the distribution of the obtained Pareto front *P* and its vicinity to the true Pareto front. *HV* is defined as the volume enclosed by *P* and the reference vector $r = (r_1, r_2, \ldots, r_m)$. *HV* can be defined as:

$$HV(P) = \bigcup_{i \in P} vol(i) \tag{34}$$

Here, $vol(i)$ represents the volume enclosed by solution $i \in P$ and the reference vector r . In this experiment, $r = (55, 50)$.

4.3 Experimental Result

SR and CDP are two mechanisms of constraint handling. Moreover, when pf = 0 the two mechanisms are equivalent [19]. Figure 1 shows different pf values in cMOEA/D when solving MEMS layout optimization problem.

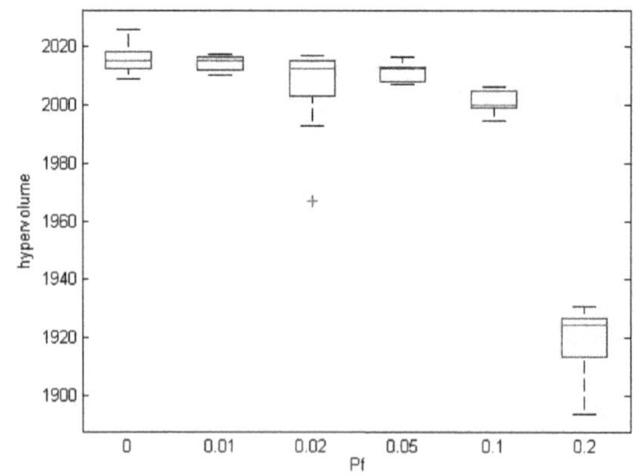

Figure 1. Box-plot of HV-metric using different pf values in 10 independent running of cMOEA/D

Table 2. HV-metric values of the solutions found by cMOEA/D using different pf value.

HV-metric	cMOEA/D	
Parameter Pf	Best	Mean
0	**2025.9**	**2015.8**
0.01	2017.3	2014.3
0.02	2017.1	2006.0
0.05	2016.7	2011.4
0.1	2006.4	2001.0
0.2	1931.0	1918.9

From figure 1 and table 2, we can know that CDP (the Pf value equals zero) works better than SR in cMOEA/D.

In the following experiments, we use CDP to deal with constraints. Figure 2 is the nondominated solutions with the maxmam H-metric in 10 runs of NSGA-II, MOEAD and CMOEAD where their constraint handling is CDP.

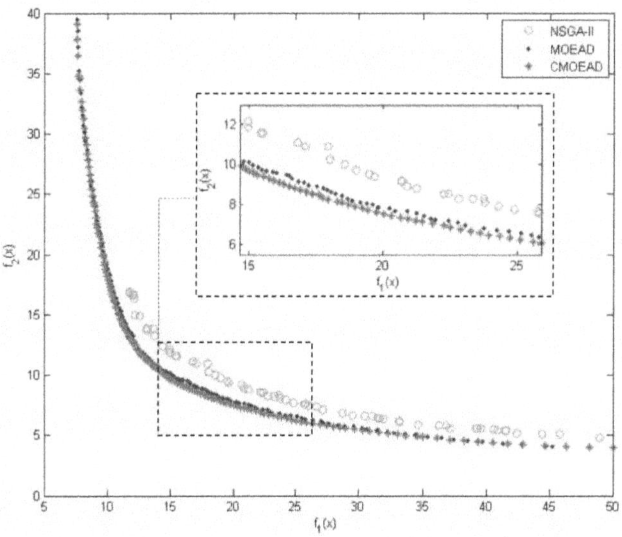

Figure 2. Plots of the nondominated solutions with the maxmam HV-metric in 10 run of NSGA-II, MOEA/D and cMOEA/D

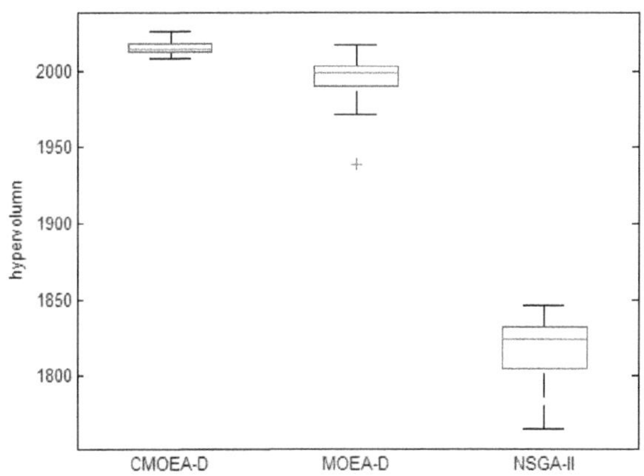

Figure 3. the boxplot about HV-metric in 10 runs of NSGA-II, MOEA/D and cMOEA/D

Table 3. HV-metric values of solutions found by cMOEA/D, MOEA/D and NSGA-II

HV-metric	cMOEA/D		MOEA/D		NSGA-II	
Instance	Best	Mean	Best	Mean	Best	Mean
MEMS	**2025.9**	**2015.8**	2017.2	1992.2	1846.3	1816.4

Figure 3 and table 3 describes the H-metric information in 10 runs of NSGA-II、MOEAD and CMOEAD.

Table 4. Average set coverage among cMOEA/D (A), MOEA/D （B） and NSGA-II（N）

C-metric	**C(A,B)**	**C(B,A)**	**C(A,N)**
	0.82	0.015	1
	C(N,A)	**C(B,N)**	**C(N,B)**
	0	1	0

Table4 presents the best of the C-metric values of the final approximations obtained by the three algorithms. The experimental results show that the proposed algorithm (cMOEA/D) outperforms the state-of-art algorithms such as NSGA-II and MOEA/D, in terms of convergence and diversity.

5. CONCLUTION

This paper proposes an improved MOEA called cMOEA/D to solve MEMS layout optimization problem. The cMOEA/D uses the frequency of individual update of sub-problems to locate the promising sub-problems. By dynamically allocating computing resources to more promising sub-problems, we can effectively improve the performance of the algorithm to find more non-dominated solutions in MEMS layout optimization. In addition, we compared two mechanisms of constraint handling, Stochastic Ranking (SR) and Constraint-domination principle (CDP). The experimental results show that CDP works better than SR and the proposed algorithm outperforms the state-of-art algorithms such as NSGA-II and MOEA/D, in terms of convergence and diversity.

The future work includes combinations of cMOEA/D with other mechanisms of constraint handling to further improve the performance of the algorithm, and test it in new applications.

6. ACKNOWLEDGMENTS

This work is supported by National Natural Science Foundation of China (Grant No. 61175073, 51375287 and 61332002).

7. REFERENCES

[1] Rosenberg B, Richards M, Langton J T, et al. Applications of multi-objective evolutionary algorithms to air operations mission planning[C]//Proceedings of the 2008 GECCO conference companion on Genetic and evolutionary computation. ACM, 2008: 1879-1886.

[2] Tapia M G C, Coello C A C. Applications of multi-objective evolutionary algorithms in economics and finance: A survey[C]//IEEE congress on evolutionary computation. 2007, 7: 532-539.

[3] Deb K, Pratap A, Agarwal S, et al. A fast and elitist multiobjective genetic algorithm: NSGA-II[J]. Evolutionary Computation, IEEE Transactions on, 2002, 6(2): 182-197.

[4] Zhang Q, Li H. MOEA/D: A multiobjective evolutionary algorithm based on decomposition[J]. Evolutionary Computation, IEEE Transactions on, 2007, 11(6): 712-731.

[5] Fonseca C M, Fleming P J. Genetic Algorithms for Multiobjective Optimization: FormulationDiscussion and Generalization[C]//ICGA. 1993, 93: 416-423.

[6] Corne D W, Jerram N R, Knowles J D, et al. PESA-II: Region-based selection in evolutionary multiobjective optimization[C]//Proceedings of the Genetic and Evolutionary Computation Conference (GECCO'2001. 2001.

[7] Zitzler E, Laumanns M, Thiele L. SPEA2: Improving the Strength Pareto Evolutionary Algorithm[J]. 2001.

[8] Ishibuchi H, Murata T. A multi-objective genetic local search algorithm and its application to flowshop scheduling[J]. Systems, Man, and Cybernetics, Part C: Applications and Reviews, IEEE Transactions on, 1998, 28(3): 392-403.

[9] Leung Y W, Wang Y. Multiobjective programming using uniform design and genetic algorithm[J]. Systems, Man, and Cybernetics, Part C: Applications and Reviews, IEEE Transactions on, 2000, 30(3): 293-304.

[10] Murata T, Ishibuchi H, Gen M. Specification of genetic search directions in cellular multi-objective genetic algorithms[C]//Evolutionary Multi-Criterion Optimization. Springer Berlin Heidelberg, 2001: 82-95.

[11] Jaszkiewicz A. On the performance of multiple-objective genetic local search on the 0/1 knapsack problem-A comparative experiment[J]. Evolutionary Computation, IEEE Transactions on, 2002, 6(4): 402-412.

[12] Runarsson T P, Yao X. Stochastic ranking for constrained evolutionary optimization[J]. Evolutionary Computation, IEEE Transactions on, 2000, 4(3): 284-294.

[13] Deb K. Multi-objective optimization using evolutionary algorithms[M]. Chichester: John Wiley & Sons, 2001.

[14] Tutum C C, Fan Z. Multi-criteria layout synthesis of mems devices using memetic computing[C]//Evolutionary Computation (CEC), 2011 IEEE Congress on. IEEE, 2011: 902-908.

[15] Fan Z, Liu J, Sorensen T, et al. Improved differential evolution based on stochastic ranking for robust layout synthesis of MEMS components[J]. Industrial Electronics, IEEE Transactions on, 2009, 56(4): 937-948.

[16] Fedder G K, Mukherjee T. Physical design for surface-micromachined MEMS[C]//Proceedings of the Fifth ACM/SIGDA Physical Design Workshop. 1996: 53-60.

[17] Fedder G K, Iyer S, Mukherjee T. Automated optimal synthesis of microresonators[C]//Solid State Sensors and Actuators, 1997. TRANSDUCERS'97 Chicago., 1997 International Conference on. IEEE, 1997, 2: 1109-1112.

[18] Zitzler E, Thiele L. Multiobjective evolutionary algorithms: a comparative case study and the strength Pareto approach[J]. Evolutionary Computation, IEEE Transactions on, 1999, 3(4): 257-271.

[19] Jan M A, Khanum R A. A study of two penalty-parameterless constraint handling techniques in the framework of MOEA/D[J]. Applied Soft Computing, 2013, 13(1): 128-148.

Epsilon Constrained Method for Constrained Multiobjective Optimization Problems: Some Preliminary Results

Zhixiang Yang, Xinye Cai,Zhun Fan
The College of Computer Science and Technology, The Department of Electrical Engineering
Nanjing University of Aeronautics and Astronautics, Shantou University
xiang052@163.com, xinye@nuaa.edu.cn, zfan@stu.edu.cn

ABSTRACT

In this paper, the ε constrained method and Adaptive operator selection (AOS) are used in Multiobjective evolutionary algorithm based on decomposition (MOEA/D). The ε constrained method is an algorithm transformation method, which can convert algorithms for unconstrained problems to algorithms for constrained problems using the ε level comparison, which compares search points based on the pair of objective value and constraint violation of them. AOS is used to determine the application rates of different operators in an online manner based on their recent performances within an optimization process. The experimental results show our proposed approach for multiobjective constrained optimization is very competitive compared with other state-of-art algorithms.

Keywords

Multiobjective evolutionary algorithm based on decomposition (MOEA/D), Adaptive operator selection, ε Constrained method, Constrained optimization problems

1. INTRODUCTION

This paper considers the following constrained multiobjective optimization problem:

$$\begin{aligned} \text{minimize} \quad & F(x) = (f_1(x), \ldots, f_m(x))^T \\ \text{subject to} \quad & g_i(x) \geq 0, i = 1, \ldots, p \\ & l_i \leq x_i \leq u_i, i = 1 \ldots, n \end{aligned} \qquad (1)$$

where $x = (x_1, \ldots, x_n)^T \in \mathbb{R}^n$ is an n dimensional vector of decision variables, the inequalities $g_i(x) \geq 0, i = 1, \ldots, p$, are constraints. l_i and u_i are the lower and upper bounds of x_i for $i = 1, \ldots, n$. The objective vector function F consists of m real-valued objective functions.

Multiobjective evolutionary algorithm based on decomposition (MOEA/D) [13] is a recent evolutionary algorithmic framework for multiobjective optimization, which explicitly decomposes a multiobjective optimization problem(MOP) into scalar optimization subproblems and solves these subproblems simultaneously by evolving a population of solutions. Its two unconstrained versions: MOEA/D-DE [11] and MOEA/D-DRA [14], work very well on unconstrained multiobjective optimization problems (e.g. [15]).

There exist many studies on solving constrained single objective optimization problems using evolutionary algorithms (EAs) [2] [8]. Among them, the ε constrained differential evolution (εDE) is one of the most popular algorithms. The εDE shows its great performance in solving constrained single objective optimization problems. The ε constrained method [5] is an algorithm transformation method, which can convert constrained optimization problems to unconstrained ones using the ε level comparison, which compares search points based on the pair of objective value and constraint violation of them. In this paper, we introduce ε constrained method into MOEA/D in order to extend it for constrained optimization problems.

Furthermore, in order to improve the efficiency of our approach, an adaptive operator selection (AOS) method is also adopted in our proposed approach. More specifically, a bandit-based AOS method (FRRMAB) is employed, which uses a sliding window to follow the dynamics of the search process.

The remainder of this paper is organized as follows. Section 2 introduces the related work of constrained multiobjective optimization. The following Section 3 is mainly dedicated to the detailed descriptions of our proposed algorithm. Experimental setting is given in Section 4. Experimental studies and discussions are detailed in Section 5. The final conclusions of this paper is in Section 5.

2. THE RELATED WORK

2.1 Tchebycheff Aggregation Function

MOEA/D needs to decompose a multiobjective problem into a number of single objective subproblems. In this paper, we use the Tchebycheff aggregation function for this purpose. It is defined as follows:

$$\begin{aligned} \text{minimize} \quad & g^{te}(x|\lambda, z^*) = \max_{1 \leq i \leq m} \{\lambda_i |f_i(x) - z_i^*|\} \\ \text{subject to} \quad & x \in S \end{aligned} \qquad (2)$$

where S is the feasible region. $z^* = (z_1^*, \ldots, z_m^*)^T$ is the reference point, i.e.,$z_i^* = \min\{f_i(x)|x \in S\}$ for each $i = 1, \ldots, m$ and $\lambda = (\lambda_1, \ldots, \lambda_m)^T$ is a weight vector, i.e., $\lambda \geq 0$ for all $i = 1, \ldots, m$ and $\sum_{i=1}^{m} \lambda_i = 1$.

GECCO'14, July 12–16, 2014, Vancouver, BC, Canada.

ACM 978-1-4503-2881-4/14/07 ...$15.00.
http://dx.doi.org/10.1145/2598394.2610012 .

2.2 Constraint violation and ε level comparisons

In the ε constrained method, constraint violation $\phi(x)$ is defined. The constraint violation can be given by the maximum of all constraints or the sum of all constraints.

$$\phi(x) = \max\{\max_j\{0, g_j(x)\}, \max_j |h_j(x)|\} \quad (3)$$

$$\phi(x) = \sum_j || \max\{0, g_j(x)\}||^p + \sum_j ||h_j(x)||^p \quad (4)$$

where p is a positive number.

The ε level comparisons are defined as an order relation on a pair of objective function value and constraint violation $(f(x), \phi(x))$. If the constraint violation of a point is greater than 0, the point is not feasible and its worth is low. The ε level comparisons are defined basically as a lexicographic order in which $\phi(x)$ precedes $f(x)$, because the feasibility of x is more important than the minimization of $f(x)$. This precedence can be adjusted by the parameter ε.

Let $f_1(f_2)$ and $\phi_1(\phi_2)$ be the function values and the constraint violation at a point $x_1(x_2)$, respectively. Then, for any ε satisfying $\varepsilon \geq 0$, ε level comparisons $<_\varepsilon$ and $\leq_\varepsilon$ between (f_1, ϕ_1) and (f_2, ϕ_2) are defined as follows:

$$(f_1, \phi_1) <_\varepsilon (f_2, \phi_2) \Leftrightarrow \begin{cases} f_1 < f_2, & \text{if } \phi_1, \phi_2 \leq \varepsilon \\ f_1 < f_2, & \text{if } \phi_1 = \phi_2 \\ \phi_1 < \phi_2, & \text{otherwise} \end{cases} \quad (5)$$

$$(f_1, \phi_1) \leq_\varepsilon (f_2, \phi_2) \Leftrightarrow \begin{cases} f_1 \leq f_2, & \text{if } \phi_1, \phi_2 \leq \varepsilon \\ f_1 \leq f_2, & \text{if } \phi_1 = \phi_2 \\ \phi_1 < \phi_2, & \text{otherwise} \end{cases} \quad (6)$$

In case of $\varepsilon = \infty$, the ε level comparisons $<_\infty$ and $\leq_\infty$ are equivalent to the ordinary comparisons $<$ and $\leq$ between function values. Also, in case of $\varepsilon = 0$, $<_0$ and $\leq_0$ are equivalent to the lexicographic orders in which the constraint violation $\phi(x)$ precedes the function value $f(x)$.

2.3 Fitness-Rate-Rank-Based Multiarmed Bandit Adaptive Operator Selection

In this section, we adopt a new bandit-based method for the to adaptively select operators. The proposed method pays particular attention to the AOS dynamic nature [9]. This consists of two modules. One is for credit assignment and the other is for operator selection.

2.3.1 Credit Assignment

In credit assignment, one needs, to address the following two issues:

1) how to measure the impact in the search process caused by the application of an operator;
2) how to assign an appropriate credit value to an operator based on this measured impact.

As for the first issue, the most commonly used approach is to directly use the raw values of the fitness improvements caused by the recent uses of the operator under assessment. However, the range of raw fitness improvements varies from problem to problem and even at the different stages of an optimization process. It is common that the raw fitness improvement value is much larger at early stages than at later ones. Therefore, as discussed in [3], the direct use of raw fitness improvement could deteriorate the algorithm's robustness. To alleviate this problem, our proposed method uses the fitness improvement rates (FIR). More specifically, the FIR achieved by an operator i at time point t is defined as

$$FIR_{i,t} = \frac{pf_{i,t} - cf_{i,t}}{pf_{i,t}} \quad (7)$$

where $pf_{i,t}$ is the fitness value of the parent, and $cf_{i,t}$ is the fitness value of the offspring. A sliding window with fixed size W is used to store the FIR values of the recently used operators. It is organized as a first-in, first-out (FIFO) queue, i.e., the FIR value of the most recently used operator is added at the tail of the sliding window, while the oldest record (the item at the head of the queue) is removed to keep the window size constant. Each slot in the sliding window stores two components:

1) the index of the operator *op* used;
2) its FIR value.

The major reason for using the sliding window is that, in dynamic AOS environments, the performance of an operator in a very early stage may be irrelevant to its current performance. The sliding window ensures that the stored FIR information is for the current situation of the search.

To address the second issue set at the outset of this subsection, we first compute $Reward_i$, the sum of all FIR values for each operator i in the current sliding window. Then, we rank all these $Reward_i$ values in a descending order. Let $Rank_i$ be the rank value of operator i, inspired by other recently proposed rank-based credit assignment schemes, and to give more chances to the best operators, we introduce a decaying factor $D \in [0, 1]$ to transform $Reward_i$ to

$$Decay_i = D^{Rank_i} \times Reward_i. \quad (8)$$

Then, we assign the following credit value to operator i:

$$FRR_{i,t} = \frac{Decay_i}{\sum_{j=1}^{K} Decay_j} \quad (9)$$

Clearly, the smaller the value of D, the larger the influence for the best operator.

Finally, at each time point t, the operator maximizing the following function is selected:

$$FRR_{i,t} + C \times \sqrt{\frac{2 \times \ln \sum_{j=1}^{K} n_{j,t}}{n_{i,t}}} \quad (10)$$

where C is a scaling factor to control the tradeoff between exploitation (the first term that favors the operators with best empirical rewards) and exploration (the square root term that favors the infrequently tried operators). $n_{i,t}$ is the number of times operator i has been applied in the recent K applications.

2.3.2 Operator Selection

Based on the received credit values, the operator selection scheme selects suitable operators to generate new solutions. This paper uses a bandit-based operator selection scheme. Our scheme is similar to that used in [3]. The major difference is that we use FRR values as the quality index instead of the average of all the rewards received so far for an operator. In addition, n_i indicates the number of times operator i has been selected in the recent W applications.

The pseudocode of our proposed bandit-based operator selection scheme is given in Algorithm 1. The combination of this operator selection with the credit assignment schemes constitutes is named as FRRMAB in our paper. It is worth noting that no operator has yet been applied at the beginning of the search; thus, we give each operator an equal chance to be selected in this case. FRRMAB is not employed until each operator has been applied at least once.

Algorithm 1: The procedure for the bandit-based operator selection

1: **if** There are operators that have not been selected **then**
2: op_t = one that uniformly randomly selected from the operators pool;
3: **else**
4: $op_t = \arg\max_{i=\{1,\ldots,K\}} (FRR_{i,t} + C \times \sqrt{\frac{2 \times \ln \sum_{j=1}^{K} n_{j,t}}{n_{i,t}}})$
5: **end**

3. THE PROPOSED ALGORITHM

3.1 Using FRRMAB to Enhance MOEA/D

Operators Pool: Many different DE mutation operators have been proposed. Four of them, which present distinct search characteristics, are chosen for the AOS in our experiments:

1) DE/rand/1

$$v^i = x^i + F \times (x^{r_1} - x^{r_2}); \quad (11)$$

2) DE/rand/2

$$v^i = x^i + F \times (x^{r_1} - x^{r_2}) + F \times (x^{r_3} - x^{r_4}); \quad (12)$$

3) DE/current-to-rand/1

$$v^i = x^i + K \times (x^i - x^{r_1}) + F \times (x^{r_2} - x^{r_3}); \quad (13)$$

4) DE/current-to-rand/2

$$v^i = x^i + K \times (x^i - x^{r_1}) + F \times (x^{r_2} - x^{r_3}) + F \times (x^{r_4} - x^{r_5}); \quad (14)$$

where x^i is called the target vector and v^i is the mutant vector. The variables $x^{r1}, x^{r2}, x^{r3}, x^{r4}$, and x^{r5} are different solutions randomly selected from P, which are also different from x^i. The scaling factor $F > 0$ controls the impact of the vector differences on the mutant vector. $K \in [0, 1]$ plays a similar role to F. For the last two mutation operators, the offspring is the direct output of mutation, where the crossover operator will not be used. For the first two mutation operators, a crossover operator is applied upon x^i and v_i for generating the offspring u^i. The binomial crossover is used in our experiments. It works as

$$u^i_j = \begin{cases} v^i_j, & \text{if } rand \leq CR \text{ or } j = j_{rand} \\ x^i_j, & \text{otherwise} \end{cases} \quad (15)$$

where $j \in \{1, \ldots, n\}$ and $rand$ is a uniformly random number from [0, 1]. The crossover rate $CR \in [0, 1]$ is a user-defined control parameter. j_{rand} is an integer randomly chosen from the set $S = 1, \ldots, n$. After the application of these DE operators, a generated offspring might undergo, with a small probability, the polynomial mutation operator.

Reward Calculation: In a recent work on AOS for selecting DE mutation operators, a DE mutation operator is rewarded based on the fitness improvement of the offspring compared with its corresponding target vector. In MOEA/D, different solutions correspond to different subproblems, and thus, different comparisons are based on different aggregations of objective functions. In this paper, if an offspring successfully replaces x^i, the DE mutation operator that generates it will receive the following reward:

$$\eta = \frac{g(x^i|\lambda^i, z^*) - g(y|\lambda^i, z^*)}{g(x^i|\lambda^i, z^*)} \quad (16)$$

where λ^i is the weight vector for subproblem i.

An operator op may receive several rewards due to its generated offspring y. We sum up all these reward values as its final reward FIR_{op}.

3.2 Controlling the ε level

Usually, the ε level is controlled according to the equation(17). The initial ε level $\varepsilon(0)$ is the constraint violation of the top θ-th individual in the initial search points. The ε level is updated until the number of iterations t becomes the control generation Tc. After the number of iterations exceeds Tc, the ε level is set to 0 to obtain solutions with minimum constraint violation.

$$\begin{aligned} \varepsilon(0) &= \phi(x_\theta) \\ \varepsilon(t) &= \begin{cases} \varepsilon(0)(1 - \frac{t}{T_c})^{cp}, & 0 < t < T_c \\ 0, & t \geq T_c \end{cases} \end{aligned} \quad (17)$$

where x_θ is the top θ-th individual. If $\theta > 1$, $\phi(x_\theta) = \theta \times \max_x \phi(x)$.

In this study, a simple scheme of setting the parameter value cp is proposed: The ε level is adjusted to be a small value $\varepsilon_\lambda = 10^{-5}$ at the generation $T_\lambda = 0.95T_c$.

$$\begin{aligned} \varepsilon(T_\lambda) &= \varepsilon(0)(1 - T_\lambda/T_c) = \varepsilon_\lambda & (18) \\ cp &= (\log \varepsilon - \log \varepsilon(0))/\log(1 - T_\lambda/T_c) & (19) \\ &= (-5 - \log \varepsilon(0))/\log 0.05 & (20) \end{aligned}$$

To avoid too small value of cp, if cp is less than $cp_{\min}$, cp is to be $cp_{\min}$ where $cp_{\min} = 3$. Also, after T_λ, in order to increase the ε level, to enlarge ε-feasible region and to search better objective values, cp is decreased and F is increased as follows:

$$\begin{aligned} cp &= 0.3cp + 0.7cp_{\min} & (21) \\ F &= 0.3F_0 + 0.7 & (22) \end{aligned}$$

3.3 Applying the ε Constrained Method and FRRMAB to MOEA/D

In this paper, we employ the ε constrained method and FRRMAB into MOEA/D-DE framework. The pseudocode of the whole algorithm is detailed in Algorithm 2.

4. EXPERIMENTAL SETTINGS AND PERFORMANCE INDICATOR

4.1 Parameters Settings

The parameters settings of our proposed approach are given as follows:

1. N: 600 for two objectives and 1000 for three objectives;

2. The number of decision variables of the test instances is set to 10;
3. $T = 0.1N$ and $n_r = 0.01N$;
4. $\delta = 0.9$;
5. In DE and mutation operators: $CR = 1.0$ and $F = 0.5$, $\eta = 20$ and $p_m = 1/n$.
6. Stopping criterion: the algorithm stops after 300,000 function evaluations for each test instance.
7. Control parameters in FRRMAB:
   Scaling factor: $C = 5.0$;
   Size of sliding window: $W = 0.5 \times N$;
   Decaying factor: $D = 1.0$.
8. Control parameters in the ε level comparison:
   T_c: 800 for two objectives and 1000 for three objectives;
   $\theta = 1.5$.

4.2 Performance Metric IGD

Let P^* be a set of uniformly distributed points along the PF. Let A be an approximate set to the PF, the average distance from P^* to A is defined as:

$$D(A, P) = \frac{\sum_{v \in P^*} d(v, A)}{|P^*|} \tag{23}$$

where $d(v, A)$ is the minimum Euclidean distance between v and the points in A. If P^* is large enough to represent the PF very well, $D(A, P)$ could measure both the diversity and convergence of A in a sense. Ten constrained MOPs (CF1 to CF10) [16] are used in our experimental studies. CMOEA/D-DE-ATP and the three best performers [10], [7], [6] in CEC 2009 MOEA competition are compared with our proposed method. All of them have been run 30 times independently for each test instance.

5. EXPERIMENTAL RESULTS AND DISCUSSIONS

Table 1 summarizes the performance of various algorithms in terms of IGD metric in statistics based on 30 independent runs. These state-of-art approaches include our proposed approach (YC) and approach proposed by Jan and Zhang(JZ [4]), and Tseng and Chen(TC [10]), Liu and li (LL [6]), and Liu et. al's (LI [7]).

It is clear to see that our proposed algorithm has the best (lowest) IGD values for CF1, CF6, and CF10. It can also be observed that our proposed approach has better performance than CMOEA/D-DE-ATP [12] on most test instances. This indicates that using FRRMAB and the ε method to MOEAD-DE is beneficial, compared with penalty function.

6. CONCLUSION

In this paper, the ε constrained method and a bandit-based AOS method FRRMAB are introduced into the MOEA /D-DE framework to tackle constrained multiobjective optimization problems. The experimental results show the proposed algorithm is very competitive on most CF test instances compared with other state-of-art approaches. The results of our proposed algorithm is very preliminary. The future works include further improvement of the performance through adopting advanced learning mechanisms.

Algorithm 2:MOEAD-εDE

Input:
1. CMOP(1);
2. a stopping criterion;
3. N: the number of subproblems; the population size of P and A;
4. a uniform spread of N weight vectors: $\boldsymbol{\lambda}^1, \ldots, \boldsymbol{\lambda}^N$;
5. T: the number of the weight vectors in the neighborhood of each weight vector.

Output: A set of non-dominated solutions EP;

Step 1 Initialization:

a) Compute the Euclidean distances between any two weight vectors and then work out the T closest weight vectors to each weight vector. For each $i = 1, \ldots, N$, set $B(i) = i_1, \ldots, i_T$ where $\lambda^{i_1}, \ldots, \lambda^{i_T}$ are the T closest weight vectors to λ^i.

b) Generate an initial population $x^1, \ldots, x^N$ by uniformly randomly sampling from the search space.

c) Initialize $z = (z_1, \ldots, z_m)^T$ by setting $z_i = \min\{f_i(x^1), f_i(x^2), \ldots, f_i(x^N)\}$.

d) Set $gen = 1$ and $\varepsilon = \varepsilon(0)$.

Step 2 Update:

For each $i = 1, \ldots, N$, do:

a) **Selection of operator:** The operator op is selected according to the **Algorithm 1**.

b) **Selection of Mating/Update Range:** Uniformly randomly generate a number $rand$ from (0,1). If $rand < \delta$, then set $P = B(i)$, otherwise $P = 1, \ldots, N$.

c) **Reproduction:** Randomly select some indexes from P, and then generate a solution y' by the application of the chosen DE mutation operator op over the selected solutions; Then apply polynomial mutation operator on y' with probability p_m, to produce the offspring y;

d) **Repair:** If an element of y is out of the boundary, its value is reset to be randomly selected value inside the boundary.

e) **Evaluate** y : $FV^y = F(y), V(y) = |\sum_{j=1}^{p} \min(g_j(y), 0)|$.

f) **Update of** z **:** For each $j = 1, \ldots, m$,if $z_j > f_j(y)$, then set $z_j = f_j(y)$.

g) **Update of Neighboring Solutions:** For each index $j \in P$, if $(g^{te}(y|\lambda^j, z), \phi(y)) <_\varepsilon (g^{te}(x^j|\lambda^j, z), \phi(x^j))$, then set $x^j = y$ and $FV^j = F(y)$.

h) **Evaluate** FIR_{op}**:** Sum up the rewards that are generated by the update of y as the FIR_{op} value.

i) **Update of FIFO queue:** The node which is combined operator op and FRR value is added at the tail of the FIFO queue. Then, the FRR values are evaluated for each operator according to the FIFO queue.

j) **Update of EP:** Remove from EP all the vectors dominated by $F(y')$. Add to EP if no vectors in EP dominate $F(y')$.

Step 3: Stopping Criteria: If stopping criteria is satisfied, then stop and output EP.

Step 4: Control the ε **level:** $\varepsilon = \varepsilon(gen)$, $\varepsilon(gen)$ is described in equation (17).

Step 5: Set $gen = gen + 1$. Go to **Step 2**.

Table 1: The Comparison of Various Algorithms in IGD. The results in **boldface** indicate the best performance

	Instance	CF1	CF2	CF3	CF4	CF5	CF6	CF7	CF8	CF9	CF10
best	YC	**0.000021**	0.0026	0.0738	0.0077	0.031	**0.0059**	0.0343	0.0678	0.0455	**0.0973**
	JZ	0.000314	0.002568	0.052966	**0.005301**	0.060908	0.007778	0.048766	0.070507	**0.039339**	0.142689
	TC	0.013854	0.004142	0.0753	0.008937	0.017565	0.009568	0.018691	0.621968	0.072071	0.117317
	LL	0.000682	0.002733	0.090844	0.008964	0.058818	0.009022	0.05351	0.047328	0.046035	0.105482
	LI	0.007061	**0.001579**	**0.038062**	0.005523	**0.007872**	0.006186	**0.010424**	**0.038785**	0.119107	0.098377
worst	YC	**0.000066**	0.026	0.2723	0.0134	0.2789	**0.0132**	0.2007	0.0827	**0.0536**	0.521
	JZ	0.001102	0.089054	0.387998	0.128202	0.47448	0.061374	0.525922	0.111194	0.061451	1.273927
	TC	0.023597	0.051815	0.142828	0.014276	**0.027832**	0.038112	0.037144	1.42867	0.096282	**0.163473**
	LL	0.001147	0.013135	0.251884	0.023999	0.192996	0.019939	0.203867	0.098487	0.058389	0.416232
	LI	0.016932	**0.003063**	**0.070731**	**0.011552**	0.039396	0.03112	**0.033821**	**0.065014**	0.206549	0.239399
mean	YC	**0.000040**	0.005	0.1771	0.0106	0.1247	**0.008**	0.0684	0.0759	0.0499	0.2309
	JZ	0.00054	0.009402	0.185618	0.015356	0.227288	0.034201	0.200548	0.086989	**0.04897**	0.325308
	TC	0.019187	0.026779	0.10446	0.011096	0.020779	0.016168	0.024695	1.08544	0.085139	**0.137648**
	LL	0.000859	0.004203	0.182905	0.014232	0.10973	0.013948	0.10446	0.060746	0.050549	0.197409
	LI	0.011311	**0.0021**	**0.056305**	**0.006995**	**0.015773**	0.01502	**0.019051**	**0.047501**	0.143432	0.162128
st.dev.	YC	**0.000012**	0.0041	0.0363	0.0014	0.0836	**0.002**	0.0406	**0.0035**	**0.0018**	0.1452
	JZ	0.000184	0.021539	0.079894	0.023468	0.116536	0.015884	0.115529	0.009889	0.006329	0.290022
	TC	0.002568	0.014715	0.015595	**0.001368**	**0.002421**	0.005985	**0.004654**	0.219108	0.008191	**0.009215**
	LL	0.00011	0.002635	0.042127	0.003293	0.030676	0.002586	0.035116	0.012972	0.003357	0.076004
	LI	0.002758	**0.000453**	**0.007573**	0.001457	0.006662	0.006462	0.006123	0.006387	0.021416	0.031621

7. REFERENCES

[1] *Proceedings of the IEEE Congress on Evolutionary Computation, CEC 2009, Trondheim, Norway, 18-21 May, 2009.* IEEE, 2009.

[2] C. A. Coello Coello. Theoretical and numerical constraint-handling techniques used with evolutionary algorithms: a survey of the state of the art. *Computer methods in applied mechanics and engineering*, 191(11):1245–1287, 2002.

[3] Á. Fialho. Adaptive operator selection for optimization. *PhD, Ecole Doctorale d'Informatique, Universite Paris-Sud, Paris*, 2010.

[4] M. A. Jan and Q. Zhang. Eee moea/d for constrained multiobjective optimization: Some preliminary experimental results. *UKCI*, 2010.

[5] K. Li, Á. Fialho, S. Kwong, and Q. Zhang. Adaptive operator selection with bandits for a multiobjective evolutionary algorithm based on decomposition. *IEEE Trans. Evolutionary Computation*, 18(1):114–130, 2014.

[6] H. lin Liu and X. Li. The multiobjective evolutionary algorithm based on determined weight and sub-regional search. In *IEEE Congress on Evolutionary Computation* [1], pages 1928–1934.

[7] M. Liu, X. Zou, Y. Chen, and Z. Wu. Performance assessment of dmoea-dd with cec 2009 moea competition test instances. In *IEEE Congress on Evolutionary Computation* [1], pages 2913–2918.

[8] T. Takahama and S. Sakai. Constrained optimization by applying the α constrained method to the nonlinear simplex method with mutations. *Evolutionary Computation, IEEE Transactions on*, 9(5):437–451, 2005.

[9] T. Takahama and S. Sakai. Efficient constrained optimization by the constrained differential evolution with rough approximation using kernel regression. In *IEEE Congress on Evolutionary Computation*, pages 1334–1341. IEEE, 2013.

[10] L.-Y. Tseng and C. Chen. Multiple trajectory search for unconstrained/constrained multi-objective optimization. In *IEEE Congress on Evolutionary Computation* [1], pages 1951–1958.

[11] J. Yao, Q. Zhang, and J. Lei. Recent developments in natural computation. *Neurocomputing*, 72(13-15):2833–2834, 2009.

[12] Q. Zhang et al. Moea/d for constrained multiobjective optimization: Some preliminary experimental results. In *2010 UK Workshop on Computational Intelligence (UKCI)*, pages 1–6, 2010.

[13] Q. Zhang and H. Li. Moea/d: A multiobjective evolutionary algorithm based on decomposition. *IEEE Trans. Evolutionary Computation*, 11(6):712–731, 2007.

[14] Q. Zhang, W. Liu, and H. Li. The performance of a new version of moea/d on cec09 unconstrained mop test instances. In *IEEE Congress on Evolutionary Computation* [1], pages 203–208.

[15] Q. Zhang, W. Liu, and H. Li. The performance of a new version of moea/d on cec09 unconstrained mop test instances. In *IEEE Congress on Evolutionary Computation* [1], pages 203–208.

[16] Q. Zhang, A. Zhou, S. Zhao, P. N. Suganthan, W. Liu, and S. Tiwari. Multiobjective optimization test instances for the cec 2009 special session and competition. *University of Essex, Colchester, UK and Nanyang Technological University, Singapore, Special Session on Performance Assessment of Multi-Objective Optimization Algorithms, Technical Report*, 2008.

Green and Efficient Energy Applications of Genetic and Evolutionary Computation (GreenGEC'14) Chairs' Welcome

We would like to express our great pleasure in welcoming you to the GECCO Workshop on Green and Efficient Energy Applications of Genetic and Evolutionary Computation (GreenGEC Workshop'14), held in conjunction with the GECCO 2014 International Conference.

A main characteristic of the studies in the area of green and energy-efficient applications is the strong connection with real-world environments and constraints. As such, there is only little place for errors and leading edge algorithms alone can be used. The potential impact and outcomes are also of foremost importance. Global increases in living standards, diminishing natural resources and environmental concerns place energy amongst the most important global issues today. On the consumer side, there is an increasing need for more efficient, smart, uses of energy, be it in large-scale computing systems and data warehouses, in homes or in office buildings. On the producer side, there is a push toward the use of sustainable, green, energy sources, which often come in the form of less reliable sources such as wind energy. In addition, future energy systems are often envisioned to be "smart", consisting of massive amounts of small generators, such as solar panels, located at consumers, effectively turning consumers into potential producers whenever they have a surplus of energy. The management, control and planning of, and efficient use of energy in (future) energy systems brings about many important challenges.

Energy systems are not only real-world systems, they are also one of the most important foundations of the modern world. Especially with the upcoming required changes to make more efficient use of energy and to shift towards a global use of sustainable, green energy sources, there are many challenges in mathematics and computer science. Real-world challenges, such as those arising in (future) energy systems, are typically highly complex because of the many aspects to be considered that are often disregarded in theoretical research such as dynamic changes, uncertainty and multiple objectives. In many situations therefore, problem-specific algorithms are infeasible or impractical. Instead, flexible and powerful approaches such as evolutionary algorithms (EAs) can often provide viable solutions. Typical real-world challenges that are addressed by EAs are of the optimization type. This covers the use of EAs to optimize issues ranging from energy consumption (e.g. scheduling, memory/storage management, communication protocols, smart sensors, etc.) to the planning and design of energy systems at many levels, ranging from small printed circuit boards to entire transmission networks.

The aim of this workshop is to bring together researchers interested in addressing challenging issues related to the use of evolutionary computation for applications in (future) energy systems. With respect to these considerations, we would like to end by thanking the authors for their contributions.

Peter A.N. Bosman   **Alexandru-Adrian Tantar**   **Emilia Tantar**

GECCO'14 Green and Efficient Energy Applications of Genetic and Evolutionary Computation (GreenGEC) Organization

Chairs: Peter A.N. Bosman *(Centrum Wiskunde & Informatica, The Netherlands)*
Alexandru-Adrian Tantar *(University of Luxembourg, Luxembourg)*
Emilia Tantar *(University of Luxembourg, Luxembourg)*

Efficiency Enhancements for Evolutionary Capacity Planning in Distribution Grids

Ngoc Hoang Luong
Centrum Wiskunde & Informatica (CWI)
Amsterdam, The Netherlands
N.H.Luong@cwi.nl

Marinus O.W. Grond
Eindhoven University of Technology (TU/e)
Eindhoven, The Netherlands
M.O.W.Grond@tue.nl

Han La Poutré
Centrum Wiskunde & Informatica (CWI)
Amsterdam, The Netherlands
Han.La.Poutre@cwi.nl

Peter A.N. Bosman
Centrum Wiskunde & Informatica (CWI)
Amsterdam, The Netherlands
Peter.Bosman@cwi.nl

ABSTRACT

In this paper, we tackle the distribution network expansion planning (DNEP) problem by employing two evolutionary algorithms (EAs): the classical Genetic Algorithm (GA) and a linkage-learning EA, specifically a Gene-pool Optimal Mixing Evolutionary Algorithm (GOMEA). We furthermore develop two efficiency-enhancement techniques for these two EAs for solving the DNEP problem: a restricted initialization mechanism to reduce the size of the explorable search space and a means to filter linkages (for GOMEA) to disregard linkage groups during genetic variation that are likely not useful. Experimental results on a benchmark network show that if we may assume that the optimal network will be very similar to the starting network, restricted initialization is generally useful for solving DNEP and moreover it becomes more beneficial to use the simple GA. However, in the more general setting where we cannot make the closeness assumption and the explorable search space becomes much larger, GOMEA outperforms the classical GA.

Categories and Subject Descriptors

I.2.8 [**Artificial Intelligence**]: Problem Solving, Control Methods, and Search

General Terms

Performance, Experimentation

Keywords

Electricity; Distribution Networks; Capacity Planning; Optimal Mixing; Linkage Learning

GECCO'14, July 12–16, Vancouver, BC, Canada.
Copyright 2014 ACM 978-1-4503-2881-4/14/07 ...$15.00.
http://dx.doi.org/10.1145/2598394.2605696.

1. INTRODUCTION

Electric distribution grids are parts of the total power system and carry the electricity from high-voltage (HV) transmission grids to the medium-voltage (MV) and low-voltage (LV) consumers. A distribution grid consists of various electric components, such as overhead power lines, underground cables, substations, transformers, meters, protection devices, etc., in which the branch configuration (i.e. lines/ cables) are of particular interest. How the cables are connected and which types of cables are chosen determine both the topology and the capacity of the grid. Distribution grids are typically constructed, maintained, and upgraded by distribution network operators (DNOs). The growth in the power demands of consumers requires DNOs to perform network reinforcements to ensure that the magnitude of the power flows that are required to satisfy consumers' demands are within the capacities of all network components. Traditionally, regarding one or multiple scenarios of forecast load growth, DNOs manually sketch a few likely network expansion plans based on engineers' expert knowledge and company-specific policies. Those plans are then evaluated for their investment cost, operational cost, and also technical feasibility, and usually the plan with the least total cost is chosen to be carried out. As distribution grids become increasingly large and complicated over time, including the introduction of new technologies, such as distributed generation or demand-side management, traditional manual generation of expansion plans is no longer thorough enough to guarantee that a good, let alone optimal, plan can be obtained from the vast search space of possible alternatives.

Optimization problems of computationally expensive evaluation functions and large search spaces often require the application of metaheuristics, such as genetic algorithms [3], simulated annealing [13], or particle swarm optimization [2]. The popular use of these classic metaheuristics in electrical engineer literature is due to, besides their general applicability and search capabilities, their straightforward implementations and wide availability in computation software (e.g. MATLAB). However, far more novel, robust developments in evolutionary computation exist, amongst which are EAs that perform linkage learning to be robust against a-priori unknown variable dependencies. These EAs are typically more involved, but offer better convergence properties. This is however more frequently tested on well-known benchmark functions rather than real-world applications, like the one we consider here. In previous, related work [8], we have applied a state-of-the-art linkage learning EA known as the Gene-pool Optimal Mixing Evolutionary Algorithm (GOMEA) [1] to the DNEP problem and obtained promising results. In this paper, we tackle the problem under a different scenario, input settings, and evaluation function. We will also present simple linkage filtering techniques aiming to improve the efficiency of GOMEA.

In real-world optimization, expert knowledge and domain-specific heuristics are often employed to disregard some "impractical" alternatives, thereby reducing the search space. Especially in the field of electricity network expansion planning, another reason is that, regarding the current legacy of already-installed network facilities, DNOs prefer conventional solutions involving an incremental number of changes to any "upside-down" reconfigurations. Expansion plans involving many big changes, such as removals of cable connections and restructuring multiple parts of the grids, are often considered as unfavorable. However, many population-based optimization algorithms often start from randomly initialized populations. Considering this, we could also generate the initial population of candidate solutions by randomly changing only a few components in the existing (starting) network. In this paper, we will study if such initialization can help to obtain acceptable solutions faster. It should be noted that in related work [6], we proposed alternative methods of reducing the size of the search space from an electrical engineering point of view by introducing engineering rules as constraints. Here we will look at search space size reduction from a more algorithmic perspective.

To this end, we solve the distribution network expansion planning problem (DNEP) by using a classic genetic algorithm (GA) and the state-of-the-art Gene-pool Optimal Mixing Evolutionary Algorithm (GOMEA) [1, 10] and study the difference in performance when using fully random population initializations as well as restricted initializations. The remainder of this paper is organized as follows. Section 2 presents the optimization model for the DNEP problem. Section 3 outlines our optimizers GA and GOMEA. Section 4 describes our efficiency enhancement techniques for solving DNEP problems. Section 5 presents the benchmark problem and exhibits experimental results. Finally, Section 6 concludes the paper.

2. DNEP OPTIMIZATION MODEL

A distribution network can be represented as a graph $G = (V, E)$, in which V is the set of m nodes (vertices) and E is the set of l branches (edges). A node can be a substation, which is usually installed with a HV/MV transformer feeding electricity from a (sub-)transmission system into the distribution grid, or a consuming unit (i.e. a customer station demanding directly MV electricity or a network station associated with an MV/LV transformer supplying LV electricity for an area of households). A branch is a connection between two nodes, which can be a power line running overhead or a cable running underground. In conventional distribution grids, the branch configuration creates feed paths for power flows from supplying substations *downward* to consuming units. In a scenario with distributed generation, such as photovoltaics at households, a consuming unit can at times become a supplying unit creating an *upward* flow feeding electricity into the grid. Nevertheless, regardless of the directions, all electric currents have to flow through cable connections, which have specific nominal capacities. Cable overload is defined as when a cable connection has to carry a power flow whose magnitude is larger than its capacity. Overload for an extended amount of time can damage the facility and causes system failures. DNOs are thus required to perform network capacity planning to assure that growths in power demand are satisfied while no overload should occur. In this regard, distribution grids may consist of various kinds of electric facilities, but for the problem of capacity planning the configurations of the cables are usually of particular interest. In this paper, we assume that DNOs perform DNEP by making decisions on how the cables are connected and which type of cable is used for each connection.

2.1 Decision Variable Codification

To solve a DNEP problem, all cable connections on which a DNO can make reinforcement decisions need to be specified. These consist of all the currently existing branches that can be upgraded and the potential branches that can be newly installed. The set of potential branches is limited by expert knowledge to dismiss impractical connections, e.g. it is uneconomical to connect two far-away nodes.

Let l be the total number of branches (i.e. both existing and potential branches), a distribution network can be represented as a vector $\boldsymbol{x}$ of l elements:

$$\boldsymbol{x} = (x_1, x_2, \ldots, x_l), \quad |x_i| \in \Omega(x_i), \quad i \in \{1, 2, \ldots, l\} \quad (1)$$

where each x_i is a categorical variable indicating which type of cable is installed at the i-th branch of the network. The set of possible alternatives of cable types $\Omega(x_i)$ that can be installed at the branch i-th is DNO-specific, which usually consists of standardized cable sizes. The value of x_i determines the status of the i-th branch:

- $x_i = id > 0$: A cable of type $id \in \Omega(x_i)$ should be installed at the i-th branch.
- $x_i = 0$: No cable should be installed at the i-th branch.
- $x_i = -id < 0$: A cable of type $id \in \Omega(x_i)$ should be installed and put into reserve status at the i-th branch. This cable connection is put into inactive state, carrying no power flow during normal operation, by opening one of the two switches at its two endings. Such cable connection is usually termed as a Normally Open Point (NOP), which is used to reconfigure the network in emergency situations.

The original distribution network is thus represented as a vector whose elements corresponding with currently existing branches receive non-zero values while elements corresponding with potential branches are set to 0.

2.2 Constraints

For a given scenario of forecast growth in power demand and, in case of distributed generation, the power generating capability at every node, the following constraints must be satisfied:

1. **Connectivity constraint**: All node should be connected, i.e. there is a feed path from a substation to a consuming unit.

2. **Voltage constraints**:

$$|V_i|^{min} \leq |V_i| \leq |V_i|^{max}, \quad i \in \{1, 2, \ldots, m\} \quad (2)$$

where $|V_i|$ is the voltage magnitude at node i. $|V_i|^{min}$ and $|V_i|^{max}$ are minimal and maximal allowed voltage magnitude at node i, respectively. All nodal voltage should stay within the allowable range.

3. **Power flow constraints**:

$$|S_i| \leq |S_i|^{max}, \quad i \in \{1, 2, \ldots, l\} \quad (3)$$

where $|S_i|$ is the magnitude of the power flow through the cable connection at the i-th branch, and $|S_i|^{max}$ is the nominal capacity of that cable. There should be no overload in normal operation.

4. **Radiality constraint**: A consuming unit should be supplied its power demand through only one single feed path in normal operation. This constraint is often employed due to security and protection policies of DNOs.

5. **Reconfigurability constraint**: When an active cable fails, the resulting short-circuit power will be disconnected by a circuit breaker to prevent damaging other components. Some parts of the network will be out of service. The DNO then reconfigures the network by closing the switches of reserve branches (i.e. NOPs) so that all power demands are supplied again. In such temporary emergency situations, the network can tolerate a mild overload for a short time due to thermal dynamics. Here, we assume the emergency capacity of a cable is 130% of its nominal capacity.

Constraints (1) and (4) can be easily verified by checking the topology of the network. To evaluate constraints (2) and (3), it is required to perform a power flow calculation (PLC) [4], which involves solving a system of non-linear equations, called the AC power flow model. A full evaluation of the constraint (5) for a network of k active cables requires k PLCs because every active cable is taken out of service at a time (i.e. to simulate a single cable fault) and it is then checked to see if closing NOPs can bring back the normal service. It is normally acceptable to simulate single cable fault only for cable connections that branching out directly a substation because these cables usually carry the heaviest loads. Nevertheless, due to performing multiple PLCs, constraint evaluation for a DNEP solution is a computationally expensive operation.

2.3 Objective Function

Solving a DNEP problem aims to minimize the net present value (NPV) of the total cost of investment $CAPEX$ and operation $OPEX$ over a planning horizon of T years. In this paper, we consider $OPEX$ as solely the cost of energy loss on cables, which depends on the load and the types of cables being used. An accurate objective evaluation requires the DNEP is solved in a dynamic planning manner, in which the optimal year t_i ($t_0 \leq t_i \leq t_T$) to perform reinforcement at a branch x_i need to be determined. Dynamic planning is typically very expensive in terms of computation effort, involving costly constraint checking for each year during the planning horizon for every candidate solution. In this paper, assuming a limited computation budget, we consider a cheaper pseudo-dynamic approach as follows.

2.3.1 OPEX Estimation

In this section, we present how to estimate the $OPEX$, i.e. the cost of energy loss, of an expansion plan $\boldsymbol{x}$ for an existing grid $\boldsymbol{x}^{origin}$. The peak loss $P_{loss}(\boldsymbol{x}, t)$ on an electricity grid $\boldsymbol{x}$ in a year t can be calculated from the result of a computationally expensive PLC for that grid regarding the peak load in that year. A less accurate, but for planning purposes commonly accepted, approach is to assume the peak loss also has a growth rate related to the load growth R as follows

$$P_{loss}^{estimated}(t) = P_{loss}(t-1) * (1+R)^2 \quad (4)$$

Given R, we can estimate the peak load at every node in each year. Regarding the currently existing configuration of the network $\boldsymbol{x}^{origin}$, we determine the year t_X that the first overload happens. The whole expansion plan $\boldsymbol{x}$, which would eventually satisfy the energy demand in the final year t_T, is then assumed to be carried out all together in the year t_X. In this regard, the year t_X would be the same for all candidate solutions $\boldsymbol{x}$'s because all expansion plans start from the same original network $\boldsymbol{x}^{origin}$. Therefore, the losses from the beginning until t_X would also be the same for all candidate solutions. The losses from the year t_X until and including the year T are different per candidate solution, depending on what types of cables are used. Therefore, we choose to estimate the peak loss $P_{loss}(\boldsymbol{x}, t)$ of an expansion plan $\boldsymbol{x}$ in year t as follows

$$P_{loss}(\boldsymbol{x}, t) = \begin{cases} P_{loss}(\boldsymbol{x}^{origin}, t) & \text{if} \quad t < t_X \\ P_{loss}^{estimated}(\boldsymbol{x}, t) & \text{if} \quad t_X \leq t < T \\ P_{loss}(\boldsymbol{x}, T) & \text{if} \quad t = t_T \end{cases} \quad (5)$$

where $P_{loss}(\boldsymbol{x}^{origin}, t)$ can be calculated in an accurate way by performing t_X PLCs once for all candidate solutions $\boldsymbol{x}$'s. $P_{loss}^{estimated}(t)$ can be estimated by performing one PLC to calculate $P_{loss}(\boldsymbol{x}, T)$ first and then using the Equation 4 to deduct backward. The yearly energy loss $E_{loss}(\boldsymbol{x}, t)$ of a grid $\boldsymbol{x}$ in year t is then computed as

$$E_{loss}(\boldsymbol{x}, t) = P_{loss}(\boldsymbol{x}, t) * T_{loss}(t) \quad (6)$$

where $T_{loss}(t)$ is the service time of peak loss, defined by the area of the yearly energy loss profile, and is input data resulting from scenarios. The $OPEX(\boldsymbol{x}, t)$ of a network $\boldsymbol{x}$ in year t is computed as

$$OPEX(\boldsymbol{x}, t) = Price * E_{loss}(\boldsymbol{x}, t) \quad (7)$$

where $Price$ is the electricity price used in analysis.

2.3.2 CAPEX Calculation

The total sum of investment cost of an expansion plan $\boldsymbol{x}$ can be easily computed by comparing $\boldsymbol{x}$ with the currently existing network $\boldsymbol{x}^{origin}$ as follows

$$Investment = \sum_{i=1}^{l} cost(x_i^{origin}, x_i) \quad (8)$$

where

$$cost(x_i^{origin}, x_i) = \begin{cases} 0 & \text{if } x_i^{origin} = x_i \\ \text{cost of } x_i & \text{if } x_i^{origin} \neq x_i \end{cases} \quad (9)$$

However, in scenario-based planning studies, the $CAPEX$ is usually computed by using the annuities method [9, 12], in which the payment for investment is converted into a series of uniform annual payments called annuities. The length of this series of payments is the economic lifetime $T^{lifetime}$ of the devices. Here, we assume that all devices have the same $T^{lifetime} = 30$ years. The annuity, i.e. the yearly payment, with a discount rate $i = 4{\cdot}5\%$ is computed as

$$Annuity = Investment * \frac{i}{1-(1+i)^{-T^{lifetime}}} \quad (10)$$

In a true dynamic expansion planning, the annuity should be computed for each invested device separately regarding its specific time of installation. However, in this paper, because we assume that all investments be carried out at the same year t_X when the first overload occurs and that all devices have the same lifetime $T^{lifetime}$, we can compute the annuity for the total investment of all devices. The $CAPEX(\boldsymbol{x}, t)$ in year t is then the annuity

$$CAPEX(\boldsymbol{x}, t) = \begin{cases} Annuity & \text{if} \quad t_X \le t \le t_X + T^{lifetime} \\ 0 & \text{else} \end{cases} \quad (11)$$

Note that due to the long lifetime, it can happen that $t_X + T^{lifetime} > t_T$. Since we only consider the cost until the end of the planning horizon t_T, the annuities of the years after the planning horizon will be disregarded. This annuities method is used to compare fairly the total costs between different scenarios [9].

2.3.3 Total Cost Objective Function

The objective of the DNEP problem is to minimize the NPV of the total cost of expansion, which consists of the operation cost $OPEX$ and the investment cost $CAPEX$, over T years with discount rate i. The objective value of a candidate solution $\boldsymbol{x}$ is thus computed as

$$f(\boldsymbol{x}) = \sum_{t=t_0}^{t_T} \frac{OPEX(\boldsymbol{x}, t) + CAPEX(\boldsymbol{x}, t)}{(1+i)^{t-t_0}} \quad (12)$$

3. OPTIMIZATION ALGORITHMS

3.1 Classical Genetic Algorithm (GA)

In this paper, we consider a popular implementation of a classical, widely-applied, GA with uniform crossover and tournament selection. First, GA starts with the random initialization of a population $\mathcal{P}$ of n candidate solutions. For a candidate solution, each decision variable x_i (i.e. a cable connection) can receive any possible value (i.e. $0, id$, or $-id$ with $id \in \Omega(x_i)$) as long as it does not downgrade the currently existing facility. All solutions are evaluated against the required constraints and objective function (Section 2.2 and 2.3). In every iteration, an offspring population $\mathcal{O}$ of n new candidate solutions are created from $\mathcal{P}$. To do this, every 2 parent solutions randomly chosen from $\mathcal{P}$ are recombined through uniform crossover to generate 2 offspring solutions. These fully constructed solutions are evaluated for their constraints and objective values. Next, the parent population $\mathcal{P}$ and the offspring population $\mathcal{O}$ are combined into a selection pool $\mathcal{P} + \mathcal{O}$ of $2n$ solutions, where a tournament selection with tournament size 4 is then performed to select n survivors. These n survivors form the new parent population $\mathcal{P}$ for the next iteration of GA.

3.2 Gene-pool Optimal Mixing Evolutionary Algorithm (GOMEA)

Although GAs can be very efficient, the conditions under which they are efficient are highly dependent on the match between the way new solutions are generated (i.e. the operators of variation), the level of dependencies between problem variables and the way the problem is encoded. If this match causes important dependencies to be disrupted during variation, GAs will exhibit poor scale-up behavior, typically requiring exponentially many evaluations to find the optimum as the problem size increases [11]. Linkage learning specifically addresses the task of figuring out, during optimization, which variables are dependent so as to better respect these dependencies during variation. If linkage learning is successful, the scale-up behavior can become extremely favorable, typically requiring only a low-polynomial number of evaluations (sometimes even sublinear) instead [7, 10].

In this paper, we also consider a linkage-learning EA to solve the DNEP problem. This EA is an instance of the GOMEA family [10]. Similar to the classical GA, GOMEA also starts with a randomly initialized population $\mathcal{P}$ of n candidate solutions, which are then evaluated against the constraints and objective function. In every iteration, a set $\mathcal{S}$ of n solutions is selected out of $\mathcal{P}$ by tournament selection with tournament size 2. A linkage model, describing dependencies among decision variables, is then learned from this set $\mathcal{S}$. Exploiting linkage structures captured by the linkage model, GOMEA performs a genetic local search-like variation operation to transform each existing solution $\boldsymbol{x}$ into a new offspring solution $\boldsymbol{o}$ in a step-wise manner. Finally, the population $\mathcal{P}$ is completely replaced by the offspring population $\mathcal{O}$ of n newly constructed solutions.

The linkage model structure of GOMEA follows the Family Of Subset (FOS) concept. Let $L = \{1, 2, \ldots, l\}$ be the set containing all decision variable indices. A FOS $\mathcal{F}$ over L is a subset of the powerset of $L : \mathcal{F} \subseteq \mathcal{P}(S)$. $\mathcal{F}$ can be written as $\mathcal{F} = \{\boldsymbol{F}^1, \boldsymbol{F}^2, \ldots, \boldsymbol{F}^{|\mathcal{F}|}\}$ where $\boldsymbol{F}^i \subseteq \{1, 2, \ldots, l\}$, $i \in \{1, 2, \ldots, |\mathcal{F}|\}$. A FOS can thus be seen as a set of linkage groups, in which each linkage group is in turn a set of decision variables indices, indicating that those variables are (inter-)dependent to some degree. In this paper, we use the Linkage Tree (LT) as the FOS model, which gives a popular instance of GOMEA, also called the Linkage Tree Genetic Algorithm (LTGA). An LT over the set L represents its linkage groups in a hierarchical manner. All l leaf nodes are singleton linkage groups, i.e. $\boldsymbol{F}^i = \{i\}, i \in \{1, 2, \ldots, l\}$, describing the univariate structure. Then, for each branch node $\boldsymbol{F}^i$ containing more than one decision variable indices, describing multivariate dependencies, there exist subsets $\boldsymbol{F}^j$ and $\boldsymbol{F}^k$ such that $\boldsymbol{F}^j \cap \boldsymbol{F}^k = \emptyset, |\boldsymbol{F}^j| < |\boldsymbol{F}^i|, |\boldsymbol{F}^k| < |\boldsymbol{F}^i|$ and $\boldsymbol{F}^j \cup \boldsymbol{F}^k = \boldsymbol{F}^i$. The root node, which contains all variable indices and is thus the set L itself, is removed from the LT because it results in copying the entire solutions when performing linkage-based recombination, which is not useful. An LT over the set L of l decision variables can be constructed by the Unweighted Pair Grouping Method with Arithmetic-mean (UPGMA) procedure in $\mathcal{O}(nl^2)$ time [5], resulting in exactly $2l - 2$ linkage groups. For more details on building the LT, please refer to the literature [1, 10].

GOMEA transforms each existing solution $\boldsymbol{x}$ into a new offspring solution $\boldsymbol{o}$ by a variation operator called Gene-pool Optimal Mixing (GOM). First, $\boldsymbol{o}$ is a direct clone from $\boldsymbol{x}$, and a backup version $\boldsymbol{b}$ of $\boldsymbol{x}$ is created. Traversing the linkage groups in the LT FOS $\mathcal{F}$, for every $\boldsymbol{F}^i \in \mathcal{F}$, a donor solution $\boldsymbol{p}$ is randomly selected from the population $\mathcal{P}$. The values of decision variables whose indices are indicated by $\boldsymbol{F}^i$ are copied from $\boldsymbol{p}$ to $\boldsymbol{o}$, if those values are different between $\boldsymbol{p}$ and $\boldsymbol{o}$ in at least one position. The constraints and objective values of this partially-altered $\boldsymbol{o}$ are evaluated and compared against the backup $\boldsymbol{b}$. If such mixing results in an improvement or an equally good solution (i.e. $fitness[\boldsymbol{o}] \geq fitness[\boldsymbol{b}]$), then the changes are accepted and also updated into the backup. Otherwise, discarding the changes, $\boldsymbol{o}$ is reverted to its backup state $\boldsymbol{b}$. Note that the acceptance criterion of equal fitness can help the search to move across a fitness plateau. When all $\boldsymbol{F}^i \in \mathcal{F}$ are traversed, an offspring solution $\boldsymbol{o}$ is fully constructed and will replace its parent solution $\boldsymbol{x}$ in the next generation.

If GOM cannot transform a solution $\boldsymbol{x}$ into a new offspring $\boldsymbol{o}$, a procedure called Forced Improvement (FI) is invoked. FI can be seen as a second round of GOM in which the donor solution is always the best-found-so-far solution $\boldsymbol{x}^{best}$. A mixing step in FI is only accepted when it results in a true improvement (i.e. $fitness[\boldsymbol{o}] > fitness[\boldsymbol{b}]$), and FI is stop as soon as such improvement is found. However, FI may never be called if there exist significant plateaus and the acceptance criterion of equal fitness in GOM simply transforms back and forth solutions of different genotypes but the same fitness value. To overcome this, if the number of subsequent generations that the best solution $\boldsymbol{x}^{best}$ does not change, termed as the no-improvement stretch (NIS), exceeds a threshold, FI is triggered. [1] suggests a threshold of $1 + \lfloor \log_{10}(n) \rfloor$. Lastly, if FI cannot transform an existing solution $\boldsymbol{x}$, the current best solution $\boldsymbol{x}^{best}$ is returned as the new offspring $\boldsymbol{o}$. Figure 1 shows pseudo-code.

```
GOMEA //population size n
  for i ∈ {1, 2, ..., n} do
    P_i ← CreateRandomSolution()
    EvaluateFitness(P_i)
  x^best ← argmax_{x∈P}{fitness[x]}
  t ← 0; t^NIS ← 0
  while ¬TerminationConditionsSatisfied do
    S ← TournamentSelection(P, n, 2)
    LearnLinkageModel(S)
    for i ∈ {1, 2, ..., n} do
      O_i ← FI-GOM(P_i)
    P ← O
    x^best ← argmax_{x∈P}{fitness[x]}
    if fitness[x^best(t)] > fitness[x^best] then
      t^NIS ← 0; x^best ← x^best(t)
    else
      t^NIS ← t^NIS + 1
    t ← t + 1
```

```
FI-GOM(x)
  b ← o ← x; fitness[b] ← fitness[o] ← fitness[x];
  changed ← false
  for i ∈ {1, 2, ..., |F|} do
    p ← Random({P_1, P_2, ..., P_n})
    o_{F^i} ← p_{F^i}
    if o_{F^i} ≠ b_{F^i} then
      EvaluateFitness(o)
      if fitness[o] ≥ fitness[b] then
        b_{F^i} ← o_{F^i}; fitness[b] ← fitness[o]; changed ← true
      else
        o_{F^i} ← b_{F^i}; fitness[o] ← fitness[b]
  if ¬changed or t^NIS > 1 + ⌊log10(n)⌋ then
    changed ← false
    for i ∈ {1, 2, ..., |F|} do
      o_{F^i} ← x^best_{F^i}
      if o_{F^i} ≠ b_{F^i} then
        EvaluateFitness(o)
        if fitness[o] > fitness[b] then
          b_{F^i} ← o_{F^i}; fitness[b] ← fitness[o]; changed ← true
        else
          o_{F^i} ← b_{F^i}; fitness[o] ← fitness[b]
      if changed then breakfor
  if ¬changed then
    o ← x^best; fitness[o] ← fitness[x^best]
```

Figure 1: Pseudo-code for GOMEA

4. EFFICIENCY ENHANCEMENTS

4.1 Restricted Initialization

Electricity grids are probably among the most complex technological networks with numerous interconnected facilities, which have been built over time. The legacy of currently existing electric components should be taken into account when conducting any real-world network expansion planning. Regarding the huge sums of investment that have been made into the current grid, network operators typically do not favor expansion plans involving radical changes, such as re-designing the grid from scratch, because this is economically unaffordable, resulting in high tariffs for consumers. Favorable solutions for DNEP problem instances in practice rather consists of incremental changes which differs from the original network in a few cable connections. Engineering heuristics and guidelines are employed to disregard impractical solutions, e.g. the addition of new cable connections should be limited, or the removal of existing connections are often discouraged. These engineering “rules of thumb” help to reduce the search space while also limit the number of changes that can be made to the current grid.

Evolutionary optimization algorithms, such as GA and GOMEA, usually start from a population of randomly generated solutions, providing an initial population of good diversity to begin with. For DNEP, this means that a complicated expansion plan of radical changes can still be obtained if doing so benefits the objective function. However, initialization can also be customized to reflect electrical-engineering expert knowledge and the assumption that only limited changes are required/desired. Initial solutions can then be direct clones of the current grid with only a limited number k of positions having different randomly generated values. We aim to investigate the balance between the computation budget and the quality of obtained solutions by experiment with different values of k that governs the size of the explorable search space of possible alternatives.

4.2 Linkage Filtering

An LT consists of $2l - 2$ linkage groups, in which not every linkage relation is necessarily beneficial in GOM if such linkages are of weak (inter-)dependencies. Filtering spurious linkage groups out of a linkage model is thus an important research topic for GOMEA. However, determining optimal filtering thresholds as in [1] often requires intensive analysis and experiments. Here, we consider a simpler filtering mechanism directly based on the sizes of linkage groups. Given that the level of changes to an existing grid that a DNO would favor is often limited, we hypothesize that large linkage groups of many variables do not contribute much to the search. As the favorable expansion plans are usually of incremental changes, it might be more computationally economical if GOMEA only attempts mixing events of small linkage groups. Therefore, larger linkage groups, which can introduce radical network restructuring, should be filtered out of the LT. We generalize this filtering mechanism by introducing a threshold L^{max}_{FOS} for the maximum size of link-

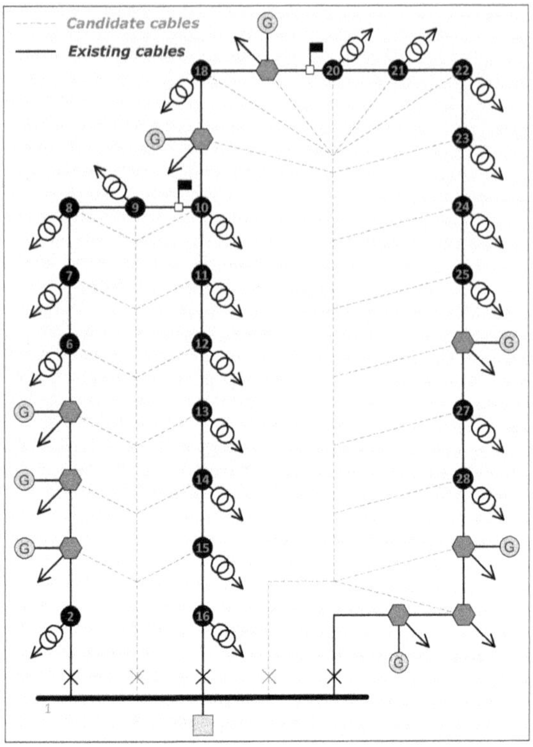

Figure 2: Topology of the benchmark network.

age groups. If a linkage group contains more than L_{FOS}^{max} variable indices, it will be ignored when GOM constructs offspring solutions. Assuming that restricted initialization will initialize the search near the optimal solution, we will experiment to see if this linkage filtering mechanism with different values of L_{FOS}^{max} can further accelerate GOMEA.

5. EXPERIMENTS

5.1 Benchmark Problem

Figure 2 shows the topology of the network that we used for benchmarking. The network is based on a real MV distribution grid containing 31 nodes and 59 branches: 30 currently existing active cable connections, 2 existing reserve cable connections (NOPs) on the 9-10 and 19-20 branches, and 27 potential connections branching out from the substation at node 1. The DNO has to make reinforcement decisions on these 59 cable connections. Note that network stations at nodes 3, 4, 5, 17, 19, 20, 29 and 31 are connected with distributed generation facilities. To evaluate an expansion plan for such an electricity grid with DGs, we need to verify the feasibility of that plan against the 2 situations that can cause the heaviest power flows on the grid as follows.

- Dominance of load: 100% peak load occurs at all nodes and all DG facilities are turned off.
- Dominance of DG: All DG facilities are turned on and operate at their full 100% generation capacity while the demand at all nodes are only 25% of the peak load.

Details about the peak loads, generation capacities of DGs, and electric cables can be found in the Appendix. Here, we consider a planning horizon of $T = 30$ years.

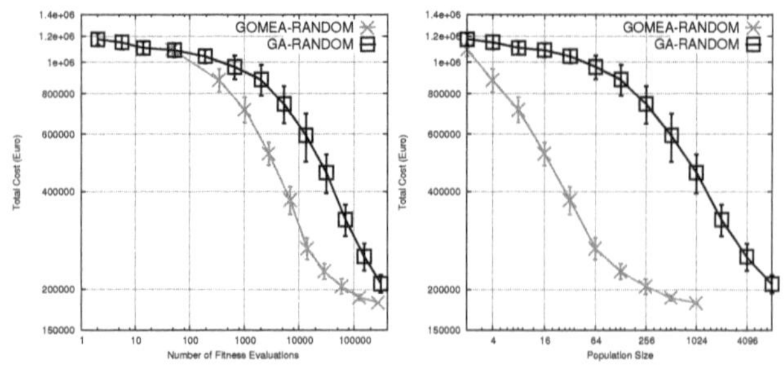

Figure 3: Performance of GA and GOMEA on solving DNEP, averaged over 30 independent runs. Vertical axis: Total cost (in EUR). Horizontal axis: Number of fitness evaluations (left) and Population size (right).

5.2 Results & Discussion

5.2.1 Random Initialization

Figure 3 compares the performance of the classical GA and GOMEA on solving a DNEP problem instance with random initialization. GOMEA clearly outperforms GA in terms of obtaining solutions of better quality using fewer network evaluations. It should be noted that GOMEA reaches near-optimal results and that although the GA seems to overtake GOMEA for even larger population sizes, this will not be the case. This will also be corroborated by results further-on in this paper. The classical GA requires much larger population sizes and longer computation time until convergence toward solutions whose fitness values are close to those found by GOMEA. The fact that the standard deviations of the results found by GOMEA are smaller than those of GA indicate the better reliability of GOMEA compared to GA. We thus propose that it can be beneficial to employ state-of-the-art EAs, which involve linkage learning, to solve industrial optimization problems rather than just relying on traditional EAs available in computation software.

5.2.2 Restricted Initialization

Figure 4 shows the performance of the classical GA and GOMEA on solving a DNEP problem instance with the restricted initialization mentioned in Section 4.1. We performed experiments for $k = 2, 4, 8, 16$ (the number of positions that a candidate solution can different in from the currently existing network). First, it can be seen that restricted initialization greatly reduces the diversity of the population, causing both optimizers GA and GOMEA to quickly converge. With a large enough population size (i.e. > 16), optimizers with restricted initialization can obtain solutions of better quality and using fewer fitness evaluations than when the same optimizers of similar population sizes are initialized randomly. Note that using too small population sizes (i.e. ≤ 16) may lead the optimizers to infeasible solutions, which can not be seen from the results in the graph. The bottom left graph in Figure 4 indicates that the best found solution is still the one obtained by GOMEA with random initialization that required longer computation time. Lastly, we concede that under the effect of restricted initialization GOMEA does not have any advantages over the classical GA for the tested network. This is likely because the number of meaningful mixing events is significantly limited with restricted initialization. While the optimum consisting of only a few incremental changes is not hard to

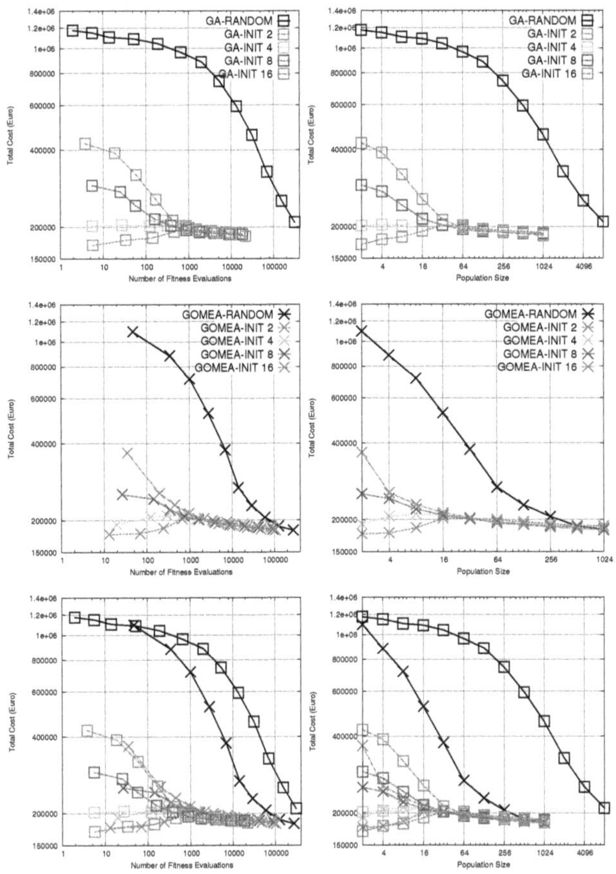

Figure 4: Performance of GA and GOMEA on solving DNEP with restricted initialization. Vertical axis: Total cost (in EUR). Horizontal axis: Number of fitness evaluations (left) and Population size(right).

find from the initial population, many more different mixing events, which are now largely superfluous, are attempted by GOMEA by traversing the whole linkage tree. Furthermore, solutions found by GOMEA and GA are of similar quality but GOMEA takes more fitness evaluations until the whole population converges. Note that the difficulty of a DNEP problem instance may be strongly related to not only the network size but also the required level of network changes needed to obtain the optimum. In this paper, our benchmark network contains 59 decision variables (i.e. cable connections) but only a small number of reinforcements (in this case, 5) are needed to transform the existing grid into the optimum. In related work [6], we reduced the search space by employing electricity expert knowledge, and obtained similar results, indicating that the initial population might be quite close to the optimum for this benchmark network.

5.2.3 *Restricted Initialization & Linkage Filtering*

Figure 5 shows the performance of GOMEA when combined with restricted initialization and linkage filtering as mentioned in Section 4. Table 1 shows an example result of GOMEA with restricted initialization of 16 different components, when coupled with linkage filtering for $L^{max}_{FOS} = 16$, i.e. removing linkage groups containing more than 16 variables out of the LT. Our simple linkage filtering slightly improves the quality of the obtained solutions. Different values

Table 1: Performance of GOMEA when coupled the restricted initialization of 16-different components and filtering of linkage groups with $L^{max}_{FOS} = 16$

	INIT 16		INIT 16-MAX 16	
Pop.Size	Objective	#Evaluations	Objective	#Evaluations
2	367624.54	35.13	355677.71	38.4
4	255586.89	196.5	253368.71	253.06
8	230316.22	445.6	223857.87	738.9
16	212774.28	971.13	200677.04	1646.86
32	203419.42	2172.5	194684.77	3543.93
64	193616.43	4820.43	189295.7	7536.06
128	190555.51	10202.93	184798.1	15573.33
256	187123.88	22471.76	183858.28	32145.13
512	184270.65	47435.8	182483.36	63931.13
1024	182506.32	104579.1	182097.35	116233.86

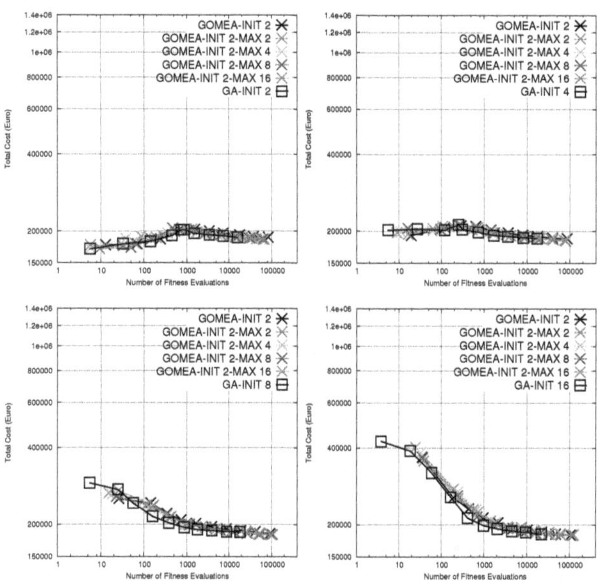

Figure 5: Performance of GOMEA in solving DNEP with restricted initialization and linkage filtering. Vert. axis: Total cost (in EUR). Horiz. axis: Number of fitness evaluations.

(2, 4, 8 or 16) of the linkage filtering threshold L^{max}_{FOS} do not result in significant differences. However, from closer observation it appears that the larger L^{max}_{FOS} is, the better the obtained solutions are. Figure 5 shows that although linkage filtering with threshold L^{max}_{FOS} improves GOMEA with restricted initialization, it is still not enough to accelerate GOMEA to outperform the restrictedly initialized classical GA. We emphasize that the better performance of GA here might be very specific to this benchmark network, where the required level of changes is very small compared to the total number of decision variables, and restricted initialization simply generates the initial population very close to the optimal solution. Therefore, future works are required to consider more complicated benchmarks with higher level of necessary changes to give a more accurate answer on the scalability of GA and GOMEA on the DNEP problem.

6. CONCLUSIONS

We measured the performance of the two population-based optimization algorithms: a classical GA, and a variant of a state-of-the-art linkage-learning EA, GOMEA, on solving the DNEP problem. Without problem-specific assumptions, starting from randomly generated populations, GOMEA was found to outperform GA. Considering DNEP common practice, we then used a restricted-initialization mechanism to reduce the size of the explorable search space and to likely have the initial population close to the optimum. With restricted initialization, GA was found to outperform GOMEA. Aiming to accelerate GOMEA, we then introduced a simple linkage filter that disregards overly large linkage groups. Although accelerations are indeed observed, this simple linkage filtering is still not enough for GOMEA outperform the simple GA in terms of number of evaluations until convergence when solving a specific DNEP problem instance. We conclude that for easy problem instances, where the optimum is close to the initial population, it is more beneficial to use the simple GA. However, in general cases, as shown in experiments with random initialization, GOMEA is found to be the better optimizer. To study the scalability of GA and GOMEA on the DNEP problem, future works also need to consider realistic, tunable and scalable distribution-network benchmarks that are more meshed and more complex.

7. REFERENCES

[1] P. A. N. Bosman and D. Thierens. More concise and robust linkage learning by filtering and combining linkage hierarchies. In *Proc. of the Genetic and Evolutionary Comp. Conf. - GECCO-2013*, pages 359–366. ACM, 2013.

[2] Y. Del Valle, G. Venayagamoorthy, S. Mohagheghi, J.-C. Hernandez, and R. Harley. Particle swarm optimization: Basic concepts, variants and applications in power systems. *IEEE Trans. on Evol. Comp.*, 12(2):171–195, April 2008.

[3] E. Diaz-Dorado, J. Cidras, and E. Miguez. Application of evolutionary algorithms for the planning of urban distribution networks of medium voltage. *Power Systems, IEEE Transactions on*, 17(3):879–884, Aug 2002.

[4] J. J. Grainger and W. D. Stevenson. *Power System Analysis*. McGraw-Hill Education, 2003.

[5] I. Gronau and S. Moran. Optimal implementations of UPGMA and other common clustering algorithms. *Information Processing Letters*, 104(6):205 – 210, 2007.

[6] M. O. W. Grond, N. H. Luong, J. Morren, P. A. N. Bosman, J. G. Slootweg, and H. La Poutré. Practice-oriented optimization of distribution network planning using metaheuristic algorithms. In *18th Power Systems Computation Conference (PSCC'14), Wroclaw, Poland*, 2014 (submitted).

[7] G. Harik, E. Cantú-Paz, D. E. Goldberg, and B. L. Miller. The gambler's ruin problem, genetic algorithms, and the sizing of populations. *Evol. Comp.*, 7:231–253, 1999.

[8] N. H. Luong, M. O. W. Grond, P. A. N. Bosman, and H. La Poutré. Medium-voltage distribution network expansion planning with gene-pool optimal mixing evolutionary algorithms. In *Biennial Int. Conf. on Artificial Evolution (EA-2013)*, pages 96–107, 2013.

[9] J. Schlabbach and K.-H. Rofalski. *Power System Engineering (chapter 4)*, pages 37–44. Wiley-VCH Verlag GmbH & Co. KGaA, 2008.

[10] D. Thierens and P. A. N. Bosman. Optimal mixing evolutionary algorithms. In *Proc. of the Genetic and Evol. Comp. Conf. - GECCO-2011*, pages 617–624. ACM, 2011.

[11] D. Thierens and D. E. Goldberg. Mixing in genetic algorithms. In *Proceedings of the 5th International Conference on Genetic Algorithms*, pages 38–47, San Francisco, CA, 1993. Morgan Kaufmann Publishers Inc.

[12] R. A. Verzijlbergh, M. O. W. Grond, Z. Lukszo, J. G. Slootweg, and M. D. Ilic. Network impacts and cost savings of controlled EV charging. *Smart Grid, IEEE Transactions on*, 3(3):1203–1212, Sept 2012.

[13] K. P. Wong. Solving power system optimization problems using simulated annealing. *Engineering Applications of Artificial Intelligence*, 8(6):665 – 670, 1995.

APPENDIX

Cable Parameters			
ID	R [Ω/km]	X [Ω/km]	C [$\mu F/km$]
1	0.257	0.085	0.38
2	0.20858	0.09592	0.3833
3	0.13517	0.10823	0.43443
4	0.08077	0.09972	0.5344
5	0.0511	0.09272	0.64103

Node Information				
Node	Load		DG	
[#]	P [kW]	Q [kVAR]	P [kW]	Q [kVAR]
1	0	0		
2	35	17		
3	1113	539	-1960	-398
4	348	216	-980	-199
5	871	286	-1960	398
6	332	109		
7	132	82		
8	170	82		
9	22	14		
10	202	98		
11	120	0		
12	88	55		
13	284	137		
14	219	136		
15	314	152		
16	185	90		
17	127	79	-980	-199
18	17	8		
19	896	434	-1960	-398
20	314	152		
21	125	77		
22	248	120		
23	85	41		
24	123	76		
25	209	130		
26	566	274	-1960	-398
27	266	129		
28	126	61		
29	360	174	-980	-199
30	273	169		
31	263	163	-980	-199

Cable Distances			
Existing		Estimated	
Branch [#]	Distance [m]	Branch [#]	Distance [m]
1-2	481	1-3	676
1-16	246	1-4	621
1-31	761	1-5	1199
2-3	96	1-6	1306
3-4	48	1-7	980
4-5	498	1-8	1465
5-6	86	1-9	1551
6-7	288	1-10	2135
7-8	935	1-11	2121
8-9	200	1-12	2121
9-10	470	1-13	1635
10-11	851	1-14	1386
11-12	220	1-15	1144
12-13	300	1-17	2218
13-14	284	1-18	2163
14-15	479	1-19	1988
15-16	846	1-20	2003
10-17	736	1-21	1751
17-18	101	1-22	1622
18-19	154	1-23	1720
19-20	283	1-24	1648
20-21	308	1-25	1535
21-22	133	1-26	1451
22-23	132	1-27	1348
23-24	138	1-28	1315
24-25	140	1-29	1057
25-26	103	1-30	1124
26-27	215		
27-28	129		
28-29	218		
29-30	136		
30-13	160		

Reinforcement Learning Based Energy Efficient LTE RAN

Joan Meseguer Llopis
Orange Polska
Warsaw
Poland
+48 797 318 373
joan.llopis@orange.com

Lukasz Rajewski
Orange Polska
Warsaw
Poland
+48 519 310 854
lukasz.rajewski@orange.com

Slawomir Kuklinski
Orange Polska and Warsaw University of Technology
Warsaw
Poland
+48 601 213 013
slawomir.kuklinski@orange.com

ABSTRACT
Reducing power consumption in LTE networks has become an important issue for mobile network operators. The 3GPP organization has included such operation as one of SON (Self-Organizing Networks) functions [1][2]. Using the approach presented in this paper the decision about turning Radio Access Network (RAN) nodes off and on, according to the network load (which is typically low at night), is taken into account. The process is controlled using a combination of Fuzzy Logic and Q-Learning techniques (FQL). The effectiveness of the proposed approach has been evaluated using the LTE-Sim simulator with some extensions. The simulations are very close to real network implementation: we used the RAN node parameters that are defined by 3GPP and simulations take into account the network behaviour in the micro time scale.

General Terms
Algorithms, Network Management, Measurements, Performance, Design, Experimentation, Theory.

Keywords
Energy savings; LTE; SON; machine learning; reinforcement learning.

1. INTRODUCTION
The new generations of mobile systems offer high bitrate streams to end users. In order to cope with such high traffic demands, the relatively small size of cells in latest mobile systems (LTE) is used, and as the consequence, the number of users per cell is limited. Small cell size causes the increased number of cells in certain area of operator network, typically in cities. The increased number of cells makes cells deployment and operation troublesome and increases the overall power consumption by RAN. In order to cope with the problem of RAN management and having in mind that human-centric management is slow and error prone, a Self-Organizing Networks concept has been developed [3]. This concept enables automation of certain RAN management functions including handover, coverage optimization, load balancing, etc. One of the SON functions, the Energy Efficient RAN (EE RAN), seamlessly turns off some radio nodes (eNodeBs), sector's carriers or node's internal blocks in order to reduce power consumption when the network load is low (typically at night). In fact the radio network is dimensioned to cope with peak traffic hours whereas it can be under-utilized in off-peak traffic time. Switching a cell (or cell sectors) off is possible if network load is low and the neighbouring cells can compensate the coverage. In case of the traffic growth the switched-off cell has to be dynamically switched on.

A holistic approach to energy savings in RAN done by 3GPP is described in [1]. In this technical report, a case study based on different scenarios is made. Some possible solutions, which depend on the given RAN topology, are also proposed in the report. The document does not describe how the EE RAN mechanisms should be implemented. Typically it is assumed that for each RAN node the decision of switching off some cells can be driven by a pre-programmed policy, which takes into account time of day (week) and network traffic patterns. Such simple approach can lead to the degradation of offered services or to low efficiency of the EE RAN mechanism. There is no doubt that the mechanism based on real traffic measurements with appropriate decision algorithm will be much more effective. In this paper, we propose to use a cognitive algorithm for EE RAN. We described the usage of an algorithm for Inter-eNodeB energy saving scenario of [1]. This scenario is based on the so-called capacity limited network, which is homogeneous (composed of a group of cells with similar size) that is presented in Figure 1. For the sake of simplicity we will consider eNodeBs with omnidirectional antennas moreover only switching off of the whole node (eNodeB) is taken into account.

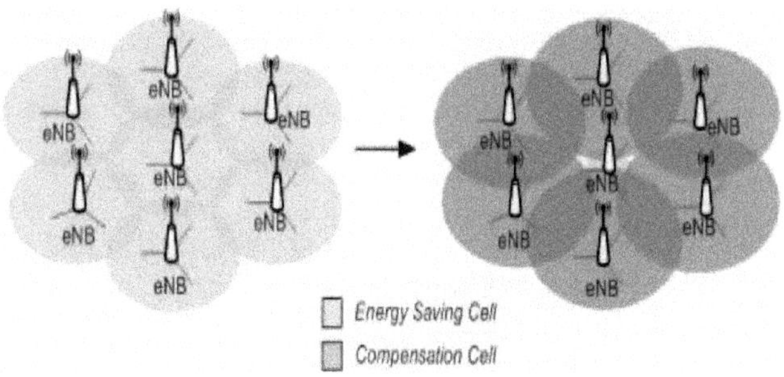

Figure 1. Inter-eNodeB energy saving use case [1]

The usage of machine learning technique automates the EE process and minimizes the degradation of offered services when the network will learn its proper behaviour. There are two situations when the cognitive approach can be applied in EE RAN. The first one is a prediction of the time when a cell can go to the dormant mode. The second one is appropriate prediction when the dormant cell has to be waked-up. If this procedure starts too early the cell will be forced again to go into the sleep state. If the cell will wake-up too late, the serious network degradation will be perceived by the users. The improper behaviour of the algorithm that is responsible for the decision will result in higher power consumption and increased signalling load – in some cases

GECCO'14, July 12–16, 2014, Vancouver, BC, Canada.
Copyright 2014 ACM 978-1-4503-2881-4/14/07…$15.00.
http://dx.doi.org/10.1145/2598394.2605694

degraded QoS can be observed as well. The switching events should happen not more often than several times per hour and this means that the switch off process does not have to be fast. On the other hand, in case of high mobility of users, the switching-on phase has to be fast.

The EE process is composed of four phases. Phase 1 lies in a continuous monitoring by each eNodeB to check if it is a candidate for switching off – potentially a preliminary decision about switching off a cell can be taken. During cell monitoring the number of active users, the cell load, time of day and other parameters related to cell activity are collected. The decision on-to-off is based on a cognitive algorithm. Phase 2 is related to the execution of the decision about switching off a cell by appropriate compensation of radio coverage by the neighbouring cells. Phase 3 is related to the monitoring of the load in the area that is compensated by the surrounding cells in order to detect a need for switching on of the sleeping cell. The set of monitored parameters related to cell activity is the same as in Phase 1. The decision about switching a cell on is taken by the cognitive algorithm likewise in Phase 1. Phase 4 concerns of restoration of the normal state of the network, i.e. turning-on the sleeping cells and does not require cognitive techniques. In our approach we used a combination of the well-known Fuzzy Logic and Q-Learning technique (FQL) to take the decision in Phases 1 and 3.

The paper is structured as follows: in section 2, the four Phases of the EE approach are explained in more detail, though the description of cognitive part of the process (i.e. phases 1 and 3) is left for the section 3. In section 4 the effectiveness of the approach is evaluated and realistic simulation results are presented. Finally, section 5 concludes the paper and suggests some further work for the improvement of proposed approach.

2. THE EE PROCESS

For switching the radio stations off and on we use two independent instances of the reinforcement learning (RL) technique combined with Fuzzy Logic in order to cope with continuous input parameters space. RL learns how to act given monitoring information regarding the environment. The parameters that are collected from each eNodeB as the input of the algorithm for all four phases of EE mechanism are presented in Table 1. In this table NAU is the number of active users [4]; the AVGTHR parameter defines the sum of each user's average throughput (downlink) and is normalized and cell's load history (LoadHist) is the aggregated load of eNodeB for the whole day.

In our EE RAN implementation a cell can be in three states [2]: NORMAL, SLEEP and COMPENSATE. When a cell has the state flag equal to NORMAL, it means that this cell is not participating in any energy saving process. The SLEEP mode indicates that the cell is turned off or restricted in physical resource usage. Finally, when the cell is in COMPENSATE mode it means that it has modified power transmission in order to provide coverage in the vicinity of the turned off cell. In our case study, QoS (Quality of Service) refers to the network performance parameters: Handover Failure (HF), Packet Loss Ratio (PLR) and Averaged Packet Delay (PDL). Handover procedure is defined in [5]. When too low received signal level is detected by the user equipment (UE) during the handover execution or due to the lack of resource at the target cell to which UE is handed over the handover failure happens. PDL parameter determines the packet delay in the downlink channel averaged during time period T, which is usually defined by the equipment vendor [4]. PLR is the number of dropped downlink packets ratio to all transmitted packets [4]. The Radio Link Failure (RLF) happens when the terminal detects radio link problems – a broken transmission [6]. Users' RxLev list is a list of measured RSRP level per each cell. Cell's RSRP is defined as the linear average over the power contributions (in Watts) of the resource elements that carry cell-specific reference signals within the considered measurement frequency bandwidth. Moreover, the following data has to be provided for proper operation of the proposed approach: RAN network topology with list of neighbors, transmitted power defaults for all RAN nodes and parameters reporting period.

Table 1. Network monitoring and configuration parameters used

Parameter	Phase	Acronym
The number of active users	1, 3	NAU
Cell load expressed in average throughput	1, 3	AVGTHR
Time of day and load history	1, 3	[Time, LoadHist]
Cell mode (NORMAL, SLEEP, COMPENSATE) with timer of the state	1, 3	[StateTimer(min), StateFlag]
Cell QoS vector: [HF, PLR, PDL]	2, 3, 4	[HF, PLR, PDL]
Radio Link Failure	2, 4	RLF
Users' RxLev (RSRP) list.	2, 4	UERxLevList
Transmission Power	2, 4	TxPower

2.1 Phase 1: Normal state

In this phase each eNodeB collects monitoring data and sends periodically the processed and averaged reports to the node that executes the EE algorithm. According to monitoring data, configuration parameters (network topology), policy parameters (network operator preferences) and history of previous decision the algorithm takes the new decision. The decision is binary and indicates a cell that should be switched off. It also indicates which cells should take part in the cell compensation procedure. The decision about switching off the cell is taken using a model-free RL (Q-Learning). The results can be positive only if all the neighbouring cells are in normal (non-compensating) state. In case when the interval time between switching a cell off and on is under a defined threshold the previous decision is seen as a failure.

2.2 Phase 2: Switching-off a cell

The phase is related to the execution of the decision about switching a cell off by appropriate compensation of radio coverage by the neighbouring cells. The process is relatively simple but has to be smooth, i.e. switching the base station off has to be preceded by proper increase of coverage of active stations. The quality of the process is evaluated by pathological network behaviour during the transition (radio link failure ratio increase, interference level increase, etc.). In the proposed approach, in order to obtain the proper compensation, a special network pilot terminal (a kind of a mobile phone) is collocated with each eNodeB. Its role is to monitor the level of the neighbouring cells signals when the cell is switched off – it helps in proper cell compensation. This terminal is useful in the case when there are no real users under the coverage of compensated area.

The switching-off operation and the consequent coverage compensation is based on a multistep procedure described below.

2.2.1 First step

This step is composed of a modification of cell state flags of the compensating cells, (i.e. NORMAL to COMPENSATE) and gradual modification of maximum power transmission of EE compensating cells and EE candidate cell. This phase can actually be divided into several sub-steps. Each sub-step determines a new value of the transmitted power (TxPower) for cells involved in the EE procedure. This procedure ensures a gradual change of the topology and thus the users should not perceive any decrease of their QoS. Number of sub-steps to apply depends on delivered QoS in terms of radio link failures (RLF), handover failures (HF) and the received signal level (RxLev) of users in the area of the dormant cell candidate as well as of the cell's pilot terminal. The first step will finish as soon as the number of users under the EE candidate cell will be equal to zero. It is important to note that a new sub-step is performed as soon as new monitoring information is received, which is determined by the network monitoring reports collection frequency.

2.2.2 Second step

Once the number of users attached to EE candidate cell is equal to zero, and the RxLev list of pilot terminals reflects normal RSRP levels from compensation cells, the state flag is set to SLEEP and the neighbouring cell list of surrounding cells of EE candidate cell must be updated in order to avoid conflicts in next handover (HO) procedures. In case of reaching this step and RSRP list of pilot terminal reflects power levels below the minimum required, the transmission power of these cells is increased by the difference of this level and the current RSRP level.

2.2.3 Third step

The EE candidate is switched off. Here two options are considered. First one, the whole eNodeB is turned off or moved to the standby mode. Second option is just the result of reducing the transmitted power to zero. This will force all the UEs to handover to neighbouring cells. In consequence the power consumed by the eNodeB's radio unit will be zero.

2.3 Phase 3: Sleeping state monitoring

This phase is related to the monitoring of the area that is compensated in order to detect a need for switching on of the sleeping cell. All cells that are compensating cells of the sleeping cell are monitored. The set of monitored parameters is the same as in Phase 1. The decision about switching a cell on uses cognitive techniques, the same algorithmic technique as used in Phase 1. Improper behaviour of the algorithm will lead to subsequent turning off the station recently turned on, i.e. the EE ping-pong effect will occur. Another measure of the success is a non-degraded QoS offered to users in the compensated area. In the case, when the interval time between switching off and on is under a defined threshold, the previous decision is seen as a failure.

2.4 Phase 4: Normal state restoration

The parameters of the switched on cells, TxPower and neighbouring cell list as well as their flags to NORMAL are restored. However, similarly to Phase 2, a gradual decrease of compensate cells' TxPower parameter is necessary as well as a gradual increase of TxPower parameter of the switched off cell. The process is non-cognitive one.

3. THE ALGORITHM

3.1 Q-Learning and Fuzzy Logic

We used Reinforcement Learning (RL) algorithm for the switching on/off of an eNodeB. From many available RL variants we have chosen the Q-learning approach due to its simplicity and its proven convergence [7]. In Q-learning, an agent (i.e. in our case the EE RAN agent) switches from one state to another by performing an action. At each state transition a reward is received which measures the quality of the action taken. The goal of the algorithm is to find the best action for each state S_t while maximizing the long-term reward. In order to achieve this, Q-learning keeps a q-value for each state-action pair. This q-value is also known as the estimation of the real-valued function $Q(S,a)$. This value function estimates the expected cumulative discounted reward of performing an action being in the state S and then following the optimal policy. At each state, the estimated q-value is updated using the formula:

$$Q_{t+1}(s_t, a_t) \leftarrow Q_t(s_t, a_t) + \alpha[r_{t+1} + \gamma Max_{|a} Q_t(s_{t+1}, a) - Q_t(s_t, a_t)] \quad (1)$$

where $\alpha \in [0,1]$ is the learning rate that defines by how much the new value is updated for the current state-action pair. It, therefore, determines the learning speed of the agent. $\gamma \in [0,1]$ is the discount factor and it influences how much the agent considers the immediate reward. The closer γ is to 1 the more it looks after the future payoffs. The reward r_{t+1} measures the quality of the action taken in a certain state (S_t) and it is calculated when the agent arrives to the next state (S_{t+1}).

In a discrete state space environment the state and action spaces are counted and each of them keeps a q value in a so called lookup table. This becomes very complex and impractical when these spaces are continuous. For this reason, the Fuzzy Logic [8] is applied to discretize the continuous input values. To keep the algorithm simple we use only three input parameters to define the cell load state S: number of active users (NAU), cell's averaged throughput (AVGTRGHP) and cell's load history (see Table 1).

$$S = [\text{NAU}, \text{AVGTHR}, \text{LoadHist}] \quad (2)$$

As mentioned before, in order to discretize the continuous space of the input variables, the data obtained from eNodeBs are fuzzified. For the fuzzification, a finite number of fuzzy labels were defined over the domain of each input variables. For the input vector, each variable will have three fuzzy labels (*Low, Medium* and *High*). A membership function that maps the same input values to a degree of truth value in the real range from 0 to 1 is assigned to each label. In this case the triangular (Medium Label) and the trapezoidal (Low and High Labels) membership function have been used with overlapping areas so that the sum of the membership functions at any point of the input space will be equal to 1.

$$\mu_{LOW}(x) = \begin{cases} 1, & x < a \\ \frac{x-b}{a-b}, & a \le x \le b \\ 0, & x > b \end{cases} \quad (3)$$

$$\mu_{MEDIUM}(x) = \begin{cases} 0, & x < a \\ \frac{x-a}{b-a}, & a \le x \le b \\ \frac{x-c}{b-c}, & b < x \le c \\ 0, & x > c \end{cases} \quad (4)$$

$$\mu_{HIGH}(x) = \begin{cases} 1, & x < a \\ \frac{x-b}{c-b}, & a \le x \le b \\ 1, & x > c \end{cases} \quad (5)$$

3.2 Selecting the candidate cell

All the parameters used by the algorithm are defined in Table 1. In order to get the best candidate cell to switch-off (Phase 1) we apply the input [NAU, AVGTHR] of each cell in a particular cell cluster to a Fuzzy Rule-Based System [9] to get a value on the output parameter., the *Quality of Candidate*, *QoC*. Likewise for the cell load related parameters, in this fuzzy system output parameter we have three fuzzy labels: Low, Medium and High. Each label is also assigned to a membership function (eq. 3-5) that maps the same input values to a degree of truth value in the real range from 0 to 1. The Table 2 consists the conjunctive rules of inference based on the observations of the network.

Table 2. Fuzzy System Rules

Input		Output
NAU	AVGTHR	QoC
L	L	H
L	M	H
L	H	M
M	L	M
M	M	L
M	H	L
H	L	L
H	M	L
H	H	L

We use the well-known max-min Mandami implication method of inference [8], which is denoted as follows:

$$\mu_{QoC}(QoC) = \max_{k}\{min[\mu_{NAU^k}(NAU), \mu_{AVGTHR^k}(AVGTHR)]\} \quad (6)$$

The result of this method is a fuzzy set so that it is yet to be calculated a final QoC discrete value. This process is known as defuzzification and in our case the so-called *centre of gravity* procedure has been applied [8].

3.3 Decision making: FQL

As mentioned before the output action is binary {0;1}. We assign the value 1 to the action of switching off and 0 for the action of switching on. When the cell is already switched on, the action 0 then means to keep the cell in the same operating state (Phase 1), i.e. the "*do-nothing*" action. Similarly, if the cell is switched off, the action 1 refers to the "*do-nothing*" action as well. In FQL, states and actions are defined using fuzzy membership functions. The continuous state variables are first transformed into a finite number of fuzzy variable membership functions. This process is called fuzzification. From these fuzzy variables, the corresponding output is calculated based on the Fuzzy Inference System (FIS). Finally the fuzzy output of the FIS is mapped back to the continuous output variable through the process of defuzzification. In general, the rule based on FIS consists of arbitrary number of different rules constructed out of AND and OR operators. A FIS has a rule based consisting of *N* rules, and the input vector *X* has *n* elements representing the input space. It typically expresses an inference as a conclusion (consequent) [9]. In our particular case we have three input variables [NAU, AVGTHR, LoadHist (time of day)] (see Table 1) with three possible labels for each one (L∈[L,M,H]) and two consequents denoted by O_p. Hence, the total number of rules is 27. Each of these rules has the following form:

$$Rule\ i\!: if \begin{bmatrix} \text{NAU} \\ \text{AVGTHR} \\ \text{LoadHist} \end{bmatrix} = \begin{bmatrix} L_1^i \\ L_2^i \\ L_3^i \end{bmatrix} then[O_p]\ is \begin{cases} 0\ with\ q_{value} = q_1 \\ 1\ with\ q_{value} = q_2 \end{cases} \quad (7)$$

As mentioned above, for each rule, O_p represents the action to be taken, and in each rule we will have 2 q-values for each action. At the beginning, all q-values will be initiated to 0. Its value will be updated after the action taken and the reward computed.

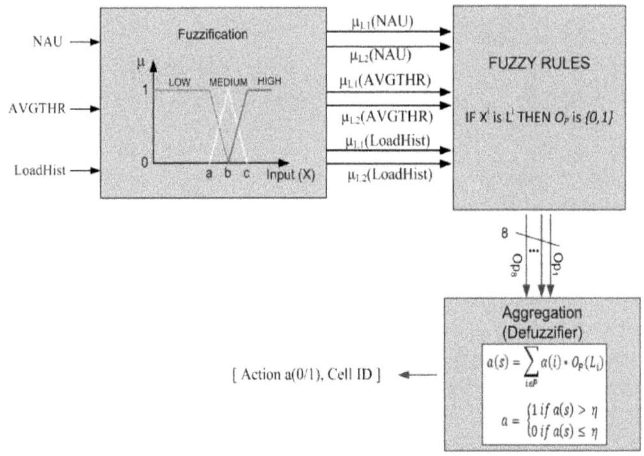

Figure 2. EE RAN Fuzzy Inference (based) system

The general structure of the developed fuzzy inference system (see Figure 2) consists of three conceptual blocks or components: a rule base, which contains a selection of fuzzy rules; a dictionary, which defines the membership functions used in the fuzzy rules; and a reasoning mechanism, which performs the inference procedure upon the rules and given facts to derive a reasonable output or conclusion. However, sometimes it is necessary to have a crisp output. In such a case the reasoning mechanism has to include the defuzzification mechanism to extract a crisp value that represents the output fuzzy set in the best way. In our case, the entire space of rule will be 27 for all the possibilities state input vector. Moreover, each input will have maximum two values of membership function (L&M or M&H). As a result, the maximum number of activated rules (with result different than zero) will be 8 for a particular input vector. Therefore, we will have 8 output values which will be fed to the defuzzification component in order to get a crisp value indicating the action to be taken. All q values, which are associated to a rule and action pair, are kept in a table in the following form:

Table 3. The Q-Learning table template

Rule	Output Action O_p	q-value
R1	1	v_{11}
	0	v_{12}
R2	1	v_{21}
	0	v_{22}
R3	1	v_{31}
	0	v_{32}
...	...	...

The Q table represents the memory of what the agent have learned through many experiences. Since Phase 1 and Phase 3 have independent FQL instances, each phase will have its own Q matrix with its own rules. Consequently we use two different rewards as well: RW_{ph1} (8) and RW_{ph3} (9) for the phases. In both cases we use a continuous reward function based on progress estimators. Progress estimators provide a measure of improvement towards an objective [9]. Moreover, the Gaussian function in both of them has been used in order to accelerate the learning process [10]. In order to update the q-value associated to the action chosen, the reward should be computed taking into consideration the action taken by the agent (O_p). Therefore, the reward functions for both Q-Learning instances are defined as follows:

$$RW_{ph1}(O_k) = \begin{cases} 1 - 2 \cdot e^{-0.5 * \frac{(W_{it} * \nabla QoS_1)^2}{\sigma_{ph1}^2}}, & O_k = O_1 \\ 2 \cdot e^{-0.5 * \frac{(W_{it} * \nabla QoS_1)^2}{\sigma_{ph1}^2}} - 1, & O_k = O_2 \end{cases} \quad (8)$$

$$RW_{ph3}(O_k) = \begin{cases} 1 - e^{-0.5 * \frac{\nabla QoS_3^2}{\sigma_{ph3}^2}}, & O_k = O_1 \\ e^{-0.5 * \frac{\nabla QoS_3^2}{\sigma_{ph3}^2}}, & O_k = O_2 \end{cases} \quad (9)$$

$$\nabla QoS = w_{HF} * HF + w_{PLR} * PLR + w_{PDL} * PDL \quad (10)$$

For both cases we have introduced the term $\nabla QoS \in \mathrm{R}^+$ (10). This term gathers all the Key Performance Indicators (KPIs) that symbolize the network's performance degradation: handover failure (HF), packet lost ratio (PLR) and averaged packet delay (PDL). The agent may switch off/on an eNodeB when the cell is under a load peak. In consequence, a global degradation of these KPIs is expected. ∇QoS_1 aggregates these KPIs during the Phase 2 and Phase 3, and ∇QoS_3 aggregates these KPIs during the Phase 3 and Phase 4. For the reward RW_{ph1} the maximum and minimum value are 1 and -1 respectively (i.e. $RW_{ph1} \in [-1,1]$). When ∇QoS_1 approaches 0, this reward will be closer to 1 for the switch-off action (O_2) and it will be near -1 for the switch-on action (O_1). On the other hand, when ∇QoS_1 is high, the switch-off action is punished with a reward close to -1 and with a value close to 1 for the switch-on action. As for the reward RW_{ph3} the maximum and minimum value are 1 and 0 respectively (i.e. $r_{t+1} \in [0,1]$). When ∇QoS_3 increases, for those active rules with action equal to O_1 and O_2, the value of RW_{ph3} will approach to 1 and 0 respectively. In the same way, when ∇QoS_3 decreases, for those active rules with action equal to O_1 and O_2, the value of RW_{ph3} will approach to 0 and 1 respectively. In equations (8) and (9), parameter σ determines the reward gradient influence area. The lower σ is the more sensitive the reward will be against an increase of ∇QoS. This parameter has been object of study during the algorithm's simulation phase since it has a big impact on its performance and convergence speed. The time window in which the reward of Phase 1 can punish the action of switching a cell off must be limited since the second FQL instance is the responsible to re-establish the normal state in case of any network performance degradation. Therefore, in equation (8), it has been added the coefficient W_{it} to the ∇QoS_1, which represents the QoS degradation impact factor for reward of phase 1 when a cell is turned off. This is shown in the following equation:

$$W_{it}(t_{sleep}) = 1 - \frac{1}{1+e^{-4*(t_{sleep} - RWimpTime)}} \quad (11)$$

The above function is the scale function with the transition from 1 to 0 at the cell sleep time (t_{sleep}) equal to $RWimpTime$. Therefore $RWimpTime$ represents the impact time of ∇QoS against the reward of Phase 1. In other words, this means that at any sleep time after $RWimpTime$ the value of this factor is 0 and in consequence value of ∇QoS will be irrelevant for the final reward, whose value will be 1 (from that time on) for the switch-off action and 0 for the switch-on action.

The first step of the FQL algorithm is to evaluate the current state of the network. A set of new values for the input variables will be provided and the degree of truth of each FIS rule i will be computed. The degree of true is the product of membership values of each input state label (L) for the specific rule i:

$$Algorithm\ Input \quad \begin{bmatrix} NAU \\ AVGTHR \\ \mathrm{LoadHist} \end{bmatrix} = \begin{bmatrix} x \\ y \\ z \end{bmatrix}$$

$$\alpha(i) = \mu_{L_i^1}(x) * \mu_{L_i^2}(y) * \mu_{L_i^3}(z) \quad (12)$$

The output action for each activated rule is denoted by O_p, and it can take only two possible values: 0 or 1. The way in which one of the actions is selected depends on whether the agent is on the learning stage (exploration stage) or exploitation stage. The exploration/exploitation policy (EEP) followed to decide which action to take is described via the equation (13). Where ε is the tradeoff between exploration and exploitation. In the exploitation phase (i.e. $\varepsilon = 1$), the agent has achieved the global optimal behaviour; thus the output chosen is the one with maximum q-value out of the two present the Q-Learning table.

$$o_p = \begin{cases} \mathrm{argmax}_{k \epsilon K}\, q(L_p, o_p^k), & with\ probability\ \varepsilon \\ \mathrm{random}_k\, o_p^k, & with\ probability\ 1 - \varepsilon \end{cases} \quad (13)$$

If α is the degree of truth for each rule and P is the total number of activated rules, the final action will be:

$$a(s) = \sum_{i \epsilon P} \alpha(i) * O_P(L_i) \quad (14)$$

where i is the number of active rule. The final action given here belongs to the continuous space with minimum value 0 and maximum 1, i.e. [0,1]. However, a final decision (whether to switch a cell off or on) is yet missing. To solve this, we have introduced a rule based on a variable threshold (η), that is:

$$a = \begin{cases} 1 \; if \; a(s) > \eta \\ 0 \; if \; a(s) \leq \eta \end{cases} \quad (15)$$

Therefore, the action to be applied depends on the final action value $a(s)$, where η shows the strictness of the current condition given (in terms of cell load) that will allow the switching-off/on of a cell. Likewise σ, the value to assign to η has been a topic of study during the simulation phase of the algorithm.

After applying the final action, the agent moves to the next state s_{t+1} and the reward will be calculated. Then the next step is to update those elements of Q-Learning table whose pair rule-action coincide with those activated rules L_p and its corresponding action chosen O_p. This is done as showed with the following equation:

$$q_{t+1}(L_p, O_p) \leftarrow q_t(L_p, O_p) + \beta * \alpha_p(s_t) * \Delta Q \quad (16)$$

First of all, before the agent applies the action, the q-value for the current state s_t must be calculated as follows:

$$Q(s_t, a(s_t)) = \sum_{p \epsilon P_s} \alpha_p(s_t) * q(L_p, O_p) \quad (17)$$

Where P_s is the set of activated rules and $q(L_p, O_p)$ is the q-value for the pair label L_p and output O_p, which is taken from the Q-Learning table. In equation (16) the quantity ΔQ is defined as the difference between the old and new value of Q(x,a(x)):

$$\Delta Q = r_{t+1} + \gamma V_t(s_{t+1}) - Q(s_t, a(s_t)) \quad (18)$$

In the above equation, r_{t+1} is the reward computed for the new state s_{t+1} (via monitoring the network status after the action is taken) and $V_t(s_{t+1})$ measures the aggregated maximum q-value achievable for the new state. The former is calculated following equations (8) or (9) and the latter is obtained from the formula shown below.

$$V_t(s_{t+1}) = \sum_{p \epsilon P_{s_{t+1}}} \alpha_p(s_{t+1}) * \text{argmax}\{q(L_p, O_p)\} \quad (19)$$

Both factors, β and γ, have range value from 0 to 1 ($0 \leq \beta < 1$ and $0 \leq \gamma < 1$). β is the learning rate which determines the influence of new information on the previous knowledge at the moment of taking a decision. The closer β is to 0 means the less learning and the closer it is to 1 means the only newest information is considered. The closer γ is to 0 the more the agent will consider only immediate rewards. If γ is closer to 1, the agent considers future reward with grater preference, willing to delay the immediate payoff.

3.4 Exploration and exploitation phases

The essence of Q-Learning is that the agent learns through experience without external supervision. This agent will explore from state to state, from transition to transition, until it reaches the goal. Each exploration process is known as an episode. In one episode the agent will move from initial state to another and so on until the goal state. In our case the goal state will be the execution of EE without a degradation of delivered QoS. Once the agent completes one episode it starts a new one. This exploration phase is also known as the training session. The longer the training is, the more global optimal way the agent will take the decisions. Based on the action taken, each episode includes two possible paths per each FQL instance. For the FQL instance of phase 1, first path belongs to the whole cycle *Phase 1 → Phase 2 → Phase 3 → Phase 4 → Phase 1* (i.e. in time *t* the agent decides to switch-off the candidate cell), and second one to the cycle *Phase 1 → Phase 1* (i.e. in time *t* the agent decides to not to switch-off the candidate cell). Once the agent finishes the execution of Phase 4, the reward (RW_{ph1}) is computed, the values of Q-table 1 are updated and the agent moves to Phase 1. Similarly to Phase 1, when the agent is in phase 3 and its FQL instance is used, the episode also includes two possible paths based on the action taken: first one belongs to the cycle *Phase 3 → Phase 3* (i.e. in time *t* the agent decides to not to switch-on the switched-off cell) and the second one to the cycle *Phase 3 → Phase 4 → Phase 1* (i.e. in time *t* the agent decides to switch-on the switched-off cell). In both cases, whenever the agent reaches the Phase 3 or Phase 1 the reward (RW_{ph3}) is computed and the values of Q-table 2 are updated.

In both FQL instances the exploration happens by the selection of a lower than 1 value of ε in EEP (eq. 13). The parameter is increased exponentially in each iteration. Once ε reaches the value of 1 only the exploitation iterations are present.

4. SIMULATIONS AND DISCUSSION

For the evaluation of the presented algorithm the LTE-Sim simulator has been used [11]. Two main modifications have been made in order to facilitate the interaction of our EE RAN agent with the simulated network. First one is the enhancement of the simulator in order to obtain of the algorithm input parameters, such: NAU, State Flag, State Timer and RLF (see Table 1). Second one is the implementation of a new traffic and mobility patterns. The simulated network's topology is composed of 7 cells with omnidirectional antennas. Each one has a radio range of 400 meters and 12 mobile terminals when the simulation starts. The initial transmission power is set to 23 dBm. Simulations are divided by simulation slots, each one representing a typical working day (from Monday to Friday). Users' traffic patterns (TP) are deterministic. For each simulation run we have set 7 slots (i.e. week). As it is shown in Figure 3 the TP for one slot (second 1-200) it can be differentiated three parts in terms of traffic load: two traffic peaks (90-100%) and one off-traffic peak (0-5%). The off-peak traffic represents cell's activity at night (e.g. 10 pm-6 am).

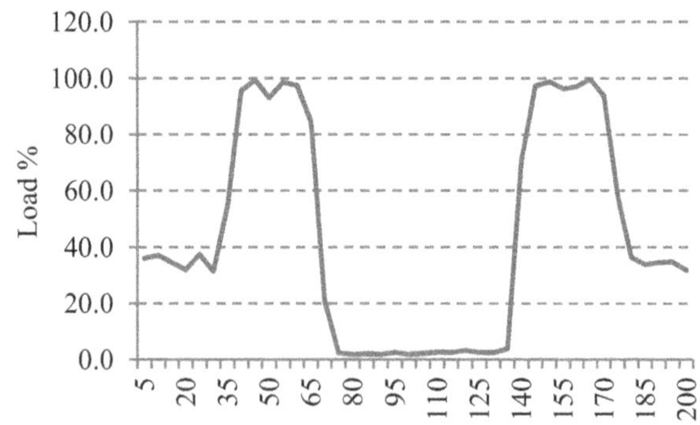

Figure 3. Users' traffic pattern

For all simulations VoIP (G.729 codec) and Video traffic models with 128Kb download transmission rate have been used. Each user receives one VoIP session and one video stream in the medium traffic intervals (approx. 0-30 and 170-200 sec.), one VoIP session in the off-peak traffic and 2 VoIP and 3 video applications at the traffic peak. User's mobility pattern is deterministic: at the peak traffic time, 90% of the users of one cell move towards some of its neighbouring cell to stay there until the time of the second traffic peak when they move back towards the initial position.

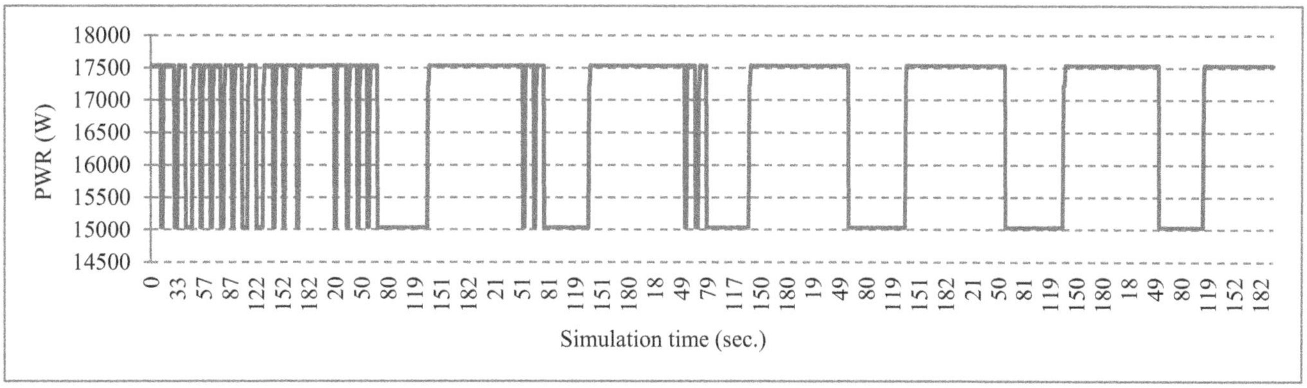

Figure 4. Power consumption for the whole network

In this way, within the simulated topology (see Fig. 1) the cell at centre would emulate the business area of a big city which usually has no users at night.

Both Q-learning instances of our algorithm (the EE RAN agents) should achieve the convergence not longer than in the first 2-3 time slots. Thus, the selection of some Q-Learning parameters (i.e. from the reward and the real-valued functions) is critical for the algorithm's convergence speed and performance. For this reason, the process of tuning of some parameters is necessary. In our case, in order to get the optimal learning parameters' values of the algorithm and robust algorithm behaviour the tuning process, which lied on changing of mutual importance of QoS parameters and learning parameters, has been very long one. The selected values of the parameters are shown in Table 4.

Table 4. Algorithm learning settings

Algorithm parameter	Parameter value
β: learning rate	0.7
γ: discount factor	0.9
ε: explotation/exploration trade-off	50% (beginning of slot 1) 100% (Slot 2-7)
W_{HF}	0.4
W_{PLR}	10.0
W_{PDL}	10.0

Table 5. Membership function thresholds

Input	a	b	c
NAU	4	12	14
AVGTHR (%)	10	50	80
QoC	0.5	0.6	0.7

Additionally, the membership functions described in equations 3-5 have been implemented using the values presented in Table 5. Algorithm performance is checked by the evaluation of the following indicators: averaged packet delay (PDL), packet loss ratio (PLR), handover failures (HF) and power consumption (PWR). Results are provided in form of charts with data changing over the simulation time (7 slots of 200 seconds each). In fact, four charts are being shown: first one shows the power consumption (in W) for the whole network, i.e. 7 cells (see Fig. 4). In this chart the EE episodes can be seen in form of down steps within the Power(t) function. The used power consumption model is described in [13]. The second, third and fourth charts (Fig. 5, 6 and 7) show the network performance via the KPIs: PDL, PLR and HOF respectively. These indicators show the network performance degradation as a consequence of the action taken by the algorithm (switch off/on the cell) when the cell is congested. If the algorithm achieves the convergence on its actions in a relatively short time, two key results are expected. First one is a decrease of switch-off events when the cell is congested while prolonging them at the time within the slot when the off-peak traffic is given. The second one is a decrease of the delivered QoS degradation along the simulation as a consequence of the less and less wrong decisions that are being taken.

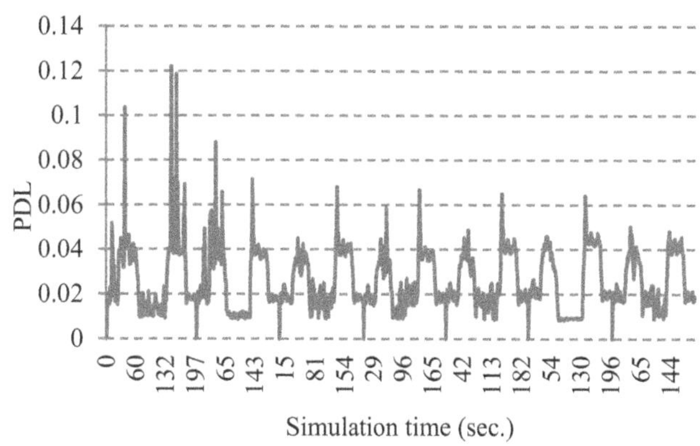

Figure 5. Averaged packet delay

Two main observations can be drawn from these charts. First one is related to the learning speed and convergence of both Q-learning instances of our agent. According to the expectations, from the third slot the agent achieves the coherence on its decisions about the proper time when a cell must enter and leave the dormant state. If we compare Fig. 4 and Fig. 3 we can see that EE episodes are aligned with the off-peak traffic interval. However, it is also noticeable that the Q-learning instance that decides about entering the dormant cell has a relatively slower learning in comparison to the instance that decides about leaving the dormant, whose convergence is achieved from second slot.

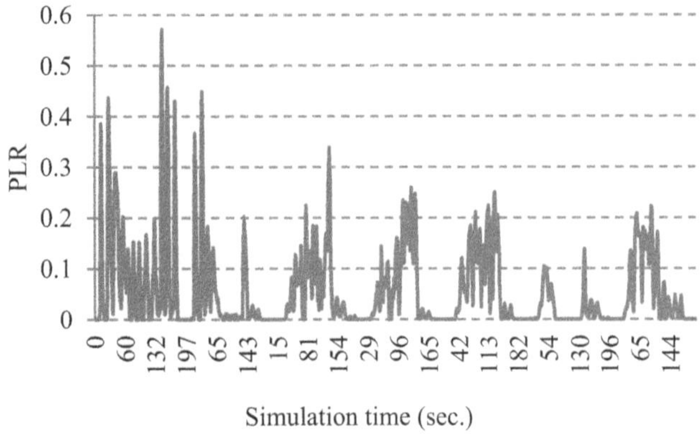

Figure 6. Packet Loss Ratio

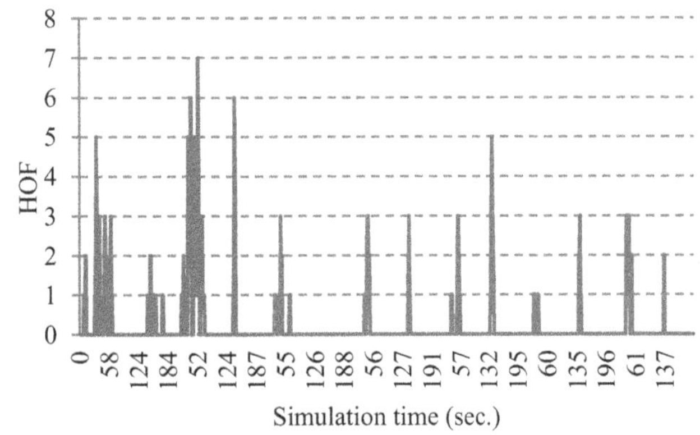

Figure 7. Handover failure

The second observation is depicted from the charts showing the network performance degradation indicators (i.e. Fig. 5-7). Here the progressive decrease of these indicators is observed. This is because of the reduction of the amount of switch-off actions during the peak traffic intervals at the time of agent's exploration.

5. CONCLUSIONS

In the paper a cognitive EE RAN approach based on machine learning has been presented. We have successfully applied the reinforcement learning to define the proper moments of switching off or on the mobile network radio stations. During simulations we have verified the proper behavior of the proposed approach via realistic simulations. In fact, the concept can be easily transferred to real networks, because it uses the network parameters that are used by real radio stations of LTE RAN as defined by 3GPP standards. Moreover, our simulations took into account all the processes which exist in real network (handovers, users' mobility, etc.). We decided to use the learning algorithm in order to have adaptive behavior of the EE RAN procedure and to avoid a design of an algorithm by an expert, however we noticed that the algorithm require a lot of efforts related to tuning it in order to obtain proper and robust behavior of the algorithm. The final result is satisfactory, but in real networks the initial learning can lead to the perceived by the users degradation of services. In the future work we intend to minimize the problem and make more simulations with differentiated users' traffic and behavior. Moreover we will use cells with directional antennas.

6. ACKNOWLEDGMENTS

The work presented in this paper has been supported by the Celtic COMMUNE project CP08-001 entitled Cognitive Network Management under Uncertainty [13]

7. REFERENCES

[1] 3GPP, "LTE; Evolved Universal Terrestrial Radio Access (E-UTRA); Potential solutions for energy saving for E-UTRAN (Release 11)", TR 36.927, 2012.

[2] 3GPP, "Technical Specification Group Services and System Aspects; Telecommunication management; Study on Energy Savings Management (ESM) (Release 10)", TR32.826, 2010.

[3] 3GPP, "Technical Specification Group Services and System Aspects; Telecommunication Management; Self-Organizing Networks (SON); Concepts and requirements (Release 10)", TS 32.500, 2010.

[4] 3GPP, "Evolved Universal Terrestrial Radio Access (E-UTRA); Layer 2 – Measurements (Release 11)", TS 36.314, 2012.

[5] 3GPP, "E-UTRA Radio Resource Control (RRC); Protocol specification (Release 11)", TS 36.331, 06.2012.

[6] 3GPP, "Evolved Universal Terrestrial Radio Access (E-UTRA); Radio Resource Control (RRC); Protocol specification (Release 12) ", TS 36.331, 03.2014.

[7] R Sutton "Reinforcement learning: An introduction" MIT Press 1998.

[8] T. J.Ross, Fuzzy logic With Engineering Applications, 2010.

[9] Mataric, M.J.: Reward functions for accelerated learning. In: Proc. of the 11th ICML. (1994) 181–189.

[10] L. Matignon et all. Reward Function and Initial Values: Better Choices for Accelerated Goal-Directed Reinforcement Learning. Artificial Neural Networks – ICANN 2006. Lecture Notes in Computer Science Volume 4131, 2006, pp 840-849.

[11] G. Piro, L. A. Grieco, G. Boggia, F. Capozzi and P. Camarda, "Simulating LTE Cellular Systems: an Open Source Framework", online, http://telematics.poliba.it/publications/2010/TVT/PiroTVT2010.pdf

[12] W. Keating, "Reducing Energy Consumption in Access Networks", August 2011. School of Electronic Engineering, Dublin City University.

[13] http://www.celtic-initiative.org/Projects/Celtic-projects/Call8/COMMUNE/commune-default.asp.

Balancing Performance, Resource Efficiency and Energy Efficiency for Virtual Machine Deployment in DVFS-enabled Clouds: An Evolutionary Game Theoretic Approach

Yi Ren
Dept. of Computer Science
University of Massachusetts
Boston, Boston, MA, USA
yiren001@cs.umb.edu

Junichi Suzuki
Dept. of Computer Science
University of Massachusetts
Boston, Boston, MA, USA
jxs@cs.umb.edu

Chonho Lee
Nanyang Technological University
Singapore
leechonho@ntu.edu.sg

Athanasios V. Vasilakos
Computer Science Dept.
Kuwait University
Safat 13060, Kuwait
th.vasilakos@gmail.com

Shingo Omura
OGIS International, Inc.
San Mateo, CA 94404, USA
omura@ogis-international.com

Katsuya Oba
OGIS International, Inc.
San Mateo, CA 94404, USA
oba@ogis-international.com

ABSTRACT

This paper proposes and evaluates a multiobjective evolutionary game theoretic framework for adaptive and stable application deployment in clouds that support dynamic voltage and frequency scaling (DVFS) for CPUs. The proposed framework, called Cielo, aids cloud operators to adapt the resource allocation to applications and their locations according to the operational conditions in a cloud (e.g., workload and resource availability) with respect to multiple conflicting objectives such as response time performance, recourse utilization and power consumption. Moreover, Cielo theoretically guarantees that each application performs an evolutionarily stable deployment strategy, which is an equilibrium solution under given operational conditions. Simulation results verify this theoretical analysis; applications seek equilibria to perform adaptive and evolutionarily stable deployment strategies. Cielo allows applications to successfully leverage DVFS to balance their response time performance, resource utilization and power consumption.

Categories and Subject Descriptors

I.2.8 [**Artificial Intelligence**]: Problem Solving, Control Methods, and Search—*Heuristic methods*; C.2.4 [**Computer-Communication Networks**]: Distributed Systems—*Distributed applications*

Keywords

Cloud computing, power-aware virtual machine placement, multiobjective optimization, evolutionary game theory

GECCO'14, July 12–16, 2014, Vancouver, BC, Canada.

ACM 978-1-4503-2881-4/14/07 ...$15.00.
http://dx.doi.org/10.1145/2598394.2605693.

1. INTRODUCTION

It is a challenging issue for cloud operators to deploy applications so that the applications can keep expected levels of performance (e.g. response time) while maintaining their utilization of resources (e.g. CPUs and bandwidth) and power consumption. In order to ensure these requirements, they are required to dynamically (re-)deploy applications by adjusting their locations and resource allocation according to various operational conditions such as workload and resource availability. This paper investigates two important properties of application deployment in clouds:

- *Adaptability*: Adjusting the locations of and resource allocation for applications according to operational conditions with respect to given objectives.
- *Stability*: Minimizing oscillations (non-deterministic inconsistencies) in making adaptation decisions.

Cielo is an evolutionary game theoretic framework for adaptive and stable application deployment in clouds that support dynamic voltage and frequency scaling (DVFS) for CPUs. This paper describes its design and evaluates its adaptability and stability. In Cielo, each application maintains a set (or a population) of deployment strategies, each of which indicates the location of and resource allocation for that application. Cielo theoretically guarantees that, through a series of evolutionary games between deployment strategies, the population state (i.e., the distribution of strategies) converges to an evolutionarily stable equilibrium, which is always converged to regardless of the initial state. (A dominant strategy in the evolutionarily stable population state is called an *evolutionarily stable strategy*.) In this state, no other strategies except an evolutionarily stable strategy can dominate the population. Given this theoretical property, Cielo aids each application to operate at equilibria by using an evolutionarily stable strategy for application deployment in a deterministic (i.e., stable) manner.

Simulation results verify this theoretical analysis; applications seek equilibria to perform evolutionarily stable deployment strategies and adapt their locations and resource allocations to given operational conditions. Cielo allows applications to successfully leverage DVFS to balance their response time performance, resource utilization and power consumption. In comparison to existing heuristics, Cielo outperforms a well-known multiobjective genetic algorithm, NSGA-II [4], while maintaining 74% less computational cost. It also exhibits 29% higher stability (lower oscillations) among different simulation runs than NSGA-II. Moreover, Cielo outperforms first-fit and best-fit algorithms (FFA and BFA), which have been widely used for adaptive cloud application deployment [1, 7, 15, 16].

2. PROBLEM STATEMENT

This section formulates an application deployment problem where M hosts are available to operate N applications. Each application is designed with three-tiered servers (Fig. 1). Using a certain hypervisor, each server is assumed to run on a virtual machine (VM) atop a host. A host can run multiple VMs. They share resources available on their local host.

Each message is sequentially processed from a Web server to a database server through an application server. A reply message is generated by the database server and forwarded in the reverse order (Fig. 1). This paper assumes that different applications utilize different sets of servers. (Servers are not shared by different applications.)

The goal of this problem is to find evolutionarily stable strategies that deploy N applications (i.e., $N \times 3$ VMs) on M hosts so that the applications adapt their locations and resource allocation to given workload and resource availability with respect to five objectives described below. (All objectives are to be minimized.)

CPU allocation: A certain CPU time share (in percentage) is allocated to each VM. (The CPU share of 100% means that a CPU is fully allocated to a VM.) It represents the upper limit for the VM's CPU utilization. This objective is computed as $\sum_{t=1}^{3} c_t$ where c_t denotes the CPU time share allocated to the t-th tier server in an application.

Bandwidth allocation: A certain amount of bandwidth (in bits/second) is allocated to each VM. It is the upper limit for the VM's bandwidth consumption. This objective is computed as $\sum_{t=1}^{3} b_t$ where b_t denotes the bandwidth allocated to the t-th tier server in an application.

Response time: This objective is indicated as the time required for a message to travel from a web server to a database server: $T^p + T^w + T^c$ where T^p denotes the total time for an application to process an incoming message from a user at three servers, T^w denotes the waiting time for a message to be processed at servers, and T^c denotes the total communication delay to transmit a message among servers. T^p, T^w and T^c are estimated with the $M/M/1$ queuing model, in which message arrivals follow a Poisson process and a server's message processing time is exponentially distributed.

T^p is computed as follows where T^p_t denotes the time required for the t-th tier server to process a message.

$$T^p = \sum_{t=1}^{3} T^p_t \qquad (1)$$

T^w is computed as follows.

$$T^w = \frac{1}{\lambda} \sum_{t=1}^{3} \frac{\rho_t^2}{1-\rho_t} \quad \text{where } \rho_t = \lambda_t \frac{T^p_t}{c_t \frac{f_t}{f_{max}}} \qquad (2)$$

λ is the message arrival rate for an application (i.e., the number of messages the application receives from users in the unit time). $\lambda = \frac{1}{3}\sum_{t=1}^{3} \lambda_t$. (Currently, $\lambda = \lambda_1 = \lambda_2 = \lambda_3$.) ρ_t is the CPU utilization of the t-th tier server. f_{max} and f_t are the maximum CPU frequency and the CPU frequency of a host that the t-th tier server resides on.

T^c is computed as follows where B is the size of a message (in bits).

$$T^c = \sum_{t=1}^{2} T^c_{t \to t'} \approx \sum_{t'=2}^{3} \frac{B \cdot \lambda_{t'}}{b_t}, \quad t' = t+1 \qquad (3)$$

Power Consumption: This objective indicates the total power consumption (in W) by the hosts that operate three VMs in an application.

$$\sum_{t=1}^{3} \{P^{f_t}_{idle} + (P^{f_t}_{max} - P^{f_t}_{idle}) \cdot c_t \cdot \frac{f_t}{t_{max}}\} \qquad (4)$$

$P^{f_t}_{idle}$ and $P^{f_t}_{max}$ denote the power consumption of a host that the t-th tier server resides on when its CPU utilization is 0% and 100% at the frequency of f_t, respectively.

Cielo considers a CPU capacity constraint: $w_i \leq 1$ for all M hosts. w_i is the total CPU share allocated to the i-th host. The violation of this constraint is computed as:

$$c^v = \sum_{i=1}^{M} (I_i \cdot (w_i - 1)) \qquad (5)$$

$I_i = 1$ if $w_i > 1$. Otherwise, $I_i = 0$.

Cielo also considers a bandwidth capacity constraint: $y_i \leq 1$ for all M hosts. y_i is the total bandwidth allocated to the i-th host (in percentage). The violation of bandwidth constraint is computed as:

$$b^v = \sum_{i=1}^{M} (I_i \cdot (y_i - 1)) \qquad (6)$$

$I_i = 1$ if $y_i > 1$. Otherwise, $I_i = 0$.

Figure 1: Three Tiers of Web, Application and Database Servers

3. EVOLUTIONARY GAME THEORY

In a conventional game, the objective of a player is to choose a strategy that maximizes its payoff. In contrast, evolutionary games are played repeatedly by players randomly drawn from a population. This section overviews key elements in evolutionary games: evolutionarily stable strategies (ESS) and replicator dynamics.

3.1 Evolutionarily Stable Strategies (ESS)

Suppose all players in the initial population are programmed to play a certain (incumbent) strategy k. Then, let a small population share of players, $x \in (0,1)$, mutate and play a different (mutant) strategy ℓ. When a player is drawn for a game, the probabilities that its opponent plays k and ℓ are $1-x$ and x, respectively. Thus, the expected payoffs for the player to play k and ℓ are denoted as $U(k, x\ell + (1-x)k)$ and $U(\ell, x\ell + (1-x)k)$, respectively.

DEFINITION 1. *A strategy k is said to be evolutionarily stable if, for every strategy $\ell \neq k$, a certain $\bar{x} \in (0,1)$ exists, such that the inequality*

$$U(k,\ x\ell + (1-x)k) > U(\ell,\ x\ell + (1-x)k) \qquad (7)$$

holds for all $x \in (0, \bar{x})$.

If the payoff function is linear, Equation 7 derives:

$$(1-x)U(k,k) + xU(k,\ell) > (1-x)U(\ell,k) + xU(\ell,\ell) \quad (8)$$

If x is close to zero, Equation 8 derives either

$$U(k,k) > U(\ell,k) \text{ or } U(k,k) = U(\ell,k) \text{ and } U(k,\ell) > U(\ell,\ell) \quad (9)$$

This indicates that a player associated with the strategy k gains a higher payoff than the ones associated with the other strategies. Therefore, no players can benefit by changing their strategies from k to the others. This means that an ESS is a solution on a Nash equilibrium. An ESS is a strategy that cannot be invaded by any alternative (mutant) strategies that have lower population shares.

3.2 Replicator Dynamics

The replicator dynamics describes how population shares associated with different strategies evolve over time [20]. Let $\lambda_k(t) \geq 0$ be the number of players who play the strategy $k \in K$, where K is the set of available strategies. The total population of players is given by $\lambda(t) = \sum_{k=1}^{|K|} \lambda_k(t)$. Let $x_k(t) = \lambda_k(t)/\lambda(t)$ be the population share of players who play k at time t. The population state is defined by $X(t) = [x_1(t), \cdots, x_k(t), \cdots, x_K(t)]$. Given X, the expected payoff of playing k is denoted by $U(k, X)$. The population's average payoff, which is same as the payoff of a player drawn randomly from the population, is denoted by $U(X, X) = \sum_{k=1}^{|K|} x_k \cdot U(k, X)$. In the replicator dynamics, the dynamics of the population share x_k is described as follows. $\dot{x}_k$ is the time derivative of x_k.

$$\dot{x}_k = x_k \cdot [U(k, X) - U(X, X)] \quad (10)$$

This equation states that players increase (or decrease) their population shares when their payoffs are higher (or lower) than the population's average payoff.

THEOREM 1. *If a strategy k is strictly dominated, then* $x_k(t)_{t\to\infty} \to 0$.

A strategy is said to be strictly dominant if its payoff is strictly higher than any opponents. As its population share grows, it dominates the population over time. Conversely, a strategy is said to be strictly dominated if its payoff is lower than that of a strictly dominant strategy. Thus, strictly dominated strategies disappear in the population over time.

There is a close connection between Nash equilibria and the steady states in the replicator dynamics, in which the population shares do not change over time. Since no players change their strategies on Nash equilibria, every Nash equilibrium is a steady state in the replicator dynamics. As described in Section 3.1, an ESS is a solution on a Nash equilibrium. Thus, an ESS is a solution at a steady state in the replicator dynamics. In other words, an ESS is the strictly dominant strategy in the population on a steady state.

Cielo maintains a population of deployment strategies for each application. In each population, strategies are randomly drawn to play games repeatedly until the population state reaches a steady state. Then, Cielo identifies a strictly dominant strategy in the population and deploys VMs based on the strategy as an ESS.

4. CIELO

Cielo maintains N populations, $\{\mathcal{P}_1, \mathcal{P}_2, ..., \mathcal{P}_N\}$, for N applications and performs games among strategies in each population. A strategy s is defined to indicate the locations of and resource allocation for three VMs in an application:

$$s(a_i) = \bigcup_{t \in 1,2,3} (h_{i,t}, c_{i,t}, b_{i,t}, f_{i,t}), \quad 1 < i < N \quad (11)$$

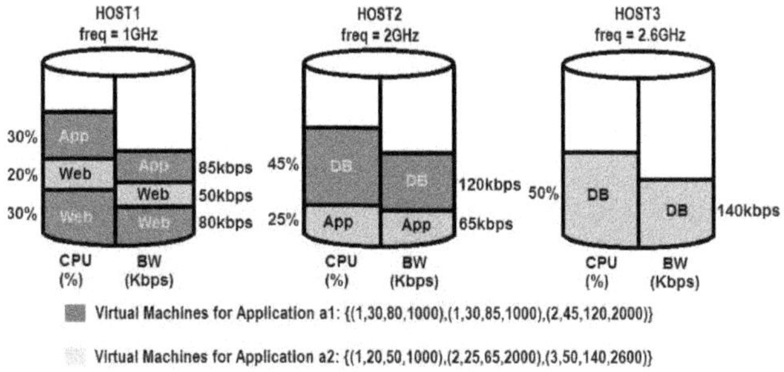

Figure 2: Example Deployment Strategies

a_i denotes the i-th application. $h_{i,t}$ is the ID of a host that operates a_i's t-th tier VM. $c_{i,t}$ and $b_{i,t}$ are the CPU and bandwidth allocation for a_i's t-th tier VM. $f_{i,t}$ denotes the CPU frequency of host $h_{i,t}$. Fig. 2 shows two example strategies for two applications (a_1 and a_2) ($N = 2$ and $M = 3$). a_1's strategy ($s(a_1)$) places the first-tier VM on host 1 ($h_{1,1} = 1$), which operates at 1 GHz CPU frequency and consumes 30% CPU share and 80 Kbps bandwidth for the VM ($c_{1,1} = 30$ and $b_{1,1} = 80$). The second-tier VM is placed on host 1 ($h_{1,2} = 1$), which consumes 30% CPU share and 85 Kbps bandwidth for the VM ($c_{1,2} = 30$ and $b_{1,2} = 85$). The third-tier VM is placed on host 2 ($h_{1,3} = 2$), which operates at 2 GHz CPU frequency and consumes 45% CPU share and 120 Kbps bandwidth for the VM ($c_{1,3} = 45$ and $b_{1,3} = 120$). Given $s(a_1)$, a_1's objective values for CPU allocation and bandwidth allocation are 105% (30 + 30 + 45) and 285 kbps (80 + 85 + 120).

Algorithm 1 Evolutionary Process in Cielo

```
1: g = 0
2: Randomly generate the initial N populations for N applications: P = {P_1, P_2, ..., P_N}
3: while g < G_max do
4:   for each population P_i randomly selected from P do
5:     P'_i ← ∅
6:     for j = 1 to |P_i|/2 do
7:       s_1 ← randomlySelect(P_i)
8:       s_2 ← randomlySelect(P_i)
9:       winner ← performGame(s_1, s_2)
10:      replica ← replicate(winner)
11:      if random() ≤ P_m then
12:        replica ← mutate(winner)
13:      end if
14:      P_i \ {s_1, s_2}
15:      P'_i ∪ {winner, replica}
16:    end for
17:    P_i ← P'_i
18:    d_i ← argmax_{s∈P_i} x_s
19:    while d_i is infeasible do
20:      P_i \ {d_i}
21:      d_i ← argmax_{s∈P_i} x_s
22:    end while
23:    Deploy VMs for the current application based on d_i.
24:  end for
25:  g = g + 1
26: end while
```

Algorithm 1 shows how Cielo seeks an evolutionarily stable strategy for each application through evolutionary games. In the 0-th generation, strategies are randomly generated for each population (Line 2). In each generation (g), a series of games are carried out on every population (Lines 4 to 24). A single game randomly chooses a pair of strategies (s_1 and s_2) and distinguishes them to the winner and the loser with respect to the objectives described in Section 2 (Lines 7 to 9). The loser disappears in the population. The winner is replicated to increase its population share and mutated with a certain rate P_m (Lines 10 to 15). Mutation randomly chooses one of three VMs in the winner and alters its $h_{i,t}$, $c_{i,t}$ and $b_{i,t}$ values at random (Line 12).

Once all strategies play games in the population, Cielo identifies a *feasible* strategy whose population share (x_s) is the highest and determines it as a dominant strategy (d_i) (Lines 18 to 22). A strategy is said to be feasible if it never violate the CPU and bandwidth capacity constraints ($c^v = 0$ in Eq. 5 and $b^v = 0$ in Eq. 6). It is said to be infeasible if $c^v > 0$ or $b^v > 0$. Cielo deploys three VMs for an application in question based on the dominant strategy.

In `performGame()` (Algorithm 1), the selection of a winner depends on the *dominance* relationship between given two strategies and their feasibility. A strategy s_1 is said to dominate another strategy s_2 (denoted by $s_i \succ s_j$) iif:

- s_1's objective values are superior than, or equal to, s_2's in all objectives, and
- s_1's objective values are superior than s_2's in at least one objectives.

A strategy s_1 is said to win over another strategy s_2 if:

- s_1 is feasible and s_2 is infeasible.
- Both s_1 and s_2 are feasible, and $s_1 \succ s_2$.
- Both s_1 and s_2 are infeasible, and s_1's constraint violation is lower than s_2's ($c^v_{s_1} + b^v_{s_1} < c^v_{s_2} + b^v_{s_2}$).

5. STABILITY ANALYSIS

This section analyzes Cielo's stability (i.e., reachability to at least one of Nash equilibria) by proving the state of each population converges to an evolutionarily stable equilibrium. The proof consists of three steps: (1) designing differential equations that describe the dynamics of the population state, (2) proving an strategy selection process has equilibria, and (3) proving the the equilibria are asymptotically (or evolutionarily) stable. The proof uses the following terms and variables.

- S denotes the set of available strategies. S^* denotes a set of strategies that appear in the population.
- $X(t) = \{x_1(t), x_2(t), \cdots, x_{|S^*|}(t)\}$ denotes a population state at time t where $x_s(t)$ is the population share of a strategy $s \in S$. $\sum_{s\in S^*}(x_s) = 1$.
- F_s is the fitness of a strategy s. It is a relative value determined in a game against an opponent based on the dominance relationship between them. The winner of a game earns a higher fitness than the loser.
- $p^s_k = x_k \cdot \phi(F_s - F_k)$ denotes the probability that a strategy s is replicated by winning a game against another strategy k. $\phi(F_s - F_k)$ is the probability that the fitness of s is higher than that of k.

The dynamics of the population share of s is described as:

$$\begin{aligned} \dot{x}_s &= \sum_{k\in S^*, k\neq s} \{x_s p^s_k - x_k p^k_s\} \\ &= x_s \sum_{k\in S^*, k\neq s} x_k\{\phi(F_s - F_k) - \phi(F_k - F_s)\} \end{aligned} \quad (12)$$

Note that if s is strictly dominated, $x_s(t)_{t\to\infty} \to 0$.

THEOREM 2. *The state of a population converges to an equilibrium.*

PROOF. It is true that different strategies have different fitness values. In other words, only one strategy has the highest fitness among others. Given Theorem 1, assuming that $F_1 > F_2 > \cdots > F_{|S^*|}$, the population state converges to an equilibrium: $X(t)_{t\to\infty} = \{x_1(t), x_2(t), \cdots, x_{|S^*|}(t)\}_{t\to\infty} = \{1, 0, \cdots, 0\}$. □

THEOREM 3. *The equilibrium found in Theorem 2 is asymptotically stable.*

PROOF. At the equilibrium $X = \{1, 0, \cdots, 0\}$, a set of differential equations can be downsized by substituting $x_1 = 1 - x_2 - \cdots - x_{|S^*|}$

$$\dot{z}_s = z_s[c_{s1}(1 - z_s) + \sum_{i=2, i\neq s}^{|s^*|} z_i \cdot c_{si}], \quad s, k = 2, ..., |S^*| \quad (13)$$

where $c_{sk} \equiv \phi(F_s - F_k) - \phi(F_k - F_s)$ and $Z(t) = \{z_2(t), z_3(t), \cdots, z_{|S^*|}(t)\}$ denotes the corresponding downsized population state. Given Theorem 1, $Z_{t\to\infty} = Z_{eq} = \{0, 0, \cdots, 0\}$ of ($|S^*| - 1$)-dimension.

If all Eigenvalues of Jaccobian matrix of $Z(t)$ has negative real parts, Z_{eq} is asymptotically stable. The Jaccobian matrix J's elements are

$$\begin{aligned} J_{sk} &= \left[\frac{\partial \dot{z}_s}{\partial z_k}\right]_{|Z=Z_{eq}} \\ &= \left[\frac{\partial z_s[c_{s1}(1 - z_s) + \sum_{i=2, i\neq s}^{|S^*|} z_i \cdot c_{si}]}{\partial z_k}\right]_{|Z=Z_{eq}} \\ & \quad for\ s, k = 2, ..., |S^*| \end{aligned} \quad (14)$$

Therefore, J is given as follows, where $c_{21}, c_{31}, \cdots, c_{|S^*|1}$ are J's Eigenvalues.

$$J = \begin{bmatrix} c_{21} & 0 & \cdots & 0 \\ 0 & c_{31} & \cdots & 0 \\ \vdots & \vdots & \ddots & \vdots \\ 0 & 0 & \cdots & c_{|S^*|1} \end{bmatrix} \quad (15)$$

$c_{s1} = -\phi(F_1 - F_s) < 0$ for all s; therefore, $Z_{eq} = \{0, 0, \cdots, 0\}$ is asymptotically stable. □

6. SIMULATION EVALUATION

This section evaluates Cielo's adaptability and stability through simulations. This paper uses a simulated cloud data center that consists of 100 hosts in a 10×10 grid topology ($M = 100$). The grid topology is chosen based on recent findings on efficient topology configurations in clouds [8, 9]. This paper also assumes five types of applications. Table 1 shows the message arrival rate (the number of incoming messages per second) and message processing time (second) for each of the five application types. This configuration follows Zipf's law. This paper simulates 40 application instances for each type (200 application instances in total; $N = 200$).

Table 1: Message Arrival Rate and Message Processing Time

Application type	1	2	3	4	5
Message arrival rate (λ)	110	70	40	20	10
Web server (T^p_1)	0.02	0.02	0.04	0.04	0.08
App server (T^p_2)	0.03	0.08	0.04	0.13	0.11
DB server (T^p_3)	0.05	0.05	0.12	0.08	0.11

This paper assumes each host is equipped with an AMD Opteron 2218 CPU, which has six frequency and voltage operating points (P-states). Table 2 shows the power consumption at each P-state under the 0% and 100% CPU utilization [10, 17]. This setting is used in Eq. 4 to compute power consumption objective values.

In Cielo, the number of strategies is 100 in each population. Mutation rate (P_m in Algorithm 1) is set to 0.01. The maximum number of generations (G_{max} in Algorithm 1) is set to 400. Every simulation result is the average with 20 independent simulation runs.

Table 2: P-states in AMD Opteron 2218

CPU frequency (f)	P^f_{idle}	P^f_{max}
1.0 GHz	34 W	68 W
1.8 GHz	51 W	80 W
2.0 GHz	55 W	84 W
2.2 GHz	66 W	89 W
2.4 GHz	90 W	97 W
2.6 GHz	96 W	108 W

Figs. 3 to 9 illustrate how Cielo evolves deployment strategies through generations and improve their objective values with respect to a given objective(s). Figs. 3 to 6 show the changes of objective values over generations when one of four objectives is considered. For example, Cielo considers the CPU allocation objective in Fig. 3.

In Fig. 3, CPU allocation decreases through generations because it is considered as the objective. Its average reaches 17.6% in the last generation, which is the best performance among Figs. 3a, 4a, 5a and 6a. The other objective values do not improve because they are not considered.

In Fig. 4, bandwidth allocation improves over time because it is considered as the objective. Its average reaches 185 Kbps in the last generation. This is the best performance among Figs. 3c, 4c, 5c and 6c. The improvement in bandwidth allocation contributes to the increase of response time because these two objectives conflict with each other.

In Fig. 5, response time improves over time because it is considered as the objective. Its average reaches 440 miliseconds in the last generation, which is the best result among Figs. 3b, 4b, 5b and 6b. As response time decreases, bandwidth allocation and power consumption increases because they are conflicting with each other.

In Fig. 6, power consumption decreases over time because it is considered as the objective. Its average reaches 150 W in the last generation, which is the best performance among Figs. 3d, 4d, 5d and 6d. For reducing power consumption, Cielo attempts to collocate as many VMs as possible on some hosts and turn off the other hosts that operate no VMs. It also attempts to run hosts at lower CPU frequencies. Fig. 10 confirms this analysis. It shows the number of hosts at each P-state in the last generation. With power consumption considered, 32 hosts are turned-off (indicated as 0 GHz), and 33 hosts run at the lowest P-state (1 GHz). Only four hosts run at the highest P-state (2.6 GHz). In Figs. 6 and 10 demonstrate that Cielo successfully leverage DVFS to reduce power consumption. Note that response time increases as power consumption decreases because they are conflicting.

Figs. 3 to 6 demonstrate that Cielo successfully evolves deployment strategies so that applications improve their objective values with respect to a given objective(s).

In Figs. 7 and 8, two objectives are considered simultaneously. All objectives are considered simultaneously in Fig. 9. As these figures show, Cielo successfully balance objective values by following the trade-offs among given objectives.

Table 3 compares Cielo with a well-known evolutionary multiobjective genetic algorithm, NSGA-II [4][1], as well as existing heuristics, FFA (first-fit algorithm) and BFA (best-fit algorithm), which have been widely used for VM placement in clouds [1, 7, 15, 16]. The table shows the minimum, average and maximum objective values in the last generation. In all objectives, Cielo outperforms NSGA-II. The largest difference is in the minimum bandwidth allocation with DVFS disabled (40%), and the smallest difference is in the maximum response time with DVFS enabled (16.60%). On average, Cielo outperforms NSGA-II by 24.19%. With DVFS disabled, FFA yields the lowest power consumption because it is designed to deploy VMs on the minimum number of hosts; however, it sacrifices the other objectives. BFA is the best in CPU allocation and the worst in power consumption because it is designed to deploy VMs on the hosts that maintain higher resource availability. With all five objectives considered, Cielo maintains balanced objective values in between FFA and BFA while yielding the best performance in response time and bandwidth allocation.

Table 4 shows the variance of objective values that Cielo and NSGA-II yield at the last generation in 20 different simulation runs. A lower variance means higher stability (or higher similarity) in objective value results (i.e., lower oscillation in objective value results) among different simulation runs. Cielo consistently maintains higher stability than NSGA-II. Cielo's average stability is 29.32% higher than NSGA-II's. This result exhibits Cielo's stability property (i.e. ability to seek evolutionarily stable strategies), which NSGA-II does not have.

Fig. 11 shows the time required for Cielo and NSGA-II to execute given numbers of generations. Simulations were carried out with a Java VM 1.7 on a Windows 8.1 PC with a 3.6 GHz AMD A6-5400K APU and 6 GB memory space. For running a single simulation (i.e., 400 generations), Cielo is 74.1% faster than NSGA-II.

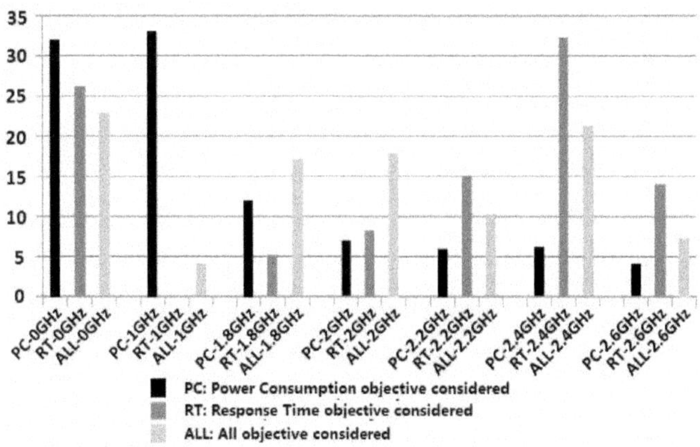

Figure 10: # of hosts at each P-state in the last generation

7. RELATED WORK

Numerous research efforts have been made to study heuristic algorithms for application placement problems in clouds (e.g., [1,3,7,13,15,16,21,23]). Most of them assume single-tier application architecture and considers a single objective. For example, in [3,13,21,23], only energy saving is considered

[1]NSGA-II and Cielo use the same population size and the same limit of generations. All other configurations are borrowed from [4].

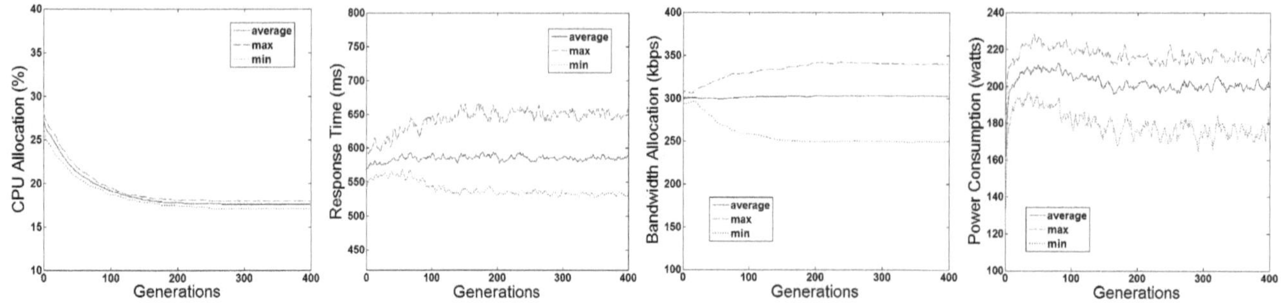

(a) CPU allocation (b) Response time (c) Bandwidth allocation (d) Power consumption

Figure 3: Configuration C_1: With the CPU Allocation Objective Considered

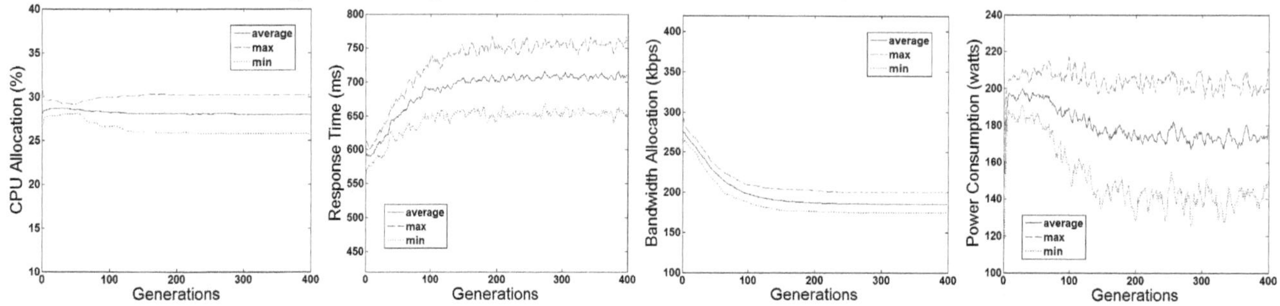

(a) CPU allocation (b) Response time (c) Bandwidth allocation (d) Power consumption

Figure 4: Configuration C_2: With the Bandwidth Allocation Objective Considered

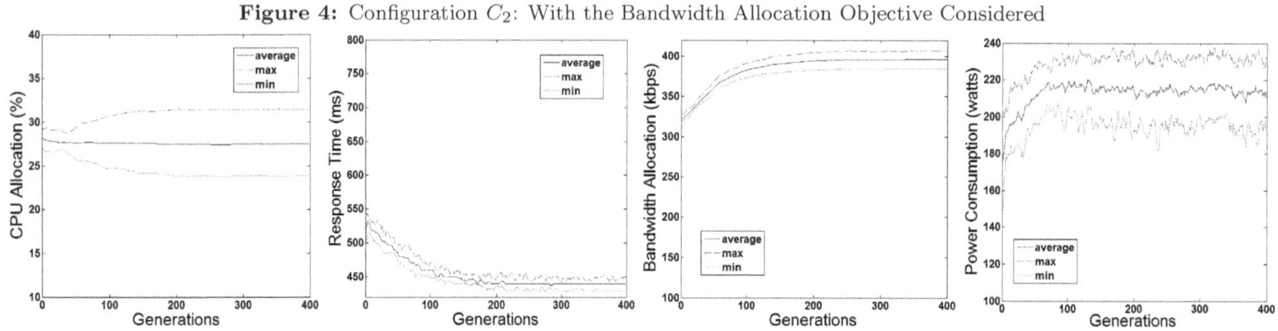

(a) CPU allocation (b) Response time (c) Bandwidth allocation (d) Power consumption

Figure 5: Configuration C_3: With the Response Time Objective Considered

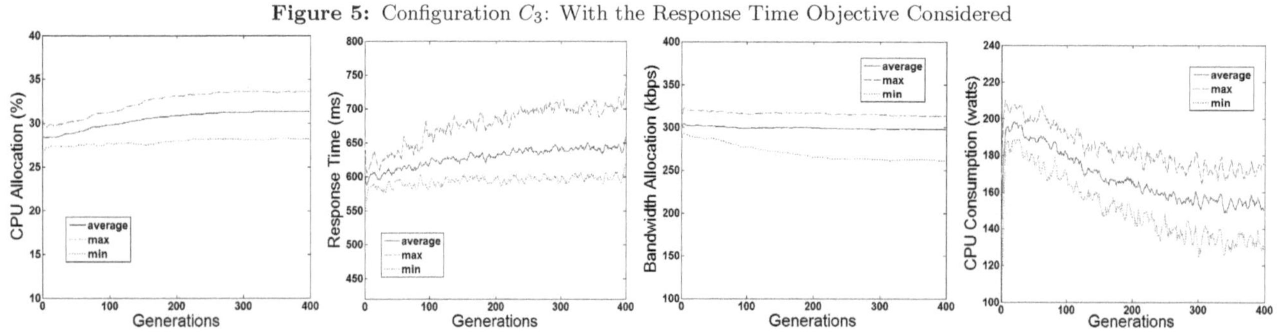

(a) CPU allocation (b) Response time (c) Bandwidth allocation (d) Power consumption

Figure 6: Configuration C_4: With the Power Consumption Objective Considered

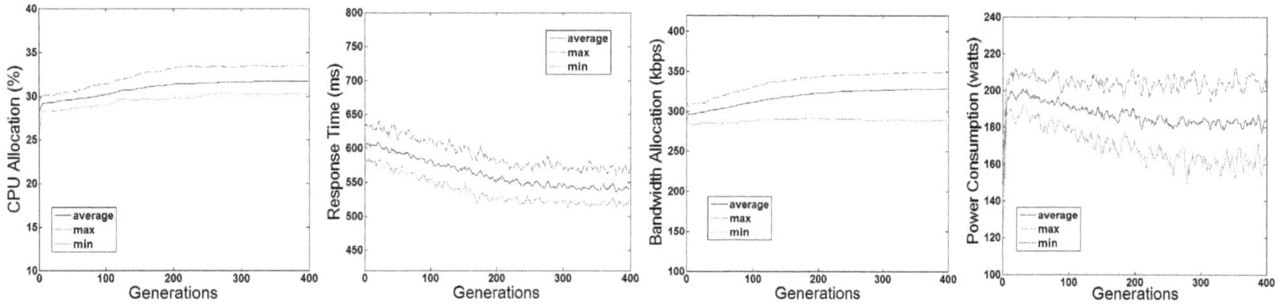

(a) CPU allocation (b) Response time (c) Bandwidth allocation (d) Power consumption

Figure 7: Configuration C_5: With the Response Time and Power Consumption Objectives Considered

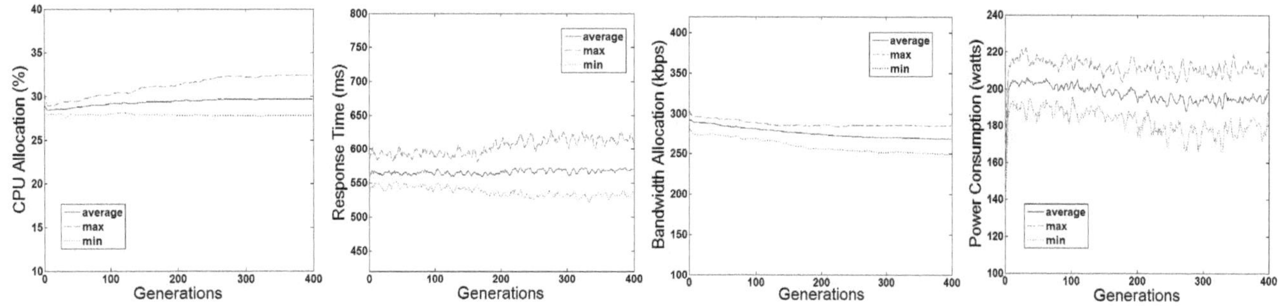

(a) CPU allocation (b) Response time (c) Bandwidth allocation (d) Power consumption

Figure 8: Configuration C_6: With the Response Time and Bandwidth Allocation Objectives Considered

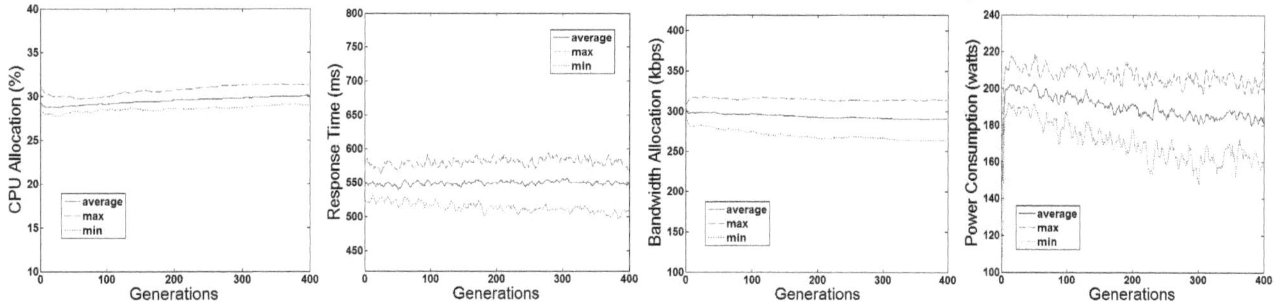

(a) CPU allocation (b) Response time (c) Bandwidth allocation (d) Power consumption

Figure 9: Configuration C_7: With All Four Objectives Considered

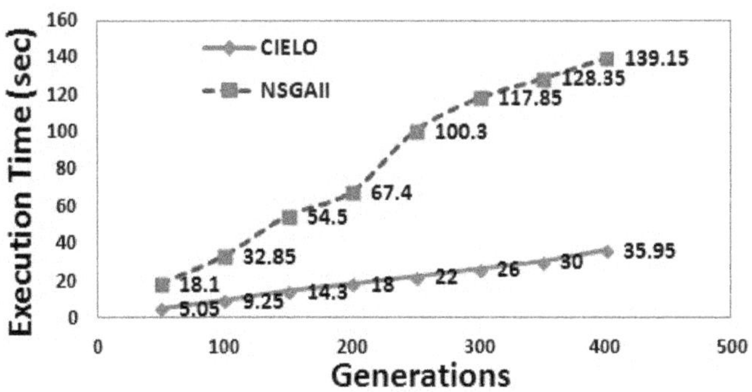

Figure 11: Computational Costs for Cielo and NSGA-II

as the objective. In contrast, Cielo assumes a multi-tier application architecture and considers multiple objectives. It is intended to reveal the trade-off relationships among conflicting objectives.

Game theoretic algorithms have been used for a few aspects of cloud computing; e.g., application placement [5, 12, 24], task allocation [18] and data replication [11]. In [5, 12, 24], greedy algorithms seek equilibria in application placement problems. This means they do not attain the stability to reach equilibria as Cielo does.

Several genetic algorithms (e.g., [19,22]) and other stochastic optimization algorithms (e.g., [2,6]) have been studied to solve application placement problems in clouds. They seek the optimal placement solutions; however, they do not consider stability. In contrast, Cielo aids applications to seek evolutionarily stable solutions and stay at equilibria.

This paper reports a set of extensions to the authors' prior work [14]. For the problem formulation, this paper considers two extra objectives (bandwidth allocation and power consumption) and an extra parameter in each deployment strategy (bandwidth allocation), all of which are not studied in [14]. This paper also considers constraints in CPU and bandwidth allocation and investigates a constraint-handling algorithm (Section 4), while no constraints are assumed in [14]. Moreover, this paper carries out larger-scale simulations with

Table 3: Performance of Cielo, NSGA-II, FFA and BFA

Objectives		Min	Avg	Max
Power consumption (W)	Cielo w/ DVFS	4,370	5,000	5,830
	Cielo w/o DVFS	8,806	9,090	9,280
	NSGA-II w/ DVFS	6,143	6,643	6,960
	NSGA-II w/o DVFS	10,032	10,033	10,036
	FFA w/o DVFS	4,380	4,380	4,381
	BFA w/o DVFS	10,090	10,103	10,127
CPU allocation (%/host)	Cielo w/ DVFS	68.4	70.4	72
	Cielo w/o DVFS	65.6	68.8	71.6
	NSGA-II w/ DVFS	85.5	86.1	86.4
	NSGA-II w/o DVFS	83.4	84.9	85.8
	FFA w/o DVFS	96.9	96.9	96.9
	BFA w/o DVFS	40.65	40.65	40.65
Bandwidth allocation (kbps/host)	Cielo w/ DVFS	430	440	450
	Cielo w/o DVFS	420	420	430
	NSGA-II w/ DVFS	530	540	550
	NSGA-II w/o DVFS	520	530	530
	FFA w/o DVFS	290	290	290
	BFA w/o DVFS	305	305	305
Response time (msec)	Cielo w/ DVFS	174.9	185.51	200.15
	Cielo w/o DVFS	172.21	190	204
	NSGA-II w/ DVFS	282.3	287	290.6
	NSGA-II w/o DVFS	287	289.37	290.75
	FFA w/o DVFS	206	206	206
	BFA w/o DVFS	203.75	203.75	203.75

Table 4: Stability of Objective Values in Cielo and NSGA-II

Objectives	Cielo	NSGA-II	Diff (%)
Power consumption (W)	150	199.3	24.73
CPU allocation (%)	17.6	28.7	38.67
Response time (ms)	440	540	18.51
Bandwidth allocation (kbps)	185.51	287.08	35.38
Average Difference (%)			29.32

more realistic configurations than [14], which uses only five hosts and simple topologies among them on a cloud that never support DVFS.

8. CONCLUSIONS

This paper proposes and evaluates Cielo, an evolutionary game theoretic framework for adaptive and stable application deployment in DVFS-enabled clouds. It theoretically guarantees that every application seeks an evolutionarily stable deployment strategy, which is an equilibrium solution under given workload and resource availability. Simulation results verify that Cielo performs application deployment in an adaptive and stable manner. Cielo outperforms existing well-known heuristics in the quality, stability and computational cost of application deployment.

9. REFERENCES

[1] H. Casanova, M. Stillwell, and F. Vivien. Virtual machine resource allocation for service hosting on heterogeneous distributed platforms. In *Proc. IEEE Int'l Parallel & Distributed Processing Symposium*, 2012.

[2] X. Chang, B. Wang, L. Jiqiang, W. Wang, and K. Muppala. Green cloud virtual network provisioning based ant colony optimization. In *Proc. ACM Int'l Conference on Genetic and Evol. Computat*, 2013.

[3] S. Chen, K. R. Joshi, M. A. Hiltunen, R. D. Schlichting, and W. H. Sanders. Blackbox prediction of the impact of DVFS on end-to-end performance of multitier systems. *ACM SIGMETRICS Performance Eval. Rev.*, 37(4), 2010.

[4] K. Deb, S. Agrawal, A. Pratab, and T. Meyarivan. A fast elitist non-dominated sorting genetic algorithm for multi-objective optimization: NSGA-II. In *Proc. Conf. Parallel Problem Solving from Nature*, 2000.

[5] N. Doulamis, A. Doulamis, A. Litke, A. Panagakis, T. Varvarigou, and E. Varvarigos. Adjusted fair scheduling and non-linear workload prediction for QoS guarantees in grid computing. *Elsevier Computer Comm.*, 30(3), 2007.

[6] Y. Gao, H. Guan, Z. Qi, Y. Hou, and L. Liu. A multi-objective ant colony system algorithm for virtual machine placement in cloud computing. *J. Computer and System Sciences*, 79(8), 2013.

[7] H. Goudarzi and M. Pedram. Energy-efficient virtual machine replication and placement in a cloud computing system. In *Proc. IEEE Int'l Conf. on Cloud Comput.*, 2013.

[8] C. Guo, G. Lu, D. Li, H. Wu, X. Zhang, Y. Shi, C. Tian, Y. Zhang, and S. Lu. Bcube: A high performance, server-centric network architecture for modular data centers. In *Proc. of ACM SIGCOM*, 2009.

[9] C. Guo, H. Wu, K. Tan, L. Shiy, Y. Zhang, and S. Lu. Dcell: A scalable and fault-tolerant network structure for data centers. In *Proc. of ACM SIGCOM*, 2008.

[10] B. Kerby. Managing data center power and cooling with AMD Opteron processors and AMD PowerNow! technology. Technical report, Dell Inc., 2007.

[11] S. Khan and I. Ahmad. A pure Nash equilibrium based game theoretical method for data replication across multiple servers. *IEEE T. Knowl. Data En.*, 21(4), 2009.

[12] S. U. Khan and C. Ardil. Energy efficient resource allocation in distributed computing systems. In *Proc. of Int'l Conf. on Distrib., High-Perf. and Grid Comp.*, 2009.

[13] D. Kliazovich, P. Bouvry, and S. U. Khan. DENS: data center energy-efficient network-aware scheduling. *Cluster Computing*, 16(1), 2013.

[14] C. Lee, J. Suzuki, A. V. Vasilakos, Y. Yamano, and K. Oba. An evolutionary game theoretic approach to adaptive and stable application deployment in clouds. In *Proc. IEEE Workshop on Bio-Inspired Algorithms for Distributed Systems*, 2010.

[15] X. Lia, Z. Qiana, S. Lua, and J. Wu. Energy efficient virtual machine placement algorithm with balanced and improved resource utilization in a data center. *Mathematical and Computer Modelling*, 58(5-6), 2013.

[16] F. Ma, F. Liu, and Z. Liu. Multi-objective optimization for initial virtual machine placement in cloud data center. *J. Infor. and Computational Science*, 9(16), 2012.

[17] J.-M. Pierson and H. Casanova. On the utility of DVFS for power-aware job placement in clusters. In *Proc. Int'l Conf. on Parallel Processing*, 2011.

[18] R. Subrata, A. Y. Zomaya, and B. Landfeldt. Game theoretic approach for load balancing in computational grids. *IEEE Trans. Parall. Distr.*, 19(1), 2008.

[19] H. A. Taboada, J. F. Espiritu, and D. W. Coit. MOMS-GA: A Multi-Objective Multi-State Genetic Algorithm for System Reliability Optimization Design Problems. *IEEE Trans. Reliability*, 57(1), 2008.

[20] P. Taylor and L. Jonker. Evolutionary stable strategies and game dynamics. *Elsevier Mathematical Biosci.*, 40(1), 1978.

[21] von Laszewski, L. Wang, A. J. Younge, and X. He. Power-aware scheduling of virtual machines in DVFS-enabled clusters. In *Proc. IEEE Int'l Conf. on Clusters*, 2009.

[22] H. Wada, J. Suzuki, Y. Yamano, and K. Oba. E3: A multiobjective optimization framework for sla-aware service composition. *IEEE Trans. Services Computing*, 5(3), 2012.

[23] Q. Wang, Y. Kanemasa, J. Li, C. A. Lai, M. Matsubara, and C. Pu. Impact of DVFS on n-tier application performance. In *Proc. ACM Conference on Timely Results in Operating Systems*, 2010.

[24] G. Wei, A. V. Vasilakos, Y. Zheng, and N. Xiong. A game-theoretic method of fair resource allocation for cloud computing services. *J. Supercomputing*, 54(2), 2009.

A Survey on Sustainability in ICT
A Computing Perspective

Alexandru-Adrian Tantar, Emilia Tantar
Interdisciplinary Centre for Security, Reliability and Trust
University of Luxembourg
4 rue Alphonse Weicker
L-2721 Luxembourg, Luxembourg
{alexandru, emilia}.tantar@uni.lu

ABSTRACT

The rise of the data centers industry, together with the emergence of large cloud computing that require large quantities of resources to be maintained, brought the need of providing a sustainable development process. Through this paper we aim to provide an introductory insight on the status and tools available to tackle this perspective within the evolutionary and genetic algorithms community. Existing advancement are also emphasized and perspectives outlined.

Keywords

evolutionary computation; sustainable ICT; energy efficiency

1. INTRODUCTION

A constant increase in the ICT sector energy consumption and the rising concern for environmental impact led to what we now refer to as sustainable computing. And while the concept may seemingly sound straightforward, it is far from being obvious, as we will later see in this paper. The sustainable computing abstraction *per se* spans a wide semantic area. Among others, it connects to energy-aware management of resources, energy efficient computing or the impact such paradigms have in other fields. At the same time, most studies only offer and, what is more, help to create an incomplete picture, e.g. by referring to resource allocation strategies or power management alone. While still relevant, such studies tend however to offer an answer that needs to fit a problem more complex than we first imagined. End of life sustainability accounts for much more than just what energy management can offer. In the following we address sustainability by laying down a series of questions and problems which, when all connected, offer a more coherent picture of the impact ICT and computing have.

As a high level definition, sustainability is often described by relying on the notion of carbon footprint. Why exactly carbon? In ordinary terms, first due to the fact that all our actions, from simply being alive, can be quantified in terms of carbon emissions, i.e. offered an idea of how green a system is. And second due to the common connection we tend to make between carbon emissions and environment destruction. A natural way of approaching sustainability, in this setup, is to reduce the (equivalent) carbon footprint, even if this only means carbon offsets, i.e. investing in areas that result in carbon emission reduction [73]. As an alternative, one may refer to a decrease in energy consumption. What these 'symbols' stand for and what they conceal, i.e. with respect to carbon footprint and energy efficiency, is in most cases more than what is delivered. For a better understanding of the entire process, one needs to think of greenhouse gas emissions, e.g. carbon dioxide, methane or nitrous oxide, or to rely on information about the nature of the energy sources used like, for example, renewable vs nuclear power. This remains however difficult to achieve due to a lack of detail in the information we have available. The percentage of nuclear power in the input energy mix is a simple example of difficult to find information. The problem is even more opaque when considering a full technology lifespan. From production to overseas delivery, operation, maintenance and, finally, replacement and disposal, any ICT component implicitly results in emissions and indirect energy, e.g. processor cooling, being consumed. Accounting such quantities is however close to impossible. Furthermore, a device like, for example, a touchscreen, may need rare earth elements for its production. The long-term impact of out of use components disposal may be at least difficult to measure, e.g. resulting toxic waste and the effort needed in removing (or isolating) such byproducts from the environment. Operation is also a complex process. Dissipated heat is a main problem and solutions vary from placing data centers in cold regions to strategies like follow the Moon [16]. Then, a different view is to consider an ICT system as being sustainable via the impact it brings in other fields like smart buildings or the design of zero-emission buildings.

A different question, when moving from the overall ICT view to algorithms, is what kind of paradigms qualify the system for the 'sustainability' or 'green' label? Would a faster algorithm, e.g. Fast-Fourier-Transform [31], imply that a given computing architecture is improved in terms of sustainability? A faster execution time is in the end equivalent to a lower energy consumption and, in a classical data center, by direct correspondence, to less emissions. All computer science research would, by this approach, be a quest for energy-efficiency and emissions reduction. Faster algorithms

GECCO'14, July 12–16, 2014, Vancouver, BC, Canada.

http://dx.doi.org/10.1145/2598394.2605695.

unfortunately only equate to more data being processed in a same time unit interval and thus to no (actual) change in terms of carbon footprint or energy reduction. For an algorithm to be considered 'green', a most commonly accepted view is that it explicitly contains terms that address issues related to energy efficiency, e.g. processor stepping.

For the remainder of this paper, we focus on the computing side of sustainability. The following sections are organized as follows. Section 2 discusses sustainability and energy efficiency in IT at different levels, e.g. data center and networking. A series of metrics and benchmarks are presented in Section 3, followed by a brief overview of evolutionary computing as used in energy efficiency and sustainability in Section 4. Section 5 concludes the paper.

2. SUSTAINABILITY AND ENERGY EFFICIENCY IN IT: LEVELS OF GRANULARITY

All domains of our everyday life are concerned with and by reducing energy consumption. For areas like, for example, in sustainable buildings, external energy input may approach zero or, in some cases, buildings may sell energy back into the network. A few notable examples are NASA's Sustainability Base [27] or the Energy Plus building in Paris [29]. When it comes to computing, however, it may not be all that simple. Also, in order to understand why energy efficiency in computing is an important issue, we first need to understand where the limits are and how we are positioned with respect to these limits.

The ICT sector is comparable to the aviation industry in terms of carbon footprint, i.e. accounting for 2% of the worldwide emissions and estimated to reach 3% by 2020 [56]. This is in fact a rough view of where ICT stands: the direct impact it has is by no means negligible. A second aspect we need to consider is related to what is commonly referred to as Moore's law [52], i.e. a doubling of the number of transistors roughly every two years. At the same time, the number of operations per joule of dissipated energy doubled every one year and a half, cf. Koomey's law[1] [36]. A last element is Maxwell's daemon and Landauer's principle [38]. Landauer's principle, only recently verified via a scientific experiment [3, 17, 12], argued that destroying information leads to energy dissipation [38]. Erasing a bit of information would thus release an amount of heat equivalent to $k_B T \ln 2$, i.e. 3×10^{-21} J (at room temperature), where $k_B = 1.3806488(13) \times 10^{-23}\mathrm{JK}^{-1}$ stands for Boltzmann's constant. And, while it may not seem the case, erasing information is a central part of how nowadays computers work. All classical computer architectures make use of what is called an irreversible gate, e.g. a NAND gate, which by concept discards information. Thus, even if we assume that all other dissipative processes are removed, a computing system that relies on irreversible gates would still release some amount of heat. This is in fact a lower and unavoidable limit. When correlated with Moore's and Koomey's laws, what follows is shattering: in a decade from now, a chip would release more heat per square centimeter than the surface of the Sun [53]. Reversible Turing machines, while not new as an idea [10], did not reach anywhere beyond the theory status for now. Thus, finding ways for dealing with heat dissipation and reducing the energy consumption in the process is essential. Heat dissipation, even if not yet at such an extreme level, is a main issue in nowadays data centers. As discussed below, a broad range of solutions are used.

2.1 Data Centers and Cloud Computing

Energy efficiency in data centers and Cloud Computing is a topic that relates to all levels, from physical design and installation to operation. The need for finding an answer to reducing cooling related consumption led, among others, to solutions that take advantage of natural factors, e.g. data centers placed in cold geographic regions [47] or that make use of wind for cooling [33]. Other examples include water-based data center designs [15], compressed air [18] or smart cooling solutions [57]. An important conclusion of most studies, while referring to operation aspects only, is that sustainable computing is mainly about energy efficiency and renewable energy sources [24]. As such, the operation of a large scale computing facility needs to be optimized at all levels, i.e. design and physical arrangement down to dynamic CPU frequency and voltage scaling. Sustainability, in addition, also needs for renewable energy to be used. The main problem one is finally faced with is operation cost (read as amount to pay for consumption) which does not always equate with what sustainability stands for. Different operators may and will prefer nuclear or coal power, for example, over solar energy due to lower costs; for a worldwide view of energy use in data centers, please refer to [35]. Also, for a taxonomy of energy-efficient data centers and cloud computing systems, refer to [8]. A follow the Sun-like approach would imply moving the load where sufficient solar (renewable for the general case) energy is available. And while this scenario implies a high percentage of green energy being used, costs are likely to be above the ones of using conventional energy. A follow the Moon strategy, at the opposite end, translates into a lower energy consumption (less cooling is required) though not always in line with where renewable energy is available [16]. Last but not least, due to a law enforcement on data transfer, any of these strategies may be fully or partially limited [16].

When looking at large scale, energy efficient computing from an algorithmic and model oriented perspective, a wide range of studies can be found in literature on, among many others, heuristics [7, 26], machine learning, e.g. neural networks, auto-regressive stochastic state transition models [59], branching processes [63, 6], stochastic programming and optimization [45, 46, 28, 41], or nature inspired algorithms [14, 9]. Among the different criteria taken into account, one can mention, energy efficiency but also performance, availability, elasticity, bandwidth or Quality of Service (QoS). A large part of the existing studies rely on discrete models alone [45, 51, 26, 58], with very few exceptions bringing continuous attributes into discussion [63, 6]. A trend towards focusing more on high-level aspects in queuing, load balancing or scheduling can be observed, also with the additional support of technologies such as frequency scaling, e.g. SpeedStep [32], Cool'n'Quiet [2], or virtualization. With respect to Cloud computing, a very concise study on details that run from low-level to infrastructure related aspects is given in [11]. Among others it reviews recent advancements and research on methods or technologies for energy efficient

[1] A large number of studies cite and refer to both Moore's and Koomey's observations as *laws*. A more correct description is that of a (linear) statistical model. Furthermore, industry also later mapped to follow this trend.

cloud and data-center operation. The authors point at, as an example, wireless and wired networks power minimization, energy efficient hardware, energy-aware scheduling in multiprocessor and grid systems, state, e.g. slowing down the processor or powering off different parts of the chip or hardware, dynamic voltage and frequency scaling, virtualization, consolidation and protocols. Full, hosted and operating system layer virtualization are also mentioned. Last, an overview of energy efficient cloud computing and energy-aware data centers is given, ending with the impact communication oriented applications have. A series of surveys on mobile cloud computing, virtualization vulnerabilities, federation of clouds, data access and integrity or low resolution security issues can also be found in [22, 5, 66, 13, 75, 37]. A more detailed discussion can be found in [68].

A separate problem from computing alone is storage. As data needs to be readily available at all times in most cases, storage devices, e.g. hard drives, and all related communication and transfer infrastructure is typically kept alive even if not used. As opposed to computing however, idle storage is considered responsible for up to 80% of the energy usage, i.e. when compared to peak operation mode. Examples of possible ways of improvement with respect to storage can be found by referring to [65].

2.2 Sustainability in Networking

A first, although not the most energy consuming part of all IT equipment comes from the standby power consumption. According to the Standby Power project, supported by the Lawrence Berkeley National Laboratory, a computer desktop consumes in average 73.97 W/day when On (idle); 27.5 W/day when Off and 1.38W/day while in a Sleep mode. Although the measurements where performed in residential appliances, this easily translates to campus networks for example. Although this seems irrelevant at first, when considering the number of IT equipment of a small to medium network, the waisted energy amount increases quickly.

The first countermeasure one can think of in a network context, comes from enabling the centralized control of the switch-on/off of the network devices. Although multiple energy efficient applications are acknowleged in the networking area, they lack scalability and depend on the ability of the network administrator of integrating them and configuring the physical network accordingly. The newly emerged Software Defined Networking (SDN) paradigm [55], promoted by the Open Networking Foundation [1], enables a centralized controller layer, that, while provided with the proper applications, can intelligently manage the unused resources, being them equipment, services or subnetworks, for example.

SDN introduces a centralized and programmable way of designing networks, that completely changes the classical distributed networking approach. It not only introduces a separation between the data plane and the control plane, but also enables the programability of the network by means of external applications. Although the Southbound Interface acknowledges the OpenFlow protocol [50] as a *de facto* standard, promoted also by the Open Networking Foundation; the Northbound Interface that ensures the interaction between the controller and the application plane is still subject of research, with no unique solution identified.

On a base functioning grounds, the protocols used for broadcasting, routing for example dictate the energy efficiency of the network. On a higher level, SDN empowers the controller with the ability of having specific applications – interfacing with the network through the north bound – that oversee/control the network sustainable characteristics. A controller can be enabled also with traffic management applications, that reduce the network load, optimize paths and thus minimize the resources consumed for handling the network traffic.

3. QUANTIFYING THE IT IMPACT – METRICS AND BENCHMARKS

The rise of the data center industry and the emergency of cloud computing infrastructures implied the need of quantifying its impact through its multiple facets. A first tool are benchmarks offering the means for a solid analysis and comparison. Next, metrics allow following the over time evolution of a given data center with respect to specified operation targets. In the follow up, an overview of the metrics recommended as best practice by the community (through for example the Green Grid Global Taskforce outputs) is provided, with an emphasize on the sustainability oriented ones, with no intent of being exhaustive. Detailed metrics overviews are available in literature (e.g. [72]) and are beyond the scope of the current paper.

3.1 Metrics for Data Centers

The usance considers a data center management needs to bridge between requirements as performance, sustainability and QoS (Quality of Service). Therefore factors as energy efficiency or performance are seen as amongst the primary ones to be quantified. Besides it has been noted that from the total energy consumption, 50% is attributed to the cooling system [64], giving rise to the need of efficient **thermal metrics**.

Data center owners and managers have also the possibility of prioritizing amongst metrics in order to serve their specific needs [48].

The common assumption considered while measuring the energy efficiency is that the resources are thoroughly allocated. Nevertheless, unsustainable solutions include also idle equipment or otherwise stated maintaining servers, storage or in general a data center with low usage.

3.1.1 Power / Energy Efficiency Metrics

Even before designing a data center, the first aspect to consider is how to measure its energy efficiency, witnessed also by the interest of both operators and policy makers. One of the leading initiatives in this area if represented by the Green Grid Taskforce on *Global Harmonization of Data Center Efficiency Metrics*. The participants of the task force represent the major players in the area U.S. Department of Energy, Save Energy Now and Federal Energy Management Programs (March 2009 – October 2012); the U.S. Environmental Protection Agency ENERGY STAR Program; the European Commission Joint Research Centre Data Centres Code of Conduct; Japan's Ministry of Economy, Trade and Industry; Japan's Green IT Promotion Council; and The Green Grid Association.

One major output of the initiative consists in the reviewing of the existing metrics and the release of new energy efficiency metrics, with the intent of providing a common ground of understanding and improve the energy use of data centers.

PUE (Power Usage Effectiveness) - the above formulation follows the last proposed one by the Global Taskforce aforementioned [54]

$$\text{PUE} = \frac{\text{total data center source energy}}{\text{IT source energy}},$$

although it is worth noting that large companies are adapting the formulation to their particular conditions, see Google [25] or Dell [60]. If we take the example of the Dell case the main difference consist in the fact that the external power delivery systems, cooling systems,lighting and so on are ignored in the computation. This can also be explained by the novelty of the guide [54].

GEC (Green Energy Coefficient) [54] - the proportion of a facility's energy that comes from green sources

$$\text{GEC} = \frac{\text{green energy used by the data center}}{\text{total data center source energy}}$$

ERF (Energy Reuse Factor) [54] - the proportion of energy that is reused outside the data centre (e.g. in campus facilities)]

$$\text{ERF} = \frac{\text{reuse energy outside of the data center}}{\text{total data center source energy}}$$

CUE (Carbon Usage Effectiveness) [54] - measures the total carbon dioxide emission equivalents (CO2e) from the energy consumption of the data center divided by the total IT energy consumption, defined as follows:

$$\text{CUE} = \text{CEF} \times \text{PUE},$$

where CEF represents the Carbon Dioxide Emission Factor (kgCO2eq/kWh) of the Data Center. It can also be seen as the ratio between the Total $C0_2$ emissions caused by the Total Data Center Energy and the IT equipment Energy.

Besides the basic metrics mentioned, also variants of them coexist. The mostly used example comes from the reciprocal of the PUE, namely the **DCIE (Datacenter Infrastructure Efficiency)**. Furthermore, when needing more granularity for PUE, the definition can be revised as:

$$\text{DCiE} = \text{CLF} + \text{PLF} + 1.0,$$

where CLF represents the Cooling Load Factor and PLF stands for the Power Load Factor, with 1.0 the normalized IT Load [4].

Various variants of the PUE have been proposed by the Green Grid association over time, e.g. PUEx, where x can take a value between 0 and 3, and depends for example on where the measurements have been made.

Extensions based on PUEx also emerged as the **GPUE (Green Power Usage Effectiveness)**, defined as

$$\text{GPUE} = \text{G} \times \text{PUEx (for inline comparison of data centers)},$$

with G being the *weighed sum of energy sources and their lifecycle KG CO2/KWh.*

The abovementioned variants are by no means exhaustive and represent only useful pointers for a novice reader eager to tackle the area and searching for the proper starting point.

3.1.2 Cooling Efficiency

Besides the energy used directly for performing computations, a large percent of a system consumption comes from the cooling part of the system.

One of the first metrics emerging in the area concerned the HVAC (Heating, Ventilation, and Air conditioning) aspect. The metric was called the **HVAC system effectiveness** [48] and is measuring the system effectivness in terms of the ratio of the IT equipment energy to the HVAC system energy. The HVAC system energy is the sum of the electrical energy for cooling, fan movement, and lately concerns any other HVAC energy use like steam or chilled water. Studies detailing the various aspects, such as airflow efficiency or quantifying the usage of air/water economizers exist in the literature [49] and [61]. In a recent taxonomy of performance metrics in data centers, the following categories have been identified:

Humidity - can produce hardware failure and increase the cooling system usage.

Thermal metrics -relate with the control of thermal parameters in the storage space

- Cooling system efficiency - seen from a holistic perspective or divided in a individual components perspective. Various characteristics can be monitored and provide useful information: airflow efficiency, the sizing of the cooling system (hard to manipulate after acquisition, erroneous usage estimation increasing also the **Total Cost of ownership** metric); air/water economizer utilization.
- Data center temperature
- British Thermal Unit
- Airflow performance index
- Air/water economizer usage

3.1.3 Performance Metrics

Various performance goals need to be met in order to obtain a sustainable computing center, often contradictory or different by nature. Take for example energy efficiency and productivity in a data center. If the first one focuses on reducing the costs needed in order to achieve a certain performance or a specific work output, productivity focuses on providing besides the already specified performance, the maximum of useful work produced given a specific amount of resources. One metric in this direction and following a holistic perspective is the **DCeP (Data Center Energy Productivity)** that is used to measure the overall performance of a specific data center in terms of productivity.

This can be synthetically expressed as:

$$\text{DCeP} = \frac{\text{useful work produced}}{\text{total source energy for producing this work}}$$

As this metric measures data center specific productivity characteristics, a generic metric able to provide a common ground for comparison between the productivity of various data centers is needed. Data center productivity proxies represent one potential alternative, although no consensus has been reached in this regard yet. Many declinations aver possible as the *Data center energy productivity (DCeP)* measured by energy checker or the sample load. Other potential alternatives include the *weighted CPU utilization – SPECpower* or the *Computed Units per Second (CUPS).*

Name	Developer	Intended use	Architecture
EnergyBench	EEMBC [20]	industrial	processors, embedded systems
SpecPower	Spec [39]	industrial	client/server architecture (for web servers)
TPC-Energy	Transaction Processing Performance Council [74]	industry	servers, disk systems, other components
JouleSort	Rivoire *et al.* [62]	academic	client/server architecture, embedded systems
SWEEP	Du Bois *et al.* [19]	both	client/server architecture

Table 1: Synthetic view of available benchmarks for energy efficiency

3.2 Available Benchmarks

In order to support researchers by enabling energy efficiency testing on data centers or cloud computing facilities, various synthetic benchmarks have been developed. The panoply of benchmarks spans over different levels of granularity, from (1) *processors*to (2) *servers* or the (3) *holistic data center perspective.*

Covering the evaluation of a single processor's energy efficiency, the Embedded Microprocessor Benchmarking Consortium (EEMBC) provides a physical infrastructure for the embedded area [20], called the EEMBC EnergyBench. The metric used to evaluate processors' energy efficiency is the commonly employed, Performance Per Watt(PPW) metric [40]. Other related metrics, more tailored for performance criteria, as the energy-delay product coexist. The later being the equivalent of performance squared per Watt. At the servers level, the SPEC Power and Performance Committee has developed the SPECPower benchmark [39]. Together with the TPC-Energy [74] proposed by the Transaction Processing Performance Council, these benchmarks enable predicting the performance per Watt in e.g., a server farm. As an addition compared with the SPECPower, TPC-Energy enables measuring the energy consumption of other system components, besides servers, as disk systems or other items that consume power [74]. The class of workloads for energy-efficiency benchmarks acknowledges also more flexible (tunable) variants, as for example the Synthetic Workloads for Energy Efficiency and Performance evaluation (SWEEP) [19]. It represents a tunable synthetic workload generator, capable of creating instances that are compute-intensive, memory-intensive, I/O-intensive, or a mix of them.

Table 1 encloses a non-exhaustive overview of the reference benchmarks providing references, targeted segment and intended audience.

4. WHERE DOES EC PLAY A ROLE?

Sustainability (optimization) problems, due to their complexity, are beyond reach for most conventional approaches. Regardless of dealing with large scale computing systems, renewable energy plants or buildings, as an example, a series of hard limitations have to be considered. All these systems are subject to complex interactions, time dependent dynamics and external perturbations [70, 71]. A classical one-snapshot approach does not suffice. What is more, the number of objectives that typically need to be met in such problems is above what most optimization paradigms can deal with. Evolutionary Algorithms (EAs), as it will be discussed in the following, are a standard solution different studies turned to, mainly due to their sheer simplicity.

Even from the setup of testing environments, by means of synthetic benchmarks, genetic algorithms play a role. They are used for example, in the search and prune of workload attributes that maximize criteria as power or temperature [34].

Among the first areas EAs were used for, even before the entire green wave, e.g. energy-efficiency in computing, buildings and so forth, communications stands out, namely in wireless sensor networks and fixed networks [30]. Then, a large number of studies focused on results in energy-aware resource allocation and scheduling. For an overview see [7, 43, 67]. Evolutionary computing was also used from thermal design [44] to live application placement [42] or workload distribution [21]. Another approach explored in detail is Dynamic Voltage and Frequency Scaling (DVFS), where the power of individual computing nodes is modulated dynamically as to reflect momentary load. A discussion of DVFS and Dynamic Frequency Islands can be found in [23]. The main axes thus cover virtualization and live migration, resource allocation, workload mitigation and low-level tuning, e.g. via DVFS.

An interesting remark is that data centers are exceedingly complex and difficult to optimize even when using evolutionary algorithms. The large number of parameters one is given with, e.g. state of all nodes, processor stepping, etc., makes the problem intractable when the system is to be optimized as a single and indivisible entity. Instead, a more realistic approach is to break the system into smaller parts like, for example, computing nodes, where hierarchical agents control the state of a given part of the system via e.g. workload negotiation or transition among states [69]. Other examples of EC algorithms used in tuning consumption vs performance and energy-aware task scheduling can be found in [14, 9].

5. CONCLUSIONS

Energy efficiency and sustainability in ICT are major problems we have not solved yet. As new technologies replace the ones now in use, advancements in, for example, renewable energies or heat dissipation, allow us to go a step further. The need for even more extensive computations and the evolution of Cloud computing shadow however the small advantage technology offers. Thus, we need to rethink the way we manage resources, how computations are made or even how data is stored and later retrieved. The different metrics presented in this paper are an important tool for understanding how different solutions scale and how effective they are. There remains however a strong need for structured data analysis with a more proactive use of runtime information. On the algorithmic side, Evolutionary Computing and the heuristic paradigms in general, play an important role when solid practical solutions are needed. The large number of parameters one needs however to tackle and the number of objectives, now beyond what the state of the art can deal with, represent a major issue. The most important conclusion of this study is however that, if addressing any of the sustainability and energy efficiency issues in, for example, data centers is delayed, we will soon reach limits that force us to restrict the current evolution of how computing is made.

Acknowledgements

Alexandru-Adrian Tantar would like to acknowledge the support offered by the National Research Fund (Fonds National de la Recherche, FNR), Luxembourg, and the Centre National de la Recherche Scientifique (CNRS), France, in the framework of the Multi-Objective Metaheuristics for Energy-Aware Scheduling in Cloud Computing Systems INTER/CNRS/11/03 Green@Cloud project. Emilia Tantar would like to acknowledge that the publication is based in parts on work performed in the framework of the CoSDN project, INTER/POLLUX/12/4434480, funded by the Fonds National de la Recherche, Luxembourg.

6. REFERENCES

[1] Open Networking Foundation. `http://www.opennetworking.org`.

[2] AMD. Cool'n'Quiet Technology. `http://www.amd.com/us/products/technologies/cool-n-quiet/Pages/cool-n-quiet.aspx`, 2004.

[3] Janet Anders, Saroosh Shabbir, Stefanie Hilt, and Eric Lutz. Landauer's Principle in the Quantum Domain. In Cooper et al. [17], pages 13–18.

[4] John Pflueger Andy Rawson and Tahir Cader. The Green Grid Data Center Power Efficiency Metrics: PUE and DCiE. `http://www.thegreengrid.org/Global/Content/white-papers/The-Green-Grid-Data-Center-Power-Efficiency-Metrics-PUE-and-DCiE#sthash.tnUhZM7e.dpuf`, Oct. 2007.

[5] Michael Armbrust, Armando Fox, Rean Griffith, Anthony D. Joseph, Randy Katz, Andy Konwinski, Gunho Lee, David Patterson, Ariel Rabkin, Ion Stoica, and Matei Zaharia. A View of Cloud Computing. *Commun. ACM*, 53(4):50–58, April 2010.

[6] Marko Bajec and Johann Eder, editors. *Advanced Information Systems Engineering Workshops - CAiSE 2012 International Workshops, Gdask, Poland, June 25-26, 2012. Proceedings*, volume 112 of *Lecture Notes in Business Information Processing*. Springer, 2012.

[7] Anton Beloglazov, Jemal Abawajy, and Rajkumar Buyya. Energy-Aware Resource Allocation Heuristics for Efficient Management of Data Centers for Cloud Computing. *Future Generation Computer Systems*, 28(5):755 – 768, 2012. Special Section: Energy efficiency in large-scale distributed systems.

[8] Anton Beloglazov, Rajkumar Buyya, Young Choon Lee, and Albert Y. Zomaya. A Taxonomy and Survey of Energy-Efficient Data Centers and Cloud Computing Systems. *CoRR*, abs/1007.0066, 2010.

[9] S. Benedict, R.S. Rejitha, and C.B. Bright. Energy Consumption-Based Performance Tuning of Software and Applications Using Particle Swarm Optimization. In *Software Engineering (CONSEG), 2012 CSI Sixth International Conference on*, pages 1 –6, sept. 2012.

[10] C. H. Bennett. Logical Reversibility of Computation. *IBM J. Res. Dev.*, 17(6):525–532, November 1973.

[11] Andreas Berl, Erol Gelenbe, Marco Di Girolamo, Giovanni Giuliani, Hermann De Meer, Minh Quan Dang, and Kostas Pentikousis. Energy-Efficient Cloud Computing. *Comput. J.*, 53(7):1045–1051, September 2010.

[12] Antoine Bérut, Artak Arakelyan, Artyom Petrosyan, Sergio Ciliberto, Raoul Dillenschneider, and Eric Lutz. Experimental verification of Landauer's principle linking information and thermodynamics. *Nature*, 483(7388):187–189, Mar 2012.

[13] Rajkumar Buyya, Rajiv Ranjan, and RodrigoN. Calheiros. InterCloud: Utility-Oriented Federation of Cloud Computing Environments for Scaling of Application Services. In Ching-Hsien Hsu, LaurenceT. Yang, JongHyuk Park, and Sang-Soo Yeo, editors, *Algorithms and Architectures for Parallel Processing*, volume 6081 of *Lecture Notes in Computer Science*, pages 13–31. Springer Berlin Heidelberg, 2010.

[14] Ying Chang-tian and Yu Jiong. Energy-Aware Genetic Algorithms for Task Scheduling in Cloud Computing. In *ChinaGrid Annual Conference (ChinaGrid), 2012 Seventh*, pages 43 –48, sept. 2012.

[15] J. Clidaras, D.W. Stiver, and W. Hamburgen. Water-based Data Center. `http://www.google.com/patents/US7525207`, April 28 2009. US Patent 7,525,207.

[16] Computer & Communications Industry Association. Cloud Computing. `http://www.ccianet.org/wp-content/uploads/library/Cloud_Computing.pdf`, 2009.

[17] S. Barry Cooper, Prakash Panangaden, and Elham Kashefi, editors. *Proceedings Sixth Workshop on Developments in Computational Models: Causality, Computation, and Physics, DCM 2010, Edinburgh, Scotland, 9-10th July 2010*, volume 26 of *EPTCS*, 2010.

[18] M.P. Czamara and O.P. Morales. Compressed Air Cooling System for Data Center. `https://www.google.com/patents/EP2554032A1?cl=en`, February 6 2013. EP Patent App. EP20,110,712,079.

[19] Kristof Du Bois, Tim Schaeps, Stijn Polfliet, Frederick Ryckbosch, and Lieven Eeckhout. SWEEP: Evaluating Computer System Energy Efficiency Using Synthetic Workloads. In *Proceedings of the 6th International Conference on High Performance and Embedded Architectures and Compilers*, HiPEAC '11, pages 159–166, New York, NY, USA, 2011. ACM.

[20] Embedded Microprocessor Benchmark Consortium (EEMBC). Energybench V1.0 Power/Energy Benchmarks. `http://www.eembc.org/benchmark/power_sl.php`.

[21] Eugen Feller, Louis Rilling, and Christine Morin. Energy-Aware Ant Colony Based Workload Placement in Clouds. In *Proceedings of the 2011 IEEE/ACM 12th International Conference on Grid Computing*, GRID '11, pages 26–33, Washington, DC, USA, 2011. IEEE Computer Society.

[22] Ian Foster, Yong Zhao, Ioan Raicu, and Shiyong Lu. Cloud Computing and Grid Computing 360-Degree Compared. *2008 Grid Computing Environments Workshop*, abs/0901.0(5):1–10, 2008.

[23] Siddharth Garg, Diana Marculescu, Radu Marculescu,

and Umit Ogras. Technology-driven Limits on DVFS Controllability of Multiple Voltage-frequency Island Designs: A System-level Perspective. In *Proceedings of the 46th Annual Design Automation Conference*, DAC '09, pages 818–821, New York, NY, USA, 2009. ACM.

[24] Greenpeace International Gary Cook. How Green is Your Cloud? Catalysing an Energy Revolution. `http://www.greenpeace.org/new-zealand/Global/international/publications/climate/2012/iCoal/HowCleanisYourCloud.pdf`, apr 2012.

[25] Google. Efficiency: How we do it. `http://www.google.com/about/datacenters/efficiency/internal/index.html#measuring-efficiency`.

[26] Hadi Goudarzi, Mohammad Ghasemazar, and Massoud Pedram. SLA-based optimization of power and migration cost in cloud computing. In *Proceedings of the 2012 12th IEEE/ACM International Symposium on Cluster, Cloud and Grid Computing (ccgrid 2012)*, CCGRID '12, pages 172–179, Washington, DC, USA, 2012. IEEE Computer Society.

[27] June A. Grant. Implementing Sustainable Practices @ NASA Ames, GreenGov Symposium, 2011 Washington, USA. `http://www.greengov2011.org/presentations/GreenFacilities/GreenGov-2011-GreenFacilities-S5-JuneGrant.pdf`, Oct 2011.

[28] Albert G. Greenberg and Kazem Sohraby, editors. *Proceedings of the IEEE INFOCOM 2012, Orlando, FL, USA, March 25-30, 2012*. IEEE, 2012.

[29] Katherine Griffiths. World's greenest office block set for Paris, The Telegraph. `http://www.telegraph.co.uk/finance/newsbysector/constructionandproperty/2781961/Worlds-greenest-office-block-set-for-Paris.html`, Jan 2008.

[30] M.N. Halgamuge, S.M. Guru, and A. Jennings. Energy Efficient Cluster Formation in Wireless Sensor Networks. In *Telecommunications, 2003. ICT 2003. 10th International Conference on*, volume 2, pages 1571–1576 vol.2, Feb 2003.

[31] Haitham Hassanieh, Piotr Indyk, Dina Katabi, and Eric Price. Nearly Optimal Sparse Fourier Transform. In *Proceedings of the Forty-fourth Annual ACM Symposium on Theory of Computing*, STOC '12, pages 563–578, New York, NY, USA, 2012. ACM.

[32] Intel White Paper 30057701. Wireless Intel SpeedStep power manager: optimizing power consumption for the Intel PXA27x processor family. Technical report, Intel, 2004.

[33] Jeremy Kirk, IDG News Service, PCWorld. HP Opens First Ever Wind-cooled Data Center. `http://www.pcworld.com/article/188996/hp_opens_first_ever_wind_cooled_data_center.html`, 2010.

[34] Ajay M. Joshi, Lieven Eeckhout, Lizy Kurian John, and Ciji Isen. Automated Microprocessor Stressmark Generation. In *HPCA*, pages 229–239. IEEE Computer Society, 2008.

[35] Jonathan G Koomey. Worldwide Electricity Used in Data Centers. *Environmental Research Letters*, 3(3):034008, 2008.

[36] Jonathan G. Koomey, Stephen Berard, Marla Sanchez, and Henry Wong. Implications of Historical Trends in the Electrical Efficiency of Computing. *IEEE Annals of the History of Computing*, 33(3):46–54, 2011.

[37] K. Kumar and Yung-Hsiang Lu. Cloud Computing for Mobile Users: Can Offloading Computation Save Energy? *Computer*, 43(4):51–56, 2010.

[38] R. Landauer. Irreversibility and Heat Generation in the Computing Process. *IBM J. Res. Dev.*, 5(3):183–191, Jul 1961.

[39] Klaus-Dieter Lange. Identifying Shades of Green: The SPECpower Benchmarks. *IEEE Computer*, 42(3):95–97, 2009.

[40] James Laudon. Performance/Watt: The New Server Focus. *SIGARCH Comput. Archit. News*, 33(4):5–13, November 2005.

[41] Wei-Ru Lee, Hung-Yi Teng, and Ren-Hung Hwang. Optimization of Cloud Resource Subscription Policy. In *Cloud Computing Technology and Science (CloudCom), 2012 IEEE 4th International Conference on*, pages 449 –455, dec. 2012.

[42] Bo Li, Jianxin Li, Jinpeng Huai, Tianyu Wo, Qin Li, and Liang Zhong. EnaCloud: An Energy-Saving Application Live Placement Approach for Cloud Computing Environments. In *Cloud Computing, 2009. CLOUD '09. IEEE International Conference on*, pages 17–24, Sept 2009.

[43] Dawei Li and Jie Wu. *Energy-aware Scheduling on Multiprocessor Platforms*. Springer Publishing Company, Incorporated, 2012.

[44] G. Li, M. Li, S. Azarm, J. Rambo, and Y. Joshi. Optimizing Thermal Design of Data Center Cabinets with a New Multi-objective Genetic Algorithm. *Distrib. Parallel Databases*, 21(2-3):167–192, June 2007.

[45] Qiang Li. Applying Stochastic Integer Programming to Optimization of Resource Scheduling in Cloud Computing. *JNW*, 7(7):1078–1084, 2012.

[46] Siva Theja Maguluri, R. Srikant, and Lei Ying. Stochastic Models of Load Balancing and Scheduling in Cloud Computing Clusters. In Greenberg and Sohraby [28], pages 702–710.

[47] Mark Gregory, BBC News. Inside Facebook's Green and Clean Arctic Data Centre. `http://www.bbc.com/news/business-22879160`, 2013.

[48] Paul A. Mathew, Srirupa Ganguly, Steve E. Greenberg, and Dale A. Sartor. Self-benchmarking Guide for Data Centers: Metrics, Benchmarks, Actions. Technical report, Lawrence Berkeley National Laboratory, Jul 2009.

[49] Sara McAllister, Van P. Carey, Amip Shah, Cullen Bash, and Chandrakant D. Patel. Strategies for Effective use of Energy-based Modeling of Data Center Thermal Management Systems. *Microelectronics Journal*, 39(7):1023–1029, 2008.

[50] Nick McKeown, Tom Anderson, Hari Balakrishnan, Guru Parulkar, Larry Peterson, Jennifer Rexford, Scott Shenker, and Jonathan Turner. OpenFlow: enabling innovation in campus networks. In *Proc. of the ACM SIGCOMM 2008 conference*, pages 38(2):69–74, 2008.

[51] M. Mezmaz, N. Melab, Y. Kessaci, Y. C. Lee, E. G. Talbi, A. Y. Zomaya, and D. Tuyttens. A Parallel

Bi-Objective Hybrid Metaheuristic for Energy-Aware Scheduling for Cloud Computing Systems. *J. Parallel Distrib. Comput.*, 71(11):1497–1508, November 2011.

[52] G. E. Moore. Cramming More Components onto Integrated Circuits. *Electronics*, 38(8):114–117, Apr 1965.

[53] Samuel K. Moore. Landauer Limit Demonstrated, IEEE Spectrum. `http://spectrum.ieee.org/computing/hardware/landauer-limit-demonstrated`, Mar 2012.

[54] The Green Grid Global Harmonization of Data Center Efficiency Metrics Task Force. Harmonizing Global Metrics for Data Center Energy Efficiency, March 2014.

[55] Open Networking Foundation. SDN architecture overview. ONF White paper, Dec. 2013.

[56] Parliament Office of Science and Technology. ICT and CO_2 Emissions. `http://www.parliament.uk/documents/post/postpn319.pdf`, Dec 2008.

[57] C.D. Patel, C.E. Bash, and A.H. Beitelmal. Smart Cooling of Data Centers. `https://www.google.com/patents/US6574104`, June 3 2003. US Patent 6,574,104.

[58] Dung H. Phan, Junichi Suzuki, Raymond Carroll, Sasitharan Balasubramaniam, William Donnelly, and Dmitri Botvich. Evolutionary Multiobjective Optimization for Green Clouds. In *Proceedings of the fourteenth international conference on Genetic and evolutionary computation conference companion*, GECCO Companion '12, pages 19–26, New York, NY, USA, 2012. ACM.

[59] J.J. Prevost, K. Nagothu, B. Kelley, and M. Jamshidi. Prediction of Cloud Data Center Networks Loads using Stochastic and Neural Models. In *System of Systems Engineering (SoSE), 2011 6th International Conference on*, pages 276 –281, june 2011.

[60] Paul Rad, Max Thoene, and Tim Webb. Best Practices for Increasing Data Center Energy Efficiency, February 2008.

[61] Jeffrey Rambo and Yogendra Joshi. Modeling of Data Center Airflow and Heat Transfer: State of the Art and Future Trends. *Distributed and Parallel Databases*, 21(2-3):193–225, 2007.

[62] Suzanne Rivoire, Mehul A. Shah, Parthasarathy Ranganathan, and Christos Kozyrakis. JouleSort: A Balanced Energy-efficiency Benchmark. In *Proceedings of the 2007 ACM SIGMOD International Conference on Management of Data*, SIGMOD '07, pages 365–376, New York, NY, USA, 2007. ACM.

[63] Victor Romanov, Aleksandra Varfolomeeva, and Andrey Koryakovskiy. Branching Processes Theory Application for Cloud Computing Demand Modeling Based on Traffic Prediction. In Bajec and Eder [6], pages 502–510.

[64] Richard Sawyer. Calculating Total Power Requirements for Data Centers, 2011.

[65] Storage Networking Industry Association (SNIA). Storage Management Initiative Specification. `http://snia.org/tech_activities/publicreview`, 2013.

[66] S. Subashini and V. Kavitha. A Survey on Security Issues in Service Delivery Models of Cloud Computing. *Journal of Network and Computer Applications*, 34(1):1 – 11, 2011.

[67] Q. Tang, S. K S Gupta, and G. Varsamopoulos. Energy-Efficient Thermal-Aware Task Scheduling for Homogeneous High-Performance Computing Data Centers: A Cyber-Physical Approach. *Parallel and Distributed Systems, IEEE Transactions on*, 19(11):1458–1472, Nov 2008.

[68] A.-A. Tantar, Anh Quan Nguyen, P. Bouvry, B. Dorronsoro, and E.-G. Talbi. Computational Intelligence for Cloud Management Current Trends and Opportunities. In *Evolutionary Computation (CEC), 2013 IEEE Congress on*, pages 1286–1293, June 2013.

[69] Alexandru-Adrian Tantar, Grégoire Danoy, Pascal Bouvry, and SameeU. Khan. Energy-Efficient Computing Using Agent-Based Multi-objective Dynamic Optimization. In JaeH. Kim and MyungJ. Lee, editors, *Green IT: Technologies and Applications*, pages 267–287. Springer Berlin Heidelberg, 2011.

[70] Alexandru-Adrian Tantar, Emilia Tantar, and Pascal Bouvry. A Classification of Dynamic Multi-objective Optimization Problems. In *Proceedings of the 13th Annual Conference Companion on Genetic and Evolutionary Computation*, GECCO '11, pages 105–106, New York, NY, USA, 2011. ACM.

[71] E. Tantar, A. Tantar, and P. Bouvry. On Dynamic Multi-Objective Optimization, Classification and Performance Measures. In *Evolutionary Computation (CEC), 2011 IEEE Congress on*, pages 2759–2766, June 2011.

[72] Lizhe Wang and SameeU. Khan. Review of Performance Metrics for Green Data Centers: A Taxonomy Study. *The Journal of Supercomputing*, 63(3):639–656, 2013.

[73] White Paper, Google. Google's Carbon Offsets: Collaboration and Due Diligence. `https://static.googleusercontent.com/media/www.google.com/en//green/pdfs/google-carbon-offsets.pdf`, 2011.

[74] Erik Young, Paul Cao, and Mike Nikolaiev. First TPC-Energy Benchmark: Lessons Learned in Practice. In Raghunath Nambiar and Meikel Poess, editors, *Performance Evaluation, Measurement and Characterization of Complex Systems*, volume 6417 of *Lecture Notes in Computer Science*, pages 136–152. Springer Berlin Heidelberg, 2011.

[75] Qi Zhang, Lu Cheng, and Raouf Boutaba. Cloud Computing: State-Of-The-Art and Research Challenges. *Journal of Internet Services and Applications*, 1:7–18, 2010.

Problem Understanding and Real World Optimisation (PURO) Chairs' Welcome

It is our great pleasure to welcome you to the *2014 GECCO Workshop on Problem Understanding and Real World Optimisation (PURO)***.** This year's workshop builds upon the success of last year's even which was organized as part of GECCO 2013, held in the VU University in Amsterdam. Last year's event was a joint workshop combining workshops on problem understanding organised by Kent McClymont of the University of Exeter and on real world optimisation organized by Emma Hart from Edinburgh Napier University. Based on the success of last year's joint workshop this year's event merges the two workshops into a single event covering both ranges of topics.

This workshop aims to provide a single forum for the presentation and discussion of works focused on optimisation problems rather than the methods for solving them. The workshop brings together the study of real-world optimisation problems with the theoretical analysis and synthesis of problems.

The workshop will focus on, but not be limited to, topics such as:

- Methods for identifying and constructing models for new optimisation problems.
- Study of real-world optimisation problems and case studies.
- Theoretical and practical analysis of optimisation problems.
- Fitness landscape analysis of real-world problems.
- Classification and ontological analysis of problems.
- Development of and technologies for building benchmark test problems.
- Technologies and theoretical works supporting the implementation, examination and application of real-world and test problems.

The call for papers attracted submissions from Asia, Canada, Europe, and the United States. The topics covered address some of the real world issues and constraints imposed by industry and the complications associated with applying highly specialised techniques to real world problems. In addition, the program includes two keynote speeches, one from an industrial perspective and the other from academia. We are very grateful to both speakers, Anna I Esparcia-Alcázar from S2 GRUPO, Spain and Darrell Whitley from Colorado State University, USA who both have extensive knowledge of biologically inspired computing techniques within both industrial and academic environments.

Kevin Sim
Edinburgh Napier University, UK

Gabriela Ochoa
University of Stirling , UK

PURO 2014 Organization

Program Chairs: Kevin Sim *(Edinburgh Napier University, UK)*
Gabriela Ochoa *(University of Stirling, UK)*

Program Committee: Kevin Sim *(Edinburgh Napier University, UK)*
Gabriela Ochoa *(University of Stirling, UK)*
Ed Keedwell *(University of Exeter., UK)*

Invited Speakers: Anna I Esparcia-Alcázar *(S2 GRUPO, Spain)*
Darrell Whitley *(Colorado State University, USA)*

Sponsor: acm SIGEVO

Supporters: Edinburgh Napier University; University of Stirling; University of Exeter; EPSRC Engineering and Physical Sciences Research Council

A Comparison of Antenna Placement Algorithms

Abhinav Jauhri
Dept. of Electrical & Computer Engineering
Carnegie Mellon University
Pittsburgh, PA, USA
ajauhri@cmu.edu

Jason D. Lohn
Dept. of Electrical & Computer Engineering
Carnegie Mellon University
Pittsburgh, PA, USA
jlohn@ece.cmu.edu

Derek S. Linden
X5 Systems
Ashburn, VA, USA
dlinden@x5systems.com

ABSTRACT

Co-location of multiple antenna systems on a single fixed or mobile platform can be challenging due to a variety of factors, such as mutual coupling, individual antenna constraints, multipath, obstructions, and parasitic effects due to the platform. The situation frequently arises where a new communication capability, and hence antenna system, is needed on an existing platform. The problem of placing new antennas requires a long, manual effort in order to complete an antenna placement study. An automated procedure for determining such placements would not only save time, but would be able to optimize the performance of all co-located antenna systems. In this paper we examine a set of stochastic algorithms to determine their effectiveness at finding optimal placements for multiple antennas on a platform. To our knowledge, this is the first study to investigate optimizing multiple antenna placement on a single platform using multiple stochastic algorithms. Of the four algorithms studied, simulated annealing and evolutionary strategy were found to be most effective in finding optimal placements.

Categories and Subject Descriptors

I.2.8 [**Aritifical Intelligence**]: Problem Solving, Control Methods, and Search—*Heuristic methods*; I.6.3 [**Simulation and Modeling**]: Applications

General Terms

Algorithms, Performance

Keywords

Antenna Placement, Placement Optimization, Genetic Algorithm, Simulated Annealing, Hill Climber, Evolutionary Strategy, Multi-Objective Optimization

1. INTRODUCTION

Antenna placement on a multi-antenna platform currently involves a manual process that is challenging, time-consuming, and may result in sub-optimal placements leading to lowered communication systems' performance. Moreover, the search space becomes exponentially large with regard to the number of antennas to be placed (|search space| $= m^n$, where m is the number of allowable placements for each antenna and n is number of antennas).

Applying an evolutionary algorithm (EA) to this problem could greatly improve this process by automatically determining acceptable antenna placements. Evolutionary algorithms encompass a variety of computer search technologies, with the Genetic Algorithm (GA) being the most well-known [10]. EAs have proven very capable in discovering high performance antenna designs and previous work has been responsible for a number of advances [9], including the seminal patent for this process and genetically-evolved antennas deployed in space [14, 16]. Additionally, our work is *highly generic* such that any type of a platform may be used to find optimal placement of antennas.

Our main contributions are:

- Applying existing stochastic algorithms to help determining optimal or near-optimal antenna placements on a platform
- Our approach is agnostic of the type of platform used
- We apply experiments on different types of platforms and antennas to demonstrate the effectiveness of different stochastic algorithms

In Section 2, we provide some related work done with finding optimal antenna placements. Section 3 formally describes the problem statement, fitness calculation, and the representation of an individual which we shall refer to as *hypothesis*. Different algorithms used in our study to find optimal antenna placements are formally described in Section 4. Experimental setup is described in Section 5. Section 6 has simulation results and comparison of algorithms. Selection of parameters for certain algorithms is also described in Section 6. In the last section, we conclude, and provide future directions for further investigation.

2. RELATED WORKS

The problem of optimizing the placement of multiple antennas on a single platform has rarely been studied, if at all. The closest research we have found concerns algorithms for locating and configuring infrastructure for cellular wireless networks with the assumption of isotropic radiation pattern, for example [25]. Another related is work used characteristic mode analysis to compute optimal antenna locations for an

GECCO'14, July 12–16, 2014, Vancouver, BC, Canada.
Copyright 2014 ACM 978-1-4503-2881-4/14/07$15.00.
http://dx.doi.org/10.1145/2598394.2605446.

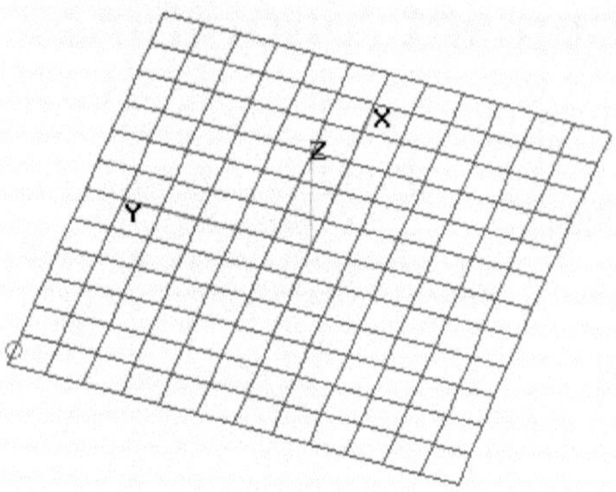

Figure 1: Platform used for test case 1 (tc1) & 4 (tc4)

antenna placed within a mobile device [24, 7]. In our work, none of the algorithms discussed have prior information of good antenna placements or type of antennas to be placed on the platform.

In addition, the related problem of co-designing antennas for a given platform (*in-situ* design) using EAs has been investigated in [15] with encouraging results. Because antenna placement bears many similarities to antenna design, we believe that such algorithms will prove effective.

3. PROBLEM FORMULATION

A platform for our problem formulation could vary from a simple rectangular box to an aircraft.

3.1 Inputs

Our inputs to an algorithm shall comprise of a platform and set of antennas each with allowable placements on the platform. Formally, a platform, P, in 3-dimensional space with its surface discretized into a regular grid with some spacing consisting of potential antenna placement points (see Figure 1). Let m denote the number of antennas to be placed on P such that $m > 1$, and let A represent the set of antennas: $A = \{A_1, ..., A_m\}$. For each antenna A_i, let L_i denote the set allowable placement coordinates $\in \mathbb{R}^3$ on P such that $\mid L_i \mid = n_i$, and $\forall i, n_i > 1$:

$$L_i = \{(x_1, y_1, z_1), ..., (x_{n_i}, y_{n_i}, z_{n_i})\}$$

Using the inputs, a *hypothesis* (**an individual is referred to as hypothesis in this paper**[1]), H, is formed by a set of m antenna locations. In other words, a hypothesis is a placement configuration i.e. a set having m placements, one for each of the m antennas, in 3-dimensional space:

$$H = \{(x_1, y_1, z_1), \cdots, (x_m, y_m, z_m)\}$$

The reader should note that the number of allowable placements for any antenna are finite. We shall elaborate how that is ensured later in Section 5.

[1]Hypotheses are described as bit strings with interpretation based on the application [20]

3.2 Fitness Evaluation

The placement optimization aims to find the best *hypothesis*, H^*, such that the radiation pattern and mutual coupling are optimal. For optimal radiation pattern, we shall minimize the difference between the free-space gain pattern (FSG) of antenna A_i, and its pattern when placed on P and in the presence of all remaining antennas (in-situ gain, or ISG). Thus, for each gain point for A_i we compute:

$$F_{RP}(A_i) = \sum_{\theta} \sum_{\phi} \| ISG_i(\theta, \phi) - FSG_i(\theta, \phi) \|^2, \quad (1)$$

where θ & ϕ define the spherical and cylindrical coordinates of a field point respectively (see *Section 5 for more information*).

For the second objective, it is desired to minimize the mutual coupling between the antennas for a given placement configuration because strong mutual coupling reduces antenna efficiency [13]. This is computed in a pairwise manner where the CP function computes the coupling between two antennas:

$$F_{MC} = \sum_{i=1}^{m-1} \sum_{j=i+1}^{m} CP(A_i, A_j) \quad (2)$$

The overall optimization for a given placement configuration is to minimize fitness, F, as follows optimal antenna placement for mobile terminals using characteristic analysis:

$$F = \alpha F_{MC} + \beta \sum_{i} F_{RP}(A_i), \quad (3)$$

where α and β are constants which satisfy: $\alpha + \beta = 1$. Values for F_{MC} and F_{RP} are positively correlated [30], and therefore we can set α and β to some value $\in [0, 1]$ without loss of generality. F will be provided by an antenna simulation software which will be introduced in Section 5.

Radiation pattern and antenna coupling are measured in decibels (dB) which is a logarithmic unit used to express the ratio between two quantities i.e. $10 \cdot \log x_1/x_2$. For radiation pattern fitness parameter, the *antenna strength* or gain shown in Eq.(1), at any given point on a sphere is the ratio of the signal strength of the antenna being tested to a perfectly isotropic antenna, expressed in dB. For coupling, the ratio compares the energy absorbed by one antenna when the another antenna is operating nearby. For our antenna placement problem, this absorption is undesirable because we want the energy to be radiated away in order to establish a communication link, and not be absorbed by a nearby antenna. This coupling thus reduces the antenna's efficiency. For example, if the coupling (F_{MC}) was -10 dB for an hypothesis instead of the best, let's say -13 dB, then this reflects a difference Δ_c of 3 dB which translates to a doubling of energy absorbed in the -10 dB case compared to the -13 dB case. Shown in Table 1 is the equivalence of overall fitness (F) to Δ_c. Also shown is the equivalence to expected gain defined as:

$$\mathbb{E}_g = \frac{1}{N \cdot m} \sum_{i}^{m} F_{RP}(A_i), \quad (4)$$

where $N = \mid \theta \mid \cdot \mid \phi \mid$.

Each test case has its specific bounds on the different fitness parameters, and therefore the equivalence values are dependent on the test case as shown Table 1.

Table 1: Equivalence of fitness to efficiency

ID	$\mathbb{E}_g$	Δ_c (dB)
tc1	872.277	0.5474
tc2	862.082	1.3034
tc3	861.845	1.5180
tc4	871.049	0.5693

For a particular test case, fitness change of 0.01 is equivalent to either the corresponding value under $\mathbb{E}_g$ column, or difference in coupling (Δ_c).

4. STOCHASTIC SEARCH ALGORITHMS

Here, we formally describe all stochastic algorithms used for experiments and comparative analysis. Following details are similar between algorithms and should be highlighted for easy reproduction of this work:

- A hypothesis used by any algorithm is similar to as defined in the previous Section 3.1.
- For any hypothesis, no two antenna placements overlap. It may be the case that two different antennas have overlapping set of allowable placements, but the formation of any hypothesis avoids such a case as it may result in imprecise calculation of fitness.
- The $fitness(H)$ function used in all four algorithms is the equivalent of Eq.(3), assuming we have its inputs i.e. F_{MC} and F_{RP}.

4.1 Genetic Algorithm

Genetic algorithms aims to model different DNA operations in nature like crossover and mutation. They have been used extensively as stochastic search procedures for numerous applications [23]. We have used elitism in our algorithm since results in [36, 26] have shown performance speed up of a GA significantly.

Operators in Antenna Placement Genetic Algorithm(AP-GA, Algorithm 1) are *one-point crossover* and *mutation*. Each pair for one-point crossover operation comprises of one hypothesis uniformly selected from the population and the other hypothesis from a tournament selection [18]. The size of the hypothesis is not arbitrarily large, and therefore it was preferred to keep the mutation restricted to just manipulating one antenna placement of an hypothesis. For arbitrarily large number of antennas, one may need to consider changing the mutation operator to manipulate more than one antenna placement. The mutation operator described in Algorithm 1 is common to all other algorithms compared in this work.

We shall discuss about intuition for selecting values of p_m and p_c in Section 6.

4.2 Evolutionary Strategy

The evolutionary strategy $(\mu + \lambda)$ [27, 8] is different from a genetic algorithm in the following ways: mutation is the primary operator here for maintaining diversity in the population since there are no crossover operations. Survivor selection is done by selecting only fittest μ hypotheses to the next generation. See Algorithm 2. A 1/7 ratio was maintained between μ and λ as suggested in [6].

Since we have a discrete set of placements (end points of wires of a platform), *mutation's* step size involves a new placement from the set of allowable placements for an antenna only. Both the antenna and its new placement are selected uniformly at random. *Mutation* operator is surely applied once on an hypothesis to generate the offspring.

Algorithm 1: AP-GA

Data: Set of placements $L = \{L_1, \cdots, L_m\}$; p - population size; p_m - percentage of population to be with mutation operator; p_c - crossover probability; e - ratio of elite population; gen_{max} - maximum number of generations

Result: H^* from P

Initialize $P \leftarrow$ generate p random hypothesis. Each hypothesis contains a placement for all m antennas. A placement is chosen uniformly from each L_i, for all antennas ;
Compute the $fitness(h_i), i = 1, \ldots, p$;
Order hypotheses in P such that $fitness(h_i) < fitness(h_j)$, where $i < j$;
$gen_{id} = 0$;
while $gen_{id} < gen_{max}$ **do**
  Elitism - Select top $e \cdot p$ hypotheses, *elites*, to add to P' ;
  Crossover - Select $((1-e) \cdot p)/2$ pairs of hypotheses. Each pair is formed by choosing one hypothesis using tournament selection and other uniformly randomly from the population. For each pair M : ;
  if $rand(0,1) < p_c$ **then**
    Apply one-point crossover operator to get two offsprings O ;
    Add O to P' ;
  else
    Add M to P' ;
  end
  Mutation - Uniformly select $p_m \cdot p$ hypothesis from P. For each, modify one uniformly at random selected antenna location to a different allowable location also selected uniformly at random ;
  Update $P \leftarrow P'$;
  Compute $fitness(h_i); i = 1, \ldots, p$, and order new population based on fitness ;
  Update $gen_{id} \leftarrow gen_{id} + 1$;
end

Algorithm 2: AP-ES

Data: Set of placements $L = \{L_1, \cdots, L_m\}$; μ; λ; gen_{max} - maximum number of generations

Result: H^* from P

Initialize $P \leftarrow$ generate μ random hypothesis ;
$gen_{id} = 0$;
while $gen_{id} < gen_{max}$ **do**
  Create λ/μ offsprings from each μ hypotheses by applying mutation operator, and add all offsprings to P ;
  Compute the $fitness(h_i), i = 1, \ldots, \lambda$;
  Keep μ best hypotheses in P, and discard remaining $\lambda - \mu$ hypotheses ;
  Update $gen_{id} \leftarrow gen_{id} + 1$
end

4.3 Simulated Annealing

Simulated annealing models thermodynamics [12] by including a temperature cooling schedule. Numerous applications [28, 5] have compared simulated annealing with evolutionary techniques. *AP-SA* (Algorithm 3) is similar to [35]. However, we perform some extra computation to determine initial temperature using an approach stated in [2].

Algorithm 3: AP-SA

Data: Set of placements $L = \{L_1, \cdots, L_m\}$; T - initial temperature; i_m - maximum iterations; $f_{cooling}$ - cooling factor
Result: H^* from P

Initialize $H \leftarrow$ generate a random hypothesis ;
Compute $fitness(H)$;
$i = 0$;
while $i < i_m$ **do**
  Mutation - Apply the operation on H as stated in Algorithm 1. Call the pertubrated/mutated hypothesis C ;
  Compute $\delta f = fitness(C) - fitness(H)$;
  if $\delta f > 0$ **then**
    Generate a random number ϵ using a uniform distribution over $[0, 1]$;
    if $\epsilon < e^{-\delta f / T}$ **then**
      $H \leftarrow C$
    end
  else
    $H \leftarrow C$;
  end
  $T \leftarrow T \cdot f_{cooling}$;
  $i \leftarrow i + 1$;
end

4.4 Hill-Climbing

Hill climbing is different from a simulated annealing since there is no cooling schedule. This makes a hill-climbing prone to getting stuck in locally optimal solutions [17, 3]. However, the ease of implementation and effectiveness in numerous optimization problems [29, 34] makes hill-climbing a popular approach for stochastic search spaces. Here is a simple hill-climbing algorithm, similar to [29], to provide a basis on how a naive random search algorithm would do on the antenna placement problem in comparison to other stochastic techniques.

Algorithm 4: AP-HC

Data: Set of placements $L = \{L_1, \cdots, L_m\}$; i_m - maximum iterations
Result: H

Initialize $H \leftarrow$ generate a random hypothesis ;
Compute $fitness(H)$;
$i = 0$;
while $i < i_m$ **do**
  Mutation - Apply the operator on H & assign the slightly perturbated hypothesis to C ;
  Compute $\delta f = fitness(C) - fitness(H)$;
  if $\delta f < 0$ **then**
    $H \leftarrow C$
  end
  $i \leftarrow i + 1$
end

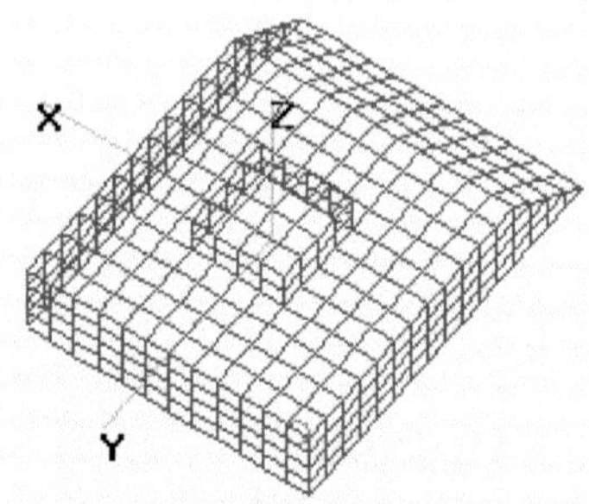

Figure 2: Platform used for test case 2 (tc2)

5. EXPERIMENTAL SETUP

We used an open source antenna modeling software called Numerical Electromagnetic Code(NEC)[4] to calculate the fitness of an hypothesis. NEC has been widely used for electromagnetic analysis and simulation work [32, 22]. Moreover, NEC provides a convenient interface to input details about platform with antennas mounted, and to collect simulation results which are mutual coupling and radiation pattern. Our application, *Evolutionary Antenna Placement*[2] (*EAP*), interacts with NEC to provide the input, and subsequently uses the output generated by NEC to calculate fitness.

For our purposes, the hypothesis is written to an input file (to be referred as N_{in}) which is used by NEC modeler to generate an output file (to be referred as N_{out}). The platform and all antennas of an hypothesis are written to N_{in} as a set of wires with a start-point and an end-point in 3-dimensional space. For instance, consider a wire represented by 2-tuple, w, of real-valued coordinates; $\{(0, 0, 0.1), (0, 0.1, 0)\}$.

Figure 2 shows the meshed platform depicting a squared plate with box and a sloped front used in test case 2 of our experiments. The platform and antenna are just a set of tuples similar to w. A square plate with box and sides fixed was the platform for test case 3 (Figure 3). Possible antenna locations, for all test cases, are defined by either start-points or end-points of platform wires. Experiments with multiple platforms highlight the technique to be *highly generic* for platforms with any shape and design.

NEC has pre-defined cards which are inserted in N_{in} to enable collection of fitness parameters. Radiation pattern, generated by the *RF* card, is calculated using a set of field points around a sphere. The number of field points in a radiation pattern is determined by the product of total number of spherical(θ) and cylindrical(ϕ) values which encompass points in a sphere. All experiments computed the radiation gain over 4140 points i.e.= $\mid \theta \mid \cdot \mid \phi \mid$.

[2]Link to code repository: `https://github.com/ajauhri/evol-ant-placement`

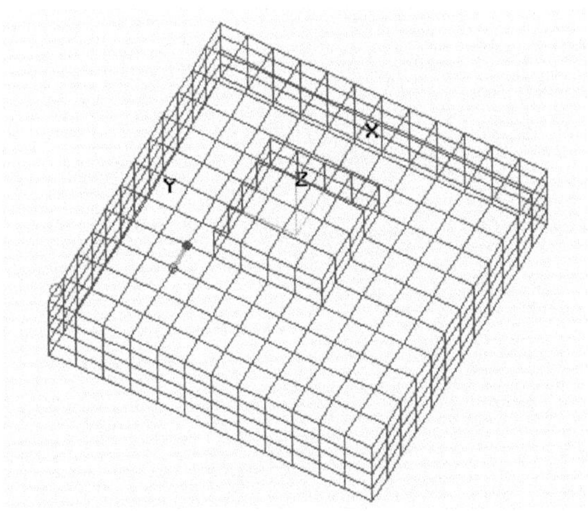

Figure 3: Platform used for test case 3 (tc3)

Table 2: Antenna Placement Test Cases

ID	Antennas	Total allowable placements[3]
tc1	2	7,056 (83x83)
tc2	3	50,625 (45x45x25)
tc3	3	126,025 (71x71x25)
tc4	4	20,736 (12x12x12x12)

For our placement study, m input files would be generated by *EAP* for an hypothesis with m antennas and with only one of the m antennas excited in each input file. Subsequently, NEC would generate m output files with performance measures. By exciting one antenna in each input file, we are able to quantify the radiation pattern of an antenna in presence of the platform and other antennas. To determine the free-space gain pattern(FSG) for an antenna, an input file is formed with just the antenna and no platform. F_{RP} is then calculated by *EAP* parsing $2m$(m files with platform and antennas; m files for free space pattern) output files generated by NEC and performing a summation over squared difference in gain between free-space and in the presence of the platform and antennas (Eq.(1)).

The second fitness parameter - mutual coupling, is generated by inserting the *CP* card in the $(m+1)th$ file generated by *EAP* . A single file is needed for NEC to generate an output file with mutual coupling results between all possible pairs of antenna placements of an hypothesis.

All test cases were subjected to the same frequency of 100 MegaHertz using the *FR* card. For a detailed description of formatting of N_{in} and N_{out} files, refer to the NEC manual [4].

6. SIMULATION RESULTS

Comparative study of algorithms is based on multiple test cases listed in Table 2. Test cases were evaluated by NEC simulator which was run in parallel using *GNU Parallel* software package [31].

Each test case was first evaluated with an exhaustive search to determine fitness for all allowable placements and antennas. The results from exhaustive search were also used to normalize fitness function values between $[0, 1]$. For all experiments $\alpha = \beta = 0.5$ in Eq.(3).

[3]Allowable placements for each antenna are provided within parenthesis

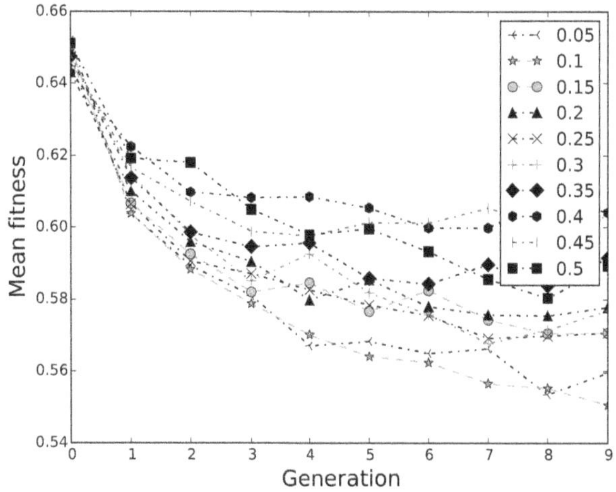

Figure 4: Mutation rates for AP-GA. The mean fitness is calculated over a population size of 500 using test case 1

Prior to collection of results, a series of trial and error runs were conducted in the case of Algorithm 1 to determine an appropriate mutation rate. Intuitively, a high mutation rate, referred as p_m in Section 4.1, drives the algorithm into a random search and renders evolutionary aspect of the algorithm weak. This is ascertained in Figure 4 where the mean fitness for each generation is shown over 10 runs of *AP-GA*. However, it is preferred to have a high value for p_c[19]. For all test cases, *AP-GA* uses $p_m = 0.1$ & $p_c = 0.6$. gen_{max} for *AP-GA* and *AP-ES* is 10.

For similuted annealing, the cooling factor was kept as $1 - \tau$, where $\tau = 0.01 \cdot m_{iters}$. Maximum iterations($m_{iters}$) were about 70% of the total allowable placements of a test case. The initial temperature calculated using technique described in [2] ranged $\in [0.23, 0.27]$.

Table 3 summarizes the average best fitness over *10* runs found by all four algorithms. The best hypothesis H^*'s fitness is shown under the *Exhaustive* algorithm column.

The reader should observe in Table 3 that effectiveness of a stochastic algorithm can be computed by the difference in the fitness found by the exhaustive search algorithm and stochastic algorithms. Formally:

$$M_{error} = \mid fitness(H^*) - \sum_{i=1}^{n=10} b_i/n \mid, \qquad (5)$$

where b_i is the best fitness of the hypothesis found in a run by the stochastic search algorithm. For a test case, this is equivalent to the difference of the cell values of *Exhaustive* column and any one of the stochastic search algorithms in Table 3. Omitted here due to brevity.

Table 3 depicts the mean fitness found by *AP-ES* for all test cases is equivalent to the optimal, H^*. This is also true for *AP-SA* for test cases 3 & 4. Hence, on such instances

Table 3: Mean Best Fitness

test case \ method	Exhaustive(H^*)	AP-GA	AP-ES	AP-SA	AP-HC
tc1	0.496 841	0.499 33	0.496 841	0.499 485	0.501 59
tc2	0.496 877	0.497 957	0.496 877	0.504 270	0.5138
tc3	0.497 47	0.497 646	0.497 47	0.497 47	0.498 728
tc4	0.499 26	0.499 26	0.499 26	0.499 26	0.499 26

these two algorithms were able to find the best hypothesis on all runs.

The other important observation is of how many number of fitness function evaluations did each algorithm take to find a good hypothesis? Evolutionary strategy and simulated annealing outperformed the genetic algorithm in terms of mean number of fitness evaluations to find the best hypothesis as seen in Table 4. These evaluations were recorded for the same runs as shown previously in Table 3. The number of evaluations recorded were until the algorithm found the best hypothesis or got stuck at some local optimal hypothesis. Number of function evaluations is more appropriate here rather than the CPU clock time as the time may vary for each machine based on the hardware configuration.

We also visualized the fitness terrain of the best hypothesis followed by each of the stochastic algorithms[4]. Such visualization is a good tool to observe the correctness of the algorithm. For instance, a simulated annealing is prone to have an event of accepting a bad hypothesis with a higher probability initially in the run and this event should happen with low probability as algorithm proceeds. For all simulated annealing graphs in Figures 5, 6, 7, & 8, we observe that the gap between any two consecutive events of such nature increases as the algorithm proceeds in the search space.

The genetic algorithm in Figure 6 accepted a worse hypothesis because of the fact that mutation could happen even in the group of elite hypothesis as stated in Algorithm 1. The elites were included in the mutation pool to maintain diversity. For evolutionary strategy and hill climbing, the fitness terrain does not have unorthodox patterns. The values in parenthesis for all population based algorithms viz. genetic algorithm and evolutionary strategy, represent the population size. They were kept at approximately the same ratio with the corresponding size of the search space in Table 2.

It may be incorrectly depicted from Table 3 that hill-climbing performed quite well for test case 3. This is not the case, since the top ten hypotheses lie within a small fitness range of [0.49747, 0.498428]. As known in general, the hill-climbing algorithm made progress only in the initial phases of the run and got stuck in local optimums for 80% of the runs for test case 3. The purpose for inclusion of such a random search algorithm was to highlight that antenna placements may not be a trivial task to solve with high probability, if the search space is large as in the case of test case 3. For smaller test cases like test case 4, hill-climbing may be appropriate.

7. CONCLUSION

A comparison of four stochastic search algorithms applied to antenna placement optimization was presented. The re-

[4]The best hypothesis's fitness curve was almost similar for all 10 runs

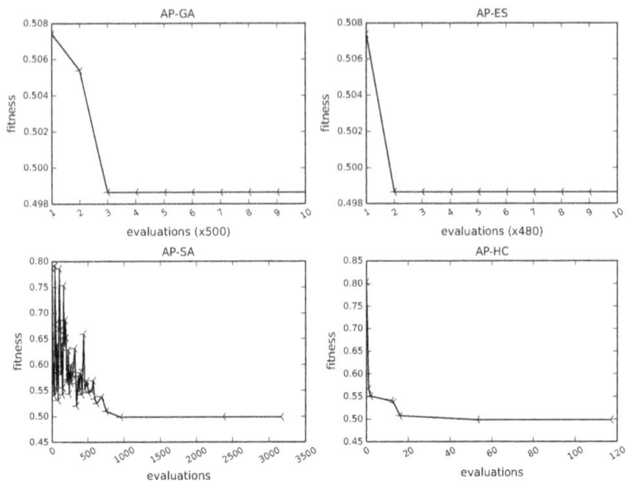

Figure 5: Test Case 1 Comparison

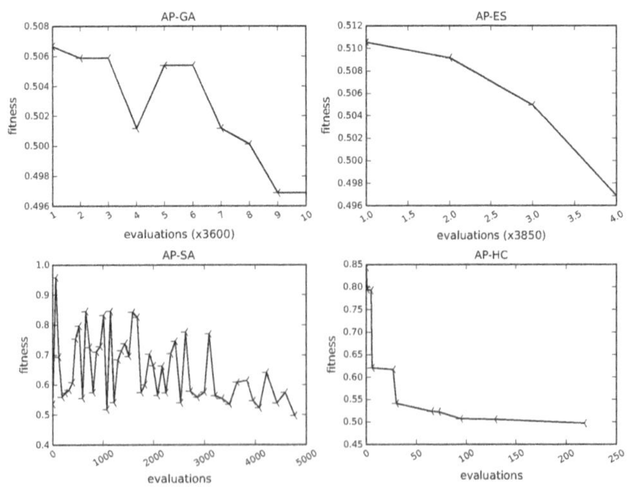

Figure 6: Test Case 2 Comparison

Table 4: Mean evaluations

test case \ method	AP-GA	AP-ES	AP-SA	AP-HC
tc1	2350	1728	667	164
tc2	31 680	11 165	1653	174
tc3	45 900	26 880	4809	227
tc4	6150	4466	423	90

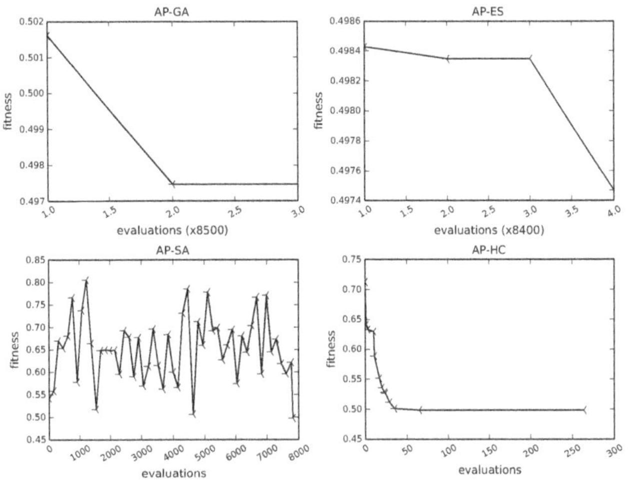

Figure 7: Test Case 3 Comparison

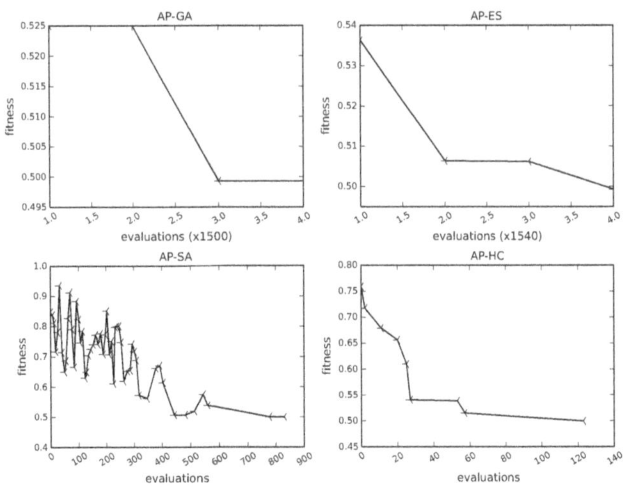

Figure 8: Test Case 4 Comparison

sults showed that a trade-off space exists: faster, less successful simulated annealing (*AP-SA*) search versus slower, more successful search by evolutionary strategy (*AP-ES*). The other generation-based algorithm (*AP-GA*) did not prove as effective as evolutionary strategy, and also much slower to find the optimal placements. Also, a random search was studied to ascertain that the antenna placement problem may not be effectively solved by a naive algorithm for large search spaces.

Our work showed that a simple formulation of the antenna placement problem and the usage of open-source technologies (NEC) can be applied effectively for a hard problem. Moreover, our methodology can be applied to any type of a platform which otherwise may be time consuming and expensive in case of large objects like satellites and aircrafts.

7.1 Future Work

Most of the stochastic algorithms presented here were elementary and there were no variations to them. For instance, scheduling problems have been effectively solved using hybrid versions of genetic algorithms [33]. Similarly, variations of algorithms mentioned here should also be looked at for the antenna placement problem.

More experiments need to be conducted for population based algorithms with different population sizes, and to statistically compare how this may affect the performance of the algorithm. Also, bigger search spaces need to be considered with more number of antennas. Other evolutionary techniques like ALPS [11], differential evolution algorithm [21], and genetic programming [1] need to be compared in terms of how quickly they find the optimal solution.

8. REFERENCES

[1] W. Banzhaf, P. Nordin, R. E. Keller, and F. D. Francone. Genetic programming: An introduction: On the automatic evolution of computer programs and its applications (the morgan kaufmann series in artificial intelligence). 1997.

[2] W. Ben-Ameur. Computing the initial temperature of simulated annealing. *Computational Optimization and Applications*, 29(3):369–385, 2004.

[3] J. Borghoff, L. R. Knudsen, and K. Matusiewicz. Hill climbing algorithms and trivium. In *Selected Areas in Cryptography*, pages 57–73. Springer, 2011.

[4] G. Burke and A. Poggio. Numerical electromagnetics code (nec)-method of moments, part iii: User's guide. *Lawrence Livermore National Laboratory*, (1), 1981.

[5] L. Davis. Genetic algorithms and simulated annealing. 1987.

[6] A. E. Eiben and J. E. Smith. *Introduction to evolutionary computing*, volume 2. Springer Berlin, 2010.

[7] C. T. Famdie, W. L. Schroeder, and K. Solbach. Optimal antenna location on mobile phones chassis based on the numerical analysis of characteristic modes. In *Microwave Conference, 2007. European*, pages 987–990. IEEE, 2007.

[8] D. B. Fogel. An introduction to simulated evolutionary optimization. *Neural Networks, IEEE Transactions on*, 5(1):3–14, 1994.

[9] R. L. Haupt and D. H. Werner. *Genetic algorithms in electromagnetics*. Wiley. com, 2007.

[10] J. H. Holland. *Adaptation in natural and artificial systems: An introductory analysis with applications to biology, control, and artificial intelligence*. U Michigan Press, 1975.

[11] G. S. Hornby. Alps: the age-layered population structure for reducing the problem of premature convergence. In *Proceedings of the 8th annual conference on Genetic and evolutionary computation*, pages 815–822. ACM, 2006.

[12] S. Kirkpatrick, D. G. Jr., and M. P. Vecchi. Optimization by simmulated annealing. *science*, 220(4598):671–680, 1983.

[13] J. Leivo and T. Vukusic. Improving the performance of strongly coupled antennas using a compensating transmission line network. 2009.

[14] D. S. Linden. Automated design and optimization of wire antennas using genetic algorithms. Technical report, DTIC Document, 1997.

[15] D. S. Linden. Wire antennas optimized in the presence of satellite structures using genetic algorithms. In *Aerospace Conference Proceedings, 2000 IEEE*, volume 5, pages 91–99. IEEE, 2000.

[16] J. D. Lohn, D. S. Linden, G. S. Hornby, A. Rodriguez-Arroyo, S. E. Seufert, B. Blevins, and T. Greenling. Evolutionary design of a single-wire circularly-polarized x-band antenna for nasa's space technology 5 mission. In *Antennas and Propagation Society International Symposium, 2005 IEEE*, volume 2, pages 267–270. IEEE, 2005.

[17] Z. Michalewicz and D. B. Fogel. *Escaping Local Optima*. Springer, 2000.

[18] B. L. Miller and D. E. Goldberg. Genetic algorithms, tournament selection, and the e ects of noise. *Urbana*, 51:61801, 1995.

[19] V. Miranda, J. Ranito, and L. M. Proenca. Genetic algorithms in optimal multistage distribution network planning. *Power Systems, IEEE Transactions on*, 9(4):1927–1933, 1994.

[20] T. M. Mitchell. *Machine Learning*. McGraw-Hill, Inc., New York, NY, USA, 1 edition, 1997.

[21] Q.-K. Pan, M. F. Tasgetiren, and Y.-C. Liang. A discrete differential evolution algorithm for the permutation flowshop scheduling problem. *Computers & Industrial Engineering*, 55(4):795–816, 2008.

[22] R. K. Pokharel, M. Ishii, and Y. Baba. Numerical electromagnetic analysis of lightning-induced voltage over ground of finite conductivity. *Electromagnetic Compatibility, IEEE Transactions on*, 45(4):651–656, 2003.

[23] Y. Rahmat-Samii and E. Michielssen. *Electromagnetic optimization by genetic algorithms*. John Wiley & Sons, Inc., 1999.

[24] J. Rahola and J. Ollikainen. Optimal antenna placement for mobile terminals using characteristic mode analysis. In *Antennas and Propagation, 2006. EuCAP 2006. First European Conference on*, pages 1–6. IEEE, 2006.

[25] L. Raisanen and R. M. Whitaker. Comparison and evaluation of multiple objective genetic algorithms for the antenna placement problem. *Mobile Networks and Applications*, 10(1-2):79–88, 2005.

[26] G. Rudolph. Evolutionary search under partially ordered sets. *Dept. Comput. Sci./LS11, Univ. Dortmund, Dortmund, Germany, Tech. Rep. CI-67/99*, 1999.

[27] H.-P. Schwefel. *Numerische Optimierung von Computer-Modellen mittels der Evolutionsstrategie: mit einer vergleichenden Einführung in die Hill-Climbing-und Zufallsstrategie*. Birkhäuser Basel, 1977.

[28] R. S. Sexton, R. E. Dorsey, and J. D. Johnson. Optimization of neural networks: A comparative analysis of the genetic algorithm and simulated annealing. *European Journal of Operational Research*, 114(3):589–601, 1999.

[29] D. B. Skalak. Prototype and feature selection by sampling and random mutation hill climbing algorithms. In *ICML*, pages 293–301. Citeseer, 1994.

[30] A. Stjernman. Antenna mutual coupling effects on correlation, efficiency and shannon capacity. In *Antennas and Propagation, 2006. EuCAP 2006. First European Conference on*, pages 1–6. IEEE, 2006.

[31] O. Tange. Gnu parallel-the command-line power tool. *login: The USENIX Magazine*, pages 42–47, 2011.

[32] T. Topa, A. Karwowski, and A. Noga. Using gpu with cuda to accelerate mom-based electromagnetic simulation of wire-grid models. *Antennas and Wireless Propagation Letters, IEEE*, 10:342–345, 2011.

[33] V. Valls, F. Ballestin, and S. Quintanilla. A hybrid genetic algorithm for the resource-constrained project scheduling problem. *European Journal of Operational Research*, 185(2):495–508, 2008.

[34] B. Xi, Z. Liu, M. Raghavachari, C. H. Xia, and L. Zhang. A smart hill-climbing algorithm for application server configuration. In *Proceedings of the 13th international conference on World Wide Web*, pages 287–296. ACM, 2004.

[35] L. Xu and E. Oja. Improved simulated annealing, boltzmann machine, and attributed graph matching. In *Neural Networks*, pages 151–160. Springer, 1990.

[36] E. Zitzler, K. Deb, and L. Thiele. Comparison of multiobjective evolutionary algorithms: Empirical results. *Evolutionary computation*, 8(2):173–195, 2000.

Hyper-Heuristic Genetic Algorithm for Solving Frequency Assignment Problem in TD-SCDMA

Chao Yang
Business School
Hunan University
Changsha, China
yangchaoedu@hnu.edu.cn

Shuming Peng
College of Information Science and Engineering
Hunan University
Changsha, China
pengshuming@hnu.edu.cn

Bin Jiang
College of Information Science and Engineering
Hunan University
Changsha, China
jiangbin@hnu.edu.cn

Lei Wang
College of Information Science and Engineering
Hunan University
Changsha, China
stone4827321@163.com

Renfa Li
College of Information Science and Engineering
Hunan University
Changsha, China
lirenfa@vip.sina.com

ABSTRACT

This paper studies the frequency assignment problem (FAP) in TD-SCDMA network of mobile communications industry in China. The problem considers finding the optimal frequency allocation scheme for carriers with a limited frequency resource, such that the entire network interference is minimized. Besides, the allocation of frequencies needs to satisfy some constraints to avoid the effect of call interference within the same cell or adjacent cell. Given the formula for calculation of the network interference, we take the FAP as a constrained optimization problem and use a hyper-heuristic genetic algorithm (HHGA) to optimize the assignment of frequencies. We first define six low-level heuristics (LLHs) search strategies based on the computation of interference, and then use genetic algorithm (GA) at a high-level to find the best combination sequence of LLH strategies to reduce interferences of the overall network. GA uses two-point crossover, uniform mutation, and Minimal Generation Gap (MGG) as the generation alternation model. In order to speed up the search, we define a Tabu table to avoid repeat search of LLHs. Compared with scatter search as one of the meta-heuristic algorithm with best performance, our experimental results on real data sets of TD-SCDMA network have shown better result.

Categories and Subject Descriptors

I.2.8 [**Artificial Intelligence**]: Problem Solving, Control Methods, and Search—*heuristic methods*; G.1.6 [**Numerical Analysis**]: Optimization—*Global optimization*

*This work was supported by grant 13JJ3049 of the Natural Science Foundation of Hunan Province, China, grant 2012FJ4131 of the Science and Technology Research Plan of Hunan Province, China and grant 2012AA01A301-1 of the National 863 High-Tech Project.

GECCO'14, July 12–16, 2014, Vancouver, BC, Canada.
 978-1-4503-2881-4/14/07…$15.00.
http://dx.doi.org/10.1145/2598394.2605445

General Terms

Algorithms, Experimentation, Performance

Keywords

TD-SCDMA; Mobile Communication Network; Frequency Assignment Problem; Hyper-Heuristic Genetic Algorithm

1. INTRODUCTION

TD-SCDMA (Time Division-Synchronous Code Division Multiple Access) network is the third generation wireless communications network developed by China. Compared with GSM (Global System for Mobile communications) network, TD-SCDMA has faster Internet speed and higher utilization of frequency resource. In China, there are more and more people choosing to use this network. Given a limited range of frequency bandwidth, operators always face the problem of finding the optimal frequency allocation scheme with minimal interference of the network. Such problem is called frequency assignment problem (FAP) in mobile communication network. Due to the limited frequency resource and the increasing size of the network, FAP has become a key issue in TD-SCDMA network [1,2,3].

Fig.1 describes the general composition of TD-SCDMA network, which mainly includes three parts: core network (CN), radio access network (RAN) and user equipments (UE) [4]. CN handles all voice calls, data connections and data exchanges within the network, and connections and routing choices with other external network. RAN processes functions associated with wireless, such as radio resource management, power control etc. [4]. UE is the receiver or transmitter of the wireless data. In these three parts, only RAN is related to FAP. As described in Fig.1, RAN is composed of radio network controller (RNC), Node B, cells and carriers [4]. RNC provides functions of mobility management, call processing, connection management, and switching mechanisms. Node B is equivalent to the function of base station in GSM [5], which provides radio services for cells. Cell represents a continuous geographic area, at which mobile services are provided. Normally, a Node B will transmit plural radio waves to multiple cells for communications, these cells are called co-station cells and such radio waves are called carriers. Each carrier should be assigned with a frequency for wireless communication and there are always multiple carriers in one cell. Among these carries, one is called main carrier (also called main frequency) and others are called secondary carrier (also called secondary frequency).

Most wireless communications of a cell are on the main carrier, the secondary carriers will not be enabled unless the business volume or the network interference on the main carrier exceeds its maximum limitation.

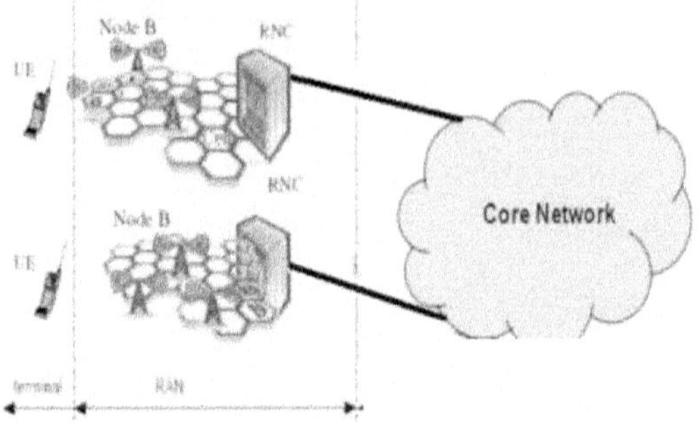

Figure 1. The General Composition of TD-SCDMA network.

In most cases of the real operations, frequencies are always reused by different carriers due to the limited frequency resources and the large requirements of the real problems. While the carries assigned with same frequencies will cause interference with each other, and such interferes would impact on call quality and data services, thus decrease the performance of the communication network. As the interference of the network varies with different frequency assignment schemes, we should find an optimal frequency assignment schema to minimize the interference of the network, so as to improve the performance of the mobile communication network.

Early scholars had regarded the frequency allocation problem as a graph coloring problem, and it was treated as a NP hard problem [6]. But this method only considered the frequency resource constraints of FAP and gave a solution without considering its quality. A high quality solution for FAP should have lower interference of the network to enable a higher quality voice call, and a balanced utilization time of all frequencies. In reality, the quality of the solution relates to every source of interference within the network environment and technical limitations. We need to find an effective way to solve FAP by considering all main factors to optimize the solution. Therefore, FAP is more like a constrained optimization problem.

There have existed contributions of FAP mostly concentrated on the GSM network, and these studies can be divided into two categories: deterministic method and heuristic method, where the latter can be further divided into meta heuristic method and hyper-heuristic method. Deterministic methods include graph coloring [7], branch cutting [8], Enumeration [9], etc. Although such methods have proved their effectiveness on dealing with small networks, they have seldom been applied to solve the large scale network problem due to the high complexity of the algorithms. Heuristic methods have proved their effectiveness on such problems [10]. Meta-heuristic methods contain tabu search [11], ant colony optimization (ACO) [5], genetic algorithm (GA) [12], scatter search (SS) [6], etc. These methods had achieved good results for solving FAP in GSM. In [6], the authors compared ACO, GA, SS and other meta-heuristic methods on a same dataset, and found that SS showed best performance for solving FAP in GSM. While these meta-heuristic algorithms had been designed for specific problems, one algorithm could not be easily applied to solve problems in different domains, so they were not generic.

Compared with meta-heuristics, hyper-heuristics have shown better perform on most optimization problems. In the literature, hyper-heuristic methods are categorized into (1) hyper-heuristics either with learning or without learning [13], or (2) constructive method and local search method [14], or (3) heuristic selection and heuristic generation [15]. Hyper-heuristic with learning changes the sequence of heuristics to call by some learning mechanism, which always achieves better performance than hyper-heuristic without learning just calling heuristics in a predetermined sequence. Local search method is more likely to find a global optimization by iteratively selecting appropriate heuristics to optimize the solution; while constructive method builds a solution incrementally by selecting heuristics. Heuristic selection selects the existing heuristics but heuristic generation can generate new heuristics from components of existing heuristics. Compared with heuristic generation, heuristic selection is independent on problem and simple to be implemented. Based on the above analysis, in this paper, we focus on hyper-heuristic with learning, local search and heuristic selection. We call this type of hyper-heuristic as hyper-heuristic in the remaining text. In contrast to meta-heuristic methods, hyper-heuristics are supposed problem independent, and easy to be implemented.

In general, hyper-heuristic methods can be divided into two layers: low level is heuristic strategies called low level heuristic (LLH), which are always some local search method based on the problems, and easy to be implemented; high level called hyper-heuristic is a selector for LLHs, which operates to find an effective LLH sequence to improve the current solution. For different optimization problems, we only need to design the LLHs according to the problems, and keep the high level unchanged. So once the hyper-heuristic (high level) has been designed, it is easy to deal with most optimization problems. In the literature, Kendall and Mohamad had proposed a hyper-heuristic method to solve FAP in GSM, they had found better solution than most other methods [16,17]. But in their work, the designed LLHs showed a slower convergence rate, and the random method used as the high level selector could not always promise a better solution. And, other works on hyper-heuristic methods to solve the FAP in mobile communication network are not so many so far.

Based on the above mentioned problems, we proposed a hyper-heuristic genetic algorithm (HHGA) in this paper to solve FAP in TD-SCDMA. In the algorithm, we designed six low level neighbor-based heuristic strategies, and use GA as the high level selector for optimizing LLH sequences. Further, we define a Tabu table to assist LLHs to avoid repeat low-level heuristic search strategy on some neighbors, through which to improve the convergence speed.

The rest of this paper is organized as follows: Chapter 2 presents the three types of frequency assignment problems in TD-SCDMA network, and gives the designed concepts, the definitions of constraints and the interference formulas in FAP; Chapter 3 introduces the generic framework of hyper-heuristic algorithm in solving optimization problems; Chapter 4 proposes a hyper-heuristic genetic algorithm for FAP in TD-SCDMA network and Chapter 5 presents and discusses the experimental results; and finally, Chapter 6 summarizes the work of this paper, and presents the future work.

2. PROBLEM DESCRIPTION

Generally, FAP contains three types of problems: (1) MS-FAP (Minimizing Span Frequency Assignment Problem), the purpose of it is to use the minimum frequency range; (2) MO-FAP (Minimizing Order Frequency Assignment Problem), it aims to use the least frequency number; (3) MI-FAP (Minimizing

Interference Frequency Assignment Problem), with its purpose to minimize the interference and improve the communication quality of the network. In this paper, we focus on the MI-FAP (The term *FAP* appears in the following text all refers to *MI-FAP*.). Before formal description of the problem, we first give some definitions and concepts related to FAP, listed in Table 1.

Table1. Definitions and Concepts Related to FAP.

Variable	Description
B	$B=\{b_1,b_2,...,b_m\}$, represents the base station set (Node B) of the network, which contains m elements.
C	$C=\{c_1,c_2,...,c_n\}$, represents a collection of cells, which contains n elements.
BC	$BC=\{bc_1,bc_2,...,bc_i,...,bc_m\}$, represents the belongs relationship between base stations and cells, where bc_i means that the collection of cells belong to the base station i.
D	$D=\{d_1,d_2,...,d_i,...,d_n\}$, represents the number of carriers that each cell has, where d_i represents that the cell i contains d_i carries.
φ_{ik}	φ_{ik} represents the frequency collection that the kth carrier of the ith cell can use, which is provided by the network operator.
f_{ik}	f_{ik} represents the frequency assigned to the kth carrier of the ith cell, $f_{ik}\in\varphi_{ik}$ .When k=1, namely f_{i1} represents the main frequency of the cell i, and other frequencies are secondary frequencies of this cell.
M	M is the interference matrix. $M[i][j]$ represents interference coefficients of cell j to cell i. This matrix is not a symmetric matrix, namely $M[i][j]\neq M[j][i](i\neq j)$.
I	The interference of the overall network, FAP should minimize the value of I.

Also, there are some constraints must be satisfied in the process of the frequency assignment. We divide these constraints into hard constraints and soft constraints. Hard constraints refer to the constraints that the solution must fulfill and those solutions met with the hard constraints are thought as feasible solutions of the problem. Soft constraints are the constraints that the solutions required to possibly satisfied, such as the utilization time of each frequency should be as close as possible, no large variance among these values. In what degree the solution meets with the soft constraints will always reflect the quality of the solution [18]. In this paper, we define and summarize the constraints of FAP in TD-SCDMA network in Table 2 [4].

Similar to GSM network, TD-SCDMA operators always split their assigned frequency bandwidth $[d_{min},d_{max}]$ into a certain number of frequencies with same intervals. These frequencies can be represented by integers like 8, 16, 24,... [17]. The task of FAP is to find a best frequency assignment schema to minimize the interference I of the entire network, with no violation of any hard constraint and satisfy the soft constraints as far as possible.

Table 2. Constraints in FAP of TD-SCDMA

Constraint type	Constraint rules	Description
Hard constraints	Limited frequency resource constraint	Each carrier can only use the frequencies provided by operator.
	Co-base station constraint	Cells of the same base station cannot have same main frequency.
	Co-cell constraint	Carriers in the same cell cannot have same frequency.
Soft constraints	Interference constraint	The less interference of the system, the better of the solution.
	Frequency distribution constraint	The utilization time of each frequency should be as close as possible, maintaining a balanced use

In this paper, we assume that two carriers would generate interference when they are assigned a same frequency. We give the equations of inference in TD-SCDMA network as follow:

$$I_{ik}=\sum_{p=1,p\neq i}^{n}\sum_{q=1}^{d_p}(M[i][p]+M[p][i])\times\alpha_{ik}^{pq},$$

$$where\ \alpha_{ik}^{pq}=\begin{cases}1, if(f_{ik}=f_{pq})\\0, else\end{cases}$$

$$I_i=\sum_{k=1}^{k=d_i}I_{ik} \qquad (1)$$

$$I=\sum_{i=1}^{n}I_i$$

In equation (1), I_{ik} represents the frequency interference of the kth carrier in cell i, calculated by the sum of interference generated between this carrier and all other carriers in the network except those carriers in cell i. The two terms of $M[i][p]$ and $M[p][i]$ are the coefficients between cell i and cell p, which represent the environment of wireless communication network between these two cells. Each pair of carriers in these two cells would share the same environment, that is, they use the same coefficients for computation of interferences. α_{ik}^{pq} describes whether the kth carrier in cell i and the qth carrier in cell p are assigned a same frequency, represented by 1 or 0. If the value is 1, then the two carriers would generate interference equivalent to the sum of $M[i][p]$ and $M[p][i]$. Or else, no interference would be generated between these two carriers. Besides, I_i is the interference of cell i, represented by the sum of all carriers' interference in cell i; and I denotes the overall interference of the network, which equals to the sum of all cells' interference.

Based on the above descriptions, the FAP of TD-SCDMA network can be taken as an optimization problem with no violation of any hard constraint:

$$\textit{Minimize } I$$
$$\textit{Subject to}$$
$$1: f_{ik} \in \phi_{ik} \quad \textit{for } i = 1 \textit{ to } n, k = 1 \textit{ to } d_i$$
$$2: \textit{if } c_i \in \mathrm{bc}_k, c_j \in \mathrm{bc}_k \textit{ then } f_{i1} \neq f_{j1} \quad \textit{for } i, j = 1 \textit{ to } n; k = 1 \textit{ to } m$$
$$3: f_{ij} \neq f_{ik} \quad \textit{for } i = 1 \textit{ to } n; j \neq k \; j, k = 1 \textit{ to } d_i$$

The above three rules are consistent with the three hard constraints in Table 2, that is, the limited frequency resource constraint, the co-base station constraint, and the co-cell constraint. In the following, we introduce the generic framework of hyper-heuristic to explain how it works to implement optimization process with problem-independent.

3. HYPER-HEURISTIC

Compared with meta-heuristic methods, hyper-heuristics are independent of the problem and have been widely applied to solve optimization problems in different domains [16]. As described in Fig.2, hyper-heuristic methods generally include two levels operations: the low level is a set of heuristics designed for local searches, which is called low level heuristics (LLHs); the high level is a selector for LLHs, which works to find the optimal solution represented by a calling sequence of LLHs. In this paper, we only focus on hyper-heuristic methods that do not make use of domain knowledge. Therefore, there exists a barrier between the low level heuristic and the high level heuristic, meaning that no domain data flow can pass through the barrier. Only the non-domain data flow, that is, the calling sequence of LLHs can be transmitted between these two levels. This design explains why hyper-heuristic methods are independent of the problem. At the low level, an evaluation function is set to give the quality of the solution, and it can also be transmitted to the high level for evaluating the hyper-heuristic algorithm.

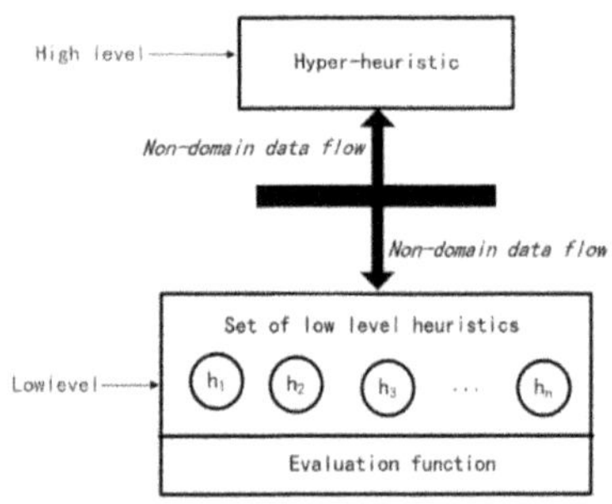

Figure 2. the framework of hyper-heuristic

The generic execution process of hyper-heuristic methods are explained as follows: first, the low level heuristics represented by h_1, h_2,..., h_n directly act on the actual problem, trying to minimize or maximize a predefined evaluation function. Next, the hyper-heuristic algorithm calls LLHs to improve the evaluation result. The evaluation result can pass through the barrier and work as the evaluation value of the high level algorithm. By keep calling LLHs with different orders and evaluating the sequences through the evaluation function, the hyper-heuristic algorithm will finally find a high quality solution with LLH sequences to solve the real problem.

When applying the hyper-heuristic method to the FAP in TD-SCDMA, hyper-heuristic at the high level deals with no domain knowledge of the FAP; it only faces a sequence of LLHs. And LLHs at the low level are general local search methods, which are carefully designed based on the actual FAP. The evaluation function at the low level is set to the overall interference of the network. The non-domain data flow represented by interference *I* can pass through the barrier between two levels, and would be evaluated by the evaluation function. Hyper-heuristic keeps calling these LLHs to minimize the interference of the network. By adjusting the calling order of LLHs, the hyper-heuristic could continuously optimize the solution.

4. HYPER-HEURISTIC GENETIC ALGORITHM for SOLVING FAP in TD- SCDMA

In the paper, we proposed a Hyper-heuristic Genetic Algorithm (HHGA) to solve the FAP in TD-SCDMA network. Following the generic framework of hyper-heuristic described in Fig.2, we first designed six LLHs of FAP at the low level, and then applied genetic algorithm as the selector of LLHs at the high level, where the chromosomes defined in GA are represented by a sequence of LLHs. In the paper, LLHs are denoted by a set of integers, where each integer represents a different LLH method. Fig.3 gives an example of chromosome in HHGA. Assume that we define four LLHs, represented by an integer set as {1,2,3,4}, the chromosome in Fig.3 would call LLHs according to the order of 2,1,3,4,1, through which to optimize the current solution.

2	1	3	4	1

Figure 3. An example of chromosome in HHGA

In the following, we will explain the design and implementation of low level heuristics and hyper-heuristic genetic algorithm.

4.1 Low Level Heuristics

Similar to the variable neighbor search (VNS) method [19], we design neighbor search-based LLHs. Each LLH starts from the current solution, and reassigns frequencies of some cells such that to find a better neighbor of the current solution. In this paper, we have designed six LLHs as follows, and the number of each LLH represents its value of the corresponding gene of a chromosome in GA. Furthermore, these LLHs can not violate any hard constraints.

1. Calculate interference of all cells according to equation (1), choose the cell with the highest interference, and then reassign the best frequency to all carriers of the cell. The best frequency for a carrier is the frequency that minimizes the interference of the carrier without changing other carriers' frequencies.
2. Same as 1, but find a better frequency. Better frequency is the frequency that the carrier reassigned with it generates less interference than the old schema.
3. Same as 1, but randomly choose a cell.
4. Same as 2, but randomly choose a cell.
5. Randomly choose a cell, and randomly choose a frequency to reassign.
6. Execute a local search for the current solution. The pseudo code of local search algorithm is given in Algorithm 1 [6].

Among these six LLHs, the fifth method is a completely random method purposing to avoid falling into local optima, and the sixth method is a local search, which aims to speed up the search process and achieve fast convergence.

Algorithm 1: Pseudo code for local search

```
input: current solution S
nextCells←{1,…,numberOfCells}
while(nextCells!=φ) do
    currentCells←nextCells
    nextCells←φ
    while(currentCells!=φ) do
        tmpCell←extract a random cell from currentCells
        neighbor←reassign frequencies of S in Cell tmpCell
        if(neighbor improves S) then
            S←neighbor
            nextCells+=cells interfered by tmpCell
            nextCells+=cells that interfere tmpCell
        end if
    end while
end while
return S
```

4.2 Hyper-heuristic Genetic Algorithm

At the high level, we use GA as selector for LLHs. For the GA operations, we use two-point crossover, uniform mutation, and Minimal Generation Gap (MGG[20]) as the generation alternation model. The execution of GA by MGG is described in Fig.4: ① First, choose two individuals from the initial population pool randomly, and take them as two parent of the next generation. ② Second, executes n_c times crossover on the selected two parent, through which $2n_c$ children generated, take them as the offspring. ③ Next, conducts uniform mutation on the offspring pool with a mutation probability p_m, and then generates a final offspring pool. ④ Finally, selects two individuals from the final offspring pool to replace the two parent selected in step 1. The two individuals are selected as: one is the best individual, and the other is chosen by a roulette way. The method of roulette selection is weighted by fitness. As each individual denotes a solution represented by a calling sequence of heuristics, and the solution corresponds to an interference value of the entire network, therefore, we define the fitness as the reciprocal of the expected interference I (Equation 1). The smaller the fitness is, the better the solution (individual).

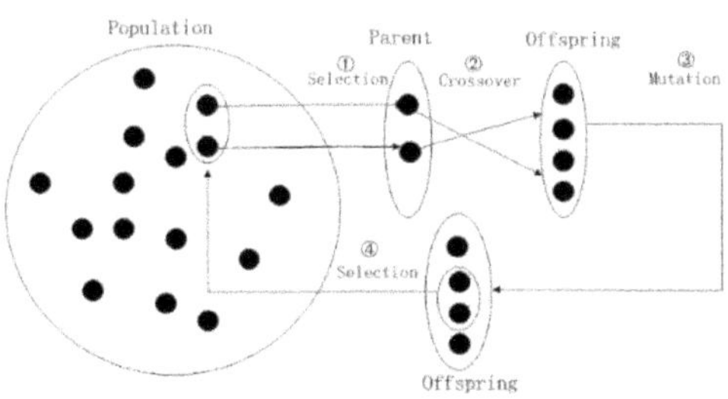

Figure 4. The Execution of GA by MGG.

Next, Algorithm 2 gives the pseudo code of HHGA for FAP in TD-SCDMA. As described in Algorithm 2, HHGA is performed in the following steps: 1) first, assume a frequency assignment task, the algorithm randomly generates a frequency assignment solution S_0, namely assigns frequencies to all the carriers randomly without violate any hard constraint, and then take S_0 as the current best solution S_{best}. 2) Generates popSize chromosomes as the GA's initial population, each chromosome is a sequence of LLHs with a fixed length L. 3) Next, randomly selects two chromosomes as parent from the initial population pool, do the crossover and mutation operations by MGG as described in Fig.4, and obtain an offspring pool. 4) For each chromosome k in the final offspring pool, applies LLHs on S_{best} according to their orders in the chromosome k, and obtains a new solution S_k. 5) For all S_k, generated in 4), compare their interferences produced by these solutions and choose two individuals with best and roulette rules to replace the parent in the initial population pool. Compare the interference produced by the best offspring solution $S_{best\_offspring}$ with the current best solution S_{best}, if it is smaller than by S_{best}, then replaces S_{best} by $S_{best\_offspring}$. 6) Repeat the steps from 3 to 5 until the predefined termination condition of GA is reached. 7) After the iteration, the algorithm returns a best solution S_{best}.

Algorithm 2: Pseudo Code for HHGA

```
Randomly generate a solution S0, Sbest←S0
Randomly generate PopSize chromosomes, which are sequences of
LLHs with a fixed length L.
while ( the termination condition of the algorithm is not reached )
    Randomly selects two chromosomes as parent from the initial
    population pool, do the crossover and mutation operations by MGG as
    described in Figure.5, and obtain an offspring pool, which contains 2nc
    chromosomes.
    for k=1 to 2nc
        Apply LLHs on Sbest according to their orders in chromosome k,
        and obtain a new solution Sk, the interference of Sk is the
        evaluation value of chromosome k. Record Sk.
    end for
    Choose two chromosomes from offspring pool to replace the parent.
    for k=1 to 2nc
        if (Interfernce(Sk)<Interfernce(Sbest))
            Sbest←Sk
        end if
    end for
end while
return Sbest
```

According to equation (1), the interference of the network is related to the interference matrix and the frequency assignment solution. Because of frequency constraints from other cells, reassignment of some cells' frequencies could not help to improve the interference of the overall network. If LLHs choose these cells to reassign, then the interference of the network could not find a better neighbor, and this search is not an effective one. In order to speed up the search process, LLHs should skip these cells. We design a Tabu table to solve this problem according to [21]. Fig.5 shows the structure of Tabu table, the base integer represents the index of a cell, and the exponent integer represents how many times this cell would not be chosen to reassign frequency. During the optimization process by HHGA, if a cell was chosen to reassign a frequency, but its interference could not be improved, this cell would be added into the Tabu table with a fixed exponent n_{max}. Each iteration the value of the exponent is reduced by 1. If the value of exponent is zero, then the cell would be removed from the Tabu table, and this cell could be chose by LLHs again. For example, 30^9 in the first grid represents that cell 30 could not be chose by LLHs in the next nine times, LLHs would skip cell 30 to speed up the searching process for better neighbors.

30^9	38^8	89^9	43^6	32^7	4^1

Figure 5. The structure of Tabu table

5. EXPERIMENTS AND ANALYSIS

5.1 Experimental Setup

The experiments select two instances of the real TD-SCDMA network of a city in China. Instance 1 is a small network which contains 560 cells, and 2679 carriers. Instance 2 is a relative large network which contains 5025 cells and 22626 carries. Fig.6 shows the topology of these two instances. In the figure, each triangle represents a cell. Instance 1 covers a circular area with radius equal to 5km while Instance 2 covers a circular area with its radius equal to 7.5km. There are 16 frequencies available for the assignment task. As scatter search (SS) algorithm has been proved as the best meta-heuristic algorithm in [6], therefore we only compare our algorithm with the SS algorithm in the paper.

Both algorithms implemented with C# programming language. The programs run on the computer with CPU 3.2GHZ, memory 2GB. Each algorithm runs 60 minutes on instance 1, and 120 minutes on instance 2. Each algorithm runs 30 trials. Table 3 gives the parameter settings of HHGA and SS algorithms.

Table 3. Parameter settings of HHGA and SS algorithms

HHGA	SS
Population size: *PopSize*=50	Population size: *PopSize*=50
Crossover times by MGG: n_c=5	Reference Set Size: *refSet size*=15
Mutation probability: p_m=0.3 Maximum skip times: n_{max}=10	solution combination method : uniform crossover [6]

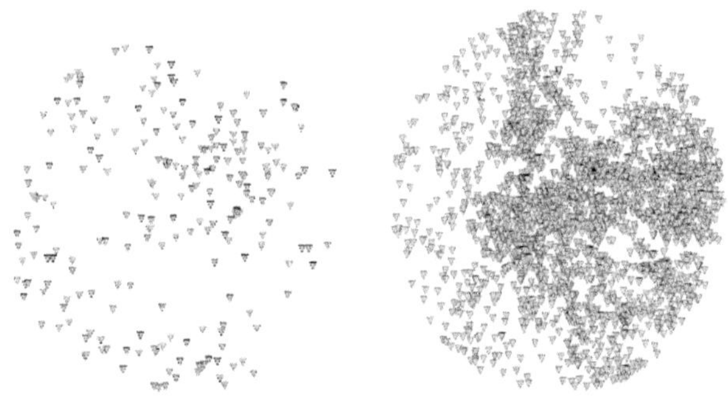

(a) Instance 1 (b) Instance 2

Figure 6. topology of instances

5.2 Results and Analysis

5.2.1 Sensitivity test of the chromosome length on GA

First, we conduct the sensitivity test of the length of the chromosome on GA, through which to compare and analyze the impact of the length of the chromosome on HHGA. The results shown in Fig.7 proved that the length of the chromosome would affect the outcome of the interference, namely HHGA is sensitive to the length of chromosome.

Based on the experimental results in Fig.7, we found that the length of chromosome equals to 30 was a better choice for the actual network data used in instance 1 while 40 was better choice for instance 2. Therefore, when applying HHGA to solve the FAP with different network scales, we must first find an appropriate value of the length of chromosome through sensitivity test. If the length of the chromosome is too long, then the rear portion of the gene in the chromosome could not be optimized from the current solution by calling LLHs. If the length of chromosome is too short, it will weaken the effect of the crossover, and cut down the diversity of GA.

5.2.2 Comparison of Optimization Results by HHGA and SS

Next, we compared the variation of interference of HHGA and SS over time with two instances, the results represented by two groups of curves were given in Fig.8 (a) and (b), where the x axis was the time slot and the y axis was the average interference of the results. By comparing the curves, we found that SS converged faster than HHGA and HHGA with tabu, but the interference of frequency assignment schema by HHGA and HHGA with tabu were smaller than SS, which proved that our proposed HHGA had a better performance than SS. The curve of HHGA with tabu is below HHGA, which proved that the tabu table speeded up the process of searching.

We discussed such results in the following: although SS increases the diversity of population by using a reference set, the diversity of the population decreased with the iteration of the algorithm, thus the result may still be trapped into local optimum. HHGA optimized the frequency assignment schema by using GA to adjust the execution order of low level heuristic strategies. In the LLHs, the solution avoids local optima by considering the influence from random factors, and the local search methods with Tabu table can speed up the search process.

Further, we executed each group of experiments 30 times and compared the variation degree of the results by two statistic indexes as the standard deviation (σ) and the standard deviation coefficient ($V\sigma$), through which to confirm a robustness of the results. As given in equation (2), $V\sigma$ is defined as the ratio of the standard deviation σ to the mean $\bar{x}$, which shows a relative variation extent and would not be affected by the unit size.

$$V\sigma = \frac{\sigma}{\bar{x}} \qquad (2)$$

The statistic results of each index were summarized in Table 4. From the results in Table 4, we found that the fluctuation of our proposed HHGA algorithm is smaller than SS, the value of $V\sigma$ were 0.20% in instance 1 and 0.30% in instance 2. The statistic results proved a robustness of our algorithm.

5.2.3 Analysis of Utilization Time of Frequencies

Finally, we analyzed the distribution of utilization time of frequencies assigned by HHGA. The results were shown in Figure.9, where the x axis represented the 16 frequencies available in the network, and the y axis gave the number of each frequency used. From the results in Figure.9, we found that the utilization times of each frequency used in both instances were very close. This result met with the soft constraints in Table 3.

From the above mentioned experiments and analysis, we can see that our proposed HHGA method has proved its effectiveness and robustness for solving the FAP in TD-SCDMA network. Furthermore, the utilization time of each frequency are very close, thus the obtained solution by HHGA is a high quality solution.

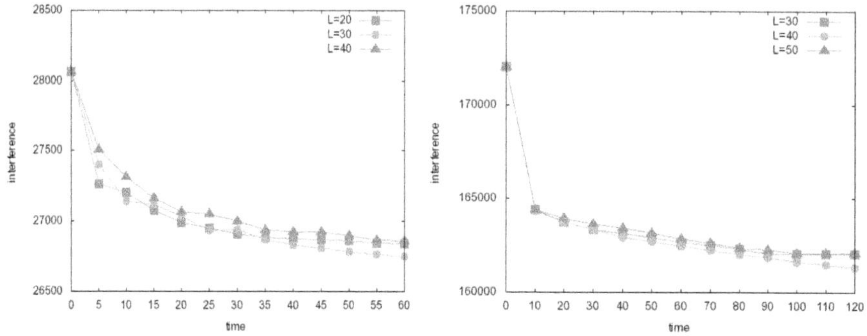

(a) Instance 1 (b) Instance 2

Figure 7. HHGA optimization process with different chromosome length

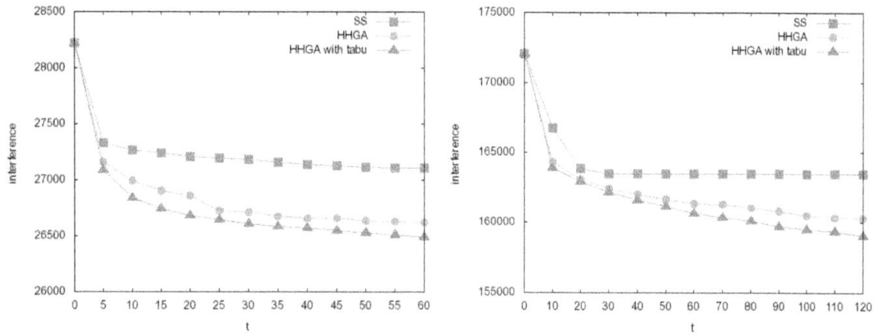

(a) Instance 1 (b) Instance 2

Figure 8. Interference curve overtime of HHGA and SS

Table 4. Average interference, standard deviation and standard deviation coefficient of the results

Algorithm	Instance 1			Instance 2		
	$\bar{x}$	σ	V_σ (%)	$\bar{x}$	σ	V_σ (%)
SS	27106.02	250.70	0.92	163494.40	590.26	0.36
HHGA	26642.89	53.04	0.20	159074.15	484.65	0.30

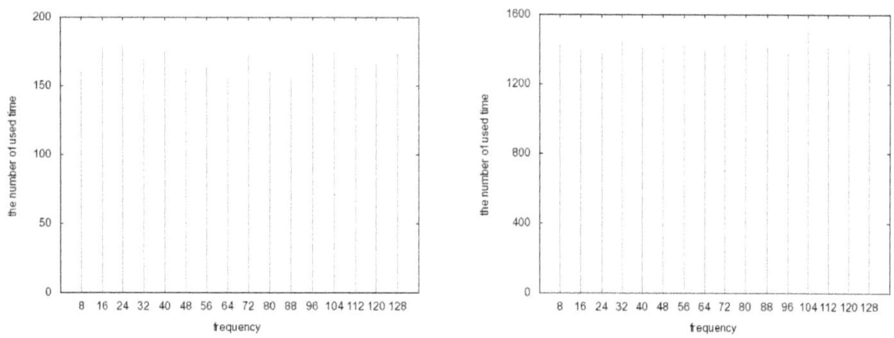

(a) Instance 1 (b) Instance 2

Figure 9. The times of each frequency used in the solution by HHGA.

6. CONCLUSION AND FUTURE WORK

This paper studies the frequency assignment problem (FAP) in TD-SCDMA network of mobile communications industry in China. The problem considers to find an optimal frequency assignment scheme for carriers with a limited frequency resource, such that the entire network interference is minimized. Besides, the allocation of frequencies needs to satisfy some constraints to avoid the effect of call interference within the same cell or adjacent cell. We define the formula for calculating the network interference, and take the FAP as a constrained optimization problem. To solve the FAP in TD-SCDMA network, we proposed a hyper-heuristic genetic algorithm (HHGA) to optimize the assignment of frequencies. We first defined six low-level heuristic

(LLH) search strategies for improving the interference of the FAP, and then applied genetic algorithm (GA) at a high-level to find the best combination sequence of LLH strategies to reduce the interferences of the TD-SCDMA network. GA used two-point crossover, uniform mutation, and Minimal Generation Gap (MGG) as the generation alternation model. Through evolution, GA found an optimal combination of LLHs to improve the interference of the network. In order to speed up the search, we defined a Tabu table to avoid repeat search of LLHs. We validated the performance of HHGA on real TD-SCDMA network data. Compared with scatter search as one of the best performance meta-heuristic algorithm, our experimental results on real data sets of TD-SCDMA network showed better result. Furthermore, in the solution obtained by HHGA, the utilization times of each frequency were very close. This result meets with the soft constraints in table 3. Therefore, this solution is a high quality solution.

In this study, the length of chromosome of GA used by HHGA is fixed. Due to the different scale and relation of networks, the length of chromosomes should be reset under different network environment. The optimal length of chromosome is not universal. For different applications of HHGA for solving FAP in TD-SCDMA network, the algorithm needs to adjust the length of the chromosome by many trials, which is a very troublesome work and not desirable in the actual optimization process. In future work, we intend to improve the algorithm so that the length of the chromosome can be adaptive. Such algorithms can be applied to different mobile communication networks, and will greatly improve the efficiency of frequency assignment.

7. REFERENCES

[1] L. Ge, J. Qiu, and M. S. Yang. Investigation of frequency and scrambler code planning for TD-SCDMA. *Mobile communication*,33(10):70-75, May 2009.

[2] Y. Chai. Genetic algorithm-based wireless network frequency planning for GSM. *Mobile communication*, 22(11): 143-146, March 2004.

[3] Y. M. Guo and L. Z. Ma. Discussion on TD-SCDMA Network Interference. *Communication technology*, 12(43)58-60, May 2010.

[4] Y. H. Duan. Wireless network design and planning for TD-SCDMA. *People post press,* Beijing, China, 2007.

[5] F. Luna, C. Blum, E. Alba, and A. J. Nebro. ACO vs EAs for solving a real-world frequency assignment problem in GSM networks. *In Proceedings of the 9th annual conference on Genetic and evolutionary computation*, pages 94-101, July 2004.

[6] F. Luna, C. Estébanez, C. León, et al. Optimization algorithms for large-scale real-world instances of the frequency assignment problem. *Soft Computing*, 15(5):975-990, May 2011.

[7] W. K. Hale. Frequency assignment: Theory and applications. *Proceedings of the IEEE*, 68(12): 1497-1514, December 1980.

[8] M. Fischetti, C.Lepschy, G. Minerva, G. Romanin-Jacur, and E. Toto. Frequency assignment in mobile radio systems using branch-and-cut techniques. *European Journal of Operational Research*, 123(2):241-255, June 2000.

[9] C. Mannino and A. Sassano. An enumerative algorithm for the frequency assignment problem. *Discrete Applied Mathematics*. 129(1):155-169, June 2003.

[10] K. I. Aardal, S. P. M. van Hoesen, A. M. C. A. Koster, C. Mannino, and A. Sassano. Models and solution techniques for frequency assignment problems. *Ann Oper Res,* 153(1):79–129, September 2007.

[11] J. K. Hao, R. Dorne, and P. Galinier. Tabu search for frequency assignment in mobile radio networks. *Journal of heuristics*, 4(1):47-62, June 1998.

[12] S. Matsui, I. Watanabe, and K. I. Tokoro. An efficient hybrid genetic algorithm for a fixed channel assignment problem with limited bandwidth. *In Proceedings of international conference on Genetic and evolutionary computation conference*, pages 2240–2251, July 2003.

[13] E. Soubeiga. Development and Application of Hyper heuristics to Personnel Scheduling. *Doctoral dissertation University of Nottingham*, June 2003.

[14] R. Bai. An Investigation of Novel Approaches for Optimising Retail Shelf Space Allocation. *Doctoral dissertation, University of Nottingham University of Nottingham*, September 2005.

[15] E. K. Burke, M. Hyde, G. Kendall, G. Ochoa, E. Özcan, and J. R. Woodward. A classification of hyper-heuristic approaches. *Handbook of Metaheuristics*, Springer,US 2010.

[16] G. Kendall and M. Mohamad. Channel assignment optimisation using a hyper-heuristic. *In Proceedings of conference on Cybernetics and Intelligent Systems*, pages 791-796, December 2004.

[17] G. Kendall and M. Mohamad. Channel assignment in cellular communication using a great deluge hyper-heuristic. *In Proceedings of 12th IEEE International Conference* , pages 769-773, November 2004.

[18] E. K. Burke, S. Petrovic, and R. C. Qu. Case-based heuristic selection for timetabling problems. *Journal of Scheduling.* 9(2):115-132, April 2006.

[19] E. K. Burke, T. Curtois, G. Post, R. Qu, and B.Veltman. A hybrid heuristic ordering and variable neighborhoods search for the nurse rostering problem. *European Journal of Operational Research*, 188(2):330-341, July 2008.

[20] I. Ono, H. Kita, and S. Kobayashi. A robust real-coded genetic algorithm using unimodal normal distribution crossover augmented by uniform crossover: Effects of self-adaptation of crossover probabilities. *In Proceedings of Genetic and Evolutionary Computation Conference,* pages 496-503, 1999.

[21] L. Han and G. Kendall. An investigation of a tabu assisted hyper-heuristic genetic algorithm Evolutionary. *In Proceedings of IEEE Congress on Evolutionary Computation*, pages 2230-2237, December 2003.

A Real-World Employee Scheduling and Routing Application

Emma Hart
Institute for Informatics and Digital Innovation
Edinburgh Napier University
Edinburgh, Scotland, UK
e.hart@napier.ac.uk

Kevin Sim
Institute for Informatics and Digital Innovation
Edinburgh Napier University
Edinburgh, Scotland, UK
k.sim@napier.ac.uk

Neil Urquhart
Institute for Informatics and Digital Innovation
Edinburgh Napier University
Edinburgh, Scotland, UK
n.urquhart@napier.ac.uk

ABSTRACT

We describe a hyper-heuristic application developed for a client to find quick, acceptable solutions to Workforce Scheduling and Routing problems. An interactive fitness function controlled by the user enables five different objectives to be weighted according to client preference. The application uses a real road network in order to calculate driving distances between locations, and is designed to integrate with a web-based application to access employee calendars.

Categories and Subject Descriptors

Computing Methodologies [**Artificial Intelligence**]: Problem Solving, Control Methods and Search

Keywords

Hyper-heuristics; interactive fitness; scheduling and routing

1. INTRODUCTION

The Workforce Scheduling and Routing Problem (WSRP) was defined in [1] as a scenario that involves the mobilisation of personnel in order to perform work related activities at different locations. Personnel are considered *flexible* in that they have variable working patterns, and *mobile* in that travelling is required between their home base and jobs, and in that travelling may involve significant times. The problem thus combines features of vehicle routing problems (VRP) that attempt to reduce distance travelled, and personnel scheduling problems that allocate work to staff to ensure that all required tasks are completed whilst respecting working patterns.

We describe software developed for a client who sell a range of software products to large companies. The client wishes to 'add value' to existing products by improving their current software to include a cheap method of creating schedules in typical WRSP situations that include time-windows, service-times and employees based from home. Rather than provide a specialised WRSP algorithm customised to each company, they wish to develop a generic algorithm that will be widely applicable in accouting for common constraints and practices, whilst recognising that some companies might operate practices that fall outside of the specification. Specifically, the aim of the software is not to search for *global* optima but to provide a simple tool that on the one hand automates the scheduling process, and on the other, provide a decision support tool for an operator. The software we developed makes use of a hyper-heuristic approach to developing a solution, and utilises an interactive fitness function to produce a single solution.

GECCO'14, July 12–16, Vancouver, BC, Canada.

http://dx.doi.org/10.1145/2598394.2605447.

2. PROBLEM DESCRIPTION

The brief required that the algorithm scheduled a set of engineers to servicing jobs that occurred at locations across Scotland. Schedules were planned for a period of one month at a time. Each of the jobs to be serviced has a planned schedule date, a *pre-schedule* tolerance and a *post-schedule* tolerance defining the earliest and latest dates the job might be scheduled, typically up to three days either side of the planned date. A company can specify whether it is possible to 'break' time-window constraints by specifying an allowable number of days. Each job has a processing time, typically between 1 and 4 hours. Each job also has a driving time which is dependent on the last position of the worker assigned to the job.

The company employs n workers, each based at their home locations which can be anywhere in Scotland. Each worker has an associated calendar that specifies their working hours over a period of one month, which may include holidays. Individual employee availability is designed to be read via a web interface that uses the Calendaring Extensions to WebDAV (CalDAV) format. This is an Internet standard allowing a client to access scheduling information on a remote server. It extends WebDAV (HTTP-based protocol for data manipulation) specification and uses iCalendar format for the data, allowing multiple client access to the same information thus allowing cooperative planning and information sharing. Availability may vary significantly across employees.

Workers always start working from home and should return to their home base at the end of each day. Some companies have a policy that a working day does not include travel time to/from the home location, while others require that travel time is factored in, therefore the algorithm must account for individual preferences. Some companies allow overtime, specifying the maximum number of overtime hours allowed.

3. ROUTING

Routing is performed using the GraphHopper library [2]. This application offers memory efficient algorithms written in Java for routing between two locations on a graph (e.g. Dijkstra and A*) using road network data provided by OpenStreetMap [3]. The OSM XML data is pre-processed into a street graph that takes account of turn and direction restrictions within the road network. GraphHopper runs on a wide variety of platforms and due to its use of Apache license can be embedded within products, making it an ideal choice for a client.

We make use of the inbuilt bidirected A* algorithm to find routes through the street graph from one latitude/longitude point to another. The client supplies data in the form of geocodes (longitude and latitude) — however, postcodes can also be used if required by looking up data released by Ordnance Survey (Crown Copyright) which contains a complete list of Postcodes and their latitute/longitude position. GraphHopper returns both the driving time and driving distance between the two locations, although we only make use of the time in the described application.

4. OBJECTIVE FUNCTION

As the application is designed to be flexible to cater for a range of client requirements, we define five different objectives that can be optimised. The rationale behind each of the objectives is explained below:

- *Idle Time - I* For a single employee, the idle time describes the ratio of time that the employee is neither working nor driving. *I* defines the average idle time over the complete schedule. Optimising this criteria is relevant in maximising employee efficiency.
- *Driving Time - D* For a single employee, this criteria measures the proportion of an employees working day that is spent driving as opposed to servicing, and thus is a measure of the productivity of an employee.
- *OverTime - O* The number of minutes worked beyond the end of the working day for each employee is calculated, and recorded as the ratio of the number of available working hours. Some clients do not allow overtime to be worked while others prefer to minimise this to reduce extra costs.
- *Unscheduled Job Time - O* Some jobs might not be able to be scheduled given the number of available employees and particularly if no overtime is allowed. This may also occur if the total time to complete a job (including driving and servicing) is greater than the working day of any employee.
- *Broken Minutes - W* For some jobs, scheduling within the tolerance period is critical. For other clients, some deviation may be tolerated, however may incur a cost.

The five objectives are combined using a weighted sum. Each of the weights can be specifed by the user according to their own preferences and can be altered interactively during the course of a run as show in in figure 1.

5. ALGORITHM

We utilise a hyper-heuristic approach that aims to reduce the amount of knowledge required in terms of the search

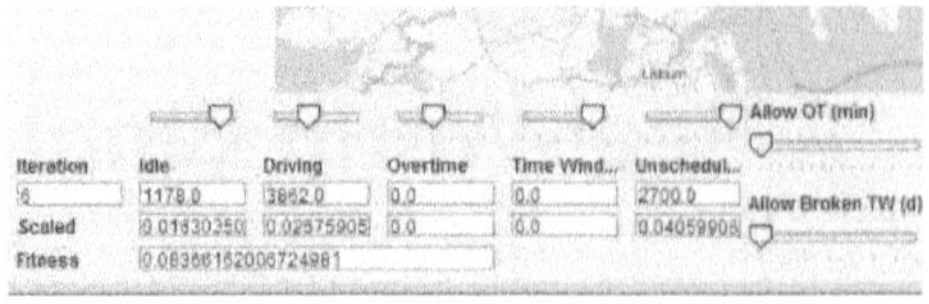

Figure 1: The sliders allow the relative weights to be adjusted during the course of a run depending on the criteria defined by the customer. The Customer can also specify the amount of allowed overtime and the maximum period by which time windows can be broken

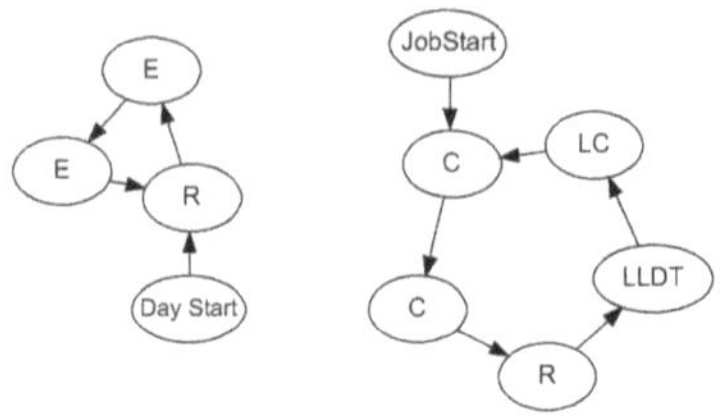

Figure 2: 2 lists of rules are maintained by each individual as a cyclic list with a predefined start point; one for the employee heuristics and the other for the job heuristics

methodology to make it easier for the client to maintain and/or develop in the future. Hyper-heuristics are well known to produce quick, acceptable solutions to problems (though rarely optimal) and our own previous work with a hyper-heuristic system called NELLI [4] suggested that combining heuristic components into a suitable sequence can lead to promising new heuristics that generalise well across sets of problems.

We define a set of low-level heuristics, shown in table 1, using intuituve knowledge of how a human might solve the problem. Using a straightforward evolutionary algorithm, we evolve two cyclic lists with pre-defined start points that define a sequence of heuristics to be used in solving the problem, each of which has a pointer indicating the current heuristic to be used.

A wrapper, defined in figure 1, controls application of heuristics. The wrapper first chooses an employee according to the current heuristic in the employee list. A job is then selected according to the heuristic defined by the pointer in the job list. The pointer is then advanced, and jobs repeatedly selected in this manner until no more jobs can be placed into the selected employees day. The pointer in the employee list is then advanced and a new employee day selected. This process is repeated until no more jobs can be scheduled. In each list, the pointer cycles back to the start of the list once it reaches the end.

A standard steady-state evolutionary algorithm is used to evolve lists, using a randomly initialised population of chromosomes. A messy crossover operator produces two new children with probability p_c, from parents selected via tournament selection. A mutation operator selects at random one of nine possible mutation operators that add, delete or swap heuristics within a sequence, or concatenate two sequences together.

Table 1: Employee Rules and Job Rules

Job Heuristic	Abreviation	Description
ClosestJob	C	based on current location of an employee
EarliestJob	E	returns job with the earliest start date (no relaxation of the time window)
EarliestJobTW	ETW	returns job with the earliest start date (including any time window relaxation)
LargestJob	L	returns job with largest processing time
LargestJobClosest	LC	returns job closest to last location from set of jobs with largest processing time
LargestJobLDT	LLDT	returns job with largest (processing time + total driving time)
RandomJob	R	returns a random job
SmallestJob	S	returns job with smallest processing time
SmallestJobClosest	SC	returns job closest to last location from set of jobs with smallest processing time
SmallestJobSDT	SSDT	returns job with the smallest (processing time + total driving time)
SmallestTwJob	STW	returns job with the smallest total time window duration

Employee Heuristic	Abreviation	Description
EarliestDayEvent	E	returns earliest available day from all employees
RandomDayEvent	R	returns a random day from a random employee
RandomNextDayEvent	RN	returns the next free day from a randomly chosen employee

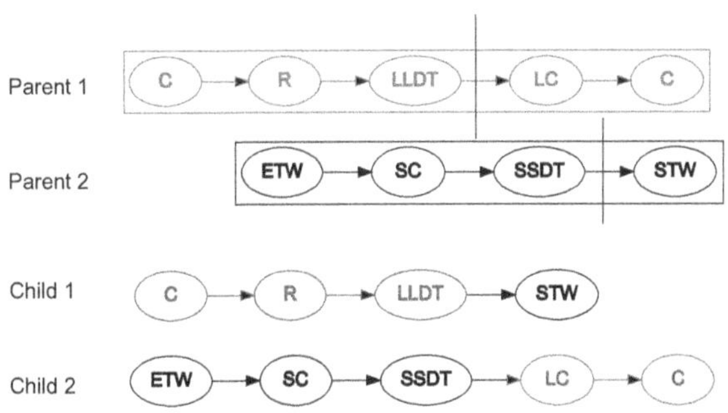

Figure 3: Crossover selects with equal probability one of the 2 heuristic lists and performs a "messy" one point crossover as shown (Shown not to benefit the EA)

Algorithm 1 Wrapper Pseudo Code

Require: EmployeeRuleList : The list of employee rules
Require: JobRuleList : The list of job rules

repeat
  select next employee rule: returns an employees free time for a day
  advance employee pointer (return to beginning at end)
  repeat
    select next job rule: returns a job that meets the constraints (overtime and time window)
    advance job pointer (return to beginning at end)
    schedule job
  until no more jobs can be placed into the selected employees day
until employees days full OR no more jobs can be placed

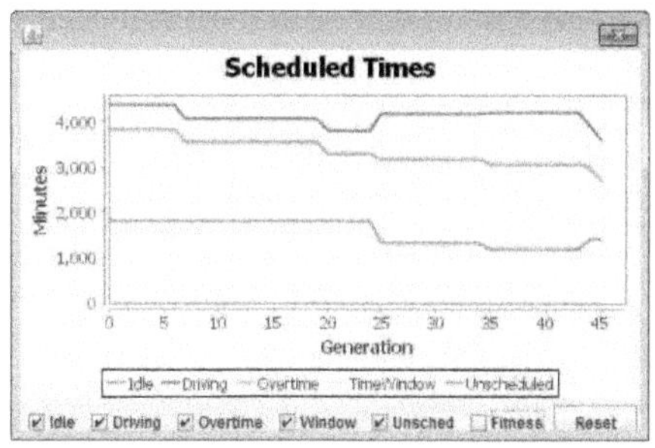

Figure 4: The plot shows the actual times for idle time, driving time, overtime, broken time windows and unscheduled jobs. The display can be switched to show the normalised weighted fitness used to drive evolution.

6. PRESENTATION OF RESULTS

In order to enable the client to interpret the results (and for them to be refined by a human scheduler if preferred) then the results need to be presented in a format that is easy to intepret.

Objectives.

Progress of the algorithm against each of the five objectives is shown in a display as in figure 4 which shows the change in each objective over time. As the sliders controlling the weighting of each objective can be controlled interactively during the course of the run, a scheduler is able to investigate alternative solutions and intuitively guide the algorithm towards their preferred objective. Note that some objectives are antaganistic, e.g. as driving time increases, idle time decreases and vice versa.

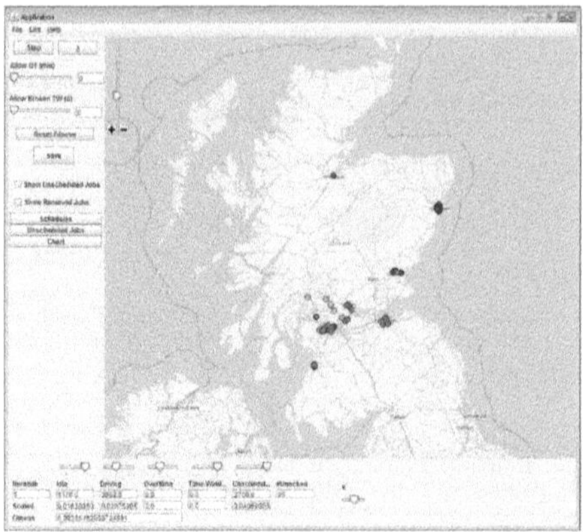

Figure 5: The Map displays the position of each employee jobs colour coded for each employee

Assignment.
Jobs assigned to each engineer are shown using a colour-coded map 5 (each colour represents an individual engineer). This gives an easy to interpret view in which it can be clearly be seen that jobs are clustered in particular geographic areas, located close to each engineers home base. Jobs tend to be clustered around the major population centres, however some jobs occur in regions that are located a considerable distance from any engineer, and require significant travelling.

Scheduling.
Schedules are displayed as the algorithm runs as indicated in Figure 6. Each vertical bar shows an employees calendar colour coded by employee. Coloured blocks indicate a jobs duration and the grey blocks indicate the corresponding driving time. In the example shown some employees have full or part days where they are not scheduled to work. This gives a visual overview of the relative amounts of driving time, servicing time, and idle time (indicated by gaps at the end of each day) for each employee. This view is for the purpose of the scheduler while running the algorithm. As previously mentioned, for each employee, calendar availability and assigned jobs are read and written using the *calDav* format from the employees own calendar, thus the scheduling information can also be viewed in calendar format as shown in figure 7 and can be manually manipulated using standard industry calendar tools if required.

7. CONCLUSION

We have described an approach that was taken to develop a WRSP application for a client. Although we are unable to present results across multiple problems due to client confidentiality, the paper illustrates a number of important points regarding the development of real-world applications. We have noted the emphasis on developing a practical solution, rather than seeking global optima. In contrast to taking a multi-objective approach, we have used a weighted objective function in order to present the client with a single solution. A map of the real road-network is used to calculate driving distances and times, and the application is able to access availability of employee calendars via a web interface. A simple search algorithm that combines heuristics is both effective and simple to understand and maintain from the

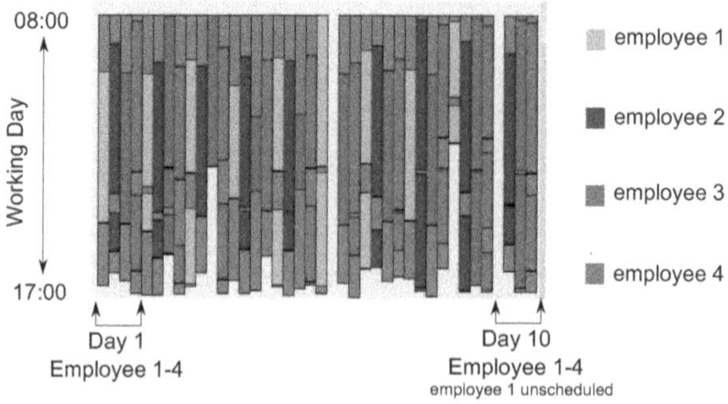

Figure 6: Each vertical bar shows an employees calendar colour coded by employee. Coloured blocks indicate a jobs duration and the grey blocks indicate the corresponding driving time. In the example shown some employees have full or part days where they are not scheduled to work. This shows the same information as is shown in the calendar application depicted in Figure 7 but is updated continuously during the course of a run.

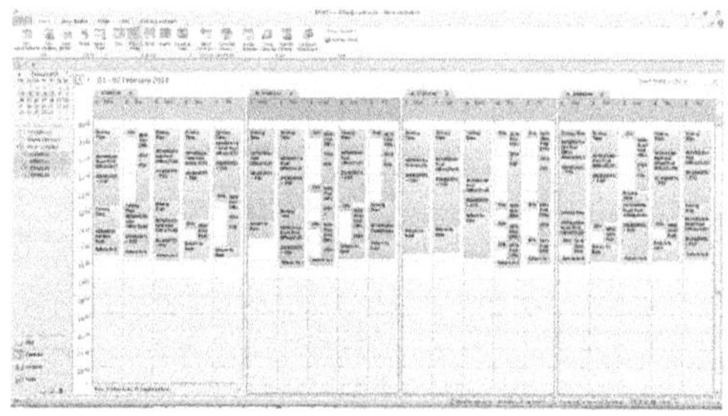

Figure 7: Output from the application is in the format of an individual ics file for each employee which can be imported into a number of Calendar applications allowing the customer to easily visualise and alter schedules manually if desired

client perspective. Finally, the algorithm can be extended in future by adding additional heuristics if required.

8. REFERENCES

[1] A Castillo-Salazar, D Landa-Silva, and R QuA. Survey on Workforce Scheduling and Routing Problems. The 9th International Conference on the Practice and Theory of Automated Timetabling (PATAT 2012), 28-31 August 2012, Son, Norway

[2] GraphHopper `http:www.graphhopper.com` applications. Ubiquity 2012 3:1–3:13.

[3] Open Street Map `http:www.openstreemap.org`

[4] Sim, K., Hart, E.: An improved immune inspired hyper-heuristic for combinatorial optimisation problems. In: GECCO '14: Proceeding of the sixteenth annual conference on Genetic and evolutionary computation conference (In Press 2014)

SecDef 2014 Workshop Chairs' Welcome

It is our great pleasure to welcome you to the all-new *2014 Workshop on Genetic and Evolutionary Computation in Defense, Security, and Risk Management (SecDef'14).* With the constant appearance of new threats, research in the areas of defense, security and risk management has acquired an increasing importance over the past few years. These new challenges often require innovative solutions and Computational Intelligence techniques can play a significant role in finding them. The workshop encouraged the submission of papers describing both theoretical developments and applications of Genetic and Evolutionary Computation and their hybrids to the following (and other related) topics:

- Cyber-crime and cyber-defense : anomaly detection systems, attack prevention and defense, threat forecasting systems, anti-spam, antivirus systems, cyber warfare, cyber fraud
- IT Security: Intrusion detection, behavior monitoring, network traffic analysis
- Corporate security, with special focus on BYOD policies and usability of security
- Risk management: identification, prevention, monitoring and handling of risks, risk impact and probability estimation systems, contingency plans, real time risk management
- Critical Infrastructure Protection (CIP)
- Advanced Persistent Threats (APTs)
- Design of military systems and sub-systems.
- Logistics and scheduling of military operations.
- Strategic planning and tactical decision making.
- Multi-objective techniques for examining tradeoffs in military, security, and counter-terrorism procedures.
- Automated discovery of tactics and procedures for site security, force protection, and consequence management.
- Other computational intelligence techniques for applications in the areas listed above.

The workshop invited completed or ongoing work, with the aim to encourage communication between active researchers and practitioners to better understand the current scope of efforts within this domain. The ultimate goal is to understand, discuss, and help set future directions for computational intelligence in security and defense problems.

As a first-year workshop, the organizers received and accepted four high-quality submissions from North America and Europe:

- *On the Role of Multi-Objective Optimization in Risk Mitigation for Critical Infrastructures with Robotic Sensor Networks* by Jamieson McCausland, Rami Abielmona, Rafael Falcon (Larus Technologies Corp., Canada); Ana-Maria Cretu (Université du Quebec en Outaouais, Canada); and Emil Petriu (University of Ottawa, Canada)
- *On Botnet Behaviour Analysis using GP and C4.5* by Fariba Haddadi, Dylan Runkel, Nur Zincir-Heywood, and Malcolm Heywood (Dalhousie University, Canada)
- *Evolutionary Based Moving Target Cyber Defense* by David John, Robert Smith, William Turkett, Daniel Canas, and Errin Fulp (Wake Forest University, USA)
- *Enforcing Corporate Security Policies via Computational Intelligence Techniques* by Antonio Mora, Paloma De las Cuevas, J.J. Merelo (University of Granada, Spain); Sergio Zamarripa, and Anna I. Esparcia-Alcázar (S2 Grupo, Spain)

We would like to thank the authors for submitting these excellent papers, and strongly encourage the broader security and defense research community to prepare and submit technical papers to future SecDef workshops. In addition, we thank ACM SIGEvo and GECCO 2014 organizers, especially Per Kristian Lehre (GECCO 2014 Workshops Chair), for their assistance. Finally, we thank Sandra Peiró from S2 Grupo for designing and setting up the workshop web site.

Anna I. Esparcia-Alcazar
Co-chair
S2 Grupo, Spain

Frank W. Moore
Co-chair
University of Alaska Anchorage, USA

Enforcing Corporate Security Policies via Computational Intelligence Techniques

Antonio M. Mora,
Paloma De las Cuevas,
Juan Julián Merelo
University of Granada
Department of Computer Architecture and Technology, ETSIIT/CITIC
Granada, Spain
{amorag,paloma,jmerelo}@geneura.ugr.es

Sergio Zamarripa,
Anna I. Esparcia-Alcázar
S2 Grupo
Valencia, Spain
{szamarripa,aesparcia}@s2grupo.es

ABSTRACT

This paper presents an approach, based in a project in development, which combines Data Mining, Machine Learning and Computational Intelligence techniques, in order to create a user-centric and adaptable corporate security system. Thus, the system, named MUSES, will be able to analyse the user's behaviour (modelled as events) when interacting with the company's server, accessing to corporate assets, for instance. As a result of this analysis, and after the application of the aforementioned techniques, the Corporate Security Policies, and specifically, the Corporate Security Rules will be adapted to deal with new anomalous situations, or to better manage user's behaviour. The work reviews the current state of the art in security issues resolution by means of these kind of methods. Then it describes the MUSES features in this respect and compares them with the existing approaches.

Categories and Subject Descriptors

I.2.6 [**Artificial Intelligence**]: Learning - Induction; D.4.6 [**Operating Systems**]: Security and Protection - Access controls; I.2.1 [**Artificial Intelligence**]: Applications and Expert Systems

Keywords

Computational Intelligence; Evolutionary Computation; Corporate Security Policies; Security Rules

1. INTRODUCTION

Security in distributed systems has been a very profitable research area from the arising of the first client/server architectures [3]. Inside this, corporate security is one of the main topics. The landscape has changed dramatically in the last years, starting with the distribution of the information (instead of being centralised in corporate servers, it has been spread among multiple machines such as portable devices, external servers, or cloud storage systems); and continuing with the so-called Bring Your Own Device (BYOD) philosophy, in which the devices that access to the system are owned by the users (company's employees), and could contain both personal and professional information.

This scenario opens up new security issues [33], which should be dealt in a different way, taking into account both (company's) data security and (user's) privacy. In order to protect them, there are defined *Corporate Security Policies*.

To deal with this new situation, a novel system is being developed (inside an European Project). It is named *MUSES*, from *Multiplatform Usable Endpoint Security System* [31], which is a device-independent end-to-end user-centric tool. It considers a set of security rules defined as specifications of the Company Security Policies, and its main feature is the ability of 'learning' from the user's past behaviour and adapt, even inferring new ones, the set of rules in order to effectively manage potential future security incidents due to the user's behaviour. Then, the system will react, in a non-intrusive way, to the potentially dangerous sequence of actions (events) that he or she is conducting at any time.

To this end MUSES will analyse the users' behaviour by means of Data Mining (DM) techniques [24] and Machine Learning (ML) methods [6], extracting a set of patterns which will be later processed by means of Computational Intelligence (CI) algorithms, mainly Evolutionary Computation methods [5, 11, 23].

This is a step beyond the current state of the art in two senses: first regarding the current security systems for managing the new BYOD scenario inside the enterprises, as it can be read in [31]; and second concerning the application of Computational or Artificial Intelligence (AI) techniques to corporate security issues, focused on (and adapted to) the users' behaviour, as will be analysed in this work.

The paper is structured as follows. Next section gives a background in the current enterprise security issues. Section 3 reviews related work regarding the application of DM, ML, AI and CI techniques to a wide range of security problems inside the enterprise, but mainly focused on the user's behaviour and the consequent security policies adaptation, which are the main advantages of MUSES. The MUSES system's features regarding the application of those techniques are described in Section 4. Then, these features are com-

GECCO'14, July 12–16, 2014, Vancouver, BC, Canada.
Copyright 2014 ACM 978-1-4503-2881-4/14/07 ...$15.00.
http://dx.doi.org/10.1145/2598394.2605438.

pared with the existing works reaching some conclusions in Section 5.

2. ENTERPRISE SECURITY

Until these days, enterprises used to follow a static Security Policy devoted to control a certain structure [4], where the Information Assets and the devices were purchased and maintained by the company. Now that corporate networks are becoming dynamic for being adapted to the BYOD philosophy, there is an additional risk because the devices that the employees use are not always company-owned. A needed security policy, or in this case, an *Information Security Policy* (ISP from now on) should deal with the way of protecting a specific organisation information against a security breach. Though there are standards, such as the ISO27002 or the Security Forum's Standard of Good Practise[1], an ISP is defined depending on the characteristics of the community/organisation that they are built for.

Normally, the enterprise network architecture was being adapted to cope with external attackers [28]. However, with the consideration of BYOD, the threat is about corporate assets being compromised due to employees' devices with vulnerabilities [34], or leaked because they are being accessed from a device connected through an unsecured (public) network.

In Figure 1 there is a proposal which can be used for the beginning of the study of solutions that may make secure such a dynamic environment. It includes the possibility of having employee-owned mobile (smartphones and tablets) and portable (laptops) devices, and also the opportunity that the employees have of connecting these devices either from inside or outside the company premises. Moreover, company information assets are constantly accessed under these conditions, considering that an information asset means every *piece of information* that has a *value* (cost depending on the risk of being lost or leaked) for the company. It can be referred to files with sensitive information, to certain mails, or even to company applications.

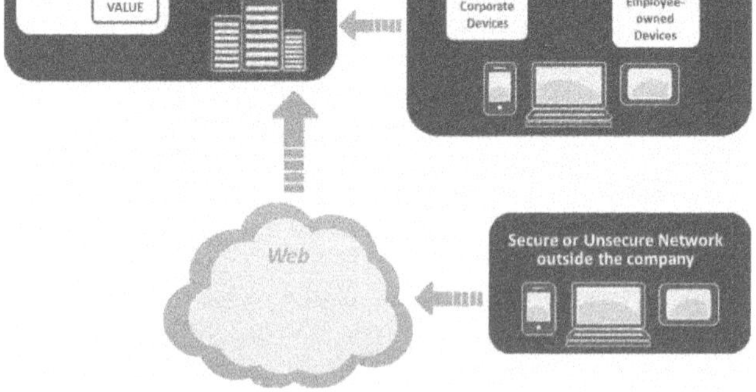

Figure 1: Architecture approach of an Enterprise Network assuming that the Company has adopted the BYOD philosophy.

The other issue to cope with is the elaboration of a good ISP, understandable for all the users of the company, and more importantly, non-intrusive for them. A lot of researchers have studied the natural tendency of employees whether to comply or not with the ISP [38, 7, 1], reaching conclusions such as the employees compliance with the security policies increases educating/training them in information security awareness [37], and decreases applying too much sanctions when a misuse or abuse occurs [17].

This situation leads to a need of protecting the organisation side, but also the users side, making non-interfering easy-to-follow ISPs, and leaving them to use their devices for personal purposes while working, without putting corporate information assets under risk. The compliance of these requirements would compose an End-to-End Security Solution (protecting both enterprise and employee), which is the aim of the MUSES project [31] (see Section 4).

[1]https://www.securityforum.org

3. STATE OF THE ART

Security is a wide area of research since the very beginning of the eighties [3]. Thousands of works have been published in a number of different issues in this topic. One of the most profiting fields is the application of Artificial Intelligence (AI) techniques to different security-based problems. This research line was started more than twenty years ago [10], and will be still open for several years further [32].

The topics addressed by the researchers are quite varied, including Data Mining (DM) [8, 22], and Machine Learning (ML) methods [12, 25], applied to many different problems.

Computational intelligence techniques have been also widely used in this area, being the most profiting methods the Evolutionary Computation (EC) metaheuristics: Genetic Algorithms (GAs) and Genetic Programming (GP).

There are several works using GAs for solving security issues, such as the intrusion detection (see [13] for a survey), the design and evaluation of security protocols [29, 43, 42], or the optimisation of different aspects related with security: IT security costs [21] and cryptographic protocols [44], to cite a few.

This work is focused on the application of different DM, ML and AI/CI techniques to a new set of security issues, which has arisen as a consequence of the new interactions between systems, and by the user's habits and behaviour (including the BYOD scenario), as it is described in Section 2. Then, the works that we are interested in are those related with the users' information and behaviour (in this scope), and the management (and adaptation) of Information or Corporate Security Policies (ISPs).

In this line, the paper by Greenstadt and Beal [14] combined biometrics signals with ML methods in order to get a reliable user authentication in a computer system. P.G. Kelley et al. [20] presented a method named *user-controllable policy learning* in which the user gives feedback to the system every time that a security policy is applied, so these policies can be refined according to that feedback to be more accurate with respect to the user's needs. This approach could be useful for a personal device, but our aim in MUSES is to have a global set of rules that could be adapted for all the users. On the other hand, policies could be created for enhancing user's privacy, as proposed by Danezis in [9], who defined a system able to infer privacy-related restrictions by means of a ML method applied in a social network environment. The idea of inferring policies will be also considered in MUSES, but in the scope of the company, and focused on ISPs.

A closer work to our approach is the one presented by Samak et al. [36], in which the authors use a clustering-based approach to infer new traffic security policies in a network. However our idea in MUSES, explained in Section 4, is to infer new Security Rules (as an specialisation of the ISPs) by means of GP.

Some other authors have applied this rule-based method for evolving (improving) a set of policies, such as Lim et al. [27, 26], who inferred new policies based in the decisions on a system, considering the user's feedback. A similar approach will be considered in MUSES, but there will be an automatic evaluation system for the new inferred rules, rather to the strict need of a user control. Moreover, these works have been tested on synthetic testbeds, but MUSES will run in real companies with real users and real data.

Finally, the work by Suarez-Tangil et al. [40], combines GP with the event correlation process which is also applied in MUSES [31]. However, their approach is designed to create the rules/engine for that process, instead of the security rules to be considered as the output of the event correlation, i.e. the decisions to be made according to the events produced and to the enterprise ISPs.

The next section briefly presents the MUSES system, and describes the techniques to be used inside it, as mechanisms for ISPs adaptation to the user's behaviour.

4. MUSES SYSTEM

As previously stated, MUSES will be a whole corporate security system aimed to deal with the new BYOD philosophy, i.e. it will manage user's accesses to the company servers from diverse own devices, which could be dangerous for several reasons, including the user's behaviour.

The defined MUSES architecture is shown in Figure 2. It is a *client/server* approach in which the *client* program will be installed in every user's mobile or portable device, independently of the platform (operating system and type of device). The *server* side would be installed in the corporate security operations centre. Both sides are connected through a secure channel (using HTTPS) over Internet.

One of the main features of this system will be the self-adaptation (to the user and context) of the set of Corporate Security Rules (specification of the ISPs). To this end, there is a component in the designed architecture (Figure 2, left side) named *MusKRS*, from MUSES *Knowledge Refinement System*. This will be run asynchronously in the server and will be in charge of analysing all the gathered information (events, context, user-related data), and adapting/refining the security rules to better deal with these events, also trying to predict future threats due to the user's behaviour.

This process will be composed by two steps: first, a Data Mining/Machine Learning procedure will be performed (in the *Data Miner* sub-component); second, a refinement and inference process will be done (in the *Knowledge Compiler* sub-component), considering the data 'extracted' in the first step, by means of Computational Intelligence techniques. It should be noticed that part of the refinement (or adaptation) of the security rules will be made using simpler methods, such as generalisation or specialisation of rules, for instance. Then, other parts of the process would be conducted using CI.

Another important fact is that MUSES will count with a human controller, normally the company Chief Security Officer (CSO), who will supervise the system activity by means of logs. Thus, adapted and inferred security rules will not be directly added to the current set of rules. Instead, they are proposed to this controller in order that he/she accepts them if they are interesting and correct. It is planned that the system will be able to 'learn' from this decisions so, after a so-called training or 'warm up' period, the rules would be directly accepted or rejected autonomously.

The following sections describe these processes: first focusing on DM techniques to be used both automatically by the KRS, and as a kind of decision-aid/monitoring tool for the CSO; second, the CI techniques are explained, mainly focusing in Evolutionary Computation approaches, since these methods perform very well, and have been widely used in security-based environments, as has been presented in Section 3.

4.1 Data Mining/Machine Learning

This task will be performed by the Data Miner module. It will take the 'raw' data from the database and will process the information, in order to yield a set of relevant data for the Knowledge Compiler sub-component or for the human controller. In the first case, this sub-component will take them as a reference in order to refine or adapt the current set of security rules (for instance, to deal with anomalous situations).

The process will be mainly non-supervised, and eventually the datasets can be huge (depending on the company's data flows), so Big Data processing methods [35] will be applied.

The DM/ML techniques will process the so-called patterns, which in this context correspond to events (and their related information) produced by the users' interactions with the system. The methods to be applied are:

- *Pattern Mining* [16]: This process will try to identify frequent or, on the contrary, anomalous patterns, in order to process them lately. The idea is that non-frequent patterns are potentially suspicious, and thus, could be of interest to be checked by the CSO or to serve as a reference for the rule-refinement process.
- *Classification* [30]: This technique tries to train a model (classifier) able to associate every pattern in the dataset to a class, so that the model could be used for assign a class for further incoming patterns with an unknown category. For instance, it could look for events (patterns) that had been marked as 'allowed' or 'denied' (according to the ISPs). When a new event arises, if it has not an assigned decision, the classifier should provide one based on the similarity with previous (and already labelled) patterns.
- *Clustering* [18]: The aim of this method is grouping the patterns considering some similarity criteria, in order to manage them as a set. This could be used for providing data visualisation mechanisms, in order to make it easier to interpret the data interaction and the distribution in clusters with respect to the different properties/features of the patterns.
- *Feature Selection* [15]: It consists on extract the most important features/variables from the data. This could be useful if we want to discard non-key features, which could be interesting in order to reduce the database weight, for improving the performance of other techniques (such as classification or clustering), and even

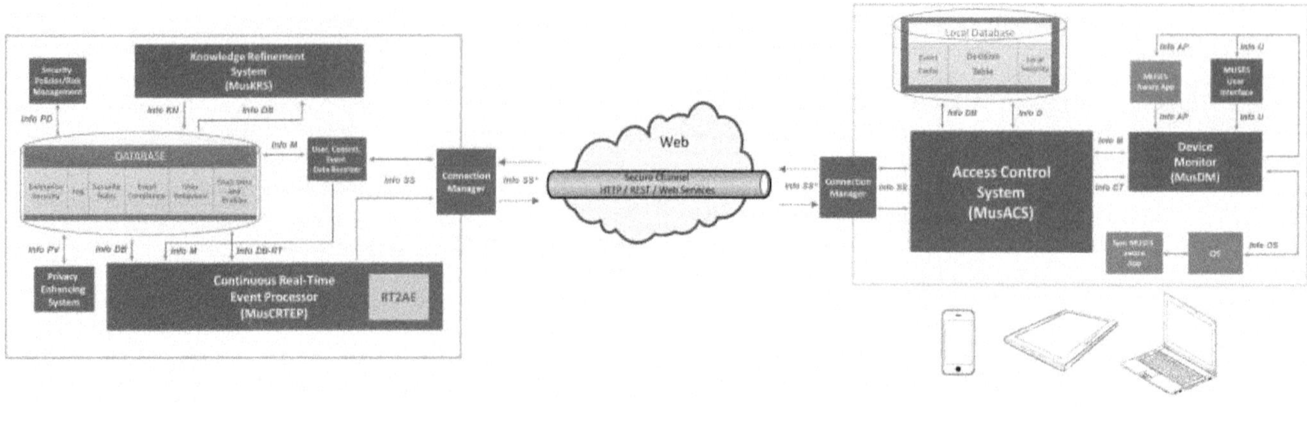

Figure 2: MUSES Architecture Overview (high-level components)

to improve the performance of whole the system, since less information would be gathered and transmitted.

- *Data Analysis*: This will provide the CSO with mechanisms to visualise interesting facts about the data, such as more frequent events, dangerous or suspicious users (according to their behaviour), more triggered rules, etc.

4.2 Computational Intelligence: Evolutionary Computation Methods

MUSES will use different EC approaches, initially, one in the DM/ML part of the process, and three in the rule-refinement/adaptation phase. They are based in GPs [23], and GAs [11].

The first evolutionary-based approach will be a *GP classification* method. This will be useful for two main reasons: first, in order to deal with the data class imbalance [19], very common in classification problems inside real systems (with real data); and second, to better manage categorical (non-numeric) data, since most of the features/variables and information gathered from the events take these kind of values.

Thus, this approach will be able to manage unbalanced datasets considering a fitness function in which a cost can be associated to the classifier accuracy at every epoch, having a penalty cost when the classifier makes a false negative (an element from the minority class which is classified as belonging to the majority class) [2]. Regarding the type of data, since GP algorithms can manage rule- or tree-based models, it will work perfectly with any categorical variable, yielding a good classifier as it has been made in other works (such as the aforementioned [2]).

The second set of EC approaches are, as stated, part of the rule-refinement (or adaptation) process. These techniques will be used for inference and optimisation, and will consider this data as a part of the process:

- The information extracted from the Data Miner subcomponent, mainly concerning the anomalous, unclassified or misclassified patterns. These are those patterns which did not match with any of the existing classes (they are quite different from the patterns belonging to those classes), so they cannot be included in any of the classes and thus they should be taken into account for a potential inference or update in the set of security rules, in order to 'cover' them.

- User-related information corresponding to those anomalous or unlabelled patterns (events). Thus, the user's ID, location and role, for instance, will be considered in order to select the applicable set of rules for that conditions.

- Context information for the same patterns, in order to also restrict the applicable set of rules considering this information.

Another useful information to consider in the refinement/adaptation process will be:

- Risk information extracted from the user profile (reputation), e.g. "Did the user received a lot of 'denies'/'allows' before?", i.e. "Is he/she trustworthy?". In case the user is not, more restrictive rules would be created for him, otherwise the corresponding rules could be 'eased' for that user.

- The information stored in logs along the system, which can, for instance, tell about how the user responds to system messages (either an action or if he gives feedback). This could result in the inference of new rules or in adaptation, in order to deal with, for instance, users that repeatedly ignore warning messages. Moreover, important log information regarding the parameters used or the decisions made in the different modules will be used for further tests of new inferred rules, as it is explained below.

So, the approaches that will be implemented are:

- *GP rule inference* method, which will generate/create new rules in order to 'cover' those situations non contemplated in the current set of rules. Thus, for instance, a new rule could be created in order to deal with the patterns to which the classifier could not assign a class. The generation will be done considering the so-called *dictionary*, i.e. a set of terms corresponding to all the possible inputs and actions in the system, which will be antecedents (conditions) and consequents in the security rules to be inferred. The evaluation of these rules will be done considering the stored log information concerning the parameters along with the actions/decisions made in every component in the system. Thus, it will be possible to 'simulate' the whole system behaviour when the new rule is included and get a value of its performance.

- *GP rule refinement* approach, which will optimise the current set of rules, adjusting the values in the conditions (antecedents), for instance. Thus, some superfluous parts on the rules and even complete rules could be removed or improved, obtaining for instance specialisations or generalisations of existing rules which could mean a better performance. The evaluation (of the whole set of security rules) will be done considering the number of unlabelled patterns that will be 'covered' after the adjustments.

- *GA optimisation* algorithm for setting up and adapting the assets' values. These are numerical representations of the importance of the corporate assets, and are considered in the Real-Time Risk and Trust Analysis process, in order to assign a risk value to every potential decision that can be made by the system. If it is possible to evaluate the partial solutions proposed by the GA, this approach could be very useful for the CSO (who is in charge of assigning and adjusting these values over time). The adaptation or adjustment concerns the change in value that an asset could have due to a loss of importance, once an event has passed (a project presentation, for instance).

5. COMPARISON AND CONCLUSIONS

As it can be seen MUSES system will go quite far in the application of DM/ML techniques, with respect to other security-aimed systems. This was explained in the previous paper [31], where the system was compared with other existing (commercial) systems.

Regarding the scientific contribution, one of the main differences with respect to previous works is the consideration of security threats 'brought' by the user's behaviour inside the system, i.e. through interaction/events, rather than more general and external threats. Moreover, the techniques to be used here will work with real data (in a real system), as a difference to some research works.

Data Mining techniques have been used by the authors in some works, but usually aiming for a specific general objective, for instance the detection of threats (botnet) [8], or the recognition of anomalies [22], but they are not linked with a following process to improve the system (the refinement phase in MUSES).

There are some proposals in which security policies are inferred or refined [9, 36], but they do not affect the ISPs as in MUSES, and they are not based in the user's behaviour in order to do this.

Genetic Programming has been previously used by several authors [40, 27], even for creating new policies or rules in a security-aimed sense, but they do not affect the ISPs and moreover, our proposed evaluation functions (completely integrated in the system) for the refinement and inference approaches are novel.

With respect to Genetic Algorithms, they have been extensively used in the literature, mainly for the detection of anomalies and intrusions rather than for optimisation, as in our case. However, there are some examples that could be used as model for our approach, such as [21, 41].

Anyway, there is room for considering some of the proposed approaches that could be added as future features for MUSES such as the analysis of users via social networks [9, 25], the optimisation of security protocols [42], the implementation of intrusion detection mechanisms [13], or the application of novel privacy-related techniques [39], which is another feature also considered in MUSES.

6. ACKNOWLEDGMENTS

This work has been mainly supported by the MUSES European project (FP7-318508). In addition to projects SIPESCA (G-GI3000/IDIF, under Programa Operativo FEDER de Andalucía 2007-2013), EvOrq (TIC-3903), CANUBE (CEI2013-P-14), ANYSELF (TIN2011-28627-C04-02) and PYR-2014-17 included in GENIL - CEI BIOTIC (Granada).

7. REFERENCES

[1] A. Al-Omari, O. El-Gayar, A. Deokar, and J. Walters. Security policy compliance: User acceptance perspective. In *45th Hawaii International Conference on System Sciences*, pages 3317–3326. IEEE Press, 2012.

[2] E. Alfaro-Cid, K. Sharman, and A. Esparcia-AlcÃ¡zar. A genetic programming approach for bankruptcy prediction using a highly unbalanced database. In M. Giacobini, editor, *Applications of Evolutionary Computing*, volume 4448 of *Lecture Notes in Computer Science*, pages 169–178. Springer Berlin Heidelberg, 2007.

[3] A. J. P. Anderson. Computer security threat monitoring and surveillance. Technical report, James P. Anderson Co., Fort Washington, PA, 1980.

[4] S. Bacik. *Information Security Management Handbook*, volume 7, chapter Security Implications of Bring Your Own Device, IT Consumerization, and Managing User Choices, pages 133–142. Sixth edition, 2013.

[5] T. Back. *Evolutionary algorithms in theory and practice*. Oxford University Press, 1996.

[6] C. Bishop. *Pattern recognition and Machine Learning.* Springer, 2006.

[7] B. Bulgurcu, H. Cavusoglu, and I. Benbasat. Information security policy compliance: an empirical study of rationality-based beliefs and information security awareness. *MIS Quarterly*, 34(3):523–548, 2010.

[8] S. Chang and T. E. Daniels. P2p botnet detection using behavior clustering & statistical tests. In *Proceedings of the 2nd ACM Workshop on Security and Artificial Intelligence*, AISec '09, pages 23–30, New York, NY, USA, 2009. ACM.

[9] G. Danezis. Inferring privacy policies for social networking services. In *Proceedings of the 2Nd ACM Workshop on Security and Artificial Intelligence*, AISec '09, pages 5–10, New York, NY, USA, 2009. ACM.

[10] J. Frank and N. U. Mda-c. Artificial intelligence and intrusion detection: Current and future directions. In *In Proceedings of the 17th National Computer Security Conference*, 1994.

[11] D. E. Goldberg. *Genetic Algorithms in search, optimization and machine learning.* Addison Wesley, 1989.

[12] N. Görnitz, M. Kloft, K. Rieck, and U. Brefeld. Active learning for network intrusion detection. In *Proceedings of the 2Nd ACM Workshop on Security and Artificial Intelligence*, AISec '09, pages 47–54, New York, NY, USA, 2009. ACM.

[13] P. Gowher Majeed and S. Kumar. Genetic algorithms in intrusion detection systems: A survey. *International Journal of Innovation and Applied Studies*, 5(3):233–240, March 2014.

[14] R. Greenstadt and J. Beal. Cognitive security for personal devices. In *Proceedings of the 1st ACM Workshop on Workshop on AISec*, AISec '08, pages 27–30, New York, NY, USA, 2008. ACM.

[15] I. Guyon and A. Elisseeff. An introduction to variable and feature selection. *J. Mach. Learn. Res.*, 3:1157–1182, 2003.

[16] J. Han, H. Cheng, D. Xin, and X. Yan. Frequent pattern mining: Current status and future directions. *Data Min. Knowl. Discov.*, 15(1):55–86, 2007.

[17] T. Herath and H. Rao. Protection motivation and deterrence: a framework for security policy compliance in organisations. *European Journal of Information Systems*, 18:106–125, 2009.

[18] A. K. Jain, M. N. Murty, and P. J. Flynn. Data clustering: A review. *ACM Comput. Surv.*, 31(3):264–323, Sept. 1999.

[19] N. Japkowicz and S. Stephen. The class imbalance problem: A systematic study. *Intell. Data Anal.*, 6(5):429–449, Oct. 2002.

[20] P. G. Kelley, P. Hankes Drielsma, N. Sadeh, and L. F. Cranor. User-controllable learning of security and privacy policies. In *Proceedings of the 1st ACM Workshop on Workshop on AISec*, AISec '08, pages 11–18, New York, NY, USA, 2008. ACM.

[21] T. Kirta and J. Kivimaab. Optimizing it security costs by evolutionary algorithms. In C. Czosseck and K. Podins, editors, *Conference on Cyber Conflict*, pages 145–160, Tallinn, Estonia, 2010. CCD COE Publications.

[22] M. Kloft, U. Brefeld, P. Düessel, C. Gehl, and P. Laskov. Automatic feature selection for anomaly detection. In *Proceedings of the 1st ACM Workshop on Workshop on AISec*, AISec '08, pages 71–76, New York, NY, USA, 2008. ACM.

[23] J. R. Koza. *Genetic Programming: On the programming of computers by means of natural selection.* MIT Press, Cambridge, MA, 1992.

[24] S. J. Lee and K. Siau. A review of data mining techniques. *Industrial Management & Data Systems*, 101(1):41–46, 2001.

[25] A. Leontjeva, M. Goldszmidt, Y. Xie, F. Yu, and M. Abadi. Early security classification of skype users via machine learning. In *Proceedings of the 2013 ACM Workshop on Artificial Intelligence and Security*, AISec '13, pages 35–44, New York, NY, USA, 2013. ACM.

[26] Y. T. Lim, P. C. Cheng, J. Clark, and P. Rohatgi. Policy evolution with genetic programming: A comparison of three approaches. In *Evolutionary Computation, 2008. CEC 2008. (IEEE World Congress on Computational Intelligence). IEEE Congress on*, pages 1792–1800, June 2008.

[27] Y. T. Lim, P. C. Cheng, P. Rohatgi, and J. A. Clark. Mls security policy evolution with genetic programming. In *Proceedings of the 10th Annual Conference on Genetic and Evolutionary Computation*, GECCO '08, pages 1571–1578, New York, NY, USA, 2008. ACM.

[28] R. Lippmann, K. Ingols, C. Scott, K. Piwowarski, K. Kratkiewicz, M. Artz, and R. Cunningham. Evaluating and strengthening enterprise network security using attack graphs. Project report ia-2, Massachusetts Institute of Technology, Lincoln Laboratory, October 2005.

[29] W. Lu and L. Traore. Detecting new forms of network intrusion using genetic programming. In *Proceedings of the 2003 Congress on Evolutionary Computation*, pages 2165–2172, 2003.

[30] J. MacQueen et al. Some methods for classification and analysis of multivariate observations. In *Proceedings of the fifth Berkeley symposium on mathematical statistics and probability*, volume 1, page 14. California, USA, 1967.

[31] A. Mora, P. De las Cuevas, J. Merelo, S. Zamarripa, M. Juan, A. Esparcia-Alcázar, M. Burvall, H. Arfwedson, and Z. Hodaie. MUSES: A corporate user-centric system which applies computational intelligence methods. In D. S. et al., editor, *29th Symposium On Applied Computing*, pages 1719–1723, 2014.

[32] B. Morel. Artificial intelligence and the future of cybersecurity. In Y. Chen, A. A. Cárdenas, R. Greenstadt, and B. I. P. Rubinstein, editors, *AISec*, pages 93–98. ACM, 2011.

[33] R. Oppliger. Security and privacy in an online world. *IEEE Computer*, 44(9):21–22, September 2011.

[34] C. Orthacker, P. Teufl, S. Kraxberger, G. Lackner, M. Gissing, A. Marsalek, J. Leibetseder, and O. Prevenhueber. Android security permissions - can we trust them? In *MobiSec Session on Smartphone Security*, Aalborg, 2011.

[35] B. Ratner. *Statistical and Machine-Learning Data Mining: Techniques for Better Predictive Modeling and Analysis of Big Data, Second Edition.* CRC Press, Inc., Boca Raton, FL, USA, 2nd edition, 2011.

[36] T. Samak and E. Al-Shaer. Synthetic security policy generation via network traffic clustering. In *Proceedings of the 3rd ACM Workshop on Artificial Intelligence and Security*, AISec '10, pages 45–53, New York, NY, USA, 2010. ACM.

[37] R. Shaw, C. Chen, A. Harris, and H.-J. Huang. The impact of information richness on information security awareness training effectiveness. *Computers & Education*, 52:92–100, 2009.

[38] M. Siponen, S. Pahnila, and A. Mahmood. *New Approaches for Security, Privacy and Trust in Complex Environments*, volume 232, chapter Employees' adherence to information security policies: an empirical study, pages 133–144. IFIP International Federation for Information Processing, 2007.

[39] A. Solanas and A. Martínez-bal. *Advances in Artificial Intelligence for Privacy Protection and Security.* World Scientific Publishing Co., Inc., River Edge, NJ, USA, 2009.

[40] G. Suarez-Tangil, E. Palomar, J. Fuentes, J. Blasco, and A. Ribagorda. Automatic rule generation based on genetic programming for event correlation. In l. Herrero, P. Gastaldo, R. Zunino, and E. Corchado, editors, *Computational Intelligence in Security for Information Systems*, volume 63 of *Advances in Intelligent and Soft Computing*, pages 127–134. Springer Berlin Heidelberg, 2009.

[41] A. Tamjidyamcholo. Genetic algorithm approach for risk reduction of information security. *International Journal of Cyber-Security and Digital Forensics (IJCSDF)*, 1(1), 2012.

[42] L. Zarza, J. Forné Muñoz, J. R. Pegueroles Vallés, and M. Soriano Ibáñez. *Advances in artificial intelligence for privacy protection and security*, chapter Genetic algorithms for designing network security protocols, pages 325–358. World Scientific, 2010.

[43] L. Zarza, J. Pegueroles, and M. Soriano. Evaluation function for synthesizing security protocols by means of genetic algorithms. In *Proceedings of the The Second International Conference on Availability, Reliability and Security*, ARES '07, pages 1207–1213, Washington, DC, USA, 2007. IEEE Computer Society.

[44] L. Zarza, J. Pegueroles, M. Soriano, and R. Martínez. Design of cryptographic protocols by means of genetic algorithms techniques. In M. Malek, E. Fernández-Medina, and J. Hernando, editors, *SECRYPT*, pages 316–319. INSTICC Press, 2006.

On Botnet Behaviour Analysis using GP and C4.5

Fariba Haddadi, Dylan Runkel, A. Nur Zincir-Heywood, and Malcolm I. Heywood
Faculty of Computer Science
Dalhousie University
Halifax, Nova Scotia, Canada
{haddadi,runkel,zincir,mheywood}@cs.dal.ca

ABSTRACT

Botnets represent a destructive cyber security threat that aim to hide their malicious activities within legitimate Internet traffic. Part of what makes botnets so affective is that they often upgrade themselves over time, hence reacting to improved detection mechanisms. In addition, Internet common communication protocols (i.e. HTTP) are used for the purposes of constructing subversive communication channels. This work employs machine learning algorithms (genetic programming and decision trees) to detect distinct behaviours in various botnets. That is to say, botnets mimic legitimate HTTP traffic while actually serving botnet purposes. To this end, two different feature sets are employed and analyzed to see how differences between three botnets – Zeus, Conficker and Torpig – can be distinguished. Specific recommendations are then made regarding the utility of different feature sets and machine learning algorithms for detecting each type of botnet.

Categories and Subject Descriptors

K.6.5 [**Management of Computing and Information Systems**]: Security and Protection—*Invasive software*

Keywords

Security; botnet detection; machine learning

1. INTRODUCTION

Botnets represent a set of compromised hosts under the remote control of a botmaster i.e., a master–slave relationship. They epitomize an approach to putting what would normally be considered legitimate users to malicious ends. As researchers propose detection mechanisms to identify botnets behaviours, botmasters upgrade their bots to defeat detection. Given the distributed nature of botnets, there are many avenues by which detection and evasion can take place. Moreover, given the widespread use of legacy systems, which remain connected to the Internet, even 'old' botnets remain effective. Hence, even after a takedown, botnets make impressive comebacks [28]. In effect, the recovery of a botnet is potentially caused by the lack of suitable upgrades to legacy systems. As reported by Fu *et al.* [15], Conficker (as a relatively older generation botnet compared to Zeus) was detected on 104 devices at the James A. Haley Veteran's Hospital in Tampa in 2013. Moreover, McAfee predicted that in 2014 attackers will target systems using the old Windows XP operating system;[1] where legacy point of sale and medical systems frequently use Windows XP.

Many existing approaches to botnet detection rely on network traffic behaviour analysis. Some of these employ Machine Learning (ML) techniques (i.e. classification and clustering) to automatically generate botnet detection models. In such systems, the first step is to represent the network traffic in a way that is meaningful for the ML techniques employed. To this end, different systems assume their own set of features [11, 16, 31, 33]. Some only use network packet headers (i.e. [11, 16]), while others take advantage of packet payloads (i.e. [31, 33]). Botnets, on the other hand, employ encryption techniques to avoid detection systems that analyze the communication information embedded in the packet payload.

In this work, we investigate a machine learning-based botnet detection mechanism that does not use packet payload information; where this is opaque when encrypted. If successful, we will therefore be able to detect botnets using encryption. To this end, two ML approaches will be employed (C4.5 decision tree induction [8] and a form of team based genetic programming (GP) [13]), with the goal of qualifying to what degree assuming different methods provides better detection coverage. Both algorithms have previously demonstrated to be effective for distinguishing between encrypted and non-encrypted traffic [9].

The approach adopted in this work is to first construct network traffic and extract the required features (attributes) using a flow exporter tool. Specifically, TCP packets are converted into a *flow* representation summarizing various properties for a group of packets associated with the same source / destination IP and port numbers as well as protocols. However, there are many properties that can be derived to characterize such flows. Depending on the tool used to construct the flow, the resulting features may be more / less effective at detecting botnet activity. Moreover, it is possi-

[1]Microsoft announced that as of 8 April 2014, Windows XP will no longer be supported. However, Windows XP is still the second most widely deployed desktop operating system.

GECCO'14, July 12–16, 2014, Vancouver, BC, Canada.

http://dx.doi.org/10.1145/2598394.2605435.

ble that botnets are using TCP flags in ways that were not intended for legitimate use [20].

Traffic from three botnets will be used: Conficker, Torpig and Zeus. These botnets have recently been associated with critical network infrastructure such as medical systems [15] or demonstrated a high infection rate. Our objectives are three-fold: 1) establish how effective a basic flow based information is for detecting each botnet; 2) to identify the most effective attributes for detecting each botnet, and 3) to make recommendations regarding signatures appropriate for detecting each botnet.

2. BACKGROUND

Many systems require supplementary information such as network alert information or several botnet binaries for the purpose of detection [21, 26, 25]. However, it is possible to detect the botnets without any additional information beyond that available in network traffic data. Yadav *et al.*, proposed a methodology to detect botnets, addressing the domain fluxing mechanism employed by the botnets such as Zeus, Conficker and Torpig [32]. To this end, they analyzed the DNS queries and the entropy of the domain names belonging to such queries. The proposed system was tested against Conficker botnet, which resulted in a promising detection and false positive rates. Haddadi *et al.*, on the other hand, designed and developed a Stateful-SBB (a co-evolutionary GP approach) based technique to detect botnets such as Conficker, employing only the command and control (C&C) domain names without any DNS group behaviour analysis [17]. However, since the systems proposed by both Yadav *et al.* and Haddadi *et al.* require access to a domain name information (i.e., packet payload information), neither are effective for botnets with encrypted packet payloads.

Botnet detection systems can be categorized based on the communication protocol they employ, the detection methods they employ or the type of data they use. Thus, some researchers apply machine learning techniques for botnet detection purposes using flow-based information (as attributes) [11, 16, 27, 14]. Given that botnets are increasingly employing encryption techniques to hide their information, then detection techniques that analyze the packet payload information can no longer be useful (e.g., [31, 33]). Researchers should therefore design frameworks that can also detect encrypted botnet behaviour. Celik *et al.*, proposed a flow-based botnet C&C activity detection system using only headers of traffic packets [11]. Specifically, they investigated the effect of calibration of time-based flow features using machine learning algorithms such as C4.5. Kirubavathi *et al.* designed specifically an HTTP-based botnet detection system using a multilayer Feed-Forward Neural network [19]. Given that HTTP-based botnets do not maintain a connection with the C&C server but periodically make a request to the C&C server (over the HTTP) to download the instructions, they extracted features related to TCP connections in specific time intervals based on the packet headers. Haddadi *et al.* designed a botnet detection approach based on botnet traffic analysis [16]. Network traces representing normal and attack traffic were generated with publicly available domain names of botnet C&C servers and legitimate web servers. NetFlow based feature extraction (only from packet headers) was used and machine learning algorithms (C4.5 and Naive-Bayes) were then employed to detect the botnets.

3. METHODOLOGY

In this work, two ML paradigms are assumed: C4.5 decision tree [8] and the symbolic bid-based (SBB) framework for evolving teams of programs to detect botnet behaviour [13]. Both of these learning algorithms generate solutions (models) that are in human readable format and therefore enable the analysis of the learned models.

Traffic features (attributes) are expressed as flows using the Softflowd tool [5]. In this case, the features are derived from packet header information alone. Therefore they can be employed for encrypted traffic classification, too. Moreover, most of the works in the literature employ a specific set of features for various botnets. However, in this work, we investigate which features can be useful to detect which type of botnet. To do so, two feature sets, namely Softflowd set.1 and Softflowd set.2, exported by Softflowd are employed and analyzed. We believe that this type of feature analysis may lead us to understand the botnet behaviors and their differences in more detail and in return could enable us to design and develop better botnet detection systems.

We evaluate our system on three botnets, namely Conficker, Torpig and Zeus. The reasons behind this are the following: most of the aggressive botnets employ encryption methods to hide their sensitive information (such as Zeus), and most of the systems such as the medical devices that Conficker and Torpig recently target have legacy operating systems. In doing so, we not only employ our proposed approach in legacy systems or medical devices but also on any device that runs on a TCP/IP network whether it is encrypted or not. Thus, the coverage is much greater than targeting a specific operating system or application.

3.1 Learning Algorithms Employed

The candidate ML algorithms go about constructing classifiers using different credit assignment policies and representations. However, both approaches share an ability to perform attribute selection is an implicit property of constructing a classifier. This property will later be used to gain insight to how botnets are communicating using HTTP.

3.1.1 C4.5 decision tree algorithm

C4.5 is a decision tree algorithm extending the earlier ID3 algorithm developed by Quinlan [8]. Decision trees are constructed through a process of deterministically splitting the training partition based on the selection of the attribute maximizing the normalized information gain. Following the addition of each split, an *IF–THEN* node is added to the current decision tree. Each branch of the tree partitions the (training) data into subsets, where the goal is to identify subsets that have the same label. Recursive application of this process incrementally constructs the decision tree until leaf nodes appear with sufficiently high normalized information gain.

In more detail, we note that the expected information or 'entropy' of a class given the exemplars, X from the training data has the form:

$$I(X) = -\sum_{i=1} f(X,i) \times log_2(f(X,i)) \quad (1)$$

where

$$f(X,i) = \frac{|\{j \in X|(j) := i|}{|X|} \quad (2)$$

A candidate split partitioning the data into partitions $X_1, , X_n$ has the entropy:

$$I_S(X) = -\sum_{k=1}^{n} \frac{|X_k|}{|X|} \times I(X_k) \quad (3)$$

The resulting information gain is the difference in entropy before and after introducing the split or $gain(X) = I(X) - I_S(X)$. The C4.5 algorithm makes use of additional normalizations to reduce biases towards unequal class representation [8]. The implementation used in this work takes the form of the WEKA 'J48' release [30].

3.1.2 SBB

The Symbiotic Bid-Based (SBB) algorithm is a form of genetic programming that builds teams of programs cooperatively while simultaneously identifying useful exemplars to learn from [13]. To do so, three distinct populations are utilized: a point population, a team population and a learner population. The learner population represents a set of symbionts (learners), which associate a GP-bidding behaviour with an action. The team population identify subsets of learners to define team membership under a variable length representation; the implication of the latter being that team size as well as composition evolves. Finally the point population denotes a subset of training data exemplars.

Host evaluation takes the following form. Each symbiont (s_j) consists of a program, $s_j.p$, and an action (class), $s_j.a \in \{1, ..., C\}$ where C denotes the maximum number of classes. All symbionts a member of the target host, h, have their program evaluated on the *same* training exemplar, x_k, (from the point population). The symbiont with the maximum output is identified or $sym^* = \arg_{sym_j \in h} \max(s_j.p(x_k))$. It is this symbiont who has 'won' the right to present its corresponding action, $sym^*.a$ as the class label on exemplar x_k. Any form of GP could be assumed for symbiont programs. In this work a linear GP representation is employed [10].

Fitness evaluation is only conducted against the current content of the point population, thus decoupling fitness evaluation from the cardinality of the entire training partition. The interaction between point and team population takes the form of Pareto archiving e.g., [12]. Thus, if an individual is not dominated by any other individual, it is set to be a part of Pareto-front. This relation is used by SBB training algorithm to determine the points and the teams that survive to the next generation.

At each generation, $Pgap$ new points are generated by sampling the training data while enforcing a heuristic to ensure all classes see equal representation in the point population. Conversely, $Hgap$ new teams are generated through variation operators (add, delete, swap and mutate) as applied to the existing teams. New symbiont programs potentially appear through mutation alone, resulting in a variable size symbiont population. That is to say, there is no symbiont 'fitness' as such, however, should a symbiont not see any host index, it is deleted. After fitness evaluation the point and team population content is deterministically ranked with $Pgap$ points and $Hgap$ teams deleted before a new generation commences.

The above ranking process utilizes Pareto archiving, thus the Pareto non-dominated teams with the highest ranks are selected. Likewise, the non-dominated points are also preserved. Meanwhile, if a point / team ranking is required in these non-dominated subsets, a form of competitive fitness sharing is employed in order to introduce a bias in favour of the points / teams that exhibit non-overlapping behaviour.

Post evolution, all the generated teams in the learning procedure are evaluated on the training data set and the one with the best performance selected as the 'champion' solution. The performance metric assumed for this purpose takes the form of the class-wise average detection rate (Eqn. (5) Section 4.2.1). The solution team is a combination of a set of learners with their corresponding GP instructions. In our evaluations, the maximum program size is set to 48. Thus, each learner in the solution can have maximum 48 instructions including the non-effective code, called introns. Given that introns were found to count for between 60% to 90% of instructions in a linear GP [10], we employ intron removal to reduce the complexity of SBB [17]. A more detailed explanation of the algorithm can be found in [13].

3.2 Data set Generation and Feature Extraction

The Hyper Text Transfer Protocol (HTTP) is one of the most common Internet protocols on account of the popularity of web applications on the Internet. Naturally, botnets have started to use this protocol to hide their malicious behaviours in the legitimate users' activities [24]. Zeus, Conficker and Torpig represent three botnets that utilize HTTP protocol for their communication purposes. These are well-known botnets where Conficker was recently reported to be seen on medical devices and is also known to be used for collecting banking information. Torpig, on the other hand, is known to be a good representative of how domain fluxing is used on the HTTP to steal financial and medical information. Finally, Zeus is one of the most destructive botnets reported which came with a new variant in 2013 after the takedown in 2012. This botnet has been collecting banking data by using man-in-the-browser keystroke logging and form grabbing but can be configured for any type of identity theft attack.

A typical advanced botnet forms in five stages: initial infection, secondary infection, connection, malicious C&C and finally update and maintenance. During stage 1, exploitation techniques are used to find victim vulnerabilities and infects the target host. Once infected the shell-code is executed on the victim machine to fetch the image of the bot binary which then installs itself on the machine (stage 2). In the third stage, the bot binary establishes the C&C channel. This channel is then used by the bot master to send the command in the malicious C&C stage. Finally, the update and maintenance stage is entered when the botmaster needs to update the bots for one reason or another.

Since, there is not a significant amount of botnet traffic publically available, we generated traffic. To this end, we designed an approach to generate the botnet traffic representing the first phase of the botnet communication which happens during the third stage of botnet lifecycle. In order to do this, we employed publicly available (from legitimate resources) lists of C&C domain names for Conficker, Torpig and Zeus. We generated the representative botnet traffic for the first phase of botnet communication by initiating HTTP based communication to the domain names reported in these publicly available lists. These lists were obtained from ZeusTracker [6], DNS-BH [3], Twitter API [29], Bonn University [2] websites. As for the representative legitimate traffic, we employed the publicly available Alexa domain lists which are based on the most popular websites from Alexa Inc. [1]. This way, both the attack and the normal traffic were generated using the publicly available domain name lists to avoid any biases in the generated traffic. The aforementioned generated botnet data sets are evaluated against the few publicly available botnet data sets in [18]. The results of this evaluation indicate that the generated traffic representing the first phase of a botnet communication is comparable to the real-life botnet traffic data sets. Moreover, since Zeus botnet leaked in 2011, there are Zeus botnet kits publically available. Therefore, we also run the Zeus botnet in a controlled environment and captured the network traffic. Furthermore, there are Zeus botnet traffic captures available at NETRESEC [4] and Snort [7] websites that we also employed in this work.

Once the traffic is collected, we convert the captured packet format traffic into Internet Protocol (IP) traffic flows using an IP Flow exporter. Flow exporters aggregates the traffic based on 5-tuple information: Source IP address, Destination IP address, Source port number, Destination port number and Protocol. Then the flow traffic is summarized in terms of some statistics such as the number of packets per flow, bytes per flow etc.

Cisco Systems introduced NetFlow to collect and aggregate IP traffic information. Given that Cisco is the leader of IP flow technology, NetFlow became an industry standard and therefore, many network equipments in the market support it. Thus, in this work, we employ of one of the open source implementations of NetFlow exporters, namely Softflowd [5].

4. EVALUATIONS AND RESULTS

As discussed earlier, our goal is first to detect various types of botnets using only flow-based features and second, to find the features that best describe the behaviour of the botnets employed. To this end, two ML algorithms are employed on two different feature sets and the solutions analyzed.

4.1 Data Sets

Softflowd is used to provide 14 flow attributes with the default parameters. All numeric attributes could be employed directly. However, the "flag" attribute is a string based feature, hence requires conversion to a numeric form prior to use by ML either SBB or C4.5. However, the numeric encoding assumed for this purpose can have a significant impact on the resulting classifier [23]. Benchmarking will therefore be conducted without the "flag" attribute (Softflowd set.1) and with (Softflowd set.2).

In the case of Softflowd set.2, six "flag"-based features are defined (Table 1). Each of the six flags are encoded using two numeric values to indicate when they are set / not set (during a communication). Table 1 summarizes the attributes that are utilized in this work. A detailed definition of the attributes can be found in Softflowd project web site [5]. Since the traffic generated/collected for each of the data sets is different, after extracting the flows, the data sets were then divided into two parts (Training and Testing) based on: (i) a $\approx$ 30(70)% breakdown for the testing (training) respectively; and (ii) keeping enough samples of each class in both of the data sets. Table 2 indicates the number of flow samples in each data set. Hereafter, we will refer to the data sets generated in our lab using the publicly available domain names as Zeus-1 (NIMS), Conficker (NIMS) and Torpig (NIMS) and the Zeus data set that is created based on the publicly available Zeus botnet kit as Zeus-2 (NIMS). On the other hand, the other botnet traffic is referred to using the download source. Hence, Zeus (Snort) is the Zeus traffic made public on the Snort web site [7] and Zeus (NETRESEC) is the botnet traffic provided on the NETRESEC web site [4].

Table 1: Employed Softflowd Features

Softflowd set.1 & 2	Softflowd set.2 only
Duration	Flag-A
Total number of packets (Pkts)	Flag-P
Total number of bytes (Byts)	Flag-R
Flows	Flag-S
Type of Service (TOS)	Flag-F
Bits per second (bps)	Flag-U
Packets per second (pps)	
Bytes per packet (Bpp)	

Table 2: Number of flows in each data set employed

Data Set	Training		Testing	
	Legit	Botnet	Legit	Botnet
Zeus-1 (NIMS)	6099	6099	2614	2614
Zeus-2 (NIMS)	611	611	262	262
Zeus (NETRESEC)	252	252	108	108
Zeus (Snort)	100	100	43	43
Conficker (NIMS)	28951	28921	12386	12416
Torpig (NIMS)	1864	1856	794	800

4.2 Performance Metrics

4.2.1 *Performance*

Typically, classifiers are evaluated using accuracy or classification rate as the fraction of all the correctly labeled instances. However, given an unbalanced data set or a multi-class data set, these metrics can be misleading. In this regard, a classwise detection rate is defined as [22]:

$$DET_c = \frac{TP_c}{FN_c + TP_c} \tag{4}$$

where $DETc$ is the class c detection rate and TPc and FNc are the True-Positive and False-Negative counts for class c. Finally, to summarize the classwise detection rates of a classifier over all classes the average DR criteria is defined by [22]:

$$Score = \frac{1}{|C|} \sum_{c \in C} DET_c \tag{5}$$

4.2.2 *Complexity*

Classifier complexity can be measured by different criteria such as memory consumption, time or the learned model by the learning algorithms. In this work, three complexity criteria are utilized: **1) training (computation) time** is employed where this is estimated on a common computing platform. **2) solution complexity**, however, a direct comparison between solutions from different representations is impractical since the underlying units of measurement are different. Therefore, the tree size for C4.5 and the program size of the solution team for SBB are considered as our units of measurement. **3) feature complexity** reflects the number of unique attributes employed per solution and potentially gives additional knowledge regarding botnet communication.

4.3 Results

Table 3 and 4 present the classification results of C4.5 and SBB employing two different feature sets, namely Softflowd set.1 and Softflowd set.2. The first feature set (Softflowd set.1) consists of the default numerical flow features exported by Softflowd whereas the second feature set (Softflowd set.2) augments the default numerical flow features with the numerically encoded TCP-Flag attributes (Section 4.1). As shown in Table 3, some of the FPRs are high when using Softflowd set.1 with C4.5 and SBB. Having said this, both of the classifiers performed equally well on Zeus-2 (NIMS), Zeus (NETRESEC), Zeus (Snort) and Conficker (NIMS) while using Softflowd set.1. On the other hand, the performance results on Torpig (NIMS) and Zeus-1 (NIMS) are much lower than the others when Softflowd set.1 is employed as the feature set. This observation indicates that Torpig and Zeus-1 (NIMS) botnets characteristics cannot be well represented by the features of Softflowd set.1.

The Softflowd set.2 feature set is then employed to investigate if TCP-flags would be beneficial to improve classification performance for Torpig (NIMS) and Zeus-1 (NIMS) specifically. Table 4 shows the results of these additional experiments. The results show that the performance of almost all of the botnets (except for Zeus (NETRESEC)) increased by at least 1% indicating that providing the TCP flags as the features to botnet classifiers can be beneficial. Surprisingly, Torpig (NIMS) results were improved by more than 30% when traffic is represented using the Softflowd set.2 feature set, implying that the six flag features of Softflowd set.2, were particularly effective at characterizing the Torpig botnet. Morever, there appears to be no disadvantage in using the Softflowd set.2 attributes.

Comparing the results over complexity criteria, Table 4, there is not much difference between the solutions based on feature complexity, i.e. the number of features used from the set given. However, there are significant differences in terms of time and solution complexities. To this end, C4.5 training time is much less than SBB training time. SBB, on the other hand, obtained smaller solutions (e.g. 88% smaller for Conficker data set) based on the solution complexity. This enables SBB to implement the solutions more efficiently. Given that such solutions need to operate at network flow speeds, simpler solutions are more advantageous, because the detection system can perform faster with less number of rule/signatures. Although, in some cases, the low complexity is caused by an under-performing solution, in others, it is a good indicator of a good solution with low complexity.

4.3.1 C4.5 solution analysis

Going beyond analyzing the classification results in terms of performance parameters such as Score, TP and FP rates, we analyzed the solutions learned by the classifiers. This

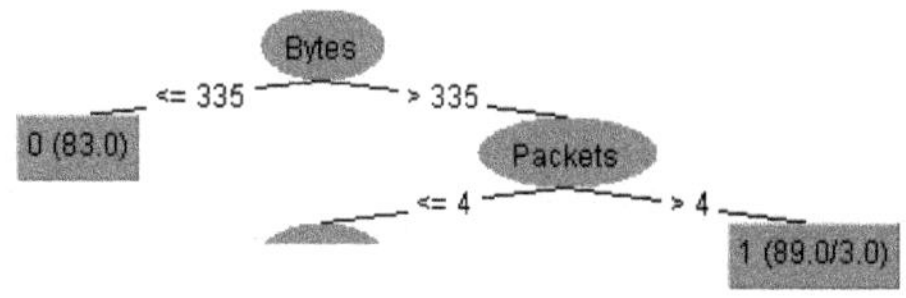

Figure 1: Part of the Zeus (Snort) C4.5 decision tree

type of analysis might give of some insights on the Zeus, Conficker and Torpig botnet behaviours.

To this end, the C4.5 solution (after training using the Softflowd set.2) for the Conficker botnet is a very complex tree (365 rules). On the other hand, C4.5 solution (after training using Softflowd set.2) for the Torpig botnet resulted in a very small tree with very high performance. As 65% of the nodes in the decision tree of the torpig botnet utilized the flag-based features (which were not included in the Softflowd set.1), we believe that Torpig probably employs these flags to tag its packets in a not-routine way. We will investigate this direction in our future work in more detail.

Additionally, we analyzed C4.5 solutions for the various Zeus botnet data sets employed in this work. Due to the high complexity of Zeus-1 (NIMS), no distinct rule could be observed rather than the very limited usage of flag-based features versus the highly used features related to the number of bytes and packets such as "Pkts" and "bps". On the other hand, the analysis of the other three Zeus botnet data sets shows that "Pkts" (i.e. the total number of packets in a flow), "Byts" (i.e. the total number of bytes in a flow), "Flag-S" (indicating the status of TCP SYN flag in the communication) and "Flag-F" (indicating the status of the TCP FIN flag in the communication) are widely utilized. To this end, in Zeus (NETRESEC), 15% of the botnet training samples were labeled using the "Flag-R" (when TCP reset flag is set in the communication) or in Zeus (Snort), 80% of the training data set is labeled based on "Pkts" and "Byts", Figure 1. Although the flag-based features are used by C4.5 to build the classification models for Zeus botnets, comparing the C4.5 results of Softflowd set.1 and set.2 shows that there are some fluctuations in the performance of the classifier from one Zeus data set to another when flag features are employed. It seems that these features do help in the identification of Zeus botnet traffic downloaded from the Snort web site as well as the Zeus-1 traffic. On the other hand, it seems like it does not help the identification of Zeus botnet traffic downloaded from the NETRESEC site nor the Zeus-2 traffic. However, in both these cases, the decrease in DR is compensated by the improvement in the FPR. This observation indicate that not all versions of the Zeus botnet (considering different data sets that may belong to different versions of this botnet) utilize the TCP flags in their communication.

4.3.2 SBB solution Analysis

In SBB, the champion team on the training dataset is selected as the final solution, which is then applied to the test dataset for performance evaluation. Under SBB the champion classifier takes the form of a team of programs. Each program is only associated with a single class label. This provides a level of task decomposition that is not possible under C4.5.

Figure 2 shows an example of a Torpig class-1 learner's

Table 3: Classification Results Using Softflowd set.1 Feature Set

	Data Set	Score	Legitimate		Botnet		Complexity		
			TPR	FPR	TPR	FPR	Time (sec)	Solution	Feature
C4.5	Zeus-1 (NIMS)	84%	86%	17%	83%	14%	0.26	485	8
	Zeus-2 (NIMS)	97%	96%	1%	99%	4%	0.01	29	5
	Zeus (NETRESEC)	97%	97%	3%	97%	3%	0.04	43	8
	Zeus (Snort)	93%	98%	12%	88%	2%	0	13	4
	Conficker (NIMS)	92%	91%	7%	93%	9%	2.71	411	6
	Torpig (NIMS)	68%	91%	55%	45%	9%	0.07	49	6
SBB	Zeus-1 (NIMS)	77%	80%	27%	73%	20%	185.56	27	5
	Zeus-2 (NIMS)	97%	96%	1%	99%	4%	176.98	42	6
	Zeus (NETRESEC)	90%	93%	13%	87%	7%	29.57	6	3
	Zeus (Snort)	98%	98%	2%	98%	2%	6.39	53	5
	Conficker (NIMS)	90%	89%	9%	91%	11%	178.10	81	7
	Torpig (NIMS)	65%	92%	63%	37%	8%	186.12	20	4

Table 4: Classification Results Using Softflowd set.2 Feature Set

	Data Set	Score	Legitimate		Botnet		Complexity		
			TPR	FPR	TPR	FPR	Time (sec)	Solution	Feature
C4.5	Zeus-1 (NIMS)	87%	90%	16%	84%	10%	0.24	457	9
	Zeus-2 (NIMS)	97%	97%	3%	97%	3%	0.01	35	9
	Zeus (NETRESEC)	96%	97%	6%	94%	3%	0.01	29	8
	Zeus (Snort)	98%	97%	1%	99%	3%	0	11	5
	Conficker (NIMS)	94%	93%	5%	95%	7%	3.41	365	10
	Torpig (NIMS)	99%	99%	1%	99%	1%	0.04	17	5
SBB	Zeus-1 (NIMS)	78%	73%	18%	82%	27%	188.252	51	8
	Zeus-2 (NIMS)	97%	94%	0%	100%	6%	161.87	14	6
	Zeus (NETRESEC)	90%	87%	7%	93%	13%	36.80	48	8
	Zeus (Snort)	100%	100%	0%	100%	0	8.22	41	8
	Conficker (NIMS)	91%	90%	9%	91%	10%	192.44	41	9
	Torpig (NIMS)	100%	100%	0%	100%	0%	109.23	60	11

instruction set which is part of the SBB's solution for the Torpig botnet i.e., a subset of the SBB solution shown in Table 4. The program's instruction count is reduced to 2 from 17 by pruning (cf., intron removal). The pruned instruction set indicates that the learner multiplies the "Bpp" (i.e. Bytes per packet) value by 0.54 *if* the "Flag-U" (indicating the urgent TCP flag) is set and returns "Bpp" value otherwise. Knowing that if this learner wins the bid over a data sample, it labels the sample as botnet, this learner's solution implies that samples with the set "Flag-U" look more suspicious and labeled as a botnet.

Using flag bits in malware communication has already been suspected by other researches [20]. Our observation supports this hypothesis for Torpig botnet on the data sets we analyzed. Overall SBB used the "Pkts" and "bps" (stands for bits per seconds) features the most for all of the botnets while for the Torpig botnet, it also utilized the "Flag-S" and "Flag-U" frequently. When SBB solutions using Softflowd set.1 and Softflowd set.2 are compared against each other, we observe similar trends to the behaviour of the C4.5 classifier. There are some fluctuations in the performance of the SBB classifier from one Zeus data set to another when flag features are employed. SBB's solutions again indicate that the versions of Zeus botnet seem to be different from one Zeus traffic file to another. For SBB flag features improve the solution performance, specially for Zeus Snort and Torpig botnets. In most cases it also introduces an improvement in the false alarm rates for SBB.

4.4 Discussion

In summary, Softflowd set.2 feature set performed better in terms of higher Score and lower FPR. Analysis of both the SBB and the C4.5 decision tree could help us to recognize the most important features of the attribute set and also the direct/indirect relationships between these features. Table 5 shows all of the features employed by each of the classifiers on each of the botnet data sets. As the table indicates, SBB and C4.5 are using different feature sets from one botnet to another. This implies that the classifiers are learning different behaviours. There are some obvious similarities/differences between the features employed by the classifiers such as: (i) almost all of the classifiers used "Pkts" and "bps". This shows the importance of these features in botnet detection, (ii) C4.5 did not use the "ToS" and "Flows" features at all while SBB used at least one of them in all types of botnet classifications, (iii) the features employed by C4.5 and SBB for Zeus (Snort) classification are almost complementary while SBB's selected feature set could obtain a 100% detection rate with a zero FPR, and (iv) in the Zeus-1 (NIMS) data set where the performance is lower than expected, the selected features by the two classifiers do not overlap much. This raises the question of whether

```
[Learner-ID: 162455, Action: 1, Instruction set size: 17, Pruned instruction set size: 2]
REG3<-Sub(REG3, REG1)
REG3<-Exp(Feature[7])
REG1<-Cos(REG6)
REG3<-Mul(REG3, Feature[7])
REG1<-Cos(REG0)
REG3<-Sub(REG3, REG5)
REG3<-Mod(REG3, Feature[7])
REG0<-Cos(Feature[13])
REG3<-Div(REG3, REG6)
REG7<-Div(REG7, REG3)
REG3<-Div(REG3, Feature[9])
REG4<-Div(REG4, Feature[13])
REG3<-Cos(Feature[10])
REG0<-Mul(REG0, Feature[7])
REG6<-Exp(Feature[0])
REG5<-Add(REG5, Feature[9])
REG1<-Mul(REG1, REG0)

[Pruned instruction set]
REG0<-Cos(Feature[13])  -----------> Uflag
REG0<-Mul(REG0, Feature[7]) -------> BPP
```

Figure 2: SBB- a sample learner instruction set with botnet label on Torpig– Softflowd set.2

the performance would increase by finding a solution that combines these two different solutions with complimentary feature sets.

Overall, our results and analysis presented in this work indicate that SBB and C4.5 learning algorithms focus on different properties of the traffic. This in return enables them to recognize different botnet behaviours. However, we think that SBB's low solution complexity makes it a better classifier when implementing a real-time botnet detection system. Finally, the two employed classifiers could detect most of the botnets with high performance while having higher than desired FPR for the Conficker and Zeus-1 botnets. Having said this, in our evaluations using a different feature set with TCP flags did help to decrease the FPR from Softflowd set.1 to Softflowd set.2 for these two botnet data sets. This indicates that a more detailed feature set analysis is necessary for these botnets. Moreover, given that different classifiers seems to work better for different botnets, i.e. different behaviours, an ensemble learning algorithm might be beneficial for future research.

5. CONCLUSIONS

A botnet is a set of compromised hosts that are under the remote control of a botmaster. Due to high infection rate and vast range of malicious activities, botnets are considered as one of the main threats against the cyber security. Since botmasters can update any phase of the botnet lifecycle at any time to defeat the detection systems, detection systems also require automatic and intelligent mechanisms to cope with the updates. In this work, we employ two machine learning algorithms, namely C4.5 and SBB, to generate botnet detection models for Zeus (different versions), Conficker and Torpig botnets automatically. Moreover, we represented the traffic using a flow exporter, namely Softflowd, to convert packets to traffic flows and extract their features. To this end, two feature sets (Softflowd set.1 and Softflowd set.2) both exported by Softflowd, are employed which enable us in revealing some of the characteristics of the aforementioned botnets behaviour.

Our first objective in this work was to investigate the possibility of detecting the aforementioned botnets using flow based features. As the results indicate, both of the classifiers performed very well using the Softflowd set.2 feature set and obtained the Score (classwise detection rate) of up to 100% for some of the botnets. This confirms the accomplishment of our first objective. To fulfill our second and third objectives which were finding the feature sets that best describe the botnets and return a solution that is suitable for a signature-based botnet detection system, the generated solutions and the features used are analyzed. The analysis determined some of the botnet characteristics. For example, given that Torpig detection models by both of the classifiers did not perform well using the Softflowd set.1 but did perform out-standing (30% increase in detection rate) using the Softflowd set.2 feature set, we believe that Torpig botnet employs the TCP flags in an abnormal way. However, we did not notice such behaviour in the Zeus or Conficker botnet solutions, which implies that these botnets do not employ such flags. Having said this, almost in all of our experiments SBB performed better than C4.5 in terms of the solution complexity.

Future work will explore what other flow features can be employed in botnet behavior analysis and their effects in terms of lowering the false alarm rates.

6. ACKNOWLEDGMENTS

This research is supported by the Natural Science and Engineering Research Council of Canada (NSERC) grant, and is conducted as part of the Dalhousie NIMS Lab at `https://projects.cs.dal.ca/projectx/`.

7. REFERENCES

[1] Alexa. http://www.alexa.com/topsites.

[2] Conficker Domain List. http://net.cs.uni-bonn.de/uploads/media/c_domains_april2009.zip.

[3] DNS-BH- Malware Domain Blocklist. http://www.malwaredomains.com/.

[4] Publicly available pcap files. http://www.netresec.com/?page=PcapFiles.

[5] Softflowd. http://www.mindrot.org/projects/softflowd/.

[6] Zeus tracker. https://zeustracker.abuse.ch/.

[7] Zeus trojan analysis. https://labs.snort.org/papers/zeus.html.

[8] E. Alpaydin. *Introduction to Machine Learning*. MIT Press, 2004.

[9] R. Alshammari, P. Lichodzijewski, M. I. Heywood, and A. N. Zincir-Heywood. Classifying ssh encrypted traffic with minimum packet header features using genetic programming. In *ACM Genetic and Evolutionary Computation Conference - Defence Applications of Computational Intelligence Workshop*, 2009.

[10] M. Brameier and W. Banzhaf. A comparison of linear genetic programming and neural networks in medical data mining. *IEEE Transaction on Evolutionary Computation*, 5:17–26, 2001.

[11] Z. B. Celik, J. Raghuram, G. Kesidis, and D. J. Miller. Salting public traces with attack traffic to test flow classifiers. In *USNIX Cyber Security Experimentation and Test (CSET) workshop*, 2011.

[12] E. D. de Jong. A monolithic archive for

Table 5: Feature Matrix

	Zeus-1 (NIMS)		Zeus-2 (NIMS)		Zeus (NETRESEC)		Zeus (Snort)		Conficker (NETRESEC)		Torpig (NIMS)	
Feature	**C4.5**	**SBB**	**C4.5**	**SBB**	**C4.5**	**SBB**	**C4.5**	**SBB**	**C4.5**	**SBB**	**C4.5**	**SBB**
Duration	✓	✓	✓	-	✓	-	-	✓	✓	-	-	✓
Packets	✓	✓	✓	✓	✓	✓	✓	-	✓	✓	-	✓
Bytes	✓	-	✓	-	✓	✓	✓	-	✓	✓	-	✓
Flows	-	-	-	✓	-	✓	-	✓	-	-	-	✓
ToS	-	✓	-	✓	-	✓	-	-	-	✓	-	✓
bps	✓	✓	✓	✓	✓	✓	-	✓	✓	✓	✓	✓
pps	✓	-	-	-	✓	✓	✓	✓	✓	✓	-	✓
Bpp	✓	✓	✓	-	✓	-	-	✓	✓	-	✓	✓
Flag-A	✓	✓	✓	-	-	-	✓	-	✓	✓	✓	✓
Flag-P	-	✓	-	✓	-	-	-	-	✓	✓	-	-
Flag-R	-	-	✓	✓	✓	-	-	✓	-	✓	-	-
Flag-S	✓	-	✓	-	✓	-	-	✓	✓	✓	✓	✓
Flag-F	✓	-	✓	-	-	✓	✓	✓	✓	-	✓	-
Flag-U	-	✓	-	-	-	✓	-	-	-	-	-	✓

pareto-coevolution. *Evolutionary Computation*, 15(1):61–93, 2007.

[13] J. Doucette, A. McIntyre, P. Lichodzijewski, and M. I. Heywood. Symbiotic coevolutionary genetic programming: A benchmarking study under large attribute spaces. *Genetic Programming and Evolvable Machines*, 13:71–101, 2012.

[14] J. Francois, S. Wang, R. State, and T. Engel. Bottrack: tracking botnets using netflow and pagerank. *Networking*, 6640:1–14, 2011.

[15] K. Fu and J. Blum. Inside risk controlling for cyberscurity risks of medical device software. *Communications of the ACM*, 56:35–37, 2013.

[16] F. Haddadi, J. Morgan, E. G. Filho, and A. N. Zincir-Heywood. Botnet behaviour analysis using ip flows with http filters using classifiers. In *7th Workshop on Bio and Intelligent Computing (AINA-BiCOM)*, 2014. in press.

[17] F. Haddadi and A. N. Zincir-Heywood. Analyzing string format-based classifiers for botnet detection: GP and SVM. In *IEEE Congress on Evolutionary Computation (CEC)*, 2013.

[18] F. Haddadi and A. N. Zincir-Heywood. Data confirmation for botnet traffic analysis. https://www.cs.dal.ca/research/techreports/cs-2014-01, February 2014.

[19] V. Kirubavathi and R. Nadarajan. Http botnet detection using adaptive learning rate multilayer feed-forward neural network. In *Information Security Theory and Practice: security, privacy and trust in computing systems and ambient intelligent ecosystems*, 2012.

[20] V. Krmicek and T. Plesnik. Detecting botnets with netflow. In *Cert Flocon*, 2011.

[21] F. Leder and T. Werner. Know your enemy: Containing conficker. The HoneyNet Project, White paper, 2009.

[22] P. Lichodzijewski and M. I. heywood. Coevolutionary bid-based genetic programming for problem decomposition in classification. *Genetic Programming and Evolvable Machines*, 9:331–365, 2008.

[23] A. Makanju, A. N. Zincir-Heywood, and E. Milios. Robust learning intrusion detection for dos attacks on wireless networks. *Intelligent Data Analysis An International Journal*, 15:801 823, 2011.

[24] Open DNS Inc. The role of DNS in botnet command and control, 2012.

[25] T. Ormerod, L. Wang, M. Debbabi, A. Youssef, H. Binsalleeh, A. Boukhtouta, and P. Sinha. Defaming botnet toolkits: A bottom-up approach to mitigating the threat. In *Emerging Security Information Systems and Technologies (SECURWARE)*, 2010.

[26] S. Shin and G. Gu. Conficker and beyond: a large-scale empirical study. In *26th Annual Computer Security Applications*, 2010.

[27] W. Strayer, D. Lapsely, R. Walsh, and C. Livadas. Botnet detection based on network behavior. *Advances in Information Security*, 36:1–24, 2008.

[28] Trend Labs- Security Intelligence Blog. Zeus/zbot malware shapes up in 2013. http://blog.trendmicro.com/trendlabs-security-intelligence/zeuszbot-malware-shapes-up-in-2013/, 2013.

[29] Twitter API. http://blog.unmaskparasites.com/2009/12/09/twitter-api-still-attracts-hackers/.

[30] weka. http://www.cs.waikato.ac.nz/ml/weka/.

[31] P. Wurzinger, L. Bilge, T. Holz, J. Goebel, C. Kruegel, and E. Kirda. Automatically generating models for botnet detection. In *14th European conference on research in computer security (ESORICS)*, 2009.

[32] S. Yadav, A. K. K. Reddy, A. L. N. Reddy, and S. Ranjan. Detecting algorithmically generated domain-flux attacks with DNS traffic analysis. *IEEE/ACM Transaction on Networking*, 20:1663–1677, 2012.

[33] H. R. Zeidanloo, A. B. Manaf, P. Vahdani, F. Tabatabaei, , and M. Zamani. Botnet detection based on traffic monitoring. In *Networking and Information Technology (ICNIT)*, 2010.

Evolutionary Based Moving Target Cyber Defense

David J. John
djj@wfu.edu

Robert W. Smith
smitrw12@wfu.edu

William H. Turkett
turketwh@wfu.edu

Daniel A. Cañas
canas@wfu.edu

Errin W. Fulp
fulp@wfu.edu

Department of Computer Science
Wake Forest University
Winston-Salem, NC 27109, USA

ABSTRACT

A Moving Target (MT) defense constantly changes a system's attack surface, in an attempt to limit the usefulness of the reconnaissance the attacker has collected. One approach to this defense strategy is to intermittently change a system's configuration. These changes must maintain functionality and security, while also being diverse. Finding suitable configuration changes that form a MT defense is challenging. There are potentially a large number of individual configurations' settings to consider, without a full understanding of the settings' interdependencies.

Evolution-based algorithms, which formulate better solutions from good solutions, can be used to create a MT defense. New configurations are created based on the security of previous configurations and can be periodically implemented to change the system's attack surface. This approach not only has the ability to discover new, more secure configurations, but is also proactive and resilient since it can continually adapt to the current environment in a fashion similar to systems found in nature.

This article presents and compares two genetic algorithms to create a MT defense. The primary difference between the two is based on their approaches to mutation. One mutates values, and the other modifies the domains from which values are chosen.

Categories and Subject Descriptors

I.2.8 [**Problem solving, Control Methods and Search**]: Heuristic methods—*genetic algorithms*; K.6.5 [**Security and Protection**]: unauthorized access

Keywords

computer security; moving target defense; directed mutation

GECCO'14, July 12–16, 2014, Vancouver, BC, Canada.
Copyright 2014 ACM 978-1-4503-2881-4/14/07 ...$15.00.
http://dx.doi.org/10.2598394.2605437 .

1. INTRODUCTION

Cyber attacks commonly initiate with a reconnaissance phase, where the adversary attempts to learn as much as possible about the potential target before launching an attack. This intelligence is very valuable, and it has been reported that a well-resourced adversary will spend approximately 45 percent of its time on this preliminary task [10]. Given the investment associated with reconnaissance and the reliance on this knowledge for a successful attack, neutralizing this attack phase has been shown to be a very successful defense strategy [7].

A Moving Target (MT) defense is a way to disrupt the attacker's attempt to learn how a system operates during the reconnaissance phase of a cyber attack. MT environments provide a diversity defense where the attack surface changes constantly. In the time it takes an attacker to perform system reconnaissance and construct an exploit, the system changes. As a consequence of the modification, the exploit will have limited impact or cause the attacker to lose confidence in the reconnoiter. In addition, an attacker acting on false or constantly changing information may expend more resources and increase the risk of being detected.

MT defenses have been successfully employed to protect computer systems at different levels. For example, address randomization is a MT defense that changes the location of certain portions of a program's memory [4, 9]. While widely implemented, this application-level defense only mitigates a certain type of attack. Another MT strategy alters network configurations to limit the usefulness of an attacker's reconnaissance [1, 14]. This MT defense operates at the infrastructure level and is somewhat effective, but it requires coordination of several resources to protect legitimate users, which is difficult. Host-level MT defenses operate at the system level and change the computer's appearance over time; however, current implementations simply cloak the system which is essentially security through obscurity.

This article describes a new type of multiple host-level MT defense that changes both the host and network attack surfaces. It does this by manipulating the settings of multiple computer's configurations directly. Using evolution-inspired techniques, the approach proactively discovers multiple functional and secure configurations and then places them in service across multiple computers during varying periods of time. As a result, the attacker faces an unpredictable computing environment which can limit the useful-

Parameter	Value Type	Description
`.htpasswd`	Binary	Allow configuration changes on a per-directory basis
`ServerTokens`	Value from a list	Controls the information about server OS and modules.
`KeepAlive`	Binary	Allow multiple requests to be sent over the same connection.
`KeepAliveTimeout`	Positive integer	Time to wait for a subsequent request before closing the connection.
`FollowSymLinks`	Binary	Allow symbolic links in a directory to be followed.
`IncludesNoExec`	Binary	Allow server side include execution.
`Indexes`	Binary	Allow automatic directory indexing.
`LimitRequestBody`	Positive integer	Limit the size of message body.
`LimitRequestFields`	Positive integer	Limit number of request HTTP header fields allowed.
`LimitRequestFieldSize`	Positive integer	Limit the size of an HTTP request header field.
`LimitRequestLine`	Positive integer	Limit the size of a client's HTTP request-line.
`autoindex_module`	Binary	Allow icons for directory listings.
`AllowOverride`	Value from a list	Controls if earlier configuration directives can be overridden.
`LimitExcept`	Value from a list	Limit request methods.

Table 1: A sample of the Apache configuration parameters used in the MT defense system. Parameter names, settings types, and brief descriptions for these 14 are shown.

ness of any reconnaissance activities. Unfortunately, finding configurations that meet these requirements is challenging. There are potentially a large number of individual configurations settings to consider, and for each one of them an administrator may not know that some are interdependent. It is also difficult to quantify the security of a computer configuration [18] since the introduction of new security vulnerabilities and functionalities can make a once secure configuration insecure.

However, evolution-based algorithms, which formulate better solutions from good solutions, are well suited for addressing such ill-formed and dynamic problems. Similar to nature, selection, crossover, and mutation processes are used over successive generations to find better solutions, or configurations, for this host-level MT system. As well, specially designed mutation operators can be developed for this system. As a result, this evolution-inspired MT approach can find secure and diverse configurations over time with appropriate feedback. This will be demonstrated with 102 parameters, taken from Apache web-server (Apache) on Red Hat Enterprise Linux 5 (RHEL5) configurations, that becomes more secure over time, while configurations maintain a level of diversity across the generations to support multiple feasible system configurations.

2. COMPUTER CONFIGURATIONS

A computer configuration is a set of parameters that govern operation. This includes operating system settings and information found in application configuration files. Furthermore, configurations can include transient data, such as the Linux `/proc` file system, or persistent data such as that found in Unix resource files. Collectively, this configuration information is a large amount of data that is often distributed across a number of files and databases.

While these parameters control how the operating system and applications perform, they also affect security. For instance, the Federal Desktop Core Configuration settings and the Consensus Security Configuration Checklist managed by NIST (National Institute for Standards and Technology) and CIS (Center for Internet Security) provide guidelines and configuration settings for various applications and operating systems [8, 16]. For example, Table 1 provides 14 Apache configuration parameters, value types, and parameter descriptions found in this checklist. Note the variety of parameter value types, which include binary, integer, and enumerated values. Furthermore, parameters can be interdependent, so a combination of settings is required to improve security [11]. For example, the NIST guidelines for Apache 2.2 identifies 4 settings to secure the `ScoreBoardFile` directive, which supports interprocess communication. Of course, other configuration parameters may have unknown impacts on security.

Although configuration guidelines can help to improve system security, they may not apply to all computer installations. A system may need certain parameter settings to remain functional, even though those settings may be deemed insecure. In addition, future security threats may render current guidelines useless. Therefore, while intermediately making configuration changes can provide a MT defense by rendering an attacker's reconnaissance ineffective, searching the large number of parameter values to find functional and secure changes is very challenging [6].

3. MOVING TARGET DEFENSE

Although searching for secure, functional, and diverse configurations is difficult, evolution-based search algorithms are well suited for these types of problem environments. Genetic Algorithms (GAs) are a type of search heuristic that naively mimic evolution [15]. Like most evolutionary algorithms, they seek better (more fit) configurations by discovering, recombining, and altering portions of current configurations to generate new ones. However, an MT environment does not aim to find a single best configuration but to ascertain and periodically implement a configuration from a set of assorted secure configurations. Before a GA can be applied to the MT problem, a genetic representation of the problem domain, methods of determining feasibility, an understanding of configuration fitness, and the design of GA operators must be carefully addressed.

3.1 Configurations as Chromosomes

In nature, an organism has a set of rules that define how it is created. These rules are encoded in genes that are connected together into long strings called chromosomes. Each gene contributes to the traits of the organism, like eye color or height, and has several different settings. Genes and their settings are usually referred to as an organism's genotype. The phenotype is the physical expression of the genotype, which is the organism itself.

In this MT defense system, GAs represent the current configuration generation as a set of chromosomes, each of which consists of multiple configuration parameter settings. Each genotype specifies a phenotypic description, though this relationship may be many to one. Consider the 14 configuration parameters shown in Table 1. There are multiple possible settings for each parameter. Therefore, each MT chromosome in this GA represents a configuration, and each generation consists of multiple MT chromosomes.

It is not necessary for the chromosomes to represent all possible configuration parameters. It may be advantageous to initially limit the number of parameters for the purposes of testing to better understand how they affect security and diversity. Over time parameters can be added to increase the search space and to find more complex configuration settings.

To be considered a potential suitable configuration, a chromosome must be feasible. For computer configurations, a chromosome is considered feasible if the configuration it represents provides the necessary functionality for the computer as defined by the user and/or administrator. For example, if the computer is a web server, then any configuration that blocks network access would be infeasible and not be enacted. Future implementations will incorporate comprehensive functionality testing, which is discussed in Section 6.

3.2 Chromosome Fitness

Chromosome fitness measures the level of security the configuration provides. While it is difficult to quantify the security of a configuration directly, it can be inferred based on the number of security events detected during operation. The evaluation of the parameter setting is based on the effect it may have on information security, specifically the effect on confidentiality, integrity, and assurance, also referred to as the CIA model [3]. Confidentiality refers to the disclosure of information to unauthorized individuals, while integrity refers to the accuracy and consistency of information, and assurance refers to the availability of information and/or services.

The security score also takes into account the difficulty of exploiting the parameter's vulnerability and the impact if the associated exploit is performed. These items can then be combined to create a Common Vulnerability Scoring System (CVSS) score: a vector of categorical scores associated with the 6 criteria of *access vector* (AV), *access complexity* (AC), *authentication* (AU), *confidentiality* (C), *integrity* (I), and *assurance* (A).

Ideally, attack information about a configured running system can be gathered, analyzed and then interpreted as chromosome fitness. However, this type of information is at best incomplete, and is likely to contain many false positives. For this research, a CVSS based rubric is applied to each parameter setting which culminates into a chromosome fitness score. This fitness score approximates knowledge on the uncertain quantity of attack information.

3.3 Genetic Algorithms

Genetic Algorithms (GAs) are a heuristic, naively mimicking evolution, to search complex or ill-formed problem spaces. GAs have been extensively researched since the 1960s, and most GA implementations use some combination of of the selection, crossover, and mutation operators [15]. These processes are among the tasks associated with the MT defense, as seen in Fig. 1. For the MT environment developed thus far, the search space is a subset of possible Apache and RHEL5 configurations, each consisting of 102 parameters. For many organisms, the selection of parents is the initial step in the creation of a child, and this sampling occurs in such a way as to bias the next generation towards the more fit individuals in the current one. The resultant offspring may have a portion of the genes from one parent and the remainder from the other. This process, crossover, encourages the propagation of discovered traits from the current generation into the next. In addition, some of the offspring's genes may be mutated, randomly changing the gene's value. The importance of mutation is its potential to introduce new traits into future generations. Using these three basic processes, selection, crossover and mutation, organisms can adapt over time.

Selection identifies members of the current chromosome pool as parents for new chromosomes. Roulette wheel selection, also known as fitness proportional selection, uses a probability distribution directly related to chromosome fitness to choose parents. The aim is to encourage chromosomes with higher fitnesses to produce even more fit offspring, while still allowing for offspring from a lesser fit parent. Tournament selection choses 4 chromosomes, has two single elimination rounds of comparisons to determine a winner. In the first round, two winners are determined through two pair comparisons, and in the last round, an overall chromosome is selected by choosing the best of the two first round winners. Tournament selection is less likely to pick chromosomes with smaller fitness values.

Possibly the most distinguishing feature of a GA is the crossover process, the combination of parent chromosomes to form a new chromosome. Therefore, a new configuration is created by combining portions of existing configurations. The crossover process implemented for this simulation is known as *two point crossover*, which has an associated probability p_c. After selecting a parent chromosome in the current generation, p_c is the probability that another chromosome from the current generation is selected and their genetic information exchanged. If two point crossover is not applied then the immediate offspring is the first parent; otherwise, two locations along a random permutation of the genes of the two selected chromosomes are identified randomly, and the genes between the two loci are traded to produce a child.

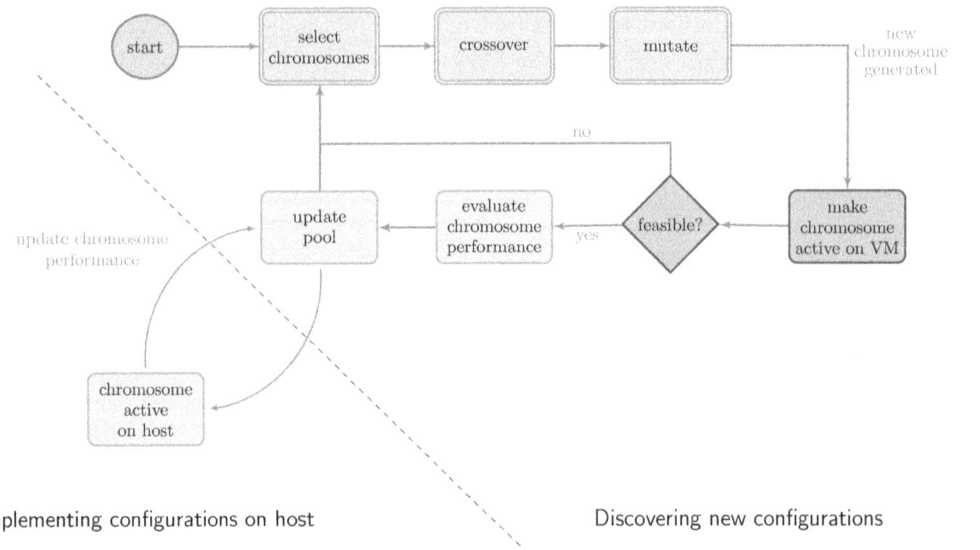

Figure 1: Flow chart of the tasks associated with the GA-based MT environment. Double-lined blocks (also in green) contain *traditional* GA processes, blocks in blue are associated with the virtual machine (VM) component, and blocks in orange are part of the assessment component.

The last process is mutation, which randomly changes settings in the offspring chromosomes. Associated with the mutation operator is a probability, p_m. The purposes of the mutation process are to maintain diversity, to allow extensive exploration of the chromosomes across the generations, and to avoid permanent fixation at any particular locus. With a probability of p_m, mutation is applied to a randomly chosen gene of a chromosome. If the rate of mutation is set too high, the resulting GA is often no better than mere random search. Mutation is not a uniform operator across the configuration parameters. Instead, it differs on a case by case basis between different parameters, according to their type and prior knowledge of acceptable or common settings. In fact, there are two mutation operators: one which applies simple changes to a parameter's value, and the other which makes changes to a parameter's domain. These two mutation operators result in two searching algorithms: the genetic algorithm with parameter value mutation (GA+PVM), and the genetic algorithm with parameter domain mutation (GA+PDM).

The parameter value mutation operator modifies the current value of a chosen chromosome's parameter based on its type. For instance, a single option which may have only one out of a number of possible values would be mutated by changing to a different option. Meanwhile a series of options, each of which may independently be turned on or off, may be modeled as a bit vector representing which options are on. Mutation would then flip a bit. Other parameters may take an integer value. In this case, mutation would randomly select a new number based on a probability distribution which takes into account which range of values the administrator believes is likely to contain secure settings.

The parameter domain mutation operator, a form of directed mutation [2], when given a chosen parameter, uses machine learning techniques to modify the domain of that parameter. If a particular parameter setting has historically been correlated with fitness decreases when adopted, or fitness increases when abandoned, the machine learning algorithm will deem it insecure. This directed mutation operator then removes that value from the parameter's domain. Additionally, if the parameter happens to be one in which a distance function can quantitatively compare settings' similarity, such as bit vectors or numbers, a support vector machine [5] is used to calculate a region of the domain surrounding known insecure values, and this entire subset of values is removed. Once a domain modification is made, then all chromosomes in the current generation must be adapted to comply with the mutated domain. The motivations for this more aggressive operator are to take advantage of the fitness function's convexity to increase the rate of fitness gain, to reduce the number of low fitness individuals in a generation, and to export information about the GA's function across generations.

The success of this MT strategy depends upon the evolution of diverse populations which are increasingly more secure. The genetic algorithm operators naturally tend to move towards a more homogeneous, less diverse, population. An adaptive selection operator, a diversity based blend of Tournament and Roulette Wheel selection, assists in keeping the populations more diverse.

The first generation of MT chromosomes is initialized randomly. Creating the next generation begins with the selection operator choosing parent chromosomes from the current chromosome pool. The crossover operator is applied to the chosen chromosomes, producing the child chromosomes. The mutation operator is then applied to each of these children, which possibly changes some of the chromosome traits (configuration parameters).

4. MOVING TARGET SYSTEM

Prior simulations have demonstrated the effectiveness of using evolution-based algorithms to discover secure and diverse configurations [6]. Based on these encouraging results, a Python-based prototype MT system has been developed

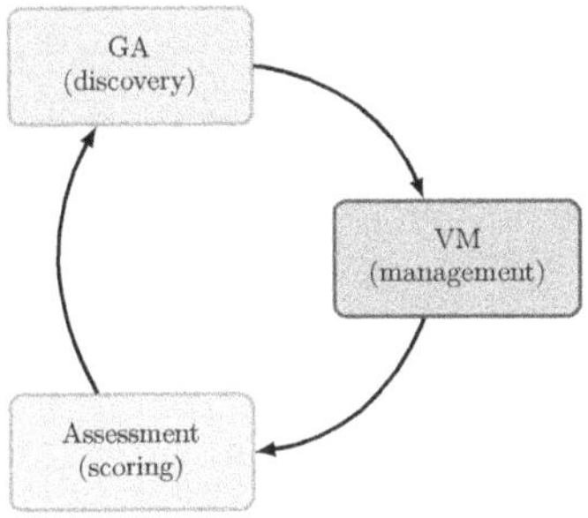

Figure 2: Three primary components of the prototype GA-based MT system and the general order of operation.

that can discover, implement, and assess configurations [12]. The prototype performs many of the core tasks necessary for a complete MT defense and will be used as the primary example for explaining system details in this section and Section 5. The evolution-based approach is designed to protect multiple machines.

The information flow of the evolutionary MT defense system is shown in Fig. 2, while the individual tasks are shown in Fig. 1. Three primary components interact to facilitate the discovery of a new generation of configuration parameters, to manage various hosts using the discovered settings, to assess the vulnerabilities of the configurations after a period of activation, and to pass along the qualitative configuration scores needed for the quantitative computation of fitness. A custom network protocol coordinates the three parts of the MT system, as well as the communication between the individual host machines and the system as a whole.

A genetic algorithm comprises the discovery component. The initiation of the MT system execution is signaled by the initialization of the first generation of MT chromosomes. In general, the current generation of chromosomes and associated fitness scores are passed to the VM management component. These Apache and RHEL5 configuration sets are applied to the virtual machines. After a period of time, the management component sends security information about the hosts to the assessment component. Using this information, the qualitative *bad*, *medium* and *good* scores are assigned based on the scoring rubric. These qualitative scores are passed along to the discovery component, which then computes the quantitative fitness scores for each chromosome in the current generation. The next generation of MT chromosomes are evolved using the genetic algorithm operators of selection, crossover and mutation. The next cycle of the MT system begins.

This MT defense system is proactive and resilient, since it constantly searches for new configurations. Converging to a single set of parameter settings is not the objective of the MT defense system since security will change as new vulnerabilities are introduced (e.g. via zero-day attacks or new software). The objective of the MT defense system is the discovery, management and assessment of generations of Apache and RHEL5 configurations.

5. SYSTEM PROTOTYPE AND RESULTS

Experimental results using the prototype will demonstrate the GA-based system, starting with arbitrary initial configu-

Range	CVSS score vector	Score
$[15, \text{MaxInt}]$	AV:N/AC:L/AU:N/C:N/I:N/A:C	204
$(5, 15)$	AC:N/AC:L/AU:N/C:N/I:N/A:P	213
$[0, 5]$	AV:L/AC:H/AU:M/C:N/I:N/A:N	600

Table 2: Rubric for the assignment of the CVSS score vector associated with potential vulnerabilities for Apache *KeepAliveTimeOut* configuration directive (parameter).

rations, can discover diverse and more secure configurations and create a viable MT defense for the web-server.

For these experiments, it is not practical to gather actual attacks to measure the security of the configuration. The Common Vulnerability Scoring System (CVSS) provides a method for measuring the security of an individual configuration parameter setting [13, 17], and thereby provides a method to estimate the number of attacks that will be successfully executed against a machine with the given parameter setting. CVSS scores parameter vulnerabilities; therefore, a configuration will have one CVSS score per parameter vulnerability, with the CIA scores all set to *none* to convey that the vulnerability is not present. Configuration security checklists, such as United States Government Configuration Baseline (USGCB) and DOD/NSA Security Technical Implementation Guidelines (STIGs), can then be used in combination with CVSS initially to assess the fitness of the configuration.

For this prototype system, MT chromosome fitness is the sum of values derived for the discovered parameter vulnerabilities associated with the configuration settings. Though not as realistic as gathering attack information, it does allow for a good basis for this initial simulation and measurement of attacks. The scoring rubric is specific to the parameters represented in the chromosomes and is based on expert knowledge about security parameter vulnerabilities, which can be found in NIST guidelines [16]. Each parameter is assigned a CVSS vector to represent the vulnerabilities it contains or the lack thereof. The algorithm then grades each vector's fields, assigning each a *bad*, *medium*, or *good* score based on the utility of that field's value. For example, the authentication metric can take values of *none*, *single*, or *multiple*, and these are graded as *bad*, *medium*, and *good*, respectively, as an attack requiring multiple authentications of credentials is preferable to one which requires only a single authentication, which is itself better than an attack which can be executed without providing any credentials at all. The rubric is intended to simulate the attacks faced by the computer on which the configuration is implemented. It is reasonable to assume that the estimated number of successful attacks is correlated with the severity of the security flaw as measured by the CVSS vector.

In order to quantify the fitness, the security categories of *bad*, *medium*, and *good* are then assigned numerical values of 1, 10 and 100, respectively, giving each parameter a set of six exponentially differing scores which yields a current population non-uniform probability distribution useful for selection. A chromosome's total fitness is the sum of the

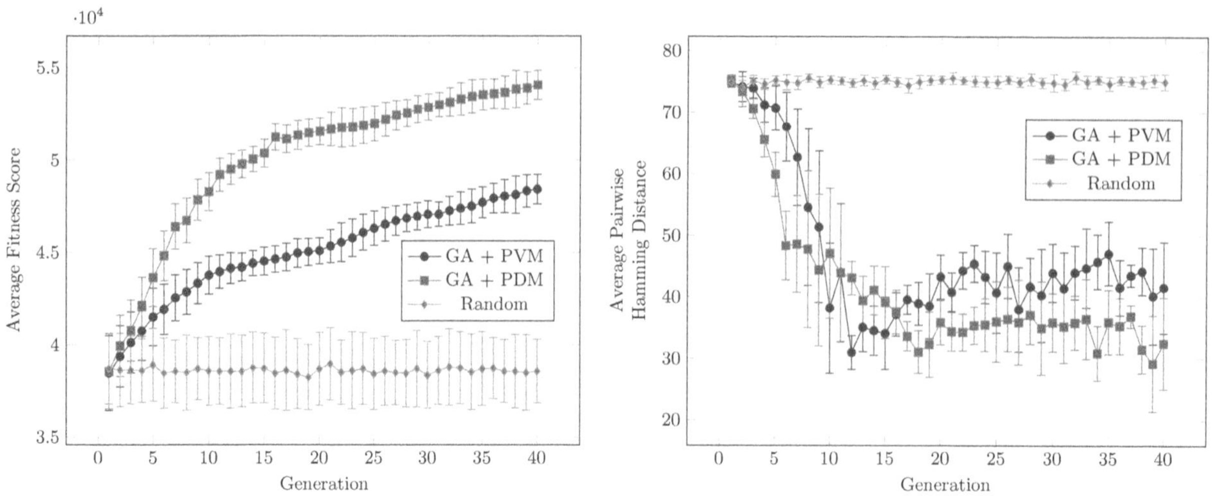

(a) Average population fitness (b) Average (sampled) diversity

Figure 3: Diversity and fitness comparisons of the genetic algorithm with parameter value mutation, the genetic algorithm with parameter domain mutation, and random search. The bars correspond to a 1 standard deviation above and below the average diversities and fitnesses, respectively. Configurations consisted of 102 parameters for an Apache 2.2 on Red Hat Enterprise Linux Revision 5.

102 individual parameter scores, and it ranges from 612 to 61,200.

As an illustration of the assignment of the CVSS vector and the computation of the fitness score, the scoring rubric for the Apache *KeepAliveTimeOut* parameter is presented in Table 2. The *KeepAliveTimeOut* parameter takes on an unsigned integer value (measured in seconds) up to MAXINT; however, only certain ranges of values are reasonable parameter settings. The CVSS score vector reflects three ranges. From the score vector, the *KeepAliveTimeOut* parameter's fitness score is computed. This rubric reflects a more secure situation when the *KeepAliveTimeOut* value does not exceed 5 seconds.

Both genetic algorithms, GA+PVM and GA+PDM, consisted of 140 chromosomes per generation. Each chromosome represented 102 parameters. The first generation was initialized randomly and allowed to evolve for 40 generations. The 40 generations simulate the application of the MT system for over a month with daily system configuration updates. The selection operation was a blend of roulette wheel and two round tournament selection, chosen with probabilities of 0.25 and 0.75, respectively. Two point crossover, with $p_c = 0.05$, and multi-faceted mutation, $p_m = 0.02$, were implemented. One genetic algorithm employed parameter value mutation, the other used parameter domain mutation.

For comparison purposes, a random search based system was also implemented. The random search system operated similarly, except that crossover was ignored, $p_c = 0$, and mutation was always applied to every parameter of every configuration, $p_m = 1$.

Two qualitative measurements provide insight into the effectiveness of the searches. The average fitness score in a generation is one performance measure of the searches. Higher fitness scores correspond to estimates of more secure web servers. Over the generations of chromosomes, more secure configurations should be indicated by an increase in the average fitnesses. The Hamming distance between two chromosomes is the number of corresponding genes with different values, and the average of these in a generation is an indicator of the expected number of parameter differences between any two chromosomes. As the genetic algorithm moves through its generations, the average Hamming distance should decrease in value, corresponding to some agreement on secure settings. However, in order to maintain chromosome diversity, the average Hamming distance must not become too small. The computation of the average Hamming distance between all pairs of chromosomes when there are a large number of genes is computationally expensive. As an alternative, a sampling technique estimates this by choosing 15 chromosomes and computing the average Hamming distance between all pairs of this subset. In this research, this approximation has been found to be an effective measurement of population diversity.

The system based on random searching was not effective in discovering diverse and more secure configurations. Fig. 3(a) shows that the average fitness score essentially remained constant across all 40 generations. The standard deviation of fitness scores is quite wide, and does not narrow over time. Fig. 3(b) shows the average Hamming distance between pairs of chromosomes, and for the random search it remains essentially constant with a value over 74, i.e. for any pair of chromosomes the expected number of gene differences is approximately 74 out of 102. The standard deviation of the average Hamming distances is quite narrow over all 40 generations.

As GA+PVM moves through the 40 generations of chromosomes guided by the evolutionary operators, the expectation is that the average chromosome fitness and diversity should increase and decrease, respectively. The average fitness score increases 25.8% from 38,458.9 to 48,415.3 across the generations. As well, the fitness standard deviations suggest that almost all the chromosomes are increasing their fitness scores. Similarly, the diversity has decreased by 44.5% from 74.9 to 33.4, which indicates that the average number of agreeing genes between pairs of Apache and RHEL5 configurations initially is 27, but in the final generation is at least 69.

For GA+PDM, similar changes in fitness and diversity of 40.2% and 56.9%, respectively, are observed. Both average Hamming distance standard deviations indicate the preservation of a diverse population of configurations. However, GA+PDM does much better than GA+PVM in terms of average fitness scores.

Increases in measured fitness correspond to more secure configurations. For any parameter, the maximum fitness score difference between a secure and insecure setting is 594 points, the difference between six partial scores of 1 and six partial scores of 100. Thus, for both GA+PVM and GA+PDM, the fitness increases of 9,956 and 15,508 over the 40 generations, shown in Fig. 3(a), indicate that, on average, configurations are susceptible to at least 16 and 25 fewer types of attack each compared to the initial generation.

Many parameters have settled to a subset of the values across all 140 chromosomes, and at least one of these values does not contain a security vulnerability. For instance, the *ServerTokens* parameter was set to a secure value in 15 of the final chromosomes using the GA+PVM. However, using parameter domain mutation, the domain of *ServerTokens* was reduced to only two values, and 42 of the chromosomes in the final generation are set with a secure value. This is illustrative of how later generations have become less vulnerable.

Although GAs tend to find better solutions, there is no guarantee that the final set of configurations will contain an optimal solution. This can be seen in Fig. 3(a), in which the fitness values are generally increasing, but not approaching a perfect score of 61,200. For instance, in the first generations of the two genetic algorithms, 2 and 18 chromosomes respectively featured a *LimitExcept* setting insecure enough to warrant a score of *complete* for each of C, I, and A. In the final generations, 6 and 11 chromosomes respectively featured this score for their *LimitExcept* setting.

The *FollowSymLinks* parameter shows remarkably different settings under the two genetic algorithms. When using parameter domain mutation, the domain of *FollowSymLinks* was reduced to one setting, the secure one. For parameter value mutation, in the final generation both possible settings for *FollowSymLinks* appeared throughout the population.

6. NEXT STEPS

In the continuing development of the evolution-based MT system, there are four improvements to be added. The first is to allow the administrator to weight the CIA scores and have that weighting be reflected in the fitness function of the GA. Secondly, the management component of the MT system must be developed to detect successful attacks. Third, currently the directed mutation operator shows much promise, and with further research there is potential of significant improvement compared to the simpler mutation operation. Fourth, it is necessary to determine the functionality of a system based on a configuration.

6.1 Prioritization of CIA Scores

At the conclusion of the monitoring of the Apache web servers configured by the chromosomes, the initial CVSS scores and information about any security events are given to the assessment component. Similar to CVSS scores, the security events are scored based on the impact on confidentiality, integrity, and assurance. The administrator can weight these three components based on their relative importance. After passing this vector to the discovery component, the GA fitness function can then compute the appropriate weighted sum.

6.2 Detection of Successful Attacks

Currently, the fitness of a chromosome is determined by the simulation of attacks using rubrics developed from CVSS information. This simulation has allowed for the development and evaluation of a prototype genetic algorithm based moving target defense. However, it is necessary for the fitness of a chromosome to reflect the exposure of a computer configured with those parameter settings to the real world. It is imperative that fitness reflect security based on detected successful attacks. Ideally, the management component captures information regarding reconnaissance. Recognition of successful attacks and reconnaissance is a difficult problem.

Attack detection will be added based on checksums that can capture a limited number of successful attacks. The base fitness of a chromosome will be the value based on the CVSS rubric. This base will be adjusted based on the detection of a successful attack and the number of generations this chromosome has been implemented without a detected successful attack.

6.3 Directed Mutation

As clearly seen in Fig. 3, the genetic algorithm using parameter domain mutation does much better in terms of fitness than the one using the parameter value mutation operator. This improvement is generally reflected over all experiments. The use of simple machine learning techniques to modify the parameters' domains is an effective mechanism. However, this modification removes a value from a parameter's domain. Once the value is removed, it can not be returned to the domain. An alternative strategy is the assignment of probability distributions associated with the values of the domain. Instead of removing a value from a domain, the probability associated with that value can be decreased, allowing for increases in probabilities for other values. As well, other machine learning strategies should be considered.

6.4 Functionality Testing

An important task of the MT defense is to test that new configurations provide the necessary functionality. Regardless of how secure a configuration may be, it cannot be considered by the system if it is unable to provide the user a minimum set of required services and capabilities. This can be achieved by leveraging research that has focused on identifying and correcting incorrect configurations [11, 19]. Many of these approaches require defining predicates (tests) that can be instrumented, such as testing for a certain webpage or measuring the response delay of a system request. It would be possible to incorporate this form of testing to provide an understanding of the functionality of the configuration.

7. CONCLUSIONS

Moving Target (MT) defenses put the system to be protected in motion, in an attempt to render the reconnaissance of the attacker useless after a period of time. This article discusses how intermittently changing system attributes directly can provide a suitable MT defense. However, finding configuration changes that maintain a functional and secure system is difficult. Configurations consist of a large number of parameters, with many of these parameters being interdependent, and may require configuration changes in concert for security to improve.

This article described how secure and diverse configurations could evolve over time based on the operational environment. Using a Genetic Algorithm (GA) and feedback about the security status of the system, this MT approach discovers configurations through a continual process of selection, crossover, and mutation. These candidate configurations can then be placed in operation over time to provide a suitable MT defense. Furthermore, the approach is resilient since it can adapt to system changes, such as the installation of new software or updates to existing applications.

Results of a prototype system show that both GAs are able to find secure configurations over the 40 generations. In addition these configurations remain diverse (configurations do differ in parameter settings), which is important for providing a MT defense. Perhaps not surprisingly, directed mutation does allow for the discovery of more secure configurations than the simpler mutation operator. Although the results are promising, more research and development are needed to reach the full potential of the system. Incorporating any feedback obtained when a configuration is made active would improve the assessment. Similarly more research is needed to measure diversity that better reflects how parameter settings are different, in terms of how they affect the system.

8. ACKNOWLEDGMENTS

The authors would like to thank Brian Lucas for his initial implementation of the GA-based MT framework as part of his 2013 Computer Science MS project at Wake Forest University.

This material is based upon work supported by the National Science Foundation (NSF) under Grant No. 1252551.

9. REFERENCES

[1] Spiros Antonatos, Periklis Akritidis, Evangelos P. Markatos, and Kotas G. Anagostakis. Defending against hitlist worms using network address space randomization. *Computer Networks*, 51:3471–3490, 2007.

[2] Stefan Berlik and Bernd Reusch. Foundations of directed mutation. In *Proceedings of the 2006 Conference on Integrated Intelligent Systems for Engineering Design*, pages 3471–3490, Amsterdam, The Netherlands, 2006. IOS Press.

[3] Matthew A. Bishop. *The Art and Science of Computer Security*. Addison-Wesley Longman, 2002.

[4] Crispin Cowan, Calton Pu, Dave Maier, Heather Hinton, Jonathan Walpole, Peat Bakke, Steve Beattie, Aaron Grier, Perry Wagle, and Qian Zhang. Stackguard: Automatic adaptive detection and prevention of buffer-overflow attacks. In *In Proceedings of the 7th USENIX Security Symposium*, pages 63–78, 1998.

[5] Nello Cristianini and John Shawe-Taylor. *An Introduction to Support Vector Machines and Other Kernel-based Learning Methods*. Cambridge University Press, 2000.

[6] Michael B. Crouse and Errin W. Fulp. A moving target environment for computer configurations using genetic algorithms. In *Proceedings of the 4th Symposium on Configuration Analytics and Automation (SafeConfig 2011)*, 2011.

[7] James F. Dunnigan and Albert A. Nofi. *Victory and Deceit: Deception and Trickery at War*. Writers Club Press, San Jose, California, USA, 2nd edition, 2001.

[8] Center for Internet Security. Security and assessment benchmarktools. `http://www.cisecurity.org/resources-publications/`.

[9] Stephanie Forrest, Anil Somayaji, and David H. Ackley. Building diverse computer systems. In *Proceedings of The 6th Workshop Hot Topics in Operating Systems*, 1997.

[10] Dorene Kewley, Russ Fink, John Lowry, and Mike Dean. Dynamic approaches to thwart adversary intelligence gathering. In *Proc. of the DARPA Information Survivability Conference & Exposition II (DISCEX '01)*, volume 1, pages 176–185, 2001.

[11] Emre Kycyman. Discovering correctness constraints for self-management of system configuration. In *Proceedings of the First International Conference on Autonomic Computing*, pages 28–35, Washington, DC, USA, 2004. IEEE Computer Society.

[12] Brian F. Lucas. An automated system for evolving secure systems. Technical report, Department of Computer Science, Wake Forest University, May 2013.

[13] Peter Mell, Karen Scarfone, and Sasha Romanosky. A complete guide to the common vulnerability scoring system version 2.0. `http://www.first.org/cvss/cvss-guide.pdf`, 2007.

[14] John Michalski, Carrie Price, Eric Stanton, Erik Lee, Kuan Seah Chua, Yip Heng Wong, and Chung Pheng Tan. Final report for the network security mechanisms utilizing network address translation LDRD project. SAND Rep. SAND2002-3613, Sandia National Laboratory, November 2002.

[15] Melanie Mitchell. *An Introduction to Genetic Algorithms*. MIT Press, Cambridge, MA, USA, 1998.

[16] NIST. Consensus security configuration checklist. `http://web.nvd.nist.gov/view/ncp/repository`.

[17] NIST. NVD common volnerability score system v2. `http://nvd.nist.gov/cvss.cfm`.

[18] Sal Stolfo, Steven M. Bellovin, and David Evans. Measuring security. *IEEE Security and Privacy*, 9:60–65, 2011.

[19] Andrew Whitaker, Richard S. Cox, and Steven D. Gribble. Configuration debugging as search: finding the needle in the haystack. In *Proceedings of the 6th conference on Symposium on Operating Systems Design & Implementation - Volume 6*, 2004.

On the Role of Multi-Objective Optimization in Risk Mitigation for Critical Infrastructures with Robotic Sensor Networks

Jamieson McCausland
Larus Technologies Corporation
58 Antares Drive Unit 1
Ottawa, Canada K2E 7W6
Tel: +1 (613) 244 8916 x215
jamieson.mccausland@larus.com

Rami Abielmona
Larus Technologies Corporation
58 Antares Drive Unit 1
Ottawa, Canada K2E 7W6
Tel: +1 (613) 244 8916 x202
rami.abielmona@larus.com

Rafael Falcon
Larus Technologies Corporation
58 Antares Drive Unit 1
Ottawa, Canada K2E 7W6
Tel: +1 (613) 244 8916 x214
rafael.falcon@larus.com

Ana-Maria Cretu
Université du Quebec en Outaouais
101 Saint-Jean-Bosco, C.P. 1250,
Gatineau (Québec) Canada
+1 (819) 595-3900 x1527
ana-maria.cretu@uqo.ca

Emil M. Petriu
University of Ottawa
800 King Edward Ave
Ottawa, Canada K1N 6N5
+1 (613) 562 5800 x2132
petriu@eecs.uottawa.ca

ABSTRACT
The use of robotic sensor networks (RSNs) for Territorial Security (TerrSec) applications has earned an increasing popularity in recent years. In Critical Infrastructure Protection (CIP) applications, the RSN goal is to provide the information needed to maintain a secure perimeter around the desired infrastructure and efficiently coordinate a corporate response to any event that arises in the monitored region. Such a response will only involve the most suitable robotic nodes and must successfully counter any detected vulnerability in the system. This paper is a preliminary study of the role played by multi-objective optimization (MOO) in the elicitation of responses from a risk-aware RSN that is deployed around a critical infrastructure. Contrary to previous studies showcasing a *pre-optimization* auctioning scheme, where the RSN nodes bid on the basis of their knowledge of the event, we introduce a *post-optimization* auctioning scheme in which the nodes place their bids knowing what their final positions along the perimeter will be, hence calling for a more informed decision at the node level. The impact of the pre- vs. post-optimization stage in a first-price sealed bid auction system over the risk mitigation strategies elicited by the RSN is evaluated and discussed. Empirical results reveal that the pre-optimization auctioning is more suitable for dense RSNs whereas the post-optimization one is preferred in sparse RSNs. To the best of our knowledge, this is the first attempt to assess the role of MOO in risk mitigation for CIP with RSNs.

Categories and Subject Descriptors
I.2.9 [**Robotics**]: – *autonomous vehicles, sensors*

General Terms
Algorithms, Measurement, Experimentation, Security

GECCO'14, July 12–16, 2014, Vancouver, BC, Canada.

Keywords
critical infrastructure protection; robotic sensor network; risk management; evolutionary multi-objective optimization; self-organization; auction protocols; computational intelligence

1. INTRODUCTION
A robotic sensor network (RSN) is a collection of autonomous, often wirelessly connected devices that are capable of sensing, communicating and actuating, both upon each other and on the environment. An RSN could be thought of as a more advanced mobile sensor network [14] in which nodes possess typical robotic features such as gripping or lifting objects. Because of the various benefits provided by their proactive and reactive capabilities, RSNs are increasingly being used in the TerrSec arena, for instance to maintain a secure perimeter around a critical infrastructure [6] [8] [9] [12] and to efficiently coordinate a corporate response to any event that arises in the monitored region.

Recently, risk-aware RSNs for critical infrastructure protection (CIP) that can react to single or multiple events were proposed in [8] and [9], respectively. Two innovative features stand behind this novel class of CIP solutions: (1) the self-organization of the RSN nodes, (i.e., the crafting of a risk mitigation response), is the outcome of a thorough risk analysis conducted on every robotic node as well as on the entire network; this analysis is driven by a group of risk features [3] which, in turn, are extracted from the raw data streams emanating from each node in the monitoring region, and (2) evolutionary MOO algorithms are used by the response coordinator (i.e., the RSN node that best perceives the event) to locally derive a set of promising candidate responses, each of which is judged according to several conflictive objectives, such as latency or cost.

When multiple concurrent events arise in the region of interest, the framework in [9] allows the RSN nodes to formulate their bids for each event by taking into account important aspects such as their current battery level, the distance to the event or the amount of redundant coverage in that area. The bids are submitted to the response coordinator for that event, which selects the winners following the first-price sealed bid auction rules and then proceeds to optimize their final locations along the perimeter. Subsequently, the winners are instructed to relocate to such positions.

Despite the encouraging results in terms of perimeter coverage and response efficiency obtained with the above approach, there are key factors in the entire risk mitigation process whose influence remains largely unexplored. One of them is the MOO component and its relation with the bidding phase. One could imagine that, under different bidding conditions and node-specific valuation systems, the responses could considerably vary, hence impacting the overall quality of the CIP solution.

This paper is a preliminary study of the role played by MOO in the elicitation of responses from a risk-aware RSN that is deployed around a critical infrastructure. Contrary to the *pre-optimization* auctioning scheme described in [8] and [9], where the RSN nodes bid on the basis of their knowledge of the event, we consider a *post-optimization* auctioning scheme in which the nodes place their bids knowing what their final positions along the perimeter will be, hence calling for a more informed decision at the node level. The impact of the pre- vs. post-optimization stage in a first-price sealed bid auction system over the risk mitigation strategies elicited by the RSN is evaluated and discussed. Empirical results reveal that the pre-optimization auctioning is more suitable for dense RSNs whereas the post-optimization one is preferred in sparse RSNs. To the best of our knowledge, this is the first attempt to assess the role of MOO in risk mitigation for CIP with RSNs.

The rest of the paper is structured as follows. Section II reviews some relevant works. Section III elaborates on the proposed post-optimization bidding scenario. Experimental results are discussed in Section IV while conclusions are outlined in Section V.

2. RELATED WORK

This section briefly reviews several works in the areas of market-based robot coordination and risk-aware robotic systems for CIP.

2.1 Market-based Robot Coordination

Market-based task allocation is a well-studied and quite successful coordination paradigm in robotics [1] [4] [5] [7-10][12]. The idea of casting different tasks in the system as auctions and letting robots bid on them to maximize their individual profit has proved valuable in improving the overall team efficiency.

Gerkey and Mataric [4] developed MURDOCH, an auction-based task allocation system which features a publish/subscribe communication model. The main goal is to create an inter-robot collaboration framework in which responses to tasks are decided in a cooperative manner. The protocol can handle robots of dissimilar types and capabilities. Only robots that are properly equipped to handle a particular task can bid in response to the corresponding broadcast auction. MURDOCH names a single winner and monitors its progress in real-time.

Mezei *et al* [10] address robot-to-robot collaboration with the goal of optimizing several objectives like communication costs, task execution costs and latency. The proposed task allocation framework relies on the aggregation of different auctions in a distributed fashion. Five auction protocols are discussed and compared to a simple auction protocol. The authors only focus on a single-robot, single-task scenario in which the cost metric is inversely proportional to the distance from the event.

Pustowka and Caicedo [12] introduce multi-robot collaboration in a surveillance application. Given a grid representation of a known environment, the goal is to have robots cover least frequently visited cells. Nearby grid cells are clustered with K-means. These clusters of cells become the tasks robots will bid for. The cost used in the utility function is the length of the path to the desired location, as computed by the A* search algorithm. The highest bidder for each task becomes the winner. This approach, however, requires full a priori knowledge of the environment and suffers from sensitivity to crucial parameters like the number of clusters (K) to be found.

Kaleci et al [5] consider a team of heterogeneous robots with three types of tasks: cleaning, carrying and monitoring. The sensing and motion models of each robot contribute to the formulation of the price and cost of a task and the authors employ two schemes to determine the auction winners. Additionally, the Hungarian algorithm is used to solve the robot-to-task assignment problem.

The above approaches illustrate the effectiveness of market-based robot cooperation. However, none of them features either MOO or risk analysis in the elicitation of candidate responses to the events. They are neither concerned with CIP.

2.2 Risk-Aware Robotic Systems for CIP

Safeguarding a critical infrastructure with an RSN typically involves appropriate situational assessment, risk detection, mitigation and prevention. The lifecycle portrayed in Fig. 1 governs the operational workflow of the RSN in this context.

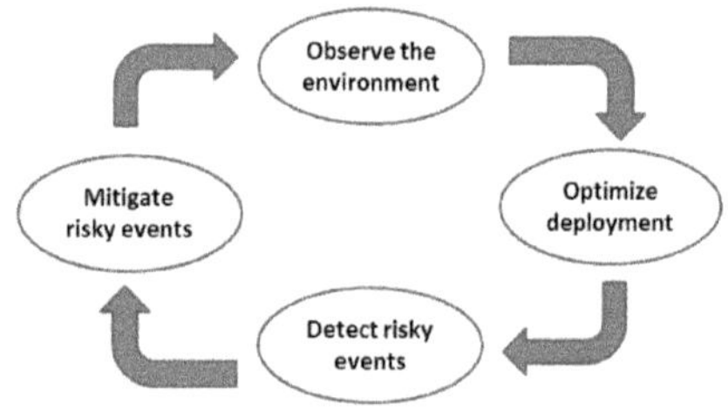

Figure 1. Lifecycle of a RSN for CIP.

An RSN for CIP is proposed in [8]. The novelty with this approach is that the RSN implements the risk management framework put forth in [2]. From the information submitted by each RSN node, three risk features are extracted: *degree of distress*, *intruder proximity factor* and *terrain maneuverability*. The overall risk posed by any RSN node is assessed on the basis of these local risk features and those nodes exceeding a permissible risk threshold are flagged as "nodes in distress" (NIDs), i.e., robotic entities likely to originate a security breach in the perimeter. The response from the RSN is to self-organize in order to maintain as much coverage as possible around the critical infrastructure while minimizing the cost of doing so. For each NID, a restricted group of candidate topologies are evolved with NSGA-II [2] as the evolutionary MOO algorithm of choice and then ranked following some network operator preferences. The network manager then decides on the most suitable response topology, which is enacted upon the environment.

The above framework could only handle a single response to a single event. That is, a network response must be effectuated before another response (such as one to another event) could be orchestrated. With this limitation in mind, the authors in [9] later augmented this approach to handle multiple concurrent events, hence creating several independent network regions which can autonomously evolve their own response sets and thus mitigate their local risks. Each response coordinator (i.e. the perimeter node that best perceives the event) initiates an auction to all RSN nodes by advertising the event location. The nodes calculate their availability by using a Sugeno fuzzy inference system (FIS) [11] and decide whether to bid or not. The response coordinator selects the winners according to the rules of the first-price sealed bid auction and then evolves their final positions with NSGA-II. Finally, the winner nodes relocate to these positions along the perimeter.

The bidding phase in [8] and [9] takes place before the actual optimization of the responses. A more informed approach would be to evolve the target perimeter locations first, advertise them to all nodes and then conduct the bidding process. This paper is aimed at gauging the impact that pre- vs. post-optimization has over the risk mitigation strategies elicited by the RSN.

3. PROPOSED METHODOLOGY

In this section, we unfold the methodological approach involving MOO and market-based robot coordination for a risk-aware RSN in a CIP scenario.

As envisioned in [8] and [9], the robotic nodes surrounding the critical infrastructure play multiple roles in the system. First, they can *detect high-risk events* that could jeopardize the integrity of the surveillance conducted by the RSN upon the region of interest. Second, they can become *auctioneers* for a particular event, which means they are responsible for advertising some event-related information to the rest of the RSN nodes, gathering the received bids and clear off the auction, i.e., announce the winner(s). Finally, they could participate as *bidders* in any auction circulating around the network.

3.1 Risk-Driven Event Detection

The RSN nodes in our study can detect two types of events that are quite relevant to the CIP context: (1) another node's failure (e.g., because of battery depletion) or (2) an attempted perimeter intrusion. Both events demand a corporate RSN response in the form of a topological self-organization, whether to fill the coverage gap brought forth by the failed node or to increase the sampling capabilities around a portion of the perimeter where the intrusion attempt might have taken place.

The Risk Management Framework (RMF) in [3] enunciated by Falcon *et al* is the backbone of the event detection phase in our study. From the raw data stream periodically submitted by each RSN node to the operations center, a parallel risk stream is dynamically extracted. This risk stream consists of a collection of user-defined *risk features* which are modeled after different constructs. In our example, each RSN node reports: (1) its current battery level, in percentage; (2) its distance, in meters, from a potential intruder and (3) the terrain maneuverability index associated with its geographical location. The distance from a potential intruder can be gauged with the help of a laser range finder in order to provide the RSN node with depth perception. The terrain maneuverability index corresponding to the node's location can be queried from the Knowledge Base of the RSN's deployment environment. In this study, a random number in [0; 1] has been used for each location. Table 1 depicts the raw-feature-to-risk-feature mapping in our CIP case study.

Table 1. Risk feature extraction

Raw Feature	Risk Feature	Modeling Construct	Parameters / Expression
Battery Level (%)	Degree of Distress ([0;1])	Fuzzy set with a triangular membership function	A = 0 B = 0 C = 100
Distance to Potential Intruder (m)	Intrusion Risk ([0;1])	Fuzzy set with a trapezoidal membership function	A = 0 B = 0 C = 1 D = 5
Geographical position (x, y)	Terrain Risk ([0;1])	Linear mapping	1 – terrain maneuverability index of the node's position

The raw data input vector submitted by each RSN node is mapped onto an output risk vector, defined as a collection of local risk values, one per risk feature. The local risk value of any risk feature is determined by applying its modeling construct and parameters/expression to the corresponding input (raw feature data) in Table 1. As per the RMF flow in [3], the overall risk assessment for an RSN unit is obtained after the application of an FIS to the collection of local risk values. For simplicity, our Mamdani-type FIS [11] consists of a single fuzzy rule that reads as follows:

```
IF Degree of Distress is DD-HIGH OR
Intrusion Risk is IR-HIGH OR
Terrain Risk in TR-HIGH THEN
Overall Risk is OR-HIGH
```

The linguistic terms DD-HIGH, IR-HIGH, TR-HIGH and OR-HIGH are modeled as fuzzy sets by taking into account the network manager's knowledge about these local risks. If the overall risk of any RSN node exceeds a user-set threshold, then it is flagged as a "node in distress" and the pursuit of a corporate risk mitigation strategy to assist that node is initiated.

3.2 Pre-Optimization Auctioning Scheme

As explained in Section 1, a market-based approach is the mechanism through which inter-robot coordination emerges in [8] and [9]. The node that best perceives the event (NID) becomes its auctioneer and starts advertising the NID's location to all remaining RSN nodes. Upon receipt of this message, an *available* RSN node (i.e., one that is not currently part of any other risk mitigation strategy) will formulate its bid and communicate it back to the auctioneer. Once all bids have been gathered, the auctioneer determines the winner(s) and begins the optimization phase to find out which among those winning nodes will be used in the response and where they should relocate.

3.2.1 Node Bidding

Each robotic node formulates its *availability metric* (bid) to the announced task by considering three major factors: its current *battery level*, its *distance to the event* and its *coverage redundancy*. A Sugeno FIS [11] is employed to render the final bid value. Figure 2 depicts the fuzzy system embedded on each robotic node.

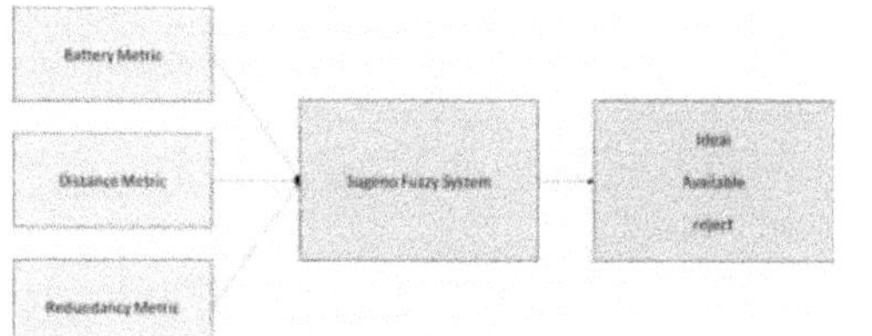

Figure 2. Sugeno fuzzy model for node bidding

The *battery metric* is an incentive to bid based on the node's remaining energy. We treat it as a linguistic variable with the following set of linguistic terms and their configurations:

- *Poor battery*: Triangular membership function with A=0.0, B=0.0 and C=0.4
- *Average battery*: Trapezoidal membership function with A=0.1, B=0.35, C=0.65 and D=0.9
- *Good battery*: Triangular membership function with A=0.6, B=1.0 and C=1.0

The *distance metric* is the node's incentive to bid based on the distance from the risk event. The closer the robotic node is to the event, the higher its motivation as it will not spend too much energy in locomotion. The normalized node-to-NID distance is the input to all the linguistic terms of this linguistic variable:

- *Far distance*: Trapezoidal membership function with A=0.0, B=0.0, C=0.65 and D = 1.0
- *Near distance*: Triangular membership function with A=0.5, B=1.0 and C=1.0

Finally, the *redundancy metric* is the node's incentive to bid given the amount of redundant coverage in its section of the perimeter, i.e., the overlap among the field of views of the RSN nodes w.r.t the set of perimeter points in that section. The more overlap, the higher the node's incentive to leave its current position and relocate somewhere else. The *redundancy metric* linguistic variable accepts a redundancy ratio as an input to its collection of linguistic terms. The redundancy ratio is the percentage of the perimeter points surveyed by this node that are also covered by nearby nodes. The linguistic terms for this fuzzy variable and their configurations are given below:

- *Low redundancy*: Triangular membership function with A=0.0, B=0.0 and C=0.4
- *Medium redundancy*: Triangular membership function with A=0.1, B=0.5 and C=0.9
- *High redundancy*: Triangular membership function with A=0.6, B=1.0 and C=1.0

The membership grade for a linguistic variable is the highest among the membership grades of its linguistic terms. Then, the availability metric of the bidder node is simply the average of the membership grades for the three linguistic variables under consideration. An ideal bidder yields 1.0 for availability while a rejection of the bid yields 0.0. All nodes not rejecting the bid submit their availabilities to the auctioneer, who then selects the winners and notifies them accordingly.

3.2.2 *Multi-Objective Optimization*

The auctioneer then proceeds to optimize the number of the winner nodes that are actually required to respond to the event and their target locations via NSGA-II [2].

3.2.2.1 *Chromosome Encoding*

Figure 3 portrays the structure of a solution (i.e. chromosome) in the MOO scheme conducted after the bidding phase has finished.

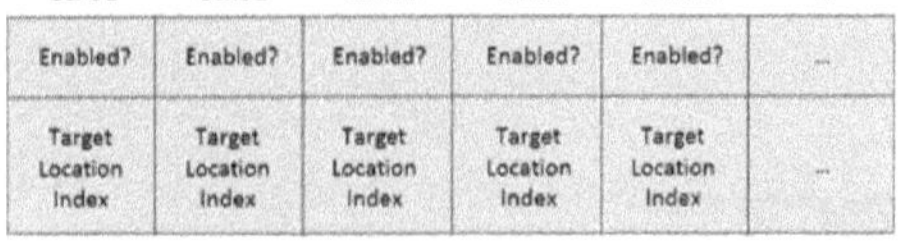

Figure 3. A two-layered chromosome encoding. The *node selection* layer decides on the inclusion of a winner node in the event response. The *target location* layer represents the index of the perimeter point where it should be relocated.

3.2.2.2 *Genetic Operators*

After two parent chromosomes are selected, crossover is probabilistically decided. Two crossover operators are proposed:

- *One-point crossover* for the node selection layer. This means that a single crossover point is randomly chosen and both parents exchange genetic segments in the node selection layer.
- *Uniform crossover* for the target selection layer. This means that genes in the target selection layer are drawn, one at a time, from a random parent, until a child chromosome is completed.

Mutation is also probabilistically decided for each population member. When a chromosome is mutated, either layer could be affected. A random gene is chosen in the node selection layer and its value is negated. On the target selection layer, if a gene is to be mutated, a new random target index on the interval of [0; *T*] will be selected, where *T* is the number of target perimeter points.

3.2.2.3 *Objective Functions*

Each population individual (risk mitigation strategy) is evaluated according to two mutually conflictive objectives: the *perimeter coverage* it provides and the *energy cost* involved in enacting its response, i.e., the energy spent in relocating all participant nodes to their target positions.

It is clear from the above description that in this pre-optimization auctioning scenario, the RSN nodes do not possess any knowledge about their final deployment along the perimeter; hence their bids are solely based on the circumstances governing their current deployment and on the location of the event.

3.3 Post-Optimization Auctioning Scheme

An interesting alternative to the aforementioned risk mitigation methodology in Section 3.2 is to conduct the optimization phase first and, based on its results, let the RSN nodes place their bids.

3.3.1 *Multi-Objective Optimization*

In this case, the auctioneer proceeds to optimize via NSGA-II the target locations of the hypothetical responders, i.e., where should the responders be placed along the perimeter so that the coverage is restored as much as possible and the amount of overlap among the responders is reduced as little as possible.

3.3.1.1 *Chromosome Encoding*

A variable-length chromosome encoding is considered, where each gene contains the <*x*, *y*> coordinates of the target location for a hypothetical responder. The cardinality of the chromosome (number of genes) varies from 1 to the maximum number of possible responders in the RSN. Figure 4 displays a response orchestrated by four RSN nodes (not decided yet).

Gene 1	Gene 2	Gene 3	Gene 4
x_1	x_2	x_3	x_4
y_1	y_2	y_3	y_4

Figure 4. A variable-length chromosome encoding the target locations of four hypothetical responder nodes

When the population is first initialized, solutions of different cardinality are injected in the population, with their coordinates within the <*x*, *y*> bounding box of the perimeter section subject to intrusion/node failure. This bounding box can be easily computed by the auctioneer prior to the execution of the NSGA-II scheme.

3.3.1.2 *Genetic Operators*

A single-point crossover operator is applied probabilistically. A single-gene mutation operator is also probabilistically enforced on each population member. The mutation is interpreted as the random generation of another <x, y> pair within the vicinity of the existing one and inside the bounding box.

3.3.1.3 *Objective Functions*

The maximization of the *perimeter coverage* achieved by the chromosome (response) and the minimization of the *overlap* among the nodes in the response stand as the two decision objectives to be evolved via NSGA-II.

3.3.2 *Node Bidding*

The bidding process in this scenario follows the same procedure outline in Section 3.2.1 with the addition of a fourth indicator: the *delta overage metric,* i.e., the difference between robot coverage at the optimized position minus the coverage of the robot at its original position. $DeltaCoverage = \{Coverage\_Optimized\_Position\} - \{Coverage\_Current\_Position\}$.

It is easy to notice that the coverage gain ratio is a more informative measure for the bidder as it takes into account the consequences of leaving the node's current location and the benefits (in terms of coverage restored) of doing so. Hence, the bidder's utility function (availability metric) is more reflective of the true internal valuation of a node in a multi-agent system. The downside is that nodes behave more selfishly and this implies that the high-risk events the network is currently experiencing might not receive a suitable degree of responsiveness.

4. EXPERIMENTAL VALIDATION

This section is devoted to the empirical validation of the proposed pre- and post-optimization auctioning schemes. We simulate a CIP scenario in Microsoft Robotics Developer Studio 4 (MRDS)[1]. The setting is a military compound with two access points at paved roads. Two different RSN deployments are investigated: a *sparse* scenario of 36 nodes and a *dense* scenario of 57 nodes, each deployed along the perimeter of the compound, thus creating a virtual fence.

The experiment simulates a single node being at risk caused by a nearly depleted battery. In the experiment, the pre- and post-optimization auctioning schemes will be compared based on: ***coverage recovery***, ***response cost***, and ***response time***.

4.1 Sparse Scenario: Pre-Optimization Case

A loss of functionality of an RSN node will most likely induce coverage gaps, thus reducing the chance of a detected intrusion. This case was explored by randomly initializing the battery levels of the robotic nodes using a uniform distribution between 20% and 100%. In the case of the *sparse* scenario, robot #23 became a NID with battery level 10% with distress risk 96.6%. A risk threshold of 90% was used, which triggered the risk event. Node #22 handles the response generation and will assume the role of *auctioneer*. Node #22 takes the role of auctioneer because of it was the closest to the NID.

[1] http://www.microsoft.com/robotics Accessed 2014-04-02.

Due to the risky state of node #23, portions of the security perimeter under its jurisdiction are at stake, i.e. $-70.119 \leq x \leq -69.817$ and $33.577 \leq y \leq 48.019$, as shown in Fig. 5. The risky region compromises the risk spatial information broadcast by robot #22 (auctioneer) to all other RSN nodes in a *task announcement message*.

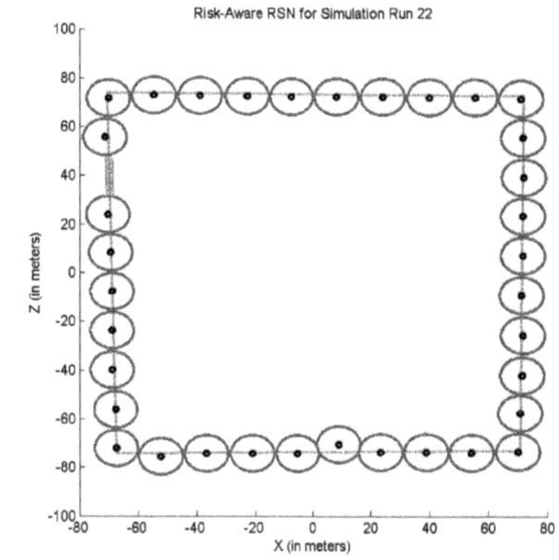

Figure 5. A two-dimensional representation of the RSN for the *sparse* scenario. Node locations are represented by small black circles. Each node's field of view is visualized by the blue circular region. Risky perimeter points are circles in green at the top left of the figure.

The RSN nodes receive the task announcement message and formulate their bids as described in Section 3.2.1. Table 2 lists the RSN nodes that did not reject the auction.

Table 2. Available bidders for the scenario in section 4.1

Node	$x_{battery}$	$x_{coverage}$	$x_{distance}$	$y_{availability}$
20	0.971	0.0	43.157	0.295
21	0.997	0.0	39.191	0.458
22	0.999	0.0	23.260	1.000
24	0.989	0.0	22.961	1.000
25	0.998	0.0	38.701	0.478

The five bidders form a candidate response group, which will be optimized using NSGA-II. The crossover and mutation probabilities were set to 0.85 and 0.1, respectively. A maximum Pareto Archive Set (PAS) size of 10 is used and the initial population contains 50 individuals. The stop criterion for the optimization is reaching 100 generations. Table 3 reports the non-dominated solutions found in the PAS once the optimization finished.

Table 3. Candidate response set for section 4.1

Response	Nr. Responders	Coverage (%)	Energy Cost (%)
1	0	83.16	0.00
2	**1**	**84.21**	**7.90**

Response 2 is selected by the network manager as the topology of choice since it has the highest coverage of 84.21% (recovery of 1.05%) at an energy cost of 0.07% (based on the battery usage model in the simulator). This solution is illustrated in Fig. 6.

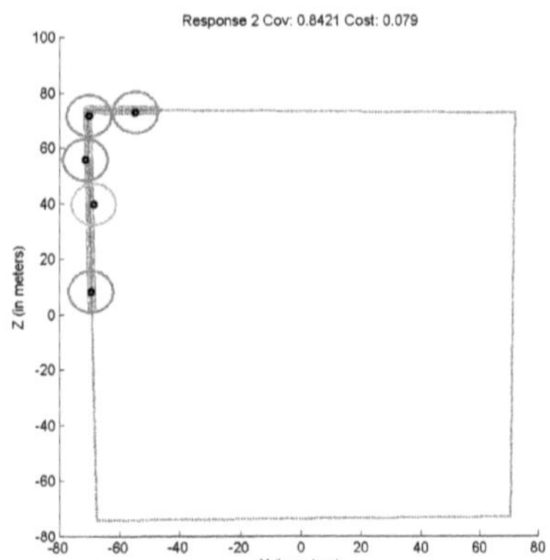

Figure 6. The RSN after response 2 in Table 3 was enforced. Only the 5 bidding nodes are displayed. Red robots remain at their original position while green robots moved to the optimized position.

The response took 50.76 seconds to generate, recovering 1.06% coverage initially lost by the NID. The responding robot executed the response with an energy cost of 7.90%.

4.2 Sparse Scenario: Post-Optimization Case

The post-optimization auctioning scheme was carried out on the exact same scenario. This time, the auctioneer optimizes the target locations of hypothetical responders first and then runs the auction. The PAS after 10 generation is shown in Table 4, which describes the optimal position, the coverage of the risk region and the number of redundant grid points surveyed by the responders.

Table 4. Candidate response set for section 4.2

Response	Solution	Coverage Risk Region (%)	Redundant Sensor Coverage (%)
1	**(-70.011, 39.667)**	**100.0**	**0**
2	(-69.810, 39.945)	100.0	0
3	(-70.090, 40.051)	100.0	0
4	(-69.985, 39.838)	100.0	0
5	(-69.919, 39.854)	100.0	0
6	(-69.896, 39.563)	100.0	0

All solutions provide the maximum coverage in the risky region with no overlap. Response 1 (in bold) is arbitrarily selected. The auction session revealed no bidders in the auctioned position, hence the nodes decided not to respond to this event, for otherwise a bigger coverage gap would have been created if they abandoned their original locations. The time taken to generate the response was 26.93 seconds.

4.3 Dense Scenario: Pre-Optimization Case

In the *dense* scenario, node #32 is flagged as a NID due to a low battery of 10% resulting in a distress risk of 96.6%. Node #33 handles the response generation and assumes the role of *auctioneer*. Node #33 takes the role of auctioneer because it is the closest node to the NID. The grid points at risk are within $-33.107 \leq x \leq -19.626$ and $73.576 \leq y \leq 73.692$ (shown in Fig. 7).

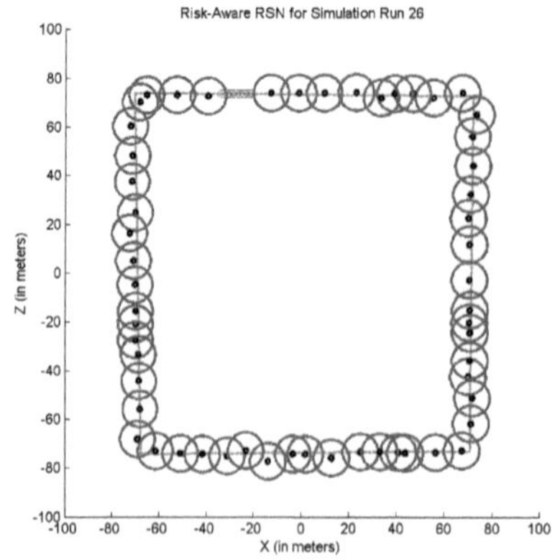

Figure 7. A two-dimensional representation of the RSN for the *dense* scenario. Risky coverage perimeter points are circles in green at the top-left of the figure.

The RSN nodes receive the task announcement message from the auctioneer and formulate their bids as portrayed in Table 5.

Table 5. Available bidders for the scenario in section 4.3

Node	$x_{battery}$	$x_{coverage}$	$x_{distance}$	$y_{availability}$
34	0.999	0.267	31.933	0.699
33	0.999	0.313	18.818	1.000
36	0.999	1.000	47.798	0.283
35	0.999	0.900	44.823	0.395
30	0.999	0.267	32.878	0.657
31	0.999	0.200	21.181	1.000
29	0.999	0.375	43.620	0.500
37	0.999	0.533	53.376	0.067

The eight bidders form a response group. Table 6 shows the PAS once the optimization has completed.

Table 6. Candidate response set for section 4.3

Response	Nr. Responders	Coverage (%)	Energy Cost (%)
1	0	89.38	0.00
2	1	90.27	0.87
3	1	92.04	2.43
4	**2**	**99.12**	**18.60**
5	2	92.92	2.88
6	1	91.15	1.08

Response 4 (in bold) offers the maximum coverage recovery and is selected as the desired response, depicted in Fig. 8.

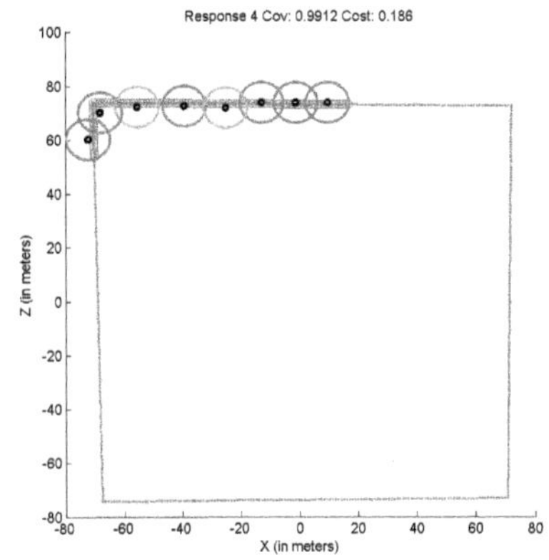

Figure 8. The RSN after response 4 in Table 6 was enforced. Only the eight bidding nodes are displayed. Robots in red remain at their original positions. Those in green move to their optimized locations.

This response took 60.50 seconds, recovered 9.74% coverage initially lost by the NID. The responding robots executed the response with an energy cost of 18.60%.

4.4 Dense Scenario: Post-Optimization Case

In this case, the response generation technique is the post-optimization auctioning for the same NID as in Section 4.3. The NSGA-II is executed over the risky region defined in the previous section as depicted in Fig. 7. The optimal position is <-23.734, 73.636>, which would recover the entire risky region with no overlap in sensor coverage. This position is auctioned by Node #33 to the entire RSN. The bids placed are tabulated in Table 7.

Table 7. Available bidders for the scenario in section 4.4

Node	$x_{battery}$	$x_{coverage}$	$x_{distance}$	$x_{deltaCov}$	$y_{availability}$
47	0.998	0.812	115.931	0.376	0.148
12	0.999	0.800	144.415	0.376	0.099
27	0.998	0.866	57.178	0.418	0.147
36	**0.999**	**0.238**	**44.664**	**0.502**	**0.409**
15	0.998	0.812	129.489	0.376	0.121
55	0.998	0.813	146.424	0.376	0.098
57	0.998	0.867	149.300	0.418	0.056
1	0.998	0.875	150.105	0.418	0.042

The auction session revealed that node #36 would be the best responder for the optimized position (bold entry in Table 7). This response is schematically depicted in Fig. 9.

The response achieved perimeter coverage of 100% (10.62%) or full recovery. This response was generated in 64.03 seconds with an energy cost of 22.33%.

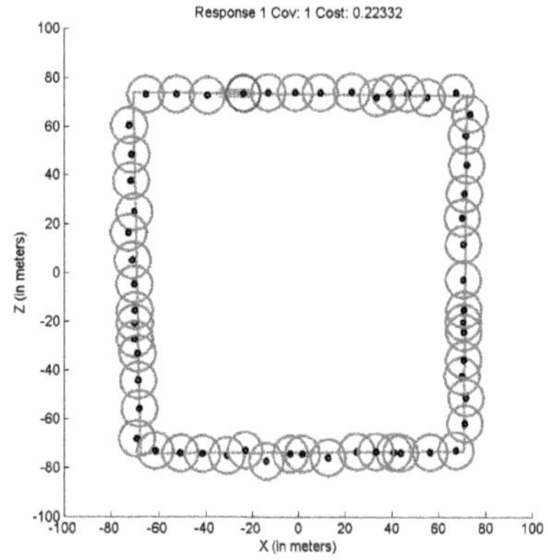

Figure 9. The RSN after node #36 responds by relocating to the target position. Robots in red remain at their original positions. The robot in blue is Node #36 at auctioned position.

4.5 Discussion

The two auctioning techniques approach the same problem from different standpoints, both using the NSGA-II evolutionary multi-objective optimizer and a fuzzy-based auction technique. In the case of the pre-optimization auctioning, a subset of the RSN nodes is gathered prior to the optimization. This set of potential responders is then evolved to determine the actual number of nodes needed to provide adequate coverage as well as their perimeter positions. On the other hand, with the post-optimization auctioning, we allow the system to determine nearly-optimal perimeter positions for hypothetical responders and their number. This information elicited by the NSGA-II is then bid out to the RSN members. The advantage witnessed with the post-optimization case is that a robot is able to use the new coverage gain versus coverage lost ratio to affect the bid process.

The response generation time in the pre-optimization case is usually longer than in the post-optimization scheme given that the former must explore all possible locations within the spatial range of all selected responder robots whereas the latter is confined to exploring the spatial region around the high-risk perimeter segment. We can expect higher response costs in the post-optimization case since the current geographical locations of the actual responders are not taken into consideration during the evolutionary process, as they are in the pre-optimization case.

The post-optimization auctioning scheme can offer superior advantages to its pre-optimization counterpart, but this depends on the density of the deployed RSN (i.e., number of nodes) and the amount of perimeter coverage overlap among them. In an RSN with fewer nodes and scarce overlap, an RSN member under the pre-optimization auctioning scheme will gladly leave its position to relocate to the event area, likely causing a coverage gap at its current location. Nodes under the post-optimization auctioning scheme will be more thoughtful about this reality and may decide not to bid at all (or bid very poorly) hence preserving the quality of the surveillance operation in their area of responsibility.

5. CONCLUSIONS

This paper has elaborated on the role played by MOO in the elicitation of different risk mitigation responses from an RSN in a CIP scenario. Two schemes have been considered. The first one establishes that the RSN nodes bid on the basis of event-related information and then the number of responders and their final locations along the perimeter are optimized. In the second one, the final locations and number of hypothetical responders are optimized first and then the bidding process takes place.

The empirical evidence seems to indicate that the pre-optimization auctioning method is preferred when the robots have low sensing ranges or there is enough coverage redundancy in the perimeter, e.g., in the case of a dense RSN. The post-optimization auctioning technique is better at handling larger robot response ranges since it does not require exploring the response region of each individual robot. It also gives RSN bidders enough coverage grounds to decide whether it is worth relocating or not, which is very helpful in the case of a sparse RSN with low coverage redundancy in order to avoid gaps due to the relocation process.

As a future research direction, we would like to measure how influential the underlying auction protocol is in the elicitation of risk mitigation strategies by an RSN. Thus far, only the first price sealed bid auction protocol has been studied. It would be interesting to shed light on what the RSN response landscape looks like when other well-known auction protocols like English, Dutch or Vickrey are enforced.

6. REFERENCES

[1] Dias, M.B., Zlot, R., Kalra, N., and Stentz, A. 2006. Market-based multirobot coordination: a survey and analysis. *Proceedings of the IEEE*. 94, 7 (July 2006), 1257-1270. DOI= http://dx.doi.org/10.1109/JPROC.2006.876939

[2] Deb, K., Pratap, A., Agarwal, S., and Meyarivan, T. 2002. A fast and elitist multiobjective genetic algorithm: NSGA-II. *IEEE Trans. Evolutionary Computation*. 6, 2 (April 2002), 182-197. DOI= http://dx.doi.org/10.1109/4235.996017

[3] Falcon, R., Abielmona, R., and Nayak, A. 2011. An evolving risk management framework for wireless sensor networks. In *Proceedings of the IEEE Int'l Conference on Computational Intelligence for Measurement Systems and Applications* (Ottawa, Canada, Sept 19-21, 2011). CIMSA'11, 1-6. DOI= http://dx.doi.org/10.1109/CIMSA.2011.6059924

[4] Gerkey, B.P., and Mataric, M.J. 2002. Sold!: auction methods for multirobot coordination. *IEEE Trans. Robotics and Automation*. 18, 5 (October 2002), 758-768. DOI= http://dx.doi.org/10.1109/TRA.2002.803462

[5] Kaleci, B. 2010. Market-based task allocation by using assignment problem. In *Proceedings of the IEEE International Conference on Systems Man and Cybernetics* (Istanbul, Turkey, October 10-13, 2010). SMC'10, 135-141. DOI= http://dx.doi.org/10.1109/ICSMC.2010.5642222

[6] Langendoerfer, P. Wireless sensor and actuator networks for critical infrastructure protection. 2011. URL: http://www.wsan4cip.eu/

[7] Li, X., Falcon, R., Nayak, A., and Stojmenovic, I. 2012. Servicing wireless sensor networks by mobile robots. *IEEE Communications Magazine*. 50, 7 (July 2012), 147-154. DOI= http://dx.doi.org/10.1109/MCOM.2012.6231291

[8] McCausland, J., DiNardo, G., Falcon, R., Abielmona, R., Groza, V., and Petriu, E. 2013. A proactive risk-aware robotic sensor network for critical infrastructure protection. In Proceedings of the *IEEE International Conference on Computational Intelligence and Virtual Environments for Measurement Systems and Applications* (Milan, Italy, July 15-17, 2013). CIVEMSA'13, 132-137. DOI= http://dx.doi.org/10.1109/CIVEMSA.2013.6617409

[9] McCausland, J., Abielmona, R., Falcon, R., Cretu, A.M., and Petriu, E. 2013. Auction-based node selection of optimal and concurrent responses for a risk-aware robotic sensor network. In *Proceedings of the IEEE International Symposium on Robotic and Sensor Environments* (Washington, USA, October 21-23, 2013). ROSE'13, 136-141. DOI= http://dx.doi.org/10.1109/ROSE.2013.6698432

[10] Mezei, I., Malbasa, V., and Stojmenovic, I. 2009. Auction aggregation protocols for wireless robot-robot coordination. In *Ad Hoc, Mobile and Wireless Networks*. LNCS 5793, 180-193. DOI= http://dx.doi.org/10.1007/978-3-642-04383-3_14

[11] Negnevitsky, M. 2005. Artificial Intelligence: a guide to intelligent systems. Pearson Education Ltd. Essex, England

[12] Pustowka, A., and Caicedo, E.F. 2012. Market-based task allocation in a multi-robot surveillance system. In *Proceedings of the 2012 Brazilian Robotics Symposium and Latin American Robotics Symposium* (Fortaleza, Brazil, October 16-19, 2012). SBR-LARS'12, 185-189. DOI= http://dx.doi.org/10.1109/SBR-LARS.2012.37

[13] Rodriguez-Canosa, G., del-Cerro G., and Cruz A.B. 2014. Detection and tracking of dynamic objects by using a multirobot system: application to critical infrastructures surveillance. *Sensors* 14, 2 (Feb 2014), 2911-2943. DOI = http://dx.crossref.org/10.3390%2Fs140202911

[14] Wang, G, Cao, G., La Porta, T., and Zhang, W. 2005. Sensor relocation in mobile sensor networks. In *Proceedings of the 24th Annual Joint Conference of the IEEE Computer and Communication Societies.* (Miami, USA, March 13-17, 2005). INFOCOM'05. 2302-2312 vol 4, DOI= http://dx.doi.org/10.1109/INFCOM.2005.1498517

2014 Evolutionary Computation for Big Data and Big Learning Workshop Chairs' Welcome

It is our great pleasure to welcome you to the *first Workshop on Evolutionary Computation for Big Data and Big Learning ECBDL'14*

We live in a time of unprecedented access to cheap and vast amounts of computational resources, which is producing a big leap forward in the fields of machine learning and data mining. We can tackle datasets of a scale (be it instances, attributes, classes, etc.) that was unimaginable some years ago, in what is well known as big data. On the other hand we can also use all these vast computational resources with the aim of understanding better our machine learning methods, by performing large scale evaluations, parameter sweeps, etc. We refer to the overall use massive on-demand computation (cloud or GPUs) for machine learning as Big Learning. Evolutionary Machine Learning techniques are perfect candidates for big learning tasks due to their flexibility in knowledge representations, learning paradigms and their innate parallelism.

In this workshop we have accepted two papers representing very different scenarios of big data and big learning. The first paper, "Evolving Relational Hierarchical Classification Rules for Predicting Gene Ontology-Based Protein Functions" by Ricardo Cerri, Rodrigo C. Barros, Alex A. Freitas and André C. P. L. F. Carvalho, focuses on an extremely complex and heterogeneous classification task, where instances have multiple classes organized hierarchically. The method is tested on real-world biological data, and explores the use of new rule representations to enhance knowledge discovery.

The second paper, "On the Application of GP to Streaming Data Classification Tasks with Label Budgets" by Ali Vahdat, Aaron Atwater, Andrew R. McIntyre, Malcolm I. Heywood, focuses on a very important topic within big data/learning, streaming data classification, in the particular scenario where access to the real annotation (classes) of data is costly, and budgets need to be specified.

Workshop organisers

- Jaume Bacardit, Newcastle University, Newcastle-upon-Tyne, UK
- Ignacio Arnaldo, Massachusetts Institute of Technology, Cambridge, MA, USA
- Kalyan Veeramachaneni, Massachusetts Institute of Technology, Cambridge, MA, USA.
- Una-May O'Reilly, Massachusetts Institute of Technology, Cambridge, MA, USA.

Evolving Relational Hierarchical Classification Rules for Predicting Gene Ontology-Based Protein Functions

Ricardo Cerri
ICMC
Universidade de São Paulo
Campus de São Carlos
Caixa Postal 668 - 13560-970
São Carlos-SP-Brazil
cerri@icmc.usp.br
\- - - - - - - -
Secretaria de Gestão Estratégica
Empresa Brasileira de Pesquisa Agropecuária
Pq. Estação Biológica - s/n
Brasília - DF
ricardo.cerri@embrapa.br

Rodrigo C. Barros
Faculdade de Informática
Pontifícia Universidade Católica do Rio Grande do Sul
Av. Ipiranga, 6681, 90619-900, Porto Alegre-RS-Brazil
rodrigo.barros@pucrs.br

Alex A. Freitas
School of Computing
University of Kent
Canterbury, Kent, CT2 7NF
A.A.Freitas@kent.ac.uk

André C. P. L. F. de Carvalho
ICMC
Universidade de São Paulo
Campus de São Carlos
Caixa Postal 668 - 13560-970
São Carlos-SP-Brazil
andre@icmc.usp.br

ABSTRACT

Hierarchical Multi-Label Classification (HMC) is a complex classification problem where instances can be classified into many classes simultaneously, and these classes are organized in a hierarchical structure, having subclasses and superclasses. In this paper, we investigate the HMC problem of assign functions to proteins, being each function represented by a class (term) in the Gene Ontology (GO) taxonomy. It is a very difficult task, since the GO taxonomy has thousands of classes. We propose a Genetic Algorithm (GA) to generate HMC rules able to classify a given protein in a set of GO terms, respecting the hierarchical constraints imposed by the GO taxonomy. The proposed GA evolves rules with propositional and relational tests. Experiments using ten protein function datasets showed the potential of the method when compared to other literature methods.

Categories and Subject Descriptors

G.3 [**Mathematics of Computing**]: Probability and Statistics—*Probabilistic algorithms*; I.2.m [**Computing Methodologies**]: Artificial Intelligence—*Miscellaneous*

Keywords

Hierarchical Multi-Label Classification, Gene Ontology, Propositional Rules, Relational Rules, Genetic Algorithms, Bioinformatics

1. INTRODUCTION

In conventional classification, an instance $\mathbf{x}_i \in X$ can be classified in only one class $c_j \in C$. However, there are more complicated classification problems, where an instance can be simultaneously classified into a set of classes $C_j \in C$. In Hierarchical Multi-Label Classification (HMC), an instance can be classified into a set of classes, and these classes are organized in a hierarchical taxonomy, having subclasses and superclasses. In this taxonomy, there is a partial order $\prec_h$ representing the superclass relationships, *i.e.*, for all $c_1, c_2 \in C, c_1 \prec_h c_2$ if and only if c_1 is a superclass of c_2.

Among the different applications of HMC, protein function prediction deserves to be highlighted. Proteins perform almost all functions in an organism. Their functions are related to cell activity, such as biochemical reactions, cell signaling, structural, and mechanical functions [6]. Protein functions are also hierarchically structured, which makes protein function prediction a typical HMC problem.

In this work, we investigate the protein function prediction problem using the Gene Ontology (GO) hierarchy. In the GO, the classes are organized in an hierarchy of terms,

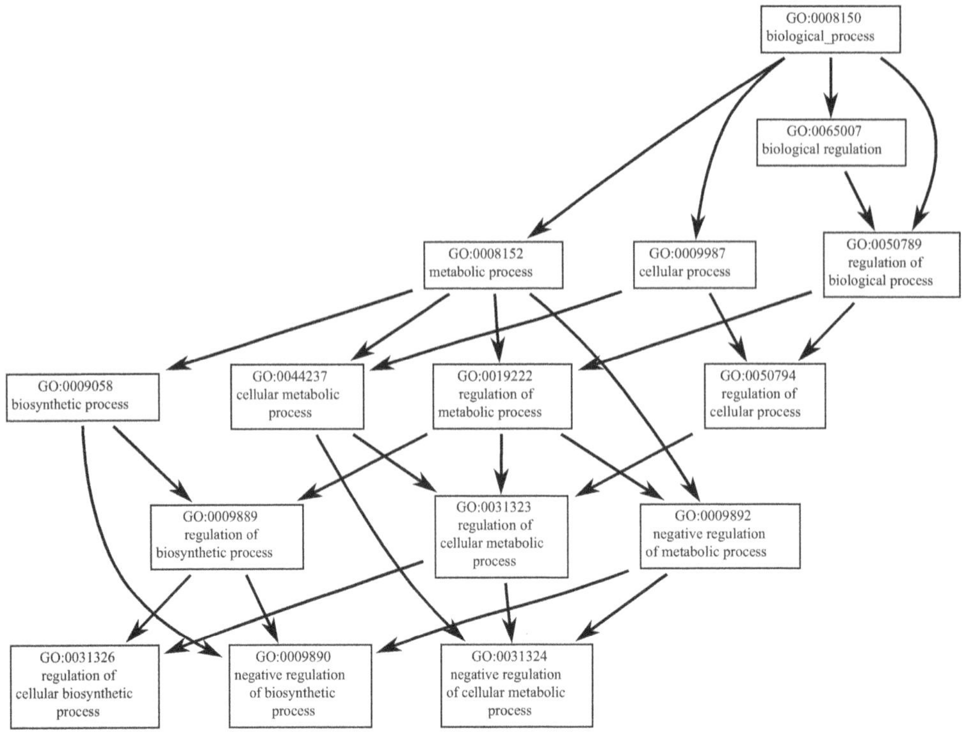

Figure 1: Part of the Gene Ontology Hierarchical Taxonomy. (Adapted from Ashburner et. al. [2])

where each term corresponds to a protein function. The GO taxonomy is organized as a Directed Acyclic Graph (DAG). It is formed by a set of three ontologies, each one covering a different domain. The domais covered are *cellular components*, *biological processes*, and *molecular functions* [2], each having thousands of classes. Figure 1 illustrates a small part of the GO taxonomy. By having thousands of classes, the protein function prediction task using the GO taxonomy is a very challenging problem. The prediction of the terms located in the deepest levels of the hierarchy is very difficult, since they have very few positive instances. In addition, an instance can be classified simultaneously in many paths of the hierarchy. When an instance is classified into a class c_j, it is classified into all superclasses of class c_j. This is the multiple inheritance interpretation, and is the correct interpretation when working with the Gene Ontology [2].

Two approaches have been used to deal with HMC problems, called local and global approaches. The local approach trains a set of classifiers, where each one is responsible for the prediction of one class or a small set of classes which are neighbors in the hierarchy. A classification for a new instance is then obtained combining the predictions provided by the individual classifiers. Any conventional classifier can be used in the local approach. In the global approach, only one classifier is trained to deal with all classes at the same time, and then the classification of a new instance is performed in just one step. Differently from the local approach, a conventional classifier cannot be used, unless adaptations are made to it in order to cope with the multi-label and hierarchical constraints [9].

In this paper, we propose a Genetic Algorithm (GA) to generate hierarchical multi-label classification rules. The method is called **R**elational **H**ierarchical **M**ulti-Label **C**lassification with a **G**enetic **A**lgorithm (RHMC-GA). It is a extended version of the method proposed in Cerri et. al. [5]. We use a new fitness function and selection operator to evolve antecedents of classification rules. The consequents of the rules are obtained using a deterministic procedure. They are represented as a class vector $\overline{\mathbf{v}}$, where each position corresponds to a class, and receives a real value interpreted as the probability of an instance being classified in the class. In addition, we evolve rules with two different kinds of tests. The first one traditionally evaluates if an attribute value A_k satisfies a test condition, *e.g.* $A_k \leq x_{i,k}$. These tests are known as propositional tests. Besides evolving rules with only propositional tests, RHMC-GA evolves rules that also compare the values of different attributes, *e.g.* $A_1 \leq A_2$. These tests are called relational tests [8].

The induction of rules containing relational tests comparing the values of two attributes is the main contribution of this paper. There are many algorithms to discover HMC rules, but none of them induce rules with relational tests. The motivation for inducing relational tests is the increasing of the expressiveness power of the rules. Also, these tests cope better with attribute interactions. However, they increase a lot the search space, which can make it more difficult to discover good rules.

The next sections are organized as follows. Section 2 reviews some works that generate HMC rules for protein function prediction; Section 3 presents our method for generating HMC rules; the experimental set up is presented in Section 4; Section 5 presents the experiments performed; finally, conclusions and future directions are presented in Section 6.

2. RELATED WORK

Not so many works proposed methods to induce HMC

rules for protein and gene function prediction in the Gene Ontology taxonomy. This section discusses some of them.

In Vens et al. [12], three methods based on the concept of Predictive Clustering Trees (PCT) were investigated. The authors proposed a global Clus-HMC method that induces a single decision tree to cope with the entire classification problem. They compared its performance with two local methods. The first method, Clus-SC, induces an independent decision tree for each class of the hierarchy, ignoring the relationships between classes. The second one, Clus-HSC, explores the hierarchical relationships between the classes to induce a decision tree for each class. Still based on PCT, the study of Schietgat et al. [11] used an ensemble technique to combine the decision trees induced by Clus-HMC.

Alves et al. [1] proposed a global method using Artificial Immune Systems (AIS) for the generation of HMC rules. The method is divided into two basic procedures: Sequential Covering (SC) and Rule Evolution (RE). The SC procedure iteratively calls the RE procedure until all (or almost all) training instances (antigens) are covered by the discovered rules. The RE procedure evolves classification rules (antibodies) that are used to classify the instances. The best antibody is added to the set of discovered rules.

In the work of Otero et al. [9], the authors proposed a global method using Ant Colony Optimization (ACO). The method discovers classification rules in the format "IF ... THEN ...", where an ACO algorithm is employed to optimize the antecedents of the rules. Basically, a sequential instance covering procedure is applied to create classification rules that cover all (or almost all) training instances. The method is initialized with an empty set of rules, and a new rule is added to the set while the number of instances not covered by any rule is higher than a given threshold.

A problem transformation method was proposed in the work of Bi and Kwok [3]. Initially, the classes of the instances are projected to a space of smaller dimension ($\mathcal{R}^m$), using kernel principal component analysis. After that, m regressors are trained. To preserve the hierarchical relationships during the projection procedure, the hierarchical constraints were incorporated to the kernel function.

A KNN-based method was proposed by Pugelj and Džeroski [10]. The authors modified the original KNN algorithm to calculate the prototype of the k-nearest neighbours of an instance. This prototype is the final classification of the instance, just like done in the PCT-based methods [12].

In the experiments performed in this work, we used the global-based method Clus-HMC and its local variants Clus-HMC and Clus-SC. These methods were proposed in [12]. We chose them because they were all applied to the datasets used in our experiments. In addition, they produce the same type of output provided by RHMC-GA and have their code available for downloading. Therefore, we could compare the prediction performances in detail. Recall that none of the above methods learns rules with relational tests.

3. RHMC-GA

Relational Hierarchical Multi-Label Classification with a Genetic Algorithm (RHMC-GA) is a global-based method for the generation of HMC rules using a Genetic Algorithm (GA). The main pseudocode of the method is presented in Algorithm 1, where a sequential covering procedure is implemented to evolve antecedents of rules. In this procedure, instances covered by a rule are removed from the training set, so that new rules can be generated with the remaining instances. The consequent of a rule is generated using a deterministic procedure considering the classes of all instances covered by the rule.

3.1 Individual Representation

Figure 2 illustrates the individual representation in RHMC-GA. Each test of an individual is represented as a 4-tuple {`FLAG`, `OP`, Δ_1, Δ_2}, where each 4-tuple is associated to a dataset attribute A. The gene `FLAG` indicates if the test over an attribute is used in the rule. If the test is used, `FLAG` receives the value 1, and 0 otherwise. Gene `OP` is the integer index of the operator used in the test. Genes Δ_1 and Δ_2 will receive values that will depend on the operators used and in the type of test used (propositional or relational). Exactly how all values are assigned will be detailed explained in the next section.

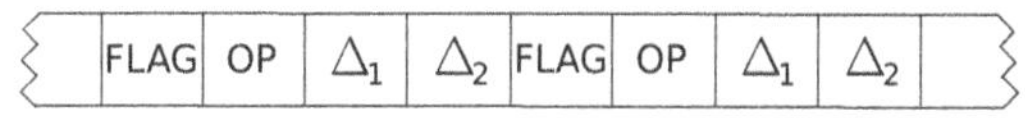

Figure 2: Representation of an Individual.

With the representation depicted in Figure 2, RHMC-GA is able to evolve rules of the form `IF` Antecedent `THEN` Consequent. The antecedent of a rule is thus formed by a conjunction of tests, and the consequent of a rule is formed by a set of GO classes, respecting the constraints of the hierarchical taxonomy. An example of rule is given below. In this example, only active tests of the rule are shown. As can be seen, a rule can be formed by both propositional and relational tests.

$$\texttt{IF } (A_1 \texttt{ OP } \Delta) \texttt{ AND } (A_3 \texttt{ OP } A_5) \texttt{ AND } (A_5 \texttt{ OP } \Delta)$$
$$\text{THEN}$$
$$\{GO_1, GO_2, GO_4, \ldots, GO_{|C|}\}$$

3.2 Population Initialization

The population in RHMC-GA is initialized using a seeding procedure, where an instance is randomly selected and transformed into a rule. Each test has a probability *pt* of being used. The operator used is randomly selected depending if the attribute is numeric or categoric.

After choosing the operator, the values to be put in the genes Δ_1 and Δ_2 depend on the operator chosen. For categorical attributes, the operators can be $=$, $\neq$, and *in*. The *in* operator verifies if a given attribute value is among a given set of values. If the operator chosen is $=$ or $\neq$, gene Δ_1 receives the index corresponding to the categoric value of the attribute in the instance being used as seed, and gene Δ_2 receives 0 (Δ_2 is not going to be used in the test). If the operator is *in*, gene Δ_1 receives the index corresponding to one of the sets of values which contain the value of attribute in the instance, and gene Δ_2 receives 0. As an example of this last procedure, if the attribute in the instance has the value `A`, and the possible values for this attribute in the dataset are `A`, `B`, and `C`, position Δ_1 receives the value corresponding to one of the sets of values which contain value `A`: {`A, B`}, {`A, C`}, and {`A, B, C`}. The set of values used is randomly chosen.

If the operator chosen corresponds to an operation over a numeric attribute, the assignment of values to genes Δ_1 and

Algorithm 1: A Genetic Algorithm to generate HMC rules.

```
procedure RHMC-GA(D,G,p,minCov,maxCov,maxNotCov,cr,mr,t,e,pt)
Input: training set D
       number of generations G
       size of population p
       minimum number of instances covered by a rule minCov
       maximum number of instances covered by a rule maxCov
       maximum number of not-covered instances maxNotCov
       crossover rate cr
       mutation rate mr
       tournament size t
       number of individuals selected by elitism e
       probability of using a test in a rule pt
Output: set of rules InducedRules
inducedRules ← ∅
while |D| > maxNotCov do
    initialPopulation ← generatePopulation(D, p, pt)
    calculateFitness(initialPopulation, D)
    currentPopulation ← initialPopulation
    bestRule ← best rule of currentPopulation according to fitness
    j ← G
    repeat
        newPopulation ← ∅
        newPopulation ← newPopulation ∪ elitism(currentPopulation, e)
        parental ← tournamentSelection(initialPopulation, t, e, p)
        offspring ← uniformCrossoverDistance(parental, cr)
        newPopulation ← newPopulation ∪ offspring
        newPopulation ← mutation(newPopulation, mr, pt)
        newPopulation ← localOperator(newPopulation, minCov, maxCov)
        currentPopulation ← newPopulation
        calculateFitness(currentPopulation, D)
        bestRule ← getBestRule(initialPopulation, bestRule)
        j ← j − 1
    until j > 0 OR ruleConvergence();
    inducedrules ← inducedRules ∪ bestRule
    remove from D all instances covered by bestRule
return inducedRules
```

Δ_2 is simpler, because numeric attribute values do not need to be indexed. In the case of operator $\geq$, gene Δ_1 receives the attribute value in the instance, and gene Δ_2 receives 0. If the operator is $\leq$, gene Δ_2 receives the attribute value in the instance, and gene Δ_1 receives 0. We use Δ_1 and Δ_2 differently depending on the operator used because we consider Δ_1 and Δ_2, respectively, as the lower and upper bounds of the attribute value. This facilitates the use of an operation testing if an attribute value is between two given values ($\Delta_1 \leq A_i \leq \Delta_2$). In this case, the values for genes Δ_1 and Δ_2 are randomly chosen in order to make the attribute value A_i satisfy the test condition.

Up to now, we have explained how the propositional rules are encoded. To encode relational rules, a modification in the above indexation scheme must be done. When comparing two attributes A_1 and A_2, we always use the operator $\leq$. However, we index it with another value, to differentiate it from the $\leq$ operator used in propositional rules. Also, the genes Δ_1 and Δ_2 receive the indexes of the attributes in the instance. Thus, if attributes A_1 and A_2 are being compared, Δ_1 and Δ_2 receive, respectively, the values 1 and 2. Recall that only numeric attributes can be compared.

The indexation of categorical values and operators is done according to Figure 3. In the Figure, a dataset with four attributes is considered. When verifying if a rule covers an instance, appropriate operations are executed according to the type of attribute (numeric and categoric), and also the index of the operation.

With the indexation scheme presented in Figure 3, a rule can be formed by any kind of test, propositional or relational, and there is no specific amount of each one of them in the rule, since the operators are randomly chosen. Still, in relational tests, all possible pairs of attributes can be compared. The indexation scheme also allows different kinds of rules to be generated by a very simple modification in the scheme. If one wishes to generate only propositional rules, he only needs to remove the operator indexed as 3 (relational operator) in the numeric indexation scheme, so that index 3 will never be chosen. On contrary, if only relational rules are desired, one needs to remove operators 0, 1 and 2 from the numeric indexation scheme, so that only index 3 will be chosen.

3.3 Evolution

The evolutionary process starts by saving the best e rules of the current population (elitism). Then, $p - e$ rules are

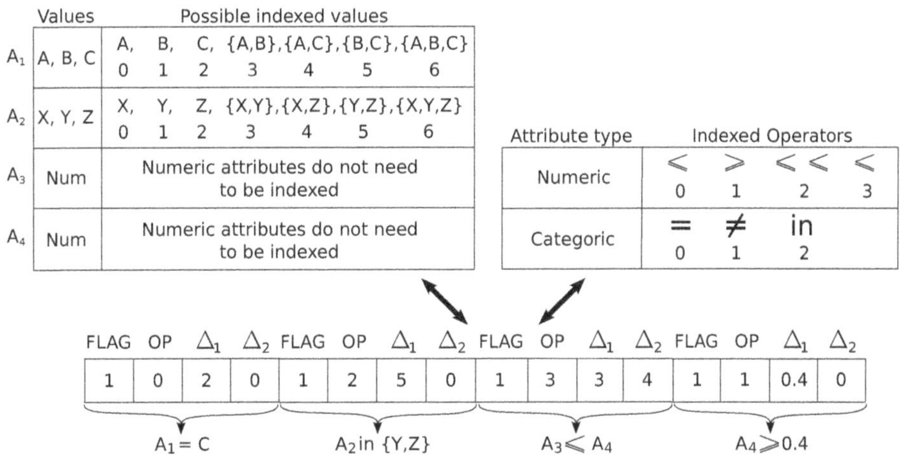

Figure 3: Indexation of operators and categorical values.

selected to be submitted to a uniform crossover operation, in order to generate an offspring. The crossover operation exchanges entires 4-tuples between the individuals. This means that crossover points are allowed to fall only in the boundaries between two 4-tuples. In order to specialize the rules in the classification of a set of instances, the crossover operation considers the distances between the consequents of the rules. The consequent of a rule represents a vector of class probabilities, and each vector position value is given by Equation 1.

$$\overline{v}_{r,j} = \frac{|S_{r,j}|}{|S_r|} \quad (1)$$

In Equation 1, $S_{r,j}$ is the set of all training instances covered by rule r, which are classified in class c_j. The set S_r contains all training instances covered by rule r. Thus, each position $v_{r,j}$ contains the proportion of instances covered by rule r, which are classified in class c_j. This can be interpreted as the probability of an instance covered by r to be classified in class c_j. Since GO terms located at levels closer to the root have more positive instances than GO terms located in deeper levels, positions in $\overline{\mathbf{v}}$ associated to terms closer to the root receive higher probability values than positions associated to deeper terms. Thus, the hierarchical constraint is guaranteed not to be violated.

Our crossover operator receives as input a list of $p-e$ rules. A rule is then removed from the list, and the weighted Euclidean distances between the consequent of this rule, and the consequents of all the other rules in the list, are calculated. The lower the Euclidean distance value between the consequents of two rules, the nearer the rules are considered to be in the search space. The two nearest rules are then removed from the list, and their antecedents are submitted to a uniform crossover to generate two child rules. The objective is to apply the crossover operator in rules that cover instances that are near in the search space, *i.e.*, instances that are classified in a similar or equal set of classes. Equation 2 gives the calculation of the weighted Euclidean distance (WED) between the consequents of two rules.

$$WED(\overline{\mathbf{v}}_1, \overline{\mathbf{v}}_2) = \sqrt{\sum_{j=1}^{|C|} w_i \times (\overline{v}_{1,j} - \overline{v}_{2,j})^2} \quad (2)$$

In Equation 2, w_j corresponds to the weight associated to the jth class in the hierarchy. Weights were associated to each class because, in the context of hierarchical classification, similarities between classes located in levels closer to the root are more important than similarities between classes located in deeper levels [12].

The weighting scheme used in RHMC-GA is the same used in the PCT-based methods [12]. After trying different schemes, the authors found out that the best one is given by Equation 3. The weight w_0 associated to a class in the first level is defined as 0.75, and the weight of a class c_j is recursively defined as the multiplication of w_0 by the mean weight of all its ancestor classes P_j.

$$w_j = w_0 \times \sum_{k=1}^{P_j} w(p_k)/P_j \quad (3)$$

After the generation of new rules, a mutation operator is applied to a percentage mr of them, randomly chosen. Each of the rules have a chance of 50% to suffer a `FLAG` mutation and a chance of 50% to suffer a restriction or generalization.

In the `FLAG` mutation, each test in the antecedent of the rule has a probability pt of being not used (gene `FLAG` exchanged from 1 to 0), or used (gene `FLAG` exchanged from 0 to 1). In the restriction/generalization operation, each used test in the rule is randomly restricted or generalized, having their values modified by using a randomly generated factor in [0, 1]. The restriction/generalization procedure is applied in order to make the tests cover a smaller/larger number of instances.

After the mutation operation, a local operator is applied in order to try to guarantee that the rules cover a minimum and maximum number of instances. This is performed to make the rules not too specific neither too general.

After the generation of a new offspring, the fitness of all rules is calculated, and the best rule is saved. This procedure is executed until the maximum number of generations is reached, or until rule convergence, *i.e.* the best rule remains the same after 10 generations. After this complete evolutionary cycle is performed, the best rule found so far is saved, and its covered instances are removed from the training data. A new population is then generated, and a new evolutionary cycle is executed. This is performed until all, or almost all, training instances are covered.

3.4 Fitness Calculation

RHMC-GA uses the variance gain [9, 12] of a rule as its fitness. The variance gain value is higher for rules which cover a more homogeneous set of instances, *i.e.*, rules that partition the training set in more homogeneous sets. In addition, the variance gain can directly cope with hierarchical multi-label data, considering the relationships between the classes [9]. The variance gain (VG) calculation is presented in Equation 4.

$$VG(r,S) = var(S) - \frac{|S_r|}{|S|} \times var(S_r) - \frac{|S_{\neg r}|}{|S|} \times var(S_{\neg r}) \quad (4)$$

As observed in Equation 4, the set S of all training instances is divided into two subsets: the set of instances covered by rule r, denoted S_r, and the set of instances not covered by rule r, denoted $S_{\neg r}$. The variance gain of a rule is obtained considering the set S, and also involves the variance (var) of the sets S_r and $S_{\neg r}$. The variance of a set of instances is defined by the sum of the mean quadratic distances between the class vector of each instance ($\mathbf{v}_i$), and the mean class label vector of all instances in the set ($\overline{\mathbf{v}}$). The variance of a set of instances S is presented in Equation 5. The distance used is the weighed Euclidean distance presented in Equation 2.

$$var(S) = \frac{\sum_{i=1}^{|S|} WED(\mathbf{v}_i, \overline{\mathbf{v}})^2}{|S|} \quad (5)$$

4. EXPERIMENTAL SET UP

In this section we present the datasets, evaluation measures, and RHMC-GA parameters used in the experiments.

4.1 Datasets

We used ten datasets where protein functions are structured according to the Gene Ontology. Details about the datasets can be found in Vens et. al. [12]. Table 1 presents the characteristics of the datasets. As can be seen, we are dealing with thousands of classes in each dataset, and all instances are assigned to more than one class simultaneously. This is, therefore, a very difficult classification task.

The datasets are available at `http://www.cs.kuleuven.be/~dtai/clus/hmcdatasets.html`, and are related to issues like phenotype data and gene expression levels.

4.2 Evaluation Measure

As explained in Section 3, the final classification of an instance is given by a vector $\overline{\mathbf{v}}$, where each position $\overline{v}_j$ corresponds to the probability of the instance being classified in class c_j. This is also true for the PCT-based methods. Thus, a threshold value must be employed in order to obtain the final prediction for an instance. If the corresponding output value $\overline{v}_j$ for a class c_j is equal to or larger than the threshold, the instance is classified into c_j. Otherwise, it is not classified into c_j. The final prediction for an instance is then given by a vector $\mathbf{v}$, where $v_j = 1$ is the instance is classified into c_j, and 0 otherwise.

The question that arises now is how to choose the optimal threshold value in order to obtain the best classification. This is a difficult task, since low threshold values lead to many classes being assigned to each instance, resulting in high recall and low precision. On the other hand, large threshold values lead to very few instances being classified, resulting in high precision and low recall.

In order to avoid the choice of a threshold, we used precision-recall curves (PR-curves) to compare the different methods. To obtain a PR-curve, different thresholds between [0,1] are applied, and thus different values of precision and recall are obtained. Each threshold then represents a point within the PR-space. We connect these points to form a PR-curve, and the area under the curve is calculated. Different methods can be compared based on their areas under the PR-curves.

In this work, we used the area under the average PR-curve ($AU(\overline{PRC})$). Given a threshold value, a precision-recall point ($\overline{Prec}, \overline{Rec}$) in the PR-space can be obtained through Equations (6) and (7). In these equations, i iterates over all classes of the hierarchy.

$$\overline{Prec} = \frac{\sum_i TP_i}{\sum_i TP_i + \sum_i FP_i} \quad (6)$$

$$\overline{Rec} = \frac{\sum_i TP_i}{\sum_i TP_i + \sum_i FN_i} \quad (7)$$

To verify the significance of the results, we employed the non-parametrical tests Friedman and Nemenyi [7]. We adopted a confidence level of 95% in the statistical tests. We used the same data partitions suggested in [12]: 2/3 of each dataset were used for inducing the rules and 1/3 for test.

4.3 RHMC-GA Parameters

The parameter values used in RHMC-GA are listed in Table 2. These parameters were obtained based on the work of Carvalho et. al. [4], and no attempts to optimize them were made. The work developed in [4] is a local-based GA to evolve rules for hierarchical, but not multi-label, problems.

The parameter *pt* (probability of using an attribute in initialization) has a different value according to the number of attributes in the dataset. It is given by $|A| \times pt = 5$, where $|A|$ is the number of attributes. Thus, the parameter value is set in order to activate on average 5 tests in the rule. We chose to start with small rules in order not to have an initial population with too many restricted rules, covering none or very few instances. This same logic is used when applying the mutation operator, with probability *pt*.

5. RESULTS AND DISCUSSION

In Table 3, we present the experiments performed using the two different types of rules induced by RHMC-GA: rules using only propositional tests and rules using propositional and relational tests.

To generate rules with relational tests, we used only the datasets whose attributes are microarray data, because it only makes sense to compare attributes of the same domain. We standardized the attributes in these datasets (mean equals 0 and standard deviation equals 1). We also executed the other methods in the standardized datasets.

The values showed in Table 3 for RHMC-GA are the mean and standard deviations after ten executions. As Clus-HMC, Clus-HSC and Clus-SC are deterministic methods, only one execution is needed. As can be seen, the $AU(\overline{PRC})$ values obtained by all methods are very low. This is considered a normal result in HMC domains, specially in the GO, where

Table 1: **Summary of datasets: number of attributes ($|A|$), number of classes ($|C|$), total number of instances (Total) and number of multi-label instances (Multi).**

Dataset	$\|A\|$	$\|C\|$	Training		Valid		Test	
			Total	Multi	Total	Multi	Total	Multi
Cellcycle	77	4122	1625	1625	848	848	1278	1278
Church	27	4122	1627	1627	844	844	1278	1278
Derisi	63	4116	1605	1605	842	842	1272	1272
Eisen	79	3570	1055	1055	528	528	835	835
Expr	551	4128	1636	1636	849	849	1288	1288
Gasch1	173	4122	1631	1631	846	846	1281	1281
Gasch2	52	4128	1636	1636	849	849	1288	1288
Pheno	69	3124	653	653	352	352	581	581
Seq	478	4130	1692	1692	876	876	1332	1332
Spo	80	4116	1597	1597	837	837	1263	1263

Table 2: Parameters used in RHMC-GA

Parameters	Values
Size of population (p)	100
Elitism rate (e)	1%
Mutation rate (mr)	40%
Crossover rate (cr)	90%
Probability of using an attribute in initialization (pt)	$\|A\| \times pt = 5$
Number of Generations (G)	100
Tournament size (t)	2
Maximum number of not-covered instances ($maxNotCov$)	10
Minimum number of instances covered by a rule ($minCov$)	10
Maximum number of instances covered by a rule ($maxCov$)	300

thousands of classes are involved, making the classification problem much more challenging.

According to Table 3, when evolving classification rules with only propositional tests, RHMC-GA obtained better results than Clus-SC in all datasets, and also outperformed Clus-HSC in some datasets. In comparison with Clus-HMC, RHMC-GA obtained competitive results in some datasets, but was, in general, outperformed.

When comparing the results using the classification rules with both propositional and relational tests, RHMC-GA still obtained better performances than Clus-SC. However, it was outperformed by Clus-HMC and Clus-SC. We can also see that the standardization of data seemed to harm the performances of the PCT-based methods, specially the local versions Clus-HSC and Clus-SC.

We can observe that the $AU(\overline{PRC})$ values obtained by RHMC-GA, when evolving these new kind of rules, were inferior to the values obtained when evolving rules with only propositional tests. This can be explained by the fact that, when comparing different attributes among themselves, the search space is largely increased. This potentially augments the possibility of finding good solutions, but also can make the classification problem more difficult, since it is more difficult to find good solutions in larger search spaces.

The fitness function employed also has a characteristic that may have harmed the RHMC-GA performance in some situations. According to Equation 4, the variance gain of a rule is maximized when the difference between the variance of S_r and $S_{\neg r}$ is minimized. However, if a very homogeneous set of training instances (instances classified in the same, or in a very similar, set or classes) is left to be covered, the fitness value can be reduced to 0. This happens when a rule which covers all instances is induced. In this case, it is a very good rule, since it covers all remaining instances belonging to a same/similar set of classes. However, its fitness value will be 0, since $\frac{|S_{\neg r}|}{|S|} \times var(S_{\neg r})$ will be 0, and the values of $var(S)$ and $\frac{|S_r|}{|S|} \times var(S_r)$ will be the same.

The individual representation is another characteristic that may have harmed the RHMC-GA performance when using relational tests. Because each 4-tuple test is associated to an attribute, when an attribute A_i associated to a given 4-tuple position i is used in a relational test, it cannot be used anymore in a propositional test.

In Table 4, we show the results of the statistical tests applied. We mark with an $*$ the comparisons where the classifier in the column obtained statistically better results than the classifier in the row.

6. CONCLUSIONS AND FUTURE WORKS

In this paper, we proposed RHMC-GA, a Genetic Algorithm to generate propositional and relational Hierarchical Multi-Label Classification Rules. We used datasets structured according to the Gene Ontology taxonomy, a directed acyclic graph (DAG) hierarchy having thousands of classes.

RHMC-GA uses a sequential covering procedure to evolve the antecedents of the rules. The consequents are deterministically obtained using the classes of the instances covered by the rules. It also tries to evolve rules specialized in the classification of a group of classes, by applying the crossover operation in rules considered near in the search space.

We showed how the RHMC-GA fitness function could have harmed the algorithm's performance in some situations. Also, we argued that the new kind of generated rules may have largely increased the search space, which can make more difficult to find good solutions.

According to the experiments, RHMC-GA obtained competitive results if compared with other methods in the literature. Although RHMC-GA was outperformed by the state-of-the-art Clus-HMC, the difference in their predictive performance was not statistically significant.

As future work, we plan to develop a better fitness function, which tries to verify if the classes of the instances were

Table 3: $AU(\overline{PRC})$ values obtained

Dataset	Only propositional tests				Dataset	Propositional and relational tests			
	RHMC-GA	Clus-HMC	Clus-HSC	Clus-SC		RHMC-GA	Clus-HMC	Clus-HSC	Clus-SC
Cellcycle	0.341 ± 0.009	0.357	0.371	0.252	Cellcycle	0.319 ± 0.016	0.358	0.344	0.243
Church	0.341 ± 0.005	0.348	0.397	0.289	Church	0.329 ± 0.008	0.340	0.374	0.267
Derisi	0.344 ± 0.003	0.355	0.349	0.218	Derisi	0.298 ± 0.015	0.353	0.346	0.208
Eisen	0.380 ± 0.004	0.380	0.365	0.270	Eisen	0.351 ± 0.017	0.389	0.338	0.271
Gasch1	0.361 ± 0.003	0.371	0.351	0.239	Gasch1	0.335 ± 0.017	0.370	0.325	0.236
Gasch2	0.351 ± 0.007	0.365	0.378	0.267	Gasch2	0.322 ± 0.022	0.369	0.352	0.266
Pheno	0.331 ± 0.002	0.337	0.416	0.316	-	-	-	-	-
Spo	0.345 ± 0.008	0.352	0.371	0.213	Spo	0.295 ± 0.028	0.351	0.315	0.214
Expr	0.361 ± 0.007	0.368	0.351	0.249	Expr	0.327 ± 0.016	0.370	0.334	0.251
Seq	0.359 ± 0.007	0.386	0.282	0.197	-	-	-	-	-

Table 4: Statistical Significance Analysis

	Only propositional tests					Propositional and relational tests			
	RHMC-GA	Clus-HMC	Clus-HSC	Clus-SC		RHMC-GA	Clus-HMC	Clus-HSC	Clus-SC
RHMC-GA					RHMC-GA				
Clus-HMC					Clus-HMC				
Clus-HSC					Clus-HSC				
Clus-SC		*	*		Clus-SC		*	*	

correctly predicted. The current fitness function only considers the variance of the sets of instances covered and not covered by the rules, but does not verify if the instances are being correctly classified. We also intent to investigate a way of evolving the consequents of the rules, and not only the antecedents. In this way, we will not only try find good antecedents, but antecedents with good consequents.

7. ACKNOWLEDGMENTS

The authors would like to thank the Brazilian research agencies FAPESP and CNPq. We would also like to thank Dr. Leander Schietgat and Dr. Celine Vens for providing support with the PCT-based methods. Ricardo Cerri is funded by grant 2009/17401-2, São Paulo Research Foundation (FAPESP).

8. REFERENCES

[1] R. Alves, M. Delgado, and A. Freitas. Knowledge discovery with artificial immune systems for hierarchical multi-label classification of protein functions. In *International Conference on Fuzzy Systems*, pages 2097–2104, 2010.

[2] M. Ashburner, C. A. Ball, J. A. Blake, D. Botstein, H. Butler, J. M. Cherry, A. P. Davis, K. Dolinski, S. S. Dwight, J. T. Eppig, M. A. Harris, D. P. Hill, L. Issel-Tarver, A. Kasarskis, S. Lewis, J. C. Matese, J. E. Richardson, M. Ringwald, G. M. Rubin, and G. Sherlock. Gene ontology: tool for the unification of biology. The Gene Ontology Consortium. *Nature Genetics*, 25(1):25–29, May 2000.

[3] W. Bi and J. Kwok. Multi-Label Classification on Tree- and DAG-Structured Hierarchies. In L. Getoor and T. Scheffer, editors, *International Conference on Machine Learning*, ICML'11, pages 17–24, New York, NY, USA, June 2011. ACM.

[4] R. Carvalho, G. Brunoro, and G. Pappa. Hcga: A genetic algorithm for hierarchical classification. In *IEEE Congress on Evolutionary Computation*, pages 933–940, June 2011.

[5] R. Cerri, R. C. Barros, and A. C. P. L. F. Carvalho. A genetic algorithm for hierarchical multi-label classification. In *Proceedings of the 27th Annual ACM Symposium on Applied Computing*, SAC '12, pages 250–255, New York, NY, USA, 2012. ACM.

[6] E. P. Costa, A. C. Lorena, A. C. P. L. F. Carvalho, and A. A. Freitas. Top-down hierarchical ensembles of classifiers for predicting g-protein-coupled-receptor functions. In *Brazilian Symposium on Bioinformatics*, volume 5167 of *Lecture Notes in Bioinformatics*, pages 35–46. Springer-Verlag, 2008.

[7] J. Demšar. Statistical comparisons of classifiers over multiple data sets. *Journal of Machine Learning Research*, 7:1–30, 2006.

[8] S. Dzeroski and N. Lavrac, editors. *Relational Data Mining*. Springer, 2001.

[9] F. Otero, A. Freitas, and C. Johnson. A hierarchical multi-label classification ant colony algorithm for protein function prediction. *Memetic Computing*, 2:165–181, 2010.

[10] M. Pugelj and S. Džeroski. Predicting structured outputs k-nearest neighbours method. In *Proceedings of the 14th international conference on Discovery science*, pages 262–276, Berlin, Heidelberg, 2011. Springer-Verlag.

[11] L. Schietgat, C. Vens, J. Struyf, H. Blockeel, D. Kocev, and S. Dzeroski. Predicting gene function using hierarchical multi-label decision tree ensembles. *BMC Bioinformatics*, 11:2, 2010.

[12] C. Vens, J. Struyf, L. Schietgat, S. Džeroski, and H. Blockeel. Decision trees for hierarchical multi-label classification. *Machine Learning*, 73:185–214, 2008.

On the Application of GP to Streaming Data Classification Tasks with Label Budgets

Ali Vahdat
Faculty of Computer Science
Dalhousie Unversity
Halifax, NS, Canada
ali.vahdat@dal.ca

Aaron Atwater
School of Computer Science
University of Waterloo
ON, Canada
aatwater@uwaterloo.ca

Andrew R. McIntyre
Faculty of Computer Science
Dalhousie Unversity
Halifax, NS, Canada
armcintyre@gmail.com

Malcolm I. Heywood
Faculty of Computer Science
Dalhousie Unversity
Halifax, NS, Canada
mheywood@cs.dal.ca

ABSTRACT

A framework is introduced for applying GP to streaming data classification tasks under label budgets. This is a fundamental requirement if GP is going to adapt to the challenge of streaming data environments. The framework proposes three elements: a sampling policy, a data subset and a data archiving policy. The sampling policy establishes on what basis data is sampled from the stream, and therefore when label information is requested. The data subset is used to define what GP individuals evolve against. The composition of such a subset is a mixture of data forwarded under the sampling policy and historical data identified through the data archiving policy. The combination of sampling policy and the data subset achieve a decoupling between the rate at which the stream passes and the rate at which evolution commences. Benchmarking is performed on two artificial data sets with specific forms of sudden shift and gradual drift as well as a well known real-world data set.

Categories and Subject Descriptors

I.2.6 [**Learning**]: Concept Learning; Parameter Learning

Keywords

Streaming data, Big data, Pareto archiving, Classification, Label budgets, Genetic programming

1. INTRODUCTION

Streaming data introduces additional challenges to the classification task that change the nature of the task in fundamental ways. A short list of potential factors of interest to this research includes, but is not limited to:

GECCO'14, July 12–16, 2014, Vancouver, BC, Canada.
Copyright 2014 ACM 978-1-4503-2881-4/14/07 ...$15.00.
http://dx.doi.org/10.1145/2598394.2611385.

Non-stationary process: The process generating the data itself might well be subject to concept drift (gradual change) or shift (sudden change). This is straightforward to address if all the data is labeled. However, this would imply that it is possible to provide such labels at the rate that the data is received. In general this is not possible, indeed, there might be a considerable cost associated with labeling.

Any time operation: Data is received on a continuous basis; whereas a machine learning (ML) algorithm should be capable of providing 'predictions' at any point in time. Dividing the data into independent training and test partitions implies knowledge about when the stream is sufficiently stationary in order to identify consistent training and test partitions, which is not possible in general. Instead, ML for streaming needs to make decisions regarding what data to use for training while always having a champion individual available for classification.

Requesting labels: Typically, some form of a windowed interface[1] is assumed in order to provide bounds on what new data can potentially be used for training purposes. Additional decisions are necessary to decide how much of this data to request labels for. Naturally, if the ML can establish that no change has appeared between the content of consecutive windows, then there is no need to request labels. In short, a balance needs achieving between too little training (in which case the ML model goes stale) versus too much (which implies that too many labels are requested).

Class imbalance: Given that only a small fraction of the data stream is available at any point in time (cf., the windowed interface to the data stream), then it is not possible to a priori stratify content. Thus, it is quite likely that the content of any data window will not be representative all possible classes. Indeed, when classes are imbalanced, it is likely that data window content will be degenerate (consist of a single class alone). Current approaches to class imbalance in GP assume an offline (batch) approach e.g., [5], thus do not directly transfer to the streaming data scenario.

[1]One of two generic window interfaces are typically assumed: 1) a sliding window – data shuffled in and out under a first-in, first-out data structure of finite length, or; 2) non-overlapping windows of finite length.

In this work we are interested in pursuing an evolutionary approach capable of addressing all three of the above properties simultaneously. In particular, we focus on the issue of change detection with label budgets in order to explicitly make label requests.

Change detection represents a label free process by which changes to the underlying process generating stream content are detected. There are at least two general aspects to the **change detection** question (detailed further in Section 2). In the first case a statistical characterization might be assumed relative to: 1) the input stream; 2) some property of the classifier architecture; or 3) the decision boundary of the classifier. All of these scenarios are potential solutions for detecting a general drift or shift to prior classification boundaries after which **label requests** would be made. However, when a previously learnt class is associated with an as yet unseen class and / or previously learnt classes are switched (as might happen when user preferences shift), there is no reference for model based change detection. This means that label requests should be driven through both knowledge of appropriate statistical characterization(s) as well as purely stochastically in order to capture switches to previously learnt classifier behaviour. Moreover, there is a limit to the number of label requests, irrespective of the source of the request i.e., a **finite label budget**.

In this work we establish a basic framework for addressing these questions under genetic programming (GP), Section 3. Such a framework consists of: 1) the sliding window interface to the stream which defines the subset of data 'available' at any point in time; 2) a sampling policy for determining which exemplars from the current sliding window are actually selected for training purposes; 3) a data subset against which a generation of the evolutionary algorithm is performed, and; 4) a data archiving policy for determining how much (if any) of the data subset is retained between generations. Naturally, it is the sampling policy that defines when exemplars labels are requested, whereas the role of the archiving policy is to retain exemplars that support the identification of 'good' GP individuals i.e., a Pareto archiving policy. A classifier is always available for providing a class label, care of the data subset that provides the basis for always being able to select a champion classifier without reference to additional label information.

Section 5 performs a benchmarking study using two artificial data sets characterized by non-stationary (gradual) drift and (sudden) shift. A third real-world data set known to include concept drift is also included. The well known Massive Online Analysis (MOA) toolbox provides a baseline classifier with labelling budget. To our knowledge this is the first time that GP has been benchmarked under the conditions of streaming data with a labelling budget. A discussion of the studies findings and future work presented in Section 6.

2. BACKGROUND AND RELATED WORK

There has been a significant body of work dedicated to streaming data scenarios under non-evolutionary ML frameworks e.g., [33, 19, 6, 20]. For brevity we will focus on the classification task alone (as opposed to clustering, item set mining or forecasting / prediction) and concentrate on the issue of change detection which lies at the centre of building ML frameworks capable of operating under label budgets. As noted in the introduction, there are three broad categories of interest, outlined as follows.

Characterizing properties specific to the model of classification: represents an approach in which properties specific to a class of ML are measured and compared to a prior reference characterization. This is particularly appropriate for decision tree architectures in which the frequency of leaf node utilization is often the property characterized [17, 24]. Naturally, the limitation in this method is that it is specific to a particular ML architecture as opposed to any ML representation.

Characterizing properties of the input data: implies that the focus of change detection is now on characterizing behaviour relative to sliding window content. Generally two sliding windows are employed. The content of a reference window is compared to that of the most recent sliding window. The principle design decision revolves around what statistic to employ e.g., Chernoff bounds [26], entropy [11, 38], Kullback–Leibler divergence [35], Hoeffding bounds [7], Fractal correlation dimension [18] or Hellinger divergence metric [15]. One significant drawback of pursuing such an approach is that it is often necessary to label the data (i.e., metrics are estimated class-wise). In addition, statistics estimated relative to the input stream are also subject to as loss of effectiveness as the dimensionality increases [40].

Characterizing properties of the label space: implies that the 'behaviour' of the classifier output is the focus of measurements. Various authors have proposed statistical characterizations of class boundary information cf., classifier confidence [30, 36]. For example, changes to classifier certainly might be detected using thresholds [31], or changes to the number of confident predictions detected [27]. Naturally, such characterizations of classifier behaviour are independent of the ML framework and potentially applicable to GP as well [34].

A remaining drawback of any of the above approaches is that they are unable to detect when a previously encountered input behaviour, $P(x)$, is associated with a new or different class label. For example, under this scenario a label space characterization would still associate $P(x)$ with the previous label, or $P(y|x)$. Likewise an input data characterization would not register any change either, as there has been no change to $P(x)$. Under these scenarios generating label requests uniformly (i.e., independently of the measurable properties) has been shown to be surprisingly effective [41]; as have hybrid approaches combining label space and uniform sampling [37]. Section 3 will discuss how such findings can be factored into an approach for applying GP to streaming data under limited label budgets.

From the particular perspective of GP there has not been a concerted effort to address streaming data requirements. The largest body of EC research has been directed towards EC in 'dynamic environments', and applications to finance in particular [14]. Financial applications generally take the form of evolving a trading agent to make buy, hold or sell decisions given some summary of the current and historical trading conditions. State-of-the-art in this case evolve both the temporal features used to characterize local historical information as well as some form of decision tree used to determine what action to apply. Unlike the streaming task of interest to this work there is no concept of a label budget. Instead trading agents are either evolved on a continuous basis [14, 25], periodically retrained [39], or make use of loss criteria to dynamically re-trigger training events [32].

Other developments from evolutionary computation (EC) include the application of learning classifier systems (LCS) to dynamic environments. Dam *et al.*, discuss the adaption of learning rates versus reinitializing the population for noisy versus non-stationary environments under the assumption that all the data is labelled [10]. Behdad and French propose an online version of LCS in which the exploit and explore cycles are reversed [4]. Moreover, various probabilistic heuristics are proposed for filling in known 'gaps' in label information. Finally, we note a recent work in which a k-NN formulation was assumed such that PSO could be used to adapt the direction in which k-NN prototype classifiers migrated under streaming data classification [9]. Again, the data must be completely labeled a priori.

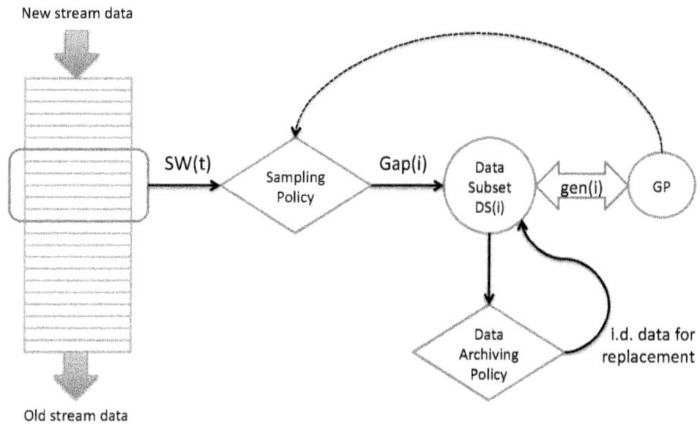

Figure 1: Components of generic architecture for applying GP to streaming data under a label budget

3. GENERIC GP STREAMING DATA ARCHITECTURE

The general architecture proposed for applying GP to streaming data under finite labelling budgets is summarized by Figure 1. The initial sliding window (SW) represents the set of exemplars that can be indexed (for training) at time, t, or $SW(t)$; whereas the sampling policy determines which exemplars are actually utilized for training purposes, or $Gap(i) \in SW(t)$; where $|Gap(i)| \leq |SW(t)|$. Only the $|Gap(i)|$ exemplars chosen are added to the Data Subset ($DS(i)$) and have their corresponding labels requested. Note also that the rate at which the sliding window updates, or t, need not be the same as the rate at which samples are taken, or i. Instead, the rate of sampling *from* the sliding window, i, defines the rate at which the Data Subset ($DS(i)$) and therefore the GP population is updated. With each new generation i, $|Gap(i)|$ exemplars are identified from the current $SW(t)$ position, and a corresponding number of exemplars from $DS(i)$ are replaced by the content of $Gap(i)$. Naturally, the degree of differentiation between stream and DS updates sets the label budget ratio.

The scheme assumed for prioritizing DS content for replacement is defined by a **Data Archiving Policy**, in this case Pareto archiving will be assumed e.g., [13]. Specifically, Pareto archiving is used to identify exemplars that distinguish between the performance of GP classifiers. Such a set of exemplars are said to be non-dominated [13]. One of the drawbacks of assuming a Pareto archiving policy, however, is that the archive of exemplars distinguishing between different GP classifiers can potentially increase to $P^2 - P$; where P is the size of the GP population. This would have implications for the overall efficiency of the algorithm. Hence, we limit the size of DS to a suitable finite value and employ a DS exemplar diversity / aging heuristic [1, 2]. The process for choosing exemplars from DS for replacement now takes one of the following forms, depending on which condition is satisfied:

- The number of exemplars forming distinctions is less than or equal to $|DS| - |Gap|$. Let the exemplars from DS that do not support distinctions be $\bar{d}$. As $|\bar{d}| \geq |Gap|$ then the DS exemplars replaced by $Gap(i)$ are selected from $\bar{d}$ alone.

- The number of exemplars forming distinctions is more than $|DS| - |Gap|$. Any exemplars not forming distinctions ($\bar{d}$) will be replaced. In addition $|Gap| - |\bar{d}|$ exemplars forming distinctions will be replaced (potentially resulting in the loss of GP classifiers i.e., no longer identified as being non-dominated). The exemplars forming distinctions are now ranked in accordance with how many other points form the same distinction and how long an exemplar has been in the archive [1, 2]. In effect exemplars supporting: 1) unique distinctions see more priority than those forming more common distinctions i.e., a form of fitness sharing or diversity maintenance, and 2) older exemplars are more likely to removed in favour of those forming more recent distinctions.

Such preference schemes were previously shown to be useful under GP streaming classification, albeit without label budgeting [3, 2, 1].

In the case of the **Sampling Policy**, Section 2 highlighted that two basic sources have been identified from the wider literature: stochastic sampling versus using classification confidence information. Classifier confidence information implies that as the certainty of the class label suggested by a classifier decreases (approaches ambiguity), then request a label. In the case of the stochastic source of label requests, this is performed uniformly relative to exemplars that are classified with certainty. The objective being to confirm that cases which are classified with certainty have not undergone some form of shift into a different class. Moreover, we also note that even requesting labels with a uniform probability (under a label budget) is often better than more sophisticated heuristics [41]. In this work we will assume the uniform sampling heuristic under a label budget for the purpose of establishing our baseline performance. Future work will introduce mechanisms to include classifier confidence, where given that multiple GP individuals are evolved, it remains to be seen how much significance is given to a single GP classifier confidence versus that of, say, the archive of non-dominated classifiers.

Finally, in order to provide **anytime classifier operation**, it is necessary to have a champion individual responsible for predicting labels for stream data at any point in time. Thus, relative to the current content of $DS(i)$ the non-dominated GP individual maximizing class-wise detection rate (DR) is assumed to be representative of the wider population. DR is estimated as follows: $\frac{1}{C}\sum_{j=[1,\dots,C]} DR(j)$; where C is the number of classes present in $DS(i)$. $DR(j) =$

$tp/(tp + fn)$; where tp and fn denote true positive and false negative counts w.r.t. class j. Note that in limiting the available candidate GP classifiers to the non-dominated set, we reduce the likelihood of selecting degenerate classifiers. This is particularly important because stream data is not stratified, whereas it is highly likely that stream data is imbalanced. Hence, it is generally not possible to make any guarantees regarding the distribution of classes appearing in any sliding window location.

The specific form of GP assumed takes the form of Symbiotic Bid-Based GP (SBB) and therefore benefits from the ability to perform task decomposition (construct a classifier as a team of programs). Studies have demonstrated that SBB is more effective than monolithic GP under (stationary) classification tasks [29], as well as under data sets with large attribute spaces [16] and data sets with high degrees of class imbalance [28]. Aside from the additional transparency of the resulting solutions, pursuing a GP teaming approach also provides an elegant solution to multi-class classification. Readers are referred to the earlier SBB papers for details of selection / variation operators and instruction set [28, 16].

Table 1: Benchmarking dataset properties

Discrete non-stationary concept shift [41]	
# of Classes per concept	5
# Attributes (# irrelevant attributes)	7 (1)
# Exemplars per 'data block'	500,000
# Exemplars over entire stream (S_{max})	6,500,000
Continuous non-stationary concept drift [17]	
# of Classes per concept	3
# Attributes (# irrelevant attributes)	11 (1)
# Exemplars per 'data block'	1,000
# Exemplars over entire stream (S_{max})	150,000
Electricity data set [23]	
# of Classes	2
# Attributes	8
# Exemplars over entire stream (S_{max})	45,312

4. EXPERIMENTAL METHODOLOGY

This section begins by establishing the approach to benchmark dataset selection (Section 4.1). Section 4.2 discusses parameterization issues for the GP approach. Section 4.3 outlines the approach adopted to performance evaluation. Finally, the alternate streaming classifier (an adaptive form of Naive Bayes with label budgeting) is summarized (Section 4.4).

4.1 Data sets

Three data sets will be employed for the purposes of benchmarking: 1) two artificially created and therefore with known degrees of non-stationary behaviour,[2] and; 2) a well known real world data set, Electricity [23], that has frequently been employed for streaming data benchmarking tasks. The basic properties of the data sets are summarized by Table 1.

Discrete concept shift dataset: adopts the approach taken in [41]. The Dataset Generator tool[3] is used to construct decision trees that specify a partitioning of the attribute space into a 5-class classification task based on randomly generated thresholds. Data is generated with a uniform p.d.f. and then assigned a class using the decision tree. A total of two concept generator decision trees (C1, C2) are used to create two sources of data. A single stream of data is then constructed block-wise with data integrated from each of the two concept generator decision trees.

Let each block consist of 500,000 exemplars, as sampled from the concept generator tuple of the form: $\langle C1\%, C2\% \rangle$. A total of 13 blocks describe the transition from purely $C1$, to purely $C2$ as follows: $\langle 100, 0 \rangle$, $\langle 100, 0 \rangle$, $\langle 100, 0 \rangle$, $\langle 90, 10 \rangle$, $\langle 80, 20 \rangle$, ... $\langle 0, 100 \rangle$. As the first 10% of the stream is made available for initial model construction, generating the first three blocks of data using concept $C1$ implies that the initial models never see anything other than concept $C1$. Moreover, blocks composed from a mixture of the two concepts assume a uniform p.d.f.

[2]Publicly available at `http://web.cs.dal.ca/~mheywood/Code/SBB/Stream/StreamData.html`

[3]Gabor Melli. The 'datgen' Dataset Generator. `http://www.datsetgenerator.com/`

Continuous concept drift dataset: adopts the approach taken in [17]. Hyperplanes are defined in a $d = 10$ dimensional space. Initial values of the hyperplane parameters are selected with uniform probability. Every $1,000$ exemplars, half of the parameters are considered for modification with a 20% chance of change. Class labels are allocated as a function of hyperplanes exceeding a class threshold. See [1] for a detailed description of the construction of this data set.

Electricity: characterizes the rise and fall of electricity demand in New South Wales (Australia) using consumption and price information for the target and neighbouring regions [23]. As such it is a two class data set (demand will either increase or decrease relative to the previous period), moreover, the distribution of classes is very imbalanced.

4.2 Parameterization of GP

The following approach will be adopted regarding the experimental methodology assumed for benchmarking GP algorithms under streaming data:

Model initialization is performed using the first 10% of the stream. This implies that relative to Figure 1, the first 10% of the generations are performed with the sliding window stationary over the initial 10% of the data set. Thereafter, the sliding window interface assumes a first-in, first-out data structure of fixed depth.

A **sliding window** of length S_{max}/i_{max} exemplars is assumed after model initialization. The remainder of the stream passes through at a constant rate (S_{max} is the ultimate length of the stream and i_{max} is the total generation count). The window is used to define the pool from which the new $|Gap(i)|$ training exemplars are sampled and their label are requested. Note that in effect this parameterization results in a *non-overlapping* sliding window. However, GP is evaluated w.r.t. the content of the Data Subset (Figure 1). Hence, there is still a 'gentle' turnover in new to old exemplar content between consecutive generations, or $\frac{|Gap|}{|DS|}$ new exemplars are introduced at each generation, where $|Gap| = 20$ and $|DS| = 120$.

Label budget is the ratio of points whose labels are requested over the stream length, or $\frac{i_{max} \times |Gap|}{S_{max}}$. In other words only $i_{max} \times |Gap|$ exemplars are requested for their label in a stream of length S_{max}. Thus, under the artificial concept shift data set (Table 1) with $S_{max} = 6,500,000$ and $i_{max} = 1,000$, then 6,500 exemplars pass between updates of the GP population, all of which are retained in the sliding window for potential sampling by the Sampling Policy. In the parameterization assumed here only $|Gap| = 20$ exemplars are sampled by the Sampling Policy to be used for training at each generation Thus, the Label Budget in this example would be $\frac{1,000 \times 20}{6,500,000} \approx 0.3\%$. Given the rather different stream lengths of the three benchmarking data sets (Table 1), two different parameterizations for i_{max} will be assumed per data set as follows:

- Concept shift data set: $i_{max} \in \{1,000; 10,000\}$;
- Concept drift and Electricity data sets: $i_{max} \in \{500; 1,000\}$

Different tapped delay line depths will be investigated in conjunction with GP. The number of taps will either be 1 (special case of no history) or always consist of 8 taps. Separate experiments will be performed with skip periods of 1, 2, 4 or 8. For example, the skip period of 2 corresponds to data instances of $[t, t-2, t-4, ..., t-14]$ where t is the index of the exemplar for which a class label is desired. Increasing the skip period increases the depth of data indexed, but reduces the resolution given a fixed number of taps. Support for a tapped delay line implies that GP indexes a matrix of #attributes × #taps and is therefore independent of the streaming framework details (Section 3).

Any remaining parameters follow from earlier work with SBB on streaming data [1, 2].

4.3 Evaluation

For comparison purposes we make use of two forms of comparator classifier: a "no change" classifier [8] and an Adaptive Naive Bayes model with label budgeting [37]; the latter is described in Section 4.4. The no change classifier was proposed as a naive 'devils advocate' approach to classification in which access to perfect label information is assumed. Specifically, it assumes that the label for exemplar t is the same as that for exemplar $t-1$, and continues with this 'prediction' until the label changes; after which the latest change in label is assumed. In short, the no change classifier is a one-bit state machine that makes no use of attribute information at all. It is known to be particularly effective (given complete access to label information) when the data stream consists of bursts of exemplars carrying the same class label [8]. However, as the number of classes and / or the degree of interleaving of class information increases, performance decreases. As such a no change classifier provides a 'feel' for how much implicit class variation exists in a stream.

Performance evaluation takes the form of an accumulative moving average metric, or prequential accuracy [12], where this is the default metric assumed by the MOA toolbox as well as being more generally used in the ML streaming literature [22]. Specifically, the prequential accuracy at exemplar t in the stream is estimated relative to all past $t-1$ exemplars as well as exemplar t, or

$$preq_t = \frac{(t-1) \times preq_{t-1} + R(t)}{t} \quad (1)$$

where $R(t) = 1$ denotes a true classification of instance t, and $R(t) = 0$ denotes otherwise. The ratio of time indexes acts as a weighting factor, enforcing a decay for older updates [22]. The resulting prequential accuracy takes the form of a curve, although current benchmarking practice also tends to compare against the final prequential accuracy estimate for $t = S_{max}$.

4.4 Adaptive Naive Bayes model

The second comparator classifier is documented in a recent study of streaming data classification under label budgets and drift detection [37], and has been made available in the Massive Online Analysis (MOA) toolbox.[4] Specifically, the Naive Bayes classifier with budgeted active learning and drift detection under the prequential evaluation task is employed. The drift detection mechanism selected was the DDM (Drift Detection Method) algorithm given by Gama *et al.*, [21] with default values for threshold (1) and step parameters (0.01). The 'random' active learning strategy was selected as it provided the baseline in [37] and is closest to the stochastic sampling policy adopted in this work. Finally the label budget parameter was varied over the range [0.05, 0.5] in 0.05 level increments.

Under this configuration a new classifier is built when the current classifier's performance begins to degrade; the current classifier is then replaced when drift is explicitly detected by the DDM. The active learning with budgeting is managed by the random selection policy where incoming points are queried for labels with the same uniform random probability as the budget parameter itself.

5. RESULTS

Figures 2, 3 and 4 provide a behavioural summary for how prequential accuracy (eqn. (1)) develops under GP during the stream w.r.t. different labelling budgets and support for various tapped delay line configurations (Section 4.2) over the three data sets (Section 4.1). In all cases each curve is the result of averaging the performance of GP over 50 runs for each configuration. Clearly a larger label budget always improves prequential accuracy, however, under the concept shift data set (Figure 2) more labels are necessary in order to provide a benefit when using a tapped delay line. This is natural as the changes are sudden, thus after the change, the data is stationary until the next sudden change. Moreover, there was a sensitivity to the taps used in the delay line under the concept shift data set, with only tap skips (2 and 4) resulting in performance improvements. Conversely, including taps was always beneficial to the concept drift and electricity data sets, with a more prominent effect under electricity (Figure 4). We also note that on the concept shift data set some regression in prequential accuracy occurs after the initial (10%) pre-training period (Figure 2). Conversely, progress on the concept drift and electricity data sets is generally monotonically increasing (Figures 3 and 4).

These figures also illustrate the performance of the "no change" classifier (Section 4.3). Both the artificial data sets illustrate the inherent weaknesses of such a classifier, with somewhat less than one class correctly classified on the concept shift data set (Figure 2), and a continuous decay experienced under concept drift (Figure 3). In the latter case, the

[4]MOA prerelease 2014.03; `http://moa.cms.waikato.ac.nz/overview/`

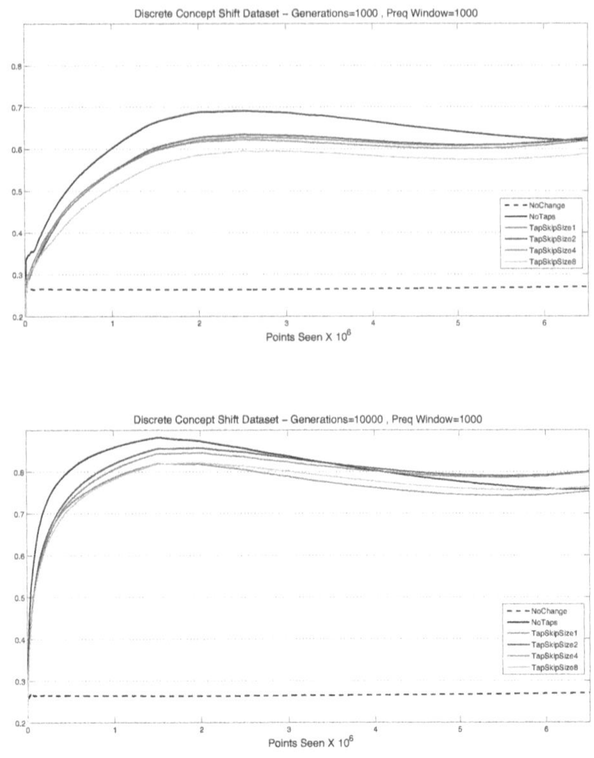

Figure 2: GP Prequential accuracy during stream. Artificial dataset with sudden concept shift. First 10% of stream (0.65×10^6 exemplars) are used to construct the initial model. Top: Label budget of $\approx 0.3\%$ or $i_{max} = 1,000$; Bottom: Label budget of $\approx 3\%$ or $i_{max} = 10,000$

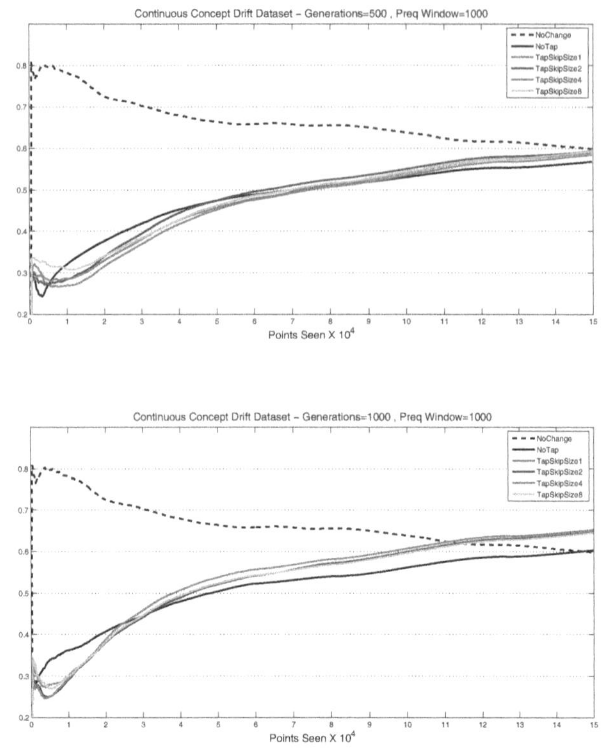

Figure 3: GP Prequential accuracy during stream. Artificial dataset with gradual concept drift. First 10% of stream (1.5×10^4 exemplars) are used to construct the initial model. Top: Label budget of $\approx 6.7\%$ or $i_{max} = 500$; Bottom: Label budget of $\approx 13.3\%$ or $i_{max} = 1,000$

no change classifier experiences an initial labelling success, but thereafter decays as no particular pattern of behaviour is evident in the labels.

Table 2 summarizes the resulting prequential accuracy in terms of mean and standard deviation for each tapped delay line configuration, label budget and data set. Note that label budgets are expressed in terms of the total stream length (Section 4.2). At each generation no more than 20 exemplars are sampled from the stream (Section 4.2). As noted above, there is a general preference for including the tapped delay line, with best cases most frequently occurring for a skip size of 4 (and no preference for a skip size of 1).

Results for the second baseline classifier, the adaptive Naive Bayesian (ANB) framework for streaming data classification under label budgets as implemented in the MOA toolkit (Section 4.4) are summarized in Figure 5. In this case label budgets are specified as a percentage of the entire stream in increments of 5 between 5 and 50 percent. These results should therefore be compared with the the GP results summarized in Table 2. Under the concept shift data set, a 3% label budget is sufficient for GP to perform better than any configuration of ANB, whereas ANB performs better than GP under the concept drift data set (both outcomes are significant at the 99% confidence interval). In the case of the Electricity data set, ANB performs better at low label budgets, but as the label budget increases there is no statistically significant difference.

6. CONCLUSION

A framework is proposed and benchmarked for applying GP to streaming data classification tasks under limited label budgets. This effectively makes GP an online algorithm able to adapt on a continuous basis to data streams created by a non-stationary source. From the perspective of scalability we note that the cost of any single GP generation is set by the cost of Pareto archiving i.e., set by the size of the data subset. Future work will continue to develop the framework to utilize additional information when deciding which exemplars to request label information for i.e., classifier confidence (see dashed line in Figure 1).

Acknowledgments

The authors gratefully acknowledge support from the NSERC CRD program (Canada).

7. REFERENCES

[1] A. Atwater. Towards coevolutionary genetic programming with Pareto archiving under streaming data. Master's thesis, Faculty of Computer Science, 2013.

[2] A. Atwater and M. I. Heywood. Benchmarking Pareto archiving heuristics in the presence of concept drift: diversity versus age. In *ACM Genetic and Evolutionary Computation Conference*, pages 885–892, 2013.

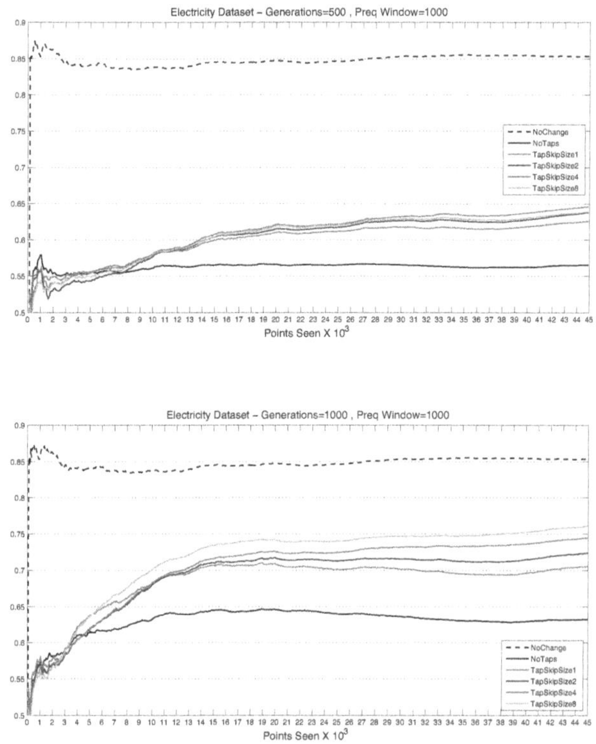

Figure 4: GP Prequential accuracy during stream. Electricity data set. First 10% of stream (4.5×10^3 exemplars) are used to construct the initial model. Top: Label budget of $\approx$ 22% or $i_{max} = 500$; Bottom: Label budget of $\approx$ 44% or $i_{max} = 1,000$

Table 2: Overall prequential accuracy of GP – Mean and standard deviation. Values in bold indicate a best case for each label budget.

Discrete Concept Shift data set				
	label budget $\approx$ 0.3%		label budget $\approx$ 3%	
TapSkip	mean	std. dev.	mean	std. dev.
none	**62.6**	5.0	75.4	5.3
1	62.0	3.3	75.9	6.0
2	62.4	3.8	80.5	4.6
4	61.8	4.1	**80.6**	4.7
8	59.2	5.1	77.1	5.5
Continuous Concept Drift data set				
	label budget $\approx$ 6.7%		label budget $\approx$ 13.3%	
none	57.4	2.7	60.3	2.2
1	57.6	3.3	65.2	2.6
2	59.8	3.8	65.0	3.3
4	59.4	4.2	**65.7**	2.4
8	**60.0**	3.2	64.6	2.6
Electricity data set				
	label budget $\approx$ 22%		label budget $\approx$ 44%	
none	56.6	2.0	63.4	1.3
1	62.3	2.4	71.1	3.2
2	63.1	2.6	72.3	2.8
4	**64.3**	3.3	75.4	3.6
8	63.2	3.3	**76.5**	3.6

[3] A. Atwater, M. I. Heywood, and A. N. Zincir-Heywood. GP under streaming data constraints: a case for Pareto archiving? In *ACM Genetic and Evolutionary Computation Conference*, pages 703–710, 2012.

[4] M. Behdad and T. French. Online learning classifiers in dynamic environments with incomplete feedback. In *IEEE Congress on Evolutionary Computation*, pages 1786–1793, 2013.

[5] U. Bhowan, M. Johnston, M. Zhang, and X. Yao. Evolving diverse ensembles using genetic programming for classification with unbalanced data. *IEEE Transactions on Evolutionary Computation*, 17(3):368–386, 2013.

[6] A. Bifet. *Adaptive Stream Mining: Pattern Learning and Mining from Evolving Data Streams*, volume 207 of *Frontiers in Artificial Intelligence and Applications*. IOS Press, 2010.

[7] A. Bifet and R. Gavalda. Learning from time-changing data with adaptive windowing. In *SIAM International Conference on Data Mining*, pages 443–448, 2007.

[8] A. Bifet, I. Žliobaitė, B. Pfahringer, and G. Holmes. Pitfalls in benchmarking data stream classification and how to avoid them. In *Machine Learning and Knowledge Discovery in Databases*, volume 8188 of *LNCS*, pages 465–479, 2013.

[9] A. Cercantes, P. Isasi, C. Gagné, and M. Parizeau. Learning from non-stationary data using a growing network of prototypes. In *IEEE Congress on Evolutionary Computation*, pages 2634–2641, 2013.

[10] H. H. Dam, C. Lokan, and H. A. Abbass. Evolutionary online data mining: An investigation in a dynamic environment. In *Studies in Computational Intelligence*, volume 51, chapter 7, pages 153–178. Springer, 2007.

[11] T. Dasu, S. Krishnan, S. Venkatasubramanian, and K. Yi. An information-theoretic approach to detecting changes in multi-dimensional data streams. In *Proceedings of the Symposium on the Interface of Statistics*, 2006.

[12] A. P. Dawid. Statistical theory: The prequential approach. *Journal of the Royal Statistical Society-A*, 147:278–292, 1984.

[13] E. D. de Jong. A monolithic archive for pareto-coevolution. *Evolutionary Computation*, 15(1):61–93, 2007.

[14] I. Dempsey, M. O'Neill, and A. Brabazon. *Foundations in Grammatical Evolution for Dynamic Environments*, volume 194 of *Studies in Computational Intelligence*. Springer, 2009.

[15] G. Ditzler and R. Polikar. Hellinger distance based drift detection for non stationary environments. In *IEEE Symposium on Computational Intelligence in Dynamic and Uncertain Environments*, pages 41–48, 2011.

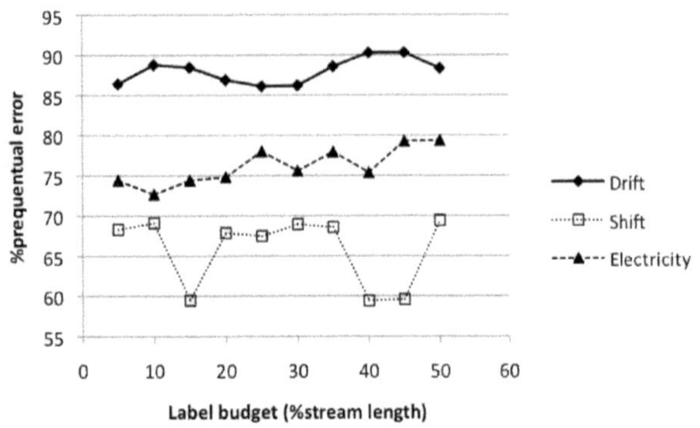

Figure 5: Overall prequential accuracy – MOA adaptive Naive Bayes.

[16] J. A. Doucette, A. R. McIntyre, P. Lichodzijewski, and M. I. Heywood. Symbiotic coevolutionary genetic programming: a benchmarking study under large attribute spaces. *Genetic Programming and Evolvable Machines*, 13(1):71–101, 2012.

[17] W. Fan, Y. Huang, H. Wang, and P. S. Yu. Active mining of data streams. In *Proceedings of SIAM International Conference on Data Mining*, pages 457–461, 2004.

[18] G. Folino and G. Papuzzo. Handling different categories of concept drift in data streams using distributed GP. In *European Conference on Genetic Programming*, volume 6021 of *LNCS*, pages 74–85, 2010.

[19] J. Gama. *Knowledge discovery from data streams.* CRC Press, 2010.

[20] J. Gama. A survey on learning from data streams: current and future trends. *Progress in Artificial Intelligence*, 1(1):45–55, 2012.

[21] J. Gama, P. Medas, G. Castillo, and P. Rodrigues. Learning with drift detection. In *Advances in Artificial Intelligence*, volume 3171 of *Lecture Notes in Computer Science*, pages 286–295, 2004.

[22] J. Gama, R. Sebastião, and P. Rodrigues. On evaluating stream learning algorithms. *Machine Learning*, 90(3):317–346, 2013.

[23] M. Harries. Splice-2 comparative evaluation: Electricity pricing. Technical report, University of New South Wales, 1999.

[24] S. Huang and Y. Dong. An active learning system for mining time changing data streams. *Intelligent Data Analysis*, 11(4):401–419, 2007.

[25] H. Iba and C. C. Aranha. *Practical applications of evolutionary computation to financial engineering*, volume 11 of *Adaptation, Learning, and Optimization.* Springer, 2012.

[26] D. Kifer, S. Ben-David, and J. Gehrke. Detecting change in data streams. In *Proceedings of the International Conference on Very Large Data Bases*, pages 180–191. Morgan Kaufmann, 2004.

[27] C. Lanquillon. Information filtering in changing domains. In *Proceedings of the International Joint Conference on Artificial Intelligence*, pages 41–48, 1999.

[28] P. Lichodzijewski and M. I. Heywood. Managing team-based problem solving with Symbiotic Bid-based Genetic Programming. In *ACM Proceedings of the Genetic and Evolutionary Computation Conference*, pages 363–370, 2008.

[29] P. Lichodzijewski and M. I. Heywood. Symbiosis, complexification and simplicity under GP. In *ACM Proceedings of the Genetic and Evolutionary Computation Conference*, pages 853–860, 2010.

[30] P. Lindstrom, B. MacNamee, and S. J. Delany. Handling concept drift in a text data stream constrained by high labelling cost. In *Proceedings of the International Florida Artificial Intelligence Research Society Conference.* AAAI, 2010.

[31] P. Lindstrom, B. MacNamee, and S. J. Delany. Drift detection using uncertainty distribution divergence. *Evolutionary Intelligence*, 4(1):13–25, 2013.

[32] A. Loginov and M. I. Heywood. On the impact of streaming interface heuristics on GP trading agents: an FX benchmarking study. In *Proceeding of the ACM Genetic and Evolutionary Computation Conference*, pages 1341–1348, 2013.

[33] J. Quinonero-Candela, M. Sugiyama, A. Schwaighofer, and N. D. Lawrence, editors. *Dataset shift in machine learning.* MIT Press, 2009.

[34] S. Rahimi, A. R. McIntyre, M. I. Heywood, and N. Zincir-Heywood. Label free change detection on streaming data with cooperative multi-objective genetic programming. In *ACM Genetic and Evolutionary Computation Conference*, pages 159–160, 2013.

[35] R. Sebastio and J. Gama. Change detection in learning histograms from data streams. In *Proceedings of the Portuguese Conference on Artificial Intelligence*, volume 4874 of *LNCS*, pages 112–123. Springer, 2007.

[36] I. Žliobaitė, A. Bifet, B. Pfahringer, and G. Holmes. Active learning with evolving streaming data. In *Proceedings of the European Conference on Machine Learning and Knowledge Discovery in Databases*, pages 597–612. Springer, 2011.

[37] I. Žliobaitė, A. Bifet, B. Pfahringer, and G. Holmes. Active learning with drifting streaming data. *IEEE Transactions on Neural Networks and Learning Systems*, 25(1):27–54, 2014.

[38] P. Vorburger and A. Bernstein. Entropy-based concept shift detection. In *Proceedings of the Sixth International Conference on Data Mining*, pages 1113–1118, 2006.

[39] G. Wilson and W. Banzhaf. Interday and intraday stock trading using PAM GP and linear GP. In A. Brabazon, O'Neill, and D. G. Maringer, editors, *Natural Computing in Computational Finance 3*, volume 293 of *SCI*, pages 191–212. Springer, 2010.

[40] X. Wu, K. Yu, W. Ding, H. Wang, and X. Zhu. Online feature selection with streaming features. *IEEE Transactions on Pattern Analysis and Machine Learning*, 35(5):1178–1182, 2013.

[41] X. Zhu, P. Zhang, X. Lin, and Y. Shi. Active learning from stream data using optimal weight classifier ensemble. *IEEE Transactions on Systems, Man, and Cybernetics – Part B*, 40(6):1607–1621, 2010.

MedGEC'14 Workshop Chairs' Welcome

Welcome to MedGEC 2014

MedGEC is the GECCO Workshop on the application of genetic and evolutionary computation (GEC) to problems in medicine and healthcare.

A dedicated workshop at GECCO continues to provide a much needed focus for medical related applications of evolutionary computation, not only providing a clear definition of the state of the art, but also support to practitioners for whom genetic and evolutionary computation might not be their main area of expertise or experience.

The Workshop has two main aims:

(i) To provide delegates with examples of the current state of the art of applications of GEC to medicine.

(ii) To provide a forum in which researchers can discuss and exchange ideas, support and advise each other in theory and practice.

This is the tenth year that this Workshop has been presented at GECCO, a reflection of the continued importance of genetic and evolutionary programming to medical applications. Presentations reflect a wide range of healthcare areas including: Medical Imaging and Signal Processing; Data Mining Medical Data and Patient Records; Clinical Expert Systems and Knowledge-based Systems; Modeling and Simulation of Medical Processes; and Clinical Diagnosis and Therapy. Despite this broad range of applications, there are common themes of interest that are important in achieving a successful solution to the problems addressed. One recurring theme is accessibility to reliable medical datasets to train, test and evaluate genetic and evolutionary algorithms. It is acknowledged that achieving a "Gold Standard" dataset is problematic, due to the difficulties in gaining access to patients and the reliance on conventional clinical evaluation, which is often subjective, and therefore, potentially unreliable. A second important theme is the choice of genetic and evolutionary algorithm employed, its suitability for the problem at hand and the benefits of alternate representations. The Workshop provides a knowledgeable and supportive forum in which these and other issues can be discussed. Although traditionally a venue for practitioners in genetic and evolutionary computation development, it is hoped that the Workshop will also attract a wider audience, such as medical practitioners and other healthcare professionals who have an interest in the use of evolutionary algorithms in medicine. The Workshop organizers are always receptive to suggestions for new themes, areas for discussion and new activities and can be contacted directly via email.

Stephen L Smith
University of York, UK
stephen.smith@york.ac.uk

Stefano Cagnoni
Universita' degli Studi di Parma, Italy
cagnoni@ce.unipr.it

Robert Patton
Oak Ridge National Laboratory, USA
pattonrm@ornl.gov

Classification of EEG Signals using a Novel Genetic Programming Approach

Arpit Bhardwaj
Indin Institute of Technology
Indore
Indore,India
phd12110102@iiti.ac.in

Aruna Tiwari
Indin Institute of Technology
Indore
Indore,India
artiwari@iiti.ac.in

M.Vishaal Varma
Indin Institute of Technology
Indore
Indore,India
cse1100121@iiti.ac.in

M.Ramesh Krishna
Indin Institute of Technology
Indore
Indore,India
ee1100220@iiti.ac.in

ABSTRACT

In this paper, we present a new method for classification of electroencephalogram (EEG) signals using Genetic Programming (GP). The Empirical Mode Decomposition (EMD) is used to extract the features of EEG signals which served as an input for the GP. In this paper, new constructive crossover and mutation operations are also produced to improve GP. In these constructive crossover and mutation operators hill climbing search is integrated to remove the destructive nature of these operators. To improve GP, we apply constructive crossover on all the individuals which remain after reproduction. A new concept of selecting the global prime off-springs of the generation is also proposed. The constructive mutation approach is applied to poor individuals who are left after selecting globally prime off-springs. Improvement of the method is measured against classification accuracy, training time and the number of generations for EEG signal classification. As we show in the results section, the classification accuracy can be estimated to be 98.69% on the test cases, which is better than classification accuracy of Liang and coworkers method which was published in 2010.

Categories and Subject Descriptors

I.2 [**Artificial Intelligence**]: Problem Solving, Search.

General Terms

Performance, Algorithms, Relaibility.

Keywords

Genetic Programming; Emperical Mode Decomposition; Globally Prime.

GECCO'14, July 12–16, 2014, Vancouver, BC, Canada.

http://dx.doi.org/10.1145/2598394.2609851

1. INTRODUCTION

Electroencephalography (EEG) [1] is the recording of electrical activity which contains information about human brain functionality and the disorders of the nervous system. Although not a brain scan as the term is usually used, the EEG, or electroencephalograph, deserves mention as one of the first ways of non-invasive observing human brain activity. An EEG is a recording of electrical signals from the brain made by hooking up electrodes to the subject's scalp. EEG accurately measures the deviations of electric signals within short period of time through multiple electrodes placed on the human scalp, the changes in these electric signals are measured in terms of voltage fluctuations of brain. The information about the human brain and neurological disorders is found through the output of the electrodes. EEG allow researchers to follow electrical impulses across the surface of the brain. An EEG can show the state of a person such as numb, awake, asleep because the characteristic patterns of current vary for the aforementioned states. One important use of EEGs has been to show how long it takes the brain to process various stimuli.

Epilepsy [3] is a brain disorder in which clusters of nerve cells, or neurons, in the brain sometimes signal abnormally. In epilepsy, the normal pattern of neuronal activity becomes disturbed, causing strange sensations, emotions, and behavior, or sometimes convulsions, muscle spasms, and loss of consciousness. The Epilepsy is characterized by sudden and recurrent malfunction of the brain which is termed *seizure*. Ictal and Interictal [2] are the medical conditions of seizure, where the period of the seizure is represented by *Ictal* and the intermediate period between two seizures is represented by *Intericatal*. However we have to make a note that Interictal differs from that of a non-seizure signal. A prediction of the Ictal from Interictal could make the patient to put away from the next seizure. It is imprecise and erroneous to detect epilepsy by visual scanning of EEG Signals. The detection of epileptic seizures, which are convulsions accompanied by impaired consciousness, in the EEG signal is a vital part in the diagnosis of epilepsy. Nonetheless, Classification between the ictal and interictal is essential for the detection of Epileptic seizures.

A wide range of methods [18] have been proposed to forecast epileptic seizure by classifying seizure and non-seizure EEG signal which employed univariate techniques, eigen spectra of space delay correlation and covariance matrices [20], Hilbert-Huang transform[8], and autoregressive modeling and least-squares parameter estimator [7]. The aforementioned techniques [7],[18] though they exhibit good sensitivity. Yet, their specificity and accuracy are not at expected level.

Genetic programming (GP) [12] is an evolutionary learning methodology that offers a great potential for classification. GP is a very flexible heuristic technique that makes it very convenient to represent complex patterns in the form of trees and graphs, therefore working with various operations and functions becomes easier. Since GP is a search and optimization algorithm, it can be easily employed as the search algorithm for generating a classifier. Since the early 1990s, there have been a number of reports [12, 19, 21] on applying GP techniques to a range of classification problems. In previous research works, many authors came up with classification of EEG signals on basis of Least Squares - Support Vector Machine (LS-SVM) [16],[1]. But the advantage of using GP over LS-SVM is that the objective function can be changed without changing the algorithm, that is instead of the Mean Absolute Error (MAE), the sum of squared errors could be used. For the SVM, such a change requires reformulating the Quadratic Programming(QP) and the optimization algorithm. Similarly, the fitness function of the GP could be defined so as to generate parsimonious [10] solutions. Although parsimony can also be obtained with the SVM [15], this again requires reformulating and re-solving the optimization problem. In short, changing the objective for a GP requires no change to the algorithm; whereas changing the objective for the SVM requires solving a new mathematical programming problem, which effectively defines a new search operator. Though GP shows lots of advantages, but still there is a need to improve the current GP life cycle, because it does not give satisfactory results for classification problems. In GP life cycle, crossover and mutation operators are the most important operator for evolving solutions but it is also considered the most devastating in nature[6]. Further, we focused our work on improving the crossover and mutation operations and demonstrating the improvements in terms of classification accuracy, number of generations and time in later sections.

In this paper, we propose the new Constructive Crossover and Mutation operations (CCM) for Genetic Programming approach and its use for the classification of the EEG Signals. To achieve this goal, we initially extract the intrinsic mode functions (IMF's) from the each EEG Signal using Empirical mode decomposition (EMD) and we use two bandwidth parameters, namely Amplitude Parameter (BAM) and Frequency Parameter (BFM) for the classification purpose. The bandwidth parameters, calculated from the respective IMF's of each EEG Signal is used as the input feature set for the Genetic Programming for the classification of the EEG signals. Finally, we propose constructive crossover and mutation operations to improve the overall GP life cycle.

The remainder of this paper is organized as follows: Section 2, describes the experimental data, and its preprocessing steps Section 3, describes the preliminaries of GP life cycle. Section 4, gives the detail description of the proposed crossover and mutation (CCM) operators. Section 5, gives the experimental results and discussion and finally Section 6 concludes the paper.

2. EXPERIMENTAL DATA

2.1 EEG signal Dataset

An EEG dataset, which is available on-line in [4] is used. It contains three classes: 1) healthy, 2) epileptic subjects during seizure-free interval (interictal), 3) epileptic subjects during seizure interval (ictal). Each case has five datasets named: O, Z, F, N, and S. Sets O and Z are obtained from healthy subjects under condition of eyes open and closed; respectively by external surface electrodes. Sets F and N are attained from interictal subjects. Set F taken from epileptogenic zone of the brain shows focal interictal activity; set N obtained from hippocampal formation of the opposite hemisphere of the brain indicates non-focal interictal activity, and set S is got from an ictal subject. Each set contains 100 single channel EEG segments of 23.6 sec duration. Sampling frequency is 173.61 Hz, so each segment contains N = 4096 samples . These EEG Signals (one from each subset) are shown in Fig 1.

2.2 Data Preprocessing

This section shows how we extract features from EEG signals to use as an input for GP. To extract the features from the EEG signal we have to follow the following steps:

2.2.1 Empirical Mode Decomposition

The empirical mode decomposition (EMD) method was developed by Huang et al. [8] to decompose functions into a superposition of natural modes, each of which could be easily analyzed for their instantaneous frequencies and bandwidths.

EMD is basically a method of breaking down a signal without leaving the time domain introduced for analysis of nonlinear and non- stationary signals. It can be compared to other analysis methods like Fourier Transforms and wavelet decomposition. The algorithm includes the following steps: 1. Calculate the IMF for each iteration using EMD on EEG signals. 2. Calculate two features namely Frequency parameter and Amplitude parameter using Hilbert transform applied on IMF's for each iteration. 3. Generate a Bandwidth parameter by combining Frequency parameter and Amplitude parameter.

2.2.2 Calculation of Intrinsic Mode functions (IMF)

Using the EMD algorithm, we obtain intrinsic mode functions (IMF), which were generated at each scale, going from fine to coarse, by an iterative procedure to locally isolate the modal behavior.

In contrast to the aforementioned Fourier transform and wavelet transform, the EMD decomposes any given data into intrinsic mode functions (IMF) and a residual function that are not set analytically and are instead determined by an analyzed sequence alone. The basis functions are in this case derived adaptively directly from input data. An IMF

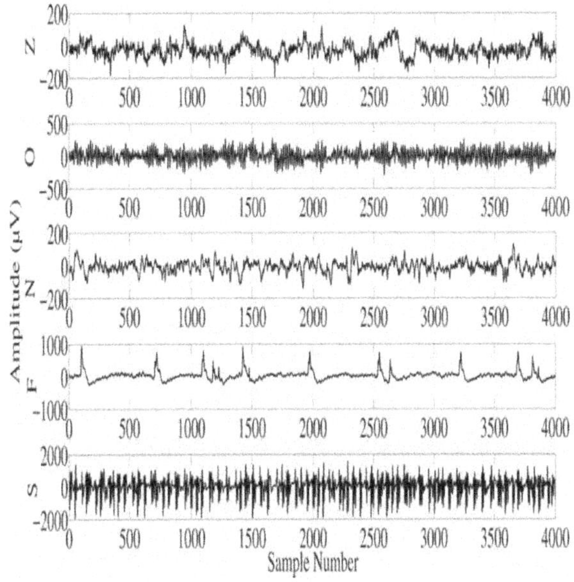

Figure 1: Example of EEG signals from each of the five subsets (Z, O, N, F, and S).

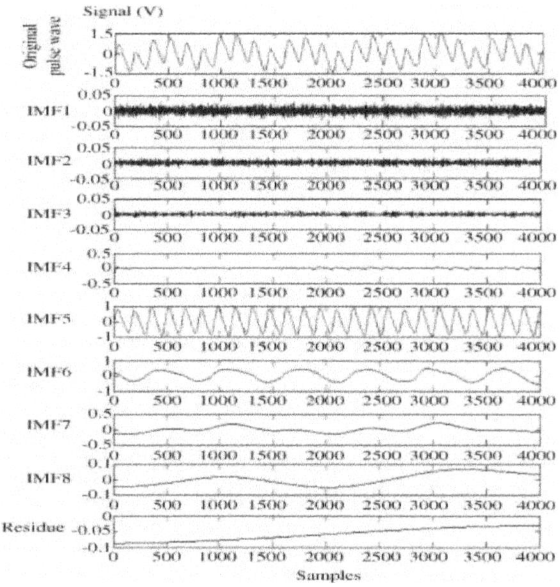

Figure 2: 8 IMF's extracted from EMD of a EEG Signal).

resulting from the EMD shall satisfy only the following requirements: 1. The number of IMF extrema (the sum of the maxima and minima) and the number of zero-crossings must either be equal or differ at most by one; 2. At any point of an IMF the mean value of the envelope defined by the local maxima and the envelope defined by the local minima shall be zero. The algorithm as proposed by Huang requires the identification of all local extrema that are further connected by cubic spline lines to produce the upper and the lower envelopes.

We use a process called sifting [13] to obtain the final IMF. The sifting process is repeated until a certain given stoppage criterion is met. This continues until all IMFs are extracted. The sifting process usually stops when the residue, for example, contains no more than two extrema. At the end of the decomposition, the original EEG Signal is represented as as the sum of IMF's and the final residue. The IMFs generated by EMD process on the 23.6 s EEG signal are shown in Fig 2. Empirical mode decomposition can successively separate the intrinsic oscillatory modes of signals into a finite number of IMFs. At the end of the decomposition, two bandwidth parameters(B_{am} and B_{fm}) are generated for every IMF [5].

2.3 Analytical Representation of EEG signal

Empirical mode decomposition can successively separate the intrinsic oscillatory modes of signals into a finite number of IMFs. At the end of the decomposition, The original EEG Signal is represented as

$$x(t) = \sum_{i=1}^{n} C_i(t) + R(t)$$

where n is the number of IMFs, Ci is the ith IMF and $R(t)$ is the final residue. The analytic signal of any real IMF A(t) is represented as:

$$A(t) = \sqrt{c^2(t) + c_H^2(t)}$$

Where $c(t)$ is the IMF and $c_H(t)$ refer to Hilbert transform of IMF. The instantaneous frequency $\omega(t)$ is defined as:

$$\omega(t) = \frac{d\varnothing(t)}{dt}$$

where $\varnothing(t)$ is instantaneous phase. Then calculate the center frequency which can be defined as:

$$< \omega > = \frac{1}{E}\int \omega |Z(\omega)|^2 \, d\omega$$

where E is the energy of analytic signal and $Z(\omega)$ is the Fourier transform of analytic signal. The amplitude parameter and the frequency parameter are defined respectively.

$$B_{am}^2 = \frac{1}{E}\int \left(\frac{dA(t)}{dt}\right)^2 dt$$

$$B_{fm}^2 = \frac{1}{E}\int \left(\frac{d\varnothing(t)}{dt} - < \omega >\right)^2 A^2(t)\, dt$$

The total bandwidth of analytic IMF x(t) is defined as:

$$B = \sqrt{B_{am}^2 + B_{fm}^2}$$

These Bam and Bfm serve as the input features for our Genetic Programming.

3. PRELIMINARIES OF GP

To build the GP based classifierfor EEG signals classification we had to follow the following steps:

3.1 Multi tree Classifier

In GP every individual is represented in the form of trees. So, for a two class problem a possible classifier or an individual is generally represented by a singletree (T). For a pattern x, the single tree is constructed for two classes as follows:

$$\begin{aligned} &if\ T(x) \geq 0, x \in class\ 1 \\ &else, x \in class\ 2 \end{aligned} \tag{1}$$

The single tree representation of the classifier is sufficient for a two-class problem. This scheme can be extended to a multicategory classification problem. In our design, every chromosome or individual will have a tree for every class. So, a possible solution or an individual for the GP is represented by c trees denoted by $(T_1, T_2, ...T_c)$. For a pattern x, the condition of belongingness corresponding to a class is given as follows:

$$if\ T_i(x) \geq 0\ and\ T_j(x) < 0\ \forall j \neq i, j \in \{1, 2, ...c\}$$
$$then\ x \in class\ i$$

3.2 Initialization

In GP, first we have to generate initial population for performing operations on it. The terminal and function sets are important components for generating the initial population. The terminal set consists of the variables and constants of the programs. The functions are several mathematical functions, such as addition, subtraction, division, multiplication. Trees for each of the individual are initialized randomly using the function set F and the terminal set T. The function set F and terminal set T used here are as follows:

$$F = \{+, -, *, /\}$$
$$T = \{feature\ variablesofEEGsignals, R\}. \quad (2)$$

Where R contains randomly generated constants in [0.0 to 10.0]. We initialize trees using the ramped half-and-half method [6]. The +, -, and * operators have their usual meanings (addition, subtraction, and multiplication), while / represents protected division, which is the usual division operator except that a divide by zero gives a result of zero. Each of these functions takes two arguments.

3.3 Fitness Measure

The most difficult and most important concept of GP is the fitness function. The fitness function determines how well a program is able to solve the problem. The GP is guided by the fitness function to search for the most efficient computer program to solve a given problem. A simple measure of fitness has been adopted for the classification problem and given as follows:

$$Fitness = \frac{n}{N} \quad (3)$$

where n= Number of Samples correctly classified and

N=Total number of training samples.

The GP is trained with the set of N number of training samples, $X_{tr} = \{x_1, x_2, ...x_N\}$. While training, the response of a tree T_i for a pattern x is expected to be as follows:

$$T_i(x) \geq 0\ if\ x\ \in\ class\ i$$
$$T_i(x) < 0\ if\ x \neq class\ i$$

In other words, a classifier with c trees is said to correctly classify a sample x, if and only if all of its trees correctly classify that sample. If we emphasize that a training sample is from class k than we say that tree T_k correctly classifies x, if $T_k(x) > 0$. On the other hand, the tree $T_{j,j} \neq_k$ is said to correctly classify x, if $T_j(x) < 0$. For each correct classification of a training sample by a classifier, its fitness is increased by 1.

Table 1: COMMON PARAMETERS FOR ALL DATASETS

Parameters	Values
Probability of Crossover Operation (P_c)	50%
Number of individuals selected for Crossover Operation	(N_c)
Probability of Reproduction Operation (P_r)	20%
Number of individuals selected for Reproduction Operation	(N_r)
Probability of Mutation Operation (P_m)	30%
Number of individuals selected for Mutation Operation	(N_m)
Population Size (k)	300
Number of Generations	40
Initial Maximum Depth	6
Initial Minimum Depth	3

3.4 Methods and Parameters

In proposed approach, we used tree structure to represent genetic programs [14]. The ramped half-and-half method [6] is used in generating programs in the initial population. The proposed crossover operator is described in the next Section. The point mutation technique [17] is used. The reproduction operator simply copied the best individuals into the population in the next generation to make sure the best individual programs are not lost during evolution.

Table 1 describes the parameters for the GP process. These parameters values are primarily chosen based on the heuristic guidelines on the choice of parameters [6] and an empirical search through initial experiments on GP with the standard crossover operator. Then, we checked those parameter values on the new approach and found that they also could do a reasonably good job.

3.5 Termination Criteria

In this approach, the learning/evolutionary process is terminated when one of the following conditions is met:

1. The number of generations reaches the maximum generations.
2. The classification problem has been solved on the training set, that is, all objects of interest in the training set have been correctly classified.

4. PROPOSED WORK

In this section, we proposed new constructive crossover and mutation operations (CCM) to improve the overall GP life

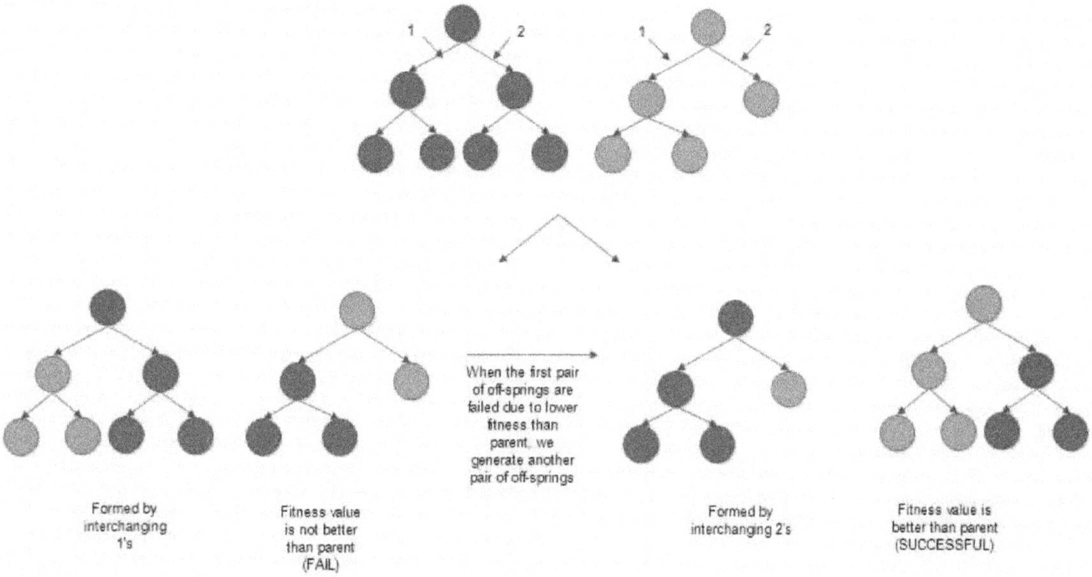

Figure 3: Constructive Crossover operation

cycle. The detailed description of both these operators are described next:

4.1 Constructive Crossover

In our GP process we first transfers the best N_r individuals from the current population to next generation by applying the reproduction operation. Then on remaining individuals we apply the crossover and mutation operation. For selecting the individuals for crossover operations, various authors applied various types of tournament [9]. The idea behind this, is to find the individual which are best for performing the crossover operations. The overall logic of finding the best parent for performing the crossover is little suspicious because of following two reasons. First is that, by just seeing the parent, nobody can guarantee the better off-springs. The second reason is that, even a individual with a lower fitness can produce better off-springs. Therefore, we propose a constructive crossover in which we we select all the individuals for crossover operation (N_c and N_m) which are left after reproduction. We make the pairs of these individuals and perform the crossover operation. We generate the off-springs from selected couple and check whether the off-springs are better than parents or not in terms of fitness. If they are better in terms of fitness, we kept them otherwise reject and repeat this process again till we get two individuals better than parent. We repeat this process for all N_c and N_m individuals. Thus, in this way we had integrated the local hill climbing method in crossover operation. We repeat this process for all the pairs.

Another concept of globally prime off-springs we had introduced in this method. That is selecting the top N_c off-springs on the basis of fitness from all the off-springs generated from crossover operation. The top N_c off-springs in terms of fitness, are present on the top N_c position in the max-heap all the remaining off-springs which are present at lower position in max-heap are deleted. A max-heap is a complete binary tree, in which the value in each internal

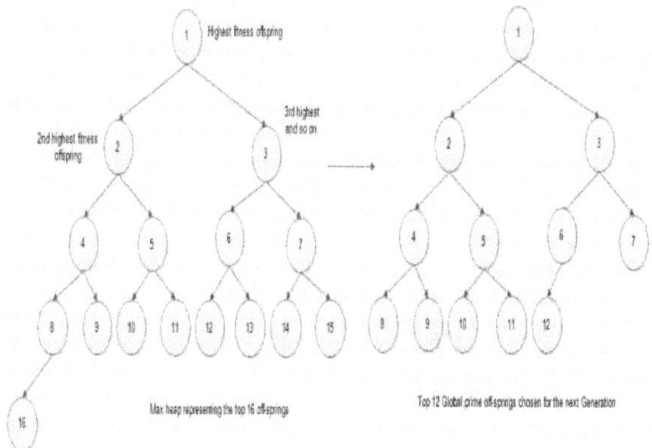

Figure 4: Selection of Global Prime Off-springs from Max-Heap

node is greater than or equal to the values in the children of that node.

To explain this approach we are presenting a small example. In this we are taking population size as 10. We are applying reproduction on 2 individuals, crossover on 6 individuals and mutation on 2 individuals. First we transfer the 2 individuals from the population by applying reproduction operator. Than 8 individuals are left, out of which we have to apply crossover on 6 individuals and mutation on 2 individuals. But, rather selecting 6 individuals for crossover we select all the 8 individuals for it and apply constructive crossover. That is, generate 16 individuals from these 8 individuals which are better than parent in terms of fitness and kept in a max-heap. Than from these 16 individuals we select the 12 globally prime off-springs of max-heap (the top 12 off-springs of max-heap). That is, top 12 individuals from these 16 individuals on the basis of fitness and delete the remaining 4 individuals. We select only 12 because the numbers of crossover individuals are 6 only. So, from them only 12 off-springs can be selected. The remaining two parents whose off-springs are not transferred to next generation are automatically selected for constructive mutation operation. The advantage of this method is that we transfer the globally prime off-springs to next generation and the parents which are not able to generate better off-springs are chosen for mutation operation.

Algorithm 1 Algorithm for Constructive Crossover

1: Begin
2: Generate initial classifier population (k).
3: Randomly select fixed percentages of the initial population for crossover crossover (P_c), mutation (P_m) and reproduction (P_r).
4: Group the total population left after reproduction (N_c and N_m) into pairs.
5: Apply Hill Climbing method that is take the parent pair and genrate off-springs from them till we get the better off-springs than parents.
6: Repeat this process for all the pairs and generate the max-heap.
7: Select the top (P_c) globaly Prime offsprings from the max-heap and delete the remaining individuals for the next generation.
8: Repeat steps 2 to 7, until we reach required number of generations or required fitness satisfaction percentage.
9: End

4.2 Constructive Mutation Operation

To further improve the GP life cycle, we propose a constructive mutation operation. In constructive mutation operation, we chose those individuals which are left after reproduction and crossover operations. Then, we apply local hill climbing search on them that is, generate the off-springs till we get the better off-springs than parents. The advantage of using constructive mutation is that we reduce the destructive nature of mutation operation by transferring only the better individuals than parents to next generation. Another advantage is that we chose the mutation parents after crossover and reproduction. So the individuals which are not good for producing better off-springs than parents are changed in our mutation.

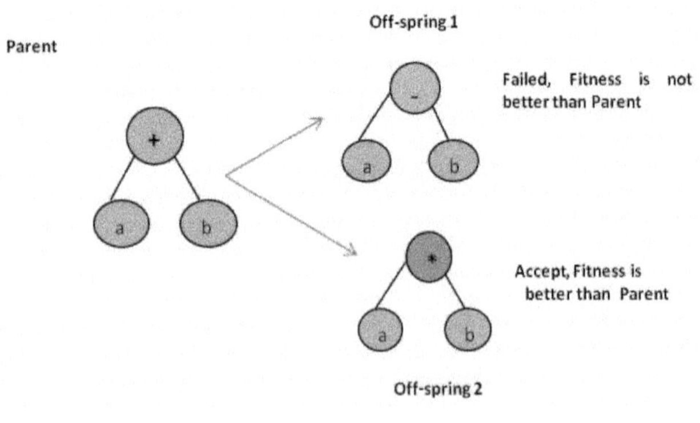

Figure 5: Constructive Mutation Operation

5. EMPERICAL RESULTS AND DISCUSSION

We have used the data described in Section 2, for our experiment. It contains three classes: 1) healthy, 2) epileptic subjects during seizure-free interval (interictal), 3) epileptic subjects during seizure interval (ictal).

Algorithm 2 Algorithm for Constructive Mutation

1: Begin
2: Generate initial classifier population (k).
3: Take the individual (N_m) which are left after reproduction and crossover operations.
4: Apply Hill Climbing method that is take the parent pair and generate off-springs from them till we get the better off-springs than parents.
5: Repeat this process for all the pairs and generate the max-heap.
6: Transfer the individual tot he next generation.
7: Repeat steps 2 to 6, until we reach required number of generations or required fitness satisfaction percentage.
8: End

5.1 Comparison with Other Approches

To evaluate the generalizability of our approach, we used 10 fold cross-validation [11] scheme (CV). Here, the data are divided into 10 parts of equal size. We use 9/10 of the data to train the GP model, and we use the remaining 1/10 of data to test the model and estimate the classification accuracy, which is how well our approach is able to classify the EEG signals. We performed 10 GP runs, each time leaving out a different 1/10 of data for testing [11]. A classification accuracy is estimated as an average across the 10 cross-validations and standard+ mean deviation of the results are calculated.

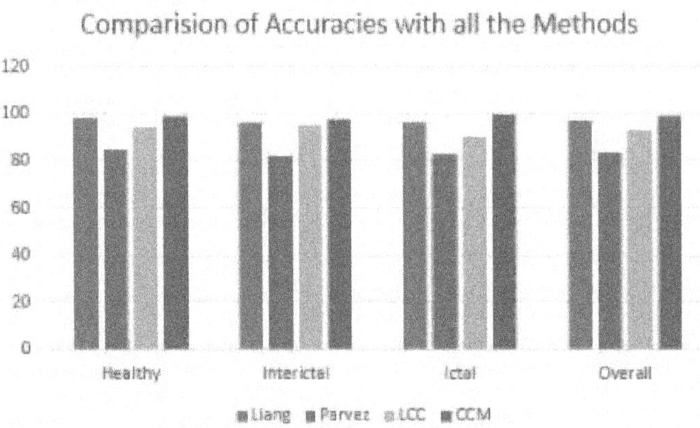

Figure 6: Comparison of Accuracies of all the classes and overall accuracies with all the methods

To compare our work we use the work of Liang et al.[16], Parvez et al.[1] and Zhang et al.[22] because Liang and Parvez had use the same dataset for classification of EEG signals and Zhang had shown the better classification accuracy by improving the crossover operator for object classification problem. Therefore, we found these works more appropriate to compare our work. Liang and Parvez, both used LS-SVM technique for the classification of EEG signals and how ever their accuracies were 97% and 83.25% respectively which is less than the accuracy achieved by CCM which is shown in Table2. The main reason for the improved accuracies is our both constructive crossover and mutation

Table 2: CLASSIFICATION ACCURACY FOR THE TEST SET WITH LIANG; PARVEZ; LCC: LOOSENESS CONTROLLED CROSSOVER; CONSTRUCTIVE CROSSOVER AND MUTATION OPERATION METHODS

Methods	Accuracy of Healthy Class	Accuracy of Interictal Class	Accuracy of Ictal Class	Overall Accuracy
Liang et al.	98.58 ± 1.13	96.43 ± 1.53	96.08 ± 1.43	97.03 ± 1.36
Parvez et al.	84.89 ± 1.18	82.25 ± 1.74	82.61 ± 1.59	83.25 ± 1.51
LCC([22])	94.47 ± 1.22	95.17 ± 1.52	89.87 ± 1.26	93.17 ± 1.33
CCM	99.19 ± 0.14	97.41 ± 1.47	99.47 ± 0.04	98.69 ± 0.55

operation. The Constructive crossover operation finds the better off-springs which help to find the optimal solution fast. The constructive mutation operation brings the diversity on those parents who have not been able to perform well in constructive crossover operation. Therefore, our both these operators work in tandem to bring the improved solution fast.

5.2 Advantage of Classifying the EEG Signals

As the EEG signals are divided into three classes. Each of this class has their properties. If a person is suffering from epilepsy then using our method its 97.41% accurate to say that he/she belongs to the interictal class and suffering from epilepsy of non-seizure and its 99.47% accurate to say that he/she belongs to the ictal class and suffering from epilepsy of seizure and these results shown tremendous improvements as compared to the other methods of Liang et al.[16], Parvez et al.[1] and Zhang et al.[22] as shown in Fig ??. In this paper, we also improved the GP life cycle by improving the crossover and mutation operations and gives the impressive result for EEG signal classification which is shown in Table 2 and 3. It improves the accuracy of the classifier with a fair amount. We further compared our work with LCC method in terms of number of generation and time required to reach the accuracy because we also uses the hill climbing method to improve the crossover operator as used in LCC method but with further changes. It is found that our method showed improvement in both the departments than LCC method. Our method has removed the issue of selecting the crossover parent by selecting all the parent for crossover which are left after reproduction. This increases the number of fitness evaluation for a single generation, but eventually we got the desired fitness in lesser number of generations than LCC, so the number of fitness evaluation required in our method is almost same as that in LCC. We reach to desired fitness in early generations than LCC because by performing the constructive crossover we transfer the globally prime off-springs which showed tremendous improvement in fitness than parent. The individuals or we can say poor parents poor parents which are not capable of generating good off-springs are used for mutation. This helps in bringing the diversity in poor individuals very early due to which the chances of getting the solution fast is improved which are demonstrated in our result which is shown in Fig 7.

6. CONCLUSIONS

The goal of this paper is to improve the crossover and mutation operations of GP for classification of EEG signals. It is successfully achieved by developing a new constructive

Table 3: COMPARISON OF NUMBER OF GENERATIONS AND TRAINING TIME FOR THE TEST SET WITH LCC: LOOSENESS CONTROLLED CROSSOVER; CONSTRUCTIVE CROSSOVER AND MUTATION OPERATION

Methods	LCC	CCM
Number of generations	22.50 ± 0.76	18.25 ± 0.25
Time(in sec)	12.84 ± 2.39	11.98 ± 0.25

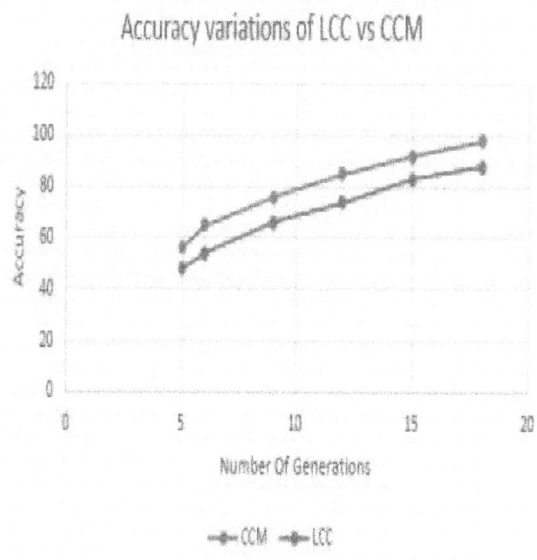

Figure 7: Comparision of Accuracies with Number of generations in LCC and CCM

crossover and mutation operators (CCM). Thus enhance the performance of GP life cycle. In this approach, a local hill climbing search method is used with crossover and mutation operators to generate better off-springs than parent. We choose all individuals which are left after reproduction to perform the crossover operations. Then we generate 2 better off-springs than parent for all the individuals. Then, we compare the off-springs of all the parent and put them in a max-heap. After that we transfer the top off-springs of max heap to next generation. In this way, we ensured that the globally Prime off-springs are transferred to the next generation. The advantage of constructive crossover is that, the best individuals are chosen for crossover and the individuals which does not perform well in crossover are chosen for constructive mutation operation. Thus, we remove the overhead of applying the tournament for selecting the crossover individuals. The constructive mutation operation also apply local hill climbing which helps in bringing the off-springs better than parents. The another advantage of constructive mutation is the poor parents who doesn't generate better off-springs are further improved by providing diversity to them. This approach is experimented and tested with EEG signal dataset and compared with the Liang, Parvez and Zhang methods. Improvements in terms of classification accuracy in the proposed approach is observed when compared with all the methods. The results suggest that this new approach outperformed all the operators in terms of the classification accuracy.

7. REFERENCES

[1] M. Z. Parvez and M. Paul. Features extraction and classification for ictal and interictal eeg signals using emd and dct. In *Computer and Information Technology (ICCIT), 2012 15th International Conference on*, pages 132–137. IEEE, 2012.

[2] Z. M. Parvez and M. Paul. Classification of ictal and interictal eeg signals. In *IASTED conference on Biomedical Engineering*, pages 791–031, 2013.

[3] S. J. Husain and K. S. Rao. Epileptic seizures classification from eeg signals using neural networks. *International Proceedings of Computer Science & Information Technology*, 37, 2012.

[4] R. G. Andrzejak, K. Lehnertz, F. Mormann, C. Rieke, P. David, and C. E. Elger. Indications of nonlinear deterministic and finite-dimensional structures in time series of brain electrical activity: Dependence on recording region and brain state. *Physical Review E*, 64(6):061907, 2001.

[5] V. Bajaj and R. B. Pachori. Classification of seizure and nonseizure eeg signals using empirical mode decomposition. *Information Technology in Biomedicine, IEEE Transactions on*, 16(6):1135–1142, 2012.

[6] W. Banzhaf, P. Nordin, R. E. Keller, and F. D. Francone. Genetic programming: An introduction: On the automatic evolution of computer programs and its applications (the morgan kaufmann series in artificial intelligence). 1997.

[7] L. Chisci, A. Mavino, G. Perferi, M. Sciandrone, C. Anile, G. Colicchio, and F. Fuggetta. Real-time epileptic seizure prediction using ar models and support vector machines. *Biomedical Engineering, IEEE Transactions on*, 57(5):1124–1132, 2010.

[8] F. Duman, N. Ozdemir, and E. Yildirim. Patient specific seizure prediction algorithm using hilbert-huang transform. In *Biomedical and Health Informatics (BHI), 2012 IEEE-EMBS International Conference on*, pages 705–708. IEEE, 2012.

[9] Y. Fang and J. Li. A review of tournament selection in genetic programming. In *Advances in Computation and Intelligence*, pages 181–192. Springer, 2010.

[10] C. Gagné, M. Schoenauer, M. Parizeau, and M. Tomassini. Genetic programming, validation sets, and parsimony pressure. In *Genetic Programming*, pages 109–120. Springer, 2006.

[11] T. Hastie, R. Tibshirani, J. Friedman, T. Hastie, J. Friedman, and R. Tibshirani. *The elements of statistical learning*, volume 2. Springer, 2009.

[12] D. Howard, S. Roberts, and R. Brankin. Target detection in sar imagery by genetic programming. *Advances in Engineering Software*, 30(5):303–311, 1999.

[13] D. Kim and H.-S. Oh. Emd: A package for empirical mode decomposition and hilbert spectrum. *The R Journal*, 1(1):40–46, 2009.

[14] J. R. Koza. *Genetic Programming: vol. 1, On the programming of computers by means of natural selection*, volume 1. MIT press, 1992.

[15] Y.J. Lee and O. L. Mangasarian. Rsvm: Reduced support vector machines. In *Proceedings of the first SIAM international conference on data mining*, pages 5–7. SIAM, 2001.

[16] S.-F. Liang, H.-C. Wang, and W.-L. Chang. Combination of eeg complexity and spectral analysis for epilepsy diagnosis and seizure detection. *EURASIP Journal on Advances in Signal Processing*, 2010:62, 2010.

[17] A. Purohit, A. Bhardwaj, A. Tiwari, and N. S. Choudhari. Removing code bloating in crossover operation in genetic programming. In *Recent Trends in Information Technology (ICRTIT), 2011 International Conference on*, pages 1126–1130. IEEE, 2011.

[18] J. Rasekhi, M. R. K. Mollaei, M. Bandarabadi, C. A. Teixeira, and A. Dourado. Preprocessing effects of 22 linear univariate features on the performance of seizure prediction methods. *Journal of neuroscience methods*, 217(1):9–16, 2013.

[19] A. Song, V. Ciesielski, and H. E. Williams. Texture classifiers generated by genetic programming. In *Evolutionary Computation, 2002. CEC'02. Proceedings of the 2002 Congress on*, volume 1, pages 243–248. IEEE, 2002.

[20] J. R. Williamson, D. W. Bliss, D. W. Browne, and J. T. Narayanan. Seizure prediction using eeg spatiotemporal correlation structure. *Epilepsy & Behavior*, 25(2):230–238, 2012.

[21] J. F. Winkeler and B. Manjunath. Genetic programming for object detection. *Genetic Programming*, pages 330–335, 1997.

[22] M. Zhang, X. Gao, and W. Lou. A new crossover operator in gp for object classification. Technical report, Technical Report CS-TR-06-02, SMSCS, VUW, Wellington, 2006.

Clarke and Parkes Error Grid Analysis of Diabetic Glucose Models obtained with Evolutionary Computation

J. Ignacio Hidalgo*
hidalgo@ucm.es

J. Manuel Colmenar *
jmcolmenar@ajz.ucm.es

Jose L. Risco-Martín*
jlrisco@ucm.es

Esther Maqueda
Endocrinology and Nutrition S.
Hospital Virgen de la Salud,
Toledo (Spain)
esthermaq@gmail.com

Marta Botella
Endocrinology and Nutrition S.
Hospital U. Príncipe Asturias,
Alcalá de Henares (Spain)
marta.botella@salud.madrid.org

Jose-Antonio Rubio
Endocrinology and Nutrition S.
Hospital U. Príncipe Asturias,
Alcalá de Henares (Spain)
joseantonio.rubio@salud.madrid.org

Alfredo Cuesta-Infante*
acuestai@ucm.es

Juan Lanchares*
julandan@ucm.es

Oscar Garnica*
ogarnica@ucm.es

*Adaptive and Bioinspired Systems Group (ABSys)
Facultad de Informática
Universidad Complutense de Madrid (Spain)

ABSTRACT

Diabetes mellitus is a disease that affects to hundreds of millions of people worldwide. Maintaining a good control of the disease is critical to avoid severe long-term complications. In recent years, a lot of research has been made to improve the quality of life of the diabetic patient, especially in the automation of glucose level control. One of the main problems that arises in the (semi) automatic control of diabetes, is to obtain a model that explains the behavior of blood glucose levels with insulin, food intakes and other external factors, fitting the characteristics of each individual or patient. Recently, Grammatical Evolution (GE), has been proposed to solve this lack of models. A proposal based on GE was able to obtain customized models of five in-silico patient data with a mean percentage average error of 13.69 %, modeling well also both hyper and hypoglycemic situations. In this paper we have extended the study of Error Grid Analysis (EGA) to prediction models in up to 8 in-silico patients. EGA is commonly used in Endocrinology to test the clinical significance of differences between measurements and real value of blood glucose, but has not been used before as a metric in obtention of glycemia models.

Categories and Subject Descriptors

I.2.8 [**Artificial Intelligence**]: Problem Solving, Control Methods, and Search—*Heuristic methods*; G.1.6 [**Numerical Analysis**]: Optimization—*Global optimization*

Keywords

Grammatical Evolution, Modeling, Diabetes

GECCO'14, July 12–16, 2014, Vancouver, BC, Canada.
Copyright 2014 ACM 978-1-4503-2881-4/14/07 ...$15.00.
http://dx.doi.org/10.1145/2598394.2609856 .

1. INTRODUCTION AND MOTIVATION

Diabetes mellitus is a disease affecting more than 366 million people worldwide. According to the World Health Organization (WHO, http://www.who.int) those figures are expected to double by 2030, so in some forums, diabetes is considered the epidemic of the XXI Century. Many factors influence the appearance of the disease, but all diabetics suffer a defect in either the secretion or in the action of insulin, which is essential for the control of blood glucose levels. The result is that cells does not assimilate sugar and, as a consequence, there is a rise in blood glucose levels, or hyperglycemia. According to the American Diabetes Association (ADA, http://www.diabetes.org/) we can distinguish four types of diabetes:

- Type 1 Diabetes (T1DM): cells do not produce insulin because of an autoimmune process. T1 diabetics needs to inject insulin or wear an insulin pump to control glucose levels.
- Type 2 Diabetes (T2DM): results from insulin resistance, where cells fail to use insulin properly, sometimes combined with an absolute insulin deficiency.
- Gestational Diabetes: appears in the gestation period in one out of ten pregnant women. Pregnancy is a change in the body's metabolism, since the fetus uses the mother's energy for food, oxygen and others. This causes a decrease in the secretion of insulin from the mother. Some T2 diabetics can control the illness only with exercise, pills or a combination of them.
- Other Types: such as problems on β -cells, genetic defects affecting insulin action, induced by drugs, genetic syndromes, etc.

It is important to maintain a good glycemic control to prevent the acute complications specific to diabetes (diabetic ketoacidosis and hypoglycemia, defined as blood glucose value lower than $70mg/dl$). Multiple studies have also demonstrated that good glycemic control prevents chronic complications (mainly nephropathy, retinopathy and microangiopathy).

Diabetic retinopathy, for instance is a leading cause of blindness in the world and visual disturbances in patients between 25 and 74 years old. regarding diabetic nephropathy, the percentage of patients who develop kidney failure has decreased significantly in recent years due to improved metabolic control, more aggressive treatment of hypertension and the use of drugs that inhibit the renin-angiotensin system: This means a reduction in the number of patients who have to be subjected to dialysis and / or kidney transplantation. In T1DM cohort of DCCT[1] / EDIC[2], less than 2 % (10 of 711) of patients treated with intensive therapy developed renal failure.

Regarding neuropathy, approximately 50 % of diabetic patients develop neuropathy. This leads to increased morbidity, including infections, ulcers and amputations. Diabetic patients are also at increased risk for cardiovascular disease (myocardial infarction, angina, silent ischemia). The coronary risk of a diabetic patient is similar to that of a person who has previously had a heart attack. The EDIC study showed that intensive therapy was able to reduce cardiovascular morbidity and mortality.

Summing up, in recent years, it has been shown that a strict glycemic control in critically ill patients improves performance and reduces medical costs [1] [14]. Unfortunately glucose levels control is a demanding and difficult task for both patients and their families. To keep good levels of blood glucose, the patient must perform regular measurements (which involves at least one puncture in each measure), insulin dose estimation, carbohydrates estimation, analyze all this information somehow and to have some capacity of prediction to know what level of glucose would have if ingested a certain amount of food or injected with a quantity of an insulin of a certain kind. In fact, the objective is to avoid not only long periods of hyperglycemia (glucose levels $\geq 120mg/dl$) but also episodes of severe hypoglycemia (glucose levels $\leq 40mg/dl$) that can lead to patient death.

One of the higher barriers for fully automatic insulin administration is the lack of individualized models of glucose levels. Recently, the application of evolutionary computation for obtaining customized models of patients, has been proposed [10]. Unlike previous approaches, that obtain averaged models, the proposal of Hidalgo et al. uses Grammatical Evolution (GE) to obtain individualized models. [10] and [11] outlined preliminary and promising results with 5 in-silico patients.

The aim of this paper is twofold. First, we would like to share the explained proposal with the audience of the MedGec Workshop, in order to receive the feedback of an expert community. Second, we have extended the work in [10] in several ways:

- We have obtained validated models for three new in-silico patients. The objective is to test the robustness of the evolutionary approach, using more variety of patients and including at least one with hypoglycemia.
- We have analyzed experimental results in terms of Error Grid Analysis (EGA) for the eight in-silico patients. EGA is commonly used in Endocrinology to test the clinical significance of differences between measurements and real value of blood glucose. We present here EGAs performed with two approaches: Clarke [3] and Parkes [17] error grids.
- We propose to apply EGA analysis in the generation and optimization of prediction models.

[1]Diabetes Control and Complications Trial

[2]Epidemiology of Diabetes Interventions and Complications

The rest of the paper is organized as follows. Section 2 gives a brief description of the related work in glycaemia models. Section 3 explains how to obtain individualized models by means of Grammatical Evolution. Section 4 presents the experimental setup, giving detailed information of the data. Section 4 also remembers the basis of EGA under both approaches, Clarke and Parkes. In Section 5 we present the experimental analysis and discussion. We conclude the paper and propose future work on Section 6.

2. RELATED WORK

Our ultimate goal is to provide a tool that allows patients to improve glucose control. As we have mentioned, glucose level control is a hard task, because patients need to perform blood glucose regular measurements, develop some ability to estimate carbohydrates units or rations, incorporate some knowledge about their personal bodies or feelings, and eventually make an insulin dose estimation. Thus, a diabetic patient needs to mentally construct the abstract model of his glucose levels and apply a kind-of algorithm to decide the insulin to be injected with each meal or at some times between two meals. One of the main problems in the automation of blood glucose levels control is the lack of reliable models in response to both insulin and the other various factors involved. We can find in the literature some approaches that provide models for the average case [21][2]. However, it is well known that each patient has a different metabolism, insulin resistance, and other features. Unfortunately, there are hardly few approaches adapted to the particularities of each patient. Other important aspect that we should have in mind is the delay between insulin administration and the appearance of insulin in the blood stream with the use of subcutaneous (SC) insulin. This delay time limits the achievable control performance on subcutaneous administration of insulin.

Most of the models in the literature apply classical modeling techniques, resulting in linear equations defined profiles, or models with a limited set of inputs [4]. There are other interesting approximations, for instance, Heusden et al. [21] proposed to use personalized information of the patient, easily accesible by the specialist or the automatic system. They construct robust models looking for improving the behavior on mismatches between estimated and real data. However, this approach is only useful with linear models and can not incorporate other important factors such as exercise or stress that clearly affect glycemias.

Apart from the mentioned works, we can find in the literature other proposals that use control models. Next, we classify them in three categories:

- **Solutions by commercial companies:** *Glucofacts Deluxe* by *Bayern*, *CoPilot Health Management System* by *Abbot*, and *MenaDiab* by *Menarini* are only some of them. Those approaches were designed to facilitate the control of diabetes. The main problem is that they work only for specific glucometers. Some of them provide also insulin recommendations, although the way the model is obtained is not available.
- **Models used in artificial pancreas systems or closed loop control models:** artificial pancreas systems are closed loop control systems trying to emulate the action of a pancreas [5] [20] . They are based on the assumption that it is possible to reach a good control with approximate models, provided that the model is related to the control objective [9][18]. The main risk is hypoglycemia as a result of excessive insulin administration and due to the lack of accurate individualized models. We can find also Autoregressive models (AR) [8][19] and protocols to improve the reliability of the models [7][5] [15].

- **Other personalized control approaches:** [12][6][13] are proposals following the clinical practice. Treatment for subjects with T1DM uses rates of basal insulin delivery, insulin to carbohydrate ratios (CHO) and individual correction factors, typically from observations of the specialist. Those models are often inaccurate, since clinical data in T1DM are not extensive enough to identify the exact models [7].

Evolutionary computation has a high potential to incorporate to the model factors that are difficult to quantify, in other words to collect system dynamics, allowing us to obtain individualized models since they are able to provide a solution for each set of data on a single patient.

3. METHODOLOGY

Figure 1 shows the proposed scheme for model induction and optimization. The scheme is based on a data set of patients with T1DM and, the result of the process are validated models of glucose. In this process, we use Grammatical Evolution (GE) to obtain a mathematical expression, which describes how glycemia varies as a function of a set of parameters. Input data set should include several observable factors that can be collected by the patient or recorded by monitoring systems. The actual level of glycaemia depends on several factors with different degrees of importance. Here, it is well known that the most important are glucose level, carbohydrate intakes and insulin injections. These are the parameters that our models do take into account to predict the future glucose level.

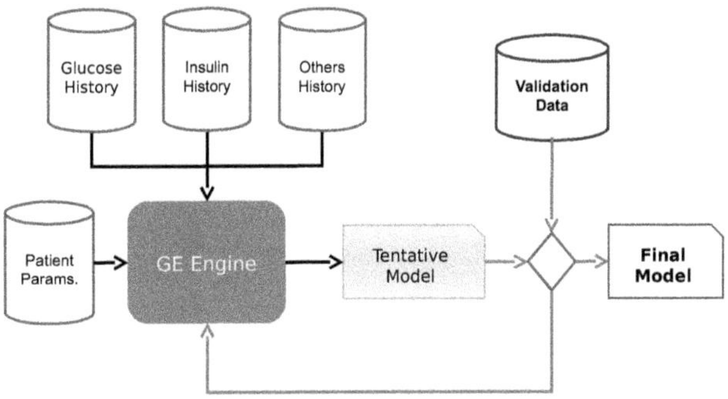

Figure 1: Model generation and optimization.

3.1 Problem description

Le us suppose that the patient is using two types of insulin, IS (Short term insulin) and IL (Long term insulin). We have registered the set of measures explained below. Given a set of measures

$$GL = \{gl_0, gl_1, \cdots, gl_n\}$$

of the glucose level of a patient, and knowing that gl_i was measured at time t_i. Given a set of intakes

$$CH = \{ch_0, ch_1, \cdots, ch_n\}$$

of carbohydrates units of a patient, and knowing that ch_i was eaten at time t_i. Given a set of injections of insulin of type S

$$IS = \{is_0, is_1, \cdots, is_n\}$$

and knowing that is_i was injected at time t_i. Given a set of injections of insulin of type L

$$IL = \{il_0, il_1, \cdots, il_n\}$$

and knowing that il_i was injected at time t_i. The problem of modeling the glucose blood level of a patient, in its simplified form, can

k	GL	CH	IS	IL
...	...	...	...	...
30	170.88974	0	0	0
31	171.55425	0	0	0
32	172.27976	0	3	12
33	173.05923	30	0	0
34	174.09018	0	0	0
...	...	...	...	...
40	237.54628	0	0	0
41	247.25104	20	0	0
42	250.72465	0	0	0
43	251.90543	0	0	0
...	...	...	...	...

Table 1: Portion of a 24-hours dataset for a in-silico patien (Joy Wilson).

be formulated as follows: Find an expression of estimated glucose values, denoted as $\widehat{GL}$

$$\widehat{GL}(k+1) = f(\widehat{GL}, CH, IS, IL), 0 \leq k \leq N \quad (1)$$

which minimizes the fitness function F, which tries to close the gap between real and estimated glucose values:

$$F = \sum_{i=0}^{n} \sqrt{(GL(i) - \widehat{GL}(i))^2}$$

Where $\widehat{GL}$ corresponds to previous estimated glucose values, CH corresponds to previously ingested carbohydrates and IS and IL correspond to previously injected insulin for both types, short and long effect. It should be noted that the model will provide estimated glucose values, denoted as $\widehat{GL}$. Hence, for each time step, estimated glucose is obtained by using previous estimated glucose values and actual carbohydrates and insulin units. Therefore, the dataset should provide input values for the variables in our glucose model proposal. Table 1 shows a reduced version of a data set for one of the in-silico patients under study.

In this way, the GE engine should be able to decide how F looks like. However, in order to guide the search of the evolutionary process, we do need a grammar that will both limit the search space and represent the behavior of the blood glucose level. Next, we detail the grammars that we studied in this work.

3.2 BNF Grammars for Modeling Glucose

Unlike traditional GAs, GE evolves a genetic code that determines the production process of this solution. The code translation process is determined by grammars represented as Backus Naur Forms (BNF) which is a notation for expressing context-free grammars. In brief, a BNF specification is a set of derivation rules, expressed in the form:

```
<symbol> ::= <expression>
```

The rules are composed of sequences of terminals and non terminals. Symbols that appear at the left are non-terminals while terminals never appear on a left side. In this case we can affirm that `<symbol>` is a non terminal and, although this is not a complete BNF specification, we can affirm also that `<expression>` will be also a non-terminal since those are always enclosed between the pair <>. So, in this case the non-terminal `<symbol>` will be replaced (indicated by `::=`) by an expression. The rest of the grammar must indicate the different possibilities.

A grammar is represented by the 4-Tuple {N, T, P, S}, being N the non-terminal set, T is the terminal set, P the production rules for the assignment of elements on N and T, and S is a start symbol which should appear in N. The options within a production rule are separated by a "|" symbol. For more details on the mapping process we refer the reader to [10] from where this last paragraph was borrowed.

The concrete form of f_{GL}, f_{CH}, f_{IS} and f_{IL} will be determined by GE engine with the help of a grammar. Figure 2 shows our first and most generic tested grammar. The three terms `<exprgluc>`, `<exprch>` and `<exprins>` correspond to f_{GL}, f_{CH} and f_{IN}, respectively, being f_{IN} a function of f_{IS} and f_{IL}. All of them are expressions that could use prefix operands like those in rule `V`, variables for each of one the terms, or combinations of them through operators in rule `VII`.

```
N = {func, expr, op, pre-op, dig, num, var}
T = { +,-,*,/, sin, cos, abs, exp, 0, 1, 2, 3, 4, 5, 6,
    7, 8, 9, 0, glucprev, chprev, insprev}
S =  {func}
P={I, II ,III ,IV ,V ,VI ,VII}

I <func> ::= glucprev <op> <expr>

II <var> ::= glucprev
        |chprev
        |insprev

III <expr> ::= <expr> <op> <expr>
|<pre-op> (<expr>)
|<var>

IV <op> ::= + | -| / | *

V <pre-op>::=sin|cos|abs|exp

VI <dig>::=0|1|2|3|4|5|6|7|8|9

VII <num>::=<dig>.<dig>|<dig>
```

Figure 2: First grammar (generic attempt).

The grammar in Figure 3 incorporates some knowledge of the problem, since we know that glucose levels rise when the patient eats and decrease when some insulin is injected into the blood flow. The general model will be approximated with expressions similar to (2), where any previous values of glucose, carbohydrates and insulin may be used. Hence, in this grammar carbohydrates are always added, while insulin values are always subtracted, as shown in rule `I`.

$$\widehat{GL}(k+1) = f_{gl}(\widehat{GL}(k-m)) + f_{ch}(CH(k-m)) - \\ -f_{in}(IS(k-m), IL(k-m)), 0 \leq m \leq k \quad (2)$$

3.3 Genetic Parameters

As with genetic programming, GE can use any search algorithm able to operate on integer or binary strings. We have selected a simple GA with single-point crossover and point mutation. Population initialization is made by randomly generating fixed integer strings. Table 2 shows the rest of the genetic and GE parameters (see [16] for more information on GE)

4. EXPERIMENTAL SETUP

In this section we describe the characteristics of the eight in-silico patients we deal with, as well as the configuration of each set of experiments. As we have explained, we predict a future value of

```
N = {func, exprgluc, gluc, exprch, varch, exprins, varins
    , op, preop, idx, cte, dgt}
T = { +,-,*,/, sin, cos, tan, exp, 0, 1, 2, 3, 4, 5, 6,
    7, 8, 9, 0, GL, CH, IS, IL, K}
S = {func}
P = {I, II ,III ,IV ,V ,VI ,VII, VIII, IX, X, XI, XII}

I     <func> ::= <exprgluc> + <exprch> - <exprins>

II    <exprgluc> ::= <preop> (<gluc>)
        |(<cte> <op> <gluc>)
        |<gluc>

III   <gluc> ::= #{GL[k_<idx>]}|#{K}

IV    <exprch> ::= <exprch> <op> <exprch>
        |<preop> (<exprch>)
        |<varch>

V     <varch> ::= #{CH[k_<idx>]}|#{K}|<cte>

VI    <exprins> ::= <exprins> <op> <exprins>
        |<preop> (<exprins>)
        |<varins>

VII   <varins> ::= #{IS[k_<idx>]}|#{IL[k_<idx>]}|#{K}
        |<cte>

VIII <op> ::=+|-|/|*
IX    <preop>::=sin|cos|tan|exp
X     <idx> ::= <dgt><dgt>
XI    <cte> ::= <dgt><dgt>.<dgt><dgt>
XII   <dgt>::=0|1|2|3|4|5|6|7|8|9
```

Figure 3: Grammar including knowledge of the problem: carbohydrates are added and insulin units are subtracted from glucose values.

Parameter	Value
Population size	100
Generations	2500
Crossover probability	0.6
Mutation probability	0.2
Tournament size	2
Max. wraps	3
Codon size	256
Chromosome length	100

Table 2: Parameters for GE experiments.

the level of glucose in the patient's blood depending on, at least, the glucose level, the carbohydrates ingested and the insulin injected. Hence we need to consider those values in our datasets.

In the target in-silico patients, data were obtained with the AIDA simulator (www2aida.org). More precisely, our data series represent measures taken each 15 minutes along the day. Table 1 shows an example of the dataset of one of the in-silico patients, named Joy Wilson . For each time step, represented in one line of the table, k is the actual time, GL is the actual glucose level, CH is the carbohydrates units ingested, IS is the short effect insulin injected and IL is the long effect insulin injected. We work with a set of in-silico patients obtained with AIDA simulator. The website of the simulator offers several characterized patients from which we selected eight of them. We have included here a more varied selection in order to better analyze the quality of the GE solutions. The glucose values for each patient were obtained by introducing different carbohydrates and insulin values and then running the simulator. The description of each one of the patients can be found on the website, but we replicate them here for the sake of clarity. The patients are the following:

Joy Wilson . This woman is on three injections of short and/or intermediate acting insulin each day, with a split-evening dose. She wants to start a family, but consistently has had quite high blood glucose levels in the early afternoon.

Howard Kistler . This 45 year old man was diagnosed as having diabetes at the age of 14. He is currently on a regimen of combined short and/or intermediate acting insulin preparations four times per day. As you can see from his home monitoring blood glucose measurements, he tends to higher blood glucose values overnight but has a low blood glucose in the mid-morning.

Steven Jones . This man is a relatively newly diagnosed insulin-dependent (type 1) diabetic patient. He has had problems maintaining his blood glucose profile on two and more recently three injections per day; so currently he is controlled on four injections per day. He tends to quite high blood glucose levels in the middle of the day, despite not eating excessively.

Elizabeth Whittaker . It has taken a lot of effort to stabilize this girl's blood glucose profile. However, she still often goes hypoglycemic in the middle of the day, especially between breakfast and lunch. She is on a slightly unusual regimen taking a short acting insulin preparation three times per day, with an intermediate acting preparation twice a day – at lunchtime and before bed.

Lizzy Laurence . This overweight 58 year old insulin-dependent (type 1) diabetic patient has had major problems losing weight. She is quite sensitive to insulin. In addition, she smokes and is at great risk of suffering a heart attack or stroke.

Mohammed Abdullah . This man often wakes with 'sweats' and feeling profoundly unwell in the middle of the night. However, his blood sugars are quite respectable when he gets up at 7:30 AM. In such a situation he needs to measure his blood glucose when he wakes in the middle of the night, feeling unwell. Clearly injecting so much insulin before he goes to bed isn't a good idea. Try adjusting his bedtime insulin and see if you can stop him going 'hypo'.

David Robins . This 18 year old insulin-dependent patient has just left home for the first time to go to the University. He isn't a very good cook and hasn't been taking good care of himself. He feels pretty awful most mornings and even going to bed early hasn't helped. He tends to quite low blood sugars in the morning, at times being at risk of going 'hypo'. See if you can adjust his insulin regimen so that his blood sugars don't run quite so low in the morning.

Hugh Allibaster . This 35 year old insulin-dependent diabetic man recently switched to using an insulin pen, injecting three 'shots' of short-acting insulin before breakfast, lunch, and dinner, while taking a single dose of long-acting insulin before going to bed. However, he hasn't quite gotten full control of his blood sugars, still tending towards high blood glucose levels overnight. How might you improve his control, through adjusting his existing insulin doses?

4.1 Error Grid Analysis

The Clarke error grid approach is used to assess the clinical significance of differences between the glucose measurement technique under test and the venous blood glucose reference measurements. The method was presented in 1986 by Clarke et al. [3] and uses a cartesian diagram to represent the values of the prediction versus the reference (actual) values. For example, if a value of 118 is predicted for a point where the real value is 90, this will be represented by the point (90, 118) in the XY cartesian graphic. In this way the diagonal, i.e. $Y = X$, represents the perfect measure, the points below and above the line indicate, respectively, overestimation and underestimation of the actual values. What is interesting in this graphic is that the XY graph is divided into a grid of zones depending on the severity of the misprediction, which is the reason of the Error Grid name. Clarke differentiated five zones in the graph (A to E), with the following meanings:

- Zone A: represents the glucose values that deviate from the reference values by 20 % or less and those that are in the hypoglycemic range (<70 mg/dl), not only the predicted value but also the reference value. Those values are clinically exact and acceptable and thus the clinical treatment will be correct.
- Zone B: represents the glucose values that deviate from the reference values by more than 20 %. In this zone we are close to unacceptable errors but the clinical treatment has a high probability of being correct. The values that fall within zone B are also clinically acceptable.
- Zones C-E: The values included in those areas are potentially dangerous, since the measure or prediction is far from being acceptable and the indicated treatment will be different from the correct. There is a high possibility of making clinically significant mistakes for values within this zones.

In 2000 Parkes et al. [17] revisited the definition of the zone and constructed a set of new error grids by using the expertise of a large panel of clinicians. They constructed new grids, differentiating for T1DM and T2DM patients. The followed method was to ask a total of 100 experts of diabetes to assign any error a category form A to E as in the Clarke error grid.

Currently, in the field of endocrinology there is not a general consensus for evaluating errors in the measurement of blood glucose for diabetics, so we use here both EGs to analyze the results.

5. EXPERIMENTAL RESULTS

Starting with the models of the eight in-silico patients, we have taken their validation data and we have obtained the Clarke and Parkes Error Grids.

Figures 4 to 11 show the experimental results on validation data and the corresponding Error Grid Analysis. Each figure is composed by four graphics. Starting from the left Figures (a) show the glucose values obtained with the best grammar-objective combination of the training phase for each patient. The actual glucose curve of the patient (in blue), the glucose value generated with the best solution of this combination (in red) and the glucose value generated with the average of the 30 solutions (in yellow) are displayed in the figure. The next two figures (b) and (c) represent the Clarke EGA for the best solution and for the average of the 30 solutions. Finally subfigures (d) show the Parkes EGA of each Patient on the validation phase.

For each patient, we have calculated the percentage that the average error of each simulation run represents in the range of the patient glucose values. The experimental results shows the quality of the models. In terms of the accuracy of the model, predicted values has an average error of 12.83 %. This results are in consonance with those presented in [10]. Once again, minimizing the average error objective does not obtain the best average results, for some of the patients.

Regarding the Error Grid Analysis, as seen in the figures, the EGA is quite good for all the in-silico patients. In the case of Clarke EG, more than 95 % of the data were found into Zone A. For Parkes EG the results are even a little bit higher. Results for patient David Robins and patient Hugh Allibaster are especially important since predict hypoglycemic values. For the first, the prediction in terms of Clarke EGA are bad. Although very close to A zone, we found several values on dangerous zones. On the other hand, results on Hugh Allibaster shows a very good prediction on low glucose values. This clearly confirms the necessity to adapt the grammars to specific cases, including other factors or allowing a small biasing in the search. This will be one of the focus of the future work.

In general, we have found that data near hypoglycemic zones are more likely to be mispredicted by our models. Hence, we will study two approaches: on the one hand, we will incorporate the EG in the object function of the optimization; on the other hand, we will study a multi-objective approach where one objective will be to fit all the data values into the A zone in both EGs.

6. CONCLUSIONS

In this paper we extend previous works were Gramatical Evolution is applied to obtain individual models of blood glucose levels in humans. Here, we present validation data for three new in-silico patients, tackling a total number of eight in-silico patients, which were taken from the AIDA simulator. Experimental results confirm that Evolutionary Computation can solve problems for a higher variety of in-silico patients and also for patients with dangerous values of glucose, i.e. hypoglycemic values.

There is still a lot of work to do, the main focus of our research is to apply the method explained in this paper to real patients. This step necessarily implies the adaptation and customization of grammars, a higher study of the fitness function and landscapes. In addition, we will consider the multiobjective optimization with both average and maximum error objective and EGAs. We will also consider to integrate fuzzy regression into the GP process.

7. REFERENCES

[1] International surviving sepsis campaign guidelines committee: Surviving sepsis campaign: international guidelines for management of severe sepsis and septic shock. *Crit Care Med*, 36:296–327, 2008.

[2] A. American-Diabetes-Association. Standards of medical care in diabetes 2010. *Diabetes Care*, 33(S1):11–61, 2010.

[3] G.-F. L. C. W. P. S. Clarke WL1, Cox D. Evaluating clinical accuracy of systems for self-monitoring of blood glucose. *Diabetes Care*, 10(5):622–628, 1987.

[4] C. Cobelli, C. Dalla Man, G. Sparacino, L. Magni, G. De Nicolao, and B. Kovatchev. Diabetes: Models, signals, and control. *Biomedical Engineering, IEEE Reviews in*, 2:54 –96, 2009.

[5] E. Dassau, H. Zisser, B. Grosman, W. Bevier, M. Percival, L. Jovanovic, and F. Doyle. Artificial pancreatic betta-cell protocol for enhanced model identification. *Diabetes*, pages A105–A106, 2009.

[6] F. El-Khatib, S. Russell, D. Nathan, R. Sutherlin, and E. Damiano. A bihormonal closed-loop artificial pancreas for type 1 diabetes. *Sci Transl Med.*, 2 (27), 2010.

[7] D. A. Finan, C. C. Palerm, F. J. Doyle, D. E. Seborg, H. Zisser, W. C. Bevier, and L. Jovanovic. Effect of input excitation on the quality of empirical dynamic models for type 1 diabetes. *AIChE Journal*, 55(5):1135–1146, 2009.

[8] A. Gani, A. Gribok, Y. Lu, W. Ward, R. Vigersky, and J. Reifman. Universal glucose models for predicting subcutaneous glucose concentration in humans. *Information Technology in Biomedicine, IEEE Transactions on*, 14(1):157 –165, jan. 2010.

[9] M. Gevers. Identification for control: From the early achievements to the revival of experiment design. In *44th IEEE Conference on Decision and Control, 2005 and 2005 European Control Conference. CDC-ECC '05*, page 12, dec. 2005.

[10] J. I. Hidalgo, J. M. Colmenar, J. L. Risco-Martin, A. Cuesta-Infante, E. Maqueda, M. Botella, and J. A. Rubio. Modeling glycemia in humans by means of grammatical evolution. *Applied Soft Computing*, (0):–, 2013.

[11] J. I. Hidalgo, E. Maqueda, J. L. Risco-Martín, A. Cuesta-Infante, J. M. Colmenar, and J. Nobel. glucmodel: A monitoring and modeling system for chronic diseases applied to diabetes. *Journal of Biomedical Informatics*, (0):–, 2014.

[12] R. Hovorka, J. M. Allen, D. Elleri, L. J. Chassin, J. Harris, D. Xing, C. Kollman, T. Hovorka, A. M. F. Larsen, M. Nodale, A. D. Palma, M. E. Wilinska, C. L. Acerini, and D. B. Dunger. Manual closed-loop insulin delivery in children and adolescents with type 1 diabetes: a phase 2 randomised crossover trial. *The Lancet*, 375:743 – 751, 2010.

[13] B. Kovatchev, C. Cobelli, E. Renard, S. Anderson, M. Breton, S. Patek, W. Clarke, D. Bruttomesso, A. Maran, S. Costa, A. Avogaro, C. D. Man, A. Facchinetti, L. Magni, G. D. Nicolao, J. Place, and A. Farret. Multinational study of subcutaneous model-predictive closed loop control in type 1 diabetes mellitus: Summary of the results. *Diabetes Sci Technol*, 4:1374–1381, 2010.

[14] J. Krinsley and R. Jones. Cost analysis of intensive glycemic control in critically ill adult patients. *Chest*, 129:644–650, 2006.

[15] H. Lee and B. Bequette. A closed-loop artificial pancreas based on model predictive control: Human-friendly identification and automatic meal disturbance rejection. *Biomedical Signal Processing and Control*, 4(4):347 – 354, 2009. Special Issue on Biomedical Systems, Signals and Control Extended Selected papers from the IFAC World Congress, Seoul, July 2008.

[16] M. O'Neill and C. Ryan. *Grammatical Evolution: Evolutionary Automatic Programming in an Arbitrary Language*. Kluwer Academic Publishers, 2003.

[17] P. S. G. B. Parkes JL, Slatin SL. A new consensus error grid to evaluate the clinical significance of inaccuracies in the measurement of blood glucose. *Diabetes Care*, 23(8):1143–1148., 2000.

[18] D. E. Rivera and S. V. Gaikwad. Systematic techniques for determining modelling requirements for siso and mimo feedback control. *Journal of Process Control*, 5(4):213 – 224, 1995. IFAC Symposium: Advanced Control of Chemical Processes.

[19] G. Sparacino, F. Zanderigo, S. Corazza, A. Maran, A. Facchinetti, and C. Cobelli. Glucose concentration can be predicted ahead in time from continuous glucose monitoring sensor time-series. *Biomedical Engineering, IEEE Transactions on*, 54(5):931 –937, may 2007.

[20] G. M. Steil, C. C. Palerm, N. Kurtz, G. Voskanyan, A. Roy, S. Paz, and F. R. Kandeel. The effect of insulin feedback on closed loop glucose control. *J Clin Endocrinol Metab*, 96:1402–1408, 2011.

[21] K. van Heusden, E. Dassau, H. Zisser, D. Seborg, and F. Doyle. Control-relevant models for glucose control using a priori patient characteristics. *IEEE Transactions on Biomedical Engineering*, 59(7):1839 –1849, july 2012.

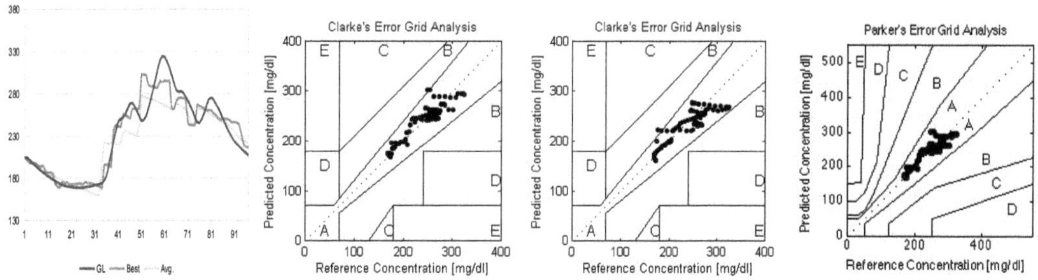

(a) Validation (b) Clarke EGA of the best (c) Clarke EGA of the Avg. (d) Parkes EGA of the best

Figure 4: Results and EGA for Joy Wilson

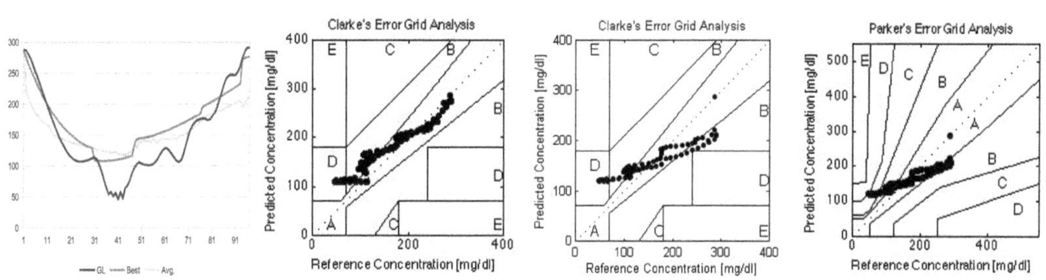

(a) Validation (b) Clarke EGA of the best (c) Clarke EGA of the Avg. (d) Parkes EGA of the best

Figure 5: Results and EGA for Howard Kistler

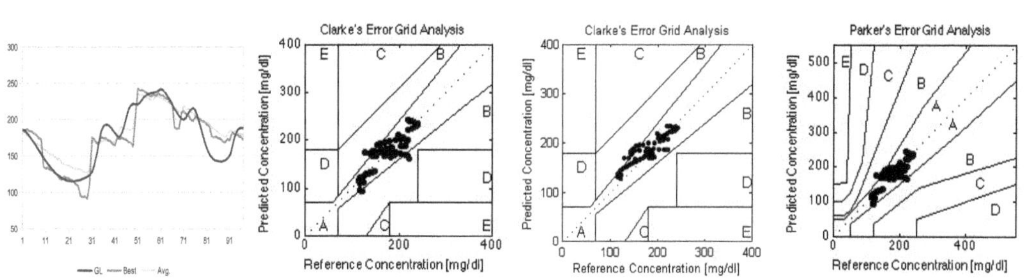

(a) Validation (b) Clarke EGA of the best (c) Clarke EGA of the Avg. (d) Parkes EGA of the best

Figure 6: Results and EGA for Steven Jones

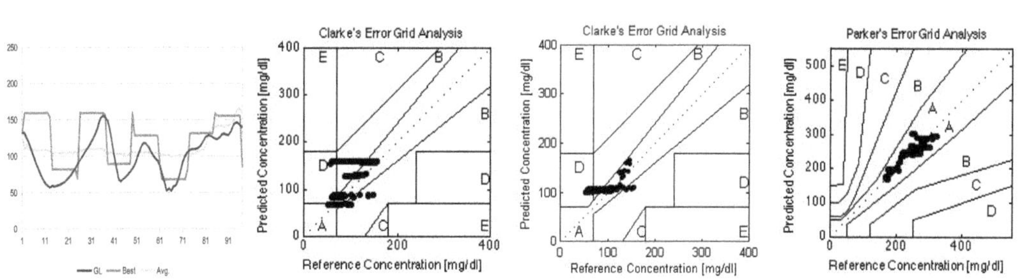

(a) Validation (b) Clarke EGA of the best (c) Clarke EGA of the Avg. (d) Parkes EGA of the best

Figure 7: Results and EGA for Elizabeth Whittaker

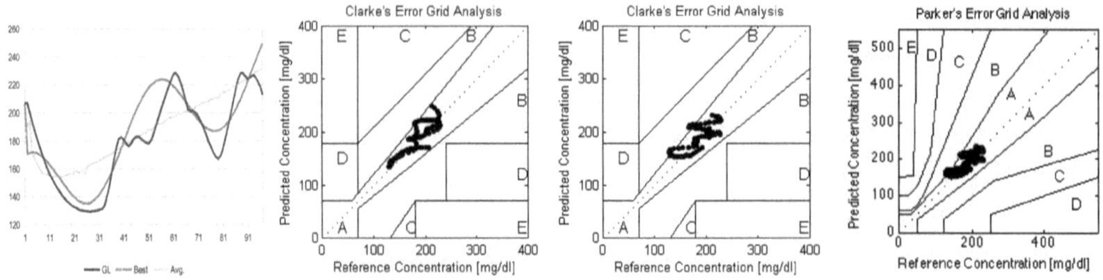

(a) Validation (b) Clarke EGA of the best (c) Clarke EGA of the Avg. (d) Parkes EGA of the best

Figure 8: Results and EGA for Lizzy Laurence

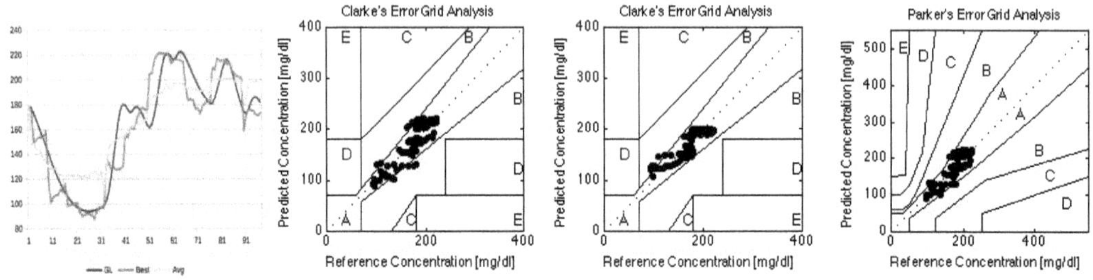

(a) Validation (b) Clarke EGA of the best (c) Clarke EGA of the Avg. (d) Parkes EGA of the best

Figure 9: Results and EGA for Mohammed Abdullah

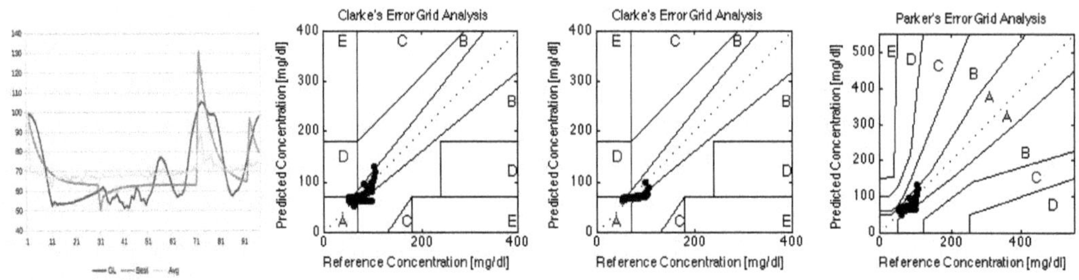

(a) Validation (b) Clarke EGA of the best (c) Clarke EGA of the Avg. (d) Parkes EGA of the best

Figure 10: Results and EGA for David Robins

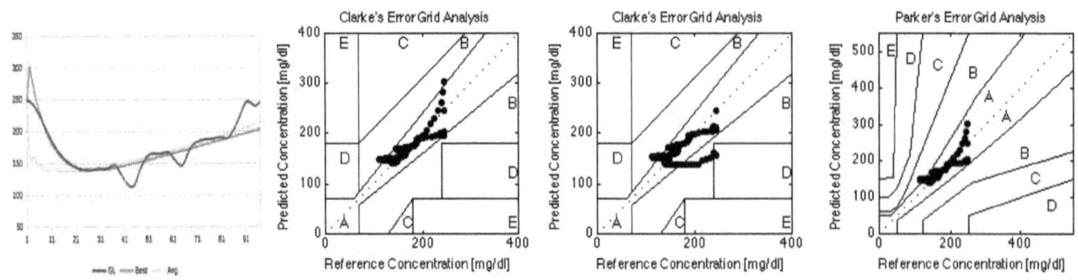

(a) Validation (b) Clarke EGA of the best (c) Clarke EGA of the Avg. (d) Parkes EGA of the best

Figure 11: Results and EGA for Hugh Allibaster

An Evaluation of Particle Swarm Optimization Techniques in Segmentation of Biomedical Images

Salim Lahmiri
Dept. of Computer Science, UQAM
Montreal, Canada
Lahmiri.salim@courrier.uqam.ca

Mounir Boukadoum
Dept. of Computer Science, UQAM
Montreal, Canada
Boukadoum.mounir@uqam.ca

ABSTRACT
Image segmentation is a common image processing step to many computer vision applications with the purpose to segment pixels into different classes. As improved variants of particle swarm optimization (PSO) algorithms, the fractional-order Darwinian particle swarm optimization (FODPSO) and Darwinian particle swarm optimization (DPSO) have been proposed for image segmentation. The purpose of this paper is to compare the segmentation performance of PSO, DPSO, and FODPSO as parametric approaches to existing methods; namely the parametric fuzzy c-means (FCM) algorithm, and the non-parametric Otsu segmentation technique with application to five biomedical images. All PSO-based experiments are conducted with twenty runs to assess the effectiveness of PSO models. The universal quality index is used to evaluate the segmentation results. The obtained experimental results showed that particle swarm based algorithms outperformed both FCM and Otsu segmentation technique.

Categories and Subject Descriptors
I.4.6 [**Image processing and computer vision**]: Segmentation.

General Terms
Algorithms;Experimentation.

Keywords
Particle swarm optimization; Fuzzy c-Means; Otsu technique; Segmentation; Biomedical images.

1. INTRODUCTION
In image processing and computer vision, image segmentation is a fundamental problem with the objective to partition an image into several subregions with homogeneous properties. The problem of image segmentation has received a large attention in biomedical applications [1]-[3]. Indeed, the automatic segmentation of biomedical images is a critical step for quantifying the changes of anatomical structures that are highly related to biological tissue diseases. For instance, global thresholding based on minimum cross entropy was adopted in [1] as a segmentation method for cuboidal cell nuclei in images of prostate tissue stained with hematoxylin and eosin, an atlas-aided fuzzy c-means (FCM-Atlas) was developed and validated in [2] to segment fibroglandular tissue and volumetric density estimation in breast MRI, and a sparse representation was adopted in [3] to fuse the multi-modality image information and incorporate the anatomical constraints for brain tissue segmentation.

Image thresholding approaches are widely used for image segmentation [4]. They can be classified into two types: optimal thresholding methods and property based thresholding methods.

Optimal thresholding methods search for the optimal thresholds by optimizing an objective function, whilst property-based thresholding methods detect the thresholds by measuring some property of the histogram [4]. Optimal thresholding methods find the thresholds that separate the gray-level regions of an image based on some discriminating criteria such as the between-class variance, entropy and cross entropy [5]. For instance, the popular Otsu's unsupervised method [6] selects optimal thresholds by maximizing the between class variance.

In general, optimal thresholding methods are simple and effective in bi-level thresholding [7]. However, they are; including Otsu's unsupervised method; inefficient in determining the optimal thresholds due to the exponential growth in computation time in when dealing with multilevel thresholding problems [7]. As an alternative, some evolutionary techniques have been adopted to solve multilevel thresholding problems; including bacterial foraging algorithm [7], particle swarm optimization [4][8], ant colony optimization [9], and more recently the fractional-order Darwinian particle swarm optimization (FODPSO) and Darwinian particle swarm optimization (DPSO) [10].

Because of its effectiveness, PSO based algorithms have received increasing interests in image segmentation [4][8][10] including its extensions; namely FODPSO and Darwinian particle swarm optimization DPSO. In [10], the DPSO and FODPSO were proposed for solving the Otsu problem for delineating multilevel threshold values. In particular, the problem of n-level thresholding is reduced to an optimization problem to search for the thresholds that maximizes a set of three objective (fitness) functions of each RGB (red-green-blue) component of the image [10]. The obtained results indicated that FODPSO is more efficient than PSO, DPSO, bacteria foraging algorithm, and genetic algorithms in the problem of segmentation of five images: airplane, hunter, butterfly, road, and a map.

The purpose of this study is to examine the effectiveness of PSO, DPSO, and FODPSO in the problem of biomedical image segmentation. Indeed, the task of determining optimal thresholds for n-level image thresholding could be formulated as a multidimensional optimization problem by using PSO-based models [10]. As a result, optimal thresholds are automatically determined by using PSO-based algorithms. For comparison purpose, the popular Otsu's unsupervised method [6] and fuzzy c-means (FCM) algorithm [11] are also used for segmentation of biomedical images used in our study. The FCM is chosen because it is more appropriate for data clustering when the boundaries

GECCO'14, July 12–16, 2014, Vancouver, BC, Canada.

ACM 978-1-4503-2881-4/14/07...$15.00.
http://dx.doi.org/10.1145/2598394.2609855

between data clusters are ill defined [12]. We notice that Otsu's approach is nonparametric since it requires no predetermined parameters, whilst FCM is parametric because the number of clusters should be set a priori. Finally, the performance of each algorithm is evaluated based on the well known universal quality index [13]. It is independent of the images being tested, the viewing conditions or the individual observers [13]. In addition, it provides a meaningful comparison across different types of image distortions [13]. Jaccard index and Dice similarity index are not considered in this study since the former is more suitable for binary images, and the latter is sensitive to homogenous data.

The rest of this paper is organized as follows. In Section 2, PSO, DPSO, FCM, Otsu technique, and the universal quality index are described. In Sections 3, results of biomedical images are presented. Finally, we conclude in Section 4.

2. METHODS

2.1 Particle Swarm Optimization

In basic PSO, a swarm of individuals, called particles, collectively moves in the search space, with each particle position representing a candidate solution to the optimization problem at hand. During the search, each particle adjusts its motion according to the best position it achieved as well as to the best ones achieved by the swarm. A fitness function is used to evaluate particle performance at each step.

In the context of image segmentation, the pixel set corresponds to the search space, and the optimal solution corresponds to maximizing the between-class (between objects in the image) variance of the distribution of intensity levels in the image. Following the notation in [10] notation, at time t each particle n moves in a search space with position x_t^n and velocity v_t^n which are dependent on local best position $\breve{x}_t^n$ neighborhood best $\breve{n}_t^n$ and global best $\breve{g}_t^n$ information as follows:

$$v_{t+1}^n = wv_t^n + \rho_1 r_1\left(\breve{g}_t^n - x_t^n\right) + \rho_2 r_2\left(\breve{x}_t^n - x_t^n\right) + \rho_2 r_2\left(\breve{n}_t^n - x_t^n\right) \quad (1)$$

$$x_{t+1}^n = x_t^n + v_{t+1}^n \quad (2)$$

where the parameters w, ρ_1, ρ_2, and ρ_3 are respectively the weights of the inertial influence, global best, local best, and neighborhood best when determining the new velocity [10]. The parameters r_1, r_2, and r_3 are vectors with uniform random numbers between 0 and 1 associated to each component of Equation 2. The fitness function φ used to evaluate the performance of the particles is given by [10]:

$$\varphi = \max_{1 < t_1 < \ldots < t_{n-1} < L} \sigma(t_j) \quad (3)$$

where, σ is the between-class variance of the image intensity distributions, t is a given threshold, L is the intensity level, and n is the number of classes into which the pixels of the image are divided (by grouping pixels in terms of their gray levels been within a specified range). More details about the fitness function are found in [10].

The PSO algorithm is summarized in Table 1 [10]. A certain number of parameters must be initialized before running it. Typically, the particle velocities are set to zero and their positions are randomly set within the boundaries of the image number of intensity levels L. For instance, the positions can be initialized as $\eta(L-X_{\min})+X_{\min}$, where η is a random variable in [0,1] and $X_{\min}$ is a predetermined parameter. In addition, the local best, neighborhood best and global best positions are initialized with the worst possible values [10], e.g., large negative numbers. As for the particle population size and iteration stopping criterion, they can be arbitrarily set or chosen depending on the nature of the problem and/or data.

Table 1. Algorithm of the PSO as in [10]

Initialize swarm: x_t^n, v_t^n, $\breve{x}_t^n$, $\breve{n}_t^n$, $\breve{g}_t^n$
Loop:
For all particles
Evaluate the fitness φ of each particle
Update : x_t^n, $\breve{n}_t^n$, $\breve{g}_t^n$
Update : v_t^n, $\breve{x}_t^n$
End
Until stopping criteria (convergence) reached

2.2 Darwinian Particle Swarm Optimization

One drawback of the PSO algorithm described in Table 1 is that it may get stuck in a sub-optimal solution region [10][14]. To avoid this situation, Tillett et al, [14] introduced the Darwinian particle swarm optimization (DPSO), an extension of the algorithm that uses natural selection to escape from local optima. In particular, the classic PSO is extended to multiple swarms where each one performs a PSO search. Thus, many swarms of test solutions coexist. At each step, a swarm that gets better results is allowed to spawn a new descendent or a particle life is extended. On the contrary, a swarm life is reduced or its particles are reduced in number if it stagnates. The state of each swarm is evaluated based on the fitness of all its particles, and the neighborhood and individual best positions of each of the particles are updated. Then, a new particle is spawned if a new global solution is found. In particular, if the swarm population falls below a minimum bound, the swarm is deleted; and the worst performing particle in the swarm is deleted if a maximum threshold number of steps ($SC_C^{\max}$) is reached without improving the fitness function. The previous steps counter is reset to a value approaching the threshold number if the particle is deleted, as follows [14]:

$$SC_c(N_{kill}) = SC_C^{\max}\left(1 - \frac{1}{N_{kill}+1}\right) \quad (4)$$

where N_{kill} is the number of particles deleted from the swarm when there is no improvement in fitness during an iteration. A new swarm is created with a probability of $p=f/S$, with f is a random number in [0,1] and S is the number of swarms [10]. Finally, a set of initial parameters is determined to run the DPSO algorithm; including the initial swarm population, minimum and maximum swarm population, initial number of swarms, minimum and maximum number of swarms, and the image number of threshold. The algorithm of the DPSO is presented in Table 2 as in [10].

Table 2. Algorithm of the DPSO as in [10]

Main program loop	Evolve swarm algorithm
For each swarm in the collection Evolve the swarm (see right column) Allow the swarm to spawn Delete failed swarms	For each particle in the swarm Update particle Fitness Update particles Best Move particle If swarm gets better Reward swarm: spawn particle: extend swarm life else Punish swarm: possibly delete particle: reduce swarm life

2.3 Fractional-order Darwinian Particle Swarm Optimization

Recently, the authors in [15] presented fractional-order (FO) DPSO or FODPSO. The idea was to use fractional calculus based on the Grünwald-Letnikov concept of fractional differential [16] to control the convergence rate of the DPSO. The fractional differential α of a given signal $x(t)$ is given by:

$$D^{\alpha}[x(t)] = \frac{1}{T^{\alpha}} \sum_{k=0}^{r} \frac{(-1)^k \Gamma(\alpha+1) x(t-kT)}{\Gamma(k+1)\Gamma(\alpha-k+1)} \tag{5}$$

where Γ, T, and r are respectively the gamma function, the sampling period, and the truncation order. Then, considering w =1, T =1, and r =4, the differential derivative of Equation 1 is written as [15][17]:

$$v_{t+1}^n = \alpha v_t^n + \frac{1}{2}\alpha v_t^n + \frac{1}{6}\alpha(1-\alpha) v_{t-2}^n + \frac{1}{24}\alpha(1-\alpha)(2-\alpha) v_{t-3}^n + \rho_1 r_1 (\breve{g}_t^n - x_t^n) + \rho_2 r_2 (\breve{x}_t^n - x_t^n) + \rho_3 r_3 (\breve{n}_t^n - x_t^n) \tag{6}$$

Thus, setting α =1 yields the standard DPSO. The parameter is closely related to the memory of the particles. If $\alpha < 1$, the particles will ignore their previous search and will probably be trapped in local solutions, whilst if $\alpha > 1$, the particles will explore more new solutions and performance will be improved [10]. The FODPSO was found to be more efficient than PSO and DPSO when the level of segmentation increases [10].

Table 3 provides the parameter values used to perform PSO, DPSO, and FODPSO searches in our study. These are the same as in [10], since they provided good results with fast processing time.

Table 3. Initial parameters as in [10]

Parameter	PSO	DPSO	FODPSO
Number of iterations	150	150	150
Population	150	30	30
ρ_1	0.8	0.8	0.8
ρ_2	0.8	0.8	0.8
w	1.2	1.2	1
V_{min}	-5	-1.5	-1.5
V_{max}	5	1.5	1.5
X_{min}	0	0	0
X_{max}	255	255	255
Min population		10	10
Max population		50	50
Number of swarms		4	4
Min swarms		2	2
Max swarms		6	6
Number of threshold		10	10
Fractal coefficient α			0.6

2.4 Fuzzy c-Means Clustering

The fuzzy c-means clustering (FCM) algorithm [11] also classifies a given data set into k clusters, but it realizes a fuzzy partition. It does so by minimizing the following objective function:

$$J_{FCM} = \sum_{j=1}^{K} \sum_{i=1}^{N} u_{ij}^m \left\| x_i^j - c_j \right\|^2 \tag{7}$$

where x and c stand respectively for the position of pixel i and the centroid of cluster j, N is the number of pixels, and K is the number of cluster, u_{ij} is a membership function, j=1,...N, and $m \in [1, \infty)$ identifies a fuzzifier [11]. Thus, the data points are partitioned into fuzzy regions using fuzzy membership grades [12]. The FCM must satisfy the constraint:

$$\sum_{j=1}^{N} u_{ij} = 1 \tag{8}$$

and the centroid of cluster j is calculated as follows:

$$c_j = \sum_{j=1}^{N} \frac{u_{ij}^m}{\sum_{k=1}^{N} u_{ik}^m} \tag{9}$$

Finally, the membership u_{ij} is updated as follows:

$$u_{ij} = \frac{\left\| x_j - c_j \right\|^{-1/(m-1)}}{\sum_{i=1}^{c} \left\| x_j - c_j \right\|^{-1/(m-1)}} \tag{10}$$

The role of the membership functions is to introduce fuzziness to the belongingness of each image pixel. As a result, each pixel belongs to all clusters, but with different degrees of membership.

2.5 Otsu Segmentation Approach

The Otsu segmentation method [6] is a threshold selection technique used to segment gray-level images by maximizing the following measure of class separability [18]:

$$D(T)=\frac{P_1(T)P_2(T)[m_1(T)-m_2(T)]^2}{P_1(T)\sigma_1^2(T)+P_2(T)\sigma_2^2(T)} \quad (11)$$

where,

$$P_1(T)=\sum_{z=0}^{T}h(z) \quad (12)$$

$$P_2(T)=1-P_1(T) \quad (13)$$

$$m_1(T)=\frac{1}{P_1(T)}\sum_{z=0}^{T}zh(z) \quad (14)$$

$$m_2(T)=\frac{1}{P_2(T)}\sum_{z=T+1}^{L-1}zh(z) \quad (15)$$

$$\sigma_1(T)=\frac{1}{P_1(T)}\sum_{z=0}^{T}[z-m_1(T)]^2h(z) \quad (16)$$

$$\sigma_2(T)=\frac{1}{P_2(T)}\sum_{z=T+1}^{L-1}[z-m_2(T)]^2h(z) \quad (17)$$

where, $z\in[0, L-1]$ is the grey-level of a pixel in the image, $h(z)$ is the normalized grey-level histogram of the image. The means of the light and dark image regions can be separated, and the variances of the two image regions can be minimized when $D(T)$ is maximized.

2.6 Evaluation Metric

For two signals x=1,…,N and y=1,…,N which are respectively the original and the test signal, the universal quality index Q [13] is given by:

$$Q=\frac{4\sigma_{xy}\bar{x}\,\bar{y}}{(\sigma_x^2+\sigma_y^2)+(\bar{x}^2+\bar{y}^2)} \quad (18)$$

Where $\bar{x}$, $\bar{y}$, σ_x, σ_y, and σ_{xy} are respectively the mean of x, mean of y, standard deviation of x, standard deviation of y, and the correlation coefficient between x and y. Alternatively, the quality index Q can be rewritten as a product of three components as follows:

$$Q=\frac{\sigma_{xy}}{\sigma_x\sigma_y}\cdot\frac{2\bar{x}\,\bar{y}}{\bar{x}^2+\bar{y}^2}\cdot\frac{2\sigma_x\sigma_y}{\sigma_x^2+\sigma_y^2} \quad (19)$$

where the first component is the correlation coefficient used to measure the degree of linear correlation between the two signals, the second component measures how close the mean luminance is between the two signals, and the third component measures how similar the contrasts of the images are [13]. For images, the quality index Q is computed as follows:

$$Q=\frac{1}{M}\sum_{i=1}^{M}Q_i \quad (20)$$

where M is the number of steps used to slide a window of size $B\times B$ which in turns moves pixel by pixel horizontally and vertically through all the rows and columns from the top-left to the bottom-right corner.

3. DATA AND RESULTS

In the present study we have used the five biomedical images: T1-weighted whole view of brain magnetic resonance image (MRI) (176×208 pixels), T1-weighted coronal view of brain MRI (176×176 pixels), T1-weighted sagittal view of brain MRI (208×176 pixels), prostate biological tissue (275×183 pixels), and breast biological tissue (631×471 pixels). They are respectively shown in Figures 1, 2, 3, 4, and 5. Since PSO and its variants are stochastic models, we performed twenty runs on each image and average and standard deviation of the universal quality index are computed. Table 4 shows the obtained results. The segmentation results are illustrated in Figures 6 to 20. Those of brain whole and coronal view are not shown because of limited space.

As indicated in Table 4, all PSO based algorithms outperformed FCM and Otsu technique in segmentation of all five images. In addition, the results indicated that PSO outperforms both DPSO and FODPSO in segmentation of prostate and breast tissue. They all obtained similar universal quality index value when used to segment brain sagittal view. Finally, both DPSO and FODPSO achieved the same performance and outperformed basic PSO when applied to the whole view of brain MRI.

In general, the obtained results are not consistent with [10] since we find that PSO outperforms both DPSO and FODPSO in segmentation of prostate and breast tissue.

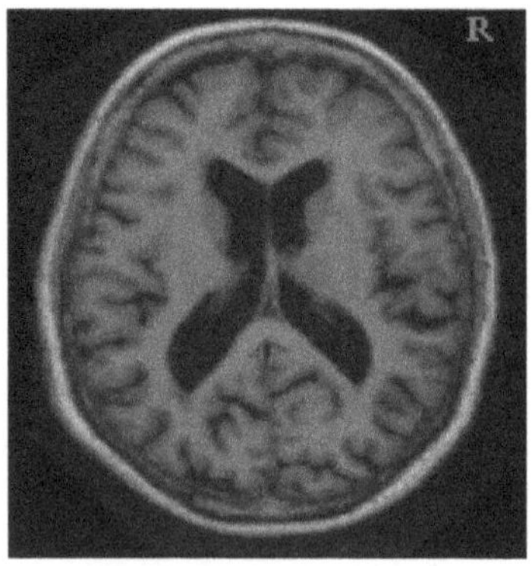

Figure 1. Whole brain MRI.

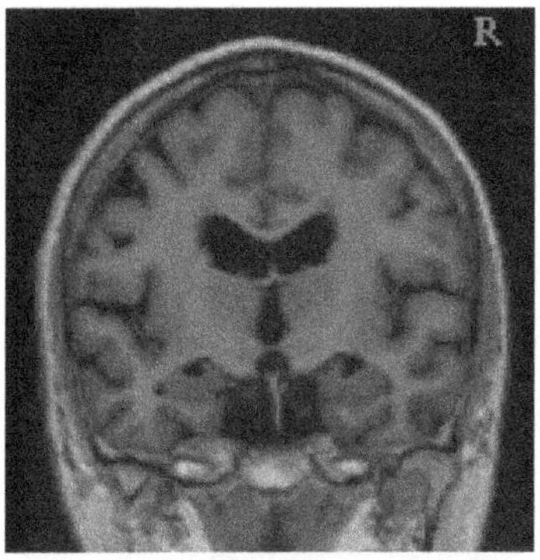

Figure 2. Coronal view of brain MRI.

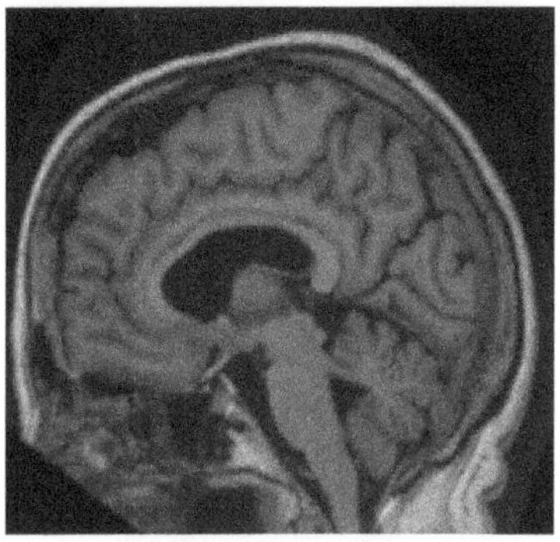

Figure 3. Sagittal view of brain MRI.

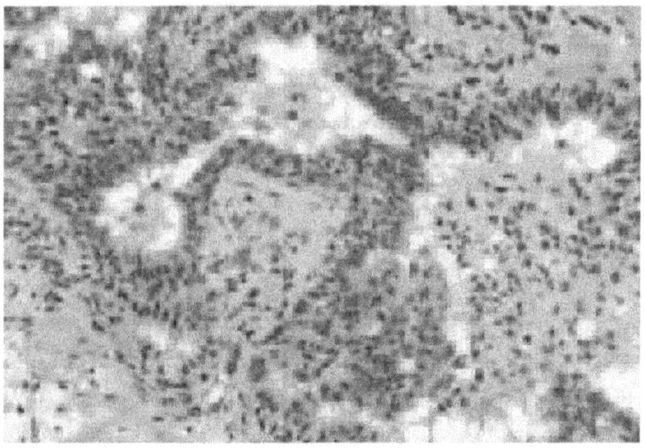

Figure 4. Prostate biological tissue.

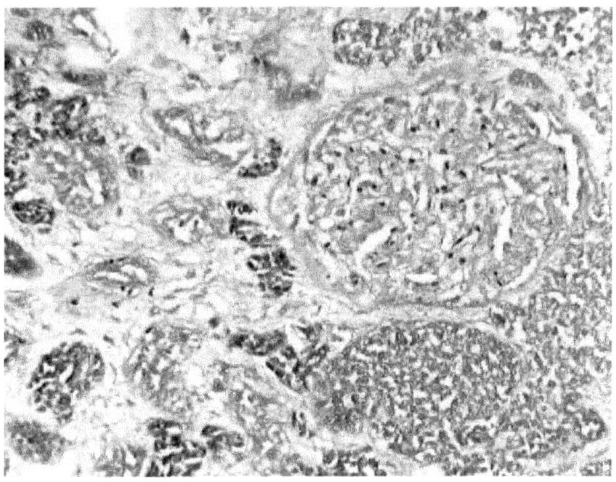

Figure 5. Breast biological tissue.

Table 4. Obtained universal quality index

	PSO	DPSO	FODPSO	FCM	OTSU
Brain Whole view	0.47±0.002	0.5±0.002	0.5±0.002	0.24	0.24
Brain Coronal view	0.53±0.002	0.53±0.002	0.53±0.002	0.24	0.05
Brain Sagittal view	0.53±0.002	0.53±0.002	0.53±0.002	0.04	0.04
Prostate	0.74±0.001	0.74±0.001	0.74±0.001	0.36	0.20
Breast	0.74±0.001	0.74±0.001	0.74±0.001	0.45	0.23

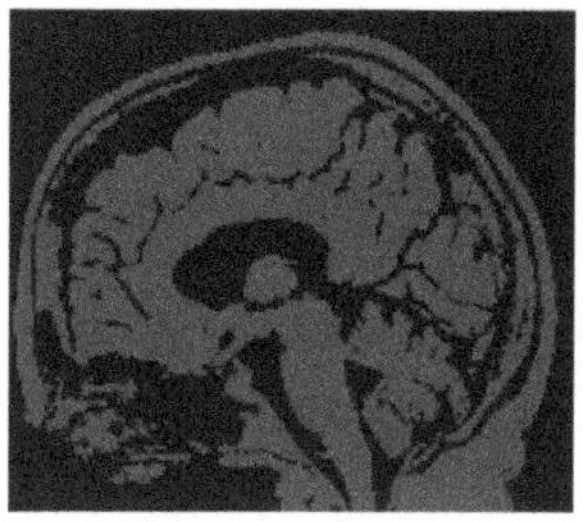

Figure 6. Sagittal view: PSO result.

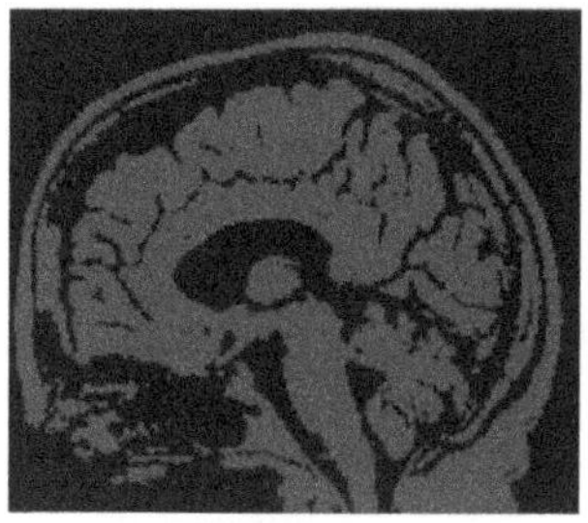

Figure 7. Sagittal view: DPSO result.

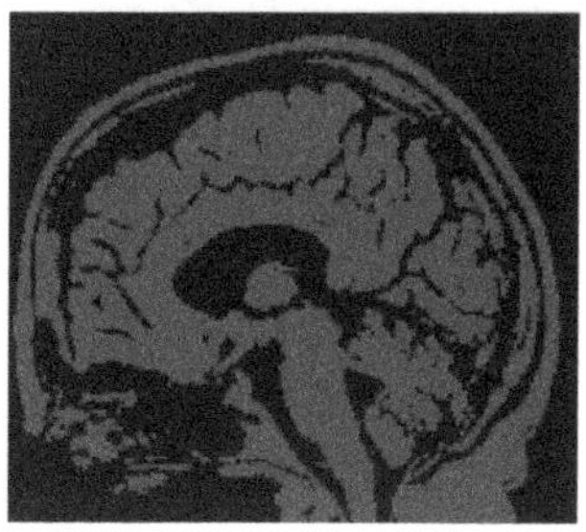

Figure 8. Sagittal view: FODPSO result.

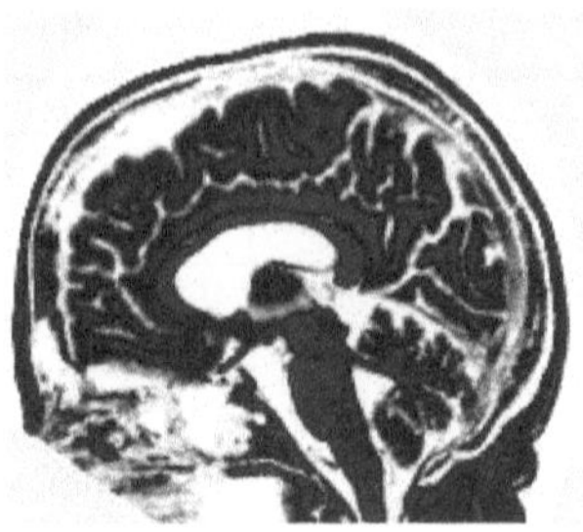

Figure 9. Sagittal view: FCM result.

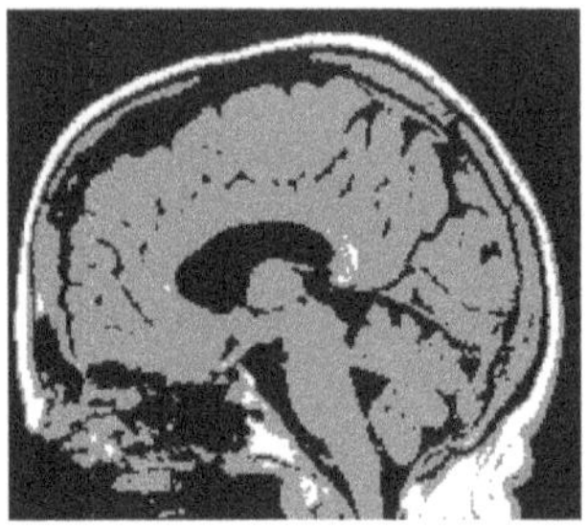

Figure 10. Sagittal view: Otsu result.

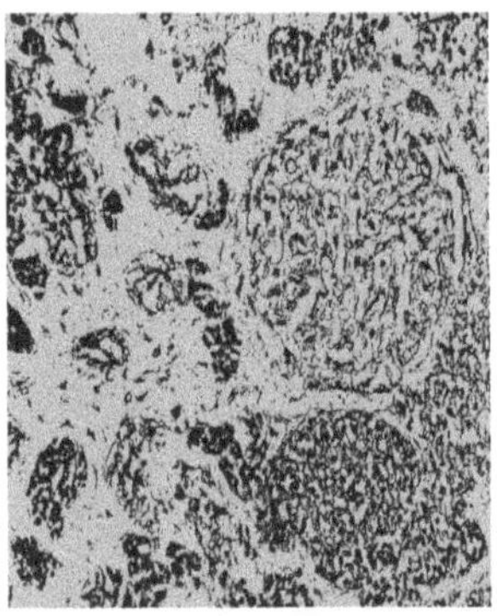

Figure 11. Prostate tissue: PSO result.

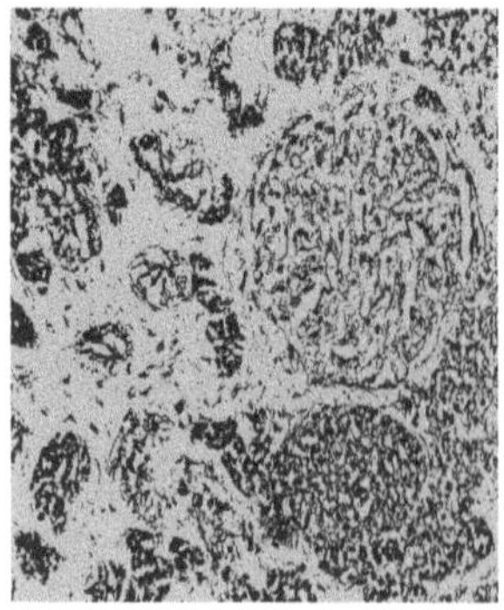

Figure 12. Prostate tissue: DPSO result.

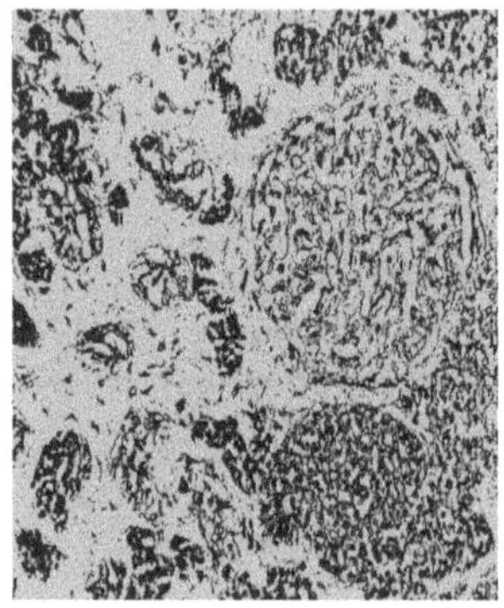

Figure 13. Prostate tissue: FODPSO result.

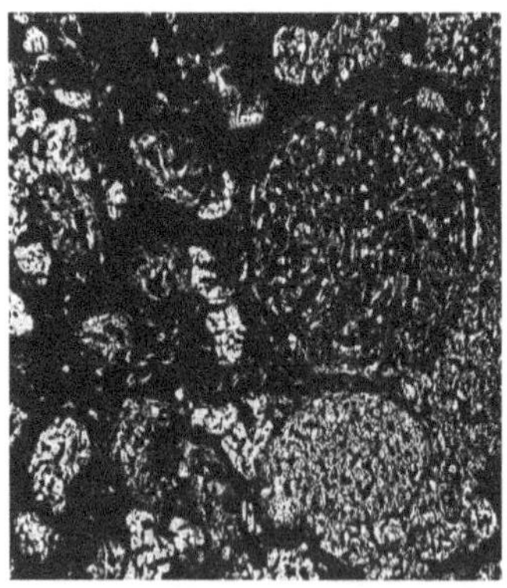

Figure 14. Prostate tissue: FCM result.

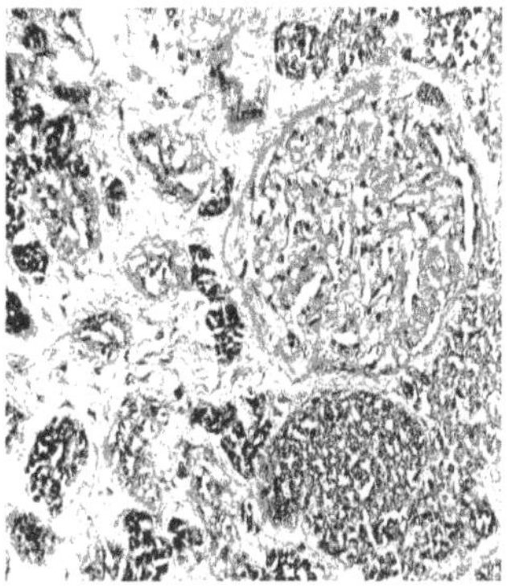

Figure 15. Prostate tissue: Otsu result.

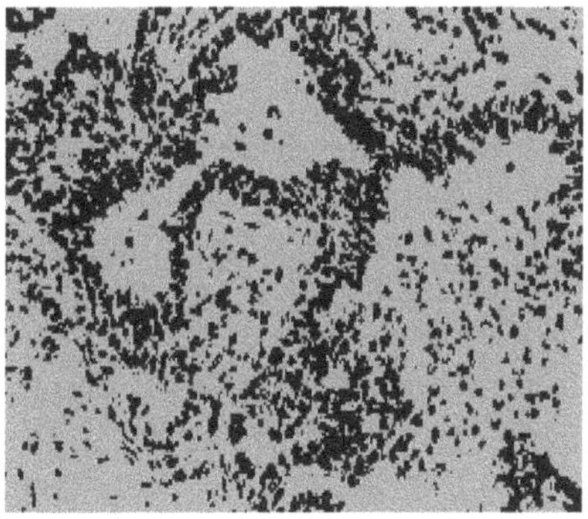

Figure 16. Breast tissue: PSO result.

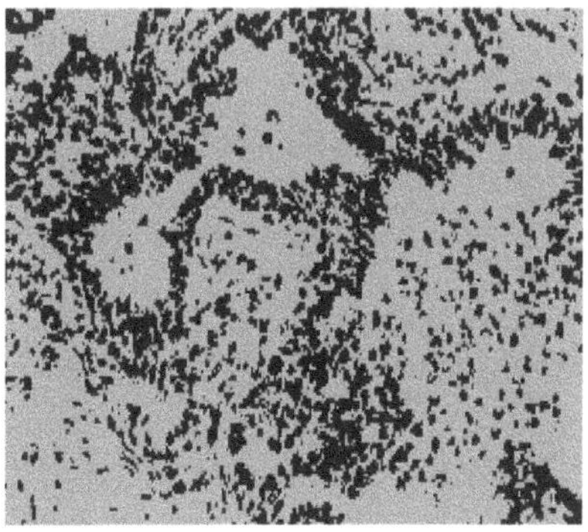

Figure 17. Breast tissue: DPSO result.

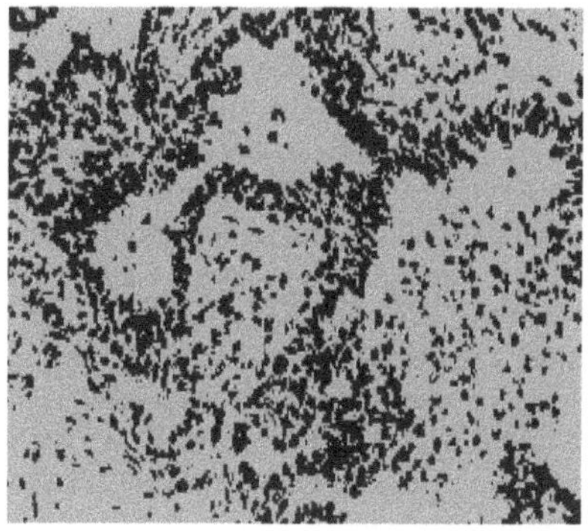

Figure 18. Breast tissue: FODPSO result.

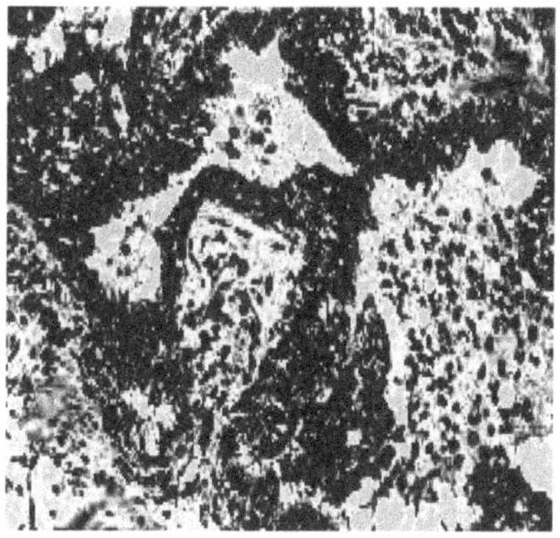

Figure 19. Breast tissue: FCM result.

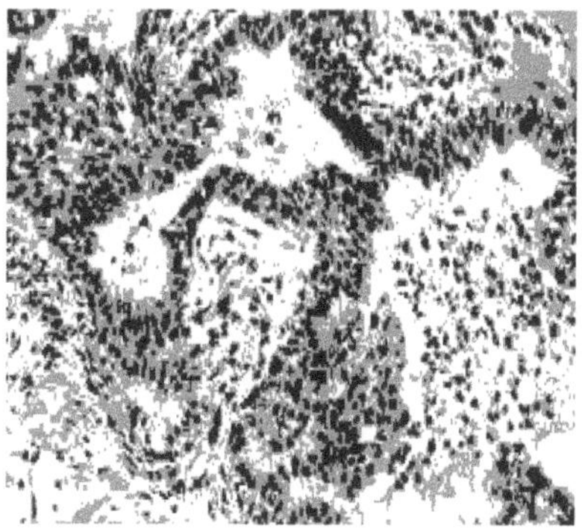

Figure 20. Breast tissue: Otsu result.

4. CONCLUSION

This study compared the performance of PSO, DPSO, FODPSO, FCM, and Otsu technique when they are used to segment different types of biological images. The main advantage of PSO, DPSO, and FODPSO is their ability to automatically determine the optimal thresholds for *n*-level image thresholding by formulating a multidimensional optimization problem. Based on the universal quality index used as performance measure, the obtained results indicated that all PSO based algorithms outperformed FCM and Otsu technique. In addition, the results indicated that in general PSO, DPSO, and FODPSO achieved similar performance. Therefore, this result suggests that the complexity of DPSO and FODPSO does not necessarily yield to large improvement in segmentation results of biomedical images.

Our future work will consider a comparison of PSO based algorithms with other evolutionary techniques. As our initial database was limited to five biomedical images, we will consider a larger database in future work for better generalization of the results.

5. REFERENCES

[1] de Oliveira, D.L.L., do Nascimento M.Z., Neves, L.A., de Godoy, M.F., de Arruda, P.F.F., and de Santi Neto, D. Unsupervised segmentation method for cuboidal cell nuclei in histological prostate images based on minimum cross entropy. *Expert Systems with Applications* 40 (2013), 7331–7340.

[2] Wu, S., Weinstein, S.P., Conant, E.F, and Kontos D. Automated fibroglandular tissue segmentation and volumetric density estimation in breast MRI using an atlas-aided fuzzy C-means method. *Med Phys.* 40 (2013); DOI: 10.1118/1.4829496.

[3] Wang, L., Shi, F., Gao, Y., Li, G., Gilmore, J.H., Lin, W., and Shen, D. Integration of sparse multi-modality representation and anatomical constraint for isointense infant brain MR image segmentation. *NeuroImage* 89 (2014) 152–164.

[4] Chander, A., Chatterjee, A., and Siarry, P. A new social and momentum component adaptive PSO algorithm for image segmentation. *Expert Systems with Applications* 38 (2011) 4998–5004.

[5] Horng, M.-H. Multilevel thresholding selection based on the artificial bee colony algorithm for image segmentation. *Expert Systems with Applications* 38 (2011) 13785–13791.

[6] Otsu, N. A threshold selection method from gray-level histograms. *IEEE Transactions on Systems, Man, Cybernetics, SMC*-9 (1979) 62–66.

[7] Sathya, P.D., and Kayalvizhi, R. Optimal multilevel thresholding using bacterial foraging algorithm. *Expert Systems with Applications* 38 (2011) 15549–15564.

[8] Maitra, M., and Chatterjee, A. A hybrid cooperative-comprehensive learning based PSO algorithm for image segmentation using multilevel thresholding. *Expert Systems with Applications* 34 (2008) 1341–1350.

[9] Zhiwei, Y., Zhaobao, Z., Xin, Y., and Xiaogang, N. Automatic threshold selection based on ant colony optimization algorithm. *In Proceedings of the International Conference on Neural Networks and Brain*, Beijing, China, Number 728–732, 2006.

[10] Ghamisi, P., Couceiro, M.S., Benediktsson, and Ferreira, N.M.F. An efficient method for segmentation of images based on fractional calculus and natural selection. *Expert Systems with Applications* 39 (2012) 12407–12417.

[11] Bezdek, J.C. 1981. Pattern recognition with fuzzy objective function algorithms. New York: Plenum Press.

[12] Nefti, S., and Oussalah, M. Probalilistic-fuzzy clustering algorithm. *In Proceedings of IEEE International Conference on Systems, Man, and Cybernetics*, 4786-4791, 2004.

[13] Wang, Z., and Bovik, A.C. A universal image quality index. *IEEE Signal Processing Letters* 9 (2002) 81-84.

[14] Tillett, J., Rao, T.M., Sahin, F., Rao, R., and Brockport, S. Darwinian particle swarm optimization. *In Proceedings of The 2nd Indian International Conference on Artificial Intelligence* (2005) 1474-1487.

[15] Couceiro, M.S., Ferreira, N.M.F., and Machado, J.A.T. In fractional order Darwinian particle swarm optimization. *In Proceedings of Symposium on Fractional Signals and Systems,* 2011.

[16] Podlubny, I. 1999. Fractional differential equations. An introduction to fractional derivatives, fractional differential equations, to methods of their solution and some of their applications. Academic Press, San Diego, CA.

[17] Couceiro, M.S., Rocha, R.P., Ferreira, N.M.F., and Machado, J.A.T. Introducing the fractional-order Darwinian PSO. *In Proceedings of SIViP* (2012) 343-350. DOI 10.1007/s11760-012-0316-2.

[18] Yan, H. Unified formulation of a class of image thresholding techniques. *Pattern Recognition* 29 (1996) 2025–2032.

Classification and Characterisation of Movement Patterns During Levodopa Therapy for Parkinson's Disease

Michael A. Lones*
Dept. of Computer Science
Heriot-Watt University
Edinburgh, UK

Jane E. Alty
Department of Neurology
Leeds General Infirmary
Leeds, UK

Phillipa Duggan-Carter
Department of Neurology
Leeds General Infirmary
Leeds, UK

Andrew J. Turner
Department of Electronics
University of York
York, UK

D. R. Stuart Jamieson
Department of Neurology
Leeds General Infirmary
Leeds, UK

Stephen L. Smith
Department of Electronics
University of York
York, UK

ABSTRACT

Parkinson's disease is a chronic neurodegenerative condition that manifests clinically with various movement disorders. These are often treated with the dopamine-replacement drug levodopa. However, the dosage of levodopa must be kept as low as possible in order to avoid the drug's side effects, such as the involuntary, and often violent, muscle spasms called dyskinesia, or levodopa-induced dyskinesia. In this paper, we investigate the use of genetic programming for training classifiers that can monitor the effectiveness of levodopa therapy. In particular, we evolve classifiers that can recognise tremor and dyskinesia, movement states that are indicative of insufficient or excessive doses of levodopa, respectively. The evolved classifiers achieve clinically useful rates of discrimination, with AUC>0.9. We also find that temporal classifiers generally out-perform spectral classifiers. By using classifiers that respond to low-level features of the data, we identify the conserved patterns of movement that are used as a basis for classification, showing how this approach can be used to characterise as well as classify abnormal movement.

Categories and Subject Descriptors

I.2.8 [**Artificial Intelligence**]: Problem Solving, Control Methods, and Search; I.5.2 [**Pattern Recognition**]: Design Methodology; I.5.4 [**Pattern Recognition**]: Applications—*Signal processing*; J.3 [**Computer Applications**]: Life and Medical Sciences

General Terms

Experimentation

*Corresponding author. Email: M.Lones@hw.ac.uk.

GECCO'14, July 12–16, 2014, Vancouver, BC, Canada.

ACM 978-1-4503-2881-4/14/07 ...$15.00.
http://dx.doi.org/10.1145/2598394.2609852.

Keywords

Classification, Genetic programming, Parkinson's disease, Time series analysis, Fourier analysis, Pattern discovery

1. INTRODUCTION

In previous work, we have focused on evolving classifiers to diagnose Parkinson's disease (PD) and other neurological conditions [12, 11, 13]. Diagnosis is, however, just the first stage of clinical management. Following diagnosis, a patient's condition needs to be carefully monitored in order to choose an appropriate medication regimen. Since many of the movement disorders associated with PD, such as tremor and bradykinesia (slowed movements), are caused by the loss of dopamine-producing neurones in the brain, patients are often prescribed dopamine replacements such as the drug levodopa. However, doses of these drugs must be carefully monitored in order to maintain a balance between treatment of the patient's symptoms and avoidance of side-effects. One of the most debilitating side-effects is levodopa-induced dyskinesia (LID), which causes involuntary spasms of the limbs, trunk, neck and face. Once LID becomes established, it is difficult to treat. A common approach to managing its occurrence is to reduce the dose of levodopa just prior to periods of severe LID, but this is difficult to monitor, as the presence and severity of LID tends to fluctuate throughout the day. Hence, there is a need for accurate measurements of the patient's symptoms, and a means to perform these measurements frequently, non-invasively, and inexpensively.

Ideally, monitoring of patients should take place during the course of their normal day-to-day activities, and recently there has been growing interest in the use of lightweight wearable devices for carrying out monitoring in this fashion. The idea is that the patient wears these devices at appropriate locations around their body. The data from the accelerometers is then passed to a portable device, which periodically checks for the presence of movement disorders, and sends this information to a clinician who can then adapt the patient's medication as appropriate. However, dyskinesias can be difficult to distinguish both from normal movement and from other types of movement disorder. Hence, the development of computational techniques that can discriminate between different classes of movement, and different severities within these classes, has become an important area of research.

In this paper, we describe the use of genetic programming for training classifiers that can identify the occurrence of tremor and LID within accelerometry data collected from wearable devices. We compare the performance of classifier models based on temporal and spectral representations of the data, and carry out analysis to identify the movement patterns used by evolved classifiers. Notably we find that classifiers trained directly on time series data are more effective than those trained on Fourier series coefficients for discriminating both tremor and LID.

2. RELATED WORK

Previous work on applying machine learning and data mining techniques to movement data collected from PD patients is reviewed in [1]. Particularly relevant are previous studies that have looked at predicting specific motor symptoms. This includes methods for measuring tremor whilst at rest [2], whilst performing specified movements [16], and during unscripted activities [15]. Several studies have also considered methods for identifying LID in movement data, whilst at rest [7], whilst performing specified movements [3], and during unscripted activities [9, 17]. In [6], the authors presented a method for detecting both tremor and dyskinesia during unscripted activities.

The work reported in this paper differs from earlier studies in our use of evolutionary algorithms and symbolic classifier models based upon low-level features of the data (e.g. raw acceleration values and Fourier coefficients), in comparison to the use of neural networks and higher-level features (such as signal energy and spectral powers over frequency ranges) in comparable studies [9, 6, 17, 15]. This is justified by our earlier work on PD diagnosis, which showed benefits in terms of interpretability and novelty discovery [12, 11], and which motivates our interest in characterising as well as classifying movement patterns. Characterisation is important, since the patterns of movement in PD are only partially understood. Better understanding of these movements may provide insight into their underlying causes, which in turn may contribute to the development of more effective treatments.

3. MATERIALS AND METHODS

3.1 Data Collection

We recruited six patients with confirmed PD for the clinical study. Lightweight devices containing integrated accelerometers and gyroscopes were fitted to the patients' legs, arms, torso, head and trunk, each able to record movement data in the three spatial and three rotational planes at a sample rate of 100Hz. An infrared camera was used to record video footage of the patients' movements. Each patient was recorded continuously for a period of 6 hours. Other than being situated in a hospital day case unit, the patients were unconstrained in their movements. Following the recording session, the video footage was analysed by two trained clinicians, who used the standard UPDRS (Unified Parkinson's Disease Rating Scale) and UDysRS (Unified Dyskinesia Rating Scale) scoring systems to mark up periods of tremor and LID within each body part with quantitative values (ranging from 0, indicating normal movements, to 4, indicating serious abnormality). Data sequences corresponding to these time periods were then extracted from the respective devices, resulting in sets of movement data corresponding to normal movement, and to tremor and LID at different clinical grades. Table 1 shows the number of data sequences in each movement class.

Tremor		Dyskinesia	
UPDRS	Count	UDysRS	Count
0	6661	0	2933
1	33	1	1227
2	61	2	1688
3	57	3	681
4	11	4	64

Table 1: Movement Data

3.2 Evolutionary Algorithm

We used implicit context representation Cartesian GP (IRCGP) to search for classifiers. IRCGP is a variant of CGP that uses a non-positional low level encoding to improve evolvability [4]. Prior to evaluation, IRCGP solutions are mapped into CGP solutions. Full details of IRCGP can be found in [11].

Evolutionary runs use a population size of 200 and a generation limit of 100. Point mutation is applied using a Gaussian distribution centred around the current value, with rates of 6% for functions and 3% for functionality profile elements (see [11]). Uniform crossover is applied with crossover points occurring with a probability of 15%.

3.3 Classifier Models

Three kinds of classifier were used: sliding window time series classifiers, long term spectral classifiers, and window-based short term spectral classifiers. In each case, classification is based on the evaluation of an evolved mathematical expression: in all cases these use up to 32 inputs, and contain up to 36 functions nodes ($\{+, -, \times, \div, \text{mean}, \text{min}, \text{max}, \text{mod}\}$) laid out on a 6×6 CGP grid. This uniformity eases comparisons, since the evolutionary algorithm is searching a space of equal size and dimensionality for each classifier model. The evolved expressions are used as follows:

Time domain classifiers For each data point, a time series is created by calculating the magnitude of acceleration at each time index. The inputs to the expression represent the acceleration values in a contiguous time series window of length 32 ($0.32s$). This window is slid along the entire time series, generating an output for each of the $L - 31$ overlapping windows, where L is the length of the time series. The classification for the time series is then the mean of these values.

Long term spectral classifiers The inputs to the expression represent spectral densities at 32 equally spaced points in the frequency range 0–50Hz. These frequencies are taken from the Fourier transform of the acceleration time series. This is calculated using the method described in [8], which involves segmenting the time series into non-overlapping windows (of length 64 in this case), applying Fourier transforms to each window, and then averaging these to produce a robust estimate of spectral density across the whole time series.

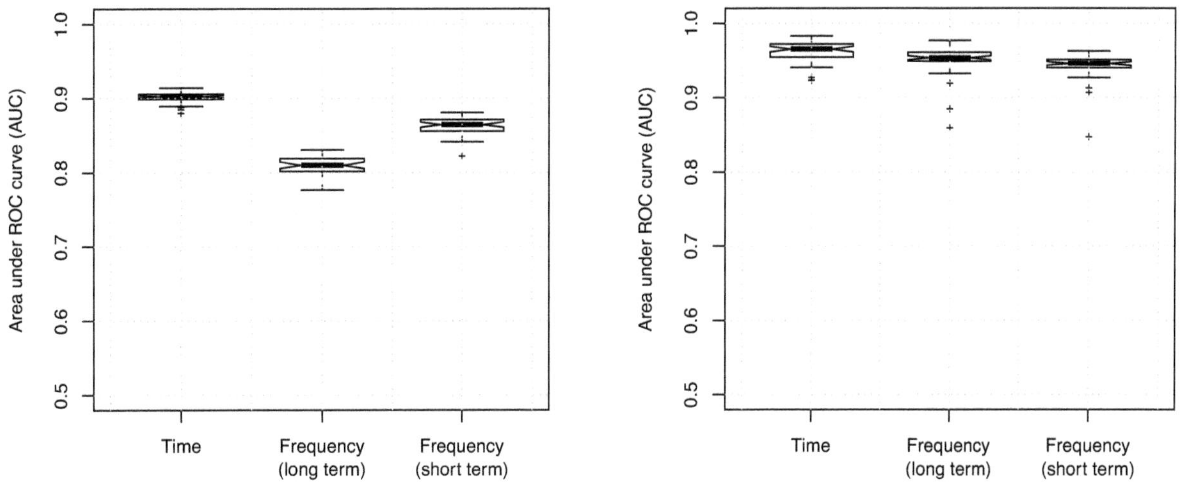

(a) Dyskinesia (b) Tremor

Figure 1: Discriminative ability of classifiers evolved to recognise dyskinesia and tremor when evaluated on the independent test sets. Notched box plots show distributions of AUC over 50 runs. Non-overlapping notches indicate a strong likelihood of statistically significant differences between means.

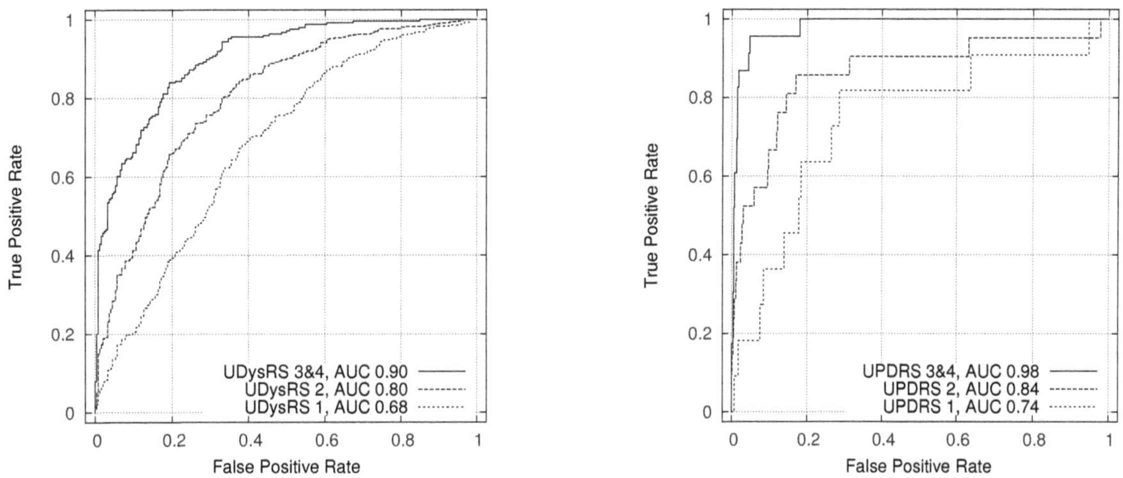

(a) Dyskinesia (b) Tremor

Figure 2: Representative ROC curves for classifiers evolved to recognise UDysRS/UPDRS level 3 and 4 dyskinesia and tremor when evaluated on the independent test sets for all UDysRS/UPDRS levels.

Short term spectral classifiers This is similar to the long term spectral classifier. However, the expression is applied independently to the Fourier transforms produced from each time series window, rather than the averaged Fourier transform. The classification for an acceleration time series is then the mean of these values.

In essence, these three classifier models operate on different views of the movement data, allowing them to recognise different kinds of pattern. The sliding window time domain classifier is designed to recognise conserved patterns of acceleration that occur during short periods of movement, the short term spectral classifier is similar, but operates in the frequency domain, and the long term spectral classifier is able to recognise stationary processes that occur over longer time periods.

3.4 Classifier Evaluation

The evolutionary algorithm is used to find diagnostic classifiers that have high predictive accuracy. This is done using an objective function that measures the area under the ROC curve (AUC) when separating classes, i.e. a classifier that maximises accuracy across all trade-offs between specificity and sensitivity. AUC is equivalent to the probability that a randomly chosen subject will be assigned to the correct class [10]. An AUC of 1 means that a classifier achieves 100% specificity and 100% sensitivity. An AUC of 0.5 indicates performance no better than random. Generally speaking, AUC>0.9 is considered excellent, and AUC>0.8 is considered good. An AUC less than 0.5 indicates the same predictive power as one with $1 - \text{AUC}$, but with a reversed ordering of the classes within its output range. To simplify

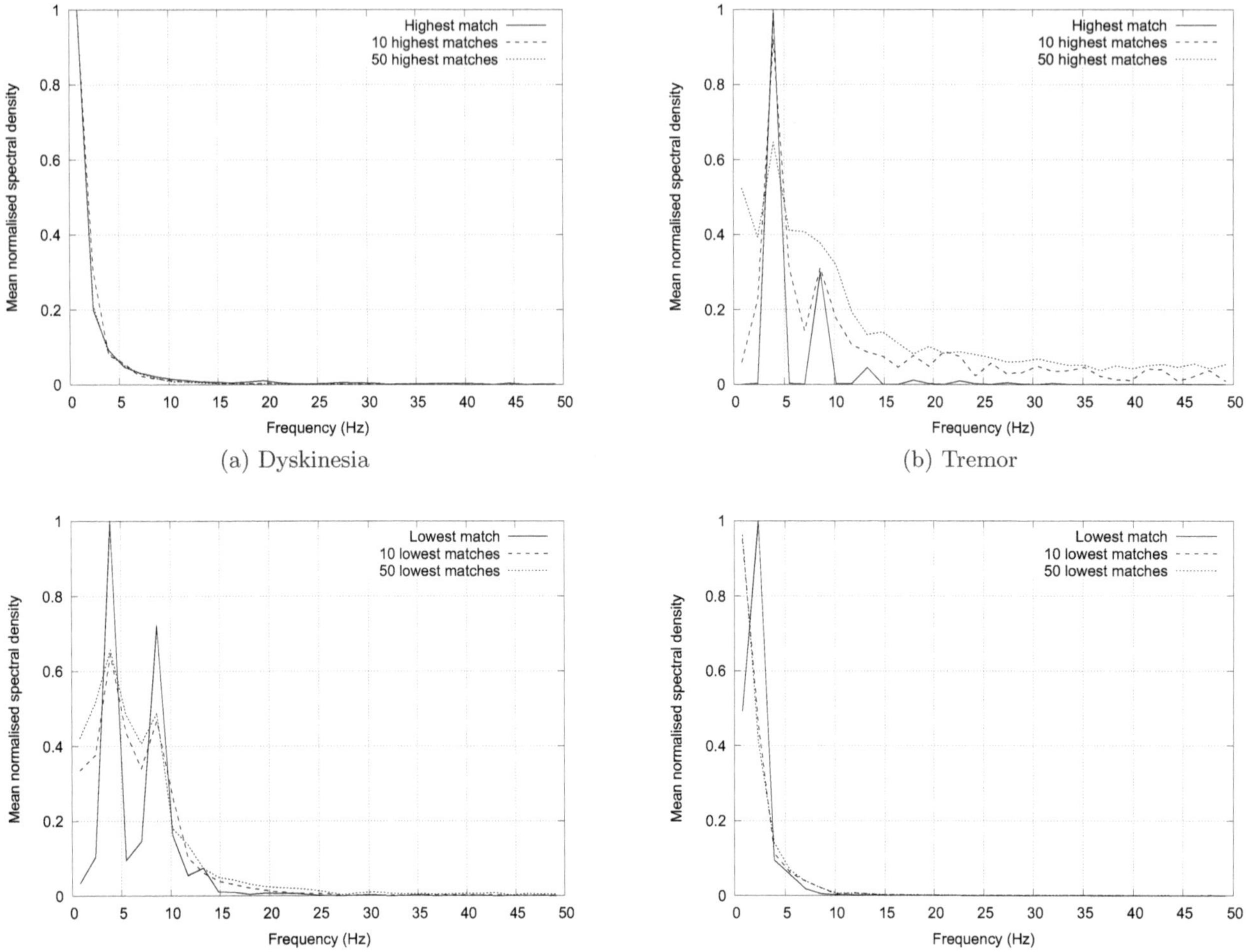

(a) Dyskinesia (b) Tremor (c) Not dyskinesia (d) Not tremor

Figure 3: Frequency responses of spectral classifiers evolved to predict dyskinesia and tremor, showing (a-b) periodograms matched as positive, (c-d) periodograms matched as negative.

the presentation of results, all AUCs are normalised to the interval [0.5,1.0].

Data classes are divided equally into three sets: a training set, a validation set, and a test set. The training set is used by the objective function. The validation set is used for early stopping, and to select the final generation solution with the highest generality. The test set is then used to give an unbiased measure of predictive accuracy for the selected solution.

4. RESULTS

We evolved two sets of classifiers: those that can recognise dyskinesia, and those that can recognise tremor. In both cases, the objective was to discriminate grade 3 (moderate) and grade 4 (severe), treated as a single class, from grade 0 (normal). Data for grades 1 (slight) and 2 (mild) were not used during training in order to focus classification on clinically significant levels of abnormal movement, and to prevent training being affected by misclassified examples (which is more likely to happen at lower grades). Note that the grade 0 set for dyskinesia contains examples of tremor in addition to normal movement, and vice versa. Hence, the evolved classifiers are expected to discriminate their movement of interest from both normal movement and other abnormal movements.

To compensate for the stochasticity of evolutionary algorithms, we carried out 50 independent runs for each combination of symptom class and classifier model. The resulting distributions of predictive accuracy are shown in Fig. 1. This shows that we obtained AUCs of around 0.9 for the best dyskinesia classifiers, and 0.98 for the best tremor classifiers. Both of these represent levels of discrimination that are likely to be useful for monitoring purposes. Fig. 2 shows ROC curves for representative examples of evolved dyskinesia and tremor classifiers. In both cases, the recognition rates are roughly proportional to clinical grade, suggesting that classifier outputs may also be useful for providing objective measurements of symptom severity.

It is notable that the time series classifiers performed, on average, significantly better than the spectral classifiers. This is most pronounced for dyskinesia, but is also true for tremor. This is an interesting result because a lot of existing classification work on both these movement types has

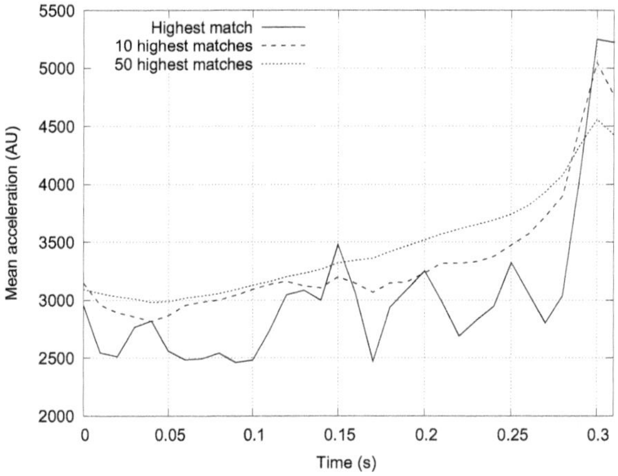

(a) Dyskinesia

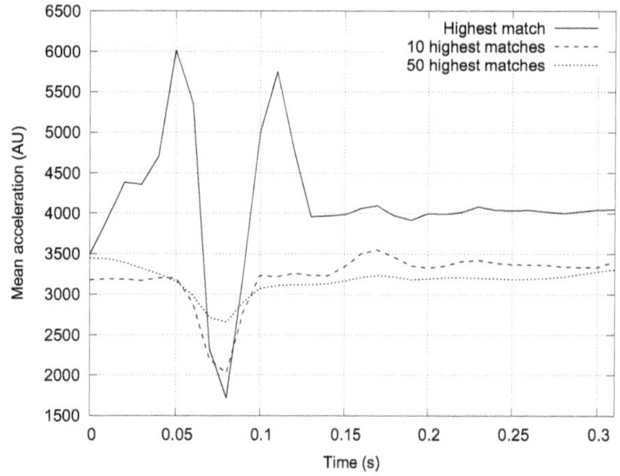

(b) Dyskinesia

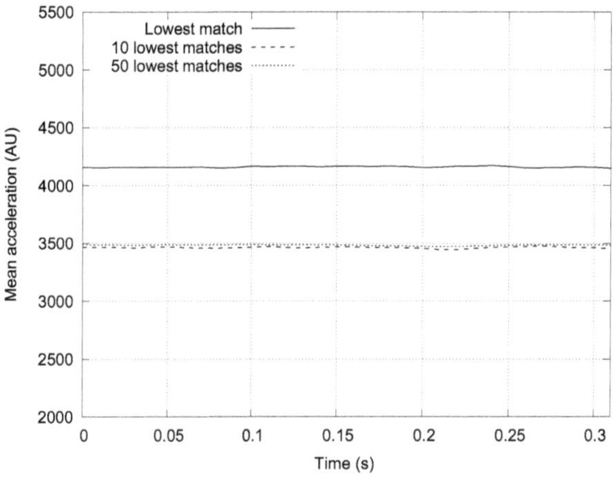

(c) Not dyskinesia

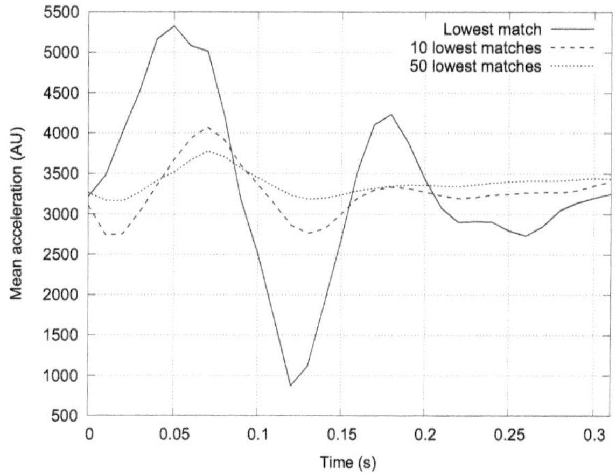

(d) Not dyskinesia

Figure 4: Acceleration patterns matched by time-domain classifiers evolved to predict dyskinesia, showing (a-b) time series windows matched as positive, (c-d) time series windows matched as negative.

focused on the frequency domain [1, 9, 14]. For tremor, a frequency analysis seems natural, since it is defined as a regular rhythmic oscillation of a body part, and the frequency ranges for different kinds of tremor are relatively well characterised. However, it is also possible to recognise oscillatory patterns in the time domain. In addition, time domain analysis makes it easier to characterise the shape of a waveform. This may underlie the performance of the time series classifiers, since the shape of the waveform may allow better separation of tremor and dyskinesia from other processes that occur within the same frequency range. For example, it has previously been observed that the frequencies associated with dyskinesia overlap with those of voluntary movements [9], especially walking.

Also notable are differences between the discriminative ability of the two spectral classifier models, particularly the observation that short term classifiers recognise dyskinesia better than long term classifiers. This suggests that dyskinesia does not occur with a constant frequency during dyskinetic periods, which reflects previous observations that periods of dyskinetic movement are intrinsically complex [5]. This is in contrast to the slightly better performance that long term classifiers show for tremor recognition, which is consistent with current understanding of the stationarity of Parkinson's tremor.

4.1 Discriminative Patterns

A benefit of using raw temporal and spectral data as a basis for classification, rather than more complex features derived from these, is the potential for identifying discriminative patterns of motor movements. In particular, it is possible to look at the data windows that lead to a strong positive or negative response from a classifier in order to identify significant over-represented patterns of movement [12]. This has more value in the time domain than the frequency domain. However, for completeness, Fig. 3 shows the periodograms which lead to strong positive and negative responses from evolved tremor and dyskinesia classifiers. It can be seen that tremor classifiers favour movements with periodograms that are dominated by spikes of around 4Hz and 8Hz. This corresponds well with the known bands of rest and action tremors. Dyskinesia classifiers, by comparison, favour periodograms with the power spectrum concentrated in the low frequencies. Again, this corresponds well with ex-

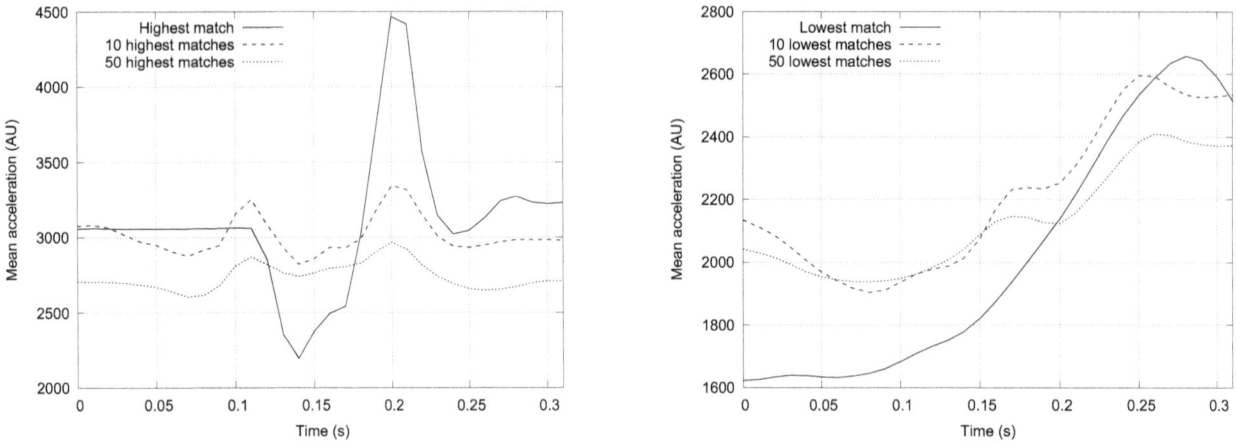

(a) Tremor (b) Not tremor

Figure 5: Acceleration patterns matched by time-domain classifiers evolved to predict tremor, showing (a) time series windows matched as positive, (b) time series windows matched as negative.

isting understanding of the frequency range of LID. It is also evident that the tremor and dyskinesia classifiers are symmetric, with the dyskinesia classifier most strongly rejecting periodograms that indicate tremor, and vice versa. This is likely to be a desirable behavior in practice, since these two movement classes are opposing indicators of levodopa dosage.

Fig. 4 shows a similar analysis from the time domain perspective, indicating over-represented patterns that occur within data windows classified strongly as dyskinesia or not dyskinesia. During the course of analysis, it was observed that classifiers evolved in different evolutionary runs often respond to different movement features in the data. For instance, the classifier whose matching behaviour is shown in Fig. 4a appears to respond strongly to the presence of a non-linear acceleration profile which starts flat and rises quickly, with a pronounced shoulder. Fig. 4b by comparison, suggests a classifier that responds to short periods of reduced acceleration during movements, with the highest matching patterns of acceleration resembling an M-shape. Some diversity is also seen in the negative responses from dyskinesia classifiers. However, Figs. 4c and 4d are representative of most. Fig. 4c suggests that constant acceleration is atypical of dyskinesia. Fig. 4d indicates the rejection of certain oscillatory patterns—most likely tremor, therefore suggesting a similar symmetric relationship to the ones seen in frequency domain classifiers. This is also supported by analysis of time domain classifiers evolved to recognise tremor (see Fig. 5), where negative responses somewhat resemble the dyskinetic acceleration profile shown in Fig. 4a.

5. CONCLUSIONS

In this paper, we have shown that genetic programming is able to design classifiers that can be used for monitoring a patient's response to levodopa therapy. We have also shown how the evolved classifiers can be analysed to identify the patterns of over-represented movement that are associated with tremor and dyskinesia.

Whilst the results seem promising, it should be born in mind that this is only an initial study involving a relatively small number of patients. Nevertheless, plans are currently underway to collect data from a larger group of patients, which will enable us to generate more robust classifiers, and also carry out a more rigorous study of the movement patterns underlying tremor, dyskinesia and other movement disorders associated with Parkinson's disease.

We can also expect to obtain better classifier performance by forming ensembles of evolved classifiers. Our previous work on Parkinson's diagnosis has shown the benefits of combining behaviourally diverse classifiers [11]. Given the diversity we have seen within the evolutionary runs in these experiments, this approach would seem particularly appropriate, especially if the movement patterns we see are complementary indicators of the underlying movement disorders.

Rather than generating a single classifier or ensemble for all patients, it may be more effective to train classifiers independently for each patient. Certainly our initial results (not reported here) seem to support this idea. Hence, in practice, we might expect the monitoring of levodopa treatment to be preceded by an initial evaluation that involves collecting movement data and training classifiers, rather than a one size fits all approach. However, such a personalised approach to medicine would be costly, especially given the growing incidence of Parkinson's disease. Nevertheless, the results presented in this paper indicate that sufficient generality can be obtained without considering patients individually.

6. ACKNOWLEDGMENTS

This work was part funded by Parkinson's UK and by the Wellcome Trust [ref: 097829] through the Centre for Chronic Diseases and Disorders (C2D2) at the University of York.

7. REFERENCES

[1] C. Ahlrichs and M. Lawo. Parkinson's disease motor symptoms in machine learning: A review. *Health Informatics*, 2, Nov. 2013.

[2] A. Bartolić, M. Šantić, and S. Ribarič. Automated tremor amplitude and frequency determination from power spectra. *Computer Methods and Programs in Biomedicine*, 94(1):77–87, Apr. 2009.

[3] P. Bonato, D. M. Sherrill, D. G. Standaert, S. S. Salles, and M. Akay. Data mining techniques to detect motor fluctuations in parkinson's disease. In *Engineering in Medicine and Biology Society, 2004. IEMBS'04. 26th Annual International Conference of the IEEE*, volume 2, pages 4766–4769. IEEE, 2004.

[4] X. Cai, S. L. Smith, and A. M. Tyrrell. Positional independence and recombination in cartesian genetic programming. In D. Hutchison et al., editors, *Genetic Programming, Proc. 9th European Conf., EuroGP 2006*, volume 3905 of *Lecture Notes in Computer Science*, chapter 32, pages 351–360. Springer Berlin Heidelberg, Berlin, Heidelberg, 2006.

[5] M. I. Chelaru, C. Duval, and M. Jog. Levodopa-induced dyskinesias detection based on the complexity of involuntary movements. *Journal of neuroscience methods*, 186(1):81–89, Jan. 2010.

[6] B. T. Cole, S. H. Roy, C. J. De Luca, and S. Nawab. Dynamic neural network detection of tremor and dyskinesia from wearable sensor data. *Annual International Conference of the IEEE Engineering in Medicine and Biology Society.*, 2010:6062–6065, 2010.

[7] J. Gour, R. Edwards, S. Lemieux, M. Ghassemi, M. Jog, and C. Duval. Movement patterns of peak-dose levodopa-induced dyskinesias in patients with parkinson's disease. *Brain Research Bulletin*, 74(1-3):66–74, Sept. 2007.

[8] D. M. Halliday, J. R. Rosenberg, A. M. Amjad, P. Breeze, B. A. Conway, and S. F. Farmer. A framework for the analysis of mixed time series/point process data–theory and application to the study of physiological tremor, single motor unit discharges and electromyograms. *Progress in biophysics and molecular biology*, 64(2-3):237–278, 1995.

[9] N. L. W. Keijsers, M. W. I. M. Horstink, and S. C. A. M. Gielen. Online monitoring of dyskinesia in patients with parkinson's disease. *Engineering in Medicine and Biology Magazine, IEEE*, 22(3):96–103, May 2003.

[10] H. C. C. Kraemer, G. A. Morgan, N. L. Leech, J. A. Gliner, J. J. Vaske, and R. J. Harmon. Measures of clinical significance. *Journal of the American Academy of Child and Adolescent Psychiatry*, 42(12):1524–1529, Dec. 2003.

[11] M. Lones, S. Smith, J. Alty, S. Lacy, K. Possin, S. Jamieson, and A. Tyrrell. Evolving classifiers to recognise the movement characteristics of parkinson's disease patients. *IEEE Transactions on Evolutionary Computation*, 2013. Published online, in press.

[12] M. A. Lones, J. E. Alty, S. E. Lacy, D. R. S. Jamieson, K. L. Passin, N. Schuff, and S. L. Smith. Evolving classifiers to inform clinical assessment of parkinson's disease. In *Computational Intelligence in Healthcare and e-health (CICARE), 2013 IEEE Symposium on*, pages 76–82. IEEE, Apr. 2013.

[13] M. A. Lones and S. L. Smith. Objective assessment of Visuo-Spatial ability using implicit context representation cartesian genetic programming. In *Genetic and Evolutionary Computation: Medical Applications*, pages 174–189. John Wiley & Sons, Ltd, 2010.

[14] K. Niazmand, A. Kalaras, H. Dai, and T. C. Lueth. Comparison of methods for tremor frequency analysis for patients with parkinson's disease. In *Biomedical Engineering and Informatics (BMEI), 2011 4th International Conference on*, volume 2, pages 693–697. IEEE, Oct. 2011.

[15] G. Rigas, A. T. Tzallas, M. G. Tsipouras, P. Bougia, E. E. Tripoliti, D. Baga, D. I. Fotiadis, S. G. Tsouli, and S. Konitsiotis. Assessment of tremor activity in the parkinson's disease using a set of wearable sensors. *Information Technology in Biomedicine, IEEE Transactions on*, 16(3):478–487, May 2012.

[16] R. Saunders-Pullman, C. Derby, K. Stanley, A. Floyd, S. Bressman, R. B. Lipton, A. Deligtisch, L. Severt, Q. Yu, M. Kurtis, and S. L. Pullman. Validity of spiral analysis in early parkinson's disease. *Movement disorders*, 23(4):531–537, Mar. 2008.

[17] M. Tsipouras, A. Tzallas, E. Tripoliti, G. Rigas, P. Bougia, D. Fotiadis, S. Tsouli, and S. Konitsiotis. On assessing motor disorders in parkinson's disease. In J. Lin and K. Nikita, editors, *Wireless Mobile Communication and Healthcare*, volume 55 of *Lecture Notes of the Institute for Computer Sciences, Social Informatics and Telecommunications Engineering*, pages 35–38. Springer Berlin Heidelberg, 2011.

Noise-aware Evolutionary TDMA Optimization for Neuronal Signaling in Medical Sensor-Actuator Networks

Junichi Suzuki
Department of Computer Science
University of Massachusetts, Boston
Boston, MA, 02125-3393, USA
jxs@cs.umb.edu

Pruet Boonma
Department of Computer Engineering
Chiang Mai University
Chiang Mai, 50200, Thailand
pruet@eng.cmu.ac.th

ABSTRACT

Neuronal signaling is one of several approaches to network nanomachines in the human body. This paper formulates a noisy optimization problem for a neuronal signaling protocol based on Time Division Multiple Access (TDMA) and solves the problem with a noise-aware optimizer that leverages an evolutionary algorithm. The proposed optimizer is intended to minimize signaling latency by multiplexing and parallelizing signal transmissions in a given neuronal network, while maximizing signaling robustness (i.e., unlikeliness of signal interference). Since latency and robustness objectives conflict with each other, the proposed optimizer seeks the optimal trade-offs between them. It exploits a nonparametric (i.e.. distribution-free) statistical operator because it is not fully known what distribution(s) noise follows in each step/component in neuronal signaling. Simulation results show that the proposed optimizer efficiently obtains quality TDMA signaling schedules and operates a TDMA protocol by balancing conflicting objectives in noisy environments.

Categories and Subject Descriptors

C.2.2 [**Computer-Communication Networks**]: Network Protocols; C.3 [**Special-purpose and Application-based Systems**]: *Signal processing systems*; I.2.8 [**Artificial Intelligence**]: Problem Solving, Control Methods, and Search—*Heuristic methods*

Keywords

Molecular communication, Neuronal networks, TDMA scheduling, Evolutionary multiobjective optimization algorithms

1. INTRODUCTION

A nanoscale system consists of one or more nanomachines, which are nanoscale devices that perform simple computation, sensing and/or actuation tasks [17, 25]. Nanomachines may be man-made devices built in the *top-down* approach, downscaling the current microelectronic and microelectromechanical technologies, or in the *bottom-up* approach, assembling synthesized nanomaterials such as graphene nanoribbons and carbon nanotubes. Alternatively, nanomachines may be *bio-hybrid*, integrating man-made nanostructures with biological materials such as DNA strands and genetically engineered cells, or *bio-enabled*, synthesizing biological materials without man-made nanostructures [9, 21].

An emerging design strategy for nanoscale systems is to *network* nanomachines for operating in larger physical spaces in higher spatial and temporal resolutions. Although individual nanomachines are limited in computation, sensing and actuation capabilities, an assembly of nanomachines can potentially organize into a "large-scale" network that spreads on centimeter to meter scale and collaboratively performs tasks that no individual nanomachines could.

Molecular communication is one of a few options to network nanomachines. It utilizes molecules as a communication medium between nanomachines [17, 25]. Due to its advantages such as inherent nanometer scale, biocompatibility and energy efficiency [9], a key application domain of molecular communication is intrabody nanonetworks where nanomachines are networked to perform sensing and actuation tasks for biomedical and prosthetic purposes. Those tasks include in-situ physiological sensing, biomedical anomaly detection, targeted drug delivery, medical operations with cellular/molecular level precision, neural signal transduction and neuromuscular implant control.

This paper focuses on molecular communication that utilizes neurons as a primary component to build intrabody nanonetworks. A neuron-based intrabody nanonetwork consists of a set of nanoscale sensor/actuator nodes and a network of neurons that are artificially formed into a particular topology It allows individual nodes to interface with neurons and communicate to other nodes with neuronal (i.e., electrochemical) signals through a chain of neurons.

This paper formulates a noisy multiobjective optimization problem for a neuronal signaling protocol, called Neuronal TDMA, and approaches the problem with a noise-aware evolutionary multiobjective optimization algorithm (EMOA). Neuronal TDMA performs single-bit Time Division Multiple Access (TDMA) scheduling for individual nodes to activate their nearby neurons and multiplex/parallelize signal transmissions in a given neuronal network.

The proposed EMOA heuristically seeks the optimal TDMA schedules (i.e., which neurons to activate and when to activate them to trigger signal transmissions) for nodes by evolving a set of solution candidates (or *individuals*) toward the optima through generations. Each individual represents a particular TDMA schedule for individual nodes. The proposed EMOA is designed to address two important issues in neuronal signaling: *interference* and *noise*. When differ-

GECCO'14, July 12–16, 2014, Vancouver, BC, Canada.

http://dx.doi.org/10.1145/2598394.2609854.

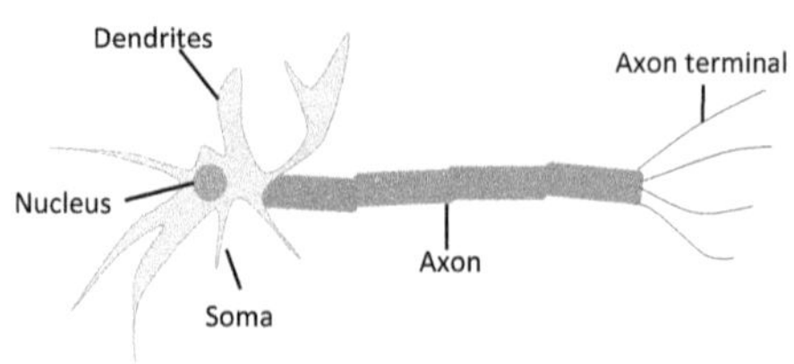

Figure 1: Structure of a neuron

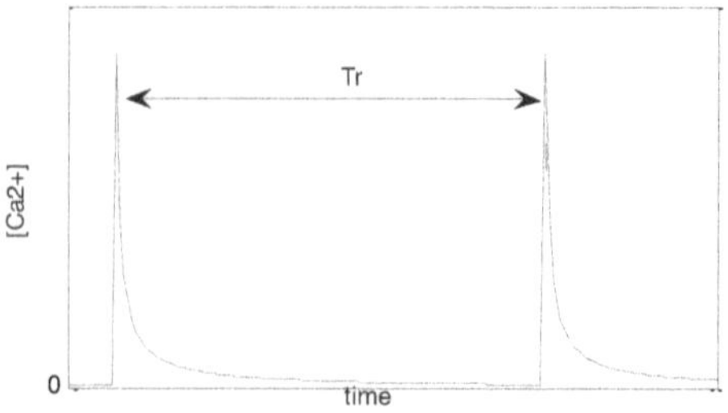

Figure 2: Intracellular Ca^{2+} concentration

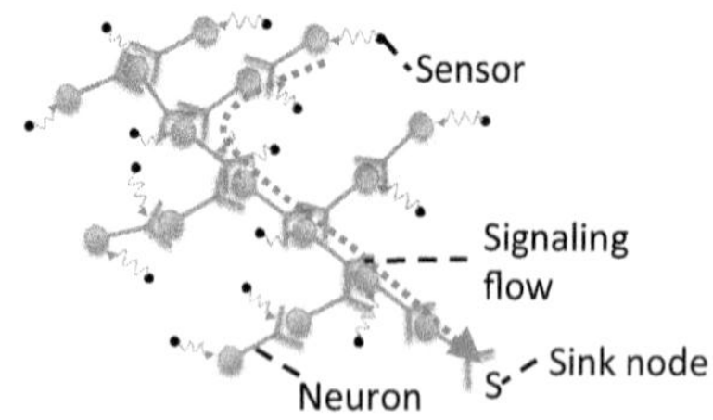

Figure 3: An Example Sensor-Actuator Network

ent signals attempt to travel through a neuron simultaneously, they *interfere* (or collide) with each other [3]. This leads to the loss or corruption of information encoded with the signals. The proposed EMOA is designed to avoid signal interference to ensure that signals reach the destination while multiplexing/parallelizing signal transmissions to improve performance measures such as signaling latency.

Neuronal signaling is inherently *noisy* [6]. For example, thermal, current and chemical noise affects the latency of signal transmission. Due to noise, the same individual (i.e., TDMA schedule) can yield different performance measures from time to time. This degenerates individual-to-individual comparison; for example, the proposed EMOA may mistakenly judge that an inferior individual outperforms a superior one. More importantly, noise can cause signal interference unexpectedly. Even if the proposed EMOA determines a *feasible* individual, which is designed to perform interference-free signaling, the individual may actually become *infeasible*, causing signal interference, due to noise.

The proposed EMOA performs a statistical noise-aware operator for individual-to-individual comparison. (Individual-to-individual comparison operators are often called *dominance* operators in the area of EMOAs.) Using the noise-aware operator, called the α-dominance, the proposed EMOA is designed to seek the Pareto-optimal individuals (TDMA schedules) with respect to conflicting optimization objectives: signaling latency and signaling robustness (unlikeliness of signal interference). Simulation results show that the proposed EMOA successfully allows Neuronal TDMA to perform signal transmissions in noisy environments and reveals the trade-offs between signaling latency and robustness. It is also verified that the α-dominance operator outperforms existing noise-aware operators.

2. RELATED WORK

Compared to other molecular communication approaches (e.g., molecular motors, calcium signaling and bacteria communication), neuron-based communication has such advantages as long distance coverage, high speed signaling (up to 90 m/s) and low attenuation in signaling [13].

Balasubramaniam et al. first examined a TDMA protocol for neuronal networks [1]. Neuronal TDMA extended it with an EMOA that considers communication performance objectives such as signaling yield and latency [26]. This paper extends [26] by considering communication robustness as well as communication performance in noisy environments.

In the area of EMOAs, there exist various existing work to handle noise/uncertainties in objective functions. Most of them take *parametric* approaches, which assume particular noise distributions in advance; for example, normal distributions [8], uniform distributions [27] and Poisson distributions [28]. Given a noise distribution, existing noise-aware dominance operators collect objective value samples from each individual in order to determine superior-inferior relationships among individuals. In contrast, the α-dominance operator assumes no noise distributions in advance because it is not fully known what distribution noise follows in each step/component in the entire neuronal signaling process.

3. BACKGROUND

This section provides preliminaries on neuronal signaling and neuron-based intrabody sensor-actuator networks.

3.1 Neuronal Signaling

Neurons are a fundamental component of the nervous system, which includes the brain and the spinal cord. They are electrically excitable cells that process and transmit information via electrical and chemical signaling.

A neuron consists of cell body (or soma), dendrites and axon (Figure 1) [3]. A soma varies from 4 to 100 micrometers in diameter. Dendrites are thin structures that arise from the soma. The length of a dendrite is up to a few hundred micrometers. Dendrites receive the majority of inputs to a neuron. An axon is a cellular extension that arises from the soma. It travels through the body in bundles called *nerves*. Its length can be over one meter in the human nerve that arises from the spinal cord to a toe.

Neurons are connected with each other to form a network(s). They communicate via *synapses*, each of which is a junction between two neurons. A synapse contains molecular machinery that allows a (presynaptic) neuron to transmit a chemical signal to another (postsynaptic) neuron. Signals are transmitted from the axon of a presynaptic neuron to a dendrite of a postesynaptic neuron. An axon transmits an output signal to a postsynaptic neuron, and a dendrite receives an input signal from a presynaptic neuron.

Presynaptic and postsynaptic neurons maintain voltage gradients across their membranes by means of voltage-gated ion channels, which are embedded in the presynaptic membrane to unbalance intracellular and extracellular concentration of ions (e.g., Ca^{2+}) [24]. Changes in the cross-membrane ion concentration (i.e., voltage) can alter the function of ion channels. If the concentration changes by a large enough amount (e.g., approx. 80 mV in a giant squid), ion channels start pumping extracellular ions inward. Upon the increase in intracellular ion concentration, the presynaptic neuron releases a chemical called a *neurotransmitter* (e.g., acetylcholine), which travels through the synapse from the presynaptic postsynaptic neuron. The neurotransmitter electrically excites the postsynaptic neuron, which in turn generates an electrical pulse called an *action potential*. This signal travels rapidly along the neuron's axon and activates synaptic connections (i.e., opens ion channels) when it arrives at the axon's terminals. This way, an action potential triggers cascading neuron-to-neuron communication.

Figure 2 shows how Ca^{2+} concentration changes in a neuron. When the concentration peaks, the neuron releases a neurotransmitter(s) and goes into a *refractory period* (T_r in Figure 2), which is the time required for the neuron to replenish its internal Ca^{2+} store. During T_r, it cannot process any incoming signals. The refractory period is approximately two milliseconds in a giant squid.

3.2 Neuron-based Intrabody Nanonetworks

This paper assumes neuronal signaling in a three-dimensional network of natural neurons that are artificially grown and formed into particular topology patterns. This assumption is made upon numerous research efforts to grow neurons on substrates [18] and form topologically-specific neuronal networks [14, 16, 20, 29].

Figure 3 illustrates a schematic neuron-based intrabody nanonetwork. It contains an artificially-grown neuronal network and several nanomachines such as sensors and a sink. Sensors utilize neuronal signaling to deliver sensor data to a sink. As a potential application, sensors may periodically monitor certain physiological status and report physiological data or biomedical anomalies to the sink. The sink may work as a transducer that converts incoming electrochemical signals to electrostatic or electromagnetic signals. Electrostatic signals may carry sensor data to an on-body (i.e., epidermal) device(s) through a body-coupled communication scheme [19, 31]. Electromagnetic signals may carry sensor data to an around-body device(s) such as a smartphone and tablet computer.

This paper assumes that nanomachines (e.g., sensor and sink nodes) interact with neuronal networks in a *non-invasive* manner. This means that it is not required to insert particular materials (e.g., carbon nanotubes) into neurons so that nanomachines can trigger and receive signals. For example, nanomachines may use chemical agents (e.g., acetylcholine and mecamylamine [1]) or light [11, 12].

Other potential applications are neurointerfaces that leverage in-situ sensing and actuation for prosthetic devices; for example, neuroprosthetic bladder control (Figure 4). In a normal bladder, a sensory nerve senses that the bladder is full of urine and transmits a sensory signal (i.e., the bladder's sense of fullness) to the brain. Whenever appropriate, the brain sends out a control signal through the spinal cord to contract the bladder, relax the sphincter and trigger urination. However, nervous system disorders (e.g., spinal cord injuries and subsequent paralysis) can disrupt those signals to/from the brain and eliminate the fullness sensation and muscle control. A person with this kind of disorder is forced to empty his/her bladder with a catheter.

In-situ sensing and actuation can help correct incontinence. In Figure 4, a particular portion of a spinal nerve, called dorsal root ganglion, is teased out and interfaced to sensor nodes. The sensors intercept neuronal signals from the nerve and forwards them to the sink node. The sink may determine whether the bladder is full, and if it is full, transmits electrostatic or electromagnetic signals to an on/around-body node(s), which in turn notify the bladder's fullness to the patient. A neurostimulator(s) connected to the nerve issues high-frequency stimulation to prevent the bladder from emptying itself. Whenever ready to urinate, the patient uses his/her on/around-body node to issue an electrostatic or electromagnetic signal to a subepidermal node, which in turn transduces the signal to a neuronal electrochemical signal and transmits it to in-situ a neurostimulator(s). Each neurostimulator delivers low-frequency stimulation or stop stimulation so that the bladder to empty. This intervention can be a less invasive alternative to the current state of the art in neuroprosthetic bladder control (e.g., [4]).

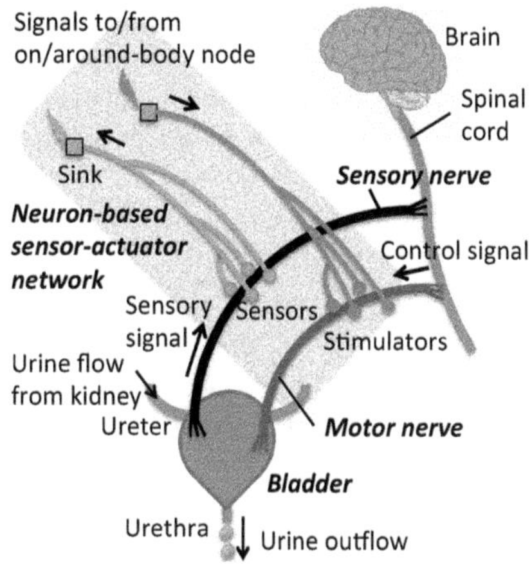

Figure 4: Neuroprosthetic Bladder Control

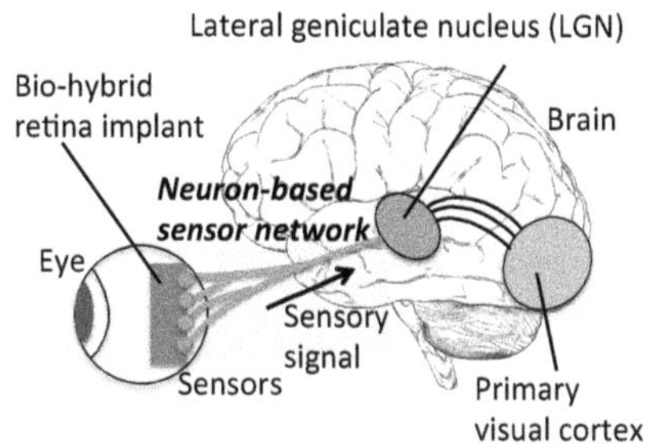

Figure 5: Neuroprosthetic Visual Pathway

Another potential neurointerface application is a bio-hybrid visual prosthesis. In a normal retina, photoreceptor cells perform phototransduction, which converts light (visible electromagnetic radiation) to electrical signals in retinal ganglion cells. Ganglion cells are located near the inner surface of the retina, and their axons extend to the brain. Those axons form the optic nerve. Ganglion cells receive visual information from photoreceptor cells by means of electrical signals and transmits it to the lateral geniculate nucleus of the thalamus, which in turn projects to the primary visual cortex in the occipital lobe.

One of treatment strategies for retinal disorders is to use retinal implants. For example, an implant proposed in [22] bypasses photoreceptor cells and stimulates the optic nerve (i.e., ganglion cells) directly with signals from a phototransduction device that is equipped with a video camera.

An emerging design approach is to bypasses the optic nerve as well as photoreceptor cells [30]. A neuron-based nanonetwork can replace the optic nerve and connect an implant with the lateral geniculate nucleus as a transplanted visual pathway (Figure 5). The implant contains nanomachines that receive signals (visual information) from a phototransduction device through a wired or wireless means. Cultured neurons are attached onto those nanomachines, and their axons are guided to the lateral geniculate nucleus. This bio-hybrid implant would be useful for patients with diseases in the optic nerve such as glaucoma and diabetic retinopathy.

4. NOISY OPTIMIZATION PROBLEM IN NEURONAL TDMA

Neuronal TDMA performs a single-bit TDMA communication that periodically assigns a *time slot* to each sensor. Sensors activate (or fire) neurons, one after the other, each using its own time slot. This allows multiple sensors to transmit signals to the sink through the shared neuronal network. Each sensor transmits a single-bit within a single time slot. This single-bit-per-slot design is based on two assumptions: (1) a signal (i.e., action potential) is interpreted with two levels of amplitudes, which represent 0 and 1, and (2) after a signal transmission, a neuron goes into a refractory period (T_r in Figure 2).

As described in Section 1, an important goal of Neuronal TDMA is to avoid signal interference, which occurs when multiple signals fire the same neuron at the same time and leads to corruption of transmitted sensor data at the sink. Signals can easily interfere with each other if sensors fire their neighboring neurons randomly. Neuronal TDMA is intended to eliminate signal interference by scheduling which sensors fire which neurons with respect to time. The proposed EMOA seeks the optimal TDMA schedules for a set of sensors in a given neuronal network.

Figure 6 shows an example neuronal network that has five neurons (n_1 to n_5) and four nodes (three sensors, s_1, s_2 and s_3, and a sink). Figure 7 illustrates an example TDMA schedule for those sensors to fire neurons. The scheduling cycle period lasts five time slots ($T_s = 5$). The sensor s_1 fires the neuron n_4 to initiate signaling in the first time slot T_1. The signal travels through n_5 in the next time slot T_2 to reach the sink. s_2 transmits a signal on n_3 in T_2. During T_2, two signals travel in the neuronal network in parallel. The duration of each time slot (T_u in Figure 7) is designed as the sum of three time periods: (1) *synaptic delay*, which is the time for neurotransmitters to travel through a synapse from a presynaptic neuron or a sensor and generate an action potential in a postsynaptic neuron, (2) *intracellular transmission delay*, which is the time for an action potential to travel within a neuron (i.e., from its dendrite terminal to its axon terminal) and (3) a refractory period.

4.1 Optimization Constraints and Objectives

The scheduling problem this paper focuses on is defined as an optimization problem where a neuron-based nanonetwork contains M sensors, $S = \{s_1, s_2, ..., s_i, ..., s_M\}$, and N neurons, $N = \{n_1, n_2, ..., n_j, ..., n_N\}$.

The proposed EMOA is designed to meet two optimization constraints. The first constraint enforces that at most one signal can pass through each neuron in a single time slot. (Otherwise, signal interference occurs.) The second constraint enforces each sensor transmits one signal during the scheduling cycle T_s A TDMA schedule is said to be *feasible* if it never violates constraints. On the contrary, it is said to be *infeasible* if it violates any of constraints. An example TDMA schedule in Figure 7 is feasible.

The proposed EMOA considers two optimization objectives: signaling latency and signaling robustness. Signaling latency (f_L) is computed with Equation 1. It indicates how soon the sink receives all signals from all M sensors. It is to be minimized.

$$f_L = max_{s_i \in S}\ t_a^{s_i} \qquad (1)$$

$t_a^{s_i}$ denotes the arrival time at which the sink receives a signal that s_i transmits. f_L determines the scheduling cycle period T_s ($T_s = f_L$). In Figure 7, $f_L = 5$.

Signlaing robustness (f_R) indicates the unlikeliness for signals to interfere with each other on shared neurons $N' = \{n'_1, n'_2, ..., n'_h, ..., n'_H\} \subset N$. Shared neurons are the neurons that sensors share to transmit their signals to the sink. In Figure 6, n_2 and n_5 are shared neurons. (s_2 and s_3 share n_2. s_1, s_2 and s_3 share n_5.) Higher robustness means lower chances of signal interference. f_R is computed with Equation 2. It is to be maximized.

$$f_R = \sum_{l=1}^{M} \sum_{m=1}^{M} \sum_{h=1}^{H} \frac{I_s}{T_u} \left(t_a^{n'_h(s_l)} - t_a^{n'_h(s_m)} \right), \quad l \neq m \qquad (2)$$

$t_a^{n'_h(s_l)}$ denotes the arrival time at which a signal from the l-th sensor s_l arrives at the h-th shared neuron n'_h. $t_a^{n'_h(s_l)} - t_a^{n'_h(s_m)} = 0$ if signals from s_l and s_m interfere on n'_h. In Figure 7, s_2's and s_3's signals pass through n_2 in T_3 and T_4, respectively. Thus, $t_a^{n_2(s_3)} - t_a^{n_2(s_2)} = T_u$. Note that $I_s = 1$ if $t_a^{n'_h(s_l)} > t_a^{n'_h(s_m)}$; otherwise, $I_s = 0$.

4.2 Impacts of Noise on Objective Functions

As described in Section 1, this paper considers noise that varies the speed and latency of signal transmissions. Major contributors to noise are variances of synaptic delay and refractory period.

Noise impacts both objective functions (Equations 1 to 2). It impacts f_F, f_L and f_R by varying t_a in Equations 1 and 2. Therefore, they are redefined as follows for signaling in noisy environments.

$$f_L^e = f_L + e_L \qquad (3)$$

$$f_R^e = f_R + e_R \qquad (4)$$

This way, noise-aware objectives are defined with additive noise (e_L and e_R), which can be positive and negative.

As t_a varies, signal interference can occur even if the *one-signal-per-slot* constraint (see Section 4.1) is satisfied. In Figure 7, s_2's signal travels on n_2 during T_3, and s_3's signal travels on n_2 during T_4. This signaling schedule satisfies the *one-signal-per-slot* constraint; however, the two signals can interfere if s_2's signal arrives at n_2 sometime in T_4 and/or if s_3's signal arrives at n_2 sometime in T_3 due to noise. This means that noise can degenerate a feasible individual (i.e., signaling schedule) to be infeasible.

5. THE PROPOSED EMOA

The proposed EMOA is designed to solve the noisy optimization problem described in Section 4. It iteratively

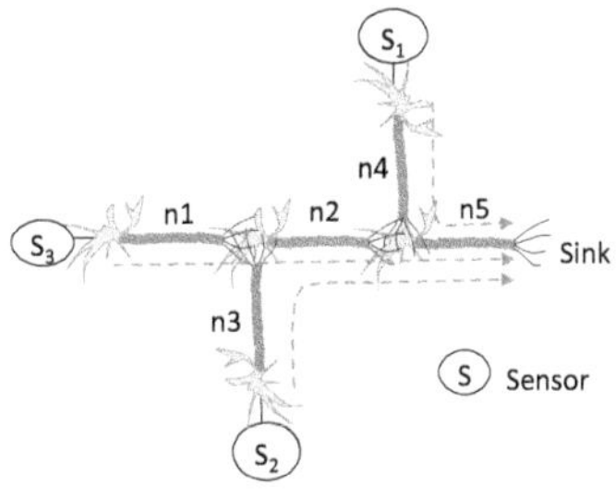

Figure 6: An Example Neuronal Network

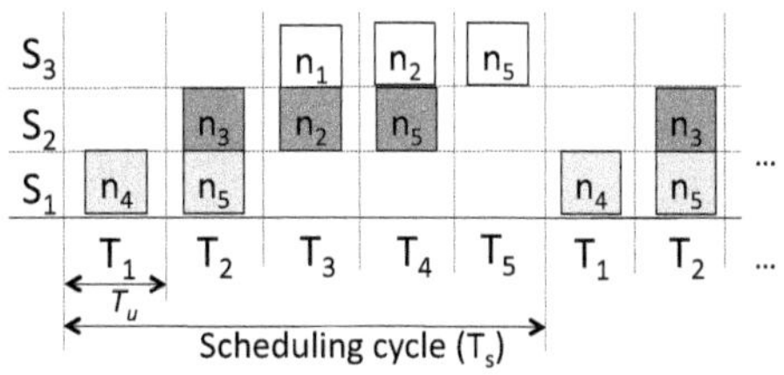

Figure 7: An Example TDMA Schedule

S_3	0	0	1	0	0
S_2	0	1	0	0	0
S_1	1	0	0	0	0
	T_1	T_2	T_3	T_4	T_5

Figure 8: An Example Individual

evolves the population of individuals (i.e., TDMA schedules) via several operators (e.g., crossover, mutation and selection operators) toward the Pareto optima.

Each individual represents a particular TDMA schedule for M sensors. Figure 8 shows the structure of an example individual, which encodes the TDMA schedule in Figure 7. In this example, s_1 fires its neighboring neuron, n_4, in the first time slot T_1. $s2$ and s_3 fire n_2 and n_1 in T_2 and T_3, respectively.

5.1 The α-Dominance Operator

This section describes the notion of α-dominance. It determines a statistical superior-inferior relationship, called the α-dominance relationship, between given two individuals using their objective value samples. It extends a classical dominance relationship [23], in which an individual i is said to *dominate* an individual j (denoted by $i \succ j$) if the both of the following conditions are hold:

- i's objective values are superior than, or equal to, j's in all objectives.
- i's objective values are superior than j's in at least one objectives.

The α-dominance operator takes objective value samples of given two individuals, estimates the impacts of noise on the samples, and determines whether it is confident enough to judge which one is superior/inferior between the two individuals. The operator determines that individual A α-*dominate* individual B (denoted by $A \succ_\alpha B$), iif:

- A's and B's objective value samples are classifiable with a statistical confidence level of α, and
- $\mathcal{C}(A, B) = 1 \wedge \mathcal{C}(B, A) < 1$.

In order to examine the first condition, the α-dominance operator classifies A's and B's objective value samples with Support Vector Machine (SVM), and measures a classification error. (See Step 1 in an example shown in Figure 9.) The error (e) is computed as the ratio of the number of miss-classified samples to the total number of samples. For evaluating the confidence level (α) in a classification error, the α-dominance operator computes the classification error's confidence interval (e_{int}):

$$e_{int} = e \pm t_{\alpha,n-1}\sigma \quad (5)$$

$t_{\alpha,n-1}$ denotes a single-tail t-distribution with α confidence level and $n-1$ degrees of freedom. n denotes the total number of samples. σ is the standard deviation of e. It is approximated as follows.

$$\sigma \cong \sqrt{\frac{e}{n}} \quad (6)$$

If e_{int} is significant (i.e., if e_{int} does not span zero), the α-dominance operator cannot classify A's and B's samples with the confidence level of α. Thus, the operator determines that A and B do not α-dominate each other. (See Step 2 in Figure 9.)

If e_{int} is not significant (i.e., if e_{int} spans zero), the α-dominance operator can classify A's and B's samples with the confidence level of α. Thus, the operator examine the aforementioned second condition. (See Step 2 in an example shown in Figure 9.) It measures $\mathcal{C}$-metric [33] with a classical notion of dominance ($\succ$) described earlier. $\mathcal{C}(A, B)$ denotes the fraction of individual B's samples that at least one sample of individual A dominates:

$$\mathcal{C}(A, B) = \frac{|\{b \in B \mid \exists a \in A : a \succ b\}|}{|B|} \quad (7)$$

If $\mathcal{C}(A, B) = 1$, all of B's samples are dominated by at least one sample of A. If $\mathcal{C}(B, A) < 1$, not all of A's samples are dominated by at least one sample of B. The α-dominance operator determines $A \succ_\alpha B$ if $\mathcal{C}(A, B) = 1$ and $\mathcal{C}(B, A) < 1$. If $\mathcal{C}(A, B) < 1$ and $\mathcal{C}(B, A) < 1$, the operator determines neither $A \succ_\alpha B$ nor $B \succ_\alpha A$. See Figure 9 as well.

Figure 9 shows an example to determine the α-dominance relationship between two individuals, A and B, with two objectives, f_1 and f_2, to be minimized. Individual A and B have seven samples each. First, the α-dominance operator classifies these 14 samples in the objective space with SVM and computes e_{int}. Suppose SVM produces a classification vector as shown in Figure 9. Two samples of B are miss-classified; $e = \frac{2}{14}$ (0.143). Thus, $\sigma \cong \sqrt{\frac{0.143}{14}} = 0.1$. Assuming the confidence level α of 95%, $e_{int} = 0.143 \pm 1.771 * 0.1 = 0.143 \pm 0.1771$. Since e_{int} spans zero, A's and B's samples are classifiable with the confidence level of 95%. This means that the aforementioned first condition is hold. In order to examine the second condition, the α-dominance operator measures $\mathcal{C}(A, B)$ and $\mathcal{C}(B, A)$. In Figure 9, $\mathcal{C}(A, B) = 1$ and $\mathcal{C}(B, A) = 2/14 < 1$. This means that the second condition

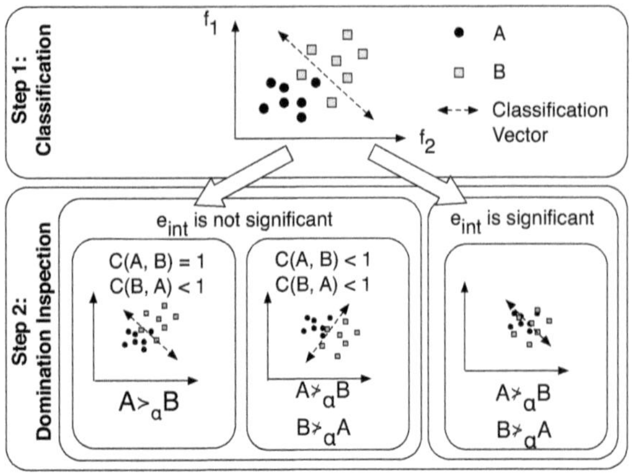

Figure 9: An Example Process to determine the α-Dominance Relationship between two individuals (A and B)

is hold. As a re result, the α-dominance operator concludes $A \succ_\alpha B$.

5.2 Evolutionary Optimization Process

Algorithm 1 shows the algorithmic structure of the proposed α-dominance based EMOA. At the *0*-th generation, P feasible individuals are randomly generated as the initial population $\mathcal{P}_0$ (Line 2).

In each generation (g), two parent individuals (p_1 and p_2) are selected from the current population $\mathcal{P}_g$ with binary tournaments (Lines 6 and 7). A binary tournament randomly takes two individuals from $\mathcal{P}_g$, compares them based on the notion of α-dominance, and chooses a superior one as a parent. With the crossover rate P_c, two parents reproduce two offspring through one-point crossover (Lines 8 to 10). Then, mutation occurs on each offspring (Lines 11 to 16). It randomly alters a neuron-firing pattern with the mutation rate P_m. Binary tournament, crossover and mutation operators are executed repeatedly on $\mathcal{P}_g$ to reproduce P offspring. The offspring ($\mathcal{O}_g$) are combined with the parent population $\mathcal{P}_g$ to form $\mathcal{R}_g$ (Line 19).

Environmental selection follows reproduction. Best P individuals are selected from $2P$ individuals in $\mathcal{R}_g$ as the next generation population ($\mathcal{P}_{g+1}$). First, the individuals in $\mathcal{R}_g$ are ranked based on the α-dominance relationships among them. Non-dominated individuals are on the first rank. The i-th rank consists of the individuals dominated only by the individuals on the $(i-1)$-th rank. Ranked individuals are stored in $\mathcal{F}$ (Line 20). $\mathcal{F}_i$ contains the individuals at the i-th rank.

Then, the individuals in $\mathcal{F}$ move to $\mathcal{P}_{g+1}$ on a rank by rank basis, starting with $\mathcal{F}_1$ (Lines 23 to 26). If the number of individuals in $\mathcal{P}_{g+1} \cup \mathcal{F}_i$ is less than P, $\mathcal{F}_i$ moves to $\mathcal{P}_{g+1}$. Otherwise, a subset of $\mathcal{F}_i$ moves to $\mathcal{P}_{g+1}$. The subset is selected based on the crowding distance metric, which measures the distribution (or diversity) of individuals in the objective space [5] (Lines 27 and 28). The metric computes the distance between two closest neighbors of an individual in each objective and sums up the distances associated with all objectives. A higher crowding distance means that an individual in question is more distant from its neighboring individuals in the objective space. In Line 27, the

Algorithm 1 Optimization Process

1: $g = 0$
2: $\mathcal{P}_g$ = Randomly generated P individuals
3: **while** g $< G_{max}$ **do**
4: $\quad \mathcal{O}_g = \emptyset$;
5: $\quad$ **while** $|\mathcal{O}_g| < P$ **do**
6: $\quad\quad p_1$ = tournament($\mathcal{P}_g$)
7: $\quad\quad p_2$ = tournament($\mathcal{P}_g$)
8: $\quad\quad$ **if** random() $\leq P_c$ **then**
9: $\quad\quad\quad \{o_1, o_2\}$ = crossover(p_1, p_2)
10: $\quad\quad$ **end if**
11: $\quad\quad$ **if** (random() $\leq P_m$) **then**
12: $\quad\quad\quad o_1$ = mutation(o_1)
13: $\quad\quad$ **end if**
14: $\quad\quad$ **if** random() $\leq P_m$ **then**
15: $\quad\quad\quad o_2$ = mutation(o_2)
16: $\quad\quad$ **end if**
17: $\quad\quad \mathcal{O}_g = \{o_1, o_2\} \cup \mathcal{O}_g$
18: $\quad$ **end while**
19: $\quad \mathcal{R}_g = \mathcal{P}_g \cup \mathcal{O}_g$
20: $\quad \mathcal{F}$ = sortByDominanceRanking($\mathcal{R}_g$)
21: $\quad \mathcal{P}_{g+1} = \{\emptyset\}$
22: $\quad i = 1$
23: $\quad$ **while** $|\mathcal{P}_{g+1}| + |\mathcal{F}_i| \leq P$ **do**
24: $\quad\quad \mathcal{P}_{g+1} = \mathcal{P}_{g+1} \cup \mathcal{F}_i$
25: $\quad\quad i = i + 1$
26: $\quad$ **end while**
27: $\quad$ sortByCrowdingDistance($\mathcal{F}_i$)
28: $\quad \mathcal{P}_{g+1} = \mathcal{P}_{g+1} \cup \mathcal{F}_i[1 : (P - |\mathcal{P}_{g+1}|)]$
29: $\quad g = g + 1$
30: **end while**

individuals in $\mathcal{F}_i$ are sorted in an descending order based on their crowding distance measures. The individuals with higher crowding distance have higher chances to be selected to $\mathcal{P}_{g+1}$ (Line 28).

5.3 Simulation Evaluation

This section evaluates the proposed EMOA through simulations. A simulated neuronal network is obtained with a two-step procedure. The first step utilizes NeuGen [7] to generate a network of N neurons. The second step forms a tree structure with those neurons based on a randomized L-ary tree construction algorithm. This algorithm generates a rooted tree in which each neuron has no more than $\mathcal{N}(L, (L+1)^2)$ child neurons. $\mathcal{N}$ denotes a normal distribution. L and $L+1$ are the mean and the standard deviation of the number of child neurons for each neuron. This paper uses a randomized 2-ary (i.e., binary) tree that contains 40 neurons and 10 sensors.

The proposed EMOA is configured with a set of parameters shown in Table 1. Q denotes the total number of time slots in an individual ($Q = 15$ in Fig. 8). Every simulation result is the average of the results from 20 independent simulations.

This simulation study considers noise that varies the time for a signal to travel through a neuron from T_u to $T_u^{'}$ as follows.

$$T_u^{'} = \beta\big(3 \times \mathcal{G}(k_1, \theta_1) + \mathcal{G}(k_2, \theta_2)\big) \times T_u \tag{8}$$

$\mathcal{G}$ denotes a gamma distribution. This noise model is designed based on existing empirical and theoretical studies on time distributions for synapitic delay and refectory period [2,10,15]. This noise ($T_u^{'} - T_u$) varies t_a in Equations 1 and 2 and in turn determines e_L and e_R in Equations 3 and 4.

Table 1: Simulation Configurations

Parameter	Value
# of objective value samples per individual	30
Confidence level (α)	0.95
Total # of generations (G_{max} in Algo. 1)	200
Population size (P in Algo. 1)	100
Crossover rate (P_c in Algo. 1)	0.9
Mutation rate (P_m in Algo. 1)	$1/Q$
Noise shape parameters k_1 and k_2 (Eq. 8)	6 and 7
Noise scale parameters θ_1 and θ_2 (Eq. 8)	0.4 and 0.5
Noise strength β (Eq. 8)	0.1

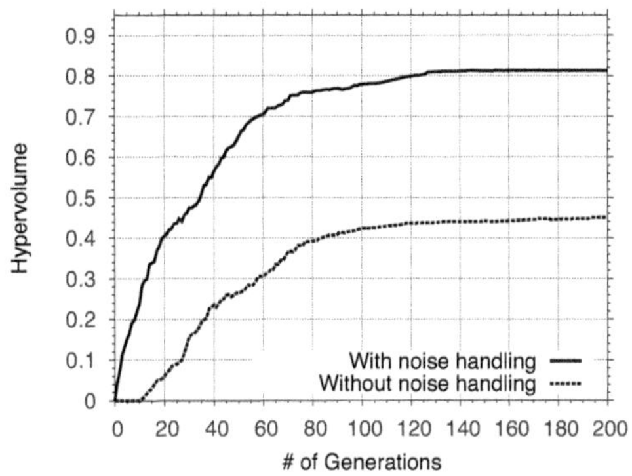

Figure 10: Hypervolume Measures with and without Noise Handling

Figure 10 illustrates how individuals increase the union of the hypervolumes that they dominate in the objective space as the number of generations grows. The hypervolume metric quantifies the optimality and diversity of individuals [32]. A higher hypervolume means that individuals are closer to the Pareto-optimal front and more diverse in the objective space. Figure 10 shows the hypervolume measures with and without the α-dominance operator. When the α-dominance operator is disabled, a classical dominance operator [23] is used in Algorithm 1. When the α-dominance operator is enabled, hypervolume measure converges around the 130th generation. When it is disabled, the proposed EMOA's convergence speed and optimization results significantly degrade. The hypervolume measure in the last generation degrades 44% with the α-dominance operator disabled. Figure 10 demonstrates that the α-dominance operator works effectively and efficiently.

Table 2 shows the average and standard deviation of each objective value that is obtained at the last generation. Figure 11 shows the objective space that plots the individuals obtained at the last generation. Those individuals approximate the Pareto front (i.e., the optimal trade-off) between signaling latency and robustness. Given the distributions of individuals in objective value ranges, signaling protocol designers can examine how they can trade one objective for another and choose a particular individual as the best TDMA schedule according to their preferences, priorities and/or constraints. For example, Figure 11 demonstrates that robustness improves 42% as signaling latency increases 20 to 30.

Table 3 depicts the hypervolume measures at the last generation where the α-dominance operator and two other noise-aware dominance operators are used with Algorithm 1.

Table 2: Objective Values

		Latency (f_L^e)	Robustness (f_R^e)
W/ Noise Handling	Mean	23.02	4.15
	Var.	6.77	0.56
W/o Noise Handling	Mean	30.43	1.33
	Var.	8.12	0.78

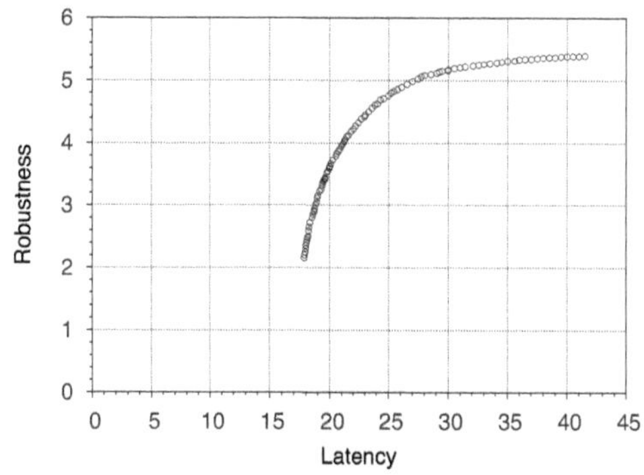

Figure 11: Latency-Robustness Tradeoff

- *Mean-based dominance operator*: It takes multiple samples, obtains mean values in different objectives and use them to rank individuals.
- *Gaussian dominance operator*: It assumes Gaussian noise in objective values in advance (c.f. Section 2) [8] and performs noise-aware ranking of individuals.

As shown in Table 3, the α-dominance operator yields the highest hypervolume measure. It outperforms a mean-based dominance operator and a Gaussian dominance operator by 44% and 37%. Through a single-tail t-test and a U-test, it is verified that the α-dominance operator significantly outperforms the other two operators with the confidence level of 95%.

6. CONCLUSIONS

This paper focuses on TDMA-based neuronal signaling and formulates a noisy multiobjective optimization problem that consists of signaling latency and robustness objectives. The problem contains environmental noise inherent in neuronal signaling. The proposed EMOA is designed to solve this problem with nonparametric (i.e.. distribution-free) statistical dominance operator. Simulation results show that the proposed EMOA handles noise well and obtains quality TDMA signaling schedules efficiently and effectively.

7. REFERENCES

[1] S. Balasubramaniam, N. T. Boyle, A. Della-Chiesa, F. Walsh, A. Mardinoglu, D. Botvich, and A. Prina-Mello. Development of artificial neuronal networks for molecular communication. *Nano Communication Networks*, 2(2-3), 2011.

[2] R. P. Betts, D. M. Johnston, and B. H. Brown. Nerve fibre velocity and refractory period distributions in nerve trunks. *J. Neurol. Neurosurg. Psychiatry*, 39(7):694–700, 1976.

[3] R. Cajal. *Histology of nervous system of man and vertebrates.* Oxford University Press, 1995.

Table 3: Comparison among Different Noise-aware Dominance Operators with Hypervolume

	Mean	Gaussian	α-dominance
Hypervolume	0.45	0.51	0.81
Difference	44%	37%	—

[4] D. J. Chew, L. Zhu, E. Delivopoulos, I. R. Minev, K. M. Musick, C. A. Mosse, M. Craggs, N. Donaldson, S. P. Lacour, S. B. McMahon, and J. W. Fawcett. A microchannel neuroprosthesis for bladder control after spinal cord injury in rat. *Sci Transl Med 6 November*, 5(210), 2013.

[5] K. Deb, S. Agrawal, A. Pratab, and T. Meyarivan. A fast elitist non-dominated sorting genetic algorithm for multi-objective optimization: NSGA-II. In *Proc. Conf. Parallel Problem Solving from Nature*, 2000.

[6] A. Destexhe. *Neuronal noise.* Springer, 2012.

[7] J. P. Eberhard, A. Wanner, and G. Wittum. NeuGen: A tool for the generation of realistic morphology of cortical neurons and neural networks in 3D. *Neurocomputing*, 70(1-3):327–342, 2006.

[8] H. Eskandari, C. D. Geiger, and R. Bird. Handling uncertainty in evolutionary multiobjective optimization: SPGA. In *Proc. IEEE Congress on Evolutionary Computation*, 2007.

[9] R. A. Freitas. Current status of nanomedicine and medical nanorobotics. *J. Computational and Theoretical Nanoscience*, 2(1):1–25, 2005.

[10] F. Gabbiani and S. J. Cox. *Mathematics for Neuroscientists.* Academic Press, 2010.

[11] N. Grossman, K. Nikolic, and P. Degenaar. The neurophotonic interface: stimulating neurons with light. *The Neuromorphic Engineer*, 2008.

[12] C. Hosokawa, Y. Sakamoto, S. N. Kudoh, Y. Hosokawa, and T. Taguchi. Femtosecond laser-induced stimulation of a single neuron in a neuronal network. *Appl. Phys. A*, 110(3), 2013.

[13] J. B. Hursh. Conduction velocity and diameter of nerve fibers. *Amer. J. Physiol.*, 127, 1939.

[14] S. B. Jun, M. R. Hynd, N. Dowell-Mesfin, K. L. Smith, J. N. Turner, W. Shain, and S. J. Kima. Low-density neuronal networks cultured using patterned polyl-L-lysine on microelectrode arrays. *Journal of Neurosci. Methods*, 160(2), 2007.

[15] B. Katz and R. Miledi. The measurement of synaptic delay, and the time course of acetylcholine release at the neuromuscular junction. *Proc. R. Soc. Lond. B. Biol. Sci.*, 161:483–495, 1965.

[16] F. Morin, N. Nishimura, L. Griscomb, B. LePioufle, H. Fujita, Y. Takamura, and E. Tamiya. Constraining the connectivity of neuronal networks cultured on microelectrode arrays with microSSuidic techniques: A step towards neuron-based functional chips. *Biosensors and Bioelectronics*, 21, 2006.

[17] T. Nakano, A. Eckford, and T. Haraguchi. *Molecular Communication.* Cambridge University Press, 2013.

[18] T. D. Nguyen-Vu, H. Chen, A. M. Cassell, R. J. Andrews, M. Meyyappan, and J. Li. Vertically aligned carbon nanofiber architecture as a multifunctional 3-D neural electrical interface. *IEEE Trans. Biomed. Eng.*, 54(6), 2007.

[19] K. Partridge, B. Dahlquist, A. Veiseh, A. Cain, A. Foreman, J. Goldberg, and G. Borriello. Empirical measurements of intrabody communication performance under varied physical configurations. In *Proc. User Interface Softw. Technol. Symp.*, 2001.

[20] S. Pautot, C. Wyart, and E. Y. Isacoff. Colloid-guided assembly of oriented 3D neuronal networks. *Nature Methods*, 5(8):735–740, 2008.

[21] P. E. M. Purnick and R. Weiss. The second wave of synthetic biology from modules to systems. *Nature Review Molecular Cell Biology*, 10:410–422, 2009.

[22] D. Shire, S. Kelly, J. Chen, P. Doyle, M. Gingerich, S. Cogan, W. Drohan, O. Mendoza, L. Theogarajan, J. Wyatt, and J. Rizzo. Development and implantation of a minimally invasive wireless subretinal neurostimulator. *IEEE Trans. Biomedical Engineering*, 56(10):2502–2511, 2009.

[23] N. Srinivas and K. Deb. Multiobjective function optimization using nondominated sorting genetic algorithms. *Evol. Computat.*, 2(3), 1995.

[24] G. Stuart, J. Schiller, and B. Sakmann. Action potential initiation and propagation in rat neocortical pyramidal neurons. *Journal of Physiology*, 505.3, 1997.

[25] T. Suda, M. Moore, T. Nakano, R. Egashira, and A. Enomoto. Exploratory research on molecular communication between nanomachines. In *Proc. ACM Genetic and Evol. Computat. Conference*, 2005.

[26] J. Suzuki, S. Balasubramaniam, and A. Prina-Mello. Multiobjective TDMA optimization for neuron-based molecular communication. In *Proc. of the 7th Int'l Conference on Body Area Networks.* September 2012.

[27] J. Teich. Pareto-front exploration with uncertain objectives. In *Proc. Int'l Conf. on Evol. Multi-Criterion Optimization*, 2001.

[28] M. Wormington, C. Panaccione, K. M. Matney, and D. K. Bowen. Characterization of structures from x-ray scattering data using genetic algorithms. *Phil. Trans. R. Soc. Lond. A*, 357(1761), 1999.

[29] C. Wyart, C. Ybert, L. Bourdieu, C. Herr, C. Prinz, and D. Chatenay. Constrained synaptic connectivity in functional mammalian neuronal networks grown on patterned surfaces. *J. Neurosci. Methods*, 117(2), 2002.

[30] T. Yagi. Biohybrid visual prosthesis for restoring blindness. *Int'l J. of Applied Biomedical Engineering*, 2(1):1–5, 2009.

[31] T. Zimmerman. Personal area networks (PAN): Near-field intra-body communication. *IBM Systems Journal*, 35(3-4), 1996.

[32] E. Zitzler and L. Thiele. Multiobjective optimization using evolutionary algorithms: A comparative study. In *Proc. Int'l Conf. on Parallel Problem Solving from Nature*, 1998.

[33] E. Zitzler and L. Thiele. Multiobjective evolutionary algorithms: a comparative case study and the strength pareto approach. *IEEE Trans. Evol. Computat.*, 3(4), 1999.

Data Based Prediction of Cancer Diagnoses Using Heterogeneous Model Ensembles - A Case Study for Breast Cancer, Melanoma, and Cancer in the Respiratory System

Stephan M. Winkler
Upper Austria University of Applied Sciences
Medical and Bioinformatics
Softwarepark 11
4232 Hagenberg, Austria
stephan.winkler@fh-hagenberg.at

Michael Affenzeller
Upper Austria University of Applied Sciences
Software Engineering
Softwarepark 11
4232 Hagenberg, Austria
michael.affenzeller@fh-hagenberg.at

Susanne Schaller
Upper Austria University of Applied Sciences
Bioinformatics
Softwarepark 11
4232 Hagenberg, Austria
susanne.schaller@fh-hagenberg.at

Herbert Stekel
General Hospital Linz
Central Laboratory
Krankenhausstraße 9
4021 Linz, Austria
herbert.stekel@akh.linz.at

ABSTRACT

In this paper we discuss heterogeneous estimation model ensembles for cancer diagnoses produced using various machine learning algorithms. Based on patients' data records including standard blood parameters, tumor markers, and information about the diagnosis of tumors, the goal is to identify mathematical models for estimating cancer diagnoses. Several machine learning approaches implemented in HeuristicLab and WEKA have been applied for identifying estimators for selected cancer diagnoses: k-nearest neighbor learning, decision trees, artificial neural networks, support vector machines, random forests, and genetic programming. The models produced using these methods have been combined to heterogeneous model ensembles. All models trained during the learning phase are applied during the test phase; the final classification is annotated with a confidence value that specifies how reliable the models are regarding the presented decision: We calculate the final estimation for each sample via majority voting, and the relative ratio of a sample's majority vote is used for calculating the confidence in the final estimation. We use a confidence threshold that specifies the minimum confidence level that has to be reached; if this threshold is not reached for a sample, then there is no prediction for that specific sample.

As we show in the results section, the accuracies of diagnoses of breast cancer, melanoma, and respiratory system cancer can so be increased significantly. We see that increasing the confidence threshold leads to higher classification accuracies, bearing in mind that the ratio of samples, for which there is a classification statement, is significantly decreased.

GECCO'14, July 12–16, 2014, Vancouver, BC, Canada.

http://dx.doi.org/10.1145/2598394.2609853.

Keywords

Cancer Diagnosis Estimation, Tumor Marker Data, Machine Learning, Data Mining, Statistical Analysis

General Terms

Algorithms, Reliability, Experimentation, Standardization

Categories and Subject Descriptors

H.2.8 [**Database Applications**]: Data mining; I.2.8 [**Artificial Intelligence**]: Heuristic methods; J.3 [**Life and Medical Sciences**]: Medical Information Systems

1. INTRODUCTION AND OVERVIEW

In this paper we present research results achieved within the research center *Heureka!*[1]: Data of thousands of patients of the General Hospital (AKH) Linz, Austria, have been analyzed in order to identify mathematical models for cancer diagnoses. We have used a medical database compiled at the central laboratory of AKH: 28 routinely measured blood values of patients are available as well as several tumor markers (substances found in humans that can be used as indicators for certain types of cancer). This paper describes research that is a continuation of the results presented at further GECCO Workshops on Medical Applications of Genetic

[1] Josef Ressel Center for Heuristic Optimization; `http://heureka.heuristiclab.com/`

and Evolutionary Computation: In [24] we reported on the data based identification of mathematical models for tumor markers (i.e., virtual tumor markers), in [25] we discussed the use of several evolutionary machine learning techniques for identifying predictors for cancer diagnoses, and in [26] we analyzed the effects of using pre-clustered data on the identification of estimation models for cancer diagnoses.

In this paper we apply an approach that is a combination of the methods described in [3] and [27], namely the use of heterogeneous model ensembles. Various machine learning methods are used separately for training estimation models; these models are combined using majority voting for calculating the final class estimation as well as a statistical confidence estimation. This confidence value can be interpreted as the trustworthiness of each single prediction based on the clearness of classifications. In [3] we described symbolic regression based ensemble modeling with confidence estimation, in [27] we used heterogeneous models for predicting the sentiment of statements based on (combinations of) keywords.

In the following section (Section 2) we describe the database we have used for our research work and also the tumors for which we have developed classifiers; we also describe the data preprocessing steps. For each tumor for which we have developed classifiers we define the sets of input variables used in this research project.

In Section 3 we give an overview of the machine learning methods applied for identifying classification models, and in Section 4 we define how final class estimations and confidence values are calculated.

In Section 5 we summarize and analyze the modeling results we have achieved using this heterogeneous model ensemble approach for learning classifiers for tumor diagnoses; we concentrate on the prediction of diagnoses of breast cancer, melanoma, and cancer in the respiratory system.

The conclusion of this paper is given in Section 6, and in the Appendix we give a overview of the machine learning methods applied in this research work.

2. DATABASE

2.1 Available Patient Data

The blood data measured at the AKH in the years 2005–2008 have been compiled in a database storing each set of measurements (belonging to one patient): Each sample in this database contains an unique ID number of the respective patient, the date of the measurement series, the ID number of the measurement, and a set of parameters summarized in Table 1; standard blood parameters are stored as well as tumor marker values and cancer diagnosis information. Patients personal data were at no time available to the authors except the head of the laboratory.

In total, information about 20,819 patients is stored in 48,580 samples. Not all values are available in all samples; there are many missing values simply because not all blood values are measured during each examination. Further details about the data set and the applied preprocessing methods can be found in [24] and [25].

2.1.1 Standard Parameters

Information about the standard parameters (general patient information and standard blood values) stored in the AKH database (which are listed in the upper part of Table 1) can be found in [13], [21], and [24], e.g.

2.1.2 Tumor Markers

In general, tumor markers (TMs) are substances found in humans (especially in the blood or in body tissues) that can be used as indicators for certain types of cancer. There are several different tumor markers which are used in oncology to detect the presence of cancer. As a matter of fact, elevated tumor marker values themselves are not diagnostic, but rather suggestive; tumor markers can be used to monitor the result of a treatment (as for example chemotherapy).

Literature discussing tumor markers, their identification, their use, and the application of data mining methods for describing the relationship between markers and the diagnosis of certain cancer types can be found for example in [10] (where an overview of clinical laboratory tests is given and different kinds of such test application scenarios as well as the reason of their production are described), [16], [5], and [29].

Table 1: List of patient data variables collected at AKH Linz: Blood parameters, standard patient information, and tumor markers.

Standard patient information and blood values
ALT, AST, BSG1, BUN, CBAA, CEOA, CH37, CHOL, CLYA, CMOA, CNEA, CRP, FE, FER, GT37, HB, HDL, HKT, HS, KREA, LD37, MCV, PLT, RBC, TBIL, TF, WBC, AGE, SEX
Tumor markers
AFP, CA 125, CA 15-3, CA 19-9, CEA, CYFRA, fPSA, NSE, PSA, S-100, SCC, TPS

2.1.3 Cancer Diagnoses

Finally, information about cancer diagnoses is also available in the AKH database: If a patient is diagnosed with any kind of cancer, then this is also stored in the database.

Our goal in the research work described in this paper is to identify estimation models for the presence of the following types of cancer:

- Malignant neoplasms in the respiratory system (RSC, cancer classes C30–C39 according to the International Statistical Classification of Diseases and Related Health Problems 10th Revision (ICD-10)),
- melanoma and malignant neoplasms on the skin (Mel, C43–C44), and
- breast cancer (BC, C50).

2.2 Data Preprocessing

Before analyzing the data and using them for training classifiers we have preprocessed the available data:

- All variables have been linearly scaled to the interval [0;1]: For each variable v_i, the minimum value min_i is subtracted from all contained values and the result is divided by the difference between min_i and the maximum plausible value $maxplau_i$; all values greater than $maxplau_i$ are replaced by 1.0.

- All samples belonging to the same patient with not more than one day difference with respect to the measurement data have been merged.
- Additionally, all measurements have been sample-wise re-arranged and clustered according to the patients' IDs. This has been done in order to prevent data of certain patients being included in the training as well as in the test data.

Before starting the modeling algorithms for training classifiers we had to compile separate data sets for each analyzed target tumor t_i: First, blood parameter measurements were joined with diagnosis results; only measurements and diagnoses with a time interval less than a month were considered. Second, all samples containing measured values for t_i are extracted. Third, all samples are removed that contain less than 15 valid values. Finally, variables with less than 10% valid values are removed from the data base.
This procedure results in a specialized data set dst_i for each tumor marker t_i. In Table 2 we summarize statistical information about all resulting data sets for the markers analyzed here; the numbers of samples belonging to each of the defined classes are also given for each resulting data set.

Table 2: Overview of the data sets compiled for selected cancer types.

Cancer Type	*Total Samples*	*Samples in Class 0*	*Samples in Class 1*	Missing Values
Breast Cancer	706	324 (45.89%)	382 (54.11%)	46.67%
Melanoma	905	485 (53.59%)	420 (46.41%)	47.79%
Respiratory System Cancer	2,363	1,367 (57.85%)	996 (42.15%)	44.76%

3. APPLIED MACHINE LEARNING TECHNIQUES

The following techniques for training classifiers have been used in this research study: Neural networks, k-nearest-neighbor classification, support vector machines, genetic programming, decision trees, and random forests.

Most of these machine learning methods have been implemented using the HeuristicLab framework [20], a framework for prototyping and analyzing optimization techniques for which both generic concepts of evolutionary algorithms and many functions to evaluate and analyze them are available; for learning decision trees the WEKA framework ([28], [9]) was used. Details of these methods are summarized in the appendix of this paper.

For all methods we have used parameter settings that were identified as the best settings by the approach described in [25]. There we have described the use of evolutionary optimization for identifying optimal modeling parameters for the here presented data collections as well as the modeling methods applied here.

Each modeling method was executed five times using 10-fold cross validation. All so created models were then applied on their respective test partitions; the final classification for each sample was calculated following the approach described in the next section.

4. ANALYSIS OF SETS OF HETEROGENEOUS MODELS

For each sample s various models are trained; models are here referred to as m_i where i represents the current model index. Subsequently, a voting over all models for each sample s is performed:

$$vote(c,s) = \mid \{m_i : m_i(s) = c\} \mid \quad (1)$$

where c represents an arbitrary, but fix class c.

The final classification fc for a sample s is calculated by using a majority voting of votes $vote(c,s)$:

$$fc(s) = \underset{c}{argmax}(vote(c,s)) \quad (2)$$

Finally, we define the confidence of classification c for a sample s (which represents the confidence towards this classification) on the basis of a set of models $\mathbf{m}$:

$$conf(c,s,\mathbf{m}) = \frac{\mid \{m_i : m_i(s) = c\} \mid}{\mid \mathbf{m} \mid}. \quad (3)$$

As we are here facing binary classification tasks, the classification confidence for any final classification fc (that is a majority vote winner and thus must have more than 50% of the votes) will always be in the interval $[0.5, 1]$.

The overall work flow followed here is graphically shown in Figure 1.

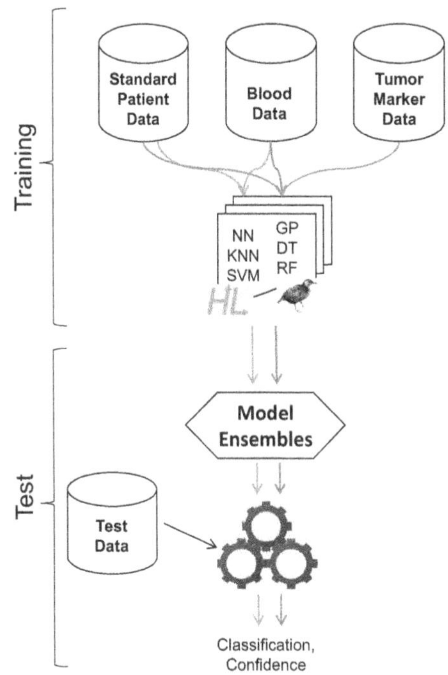

Figure 1: General work flow of the hybrid ensemble modeling approaches pursued in this research work.

In the empirical tests documented in the following sections we use a confidence threshold $\theta \in [0 \ldots 1]$. If the confidence for a sample's classification is smaller than this threshold, then there is no estimation statement for this sample. As a consequence, the ratio of samples for which a classification statement is given will be below 100%; we expect this samples coverage ratio to decrease for increasing values of θ.

5. EMPIRICAL TESTS

We have trained classification models using neural networks, k-nearest-neighbor classification, support vector machines, genetic programming, decision trees, and random forests; for all methods we have used parameter settings that were identified as "optimal" as described in [25]. As for all parameters the optimal values were given as average values and their respective variance, we have drawn each parameter independently and randomly within the range $\pm\sigma$ around its average optimal value.

As tumor diagnosis predictions are especially valuable if no tumor marker information is needed, we have trained estimation models both using all variables as well as not using tumor markers at all; this approach is in accordance to the test evaluations presented in [25] and [26].

Each modeling method was executed five times using 10-fold cross validation; all so created models were then combined to model ensembles and applied on their respective test partitions. The final classification for each sample was calculated following the approach described in Section 4.

In Tables 3, 4, and 5 we summarize the so achieved test classification accuracies and samples coverage ratios.

In Figures 2, 3, and 4 we show a graphical analysis of samples coverage vs. test accuracies for each modeled diagnosis prediction with varying confidence threshold θ.

In Figure 5 we graphically show overviews of the achieved test classification accuracies using different modeling approaches: Machine learning methods in combination with evolutionary parameters and feature set optimization were applied in the here used data as described in [25], a combination of clustering and machine learning algorithms was used as described in [26], and here we used hybrid model ensembles.

The most important insights we get here are the following ones:

- As expected, the ratio of covered samples decreases with increasing θ.
- The most important result is that for all three analyzed test cases, i.e., for the prediction of all three kinds of tumor, the test accuracy is significantly increased with increasing the confidence threshold θ. This holds for all analyses shown in this paper for both modeling & test approaches (using all variables as well as not using tumor markers).
- In detail, for **breast cancer** diagnosis modeling we see:
  - For BC diagnosis estimation using all variables, the test classification reaches 81.6% for $\theta = 0.5$ (i.e., for all samples) and can be increased to 87.3% by setting $\theta = 1.0$; this decreases the samples coverage ratio to 72%. The so reached accuracy is higher than the values reported in previous studies with the here used data set ranging from 79.3% to 84.2%.
  - For BC diagnosis estimation not using tumor markers, the test classification can be increased to 78.8% by setting $\theta = 1.0$; this decreases the samples coverage ratio to an approximately same extent, namely to 73%. The so reached accuracy is also higher than the values reported in previous studies with the here used data set ranging from 70.6% to 78.2%; still, in this case the performance increase is not as significant as when using all variables.
- For **melanoma** diagnosis estimation modeling we see:
  - For melanoma diagnosis estimation using all variables, the test classification reaches 75.9% for $\theta = 0.5$ (i.e., for all samples) and can be increased to 82.8% by setting $\theta = 1.0$; this decreases the samples coverage ratio, to 79.7%. In previous studies we have seen test classification accuracies for melanoma diagnosis ranging from 67.7% to 80.3%.
  - For melanoma diagnosis estimation not using tumor markers, the test classification can be increased to 80.4% by setting $\theta = 1.0$; this decreases the samples coverage ratio to an approximately same extent, namely to 78.3%. The so reached accuracy is also higher than the values reported in previous studies with the here used data set ranging from 66.8% to 78%.
- Finally, for the modeling of diagnosis of **cancer in the respiratory system** we see in detail:
  - For RSC diagnosis estimation using all variables, the test classification reaches 92.4% for $\theta = 0.5$ (i.e., for all samples) and can be increased to 94.1% by setting $\theta = 1.0$; this decreases the samples coverage ratio, but not very dramatically, namely to 95.2%. In previous studies we have seen RSC test classification accuracies ranging from 88.3% to 94.1%.
  - Surprisingly, for RSC diagnosis estimation not using tumor markers, setting $\theta = 1.0$ leads to an almost equal classification accuracy, namely 94%; this decreases the samples coverage ratio slightly more than using all variables, namely to 88.5%. The so reached accuracy is also higher than the values reported in previous studies with the here used data set ranging from 84.7% to 93.3%.

6. CONCLUSION

In this paper we have described an approach for estimating tumor diagnoses using heterogenous model ensembles. These model ensembles are compiled using various machine learning techniques, and we attribute each final classification with a confidence value.

Empirical tests have shown that this approach leads to higher accuracies of estimations of diagnoses of breast cancer, melanoma, and cancer in the respiratory system. Especially when using high confidence thresholds, i.e., when following a maximally conservative approach, the ratio of correct estimations is significantly increased. Still, we have to keep in mind that this approach reduces the ratio of samples for which a classification statement is given.

Acknowledgments

The work described in this paper was done within the Josef Ressel Center for Heuristic Optimization (*Heureka!*) sponsored by the Austrian Research Promotion Agency (FFG).

Table 3: Statistics of model ensembles for breast cancer diagnosis prediction. The confidence threshold θ is varied from 0.5 to 1.0, for each θ we give samples coverage ratios as well as classification accuracies.

Confidence threshold θ	All variables		No tumor markers	
	Samples coverage	Test accuracy	Samples coverage	Test accuracy
0.5	1.000	0.816	1.000	0.732
0.6	0.973	0.820	0.978	0.730
0.7	0.842	0.842	0.938	0.735
0.8	0.815	0.849	0.891	0.752
0.9	0.763	0.855	0.834	0.764
1.0	0.720	0.873	0.730	0.788

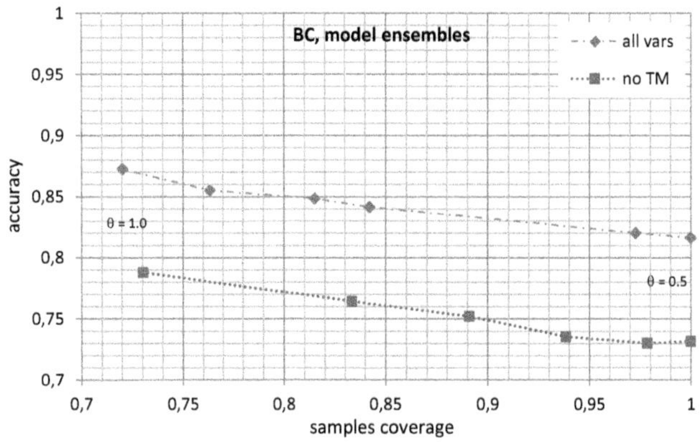

Figure 2: Graphical analysis of samples coverage and test accuracies for BC diagnosis prediction with varying confidence threshold θ.

Table 4: Statistics of model ensembles for melanoma diagnosis prediction. The confidence threshold θ is varied from 0.5 to 1.0, for each θ we give samples coverage ratios as well as classification accuracies.

Confidence threshold θ	All variables		No tumor markers	
	Samples coverage	Test accuracy	Samples coverage	Test accuracy
0.5	1.000	0.759	1.000	0.762
0.6	0.980	0.764	0.982	0.766
0.7	0.941	0.772	0.955	0.772
0.8	0.901	0.785	0.923	0.774
0.9	0.862	0.795	0.862	0.786
1.0	0.797	0.828	0.783	0.804

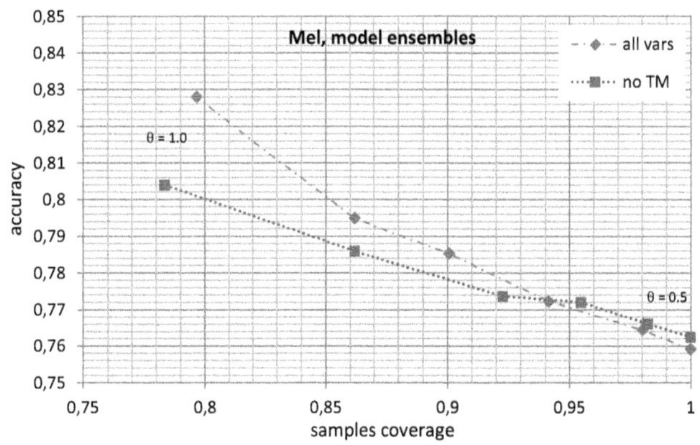

Figure 3: Graphical analysis of samples coverage and test accuracies for melanoma diagnosis prediction with varying confidence threshold θ.

Table 5: Statistics of model ensembles for prediction of diagnoses of cancer in the respiratory system. The confidence threshold θ is varied from 0.5 to 1.0, for each θ we give samples coverage ratios as well as classification accuracies.

Confidence threshold θ	All variables		No tumor markers	
	Samples coverage	Test accuracy	Samples coverage	Test accuracy
0.5	1.000	0.924	1.000	0.899
0.6	0.994	0.925	0.992	0.901
0.7	0.983	0.927	0.975	0.907
0.8	0.974	0.931	0.944	0.922
0.9	0.965	0.935	0.915	0.933
1.0	0.952	0.941	0.885	0.940

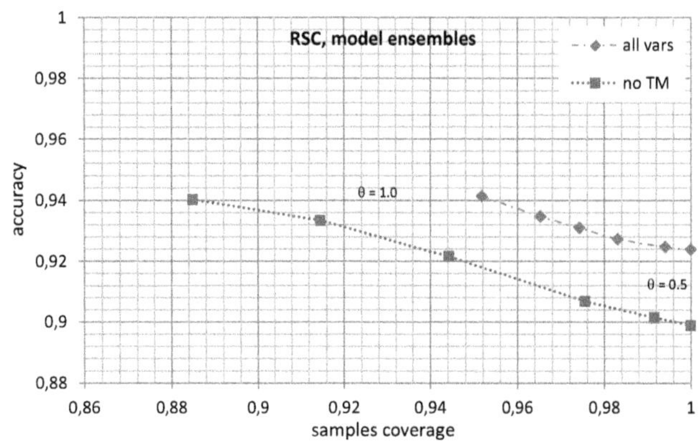

Figure 4: Graphical analysis of samples coverage and test accuracies for RSC diagnosis prediction with varying confidence threshold θ.

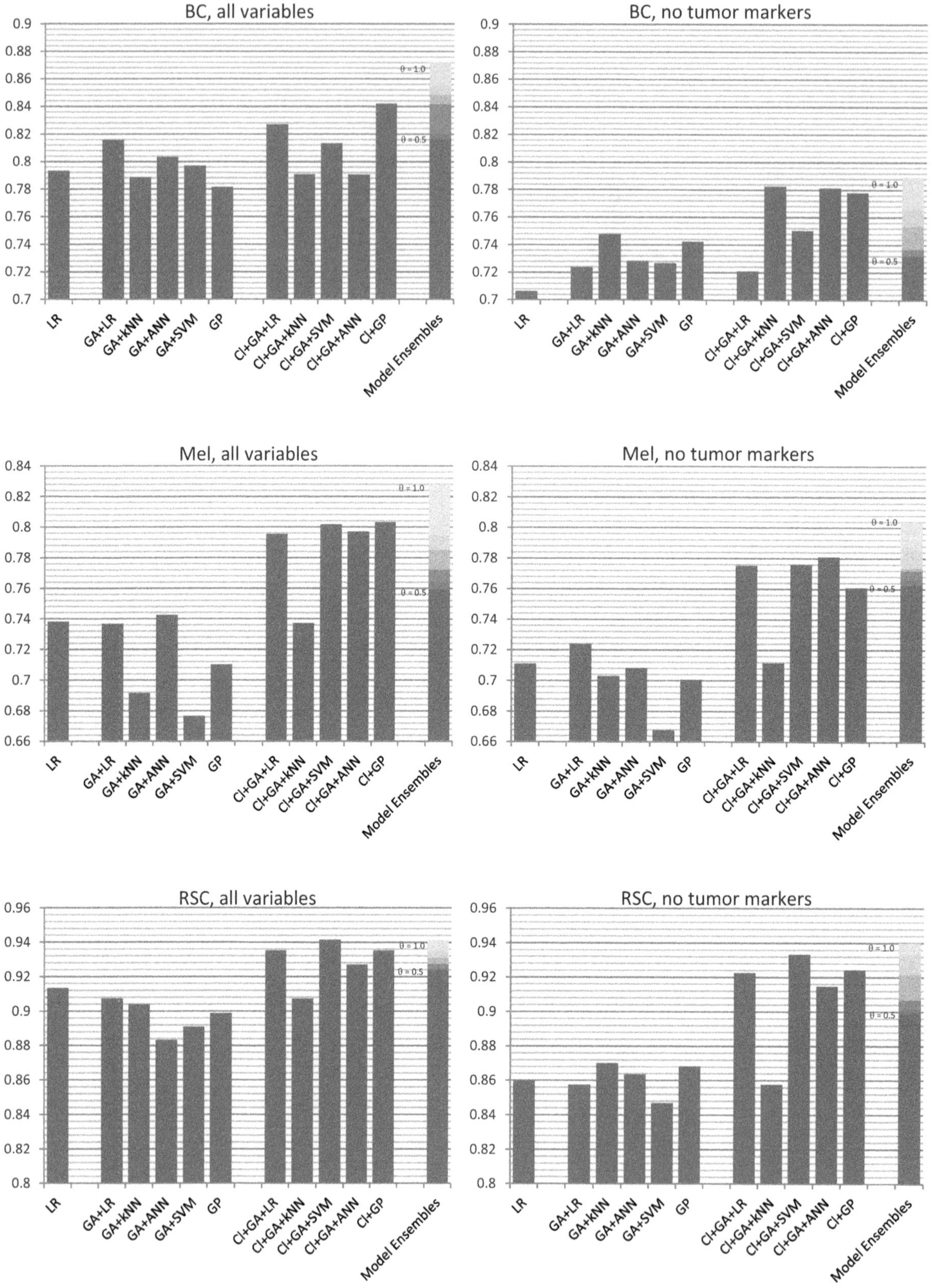

Figure 5: Comparison of results achieved for diagnosis estimation of breast cancer, melanoma, and cancer in the respiratory system: Results using linear regression (LR) [25], machine learning methods optimized by evolutionary algorithms (GA+LR, ..., GA+SVM) [25], genetic programming (GP) [25], a combined approach including clustering and machine learning (Cl+GA+LR, ..., Cl+GP) [26], and heterogeneous model ensembles as presented in this paper are compared.

7. REFERENCES

[1] M. Affenzeller and S. Wagner. SASEGASA: A new generic parallel evolutionary algorithm for achieving highest quality results. *Journal of Heuristics - Special Issue on New Advances on Parallel Meta-Heuristics for Complex Problems*, 10:239–263, 2004.

[2] M. Affenzeller, S. Winkler, S. Wagner, and A. Beham. *Genetic Algorithms and Genetic Programming - Modern Concepts and Practical Applications.* Chapman & Hall / CRC, 2009.

[3] M. Affenzeller, S. M. Winkler, H. Stekel, S. Forstenlechner, and S. Wagner. Improving the accuracy of cancer prediction by ensemble confidence evaluation. *Lecture Notes in Computer Science*, 8111:316–323, 2013.

[4] W. Banzhaf and C. Lasarczyk. Genetic programming of an algorithmic chemistry. In U. O'Reilly, T. Yu, R. Riolo, and B. Worzel, editors, *Genetic Programming Theory and Practice II*, pages 175–190. Ann Arbor, 2004.

[5] N. Bitterlich and J. Schneider. Cut-off-independent tumour marker evaluation using ROC approximation. *Anticancer Research*, 27:4305–4310, 2007.

[6] L. Breiman. Random forests. *Machine Learning*, 45(1):5–32, 2001.

[7] C.-C. Chang and C.-J. Lin. *LIBSVM: a library for support vector machines*, 2001. Software available at `http://www.csie.ntu.edu.tw/~cjlin/libsvm`.

[8] R. O. Duda, P. E. Hart, and D. G. Stork. *Pattern Classification.* Wiley Interscience, 2nd edition, 2000.

[9] M. Hall, E. Frank, G. Holmes, B. Pfahringer, P. Reutemann, and I. H. Witten. The weka data mining software: An update. *SIGKDD Explorations*, 11(1), 2009.

[10] J. A. Koepke. Molecular marker test standardization. *Cancer*, 69:1578–1581, 1992.

[11] S. Kotsiantis. Supervised machine learning: A review of classification techniques. *Informatica*, 31:249–268, 2007.

[12] J. R. Koza. *Genetic Programming: On the Programming of Computers by Means of Natural Selection.* The MIT Press, 1992.

[13] M. LaFleur-Brooks. *Exploring Medical Language: A Student-Directed Approach.* St. Louis, Missouri, USA: Mosby Elsevier, 7th edition, 2008.

[14] O. Nelles. *Nonlinear System Identification.* Springer Verlag, Berlin Heidelberg New York, 2001.

[15] J. R. Quinlan. *C4.5: Programs for Machine Learning.* Morgan Kaufmann Publishers, 1993.

[16] A. J. Rai, Z. Zhang, J. Rosenzweig, I. ming Shih, T. Pham, E. T. Fung, L. J. Sokoll, and D. W. Chan. Proteomic approaches to tumor marker discovery. *Archives of Pathology & Laboratory Medicine*, 126(12):1518–1526, 2002.

[17] M. Segal. *Machine Learning Benchmarks and Random Forest Regression.* Center for Bioinformatics & Molecular Biostatistics, 2004.

[18] V. Vapnik. *Statistical Learning Theory.* Wiley, New York, 1998.

[19] S. Wagner and M. Affenzeller. SexualGA: Gender-specific selection for genetic algorithms. In N. Callaos, W. Lesso, and E. Hansen, editors, *Proceedings of the 9th World Multi-Conference on Systemics, Cybernetics and Informatics (WMSCI) 2005*, volume 4, pages 76–81. International Institute of Informatics and Systemics, 2005.

[20] S. Wagner, G. Kronberger, A. Beham, M. Kommenda, A. Scheibenpflug, E. Pitzer, S. Vonolfen, M. Kofler, S. Winkler, V. Dorfer, and M. Affenzeller. *Advanced Methods and Applications in Computational Intelligence*, volume 6 of *Topics in Intelligent Engineering and Informatics*, chapter Architecture and Design of the HeuristicLab Optimization Environment, pages 197–261. Springer, 2014.

[21] P. W. Williams and H. D. Gray. *Gray's anatomy.* New York: C. Livingstone, 37th edition, 1989.

[22] S. Winkler, M. Affenzeller, and S. Wagner. Using enhanced genetic programming techniques for evolving classifiers in the context of medical diagnosis - an empirical study. *Genetic Programming and Evolvable Machines*, 10(2):111–140, 2009.

[23] S. M. Winkler. *Evolutionary System Identification - Modern Concepts and Practical Applications.* PhD thesis, Institute for Formal Models and Verification, Johannes Kepler University Linz, 2008.

[24] S. M. Winkler, M. Affenzeller, W. Jacak, and H. Stekel. Classification of tumor marker values using heuristic data mining methods. In *Proceedings of the GECCO 2010 Workshop on Medical Applications of Genetic and Evolutionary Computation (MedGEC 2010)*, 2010.

[25] S. M. Winkler, M. Affenzeller, W. Jacak, and H. Stekel. Identification of cancer diagnosis estimation models using evolutionary algorithms – a case study for breast cancer, melanoma, and cancer in the respiratory system. In *Proceedings of the GECCO 2011 Workshop on Medical Applications of Genetic and Evolutionary Computation (MedGEC 2011)*, 2011.

[26] S. M. Winkler, M. Affenzeller, and H. Stekel. Evolutionary identification of cancer predictors using clustered data - a case study for breast cancer, melanoma, and cancer in the respiratory system. In *Proceedings of the GECCO 2013 Workshop on Medical Applications of Genetic and Evolutionary Computation (MedGEC 2013)*, 2013.

[27] S. M. Winkler, S. Schaller, V. Dorfer, M. Affenzeller, G. Petz, and M. Karpowicz. Data based prediction of sentiments using heterogeneous model ensembles. *submitted to Soft Computing*, 2014.

[28] I. H. Witten and E. Frank. *Data Mining: Practical machine learning tools and techniques.* Morgan Kaufmann, 2nd edition, 2005.

[29] L. Zhong, X. Zhou, K. Wei, X. Yang, C. Ma, C. Zhang, and Z. Zhang. Application of serum tumor markers and support vector machine in the diagnosis of oral squamous cell carcinoma. *Shanghai Journal of Stomatology*, 17(5):457–460, 2008.

APPENDIX: MACHINE LEARNING METHODS APPLIED IN EMPIRICAL TEST STUDY

Most of these machine learning methods have been implemented using the HeuristicLab framework[2] [20], a framework for prototyping and analyzing optimization techniques for which both generic concepts of evolutionary algorithms and many functions to evaluate and analyze them are available; for learning decision trees the WEKA framework[3] ([28], [9]) was used. Details about the HeuristicLab implementation of these methods can for example be found in [2], [22], [20], [24], and [25].

7.1 k-Nearest-Neighbor Classification

Unlike other data based modeling methods, k-nearest-neighbor classification [8] works without creating any explicit models. During the training phase, the samples are simply collected; when it comes to classifying a new, unknown sample x_{new}, the sample-wise distance between x_{new} and all other training samples x_{train} is calculated and the classification is done on the basis of those k training samples (x_{NN}) showing the smallest distances from x_{new}.

In the context of classification, the numbers of instances (of the k nearest neighbors) are counted for each given class and the algorithm automatically predicts that class that is represented by the highest number of instances (included in x_{NN}). In the test series documented in this paper we have applied weighting to kNN classification: The distance between x_{new} and x_{NN} is relevant for the classification statement, the weight of "nearer" samples is higher than that of samples that are "further away" from x_{new}.

7.2 Decision Tree Learning

The C4.5 algorithm, an extension of the ID3 tree learning method, is designed to generate decision trees that can be used as classifiers ([15], [11]). On the basis of given training data, the C4.5 algorithm uses information entropy provided by the available samples' features; it iteratively constructs decision trees consisting of nodes that use those attributes that most effectively split the given samples into subsets of samples belonging to the same class. In this research context we have used the J48 implementation of C4.5 available in the Weka data mining framework.

7.3 Artificial Neural Networks

For training artificial neural network (ANN) models, feed-forward neural networks with one hidden layer (with sigmoid neurons) and one linear output neuron were created using backpropagation; theoretical background and details can for example be found in [14] (Chapter 11, "Neural Networks"). We have applied ANN training algorithms that use internal validation sets, i.e., training algorithms use 30% of the given training data as validation data and eventually return those network structures that perform best on these internal validation samples.

7.4 Support Vector Machines

Support vector machines (SVMs) are a widely used approach in machine learning based on statistical learning theory [18]. The most important aspect of SVMs is that it is possible to give bounds on the generalization error of the models produced, and to select the corresponding best model from a set of models following the principle of structural risk minimization [18].

In this work we have used the LIBSVM implementation described in [7], which is used in the respective SVM interface implemented for HeuristicLab; here we have used Gaussian radial basis function kernels with cost parameter c ($c \in [0, 512]$) and the γ parameter of the SVM's kernel function ($\gamma \in [0, 1]$).

7.5 Random Forest Classification

Random forests (RFs, [6]) are ensembles of decision trees, each depending on randomly chosen samples and features. The best known algorithm for inducing random forests was first described in [6] combining bagging and random feature selection:

- For each tree in the forest, a certain number of input variables is used to determine the decision at a node of the tree.
- A certain number of samples is randomly drawn from the training data base; the rest of the samples is used as internal validation set for estimating the model's prediction error (out-of-bag error).

RFs are a very popular machine learning method as they are known to be one of the most accurate learning algorithms available [17], robust against overfitting, and widely considered a very efficient machine learning method.

7.6 Genetic Programming

As an alternative to the approach described in the previous sections we have also applied a classification algorithm based on genetic programming (GP) [12] using a structure identification framework described in [23] and [2], in combination with strict offspring selection; this GP approach has been implemented as a part of HeuristicLab.

We have used the following parameter settings for our GP test series: The mutation rate was set to 20%, gender specific parents selection [19] (combining random and roulette selection) was applied as well as strict offspring selection [1] (OS, with success ratio as well as comparison factor set to 1.0). The functions set described in [23] (including arithmetic as well as logical ones) was used for building composite function expressions.

In addition to splitting the given data into training and test data, the GP based training algorithm implemented in HeuristicLab has been designed in such a way that a part of the given training data is not used for training models and serves as validation set; in the end, when it comes to returning classifiers, the algorithm returns those models that perform best on validation data. This approach has been chosen because it helps to cope with over-fitting; it is also applied in other GP based machine learning algorithms as for example described in [4].

[2] http://dev.heuristiclab.com

[3] http://www.cs.waikato.ac.nz/ml/weka/

GECCO'14 Symbolic Regression and Modeling Chairs' Welcome

It is our great pleasure to welcome you to the 6th 2014 GECCO Workshop on Symbolic Regression and Modeling. Over the past five workshops, we have had interesting presentations and fantastic discussions around symbolic regression, genetic programming, and the increasing demands and opportunities to impact science and industry. The workshop has spawned new research and lead to many new collaborations. We are looking forward to another great workshop with four accepted papers and one invited talk.

Symbolic Regression and Modeling is used to designate the search for symbolic descriptions, usually in the language of mathematics, to describe and predict numerical data in diverse fields such as industry, economics, finance and science.

Symbolic modeling captures the field of symbolic regression: a genetic programming based search technique for finding symbolic formulae on numerical data in order to obtain an accurate and concise description of that data in symbolic, mathematical form. In the evolutionary computation field it also captures learning classifier systems, if and when they are applied to obtain specific interpretable results in the field of interest.

The key discriminator of producing symbolic results over numerical results is the ability to interpret and analyze the results, leading either to acceptance by field experts, or to heightened understanding of the theory in the field of application. Interpretation is key, and the workshop will focus heavily on this. The workshop will focus on advances in using symbolic modeling for real world problems in industry, economics, finance and science.

The invited talk to be presented at the workshop is by David Medernach from the University on the topic of training data sampling approaches in symbolic regression modeling.

Steven Gustafson
GECCO-Workshop'14 Chair
GE Global Research, USA

Ekaterina Vladislavleva
GECCO-Workshop'14 Chair
Evolved Analytics, Belgium

A Mathematical Model of a Cold Rolling Mill by Symbolic Regression alpha-beta

L. A. Alvarado
FIME-UANL
Av. Universidad S/N, CP. 64400, San Nicolás de los Garza, Nuevo León, México.
luis.alvarado.yanez@gmail.com

L. M. Torres-Treviño
FIME-CIIDIT-UANL
Av. Universidad S/N, CP. 64400,
San Nicolás de los Garza, Nuevo León, México.
luis.torrestv@uanl.edu.mx

F. Gonzalez
Ternium México
Av. Los Angeles 325 Ote.
San Nicolás de los Garza, N.L., México
fgonzalezgzz@ternium.com.mx

L. Nieves
Ternium México
Av. Los Angeles 325 Ote.
San Nicolás de los Garza, N.L., México
lnieves@ternium.com.mx

ABSTRACT

Improvement of processes in metallurgical industry is a constant of competitive enterprises, however, changes made in a process are risky and involves high cost and time, considering this, a model can be made even using inputs usually not presented in real process and its analysis could be useful for the improvement of the process. In this work, a mathematical model is built using only experimental data of a four high tandem cold rolling mill, a set of input variables involving characteristics of the process. The performance of the model is determined by residual analysis considering new data. Results are a non black box model with a good performance; by this way, the model is a good representation of the process under study.

Categories and Subject Descriptors

I.28 [**Problem Solving, Control Methods, and Search**]:

General Terms

Algorithms

Keywords

Symbolic regression; modelling; rolling mill

1. COLD ROLLING MILL

Cold rolling is one of the most important processes in an integrated steelworks because it increases the strength of the material, improves accuracy in controlling sizes, and produces thinner gauge products with a bright smooth surface. On this basis, continuous improvement in quality is one of the most important themes in cold rolling. Customer expectations like product accuracy and tighter tolerances have become extremely important control items. In a Cold Rolling Process many parameter are involved to reduce the thickness of the material and this parameters had a great influence in the quality features of the final product. The goal of this paper is present a good model of this process using symbolic regression α-β. Below in Figure 1 is the structure of a Cold Rolling Model:

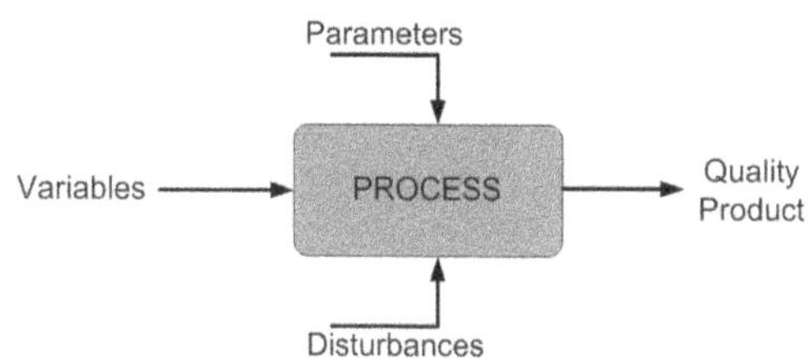

Figure 1: ***Block diagram of Cold Rolling Model.***

In cold rolling mills to reduce the thickness the metal is exposed to several forces of compress and tension. That make the crystals of the grain structure of the metal be strained. The applied forces in a cold rolling mill must be equally distributed through the width of the sheet to have a uniform deformation in the length. The applied forces depend of several factors that have a non linear relationship. But all are known and can be measurable.

1.1 Intelligent Systems in Cold Rolling Mill

Nowadays, Neural Networks (NN) was used to improve the optimization of parameters in open loop controls in rolling mills[2]. As well as prediction of features like Flow stress, yield stress, the rolling force and rolling torque[4, 1, 11, 6, 12].

Evolutionary computing techniques show significant mod-

GECCO'14, July 12–16, 2014, Vancouver, BC, Canada.

http://dx.doi.org/10.1145/2598394.2609858.

Table 1: α operator parameters and its related mathematical functions.

α operator	mathematical operation
1	$(k_1x + k_2)$
2	$(k_1x + k_2)^2$
3	$(k_1x + k_2)^3$
4	$(k_1x + k_2)^{-1}$
5	$(k_1x + k_2)^{-2}$
6	$(k_1x + k_2)^{-3}$
7	$(k_1x + k_2)^{1/2}$
8	$(k_1x + k_2)^{1/3}$
9	$\exp(k1x + k_2)$
10	$\log(k1x + k_2)$
11	$\sin(k1x + k_2)$
12	$\cos(k1x + k_2)$
13	$\tan(k1x + k_2)$

eling capabilities on handling complex non-linear systems modeling. Symbolic regression modeling via genetic programming is used to develop relatively simple mathematical models[5]. Otherwise, a genetic algorithm has been used in order to design new hot rolling schedules with lower energy consumption through a reduction in the total roll power[7]. In cases of multi objective optimization genetic algorithms are used to minimize the overall standard deviations in terms of each of the properties during the entire rolling campaign[3].

2. SYMBOLIC REGRESSION α-β

In this approach, a mathematical equation is represented by the combination of α and β operators. An α operators is defined as a function that requires only one argument and applies only one mathematical operation. Considering a review of several mathematical models of real processes, 13 operations are chosen as α operators (see Table 1). An α operator uses two real number parameters called $k1$ and $k2$ and an integer that describes the mathematical operation. The α operator is defined as follows:

$$Opr_\alpha(x, k_1, k_2) = \alpha(k_1 * x + k_2) \quad (1)$$

where x is an input variable and α is an operation. Depending of the α operator selected, a specific mathematical operation that requires only one argument is executed; e.g., if α=1 then the operation made is $(k1*x+k2)$, if α= 13 then the operation made is $tan(k1 * x + k2)$. α operator can be represented as an integer number. A β operator is defined as a function that require two arguments and makes the four basic arithmetic operations β=c so a β operator equal to 1 imply the plus operator or $\beta(a, b) = a+b$, and $\beta(a, b) = a/b$ if β=4.

A basic configuration can be defined when an α operator is assigned per input variable then an β operator is used to connect two α operators (2). Usually, a simple configuration in majority of the cases is enough for the regression.

$$y = \beta_{n-1}(...\beta_2(\beta_1(\alpha_1(x_1), \alpha_2(x_2)),)), ...\alpha_n(x_n)) \quad (2)$$

In this work, connectivity can be controlled by a binary variable to select the number of α operators per input variable that can be used, inclusive any variable could be not required if this is the case. A maximum of three alpha operators per variable is determined, so if there are two variables, a configuration with six alpha operators and five beta operators are defined as a core configuration as is shown in Equation 3. Depending de number of input variables a core configuration is used.

$$\begin{aligned} y = \; & \beta_5(\beta_4(\beta_3(\beta_2(\beta_1(b_1\alpha_1(x_1k_{11} + k_{21}), b_2\alpha_2(x_1k_{12} + k_{22})), \\ & b_3\alpha_3(x_1k_{13} + k_{23})), b_4\alpha_4(x_2k_{14} + k_{24})), \\ & b_5\alpha_5(x_2k_{15} + k_{25})), b_6\alpha_6(x_2k_{16} + k_{26})) \end{aligned} \quad (3)$$

The representation depends of the configuration used or the number of variables required. The number of variables determine the core configuration as was mention above. A vector with normalised real numbers can be used to represents the connectivity or the number of alpha operators per variable, the alpha and beta operators and the k parameters of the alpha operators. As an example consider the core configuration for two variables, the following parameters can be extracted: Connectivity parameters are b_1, b_2, b_3, b_4, b_5, b_6 and belongs to a binary vector; operators parameters are α_1, α_2, α_3, α_4, α_5, α_6, β_1, β_2, β_3, β_4, β_5 and they are integers; and real parameters are k_{11}, $k_{21}k_{12}$, k_{22},k_{13}, k_{23},k_{14}, k_{24},k_{15}, k_{25},k_{16}, k_{26}. A single real number is used for connectivity because this number is converted to an integer value, then it is converted again in a binary vector and extract the b values using their corresponding position of the elements of the binary vector. k parameters is assigned directly the real value of the representation vector. Every α and β operators are integers, so is required the following formulation to get its value from the representation V:

$$\alpha = \lceil V(i) * 13 \rceil \quad (4)$$

$$\beta = \lceil V(i) * 4 \rceil \quad (5)$$

where $\lceil . \rceil$ is the ceiling function. There are 13 α operators defined in table 1 and 4 β operators (basic algebraic operations)

Consider the following example of decoding; the vector of parameters is V=[0.432 0.963 0.529 0.043 0.294 0.284 0.786 0.569 0.156 0.561 0.315 0.722 0.518 0.201 0.715 0.017 0.911 0.306 0.275 0.797 0.562 0.898 0.021 0.793]

Connectivity is defined in $V(1)$, we have $\lceil (0.482{*}2^{2*3-1}) \rceil = \lceil 15.424 \rceil$ two variables and three alpha operators per variable, zero is considered a non connection. Binary vector is [0 0 1 0 1 1] where variable x_1 is connected by one α operator and variable x_2 is connected by two α operators.

Every alpha and beta operator is extracted by decoding every element of the vector V.

$\alpha_1 = \lceil V(2) * 13 + 0.5 \rceil = \lceil (0.963 * 13) \rceil = 13$ this represents a tan function.

$\alpha_2 = \lceil V(3) * 13 + 0.5 \rceil = \lceil (0.529 * 13) \rceil = 7$ this represents an exponential to -2 function.

$\alpha_3 = \lceil V(4) * 13 + 0.5 \rceil = \lceil (0.043 * 13) \rceil = 1$ this represents a linear function.

$\alpha_4 = \lceil V(5) * 13 + 0.5 \rceil = \lceil (0.294 * 13) \rceil = 4$ this represents an inverse function.

$\alpha_5 = \lceil V(6) * 13 + 0.5 \rceil = \lceil (0.284 * 13) \rceil = 4$ this represents an inverse function.

$\alpha_6 = \lceil V(7) * 13 + 0.5 \rceil = \lceil (0.786 * 13) \rceil = 11$ this represents a sin function.

$\beta_1 = \lfloor (V(8) * 4 + 0.5) \rfloor = \lfloor (0.569 * 4) \rfloor = 3$ this represents a multiplication.

$\beta_2 = \lfloor (V(9) * 4 + 0.5) \rfloor = \lfloor (0.156 * 4) \rfloor = 1$ this represents an addition.

$\beta_3 = \lfloor (V(10) * 4 + 0.5) \rfloor = \lfloor (0.461 * 4) \rfloor = 2$ this represents a subtraction.

$\beta_4 = \lfloor (V(11) * 4 + 0.5) \rfloor = \lfloor (0.315 * 4) \rfloor = 2$ this represents a subtraction.

$\beta_5 = \lfloor (V(12) * 4 + 0.5) \rfloor = \lfloor (0.722 * 4) \rfloor = 3$ this represents a multiplication.

Finally, parameters $k_{1i} = V(i)\ k_{2i})V(i+1)$ where $i = 13, 15, 17, 19, 21, 23$ by this way we have the following mathematical model based on core configuration:

$$y = x_1 - (x_2^{-1} * sin(x_2)) \tag{6}$$

In this work, Evonorm is used to solve the problem of selection the suitable parameters (k's), the connectivity and integers to define α and β operations.

2.1 Evolutionary algorithm Evonorm

Evonorm is an easy way to implement an estimation of distribution algorithm [9, 10]. As a evolutionary algorithm selection of new individuals and the generation of a new population is used; however, the crossover and mutation mechanism is substituted by an estimation of parameters of a normal distribution function. The following steps are used in Evonorm:

1. Evaluation of a population P.
2. Deterministic selection of individuals from P to PS.
3. Generation of a new population using PS

A population P is a matrix of size I_p (total of individuals) and D_r (total of decision variables). A solution is a set of decision variables and this set is represented as a real vector. Every row of the population P represents a set of decision variables. The selection mechanism is deterministic because the most fittest individuals are selected. Usually the number of selected individuals are lower than the number of the original population, usually a twenty or ten percent of the total population. A random variable with normal distribution is estimated per decision variable, so a marginal distribution function is used. Two parameters are estimated, the mean and the standard deviation, that is determined using the values of the selected individuals. The population of selected individuals is a matrix Ps of size I_s (total of individuals selected) and D_r. The equations (7, 8) are used to calculate the mean and standard deviation considering every vector of the population Ps.

$$\mu_{pr} = \sum_{k=1}^{I_s} (Ps_{pr,k})/I_s \tag{7}$$

$$\sigma_{pr} = \sqrt{(}\sum_{k=1}^{I_s} (Ps_{pr,k} - \mu_{pr})^2)/I_s \tag{8}$$

where $pr = 1..D_r$

A new population is generated using the estimated normal random variables. This is a stochastic process;, however, an heuristic is used to maintain an equilibrium between exploration and exploitation, so new solutions can be found not necessarily near of the mean calculated. The best solution found Ix at the moment is involved in the generation so in the 50% percent of the times the mean is used in the calculations and in the other 50% percent of the time the best solution found Ix is used as a mean as is shown in the following equation:

$$P_{i,pr} = \begin{cases} N(\mu_{pr}, \sigma_{pr}) & U() > 0.5 \\ N(Ix_{pr}, \sigma_{pr}) & otherwise \end{cases} \tag{9}$$

The random variable $U()$ has a uniform distribution function, $N()$ is a random variable with a normal distribution function.

2.2 Residual analysis

One effective way to validate a regression model is to collect new experimental data to determine how well the model performs in practice [8]. The most simple measure is the residual calculated as the difference $(e(i))$ between new observations made by the response of the process $y(i)$ and predicted response generated by the regression model made $\hat{y}(i)$ (equation 10).

$$e(i) = y(i) - \hat{y}(i) \tag{10}$$

The PRESS (prediction error sum of squares) is a measure of how well a model works to predict new data. Usually a small value of PRESS is desirable (11). In this case, the PRESS is obtained using cross validation.

$$PRESS = \sum_{i=1}^{n} (y(i) - \hat{y}(i))^2 \tag{11}$$

The percentage of variability R^2_{pred} is a measurement for indicating the efficiency of the model to predict new observations. A value near of one is desirable on this indicator (12).

$$R^2_{prec} = 1 - \frac{\sum_{i=1}^{n} (y(i) - \hat{y}(i))}{y'y - (\sum_{i=1}^{n} y(i))^2} \tag{12}$$

2.3 Model selection and optimization

Complexity is determinate adding all the α and β operators used in the chosen configuration. $Cx = \sum_{i=n}^{n} (\alpha_1 + \alpha_2 + \cdots + \alpha_n + \beta_1 + \beta_2 + \cdots + \beta_{n-1})$. Percentage of variability R^2_{prec} is calculating with 20% of non used data for model building. A selection with lower complexity and with near to one variability percentage is preferred. The objective function uses complexity, mean square error, and connectivity and all of them are minimized.

3. MODELING COLD ROLLING MILL

Cold rolling mill process has a total of 60 inputs, however, many of them do not contribute in output response (Table 2). The variables can be grouped in two categories, inputs related with products and inputs variables related with process characteristics (Figure 2).

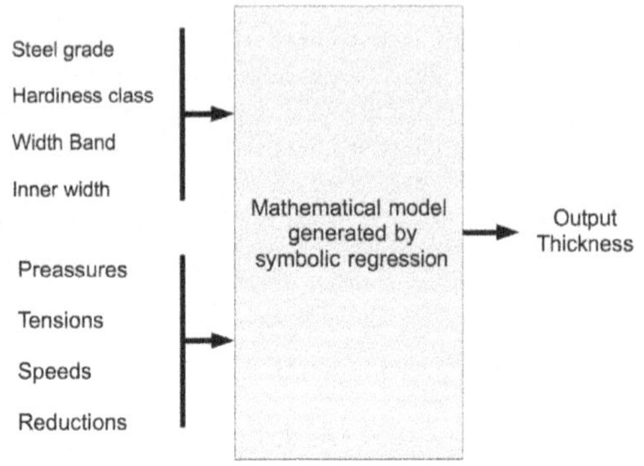

Figure 2: ***Inputs and output of the cold rolling model.***

Type	Number	Name
Inputs	1	SteelGrade
	2	Hardness_Class
	3	WidthBand
	4	Inner_Width
	5	Pressure_1
	6	Pressure_2
	7	Pressure_3
	8	Pressure_4
	9	Tension_Payoff
	10	Tension_1_2
	11	Tension_2_3
	12	Tension_3_4
	13	Tension reel
	14	Speed_1
	15	Speed_2
	16	Speed_3
	17	Speed_4
	18	Reduction_1
	19	Reduction_2
	20	Reduction_3
	21	Reduction_4
Output	1	Output_Thickness

Table 2: Process Inputs and Output

A basic configuration is used considering one α operator per input variable. Considering this, a total of 84 parameters must be used to estimate 42 k parameters, 21 alpha, 20 beta operators and one integer used for connectivity. Considering 500 records, an 80 % percentage of them was chosen for building and the rest for validations and calculation of statistical indicators from residual analysis. Evonorm algorithm was used considering a population of 100 individuals, 10 are chosen for selection and run for 100 generations. The algorithm was run five times. The best solution in terms of statistical indicators was chosen.

Table 3: Results of the residual analysis of solution selected.

MSE	R^2_{pred}	PRESS
0.0095267	0.9880336	0.7430802

Vector of connectivity is $B = [\,1\;0\;0\;1\;0\;0\;1\;1\;1\;0\;0\;1\;1\;1\;1\;0\;0\;0\;1\;0\;1\,]$ where some input variables are not required or has a low influence in output response. Results of α and β operations required are shown in Table 1 and Table ?? respectively. Coding the solution, the mathematical model generated is shown in equation 13. This model is useful for simulations of operation conditions, inquiring specific conditions to determine its effects on thickness, changes of reductions, tension and pressure. The model can be used to establish output thickness considering other products not used in training because different products has different steel grade or hardiness and some of them require a specific width band.

$$y(x_3, x_7, x_8, x_9, x_{11}, x_{14}, x_{16}, x_{18}, x_{19}, x_{21}) = ((((((((((((((((((+(0.5847666 * x_3 + 0.6593538)^3))))+ (0.43712 * x_7 + 0.3346624)^2) + (0.7857256 * x_8+ 0.2255187)) * (0.2336883 * x_9 + 0.9180191)))+ (0.9875162 * x_{11} + 0.5309005)))) + (0.3485697 * x_{14}+ 0.0419397))) + (0.0234704 * x_{16} + 0.5189331)^2))+ (0.6363647 * x_{18} + 0.4944638)^(- 1)) * (0 * x_{19}+ 0.8175074)^2)) + cos(0.4328817 * x_{21} + 0.3899872)) \quad (13)$$

4. CONCLUSION AND FUTURE WORK

This work presents a practical application of a symbolic regression to generate mathematical models from records of data of a cold rolling mill. Symbolic regression α β eliminates some variables, reducing number of input variables and making the mathematical model simpler. The generation of data about the process is intensive, above of 50,000 records by day. Analysis of the information to establish a set of conditions is too complex and requires experience of the user; however, the model generates gives clues about the performance of the process and considering the high values of statistical indicators, the model is accurate in the prediction. As a future work is the use of flatness as quality in place of thickness, and improve the process considering the mathematical model by means of optimization.

5. ACKNOWLEDGMENTS

We would like to thank CONACYT for the support that gives students in the research area, it would of been impossible to achieve this work without this sustain. Besides we stay in gratitude with Ternium for all the economic support, facilities and the magnificent cathedra that gives place to this side to side works. To Luis Leduc for all the advices about rolling process and the administration of the cathedra.

6. REFERENCES

[1] M. Bagheripoor and H. Bisadi. Application of artificial neural networks for the prediction of roll force and roll

torque in hot strip rolling process. *Applied Mathematical Modelling*, 37(7):4593 – 4607, 2013.

[2] J. L. Calvo-Rolle, J. L. Casteleiro-Roca, H. Quintín, and M. del Carmen Meizoso-Lopez. A hybrid intelligent system for {PID} controller using in a steel rolling process. *Expert Systems with Applications*, 40(13):5188 – 5196, 2013.

[3] N. Chakraborti, B. S. Kumar, V. S. Babu, S. Moitra, and A. Mukhopadhyay. A new multi-objective genetic algorithm applied to hot-rolling process. *Applied Mathematical Modelling*, 32(9):1781 – 1789, 2008.

[4] S. K. Das. Neural network modelling of flow stress and mechanical properties for hot strip rolling of trip steel using efficient learning algorithm. *Ironmaking and Steelmaking*, 40:298–304, 2013.

[5] H. Faris, A. Sheta, and E. ÃŰznergiz. Modelling hot rolling manufacturing process using soft computing techniques. *International Journal of Computer Integrated Manufacturing*, 26(8):762–771, 2013.

[6] J. Ghaisari, H. Jannesari, and M. Vatani. Artificial neural network predictors for mechanical properties of cold rolling products. *Advances in Engineering Software*, 45(1):91 – 99, 2012.

[7] M. A. M. . C. A. C. A. A. J. L. A. J. (Marquez, Itziar); Arribas. Optimisation of total roll power using genetic algorithms in a compact strip production plant. *International journal of materials research*, 104:686–696, 2013.

[8] D. C. Montgomery. *Introduction to Linear Regression Analysis*. John Wiley and Sons, 2007.

[9] L. M. T.-T. no. Evonorm, a new evolutionary algorithm to continuous optimization. In *Workshop on Optimization by Building and Using Probabilistic Models (OBUPM) Genetic and Evolutionary Computation Conference (GECCO)*, 2006.

[10] L. T.-T. no. Evonorm: Easy and effective implementation of estimation of distribution algorithms. *Journal of Research in Computing Science*, 23:75–83, 2006.

[11] N. Reddy, B. Panigrahi, and J. Krishnaiah. Modeling mechanical properties of low carbon hot rolled steels. In J. C. Bansal, P. Singh, K. Deep, M. Pant, and A. Nagar, editors, *Proceedings of Seventh International Conference on Bio-Inspired Computing: Theories and Applications (BIC-TA 2012)*, volume 202 of *Advances in Intelligent Systems and Computing*, pages 221–228. Springer India, 2013.

[12] P. Saravanakumar, V. Jothimani, L. Sureshbabu, S. Ayyappan, D. Noorullah, and P. Venkatakrishnan. Prediction of mechanical properties of low carbon steel in hot rolling process using artificial neural network model. *Procedia Engineering*, 38(0):3418 – 3425, 2012. {INTERNATIONAL} {CONFERENCE} {ON} {MODELLING} {OPTIMIZATION} {AND} {COMPUTING}.

Predict the Performance of GE with an ACO Based Machine Learning Algorithm

Gopinath Chennupati
BDS Group
CSIS Department
University of Limerick, Ireland
gopinath.chennupati@ul.ie

R. Muhammad Atif Azad
BDS Group
CSIS Department
University of Limerick, Ireland
atif.azad@ul.ie

Conor Ryan
BDS Group
CSIS Department
University of Limerick, Ireland
conor.ryan@ul.ie

ABSTRACT

The quality of the evolved solutions of an evolutionary algorithm (EA) varies across different runs and a significant percentage of runs can produce solutions of undesirable quality. These runs are a waste of computational resources, particularly in difficult problems where practitioners have time bound limitations in repeating runs.

This paper proposes a completely novel approach, that of a *Run Prediction Model* (RPM) in which we identify and terminate evolutionary runs that are likely to produce low-quality solutions. This is justified with an Ant Colony Optimization (ACO) based classifier that learns from the early generations of a run and decides whether to continue or not.

We apply RPM to Grammatical Evolution (GE) applied to four benchmark symbolic regression problems and consider several contemporary machine learning algorithms to train the predictive models and find that ACO produces the best results and acceptable predictive accuracy for this first investigation. The ACO discovered prediction models are in the form of a list of simple rules. We further analyse that list manually to tune them in order to predict poor GE runs.

We then apply the analysed model to GE runs on the regression problems and terminate the runs identified by the model likely to be poor, thus increasing the rate of production of successful runs while reducing the computational effort required. We demonstrate that, although there is a high bootstrapping cost for RPM, further investigation is warranted as the mean success rate and the total execution time enjoys a statistically significant boost on all the four benchmark problems.

Categories and Subject Descriptors

I.2.8 [**Artificial Intelligence**]: Problem Solving, Control Methods, and Search - Heuristic methods

General Terms

Algorithms, Applications

GECCO'14, July 12–16, 2014, Vancouver, BC, Canada.

http://dx.doi.org/10.1145/2598394.2609860.

Keywords

Grammatical Evolution; Ant Mining; Machine Learning; Symbolic Regression; Training Set;

1. INTRODUCTION

Experiments in evolutionary computation (EC) follow a common practice of running the algorithm multiple times in order to obtain statistically significant data, particularly when the likelihood of achieving a solution of a certain quality is only estimated through a large number of runs. However, as problems get increasingly computationally expensive, the computational resources are best utilised if the Evolutionary Algorithm (EA) consistently generates solutions of desirable quality and the runs producing poor solutions are minimised. For example [21, 26, 33] are all more concerned with producing a single *useful* result rather making statistical affirmations about their ability to emulate the same result.

This paper details a pilot study into a mechanism to better utilise resources for EC by predicting which runs are most likely to fail and discontinuing them early on. Our technique will work with essentially all other techniques for improving GE (or Genetic Programming (GP)), such as Linear Scaling [11] and No Same Mates (NSM) [9]. We apply an ACO [6] induced prediction model to estimate the end of run performance based on the information gathered in the first few generations of GE. Then, we only allow the run to continue if it is predicted to be *successful* and terminate the remaining runs. This improves the rate of success while reducing the total amount of time significantly.

In this paper we establish the use of $cAnt-Miner_{PB}$ [18], an ACO based classifier that produces a model to predict the performance of GE; the results indicate that the predictive model effectively improves the proportion of successful GE runs on a selection of symbolic regression problems. The training data required for the classifier describes the *changes* in different parameters (such as fitness, genome lengths) at the early stages of an evolutionary cycle of GE, that is, how fast does a particular measure change. The ants then devise a rule based classification model that has been further scrutinized to select the best combination of rules to predict the performance. The predictive model thus produced is then used during the prediction of the evolutionary cycle of a given run. Finally, the runs that are predicted to be poor are immediately halted, freeing more resources for higher quality runs. Our approach in predicting the run time performance is novel: to the best of our knowledge, this is the first attempt to employ an ACO classifier to predict the performance of an EA run along with a detailed understanding of how we use an ACO based classifier for model discovery in the current context.

The rest of the paper is laid out as follows: section 2 introduces GE, some previous approaches to improve the quality of evolutionary search with GE, describes the ACO and, presents the novel approach to predict the GE runs; section 4 details the selection of problems for this study, the experimental setups and the results achieved; section 5 analyses the ACO based predictive models; and finally, section 6 concludes the paper and outlines our future aspirations.

2. BACKGROUND

GE [25] is an evolutionary algorithm that evolves computer programs in an arbitrary language. Unlike standard GP [14], GE endorses genotypes to phenotypes distinction through grammars to generate the computer programs; a genotype is a variable length binary string genome whereas the phenotype is a computer program in a language defined by a CFG of choice specified in Backus Naur Form (BNF).

GE uses a simple *mapping* process to convert the genotypes to phenotypes. In GE, a genotype is a string of 8 bit integers each integer termed a *codon*; each of these codons helps mapping a derivation tree from the selection of production rules in the CFG. To facilitate this, each codon selects a production rule from the given grammar as follows:
Rule=(Codon Integer Value)%(# rules of this non-terminal) where *Rule* is an index to a production rule that is applicable in the present context of mapping a derivation. Naturally, the codons that appear earlier in the genome shape the derivation tree so that the codons appearing later only select rules as required by the partially generated derivation tree. Thus, there is a left to right dependency in how the codons in a GE genome are interpreted by the GE mapping process; therefore, if we change a codon at the start of the genome, the interpretation of the codons appearing later changes. Thus the effect of the change at the start of the genome *ripples* through the rest of the genome; correspondingly, the one point crossover in GE is called the *ripple crossover* [13]. If the mapping remains incomplete, then a special operator, *wrapping*, can be used to reuse the genotype from the start.

It is possible that the mapping can finish before using the entire genotype. Thus, in GE, the *actual length* of a genotype may be different from the *effective length* which is the number of codons mapped. The actual length of a genome is usually longer than the effective length, on any problem. A complete description of GE can be found in [20].

Note that the nature of GE mapping easily allows us to use both the actual and effective lengths of the genomes as inputs to our predictive model, while in GP, it is not trivial to distinguish between functional and non-functional parts of the genome[1]. This is why we currently use GE, and will later extend the work to GP.

2.1 Run Improvement

The efforts to improve the performance of GP date back to its inception; GE being a form of GP [14], can also benefit from a number of such approaches. Typically, this work tries to improve the success rate of the results, which, in turn, impacts the total execution time.

For example, Keijzer [10] improved GP based symbolic regression results using interval arithmetic and linear scaling. An improved GP search was presented in [9] for the symbolic regression problems with an analysis on crossover and diversity. [15, 23] proposed improvement techniques that work by killing the bloating individuals which occur at the later stages of the evolutionary cycle. Tsakonas et al. [31] applied kill tournaments [28], replacing the worst (fitness) individual with the best, in predicting the classification rules with GP. Work shown in [1, 7] improved the quality of GP on symbolic regression problems.

Although this is just a tiny subset of vast amount of research, in general, they all have the same focus, that is to make the best out of the available genetic material. This paper attempts to ensure that the available genetic material is as good as it can be, so that all these methods should be able to benefit from it.

2.2 Predicting The Quality of Runs

There are many possible reasons for a run to fail to achieve good quality solutions, but many manifest themselves in the form of the premature convergence [14] of the population to a sub-optimal solution leaving little diversity in the population to explore new solutions. In the case of GE, Keijzer et al. [13] showed that the *ripple* crossover (a variant of one-point crossover specific to GE) delays premature convergence. However, GE suffers from the problem of locality [24] that worsens the search results.

Some studies suggested that multiple independent runs could result in useful solutions. For example [27] argued that multiple small runs can reach global solutions with fewer function evaluations than a single run for a genetic algorithm (GA).

The quality can be improved by proposing modifications to the search process as explained in literature or by performing multiple isolated runs [27], but, a different solution is to some how catch the runs that fail to produce high-quality solutions and kill them. We accomplish this goal by predicting the success or otherwise of a GE run using an ACO based machine learning algorithm. As a result, we find that, along with an improvement in the final result of run, our approach reduces the execution time using fitness prediction that leverages the difference between the individuals in the current and past generations.

A key difference with this work is that we are more concerned with producing a small number of high quality runs than producing a large number of statistically useful runs. However, RPM can operate in tandem with virtually any system from the literature.

2.3 Ant Miner Overview

ACO [6] is an optimization meta-heuristic inspired by the foraging and pheromone strategies of real ants. In essence, ants cooperate each other in the form of colonies in order to find an optimal solution to a given problem. For example, if we consider the travelling salesman problem (TSP): ants start from a random city (vertex) and then select the routes (edges) to add new cities that iterative process, in return, produces a solution in the form of pheromones present on the edges. Many researchers have applied ACO to a number of optimization problems and classification is one such domain.

[1]This is not to say that GE cannot produce useless parts of the genome, e.g. (X*0). However, identifying this is beyond the scope of this work.

The first ACO based classification algorithm, *Ant-Miner*, was introduced in [22] that dealt only with the nominal attributes in a given data set. Ant-Miner produces a list of *IF-THEN* classification rules of the form *IF BFC <= 0.0268 THEN no*. Following this, several variations were proposed, some dealt with pheromone update strategies and heuristic information [17], others with discovering fuzzy classification rules [8]. One such extension is $cAnt-Miner_{PB}$ [18], showed much better accuracy with a list quality function that can deal with the numerical attributes also.

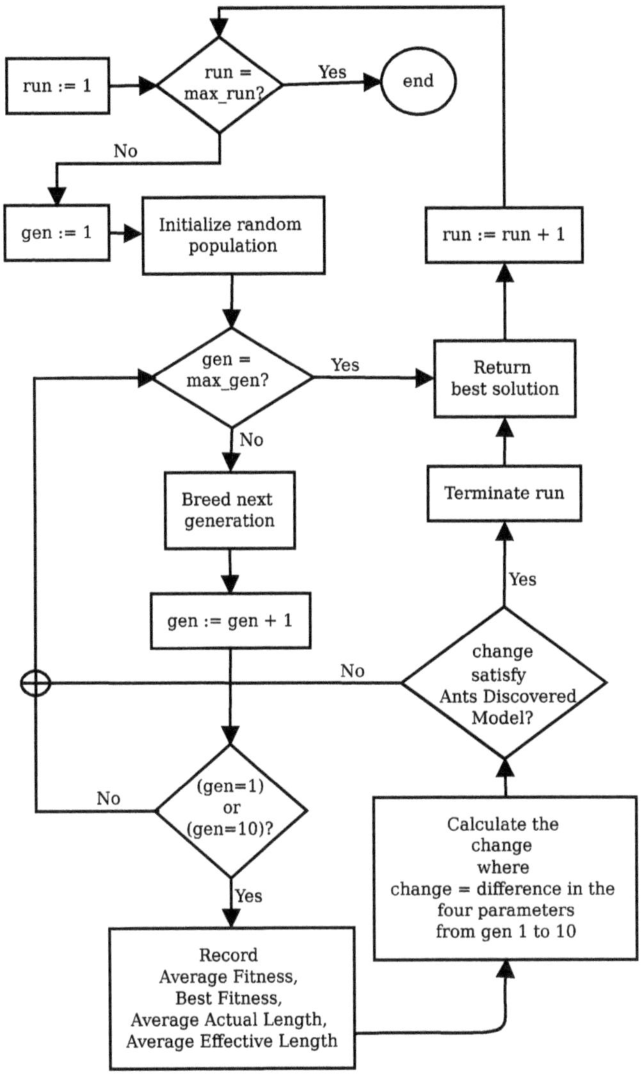

Figure 1: The flowchart for the RPM applied GE that predicts the performance of GE runs.

$cAnt-Miner_{PB}$ algorithm starts with an empty rule list and the training set in each iteration and, repeated until the maximum number of iterations reached or the algorithm converges. The ant then creates a rule from the data points in the training set. There after, the ant prunes the rule and removes all the covered data points from the training set. This process is repeated until the remaining data points in the training set become less than the user specified number of uncovered training points. This way a rule list is prepared in each iteration. The quality of the current list of rules is compared with the previous list of rules, and replaces if the current list is better than the best so far. This way, ants construct a list of best rules. A data point is considered correctly classified if the predicted class value is same as the actual class value. $cAnt-Miner_{PB}$ has produced competitive results when compared against the state-of-the-art machine learning methods. With this motivation for the first time we employ $cAnt-Miner_{PB}$ to improve the quality of GE results as proposed in this paper.

3. THE RUN PREDICTION MODEL

This section describes an overview of the ACO learning process in predicting the GE runs then, the implementation details of the novel approach. The ACO based learning algorithm uses the training data (shown in section 4.1), that discovers a prediction model. The model takes GE evolutionary cycle as an input then, tries to identify the quality of the solution attainable at the end of a GE run. This way, the model allows only the *promising* runs to continue and terminates the remaining runs early.

Figure 1 presents the flowchart of run prediction model (RPM) applied GE. Except for a small change to interrupt the execution of GE, the proposed approach follows the standard GE algorithm. The variable *gen* stands for the current generation number. In summary, the proposed approach starts with an initial random population of individuals. Then, the next generation of individuals are evolved iteratively performing genetic operations, mapping the genotypes to phenotypes, evaluating the fitness of the phenotypes, incrementing the generation count. During this process a new step, the algorithm records the change in the parameters: best fitness, average fitness, average actual length and, average effective length; we note the change in these parameters that records the difference (change) from generation 1 to 10. This change in the respective parameters is used to identify the success or failure of a GE run. An interesting question here is that what if we consider the difference between generation 1 and 5 or generation 1 and 20? The former, in fact achieves a better optimization in the execution time while the calculated change resulted in an approximately zero difference in most of the runs, that in turn resulted in omitting this choice. With the latter possibility, we end up with less optimization in total execution time. Considering these factors into count, we leaned towards experimenting with the difference between generations 1 and 10. If the change in any one or all of the recorded parameters satisfy the conditions in the ACO classifier discovered model then, that run is terminated recording the best so far fitness that helps for the comparison. Otherwise, the algorithm continues to run reporting the best of run result. This process is repeated until the maximum number of runs have reached.

4. EXPERIMENTS

This section describes the regression problems and the generated training data for the respective problem, the experimental approach and the results.

4.1 Problems and Training data

We followed the experimental procedure explained in [3] in preparing the data sets for the four symbolic regression problems.

Table 1: The problem set considered. The "yes" column counts the number of runs producing results above the threshold; the "no" column counts the runs that remained below the threshold.

#	Problem:Source	no	yes	Success threshold (Best Fitness <)
f_1	$(1+x)^3$:[5]	590	410	0.7
f_2	$x^4 - x^3 - y^2 - y$:[30]	606	394	0.65
f_3	$x^3 - y^3 - y - x$:[30]	848	152	0.7
f_4	x^y:[29]	518	482	1

Table 1 describes the experimental problems and the data sets used in this paper. The first column in Table 1 gives an index to the problem; henceforth, we use this index to refer to the corresponding problem. The second column gives the target function in each problem; we also cite the source of the problem from the GP literature.

For each problem, a training set has been prepared to train the ACO algorithm. Each data set contains 1000 data points that are classified with two (*yes, no*) labels. The number of *yes, no* class labels are presented in third and fourth columns for the respective problem. The classification of a data point depends upon the user defined success threshold, Best Fitness (BF). For problem f_1, if $BF > 0.7$ then those data points belong to *yes* class, *no* otherwise. Since, the regression problems are hard to solve and the solution evolved by an EA varies largely from a problem to problem, we consider a different threshold value as a success measure on each problem. All the attributes in the resulting data sets are continuous with no duplicates.

Table 2: A brief description of the data sets used in the experiments. BFC (Best Fitness Change), AFC (Average Fitness Change), AALC (Average Actual Length Change), AELC (Average Effective Length Change), are the attributes of the data set with the data points that represent the change from generation 1 to 10.

BFC	AFC	AALC	AELC	Class
0.0220119	0.0481755	2.005	-18.995	no
0.0530694	0.0641799	6.105	-12.565	yes
⋮	⋮	⋮	⋮	⋮
0.0868888	0.0622562	10.945	-17.825	no

Table 2 presents an example description of f_1 training set. The data set contains four attributes: BFC, AFC, AALC, AELC that represent the change in the respective parameters between generation 1 and generation 10. The two fitness related attributes (BFC and AFC) are intuitive; however, these are not the only possible attributes, and later work will examine more. The data sets were prepared recording the change in the respective attributes and classifying them as per the threshold values defined in Table 1 for the respective problem. Although the computational effort in preparing the training sets is rather high for this preliminary investigation, it has resulted highly in improving the success rate and optimizing the execution time with the help of the proposed run prediction model.

4.2 Experimental Approach and Results

We have conducted two sets of experiments. In the first set, we compare the predictive accuracy of the ACO based classifier with those produced by a number of contemporary machine learning algorithms. We find that the ACO based classifier outperforms the benchmark machine learning methods. Next, we apply the ACO devised models to actual GE runs after a manual inspection in order to detect and terminate poor runs and present the results showing the efficacy of the proposed approach.

Listing 1: Ant discovered model for problem f_1

```
IF AALC <= -12.8875 THEN no;
IF BFC <= 0.0268 THEN no;
IF AELC <= -23.31 THEN yes;
IF AFC > 0.0731 THEN yes;
IF 0.0614 < AFC <= 0.0633 THEN no;
IF AELC <= -21.725 THEN yes;
IF AELC <= -20.99 THEN no;
IF AALC <= -6.035 THEN yes;
IF 7.2475 < AALC <= 8.3425 THEN no;
IF BFC <= 0.0268 THEN no;
IF AFC <= 0.0534 THEN no;
IF BFC > 0.0656 THEN yes;
IF AELC > -17.7924 AND
   AALC > -1.5025 THEN yes;
IF BFC > 0.0558 THEN no;
IF BFC > 0.0496 AND
   AFC <= 0.0613 THEN yes;
IF AFC > 0.0558 AND
   AELC > -22.855 THEN no;
IF BFC > 0.0292 THEN yes;
IF <empty> THEN yes;
```

4.2.1 Discovered Models

We ran $cAnt - Miner_{PB}$ mining algorithm on all the four data sets to generate four different predictive models, one for each problem. The set parameters for the algorithm were: *ant_colony_size* = 5, *iterations* = 500, *minimum_cases_per_interval* = 10, and, *evaporation_probability* = 0.9. A complete description of these parameters can be found in [22].

The ant learning algorithm discovered four prediction models, one for each problem. For example, Listing 1 presents the ant discovered model for problem f_1, the remaining models are concealed owing to the space restrictions. In the model, each line that starts with an *IF* keyword and ends with *;* (semi-colon) represents a rule. All the models consist of the best list of rules derived by ants. Note that the rules in the models are simple enough for a manual inspection and analysis. As the focus of the paper is to predict the *poor* runs that fail to produce high-quality solution, we consider the rules that predict the class value *no* from the discovered rule list.

Examining the classification model shown in Listing 1, ants devised a manageable number of rules with a single attribute alone or in combination of more than one attribute and a class. While it is difficult to identify clearly which rule of the model suits best in run prediction, we manually explored different possibilities of these rules on the training data set of the respective problem in order to identify the best combination of rules.

Table 3: Comparison of accuracy measure (*mean* [*standard deviation*]) in %, among J48, ZeroR, $cAnt\text{-}Miner_{PB}$, PART and JRip measured by applying 10-fold cross-validation. The value of the most accurate algorithm is shown in bold for a given data set with the Wilcoxon tests at $\alpha = 5\%$.

Problem	J48	ZeroR	$cAnt - Miner_{PB}$	PART	JRip
f_1	58.4 [0.49]	54.12 [0.95]	**78.72 [0.84]**	57.85 [0.63]	59.18 [0.81]
f_2	60.61 [0.89]	60.25 [1.32]	**69.32 [0.61]**	61.19 [1.58]	62.60 [1.02]
f_3	79.44 [0.35]	78.43 [0.26]	**86.96 [0.45]**	80.88 [1.01]	80.24 [0.56]
f_4	54.21 [0.54]	51.82 [0.64]	**68.12 [0.99]**	56.10 [0.38]	58.50 [0.47]

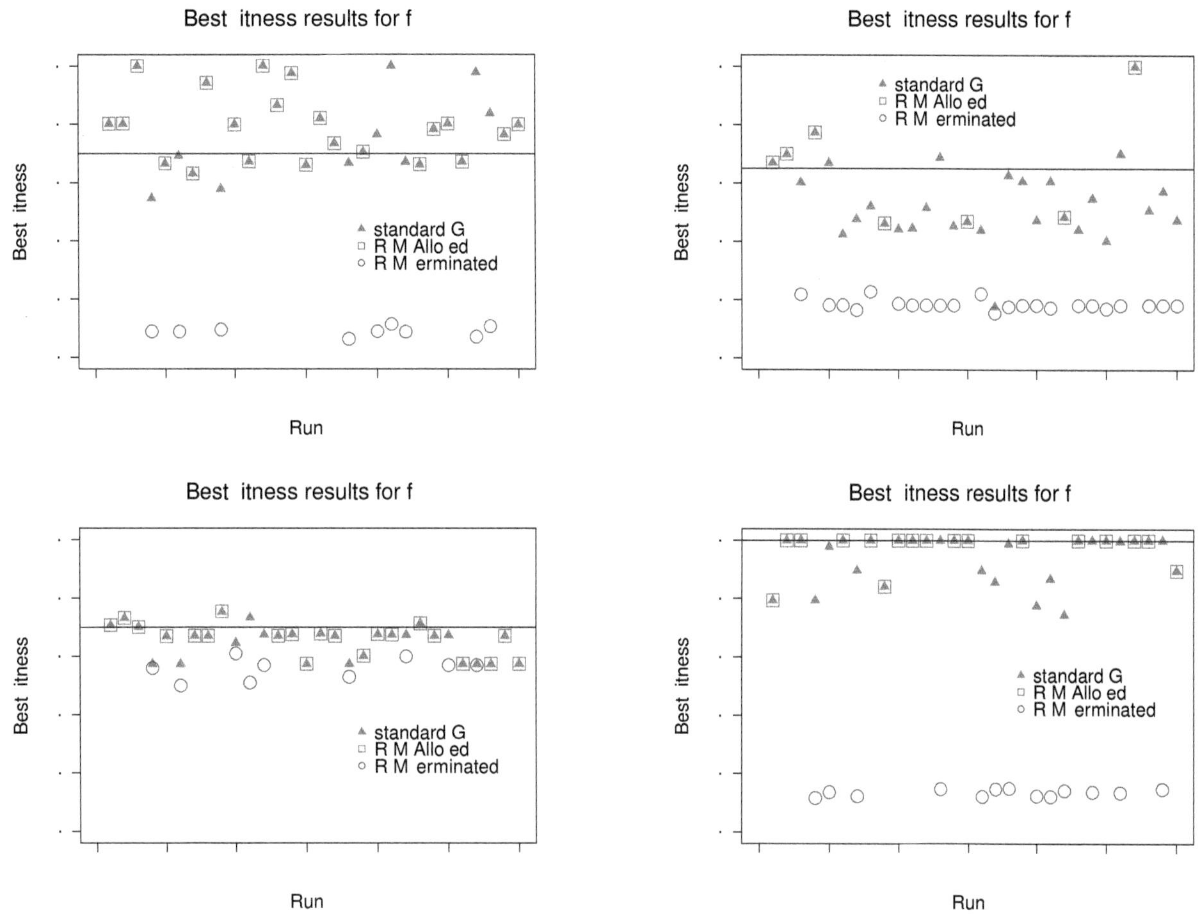

Figure 2: The best fitness measure of standard GE (shown in triangles) vs. RPM applied GE (shown in squares and circles) on the four symbolic regression problems. The end of run results of all four problems illustrate an improvement in the quality of runs after applying the prediction model.

Table 4: A comparison in the success rate of the standard GE vs. Run Prediction Model (RPM) applied GE out of 30 evolutionary runs on each approach.

Problem	GE		GE+RPM		
	# of successful runs	% of success	# of successful runs	% of success	terminated runs
f_1	18	56.66	15	71.43	9
f_2	7	23.33	3	65.15	23
f_3	6	20.00	5	23.81	9
f_4	17	56.66	12	70.59	13

Table 5: Selected rules for run prediction.

Problem	Selected Rule(s)
f_1	if(bfc <= 0.027)
f_2	if((bfc > 0.022) && (afc > 0.087))
f_3	if(aalc > 5.97)
	if((bfc <= 0.19) && (aelc > 3.84))
f_4	if(bfc > 0.035) and
	if((aalc < -17.79) && (aelc > -22.85))

Table 5 presents the selected rules from the manual analysis on all the problems and shows the simplicity of the selected rules. We focused on the rules that can identify the low-quality run only. In fact the selected list of rules may sometimes fail to exactly find the poor solution producing runs as is the case that it might try to terminate a few useful runs also. We treat this as the error exerted by the prediction that we explain it in detail later in section 5.

Table 3 compares the predictive accuracy achieved by $cAnt - Miner_{PB}$ with some state of the art classification algorithms on the four data sets considered in this study. Each entry in Table 3 shows the mean accuracy measure (in %) followed by the standard deviation, calculated as a result of 10-fold cross-validation. $cAnt - Miner_{PB}$ exhibited significantly better predictive accuracy than its counter parts when performed the Wilcoxon two-tailed significance tests at a significance level of $\alpha = 5\%$. Overall, $cAnt - Miner_{PB}$ models exhibit significantly better predictive accuracy outperforming the remaining classifiers on all the four data sets.

4.2.2 *Impact of Predictors*

With the predictors generated, the next step was to establish how effective they were. We assess the effectiveness of the predictors by conducting the next set of experiments in two steps. We used libGE [19], an open source framework for GE in C++. In the first step, all four problems were run with standard GE system recording the best fitness at the end of run. Similarly, in the second step, the same problems were run with RPM applied GE system recording the best fitness and, terminating the runs that satisfy the respective model of the corresponding problem. Finally, a comparative analysis has been presented with the results obtained in both the steps.

The following parameters were kept consistent in both the experimental setups. The parameters were: *number of runs* = 30, *population size* = 200, *number of generations* = 120, *crossover probability* = 0.9, *mutation probability* = 0.01, randomly initialized the initial population with a *minimum genotype length* of 15, *maximum length* of 25, *seed* value was incremented for each run, and a steady state replacement strategy. We used an *S-Lang* evaluator for the fitness evaluation. A run in this experimental settings is considered as long (with 120 generations) when compared to the standard GE settings (50 generations). The main reason for this setting is that [2] showed that a single large run reaches the global solution faster than multiple small runs saving the computational resources.

Figure 2 shows the best fitness measure for 30 runs that summarizes the results comparing the standard GE system with that of the run prediction model applied GE. Standard GE results are shown in triangles, whereas the model applied GE results are represented with squares and circles. In that, the circles represent the terminated runs, whereas the squares represent the model allowed runs that completed their execution. At $BestFitness = 0.70$ there exists a black straight line parallel to x-axis. This represents the success measure (defined in section 4.1) on the respective problems, if the end of run result is greater than that value then it is a high-quality run, or else a low-quality run. Some of the squares and the triangles in Figure 2 overlap each other. This is due to the fact that the proposed approach tries to predict the success or failure of a run without making any modifications to the GE search process. This results in an improvement in the success rate of the GE results.

The results shown in Table 4 summarizes the number of successful (high-quality) runs and, the rate of success for 30 runs with standard GE and RPM applied GE approaches. In addition to this the count of terminated runs resulted from the run prediction model are reported. The RPM+GE exhibits significant improvement in the % of successful results over standard GE on all the four problems. While f_3 enjoys only a small (but still statistically significant) improvement of 3.81%, the remaining three problems f_1, f_2 and f_4 exhibit 14.77%, 41.82%, and 13.93% respectively. Notice that f_2 exhibits huge jump in the success rate; it is because, the model has identified 23 runs as the *poor* runs and terminated. This behaviour of the model requires us to consider how many *good* runs are killed by the model? We explain the answer later in section 5 with an analysis on the inherent error of the new prediction approach.

Table 6: Statistical test results for the total execution time of standard GE (T_{GE}) vs. that of RPM applied GE (T_{GE+RPM}) over 30 runs. Note that the "Yes" represents that the model applied GE performed significantly better than standard GE with Wilcoxon Signed rank test at $\alpha = 5\%$. When there is significant difference, *A* measure value is shown, otherwise (-).

Problem	Significant	A measure	T_{GE} (in sec)	T_{GE+RPM} (in sec)
f_1	No	-	91.83	66.78
f_2	Yes	0.831	88.24	25.43
f_3	Yes	0.661	87.65	61.93
f_4	Yes	0.692	87.73	52.31

Since the amount of processing time required to evolve the solution is one of the major concerns in EA, we illustrate the total execution time results as shown in Table 6, whereas T_{GE} stands for total execution time of standard GE and T_{GE+RPM} stands for the total execution time of the RPM applied GE. We observe that the proposed approach reduces the time on all the problems. Execution time reduction in f_1 is insignificant as a result of the Wilcoxon test, whereas it is significant for the remaining three problems. The non-parametric Wilcoxon Signed Rank test states whether the model applied GE is significantly better or not, but it fails to state how much better it is. We use *Vargha-Delaney A* [32] measure that tells us the probability that the model applied GE achieve better performance over the standard GE. When the A measure is above 0.5, standard GE outperforms the model applied GE. When it is 0.5, both are equal, otherwise, the model applied GE outperforms the standard GE. The A measure tells us that run prediction model applied GE outperforms standard GE, 83.16%, 66.11% and, 69.17% of times on f_2, f_3 and f_4 respectively.

From the results shown in Table 4 and 6, we conclude that the rate of success of GE has increased while reducing the total execution time on the respective regression problems with the introduction of the new run prediction approach.

5. DISCUSSION

Recall that the proposed RPM+GE inherently exerts error so that it misclassified a few GE runs as either low-quality or high-quality runs and terminates or allows to continue the execution. We describe this issue of the model incorrect predictions in this section.

Table 7: RPM applied GE predictions on the four benchmark problems.

Problem	TP	FP	FN	TN
f_1	15	6	3	6
f_2	3	4	4	19
f_3	5	16	1	8
f_4	12	5	5	8

Table 7 shows the prediction results of the four RPM applied GE problems. The terms are defined as follows: *TP* is the actual number of correctly identified high-quality runs, *FP* is the number of runs that are actually low-quality but identified as high-quality, *FN* is the number of runs that are actually high-quality but identified as low-quality, *TN* is the number of runs that are actually low-quality and identified as low-quality. The results shown in Table 7 describe that there is a possibility that the model terminates a few number of successful runs (FN), even though, the results in Table 4 confirm the improvement in the success rate. Considering FP rate, problem f_3 has high FP rate. If we refer back to Figure 2, we note that most of these runs fall just short of crossing the threshold. Therefore, we need a too sensitive predictor to classify such points as negative examples. As it is, this performance is not a disaster if we allow for a small margin of error around the threshold.

In summary, the analysis clearly suggests that the ACO discovered models are simple enough to analyse and easy to use in an EA run prediction. Combined use of ACO with EA produced a reasonably good prediction system. As a result, a significant improvement has been observed in the number of successful runs while significantly reducing the total execution time.

6. CONCLUSIONS

We have successfully accomplished the set goals of improving the quality of the solution as well as optimizing the speed of execution by employing an ACO based classification with the introduction of the new run prediction approach. This approach was more akin to reduce the total execution time while improving the rate of success. This work can have huge implications for scaling EC algorithms which, due to their stochastic nature, often confront prediction when it comes to the length of the runs. One assumption that we have made is the existence of good predictive data.

The next step will be concerned with bootstrapping the system, and we are currently examining two approaches. First, the use of data produced on smaller but related versions of the problem, similar to the technique used in [12] will be examined. Although not perfect, this could get over the initial bootstrapping phase, particularly if the problem being tackled is a scaled up version of the one the data came from.

Secondly, and probably in tandem with the first method, we will investigate rapidly retraining the predictors during the runs as increasingly more data becomes available, similar to work by [4, 16, 26]. This would facilitate increasingly accurate predictors as more data becomes available.

7. REFERENCES

[1] R. M. A. Azad and C. Ryan. Abstract functions and lifetime learning in genetic programming for symbolic regression. In *Proceedings of the Twelth International Conference on Genetic and Evolutionary Computation Conference, GECCO'10*, pages 893–900, 2010.

[2] E. Cantú-Paz and D. Goldberg. Are multiple runs of genetic algorithms better than one? volume 2723 of *LNCS*, pages 801–812. Springer, Berlin, Heidelberg, 2003.

[3] G. Chennupati, C. Ryan, and R. M. A. Azad. An empirical analysis through the time complexity of GE problems. In R. Matousek, editor, *19th International Conference on Soft Computing, MENDEL'13*, pages 37–44, Brno, Czech Republic, jun, 26-28 2013.

[4] D. Costelloe and C. Ryan. On improving generalisation in genetic programming. In L. Vanneschi, S. Gustafson, A. Moraglio, I. Falco, and M. Ebner, editors, *Genetic Programming*, volume 5481 of *LNCS*, pages 61–72. Springer, Berlin, Heidelberg, 2009.

[5] J. M. Daida, R. R. Bertram, S. A. Stanhope, J. C. Khoo, S. A. Chaudhary, O. A. Chaudhri, and J. A. I. Polito. What makes a problem gp-hard? analysis of a tunably difficult problem in genetic programming, 2001.

[6] M. Dorigo and T. Stützle. *Ant colony optimization*. MIT Press, 2004.

[7] J. Fitzgerald, R. M. A. Azad, and C. Ryan. A bootstrapping approach to reduce over-fitting in genetic programming. In *Proceeding of the Fifteenth Annual Conference Companion on Genetic and Evolutionary Computation Conference Companion*, pages 1113–1120, 2013.

[8] M. Galea and Q. Shen. Simultaneous ant colony optimization algorithms for learning linguistic fuzzy rules. In A. Abraham, C. Grosan, and V. Ramos, editors, *Swarm Intelligence in Data Mining*, volume 34 of *Studies in Computational Intelligence*, pages 75–99. Springer, Berlin, Heidelberg, 2006.

[9] S. Gustafson, E. Burke, and N. Krasnogor. On improving genetic programming for symbolic regression. In *IEEE Congress on Evolutionary Computation*, volume 1, pages 912–919, 2005.

[10] M. Keijzer. Improving symbolic regression with interval arithmetic and linear scaling. In C. Ryan, T. Soule, M. Keijzer, E. Tsang, R. Poli, and E. Costa, editors, *Genetic Programming*, volume 2610 of *LNCS*, pages 70–82. Springer, Berlin, Heidelberg, 2003.

[11] M. Keijzer. Scaled symbolic regression. *Genetic Programming and Evolvable Machines*, 5(3):259–269, 2004.

[12] M. Keijzer, C. Ryan, and M. Cattolico. Run transferable libraries - learning functional bias in problem domains. In K. Deb, editor, *Proceedings of the Genetic and Evolutionary Computation Conference*, volume 3103 of *LNCS*, pages 531–542. Springer, Berlin, Heidelberg, 2004.

[13] M. Keijzer, C. Ryan, M. O'Neill, M. Cattolico, and V. Babovic. Ripple crossover in genetic programming. In J. Miller, M. Tomassini, P. Lanzi, C. Ryan, A. Tettamanzi, and W. Langdon, editors, *Genetic Programming*, volume 2038 of *LNCS*, pages 74–86. Springer, Berlin, Heidelberg, 2001.

[14] J. R. Koza. *Genetic Programming: On the Programming of Computers by Means of Natural Selection*. MIT Press, Cambridge, MA, USA, 1992.

[15] J. R. Koza, S. Al-Sakran, and L. Jones. Cross-domain features of runs of genetic programming used to evolve designs for analog circuits, optical lens systems, controllers, antennas, mechanical systems, and quantum computing circuits. In *Proceedings of NASA/DoD Conference on Evolvable Hardware*, pages 205–212, 2005.

[16] K. Krawiec and J. Swan. Pattern-guided genetic programming. In *Proceeding of the Fifteenth Annual Conference on Genetic and Evolutionary Computation Conference*, pages 949–956, 2013.

[17] D. Martens, M. De Backer, R. Haesen, J. Vanthienen, M. Snoeck, and B. Baesens. Classification with ant colony optimization. *IEEE Transactions on Evolutionary Computation*, 11(5):651–665, 2007.

[18] M. Medland and F. E. B. Otero. A study of different quality evaluation functions in the cant-miner(pb) classification algorithm. In *Proceedings of the fourteenth international conference on Genetic and evolutionary computation conference, GECCO '12*, pages 49–56, 2012.

[19] M. Nicolau and D. Slattery. libge - grammatical evolution library. http://bds.ul.ie/libGE/index.html, 2006.

[20] M. O'Neill and C. Ryan. *Grammatical Evolution: Evolutionary Automatic Programming in an Arbitrary Language*. Kluwer Academic Publishers, Norwell, MA, USA, 2003.

[21] U.-M. O'Reilly, M. Wagy, and B. Hodjat. Ec-star: A massive-scale, hub and spoke, distributed genetic programming system. In R. Riolo, E. Vladislavleva, M. D. Ritchie, and J. H. Moore, editors, *Genetic Programming Theory and Practice X*, pages 73–85. Springer New York, 2013.

[22] R. Parpinelli, H. Lopes, and A. Freitas. Data mining with an ant colony optimization algorithm. *IEEE Transactions on Evolutionary Computation*, 6(4):321–332, 2002.

[23] R. Poli. A simple but theoretically-motivated method to control bloat in genetic programming. In *Proceedings of the 6th European Conference on Genetic Programming*, EuroGP'03, pages 204–217. Springer, Berlin, Heidelberg, 2003.

[24] F. Rothlauf and M. Oetzel. On the locality of grammatical evolution. In *Proceedings of the 9th European Conference on Genetic Programming*, EuroGP'06, pages 320–330. Springer, Berlin, Heidelberg, 2006.

[25] C. Ryan, J. J. Collins, and M. O'Neill. Grammatical evolution: Evolving programs for an arbitrary language. In W. Banzhaf, R. Poli, M. Schoenauer, and T. C. Fogarty, editors, *Proceedings of the First European Workshop on Genetic Programming*, volume 1391 of *LNCS*, pages 83–95. Springer, 1998.

[26] C. Ryan, M. Keijzer, and M. Cattolico. Favourable biasing of function sets using run transferable libraries. In U.-M. O'Reilly, T. Yu, R. Riolo, and B. Worzel, editors, *Genetic Programming Theory and Practice II*, volume 8, pages 103–120. Springer US, 2005.

[27] R. Shonkwiler. Parallel genetic algorithms. In *ICGA*, pages 199–205. Morgan Kaufmann, 1993.

[28] J. Smith and F. Vavak. Replacement strategies in steady state genetic algorithms: static environments. In W. Banzhaf and C. Reeves, editors, *Foundations of Genetic Algorithms 5*, pages 219–234, 1999.

[29] M. Streeter and L. Becker. Automated discovery of numerical approximation formulae via genetic programming. *Genetic Programming and Evolvable Machines*, 4(3):255–286, 2003.

[30] A. Topchy and W. F. Punch. Faster genetic programming based on local gradient search of numeric leaf values. In L. Spector, E. D. Goodman, A. Wu, W. B. Langdon, H.-M. Voigt, M. Gen, S. Sen, M. Dorigo, S. Pezeshk, M. H. Garzon, and E. Burke, editors, *Proceedings of the third international conference on Genetic and evolutionary computation conference, GECCO '01*, pages 155–162, San Francisco, California, USA, 7-11 July 2001. Morgan Kaufmann.

[31] A. Tsakonas, G. Dounias, J. Jantzen, H. Axer, B. Bjerregaard, and D. G. von Keyserlingk. Evolving rule-based systems in two medical domains using genetic programming. *Artificial Intelligence in Medicine*, 32(3):195–216, 2004.

[32] A. Vargha and H. D. Delaney. A critique and improvement of the "cl" common language effect size statistics of mcgraw and wong. *Journal of Educational and Behavioral Statistics*, 25(2):101–132, 2000.

[33] D. Wilson, K. Veeramachaneni, and U.-M. O'Reilly. Cloud scale distributed evolutionary strategies for high dimensional problems. In *Proceedings of the 16th European Conference on Applications of Evolutionary Computation*, EvoApplications'13, pages 519–528, Berlin, Heidelberg, 2013. Springer-Verlag.

Genetic Programming with Data Migration for Symbolic Regression

Michael Kommenda[1,2], Michael Affenzeller[1,2],
Bogdan Burlacu[1], Gabriel Kronberger[1], Stephan M. Winkler[1]

[1]University of Applied Sciences Upper Austria
Heuristic and Evolutionary Algorithms Laboratory
Softwarepark 11, 4232 Hagenberg, Austria

[2]Johannes Kepler University Linz
Institute for Formal Models and Verification
Altenbergerstr. 69, 4040 Linz, Austria

{michael.kommenda, michael.affenzeller, bogdan.burlacu,
gabriel.kronberger, stephan.winkler}@fh-hagenberg.at

ABSTRACT

In this publication genetic programming (GP) with data migration for symbolic regression is presented. The motivation for the development of the algorithm is to evolve models which generalize well on previously unseen data. GP with data migration uses multiple subpopulations to maintain the genetic diversity during the algorithm run and a sophisticated training subset selection strategy. Each subpopulation is evaluated on a different fixed training subset (FTS) and additionally a variable training subset (VTS) is exchanged between the subpopulations at specific data migration intervals. Thus, the individuals are evaluated on the unification of FTS and VTS and should have better generalization properties due to the regular changes of the VTS.

The implemented algorithm is compared to several GP variants on a number of symbolic regression benchmark problems to test the effectiveness of the multiple populations and data migration strategy. Additionally, different algorithm configurations and migration strategies are evaluated to show their impact with respect to the achieved quality.

Categories and Subject Descriptors

I.2.2 [**Automatic Programming**]: Program synthesis; I.2.8 [**Problem Solving, Control Methods, and Search**]: Heuristic Methods

General Terms

Algorithms, Experimentation

Keywords

Symbolic Regression, Multi-population Genetic Programming, Generalization

GECCO'14, July 12–16, 2014, Vancouver, BC, Canada.

ACM 978-1-4503-2881-4/14/07 ...$15.00.
http://dx.doi.org/10.1145/2598394.2609857.

1. INTRODUCTION

Symbolic regression is the task of finding a model in the form of a mathematical expression describing the relation between a dependent variable and several independent ones as accurately as possible. Symbolic regression problems are commonly solved by genetic programming [8], a population-based and meta-heuristic optimization method for evolving a program that solves a given task. In the case of symbolic regression the program is a mathematical expression and the objective function is the correlation between the model's estimates of the dependent variable and its true values. The main advantages of symbolic regression by genetic programming are that the structure of the model does not have to be predefined, its implicit feature selection strategy [12], and the interpretability of the evolved mathematical expressions [1].

Symbolic regression is regarded as a supervised machine learning task and could produce models with weak generalization properties on unseen data. A common approach to counteract this phenomenon is to restrict the complexity of the produced models and to determine optimal algorithm parameter settings by cross-validation. However, determining optimal parameter settings is quite hard for stochastic algorithms such as symbolic regression by genetic programming, due to the occuring variations in terms of result quality for repeated algorithm executions.

Another common approach to improve the generalization properties of the produced models, which is especially suited for GP, is changing the samples used for fitness calculation regularly to avoid a too strong adaption of the models to the presented training samples. This can be done either by random subset selection [4, 5] or more specialized techniques such as coevolution [11, 6]. An approach similar to the random subset selection technique is presented in this publication and combined with a multi-population genetic programming algorithm.

Multi-population Evolutionary Algorithms

The first coarse-grained parallel and distributed evolutionary algorithms [13, 18] were developed to speed up the evolutionary process by evolving multiple populations in parallel on different machines. If no information exchange happens between the populations, the distributed algorithm is equivalent to executing multiple repetitions of a single population algorithm sequentially and aggregating the results.

One common approach to exchange information between the subpopulations is to copy or move individuals among the subpopulations according to a predefined topology at specific intervals.

The motivation behind the development of evolutionary algorithms with multiple populations, in addition to reducing the execution time, is to explore different regions of the search space simultaneously and thus, maintaining the overall genetic diversity during the algorithm execution. The genetic information present in the subpopulation is exchanged at specific intervals and this is referred to as migration. During migration a certain part of the population (e.g., the best, worst, most diverse, or random individuals) is selected and inserted in another subpopulation, where for example the worst individuals are replaced. Migration is performed according to a spatial topology of the subpopulations [2], which stays constant during the algorithm execution. Popular examples of such a topology are unidirectional or bidirectional ring topologies, but also others like grids or hyper cubes can be used.

Another advantage of multi-population evolutionary algorithms is that building blocks of the final solution can be evolved in different subpopulations and assembled by combining migrated individuals containing these building block [17, 14]. Although the concept of multiple populations for evolutionary algorithms has been originally developed for genetic algorithms, it is easily adapted to genetic programming.

The subsequent parts of the publication are organized as follows: Section 2 introduces the algorithm modifications and the resulting consequences. In Section 3 a detailed experiment plan including a description of the used benchmark problems and parameter settings is given and the obtained results are presented and discussed in Section 4. Finally, Section 5 concludes this publication and explains possible shortcomings and necessary further test and developments to improve the methodology.

2. METHODS

Multi-population evolutionary algorithms explore different regions of the search space simultaneously and individual migration maintains the population diversity during the algorithm execution [14]. Additionally, multiple populations allow an easy integration of advanced sampling strategies for training subset selection and should lead to increased generalization capabilities of the evolved models.

We have combined these ideas into a multi-population genetic programming algorithm for symbolic regression, where each subpopulation is evolved on different parts of the training data. The distribution of the training data is performed during the initialization of the algorithm and the selected training subset, denoted as *FixedTrainingSubset* (FTS), stays constant during the algorithm execution. If the reciprocal of the number of subpopulations is equal to the relative amount of the FTS, the whole training data is divided evenly (without any overlaps) across the subpopulations. Alternatively, if the size of the FTS is smaller, not every sample of the training data will be covered and if it is larger, the individual subsets will overlap. If no individual migration is included, this algorithm performs exactly the same as standard genetic programming, applied multiple times on different parts of the training data, with an aggregation of the obtained results.

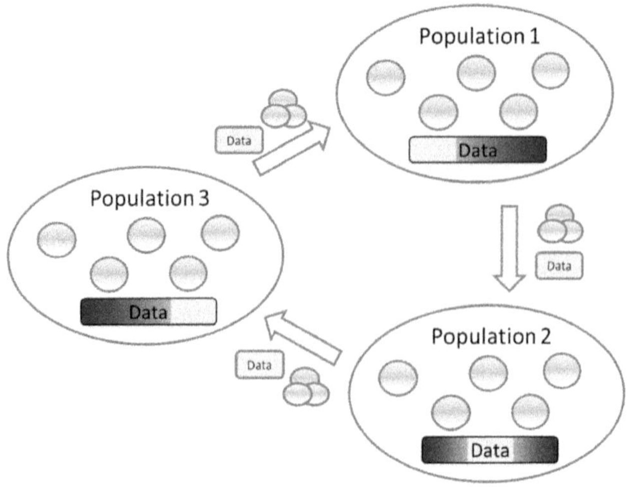

Figure 1: Multipopulation GP with data migration.

An unidirectional ring structure is used as the migration topology of the algorithm and the best individuals are moved to the clockwise neighbor of the current subpopulation.The number of immigrated and emigrated individuals are the same for each subpopulation and therefore the size of each subpopulation stays constant during the algorithm execution. The migrated individuals are evaluated on different parts of the training data and are expected to have better generalization capabilities compared to individuals evolved on a constant subset of the training partition.

A drawback of using only a fixed training subset to evaluate the individuals is that only migrated individuals are trained on different parts of the training data. Individuals that are never migrated are always evaluated on the same training subset and are more likely to generalize poorly. Another aspect is that migrated individuals have to be reevaluated on the FTS of the new subpopulation, so that selection is not mislead by outdated fitness information. The reevaluation could lead to a drastic change in the fitness and to diminish this effect a data migration step (in addition to individual migration) has been included in the multi-population algorithm.

As a result, the fitness of an individual is calculated on samples included in the FTS and an changing *VariableTrainingSubset* (VTS). The VTS is initially chosen as a consecutive part of the training data adjoining the FTS. These two subsets never overlap to avoid the repeated evaluation of training samples. At a specific data migration interval, which by default is equal to the individual migration interval, the VTS is migrated to another subpopulation. By using a fixed and variable training subset for every subpopulation the generalization properties of the evolved individuals should be increased. At the same time the genetic diversity is maintained by migrating the individuals and the algorithm should be able to produce better solutions compared to single population variants. Figure 1 depicts the algorithm, where the training data is distributed evenly across the subpopulations.

As a consequence of evaluating the fitness of an individual only on parts of the training data, the individual with the highest fitness does not have to be the best individual on the whole training data. This causes problems when the best model has to be selected as the algorithm result. Therefore, after the algorithm is finished, every individual in the final population is reevaluated on the whole training data, so that the fitness reflects the model's fit on the training partition. The algorithm steps of the multi-population genetic programming algorithm with data migration for symbolic regression are given as pseudo code in Algorithm 1.

Algorithm 1 Multi-population GP with data migration.

```
for each Subpopulation do
    Assign fixed training subset FTS
    Assign variable training subset VTS
    Generate random individuals
    Evaluate individuals on FTS ∪ VTS
end for

generations ← 0
while generations <maxGenerations do
    for each subpopulation do
        Generate offspring from selected parents
        Evaluate offspring on FTS ∪ VTS
        Replace parents with newly generated offspring
    end for
    if Migrate individuals? then
        Comment: Data changes for migrated individuals
        Migrate best individuals to the next subpopulation
        Reevaluate migrated individuals on new data
    end if
    if Migrate data? then
        Comment: Data changes for all individuals
        Migrate VTS to the next subpopulation
        Reevaluate all individuals
    end if
    generations ← generations + 1
end while

Reevaluate all individuals on whole training data
return Best individual
```

3. EXPERIMENTS

We tested the multi-population GP algorithm with data migration on several synthetic benchmark problems to examine the effects regarding the generalization properties of the resulting models. The problems were taken from the recommended GP benchmark problems[1] [16] and additionally the Poly-10 [10], the Friedman-1, and the Friedman-2 [3] problems were included. A detailed description of the used benchmark problems, including the data generating formula and the number of training and test samples, is given in Table 2.

Algorithm Configurations

For the first experiment four different algorithm configurations were tested: single-population genetic programming (GP), single-population genetic programming with data migration (GP+DM), multi-population genetic programming (MultiPop GP), and multi-population genetic programming with data migration (MultiPop GP+DM). In contrast to the configurations without data migration, the ones with data migration use only a certain part of the available training data for fitness calculation.

The configurations with data migration use 20% of the available training data as fixed training subset (FTS) and 20% as variable training subset (VTS) that is altered during the algorithm execution with a data migration interval of 5 generations. Both multi-population algorithms are configured to include 5 subpopulations and an individual migration interval of 5 generations. Therefore, the MultiPop GP + DM algorithm migrates individuals and data always simultaneously.

Additionally, to the comparison of the achieved qualities of the different algorithms, the influence of data migration on the algorithm is investigated. Based on the MultiPop GP+DM algorithm, we performed tests with both, individual and data migration, with only one of the migration types, and with no migration at all between the different subpopulations. For all configurations the fixed training subset is used and contains 20% of the available training data as stated above.

Table 1: Algorithmic settings common for all algorithms.

Parameter	Value
Tree initialization	PTC2 [9]
Maximum tree length	200 Nodes
Population size	500 Individuals
Elites	1 Individual
Selection	Tournament selection
	Group size 4
Crossover probability	100%
Crossover operator	Subtree crossover
Mutation probability	25%
Mutation operators	Single point mutation
	Remove branch
	Replace branch
Fitness function	Coefficient of determination R^2
Termination criterion	100 Generations
Terminal symbols	*Constant*, $weight * variable$
Function symbols	Binary functions$(+, -, \times, /)$

Further specific algorithm settings are described textually.

Parameter settings

The parameter settings that are common to all configurations are listed in Table 1. For all configurations that use multiple subpopulations, 5 subpopulations with a size of 100 were used, so that the total number of individuals stays constant regardless of using a single or multiple populations.

The fitness function for all GP algorithms is the coefficient of determination R^2 (Equation 1), which is defined between [0,1]. The R^2 automatically takes linear transformations of the models into account to achieve the best possible fit on the data, but as a consequence the models have to be scaled linearly before other quality values (e.g., mean square error, average relative error, ...) can be calculated. The result of a GP run is the best model in the last generation evaluated on the whole training partition.

[1]`http://www.gpbenchmarks.org/wiki/index.php?title=Problem_Classification`

Table 2: **Definition of benchmark problems and training and test ranges.**

Name	Function	Training	Test
Nguyen-12	$f(x,y) = x^4 - x^3 + 0.5y^2 - y$	200 samples	1000 samples
Keijzer-14	$f(x,y) = \frac{8}{2+x^2+y^2}$	200 samples	798 samples
Vladislavleva-5	$f(x_1,...,x_3) = 30\frac{(x_1-1)(x_3-1)}{x_2{}^2(x_1-10)}$	300 samples	2700 samples
Poly-10	$f(x_1,...,x_{10}) = x_1x_2 + x_3x_4 + x_5x_6 + x_1x_7x_9 + x_3x_6x_{10}$	250 samples	250 samples
Pagie-1	$f(x,y) = \frac{1}{1+x^{-4}} + \frac{1}{1+y^{-4}}$	676 samples	1000 samples
Friedman-1	$f(x_1,...,x_{10}) = 0.1\exp(4x_1) + \frac{4}{1+\exp(-20(x_2-0.5))} + 3x_3 + 2x_4 + x_5 + \text{Noise}$	500 samples	5000 samples
Friedman-2	$f(x_1,...,x_{10}) = 10\sin(\pi x_1 x_2) + 20(x_3 - 1/2)^2 + 10x_4 + 5x_5 + \text{Noise}$	500 samples	5000 samples

$$R^2(x,y) = \frac{\text{Cov}(x,y)^2}{\text{Var}(x) * \text{Var}(y)} \quad (1)$$

All the benchmark problems, algorithms and extensions in this publication are implemented in HeuristicLab [15], an open source framework for heuristic optimization.

4. RESULTS

The results presented in this section were aggregated over 50 repetitions for every algorithm configuration to take the stochasticity of the algorithms into account and report the coefficient of determination R^2 on the training and test data.

Table 3 reports the median, the average, and the standard deviation of the quality of the best models generated by repeated algorithm executions on all benchmark problems. In the first two columns standard genetic programming (GP) using the whole training data is compared to single-population genetic programming with data migration (GP+DM), where the first 20% of the training data are used as fixed training subset (FTS) and another 20% are used as variable training subset (VTS). The last two columns show the achieved qualities of multi-population genetic programming without (MultiPop GP) and with data migrations (MultiPop GP+DM), where the same parameters for data migration were applied as in the single-population case.

When comparing GP with GP+DM, the training results produced by GP are slightly better, but in turn the better test results are obtained by GP+DM. The largest differences occur on the Poly-10 and Pagie-1 datasets, where neither of the two algorithms was able to find any model describing the data generating formula very well. The obtained results with multi-population algorithms are in general better compared to the single-population ones (e.g., Nguyen-12, Pagie-1, Friedman-1).

The picture for the influence of the data migration on the multi-population algorithm variants is similar to the single-population ones. Again, the training results are better without data migration and the test results are better with data migration, but these differences are rather small. Although the improvements in terms of the quality for the data migration algorithms are not very high, it is interesting to observe that apparently it is not necessary to use all available training samples for the fitness of an individual during the algorithm execution and still well-fitting models are created.

Migration strategies

After this first experiment we investigated the influence of the different migration strategies incorporated in the algorithm. Table 4 summarizes the obtained results (median, average and standard deviation) for the multi-population algorithm with four different configurations, where 20% of the training samples were used as FTS. The first column shows the results for the MultiPop GP+DM runs, in the second column the algorithm was configured to use no data migration (VTS=0%), but individual migration and vice versa in the third column (VTS=20%, no individual migration). In the last column the results are stated with no migration at all, which is equivalent to repeating a single-population algorithm for every different FTS and reporting the best model on the whole training of all repetitions.

The worst results when using only a subset of the available data for each subpopulation were obtained by using no migration at all. The picture is not as clear when only data or individual migration are used, but in general it is slightly better to use data instead of individuals migration. However, the best performing strategy is the MultiPop GP+DM with data and individual migration, especially on the harder problems (Poly-10 - Frieman-2).

5. DISCUSSION & OUTLOOK

In this publication a new multi-population genetic programming algorithm for symbolic regression is presented. The main innovation is that every subpopulation is evolved on a different, fixed training subset (FTS) and a changing variable training subset (VTS). Additionally, the VTS is exchanged between the subpopulations by migration according to an unidirectional ring topology. The intended benefits of the developments were that multiple populations promote the genetic diversity and hence, the algorithm learns better on the presented data. At the same time data migration should prevent the algorithm from producing overfit models by changing the data used for fitness calculations and thus, models with better generalization properties should be evolved. Another benefit of using only a subset of the training data for fitness evaluation is that the execution time of the algorithm is reduced, which is important when dealing with large datasets.

The shown results obtained by the new algorithm are encouraging in the sense that the results are as good or slightly better as the results obtained by multi-population genetic programming and for the Pagie-1 benchmark problem the multi-population GP with data migration clearly outperformed all other tested algorithm variants. However, the presented algorithm should be tested on further problems to highlight its advantages and drawbacks. Furthermore, the influence of different parameter settings, especially regarding the impact of the sizes of the two training subsets, whether individual and data migration should be performed simultaneously or asynchronously, and other possible migration topologies is subject to further research.

Another interesting idea for further developments is to combine data migration with offspring selection genetic programming and constant optimization [7], because this algorithm variant achieves better results on symbolic regression problems compared to standard GP. A drawback of the enhanced learning abilities is that the algorithm tends to adapt on the presented data to well and thus, it is more likely that overfit models are produced. Hence, data migration could be an appropriate extension to diminish these effects.

6. ACKNOWLEDGMENTS

The work described in this publication was partly done within the Josef Ressel Centre for Heuristic Optimization *Heureka!* sponsored by the Austrian Research Promotion Agency (FFG).

7. REFERENCES

[1] M. Affenzeller, S. Winkler, G. Kronberger, M. Kommenda, B. Burlacu, and S. Wagner. Gaining deeper insights in symbolic regression. In R. Riolo, J. H. Moore, and M. Kotanchek, editors, *Genetic Programming Theory and Practice XI*, Genetic and Evolutionary Computation. Springer, 2014.

[2] E. Cantú-Paz. A survey of parallel genetic algorithms. *Calculateurs paralleles, reseaux et systems repartis*, 10(2):141–171, 1998.

[3] J. H. Friedman. Multivariate adaptive regression splines. *The annals of statistics*, pages 1–67, 1991.

[4] C. Gathercole and P. Ross. Dynamic training subset selection for supervised learning in genetic programming. In *Parallel Problem Solving from Nature-PPSN III*, pages 312–321. Springer, 1994.

[5] I. Goncalves, S. Silva, J. B. Melo, and J. M. B. Carreiras. Random sampling technique for overfitting control in genetic programming. In A. Moraglio, S. Silva, K. Krawiec, P. Machado, and C. Cotta, editors, *Proceedings of the 15th European Conference on Genetic Programming, EuroGP 2012*, volume 7244 of *LNCS*, pages 218–229, Malaga, Spain, 11-13 Apr. 2012. Springer Verlag.

[6] R. Harper. Spatial co-evolution in age layered planes (SCALP). In *IEEE Congress on Evolutionary Computation (CEC 2010)*, Barcelona, Spain, 18-23 July 2010. IEEE Press.

[7] M. Kommenda, G. Kronberger, S. Winkler, M. Affenzeller, and S. Wagner. Effects of constant optimization by nonlinear least squares minimization in symbolic regression. In *Proceeding of the fifteenth annual conference companion on Genetic and evolutionary computation conference companion (GECCO2013)*, pages 1121–1128. ACM, 2013.

[8] J. R. Koza. *Genetic Programming: On the Programming of Computers by Means of Natural Selection.* MIT Press, Cambridge, MA, USA, 1992.

[9] S. Luke. Two fast tree-creation algorithms for genetic programming. *IEEE Transactions on Evolutionary Computation*, 4(3):274–283, Sept. 2000.

[10] R. Poli. A simple but theoretically-motivated method to control bloat in genetic programming. In *Proceedings of the 6th European conference on Genetic programming*, EuroGP'03, pages 204–217, Berlin, Heidelberg, 2003. Springer-Verlag.

[11] M. D. Schmidt and H. Lipson. Coevolution of fitness predictors. *Evolutionary Computation, IEEE Transactions on*, 12(6):736–749, 2008.

[12] S. Stijven, W. Minnebo, and K. Vladislavleva. Separating the wheat from the chaff: on feature selection and feature importance in regression random forests and symbolic regression. In S. Gustafson and E. Vladislavleva, editors, *3rd symbolic regression and modeling workshop for GECCO 2011*, pages 623–630, Dublin, Ireland, 12-16 July 2011. ACM.

[13] R. Tanese. Distributed genetic algorithms. In *Proceedings of the third international conference on Genetic algorithms*, pages 434–439. Morgan Kaufmann Publishers Inc., 1989.

[14] M. Tomassini, L. Vanneschi, F. Fernández, and G. Galeano. A study of diversity in multipopulation genetic programming. In *Artificial Evolution*, pages 243–255. Springer, 2004.

[15] S. Wagner, G. Kronberger, A. Beham, M. Kommenda, A. Scheibenpflug, E. Pitzer, S. Vonolfen, M. Kofler, S. Winkler, V. Dorfer, and M. Affenzeller. *Advanced Methods and Applications in Computational Intelligence*, volume 6 of *Topics in Intelligent Engineering and Informatics*, chapter Architecture and Design of the HeuristicLab Optimization Environment, pages 197–261. Springer, 2014.

[16] D. R. White, J. McDermott, M. Castelli, L. Manzoni, B. W. Goldman, G. Kronberger, W. Jaskowski, U.-M. O'Reilly, and S. Luke. Better GP benchmarks: community survey results and proposals. *Genetic Programming and Evolvable Machines*, 14(1):3–29, Mar. 2013.

[17] D. Whitley, S. Rana, and R. B. Heckendorn. The island model genetic algorithm: On separability, population size and convergence. *Journal of Computing and Information Technology*, 7:33–48, 1999.

[18] D. Whitley and T. Starkweather. Genitor ii: A distributed genetic algorithm. *Journal of Experimental & Theoretical Artificial Intelligence*, 2(3):189–214, 1990.

Table 3: Training and test qualities given as the coefficient of the determination R^2 between the estimates of the best training solution returned by the algorithm and the target values. The shown values are the median (first row), average (second row), and standard deviation (third row) of 50 repetitions of every algorithm variant.

	GP		GP + DM		MultiPop GP		MultiPop GP + DM	
	Training	**Test**	Training	**Test**	Training	**Test**	Training	**Test**
	0.993	**0.991**	0.990	**0.987**	0.992	**0.989**	0.994	**0.993**
Nguyen-12	0.993	**0.902**	0.990	**0.939**	0.992	**0.922**	0.993	**0.958**
	0.004	**0.200**	0.005	**0.129**	0.004	**0.175**	0.004	**0.146**
	0.993	**0.987**	0.992	**0.987**	0.996	**0.992**	0.995	**0.989**
Keijzer-14	0.991	**0.890**	0.989	**0.920**	0.993	**0.931**	0.992	**0.965**
	0.008	**0.218**	0.009	**0.185**	0.007	**0.189**	0.007	**0.092**
	0.982	**0.946**	0.995	**0.989**	0.994	**0.989**	0.997	**0.994**
Vladislavleva-5	0.966	**0.808**	0.962	**0.878**	0.978	**0.904**	0.982	**0.897**
	0.042	**0.291**	0.058	**0.216**	0.031	**0.209**	0.036	**0.233**
	0.503	**0.247**	0.403	**0.230**	0.521	**0.284**	0.517	**0.475**
Poly-10	0.537	**0.311**	0.500	**0.320**	0.559	**0.347**	0.531	**0.416**
	0.123	**0.207**	0.165	**0.241**	0.149	**0.255**	0.167	**0.251**
	0.866	**0.271**	0.651	**0.207**	0.902	**0.386**	0.507	**0.456**
Pagie-1	0.839	**0.456**	0.680	**0.346**	0.862	**0.465**	0.596	**0.473**
	0.095	**0.370**	0.176	**0.333**	0.085	**0.338**	0.263	**0.339**
	0.754	**0.760**	0.735	**0.739**	0.768	**0.780**	0.754	**0.776**
Friedman-1	0.755	**0.685**	0.730	**0.666**	0.761	**0.734**	0.751	**0.759**
	0.016	**0.141**	0.034	**0.158**	0.768	**0.105**	0.018	**0.060**
	0.799	**0.759**	0.785	**0.744**	0.809	**0.781**	0.795	**0.764**
Friedman-2	0.801	**0.735**	0.787	**0.717**	0.812	**0.761**	0.795	**0.750**
	0.042	**0.102**	0.039	**0.113**	0.033	**0.074**	0.029	**0.071**

Table 4: Training and test qualities given as the coefficient of the determination R^2 between the estimates of the best training solution returned by the algorithm and the target values. The shown values are the median (first row), average (second row), and standard deviation (third row) of 50 repetitions of the algorithm with different migration strategies.

	MultiPop GP + DM		No data migration		No individual migration		No migration	
	Training	**Test**	Training	**Test**	Training	**Test**	Training	**Test**
	0.994	**0.993**	0.990	**0.984**	0.991	**0.991**	0.986	**0.980**
Nguyen-12	0.993	**0.958**	0.987	**0.943**	0.991	**0.973**	0.983	**0.914**
	0.004	**0.146**	0.008	**0.148**	0.004	**0.069**	0.010	**0.187**
	0.995	**0.989**	0.991	**0.980**	0.992	**0.989**	0.982	**0.974**
Keijzer-14	0.992	**0.965**	0.960	**0.865**	0.991	**0.982**	0.957	**0.835**
	0.007	**0.092**	0.123	**0.258**	0.005	**0.029**	0.093	**0.278**
	0.997	**0.994**	0.986	**0.960**	0.984	**0.942**	0.962	**0.871**
Vladislavleva-5	0.982	**0.897**	0.954	**0.851**	0.971	**0.807**	0.941	**0.745**
	0.036	**0.233**	0.056	**0.218**	0.031	**0.295**	0.062	**0.299**
	0.517	**0.475**	0.303	**0.199**	0.472	**0.262**	0.221	**0.055**
Poly-10	0.531	**0.416**	0.341	**0.243**	0.483	**0.323**	0.217	**0.110**
	0.167	**0.251**	0.156	**0.206**	0.134	**0.225**	0.157	**0.162**
	0.507	**0.456**	0.496	**0.429**	0.849	**0.607**	0.454	**0.165**
Pagie-1	0.596	**0.473**	0.474	**0.338**	0.739	**0.562**	0.323	**0.221**
	0.263	**0.339**	0.125	**0.192**	0.184	**0.333**	0.201	**0.206**
	0.754	**0.776**	0.715	**0.736**	0.741	**0.760**	0.708	**0.712**
Friedman-1	0.751	**0.759**	0.718	**0.720**	0.740	**0.752**	0.699	**0.614**
	0.018	**0.060**	0.031	**0.085**	0.028	**0.043**	0.053	**0.191**
	0.795	**0.764**	0.753	**0.733**	0.775	**0.742**	0.737	**0.707**
Friedman-2	0.795	**0.750**	0.761	**0.723**	0.780	**0.721**	0.736	**0.616**
	0.029	**0.071**	0.040	**0.089**	0.031	**0.093**	0.051	**0.179**

Identification and Prediction using Symbolic Regression Alpha-beta: Preliminary Results

L. M. Torres-Treviño
Facultad de Ingeniería Mecánica y Eléctrica, Universidad Autónoma de Nuevo León-CIIDIT
Av. Universidad S/N, CP. 64400, San Nicolás de los Garza, Nuevo León, México.
luis.torrestv@uanl.edu.mx

ABSTRACT

A novel approach is proposed for generating equations from measured data of dynamic processes. A composition of unary (alpha) and binary (beta) functions is represented by a real vector and adapted by an evolutionary algorithm to build mathematical equations. The equations can be used for identification and prediction considering a mathematical model with specific number of inputs and outputs. Three cases are used for illustration of the approach where mathematical models and plots of theirs performance are presented with promising results.

Categories and Subject Descriptors

I.28 [**Problem Solving, Control Methods, and Search**]:

General Terms

Algorithms

Keywords

Symbolic regression; process identification; prediction

1. INTRODUCTION

Several processes in industry are dynamic non linear systems and a modeling of such systems in most of the cases it is required for identification and prediction. A model can be useful for analysis, control, optimization, supervision and fault diagnosis. Symbolic regression has been used for identification and prediction, per example, the work of Ly and Lipson [1] propose a multimodal symbolic regression to construct non-linear mathematical model for describing hybrid dynamical systems using data collection. Sharifi and Massoudieh propose an evolutionary data-driven model using a NSGA multiobjective genetic algorithm for discovering models considering a wash-off and building of suspended solids in highway run-off [2]. Chaotic system identification is a complex task and symbolic regression has been used for model generation. An hybrid genetic programming algorithm based on evolution strategies is used for generating a model from Lorenz attractor data [3]. Patelli and Ferariu propose the use of an elite based multiobjective Genetic Programming (GP) for non-linear identification of an industrial plant [5].

Traditionally, non linear autoregressive models and neural networks has been used for non linear dynamic identification; however, hybrids systems using genetic programming variants has been proposed. In the work of Coelho and Pessoa use a GP for selecting the structure for system identification and combines crossover and mutation with orthogonal least squares algorithm to estimate the contribution of the branches of the tree. This GP non linear autoregressive with exogenous inputs modelling is used for identification of a ball and tube system [6].

A similar work made by Xiao-Lei and Bay [7] where a NARX and a non linear autoregressive moving average with exogenous input (NARMAX) polynomial models with a multi-population genetic programming are used for handling complex stochastic nonlinear system identification.Time series prediction using symbolic regression has been used successfully, inclusive with the presence of multiple-time scale dynamics as is shown in the work of Cornforth and Lipson [4]. A summary of non linear model identification can be found in the work of Winkler et al. [8].

The principal problem with symbolic regression for identification and prediction problems is the use of genetic programming that requires in most of the cases special programming languages and procedures. Some authors have proposed alternatives to reduce this problem. Luo and Zhang [9] proposes the use of a Parse-matrix evolution to solve some regression problems. Kotanchek et al. proposes balancing algorithms to sort the data records before the use of a Pareto genetic programming and used for model building and identification of a data set of economic, political, social, geographic data collected [10].

The paper is organized as follows: In section 2, a description of symbolic regression alpha-beta is made including fitness function. In section 3, an illustration of the proposal approach is made considering three cases of identification and prediction are made using experimental data. Results and conclusions will be given in section 4 and 5 respectively.

2. SYMBOLIC REGRESSION α-β

In this work, a new form of symbolic regression is proposed where a core configuration based on simple operations called α β, the selection of operations and parameters is made by

GECCO'14, July 12–16, 2014, Vancouver, BC, Canada.

http://dx.doi.org/10.1145/2598394.2609859.

Table 1: α operator parameters and their related mathematical functions.

α operator	mathematical operation
1	$(k_1x + k_2)$
2	$(k_1x + k_2)^2$
3	$(k_1x + k_2)^{1/2}$
4	$(k_1x + k_2)^{-1}$
5	$\exp(k_1x + k_2)$
6	$\log(k_1x + k_2)$
7	$(k_1x + k_2)^{-2}$
8	$(k_1x + k_2)^3$
9	$(k_1x + k_2)^{-3}$
10	$(k_1x + k_2)^{1/3}$
11	$\sin(k_1x + k_2)$
12	$\cos(k_1x + k_2)$
13	$\tan(k_1x + k_2)$

an evolutionary algorithms. Connectivity and complexity is involved in the search so the use of this form of symbolic regression is very simple [11, 12].

2.1 Operators and core configuration

An α operators is defined as a unary and simple mathematical function that requires only one argument. Considering a review of several mathematical models of real processes, 13 operations are chosen as α operators (see Table 1). An α operator uses two real number parameters called $k1$ and $k2$ and an integer that describes the mathematical operation.

A β operator is defined as a binary function that requires two arguments and makes the four basic arithmetic operations. A maximum of three alpha operators per variable is used, so if there are two variables, a configuration with six alpha operators and five beta operators are defined as a core configuration as is shown in equation (1). Depending de number of input variables a core configuration is used.

$$\begin{aligned} y = \; & \beta_5(\beta_4(\beta_3(\beta_2(\beta_1(b_1\alpha_1(x_1k_{11} + k_{21}), b_2\alpha_1(x_1k_{12} + k_{22})), \\ & b_3\alpha_1(x_1k_{13} + k_{23})), b_4\alpha_1(x_2k_{14} + k_{24})), \\ & b_5\alpha_1(x_2k_{15} + k_{25})), b_6\alpha_6(x_2k_{16} + k_{26})) \end{aligned} \tag{1}$$

The representation depends of the core configuration used or the number of variables required. The number of variables determine the core configuration as was mention above. A vector with normalized real numbers can be used to represents the connectivity or the number of alpha operators per variable, the α and β operators and the k parameters of the alpha operators. A single real number is used for connectivity because this number is converted to an integer value, then it is converted again in a binary vector and extract the b values using their corresponding position of the elements of the binary vector.

k parameters is assigned directly the real value of the representation vector.

Every α and β operators are integers, so is required the following formulation to get its value from the representation V:

$$\alpha = \lceil V(i) * 13 \rceil \tag{2}$$

$$\beta = \lceil V(i) * 4 \rceil \tag{3}$$

where $\lceil . \rceil$ is the ceiling function. There are 13 α operators defined in table 1 and four β operators (basic algebraic operations)

In this work, Evonorm is used to solve the problem of selection the suitable parameters (k's), the connectivity and integers to define α and β operations.

2.2 Evolutionary algorithm Evonorm

Evonorm is an easy way to implement an estimation of distribution algorithm [13, 14]. As a evolutionary algorithm selection of new individuals and the generation of a new population is used; however, the crossover and mutation mechanism is substituted by an estimation of parameters of a normal distribution function. The following steps are used in Evonorm:

1. Evaluation of a population P.
2. Deterministic selection of individuals from P to PS.
3. Generation of a new population using PS

A population P is a matrix of size I_p (total of individuals) and D_r (total of decision variables). A solution is a set of decision variables and this set is represented as a real vector. Every row of the population P represents a set of decision variables. The selection mechanism is deterministic because the most fittest individuals are selected. Usually the number of selected individuals are lower than the number of the original population, usually a twenty or ten percent of the total population. A random variable with normal distribution is estimated per decision variable, so a marginal distribution function is used. Two parameters are estimated, the mean and the standard deviation, that is determined using the values of the selected individuals. The population of selected individuals is a matrix Ps of size I_s (total of individuals selected) and D_r. The equations (4, 5) are used to calculate the mean and standard deviation considering every vector of the population Ps.

$$\mu_{pr} = \sum_{k=1}^{I_s} (Ps_{pr,k})/I_s \tag{4}$$

$$\sigma_{pr} = \sqrt{(}\sum_{k=1}^{I_s} (Ps_{pr,k} - \mu_{pr})^2)/I_s \tag{5}$$

where $pr = 1..D_r$

A new population is generated using the estimated normal random variables. This is a stochastic process;, however, an heuristic is used to maintain an equilibrium between exploration and exploitation, so new solutions can be found not necessarily near of the mean calculated. The best solution found Ix at the moment is involved in the generation so in the 50% percent of the times the mean is used in the calculations and in the other 50% percent of the time the best solution found Ix is used as a mean as is shown in the following equation:

$$P_{i,pr} = \begin{cases} N(\mu_{pr}, \sigma_{pr}) & U() > 0.5 \\ N(Ix_{pr}, \sigma_{pr}) & otherwise \end{cases} \tag{6}$$

The random variable $U()$ has a uniform distribution function, $N()$ is a random variable with a normal distribution function.

2.3 Fitness function

An evaluation value of every individuals depends on complexity, and accuracy of the model. Complexity is determinate adding all the α and β operators used in the chosen configuration. Mean square error (Equation 7) is used as second objective; however, both complexity and MSRES are weighted to use only one objective function. The criteria is both the minimization of complexity and mean square error.

$$MSRES = \sum_{i=1}^{n} (y(i) - \hat{y}(i))^2 \quad (7)$$

where $y(i)$ is the response of the process and $\hat{y}(i)$ is the predicted response generated by the regression model proposed and n is the total of testing data.

3. IDENTIFICATION AND PREDICTION OF NONLINEAR DYNAMICAL PROCESSES

Identification and prediction of the non-linear dynamic systems requires similar architectures. The number of inputs depends on the number of delay used on input and output signals treating the problem as a regression one. A typical architecture is shown in Figure 1.

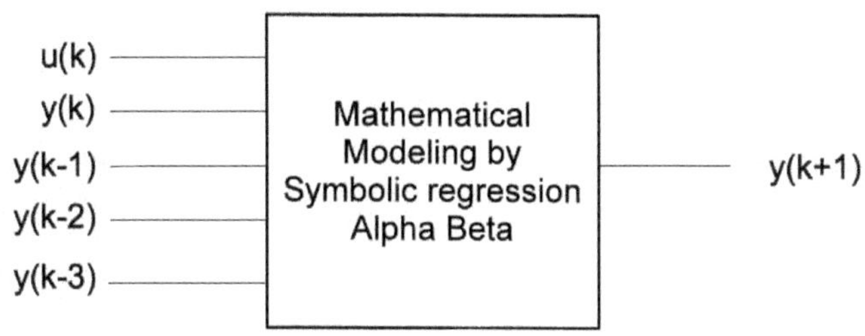

Figure 1: A common architecture used in symbolic regression α β for identification and prediction.

3.1 Cases

Three case can be found in literature, first it is the identification of the systems modelled by (8) and (9) and third it is the prediction on Box-Jenkins furnace.

Process 1

$$y(k+1) = \frac{y(k)y(k-1)[y(k) - 0.5]}{1 + y^2(k) + y^2(k-1)} + x(k) \quad (8)$$

Process 2.

$$y(k+1) = 0.3y(k) + 0.6y(k-1) + f(x(k)) \quad (9)$$

These two discrete processes have an specific input signal. In (8), $x(k) = \sin(2\pi k/25)$. In (9), $f(x(k)) = 0.6\sin(\pi x(k)) + 0.3\sin(3\pi x(k)) + 0.1\sin(5\pi x(k))$ with its input $x(k) = \sin(2\pi k/200)$. The initial condition in all cases is $y(0) = 0$. For identification of the first two cases a core configuration of three variables is used (10). In third case, a core configuration of four inputs is used (11).

$$y(k+1) = SRAB(u(k), y(k), y(k-1)) \quad (10)$$

$$y(k+1) = SRAB(u(k), y(k), y(k-1), y(k-2)) \quad (11)$$

4. RESULTS

An Evonorm algorithm with 100 individuals where 10 of them are selected during 50 generations. These setting are used in all three cases. A set of building and testing data is generated or recorded where a high percentage of data are used for building the model and the rest are used for testing. Ten runs are used and the solution with lower mean square error was chosen.

4.1 First case

The performance of the model using testing data as is shown in Figure (2). Mathematical model is shown in Equation 12. A total of 5000 data were used for building and 200 for testing. Mean square error on testing data is 0.0007307 considering testing data.

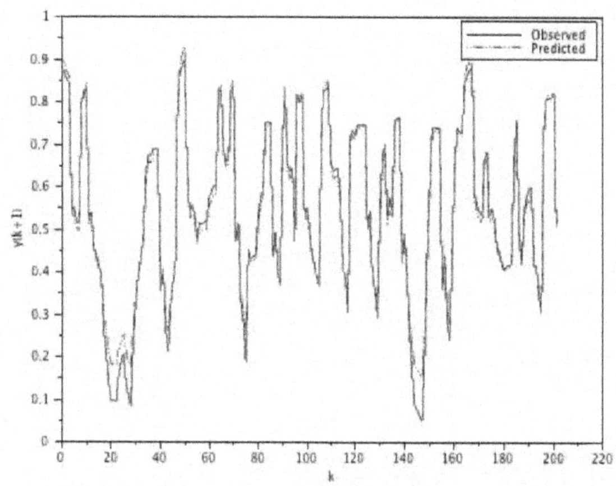

Figure 2: Performance of the best model found versus the real output response.

$$\begin{aligned} y = \; & ((k_{11}u(k) + k_{21}) - (k_{13}u(k) + k_{23})) \\ & (k_{14}y(k) + k_{24})^2 + (k_{15}y(k) + k_{25})^2 - \\ & (k_{18}y(k-1) + k_{28}) + (k_{19}y(k-1) + k_{29}) \end{aligned} \quad (12)$$

where k_{11}=0.9809215, k_{21} = 0.6328762, k_{13}= 0.4296275, k_{23} =0.0722073, k_{14} = 0.3753558, k_{24} = 0.0120735, k_{15} = 0.4772979, k_{25} = 0.5380167, k_{18} = 0.5925161, k_{28} = 0.4077315, k_{19} =0.6232973, and k_{29} = 0.2440728.

4.2 Second case

The performance of the model using testing data as is shown in Figure (3). A total of 3000 data were used for building and 200 for testing. Mathematical model is shown in Equation 13. Mean square error on testing data is 0.0018459 considering testing data.

$$\begin{aligned} y = \; & ((k_{11}u(k) + k_{21})^{1/2} - \exp(k_{14}y(k) + k_{24}) \\ & -(k_{15}y(k) + k_{25})^{-1} + \exp(k_{16}u(k) + k_{26}) \\ & +(k_{17}y(k-1) + k_{27})^{1/2} - (k_{18}y(k-1) + k_{28})^{1/2} \end{aligned} \quad (13)$$

where k_{12} = 0.4232765, k_{22}= 0.9903058, k_{14}= 0.1049508, k_{24}= 0.6088263, k_{15}= 0.3934277, k_{25}= 0.7465172, k_{16} = 0.2367586, k_{26}= 0.7177606, k_{17} = 0.3027999, k_{27}= 0.5093251, k_{19}= 0.1463342, and k_{29} = 0.4300170.

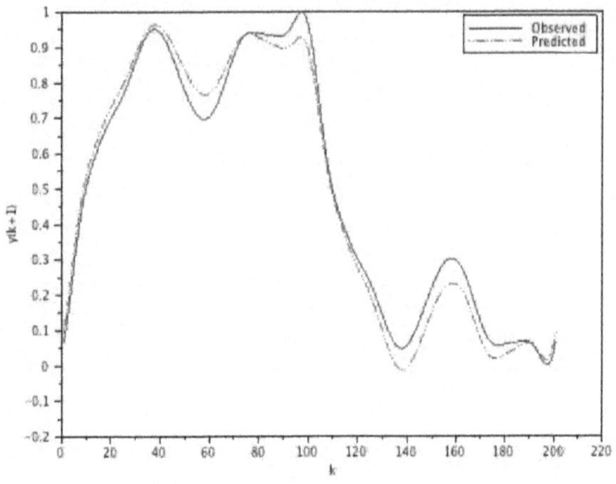

Figure 3: Performance of the best model found versus the real output response.

4.3 Third case

The performance of the model using testing data as is shown in Figure (4). 200 data were used for building 98 for testing. Mathematical model is shown in Equation 14. Mean square error on testing data is 0.0002214 considering testing data.

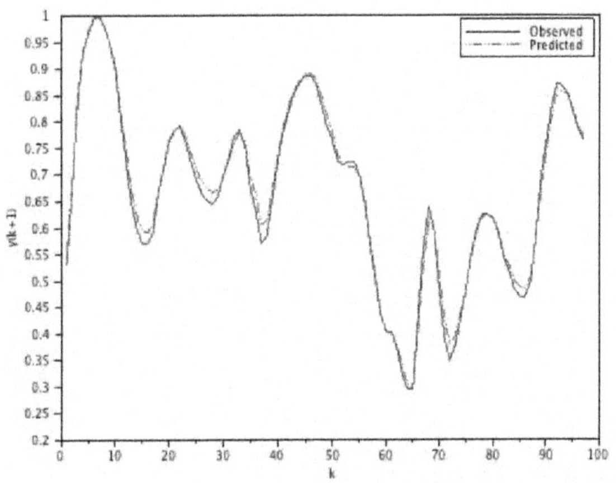

Figure 4: Performance of the best model found versus the real output response.

$$\begin{aligned} y = & -(k_{13}u(k) + k_{23})^2 + (k_{14}y(k) + k_{24}) \\ & - \log(k_{16}y(k) + k_{26})^2 + \log(k_{18}y(k-1) + k_{28}) \\ & -(k_{110}y(k-2) + k_{210}) + (k_{112}y(k-2) + k_{212}) \end{aligned} \quad (14)$$

where k_{13}=0.1070782, k_{23} = 0.2730927, k_{14} = 0.9421514, k_{24} = 0.5979528, k_{16}=0.0842617, k_{26} = 0.0292099, k_{18}= 0.0568625, k_{28} = 0.2968381, k_{110}= 0.4361714, k_{210} = 0.7237257, k_{112}=0.7237689, k_{212} = 0.1376476.

5. CONCLUSION AND FUTURE WORK

These preliminary results illustrate the possibility to use symbolic regression α β for identification and prediction problems. The approach selects the parameters, complexity and connectivity generating feasible mathematical models; however, the core configuration most be given depending of the number of input variables that must be initially give. Improvement considering fitness and complexity requires multi-objective optimization and a weighting mechanism was used for simplicity and generate practical models; however, it is possible to use related algorithms to generate a Pareto front considering different alternatives of models by complexity and connectivity and let the final selection to the user. Finally, a comparison with other approaches will open an opportunity to improve the proposal. All of these stuff is considered as a future work.

6. REFERENCES

[1] Ly, Daniel L.; Lipson, Hod Learning Symbolic Representations of Hybrid Dynamical Systems Journal of machine learning research Volume: 13 (2012) 3585-3618

[2] Zelinka, Ivan; Skanderova, Lenka; Chadli, Mohammed; et al. Evolutionary Identification and Synthesis of Predictive Models. Conference: Nostradamus Conference Location: Ostrava, Czech Republic, SEP, 2012 Sponsor(s): IT4 Innovat; VSB Tech Univ Ostrava; MIR Lab; Ctr Chaos & Complex Networks; Journal Unconvent Comp Nostradamus: Modern methods of prediction, modeling and analysis of nonlinear systems. Advances in Intelligent Systems and Computing. Volume: 192 (2013) 261-272

[3] Brandejsky, Tomas Symbolic regression of deterministic chaos Book Editor(s): Matousek, R. 17th International Conference on Soft Computing Meldel 2011 Location: Brno, Czech Republic Date: JUN 15-17, 2011 Mendel 2011 - 17th International conference on soft computing book Series:: Mendel (2011) 90-93

[4] Cornforth, Theodore W.; Lipson, Hod Symbolic Regression of Multiple-Time-Scale Dynamical Systems Book Editor(s): Soule, T Conference: 14th International Conference on Genetic and Evolutionary Computation Conference (GECCO) Location: Philadelphia, PA JUL 07-11, 2012 Proceedings of the fourteenth international conference on genetic and evolutionary computation conference. DOI: 10.1145/2330163.2330266 (2012) 735-740

[5] Patelli, Alina; Ferariu, Lavinia Elite Based Multiobjective Genetic Programming in Nonlinear Systems Identification Advances in Electrical and Computer Engineering. Volume: 10, Issue:1. DOI: 10.4316/AECE.2010.01017. (2010) 94-99

[6] Coelho, Leandro dos Santos; Pessoa, Marcelo Wicthoff Nonlinear model identification of an experimental ball-and-tube system using a genetic programming approach Mechanical Systems and Signal Processing. Volume: 23, Issue: 5 DOI: 10.1016/j.ymssp.2009.02.005 (2009) 1434-1446

[7] Yuan Xiao-lei; Bai Yan Stochastic Nonlinear System Identification Using Multi-objective Multi-population Parallel Genetic Programming. IEEE Conference: 21st

Chinese Control and Decision Conference Location: Guilin, PEOPLES R CHINA Date: JUN 17-19, 2009 Sponsor(s): NE Univ; IEEE Ind Elect Singapore Chapter; Guilin Univ Elect Technol; IEEE Control Syst Soc; IEEE Ind Elect Soc Source: CCDC 2009: 21ST Chinese Control and Decision Conference, vols 1-6, (2009) 1148-1153.

[8] Winkler, Stephan; Affenzeller, Michael; Wagner, Stefan; et al. Using Genetic Programming in Nonlinear Model Identification Editors: Alberer, D; Hjalmarsson, H; DelRe, L Workshop on Identification for Automotive Systems Location: Johannes Kepler Univ Linz, Linz, AUSTRIA Date: JUL 15-16, 2010 Identification for Automotive Systems Book Series: Lecture Notes in Control and Information Sciences. Volume: 418 (2012) 89-109

[9] Luo, Changtong; Zhang, Shao-Liang Parse-matrix evolution for symbolic regression Engineering Applications of Artificial Intelligence. Volume: 25 Issue: 6 DOI: 10.1016/j.engappai.2012.05.015 (2012) 1182-1193

[10] Brandejsky, Tomas and Matousek, R Symbolic Regression of Deterministic Chaos 17th International Conference on Soft Computing MENDEL 2011 Location: Brno, CZECH REPUBLIC Date: JUN 15-17, 2011 Sponsor(s): B & R Automat CZ Ltd; Humusoft Ltd; AutoCont CZ Ltd Mendel 2011 - 17th International conference on soft computin. Book Series: Mendel (2011) 90-93

[11] Luis M. Torres-Treviño Symbolic Regression Using alpha, beta Operators and Estimation of Distribution Algorithms: Preliminary Results 3rd symbolic regression and modeling workshop for GECCO 2011 July 12-16, 2011, Dublin, Ireland. Distributed on CD-ROM at GECCO-2011.

[12] L. M. Torres-Treviño , I. Escamilla, B. González, R. Praga-Alejo & P. Pérez-Villanueva Modeling cutting machining process using symbolic regression alpha -beta The International Journal of Advanced Manufacturing Technology Noviembre 2012. ISSN 0268-3768 ISSN 0268-3768. DOI 10.1007/s00170-012-4655-5 The International Journal of Advanced Manufacturing Technology: Volume 67, Issue 9 (2013) 2351-2366

[13] L. Torres-T., (2006) Evonorm, a new evolutionary algorithm to continuous optimization, Workshop on Optimization by Building and Using Probabilistic Models (OBUPM) Genetic and Evolutionary Computation Conference (GECCO).

[14] L. Torres-Treviño , Evonorm: Easy and effective implementation of estimation of distribution algorithms,Journal of Research in Computing Science, 23, (2006) 75–83.

Automated Design of Algorithms and Genetic Improvement: Contrast and Commonalities

Saemundur O. Haraldsson
University of Stirling
Stirling, Scotland, UK
soh@cs.stir.ac.uk

John R. Woodward
University of Stirling
Stirling, Scotland, UK
jrw@cs.stir.ac.uk

Categories and Subject Descriptors

I.2.2 [**Automatic Programming**]: Program modification

ABSTRACT

Automated Design of Algorithms (ADA) and Genetic Improvement (GI) are two relatively young fields of research that have been receiving more attention in recent years. Both methodologies can improve programs using evolutionary search methods and successfully produce human competitive programs. ADA and GI are used for improving functional properties such as quality of solution and non-functional properties, e.g. speed, memory and, energy consumption. Only GI of the two has been used to fix bugs, probably because it is applied globally on the whole source code while ADA typically replaces a function or a method locally. While GI is applied directly to the source code ADA works ex-situ, i.e. as a separate process from the program it is improving.

Although the methodologies overlap in many ways they differ on some fundamentals and for further progress to be made researchers from both disciplines should be aware of each other's work.

Keywords

Automated Design of Algorithms (ADA), Genetic Improvement (GI), Genetic Programming (GP), Abstract Syntax Tree (AST), Genetic Algorithm (GA), Search Based Software Engineering (SBSE), Genetic Algorithm (GA)

1. INTRODUCTION

Recent decades has seen surge in the development of Metaheuristics [10] and Hyper-heuristics [7] where the latter could be defined as a special case of Automated Design of Algorithms (ADA). ADA is a general methodology employing search methods to improve or discover algorithms for computational problems. It generates algorithms by sampling the large, discontinuous and complex space of programs.

GECCO'14, July 12–16, 2014, Vancouver, BC, Canada.

ACM 978-1-4503-2881-4/14/07 ...$15.00.
http://dx.doi.org/10.1145/2598394.2609874.

GI has seen some progress due to the well-established Search Based Software Engineering (SBSE) [27, 26] with initiatives in automating many key aspects of software engineering [22]. SBSE applies computational search to software engineering problems and GI is the special case of automatic software adjustment methods working directly on the source code. The idea is that the source code acts as the genetic material and can be rearranged to improve the program for a given objective. The need to decrease the cost of maintenance in the development of software is very important since it is usually the largest part of the software life cycle. Automating the maintenance process would more than likely reduce the cost considerably and give developers more time and money to focus on more qualitative features of programs.

Recent years have seen research that can be defined as ADA and GI gaining momentum and an increase in number of publications. The two fields have much in common but they can be divided by their application and definition. They apply same and similar methods, typically Genetic Programming (GP) or other metaheuristics. They are often used for identical objectives, e.g. speed or accuracy, albeit those objectives sometimes have different evaluation criteria. For example to measure speed both CPU time and number of iterations until a sufficient solution has been reached are used. The time is ripe to synchronize their terminologies and thus recognize the opportunities that lie in the inevitable crossing of the two methodologies.

The reminder of this paper will firstly give an overview of ADA and GI in sections 2 and 3 respectively. In section 4 the two methodologies will be compared by highlighting their similarities and differences. In section 5 the paper will be summarized and it will conclude in section 6.

2. AUTOMATED DESIGN OF ALGORITHMS

In this section we will define ADA and give examples of its applications and opportunities. Designing algorithms is a complex and sometimes unintuitive search and the automation of that process is therefore necessary and often inevitable. Algorithms are defined as a set of stepwise instructions for general problem solving and each algorithm can be viewed as a recipe for tackling a specific type of problem. When designing an algorithm one can either do it bottom-up by defining a general outline and filling in with appropriate components or start with an already functioning algorithm and adjust it for ones needs. Given a certain abstraction each algorithm can be altered and adjusted in three ways.

- By *replacing* components with an alternative [55]. In its simplest form this is done by selecting from a set of suitable replacement components which confines the search for a better algorithm to a discrete and finite space. An example of this might be to have a evolutionary algorithm and a set of predefined selection methods to choose from, such as elitist selection and tournament selection. Another approach is to evolve or generate replacement components and depending on multiple aspects such as, component representation, generation method and the original algorithm this can easily become very complex and impossible for exhaustive search.

- By *reordering* the application of the components [12]. Given certain restrictions, where the algorithm needs to be initiated and what it returns must be of specific type, this way is a special case of a permutation problem.

- *Parameter tuning*, i.e. changing the amount of any or each component [49]. E.g. altering the likelihood of mutation in a Genetic Algorithm (GA). Even if this is not in the strictest sense a design problem, it should be combined with the other two ways whenever possible. When comparing the newly designed algorithm with its predecessor, both subjects should perform at optimal capacity given the evaluation criteria.

The combined search space for those three ways can be vast, discontinuous, non-linear and/or multidimensional. Not to mention the difficulties with selecting and presenting the fitness which guides the search. In machine learning literature an objective of finding or making new algorithms has typically been to generalize them as much as possible, given a certain domain [41, 48]. Recent research and in particular ADA research has however suggested that automating the process reveals opportunities to specialise the algorithms to a certain problem class [8, 55, 56]. A problem class is a probability distribution over all instances of a given domain, e.g. Travelling Salesman Problem (TSP), timetabling and bin packing. The current access to computational resources can give us millions of variations of each algorithm in seconds and thus we should not be limiting the search for the one algorithm that solves all or a "Jack-of-all-Trades" [8]. Then we can create general frameworks that can be adjusted to produce algorithms for a wide variety of computational problems. There could be a general framework that generates algorithms to solve problems where the solution representation and another for problems where the solution representation is bit-strings. When the algorithm being designed is a search or an optimization algorithm the main objective of the fitness function is typically to improve a functional property that is evaluated as the fitness of the best solution found by the evolved algorithm [4, 13, 18, 19, 29]. Speed has also been of interest for others [21] as well as combinations of both where GP was used to evolve search heuristics [21], and novel matrix multiplication methods where discovered with GA [31].

2.1 Definition of Automated Design of Algorithms

We define ADA as a general methodology for using search methods to improve or discover algorithms for any given computational problem. When generating complete algorithms the amount of information provided can be as little as only a set of problems, their required output data type and a selection of primitive instructions or functions to assemble the algorithm from. Generating algorithms can also be done by using an existing algorithm and adjust it to serve either a different purpose or just to improve it for its current purpose. The algorithm in question must be suitable for a partition into blocks or components that can be replaced by a function with the same type signature, such that the original algorithm can serve as a template or scaffold.

Given this definition, research from as early as the 1990's can be categorized as ADA e.g. where [4] use GP to evolve annealing schedule for a simulated annealing algorithm. Hyper-heuristics to generate heuristics is a sub-field of ADA, as they are defined to be a heuristic search in the space of heuristics [11]. The definition of ADA is broad and its application is included in many well established fields of research, such as machine learning [30], data mining [45] and operation research [6]. Many of those fields are overlapping and sometimes the line between them is not distinct. Therefore it is necessary to give a more general platform for discussion and debate so that progress can be made.

The last decade has seen rapid increase in the frequency of research that falls under the definition of ADA and because of that, effort has been made to gather relevant publications in this paper. There is shortage in the literature of solid categorization of research that is ADA which makes it difficult to guarantee that a published algorithm or methodology is indeed novel. Completely different names and terminology for similar things are somewhat scattered, so extensive comparison is difficult. The Workshop on the Automated Design of Algorithms in the annual Genetic and Evolutionary Computation Conference (GECCO) has been held since 2011 and serves as an international platform for exchanging ideas[1].

2.2 Applications of Automated Design of Algorithms

ADA has been used in many different and creative ways. We now examine component replacement and reordering. We do not however examine automatic parameter tuning as there is already a vast literature on that [3, 15].

2.2.1 Component replacement

The most common example of ADA is where an algorithm is improved by selecting one of its components and replacing it with an automatically designed alternative. The component is usually something that can be easily replaced by a function due to its place in the program where it has known input and output data type. Some examples of such components are:

- Annealing schedule for the simulated annealing algorithm [4].

- Selection heuristic for bin packing problems [9] and vehicle routing algorithm [12].

- Scheduling rules for job shop scheduling [43].

- Flowtime estimators for job shop scheduling [42].

[1] `http://www.sigevo.org/gecco-2011/workshops.html#ecdga`

- Variable-selection heuristic for Boolean Satisfiability (SAT) solvers [19, 20].

For each of these applications note that the components being designated for replacements can be easily isolated in the algorithm structure. Then they can be replaced by any arbitrary function so long as that function has the same type signature as defined by the original component. Note also that each of these examples are relatively small algorithms and components that can be expressed in a few lines of code but still the search space for ADA is huge and complex. The annealing schedule can for example be replaced with any function that returns a double precision variable on the closed interval between zero and one [4]. GP has proved to be very effective in evolving the replacement [55] and its ability to generate small but complex programs makes it the primary method for these types of ADA. Also, the abstraction and a careful selection of the GP function set allows an easy way of guaranteeing error free compilation and termination, e.g. if the function set only contains Turing complete operators [44]. The evolution of the replacement always takes place ex situ i.e. it is a search process that runs separate from the original algorithm. It typically takes place in parallel and with a representation that does not need to be identical to the original algorithm's representation. The outcome of that process is evaluate by either converting the component into the original source language before substituting the evolved code into the original program or building a wrapper function to interpret.

2.2.2 *Component reordering*

ADA has not to the authors' best knowledge been applied as a permutation problem but only in combination with the replacement idea and with a given framework for scaffolding [14]. The scaffolding method is another ADA application that uses an existing algorithm framework as a template and finds the best combination of a finite number of predefined alternatives for each place in the scaffold. This method was used to evolve multiple meta-heuristics for a vehicle routing problem. A general outline of the simplex variant called a push/pull algorithm was used as a template and the components were extracted from three established and widely used algorithms to serve as the blocks that could be put into the scaffold [12].

The search space of ADA has also been widened by extracting components from many different algorithms to use them as building blocks [39, 45]. Allowing the structure to evolve with minimal restrictions as well as the what the structure contains, i.e. the blocks can be stacked in any order with the only limitation being that the output is meaningful. While one describes a general automation process for various data mining algorithm [45], the other evolves a structure of a black-box algorithm that tackles the Deceptive Trap problem [39]. Both papers rely on grammatical evolution which describes the restrictive condition each block has, such as what blocks can precede and follow other blocks. These conditions are primarily based on the blocks data signatures.

3. GENETIC IMPROVEMENT

Human programmers working in industry cannot be expected to optimize their software with respect to non-functional properties within a given budget or available project time frame [5]. The software development life cycle is a iterative process where the program is constantly undergoing improvements. Whether it is bug fixing, speed up, memory optimization, platform specific adaptation or many more examples. This process is carried out by human programmers that are usually only experts on a few platforms, languages or environments. End users are vaguely aware of this process when their device prompts them to update but for developers this is a cycle of often tiny tweaks and minor improvements. Moreover because programmers, without automated tools, are limited by trial and error methods and they can only view a small portion of the space of all available adjustments those updates could have to be reverted in later cycles.

Many methods have been proposed to counteract software's inevitable high maintenance cost, substandard releases with annoyingly frequent updates and other maintenance problems. One promising approach developed in the recent decade suggests automation in one or all aspects, employing SBSE [28] methods. More specifically evolutionary search methods such as GP have been used to explore program variants. GI is one of these SBSE methods that has in recent years been surfacing as the conquering automatic improvement candidate in the software engineering literature.

Since GI involves adjusting an already functioning software it is often highly susceptible to producing compiler errors non-terminating programs. That is anticipated and methods to handle it usually involve some kind of penalty such that it has little to no possibility to survive to the next iteration [54]. Other methods employ direct elimination, by discarding them entirely from the population of programs being evaluated [36, 50]. Although solutions have been suggested to this using reflective properties of certain programming languages and an *actor model* [50].

In this paper variants of GI will be divided into 4 categories based on their application domain.

- Bug fixing, probably its most common application.
- Increasing speed, which has always been of much interest maybe because of easy evaluation.
- Migration and transplantation. Migrating software from one platform to another, transplanting a code segment or a functionality from on program to another.
- Dynamic adaptive software improvement where the program is improved while it is being used.

3.1 Definition of Genetic Improvement

GI is the name given to automatic software adjustment methods that operate directly on the source code, treating it as the genetic material. These operations may for example consist of copying, deleting and swapping lines of code. An existing software's source code is used as the building material for the improvements, meaning that it is assumed the software already possesses sufficient expressions [24, 33]. The search is therefore limited to all variants of said software code, albeit those variants can be of variable length because expressions can be duplicated or deleted. The pool of genetic material can however be expanded with transplantation from other programs, either multiple variants of the same program or other programs that have desirable features. Code transplantation has been used to expand the pool of genetic material with already existing variants of the software that was being improved. Two award winning and manually improved variants of the MiniSAT solver introduced enough new genetic material to improve the performance of the original beyond the donor programs [46].

The automation involves applying some search method in the program space driven by the objectives set by the developer. While these objectives are relatively easy to define, finding an effective fitness function can pose a real problem [16] because the software must maintain its correct functionality. The correctness of an improvement is found either by comparing the output with the output of the original software as an oracle [34, 2] or by evaluating its performance on a suite of test cases that has already been run on the original code. The fitness is then monitored during compilation and runtime by instrumentation, simple timing mechanisms or whatever the objective defines. Given that the search space is highly noisy [32] evolutionary methods have been preferable over others. Particularly GP with grammatical representation, again for its ability to represent and evolve programs.

As with ADA, some focus of GI has recently been turned towards specialisation of software rather than generalization [23, 24, 46]. With increasing computational resources and constantly better methods for improvement, making multiple variants of a software and maintaining them is more viable than before. A program that is fast but energy inefficient might be acceptable for a desktop computer but the user might be willing to consider slower but energy saving variant for his laptop in order to extend the usage of the battery before needing to be recharged.

Earlier in GI the typical approach to evolve improvements was to maintain multiple copies of the program in a population but that was shortly discarded in favour of maintaining a population of edits. Each edit describes changes that should be made to the original program before evaluation. This approach is much more memory efficient and makes explaining the changes to the software developer easier, although the extra effort of applying the changes must be made before each evaluation.

3.2 Applications of Genetic Improvement

The appeal of GI is that the process of optimization does not need a model because the software is its own substrate. Therefore the evaluation process does not give an approximation of how the software will perform but potentially an accurate vision. Unlike other engineering practices where e.g. structural loads are approximated in civil engineering and productivity is estimated in industrial engineering with models. GI in software engineering makes it possible to monitor the effects of every small change directly which makes it well suited for fixing faulty programs.

3.2.1 Bug Fixing

GI has been extensively applied to automatic bug fixing where test cases were used to identify nodes in the AST that might be faulty and successfully focus an evolution of patches [17, 52]. They were able to repair multiple different bugs in 20 legacy C programs. Further progress was then made where test suite optimization was used to improve the fitness evaluation of the fixes [16, 51]. Their success has spurred further research into other domains and programming languages such as Python [1] where a novel patch representation was introduced. The work of Weimer et al. has since then culminated in a framework called GenProg [38]. It also built on the Python novel patch representation [1] by changing the representation to edits from ASTs to be able to scale properly to larger programs. GenProg was reported to fix 55 of 105 known bugs for about US $8 each in 8 open-source programs [37]. Therefore giving plenty of evidence for the merit of GI as an automatic software repair method.

3.2.2 Increasing Speed

GI is appropriate for improving non-functional properties of an existing software when there is sufficiently good test suit available. The original version of the software can act as an oracle to maintain proper functionality [34, 2] alongside evaluation. The non-functional property that is probably most popular to improve has to be speed since its evaluation is quite uncomplicated and comparison is easy.

Strongly typed GP was successfully applied on small programs with seeding [2, 54]. That work also introduced multi-objective approach to the improvement process by allowing some error while searching for faster alternatives to the original seed. Later the speed improvements were generalised to other non-functional properties specifically for low-resource systems [53].

Larger systems have been optimized for speed in [36] where Bowtie2, a DNA sequencing system that is made up of approximately 50k lines of C++ code. A 70 fold speed up on specialized DNA sequences was reported without decreasing functionality by evolving edits with grammatical evolution. The same framework and methodology was used to improve the computational time of the boolean satisfiability (SAT) solver, MiniSAT, with moderate success [47]. Later a significant speed gain was observed when the genetic pool was widened with multiple versions of the solver software [46].

3.2.3 Migration and transplantation

Code transplantation has been suggested in [25] for reverse engineering purposes such as inserting a feature from one system into another. It seems that GI has the tools and right approach to accomplish this task automatically by using GP and appropriate representation. Transplantation has been reported with success, although it was not between systems or software but between different versions of the same software [46]. Proper automatic code transplantation between systems written in the same language or even systems written in different languages has yet to be made but migrating software from one environment to another has seen success.

The migration and complete a repurposing was accomplished in [34] where CUDA C++ code was adapted for the gzip functionality to run on parallel processes, accelerating the function considerably in the process. The CUDA C++ code, StereoCamera system, was also migrated to parallel graphics hardware and gained from 5% to a factor of 6.8 speed up [35].

3.2.4 Dynamic adaptive approach

Attaining dynamic adaptivity means to be able to improve the software while it is in use and therefore potentially being able to reduce maintenance costs to absolute minimum. If the software can improve itself that also means that downloading updates could be eliminated thus using bandwidth and data charges for other more productive or entertaining means. Some methods have been suggested such as the semi online approach in [23] where it is proposed that optimization of non-functional properties could happen on mobile devices while charging. A more dynamically online stance is suggested and implemented in [50] with a web service running on the Java Virtual Machine (JVM) and utilizing the reflection abilities of the Scala programming language.

4. DISCUSSION AND CONTRAST

Although the broadest definition of an algorithm includes the simplest instructions that can be executed with a pen and paper, the automation is only possible for when those instructions have been implemented into a software. As such we can view ADA as a specific software improvement methodology and compare it with the field of GI. This section will first compare similarities and then compare differences. So that one might be better equipped to make the decision which one to use for a given problem. This is not a trivial decision.

4.1 Similarities

The apparent similarities are firstly that both methodologies are driven by the need to automatically improve or adapt software and therefore they partly share a domain. ADA and GI both work on either existing software or a software framework where the functionality is known and at least the minimal number of components that are needed for that functionality are known and available. ADA has mainly been used to evolve small functions from scratch as a replacement component for a bigger algorithm and although GI sometimes operates on large scale systems, its output is usually small set of edits to that system. So typically the output from both methodologies are relatively small such as a few edits or a function that can be expressed in a few lines of code.

GI has been successfully applied to accelerate the MiniSAT solver and so has ADA, although the ADA only required access to the heuristic selection operator.

Last but not least the part of the shared domain of computer programs is highly complex and large and the task of searching it is consequently complex. GI and ADA both employ evolution for that search which make them comparatively resource consuming both in terms of CPU time and memory.

4.2 Difference

The most notable difference is that GI is applied in-situ or directly to the source code while ADA works ex-situ, i.e. evolves a function that is injected into the original code. GI makes small changes, sometimes many small changes that do not have to be constrained to a small region of the source code. ADA's improvement of an existing program on the other hand is a replacement of a certain call or statement in the source and is thus limited to the places where that call is made.

As observed GI and ADA evolve small edits and functions respectively but the main difference is that the GI's edits are human readable while ADA's functions are often quite unintuitive and cannot be explained simply. This can possibly be the cause for their difference in sub-domain application, where ADA is commonly used to improve heuristics [4, 9, 12, 19, 20, 43], data mining, and machine learning algorithms [30, 45]. GI is applied to software in general, although it improves MiniSAT [46] and a classification algorithm [2] it is not limited to algorithms and has fixed bugs in legacy programs [17, 52] and 20 other open-source programs [37].

ADA has typically been used to evolve small functions but those can be relatively large compared to the whole software when the program is a heuristic. GI's successes are typically reported on a larger systems and therefore suggesting that it fairs better when it has access to a larger gene pool of potential changes. The difference here lies in how the methodologies use the ASTs, GI alters the whole AST while ADA takes one node or a cluster of nodes and replaces them. For that reason GI has been used more often for automatically repairing software since it can make small changes in the software that are separated by many lines or even files in the code. Changes that potentially fix a fault that a human could not find because the bug's location might not be co-located with the fault it causes or the fault is caused by a series of bugs that are dispersed in different sections of the code. ADA would probably not be able to fix the latter kind of fault with its limited scope into the original software. Similarly for non-functional properties such as speed or memory usage, GI might find solutions that are not confined to a single node or a cluster of nodes in the AST. Sometimes those improvements are just to turn off non-vital functionalities of the original software [36]. Also, although the two methodologies have the objective to speed up a software in common, they usually approach the task from different angles. While GI tries to speed up programs by finding variants of the original software, ADA's approach is often to make the algorithm find a better solution sooner.

A side effect of the GI process is that it produces lots of faulty individuals out of scope, semantically incorrect or non terminating, while ADA can more easily be applied so that all individuals compile and terminate. For some, a few faulty program variants while iterating over many is considered to be an annoyance but nothing to be concerned about and it has been argued that it does not affect the evolution to much [36]. Others suggest using better approaches with reflection and agent based coding to prevent these side effects [50].

5. SUMMARY

This paper has given a brief overview of the fields of ADA and GI. Where some examples of usage and application were talked about as well as their merits and shortcomings, limitations and some opportunities. At last their similarities and differences were highlighted while trying to give some idea of when one should be chosen over the other.

The following bullet points highlight the main findings of this paper and overall what is observed is that the two fields are very similar and share many characteristics but they still differ in a fundamental way.

- ADA and GI both produce human compatible outputs, i.e. they improve upon existing software and even successfully improve a program [2] that has been manually improved multiple times.
- ADA and GI both typically apply GP or other evolutionary methods to generate changes. Although ADA has been using it in the more traditional sense [32] while GI converted to evolving edit lists as they are less memory consuming and more easily explainable to humans.

[2]For example MiniSAT [46, 19, 20]

- Current application of GI can produce faulty and non-terminating programs in the process of finding improved variants while ADA generates syntactically correct terminating code.
- ADA is used to improve functional and non-functional properties while GI's focus has typically been non-functional properties although with different approach than ADA. ADA's approach to speed up has been to improve the convergence of an algorithm to a good solution and GI has been used to optimize the code structure, i.e. in what sequence the statements are executed. Also, only GI has been used to fix bugs.
- ADA and GI share a general domain where they are both used to improve software but ADA has only been used on heuristics and machine learning and data mining algorithms.

6. CONCLUSIONS

ADA and GI are two related fields which are similar and are both at an early stage of their development but an increase in use by researchers and industry alike is to be expected. It would probably be beneficial for further progress for researchers in either discipline to be aware of each other's work. The former is mainly manned by computer scientists while the latter consists of mainly software engineers. They share a domain but the approach and applicability are quite different.

The search method of choice for both fields is GP and recently it has been accused of tackling toy problems [40] so ADA and GI offer a rich domain of real world problems which will necessitate improvements in GP, the search technology. The usage of GP is also different between the fields where representation of improvements and objectives are often not the same.

When fixing bugs, GI is preferable for its ability to make small but significant changes to a software and ADA when the task at hand is to find novel components for a computational method. For accelerating software the choice of method depends on the software, if the software is an easily compartmentalized algorithm it seems that ADA could be better but for a general software GI might be more suitable. Because GI can work on a more fine grained level of the software and does not have to be focused on one particular AST node or a cluster of nodes.

7. REFERENCES

[1] T. Ackling, B. Alexander, and I. Grunert. Evolving Patches for Software Repair. In *GECCO'11, 13th annual conference on Genetic and evolutionary computation*, pages 1427–1434, Dublin, Ireland, July 2011. ACM.

[2] A. Arcuri, D. R. White, J. Clark, and X. Yao. Multi-objective improvement of software using co-evolution and smart seeding. In X. Li, M. Kirley, M. Zhang, D. Green, V. Ciesielski, H. Abbass, Z. Michalewicz, T. Hendtlass, K. Deb, K. Tan, J. Branke, and Y. Shi, editors, *7th International Conference, SEAL 2008*, Lecture Notes in Computer Science, pages 61–70, Melbourne, Australia, Dec. 2008. Springer Berlin Heidelberg.

[3] M. Birattari, Z. Yuan, P. Balaprakash, and T. Stützle. F-Race and iterated F-Race: An overview. In T. Bartz-Beielstein, M. Chiarandini, L. Paquete, and M. Preuss, editors, *Experimental Methods for the Analysis of Optimization Algorithms*, chapter 13, pages 311–336. Springer Berlin Heidelberg, Berlin, Heidelberg, 2010.

[4] A. Bölte and U. W. Thonemann. Optimizing simulated annealing schedules with genetic programming. *European Journal of Operational Research*, 92(2):402–416, July 1996.

[5] F. P. Brooks. *The Mythical Man-Month, Essays on Software Engineering, Anniversary Edition.* Addison Wesley, 1995.

[6] E. Burke, M. Hyde, G. Kendall, and J. Woodward. Genetic Programming Hyper-Heuristic Approach for Evolving Two Dimensional Strip Packing Heuristics. *IEEE Transactions on Evolutionary Computation*, 14(6):942–958, 2010.

[7] E. K. Burke, M. Hyde, G. Kendall, G. Ochoa, E. Özcan, and J. R. Woodward. A classification of hyper-heuristic approaches. In M. Gendreau and J.-Y. Potvin, editors, *Handbook of Metaheuristics*, volume 146 of *International Series in Operations Research & Management Science*, pages 449–468. Springer US, 2010.

[8] E. K. Burke, M. Hyde, G. Kendall, and J. Woodward. Automatic Heuristic Generation with Genetic Programming : Evolving a Jack-of-all-Trades or a Master of One. In *GECCO'07, 9th annual conference on Genetic and evolutionary computation*, pages 1559–1565, New York, New York, USA, 2007. ACM.

[9] E. K. Burke, M. R. Hyde, and G. Kendall. Grammatical Evolution of Local Search Heuristics. *IEEE Transactions on Evolutionary Computation*, 16(3):406–417, June 2012.

[10] E. K. Burke and G. Kendall. *Search Methodologies.* Springer US, Boston, MA, 2005.

[11] E. K. Burke, G. Kendall, J. Newall, E. Hart, P. Ross, and S. Schulenburg. Hyper-heuristics: An emerging direction in modern search technology. In *Handbook of Metaheuristics*, International Series in Operations Research & Management Science, pages 457–474. Springer US, 2003.

[12] Y. Caseau, F. Laburthe, and G. Silverstein. A meta-heuristic factory for vehicle routing problems. In *5th International Conference, Principles and Practice of Constraint Programming, CP'99*, Lecture Notes in Computer Science, pages 144–159, Alexandria, VA, USA, 1999. Springer Berlin Heidelberg.

[13] L. Diosan, M. Oltean, and L. Dio. Evolving crossover operators for function optimization. In *9th European Conference on Genetic Programming, EuroGP 2006*, Lecture Notes in Computer Science, pages 97–108, Budapest, Hungary, 2006. Springer Berlin Heidelberg.

[14] J. Drake, N. Kililis, and E. Özcan. Generation of VNS components with grammatical evolution for vehicle routing. In K. Krawiec, A. Moraglio, T. Hu, A. ÃĚ. Etaner-Uyar, and B. Hu, editors, *16th European Conference, EuroGP 2013, April 3-5*, Lecture Notes in Computer Science, pages 25–36, Vienna, Austria, 2013. Springer Berlin Heidelberg.

[15] A. E. Eiben and S. K. Smit. Evolutionary Algorithm Parameters and Methods to Tune Them. In Y. Hamadi, E. Monfroy, and F. Saubion, editors, *Autonomous Search*, chapter 2, pages 15–36. Springer Berlin Heidelberg, Berlin, Heidelberg, 2012.

[16] E. Fast, C. L. Goues, S. Forrest, and W. Weimer. Designing better fitness functions for automated program repair. In *GECCO '10 Proceedings of the 12th annual conference on Genetic and evolutionary computation*, pages 965–972, Portland, Oregon, USA, 2010. ACM.

[17] S. Forrest, T. Nguyen, W. Weimer, and C. Le Goues. A genetic programming approach to automated software repair. In *11th Annual conference on Genetic and evolutionary computation, GECCO'09*, pages 947–954, New York, New York, USA, 2009. ACM.

[18] W. Fu, M. Johnston, and M. Zhang. Automatic construction of invariant features using genetic programming for edge detection. In *25th Australasian Joint Conference, AI 2012: Advances in Artificial Intelligence*, number 2 in Lecture Notes in Computer Science, pages 144–155, Sydney, Australia, 2012. Springer Berlin Heidelberg.

[19] A. Fukunaga. Automated Discovery of Composite SAT Variable-Selection Heuristics. In *The 18th National Conference on Artificial Intelligence*, pages 641–648, Edmonton, Canada, 2002. The AAAI Press.

[20] A. S. Fukunaga. Evolving local search heuristics for SAT using genetic programming. In K. Deb, editor, *Genetic and Evolutionary Computation - GECCO 2004*, volume 3103 of *Lecture Notes in Computer Science*, pages 483–494, Seattle, WA, USA, June 2004. Springer Berlin Heidelberg.

[21] A. S. Fukunaga. Automated discovery of local search heuristics for satisfiability testing. *Evolutionary Computation*, 16(1):31–61, Jan. 2008.

[22] M. Harman, E. Burke, J. Clark, and X. Yao. Dynamic adaptive search based software engineering. In *International Symposium on Empirical Software Engineering and Measurement*, 2012.

[23] M. Harman, Y. Jia, W. B. Langdon, J. Petke, I. H. Moghadam, S. Yoo, and F. Wu. Genetic Improvement for Adaptive Software Engineering (keynote paper). In G. Engels, editor, *SEAMS '14*, Hyderabad, India, 2014. ACM.

[24] M. Harman, W. B. Langdon, Y. Jia, D. R. White, A. Arcuri, and J. A. Clark. The GISMOE challenge: Constructing the pareto program surface using genetic programming to find better programs (keynote paper). In *27th IEEE/ACM International Conference on Automated Software Engineering*, pages 1–14, Essen, Germany, Sept. 2012. ACM.

[25] M. Harman, W. B. Langdon, and W. Weimer. Genetic programming for Reverse Engineering. In *WCRE'13 20th Working Conference on Reverse Engineering*, pages 1–10, Koblenz, Germany, Oct. 2013. IEEE.

[26] M. Harman, S. Mansouri, and Y. Zhang. Search based software engineering: A comprehensive analysis and review of trends techniques and applications. *University College London, Tech. Rep. TR-09-03*, pages 1–78, 2009.

[27] M. Harman, S. A. Mansouri, and Y. Zhang. Search-based Software Engineering: Trends, Techniques and Applications. *ACM Computing Surveys*, 45(1):1–61, Nov. 2012.

[28] M. Harman, P. McMinn, J. T. de Souza, and S. Yoo. Search based software engineering: Techniques, taxonomy, tutorial. *Empirical Software Engineering and Verification*, 7007:1–59, 2012.

[29] L. Hong, J. Woodward, J. Li, and E. Özcan. Automated design of probability distributions as mutation operators for evolutionary programming using genetic programming. In *16th European Conference, EuroGP 2013*, Lecture Notes in Computer Science, pages 85–96, Vienna, Austria, 2013. Springer Berlin Heidelberg.

[30] U. Johansson, R. König, and L. Niklasson. Genetically evolved kNN ensembles. *Data mining*, 8:299–313, 2010.

[31] A. Joó, A. Ekart, and J. Neirotti. Genetic algorithms for discovery of matrix multiplication methods. *IEEE transactions on evolutionary computation*, 16(5):749–751, 2012.

[32] J. R. Koza. *Genetic Programming, on the programming of computers by means of natural selection.* The MIT Press, 1992.

[33] W. B. Langdon. Genetic improvement of programs (Keynote). In *18th International Conference on Soft Computing, MENDEL'12*, pages 7–12, 2012.

[34] W. B. Langdon and M. Harman. Evolving a CUDA kernel from an nVidia template. In P. Sobrevilla, editor, *IEEE Congress on Evolutionary Computation*, pages 1–8, Barcelona, Spain, July 2010. IEEE.

[35] W. B. Langdon and M. Harman. Genetically improved CUDA C++ software. In M. Nicolau, K. Krawiec, and M. Heywood, editors, *17th European Conference on Genetic Programming, EuroGP 2014*, Lecture Notes in Computer Science, pages 1–12, Granada, Spain, 2014. Springer Berlin Heidelberg.

[36] W. B. Langdon and M. Harman. Optimising Existing Software with Genetic Programming. *IEEE Transactions on Evolutionary Computation*, PP(99):1–18, 2014.

[37] C. Le Goues, M. Dewey-Vogt, S. Forrest, and W. Weimer. A systematic study of automated program repair: Fixing 55 out of 105 bugs for $8 each. In *2012 34th International Conference on Software Engineering (ICSE)*, pages 3–13, Zurich, Swiss, June 2012. IEEE.

[38] C. Le Goues, T. Nguyen, S. Forrest, and W. Weimer. GenProg: A Generic Method for Automatic Software Repair. *IEEE Transactions on Software Engineering*, 38(1):54–72, 2012.

[39] M. A. Martin and D. R. Tauritz. Evolving black-box search algorithms employing genetic programming. In *GECCO'13, 15th annual conference on Genetic and evolutionary computation*, pages 1497–1504, Amsterdam, The Netherlands, July 2013. ACM Press.

[40] J. Mcdermott, D. R. White, S. Luke, L. Manzoni, M. Castelli, L. Vanneschi, W. Jaśkowski, K. Krawiec, R. Harper, K. D. Jong, and U.-M. O'Reilly. Genetic Programming Needs Better Benchmarks. In *GECCO'12, 14th annual conference on Genetic and evolutionary computation*, pages 791–798, Philadelphia, Pennsylvania, USA, July 2012. ACM.

[41] T. M. Mitchell. *Machine Learning*. McGraw Hill, 1997.

[42] S. Nguyen, M. Zhang, M. Johnston, and K. C. Tan. Evolving reusable operation-based due-date assignment models for job shop scheduling with genetic programming. In *15th European Conference, EuroGP 2012*, Lecture Notes in Computer Science, pages 121–133, Málaga, Spain, 2012. Springer Berlin Heidelberg.

[43] S. Nguyen, M. Zhang, M. Johnston, and K. C. Tan. Learning iterative dispatching rules for job shop scheduling with genetic programming. *The International Journal of Advanced Manufacturing Technology*, 67(1-4):85–100, Feb. 2013.

[44] P. Nordin and W. Banzhaf. Evolving Turing-Complete Programs for a Register Machine with Self-modifying Code. In *Genetic algorithms: proceedings of the sixth international conference (ICGA95)*, pages 318–325. Morgan Kaufmann, 1995.

[45] G. L. Pappa and A. A. Freitas. *Automating the Design of Data Mining Algorithms*. Natural Computing Series. Springer Publishing Company, Heidelberg, 1st edition, 2009.

[46] J. Petke, M. Harman, W. B. Langdon, and W. Weimer. Using Genetic Improvement & Code Transplants to Specialise a C++ Program to a Problem Class. In M. Nicolau, K. Krawiec, and M. Heywood, editors, *17th European Conference on Genetic Programming, EuroGP 2014*, Lecture Notes in Computer Science, Granada, Spain, 2014. Springer Berlin Heidelberg.

[47] J. Petke, W. B. Langdon, and M. Harman. Applying Genetic Improvement to MiniSAT. In G. Ruhe and Y. Zhang, editors, *5th International Symposium, SSBSE 2013*, Lecture Notes in Computer Science, pages 257–262, St. Petersburg, Russia, Aug. 2013. Springer Berlin Heidelberg.

[48] R. Sedgewick and K. Wayne. *Algorithms*. Addison Wesley, Westford, Massachusetts, USA, 4th edition, 2011.

[49] S. Smit and A. Eiben. Comparing parameter tuning methods for evolutionary algorithms. In *2009 IEEE Congress on Evolutionary Computation*, pages 399–406, Trondheim, May 2009. IEEE.

[50] J. Swan, M. G. Epitropakis, and J. R. Woodward. Gen-O-Fix: An embeddable framework for Dynamic Adaptive Genetic Improvement Programming. Technical Report January, Department of Computing Science and Mathematics, University of Stirling, Stirling, UK, 2014.

[51] W. Weimer, S. Forrest, C. Le Goues, and T. Nguyen. Automatic Program Repair with Evolutionary Computation. *Communications of the ACM*, 53(5):109–116, 2009.

[52] W. Weimer, T. Nguyen, C. Le Goues, and S. Forrest. Automatically finding patches using genetic programming. In *2009 IEEE 31st International Conference on Software Engineering*, pages 364–374, Vancouver, Canada, 2009. IEEE.

[53] D. R. White. *Genetic Programming for Low-Resource Systems*. Phd, University of York, 2009.

[54] D. R. White, A. Arcuri, and J. a. Clark. Evolutionary Improvement of Programs. *IEEE Transactions on Evolutionary Computation*, 15(4):515–538, Aug. 2011.

[55] J. Woodward and J. Swan. The automatic generation of mutation operators for genetic algorithms. In G. L. Pappa, J. Woodward, M. R. Hyde, and J. Swan, editors, *GECCO'12, 14th annual conference on Genetic and evolutionary computation*, pages 67–74, Philadelphia, Pennsylvania, USA, 2012.

[56] J. R. Woodward and J. Swan. Automatically designing selection heuristics. In *GECCO'11, 13th annual conference on Genetic and evolutionary computation*, page 583, New York, New York, USA, 2011. ACM Press.

A Step Size Based Self-Adaptive Mutation Operator for Evolutionary Programming

Libin Hong
School of Computer Science,
University of Nottingham P.R.C
Libin.hong@nottingham.edu.cn

John H. Drake
School of Computer Science,
University of Nottingham P.R.C
John.drake@nottingham.edu.cn

Ender Özcan
School of Computer Science,
University of Nottingham U.K
Ender.ozcan@nottingham.ac.uk

ABSTRACT

The mutation operator is the only genetic operator in Evolutionary Programming (EP). In the past researchers have nominated Gaussian, Cauchy, and Lévy distributions as mutation operators. According to the No Free Lunch theorem [9], no single mutation operator is able to outperform all others over the set of all possible functions. Potentially there is a lot of useful information generated when EP is ongoing. In this paper, we collect such information and propose a step size based self-adaptive mutation operator for Evolutionary Programming (SSEP). In SSEP, the mutation operator might be changed during the evolutionary process, based on the step size, from generation to generation. Principles for selecting an appropriate mutation operator for EP is proposed, with SSEP grounded on the principles. SSEP is shown to outperform static mutation operators in Evolutionary Programming on most of the functions tested. We also compare the experimental results of SSEP with other recent Evolutionary Programming methods, which uses multiple mutation operators.

Keywords

Evolutionary Programming; Step Size; Mutation Operator; Self-Adaptive; Function Optimization; Convergence.

1. INTRODUCTION

Evolutionary Programming (EP) is a branch of Evolutionary Computation used to evolve numerical values, in an attempt to find a global optimum of a function. The only genetic operator available in an EP system is mutation. Probability distributions used as mutation operators in EP include Gaussian, Cauchy and Lévy, among others. Classical Evolutionary Programming (CEP) [10] uses Gaussian mutation, while Fast Evolutionary Programming (FEP) [10] uses Cauchy mutation. For Evolutionary Programming methods using Lévy distribution as a mutation operator (LEP) [4], it is also possible perform Gaussian or Cauchy mutation through the settings of the α parameter.

GECCO'14, July 12–16, 2014, Vancouver, BC, Canada.
Copyright 2014 ACM 978-1-4503-2881-4/14/07 ...$15.00.
http://dx.doi.org/10.1145/2598394.2609873.

In recent years, many improvements to EP have been proposed. Improved FEP (IFEP) [11], mixes mutation operators, and uses both Gaussian and Cauchy mutations. Later a mixed mutation strategy (MSEP) [2] was proposed: four mutation operators are used and the mutation operator is selected according to their probabilities during the evolution. In 2010 MSEP with local fitness landscape (LMSEP) [8] was proposed: based on MSEP, local fitness landscape is considered. Ensemble Strategies with Adaptive Evolutionary Programming [7] was also proposed in 2010: each mutation operator has an associated population, with every population benefiting from every function call. In 2013, researchers proposed to automatically design the mutation operator for EP using Genetic Programming [3].

This paper proposes a novel method, using a self-adaptive mutation operator to keep the convergence rate stable for EP throughout the evolutionary process. From previous research and our observations, useful information is collected to help EP make a decision which mutation operator to use at each generation. We propose principles to design an algorithm which utilises this information. According to the principles, a step size based self-adaptive mutation operator for Evolutionary Programming (SSEP) is presented.

Section 2 introduces function optimization and the EP algorithm. In Section 3 we describe the principles used to design the SSEP mutation operator. Section 4 provide the details of the EP designed by the principles. In Section 5 we present and compare the experimental results of Gaussian, Cauchy, and Lévy mutation with the SSEP. We also compare SSEP to the MSEP and LMSEP methods take from the literature. In Section 6 we discuss and explain future work. Section 7 summarizes and concludes the article.

2. FUNCTION OPTIMIZATION BY EVOLUTIONARY PROGRAMMING

Global minimization in $\mathbb{R}^n$ can be formalized as a pair (S, f), where $S \in \mathbb{R}^n$ is a bounded set on $\mathbb{R}^n$ and $f : S \to \mathbb{R}$ is an n-dimensional real-valued function. The aim is to find a point $x_{\min} \in S$ such that $f(x_{\min})$ is a global minimum on S. More specifically, it is required to find an $x_{\min} \in S$ such that

$$\forall x \in S : f(x_{\min}) \le f(x)$$

Here f does not need to be continuous or differentiable but it must be bounded. The algorithm of EP is implemented as follows [1, 10]:

1. *Generate the initial population of p individuals, and set $k = 1$. Each individual is taken as a pair of real-valued*

vectors, (x_i, η_i), $\forall i \in \{1, \cdots, \mu\}$. The initialization value of the strategy parameter η is set to 3.0.

2. *Evaluate the fitness value for each (x_i, η_i), $\forall i \in \{1, \cdots, \mu\}$.*

3. *Each parent (x_i, η_i), $\forall i \in \{1, \cdots, \mu\}$, creates λ/μ offspring on average, so that a total of λ offspring are generated: for $i=1, \cdots, \mu$, $j=1, \cdots, n$.*

$$x_i'(j) = x_i(j) + \eta_i(j)D_j \tag{1}$$

$$\eta'(j) = \eta_i(j)exp(\gamma' N(0,1) + \gamma N_j(0,1)) \tag{2}$$

The above two equations are used to generate new offspring. Objective function is used to calculate the fitness value, the survival offspring is picked up according to the fitness value. The factors γ and γ' have set to $(\sqrt{2\sqrt{n}})^{-1}$ and $(\sqrt{2n})^{-1}$.

4. *Evaluate the fitness of each offspring (x_i', η_i'), $\forall i \in \{1, \cdots, \mu\}$, according to $f(x')$.*

5. *Conduct pairwise comparison over the union of parents (x_i, η_i) and offspring (x_i', η_i'), $\forall i \in \{1, \cdots, \mu\}$. Q opponents are selected randomly from the parents and offspring for each individual. During the comparison, the individual receives a "win" if its fitness is no greater than those of opponents.*

6. *Pick the μ individuals out of parents and offspring, $i \in \{1, \cdots, \mu\}$, that have the most wins to be parents, to form the next generation.*

7. *Stop if the stopping criterion is satisfied; otherwise, k++ and goto Step3.*

If D_j in Eq.(1) is the Gaussian distribution, then the algorithm is CEP [10]. If D_j is the Cauchy distribution, it is FEP [11]. If D_j is the Lévy distribution, it is LEP [4]. The above algorithm acts as a template for SSEP, which is the contribution of this paper.

3. PRINCIPLES OF A STEP SIZE BASED SELF-ADAPTIVE MUTATION OPERATOR

In this section we introduce the principles used to design SSEP and explain how it works. The idea of SSEP is inspired by a driver tuning an analogue car radio. A driver will usually tune the radio in a wide range to search channels, and several channels may be discovered. Once the driver decides which channel to listen to, he will adjust the radio slightly to make the signal more clear. We try to design an EP system that moves in the search space with a long step size at the beginning, and uses a short step size later on in the search, where step size is the distance between a 'survived' offspring and its parent.

Liang et al. [5, 6] proposed to control the lower bound of offspring in order to improve the performance in EP, and noted that self-adaptation may rapidly lead to a search step size that is far too small to explore the search space any further. This is known as *loss of step size control.* Liang et al. [5, 6] also analyse how the step size control was lost. In this paper we propose to change the mutation operator in EP based on the step size that the parent jumped, rather than control the lower bound.

Yao et al. [11] point out that Cauchy mutation is more likely to generate an offspring further away from its parent than Gaussian mutation. In other words, Gaussian offers better performance if the parent is close to the global optimum, otherwise Cauchy mutation is a better choice for EP.

From a large number of EP experiments we observed an interesting phenomena: when using a static mutation operator in EP, usually more offspring survive in early generations and less offspring survive in later generations of the run. According to previous research conclusions and our own observations, we believe that in early generations of function optimization, a long step size mutation operator is necessary, as it guarantees more of the search space can be covered. However, once the individuals are close to the global optimum, a long step size mutation operator should be replaced by a short step size mutation operator in order to keep the convergence rate of the run consistent in later generations. But how 'short' is short enough? In previous research, a standard normal distribution $N(0,1)$ represents a short step size mutation operator. In our experiments we use $N(0, 0.1)$ or $N(0, 0.01)$ as 'short' step size mutation operators.

3.1 Symbols Used in Principles

Below are the symbols used in the principles:

1. S_k: a single value representing the single step size at each generation k. In EP, after tournament selection at each generation, the new population consists of both parents and offspring. The offspring which appear in the new population are known as "survived" offspring, S_k is calculated as the mean value of the jumped step size of all "survived" offspring. This value will be updated at each generation (in Algorithm 2 line 8), $\forall k \in \{1, \cdots, n\}$ where n is the maximum generation of EP.

2. S_H_k: a single value representing the average step size from generation 1 to the current generation k. This value is calculated as $mean(S_1...S_k)$ where k is current generation number. This value is also updated at each generation (in Algorithm 2 line 10).

3. $N(\mu, \sigma^2)$: Gaussian distribution, in SSEP ($\mu = 0, \sigma^2 = 0.1$) or ($\mu = 0, \sigma^2 = 0.01$) is used according to the principles.

4. C: represents the Cauchy distribution.

5. T: the distance coefficient. When S_k is very small, it helps EP to have sufficient generations with a long step size mutation operator to prevent it from falling into local optimum. In our experiments, the value of T for each function is given in Table 2. The values of T we set for SSEP are empirically determined.

3.2 Principles for SSEP

The following are the principles for SSEP:

1. If $S_k \in (1e-4, 1e-2]$ at the current generation and $S\_H_k \geq S_k \times T$, set a σ^2=0.1 for $N(0, \sigma^2)$, and use $N(0, 0.1)$ as the mutation operator for EP.

2. If $S_k \in (0, 1e-4]$ at the current generation and $S\_H_k \geq S_k \times T$, set σ^2=0.01 for $N(0, \sigma^2)$, and $N(0, 0.01)$ is selected as mutation operator for EP.

3. If $S\_H_k \geq 1$ or $S\_H_k \leq S_k \times T$, C is selected as mutation operator for EP.

4. For all other cases, σ^2 is set as S_H_k for $N(0, \sigma^2)$, and $N(0, S\_H_k)$ is selected as the mutation operator for EP.

Previous works in the literature often use standard normal distribution $N(0, 1)$ as a short step size mutation operator.

However according to our observations, the random values generated by $N(0,1)$ are not 'short' enough to keep convergence rate stable in later stages of EP. This is a particular problem when the population is 'very close' to the global optimum. Hence we use principle 1 and 2 to keep the convergence rate stable in later generations of EP. In SSEP, $S\_H_k = 1$ is a watershed, $S\_H_k \geq 1$ represents more offspring survived using long step size mutation operator. As a result we will use a mutation operator that can generate long step size values for the next generation, hence we propose principle 3.

Table 1 Parameter settings for EP.

Parameter	Settings
DIM	n in Table 3
POPNO	100

Algorithm 1 Algorithm to calculate step size for each population

```
DIM /*Initial dimensional size*/
POPNO /*Initial population number*/
pop[POPNO × 2][DIM]
/*Parents and offsprings in current generation*/
for i : POPNO do
   indStepSize = 0;
   for j : DIM do
      /*Calculate step size for each individual*/
      temp(i, j) = pop[i][j] - pop[POPNO + i][j]
      /*Calculate total step size for all individuals*/
      indStepSize += abs(temp(i, j))
   end for
   /*Calculate average step size for pop[i]*/
   popStepSize(POPNO + i) = indStepSize/DIM
end for
```

4. DETAILS OF SSEP IMPLEMENTATION

In this section we list the the pseudo-code of the SSEP algorithm designed according to the principles in Section 3.2.

Algorithm 1 is used to calculate the step size of the population at each generation of EP. The updating of S_k and S_H_k in Algorithm 2 will use the data prepared in this algorithm. Algorithm 1 is injected in between step 4 and step 5 of the EP algorithm introduced in Section 2.

Algorithm 2 implements the principles proposed in Section 3.2. Algorithm 2 is injected in between step 6 and step 7 of the EP algorithm introduced in Section 2.

5. EXPERIMENTAL RESULTS AND DISCUSSION

In previous work, most researchers have tested their algorithms on a benchmark suite of 23 functions [10]. In this paper, we use the first 10 (see Table 3).

Table 3 lists the functions used in this paper. In the function suite, f_1-f_7 are unimodal functions and f_8-f_{10} are multimodal functions.

Algorithm 2 Algorithm to implement SSEP

```
for i : POPNO do
   if pop[i] is offspring then
      totalPopStepSize += popStepSize[i]
      survivedOffspringNo ++
   end if
end for
/*update S_k*/
S_k = totalPopStepSize/survivedOffspringNo
/*update S_H_k*/
S_H_k = mean(S_1...S_k);
/*Initial T*/
if S_k < 1e − 2 and S_k > 1e − 4 and S_H_k ≥ S_k × T then
   /*If mutation type is 2, use N(0, σ^2) as mutation operator*/
   muttype ← 2
   σ^2 ← 0.1
else if S_k ≤ 1e − 4 and S_k < 0 and S_H_k ≥ S_k × T then
   muttype ← 2
   σ^2 ← 0.01
else if S_H_k ≥ 1 or S_H_k ≤ S_k × T then
   /*If mutation type is 1, use C as mutation operator*/
   muttype ← 1
else
   muttype ← 2
   σ^2 ← S_H_k
end if
```

The results of SSEP are given for each function in Table 4, alone with the results of various previous methods taken from the literature.

Table 5 shows the results of a Wilcoxon Signed-Rank Test within a 95% confidence interval between SSEP and other methods from literature. In this table, "≥" and "≤" indicate that SSEP performs better or worse on average respectively, compared to a particular existing method. In the case that this difference is statistically significant, ">" and "<" are used.

5.1 Analysis and Comparisons

The results in Table 4 show that SSEP gives the best performance when compared with using a static mutation operator on f_1, f_2, f_4 and f_7. The results of the 2-tailed Wilcoxon Signed-Rank Tests given in Table 5, show a statistically significant difference between SSEP and CEP, FEP and the LEP variations. SSEP also beats some of the static mutation operators on f_6, f_8 and f_{10}. We notice that SSEP has good performance on f_{10}, the original experimental data shows that the mean fitness value in final generation reaches a level of 10^{-5} more than 30 times over 50 runs.

The new methods proposed have successfully kept the convergence rate stable for some of the functions, not only in early generations, but also in later generations of EP. In general, SSEP outperforms EP methods using static mutation operators, such as FEP, CEP and LEP. The only function on which SSEP has worst results is f_5. This may be because the principles used are either over-fitting or under-fitting and is discussed in future work.

Table 2 Settings of T for $f_1 - f_{10}$.

f_n	f_1	f_2	f_3	f_4	f_5	f_6	f_7	f_8	f_9	f_{10}
T	$1.5e+2$	$1.0e+2$	$1.5e+2$	$1.0e+2$	$1.5e+2$	$1.5e+2$	$1.5e+2$	$1.5e+2$	$1.5e+2$	$1.5e+2$

Table 3 The 10 functions used in our experimental studies, where n is the dimensional size of the function, f_{min} is the minimum value of the function, and $S \subseteq \mathbb{R}^n$.

Function	n	S	f_{min}
$f_1(x) = \sum_{i=1}^{n} x_i^2$	30	$[-100, 100]^n$	0
$f_2(x) = \sum_{i=1}^{n} \mid x_i \mid + \prod_{i=1}^{n} \mid x_i \mid$	30	$[-10, 10]^n$	0
$f_3(x) = \sum_{i=1}^{n} (\sum_{j=1}^{i} x_j)^2$	30	$[-100, 100]^n$	0
$f_4(x) = \max_i \{\mid x_i \mid, 1 \leq i \leq n\}$	30	$[-100, 100]^n$	0
$f_5(x) = \sum_{i=1}^{n} [(x_{i+1} - x_i^2)^2 + (x_i - 1)^2]$	30	$[-30, 30]^n$	0
$f_6(x) = \sum_{i=1}^{n} (\lfloor x_i + 0.5 \rfloor)^2$	30	$[-100, 100]^n$	0
$f_7(x) = \sum_{i=1}^{n} i x_i^4 + random[0, 1)$	30	$[-1.28, 1.28]^n$	0
$f_8(x) = \sum_{i=1}^{n} -x_i \sin(\sqrt{\mid x_i \mid})$	30	$[-500, 500]^n$	-12569.5
$f_9(x) = \sum_{i=1}^{n} [x_i^2 - 10cos(2\pi x_i) + 10]$	30	$[-5.12, 5.12]^n$	0
$f_{10}(x) = -20\exp(-0.2\sqrt{\frac{1}{n}\sum_{i=1}^{n} x_i^2}) - \exp(\frac{1}{n}\sum_{i=1}^{n}\cos 2\pi x_i) + 20 + e$	30	$[-32, 32]^n$	0

Table 4 The results of SSEP, FEP, CEP and LEP with α=(1.2,1.4,1.6,1.8) on f_1-f_{10}, "Mean" indicates the mean best fitness values found in the last generation over 50 runs, "Best" indicates the best fitness value in last generation in 50 runs, "Std Dev" stands for standard deviations.

f_n		SSEP	FEP	CEP	$\alpha = 1.2$	$\alpha = 1.4$	$\alpha = 1.6$	$\alpha = 1.8$
f_1	Mean	**1.1679E-07**	4.8402E-04	5.8365E-05	2.5452E-04	1.7666E-04	1.3584E-04	1.0588E-04
	Best	**6.9710E-09**	3.0336E-04	2.7631E-05	1.4416E-04	8.5229E-05	8.1850E-05	7.6026E-05
	Std Dev	(2.15E-07)	(7.27E-05)	(2.36E-05)	(4.49E-05)	(3.66E-05)	(2.83E-05)	(1.70E-05)
f_2	Mean	**2.4397E-04**	6.8787E-02	2.2292E-02	5.2286E-02	4.2083E-02	3.6502E-02	3.3497E-02
	Best	**2.0062E-04**	5.5150E-02	1.9973E-02	4.5706E-02	3.4859E-02	3.1018E-02	2.8360E-02
	Std Dev	(1.67E-05)	(5.61E-03)	(1.28E-03)	(3.15E-03)	(2.84E-03)	(2.50E-03)	(2.03E-03)
f_3	Mean	7.9868E-03	1.2047E-02	7.4353E-03	6.1633E-03	5.9409E-03	**4.2044E-03**	5.4785E-03
	Best	2.4046E-03	2.9402E-03	**1.3768E-04**	1.1369E-03	6.3364E-04	4.1240E-04	4.0410E-04
	Std Dev	(6.50E-03)	(1.10E-02)	(1.14E-02)	(5.06E-03)	(1.44E-02)	(5.42E-03)	(1.00E-02)
f_4	Mean	**8.8458E-04**	6.6422E-03	1.2984	5.9469E-03	2.97E-02	2.4820E-01	5.5215E-01
	Best	**2.0549E-05**	5.0559E-03	1.8176E-01	4.4390E-03	3.7107E-03	3.4234E-03	3.6725E-03
	Std Dev	(1.99E-03)	(6.73E-04)	(9.67E-01)	(1.34E-03)	(1.06E-01)	(5.29E-01)	(6.86E-01)
f_5	Mean	32.0200	25.8343	5.9900	15.2293	9.0767	**5.5955**	7.5573
	Best	0.1599	0.0431	0.0787	0.0416	0.0578	**0.0203**	0.0305
	Std Dev	(34.10)	(28.96)	(11.90)	(23.72)	(11.82)	(5.30)	(11.66)
f_6	Mean	**0**	**0**	119.72	**0**	**0**	0.08	26.28
	Best	**0**	**0**	**0**	**0**	**0**	**0**	**0**
	Std Dev	(0)	(0)	(402.51)	(0)	(0)	(0.27)	(154.00)
f_7	Mean	**7.5877E-03**	8.6825E-03	1.9285E-02	8.4072E-03	1.0126E-02	1.2125E-02	1.3827E-02
	Best	0.0040	0.0039	0.0095	**0.0029**	0.0047	0.0052	0.0048
	Std Dev	(2.11E-03)	(2.27E-03)	(6.14E-03)	(2.56E-03)	(2.80E-03)	(4.08E-03)	(4.66E-03)
f_8	Mean	-11087.73	**-11363.42**	-7974.68	-10553.20	-10261.56	-9522.00	-8807.46
	Best	**-12095.73**	**-12095.73**	-9330.51	-11500.51	-11049.53	-10832.39	-10215.79
	Std Dev	(376.22)	(344.28)	(640.90)	(367.01)	(486.21)	(579.09)	(633.00)
f_9	Mean	47.73	**3.8752E-02**	79.40	4.7913E-02	2.12	20.64	67.03
	Best	0.0329	0.0413	60.6957	**0.0297**	2.0129	20.9487	66.6733
	Std Dev	(28.09)	(5.34E-03)	(22.79)	(0.14)	(1.35)	(8.89)	(20.21)
f_{10}	Mean	0.1661	0.0160	8.1118	0.0118	**0.0113**	1.1340	5.0703
	Best	**5.4074E-05**	1.2613E-02	9.3137E-01	8.4018E-03	8.0068E-03	7.7945E-03	5.7543E-03
	Std Dev	(5.80E-01)	(1.45E-03)	(3.29)	(1.32E-03)	(3.30E-03)	(1.29)	(3.65)

Table 5 2-tailed Wilcoxon Signed-Rank Test comparing SSEP with FEP, CEP and LEP with $\alpha = (1.2, 1.4, 1.6, 1.8)$ on f_1-f_{10}.

f_n	Number of Generations	vs FEP	vs CEP	vs $\alpha = 1.2$	vs $\alpha = 1.4$	vs $\alpha = 1.6$	vs $\alpha = 1.8$
f_1	1500	$>$	$>$	$>$	$>$	$>$	$>$
f_2	2000	$>$	$>$	$>$	$>$	$>$	$>$
f_3	5000	$>$	$\leq$	$\leq$	$<$	$<$	$<$
f_4	5000	$>$	$>$	$>$	$>$	$>$	$>$
f_5	20000	$\leq$	$<$	$<$	$<$	$<$	$<$
f_6	1500	$=$	$>$	$=$	$=$	$=$	$>$
f_7	3000	$>$	$>$	$\geq$	$>$	$>$	$>$
f_8	9000	$<$	$>$	$>$	$>$	$>$	$>$
f_9	5000	$<$	$>$	$<$	$<$	$<$	$>$
f_{10}	1500	$<$	$>$	$<$	$<$	$>$	$>$

Table 6 Comparison of SSEP, MSEP and LMSEP, means and (standard deviations

f_n	Number of Generations	SSEP	LMSEP [8]	MSEP [8]
f_1	1500	**1.1679E-07** (2.15E-07)	3.803E-05 (7.97E-05)	6.209E-05 (1.61E-04)
f_2	2000	**2.4397E-04** (1.67E-05)	1.556E-03 (9.37E-04)	8.226E-02 (4.35E-01)
f_4	5000	**8.8458E-04** (1.99E-03)	0.767 (1.09)	0.629 (1)
f_6	1500	0 (0)	**0** (0)	43.8 (126)
f_7	3000	**7.5877E-03** (2.11E-03)	3.514E-02 (1.85E-02)	3.56E-02 (1.74E-02)
f_9	5000	**47.73** (28.09)	61.39 (13.18)	63.44 (13.8)
f_{10}	1500	1.661E-01 (5.80E-01)	**1.956E-03** (1.76E-03)	6.498 (2.49)

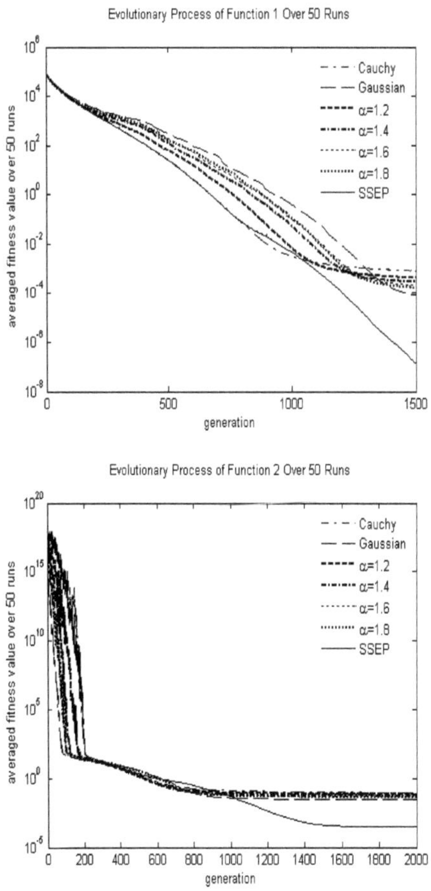

Figure 1 Evolutionary Process of $f1$, $f2$.

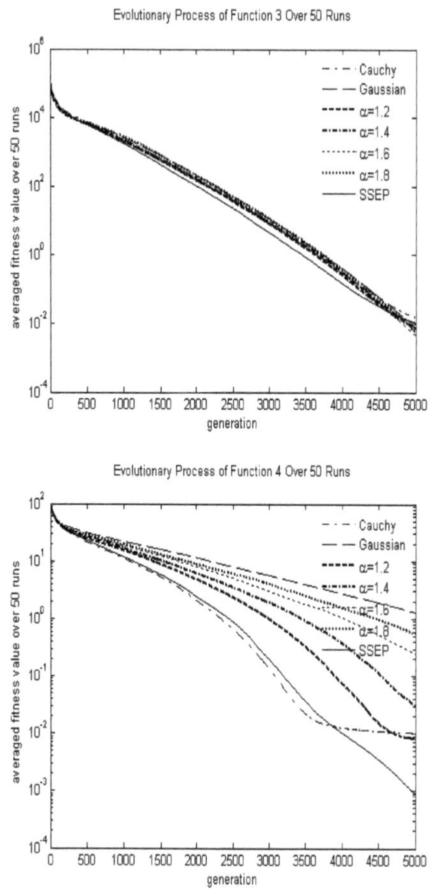

Figure 2 Evolutionary Process of $f3$, $f4$.

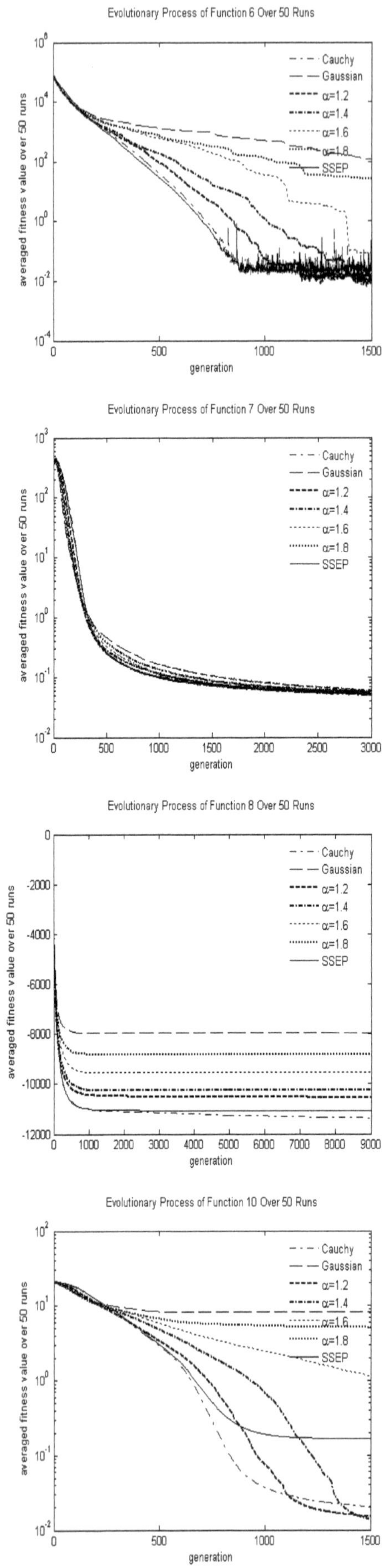

Figure 3 Evolutionary Process of $f6, f7, f8, f10$.

In Figure 1, 2 and 3 , we plot the averaged fitness value over 50 runs at each generation. SSEP shows its consistent convergence rate throughout evolutionary process on f_1, f_2 and f_4.

5.2 Comparison of EP Use None Static Mutation Operator

We list the experimental data of SSEP, MSEP and LMSEP in Table 6. Both MSEP and LMSEP do not use a static mutation operator strategy. SSEP offers better performance on f_1, f_2, f_4, f_7 and f_8.

Note: Shen et al. [8] does not provide results for f_3, f_5 and f_8, so it is only possible to make comparisons on f_1, f_2, f_4, f_6, f_7, f_9 and f_{10}.

6. DISCUSSION AND FUTURE WORK

The main aim of this paper is to implement an algorithm which is capable of selecting a mutation operator for EP at each generation.

We have tested SSEP, using single step size S_k at each generation, history step size S_H_k from generation 1 to current generation k as a self-adaptive factor to pick an appropriate mutation operator for the next generation of EP. The distance coefficient T is used to control SSEP, trying to avoid falling into local optimum in early generations of EP.

So far we have compared it with the static mutation operators used in CEP [10], FEP [10] and LEP [4]. We also compared SSEP to MSEP [2] and LMSEP [8], which both use multiple mutation operators. Several principles are proposed to implement SSEP. Later work will focus on improving the principles in order to fit more functions, hopefully improving the accuracy of the self-adaptive mutation operator.

Another extension in SSEP is to examine how the distance coefficient T affects the convergence speed on different functions. Search space is not considered in the current principles. We believe that the search space of functions is another important factor of self-adaptive mutation operators worthy of future investigation. Currently SSEP works on the same dimensional size for all functions, we are also planning to investigate how SSEP works on functions with different dimensional sizes.

SSEP does not show good performance on some functions, especially f_5, this suggests that the principles are not robust enough. Regardless of this dilemma we have proposed principles and designed an algorithm which outperforms existing EP systems with static mutation operators and dynamic mutation operators on most of the functions tested.

One possible criticism of this method is that the principles do not fit all of the functions tested so far. This is because some important factors that affect the selection of mutation operators is omitted. In future, we will collect as much useful information as possible throughout the evolutionary process to make SSEP more accurate and robust.

7. SUMMARY AND CONCLUSIONS

Evolutionary Programming is a robust method of solving numerical optimization problems. In the past it has involved using probability distributions (Gaussian, Cauchy and Lévy, etc) as the unique mutation operator. Recently multiple mutation operators have been adopted in EP methods, such as IFEP [11], MSEP [2] and LMSEP [8]. EP with a static mutation operator usually keeps high convergence rate in early generations, but less offspring survive in tournament selection in later generations. In this paper, we propose principles to keep the high convergence rate not only in early generations of EP, but also in later generations. According to the principles, an algorithm is presented and injected into EP, to help EP adaptively select appropriate mutation operators at each generation throughout the evolutionary process.

SSEP is inspired by the process of tuning an analogue car radio, when a driver usually tunes the radio in a wide range to search for a channel, before slightly adjusting the radio to get a clear signal. SSEP moves in the search space with a long step size mutation operator at beginning and uses a short step size mutation operator towards the end of the search.

From the experimental results, SSEP shows good performance on a set of 10 benchmark functions. The initial results are highly encouraging, we cannot claim that our principles can fit over all functions from the literature, but our principles are successful on some functions, outperforming existing EP methods.

8. REFERENCES

[1] T. Bäck and H.-P. Schwefel. An overview of evolutionary algorithms for parameter optimization. *Evolutionary Computation*, 1:1–23, 1993.

[2] H. Dong, J. He, H. Huang, and W. Hou. Evolutionary programming using a mixed mutation strategy. *Information Science*, 177:312–327, 2007.

[3] L. Hong, J. Woodward, J. Li, and E. Özcan. Automated design of probability distributions as mutation operators for evolutionary programming using genetic programming. In *Genetic Programming*, volume 7831 of *Lecture Notes in Computer Science*, pages 85–96. Springer Berlin Heidelberg, 2013.

[4] C.-Y. Lee and X. Yao. Evolutionary programming using mutations based on the lévy probability distribution. *IEEE Transactions on Evolutionary Computation*, 8:1–13, 2004.

[5] K.-H. Liang, X. Yao, Y. Liu, C. Newton, and D. Hoffman. An experimental investigation of self-adaptation in evolutionary programming. In V. Porto, N. Saravanan, D. Waagen, and A. Eiben, editors, *Evolutionary Programming VII*, volume 1447 of *Lecture Notes in Computer Science*, pages 291–300. Springer Berlin Heidelberg, 1998.

[6] K.-H. Liang, X. Yao, and C. S. Newton. Adapting self-adaptive parameters in evolutionary algorithms. *Applied Intelligence*, 15(3):171–180, 2001.

[7] P. N. S. Rammohan Mallipeddi, S. Mallipeddi. Ensemble strategies with adaptive evolutionary programming. *Information Science*, 180:1571–1581, 2010.

[8] L. Shen and J. He. A mixed strategy for evolutionary programming based on local fitness landscape. In *Evolutionary Computation (CEC), 2010 IEEE Congress on*, pages 1–8, July 2010.

[9] D. H. Wolpert and W. G. Macready. No free lunch theorems for optimization. *IEEE Transactions on Evolutionary Computation*, 1(1):67–82, 1997.

[10] X. Yao and Y. Liu. Fast evolutionary programming. *Proceedings of the Fifth Annual Conference on Evolutionary Programming, MIT Press*, pages 451–460, 1996.

[11] X. Yao, Y. Liu, and G. Lin. Evolutionary programming made faster. *IEEE Transactions on Evolutionary Computation*, 3:82–102, 1999.

A Problem Configuration Study of the Robustness of a Black-Box Search Algorithm Hyper-Heuristic

Matthew A. Martin
Natural Computation Laboratory
Department of Computer Science
Missouri University of Science and Technology
Rolla, Missouri, U.S.A.
mam446@mst.edu

Daniel R. Tauritz
Natural Computation Laboratory
Department of Computer Science
Missouri University of Science and Technology
Rolla, Missouri, U.S.A.
dtauritz@acm.org

ABSTRACT

Black-Box Search Algorithms (BBSAs) tailored to a specific problem class may be expected to significantly outperform more general purpose problem solvers, including canonical evolutionary algorithms. Recent work has introduced a novel approach to evolving tailored BBSAs through a genetic programming hyper-heuristic. However, that first generation of hyper-heuristics suffered from over-specialization. This paper presents a study on the second generation hyper-heuristic which employs a multi-sample training approach to alleviate the over-specialization problem. In particular, the study is focused on the affect that the multi-sample approach has on the problem configuration landscape. A variety of experiments are reported on which demonstrate the significant increase in the robustness of the generated algorithms to changes in problem configuration due to the multi-sample approach. The results clearly show the resulting BBSAs' ability to outperform established BBSAs, including canonical evolutionary algorithms. The trade-off between a priori computational time and the generated algorithm robustness is investigated, demonstrating the performance gain possible given additional run-time.

Categories and Subject Descriptors

I.2.8 [**Artificial Intelligence**]: Proglem Solving, Control Methods, and Search; I.2.2 [**Artificial Intelligence**]: Automatic Programming– *program synthesis*

General Terms

Algorithms, Design

Keywords

Black-Box Search Algorithms, Evolutionary Algorithms, Genetic Programming, Hyper-Heuristics

GECCO'14, July 12–16, 2014, Vancouver, BC, Canada.

http://dx.doi.org/10.1145/2598394.2609872.

1. INTRODUCTION

Practitioners tend to be interested in solving a particular problem class which may fall anywhere on the continuum from a single instance problem to an arbitrarily large problem class. However, progress in the field of meta-heuristics has typically been aimed at solving increasingly varied problem classes. There is a clear need for meta-heuristics tunable to the needs of practitioners in terms of the scope of the problem classes of interest, whether that be solving solely instances of MAXSAT with a fixed clause length and set number of variables, or arbitrary MAXSAT instances.

A novel approach to creating BBSAs through a hyper-heuristic using Genetic Programming (GP) demonstrated that there are problem classes for which BBSAs can be evolved which significantly outperform established BBSAs, including canonical the Evolutionary Algorithm (EA) [12]. That approach, however, had the drawback of tending to overspecialize the BBSAs to outperform established algorithms only on the trained problem configurations.

This paper presents a study on the second generation hyper-heuristics employing a multi-sample training approach which drastically decreases the probability of evolving BBSAs that suffer from over-specialization [13]. It is focused on the affect that the multi-sample approach has on the problem configuration landscape. An investigation is presented on the trade-off between the extra a priori computational time due to increasing sampling size and the increased robustness of the generated BBSAs in terms of lower variation in performance when varying the problem configuration. This is of critical importance to practitioners who need to be able to rely on the consistency of the generated BBSAs on all instances of their problem class of interest.

The goal of the research reported in this paper is to show that increasing the multi-sampling level increases the robustness of the generated BBSAs. Two primary measures of robustness are employed [7], as seen in Figure 1. The first is *fallibility*; if this value is large, it means that the BBSA can have a large difference in performance depending on the location on the problem configuration landscape. The second measure is *applicability*; it indicates the size of the problem configuration space in which the BBSA performs better than a threshold value. For a BBSA to be highly robust, it should have a small fallibility and a large applicability.

2. RELATED WORK

Most previous work on employing evolutionary computing to create improved BBSAs has focused on tuning parame-

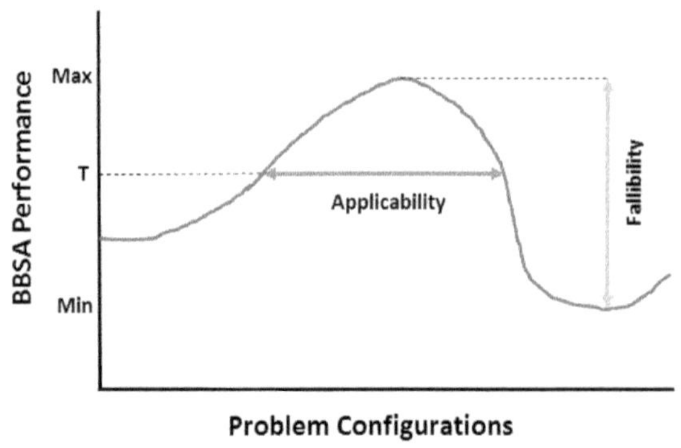

Figure 1: This figure demonstrates the concepts of Applicability and Fallibility. Applicability is the proportion of the problem configuration space that a BBSA can perform higher than a given threshold value. Fallibility is the difference between the highest and lowest performing problem configurations.

ters [16] or adaptively selecting which of a pre-defined set of operators to use and in which order [15]. The latter employed Multi Expression Programming to evolve how, and in what order, the EA used selection, mutation, and recombination. This approach used four high level operations: Initialize, Select, Crossover, and Mutate. These operations were combined in various ways to evolve a better performing EA. Later this approach was also attempted employing Linear GP [4, 5, 14]. While this allowed the EA to identify the best combination of available selection, recombination, and mutation operators to use for a given problem, it was limited to a predefined structure.

A more recent approach to evolving BBSAs employed Grammatical Evolution (GE) [10] which uses a grammar to describe structure, but is constrained to the canonical EA model. In later work [11], due to the computational load necessary for evaluating algorithms, a study was presented on how restricting the computational time for evaluating the evolved algorithms affects the structure.

First attempts at applying GP to the generation of BBSAs was to evolve individual EA operators [1, 6]. The primary effort has been to create improved EA variation operators [1, 6, 9, 19]. Some work has been done on evolving EA selection operators [17, 18].

Burke et al. described a high-level approach to evolving heuristics [2]. That approach was extended to evolve entire BBSAs of indiscriminate type [12]. This paper describes an improvement on that extension employing multi-sample evaluation to increase the robustness of the produced BBSAs.

3. METHODOLOGY

The specific focus of the research reported in this paper is to demonstrate the significant increase in the robustness of the generated algorithms to changes in problem configuration due to the multi-sample approach. GP was employed to evolve the algorithms where fitness was based upon the performance averaged over a set of training problem configurations.

3.1 Parse Tree

In order to condense the quantity of code needed to be evolved, the common iterative nature of BBSAs is exploited by representing a single iteration of a BBSA rather than the entirety of the algorithm. A parse tree is used to represent the iteration for the evolutionary process such that standard GP operators will work effectively.

Each non-terminal node will take one or more sets of solutions (including the empty set or a singleton set) from its child node(s), perform an operation on the sets(s) and then return a single set of solutions. The nodes continue operating in a post-order fashion and the set that the root node returns will be stored as the 'Last' set which can be accessed in future iterations to facilitate population-based BBSAs. The terminal nodes can either be sets of previous solutions or a set of randomly generated solutions. The sets include the 'Last' set as well as auxiliary sets which will be explained in Section 3.2.4. An example of a BBSA represented as a parse tree and related code representation are shown in figures 2 and 3.

3.2 Nodes

The non-terminal nodes that compose these trees are operations extracted from pre-existing algorithms. The nodes are broken down into selection, variation, set-manipulation, terminal, and utility nodes. The following subsections describe the operations employed of each type for the experiments reported in this paper.

3.2.1 Selection Operation Nodes

Two principal selection operations were employed in the experiments. The first of these is k-tournament selection with replacement. This node has two parameters, namely k and the number of solutions selected, the second is *count* which designates the number of solutions passed to the next node. The second selection operation employed is truncation selection. This operator takes the n best solutions from the set passed to it, n being one of its parameters.

3.2.2 Variation Operation Nodes

For the experiments, three primary variation operations are used; the first one is standard bit-flip mutation. This operation has a single argument, *rate*, which is the probability that a given bit is flipped. The second operation is the standard uniform recombination with an arbitrary number of parents. This operation has a single argument, *count*, which designates the number of children generated. The final primary variation operation is diagonal crossover [8] which returns the same number of solutions as are passed in. This variation node has one parameter, n, which determines the number of points used by the crossover operation.

3.2.3 Set Operation Nodes

The experiments reported in this paper employ two distinct set operations. The first is the union operation. This node takes two sets of solutions and returns the union of the sets passed into it. The other operation is the save operation called "Make Set". This operation saves a copy of the set passed into it. This set can be used elsewhere in the algorithm as explained in Section 3.2.4.

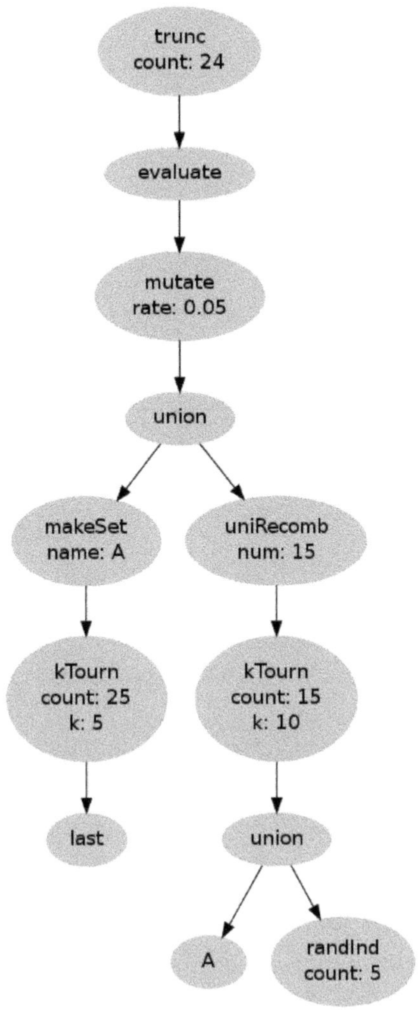

Figure 2: Example Parse Tree

```
Last = [initialize population]
evaluate(Last)
A = [ ]
while termination condition not met do
    X = kTournament(Last, k = 5,count =25)
    A = X
    Y = randInd(count = 5)
    Y = A + Y
    Y = kTournament(Y,k = 10, count = 15)
    Y = uniformRecombination(Y, count = 15)
    Z = X+Y
    Z = mutate(Z, rate = 5%)
    evaluate(Z)
    Last = truncate(Z, 24)
end while
evaluate(Last)
```

Figure 3: Example Parse Tree Generated Code

3.2.4 *Terminal Nodes*

The terminal nodes in this representation are sets of solutions. They can either be the 'Last' set returned by the previous iteration, a set that was created by the save operation, or a set of randomly created solutions. The saved sets persist from iteration to iteration such that if a set is referenced before it has been saved in a given iteration, it will use the save from the previous iteration. At the beginning of each run, the saved sets are set to the empty set and the 'Last' set is set to a randomly generated population of solutions. The randomly generated set of solutions terminal node creates a set of n solutions, n being one of its parameters, and returns that to its parent node.

3.2.5 *Utility Nodes*

There is currently one utility operation employed for use in the experiments. This node is the evaluation node which evaluates all of the solutions that are passed into it. Operations that can be added to this group in the future can include looping nodes and conditional nodes.

3.3 Meta-Algorithm

GP is employed to meta-evolve the BBSAs. The two primary variation operators employed are the standard subtree crossover and mutation altered to make the maximum number of nodes being added a user defined value. Another mutation operation was added to this algorithm that with equal chance randomizes the size of the initial 'Last' set or selects a random node from the parse-tree and randomizes the parameters if it has any; if the node does not have any parameters, the mutation is executed again. To ensure that the genetic program produces good BBSAs, the ones which do not evaluate any solutions are discarded upon generation.

3.3.1 *Black-Box Search Algorithm*

Each individual in the GP population encodes a BBSA. To evaluate the fitness of an individual, its encoded BBSA is run for a user-defined number of times. Each run of the BBSA begins with population initialization, followed by the parse-tree being repeatedly evaluated until one of the termination criteria is met. Once a run of the BBSA is completed, the 'Last' set and all saved sets are evaluated to ensure that the final fitness value is representative of the final population. Logging is performed during these runs to track when the BBSA converges and what the average solution quality and best current solution is.

The fitness of a BBSA is estimated by computing the fitness function that it employs on the solutions it evolves averaged over multiple runs. Parsimony pressure is added to temper the growth of the parse trees. The parsimony pressure is calculated by multiplying the number of nodes in a tree by a user defined value. The parsimony pressure is subtracted from the best solution in the final population averaged over all runs to get the fitness of the BBSA.

Learning conditions were added to terminate poor solutions before they are fully evaluated in order to ameliorate the very computationally intensive nature of hyper-heuristics analogously to [11]. This is accomplished by applying four limiting factors. First of all, if a BBSA exceeds the maximum number of evaluations, then it will automatically be terminated mid-run. Secondly, there is a maximum number of iterations that the BBSA may perform before it will halt. This addition of an iteration limit adds pressure

Number of Samples	Bit-Length	Trap Size
1	100	5
2	200	5
3	105	7
4	210	7
5	300	5

Table 1: Problem Configurations for Multi-Sampling Test. Each test includes prior tests' problem configurations; e.g., the run in which there are two problem configurations uses the first two problem configurations shown.

to evolve algorithms with more evaluations per iteration. Thirdly, the algorithm counts the relative number of operations performed. Each node represents an operation, and these operations can take a significant amount of time to perform. A weight is associated with each node that represents an estimation of how many operations that node takes per input solution. Once a node is executed, that weight is added to a running total of the operations for that run. Once the limit is reached, the run will end. This is to prevent inefficient algorithms which despite evaluating few solutions incur a high computational cost. The fourth method terminates algorithms which have converged based on not having improved in i iterations.

3.3.2 Multi-Sampling

A major issue identified in [12] is the problem of over-specialization when training on a single problem configuration of a given problem class. Following the approach suggested in [12], the BBSAs are executed on multiple problem configurations of the problem class of interest. On each problem configuration, the BBSAs run a user-specified number of times. This addition allows the user to control the robustness of the generated BBSA. If the user requires a BBSA that performs very consistently, then running the algorithm with more problem configurations is beneficial.

3.3.3 External Verification

To assure that the performance of the evolved BBSA is consistent with its performance reported during evolution, executable code is generated to represent the parse tree as a full BBSA. This is done to externally verify that the performance that the GP shows for a given BBSA is accurate when actually implemented. The generated code is used in all of the experiments to insure unbiased execution of the BBSAs. An example of a parse tree and pseudo-code generated can be found in Figure 2 and Figure 3. This verification was employed for the testing of the BBSAs in all experiments.

4. EXPERIMENTS

To demonstrate that employing multi-sample evaluation of the BBSA reduces the probability of over-specialization, the algorithm was run on a series of multi-sampling levels, where a level is defined by the number of training problem configurations it samples. Once the BBSA has been evolved with a given multi-sampling level, it is tested on a superset of problem configurations to determine the preliminary robustness of the BBSA and to demonstrate that they can out perform a standard EA.

Bit-Length	Trap Size
100	5
200	5
105	7
210	7
300	5
99	9
198	9
150	5
250	5
147	7
252	7

Table 2: Problem Configurations that were used to test the robustness of the BBSA.

Parameter	Value
Population Size	50
Children per Generation	20
Parent Selection k	15
Recombination	Uniform
Mutation Rate	5%
Survival Selection	Truncation

Table 3: EA Configurations

The classic Deceptive Trap problem [3] is employed as benchmark in this paper. It divides a bit-string into traps of size j bits each which are scored using the following equation where t is equal to the sum of the bit values in the trap.

$$trap(t) = \begin{cases} j - 1 - t & (t < j) \\ j & (t = j) \end{cases}$$

This problem was chosen to compare the results in this paper with those in [12], where BBSAs were evolved and suffered from over-specialization.

The BBSAs were evolved with a multi-sampling level from one to five. The problem configurations are shown in Table 1. Each run includes the problem configurations from the runs before; e.g., the runs with two samples use the problem configurations from the first two rows. For each evolved BBSA, code was generated to determine its robustness externally from the evolution. To test the preliminary robustness of the generated BBSAs, they were run on a super-set of problem configurations as shown in Table 2. This set includes the training set to validate that the fitness found during evolution is accurate.

The EA has an initial population of 50 and generates 20 children each generation. It uses k-Tournament with replacement for parent selection with k being 15, uniform recombination, bit-flip mutation with a 5% rate, and truncation survivor selection. The EA parameter settings are summarized in Table 3. These values were selected to be similar to those in [12] with minor hand tuning to perform well with the first problem configuration shown in Table 1.

For these experiments, four BBSAs were evolved at each multi-sampling level. During the evolution each problem configuration was run five times. Meaning that in the experiment with multi-sampling level one, each BBSA evaluation is five runs where with multi-sampling level five, each

Parameter	Value
Evaluations	5000
Initial Population	100
Children per Generation	40
k-Tournament	8
Sub-Tree Crossover Probability	30%
Sub-Tree Mutation Probability	30%
Alternate Mutation Probability	40%
Alternate Mutation Depth	5
Parsimony Pressure	0.001
Maximum Operations	5,000,000
Maximum Iterations	10,000
Maximum Evaluations in BBSA	100,000

Table 4: GP Configurations

BBSA evaluation is twenty-five runs. All of the testing data was produced by executing the code generated by the meta-algorithm. Each of the evolved BBSAs were executed 30 times for each of the problem configurations. Each algorithm was run for 100,000 evaluations. These results were compared to an EA executed 30 times for each of the problem configurations.

After collecting results from the first experiment which was focused on determining the preliminary robustness increase caused by multi-sampling, a secondary experiment was run to study the effect of multi-sampling on the performance landscape across a wide set of problem configurations. The areas of interest in this experiment are the problem configurations that were significantly different from the trained problem configurations. The BBSA with the largest fallibility, where fallibility indicates the difference between best and worst performance on the test problem configurations, was selected from each multi-sampling level to demonstrate a worst case scenario. These BBSAs, along with an EA, were run on all problem configurations with k from 4 to 20 inclusive and bit-lengths from roughly 70 to 500. The algorithms were run five times on each problem configuration.

All of the experiments were conducted under the same settings. The meta-algorithm was run for 5000 evaluations. The initial population was 100 individuals and each generation 40 new individuals were created. k-tournament selection with replacement and $k = 8$ was employed for parent selection. The sub-tree crossover and mutation operations had 30% chance of being used while the alternate mutation had a probability of 40%. The parsimony pressure for the tree size was 0.001. The maximum number of operations the BBSAs could use was 5,000,000, the maximum number of iterations was 10,000, and the maximum number of evaluations in the BBSA was 100,000. All the parameter settings for the meta-algorithm are summarized in Table 4. Due to the high computational cost of running hyper-heuristics, only minimal tuning of the meta-algorithm is feasible.

For the generation of the BBSAs, heuristic constraints were employed to limit various parameters to reasonable values. The maximum number of individuals in the initial population was set to 50. The range of individuals selected by selection nodes was set to be from 1 to 25 inclusive. The range of the k value used for the k-tournament is from 1 to 25 inclusive. The range of the number of points for diagonal crossover is from 1 to 25 points inclusive. All the parameter settings for the BBSA are summarized in Table 5.

Parameter	Value
Runs per Problem Configuration	5
Maximum Initial Population	50
k Value Range	[1,25]
Number of Selected Individuals Range	[1,25]
Crossover Points Range	[1,25]
Randomly Generated Set Size Range	[1,25]
Children for Uniform Recombination Range	[1,25]

Table 5: Black-Box Search Algorithm Settings

Level	Run	Train Fit.	Test Fit.	Fallibility
1	1	1.0	0.976	0.094
1	2	1.0	0.999	8.33 E-3
1	3	0.944	0.883	0.082
1	4	0.976	0.894	0.224
2	1	0.997	0.996	0.023
2	2	0.992	0.959	0.130
2	3	0.966	0.970	0.054
2	4	0.979	0.947	0.120
3	1	0.965	0.966	0.050
3	2	0.984	0.980	0.065
3	3	0.899	0.886	0.059
3	4	0.926	0.898	0.073
4	1	0.976	0.999	5.00 E-3
4	2	0.973	0.969	.0903
4	3	0.982	0.975	0.059
4	4	0.993	0.999	5.00 E-3
5	1	0.973	0.977	0.050
5	2	0.893	0.879	0.035
5	3	0.850	0.850	0.045
5	4	0.955	0.986	0.029

Table 6: BBSA Experimental Results

5. RESULTS

The first experiment's results are summarized in Table 6. This table shows the fitness of the BBSAs at the end of evolution labelled as the 'Training Fit.'. The 'Test Fit.' is the averaged fitness across the testing set of problem configurations shown in Table 2. The 'Fallibility' field is the difference between the best and worst performing problem configuration for a given BBSA. As this number decreases, the BBSA can be said to be a more robust algorithm.

The comparison between the EA and the evolved BBSAs is shown in Table 7. The $-$ column represents the number of problem configurations that the EA performed better on than the BBSA. The $\sim$ column represents the number of problem configurations that there was no statistical difference between the EA and the BBSA. The $+$ column represents the number of problem configurations that the EA performs worse on than the BBSA. The t-test with $\alpha = 0.05$ was used to determine the statistically better algorithm.

To study the effect of multi-sampling on the performance landscape across a wide set of problem configurations, 3-dimensional plots were generated that represent the quality of solutions that can be found using different problem configurations. Figures 4-8 show the least robust BBSA evolved

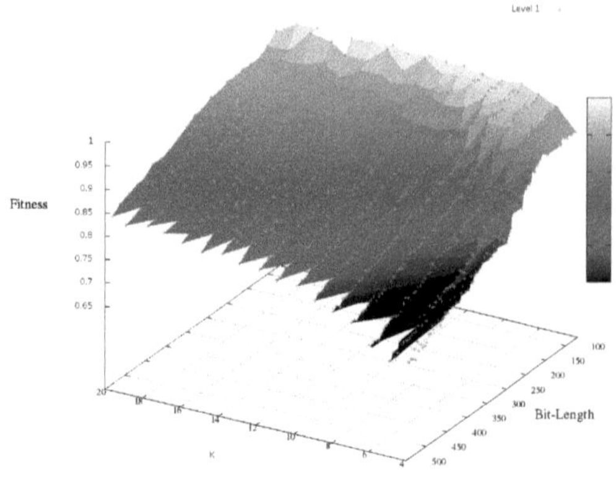

Figure 4: The worst BBSA found for multi-sampling level one, run on the problem configuration space.

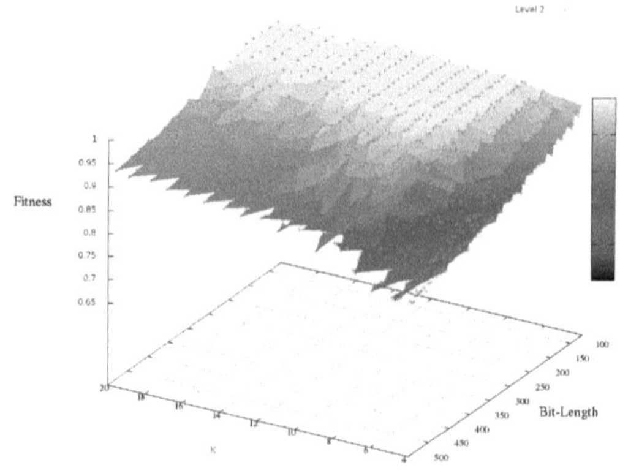

Figure 5: The worst BBSA found for multi-sampling level two, run on the problem configuration space.

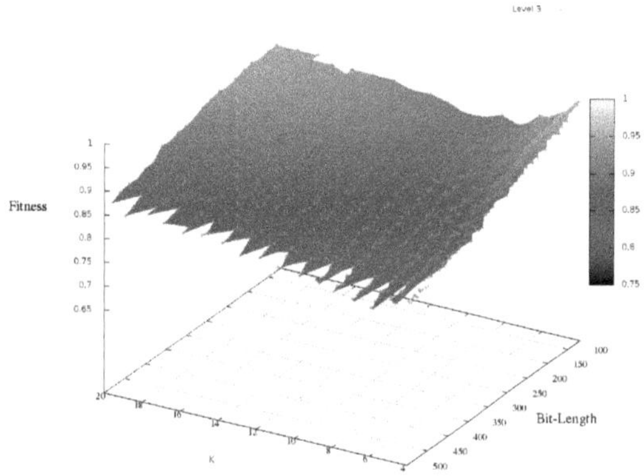

Figure 6: The worst BBSA found for multi-sampling level three, run on the problem configuration space.

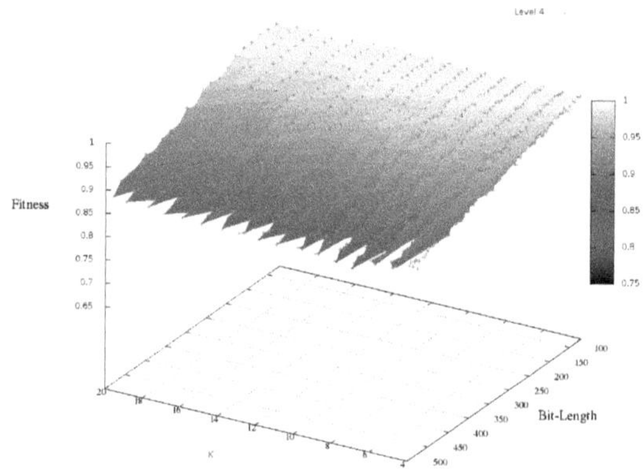

Figure 7: The worst BBSA found for multi-sampling level four, run on the problem configuration space.

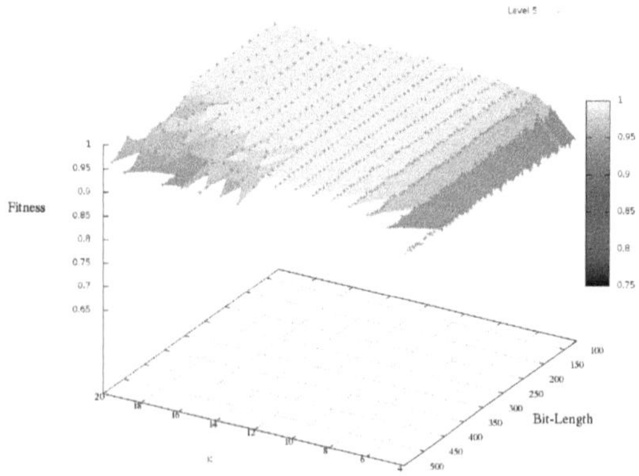

Figure 8: The worst BBSA found for multi-sampling level five, run on the problem configuration space.

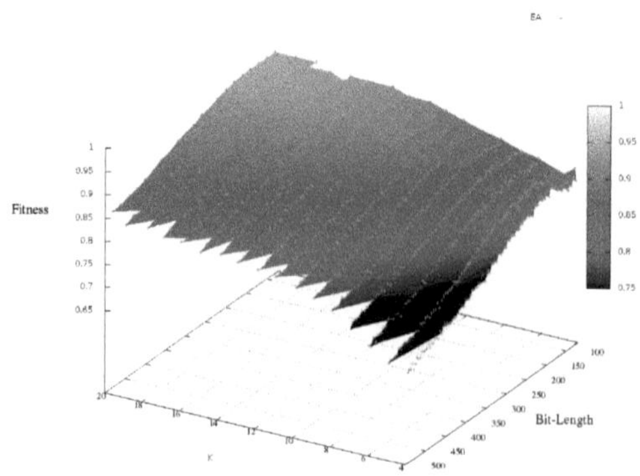

Figure 9: A standard EA run on the problem configuration space.

Level	Run	+	~	−
1	1	11	0	0
1	2	11	0	0
1	3	11	0	0
1	4	6	2	3
2	1	11	0	0
2	2	11	0	0
2	3	11	0	0
2	4	11	0	0
3	1	11	0	0
3	2	11	0	0
3	3	11	0	0
3	4	11	0	0
4	1	11	0	0
4	2	11	0	0
4	3	11	0	0
4	4	11	0	0
5	1	11	0	0
5	2	10	1	0
5	3	7	4	0
5	4	11	0	0

Table 7: This table is a summary of the comparison of the evolved BBSA and the standard EA.

at each multi sampling level. Figure 9 shows the baseline of a standard EA. These plots were generated averaging over five runs on each problem configuration.

6. DISCUSSION

The goal of the research reported in this paper is to show that increasing the multi-sampling level increases the robustness of the generated BBSAs. The two measurements of robustness that we chose to use were applicability and fallibility. Applicability is the size of the problem configuration space in which the BBSA performed higher than a given threshold value. Fallibility is the difference between the best and worst performing problem configuration. As the applicability increases and the fallibility decreases, the robustness of the BBSA increases. The results presented show that both of these happen as the multi-sampling level is increased.

T-tests were run on the selected testing problem configurations, the results of which are shown in Table 7. It can be seen that one of the BBSAs that was evolved with multi-sampling level one performed worse than the EA. From a practitioner's standpoint, this result would seem very surprising compared to its trained fitness. The runs of multi-sampling level five performed consistent with the trained fitness when compared to the EA.

Figure 4 shows the performance of the least robust BBSA found using multi-sampling level one when run on a wide variety of problem configurations. As can be seen, the BBSA performs well in the immediate area around the problem configuration that it was trained on ($k = 5$, $bit - length = 100$). Unsurprisingly, as the problem configuration gets farther away from the trained problem configuration, the fitness decreases. This algorithm performs similarly to other algorithms that are tuned to specific problem configurations. When compared to how the EA performs on the same problem configuration space in Figure 9, the BBSA outperforms the EA in problem configurations near the trained problem configuration, but performs at near the same level as the distance increases. As can be seen in figures 4-8, the variance in performance of the algorithm decreases as the multi-sampling level increases.

Training a BBSA on a larger number of training problem configurations improves the performance of the BBSA. However, in most cases, the improved performance is restricted to problem configurations that are relatively close to the trained problem configurations. These results look similar to the results shown in Figure 4 where near the trained problem configuration the BBSA performs well, but as the problem configuration differs more from the trained problem configuration, the BBSA performs poorly.

When multi-sampling is performed during the generation of the algorithm rather than solely the parameter tuning, the increased performance of the algorithm can be generalized to larger portions of the problem configuration space. As can can be seen in figures 4-8, the fallibility decreases as the multi-sample level increases. Note that the training sets that these algorithms were evolved on had problem configurations with k ranging from 5 to 7 and a $bit - length$ ranging from 100 to 300 and the problem configuration space shown in figures 4-8 includes a k from 4 to 20 and a $bit-length$ from approximately 75 to 500. This demonstrates the enhanced robustness of the BBSAs evolved with a higher multi-sampling level. This robustness is superior to that of strictly parameter optimization of a BBSA due to its ability to generalize to problem configurations much different to those trained on.

There was a case in which a BBSA evolved with a multi-sampling level of one, when tested, was shown to be robust. As in previous work [12], there is always the potential of producing a robust algorithm trained on a single sample; however, this is highly unreliable and the method introduced in this paper significantly increases the probability of evolving a robust BBSA.

One drawback of this method is the increased computational time that it requires. One cause of this increase are the additional runs that are necessary during the evaluation of a given BBSA. This extra computational time increases linearly with the multi-sampling level. It was noticed during testing and in the final results, that the experiments run at a higher multi-sampling level can have a lower average fitness. Due to this result, a trend in the applicability is not statistically discernible. As is shown in Table 6, the BBSAs evolved at multi-sampling level five had the lowest trained fitness. This is believed to be caused by the increased difficulty of finding an algorithm that performs well on all of the training problem configurations. These two aspects cause the computational time increase of $\Omega(L)$, with L being the multi-sampling level.

7. CONCLUSIONS

The research reported in this paper demonstrates that employing the proposed multi-sampling method tends to increase the robustness of evolved BBSAs. This method is shown to not only generate BBSAs that generalize to the problem configuration space close to the trained problem configurations, but to create BBSAs that have generalized to a much wider area of the problem configuration landscape. Though it is possible to evolve robust algorithms without using the multi-sampling method, it is shown that with a higher multi-sampling level, the general robustness of the evolved BBSA is increased along with the certainty that the evolved BBSA will indeed be robust.

The predominant disadvantage to this method is the increased computational time that is necessary to evolve high-performance BBSAs when using high multi-sampling levels. However, it is shown that it is possible to evolve high-performance BBSAs when using high multi-sampling levels that are also robust as shown in Table 6.

8. FUTURE WORK

The next step to improve upon the proposed approach is to perform run-time analysis of the BBSAs. This will help reveal what features cause the BBSAs to run slower compared to others. This allows the computational time necessary for running with a higher multi-sampling level to decrease which will make this approach more feasible for practitioners.

This multi-sampling approach also needs to be tested on a larger variety of problem classes to better understand how the multi-sampling level affects the robustness of evolved BBSAs. A larger variety of node operations may have to be added to allow this approach to create well-performing BBSAs. As well as testing this approach on other problem classes, an in depth study should be conducted to determine the correlation between the proximity of the training classes and the robustness of the resulting BBSAs.

Finally, multi-objective optimization should be introduced into the meta-algorithm such that it is capable of creating BBSAs that are not only robust, but quick to converge as well. This is necessary to enable the proposed method to evolve human-competitive BBSAs.

9. REFERENCES

[1] P. J. Angeline. Two Self-Adaptive Crossover Operators for Genetic Programming. In P. J. Angeline and K. E. Kinnear, Jr., editors, *Advances in Genetic Programming*, pages 89–109. MIT Press, Cambridge, MA, USA, 1996.

[2] E. Burke, M. Hyde, G. Kendall, G. Ochoa, E. Ozcan, and J. Woodward. Exploring Hyper-heuristic Methodologies with Genetic Programming. In C. Mumford and L. Jain, editors, *Computational Intelligence*, volume 1 of *Intelligent Systems Reference Library*, pages 177–201. Springer, 2009.

[3] K. Deb and D. Goldberg. Analyzing Deception in Trap Functions. In *Proceedings of FOGA II: the Second Workshop on Foundations of Genetic Algorithms*, pages 93–108, 1992.

[4] L. Dioşan and M. Oltean. Evolutionary Design of Evolutionary Algorithms. *Genetic Programming and Evolvable Machines*, 10(3):263–306, Sept. 2009.

[5] L. S. Diosan and M. Oltean. Evolving Evolutionary Algorithms Using Evolutionary Algorithms. In *Proceedings of GECCO 2007 - Genetic And Evolutionary Computation Conference*, GECCO '07, pages 2442–2449, New York, NY, USA, 2007. ACM.

[6] B. Edmonds. Meta-Genetic Programming: Co-evolving the Operators of Variation. CPM Report 98-32, Centre for Policy Modelling, Manchester Metropolitan University, UK, Aytoun St., Manchester, M1 3GH. UK, Jan. 1998.

[7] A. Eiben and S. Smit. Parameter tuning for configuring and analyzing evolutionary algorithms. *Swarm and Evolutionary Computation*, 1(1):19 – 31, 2011.

[8] A. E. Eiben and C. H. van Kemenade. Diagonal Crossover in Genetic Algorithms for Numerical Optimization. *Journal of Control and Cybernetics*, 26(3):447–465, 1997.

[9] B. W. Goldman and D. R. Tauritz. Self-Configuring Crossover. In *Proceedings of GECCO 2011 - Genetic And Evolutionary Computation Conference*, GECCO '11, pages 575–582, New York, NY, USA, 2011. ACM.

[10] N. Lourenço, F. Pereira, and E. Costa. Evolving Evolutionary Algorithms. In *Proceedings of GECCO 2012 - Genetic And Evolutionary Computation Conference*, GECCO Companion '12, pages 51–58, New York, NY, USA, 2012. ACM.

[11] N. Lourenço, F. B. Pereira, and E. Costa. The Importance of the Learning Conditions in Hyper-heuristics. In *Proceeding of the Fifteenth Annual Conference on Genetic and Evolutionary Computation Conference*, GECCO '13, pages 1525–1532, New York, NY, USA, 2013. ACM.

[12] M. A. Martin and D. R. Tauritz. Evolving Black-box Search Algorithms Employing Genetic Programming. In *Proceeding of the Fifteenth Annual Conference Companion on Genetic and Evolutionary Computation Conference Companion*, GECCO '13 Companion, pages 1497–1504, New York, NY, USA, 2013. ACM.

[13] M. A. Martin and D. R. Tauritz. Multi-Sample Evolution of Robust Black-Box Search Algorithms. In *Proceeding of the Sixteenth Annual Conference Companion on Genetic and Evolutionary Computation Conference Companion*, GECCO '14 Companion, New York, NY, USA, 2014. ACM.

[14] M. Oltean. Evolving Evolutionary Algorithms Using Linear Genetic Programming. *Evolutionary Computation*, 13(3):387–410, Sept. 2005.

[15] M. Oltean and C. Grosan. Evolving Evolutionary Algorithms Using Multi Expression Programming. In *Proceedings of The 7th European Conference on Artificial Life*, pages 651–658. Springer-Verlag, 2003.

[16] S. Smit and A. Eiben. Comparing Parameter Tuning Methods for Evolutionary Algorithms. In *IEEE Congress on Evolutionary Computation, 2009. CEC '09*, pages 399–406, May 2009.

[17] E. Smorodkina and D. Tauritz. Toward Automating EA Configuration: the Parent Selection Stage. In *IEEE Congress on Evolutionary Computation, 2007. CEC '07*, pages 63–70, Sept. 2007.

[18] J. R. Woodward and J. Swan. Automatically Designing Selection Heuristics. In *Proceedings of GECCO 2011 - Genetic And Evolutionary Computation Conference*, GECCO '11, pages 583–590, New York, NY, USA, 2011. ACM.

[19] J. R. Woodward and J. Swan. The Automatic Generation of Mutation Operators for Genetic Algorithms. In *Proceedings of GECCO 2012 - Genetic And Evolutionary Computation Conference*, GECCO Companion '12, pages 67–74, New York, NY, USA, 2012. ACM.

Benchmarks That Matter For Genetic Programming

John Woodward
Computing Science and Mathematics
University of Stirling
FK9 4LA Scotland UK
jrw@cs.stir.ac.uk

Simon Martin
Computing Science and Mathematics
University of Stirling
FK9 4LA Scotland UK
spm@cs.stir.ac.uk

Jerry Swan
Computing Science and Mathematics
University of Stirling
FK9 4LA Scotland UK
jsw@cs.stir.ac.uk

ABSTRACT

There have been several papers published relating to the practice of benchmarking in machine learning and Genetic Programming (GP) in particular. In addition, GP has been accused of targeting over-simplified 'toy' problems that do not reflect the complexity of real-world applications that GP is ultimately intended. There are also theoretical results that relate the performance of an algorithm with a probability distribution over problem instances, and so the current debate concerning benchmarks spans from the theoretical to the empirical.

The aim of this article is to consolidate an emerging theme arising from these papers and suggest that benchmarks should not be arbitrarily selected but should instead be drawn from an underlying probability distribution that reflects the problem instances which the algorithm is likely to be applied to in the real-world. These probability distributions are effectively dictated by the application domains themselves (essentially data-driven) and should thus re-engage the owners of the originating data.

A consequence of properly-founded benchmarking leads to the suggestion of meta-learning as a methodology for automatically designing algorithms rather than manually designing algorithms. A secondary motive is to reduce the number of research papers that propose new algorithms but do not state in advance what their purpose is (i.e. in what context should they be applied). To put the current practice of GP benchmarking in a particular harsh light, one might ask what the performance of an algorithm on Koza's lawnmower problem (a favourite toy-problem of the GP community) has to say about its performance on a *very* real-world cancer data set: the two are completely unrelated.

Keywords

genetic programming (GP), evolutionary computation, function optimization, machine learning, meta-learning, hyper-heuristics, no free lunch theorems (NFL).

GECCO'14, July 12–16, 2014, Vancouver, BC, Canada.

ACM 978-1-4503-2881-4/14/07
http://dx.doi.org/10.1145/2598394.2609875 ...$15.00.

1. INTRODUCTION

The aim of this paper is to highlight an emerging crisis in GP by connecting a number of recently published papers: benchmarking is poorly practiced in the GP community. We describes a methodology [4] that offers a natural solution to this crisis (one to which GP itself is ideally suited). [11, 9, 20, 33]. We summarize each of these four papers in the following points.

- Machine learning has become largely disconnected from the communities of domain experts who provided the data sets in the first place [33].
- GP lacks decent benchmark problems and has been singled-out as having elevated the status of toy problems as an effective test bed, many papers being published do not even tackle real-world problems [20, 34].
- Recent theoretical results link the performance of an algorithm with the probability distribution from which the problem instances are drawn [9, 26].
- Meta-learning [11, 23], and in particular the use of GP as a hyper-heuristic to automatically design algorithms [4], offers a natural vehicle to address the issue of how to design an algorithm for a problem class (i.e. probability distribution over problem instances) at hand, and therefore provide a new set of interesting benchmarks.

The contribution of this paper is not a new algorithm, theorem or application, but to drive the current debate about GP benchmarks, and emphasize the emerging trend in hyper-heuristics for automated design as a way-forward. The suggestion is, in view of recent theoretical results, is that GP can be employed in a hyper-heuristics framework to automatically design algorithms for problem instances drawn from a probability distribution.

In the remainder of the introduction we consider the purpose of metaheuristics and how that purpose is demonstrated by the practice of benchmarking. We then consider a recent NFL result relevant to benchmarking [9, 26], and a related issue in GP, namely that GP cannot alter its own search bias from one problem instance to the next and therefore cannot tune itself to the benchmark problem class [36]. We use the terms algorithm and metaheuristic interchangeably, as we do with problem instance and (objective) function.

1.1 Metaheuristics.

Metaheuristics [31, 19] sample intractably large search spaces so there is a trade-off when deciding which metaheuristic to apply to given problem instances. It is intended that a metaheuristic returns a "good enough, soon enough, cheap enough" solution to the current problem instance [3]. However, metaheuristics offer little in the way of guarantees about either the *quality* of the solution, or the *quantity* of computational time required.

The metaheuristic research literature is peppered with largely biologically inspired papers which begin "we propose a novel algorithm ..." [29], but rarely is it said what purpose the algorithm serves, that is, on what problem class (probability distribution of problem instances) will the proposed algorithm outperform other algorithms. While there has been some theoretical progress in understanding the behaviour of metaheuristics and GP in particular [24], the field is still largely empirical and the most common way to compare metaheuristics is still benchmarking.

1.2 Benchmarking.

Benchmarking is the practice of taking a set of problem instances, often from a diverse set of domains, and demonstrating an algorithm's performance on this set, comparing it with the performance of other algorithms. The typical approach by academic researchers is to propose a new algorithm and then compare it to other state-of-the-art algorithms in the research literature by comparing their performance on benchmarks.

A central assumption of machine learning is the test data is drawn from the same distribution as the training data [10]. It will become apparent in this paper that benchmark problem instances should be drawn from the same distribution as the real-world problem instances. In other words, if we employ GP as a hyper-heuristic to automatically design algorithms the test benchmark problem instances should be drawn from the same distribution as the training instances. It is stated that there is a hyper-focus on benchmark data sets [33], and that GP has a "toy-problem problem"; often benchmark problem instances are too simple [20]. In a similar vein to [20], this paper is not a list of benchmark recommendations, but is instead aimed at contributing to the debate.

1.3 No Free Lunch.

NFL results have been expressed informally as statements such as "over all problems, no optimization algorithm outperforms any other", or " no machine learning algorithm generalizes better than any other over the space of all problems". These results have been largely ignored by practitioners as we are rarely interested in the set of all problems. However, a new result [9, 26] (which we formally present in Section 3) states that for a given algorithm and *any* probability distribution over a set of functions, that there exists another algorithm and probability distribution with identical performance. Importantly, this result *does not depend on a uniform distribution*, as many previous NFL interpretations have done. We can ask ourselves what are the implications of this result regarding benchmarking. One implication of this result it that we should state (in some way) what probability distribution of problem instances the metaheuristic is intended for. Or to phrase it another way, a metaheuristic should not be proposed without being associated with a problem class (probability distribution over problem instances). A metaheuristic should be fit-for-purpose, that purpose being defined by the problem class. Therefore a metaheuristic should not be proposed in isolation but in the context of a problem class.

1.4 Genetic Programming.

GP is a metaheuristic which operates on a space of programs. As GP offers a way to automatically generate programs (with loops and conditional statements), there are many potential applications, perhaps more so than other machine learning techniques because GP can evolve anything representable on a computer (cf. decision trees which are a limited representation).

GP borrows concepts from natural evolution: organisms *adapt* to fit their environment. In the case of GP, this means that programs evolve to fit the problem instance and the fittest programs survive. It is true that the *population of programs* adapts when GP is applied to a single problem instance, but *the way* GP searches from one problem instance to the next typically does not (cannot) alter [36]. Therefore, if we select a GP algorithm, it may perform poorly on those particular problem instances, and the GP algorithm has no way to improve its performance on future problem instances (except for intervention by a human programmer). In other words, the behaviour of GP is completely determined by the bias provided by its human designer. However, a meta-learning system, such as GP as a hyper-heuristic [4] can do this off-line. On a training set GP can alter bias, which is then fixed in a testing phase [38, 37, 12].

The outline of the remainder of this article is as follows. In Section 2 we connect together a number of recent papers relating to metaheuristics, GP, meta-learning and NFL. Section 3 presents a mathematical framework and theorems illustrating the trade-off between metaheuristic performance and problem classes. In Section 4 we give examples of problem classes pertaining to bin-packing and the traveling salesman problem. In Section 5 we summarize the argument that benchmarks need to be relevant, not isolated, and that meta-learning and hyper-heuristics to generate heuristics can address this.

2. BACKGROUND WORK

2.1 Reconnecting Machine Learning To The Real-world.

The academic practice of machine learning has become disconnected from the communities which originally supplied the data sets [33]. Thus, as these communities rarely communicate, there is little long-term benefit to the application-domain community (or in fact the machine learning community itself). Wagstaff [33] concludes that progress in the field of machine learning has little impact on the community that initially supplied the actual data set. Data sets are simply treated as rows and columns of numerical data to be freely downloaded and the real-world *context* of the data has been lost.

2.2 Realistic Benchmarks for Genetic Programming.

McDermott et al. [20] criticize the lack of rigor in the choice of benchmark problem instances. The standard, often-used problem instances (so-called toy problems, where the optimal solutions are often *known* in advance) do not reflect the complexities which are experienced when tackling real-world problems, where the optimal solutions are often *not known*. This defeats the whole purpose of applying a metaheuristic to a problem as the solution (global optimum) is already known.

The development of a machine learning algorithm is typically a three stage process; training, testing and application [22]. In the training stage, the algorithm learns by adjusting its bias (probability distributions). Its performance is confirmed on an independent test set to check that over-fitting is not a problem (i.e. we have generalized beyond the training set). Once this stage has been passed to the satisfaction of the GP researcher, then the algorithm can be applied problem instances from the application domain. The set of training and testing instances should represent the application instances, and therefore we should make some attempt to describe what characterizes these problem instances, for example their source (see 4). Johnson [18] states; "use instance test-beds that can support general conclusions". So if we demonstrate the utility of a metaheuristic on a set of test problem instances, then it follows that this set should be drawn from the same probability distribution as in the application stage as is common practice in the machine learning community, but no so much the optimization community. It seems as if GP has become separated from the third, and arguably the most important part of the developmental process; the application.

2.3 No Free Lunch And Benchmarking With Problem Classes.

NFL effectively states that given a uniform distribution over the set of *all* problem instances, no single algorithm outperforms any other [35]. This sounds like a negative and defeatist result, as it comprehensively covers *all* functions. NFL holds for cross-validation [39] and early-stopping [6], two major sources of bias in machine learning. We are not aware of a NFL result for feature selection [2], for example, but nor would we be surprised if one existed. However feature selection, which is based on information theory, remains a useful bias in practice, as are cross-validation and early-stopping.

NFL has become the holy grail in some research communities [14], and been called a "show-stopper" [11] (which was firmly answered in the negative and on which this paper builds its implications). NFL applies to a vanishingly small number of the subsets of all functions and is unlikely to apply to real-world situations [15, 16, 17]. It has conclusively been shown by theoretical analysis, that on restricted sets of problems, one algorithm *does* outperform another [7, 8]. We advocate that these restrictions should be imposed by the application domain itself. In this paper we interpret "restricted sets of problems" as probability distributions over problem instances (i.e. problem classes).

Links have been made between the performance of an algorithm and the probability distribution over benchmark problem instances [9, 26]. An earlier similar result connects the performance of an algorithm on a single problem instance [28]. Essentially two search algorithms (which are permutations of one another), and two functions (which are the inverse permutations of one another), have identical and therefore indistinguishable performance. Further results have been obtained concerning the use of arbitrary benchmarks to evaluate randomized algorithms [9, 26].

2.4 Bias In Algorithms And Problem Classes.

Mitchell [21] defines bias as any basis (probability) for choosing one generalization over another, other than strict consistency with the observed training problem instances. Specifying a bias is equivalent to specifying an algorithm as we are only interested in the output of the algorithm (i.e. what it does, not how it does it). Bias determines which items in the search space the algorithm will visit. Mitchell [21] states that there needs to be a bias in order to learn. Similarly, there must be bias over the problem class if there is anything to be learnt about the problem instances on *average*.

A problem class F is a probability distribution over problem instances $F = (p_f(f_1), \ldots, p_f(f_i), \ldots)$. Each time an algorithm is executed, it will return the best solution it has found. If we consider an algorithm as a stochastic search process then when the is algorithm executed again, it may yield a different solution. The *bias* of an algorithm a on a function f is the probability that a will return a given solution. This notion of problem classes and algorithms seen as probability distributions corresponds to the geometric perspective in [35] and Lemma 1 in [11]. Essentially, to gain good performance of an algorithm on a problem class, we want the bias of the algorithm to align with the bias of the problem class. We want the algorithm to sample the space with high probability, were we expect solutions to be found. If we increase the probability of an algorithm sampling some region(s) of the search space, then it follows that the probability of sampling the remainder of the search space will decrease (as probability is conserved). We want the algorithms to visit part of the search space solutions are likely to reside, given the problem class at hand.

2.5 From No Free Lunch To Meta-learning.

NFL is of little relevance to research in machine learning (who is interested in learning or optimizing a white noise effectively random function [13]). However, NFL *does* make the contribution that whenever an algorithm performs well on some problem instances, then it must perform poorly on some other problem instances [11]. In the absence of bias, enumerating a set of fixed-arity binary functions demonstrates that, given a subset of input-output pairs (i.e. the training set) then it is impossible to generalize over the remaining input-output pairs, (i.e. the testing set) [11]. This result is referred to as Conservation of Generalization [27]. [11] further make the claim that this theorem supports the argument for meta-learning.

Let us take the example of classification [10]. The task is to design a classifier, which maps an example e to a class c (i.e. $f(e) = c$). Domain experts may well be interested in the problem of designing a classifier for a single problem (e.g. automatic number plate recognition: mapping photographs of vehicle licence plates to the plate number). However, as machine learning researchers we are usually interested in a method of producing classification algorithms [22, 25]. Given that we (metaheuristic researchers) are interested in, not a single classification problem, but many, this gives us a probability distribution of problem instances F (i.e. a problem class). In [11] the following Lemma is proved: knowing F, the probability of encountering an arbitrary function f, is equivalent to knowing $p(c|e)$, the probability of class membership for an arbitrary example e. The question then is how to arrive at $p(c|e)$, and one answer is meta-learning to which we now turn our attention.

2.6 Meta-learning

Meta-learning (also called 'learning to learn' [32] and hyper-heuristics [4]) is the idea that the base-level learns about single problem instances, and the meta-level learns about the problem class (i.e. a sample of problem instances drawn from the probability distribution associated with the problem class) [32]. In principle there is no difference between learning at the base-level and meta-level. Therefore just as a central assumption in machine learning is that the training and test data at the base-level are drawn from the same probability distribution, so too should the training and test instances be drawn from the same probability distribution (i.e. problem class). In both cases the search process can be thought of as being conducted over a set of items in a search space. In the former, the set of items being solutions to a problem instance, and the latter either being learning algorithms or some component (e.g. parameters) of the learning algorithm [1]. The meta-level learns invariants of the problem class. Consider the example of problem instances of face recognition of individual people. An invariant common across all face recognition tasks include translational and rotational invariance (i.e. if any face, is rotated or translated, it is still the same face) [32]. If an automated learning system is to learn about a set of related problem instances, then we should ask what we suspect these instances have in common. Just as we would not expect a machine learning algorithm to learn a source of random noise, nor should we expect algorithms to perform well on unrelated (i.e. randomly selected) problem instances. Meta-learning offers a way of automatically building learning algorithms in response to a specific problem class.

3. A MATHEMATICAL FRAMEWORK

We begin this section with a presentation of an established framework for search operators [28, 30, 17]. The two theorems below are taken from [26, 9]. Let X and Y be finite sets and $f : X \to Y$ be *an objective function* (i.e. $y = f(x)$), and $\mathcal{F}$ is the set of all such functions. The domain X and co-domain Y are fixed but f may vary. Let σ be a permutation. As $|X|$ and $|Y|$ are finite, so too is $|\mathcal{F}|$. Define a *trace* T_m (of size m $(0 \leq m \leq |X|)$) corresponding to f to be a sequence of pairs $(x, y) \in X \times Y$ where x components are unique. Note $T_{|\mathcal{F}|} \equiv f : X \to Y$ as $T_{|\mathcal{F}|}$ contains all the information about f i.e. $T_{|\mathcal{F}|}$ is effectively a look-up-table for f. X^m has corresponding projections $T^x_m : T_m \to X^m$ and $T^y_m : T_m \to Y^m$.

$T_m = [(x_0, f(x_0)), \ldots, (x_m, f(x_m))]$
$T^x_m = [(x_0), \ldots, (x_m)]$
$T^y_m = [(f(x_0)), \ldots, (f(x_m))]$

A trace is a list of the sampled items x_i in the search space X, together with their associated objective values $f(x_i)$. T^x_m is a list of unique items visited (i.e. a permutation of X) and T^y_m is the list of the corresponding objective values.

We define a *search operator* as a function $a : T_m \to X$ which takes a trace T_m and returns x with $x \notin T^x_m$. Thus, application of the search operator a on the objective function f builds a longer trace.

$$T_{m+1} = T_m \oplus (a(T_m), f(a(T_m)))$$

where $\oplus$ appends $(a(T_m), f(a(T_m)))$ to the end of T_m We define a *performance vector* $v_m(a, f) = T^y_m$ (i.e. the performance vector is a list of values in Y, corresponding to the order in which the domain values are sampled in X). We define a *performance measure* $M : v_m \to \mathbb{R}$. We define a *problem class* F to be a probability distribution over $f \in \mathcal{F}$, i.e. the probability $F(f)$ of encountering f as a function optimization problem. The overall performance measure $M_0(a)$ is given by:

$$M_0(a) = \sum_{f \in \mathcal{F}} F(f) M(v(a, f))$$

[30] (i.e. the performance measure is now simply the weighted sum of the performance on each individual function, weighted by the probability of sampling that function). We define a *probabilistic performance vector* $V_m(A, F)$ where the i component of $V_m(A, F)$, is the average of the ith component of T^y_m, generated from the pair (a, f) with a and f drawn from A and F We say an NFL result applies to F if and only if $M_0(a) = M_0(b)$ for any pair of search operators a and b.

Theorem 1. Given an objective function f, a search operator a, a permutation σ and m $(0 \leq m \leq |X|)$

$$v_m(\sigma(a), f) = v_m(a, \sigma(f))$$

This result is summed up as follows. a search operator $\sigma(a)$ applied to a function f and a search operator a applied to a function $\sigma(f)$ have the same performance as they produce identical y-component traces T^y_m.

Theorem 2. Given a probability distribution F over the set of all functions $\mathcal{F}$, and a probability distribution A over the set of all search operators $\mathcal{A}$, and m with $(0 \leq m \leq |X|)$, there exists a probability distribution $G = F(\sigma)$ over all functions, and a probability distribution $B = A(\sigma)$ over the set of all search operators such that

$$V_m(A, F) = V_m(B, G)$$

In short, the implication of this theorem is the bias of an algorithm needs to align with the bias of the probability distribution over functions.

4. DISCUSSION

In this section we discuss two examples (traveling salesman problem (TSP) and bin packing) of application domains that naturally give rise to problem classes. As it has been established in the previous section, from a theoretical point of view it only makes sense to compare algorithms on problem instances drawn from a given probability distribution. As we do not have explicit access to these distributions, we have to do with samples taken from them, as is done in machine learning.

4.1 Bin Packing As An Example Of Problem Classes.

Let us consider how problem classes arise naturally in the real-world. Imagine two logistics companies, each with a different customer base. These will each give rise to two different sets of bin-packing problem instances (associated with two different probability distributions of item sizes) and therefore can be considered to be drawn from two bin-packing problem classes. The two companies are therefore the source of two different problem classes.

To put benchmarking in the specific terms of the domain of online bin-packing, there should not be a "standard" set of benchmarks, as the problem instances we solve will belong to specific probability distributions of item sizes. While we can have a "general" (all round) bin-packing solver i.e. one trained on a uniform distribution of item sizes in the range, there is always room for specialization if we have information about the problem class (i.e. given we have items in the range [lower bound, upper bound]). It has been shown that bin packing algorithms that were automatically designed for a specific problem class outperform bin packing algorithms that were designed for different problem classes [5]. Furthermore, we can train our algorithm on bin packing problem instances of a known range of sizes, and test the algorithm on problem instances with the *same* range of sizes but different number of items while still achieving scalable performance.

4.2 Traveling Salesman Problem As An Example Of Problem Classes.

The Traveling Salesman Problem (TSP) is the problem of finding a tour that visits all cities in a set only once, while minimizing the total distance travelled. TSP problem instances could be generated by the following two different methods. One TSP problem class corresponding to points uniformly distributed in the unit square. It turns out, one can obtain very good estimates of what the expected value of that bound (i.e. tour length) is for any number of cities [18]. An alternative TSP problem class could be cities distributed according to a Gaussian distribution over the unit circle. Either a theoretical or empirical analysis would give expectation values for any number of cities assuming a given TSP problem class (i.e. probability distribution over TSP instances).

Let us extend the artificial example of square and circular TSP problem classes to a real-world situation. An example of a real-world TSP problem class would be having delivery points distributed according to a population density of customers for a given company. A set of TSP problem instances generated by different company (possibly is a different location) will, more than likely, have a different probability distribution associated with it. And it is this difference in probability distributions which will give one algorithm leverage over another. To really emphasize the point that real problem instances are grounded in a problem class, it is hard to see how a TSP instance could arise without being in the context of other TSP instances. There are rarely one-off TSP instances we want to solve, but typically a whole sequence of TSP instances generated by a single source (e.g. a logistics company).

4.3 The Comparison of Algorithms On Problem Classes.

One measure of the performance of an algorithm is to examine its behaviour on a single problem instance. However, it does not make sense to compare single runs of an algorithm, as they are stochastic so need to be executed multiple times. Neither are we typically interested in a single problem instance anyway [7], but typically a set of problem instances [32]. We could compare two stochastic algorithms by repeatedly executing them on a single problem instance. However, this is somewhat artificial as we only want to execute an algorithm once on a given problem instance. It seems to make more sense to compare our algorithms on multiple problem instances drawn from a problem class (i.e. one algorithm is only run once on one problem instance).

Also when developing metaheuristics, it is tempting to test them on benchmark problem instances during the development (training) stage. And if the performance is poor we reengineer the metaheuristic. However, if a problem instance is used in the development stage, it should not later be used again to demonstrate the utility of the metaheuristic. In other words we should adopt a strict machine learning regime, which separates training and testing problem instances. A set of benchmark instances should therefore be representative of the underlying problem class of interest, which are used in the development stage to learn about the problem class, and a separate set of test problem instances are used to show something of use has been learned in the training phase which can be used in the testing phase. In short, training and testing instances should be separate and not contaminate one another. Developing a metaheuristic by using problem instances in the training phase, and then using those instances in the testing phase to demonstrate the performance of the algorithm for the purposes of publication is equivalent in machine learning to over-fitting.

4.4 Sampling To Estimate Probability Distributions.

We usually do not have explicit access to the probability distribution over the set of problem instances, except in the case of toy problems (where we can define our own probability distribution). We can only obtain samples of problem instances from real-world problem classes. By the law of large numbers, as we sample more and more problem instances we will gain more information and tend towards the expected probability distribution. Thus, while we do not have explicit access to the probability distribution responsible for the problem class, increasing the sample size will give a better and better approximation.

5. SUMMARY AND CONCLUSION

We have argued for the utilization of realistic benchmarks for GP based on a number of recent papers. Firstly [33] observes a proliferation of machine learning papers that evaluate new algorithms on a handful of *isolated* benchmark data sets and those improvements are not fed-back to the originators of the data. As machine learning researchers, we should remind ourselves of the importance of feedback, as it is a fundamental mechanism in the machine learning process itself.

Secondly, GP is singled out as a particularly bad example of machine learning practice where toy problems have enjoyed attention they do not rightly warrant [20]. They make a number of recommendations for establishing properties that a suite of benchmark instances should have, some of which are inconsistent with the approach advocated in this paper. The main objection being that there should not be a standard benchmark suite, but a set of problem instances dictated directly by the real-world problem instances one is attempting to solve. In other words, isolated context-free individual benchmark problem instances of are little use. What is needed are problem instance generators (i.e. a probability distribution from which problem instances are drawn). This would reduce the chances of over-tuning a metaheuristic to a given problem instance.

Thirdly, a theoretical result in [9, 26] links the performance of an algorithm with instances drawn from a probability distribution. One of the consequences of this is that the bias of an algorithm needs to align with the bias of a probability distribution over problem instances [11, 35]. The outcome of this is that an algorithm should be tuned to a problem class to obtain better than average performance. When the bias of an algorithm precisely aligns with the problem class, then that is the best algorithm for that problem class.

Finally, a solution is provided to the problem of designing algorithms tailored to a specific problem class; meta-learning [11] and hyper-heuristics [4]. While base-level learning is concerned with solving a specific problem instance, meta-level learning is concerned with solving many problem instances from a problem class (i.e. learning about the problem class). In other words, a meta-level provides a channel through which learning from problem instance in a training set can be retained to improve performance on problem instances in the application stage.

In short, it does not make sense to nominate an algorithm without simultaneously nominating the set of problem instances to which it is to be applied (i.e. an algorithm is appropriate *for* a problem class). By analogy with the inspiring metaphor of GP, just as organisms evolve in response to environmental changes (i.e. survival of the fittest), and objects are engineered in response to needs (i.e. fit for purpose), so too should we automatically design algorithms in response to grounded benchmark instances (i.e. drawn from a probability distribution).

There are at least two reasons why we would want to employ meta-learning. Firstly, we could manually generate new algorithms (i.e. 'hand-coding'), and test them on said benchmarks (which seems to be the most widely adopted approach). However, this itself is just a generate-and-test approach (no different to GP itself) that can be automated. Secondly, with real-world problems, the probability distribution of problem instances is likely to change over time, so rather than having to hand-code new algorithms in response to this change, they can be generated on demand for a new set of benchmark instances.

We hope that this paper goes some way of addressing the issues raised in [33, 20]. We provided support for engaging with real-world problems via the adoption of meta-learning as a problem domain for GP.

6. REFERENCES

[1] Juergen Branke and Jawad Asem Elomari. Meta-optimization for parameter tuning with a flexible computing budget. In *Proceedings of the fourteenth international conference on Genetic and evolutionary computation conference*, GECCO '12, pages 1245–1252, New York, NY, USA, 2012. ACM.

[2] Gavin Brown. A new perspective for information theoretic feature selection. In *International Conference on Artificial Intelligence and Statistics*, pages 49–56, 2009.

[3] Edmund Burke, Graham Kendall, Jim Newall, Emma Hart, Peter Ross, and Sonia Schulenburg. Hyper-heuristics: An emerging direction in modern search technology. In Fred Glover, Gary Kochenberger, and Frederick S. Hillier, editors, *Handbook of Metaheuristics*, volume 57 of *International Series in Operations Research and Management Science*, pages 457–474. Springer New York, 2003.

[4] Edmund K Burke, Mathew R Hyde, Graham Kendall, Gabriela Ochoa, Ender Ozcan, and John R Woodward. Exploring hyper-heuristic methodologies with genetic programming. In *Computational intelligence*, pages 177–201. Springer Berlin Heidelberg, 2009.

[5] Edmund K. Burke, Matthew R. Hyde, Graham Kendall, and John Woodward. Automatic heuristic generation with genetic programming: evolving a jack-of-all-trades or a master of one. In *GECCO '07: Proceedings of the 9th annual conference on Genetic and evolutionary computation*, volume 2, pages 1559–1565, London, 7-11 July 2007. ACM Press.

[6] Zehra Cataltepe, Yaser S. Abu-Mostafa, and Malik Magdon-Ismail. No free lunch for early stopping. *Neural Comput.*, 11:995–1009, May 1999.

[7] Stefan Droste, Thomas Jansen, and Ingo Wegener. Perhaps Not a Free Lunch But At Least a Free Appetizer. In Wolfgang Banzhaf, Jason Daida, Agoston E. Eiben, Max H. Garzon, Vasant Honavar, Mark Jakiela, and Robert E. Smith, editors, *Proceedings of the Genetic and Evolutionary Computation Conference GECCO-1999*, pages 833–839, San Francisco, CA, 1999. Morgan Kaufmann Publishers, Inc.

[8] Stefan Droste, Thomas Jansen, and Ingo Wegener. Optimization with randomized search heuristics - the (a)nfl theorem, realistic scenarios, and difficult functions. *Theor. Comput. Sci.*, 287(1):131–144, 2002.

[9] Edgar A. Duéñez Guzmán and Michael D. Vose. No Free Lunch and Benchmarks. *Evolutionary Computation*, pages 1–20, March 2012.

[10] Peter Flach. *Machine Learning: The art and science of algorithms that make sense of data*. Cambridge University Press, September 2012.

[11] C. Giraud-Carrier and F. Provost. Toward a Justification of Meta-learning: Is the No Free Lunch Theorem a Show-stopper? In *Proceedings of the ICML-2005 Workshop on Meta-learning*, pages 12–19, 2005.

[12] Libin Hong, John Woodward, Jingpeng Li, and Ender Ozcan. Automated design of probability distributions as mutation operators for evolutionary programming using genetic programming. In Krzysztof Krawiec, Alberto Moraglio, Ting Hu, A. Sima Uyar, and Bin Hu, editors, *Proceedings of the 16th European Conference on Genetic Programming, EuroGP 2013*, volume 7831 of *LNCS*, pages 85–96, Vienna, Austria, 3-5 April 2013. Springer Verlag.

[13] Marcus Hutter. *Universal Artificial Intelligence: Sequential Decisions based on Algorithmic Probability*. EATCS. Springer, Berlin, 2005. 300 pages, http://www.hutter1.net/ai/uaibook.htm.

[14] Marcus Hutter. A complete theory of everything (will be subjective). *Algorithms*, 3(4):329–350, 2010.

[15] Christian Igel and Marc Toussaint. On classes of functions for which no free lunch results hold. *Inf. Process. Lett.*, 86(6):317–321, 2003.

[16] Christian Igel and Marc Toussaint. Recent results on no-free-lunch theorems for optimization. *CoRR*, cs.NE/0303032, 2003.

[17] Christian Igel and Marc Toussaint. A no-free-lunch

theorem for nonuniform distributions of target functions. *Journal of Mathematical Modeling and Algorithms*, page 313, 2004.

[18] D. S. Johnson. A Theoretician's Guide to the Experimental Analysis of Algorithms. In *5th and 6th DIMACS Implementation Challenges*. American Mathematical Society, 2002.

[19] Sean Luke. *Essentials of Metaheuristics*. Lulu, second edition, 2013. Available for free at http://cs.gmu.edu/~sean/book/metaheuristics/.

[20] James McDermott, David R. White, Sean Luke, Luca Manzoni, Mauro Castelli, Leonardo Vanneschi, Wojciech Jaskowski, Krzysztof Krawiec, Robin Harper, Kenneth De Jong, and Una-May O'Reilly. Genetic programming needs better benchmarks. In *GECCO '12: Proceedings of the fourteenth international conference on Genetic and evolutionary computation conference*, pages 791–798, Philadelphia, Pennsylvania, USA, 7-11 July 2012. ACM.

[21] Tom M. Mitchell. The need for biases in learning generalizations. Technical report, Rutgers University, New Brunswick, NJ, 1980.

[22] Gisele L. Pappa and Alex A. Freitas. *Automatically Evolving Data Mining Algorithms*, volume XIII of *Natural Computing Series*. Springer, 2010.

[23] Gisele L Pappa, Gabriela Ochoa, Matthew R Hyde, Alex A Freitas, John Woodward, and Jerry Swan. Contrasting meta-learning and hyper-heuristic research: the role of evolutionary algorithms. *Genetic Programming and Evolvable Machines*, pages 1–33.

[24] Riccardo Poli, Leonardo Vanneschi, William B. Langdon, and Nicholas Freitag Mcphee. Theoretical results in genetic programming: The next ten years? *Genetic Programming and Evolvable Machines*, 11(3-4):285–320, September 2010.

[25] J. Ross Quinlan. *C4.5: Programs for Machine Learning*. Morgan Kaufmann Publishers Inc., San Francisco, CA, USA, 1993.

[26] Jonathan E. Rowe and Michael D. Vose. Unbiased black box search algorithms. In *GECCO*, pages 2035–2042, 2011.

[27] C. Schaffer. A conservation law for generalization performance. In *Proceedings of the Eleventh International Conference on Machine Learning*, pages 259–265. Morgan Kaufmann, 1994.

[28] C. Schumacher, M. D. Vose, and L. D. Whitley. The no free lunch and problem description length. In *Proceedings of the Genetic and Evolutionary Computation Conference (GECCO-2001)*, pages 565–570. Morgan Kaufmann, 2001.

[29] Kenneth Sörensen. Metaheuristics the metaphor exposed. *International Transactions in Operational Research*, 2013.

[30] Matthew J. Streeter. Two broad classes of functions for which a no free lunch result does not hold. In *Proc. Genetic and Evolutionary Computation Conference GECCO-2003*, pages 1418–1430. Morgan Kaufmann, 2003.

[31] El-Ghazali Talbi. *Metaheuristics - From Design to Implementation*. Wiley, 2009.

[32] Sebastian Thrun and Lorien Pratt, editors. *Learning to learn*. Kluwer Academic Publishers, Norwell, MA, USA, 1998.

[33] Kiri Wagstaff. Machine learning that matters. *CoRR*, abs/1206.4656, 2012.

[34] David R White, James McDermott, Mauro Castelli, Luca Manzoni, Brian W Goldman, Gabriel Kronberger, Wojciech Jaśkowski, Una-May Oï£¡Reilly, and Sean Luke. Better gp benchmarks: community survey results and proposals. *Genetic Programming and Evolvable Machines*, 14(1):3–29, 2013.

[35] D. H. Wolpert and W. G. Macready. No free lunch theorems for optimization. *Evolutionary Computation, IEEE Transactions on*, 1(1):67–82, April 1997.

[36] John R Woodward. The necessity of meta bias in search algorithms. In *Computational Intelligence and Software Engineering (CiSE), 2010 International Conference on*, pages 1–4. IEEE, 2010.

[37] John R. Woodward and Jerry Swan. The automatic generation of mutation operators for genetic algorithms. In Gisele L. Pappa, John Woodward, Matthew R. Hyde, and Jerry Swan, editors, *GECCO 2012 2nd Workshop on Evolutionary Computation for the Automated Design of Algorithms*, pages 67–74, Philadelphia, Pennsylvania, USA, 7-11 July 2012. ACM.

[38] John Robert Woodward and Jerry Swan. Automatically selection heuristics. In *Proceedings of the 13th annual conference companion on Genetic and evolutionary computation*, GECCO '11, pages 583–590, New York, NY, USA, 2011. ACM.

[39] Huaiyu Zhu and Richard Rohwer. No free lunch for cross-validation. *Neural Comput.*, 8:1421–1426, October 1996.

MetaDeeP'14 Chairs' Welcome

The widespread adoption of 'Design Patterns' heralded a revolution in the software industry, offering a catalog of designs that cut across lower-level concerns such as choice of programming language, platform etc.

In a similar manner, we anticipate that the identification of "cross-cutting abstractions" within metaheuristic theory and practice will afford new and unifying perspectives on a field that has become dominated by metaphor and is in danger of increasingly fragmentation.

Despite this being the first MetaDeeP workshop, we are happy to say that there were a total of 15 submissions, of which 10 have been accepted. Each submission was reviewed by at least two program committee members. One of the main goals for this initial Workshop is to attempt consensus on what the metaheuristics community might usefully obtain from a pattern-based approach. To this end, the range of presentation topics is intentionally diverse, and includes:

- Metaheuristic applications of pre-existing design patterns (e.g., Composite, Template Method).
- New patterns specific to metaheuristics (e.g., Representative, Repair, Tagging).
- Methodological case studies (statistical testing and interactive fitness measures).

The longer-term motivation behind the Workshop is twofold:

1. Educational: In adopting a 'pattern-based' perspective, we're additionally seeking to decompose good research practice by cutting 'horizontally' across frameworks and methodologies, looking to abstract out aspects that have yet to be folded back into the mainstream. This can be seen as serving an educational purpose: "how best to convey the practicalities of metaheuristic engineering to the uninitiated?".

2. Facilitating automation: the "Problem Statement" aspect of the design pattern format essentially gives heuristic preconditions for the application of a pattern. This lends itself well to the process of component selection/generation. Since this is an essential part of the automated design of metaheuristics, what we'd really like is to be able to convey this heuristic information declaratively (i.e., so that even a computer can understand it). The ultimate goal is to use this information to help reformulate metaheuristic design as a problem of (potentially dynamic) software component assembly.

Above all, we envision this initiative as primarily bottom-up, driven by ideas and needs of the community rather than by any arbitrary assumptions. A panel discussion will following the paper presentations and we will attempt to provide a platform for the range of opinions expressed by those present.

Thanks are due to all who submitted papers. We encourage everyone with an interest in "metaheuristics in the large" to attend and help shape the future of this exciting new initiative.

Jerry Swan
University of Stirling, UK

Krzysztof Krawiec
Poznan University of Technology, Poland

MetaDeeP'14 Organization

General Chairs:
Jerry Swan (University of Stirling, UK)
Krzysztof Krawiec (Poznan University of Technology, Poland)
John Woodward (University of Stirling, UK)
John Clark (University of York, UK)
Chris Simons (University of the West of England, UK)

Program Chairs:
Jerry Swan (University of Stirling, UK)
Krzysztof Krawiec (Poznan University of Technology, Poland)
John Woodward (University of Stirling, UK)
John Clark (University of York, UK)
Chris Simons (University of the West of England, UK)

Sponsor: acm SIGEVO

Supporters:

EPSRC
Engineering and Physical Sciences Research Council

EXCELLENCE IN SCIENCE
THE ROYAL SOCIETY

Structural stigmergy: A speculative pattern language for metaheuristics

Ben Kovitz
Fluid Analogies Research Group
Indiana University
512 North Fess Avenue
Bloomington, Indiana 47408 USA
bkovitz@indiana.edu

Jerry Swan
Computing Science and Mathematics
University of Stirling
FK9 4LA Scotland UK
jerry.swan@cs.stir.ac.uk

ABSTRACT

To construct graphs whose quality results from complicated relationships that pervade the entire graph, especially relationships at multiple scales, follow a strategy of repeatedly making local patches to a single graph. Look for small, easily recognized flaws in local areas of the graph and fix them. Add tags to the graph to represent non-local relationships and higher-level structures as individual nodes. The tags then have easily recognized flaws that relate to non-local and higher-level concerns, enabling local patching to set off cascades of local fixes that address those concerns.

Categories and Subject Descriptors

I.2.8 [**Problem Solving, Control Methods, and Search**]: [Heuristic methods]; G.1.6 [**Optimization**]: [Stochastic programming]

General Terms

Algorithms, Design

Keywords

metaheuristics; stigmergy; design patterns

1. FIVE PATTERNS

1.1 Local patching

In search problems where each candidate solution is a graph in which the goodness of a solution results from complicated relationships that pervade the entire graph, **often it's easy for a person to identify local flaws and ways to fix them but hard to design a fitness function that provides a workable gradient to go from poor to good solutions.**

For example, an analog circuit is a complicated graph in which the nodes are electronic components and the edges are electrical connections between those components. Some simple flaws in a circuit design: an integrated circuit's V_{CC} pin isn't connected to the supply voltage; an electrolytic capacitor is connected in reverse polarity; a component isn't connected to anything at all. These flaws all have simple and obvious fixes. But the relationships between components to make a correct or acceptable circuit are subtle and complex: waveforms and timings result from feedback loops between components and must be chosen correctly to orchestrate the activity of other components, etc. Almost any random variation made to a circuit renders it completely inoperable. Consequently, it's hard to design a fitness function without large plateaus and bad local minima.

Therefore:

Instead of maintaining a population of graphs, **maintain a single graph. Make a "library of patches": a collection of types of small, local flaws together with simple ways to fix them. On each iteration of the search, choose one flaw randomly and fix it.**

Each flaw should be computationally cheap to recognize: ideally, by examining a single node and its immediate connections. No flaw can pertain to a single node alone. Every flaw should pertain to a node's relationship to its neighbors.

There should be more than one way to fix many of the flaws. For example, a completely unconnected component simply needs to connect to *something.* Make the system choose randomly among the fixes available in the circuit as it stands now.

Ideally, each fix consists of an operation on a single node or edge: creating, modifying, or deleting a node, or creating, modifying, or deleting an edge connecting two nodes.

Consequences:

1. Most changes improve the graph.

As the search runs, consecutive changes appear scattered about the graph, each bringing the graph closer to a good graph. But they don't necessarily result directly in a graph that, considered as a whole, is any better. For example, even after making a number of connections, a circuit design might still not work at all.

2. Fixing one flaw often creates a new flaw.

For example, hooking up an LED to a positive voltage and ground without also adding a pull-up resistor is likely to send too much current through the LED.

3. The detected flaws become progressively more specific to their context.

For example, if an electrolytic capacitor wasn't connected to anything at all, detecting that flaw might trigger the

GECCO'14, July 12–16, 2014, Vancouver, BC, Canada.

ACM 978-1-4503-2881-4/14/07 ...$15.00.
http://dx.doi.org/10.1145/2598394.2609845.

patch "hook it up to any component that can connect with a capacitor." Once connected to one component, its flaw is that it needs another connection, having something to do with the other component. Once connected to two components, the capacitor might be connected with the wrong polarity, triggering a patch to reverse its connections.

4. There's no tendency to converge on a particularly good graph, only a "reasonable" graph.

This may be OK for some searches, such as a search for a valid solution which can be defined entirely in terms of local relationships between nodes. For many searches, though, we want to find better and better graphs as defined by some set of criteria, such as operating characteristics of a circuit. See "Goal tags" (sec. 1.4) for how to address this.

1.2 Change creates salience

Often a sequence of several small changes in one place is needed to do much good. But the first change doesn't get followed up because the attention of the system is distributed equally everywhere.

For example, a voltage regulator needs a capacitor and resistor, a power source, and an output which matches the voltage needed by the integrated circuit(s) whose voltage it regulates. The regulator's output is itself a function of the capacitor and resistor that it's connected to. If only one of these fixes is done and then ignored, the other components will have flaws of their own, which might trigger incompatible fixes.

Therefore:

Associate a level of salience with every node. Give it a boost whenever that node or its edges are modified. And let it decay on every search step when it's not modified. When randomly choosing nodes to fix, give higher probability to the more-salient nodes.

When a node has no flaws, it won't get modified, providing opportunity for decay. A node also won't be modified while attention is on far-off nodes in the graph, even if that node has a flaw.

Consequences:

1. Flaw-fixing tends to happen in local cascades.

Fixing one flaw tends to create a new flaw in the same node or an adjacent node. That flaw triggers another fix, and so on.

2. Sometimes the system flounders, undoing a fix it just made for one node because of the flaw that it created for a neighboring node.

Floundering is not necessarily bad. The resulting instability creates a variety of opportunities for other nodes to make a connection with one of the floundering nodes. This fixes more of the node's potential flaws, resulting in greater stability. To counter floundering of a more pernicious sort, see "When you're stuck, break something" (sec. 1.5).

3. Distant parts of the graph can build up internally coherent but mutually incompatible subgraphs.

This is partly addressed in the next pattern, and partly in "When you're stuck, break something" (sec. 1.5).

1.3 Tags

Most relationships of interest are not local. Making a good decision regarding one node requires knowledge of how that node fits into a larger structure, and even how that larger structure fits into yet larger structures.

Therefore:

Attach tags to nodes, groups of nodes, and nodes with an important relationship between them.

Tags are "administrative" nodes, which represent non-local knowledge where it's needed. You must define a "library of tags" and situations they apply to. And you must extend the "library of patches" to include flaws involving tags and what's needed to fix them.

For example, a group of several electronic components might produce a certain waveform. This group should be tagged as "generating a waveform". It's a flaw for this tag to lack an appropriate power source, to lack a receiving component or module into which to feed the waveform, or for its frequency to be unsuitable for that required by the receiving component.

If certain kinds of nodes must be arranged in a certain sequence, tags can indicate where in the sequence they occur. For example, it's a flaw for an English sentence to end with "the", so, in a program that constructs sentences, the last word in a sentence might get a special tag.

In some problems, tags can themselves be part of the solution in addition to performing an administrative role (e.g. Copycat, sec. 3.1).

Consequences:

Relationships between aspects of the graph that exist on a larger scale than a single node drive the search.

A tag that binds several nodes into a group can have neighbors that are also tags, which bind other groups together. Now, from the standpoint of local patching, the high-level structures and their relationships are local, too. Tags that designate relationships of interest can have tags as neighbors, and consequently flaws in relation to those neighbors, and consequently set off new cascades of local patching.

1.4 Goal tags

Internal coherence alone is not enough to make a practical metaheuristic. There must be a way to drive the graph toward predefined objectives.

Therefore:

Represent objectives with "goal tags": tags that are flawed when they don't connect with nodes that implement the objective.

For example, a goal tag for a circuit to generate a sine wave would be flawed when it lacks connection to a tag that describes an output waveform. Upon connection with such a tag, there might still be a flaw because the waveform doesn't match the shape or frequency specified in the goal tag. This flaw sets off a cascade of changes to the waveform tag's other neighbors.

Consequences:

The goal tags provide "top-down" pressure to direct the search, balancing the opportunistic "bottom-up" pressures that come from looking for ways to connect the lowest-level nodes.

At the start of a search, the goal tags' flaws can't be satisfied, because the tags representing the high-level structures and relationships they need to connect to don't exist. To fix this flaw, the program makes a tag for the relevant kind of structure or relationship, just without the structure or relationship existing. This is a flaw for the new tag, which creates pressures to build up the needed kinds of structures.

1.5 When you're stuck, break something

Sometimes, two large parts of the graph are each internally coherent but they conflict with each other, and there's no way to tell which one is "wrong".

In this situation, most of the nodes have few flaws left to fix, except the goal tags are not satisfied or only poorly satisfied. Each local patch seems to do as much damage as good. Small changes to either part of the graph make that part locally worse. Neither part of the graph offers a path of locally beneficial changes to produce a global improvement.

Therefore:

Monitor the rate of local improvement throughout the graph. When it stops, arbitrarily unlink or destroy a large, connected part of the graph.

Since there's no way to tell which part should be destroyed, the best you can do is arbitrarily destroy one of them, so something new can grow in its place, hopefully influenced by and more harmonious with the remaining part.

On the other hand, if you have enough domain knowledge to program an educated guess about which part should be destroyed, you can implement "competition". When a node tries to fix its own flaw by linking to a node that's already linked, it must dislodge the competitor. The system can give varying weights to the first node's fix, the creation of a flaw for the competing node, and the effect on the node connected to. The winner is determined by these weights; the loser is disconnected and will have to find some other way of getting the connection it needs. Or if the loser is a group, the group tag can be removed, releasing the contained nodes to build a fresh structure. The weights can reflect how long a connection has been in existence, how long each node has been flawed, and how serious the flaws are.

Consequences:

The search cycles between slow construction and fast destruction.

With competition, subgraphs tend to prevail if they can contribute to the global goals, and tend to be destroyed if they can't.

There is, however, no way to tell in advance if breaking up a large part of the graph will lead to something better or not. It's possible for the program to find the best graph it will ever find, break it up because it can't improve it, and never find it again.

2. CONSEQUENCES FOR THE DESIGNER

1. The problem becomes more tractable for the metaheuristic designer.

Local flaws are very easy to understand and think of how to fix. As you watch the search in progress, you see simple flaws that are not being addressed, and you think of new additions to the library of patches and the library of tags. In effect, you patch up flaws in the metaheuristic as you find them, not so different from what the metaheuristic does. Criticizing, nit-picking, and patching is much easier than coming up with an elegant theory.

You never have to invent a fitness function. You just define various kinds of connections that you want to see in a solution graph.

2. You can add all the domain knowledge you like.

For example, a circuit-design metaheuristic can exploit as much electronics knowledge and circuit-design know-how as you can find. You keep adding it a little bit at a time, by translating it into the language of tags and flaws.

3. Because of that, the metaheuristic tends to acquire both human-like common sense and human-like blind spots.

Genetic algorithms sometimes discover bizarre circuits that no human engineer ever would—like circuits where one part is not connected but that don't work if the unconnected part is removed [11]. This is both good and bad, but in practice it's usually bad. The good is that such searches don't have the blind spots that sometimes prevent humans from seeing excellent solutions. The bad is that bizarre solutions often exploit dependencies that make them impractical. For example, the above-cited circuit worked by exploiting thermal properties resulting from the manufacturing quirks of a single FPGA chip. When tried in another FPGA of the exact same model, the circuit design didn't work.

4. You must manually adjust global parameters.

Boosting salience, decaying salience, weighting the importance of flaws, determining when local improvement has petered out—all these involve choosing constants with far-reaching effects on the performance of the program. If these global parameters aren't just right in relation to each other, the system can spend all of its time stuck on a bad solution, abandon excellent solutions, break up nascent solutions before they've had a chance, etc. This sounds like the kind of problem that a metaheuristic could help solve. To date, though, programs that do structural stigmergy with local patching (sec. 3) have gotten their global parameters set by somewhat laborious manual tuning.

3. EXAMPLES

Because these are speculative patterns, there are few examples of metaheuristics that use them. These patterns are found mostly in biology (sec. 4) and in blackboard systems [2]. Blackboard systems model collaboration of different experts on the solution to a problem. All can see and edit the current version of the solution. We briefly describe Copycat, a blackboard-like system that demonstrates local patching and tagging especially well.

3.1 Copycat

The Copycat program [8] makes analogies between strings of letters. Given an example of changing one letterstring to another, such as `abc` → `abd`, Copycat will attempt to "do the same thing" to another given string. Attempting to make the analogous transformation to `iijjkk`, it might come up with `iijjll`, `iijjkl`, `iijjdd`, `ijl`, or other choices, depending on how it mapped the example to the given string and what rule it came up with to explain the example.

Flexible analogy-making faces problems fundamental to all metaheuristics: the number of possible choices is vast, only a fairly small number of them are reasonable, it's hard to tell whether a bad candidate solution is near or far from a good one, and one must often settle for a solution that is less than ideal. In addition, there is no way to define a simple fitness function for all possible letterstring analogies. The set of possible relationships is just too vast and irregular.

Copycat makes extensive use of tags, in particular tags that define groups and tags that define sequences in terms of successor or predecessor relationships. Given the example pqqp → qppq and the start string gghijj, Copycat could tag gg and jj as groups. This would influence the choice of mapping from pqqp, perhaps favoring mapping the first p to the gg and the second p to the jj, perhaps leading to a result of hggjji. Or Copycat might tag the successor relationships gg→h→i→jj, leading it to tag the initial string with successor/predecessor relationships: p→q–q←p. It might then convert the input string to an analogously symmetric "hill": gghijjjjihgg.

All the parts of the solution grow together, each tag setting off searches for ways to make an analogous tag elsewhere or ways to define a mapping rule to make use of the tags. Tentatively considered mapping rules set off searches for appropriate ways to tag the letters. Nodes become "unhappy" due to inappropriate positioning in the solution graph, triggering searches for ways to repair the problem. Competitions (as in sec. 1.5) determine when one node can dislodge another. A global "temperature" tracks overall satisfaction with the current solution, and affects the probability of a "breaker" randomly destroying part of the solution.

A spreading-activation network called the "slipnet" directs the search top-down, complementing the bottom-up search of nodes looking for appropriate links. When a node in the slipnet becomes active, the corresponding type of node in the "workspace" (the tentative solution now being worked on) is deemed most relevant to the search right now, giving actions ("codelets") related to nodes of that type higher urgency. The slipnet also models something not covered above: the ability of concepts to "slip", or adjust their meaning to fit what's currently feasible to achieve in the workspace.

4. BIOLOGICAL INSPIRATION

4.1 Stigmergy

The biological phenomenon of stigmergy has been a fertile source of inspiration for metaheuristics [3]. Stigmergy is the stimulation to act resulting from effects in the environment of actions already completed. For example, when termites are building a nest, the parts of the nest already built stimulate the termites to perform the next steps toward completing the nest. Each insect decides what to do next only by sensing stimuli that are present and nearby. Pheromones left by ants while searching for food are a natural tag: a sign left in the environment rather than simply a side-effect of action.

Ant-colony optimization [4] was, of course, inspired by ants—as was Copycat [5]. Stigmergy in ant-colony optimization is limited to attaching tags ("pheromones") to edges of a graph in order to steer the search toward favorable variations. We define the term *structural stigmergy* here to mean specifically the building of hierarchical structures by local patching. This requires both building upon or correcting partial structures and tagging partial structures to make non-local information local.

John Holland has discovered a wide variety of tags in complex adaptive systems, especially tags that define or distinguish groups ("aggregates"). A particularly relevant example is the use of a flag to rally an army or political group [6, p. 13]. The group members' attachment to a symbol enables them to be led as if they were a single entity. Yet each member makes locally appropriate decisions, helping the group goal according to his or her own skills and opportunities.

4.2 Stigmergy in human life

Stigmergy occurs in human life at least as much as it occurs in social insects [10]. In addition to natural side-effects of action, such as trails of worn vegetation left by walking and the spread of information in a marketplace through individual negotiations, humans deliberately leave signs in their environment that represent information in terms of conventional symbols. For example, road signs direct traffic, advertisements connect buyers with sellers, and of course all writing is signs deposited in the environment to carry information. We should not be surprised that when people notice something wrong in other people's writing, they often feel an immediate urge to correct it [9].

Wikipedia is made entirely by stigmergy. Each editor edits without consulting others, stimulating other editors to make corrections or improvements [7]. Wikipedia articles have "tags" explicitly noting the presence of problems: non-neutral point of view, lack of cited sources, etc. These tags stimulate other editors to correct the problems noted.

Christopher Alexander's concept of a "pattern language" is itself a form of structural stigmergy. Each pattern is a way of solving a recurring problem: a conflict between forces (drives to action) that arises in a situation [1, ch. 14]. Building is a process of repair [1, ch. 24], making local changes to fix local problems.

The enormous success of structural stigmergy in nature suggests that it's both workable and effective for many hard problems. It demands little at each decision-point, and it produces structures that cohere at all levels and fit external pressures such as an environment or a set of objectives.

5. REFERENCES

[1] ALEXANDER, C. *The Timeless Way of Building.* Oxford University Press, 1979.

[2] CRAIG, I. *Blackboard systems.* Intellect Books, 1995.

[3] CRINA, G., AND AJITH, A. Stigmergic optimization: Inspiration, technologies and perspectives. In *Stigmergic optimization.* Springer, 2006, pp. 1–24.

[4] DORIGO, M., AND STÜTZLE, T. *Ant Colony Optimization.* Bradford, 2004.

[5] HOFSTADTER, D. R., MITCHELL, M., ET AL. The Copycat project: A model of mental fluidity and analogy-making. *Advances in connectionist and neural computation theory 2*, 31-112 (1994), 29–30.

[6] HOLLAND, J. H. *Hidden order: How adaptation builds complexity.* Basic Books, 1995.

[7] LIH, A. Long live Wikipedia? In *A Companion to New Media Dynamics*, J. Hartley, J. Burgess, and A. Bruns, Eds. Wiley, 2013, pp. 185–190.

[8] MITCHELL, M. *Analogy-Making As Perception: A Computer Model.* MIT Press, 2002.

[9] MUNROE, R. Duty calls. https://xkcd.com/386/. Accessed: 4-Apr-2014.

[10] PARUNAK, H. V. D. A survey of environments and mechanisms for human-human stigmergy. In *Environments for Multi-Agent Systems II.* Springer, 2006, pp. 163–186.

[11] THOMPSON, A., LAYZELL, P., AND ZEBULUM, R. Explorations in design space: Unconventional electronics design through artificial evolution. *Evolutionary Computation, IEEE Transactions on 3*, 3 (1999), 167–196.

Tagging in Metaheuristics

Ben Kovitz
Fluid Analogies Research Group
Indiana University
512 North Fess Avenue
Bloomington, Indiana 47408 USA
bkovitz@indiana.edu

Jerry Swan
Computing Science and Mathematics
University of Stirling
FK9 4LA Scotland UK
jerry.swan@cs.stir.ac.uk

ABSTRACT

Could decisions made during some search iterations use information discovered by other search iterations? Then store that information in *tags:* data that persist between search iterations.

Categories and Subject Descriptors

I.2.8 [**Problem Solving, Control Methods, and Search**]: [Heuristic methods]; G.1.6 [**Optimization**]: [Stochastic programming]

General Terms

Algorithms, Design

Keywords

metaheuristics; tags; design patterns

1. TAGGING

1.1 Problem

When early decisions in a sequence affect what is possible in later decisions, the early decisions can usually be made better if informed by the results of later decisions.

Benefit of hindsight occurs in two ways in metaheuristics: when constructing candidate solutions that are themselves sequences of decisions, such as paths or graphs (constructive search), and when choosing which of a set of variations of candidate solutions are most likely to be fruitful (perturbative search).

An example in a constructive search: When attempting to construct a short path through a graph, each decision is the choice made, at one vertex, of which edge to follow to reach the next vertex. A poor decision at an early vertex can limit all decisions made at later vertices to constructing unacceptably long paths. But there's no way to know this before exploring them.

GECCO'14, July 12–16, 2014, Vancouver, BC, Canada.

ACM 978-1-4503-2881-4/14/07 ...$15.00.
http://dx.doi.org/10.1145/2598394.2609844.

An example in a perturbative search: A genetic algorithm searching a high-dimensional space for an $\vec{x}$ that produces a minimal $f(\vec{x})$ can produce many more variations (mutations and crossovers) in each generation than it can feasibly explore in that generation. Some lead to fruitful regions of the fitness landscape and others don't. There's no informed way to choose which variations are most worth exploring without actually exploring them.

In iterative searches, previous explorations of sequences of decisions have often passed through the same decision points and already discovered results of some of the available choices.

A real-life illustration: While searching for a path out of a cave, you might come to the same branching point many times without realizing you'd been there before. To keep yourself from re-exploring a branch that leads only to a dead end, you could write "dead end" on the wall the first time you backed out of it. The wall at the start of that branch is the most convenient place for this information, since that's the exact place where you need it.

1.2 Solution

During or immediately after exploring each decision sequence, record just-discovered facts which can benefit later searches. Store them in a way that makes them easy to look up when they are most likely to be relevant, such as when a later search reaches a decision point that was crossed during the current search.

Such records are called "tags", "pheromones", "annotations", or "descriptors". Tags form a secondary level of description beyond that of the candidate solutions themselves, suggesting which directions of search are most promising.

The simplest kinds of tags are markers that a solution has already been explored, as in tabu search (section 2.1), or a single number such as the average fitness of previous paths that passed through a given edge, as in ant-colony optimization (section 2.2).

There is, however, no upper limit to the complexity of the information that can be stored in a tag. Tags can hold any kind of information about results discovered so far, relevant facts from the problem domain, or any kind of estimate of the promisingness of a line of exploration. For example, a classification algorithm might tag several items as a single group, reflecting the hypothesis that the differences between them are unimportant and should be left out of the classification. Upcoming searches can build upon that hypothesis, perhaps adding further tags linking it to other hypotheses.

Eventually that hypothesis may be rejected and then the tag will be removed or itself tagged as a "dead end".

1.3 Consequences

1. The fitness landscape becomes progressively more hill-shaped (less "rugged") as more searches occur.

Each tag functions as a sign pointing the way toward more-fruitful searches or away from less-fruitful searches. Future searches skip over alternatives that appear good on the basis of information local to a decision point but that information from elsewhere suggests will lead to poor results. Thus the tags provide a communication channel from decisions that come later on a path to decisions that come earlier. Each tag expands the "local" knowledge available at each decision point to include some "global" knowledge of the region of the fitness landscape that each choice leads to.

2. An explicit representation of promisingness of different lines of exploration grows and improves, separately from evaluation of solutions.

In effect, the tags co-evolve with the candidate solutions. Tags direct and prioritize future searches, and future searches find information that helps make and refine the tags.

3. A certain proportion of computational capacity will be devoted to the overhead of maintaining, accessing, and interpreting the tags.

Since tag-related computation occurs on each iteration of a search, it slows down the algorithm's main inner loop. As long as recording and interpreting tags is cheaper than rediscovering the information in them, tags are likely a worthwhile addition to most metaheuristics.

4. Tags can encode domain knowledge.

One of the defining properties of metaheuristics is their problem-domain independence. However, it is well-known that domain knowledge is the key to ensuring the tractability of precisely the kinds of problems we wish to address with metaheuristics.

A set of tags provides a way for a search to capitalize on domain knowledge when it's determined to be relevant. For example, a metaheuristic for laying out components on a printed-circuit board can exploit a tag that certain pins are ground pins, and favor exploring layouts that orient the components so their ground pins are all on the same side.

2. EXAMPLES

2.1 Tabu search

Tabu search [4] maintains a memory of candidate solutions that have been recently evaluated, declaring a "tabu" against evaluating them again until sufficient new candidates have been explored. This keeps the exploration of variations in a perturbative search from repeatedly rediscovering the same local minima.

Some forms of tabu search tag specific elements of candidate solutions that have recently been varied, declaring a tabu against varying them again too soon ("recency-based memory"). This temporarily holds the search within or outside a neighborhood of solutions.

Other forms of tabu search ("frequency-based memory") track how many times a certain solution element has been present in explored solutions or how many times an element has been changed, swapped, deleted, etc. These tags last many search iterations, and can identify features of the fitness landscape such as that a certain element has a large or a small effect on fitness. This information suggests important aspects of the structure of the fitness landscape, such as where are the paths between regions with very different properties. This helps the algorithm choose between intensification and diversification strategies and tune them appropriately.

An illustration of the injection of explicit domain knowledge to a tabu-search algorithm for finding maximal subgraph isomorphisms between two finite-state automata is given in [9]. Since a node representing an accepting state can't map to a node representing a non-accepting state, any such mapping is declared permanently tabu.

2.2 Ant-colony optimization

Ant-colony optimization (ACO) [2] searches for the best paths through a graph by tagging each edge with a "pheromone": a number that correlates with the overall quality of recently searched paths that contained that edge. While constructing a new path, the algorithm favors edges with high pheromone numbers. Thus when choosing which parts of a path to vary, the algorithm tends to vary edges from bad paths more and edges from good paths less. The pheromones decay in order to prevent the search from converging too quickly on a suboptimal path.

ACO has a particular advantage in problems where the properties of the graph change while the algorithm is running. The pheromones change right along with the introduction, removal, or re-weighting of edges, directing the search toward the paths that are most favorable right now. This illustrates the advantage of maintaining a description separate from that of the candidate solutions and their fitness. The pheromones redirect the gradient of the search by amplifying information about which search *directions* are most fruitful. The fitnesses of candidate solutions alone don't contain this information.

A simple way to add domain knowledge to an ACO algorithm is to reduce the pheromone level for known bad elements of a solution. For example, in the Euclidean Traveling Salesman Problem, a path with a pair of crossed edges is known to be longer than the same path with those edges uncrossed [1, p. 1-12]. Simply reducing the pheromone level on edges that recently crossed speeds up the basic algorithm by several hundred times on standard large problems [10].

2.3 Model-driven searches

Another kind of tag consists of an explicit model of the problem domain or the fitness landscape, updated as candidate solutions are inspected and evaluated. For example, estimation-of-distribution algorithms [7] maintain an approximate map of the fitness landscape. This map takes the form of a probability distribution over the set of all possible solutions, where higher probability densities indicate regions where fitnesses tend to run high. Each time a candidate solution is evaluated, the algorithm adjusts the probability distribution to more closely match the fitnesses actually found. Instead of choosing new candidate solutions by varying old ones, these algorithms simply choose by sampling the current probability distribution.

3. OTHER KINDS OF TAGS

This pattern does not explain all kinds of tags.

A kind of tag that occurs in genetic programming serves as a label for a code fragment [8]. This enables another part of the program to refer to it—say, to call it as a subroutine. This, in turn, facilitates the evolution of a modular architecture, which in turn facilitates evolvability. Without tagged code fragments, reference from one part of a program to another has to rely on mechanisms that are much more easily broken by mutation and crossover. For example, referring a certain number of instructions ahead or backward, or to an absolute location in a program, will likely produce a completely useless program whenever an instruction is inserted or deleted.

Reference tags are made even more robust by being inexact. When a program branches to an inexact tag, the interpreter simply finds the best match. This enables tagged modules and code that refers to them to evolve fairly independently without breaking each other. Almost-duplicate modules can coexist in the same program and eventually specialize for different purposes. Eventually they can get distinct tags that other parts of the program can evolve to take advantage of, but a reference won't break completely if it doesn't specify exactly the right tag.

A dizzying variety of tags are found in complex adaptive systems [5]. Cell-adhesion molecules dictate when a cell adheres to other cells and what other kinds of cells it adheres to; they play a fundamental role in growth and in the immune system [3]. Every colony of the African weaver ant has a distinct scent, which enables ants to tell if they're in their own colony or a foreign one [6]. Company logos enable customers to easily recognize businesses, and uniforms help them tell who are the employees and who are the customers.

Like the tags described in the first two sections of this paper, reference tags, group tags, timing tags, etc. are "administrative overhead" that guides the activity of the system. These tags are different in that they primarily serve the purpose of coordination between different parts of a candidate solution or between different agents. They don't primarily record knowledge gained in previous search iterations to save the system from having to rediscover it.

4. REFERENCES

[1] Applegate, D., Bixby, R., Chvátal, V., and Cook, W. *The Traveling Salesman Problem: A Computational Study*. Princeton Series in Applied Mathematics. Princeton University Press, 2011.

[2] Dorigo, M., and Stützle, T. *Ant Colony Optimization*. Bradford, 2004.

[3] Edelman, G. *Topobiology: An Introduction to Molecular Embryology*. Basic Books, 1993.

[4] Glover, F., and Laguna, M. *Tabu Search*. Springer US, 1997.

[5] Holland, J. H. *Hidden order: How adaptation builds complexity*. Basic Books, 1995.

[6] Hölldobler, B., and Wilson, E. O. Colony-specific territorial pheromone in the african weaver ant Oecophylla longinoda (Latreille). *Proceedings of the National Academy of Sciences 74*, 5 (1977), 2072–2075.

[7] Larrañaga, P. A review on estimation of distribution algorithms. In *Estimation of distribution algorithms*. Springer, 2002, pp. 57–100.

[8] Spector, L., Martin, B., Harrington, K., and Helmuth, T. Tag-based modules in genetic programming. In *Proceedings of the 13th annual conference on Genetic and evolutionary computation* (2011), ACM, pp. 1419–1426.

[9] Swan, J., Harman, M., Ochoa, G., and Burke, E. Generic software subgraph isomorphism. In *Proceedings of the 4th International Symposium on Search Based Software Engineering (SSBSE '12) - Fast Abstracts* (2012).

[10] Wang, C.-X., Cui, Y.-A., Li, X., Chen, H., and Cui, D.-W. A novel ant colony system based on traditional chinese medicine theory. *International Journal of Computer Science and Network Security 6*, 5 (May 2006), 153.

Metaheuristic Design Pattern: Candidate Solution Repair

Krzysztof Krawiec*
Institute of Computing Science
Poznan University of Technology
60965 Poznan, Poland
krawiec@cs.put.poznan.pl

ABSTRACT

In metaheuristic algorithms applied to certain problems, it may be difficult to design search operators that guarantee producing feasible search points. In such cases, it may be more efficient to allow a search operator to yield an infeasible solution, and then turn it into a feasible one using a repair process. This paper is an attempt to provide a broad perspective on the candidate solution repair and frame it as a metaheuristic design pattern.

Categories and Subject Descriptors

I.2.8 [**Artificial Intelligence**]: Problem Solving, Control Methods, and Search—*Heuristic methods*

Keywords

metaheuristic algorithms; solution repair; search operators; feasibility

1. PROBLEM STATEMENT

Many problems solved with metaheuristic algorithms are *constrained*, i.e., problem formulation includes conditions (usually logical predicates) that have to be fulfilled by a candidate solution to be *feasible*. As a result, the entire search space S of candidate solutions is partitioned into *feasible solutions* $F \subset S$ and *infeasible solutions* $I \subset S$, $F \cap I = \emptyset$.

As the goal is to find the optimal *and* feasible solution (or, more often in practice, a well-performing suboptimal and feasible solution), it is desirable to traverse S using search operators that are guaranteed to produce feasible solutions (i.e., $s : S \to F$). However, designing operators with this guarantee can be challenging, for instance when feasible solutions are few and far in between (i.e., the ratio $|F|/|S|$ is small), or when the structure of S is such that the feasible solutions are frequently neighbored by the infeasible ones.

*Research conducted during K. Krawiec's stay at the ALFA Group, Computer Science and Artificial Intelligence Laboratory (CSAIL), MIT.

GECCO'14, July 12–16, 2014, Vancouver, BC, Canada.

ACM 978-1-4503-2881-4/14/07 ...$15.00.
http://dx.doi.org/10.1145/2598394.2609847 .

Moreover, even if such an operator can be designed, then it may be biased in an undesirable way (in the sense of the probability distribution of produced candidate solutions).

This makes it necessary to equip an algorithm with some means of handling the infeasible solutions. Discarding them is rarely a good idea for at least two reasons. Firstly, with the discarded candidate solutions some knowledge gathered in hitherto search is also lost. Secondly, this may prevent the algorithm from visiting the yet unexplored and potentially promising parts of the search space. As an alternative, one may extend the definition of the objective function so that it works 'reasonably' beyond the feasible region; for instance, an infeasible candidate solution to a knapsack problem may be evaluated according to how much it violates the knapsack capacity ([4], p. 149). For many problems however coming up with such an extended and uncontroversial objective function may be difficult.

Another way of handling infeasible solutions is penalization by introducing appropriate terms into objective function f, or by defining additional objectives that implement constraint violation measures. This proceeding assumes however that f can be applied to unfeasible solutions, i.e., that the constraints are in some sense *soft*. Though this is often technically true (e.g., in many continuous optimization benchmarks f is defined in almost entire $\mathbb{R}^n$ space), f applied to an unfeasible solution may return a nonsensical value and potentially deceive the search process. This can be solved by not applying f to infeasible solutions altogether, i.e., by relying on penalties alone for such candidate solutions, but this typically implies that an infeasible solution will be always considered as worse than any feasible solution, which can again prevent exploration of certain parts of the search space.

2. THE SOLUTION

In the face of above controversies, it has been often recommended to *repair* the unfeasible solutions. A repair operator is any operator O guaranteed to fulfill

$$O(x) \in F$$

for any given infeasible solution $x \in I$.

There are at least two major ways in which such an operator can be employed:

1. In the most obvious scenario, the resulting repaired solution $x' = O(x)$ replaces the infeasible one, and the latter one is discarded. This proceeding is useful in problems where the objective function is capable of evaluating infeasible solutions. For instance, in

the Traveling Salesperson Problem (TSP), one can still calculate route length even if it visits some cities more than once [10].

2. One can alternatively use the repaired solution $x' = O(x)$ only as a means for obtaining the value of $f(x)$, which otherwise could not be calculated [5]. More specifically, x remains a working solution, but receives the objective value of its repaired version, i.e.:

$$f(x) = f(O(x)) \quad (1)$$

3. CONSEQUENCES

The availability of a repair operator for a given problem has several implications. Firstly, it gives the experimenter more freedom in designing search operators, which do not have to always produce feasible solutions anymore. In some cases, it may pay off to design search operators that *notoriously* yield infeasible solutions, in which case repair becomes a norm rather than an exception, and the repair operator gets to be a more important 'search driver' than the primary search operator(s).

Using repair only to obtain an 'evaluable proxy' (case 2 in Section 2) has particularly interesting consequences. In principle it allows conducting search as if there were no constraints, i.e., in the space S of all candidate solution rather than in the subspace F of feasible solutions only. As a consequence, the search trajectory can traverse the subspace of infeasible solutions I and remain there for several iterations (provided the search operators can work there). This potentially allows the algorithm to find 'shortcuts' to parts of F that would be hard (or even impossible) to reach via a path of feasible solutions only. On the other hand, such a policy involves the risk of diverging from F so far that the evaluation proxies obtained by repair ($O(x)$ in Eq. (1)) cease to provide useful information about the search gradient. In general, whether this policy pays off depends on the structure of the search space, characteristics of repair operator, and informativness of fitness function.

Though usually a necessity, solution repair can be seen in a broader context as a way to make a search process more *responsive* to the feedback resulting from the evaluation of candidate solutions. On the other hand, the information about constraint violation can be considered as a manner of making the search process more *informed*.

Note that repair in the above sense can be seen as yet another search operator, capable of operating in I (as opposed to conventional search operators which normally are required to work only in F). Therefore, the characteristics of a repair operator becomes a (potentially important) part of algorithm's *search bias*.

In the context of evolutionary computation, the two modes of operation listed in the previous section can be respectively deemed *Lamarckian repair* and *Baldwinian repair*, as the former one employs the feedback received from the environment (i.e., the information about violating a constraint) to explicitly modify (replace) the solution, while in the latter scenario the only effect is in the objective (fitness) value.

Sometimes it may be difficult to delineate repair from other components of a metaheuristic algorithm. In some cases, repair is an indispensable element of genotype-phenotype mapping. For instance in grammatical evolution [8], solutions (genotypes) are vectors of numbers, each of them determining the choice of a grammar production to be used when deriving the phenotype (program). When such a number is greater than the number of productions available at a given stage of program derivation, it is to be treated by a modulo n operator. That operator can be seen as a repair operator in this context.

A general concept related to repair is *embedding*. The space of feasible solutions can be seen as embedded in a greater space of all candidate solutions reachable by means of the search operator(s). For instance an n-argument Boolean function can be uniquely represented by a look-up table of 2^n values 0 and 1. One can embed this space in the $[0,1]^{2^n}$ hypercube, in which only the corners of the hypercube correspond to the feasible solutions. In this setting, repair is the collapse from the latter space to nearest lower space representative (where the notion 'nearest' would be explicitly or implicitly implemented by the repair algorithm). In general, the embedding space can feature a different number of dimensions (typically higher) than the embedded space. However, such embeddings can be considered also for dimensionless (i.e., non-vector) spaces, for instance spaces of programs.

4. EXAMPLES

- Numerical optimization abounds in various methods for solution repair (see, e.g., [5] for a review).
- A simple form of solution repair is clamping (trimming) the value of a modified variable to a predefined range (domain). Though in most cases the ranges are part of problem statement, sometimes the reasons are more subtle. For instance in [9], we clamp the variables representing the parameters of Othello strategies. However, we do so not because the fitness function is *inherently* unable to handle the values outside the interval, but to avoid an uncontrolled growth of variables that may not bring qualitative changes in players' behavior (because candidate solutions are functionally equivalent up to linear scaling). Thus, infeasibility is not the only motivation for repair.
- Crossover can be a significant source of infeasible offspring, in particular in metaheuristic search algorithms with discrete representation encodings. For example, in Grouping Genetic Algorithms [1], crossover of two parents with permutation encodings is highly likely to produce an infeasible offspring. In such cases, solution repair becomes an integral part of the crossover operation.
- Intron removal in genetic programming (GP, e.g., [2]) can be considered as a form of repair (notwithstanding that it has been shown that some amount of introns may be beneficial for GP search).
- Simplification algorithms used in certain variants of genetic programming to reduce solution size (e.g., [6, 7]) can be seen as as a form of repair: they do not affect the semantics of a program, but change its syntax and thus make it possible for it to meet, e.g., an upper limit imposed on program size.
- Methods have been proposed that avoid solution repair by using the information on constraint violation to guide the search process [3].

- Repair is applicable also in presence of weak constraints. For instance in GP, the program size limit is intended to avoid expensive evaluation and excessive memory occupancy rather than to principally exclude certain programs as infeasible. A program that slightly violates this constraint but commits low error can be still considered attractive. In this context, repair interestingly becomes an operator that transforms the 'less desirable' candidate solutions into the more desired ones.

Acknowledgment

The author would like to thank the reviewers for constructive remarks and acknowledges financial support from the Polish-U.S. Fulbright Commission and from National Science Centre grant no. DEC-2011/01-/B/ST6/07318.

5. REFERENCES

[1] Emanuel Falkenauer. *Genetic Algorithms and Grouping Problems.* John Wiley & Sons, Inc., New York, NY, USA, 1998.

[2] Thomas Haynes. Duplication of coding segments in genetic programming. In *Proceedings of the Thirteenth National Conference on Artificial Intelligence*, volume 1, pages 344–349, Portland, USA, 4-6 August 1996. AAAI Press / MIT Press.

[3] Nanlin Jin, Edward Tsang, and Jin Li. A constraint-guided method with evolutionary algorithms for economic problems. *Applied Soft Computing*, 9(3):924–935, 2009.

[4] Sean Luke. *Essentials of Metaheuristics.* lulu.com, first edition, 2009. Available at http://cs.gmu.edu/~sean/books/metaheuristics/.

[5] Z. Michalewicz. A survey of constraint handling techniques in evolutionary computation methods. In John R. McDonnell, Robert G. Reynolds, and David B. Fogel, editors, *Proc. of the 4th Annual Conf. on Evolutionary Programming*, pages 135–155, Cambridge, MA, 1995. MIT Press.

[6] Alberto Moraglio, Krzysztof Krawiec, and Colin Johnson. Geometric semantic genetic programming. In Christian Igel, Per Kristian Lehre, and Carsten Witt, editors, *The 5th workshop on Theory of Randomized Search Heuristics, ThRaSH'2011*, Copenhagen, Denmark, July 8-9 2011.

[7] Alberto Moraglio, Krzysztof Krawiec, and Colin G. Johnson. Geometric semantic genetic programming. In Carlos A. Coello Coello, Vincenzo Cutello, Kalyanmoy Deb, Stephanie Forrest, Giuseppe Nicosia, and Mario Pavone, editors, *Parallel Problem Solving from Nature - PPSN XII*, volume 7491 of *Lecture Notes in Computer Science*, pages 21–31. Springer, 2012.

[8] Conor Ryan, J. J. Collins, and Michael O'Neill. Grammatical evolution: Evolving programs for an arbitrary language. In W. Banzhaf, R. Poli, M. Schoenauer, and T. C. Fogarty, editors, *First European Workshop on Genetic Programming 1998*, pages 83–95, Berlin, 1998. Springer.

[9] M. Szubert, W. Jaśkowski, and K. Krawiec. On scalability, generalization, and hybridization of coevolutionary learning: A case study for othello. *Computational Intelligence and AI in Games, IEEE Transactions on*, 5(3):214–226, 2013.

[10] Tim Walters. Repair and brood selection in the traveling salesman problem. In Agoston E. Eiben, Thomas Bäck, Marc Schoenauer, and Hans-Paul Schwefel, editors, *Parallel Problem Solving from Nature - PPSN V*, pages 813–822, Berlin, 1998. Springer. Lecture Notes in Computer Science 1498.

Metaheuristics in Nature-Inspired Algorithms

Michael A. Lones
School of Mathematical and Computer Sciences
Heriot-Watt University, Edinburgh, UK
m.lones@hw.ac.uk

ABSTRACT

To many people, the terms nature-inspired algorithm and metaheuristic are interchangeable. However, this contemporary usage is not consistent with the original meaning of the term metaheuristic, which referred to something closer to a design pattern than to an algorithm. In this paper, it is argued that the loss of focus on true metaheuristics is a primary reason behind the explosion of "novel" nature-inspired algorithms and the issues this has raised. To address this, this paper attempts to explicitly identify the metaheuristics that are used in conventional optimisation algorithms, discuss whether more recent nature-inspired algorithms have delivered any fundamental new knowledge to the field of metaheuristics, and suggest some guidelines for future research in this field.

Categories and Subject Descriptors

I.2.8 [**Artificial Intelligence**]: Problem Solving, Control Methods, and Search

General Terms

Theory

Keywords

Metaheuristics, design patterns

1. INTRODUCTION

Metaheuristic is a widely used, but under-appreciated, term. In common usage, it is often used as a synonym for a search or optimisation algorithm. However, this was not the intention of the term's originator, who used it to refer to general ideas of how to carry out search, rather than specific implementations. A true metaheuristic is like a design pattern, in that it encapsulates knowledge that may be applied to the design of a range of specific optimisation algorithms. Likewise, there is no reason why a particular algorithm can not implement multiple metaheuristics, making use of complementary ideas of how to search for optima within solution landscapes.

Over the last decade, there has been an explosion in the development of new nature-inspired optimisation algorithms [6], a practice which has received significant criticism [5]. Even if we ignore the more superfluous of these, we are still left with a seemingly diverse group of nature-inspired algorithms in common use. Add in more traditional derivative-free optimisation algorithms [1, 3] and the range of options may seem overwhelming for a practitioner trying to solve a particular problem. It is perhaps no wonder that people from outside the field of metaheuristics sometimes use algorithms which do not seem optimal for the task at hand.

It is arguable that the main problem is not the runaway invention of new algorithms, but rather the way in which new algorithms are presented. Close inspection reveals that many of these algorithms do introduce new ideas. However, by focusing on the modeling of the domain processes by which they are inspired, their authors often fail to identify the more general metaheuristics upon which these processes are based, and as a consequence, rarely relate this knowledge back to our wider understanding of how to carry out search. Hence, we get a proliferation of new algorithms, but no proliferation of new knowledge.

The main aim of this paper is to identify metaheuristics underlying nature-inspired optimisation algorithms. This is done by identifying the implicit metaheuristics used by these algorithms and, through reference to these metaheuristics, highlighting the relationships between different optimisation algorithms. The hope is that this will contribute to our wider understanding of metaheuristics and offer some guidance to practitioners overwhelmed by the expansive literature. It is also hoped that this paper will cast some light on recent developments in nature-inspired algorithms, and offer guidelines for future developments.

The paper is organised as follows[1]: beginning with a review of local search metaheuristics, this is followed by discussion of the most commonly used nature-inspired optimisation algorithms: evolutionary algorithms, particle swarm optimisation and ant colony optimisation. After this, some recent nature-inspired algorithms are reviewed, and related to the metaheuristics we identified in previous sections. The paper concludes by offering some guidelines for those looking to develop new nature-inspired optimisation methods.

[1]Note, due to limited space, some citations are made to collections and review papers rather than primary sources.

GECCO'14, July 12–16, 2014, Vancouver, BC, Canada.

ACM 978-1-4503-2881-4/14/07 ...$15.00.
http://dx.doi.org/10.1145/2598394.2609841.

Neighbourhood Search

Intent: Find new solutions by exploring those that are a step change—*a move*—away from the current one. A move could be anything from flipping a single bit to randomly replacing the entire solution.

Motivation: To explore variants of a known solution.

Applicability: Whenever a suitable neighbourhood can be defined.

Examples: Particular heuristics can be generated by considering different neighbourhoods, and by sampling these neighbourhoods in different ways.

Hill Climbing

Intent: Follow a sequence of local improvements in order to find a locally optimal solution. A single move is performed at each step. If this leads to a better solution, the algorithm then moves on to explore a variant of this new solution, otherwise it remains at the original point and considers a different move.

Motivation: To improve upon an existing solution.

Applicability: Whenever neighbourhood search can be performed and where solutions can be assigned an objective value.

Accepting Negative Moves

Intent: Allow moves to worse solutions.

Motivation: To prevent convergence to local optima when carrying out hill climbing.

Examples: Implementations include threshold accepting and simulated annealing [1]. The latter reduces the probability of accepting negative moves as the search process approaches the global optimum.

Multi-Start

Intent: Restart the search process in a different region once it has converged at a local optimum. After this has been repeated a number of times, the best local optimum seen is returned.

Motivation: To explore the search space more widely.

Applicability: May not be suitable for large search spaces with sparse optima.

Examples: Restart points may be random. An alternative approach, used by iterated local search [1], is to estimate the distance between neighbouring optima and apply a move of this magnitude from the current local optimum.

Adaptive Memory Programming

Intent: Use memory of past search experience to guide future search.

Motivation: The original motivation was to prevent cyclic patterns of search when attempting to escape local optima.

Applicability: Requires memory. May not be applicable in highly dynamic search landscapes, where memory of previous search may be misleading.

Examples: Adaptive memory programming is a generalisation of ideas developed in tabu search. The simplest forms of tabu search maintain a short fixed-length FIFO list, which stores recent moves or types of moves. These moves are then prohibited until they leave the list. There are many variants of this idea, including the use of long term memory, and the use of aspiration criteria to revoke tabus [1]. Many nature-inspired algorithms, including evolutionary algorithms, also carry out a form of adaptive memory programming, using a population of search points as their memory.

Figure 1: Local search metaheuristics

2. LOCAL SEARCH ALGORITHMS

Before considering nature-inspired algorithms, it is first instructive to review some of the common metaheuristics used by more traditional optimisation algorithms (see Fig. 1). Most of these are local search algorithms, which consider a single search point at a time during the search process. Fundamental to all these algorithms is the **neighbourhood search** metaheuristic. Many local search algorithms are concerned with finding trajectories that lead towards local optima. A general metaheuristic for achieving this is **hill climbing**. However, in most cases the local optimum will not be the global optimum. To address this, there are a number of metaheuristics that can be used to encourage wider exploration of the search space. Two simple, and widely used, ones are **accepting negative moves** and **multi-start**. Another popular method, and the originator of the term metaheuristic, is tabu search. This is now often referred to using the more general term **adaptive memory programming**.

3. EVOLUTIONARY ALGORITHMS

Evolutionary algorithms (EAs) [1, 4] are an abstract model of biological evolution, in which a population of candidate solutions is iteratively exposed to analogues of natural selection and genetic variation. The basic procedure is as follows: the initial population is a random sample of search points, a selection mechanism then discards search points with poor objective value, and variation operators derive new search points from those that remain. This new population then replaces the previous population, and the process of selection and variation is repeated until an optimal solution is found, or some other termination criterion is met.

Interestingly, EAs use all the metaheuristics described in the previous section. Mutation carries out a **neighbourhood search**, elitism supports **hill climbing**, stochastic selection means that the algorithm can **accept negative moves**, the use of many starting points resembles **multi-start**, and the population uses previous search points to guide future search, making it a form of **adaptive mem-**

Population-Based Search

Intent: Multiple, cooperating search processes that are typically executed in parallel.

Motivation: The sharing of information at intermediate stages of search helps guide convergence to global optima.

Applicability: Usually less efficient than local search when applied to relatively easy problems.

Examples: In an EA, sharing is implemented indirectly through the selection mechanism, which spreads information about relative fitness, and directly through the recombination operator. Whilst EAs popularised this metaheuristic, it is also also used by other optimisation algorithms—such as scatter search [1]—which are not modelled upon natural processes.

Intermediate Search

Intent: Explore the region between two or more previously visited search points, each of which is known to have a relatively high objective value.

Motivation: To explore solutions with properties derived from more than one good solution. Originally motivated by genetic crossover in biology.

Applicability: Particular implementations may not be suitable for particular search spaces.

Examples: Recombination, or crossover, is the best known example of this metaheuristic. A related approach, termed path relinking [1], has more recently been introduced to tabu search and scatter search. This is to some extent a generalisation of crossover that involves finding new (relinked) paths between known solutions and exploring the neighbourhood of this path.

Figure 2: EA metaheuristics

Directional Search

Intent: Identify productive directions within the search space, and then carry out moves accordingly.

Motivation: For PSO, animal foraging behaviours.

Applicability: PSO requires a metric space. Gradient methods require a differentiable objective function.

Examples: In PSO, productive search directions are estimated from the locations of good solutions (also resembling intermediate search). Directional search may also be guided by other sources of knowledge. For example, gradient ascent uses derivatives of the objective function to identify productive search directions. Where the objective function is not known, estimates of its derivatives can be used. An example of this is the CMA-ES algorithm [4], an evolution strategy that estimates second derivatives, using this knowledge to bias the mutation operator.

Variable Neighbourhood Search

Intent: Search different neighbourhoods around the location of a known local optimum.

Motivation: The local optimum in one neighbourhood may not be the local optimum in another.

Applicability: Requires multiple neighbourhoods.

Examples: The variable neighbourhood search algorithm [1] does this by iteratively increasing the neighbourhood size, exploring moves of increasing magnitude from the current local optimum. Although PSO takes a less structured approach, different particles approaching the current best known search point will tend to have different velocities, in effect exploring neighbourhoods of different magnitude around this point.

Figure 3: PSO metaheuristics

ory programming. However, EAs are also notable for introducing a new metaheuristic: **population-based search** (Fig. 2). The use of recombination in EAs is also distinctive, and has likewise promoted interest in a more general metaheuristic, the idea of **intermediate search** (Fig. 2).

4. PARTICLE SWARM OPTIMISATION

Particle swarm optimisation (PSO) [4] models group foraging. As for an EA, an initial population of search points is randomly sampled. Unlike an EA, each search point is explicitly associated with a search process, which also has a velocity and a memory of the best point it has seen so far. For each iteration, each search process updates its velocity so that its path veers slightly towards the best solutions seen by a subset of the search processes. It then applies this velocity to its current search point in order to derive a new search point. This method of exploring new search points continues until a termination criterion is met.

PSO has significant commonalities with EAs, including the use of **population-based search** and **intermediate search**. However, arguably the most distinctive feature of PSO is the use of **directional search** (Fig. 3). A further distinctive aspect of PSO is how it extends directional search with the notion of search velocity. In the original PSO paper, this is described as a means of promoting exploration over exploitation when carrying out directed search, primarily by allowing a particle to overshoot its target. However, it can also be seen as a combination of directional search with another metaheuristic that has recently developed some popularity, **variable neighbourhood search** (Fig. 3).

5. ANT COLONY OPTIMISATION

Ant colony optimisation (ACO) [1] is motivated by the way in which ants share their foraging experience. The idea is that search processes mark paths through the search space that lead to regions of high objective value. Marking up is done using an analogue of pheremone concentration, typically in three ways: the path that leads to the best solution is reinforced to promote followers, paths traversed by search processes are decayed to promote diversity, and all paths decay through evaporation to allow forgetting.

ACO revisits a number of the metaheuristics already discussed, notably **population-based search** and **directional search**. However, the idea of marking up the search space (often referred to as stigmergy) is distinctive. Whilst it could be described as **adaptive memory programming**, it also

Search Space Mapping

Intent: Construct a map to guide search processes that are traversing the search space.

Motivation: For ACO, ant foraging behaviour.

Applicability: Standard ACO is only applicable to discrete optimisation, though generalisations do exist.

Examples: In the case of ACO, the map takes the form of a probabilistic overlay that points towards regions of productive search. An overlay approach is also used in guided local search [1], where it modifies the underlying objective values, pointing search away from solutions with features considered undesirable. Another approach to mapping, used by branch-and-bound methods such as DIRECT [3], is to divide the search space into partitions, directing search towards partitions known to contain fit solutions.

Figure 4: ACO metaheuristic

represents a more specific metaheuristic principle concerned with **search space mapping** (Fig. 4).

6. EMERGING ALGORITHMS

EAs, PSO, ACO, and their variants, still dominate the field of nature-inspired optimisation. However, many recent nature-inspired algorithms have developed a substantial following. Some of the most popular include:

The artificial bee colony algorithm (ABC) [6] (>1000 citations) models honey bee foraging. It explores a fixed number of regions within the search space at any one time. The number of search processes in each region is determined by relative fitness. Search continues in a region whilst fitter solutions continue to be found; otherwise, a new region is randomly sampled.

Bacterial foraging optimization (BFO) [2] (>1000 citations) models *E. coli* colonies. Like PSO, it uses a population of search processes. Each performs a random walk composed of straight segments followed by random direction changes. Segment length is proportion to search gradient, so bigger steps are taken in productive directions. Objective values are overlaid by a crowding term, whose effect is to draw the random walks towards one another. A dispersal routine randomly reallocates a subset of search points.

Firefly algorithm (FA) [6] (>500 citations) is similar to PSO, and loosely motivated by the grouping behaviour of fireflies. Compared to PSO, the main differences are the lack of search velocities and the use of an inverse-square law to guide interactions between all search processes. This leads to more localised interactions and a consequent tendency to form multiple regions of search.

Cuckoo search (CS) [6] (>500 citations) uses a small population of solutions. At each step, a poor solution is replaced either randomly or by using a 'Lévy flight' applied to another, randomly selected, solution. Lévy flights are a kind of random walk with step sizes generated from a heavy-tailed probability distribution that has been shown optimal for exploring sparse foraging environments.

Each of these algorithms carries out a **population-based search**. ABC and CS make explicit use of **hill climbing** and **multi-start** strategies, and are the only algorithms not to use **intermediate search** or **directional search** metaheuristics. BFO carries out both a **variable neighbourhood search** and **search space mapping**. Random walks are used in both BFO and CS, and could be considered as a novel metaheuristic. FA, on the other hand, has little to distinguish it from PSO, with the inverse-square law having a similar effect to crowding and fitness sharing in EAs, and the use of multi-swarms in PSO. However, there is scope for recognising this general group of search balancing mechanisms as a metaheuristic, since they are often central to solving multimodal problems.

7. DISCUSSION

Arguably the main contribution of recent nature-inspired algorithms has not been to develop new metaheuristics, but rather to investigate new ways of combining metaheuristics that we already know about. However, this is typically done in an *ad hoc* fashion, with no explicit identification of the metaheuristics being used, and little understanding of why they are being combined. To address this issue, we might suggest the following considerations for the future:

Explicitly identifying metaheuristics would help spread knowledge, bring cohesion to the field, and make algorithmic descriptions more accessible. This paper is a small step in this direction, but more work is required to identify and express the metaheuristics in current use and the relationships between them.

When to combine metaheuristics is currently unclear. It is likely that different combinations are suitable for different problems. However, there is limited theoretical understanding, and experimental studies are generally done at the algorithmic level. Again, explicit identification of metaheuristics would help to develop this knowledge.

Hyper-metaheuristics could build upon the success of hyperheuristics [1], automatically evaluating different combinations of metaheuristics to produce new general-purpose algorithms, and addressing the *ad hoc* manner in which combinations are currently explored.

Design patterns, whilst distinct from metaheuristics, help to formalise implementations and mechanisms for combining metaheuristics [4](ch. 29), promoting thinking at the metaheuristic level. The documentation conventions of design patterns could also be adapted to metaheuristics, providing a method for standardisation and expressing ontologies.

8. REFERENCES

[1] M. Gendreau and J. Y. Potvin. *Handbook of Metaheuristics*. Springer, 2nd edition, 2010.

[2] K. M. Passino. Biomimicry of bacterial foraging for distributed optimization and control. *Control Systems, IEEE*, 22(3):52–67, June 2002.

[3] L. Rios and N. Sahinidis. Derivative-free optimization. *Journal of Global Optimization*, 56(3):1247–1293, 2013.

[4] G. Rozenberg, T. Bäck, and J. N. Kok. *Handbook of Natural Computing*. Springer, Berlin, Heidelberg, 2012.

[5] K. Sörensen. Metaheuristics—the metaphor exposed. *Intl. Trans. in Op. Res.*, Feb. 2013. online version.

[6] X. S. Yang. *Nature-Inspired Metaheuristic Algorithms*. Luniver Press, 2nd edition, 2010.

A Template for Designing Single-Solution Hybrid Metaheuristics

Manuel López-Ibáñez
IRIDIA, CoDE,
Université Libre de Bruxelles
Brussels, Belgium
manuel.lopez-ibanez@ulb.ac.be

Franco Mascia
IRIDIA, CoDE,
Université Libre de Bruxelles
Brussels, Belgium
fmascia@ulb.ac.be

Marie-Éléonore Marmion
LIFL, Université Lille 1
Lille, France
marie-eleonore.marmion@inria.fr

Thomas Stützle
IRIDIA, CoDE,
Université Libre de Bruxelles
Brussels, Belgium
stuetzle@ulb.ac.be

ABSTRACT

Single-solution metaheuristics are among the earliest and most successful metaheuristics, with many variants appearing in the literature. Even among the most popular variants, there is a large degree of overlap in terms of actual behavior. Moreover, in the case of hybrids of different metaheuristics, traditional names do not actually reflect how the hybrids are composed. In this paper, we discuss a template for single-solution hybrid metaheuristics. Our template builds upon the Paradiseo-MO framework, but restricts itself to a predefined structure based on iterated local search (ILS). The flexibility is given by generalizing the components of ILS (perturbation, local search and acceptance criterion) in order to incorporate components from other metaheuristics. We give precise definitions of these components within the context of our proposed template. The template proposed is flexible enough to reproduce many classical single-solution metaheuristics and hybrids thereof, while at the same time being sufficiently concrete to generate code from a grammar description in order to support automatic design of algorithms. We give examples of three IG-VNS hybrids that can be instantiated from the proposed template.

Categories and Subject Descriptors

I.2.8 [**Computing Methodologies**]: Artificial Intelligence—*Problem Solving, Control Methods, and Search*

General Terms

Algorithms

GECCO'14, July 12–16, 2014, Vancouver, BC, Canada.

ACM 978-1-4503-2881-4/14/07 ...$15.00.
http://dx.doi.org/10.1145/2598394.2609846 .

Keywords

Automatic Algorithm Configuration, Automatic Algorithm Design, Local Search, Metaheuristics

1. PROBLEM STATEMENT

Single-solution metaheuristics are those metaheuristics that consider a single solution at each step instead of a population of solutions [3]. These include classical local search algorithms, such as iterated local search (ILS) [7], simulated annealing (SA) [6], variable neighborhood search (VNS) [2], among others; and also classical evolution strategies such as (1+1)-ES and (1,1)-ES [1].

Given the large number of single-solution metaheuristics proposed in the literature, it is not surprising that very similar proposals are discussed under different names. For example, *iterated greedy* (IG) [10] is fundamentally equivalent to *ruin-and-recreate* (RR) [11] and *large-neighborhood search* (LNS) [9]. This duplication is problematic for two reasons: (1) it artificially divides the research concerning these algorithms leading to a lack knowledge sharing and a duplication of efforts, and (2) it makes more difficult for practitioners to understand the state-of-the-art and identify the best algorithm for their particular problem.

A related but different problem arises when well-known algorithms are slightly modified or hybridized with other metaheuristics. For instance, ILS could be augmented with the Metropolis acceptance criterion typical of SA. In such a case, depending on the point of view, it could be considered either a hybrid of ILS and SA or an SA with a large neighborhood and a local search intensification. Both views basically describe the same algorithm.

We believe that previous approaches suffer from an excessive flexibility [4, 14]. They attempt to instantiate almost any possible algorithm, which leads to a high degree of flexibility, but allows defining the same algorithm in multiple equivalent ways. Nonetheless, our proposal is not a radical departure from existing approaches, since our goal is to synthesize the accumulated knowledge about which single-solution metaheuristics, and which of their components, have been shown to work well on various problems.

In particular, we build directly on top of the Paradiseo-MO C++ framework [4] by reusing many of its underlying components, although other underlying frameworks and programming languages may be used to implement the template described here.

2. SOLUTION

Our proposal sacrifices some of the flexibility of Paradiseo-MO for simplicity by pre-defining an algorithmic structure based on ILS (Fig. 1). A classical ILS algorithm is composed of a perturbation, a local search, an acceptance criterion and a termination criterion. However, in our template, these components are much more general than those found in classical ILS algorithms. Moreover, the components may influence each other by updating a common state, which may represent a strength parameter in the case of perturbation, a temperature in the case of the Metropolis acceptance criterion, a history of previous solutions, a tabu list, etc.[1]

We define a perturbation as a stochastic move within a particular neighborhood. A perturbation is often defined in terms of a strength parameter, which may be dynamically adjusted. The neighborhood of the perturbation may also be the solutions that can be reached in a certain number of consecutive moves. In that case, the strength parameter defines the number of moves for each perturbation. The class of perturbations includes not only classical random swap moves, but also the complex destruction-reconstruction moves typical of IG (and by extension, RR and LNS). The key feature of a perturbation is that it is stochastic, that is, applying the same perturbation twice with the same strength to the same solution is likely to produce different solutions. Moreover, perturbations may react to a new solution being accepted as the current one by adjusting the strength.

An acceptance criterion is defined as a procedure that takes the current solution and a new solution and returns either one of them or a previously found one. The solution returned then becomes the current solution. Examples of acceptance criteria are: accept always the new solution, which is typical of restart mechanism; accept only if improving, which is typical of ILS and VNS, and Metropolis acceptance, which is the acceptance criterion used in the classical SA. Some of these acceptance criteria, such as the Metropolis one, have internal parameters.

A local search, in our template, is defined as any classical iterative improvement plus the ILS itself. Iterative improvement algorithms are not based on stochastic perturbations as defined above, but on a systematic search within a neighborhood. Therefore, they are not part of the algorithms that can be instantiated from our ILS template. Moreover, iterative improvement algorithms are often problem-specific in order to make use of particular speed-ups when systematically exploring a neighborhood. Since the ILS contains a local search, and the local search can be an ILS, this recursive definition allows hybridizing different types of single-solution metaheuristics within a single algorithm. The idea of defining hybrid ILS algorithms by means of a recursive definition has already been explored in the literature in the context of the traditional ILS definition [5]. More generally, the idea that a template for local search should have a recursive definition is even older [14]. Recently, the same ideas have been applied to hyperheuristics templates [12, 13].

[1]In the case of Paradiseo-MO, this state is not passed explicitly between functions as in Fig. 1, but implemented in terms of relationships between different objects.

ILS Algorithm
1: s_0 := Initialization()
2: s^* := ILS(s_0)
3: **return** s^*

Function ILS(s_0)
Require: Perturbation, LS, Acceptance, Termination
1: s^* := LS(s_0, $State$)
2: **repeat**
3: s' := Perturbation(s^*, $State$)
4: s' := LS(s', $State$)
5: s^* := Acceptance(s', s^*, $State$)
6: **until** Termination($State$)
7: **return** s^*

Figure 1: The iterated local search (ILS) template.

Finally, the termination criterion is defined as a function that returns true when the main loop of ILS should stop. It can be a time limit, a number of iterations or another condition. In the case of an ILS embedded within another ILS, the termination condition of the ILS at the lower level is often a function, such as a fraction of time, of the termination condition of the upper level.

3. CONSEQUENCES

Despite being more restricted than the general framework given by Paradiseo-MO [4], the above template can instantiate a large number of classical single-solution metaheuristics, including SA, ILS, IG, VNS, etc. Moreover, it can combine components of them in a flexible (but not entirely arbitrary) way. We will discuss some examples below.

One of the consequences of such a framework is to move away from describing algorithms in terms of similarities with other algorithms, which is actually a subjective view that depends on our own background, towards describing algorithms in terms of the components that they use. That is, a SA-VNS hybrid could be implemented in various ways, but an algorithm that uses a perturbation with a dynamically increasing strength and a Metropolis acceptance criterion has always the same structure in the template proposed above.

Another consequence is that, except for a few problem-specific components, generating a hybrid single-solution metaheuristic is a matter of choosing how many levels of ILS we wish to have and which components should appear at each level. This property allowed us to generate code in a procedural manner from a grammar description of the above template and to find the best instantiation using an off-the-shelf automatic algorithm configuration tool [8].

4. EXAMPLES

As an example, let us consider a hybrid IG-VNS. Such a name on its own is not very helpful, since what is exactly a hybrid IG-VNS depends on the actual components and how they are combined. In terms of our ILS template, we have at least the following three possibilities:

IG that restarts from solutions increasingly distant from the best-so-far. In this case, there is an IG algorithm that, after not improving the best-so-far solution for a while, applies a perturbation to it and restarts the IG algorithm from the perturbed solution. Every time such a restart occurs without improving the best-so-far solution, the perturbation applied is stronger. This corresponds to a two level ILS, where the perturbation of the inner ILS is of the type destruct-reconstruct, whereas the perturbation of the outer ILS is a partial reinitialization of the best-so-far solution with a strength that increases as long as no new best-so-far solution is found.

IG with increasingly stronger destruction-reconstruction. This corresponds to a single level ILS, where the perturbation is of type destruct-reconstruct, but the strength of the perturbation increases as long as no new best-so-far solution is found.

IG with a VNS as subsidiary local search. This corresponds to a two level ILS, where the perturbation of the outer level is of the type destruct-reconstruct and the inner level is a classical VNS algorithm.

The above examples show that complex hybrid algorithms can be described in terms of very few components based on the template proposed above.

5. REFERENCES

[1] H.-G. Beyer and H.-P. Schwefel. Evolution stratagies: a comprehensive introduction. *Natural Computing*, 1: 3–52, 2002.

[2] P. Hansen and N. Mladenovic. Variable neighborhood search: Principles and applications. *European Journal of Operational Research*, 130(3):449–467, 2001.

[3] H. H. Hoos and T. Stützle. *Stochastic Local Search—Foundations and Applications.* Morgan Kaufmann Publishers, San Francisco, CA, 2005.

[4] J. Humeau, A. Liefooghe, E.-G. Talbi, and S. Verel. ParadisEO-MO: From fitness landscape analysis to efficient local search algorithms. *Journal of Heuristics*, 19(6):881–915, June 2013.

[5] M. S. Hussin and T. Stützle. Hierarchical iterated local search for the quadratic assignment problem. In M. J. Blesa et al., editors, *Hybrid Metaheuristics*, volume 5818 of *LNCS*, pages 115–129. Springer, 2009.

[6] S. Kirkpatrick, C. D. Gelatt, and M. P. Vecchi. Optimization by simulated annealing. *Science*, 220: 671–680, 1983.

[7] H. R. Lourenço, O. Martin, and T. Stützle. Iterated local search. In F. Glover and G. Kochenberger, editors, *Handbook of Metaheuristics*, pages 321–353. Kluwer Academic Publishers, Norwell, MA, 2002.

[8] M.-E. Marmion, F. Mascia, M. López-Ibáñez, and T. Stützle. Automatic design of hybrid stochastic local search algorithms. In M. J. Blesa et al., editors, *Hybrid Metaheuristics*, volume 7919 of *LNCS*, pages 144–158. Springer, 2013.

[9] D. Pisinger and S. Ropke. Large neighborhood search. In M. Gendreau and J.-Y. Potvin, editors, *Handbook of Metaheuristics*, volume 146 of *International Series in Operations Research & Management Science*, pages 399–419. Springer, New York, NY, 2 edition, 2010.

[10] R. Ruiz and T. Stützle. A simple and effective iterated greedy algorithm for the permutation flowshop scheduling problem. *European Journal of Operational Research*, 177(3):2033–2049, 2007.

[11] G. Schrimpf, J. Schneider, H. Stamm-Wilbrandt, and G. Dueck. Record breaking optimization results using the ruin and recreate principle. *Journal of Computational Physics*, 159(2):139 – 171, 2000.

[12] J. Swan, E. Özcan, and G. Kendall. Hyperion - a recursive hyper-heuristic framework. In C. A. Coello Coello, editor, *Learning and Intelligent Optimization, 5th International Conference, LION 5*, volume 6683 of *LNCS*, pages 616–630. Springer, 2011.

[13] J. Swan, J. Woodward, E. Özcan, G. Kendall, and E. Burke. Searching the hyper-heuristic design space. *Cognitive Computation*, 6(1):66–73, Mar. 2014.

[14] R. J. M. Vaessens, E. H. L. Aarts, and J. K. Lenstra. A local search template. *Computers & Operations Research*, 25(11):969–979, 1998.

The Executable Experimental Template Pattern for the Systematic Comparison of Metaheuristics

[Extended Abstract]

Geoffrey Neumann
Computing Science and Mathematics
University of Stirling
FK9 4LA Scotland UK
gkn@cs.stir.ac.uk

Jerry Swan
Computing Science and Mathematics
University of Stirling
FK9 4LA Scotland UK
jsw@cs.stir.ac.uk

Mark Harman
Department of Computer Science
University College London,
London, WC1E 6BT, UK.
mark.harman@ucl.ac.uk

John A. Clark
Department of Computer Science and YYCSA
University of York
York, YO10 5GH, UK.
john.clark@cs.york.ac.uk

Categories and Subject Descriptors

I.2 [**Computing Methodologies**]: Artificial Intelligence; I.2.8 [**Problem Solving, Control Methods, and Search**]: [Heuristic Methods]

Keywords

Statistical Significance, Hypothesis Testing, Effect Size

1. PROBLEM STATEMENT

In order to establish the effectiveness of a new metaheuristic it is necessary to compare it against a base case (e.g. some version of the metaheuristic without the new functionality under consideration or a metaheuristic representing the state-of-the-art).

This is an area that is fraught with difficulty for several reasons. Firstly, for some metaheuristics there are many parameters that may require manual tuning (e.g. mutation or crossover rate [8]). As there is a tendency to tune these parameters to obtain the best possible performance for a new metaheuristic it is difficult to differentiate between a genuine advantage and the effect of tuning.

Secondly, since metaheuristics are stochastic, it is important to distinguish genuine improvements in the performance of a metaheuristic from apparent improvements arising from chance. There are a wide variety of statistical tests for this purpose, many of which have certain preconditions regarding the nature of the data (e.g. assumptions of normality). It is desirable that a statistical test is chosen which is appropriate for the results, and yet metaheuristic researchers are often not sufficiently knowledgeable to make this decision [2] [9].

This paper focusses primarily on a solution to the second of these problems, but also describes how this solution may be incorporated into a wider framework for testing a new metaheuristic.

GECCO'14, July 12–16, 2014, Vancouver, BC, Canada.

ACM 978-1-4503-2881-4/14/07 ...$15.00.
http://dx.doi.org/10.1145/2598394.2609850.

2. THE SOLUTION

We are developing an automated system for comparing metaheuristics. We claim that this would be of benefit, both in ensuring good practice in the assessment of new metaheuristics and as part of the wider goal of automating the metaheuristic design process. A framework for automatically choosing and carrying out statistical tests, based on the nature of the data, forms a key part of such a system.

The approach proposed in this paper is an application for systematic comparison of experimental results. For simplicity, we will restrict discussion to comparison of a pair of experiments, since the nontransitive effects that may result from comparing multiple experiments [12] would detract from the essential points we wish to convey. We will also initially focus solely on real valued data, although nomimal data may be considered at a later date. This will ultimately form the 'Core Layer' of a framework for the systematic comparison of metaheuristics. We term this framework as an 'Executable Experimental Template' (EET) which is an instance of a Template Method Pattern whereby a skeleton structure is defined which defers to user-specified callbacks which are invoked at key points in the skeleton. Each statistical test, for example, constitutes one subclass [7].

The EET framework consists of three layers. Although the 'Core Layer' is the focus of this paper, all three layers are briefly outlined below:

1. 'Core Layer': Responsible for determining whether two datasets are different to a statistically significant extent and what the effect size of this difference is.

2. 'Experimental Layer': Responsible for planning and conducting experiments. In the case of metaheuristics, it should be able to conduct the experiments necessary to determine whether there is a difference in performance between different techniques. Given two datapoint-generating procedures f_a and f_b (potentially paired), this layer will initially generate k datapoints, producing two sets of fitness scores $\mathbf{a}$ and $\mathbf{b}$. Although we are working in the domain of metaheuristic development, without loss of generality, f_a and f_b can be any stochastic functions able to generate data points. The functionality of the 'Core Layer' is invoked to determine whether $\mathbf{a}$ and $\mathbf{b}$ are significantly different and the size of the effect observed. If the 'Core Layer' is unable to find a statistically significant difference between the two sets of results then the 'Experimental Layer' may decide to run further tests to obtain more results. This increases the probability that a significant p value will be obtained but, in doing so, increases the risk that two techniques will be judged to be significantly different even when the difference is minimal. This concern is addressed by ensuring that the 'Core Layer' carries out effect size tests in addition to p value tests.

3. 'Sensitivity Layer': Responsible for establishing how senstive a datapoint generator is to its choice of parameters. This layer is provided with a *parameter schema* that describes the set of permissible parameter values, (e.g. mutation or crossover probabilities when the datapoint generator is a genetic algorithm). This layer samples the search space of parameters by generating datapoints from different parameter settings. These will be compared using the 'Experimental Layer'. The underlying intention is to allow fair comparision of the 'tunability' of metaheuristics in terms of: a) the robustness of metaheuristics w.r.t. their parameter settings b) the number of samples required to achieve equivalent results. The process of automated parameter tuning to ensure the fair comparison of algorithms has precedent in the work of Wang et al [18].

The EET framework has the following design criteria:

1. Portability: It should be widely portable and easily deployed. Conforming to these requirements will ensure maximum adoption and enable EETs to become a standard.

2. Familiarity: It should use a widely-accepted implementation for statistical tests.

3. Recordability: Every decision made by an EET (as well as the outcome of every test) should be recorded and made available to the user. This will enable the user to publish a complete account of all testing carried out and so will help to ensure complete transparency for all published results.

4. Controllability: Although the system should be able to function without user input, it should also be possible for the user to take manual control of any part of the process. Where a decision cannot be made automatically the system should inform the user and prompt for further action.

5. Plugability: The user should be able to modify EETs to reflect their own preferences in areas such as the choice of statistical test. They should be able to add new tests or new preconditions, to remove tests or to change the way in which tests are selected. Although EETs will have a default configuration suitable for most users, those who have expertise in a particular area should be able to construct versions of EETs that are most suitable for their requirements.

In order to satisfy the portability and familiarity requirements, the EETs are implemented in the Java programming language. All statistical tests are carried out using R, a popular statistical language providing standard implementations of many statistical tests [15]. This is a natural implementation as Java provides RJava, an interface to R. Java itself has the advantage of being a widely used and platform independent language.

2.1 The 'Core Layer'

This layer takes the form of a rule-based system for hypothesis testing. It takes as input two datasets (viz. 'Dataset A' and 'Dataset B'). It may be used to compare a new metaheuristic (Metaheuristic A) against a baseline metaheuristic, (Metaheuristic B). In this case Dataset A will consist of a vector of fitnesses achieved by Metaheuristic A and Dataset B will be the corresponding vector for Metaheuristic B. The purpose of this layer is to find a statistical test which is able to correctly reject the null hypothesis if and only if there is a significant difference between the two datasets. The null hypothesis in this case is that there is no such difference and that both datasets are drawn from the same distribution. This test should have sufficient power to avoid making type II errors [14] without making inaccurate assumptions about the data, increasing the risk of type I errors.

In order to identify the appropriate test, the datasets are examined for the following characteristics:

- Whether both datasets follow a normal distribution.
- Whether both datasets have a similar variance or whether this varies between the two datasets, in which case the two datasets are said to *heteroscedastic*.
- If one or both datasets are skewed, whether the extent and direction of skew is similar in both datasets.
- Whether the level of kurtosis is similar in both datasets.
- Whether either dataset contains missing data.
- Whether the size of both datasets is the same or whether there is a difference. If there is a difference then the two datasets are said to be *unbalanced*.

These characteristics are used in a decision tree to choose the appropriate statistical test (i.e. a test which does not make an assumption which contradicts an observed characteristic).

We do not claim this list to be complete: rather it will be revised according to feedback from the empirical methods community. It should be noted that, although some research has already been carried out on automating the process of statistical testing [10] we are not aware of any complete solutions. That is to say, a solution that takes into account all of these considerations and that can be integrated into a wider automated experimental framework.

Having decided on a test, the EET performs the test and outputs the corresponding p value. If this p value is below the level of confidence specified by the user, then this is interpreted as a rejection of the null hypothesis. Although the p value on its own is useful for determining statistical significance, it can be misleading when the number of runs is large. In this situation the p value will likely be low even when two experimental treatments differ to only a very slight degree. For this reason it is necessary to supplement a statistically significant p value with a measure of effect size in order to give an indication of the magnitude of difference between the two metaheuristics [1]. The 'Core Layer' of the EET framework therefore also chooses and carries out an appropriate effect size test and outputs the results of this test too.

Because of the number of characteristics to be taken into consideration and the fact that many of them require their own tests, the process of choosing an appropriate statistical test may become complex and time consuming. For this reason, it is highly desirable that a simple and efficient test should occupy the root of the decision tree and that further tests should only take place when the results of this test are unsatisfactory. The Cliff test was chosen for this purpose due to its simplicity and because it makes no assumptions about the data [5]. This test produces an effect size (d). d is simply the number of possible comparisons between the two datasets that return in Dataset A's favour subtracted from the number of comparisons that return in Dataset B's favour. This is then divided by the total number of possible comparisons. d will be in a range -1.0 to +1.0, with values close to 0 indicating little difference between the two samples. A d value close to -1.0 or +1.0 indicates both a high probability that the two datasets are from different distributions and provides a measure of effect size similar to the Vargha-Delaney $\hat{A}_{12}$ measure recommended elsewhere [2]. Because of this, by initially using the Cliff test, EETs do not necessarily need to identify and carry out either an ideal test for statistical significance or an ideal test for effect size.

3. AN EXAMPLE: CHOOSING AND CARRYING OUT STATISTICAL TESTS

This section illustrates the behaviour of the 'Core Layer'. As previously mentioned, the schematic provided here is simply an example produced from the rules existing in our current, standard implementation of the EET framework. These rules may change due to further feedback from the empirical methods community. It is also a key requirement that the specific tests used and the decisions made are plugable modules. This is so that the user is able to adapt the default EET configuration to their needs.

We will assume that this layer is presented with two datasets, Dataset A and Dataset B. Let us assume that these two datasets have the attributes specified in Table 1.

To establish whether there is a significant difference between these two datasets, the Cliff test is first employed. As discussed above, this is the EET framework's default test as it has no preconditions and so is suitable for any two datasets. The result of this test will be returned to the user (who may be either a human researcher or the 'Experimental Layer' of the framework). If the user is not satisfied with the outcome of the Cliff test then the following steps

Table 1: Datasets

Attribute	Dataset A	Dataset B
Dataset Size	35	60
Distribution Type	Normal	Not Normal
Heteroscedastic	Yes	Yes
Missing Data	No	No

will be completed. The outcome of these steps will be a p value indicating the statistical significance of the difference between the two sets and a measure of effect size, indicating the magnitude of the difference between the two sets.

1. First of all, the number of data points in each dataset will be counted. If either dataset contains fewer data points than a pre specified threshold then a warning will be returned to the user. For example: with fewer than 20 data points determining whether the data is normally distributed can be difficult [16]. As normality is a prerequisite for many statistical tests, this may lead to an inappropriate test being chosen. A low number of datapoints may also reduce the probability that a statistically significant difference can be found [1].

2. It will then be determined whether or not the data is normally distributed. A decision tree within EETs will be used to choose an appropriate normality test:
   (a) For Dataset A the Shapiro-Wilk test will be used. This has been shown to perform better than several well known alternatives for a dataset size of between 20 and 40 [16].
   (b) For Dataset B the Shapiro-Francia test will be used as it has been shown to perform better than the Shapiro-Wilk test for dataset sizes above 40 [17].

3. Once it has been established that Dataset A does follow a normal distribution but Dataset B does not, a test will need to be carried out to determine whether the data is heteroscedastic or not. This will be the case if the two datasets have a different variance. Again, a decision tree within EETs is used to determine an appropriate check for heteroscedasticity.
   (a) For this decision the main consideration is whether the data is normally distributed. As in this case it is not, a common check for heteroscedasticity, the Bartlett test, is not suitable as it relies on both datasets following a normal distribution. Brown and Forsythe discuss a number of alternatives [3], including several variations of the Levene test, which may be used instead.

4. In this case, a reliable test for heteroscedasticity should show that the data that we are using is heteroscedastic.

5. It is now known that two preconditions that some statistical tests rely on, i.e. that both datasets are normally distributed and that there is no heteroscedasticity, are not met. This information will be used by the main decision tree that is used to decide on a statistical test:
   (a) In the absence of normality, a nonparametric test is likely to be more reliable than a parametric

test. The Mann-Whitney U test, a popular non-parametric test, will be considered [13].

   (b) The U test will be rejected when heteroscedasticity is considered as it is sensitive to heteroscedasticity. A more robust test, such as the Brunner-Munzel test [4] will be chosen.

6. Having chosen a test, the p value will be obtained.

7. If the p value is below the threshold, the datasets will be judged to be different to a statistically significant extent. An effect size test will now be chosen in a similar manner to how the significance test was chosen.

4. CONSEQUENCES

- **Decreased human effort** EETs allow further automation of the time-consuming process of parameter tuning and choosing an appropriate statistical test can now be achieved automatically.
- **Less dependence on the knowledge of the researcher** The necessary statistical knowledge is embedded within EETs.
- **A step towards fully-automated metaheuristic development** If a generative hyperheuristic [6] is integrated into EETs then the complete process of developing and testing metaheuristics may be automated.
- **Helps to ensure complete transparency in experimental methods** EETs will generate a report detailing every decision that was made and the grounds on which it was made. For example, suppose that a normality test is carried out in order to choose the most appropriate statistical test. Details of which normality test was used and how it was chosen, the resulting normality score and how this affected subsequent decisions will all be included in the report. This report will be in latex so that a complete, standardized and unambiguous account of statistical testing can be easily incorporated into publications for peer review.
- **Helps to ensure reproducibility** By making experimental conditions explicit it will be easier to recreate these experiments.
- **Helps to ensure a standard practise in the analysis of results** In current research, experimentation is often carried out in an informal and *ad hoc* manner [11]. A recent study by Arcuri found a lack of consistency in the quality of statistical testing [1]. In many cases the number of data points was insufficient and sometimes statistical testing was omitted altogether. By automating the process of statistical testing EETs will bring much needed standardization to this area.
- **Standardization and transparency in parameter tuning** The 'Sensitivity Layer' also encourages standardization and full transparancy in the process of parameter tuning. EETs produce a report which will enable researchers to provide complete, detailed and standardized information on how a new metaheuristic performs under different parameter settings. This will both confirm that the performance has been fairly assessed and provide information on metaheuristic robustness and the amount of parameter tuning that is required to produce good performance.

5. REFERENCES

[1] A. Arcuri and L. Briand. A practical guide for using statistical tests to assess randomized algorithms in software engineering. In *ACM/IEEE Int. Conf. on Software Engineering (ICSE)*, pages 1–10, 2011.

[2] Andrea Arcuri and Lionel Briand. A hitchhiker's guide to statistical tests for assessing randomized algorithms in software engineering. *Software Testing, Verification and Reliability*, 2012.

[3] Morton B Brown and Alan B Forsythe. Robust tests for the equality of variances. *Journ. of the American Statistical Association*, 69(346):364–367, 1974.

[4] Edgar Brunner and Ullrich Munzel. The nonparametric behrens-fisher problem: Asymptotic theory and a small-sample approximation. *Biometrical Journ.*, 42(1):17–25, 2000.

[5] Norman Cliff. Dominance statistics: Ordinal analyses to answer ordinal questions. *Psychological Bulletin*, 114(3):494, 1993.

[6] G. Kendall G. Ochoa E. Özcan E.K. Burke, M. Hyde and J. R. Woodward. *A Classification of Hyper-heuristic Approaches*, chapter Handbook of Meta-Heuristics, pages 449–468. Kluwer, 2010.

[7] Erich Gamma, Richard Helm, Ralph Johnson, and John Vlissides. *Design patterns: elements of reusable object-oriented software*. Pearson Education, 1994.

[8] Greffenstette. Optimization of control parameters for genetic algorithms. In *IEEE Trans. Syst. Man Cybern. SMC-16*, volume 1, pages 122–128, Jan/Feb 1986.

[9] Phil Souza Jerffeson Teixeira de Harman, Mark McMinn and Shin Yoo. Search based software engineering: Techniques, taxonomy, tutorial. In Bertrand Meyer and Martin Nordio, editors, *Empirical software engineering and verification: LASER 2009-2010*, pages 1–59. Springer, 2012. LNCS 7007.

[10] W.M. Hathaway. Automated hypothesis testing, February 5 2013. US Patent 8,370,107.

[11] John N Hooker. Needed: An empirical science of algorithms. *Operations Research*, 42(2):201–212, 1994.

[12] Sean Luke. *Essentials of Metaheuristics*. Lulu, second edition, 2013. Available for free at http://cs.gmu.edu/~sean/book/metaheuristics/.

[13] Henry B. Mann and Donald R. Whitney. On a test of whether one of two random variables is stochastically larger than the other. *The annals of mathematical statistics*, 18(1):50–60, 1947.

[14] J. Neyman and E. S. Pearson. On the Use and Interpretation of Certain Test Criteria for Purposes of Statistical Inference: Part I. *Biometrika*, 20A(1/2):175–240, July 1928.

[15] R Core Team. *R: A Language and Environment for Statistical Computing*. R Foundation for Statistical Computing, Vienna, Austria, 2013.

[16] Martin B Shapiro, Samuel S Wilk and Hwei J Chen. A comparative study of various tests for normality. *Journ. of the American Statistical Association*, 63(324):1343–1372, 1968.

[17] Samuel S Shapiro and RS Francia. An approximate analysis of variance test for normality. *Journ. of the American Statistical Association*, 67(337):215–216, 1972.

[18] Tiantian Wang, Mark Harman, Yue Jia, and Jens Krinke. Searching for better configurations: a rigorous approach to clone evaluation. In *European Software Engineering Conf. and the ACM SIGSOFT Symposium on the Foundations of Software Engineering, ESEC/FSE'13*, Saint Petersburg, Russian Federation, August 2013. ACM.

Metaheuristic Design Pattern: Interactive Solution Presentation

Mark R.N. Shackelford
Custom Software Development
Domestic and General Insurance
Brighton BN1 3FD
United Kingdom
mark.shackelford@domesticandgeneral.com

Christopher L. Simons
Department of Computer Science & Creative Technology
University of the West of England
Bristol BS16 1QY
United Kingdom
chris.simons@uwe.ac.uk

1. PROBLEM STATEMENT

In interactive metaheuristic search, the human helps to steer the trajectory of search by providing qualitative evaluations of solution individuals in the population. Given that much meta-heuristic search is typically population-based, it is challenging to design the presentation of solutions such that the human can provide effective qualitative evaluation [1]. Naively presenting each individual in a large population at each generation causes evaluation fatigue and a subsequent non-linearity of user focus making search trajectory inconsistent and ineffective [2].

Interactive search relies either on solely user-provided qualitative evaluation or a combination of user qualitative evaluation and machine-based quantitative fitness measures. User qualitative evaluation is often "multi-subjective" in that many fitness concerns are simultaneously evaluated [3]. Some evaluative concerns may be explicitly articulated by the user, although others are implicit. Thus the design of solution individual presentation is challenging but crucial to interactive metaheuristic search.

2. THE SOLUTION

Interactive Solution Presentation increases the focus and value of a single user interaction. A number of presentational mechanisms are available to achieve this, and these are grouped into potential design pattern abstractions:

2.1 Reduced Population Size

- *Rank-based presentation:* reduce population size significantly but present all candidate solutions in the population for rank ordering. User evaluation consists of placing candidate solutions in rank order rather than making absolute evaluations. Fitness values can be assigned to individuals in proportion to their rank.

2.2 Selected Individuals from Large Population

- *Banded presentation:* maintain a large population size but divide the population into N bands, where N is a suitably small number of solutions to present. One solution from each band is selected at random for presentation. The user evaluation of fitness for the band representative solution can be used to scale the original fitness values of all solutions in the band.
- *Partial sequential presentation:* maintain a large population size p, but select a reduced number for presentation at every p/N solutions from the population in fitness order, where N is suitably small number of solutions to present. Only the selected individuals have their fitness changed.
- *Partial random presentation*: maintain a large population size but select N solutions at random, where N is a suitably small number of solutions to present, and as with Partial Sequential presentation, only the selected individuals are changed.
- *Cluster representative presentation:* maintain a large population size but present a subset of the population to the user by eliminating solutions considered to be similar to their neighbors in the search space by means of 'clustering' algorithm based on some measure of distance between individuals. Those individuals presented to the user are thus considered to be representative of their close neighbors in the search landscape. Fitness values are assigned to individuals in proportion to their distance from the qualitatively evaluated individuals.
- *Surrogate presentation:* maintain a large population size but reduce the number of individuals presented to the user by applying 'quick and dirty' quantitative measures as surrogates of user evaluation to eliminate candidate solutions anticipated to be of little utility to the user.

2.3 Multiple Generations between Interactions

- *Fixed presentation interval:* present individuals from the population to users only after a fixed number of computational search iterations have elapsed rather than every iteration.
- *Fitness proportionate presentation interval:* present individuals to users at dynamic numbers of computational search iterations in proportion to overall population fitness. Where user evaluation is combined with computational quantitative calculation of fitness measures, early iterations of search rely on computational calculations. However, as iterations progress, the influence of user evaluation is more pronounced as population fitness increases.

3. CONSEQUENCES

For interactive search where qualitative user evaluation is the sole means of candidate solution fitness measurement, Reduced Population Size (e.g. *rank-based presentation)* can be beneficial. Conversely, for interactive search where qualitative user

GECCO '14, July 12 - 16 2014, Vancouver, BC, Canada

ACM 978-1-4503-2881-4/14/07...$15.00.
http://dx.doi.org/10.1145/2598394.2609849

evaluation is combined with computational quantitative fitness calculation, Selected Individuals (e.g. *banded, cluster representative* or *surrogate presentation)* can be valuable. For interactive search where large numbers of iterations are required for effective exploration of the search space, Multiple Generations (e.g. *fixed presentation interval* and *fitness proportionate presentation interval*) can beneficial.

Two competing forces drive a significant trade-off in interactive solution presentation. Firstly, it's important to minimize user evaluation fatigue, which requires that evaluation is effective in influencing the search trajectory to arrive swiftly at promising individuals and regions of search space. However, it's also important to maintain diversity in the population to ensure satisfactory exploration of the search space. *Banded, partial sequential, partial random, cluster representative* and *surrogate presentation* can all be useful when balancing this trade-off.

4. EXAMPLES

4.1 Rank-based Presentation

This has been widely used in a variety of interactive metaheuristic search applications. For instance, rank-based presentation has been used for large, real-world resource constrained multiple-project scheduling problems involving complex quality criteria [4]. Up to 25 evolving schedules are presented (as Gannt charts or Resource profiles) for ranking which enables the search to be guided by both the standard schedule quality criteria and also the master scheduler's non-formalized knowledge and experience. Rank-based presentation has also been used in the interactive evolution of user interfaces in the XUL interface definition language [5]. Rather than overload the user, the top fittest ten of a population of 100 interfaces are presented to the user, but the user has only to pick two for ranking. A further application of rank-based presentation can be seen in the adaptive surface inspection of hot freshly rolled steel sheets via interactive evolution [6]. An evolutionary strategy approach is used to generate eight offspring from a single parent individual image. When an engineer inspects the surfaces, images may be inspected side-by-side, and the eight individual images are ranked by the user scoring each image on a scale of 0 to 10. In a further different rank-based approach, the layout of a simple planar graph is evolved interactively by co-evolving a set of weights to take account of personal users' preferences based on the ranking of individual graph layouts [7].

4.2 Small Populations

An example of small populations of individuals presented to user for ranking relates to conceptual bridge design [8]. In this example, small populations (i.e. 20) of individual bridge designs comprising simple horizontal span bridges with and without support and angled span bridges with supports are presented to the user for ranking. Quantitative fitness measures relating to both the structural integrity and aesthetics of the bridge designs are combined with user-assigned ranking fitness to steer the search trajectory. In an example in the field of software engineering, rank-based presentation has been used in an interactive genetic algorithm for software re-modularization [9]. Two ranking presentation mechanisms are trialed. In the first mechanism, a number of individual software component pairs are presented to the user who simply ranks them as part of the same module or not. In the second, small modules containing a single software component are presented and the user is asked to rank other modules as the most appropriate to act as a placeholder for the component.

A further example of small populations of individuals being presented to users for ranked evaluation involves ergonomic chair design [10]. In this example, qualitative designer rankings of chair designs are combined with quantitative fitness measures relating to the structural integrity of chairs to steer the search trajectory. In a further example, rank-based presentation is also used with small population sizes for combining morphological fitness (e.g. fractal symmetries) with aesthetic fitness in jewelry design [11]. Indeed, small population sizes (i.e. < 10) have been recommended for interactive evolutionary computing to facilitate rank-based presentation [12].

4.3 Partial Presentation

Examples of *banded-presentation*, *partial sequential presentation* and *partial random presentation* can be found in interactive evolutionary search for drug discovery [13]. In this example, the goal is not to find an optimal solution or even a molecule that could be synthesized by a chemist, but rather to enable the user to explore the drug molecule design search space to arrive at fruitful candidate solutions that might be outside the user experience. The main intention with these methods is to maintain diversity (by keeping a large population) whilst at the same time allowing interactive fitness on a limited number of individuals.

4.4 Cluster Representative Presentation

This technique has been used in numerous engineering design domains where Cluster-Oriented Genetic Algorithms (COGAs) [14],[15] have been used in interactive search to identify high-performance regions of complex, multi-dimensional engineering design search spaces.

4.5 Surrogate Presentation

This interactive technique has been explored in a variety of search-based software testing systems where the user and computational search combine to generate effective test cases [16]. An 'Interaction Handler' component displays potential solutions to the user and collects feedback which is subsequently exploited to enable a dynamic preliminary selection of potential solutions for future presentation. In another example, decision maker preferences are exploited to enable strictly monotone progressively approximated value functions [17]. This preference-based approximated value function is used to select a subset of population individuals which are then evaluated by the decision maker in pair-wise comparisons. Surrogate presentation has also been used in the interactive search for early lifecycle software designs [18], where surrogate measures of software design elegance are used to select individuals from a large sized population for designer evaluation. In a further example of interactive genetic algorithm-based design of fashion garments, a surrogate model of user evaluation is used to alleviate user fatigue by building a classifier and a regressor to approximate the designer's cognition [19]. Two reliable training sets based on user evaluation are obtained, and then support vector classification and regression machines are trained as surrogate models. The input trained samples are the individuals evaluated by the user, and the output training samples of the classifier and the regressor are the widths and centers of individuals' fuzzy fitness assigned by the user, respectively.

4.6 Fixed Presentation Interval

Recommended by Kamalian et al. [20] as a concept to reduce user evaluation fatigue (in addition to reducing the number of individuals for user evaluation), fixed presentation interval has also been applied to interactive search-based software testing of embedded software systems [21].

4.7 Fitness Proportionate Presentation

This has been shown to be effective in interactive search for early lifecycle software designs [18], [22]. Quantitative computational calculations minimizing design coupling are combined with interactive user evaluation of design elegance. Initially, the number of iterations between user evaluations is high but as design coupling is minimized, the number of iterations between user evaluation decreases as qualitative assessments of design elegance increasingly steer search.

5. REFERENCES

[1] Tagaki, H. (2001) Interactive Evolutionary Computation: A Fusion of the Capabilities of EC Optimisation and Human Evaluation. *Proceedings of the ACM.* 78(9), 1275-1296.

[2] Shackelford, M.R.N. (2005) Implementation Issues for an Interactive Evolutionary Computation System. *Proceedings of the 2005 Genetic and Evolutionary Computation Conference (GECCO '05)*, 1045-1051, ACM Press.

[3] Miettinen, K.M. (1998) *Nonlinear Multiobjective Optimization.* Kluwer Academic Publishers.

[4] Shackelford M.R.N. and Corne, D. (2001) Collaborative Evolutionary Multi-project Resource Scheduling. *Proceedings of the 2001 Congress on Evolutionary Computing, vol. 2,* 1131-1138, IEEE Press.

[5] Quiroz, J.C., Louis, S.J. and Dascalu, S.M. (2007) Interactive Evolution of XUL User Interfaces. *Proceedings of the 2007 Annual Conference on Genetic and Evolutionary Computation (GECCO '07)*, 2151-2158, ACM Press.

[6] Caleb-Solly, P. and Smith, J.E. (2007) Adaptive Surface Inspection via Interactive Evolution. *Image and Vision Computing*, 25(7), 1058-1072.

[7] Barbosa, H.J. and Barreto, A.M. (2001) An Interactive Genetic Algorithm with Co-evolution of Weights for Multi-objective Problems. *Proceedings of the 2001 Annual Conference on Genetic and Evolutionary Computing (GECCO '01)*, 203-210, Morgan Kaufman.

[8] Machwe, A.T. and Parmee, I.C. (2007) Multi-objective Analysis of a Component-based Representation within an Interactive Evolutionary Design System. *Engineering Optimisation.* 39(5), 591-613.

[9] Bavota, G., Carnevale, F., De Lucia, A., Di Penta, M. and Oliveto, R. (2012) Putting the Developer in-the-loop: An Interactive GA for Software Re-modularization. *Proceedings of the 4th International Symposium on Search-Based Software Engineering (SSBSE 2012), LNCS 7515,* 75-89, Springer-Verlag, Heidelburg, Berlin.

[10] Brintrup, A.M., Ramsden, J., Takagi, H. and Tiwiri, A. (2008) Ergonomic Chair Design by Fusing Qualitative and Quantitative Criteria Using Interactive Genetic Algorithms. *IEEE Transactions on Evolutionary Computation.* 12(3), 343-354.

[11] Wannarumon. S., Bohez, E.L.J. and Annanon, K. (2008) Aesthetic Evolutionary Algorithm for Fractal-based User-cenered Jewely Design. *Artificial Intelligence for Engineering Design, Analysis and Manufacturing.* 22(1), 19-39.

[12] Bentley, P. (1999) An Introduction to Evolutionary Design by Computers. In *Evolutionary Design by Computer* (Bentley, P. Ed.), 1-73, Morgan Kaufmann.

[13] Shackelford, M.R.N. (2014) Evolutionary Algorithm for Drug Discovery Interim Design Report. Online: http://arxov.org/abs/1403.4871

[14] Parmee, I.C., Cvetkovic, D, Watson, A.H. and Bonham, C.R. (2000) Multiobjective Satisfaction within an Interactive Evolutionary Design Environment. *Evolutionary Computation.* 8(2), 197-222.

[15] Bonham, C.R. and Parmee, I.C. (2004) Developments of the Cluster-Oriented Genetic Algorithm (COGA). *Engineering Optimisation.* 36(2), 249-279.

[16] Marculescu, B., Feldt R. and Torkar, R. (2012) A Concept for an Interactive Search-Based Software Testing System. *Proceedings of the 4th International Symposium on Search-Based Software Engineering (SSBSE 2012), LNCS 7515,* 273-278, Springer-Verlag, Heidelburg, Berlin.

[17] Deb, K., Sinha, A., Korhonen, P.J and Wallenius, J. (2010) An Interactive Evolutionary Multiobjective Optimization Method Based on Progressively Approximated Value Functions. *IEEE Transactions on Evolutionary Computation.* 14(5), 723-739.

[18] Simons, C.L. and Parmee, I.C. (2012) Elegant Object-oriented Software Design via Interactive Evolutionary Computation. *IEEE Transactions on Systems, Man, and Cybernetics, Part C: Applications and Reviews.* 42(6), 1797-1805.

[19] Sun, X, Gong, D. and Li, S. (2009) Classification and Regression-based Surrogate Model-assisted Interactive Genetic Algorithm with Individual Fuzzy Fitness. *Proceedings of the 2009 Annual Conference on Genetic and Evolutionary Computation (GECCO '09)*, 907-914, ACM Press.

[20] Kamalian, R., Yeh, E., Zhang, Y., Agogino, A. and Takagi, H. (2006) Reducing Human Fatigue in Interactive Evolutionary Computation through Fuzzy Systems and Machine Learning Systems. *Proceedings of the 2006 IEEE International Conference on Fuzzy Systems*, 678-684, IEEE Press.

[21] Marculescu, B., Feldt R. and Torkar, R. (2013) Objective Re-Weighting to Guide an Interactive Search-Based Software Testing System. *Proceedings on the 12th International Conference on Machine Learning and Applications*, in press, IEEE Press.

[22] Simons, C.L., Smith, J.E. and White, P. (2012) Interactive Ant Colony Optimization (iACO) for Early Lifecycle Software Design. Online: http://arxiv.org/abs/1212.5461

The 'Representative' Metaheuristic Design Pattern

Jerry Swan
Computing Science and Mathematics
University of Stirling
FK9 4LA Scotland UK
jsw@cs.stir.ac.uk

Zoltan A. Kocsis
Computing Science and Mathematics
University of Stirling
FK9 4LA Scotland UK
zak@cs.stir.ac.uk

Alexei Lisitsa
Department of Computer Science
University of Liverpool
L69 7ZF UK
A.Lisitsa@liverpool.ac.uk

Categories and Subject Descriptors

I.1 [**SYMBOLIC AND ALGEBRAIC MANIPULATION**]: General|Expressions and Their Representation|Simplification of expressions.

Keywords

Term Rewriting; Design Patterns; Evolutionary Computing; Metaheuristics.

1. PROBLEM STATEMENT

The 'Representative' pattern is applicable when it is desirable to eliminate redundancy in the search process:

- It is often the case that some function f of interest in optimization gives a many-to-one mapping, i.e. it induces equivalence classes over the image of f. If f is a fitness function, this can lead to plateaus in the fitness landscape.
- It may be that the elimination of redundancy allows search to be performed in a smaller ('quotient') space that can be searched using methods (possibly even *exact* techniques) not applicable to the original space.
- In the case of GP-trees, syntactically inequivalent but semantically equivalent representations (e.g. $x+x, 2*x$) can lead to a lack of gradient in genotype-to-phenotype mappings, which *may* make the space of programs harder to search effectively.

2. THE SOLUTION

Transform representations into a normal or canonical form.

It is useful here to adopt the terminology of the computer algebra community in distinguishing between these forms [6]. Consider some representation $\mathcal{R}$ with equivalence relation $\sim$. Syntactic equivalence on $\mathcal{R}$ is denoted by $\equiv$.
For some distinguished element $0_{\mathcal{R}} \in \mathcal{R}$, a *normal form* of $\mathcal{R}$ is the output of a procedure $N : \mathcal{R} \to \mathcal{R}$ such that for all $x \in \mathcal{R}$

$$N(x) \sim x$$

GECCO'14, July 12–16, 2014, Vancouver, BC, Canada.

ACM 978-1-4503-2881-4/14/07 ...$15.00.
http://dx.doi.org/10.1145/2598394.2609842.

$$x \sim 0_{\mathcal{R}} \implies N(x) \equiv N(0_{\mathcal{R}})$$

A *canonical form* of $\mathcal{R}$ is the output of a procedure $C : \mathcal{R} \to \mathcal{R}$ such that for all $x, y \in \mathcal{R}$

$$C(x) \sim x$$

$$x \sim y \implies C(x) \equiv C(y)$$

Since canonical implies normal but not conversely, even if both forms exist it is generally less computationally-expensive to compute normal forms. For example, the normal form procedure for univariate polynomials is given by recursively distributing products over sums, collecting like terms and eliminating terms with zero coefficients. In this case, the canonical form requires the additional step of applying a fixed ordering to terms (i.e. by degree-order). For boolean functions, both DNF and CNF are ubiquitous normal forms. If we fix the ordering of propositional letters and consider minimal equivalents, one may obtain a canonical form. Moreover, boolean polynomials (a.k.a. Zhegalkin polynomials [17]) may serve as an alternative algebraic normal form (ANF). Note also that functions on fixed-width integers (e.g. 32-bit) can be treated as boolean functions. Table 1 gives references for representative forms for a variety of structures. The existence of normal and canonical forms (jointly, 'representative forms' hereafter) depends on the algebraic properties of the representation. The representative forms of many structures of interest in metaheuristics can found via the application of *term rewriting* [2], which proceeds via the iterated application of a *Term Rewriting System* (TRS). For a set of elements of a structure of type S (e.g. polynomials, operators etc), let the set of all possible combinations of elements of S (e.g. expression trees, operator sequences etc) be denoted by Σ^*. A *rewriting system* $(\mathcal{S}, <)$ is then a set of ordered pairs $(l, r) \in \Sigma^* \times \Sigma^*$ subject to the condition $l < r$, where $<$ is a *reduction ordering* that determines which of two expressions is to be considered 'more simple'. The elements of $\mathcal{S}$ are called *rewrite-rules.* and the idea is that we can replace occurrences of l in a r in the hope of that we will eventually arrive at a maximally simplified expression. Under certain conditions on $<$ [2], this hope is justified: the iterated application of rewrite rules will always yield a unique representative. Such a rewriting system is said to be *confluent*.

3. THE CONSEQUENCES

- Transformations into representative form can be used to reduce the size of the state-space graph. By converting solution states (or operator sequences, as per the example below) into their representative forms, one is

Algebraic Structure	Representative Algorithm
Monoid or Group	[8]
Boolean function	[3]
Polynomial	[6, 11]
Polynomials modulo an Ideal	[4]
Rational function	[6, 11]
Truncated power series	[11]

Table 1: Computing representatives of various algebraic structures

effectively working in a smaller (a.k.a. quotient) search space.

- Elimination of redundancy is not necessarily advantageous. Reduction to representative form by removing non-functional elements from evolutionary computation (e.g. $0 * s$ for any subexpression s) can reduce neutrality in genotype-to-phenotype mappings. The presence of such redundancy is argued by some to be desirable [16], since it is argued that non-functional nodes can nonetheless contribute to good quality solutions in subsequent generations. However, there is no consensus in this respect [10].

4. EXAMPLES

- In [14], a canonical form for rational functions over $\mathbb{Q}$ is given in terms of their roots. In constrast to the corresponding GP-tree, it is possible to make small changes to this representation.
- Finite state automata are a ubiquitous representation in evolutionary computation [9]. It is well-known that there is a unique canonical form for Deterministic Finite-state Automata (subject to the imposition of a specified ordering on transitions), and there are a number of DFA-minimization algorithms (having $O(n * log(n))$ average-case behaviour) for achieving this. An empirical comparison of several of these algorithms is given in [1].
- Binary decision diagrams provide a canonical form for boolean functions [3]. In [15], Genetic Programming is augmented via the use of binary-decision diagrams to share isomorphic sub-graphs across the population, thereby solving the 20-multiplexer problem.
- Techniques such as tabu search have traditionally exploited domain knowledge about operators (e.g. prohibiting the inverse of an operation for some number of iterations). Any set of operators can be considered as a *monoid* under concatenation, and we can use the *Knuth Bendix Algorithm* to convert a sequence of operators into its length-minimal canonical form [13]. By this means, as an offline activity it is possible to eliminate all operator sequences that represent cycles in the state-space graph.
- The λ-calculus with β-reduction as a rewrite rule is confluent, so normal forms are unique whenever they exist [5].Normally, uniqueness is up to renaming of bound variables only, but it can be extended to syntactic equality using the method of de Bruijn indices [7]. There are multiple algorithms for finding normal forms, their differences in reduction strategy dictated by the distinction between *lazy* and *eager* evaluation in functional programming languages. A non-deterministic optimal algorithm for finding normal forms is given in [12].

5. REFERENCES

[1] Marco Almeida, Nelma Moreira, and Rogério Reis. On the performance of automata minimization algorithms. Tech report, Universidade do Porto, 2007.

[2] Franz Baader and Tobias Nipkow. *Term Rewriting and All That*. Cambridge University Press, New York, 1998.

[3] Randal E. Bryant. Graph-based algorithms for boolean function manipulation. *IEEE Trans. Comput.*, 35(8):677–691, August 1986.

[4] Bruno Buchberger. An algorithm for finding the basis elements of the residue class ring of a zero dimensional polynomial ideal. *J. Symb. Comput.*, 41(3-4):475–511, 2006.

[5] Alonzo Church and J. B. Rosser. Some properties of conversion. *Transactions of the American Mathematical Society*, 39(3):pp. 472–482, 1936.

[6] James Harold Davenport, Y Siret, E. Tournier, and A. Davenport. Computer algebra : systems and algorithms for algebraic computation, 1993.

[7] N.G de Bruijn. Lambda calculus notation with nameless dummies. *Indagationes Mathematicae (Proceedings)*, 75(5):381 – 392, 1972.

[8] D. B. A. Epstein, D. F. Holt, and S. E. Rees. The use of Knuth-Bendix methods to solve the word problem in automatic groups. *J. Symb. Comput.*, 12(4-5):397–414, October 1991.

[9] L.J. Fogel, A.J. Owens, and M.J. Walsh. *Artificial intelligence through simulated evolution*. Wiley, Chichester, WS, UK, 1966.

[10] Edgar Galván-López, Riccardo Poli, Ahmed Kattan, Michael O'Neill, and Anthony Brabazon. Neutrality in evolutionary algorithms... what do we know? *Evolving Systems*, 2(3):145–163, 2011.

[11] Keith O. Geddes, Stephen R. Czapor, and George Labahn. *Algorithms for computer algebra*. Kluwer, 1992.

[12] John Lamping. An algorithm for optimal lambda calculus reduction. pages 16–30. ACM Press, 1990.

[13] J. Swan, M. Edjvet, and E. Özcan. Augmenting metaheuristics with rewriting systems. Technical Report CSM-197, Computing Science and Mathematics, University of Stirling, Stirling FK9 4LA, Scotland, January 2014.

[14] John R. Woodward and Ruibin Bai. Canonical representation genetic programming. In *GEC Summit*, pages 585–592, 2009.

[15] Masayuki Yanagiya. Efficient genetic programming based on binary decision diagrams. In *1995 IEEE Conference on Evolutionary Computation*, volume 1, pages 234–239, Perth, Australia, 29 November - 1 December 1995. IEEE Press.

[16] Tina Yu and Julian Miller. Finding needles in haystacks is not hard with neutrality. In James A Foster et al, editors, *Genetic Programming*, volume 2278 of *Lecture Notes in Computer Science*, pages 13–25. Springer, 2002.

[17] Ivan Ivanovich Zhegalkin. On the technique of calculating propositions in symbolic logic. *Matematicheskii Sbornik*, 43:9–28, 1927.

Template Method Hyper-heuristics

John Woodward
Computing Science and Mathematics
University of Stirling
FK9 4LA Scotland UK
john.woodward@cs.stir.ac.uk

Jerry Swan
Computing Science and Mathematics
University of Stirling
FK9 4LA Scotland UK
jerry.swan@cs.stir.ac.uk

1. PROBLEM STATEMENT

The optimization literature is awash with metaphorically-inspired metaheuristics and their subsequent variants and hybridizations. This results in a plethora of methods, with descriptions that are often polluted with the language of the metaphor which inspired them [8]. Within such a fragmented field, the traditional approach of manual 'operator tweaking' makes it difficult to establish the contribution of individual metaheuristic components to the overall success of a methodology.

Irrespective of whether it happens to best the state-of-the-art, such 'tweaking' is so labour-intensive that does relatively little to advance scientific understanding. In order to introduce further structure and rigour, it is therefore desirable to not only to be able to specify entire *families* of metaheuristics (rather than individual metaheuristics), but also be able to generate and test them. In particular, the adoption of a *model agnostic* approach towards the generation of metaheuristics would help to establish which metaheuristic components are useful contributors to a solution.

2. THE SOLUTION

In [7], Krasnogor shows how families of algorithms can be specified in terms of the well-known *template method pattern* [4]. The template-method is a definition of an algorithm 'skeleton' within which the interaction of a collection of abstractly-specified components is orchestrated. Components can be thought of as classes/procedures/functions in object-oriented/procedural functional programming terms. The hard-coded backbone restricts the set of possible algorithms expressed by the template, while the abstract component specification allows for variant implementations within the specified constraints.

Given the requirement to not only specify the members of a family of metaheuristics, but also to *generate* them, the behavioural constraint imposed on the components by the template method is of relevance for two main reasons:

GECCO'14, July 12–16, 2014, Vancouver, BC, Canada.

ACM 978-1-4503-2881-4/14/07...$15.00.
http://dx.doi.org/10.1145/2598394.2609843 ...$15.00.

Firstly, automatic algorithm synthesis methods such as Genetic Programming (GP) are not yet capable of evolving complete programs from scratch (i.e. those which require nested loops, indexed memory and other control structures such as switch statements). In current practice, GP is best employed to evolve *expressions*, i.e. small mathematical functions or logical expressions. To facilitate the creation of larger programs, the fixed part of a hyper-heuristic template can be seen as providing the orchestrating control structures. A simple example would be with the skeleton providing an iterative procedure (e.g. a for-loop with appropriate bounds), and the variant implementation of the iteration body providing by GP (e.g. the body of the for-loop). This is true of many of the examples in Section 4.

Secondly, Template-Method Hyper-heuristics allows a metaheuristic to be automatically tuned to the set of problems of specific interest. A consequence of the No Free Lunch (NFL) theorems [6] is that no 'universal' optimizer exists, and hence metaheuristics must be specialised on a problem-specific basis. One approach to this to use is meta-learning [5] to adapt a heuristic to the problem instances to which it will be exposed. This employs the traditional machine-learning style of splitting a set of problem instances into disjoint training and testing sets [1] as practiced in [10, 9]. A consequence of NFL is that metaheuristics should not be 'designed' in isolation from a problem domain but designed (and most importantly their performance cited) in the context of some representative problem instances.

As a concrete example of an algorithm template, consider a framwork for a simple evolutionary algorithm. In generative terms, for population P and population history H (the latter being a list of successive populations), we can consider the framework to be parameterized by five variant methods:

$$\begin{aligned} initialization &: Void \to P \\ selection &: P \times H \to P \\ variation &: P \times H \to P \\ succession &: P \times H \to P \\ termination &: H \to Bool \end{aligned}$$

In general, we can either elect to search the entire design space defined by this framework (e.g. by simultaneously searching for good versions of all the variant components) or else fix one or more components and generate the others. Section 4 gives examples where the selection operator and mutation operators are evolved.

3. CONSEQUENCES

- 'Tuned to the problem'. If the heuristic is designed

```
procedure evolve
begin
  pop = initialization()
  history = []
  repeat
    parents =  selection( pop, history )
    offspring =  variation( parents, history )
    pop  = succession( offspring, history )
    history =  history.append( pop )
  until termination( history )
end
```

in the context of representative problem instances, the resulting heuristic will be expected to perform well on problem instances drawn from a similar probabality distribution as the problem instances in the training phase. Equally there will be a degradation in performance if the training does not reflect the testing [3].

- 'Algorithm agnostic'. Given a palette of metaheuristic components, the ones that are best suited to the problem instances under consideration will have a greater chance of appearing in the resulting heuristic.
- 'Human competitive performance'. The heuristics produced by this method will produce results which are competitive with already existing human designed heuristics. Indeed, we have the choice of initialzing the search process with already existing heuristics and therefore the design process can be thought of as *improving* algorithms, rather than inventing them from *scratch.*
- 'Decreased human effort'. There is a financial cost involved in developing a heuristic. If we continue to manually design heuristics, this price will increase inline with inflation. However, if we harness automatic design, this price is likely to fall as processor speeds increase roughly with Moore's law. Therefore, if this method of automatic design that we advocate is adopted [2], this monetray cost is expected to fall in the long term.

4. EXAMPLES

Evolving Mutation Operators For Genetic Algorithms Two well-known GA mutation operators on bit-strings are one-point (which alters a single bit in the bit-string) and uniform mutation (which alters all bits in the bit-string with a fixed probability). The well-known GA template can be parameterized by its mutation operator, which can be considered as a procedure with type signature $mutation : \mathbb{B}^n \rightarrow \mathbb{B}^n$. In [9] GP is used to automatically generate a mutation operator that outperforms both one-point and uniform mutation. Key to the success of this approach is setting up the orchestrating template so that operators known to be effective are easily generated by GP or can be encoded easily by a human programmer (e.g. the ability to express one-point and uniform mutation as degenerate cases).

Evolving Selection Operators Similarly, as with the case of mutation abovef selection operators are commonly implemented as either fitness-proportional (which assigns a selection value in proportion to absolute fitness f) or rank selection (which assigns a selection value according to its rank index r in the sorted population of bit-strings). One generalization of these two selection operators is a selection function $selection : \mathbb{R}^2 \rightarrow \mathbb{R}$ which takes as arguments the absolute fitness f and the rank index r and assigns a selection value to each bit-string in the population. Clearly, by returing just the first argument we have fitness-proportional selection, and by returning just the second argument we have rank selection. In [10], GP (with f and r in its terminal set) is used to develop a new selection operator that outperforms both of these two standard selection operators.

5. REFERENCES

[1] Mauro Birattari, Mark Zlochin, and Marco Dorigo. Towards a theory of practice in metaheuristics design: A machine learning perspective. *ITA*, 40(2):353–369, 2006.

[2] Edmund K. Burke, Mathew R. Hyde, Graham Kendall, Gabriela Ochoa, Ender Ozcan, and John R. Woodward. Exploring hyper-heuristic methodologies with genetic programming. In Christine L. Mumford and Lakhmi C. Jain, editors, *Computational Intelligence*, volume 1 of *Intelligent Systems Reference Library*, chapter 6, pages 177–201. Springer, 2009.

[3] Edmund K. Burke, Matthew R. Hyde, Graham Kendall, and John Woodward. Automatic heuristic generation with genetic programming: evolving a jack-of-all-trades or a master of one. In Dirk Thierens et al., editor, *GECCO '07: Proceedings of the 9th annual conference on Genetic and evolutionary computation*, volume 2, pages 1559–1565, London, 7-11 July 2007. ACM Press.

[4] Erich Gamma, Richard Helm, Ralph Johnson, and John Vlissides. *Design Patterns: Elements of Reusable Object-oriented Software.* Addison-Wesley Longman Publishing Co., Inc., Boston, MA, USA, 1995.

[5] C. Giraud-Carrier and F. Provost. Toward a Justification of Meta-learning: Is the No Free Lunch Theorem a Show-stopper? In *Proceedings of the ICML-2005 Workshop on Meta-learning*, pages 12–19, 2005.

[6] Christian Igel. No free lunch theorems: Limitations and perspectives of metaheuristics, 2014.

[7] N. Krasnogor. Memetic algorithms, 2009.

[8] Kenneth Sörensen. Metaheuristics–the metaphor exposed. 2012.

[9] John R. Woodward and Jerry Swan. The automatic generation of mutation operators for genetic algorithms. In Gisele L. Pappa, John Woodward, Matthew R. Hyde, and Jerry Swan, editors, *GECCO 2012 2nd Workshop on Evolutionary Computation for the Automated Design of Algorithms*, pages 67–74, Philadelphia, Pennsylvania, USA, 7-11 July 2012. ACM.

[10] John Robert Woodward and Jerry Swan. Automatically designing selection heuristics. In Gisele L. Pappa, Alex A. Freitas, Jerry Swan, and John Woodward, editors, *GECCO 2011 1st workshop on evolutionary computation for designing generic algorithms*, pages 583–590, Dublin, Ireland, 12-16 July 2011. ACM.

The 'Composite' Design Pattern in Metaheuristics

John Woodward
Computing Science and Mathematics
University of Stirling
FK9 4LA Scotland UK
john.woodward@cs.stir.ac.uk

Jerry Swan
Computing Science and Mathematics
University of Stirling
FK9 4LA Scotland UK
jsw@cs.stir.ac.uk

Simon Martin
Computing Science and Mathematics
University of Stirling
FK9 4LA Scotland UK
spm@cs.stir.ac.uk

Categories and Subject Descriptors

I.2 [**ARTIFICIAL INTELLIGENCE**]: Problem Solving, Control Methods, and Search|Heuristic methods.

Keywords

Design Patterns; Evolutionary Computing; Metaheuristics; Hyper-heuristics; Classifiers.

1. THE 'COMPOSITE' DESIGN PATTERN

Introduced in [13], the 'Composite' Design Pattern can be observed whenever some 'aggregator' object can be considered to share behavioural commonalities with the entities from which it is composed. It therefore offers a concise means of describing functional [9] or structural recursion [5], which are of course ubiquitous in computer science and software engineering. In computer science, the prototypical example is a recursive data structure such as a tree, defined inductively either as an empty node or else as a node having a list of nodes as its children. In software engineering, an example is a concept such as Displayable, instances of which might include OKButton, (which can directly display itself), or Window which might display itself by asking all the Displayables it contains to display themselves in turn. Figure 1 shows the class diagram for a prototypical example of the composite pattern [13].

It is useful to be able to identify Composite relationships within metaheuristics for several reasons:

- Ease of communicating entity relationships — the same motivation for factoring patterns from software architectures.
- Facilitating automation — a composite implicitly defines a 'grammar template' for the generation of new metaheuristic components.

In general, the pattern is applicable whenever either or both of the following apply:

GECCO'14, July 12–16, 2014, Vancouver, BC, Canada.

ACM 978-1-4503-2881-4/14/07 ...$15.00.
http://dx.doi.org/10.1145/2598394.2609848.

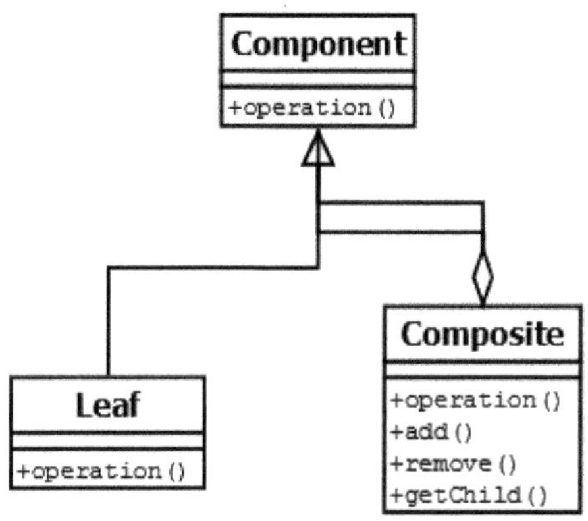

Figure 1: UML class diagram of composite pattern

- Decisions can incorporate information obtained by a diverse range of techniques (e.g. ensemble methods, selective hyper-heuristics).
- The granularity at which decisions are made imposes a notion of hierarchy that can be expressed by aggregation (e.g. multi-level search).

In their most general form, the behaviour of instances of the Composite pattern might be expressed by a collection of functions (e.g. isLeaf(), numChildren(),display() etc). In the case where the behaviour to be aggregated consists of a single function f (as is often the case in metaheuristics, as demonstrated by the above example), with signature

$$f(t_1 : T_1, t_2 : T_2, \ldots, t_n : T_n)$$

where $T_1 \ldots T_n$ are the types of the formal arguments, then the value of composite function f_c (with k children with functions $f_1 \ldots f_k$ respectively, each with the same signature as f_c) can be expressed in general as:

$$f_c(t_1 : T_1, t_2 : T_2, \ldots, t_n : T_n) \triangleq_{def} g(t_1, t_2, \ldots, t_n, f_1, \ldots, f_k)$$

where the implementation of g may elect to invoke any or all of $f_1, \ldots, f_k$ as some arbitrary function of actual parameter values $t_1, \ldots, t_n$. Such a formulation clearly lends itself to automation, e.g. via genetic programming [20] or decision tree induction [26].

Below, we give two detailed examples of the 'Composite' pattern in metaheuristics (viz. 'Hyper-heuristic as composite metaheuristic' and 'Composition of Classifiers'). These (and the 'composite function' scheme just described) are merely exemplars: if the above criteria apply, then the pattern is of potential value across the entire spectrum of metaheuristic concerns (e.g. clustering, dimensionality reduction etc).

2. HYPER-HEURISTICS AS COMPOSITE METAHEURISTICS

2.1 Problem statement

The uniform treatment of a collection of operators is likely to be useful when:

- It is necessary to escape the combined basins of attraction of a cluster of local minima. The required perturbation strength should therefore ideally be dynamically determined (e.g. as in the 'breakout local search' metaheuristic [?]).
- It is desirable (as is the case with multi-level search) to treat perturbation as a heirarchical aggregation of lower-level perturbations (grounding of course in primitive operators that directly affect solution state).
- We wish to clarify the relationship between hyper-heuristics and the operators they invoke or generate. Hyper-heuristics can be described as "heuristics for searching the space of heuristics", and (in the form of *selective hyperheuristics*) can be seen as imposing a homogeneous perspective on the heterogeneous selection of operators.
- A more expansive (yet concrete) definition of hyper-heuristic is required in order to facilitate the creation of solvers that can act with greater autonomy. Although hyper-heuristics have been categorized as selective or generative [4], there is no necessity for solvers to be restricted *a priori* to only one of these categories.

The 'Composite' pattern is applicable precisely when we wish to treat entities and collections of entities in such a uniform manner. Explicit acknowledgement of the presence of the composite pattern allows the relationship between the levels of operator application to be formally clarified.

2.2 The solution

Let S denote solution-state and let $[S]$ be a list of same. We start by formally defining an operator. For generality, it is convenient to operate on traces (i.e. a time-series of solution states) rather than single states — this allows the operator to act as a function of solution history (e.g. in the manner of tabu search). Define an operator to be a function with signature

$$O_S : [S] \to [S]$$

where the argument represents the trace of solution-states and the result represents the extension of the trace obtained by applying the operator. Following [29], we can then define a hyper-heuristic to be a function with the following signature:

$$\mathcal{H}_S : [S] \times [O_S] \to [S] \times [O_S]$$

i.e. $\mathcal{H}_S$ takes a list of solutions and a list of operators as input, and produces as output a (potentially updated) list of solutions and operators. It is clear that this suffices to represent both selective and generative hyper-heuristics: the former may update only the solution list, the latter the operator list.

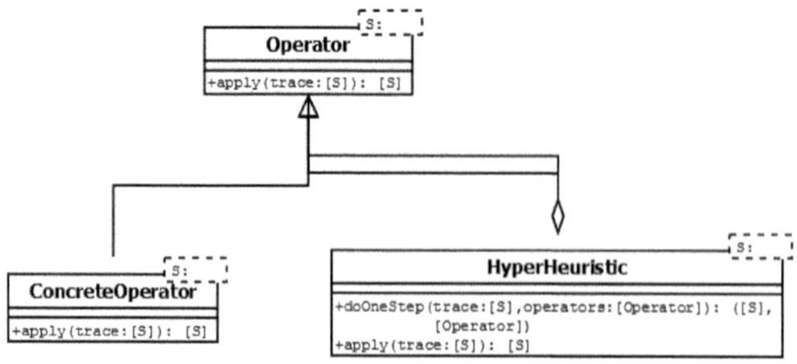

Figure 2: UML class diagram of composite hyper-heuristic

We consider $\mathcal{H}_S$ to be *parameterized* by S, i.e. it is associated with a specific type of solution-state (e.g. bit-strings, permutations etc). There is of course no necessity for S to be a data-type: it may itself be a function. In particular, S may itself be a meta- or hyper-heuristic: if we take S to be $\mathcal{H}_T$ for some solution-type T, then $\mathcal{H}_{\mathcal{H}_T}$ expresses a multi-level search over T. This recursive structure is well-known to be characteristic of the composite pattern. Figure 2 gives an instantiation of the Composite pattern for hyper-heuristics. From this diagram, we can see that a hyper-heuristic IS-A Operator and USES-A sequence of operators. Since we can consider metaheuristics (e.g. tabu search, simulated annealing etc) to be synonymous in both behavioural and signature terms with the definition of operator, we can consider hyper-heuristic to be a composite metaheuristic.

2.3 Examples

- In their description of local search frameworks, Lourenço et al. [22] note the potential for nesting of operators, thereby implicitly alluding to this pattern.
- The HYPERION framework [28] uses the class decomposition above to allow the same source code to express both metaheuristic and hyper-heuristic, depending on the choice of the type S.
- In multi-level search, the appropriate level of nesting cannot usually be determined *a priori*, but the polymorphic relationship between OPERATOR and HYPER-HEURISTIC means that the nesting of levels can be *dynamic*, i.e. determined as a function of search progress at any given level.

3. COMPOSITION OF CLASSIFIERS

3.1 Problem Statement

Supervised machine learning seeks methods to find classifiers which map features to class labels. Since many machine learning algorithms are stochastic [23, 6], they produce different models (classification, prediction, function approximation, etc. herein referred to as classifier)[1] each time they are used. One option is to execute the learning algorithm multiple times and take the single 'best' classifier. However, we might be able to benefit from the composition of

[1]is this not at odds with the simple notion of 'mapping features to class labels'?

multiple classifiers (commonly referred to elsewhere in the literature as an *ensemble*) to produce a better-performing overall classifier. There is also the possibility of selecting a poor classifier. These points raise the following four questions:

- How to combine the classifier outputs to compute an overall classification?
- How to generate multiple diverse classifiers to produce a well-performing ensemble?
- How to set the parameters of machine learning algorithms?
- How can we build high quality classifiers more efficiently in the new era of big data and parallel processing?

While many algorithms used to train classifiers are stochastic, there are a number of exceptions including C4.5 for decision trees, Naive Bayes, and Support Vector Machines [6].

3.2 The Solution

One solution to the problem of randomness in classifier training is to adopt well-founded statistical techniques to perform any or all of: combine classifiers; sample the data set; sample the features and generate diverse classifiers. There are a number of methods available which allow us to combine separate classifiers into a single classifier and as machine learning is largely statistical (in respect of both the algorithms to train classifiers and the actual data [16]) it makes sense to turn to a statistical technique to alleviate this issue.

One of the basic tasks of statisticians is to sample a tiny subset of a population in order to estimate the true statistics of the entire population. Likewise, since machine learning algorithms automatically sample a space of classifiers, ensemble techniques allow us to combine them to provide a better reflection of the entire population of classifiers. The law of large numbers dictates that as the sample size increases, the ensemble will converge to better estimates of the true underlying statistics.

Classifiers are functions mapping features to class labels. We can employ one of the following methods to map the outputs of single classifiers to an output for the entire ensemble:

- Majority vote: The entire set of classifiers vote on a class, and the class which receives the most votes is taken.
- Averaging: If the outputs of each classifier are a real number then the outputs can be averaged.
- Weighted average: Each classifier is assigned a weight according to its 'expertise'. When the averaging is done more emphasis is placed on the classifiers with a higher weight.
- Algebraic combiners: real-valued outputs of classifiers are combined through statistical expressions such as sum, mean, product, median, minimum, maximum.

Classifiers in an ensemble should be *diverse*, i.e. they should make different errors and be independent or negatively correlated. There are a number of ways a diverse set of classifiers can be generated from the given dataset. The most obvious is to re-run the machine learning algorithm: however there are more effective methods available, including:

- Bagging (bootstrap aggregation) creates a diverse set of classifiers based on different random samples (usually with replacement) taken from the original dataset [11, 10]. Each classifier is trained on a different subset of the data. As an example, random forests [2] are a combination of classifiers. Each classifier is a tree-model, hence the name random forests. The generalization error of the whole forest tends towards a limit as the number of trees increases, by the law of large numbers. The Kinect motion sensing alogorithm for the Xbox gaming console uses decision tree classifiers [10].
- Boosting adjusts the probability of sampling misclassified data. Thus, misclassified data is more likely to be considered in the training of subsequent classifiers. However, boosting only applies to binary classification but this issue can be addressed by the AdaBoost algorithm [12].
- Stacked Generalization trains multiple levels of classifiers [30]. An ensemble is trained creating level-1 classifiers. The outputs from level-1 are then used to train an ensemble of level-2 classifiers. The outputs from level-1 classifiers can be thought of as features on which level 2 classifiers can make decisions.
- Mixture of Experts generates several classifiers whose outputs are combined through a rule which typically trained using the expectation maximization (EM) algorithm [18]. A hierarchical mixture of experts can be obtained by combining several mixture-of-experts models [19].

Just as bagging and boosting sample subsets of instances, we can also select subsets of features to build diverse set classifiers. Generating different classifiers from randomly-selected subsets of feature is known as the random subspace method [17]. This is particularly useful when unstable machine learning representations are used. Unstable learners are those sensitive to differences in the training data set and include decision trees while stable learners are those less sensitive to differences in the training data set and include nearest neighbour [8].

3.3 Consequences

3.3.1 Generation of Diverse Classifiers

As remarked above, classifiers in an ensemble must be diverse. This can be achieved either by altering parameters that determine the architecture of a classifier, or how the space of classifiers is sampled. With an artificial neural network (ANN) [1], this can be achieved by choosing different initial weights, different numbers of hidden nodes or different learning rules. With Evolutionary Computation methods such as genetic programming [20], we choose different numerical parameters such as population size and number of generations, but also different crossover and mutation operators [7]. In fact, when training a diverse set of classifiers intended for an ensemble, our ignorance about appropriate values for parameter settings is turned into an advantage as we are forced to explore different parameter settings, each combination of parameter settings potentially creating a different classifier.

3.3.2 Statistically better behaviour

One major benefit of an ensemble approach is that the combined classifier is the result of all the existing classifiers. Rather than discarding any suboptimal classifiers generated during preliminary parameter setting experiments, they can all contribute to the ensemble. Since the final ensemble results from a larger sample of classifiers, it is more robust: a single execution of a machine learning algorithm may or may not produce an acceptable classifier. However, combining multiple classifiers, each of which came from an independent execution of a machine learning algorithm, is less likely to succumb to statistical fluctuation [8].

An ensemble also exhibits the desirable property of graceful degradation. ssuming a large number of classifiers, should a small number of them fail, the whole ensemble will not fail catastrophically. ANNs also share this property, which was originally modelled on the gradual reduction of brain function (and the lack of a 'grandmother' neuron) [27].

3.3.3 Integration of different types of classifier

Part of the broad appeal of ensembles is the integration of different types of classifier. For example a decision tree might be trained by C4.5, and an ANN might be trained by back-propagation [24]. Combining these different types of classifier into an ensemble may have more benefit than combining classifiers of the same type, as each approach will have a different bias. Separate researchers with expertise in different sub-fields of machine learning can collaborate by contributing classifiers to an ensemble. Different machine learning researchers do not need to understand the training method of each other's technique as the classifiers can be inserted directly into the ensemble.

3.3.4 Learning Classifier Systems

Learning Classifier Systems offer an interesting solution to the question of how to build a system of classifiers. A set of classifiers is evolved, but each one is 'guarded' by a rule stating which part of the input space it applies to. These condition-action pairs, as they are called in the Learning Classifier Systems literature, can be guarded by relatively simple conditions such as ternary-schema matching or by more complex S-expressions. Thus a single classifier can be considered to be an expert in classifying parts of the feature space. The relationship between Learning Classifier Systems and ensembles has already been investigated [3].

3.3.5 Confidence

With a single classifier it is difficult to say what confidence we have in the classification. The outcome of a single classification task is Boolean and we have no further information to make any judgement about the confidence of the classification. However if we have a set of classifiers, we can also give some indication of our certainty in our prediction. For example, imagine we have one hundred binary classifiers. In one case, if we have 99 votes for true and 1 vote for false we can be more confident than if we only received 51 votes for true and 49 votes for false. An ensemble is a probabilistic model which allows us to perform classification and report our confidence in this classification. Thus, we can estimate the posterior probabilities of the classification decisions [25]. It should also be emphasized that combining classifiers does not guarantee an improvement in performance when compared to the best classifier in the ensemble[2] and of course high confidence does not imply that the classification is correct.

3.3.6 Levels of Measurement

Using statistics as a fundamental foundation, an ensemble should be able to deal with different levels of measurement (Discrete, Categorical, Nominal, and Ordinal data). [31] defines three types of classifier outputs[3].

- Abstract-level output: output is a unique class label for each input.
- Rank-level output: output is a list of ranked class labels for each input.
- Measurement-level output: output is a vector of real-valued measures representing estimates of class posterior probabilities.

3.3.7 Statistics and Machine Learning

There is a tension between statistics and machine learning. Statisticians follow at least a two-stage process when fitting a model to the data (i.e. constructing a classifier):

- Examine data manually and choose a model (e.g. a polynomial of a given degree).
- Choose the best parameters for the model (e.g. by least squares).

Some machine learning techniques attempt to automate the model selection process itself, selecting the most appropriate parameters. For example ANN can represent any continuous, differentiable function, and is not constrained to a highly restricted model [1]. Similarly Genetic Programming can construct any computable function if the function set is expressive enough, while simultaneously choosing any numerical parameters the model requires [24]. In machine learning a model (i.e. a classifier mapping features to class labels) is ratified by A/B testing where the dataset is partitioned into two disjoint sets:

- The training set is used to train the classifier.
- The testing set confirms the validity of the classifier.

Classifiers chosen manually by statisticians are clearly human-understandable. Machine learning techniques may generate more accurate classifiers but be more difficult to interpret. For example, a linear model is easy to understand while ANNs have no such simple interpretation [27]. An ensemble approach offers a seamless marriage between traditional statistical approaches and contemporary machine learning techniques, potentially reconciling some of these tensions. For example, an ensemble could consist of a number of human-selected classifiers and a number of classifiers trained with machine learning techniques. Depending on our perspective, we could increase the weight of the human selected

[2]Is this not at odds with some of the above statements
[3]How do these relate to the above 'levels of measurement'?

classifiers if we demand explanations of the data. If we alternatively demand accuracy, we could increase the weight of the machine learning trained classifiers. In other words, the weights of the different kinds of classifiers provide a sliding scale between the manual and automatic approaches to classification.

3.4 Classifier Outputs as Features

In machine learning, features are aggregate information extracted from the raw data of the application domain, the motive being that features are easier for machine learning algorithms to handle than raw data. For example: eye colour of a person could consist of the set {blue, brown, hazel, green} could be extracted from the RGB colour pixels in a photograph which is subject to noise; or a person's height could be discretized into the set {short, medium, tall}. These features are units of information that the machine learning algorithms and the classifiers they produce receive as input. Features form the basis space, from which subsets of features can be selected to reduce the dimensionality of the problem [15] or more aggregate features can be constructed [21].

Classifiers can be considered as a feature-space mapping from the original features to the space of class labels. Similarly, data points in the input space can be used to classify unseen data based on its distance to existing data points, e.g. by using the kth nearest neighbour classifier. However instead of using the entire dataset, a subset of the initial set of data points can be used, and therefore mapping the original data to a subset can be considered as reducing the number of features [14].

3.5 Ensembles of Linear Classifiers

Ensembles of linear classifiers can learn non-linear decision boundaries. Linear classifiers place a linear decision boundary across the feature space. For example, perceptrons can only express linearly separable decision boundaries and are the 'computational unit' in ANNs. An ANN is similar to an ensemble of perceptrons, with a layer of classifiers feeding into a threshold function (typically a sigmoid function). Assuming three-layer feed-forward architecture, we can think of the first layer as an ensemble. Similarly, the outputs from the second layer can be considered to be a set of classifications which are combined in the third layer. However, it must be remembered that in the case of ensembles each classifier is produced independently, whereas in the case of ANN, perceptrons may not be learned independently.

There is thus a parallel between ANNs and ensembles. A linear classifier places a linear decision boundary across the feature space, and cannot express non-linear decision boundaries. However, and ensemble of linear classifiers can express a convex decision boundary. A single perceptron can only learn and express a linear decision boundary and can never learn to express the logical function XOR (or the general parity problem). It was later discovered that a second layer of perceptrons could express convex decision boundaries, and a third layer could express concave decision boundaries [1]. Perhaps if ensemble approaches had been more prevalent in the 1960s, it would not have taken 20 years between the development of perceptrons and multilayer ANN [27]

3.6 Big Data and Parallelism

Ensemble techniques are increasingly important for big data analysis and parallel processing. Techniques for dealing with classification should scale with data volume. Large amounts of data can be sampled and classifier training algorithms can be run on physically separate processors, before being combined into an ensemble. Bagging is particularly disposed to dealing with large amounts of data as it is a divide-and-conquer approach to training a classifier that can be parallelized.

Once a set of classifiers is learned, if more data instances arrive, we do not need to train an entirely new ensemble from scratch. Classifiers which are typically learned off-line on a batch of data, can thus be learned on new sets of data instances upon arrival, and be integrated into the ensemble. We can simply add new classifiers trained on the new data, and include them in the ensemble without altering the existing classifiers. This is of increased importance with larger and incrementally-growing datasets. In summary, both the training of classifiers and the classification of data can be parallelized.

4. REFERENCES

[1] Christopher M. Bishop. *Pattern Recognition and Machine Learning (Information Science and Statistics)*. Springer-Verlag New York, Inc., Secaucus, NJ, USA, 2006.

[2] Leo Breiman. Random forests. *Machine learning*, 45(1):5–32, 2001.

[3] Gavin Brown, Tim Kovacs, and James AR Marshall. Ucspv: principled voting in ucs rule populations. In *Proceedings of the 9th annual conference on Genetic and evolutionary computation*, pages 1774–1781. ACM, 2007.

[4] E.K. Burke, M. Hyde, G. Kendall, G. Ochoa, E. Ozcan, and J. R. Woodward. *A Classification of Hyper-heuristic Approaches*, chapter Handbook of Meta-Heuristics, pages 449–468. Kluwer, 2010.

[5] R. M. Burstall. Proving Properties of Programs by Structural Induction. *The Computer Journal*, 12(1):41–48, February 1969.

[6] David Corne, Marco Dorigo, Fred Glover, Dipankar Dasgupta, Pablo Moscato, Riccardo Poli, and Kenneth V. Price, editors. *New Ideas in Optimization*. McGraw-Hill Ltd., UK, Maidenhead, UK, England, 1999.

[7] Tianxiang Cui, Jingpeng Li, John R. Woodward, and Andrew J. Parkes. An ensemble based genetic programming system to predict english football premier league games. In P. N. Suganthan, editor, *2013 IEEE Symposium Series on Computational Intelligence*, pages 138–143, Singapore, 16-19 April 2013. IEEE.

[8] Thomas G. Dietterich. Ensemble methods in machine learning. In *MULTIPLE CLASSIFIER SYSTEMS, LBCS-1857*, pages 1–15. Springer, 2000.

[9] E.W. Dijkstra. Recursive programming. *Numerische Mathematik*, 2(1):312–318, 1960.

[10] Peter Flach. *Machine Learning: The Art and Science of Algorithms That Make Sense of Data*. Cambridge University Press, New York, NY, USA, 2012.

[11] Yoav Freund and Robert E Schapire. A decision-theoretic generalization of on-line learning and an application to boosting. *Journal of computer and system sciences*, 55(1):119–139, 1997.

[12] Yoav Freund, Robert E Schapire, et al. Experiments with a new boosting algorithm. In *ICML*, volume 96, pages 148–156, 1996.

[13] Erich Gamma, Richard Helm, Ralph Johnson, and John Vlissides. *Design patterns: elements of reusable object-oriented software*. Addison-Wesley Longman Publishing Co., Inc., Boston, MA, USA, 1995.

[14] Roberto Gil-Pita and Xin Yao. Evolving edited k-nearest neighbor classifiers. *Int. J. Neural Syst.*, 18(6):459–467, 2008.

[15] Isabelle Guyon. An introduction to variable and feature selection. *Journal of Machine Learning Research*, 3:1157–1182, 2003.

[16] Trevor Hastie, Robert Tibshirani, Jerome Friedman, T Hastie, J Friedman, and R Tibshirani. *The elements of statistical learning*, volume 2. Springer, 2009.

[17] Tin Kam Ho. The random subspace method for constructing decision forests. *Pattern Analysis and Machine Intelligence, IEEE Transactions on*, 20(8):832–844, 1998.

[18] Robert A Jacobs, Michael I Jordan, Steven J Nowlan, and Geoffrey E Hinton. Adaptive mixtures of local experts. *Neural computation*, 3(1):79–87, 1991.

[19] Michael I. Jordan. Hierarchical mixtures of experts and the em algorithm. *Neural Computation*, 6:181–214, 1994.

[20] John R. Koza. *Genetic Programming: On the Programming of Computers by Means of Natural Selection*. MIT Press, Cambridge, MA, USA, 1992.

[21] Huan Liu and Hiroshi Motoda. *Feature Extraction, Construction and Selection: A Data Mining Perspective*. Kluwer Academic Publishers, Norwell, MA, USA, 1998.

[22] Helena R. Lourenço, Olivier C. Martin, and Thomas Stützle. Iterated local search. In *Handbook of Metaheuristics, volume 57 of International Series in Operations Research and Management Science*, pages 321–353. Kluwer Academic Publishers, 2002.

[23] Sean Luke. *Essentials of Metaheuristics*. Lulu, second edition, 2013. Available for free at http://cs.gmu.edu/~sean/book/metaheuristics/.

[24] Thomas M. Mitchell. *Machine Learning*. McGraw-Hill, Inc., New York, NY, USA, 1 edition, 1997.

[25] Michael Muhlbaier, Apostolos Topalis, and Robi Polikar. Ensemble confidence estimates posterior probability. In Nikunj C. Oza, Robi Polikar, Josef Kittler, and Fabio Roli, editors, *Multiple Classifier Systems*, volume 3541 of *Lecture Notes in Computer Science*, pages 326–335. Springer, 2005.

[26] J. Ross Quinlan. Induction of decision trees. *Machine Learning*, 1(1):81–106, 1986.

[27] D. E. Rumelhart and J. L. McClelland. *Parallel Distributed Processing: Explorations in the Microstructure of Cognition, Vol. 1: Foundations*. MIT Press, 1986.

[28] Jerry Swan, Ender Özcan, and Graham Kendall. Hyperion - a recursive hyper-heuristic framework. In Carlos A. Coello, editor, *Learning and Intelligent Optimization*, volume 6683 of *Lecture Notes in Computer Science*, pages 616–630. Springer Berlin Heidelberg, 2011.

[29] Jerry Swan, John Woodward, Ender Özcan, Graham Kendall, and Edmund Burke. Searching the hyper-heuristic design space. *Cognitive Computation*, 2013.

[30] David H. Wolpert. Stacked generalization. *Neural Networks*, 5:241–259, 1992.

[31] Lei Xu, Adam Krzyzak, and Ching Y Suen. Methods of combining multiple classifiers and their applications to handwriting recognition. *Systems, Man and Cybernetics, IEEE Transactions on*, 22(3):418–435, 1992.

NSGA-II Implementation Details May Influence Quality of Solutions for the Job-Shop Scheduling Problem

Maxim Buzdalov
ITMO University
49 Kronverkskiy prosp.
Saint-Petersburg, Russia
buzdalov@rain.ifmo.ru

Irina Petrova
ITMO University
49 Kronverkskiy prosp.
Saint-Petersburg, Russia
petrova@rain.ifmo.ru

Arina Buzdalova
ITMO University
49 Kronverkskiy prosp.
Saint-Petersburg, Russia
afanasyeva@rain.ifmo.ru

ABSTRACT

The helper-objective approach for solving the job-shop scheduling problem using multi-objective evolutionary algorithms is considered.

We implemented the approach from the Lochtefeld and Ciarallo paper using NSGA-II with the correct implementation of the non-dominated sorting procedure which is able to work with equal values of objectives. The experimental evaluation showed the significant improvement of solution quality.

We also report new best results for 16 out of 24 problem instances used in the considered paper.

Categories and Subject Descriptors

G.1.6 [**Numerical Analysis**]: Optimization

General Terms

Algorithms, Performance

Keywords

job-shop, helper-objectives, auxiliary objectives, NSGA-II

1. INTRODUCTION

The job-shop scheduling problem consists of n jobs and m machines. Each job i has at most m operations. Each operation has a specified machine and processing time. The processing order of the operations is predefined. Each machine can process only one operation at time. An operation can not be interrupted once it is started. No two operations of a job can be processed simultaneously. To solve the job-shop problem means to schedule the operations on the machines to minimize the measure of scheduling. There exists several ways to measure scheduling, i.e. makespan or total flow-time. The latter is used in this paper and calculated as the sum of flowtimes for all jobs.

GECCO'14, July 12–16, 2014, Vancouver, BC, Canada.
ACM 978-1-4503-2881-4/14/07.
http://dx.doi.org/10.1145/2598394.2602288.

Jensen [5] first applied multi-objectivization approach to the job-shop scheduling problem. Along with the target objective (the sum of all flowtimes), he introduced *helper-objectives*, which are individual flowtimes or sums of several flowtimes. The target objective and one or several helper-objectives were optimized using a multi-objective evolutionary algorithm, namely, NSGA-II [2]. The time budget for each run was divided into equal intervals, and for each interval helper-objectives were selected at random.

Later, Lochtefeld and Ciarallo [6] presented their deterministic helper-objective optimization strategy for solving the job-shop scheduling problem. In their paper, it was advised to sort the jobs by their minimum possible flowtime and join the adjacent jobs into equally sized groups to produce helper-objectives (each helper objective is the sum of flowtimes for the corresponding jobs). To be as much compatible with Jensen [5] as possible, for the sake of result comparison, they also used an implementation of NSGA-II. Their approach was shown experimentally to be quite efficient, and best known results for several problem instances were updated.

Unfortunately, neither Jensen, nor Lochtefeld and Ciarallo left any source code in the public domain to reproduce the results of experiments. When we were implementing our own approach to multi-objectivization, described in [7], we couldn't reproduce the results from [6] and had to compare our approach with our implementation of the approach from [6], which produced worse results than the original implementation.

One more difficulty comes from the multi-objective evolutionary algorithm, NSGA-II [2], used in both papers. Jensen, the author of the first paper [5], is also an author of the fast non-dominated sorting technique [4], which he seemed to use in his research. It is probably that Lochtefeld and Ciarallo also used his implementation. However, it suffers from treating equal values of objectives wrong, which was fixed by Fortin et al only very recently [3]. This means that some of the problems with reproducing the results may be related to quirks of implementations of the non-dominated sorting algorithm.

2. EXPERIMENT RESULTS

We performed 1000 runs of our implementation of the NSGA-II-based solver for the job-shop scheduling problem. The non-dominated sorting procedure is implemented as in [3]. The solver configuration, such as genetic operators and the number of iterations, and the problem instances used are the same as in [6]. We compared three helper-

Instance	Size	Best known solution	Original 1 JPH	Original 2 JPH	Original $\lfloor N/2 \rfloor$ JPH	New 1 JPH	New 2 JPH	New $\lfloor N/2 \rfloor$ JPH	New best solution
la01	10 × 5	4832	2.297	2.431	2.992	1.386	1.645	2.222	4832
la02	10 × 5	4459	3.111	3.177	2.447	2.550	2.548	2.051	4459
la06	15 × 5	8694	4.941	4.503	3.828	5.087	4.660	3.503	8635
la07	15 × 5	8174	5.425	5.245	5.091	5.770	5.709	5.249	8174
la11	20 × 5	14 756	5.537	5.484	5.027	5.941	5.840	5.005	14 629
la12	20 × 5	12 403	6.252	6.034	4.893	6.970	6.713	5.190	12 373
la16	10 × 10	7393	4.230	3.993	4.449	3.381	3.561	3.478	7393
la17	10 × 10	6555	3.555	3.696	2.617	2.366	2.649	2.088	6537
la21	15 × 10	12 942	4.489	4.320	4.537	3.993	3.954	3.850	12 649
la22	15 × 10	12 106	4.581	5.182	4.337	4.004	4.147	3.917	11 890
la26	20 × 10	20 234	5.290	5.480	5.924	5.515	5.621	5.268	20 013
la27	20 × 10	20 764	5.321	5.428	5.768	5.521	5.750	5.546	20 764
la31	30 × 10	39 007	5.321	5.815	6.123	6.466	6.373	6.019	39 004
la32	30 × 10	42 189	4.863	4.728	5.026	5.914	5.539	4.556	41 740
la36	15 × 15	17 073	5.052	5.348	4.943	3.963	4.257	4.318	16 793
la37	15 × 15	17 886	5.114	5.337	5.321	4.346	4.549	4.874	17 787
ft10	10 × 10	7501	6.822	6.456	7.627	5.142	5.406	5.839	7501
ft20	20 × 5	14 279	7.616	7.320	8.633	7.560	7.221	6.874	14 156
swv01	20 × 10	20 688	9.768	10.301	13.259	9.427	9.622	11.691	20 688
swv02	20 × 10	21 682	8.334	9.956	10.867	7.726	8.472	8.936	21 670
swv06	20 × 15	28 863	7.022	7.669	9.782	6.840	7.212	9.686	28 691
swv07	20 × 15	27 385	7.937	8.403	10.834	7.734	8.134	10.191	27 166
swv11	50 × 10	108 842	8.912	9.991	13.068	7.425	8.609	11.506	108 014
swv12	50 × 10	109 128	8.737	10.912	13.750	8.575	9.645	11.659	109 128

Table 1: Experimental results. JPH means the number of jobs per helper. In "original–new" columns, average percentages are presented, the percentage of the result X is $(X - B)/B$, where B is the previously best known solution for that problem instance. Gray cells specify which optimizer produced better average percentage, dark-gray cells show the best average percentage. In the last column, the updated best known solutions are marked gray.

objective configurations — one, two and $\lfloor N/2 \rfloor$ jobs per helper. The results are presented in Table 1.

One can see that in 54 out of 72 cases the new implementation is better. For 20 out of 24 problem instances, the best average percentage is shown by the new implementation. For 16 out of 24 problem instances we updated the best known results (the gray cells in the right column of Table 1).

Source code for experiments is available at GitHub [1].

This work was financially supported by the Government of Russian Federation, Grant 074-U01.

3. REFERENCES

[1] Source code for experiments (a part of this paper). URL: https://github.com/mbuzdalov/papers/tree/master/2014-gecco-lba-jobshop.

[2] K. Deb, A. Pratap, S. Agarwal, and T. Meyarivan. A Fast Elitist Multi-Objective Genetic Algorithm: NSGA-II. *Transactions on Evolutionary Computation*, 6:182–197, 2000.

[3] F.-A. Fortin, S. Grenier, and M. Parizeau. Generalizing the Improved Run-time Complexity Algorithm for Non-dominated Sorting. In *Proceeding of the Fifteenth Annual Conference on Genetic and Evolutionary Computation Conference*, GECCO '13, pages 615–622. ACM, 2013.

[4] M. T. Jensen. Reducing the Run-time Complexity of Multiobjective EAs: The NSGA-II and Other Algorithms. *Transactions on Evolutionary Computation*, 7(5):503–515, 2003.

[5] M. T. Jensen. Helper-Objectives: Using Multi-Objective Evolutionary Algorithms for Single-Objective Optimisation: Evolutionary Computation Combinatorial Optimization. *Journal of Mathematical Modelling and Algorithms*, 3(4):323–347, 2004.

[6] D. F. Lochtefeld and F. W. Ciarallo. Helper-Objective Optimization Strategies for the Job-Shop Scheduling Problem. *Applied Soft Computing*, 11(6):4161–4174, 2011.

[7] I. Petrova, A. Buzdalova, and M. Buzdalov. Improved Helper-Objective Optimization Strategy for Job-Shop Scheduling Problem. In *Proceedings of the International Conference on Machine Learning and Applications*, volume 2, pages 374–377. IEEE Computer Society, 2013.

Some Measurements on the Effects of the Curse of Dimensionality

Stephen Chen
School of Information Technology
York University
Toronto, Canada
1-416-736-2100 x:30526
sychen@yorku.ca

James Montgomery
School of Engineering and ICT
University of Tasmania
Hobart, Australia
61-3-6226-7294
james.montgomery@utas.edu.au

Antonio Bolufé-Röhler
School of Mathematics and CS
University of Havana
Havana, Cuba
53-5-242-0064
bolufe@matcom.uh.cu

ABSTRACT

The existence of the curse of dimensionality is well known, and its general effects are well acknowledged. However, perhaps due to this colloquial understanding, specific measurements on the curse of dimensionality and its effects are not as extensive. In continuous domains, the volume of the search space grows exponentially with dimensionality. Conversely, the number of function evaluations budgeted to explore this search space usually grows only linearly. New experiments show that particle swarm optimization and differential evolution have super-linear growth in convergence time as dimensionality grows. When restricted by a linear growth in allotted function evaluations, this super-linear growth in convergence time leads to a decrease in the allowed population size.

Categories and Subject Descriptors

I.2.8 [**Artificial Intelligence**]: Problem Solving, Control Methods, and Search – *Heuristic methods*

General Terms

Algorithms

Keywords

Curse of dimensionality, large scale global optimization.

1. INTRODUCTION

Our intuitive understanding of population-based heuristic search techniques is often based on examples formed in two dimensions. Of note, particle swarm optimization (PSO) starts with an image of birds circling in towards a food source in a corn field [1]. As we picture the 15-30 birds involved with this original conceptualization, we can imagine how the proposed search technique will achieve excellent coverage of the search space. However, these intuitive ideas can be inaccurate and even misleading in higher dimensional search spaces.

GECCO'14, July 12–16, 2014, Vancouver, BC, Canada.
ACM 978-1-4503-2881-4/14/07.
http://dx.doi.org/10.1145/2598394.2602271

A simple guideline from differential evolution (DE) is to use a population size (n) that is ten times the dimensionality (d) of the search space [2]. However, going from d = 2 to d = 42 can increase the size of the search space by a factor of about 10^{12}. Whereas we might imagine 20 birds being able to fully explore a 10m x 10m courtyard, we should have a different visualization of 420 birds in an area similar to the size of the Atlantic Ocean.

Despite this increasing sparseness in the coverage of the search space, popular guidelines for the recommended size of the population in PSO and DE include constant sized (e.g. [3] for PSO) and linearly increasing sizes (e.g. [2][4] for DE). The following experiments show that even these population sizes can become too large to allow convergence when PSO and DE are applied to large scale global optimization (i.e. $d \geq 1000$).

2. PARTICLE SWARM OPTIMIZATION

The experiments measure what it takes for PSO and DE to converge "close" to the optimum on sphere. The sphere function is chosen because it is the simplest (unimodal) baseline function used in many benchmark sets. If a search technique is unable to reach the optimum on sphere, the error on sphere suggests a minimum error that will exist for any (local) optimum on a deceptive (multi-modal) problem.

The current implementation of sphere uses the range of +/– 100 and the limit of 10,000 * d function evaluations. Starting with uniform random solutions on this range, we record the number of function evaluations required to first produce a solution within the +/– 0.1 hypercube around the origin (where the un-shifted global optimum is located). Thirty independent trials are run for each data point. Since variations amongst the trials were negligible (with the excess of trials mostly to confirm the key trends), only averages of the converged trials are presented.

The first set of experiments is a 10 by 10 grid – dimensions d from 50 to 500 in steps of 50 and population sizes n from 50 to 500 also in steps of 50. The average number of generations (i.e. function evaluations divided by population size) to first find a solution within the target hypercube is reported in Table I. In general, the number of generations required for convergence is mostly constant with respect to population size with a slight benefit (i.e. fewer generations required) for larger values of n. However, the approximate growth rate in generations required to converge as a function of dimensions d is faster than a linear function with a constant of 1. Since the allowed function evaluations increases linearly (i.e. function evaluations = 10,000 * d), the growth rate in generations eventually eclipses the growth rate in function evaluations. PSO with n = 450 cannot converge for $d \geq 450$ dimensions, and n = 500 fails for $d \geq 250$ dimensions.

Table 1. Number of generations required by PSO to converge on the sphere function.

n	Dimensions (d)									
	50	100	150	200	250	300	350	400	450	500
50	959.4	1982.9	3099.6	4251.3	5465.6	6816.1	8121.4	9346.4	10807.0	12361.0
100	935.9	1961.3	3047.1	4212.2	5416.2	6653.1	7905.1	9234.7	10579.8	11899.0
150	924.4	1963.1	3053.3	4174.4	5371.7	6611.6	7879.1	9180.5	10480.0	11870.7
200	920.1	1942.8	3021.8	4177.8	5348.0	6562.4	7830.4	9107.8	10436.3	11738.2
250	920.6	1944.1	3015.7	4148.9	5335.3	6559.6	7814.1	9078.4	10416.2	11776.3
300	918.2	1932.7	3016.9	4134.9	5299.7	6563.9	7763.8	9059.8	10439.3	11739.0
350	914.2	1938.3	3008.6	4129.6	5296.7	6557.4	7793.1	9045.3	10392.5	11692.9
400	900.5	1918.4	3003.2	4118.1	5307.1	6548.5	7805.5	9069.5	10312.4	11685.8
450	909.4	1919.1	3016.5	4121.0	5284.3	6504.5	7710.9	8821.3	-	-
500	913.3	1929.3	2971.6	3974.0	-	-	-	-	-	-

The observation that the resources required for convergence grow super-linearly with dimensions is more easily seen in Figure 1. The blue diamonds indicate the actual number of generations required to first produce a solution within the target hypercube, and the red crosses indicate a linear extrapolation of the first point for $d = 50$ and the origin.

3. DIFFERENTIAL EVOLUTION

A similar super-linear growth rate in the number of generations required for convergence is also observed in DE. In Figure 2, a standard DE/rand/1/bin is tested on sphere using a target hypercube of +/− 1, $n = 50$, and $F \in \{0.5, 0.6, 0.7, 0.8\}$. The shaded area represents generation counts above the maximum imposed by the FE limit. These results also indicate that lowering F can lead to improved search efficacy – the curves from top to bottom have $F = 0.8$, 0.7, 0.6, and lastly 0.5. However, while the trend in the plot suggests that continuing to reduce F would produce further improvements, experiments with $F = 0.4$ resulted in premature convergence for all $d > 50$. The balance between allowing the population to contract (so that it can make effective exploratory moves) while maintaining sufficient diversity is evidently critical to DE's success, but can be difficult to achieve.

4. SUMMARY

Since the budget of function evaluations usually grows only linearly with dimension d, it becomes clear that for any population size n, there will eventually be a problem size d for which this linear budget of function evaluations (e.g. 10,000 * d) will become insufficient to achieve a desired level of convergence. For large scale global optimization, the trends in Figures 1 and 2 suggest that populations sizes will have to become much smaller than the problem dimensionality (i.e. $n \ll d$) to ensure convergence in a reasonable amount of time. This limitation may affect the performance of PSO and DE in high dimensional search spaces.

5. REFERENCES

[1] Kennedy, J. and Eberhart, R. C. 1995. Particle swarm optimization. In *Proceedings of the IEEE International Conference on Neural Networks* (Perth, Australia, Nov 27-Dec 01, 1995). ICNN'95. IEEE Press, Piscataway, NJ, 1942-1948. DOI= http://dx.doi.org/10.1109/ICNN.1995.488968.

[2] Storn, R. 1996. On the usage of differential evolution for function optimization. In *Proceedings of the 1996 Biennial Conference of the North American Fuzzy Information Processing Society* (Berkeley, USA, June 19-22, 1996). NAFIPS'96. IEEE Press, Piscataway, NJ, 519-523. DOI= http://dx.doi.org/10.1109/NAFIPS.1996.534789.

[3] Bratton, D. and Kennedy, J. 2007. Defining a standard for particle swarm optimization. In *Proceedings of the Swarm Intelligence Symposium* (Honolulu, USA, April 01-05, 2007). SIS'07. IEEE Press, Piscataway, NJ, 120-127. DOI= http://dx.doi.org/10.1109/SIS.2007.368035.

[4] Mallipeddi, R. and Suganthan, P. N. 2008. Empirical study on the effect of population size on differential evolution algorithm. In *Proceedings of the IEEE Congress on Evolutionary Computation* (Hong Kong, June 01-06, 2008). CEC'08. IEEE Press, Piscataway, NJ, 3663-3670. DOI= http://dx.doi.org/10.1109/CEC.2008.4631294.

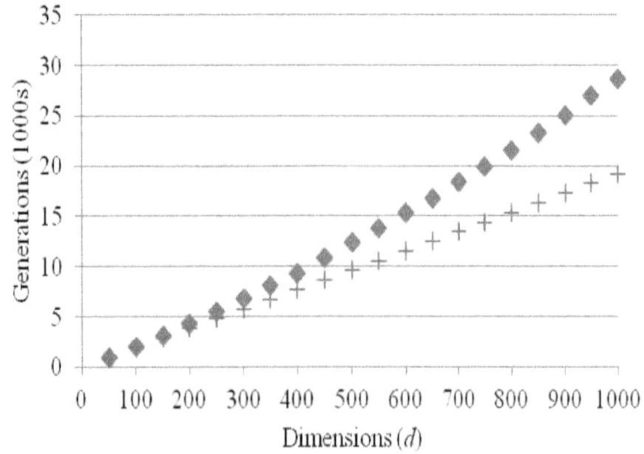

Figure 1. Convergence time grows super linearly in PSO.

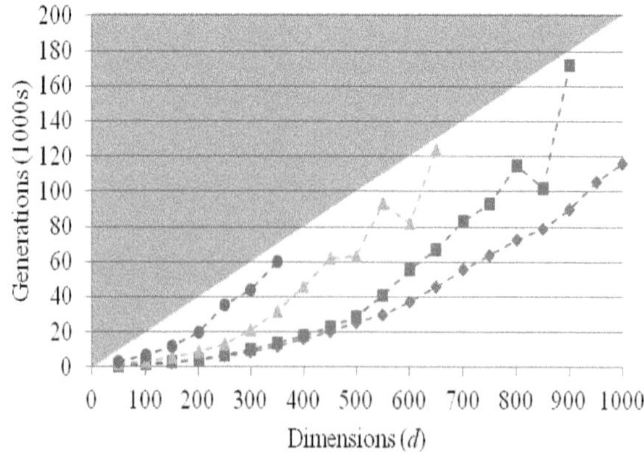

Figure 2. Convergence time grows super linearly in DE.

A Fast Genetic Algorithm for the Flexible Job Shop Scheduling Problem

Marcin Cwiek
Future Processing
Bojkowska 37A
44-100 Gliwice, Poland
mcwiek@future-processing.com

Jakub Nalepa
Institute of Informatics
Silesian University of Technology
Akademicka 16
44-100 Gliwice, Poland
jakub.nalepa@polsl.pl

ABSTRACT

This paper presents a fast genetic algorithm (GA) for solving the flexible job shob scheduling problem (FJSP). The FJSP is an extension of a classical NP-hard job shop scheduling problem. Here, we combine the active schedule constructive crossover (ASCX) with the generalized order crossover (GOX). Also, we show how to divide a population of solutions in the high-low fit selection scheme in order to guide the search efficiently. An initial experimental study indicates high convergence capabilities of the proposed GA.

Categories and Subject Descriptors

I.2.8 [**Artificial Intelligence**]: Problem Solving, Control Methods, and Search—*Heuristic methods*

General Terms

Algorithms

Keywords

Genetic algorithm; randomized crossover; flexible job shop scheduling problem

1. INTRODUCTION

The job shop scheduling problem (JSP) is a classical NP-hard optimization problem. It consists in finding a schedule σ for completing n jobs J_i, $i \in \{1, 2, \ldots, n\}$, on m machines M_j, $j \in \{1, 2, \ldots, m\}$. Each job J_i is composed of h operations $o_{i,j}^k$, $k \in \{1, 2, \ldots, h\}$, which must be executed in a pre-defined order, and $o_{i,j}^k$ should be run on M_j. Execution time of each $o_{i,j}^k$ is given as $\tau_{i,j}^k$. The objective of the JSP is to minimize the total time of completing all jobs, usually referred to as the *makespan*. σ must be feasible, i.e., the operations of each job must be executed in the defined order.

In this paper we consider an extension of the JSP, called the flexible job shop scheduling problem (FJSP). In the FJSP, an operation o_i^k (the *k-th* operation of the *i-th* job) can be processed by more than one machine M_j, $j \in \{1, 2, \ldots, m\}$.

The JSP, along with its numerous variants, are of a wide practical applicability, thus they have been extensively studied over the years. Due to the NP-hardness of the FJSP, a number of heuristic algorithms were proposed to solve it in acceptable time [1,3–5].

The paper is organized as follows. Section 2 outlines the genetic algorithm to solve the FJSP. The experimental study is reported in Section 3. Section 4 concludes the paper.

GECCO'14, July 12–16, 2014, Vancouver, BC, Canada.
ACM 978-1-4503-2881-4/14/07.
http://dx.doi.org/10.1145/2598394.2602280.

Algorithm 1 A genetic algorithm for the FJSP.

1: Generate a population of N feasible solutions;
2: *done* $\leftarrow$ false; $\mathcal{C} \leftarrow \emptyset$;
3: **while not** *done* **do**
4: Determine N pairs (σ_A, σ_B); ▷ Pre-selection
5: **for all** (σ_A, σ_B) **do**
6: $\mathcal{X} \leftarrow$ SelectCrossoverOperator$(\mathcal{P}_A, \mathcal{P}_G)$;
7: $\sigma_c \leftarrow$ Crossover$(\sigma_A, \sigma_B, \mathcal{X})$;
8: $\sigma_c \leftarrow$ Mutate$(\sigma_c, \mathcal{P}_m)$;
9: UpdateChildPool$(\mathcal{C}, \sigma_c)$;
10: **end for**
11: Form the next population; ▷ Post-selection
12: *done* $\leftarrow$ CheckStoppingCondition();
13: $\mathcal{C} \leftarrow \emptyset$;
14: **end while**
15: **return** best solution;

2. GENETIC ALGORITHM OUTLINE

In the proposed GA, a population of N randomly generated feasible solutions (Alg. 1, line 1) evolves in time. In this paper we aim at minimizing the makespan, which is the primary objective of the FJSP. Once the initial population is generated, N pairs of parents (σ_A,σ_B) are determined for the crossover (line 4). We utilize the high-low fit (HLF) selection which has high exploration capabilities [2]. In HLF, the population is sorted and divided into two parts. A parent σ_A is selected from the well-fitted part ($\epsilon \cdot N$ individuals, $0 < \epsilon < 1$), and σ_B from the other part. Here, ϵ affects the exploration and exploitation capabilities of the GA.

Then, the crossover operator is selected (line 6). Here, the ASCX [1] is chosen with the probability $\mathcal{P}_A$, and the GOX with the probability $\mathcal{P}_G$, where $\mathcal{P}_A + \mathcal{P}_G = 1$. The parents σ_A and σ_B are crossed-over (line 7) and the child σ_c is mutated using the scramble mutation with the probability $\mathcal{P}_m$ which is decreased in time (line 8). The child σ_c is added

Table 1: **The minimum makespan obtained using the GA for mt10 and mt20 (best shown in boldface).**

$\mathcal{P}_A \downarrow$	$\epsilon \rightarrow$	0.05	0.10	0.15	0.20	0.25	0.30	0.35	0.40	0.45
0.10	mt10	971	971	976	993	976	1002	993	1017	1016
0.30	mt10	952	967	967	971	974	977	983	990	994
0.50	mt10	967	967	967	967	967	971	971	976	971
0.70	mt10	967	967	971	971	971	973	971	971	967
0.90	mt10	**941**	967	967	981	974	971	993	989	996
0.10	mt20	1293	1293	1317	1314	1313	1316	1318	1301	1332
0.30	mt20	1237	1251	1291	1316	1307	1282	1304	1279	1314
0.50	mt20	1199	1220	1233	1253	1261	1285	1309	1298	1320
0.70	mt20	**1195**	1200	1213	1223	1228	1238	1250	1274	1271
0.90	mt20	1233	1216	1213	1205	1205	1205	1205	1211	1230

to the child pool $\mathcal{C}$ (line 9). Then, the next population is composed of the children residing in $\mathcal{C}$, and the elitist strategy is applied (line 11). Finally, the best individual from the last population is returned (line 15).

3. EXPERIMENTAL RESULTS

The GA was implemented in C# and run on an Intel Core 2 Quad Q9300 (3 GB RAM) computer. Its parameters were set to the following values: $N = 100$, $\mathcal{P}_m = 0.3$, $\tau = 20$ sec., where τ is the maximum execution time. The GA was tested on two benchmark tests[1], namely mt10 and mt20. Each test was run 10 times for each GA configuration.

The minimum makespan obtained using the GA is presented in Tab. 1. Here, the HLF parameter ϵ was subject to change, along with the probability of applying the ASCX ($\mathcal{P}_A$). The experimental results prove that the convergence capabilities of the GA are strongly influenced by ϵ and $\mathcal{P}_A$. Here, selecting parents from a relatively small set of well-fitted individuals (see $\epsilon = 0.05$) allowed for crossing them over with a larger number of other ones (i.e., σ_A was drawn from the $\epsilon \cdot N$ best individuals). Thus, the probability of improving the best solutions in the population increased. The search was guided fast towards the best regions of the search space by exploiting a small number of the best individuals.

The makespan averaged for 10 runs of each GA configuration is presented in Figs. 1–2, for mt10 and mt20, respectively. The results show that the exploitation of a small number of best individuals help converge to the solutions of the highest quality in short time. Moreover, the ASCX operator should be preferred to guide the search efficiently.

4. CONCLUSIONS AND FUTURE WORK

We presented a fast GA to solve the FJSP. The initial results confirm that the search can be guided by randomizing the proportion of the applied crossover operators. Also, we showed the influence of the high-low fit parameter on the convergence capabilities of the GA. Our ongoing research includes performing full benchmark tests of the proposed GA, and designing a memetic algorithm to solve the FJSP. Also, we aim at implementing a parallel version of the GA.

5. ACKNOWLEDGMENTS

This work has been partially supported by the European Regional Development Fund under Operational Programme Innovative Economy 2007–2013, based on the Agreement No. UDA-POIG.01.04.00-24-138/11-01.

[1]See `http://www.idsia.ch/~monaldo/fjsp.html`.

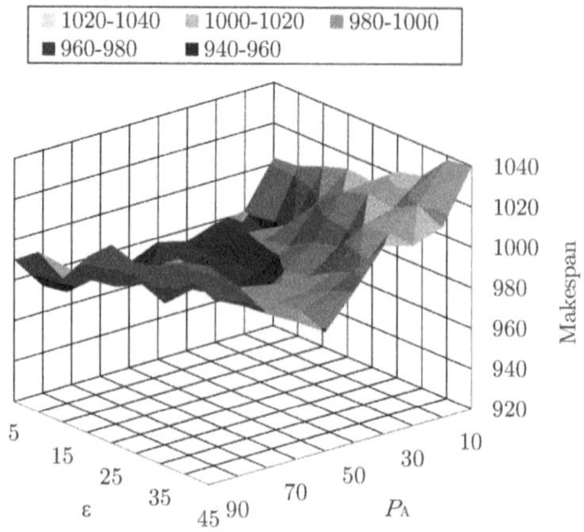

Figure 1: Average makespan for the mt10 problem (ϵ and $\mathcal{P}_A$ are given in %).

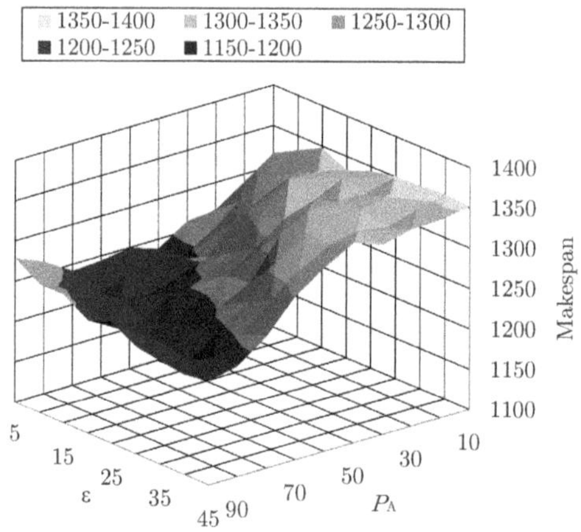

Figure 2: Average makespan for the mt20 problem (ϵ and $\mathcal{P}_A$ are given in %).

6. REFERENCES

[1] C. Dimopoulos and A.M. Zalzala. Recent developments in evolutionary computation for manufacturing optimization: problems, solutions, and comparisons. *IEEE T. Evolut. Comput.*, vol. 4, no. 2, pp. 93 – 113, 2000.

[2] M. Kawulok and J. Nalepa. Support Vector Machines Training Data Selection Using a Genetic Algorithm, in *S+SSPR 2012*, ser. LNCS, vol. 7626. Springer, 2012, pp. 557–565.

[3] M. A. Perez and F. M. Raupp. A Newton-based heuristic algorithm for multi-objective flexible job-shop scheduling problem. *J. of Intell. Manuf.*, pp. 1–8, 2014.

[4] C. R. Scrich, V. A. Armentano, and M. Laguna. Tardiness minimization in a flexible job shop: A tabu search approach. *J. of Intell. Manuf.*, vol. 15, no. 1, pp. 103–115, 2004.

[5] W. Xia and Z. Wu. An effective hybrid optimization approach for multi-objective flexible job-shop scheduling problems. *Comp. and Ind. Eng.*, vol. 48, no. 2, pp. 409 – 425, 2005.

Genetic Algorithms for Evolving Deep Neural Networks

Omid E. David
Bar-Ilan University
Ramat-Gan 52900, Israel
mail@omiddavid.com

Iddo Greental
Tel Aviv University
Tel Aviv 69978, Israel
iddo.greental@gmail.com

ABSTRACT

In recent years, *deep learning* methods applying unsupervised learning to train deep layers of neural networks have achieved remarkable results in numerous fields. In the past, many genetic algorithms based methods have been successfully applied to training neural networks. In this paper, we extend previous work and propose a GA-assisted method for deep learning. Our experimental results indicate that this GA-assisted approach improves the performance of a deep autoencoder, producing a sparser neural network.

Categories and Subject Descriptors: I.2.6 [Artificial Intelligence]: Learning—*Connectionism and neural nets*

General Terms: Algorithms.

Keywords: Genetic algorithms, Deep learning, Neural networks, Autoencoders

1. INTRODUCTION

While the motivation for creating deep neural networks consisting of several hidden layers has been present for many years, supported by a growing body of knowledge on the deep architecture of the brain and advocated on solid theoretical grounds [1, 3], until recently it was very difficult to train neural networks with more than one or two hidden layers.

Recently, *deep learning* methods which facilitate the training of neural networks with several hidden layers have been the subject of increased interest, owing to the discovery of several novel methods. Common approaches employ either *autoencoders* [2, 10] or *restricted Boltzmann machines* [5, 8, 9] to train one layer at a time in an unsupervised manner.

In the past, genetic algorithms have been applied successfully to training neural networks of shallow depths (one or two hidden layers) [11]. In this paper we demonstrate how genetic algorithms can be applied to improve the training of deep autoencoders.

2. DEEP AUTOENCODERS

In this section, we briefly describe autoencoders and explain how they are used in the context of deep learning.

GECCO'14, July 12–16, 2014, Vancouver, BC, Canada.
ACM 978-1-4503-2881-4/14/07.
http://dx.doi.org/10.1145/2598394.2602287 .

An autoencoder is an unsupervised neural network which sets the target values (of the output layer) to be equal to the inputs, i.e., the number of neurons at the input and output layers is equal, and the optimization goal for output neuron i is set to $y_i = x_i$, where x_i is the value of the input neuron i. A hidden layer of neurons is used between the input and output layers, and the number of neurons in the hidden layer is usually set to fewer than those in the input and output layers, thus creating a bottleneck, with the intention of forcing the network to learn a higher level representation of the input. The weights of the encoder layer (W) and the weights of the decoder layer (W') can be *tied* (i.e., defining $W' = W^T$).

Autoencoders are typically trained using backpropagation. When an autoencoder's training is completed, we can discard the decoder layer, fix the values of the encoder layer (so the layer can no longer be modified), and treat the outputs of the hidden layer as the inputs to a new autoencoder added on top of the previous autoencoder. This new autoencoder can be trained similarly. Using such layer-wise unsupervised training, deep stacks of autoencoders can be assembled to create deep neural networks consisting of several hidden layers (forming a *deep belief network*). Given an input, it will be passed through this deep network, resulting in high level outputs. In a typical implementation, the outputs may then be used for supervised classification if required, serving as a compact higher level representation of the data.

3. GA-ASSISTED DEEP LEARNING

Genetic algorithms (GA) have been successfully employed for training neural networks [11]. Specifically, GAs have been used as substitute for the backpropagation algorithm, or used in conjunction with backpropagation to improve the overall performance.

We now propose a simple GA-assisted method which (according to our initial results presented in the next section) improves the performance of an autoencoder, and produces a sparser network.

When training an autoencoder with tied weights (i.e., the weights of the encoding layer are tied to those of the decoding layer), we store multiple sets of weights (W) for the layer. That is, in our GA population each chromosome is one set of weights for the autoencoder. For each chromosome (which represents the weights of an autoencoder), the root mean squared error (RMSE) is calculated for the training samples (the error for each training sample is defined as the difference between the values of the input and output layers). The fitness for chromosome i is defined as $f_i = 1/RMSE_i$. After calculating the fitness score for all the chromosomes, they are sorted from the fittest to the least fit. The weights of the high ranking chromosomes are updated using backpropagation, and the lower ranking chromosomes are removed from the population. The removed chromosomes are replaced by the offsprings of the high ranking chromosomes. The selection is performed uniformly with each of the remaining chromosomes having an equal probability for selection (regardless of the fitness values of the chromosomes, i.e., the fitness score is used only for determining which chromosomes are removed from the population). Given two parents, one offspring is created as follows: Crossover is performed by randomly selecting weights from the parents, and mutation is performed by replacing a small number of weights with zero.

Gradient descent methods such as backpropagation are susceptible to trapping at local minima. Our method assists backpropagation in this respect, reducing the probability of trapping at local minima. Additionally, mutating the weights to zero encourages sparsity in the network (fewer active weights). Sparse representations are appealing due to information disentangling, efficient variable-size representation, linear separability, and distributed sparsity [4].

Note that when training of an autoencoder is complete, the values of the best chromosome are selected for that autoencoder. These values are fixed and shared amongst all chromosomes when a new autoencoder layer is added on top of the previously trained layer. Thus, each chromosome contains only the values of the layer currently being trained.

4. EXPERIMENTAL RESULTS

For our experiments we used the popular MNIST handwritten digit recognition database [7]. In the MNIST dataset, each sample contains 784 pixels (28x28 image), each having a grayscale value between 0 to 255 (which we scale to a 0 to 1 range). Each sample also contains a target classification label (between 0 and 9), which is used for the subsequent supervised classification phase (using the high level representations generated by the unsupervised autoencoder).

Our deep neural network uses a stack of 5 layers. The first layer has 784 neurons, followed by four higher level layers consisting of 500, 250, 100, and 50 neurons. Each layer is trained separately, with the next layer added only once training is complete: first we train the 784-500 layer, then use the 500 output neurons as inputs to the 500-250 layer, and similarly for the 250-100 and 100-50 layers.

The GA implementation uses a population of 10 chromosomes. In each generation, the five worst chromosomes (half the population) are removed and replaced by the offsprings of the five best chromosomes. We used crossover and mutation rates of 0.8 and 0.01 accordingly.

To compare the performance of our GA-assisted method with traditional backpropagation, we ran both methods under similar conditions. First, we ran the traditional backpropagation version 10 times and selected the result with the least reconstruction error (best tuned). Next, we ran the GA-assisted method only once, allowing the same total runtime as the previous method. Comparing the reconstruction errors of the two approaches, the GA-assisted method consistently yielded a smaller reconstruction error, as well as a sparser network.

In order to compare the classification accuracy of the two methods, we ran 10,000 new test samples through the two trained networks and recorded the 50 output values for each sample. Recall that in this test phase the weights of the network are already fixed, hence an input sample of 784 values is passed through the layers of 500, 250, 100, and 50 neurons without modifying their weights. The representation quality of the networks can be compared by applying supervised classification to the higher level values produced by the 50 neurons of the output layer. We used SVM classification with a radial basis function (RBF) kernel. Using SVM, the traditional autoencoder achieved a 1.85% classification error, while the GA-assisted method's classification error was 1.44%.

5. CONCLUDING REMARKS

In this paper we presented a simple GA-assisted approach, which according to our initial results improves the performance of a deep autoencoder. While our implementation used an autoencoder, the same method is applicable to other forms of deep learning such as restricted Boltzmann machines (RBM).

In recent years, several improvements upon traditional autoencoders and RBM have been proposed which improve their generalization. Such improvements include *dropout* [6], which randomly disables some neurons during training, *dropconnect* [13], which randomly disables some weights during training, and *denoising autoencoders* [12], which randomly add noise by removing a portion of the training data. The improved performance of the GA-assisted autoencoder could arise from a similar principle, since mutation randomly disables some of the weights during training. It is important to compare the GA-assisted approach to the above mentioned alternative improvements in future research.

6. REFERENCES

[1] Y. Bengio and Y. LeCun. Scaling learning algorithms towards AI. *Large Scale Kernel Machines.* MIT Press, 2007.

[2] Y. Bengio, P. Lamblin, D. Popovici, and H. Larochelle. Greedy layer-wise training of deep networks. *Advances in Neural Information Processing Systems 19*, pages 153–160. MIT Press, 2007.

[3] Y. Bengio. Learning deep architectures for AI. *Foundations and Trends in Machine Learning*, 2(1):1–127, 2009.

[4] X. Glorot, A. Bordes and Y Bengio. Deep sparse rectifier neural networks, *14th International Conference on Artificial Intelligence and Statistics*, pages 315–323, 2011.

[5] G.E. Hinton, S. Osindero, and Y.W. Teh. A fast learning algorithm for deep belief nets. *Neural Computation*, 18:1527–1554, 2006.

[6] G.E. Hinton, N. Srivastava, A. Krizhevsky, I. Sutskever, and R. Salakhutdinov. Improving neural networks by preventing co-adaptation of feature detectors. *CoRR* abs/1207.0580, 2012.

[7] Y. LeCun, L. Bottou, Y. Bengio, and P. Haffner. Gradient-based learning applied to document recognition. *Proceedings of the IEEE*, 86(11):2278–2324, 1998.

[8] G.E. Hinton and R. Salakhutdinov. Reducing the dimensionality of data with neural networks. *Science*, 313(5786):504–507, 2006.

[9] H. Lee, C. Ekanadham, and A. Ng. Sparse deep belief net model for visual area V2. *Advances in Neural Information Processing Systems 20*, pages 873–880, MIT Press, 2008.

[10] M. Ranzato, C.S. Poultney, S. Chopra, and Y. LeCun. Efficient learning of sparse representations with an energy-based model. *Advances in Neural Information Processing Systems 19*, pages 1137–1144. MIT Press, 2007.

[11] J.D. Schaffer, D. Whitley, and L.J. Eshelman. Combinations of genetic algorithms and neural networks: a survey of the state of the art. *International Workshop on Combinations of Genetic Algorithms and Neural Networks*, pages 1–37, 1992.

[12] P. Vincent, H. Larochelle, I. Lajoie, Y. Bengio, and P. Manzagol. Stacked denoising autoencoders: Learning useful representations in a deep network with a local denoising criterion. *Journal of Machine Learning Research*, 11:3371-3408, 2010.

[13] L. Wan, M.D. Zeiler, S. Zhang, Y. LeCun, and R. Fergus. Regularization of neural networks using dropconnect. *International Conference on Machine Learning*, pages 1058–1066. JMLR.org, (2013)

A Modified Gravitational Search Algorithm for Continuous Optimization

Emerson Hochsteiner de Vasconcelos Segundo
Mechanical Eng. Grad. Program, Pontifical Catholic University of Parana, Curitiba, PR, Brazil
e.hochsteiner@gmail.com

Gabriel Fiori Neto
Industrial and Systems Eng. Graduate Program (PPGEPS), Pontifical Catholic University of Parana (PUCPR), Curitiba, PR, Brazil
meudeu@gmail.com

Andre Mendes da Silva
Mechatronics Engineering Undergraduate Program, Pontifical Catholic University of Parana, Curitiba, PR, Brazil
andremendes1991@gmail.com

Viviana Cocco Mariani
Mechanical Engineering Graduate Program, Pontifical Catholic University of Parana, and Electrical Engineering, Federal University of Parana, Curitiba, PR, Brazil
viviana.mariani@pucpr.br

Leandro dos Santos Coelho
Industrial and Systems Eng. Graduate Program, Pontifical Catholic University of Parana, and Electrical Engineering, Federal University of Parana, Curitiba, PR, Brazil
leandro.coelho@pucpr.br

ABSTRACT

The gravitational search algorithm (GSA) is a stochastic population-based metaheuristic inspired by the interaction of masses via Newtonian gravity law. In this paper, we propose a modified GSA (MGSA) based on logarithm and Gaussian signals for enhancing the performance of standard GSA. To evaluate the performance of the proposed MGSA, well-known benchmark functions in the literature are optimized using the proposed MGSA, and provides comparisons with the standard GSA.

Categories and Subject Descriptors

G.1.6 [**Mathematics of Computing**]: Optimization—*Global Optimization*; I.2.8 [**Artificial Intelligence**]: Problem Solving, Control Methods, and Search—*Heuristic methods*

Keywords

Gravitational Search Algorithm; Optimization

1. INTRODUCTION

Gravitational search algorithm (GSA), proposed by Rashedi et al. [1], is a versatile population-based metaheuristic recently proposed inspired on the law of gravity and mass interaction for global optimization. There are several advanced GSA variants available in the literature to obtain better performance than the original GSA, such as approaches based chaos theory [2], oppositional operator [3], and quantum bits [4].

In this paper, we propose a modified GSA (MGSA) by introducing a new operator to update the velocities to diminish premature convergence and local minima for a minimization problem. In this context, the main purpose of this paper is to verify that the search ability of GSA can be enhanced by modification to update the velocities logarithm and Gaussian signals instead to uniform distribution signals. GSA and MGSA are used to optimize well-known benchmark functions and some simulation results are compared. Obtained results confirm the efficiency of the proposed MGSA.

The remainder of this paper is organized as follows: In Section 2 we provide a brief summary of GSA and explains the MGSA. Section 3 introduces the well-known benchmark functions and optimization results. Finally, we provide conclusions in Section 4.

2. GRAVITATIONAL SEARCH ALGORITHM

In GSA, agents are considered as objects and their performance are measured by their masses, with all objects attracting each other by the gravity force, while this force causes a global movement of all objects towards the objects with heavier masses [3]. This approach provides an iterative method that simulates mass interactions, and moves through a multi-dimensional search space under the influence of gravitation.

To describe the GSA, consider a system with N agents (masses) in which the position of the ith agent is represented by:

$$X_i = \left(x_i^1 \ldots x_i^d \ldots x_i^n\right), \quad i = 1,2,\ldots,N \tag{1}$$

where n is the search space dimension and x_i^d defines the position of the ith agent in the dth dimension. At any time (or current iteration) t the force acting between the ith mass and the jth mass based on Newtonian gravitation theory is defined as [3]:

$$\mathbf{f}_{ij}(t) = G(t)\frac{M_i(t)\cdot M_j(t)}{R_{ij}(t)+\varepsilon}\left(\mathbf{x}_j(t) - \mathbf{x}_i(t)\right) \tag{2}$$

where $G(t)$ is parameter which is reduced during iterations according to

$$G(t) = G_O e^{-\alpha \cdot \frac{t}{\max\_t}} \tag{3}$$

where max_t is the maximum of iterations, α is a constant value, M is the mass, R_{ij} is the distance and ε is a small value. It is then assumed that the total force acting on a mass is a randomly weighted sum of the individual forces (2), thus:

GECCO'14, July 12–16, 2014, Vancouver, BC, Canada.
ACM 978-1-4503-2662-9/14/07.

$$\mathbf{f}_i(t) = \sum_{j=1, j \neq i}^{N} r_j \cdot \mathbf{f}_{ij}(t) \tag{4}$$

where r_j is a uniformly distributed random number in the interval [0,1]. This allows the update of velocities and positions according to [3]:

$$\begin{aligned} \mathbf{v}_i(t+1) &= r_i \cdot \mathbf{v}_i(t) + \mathbf{a}_i(t) \\ \mathbf{x}_i(t+1) &= \mathbf{x}_i(t) + \mathbf{v}_i(t+1) \end{aligned} \tag{5}$$

where

$$\mathbf{a}_i(t) = \frac{\mathbf{f}_i(t)}{M_i(t)} \tag{6}$$

After this step masses are updated according to:

$$\begin{aligned} m_i(t) &= \frac{f_i(t) - w(t)}{b(t) - w(t)} \\ M_i(t) &= \frac{m_i(t)}{\sum_{j=1}^{N} m_j(t)} \end{aligned} \tag{7}$$

where b and w indicate the best and worst objective function values and f is the objective function. The procedure is then repeated until some convergence criterion is satisfied. Summarizing, the classical GSA is composed of following steps:

(i) Randomized initialization of the agents including positions and velocities using uniform distribution;

(ii) Fitness evaluation for each agents;

(iii) Update $G(t)$, $b(t)$, $w(t)$ and $M_i(t)$;

(iv) Calculation of the total force in different directions;

(v) Calculation of acceleration and velocity;

(vi) Updating agents' position;

(vii) Repeat steps (ii) to (vi) until a given stopping criterion related to the number of objective function evaluations is reached.

(viii) Return the best fitness computed at final iteration as a global fitness and the positions of the corresponding agent at specified dimensions as the global solution of that problem.

To improve the performance of GSA, a logarithm and Gaussian updating of the r_i is incorporated into MGSA by means of utilizing a modified version of the equation (5) given by following procedure:

if $ru > 0.5$ then $r_i \cdot = \ln(1/rd)/8$ else $r_i \cdot = 0.3 + 0.1 \cdot rg$

where ru and rd are uniformly distributed random numbers in the interval [0,1], and rg is a normally distributed pseudorandom number with mean 0 and standard deviation 1.

3. COMPUTATIONAL RESULTS

In order to test the performance of the proposed MGSA, two well-known benchmark functions are evaluated in N = 30 dimensions (50 runs). For all runs, we used the following parameters in GSA and MGSA: population size is set to 100 agents, stopping criterion (max_t) is equal to 3,000 iterations, G_0, is set to 100, and $\alpha = 20$. Figure 1 shows mean best objective function (for the best solution) for the GSA and MGSA with 30 independent runs for the benchmark functions. It is evident from the Figure 1 that the MGSA is able to give better convergence trends for the Rosenbrock and Rastrigin functions.

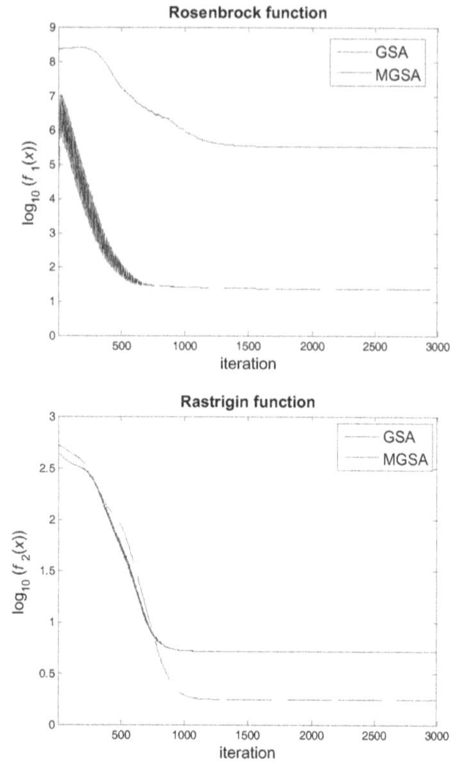

Figure 1. Comparison of mean best objective function (30 runs) for the GSA and MGSA.

4. CONCLUSION

In this paper, the proposed MGSA has been successfully implemented to solve two benchmark functions. It has a flexible and well-balanced mechanism for enhancing exploration and exploitation abilities. Simulation results show that MGSA achieves promising results and outperforms the classical GSA. In the future we may examine the performance of MGSA for other continuous optimization problems.

5. REFERENCES

[1] E. Rashedi, H. Nezamabadi-pour, and S. Saryazdi, 2009, GSA: A gravitational search algorithm, *Information Sciences*, 179(13):2232-2248.

[2] S. Gao, C. Vairappan, Y. Wang, Q. Cao and Z. Tang, 2014, Gravitational search algorithm combined with chaos for unconstrained numerical optimization, *Applied Mathematics and Computation,* 231:48-62.

[3] L. S. Coelho, V. C. Mariani, N. Tutkun and P. Alotto, 2014, Magnetizer design based on a quasi-oppositional gravitational search algorithm, *IEEE Transactions on Magnetics*, 50(2):705-708.

[4] B. Ji, X. Yuan, Z. Chen and H. Tian, 2014, Improved gravitational search algorithm for unit commitment considering uncertainty of wind power, *Energy*, 67:52-62.

Bat-Inspired Optimization Approach Applied to Jiles-Atherton Hysteresis Parameters Tuning

Leandro dos Santos Coelho
Industrial and Systems Eng. Grad. Program, Pontifical Catholic University of Parana, and Electrical Engineering, Federal University of Parana, Curitiba, PR, Brazil
leandro.coelho@pucpr.br

Viviana Cocco Mariani
Mechanical Eng. Grad. Program, Pontifical Catholic University of Parana, and Electrical Engineering, Federal University of Parana, Curitiba, PR, Brazil
viviana.mariani@pucpr.br

Helon Vicente Hultmann Ayala
Industrial and Systems Eng. Graduate Program (PPGEPS), Pontifical Catholic University of Parana (PUCPR), Curitiba, PR, Brazil
helonayala@gmail.com

Andre Mendes da Silva
Mechatronics Eng. Undergraduate Program, Pontifical Catholic University of Parana, Curitiba, PR, Brazil
andremendes1991@gmail.com

Nelson Jhoe Batistela
GRUCAD-EEL-CTC, Federal University of Santa Catarina (UFSC), Florianopolis, SC, Brazil
jhoe@grucad.ufsc.br

Jean Vianei Leite
GRUCAD-EEL-CTC, Federal University of Santa Catarina (UFSC), Florianopolis, SC, Brazil
jean@grucad.ufsc.br

ABSTRACT
Recently, it was proposed a new metaheuristic optimization approach namely bat algorithm (BA), which is based on the fascinating capability of microbats in to find their prey and discriminate different types of insects even in complete darkness. In this paper, we introduce a novel enhanced hybrid approach combining BA with a mutation style operator from differential evolution and beta probability distribution (BADEBD) and report its performance on to identification of the 10 hysteresis parameters for the 2-dimensional Jiles-Atherton hysteresis modeling to a material under rotational excitation. Compared with the classical BA, the proposed BADEBD performs better in terms of the solution accuracy and the convergence rate.

Categories and Subject Descriptors
G.1.6 [**Mathematics of Computing**]: Optimization—*Global Optimization*; I.2.8 [**Artificial Intelligence**]: Problem Solving, Control Methods, and Search—*Heuristic methods*

Keywords
Bat Algorithm; Differential Evolution, Hysteresis Parameters

1. INTRODUCTION
A promising recent paradigm is the bat algorithm (BA) proposed by Yang [1], which is based on the fascinating capability of microbats in to find their prey and discriminate different types of insects even in complete darkness based on echolocation features. On the other hand, differential evolution (DE) [2] is arguably one of the most powerful stochastic real-parameter optimization algorithms of current interest. This paper suggests a novel combination of BA with a mutation style operator from DE and beta probability distribution (BADEBD) for Jiles-Atherton (J-A) hysteresis model parameters estimation of a material under rotational excitation. Results show the potential of the BADEBD as an efficient search technique for optimization of J-A hysteresis parameters.

GECCO'14, July 12–16, 2014, Vancouver, BC, Canada.
ACM 978-1-4503-2662-9/14/07.

The rest of this manuscript is structured as follows. Section 2 provides an overview of the BA and BADEBD. The performance of the optimization algorithms for the J-A hysteresis modeling is presented in Section 3 while Section 4 concludes the paper with final remarks.

2. BAT ALGORITHM
Bats have been known to be mysterious creatures that exhibit an interesting ability to navigate their environments and capture preys without relying on their eyesight by using the echolocation technique. BA is inspired from the echolocation of microbats and the its basic procedure involves the following steps [1]:

Step 1: Initialize the bat population, where for each bat (i), its position x_i^t and velocity v_i^t in a d-dimensional search space should be initialized;

Step 2: Define the pulse frequency F_i at x_i^t ;

Step 3: Initialize the pulse rates r_i^t and the loudness A_i^t ;

Step 4: Generate new solutions by adjusting frequency, and updating velocities and locations/solutions;

Step 5: Evaluate the objective function of the bat population;

Step 6: Rank the bats and find the current best x^*;

Step 7: Repeat *Steps 4-6* until a given stopping criterion related to the number of objective function evaluations is reached.

The adopted equations in the *Steps* 1 to 7 are given by [3]:

$$F_i = F_{\min} + (F_{\max} - F_{\min}) \cdot \beta \tag{1}$$

$$v_i^t = v_i^{t-1} + \left(x^* - x_i^{t-1}\right) \tag{2}$$

$$x_i^t = x_i^{t-1} + v_i^t \tag{3}$$

$$x_{i,new}^t = x_{i,old}^{t-1} + \varepsilon \cdot \left\langle A_i^{t-1} \right\rangle \tag{4}$$

$$A_i^t = \alpha \cdot A_i^{t-1}, r_i^t = r_i^0 \cdot \left(1 - e^{-\gamma t}\right) \tag{5}$$

where $\beta \in [0,1]$, $r \in [0,1]$ and $\varepsilon \in [-1,1]$ are random vectors drawn from uniform distribution. F_i is the ith bat emission frequency, $F_{\min}$ and $F_{\max}$ the frequency's lower and upon bounds respectively. v_i^t is the ith bat velocity vector at the iteration t, x_i^t the ith bat position vector at the ith iteration. Besides, $x_{i,old}^t$ is the same of x_i^t in equation (3), but after the use of (4), it is stored in the same memory position but denoted, as $x_{i,new}^t$. Finally, α and γ are parameters to be set before the run. In this work, their values are assigned to 0.9, for both cases.

On the other hand, to improve the performance of classical BA by balancing the exploration and exploitation, in the proposed BADEBD, we have induced a DE's mutation operator [2] in the *Step 4* of the traditional BA instead of the utilization of velocity v_i in each bat. Mutation operation integrated in the BADEBD is carried out by the arithmetical combinations of the selected bats, but using a mutation rate generated by a beta distribution in range [0,1]. The mutation operation is a powerful strategy to diversify the bats population and improve the BADEBD's performance to avoid the premature convergence.

3. OPTIMIZATION RESULTS

In order to solve the optimization problem, the vector J-A model is considered in its two-dimensional version (x,y) so it is necessary 10 parameters (five for the transverse and five for the rolling direction) for the modelling of an anisotropic material: saturation magnetization M_S, parameters a and α related to the anhysteretic Langevin function, c related to the reversible magnetization and k related to the irreversible magnetization. Experimental data, obtained from a Rotational Single Sheet Tester (RSST) [4] are used in the curve fitting. In this paper, it is adopted in the optimization procedure the minimization of an objective function F given by the sum of the Mean Squared Errors (MSE) between calculated and measured curves in the two-dimensional version (x,y), i.e., $F = \text{MSE}x + \text{MSE}y$.

We adopted the following control parameters for tested BA and BADEBD: number of independent runs is 30, the population size is 25 bats, the maximum of generations is equal to 300. In the setup of the BA is adopted both loudness and pulse rate equal to 0.5. In the BADEBD approach, both loudness and pulse rate are generated with uniform distribution in range [0,1].

Table 1 presents the simulation results of objective function F of best solution after 7,500 objective function evaluations (in 30 runs). A result with Boldface means the best value found in Table 1. Fig. 1 showed measured and calculated curves with the best J-A parameters set in terms of F value obtained using BADEBD. Furthermore, Table 2 shows the obtained J-A model parameters. In terms of mean and minimum F values, the BADEBD found best values than the tested traditional BA. The best solution of the BADEBD was with F=4422.8 (MSEx=784.6 and MSEy=3638.2) with error between experimental and calculated losses of 1.49%. The results of the J-A hysteresis model with BADEBD are found to be in good agreement with the measured ones. Through the application of the BADEBD was revealed promising to obtain an optimized parameters set for the J-A vector hysteresis model.

Table 1. Optimization results of F for the J-A model

Optimization Method	Objective function F of best solution (bat)			
	Maximum (Worst)	Mean	Minimum (Best)	Std. Dev.
Classical BA	8908.4	6373.2	5089.6	1497.3
BADEBD	5564.3	**4824.7**	**4422.8**	411.5

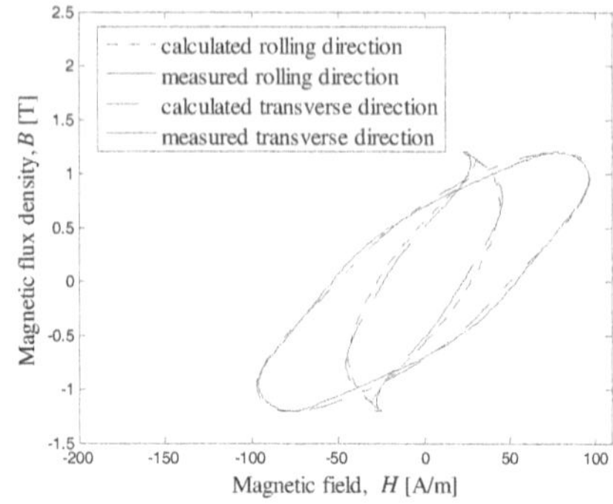

Figure 1. Calculated (solution of BADEBD) and measured *B-H* curves for the material under rotational excitation.

Table 2. Parameters for the J-A model obtained by BADEBD

Variable	Rolling direction (x)	Transverse direction (y)
M_S	1.390×10^6 [A/m]	2.498×10^6 [A/m]
k	3.399×10^1 [A/m]	5.556×10^1 [A/m]
c	2.050×10^{-1}	9.500×10^{-2}
a	8.467×10^1 [A/m]	2.477×10^2 [A/m]
α	2.609×10^{-4}	2.480×10^{-4}

4. CONCLUSION AND FUTURE WORK

In this paper, the proposed BADEBD algorithm has been successfully implemented to solve a J-A modeling problem. Simulation results have shown significant solutions for the proposed BADEBD in the case of J-A hysteresis model parameters estimation for the RSST when compared with the classical BA. In the future work the proposed BADEBD will be applied to benchmark optimization problems and practical applications such as transformers design optimization.

5. REFERENCES

[1] X. S. Yang, 2010. A new bat-inspired algorithm, In *Nature Inspired Cooperative Strategies for Optimization (NICSO)*, Springer, Studies in Computational Intelligence, 284:65-74.

[2] R. Storn and K. V. Price, 1995. Differential evolution - A simple and efficient adaptive scheme for global optimization over continuous spaces, *Technical Report TR-95-012*, International Computer Science Inst., Berkeley, CA, USA.

[3] T. C. Bora, L. S. Coelho and L. Lebensztain, 2012. Bat-inspired optimization for the brushless DC wheel motor problem, *IEEE Transactions on Magnetics*, 48(2):947-950.

[4] P. A. da Silva Jr, 2007. Workbench for assays of ferromagnetic materials in single sheet under rotational fields, PhD Thesis (in Portuguese), Federal University of Santa Catarina (UFSC), Florianopolis, SC, Brazil.

Portfolio Optimization Using an Integer Genetic Algorithm

Javier Fernández-Rendón
Facultad de Ciencias, UNAM
Mexico City, Mexico
ferjavi7@hotmail.com

Katya Rodríguez-Vázquez
IIMAS, UNAM
Mexico City, Mexico
katya.rodriguez@iimas.unam.mx

ABSTRACT

The portfolio selection is an essential component of fund administration because it contributes to economic growth of the investor. Many of the related works use the Markowitz's mean–variance portfolio selection model approach to solve this optimization problem. However, the use of continuous variables in this approach does not allow us to implement directly the obtained solutions because assets cannot be divided. This paper presents a portfolio selection model that involves integer variables, allowing a more realistic treatment. Due to the complexity of this mixed–integer nonlinear programming problem, a corresponding genetic algorithm is used to solve it.

Categories and Subject Descriptors

I.2.8 [**Artificial Intelligence**]: Problem Solving, Control Methods, and Search—*heuristic methods, genetic algorithms*; G.1.6 [**Numerical Analysis**]: Optimization—*constrained optimization, integer programming, nonlinear programming*; J.1 [**Administrative Data Processing**]: Financial

Keywords

Portfolio optimization, Markowitz model, Non–linear integer programming, Genetic algorithm

1. PROBLEM FORMULATION

The Markowitz's modern portfolio theory [3, 4] has made a new paradigm of portfolio selection problem in which the investor wants to form a portfolio with the lowest level of risk at a given desired expected return. This optimization problem consists in determining the optimal investing weight of each asset. However, this model assumes a perfect market in which assets can be divided infinitely and therefore can be traded in any fraction. Due to this strong assumption, this model cannot be implemented in practice and only gives an investment portfolio construction approximation. This approximation can be made with adjustments in the obtained solutions, commonly rounding this values. But this can lead to some issues. The first one is that previously obtained values of risk and expected return of the portfolio may have changed. And the second one is regarding the allocation of capital since it could exceed the available capital or it could stay well below this (a problem in stock markets, because there exist a minimum investment capital).

In order to handle these issues and look for more practical results, a model (based on Markowitz's model) which involves integer variables is here presented. This model takes into account the unit price of the assets and a minimum investment capital proportion to give a more realistic approach of portfolio selection. Let:

n	be the total number of assets available
μ_i	be the expected return of asset i ($i = 1, \dots, n$)
σ_{ij}	be the covariance between assets i and j ($i = 1, \dots, n$; $j = 1, \dots, n$)
r^*	be the minimum desired expected return of investor
C	be the total available capital (monetary terms)
p	be the minimum proportion of capital to be invested
c_i	be the price of asset i (monetary terms)
x_i	be the number of asset i which model suggest to purchase (non–negative integer variable)

Then the proposed model is formulated as:

$$\min \sqrt{\sum_{i=1}^{n}\sum_{j=1}^{n} c_i\, x_i\, c_j\, x_j\, \sigma_{ij}} \tag{1}$$

$s.t.$

$$\sum_{i=1}^{n} c_i\, x_i\, \mu_i \geq r^*\, C \tag{2}$$

$$\sum_{i=1}^{n} c_i\, x_i \leq C \tag{3}$$

$$\sum_{i=1}^{n} c_i\, x_i \geq p\, C \tag{4}$$

$$x_i \geq 0 \text{ and integer}, \quad i = 1, \dots, n \tag{5}$$

Eq. 1 is the objective function which determines the risk and it should be minimized. Eq. 2 ensures the desired minimum expected return of investor. Eq. 3 indicates the maximum capital allocation, whereas eq. 4 indicates the minimum capital allocation. Finally, eq. 5 indicates that x_i is a non–negative integer variable (i.e., no short sale is allowed).

GECCO'14, July 12–16, 2014, Vancouver, BC, Canada.
ACM 978-1-4503-2881-4/14/07.
http://dx.doi.org/10.1145/2598394.2602278.

2. GENETIC ALGORITHM DEFINITION

Since Genetic Algorithms (GAs) allow the treatment of very complex problems, such as mixed–integer nonlinear programming problems, a corresponding GA is proposed in order to deal with the portfolio optimization model here presented.

The design of the proposed GA is described as follows. The individuals are represented by an integer string values (as such are defined the decision variables); thus, each individual represents a portfolio investment where ith component indicates the number of ith asset to be bought. These values must be between 0 and $\lfloor \frac{C}{c_i} \rfloor$ in order to limit the search space.

For the evaluation of individuals the standard deviation as risk measure plus a penalty for each violated constraint are considered. This penalization is assigned depending on the amount of violation for each constraint of the problem and is expressed in terms of r^*, n and a penalty coefficient.

The selection process uses both a linear ranking [1] and a roulette wheel selection method [2] for prevents premature convergence. In addition, to preserve the fittest individual of the generation elitism is used.

As genetic operators, the intermediate recombination and the BGA mutation [5] are considered, both with rounding values for preserving representation of individuals. Also a repair strategy is implemented for those solutions that get out of the bounded search space assigning them the nearest limit value.

Finally, parameters are set as follows: a population size of 80 individuals, a total number of 10,000 generations, a crossover probability of 0.9 and a mutation probability of $1/n$ (the recommended for the BGA mutation method).

3. EMPIRICAL RESULTS

A portfolio optimization problem with a total number of 165 assets, with a sample historical data of 419 daily returns,[1] is formulated by proposed model considering an available capital of \$100,000 and setting a 99% of this capital as a minimum required investment.

As it can see in Figure 1, both efficient frontiers one obtained by the defined GA and the other one obtained by means of rounding method to adjust the *MATLAB* generated solutions[2] are presented. Here the risk of *MATLAB* solutions is lower than the obtained by the defined GA; however the average investment of adjusted solutions is \$98,619.87 (with a minimum of \$93,662.26 and a maximum of \$105,246.61) which implies the risk reduction but also infeasible solutions. On the other hand, the average investment of GA solutions is \$99,977.54 (with a minimum of \$99,753.02 and a maximum of \$99,999.96); thus, they are feasible solutions with slightly higher risk.

4. CONCLUSIONS

In this paper, a portfolio selection model based on Markowitz's model is proposed. The presented model involved integer variables and a minimum capital investment constraint for a more realistic treatment of portfolio optimization. A corresponding GA is defined due to the proposed

[1]By convention, the standard deviations and expected returns have been annualized in order to obtain the annual volatility and the expected annual return of the portfolio.

[2]Using the Financial Toolbox.

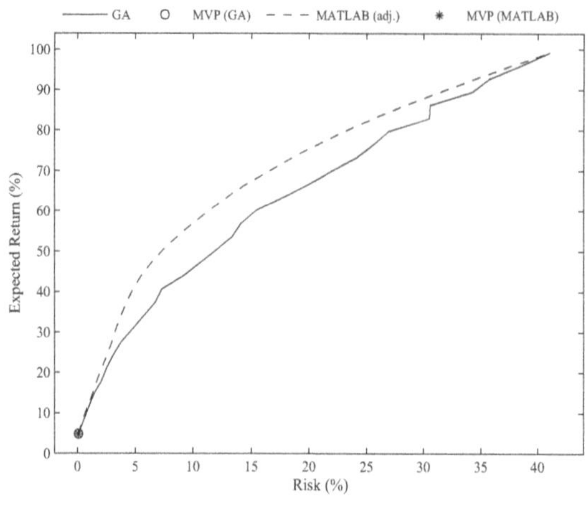

Figure 1: GA Efficient Frontier vs. MATLAB (adj.) Efficient Frontier.

model complexity. The results show a good performance of the proposed GA.

Finally, in a future research, asset lots investment, buy–in threshold, cardinality and capitalization sector constraints with transaction costs and other risk measures will be considered.

5. REFERENCES

[1] J. E. Baker. Adaptive Selection Methods for Genetic Algorithms. In J. J. Grefenstette, editor, *Proceedings of the First International Conference on Genetic Algorithms and Their Applications*, pages 101–111, Hillsdale, NJ, USA, 1985. Lawrence Erlbaum Associates.

[2] D. E. Goldberg. *Genetic Algorithms in Search, Optimization and Machine Learning.* Addison-Wesley, Boston, MA, USA, 1989.

[3] H. M. Markowitz. Portfolio Selection. *The Journal of Finance*, 7(1):77–91, 1952.

[4] H. M. Markowitz. *Portfolio Selection: Efficient Diversification of Investments.* Yale University Press, USA, 1959.

[5] H. Mühlenbein and D. Schlierkamp-Voosen. Predictive Models for the Breeder Genetic Algorithm I. Continuous Parameter Optimization. *Evolutionary Computation*, 1(1):25–49, 1993.

Towards the Automated Generation of Term-Weighting Schemes for Text Categorization

Mauricio Garcia, Hugo J. Escalante, Manuel Montes, Alicia Morales, Eduardo Morales
INAOE, Luis Enrique Erro 1, Puebla, 72840, Mexico
{mauricio.garcia, hugojair, mmontesg, a.morales, emorales}@inaoep.mx

ABSTRACT

This paper describes ongoing research on the use of genetic programming to learn term-weighting schemes to be used for text classification. A term-weighting scheme (TWS) determines the way in which documents are represented before applying a text classification model. We propose a genetic program that aims at learning an effective TWS that can improve the performance in text classification. We report preliminary experimental results that give evidence of the validity of the proposal.

Categories and Subject Descriptors

I.2.7 [**Artificial Intelligence**]: Natural Language Processing—*Text analysis*

Keywords

GP; Text classification; Representation learning.

1. INTRODUCTION

Text classification (TC) is the task of associating documents with predefined categories that are related to their content. TC is an important and active research field because of the large number of digital documents available and the consequent need to organize them. TC is a typical problem that has been approached with pattern classification methods, where documents are represented as numerical vectors and standard classification methods (e.g., SVM, KNN) are applied. A crucial component of TC systems is the TWS, which specifies how a document is represented in a way that classifiers can be applied.

Given a TWS, a document d_i is represented by a numerical vector $\mathbf{w}_i$ of length equal to the size of the vocabulary V (the set all the different terms/words that appear in a corpus). Each element $w_{i,j}$, $j = 1, \ldots, |V|$, of $\mathbf{w}_i$ indicates how relevant word j is for describing the content of document i, the value of $w_{i,j}$ is deterimed by the TWS. Many TWS have been proposed so far, including unsupervised (e.g., Boolean and TFIDF) and supervised schemes (e.g., TF-IG and TF-CHI). Unsupervised TWS are the most used ones, for example, under the Boolean TWS $w_{i,j} = 1$ iff word j appears in document i and 0 otherwise. Under the term-frequency (TF) TWS, $w_{i,j} = \#(i,j)$, where $\#(i,j)$ accounts for the times word j appears in document i. On the other hand, supervised term-weighting schemes aim at incorporating discriminative information into the weighting scheme. For instance in the TF-IG scheme, $w_{i,j} = \#(i,j) \times I(j)$, is the product of the TF weight for word j and document i with the information gain of word j ($I(j)$). In this way, the discrimination power of each word is taken into account for the document representation.

Although acceptable performance has been reported with existing TWS, it is still an art determining the adequate TWS for a particular data set. Besides, one should note that most term weighting schemes are combinations of other word-document (e.g., $\#(i,j)$) and/or word (e.g., $I(j)$) weighting factors. Hence, it is worth asking ourselves whether better weighting schemes than the ones proposed so far can be obtained by merging the already known TWS. In this direction, this paper presents preliminary results on the use of genetic programming for learning TWSs to be used in TC tasks. A genetic program is proposed in which a set of basic TWSs (terminals) are combined through arithmetic operators in order to generate alternative schemes that can improve the classification performance. We report experimental results in a number of data sets that show the proposed formulation is a promising solution to term-weighting learning.

To the best of our knowledge, this is the first effort trying to learn TWSs from existing ones. The most related work is that from [1], where genetic programming is used to evolve weighting schemes for information retrieval. The main differences rely in that: we focus on TC instead on information retrieval; we learn TWS for a data set using the data set itself (not requiring additional collections as in [1]); we maximize the classification performance using labeled training samples, instead of requiring queries and the corresponding relevance-judgments, which are rather difficult to obtain.

2. LEARNING TWS

For learning TWS we propose a genetic program with standard tree-representation using as terminals a set of basic TWSs widely used in the TC literature [2, 3], see Table 1. The genetic program will learn how to combine basic TWSs to generate better schemes for TC. We consider term-document TWSs (e.g., $\mathbf{W}_5$, $\mathbf{W}_6$, $\mathbf{W}_{21}$), term weights (e.g.,

GECCO'14, July 12–16, 2014, Vancouver, BC, Canada.
ACM 978-1-4503-2881-4/14/07.
http://dx.doi.org/10.1145/2598394.2602286.

$\mathbf{W}_3$, $\mathbf{W}_4$) and constants (e.g., $\mathbf{W}_1$). Each (non-constant) terminal is a matrix of size $m \times n$, with m the number of training documents and n the number of terms. Term-document TWSs are matrices already, for term weights we generate a matrix where each row is the corresponding term-weight vector (constants are treated as scalar constants). The function set for combining these terminals is the set of arithmetic operators: $\{+, -, *, /, \log_2 x, \sqrt{x}, x^2\}$. The population is initialized with Ramped Half-and-Half and the selection method was half-elitism. Standard mutation and crossover operators were considered.

Table 1: Terminal set

Variable	Meaning
$\mathbf{W}_1$	$\|D\|$, Constant array that stores the total number of documents.
$\mathbf{W}_2$	$\|W\|$, Constant array that stores the total terms.
$\mathbf{W}_3$	C, Matrix containing in each row vector Chi^2.
$\mathbf{W}_4$	I, Matrix containing in each row vector IG.
$\mathbf{W}_5$	$TF-IDF$, An array containing the TF-IDF term weighting.
$\mathbf{W}_6$	TF, An array containing the TF term-weighting.
$\mathbf{W}_7$	FGT, Array containing the global frequency of terms in the document.
$\mathbf{W}_8$	TP, Matrix containing in each row vector of True Positives.
$\mathbf{W}_9$	FP, Matrix containing in each row vector of False Positives.
$\mathbf{W}_{10}$	TN, Matrix containing in each row vector of True Negatives.
$\mathbf{W}_{11}$	FN, Matrix containing in each row vector of False Negatives.
$\mathbf{W}_{12}$	*Accuracy*, Matrix containing the Accuracy per FP (term, class).
$\mathbf{W}_{13}$	*Accuracy_Balance*, Matrix containing the AC_Balance each (term, class).
$\mathbf{W}_{14}$	BNS, An array that contains the value for each BNS per (term, class).
$\mathbf{W}_{15}$	*DFreq*, DocumentFrecuency matrix containing the value for each (term, class).
$\mathbf{W}_{16}$	*FMeasure*, FMeasure matrix containing the value for each (term, class).
$\mathbf{W}_{17}$	*OddsRatio*, An array containing the OddsRatio term-weighting.
$\mathbf{W}_{18}$	*Power*, Matrix containing the Power value for each (term, class).
$\mathbf{W}_{19}$	*ProbabilityRatio*, Matrix containing the ProbabilityRatio each (term, class).
$\mathbf{W}_{20}$	*Max_Term*, Matrix containing the vector with the highest repetition for each term.
$\mathbf{W}_{21}$	RF, Matrix containing the RF vector.
$\mathbf{W}_{22}$	$RF * TF$, Array containing $RF * TF$ (element by element)

As fitness function we use the TC performance of a linear SVM when using the documents represented by the TWS obtained from each individual. The fitness function is estimated using $k-$fold cross validation ($k = 3$) over a subset of the original training documents this in order to reduce the computational cost and avoid overfitting (to some extent). The TWS achieving the highest classification performance is returned by the genetic program, this TWS is then evaluated in a test data set, that was not used during the optimization process.

3. EXPERIMENTAL RESULTS

We performed experiments in a suite of benchmark data sets. On the one hand, we consider 2 thematic categorization (TC) and 6 authorship attribution (AA) data sets, see Table 2. In AA the categories are authors, hence the problem is to associate documents with authors. We applied the proposed GP for 50 generations in each of these data sets, using a population size of 50 individuals.

Table 2: Data sets considered for experimentation.

Type	Data set	Authors	Terms	Train	Test
TC	20 Newsgroup	20	61188	11269	7505
TC	Reuters	8	5310	5459	2179
AA	Business	6	10550	85	90
AA	Cricket	4	10044	98	60
AA	Football	3	8620	52	45
AA	Poetry	6	8016	145	55
AA	Travel	4	11581	112	60
AA	CCA	10	15587	500	500

Tables 3 and 4 show the average classification performance (macro f_1 measure) of an SVM in the test partitions when using the TWSs learned with the genetic program, when using the top 1000 most frequent terms and when using all of the terms, respectively. We report the average (across TC, AA and overall, data sets) performance obtained by the different weighting schemes. We report the performance of the best TWS learned by GP for both TC and AA data sets. It can be seen that in average the TWSs learned with the genetic program obtain better average performance than standard schemes (rows 1-5). This result holds for experiments using the top 1000 most frequent terms or when all of the terms were considered, although the classification performance is higher when all features are used. Different TWS were selected for each data set, although we cannot show the learned TWSs it is worth mentioning that most learned schemes contained a few terminals.

Table 3: Results 1000 features

	Baseline	Average AA		Average TC		Overall average	
		Fscore	Std	Fscore	Std	Fscore	Std
1	TF	0.7606	0.1219	0.6592	0.2596	0.7353	0.1498
2	Boolean	0.7639	0.1484	0.6602	0.2313	0.738	0.1602
3	TF-IDF	0.7576	0.059	0.6789	0.2017	0.7379	0.0981
4	RF*TF	0.7606	0.1219	0.6592	0.2596	0.7353	0.1498
5	CHI*TF	0.7339	0.1067	0.6767	0.2166	0.7196	0.1246
6	IG*TF	0.735	0.1143	0.6513	0.1952	0.7141	0.1276
7	GP - Best TC	**0.8108**	**0.1532**	0.6746	0.2431	**0.7768**	**0.1708**
8	GP - Best AA	0.7996	0.1136	**0.7055**	**0.2281**	0.7761	0.1362

Table 4: Results all features

	Baseline	Average AA		Average TC		Overall average	
		Fscore	Std	Fscore	Std	Fscore	Std
1	TF	0.785	0.1136	0.7193	0.1601	0.7686	0.1175
2	BOW	0.7783	0.199	0.7464	0.1394	0.7703	0.1769
3	TF-IDF	0.7305	0.0576	0.7602	0.0894	0.7379	0.0608
4	TF*RF	0.785	0.1136	0.7194	0.16	0.7686	0.1175
5	CHI*TF	0.7583	0.1243	0.7256	0.158	0.7501	0.1218
6	IG*TF	0.7601	0.1235	0.688	0.1458	0.7421	0.1226
7	GP - Best TC	**0.8116**	**0.1667**	0.749	0.1416	**0.7959**	**0.1534**
8	GP - Best AA	0.7895	0.1709	**0.7832**	**0.1203**	0.7879	0.1514

4. CONCLUSIONS

We described a novel method to learn TWSs via Genetic Programming. This method generated TWSs that showed better classification performance than standard schemes, outperforming state-of-art TWSs by a substantial margin. The improvements hold for both: TC and AA data sets, hence we can argue that the proposed approach has appealing robustness and generalization features.

Acknowledgements. This work was partially supported by the LACCIR programm under project ID R1212LAC006. Mauricio García-Limón was supported by CONACyT with scholarship No. 345683.

5. REFERENCES

[1] R. Cummins and C. O'Riordan. Evolving local and global weighting schemes in information retrieval. *Information Retrieval*, 9:311–330, 2006.

[2] G. Forman. An extensive empirical study of feature selection metrics for text classification. *J. of Mach. Learn. Res.*, 3:1289–1305, 2003.

[3] M. Lan, C. L. Tan, J. Su, and Y. Lu. Supervised and traditional term weighting methods for automatic text categorization. *Trans. PAMI*, 31(4):721–735, 2009.

A Genetic Algorithm for Linear Ordering Problem Using an Approximate Fitness Evaluation

Jinhyun Kim
School of Computer Science & Engineering
Seoul National University
1 Gwanak-ro, Gwanak-gu
Seoul, 151-744 Korea
jh@soar.snu.ac.kr

Byung-Ro Moon
School of Computer Science & Engineering
Seoul National University
1 Gwanak-ro, Gwanak-gu
Seoul, 151-744 Korea
moon@snu.ac.kr

ABSTRACT

Genetic algorithms are widely used to solve combinatorial optimization problems, but they often take a long time. Usually, generating and evaluating a large number of different solutions spend most of the running time. We propose a genetic algorithm for the linear ordering problem which uses an approximate fitness evaluation. We use a part of the edges to compute the fitness function value, and the number of the edges for this is gradually increased during the evolutionary process. We present experimental results on the benchmark library LOLIB. The approximation scheme reduced the running time without loss of solution quality in general.

Categories and Subject Descriptors

G.1.6 [**Numerical Analysis**]: Optimization—*Global optimization*; G.2.2 [**Discrete Mathematics**]: Graph Theory—*Graph algorithms*

General Terms

Algorithms

Keywords

Genetic algorithm, fitness approximation, linear ordering problem

1. INTRODUCTION

Let $G = (V, E)$ be a directed graph with N vertices and M edges, and $w(u, v)$ be the weight of an edge from vertex u to v. The linear ordering problem(LOP) is to find a linear ordering of vertices $\langle v_1, v_2, \cdots, v_N \rangle$ which maximizes the fitness function

$$f(\langle v_1, v_2, \cdots, v_N \rangle) = \sum_{i=1}^{N} \sum_{j=i+1}^{N} w(v_i, v_j).$$

GECCO'14, July 12–16, 2014, Vancouver, BC, Canada.
ACM 978-1-4503-2881-4/14/07.
http://dx.doi.org/10.1145/2598394.2602282.

If the graph does not contain a cycle, then a topological ordering is an optimal solution; if not, the problem is equivalent to feedback arc set problem(FASP) which tries to remove minimal edges from the graph in order to make the graph acyclic.

LOP, FASP, and several other related problems have been studied for a long time [1]. And these problems have a number of applications in various fields [3]. The problem is known to be NP-hard and many metaheuristic approaches, including evolutionary approaches have been proposed [2]. It is known that genetic algorithms are suitable for solving combinatorial optimization problems. But usually they are slow since a large number of candidate solutions are generated and evaluated during the evolutionary process.

In this paper, we propose a genetic algorithm for LOP which evaluates an approximate fitness value. In the early generation of the GA, only a portion of the edges are used to evaluate the fitness. We increase the number of used edges from 0 to M over time. The proposed algorithm was tested on well-known instances. Experimental results show that the proposed approach reduces the running time without losing the quality of the solutions.

2. THE PROPOSED METHOD

We use a typical GA to solve the problem.

- **Population**: The population consists of 100 permutations, each representing a linear ordering of the vertices. We generate 20 offspring in each generation. Among the 120 solutions, the best 100 solutions form the population of the next generation.
- **Selection**: We randomly pick two solutions, and return the better one with probability 80%, and the worse one with probability 20%.
- **Crossover**: We use order based crossover [3]. First, each gene is copied from one of the two parents. Then we pick some genes and reorder them with respect to their order in the other parent. The probability for each gene to be picked is 50%.
- **Mutation**: Each gene has 1% chance of mutation, and the selected genes are randomly shuffled.
- **Stopping Criterion**: The GA runs for a fixed number of generations and stops. The number of generations K depends on the characteristic of the instance.

To compute the fitness directly, all N^2 pairs of vertices has be considered. By considering the edges of the graph, the fitness can be rewritten as

$$\sum_{(u,v)\in E} w(u,v)R(u,v).$$

R is a binary relation on V and $R(u,v)$ is defined to be 1 if u comes before v in the ordering, and 0 otherwise.

To approximate the fitness, we use the subset $E' \subseteq E$ which has M' edges, and compute the summation only for $(u,v) \in E'$. The accuracy of the approximation is controlled by the size of E'; it is more accurate if the size is close to M. We set the size to be 0 in the first generation, and to be M in the half-way point. During the first half of the GA, the size is gradually and linearly increased as the generation progresses. In the second half, the GA is as same as the one using exact fitness evaluation. The GA travels the search space almost randomly in the earlier generations, and it gradually finds the right direction later.

The edges in E' need to be changed at each time of the fitness evaluation. GA could easily be stuck in a local optimum, if E' has only few edges in it and it is being kept similar for a while. However, it is inefficient to randomly choose M' edges all the time. It takes time to generate a random number, and shuffling the set of edges diminishes the cache utilization. Instead, we only change some part of the elements in E'. We first randomly shuffle the list of edges, and the first M' edges form the subset E'. We exchange $0.005 \times M$ random pairs of edges at each time of evaluation; the ith and the jth edges(i, j are randomly picked from $\{1, 2, \cdots, M'\}$ and $\{1, 2, \cdots, M\}$).

3. EXPERIMENTAL RESULTS

The proposed algorithm was tested on the a widely used benchmark library LOLIB [2]. There are 485 instances, comprising both real-world instances and randomly generated ones. Among them, we selected the instances with sizes $N = 50, 100, 150, 200, 250$, since there exist a sufficient number of instances having those sizes. An instance having an error, `N-t65f11xx_150`, was excluded.

The number of generations K was selected in order to guarantee that the population is converged after K generations. We assume that the population is converged if no change is made to the population for 100 generations. An appropriate value of K for each instance was chosen after a sufficient number of experiments.

We conducted experiments with 4 different kinds of GAs. Two of them are the GA using exact fitness(`EXACT-K`) and the proposed GA using an approximate fitness(`APPROX-K`). The other two GAs run for $2K$ generations, and each of them uses either exact(`EXACT-2K`) or approximate fitness(`APPROX-2K`). We measured the fitness value of an optimal solution found and the running time for each run. We conducted 100 runs for each instance and each algorithm, and computed the average result.

Table 1 shows the comparison between `APPROX` algorithms and `EXACT` algorithms. For each instance, we compute the relative fitness and time. The relative fitness is the ratio of the average fitness value obtained by the algorithm with approximation to the average fitness value obtained by the algorithm without approximation. The relative time is computed similarly. Then, we averaged the relative values over the instances with the same size.

Table 1: Comparing the performance of the algorithms in terms of fitness and time. `APPROX-K` was compared to `EXACT-2K`, and `APPROX-2K` was compared to `EXACT-2K`.

N	APPROX-K to EXACT-K		APPROX-2K to EXACT-2K	
	fitness	time	fitness	time
50	0.9990	0.9819	1.0001	0.9821
100	1.0001	0.9426	1.0004	0.9446
150	0.9989	0.9595	0.9998	0.9595
200	1.0015	0.9346	1.0013	0.9342
250	0.9966	0.9905	0.9983	0.9907

By using the approximate fitness evaluation, the running time was reduced for both of the cases with K and $2K$. However, the quality of an optimal solution found did not changed significantly by using the approximation scheme. In fact, it was even better for some of the instances.

The relative performance of `APPROX-2K` was slightly better than that of `APPROX-K`. Note that the genetic algorithm was converged in K generations. This suggests that, when running a genetic algorithm with sufficiently large number of generations, the approximation scheme helps to escape from a local optimum. Using the approximate fitness evaluation gives a chance of accepting a worse solution, and the probability gradually decreases during the space search. The same idea is often used in some metaheuristics, and the representative one of them is simulated annealing.

4. CONCLUSION

In this paper, we proposed a genetic algorithm for LOP which uses the subset of edges to compute the approximate fitness value of a solution. The accuracy of the approximation was gradually increased the first half of the evolution, and exact fitness was used in the second half. The preliminary experimental results showed that the running time was decreased, but the performance was not harmed as well. The proposed scheme seems to be useful when the number of generations is large enough.

5. ACKNOWLEDGMENTS

This work was supported by the Engineering Research Center of Excellence Program of Korea Ministry of Science, ICT & Future Planning(MSIP) / National Research Foundation of Korea(NRF) (Grant NRF-2008-0062609). The ICT at Seoul National University provided research facilities for this study.

6. REFERENCES

[1] M. Grötschel, M. Jünger, and G. Reinelt. A cutting plane algorithm for the linear ordering problem. *Operations Research*, 32(6):1195–1220, 1984.

[2] R. Martí, G. Reinelt, and A. Duarte. A benchmark library and a comparison of heuristic methods for the linear ordering problem. *Comput. Optim. Appl.*, 51(3):1297–1317, Apr. 2012.

[3] T. Schiavinotto and T. Stützle. The linear ordering problem: Instances, search space analysis and algorithms. *Journal of Mathematical Modelling and Algorithms*, 3(4):367–402, 2005.

ABC+ES: A Novel Hybrid Artificial Bee Colony Algorithm with Evolution Strategies

Marco A. F. Mollinetti
University Centre of Pará, Laboratory of Natural Computing (LCN)
Belém, Brazil
marco.mollinetti@gmail.com

Daniel Leal Souza
Federal University of Pará (UFPA), Institute of Exact and Natural Sciences(ICEN)
Belém, Brazil
daniel.leal.souza@gmail.com

Otávio Noura Teixeira
University Centre of Pará, Laboratory of Natural Computing (LCN)
Belém, Brazil
onoura@gmail.com

ABSTRACT

This paper has the purpose of presenting a new hybridization of the Artificial Bee Colony Algorithm (ABC) based on the evolutionary strategies (ES) found on the Evolutionary Particle Swarm Optimization (EPSO). The main motivation of this approach is to augment the original ABC in a way that combines the effectiveness and simplicity of the ABC with the robustness and increased exploitation of the Evolution Strategies.

The algorithm is intended to be tested on two large-scale engineering design problem and its results compared to other optimization techniques.

Categories and Subject Descriptors

I.2.8 [**Artificial Intelligence**]: Problem Solving, Control Methods, and Search – Heuristic methods

General Terms

Algorithms, Theory

Keywords

Swarm Intelligence; Artificial Bee Colony; Evolution Strategies; Hybrid Metaheuristic; Constrained Optimization

1. INTRODUCTION

In the last years, a vast number of modifications of the Artificial Bee Algorithm were made by researchers involving many kinds of approaches [4].

In order to create a new hybridization of the algorithm that has never been made, a hybrid version of the ABC involving Evolution Strategies (ES) found on the work of [5] concerning the Evolutionary Particle Swarm Optimization(EPSO) has been created.

The Artificial Bee Colony algorithm (ABC) is a metaheuristic that simulates the foraging behaviour of honey bees, created from the work of [3]. The ABC is well-known for being a simple and effective algorithm for both constrained and unconstrained problems, being used on both constrained and unconstrained optimization problems [1]. Although this popular algorithm is effective, it has been empirically indicated that the ABC when applied to constrained optimization problems produces solutions that are not entirely robust, displaying high variance and mean values.

One of the optimization techniques that are most well-known for its large use in the field of engineering is the Particle Swarm Optimization (PSO). One of its variations that is noteworthy is the Evolutionary Particle Swarm Optimization (EPSO) [5] where it consists of a variant of the PSO in which employs operations from evolutionary strategies such as replication, mutation and selection. The EPSO through the evolutionary strategies achieves a very high convergence rate albeit maintaining a good quality for its solution.

The new Algorithm has the same Bees cycles as of the ABC, however the position update formula for the onlooker and employed bees are expanded according to the movement formula of the EPSO and replicas are made of the original bee as part of the ES. Also, new behavioural mechanisms for the selection of onlooker bees and abandonment of scout bees were made in order to further optimize the algorithm.

2. A BRIEF OVERVIEW OF THE ABC+ES

After observing that even though the original ABC is able to produce very good results for continuous unconstrained optimization problems, for the constrained counterparts, it has been empirically proven that for such problems, the ABC often displays a high standard deviation and variance values in comparison to others optimization techniques like the Particle Swarm Optimization (PSO) and the Differential Evolution (DE). Following such observations, a hybridization of the ABC has been devised with the intention of increasing the algorithm robustness as well as to produce even better solutions, thus resulting in an new algorithm that has either ES and ABC.

The ABC+ES follows the Evolution Strategies present in the EPSO where the solution is replicated n times and then mutated with various goals, such as to provide an increased exploration in the solution space because of the high variability rate, raise the convergence rate due to the fact that the clones will be trying to further improve a solution that has already been improved, and lastly to increase the quality of the solutions in the same cycle.

GECCO'14, July 12–16, 2014, Vancouver, BC, Canada.
ACM 978-1-4503-1964-5/14/07.
http://dx.doi.org/10.1145/2598394.2602277 .

The Evolution Strategies is also responsible for a feature present on constrained optimization problems that is, an infeasible solution might as well become a viable solution with a small push from one of the parameters values. Such possibility is much present in this case since the mutation operation is likely to perform a minor modification on one random chosen parameter, thus making a solution transform from infeasible to feasible, although on some cases it may further improve an already optimum value. Equation 1 shows the mutation for the replicas of the solution ($\gamma_m^{*}{}^{*}$).

$$\gamma_m^* = \gamma_m + (1 + \sigma N(0,1)) \quad (1)$$

The new position update formula for the ABC+ES as seen on 2 is the same as the ABC with the addition of a portion of the EPSO movement formula. Given the absence of an individual component like the one found on PSO, the new position update equation tends to guide the source towards the global best only having in reference the global component P_g via a social weight that undergoes mutation γ_m^* which forces the solution to converge to the global best (P_g).

$$X_m^{(t+1)} = X_m^{(t)} + \varphi * (X_m^{(t)} - X_k^{(t)}) + \gamma_m^*(P_g^* - X_m^{(t)}) \quad (2)$$

Aside from the new position update formula, other modifications were: a new selection mechanism has been created where it replaces the simple tournament selection with an elitism favoured variation where it consists of creating a pool where it contains the winner solutions — that can be present multiple times in the pool— of n tournaments of two or four participants; and a new policy for the scout bees cycle where if multiples solutions reach the limit value at the same time, only one will have its values rerolled. However, if a solution reach a threshold value, which is 1.5 times the limit value, all of the solutions that are abandoned will have new values generated.

3. RESULTS

The ABC+ES has been tested on two constrained optimization problems, that also are engineering problems that is widely used in scientific literature, the Design of a Pressure Vessel (DPV) and Minimization of the Weight of a Tension/Compression Spring (MWTCS). The results obtained for each problem are shown below on Table 1 and on Table 2.

Table 1: Comparison of Results for the DPV

Variables	ABC+ES	[7]	[2]
$X_1(T_s)$	0.785258	0.812500	0.812500
$X_2(T_h)$	0.390208	0.437500	0.437500
$X_3(R)$	40.686332	42.092732	42.097398
$X_4(L)$	196.341524	195.678619	176.654050
G_1	-0.000012	-0.000110	-0.000020
G_2	-0.002061	-0.035935	-0.035891
G_3	-7198.483555	-1337.994634	-27.886075
G_4	-201.981720	-63.052220	-63.345953
Violations	0	0	0
Fitness	5933.919333	6066.029360	6059.946300

Table 2: Comparison of results for the MWTCS

Variables	ABC+ES	[6]	[7]
$X_1(d)$	0.050000	0.050000	0.500250
$X_2(D)$	0.282023	0.282023	0.280748
$X_3(P)$	2.000000	2.000000	2.036163
G_1	-0.000000	-0.000000	-0.002840
G_2	-0.235327	-0.235327	-0.249450
G_3	-43.146137	-43.146145	-42.176000
G_4	-0.778651	-0.778651	-0.780140
Violations	0	0	0
Fitness	0.002820	0.002820	0.002836

4. CONCLUSION

The ABC+ES was able to produce better results compared to the others, indicating that it presents: a higher convergence rate due to the replications of the bees, allowing a further exploration of the search space; an improved quality of solutions because of the mutation factor of the replicas that may improve an already optimum solution; lastly, a fix of the issue brought by the ES that causes the algorithm to have many solutions trapped at local optima on later iterations, since the ABC+ES overcomes the problem by utilizing the classical position update formula for the original bee.

The next step for this algorithm is to: execute more tests with engineering design functions as well as other kinds of problems such as Real Valued Parameter Function Problems, Knapsack Problem and Real-World Problems; design a multi-swarm model to be run under CUDA architecture; and further study of the behaviour of the onlooker bees based on social aspects of the Game Theory from the work of [7] .

References

[1] B. Akay and D. Karaboga. "Artificial Bee Colony Algorithm for Large-Scale Problems and Engineering Design Optimization". In: *Journal of Intelligent Manufacturing* 23.4 (2012), pp. 1001–1014.

[2] Q. He and L. Wang. "An Effective Co-evolutionary Particle Swarm Optimization for Constrained Engineering Design Problems". In: *Engineering Applications of Artificial In- telligence* (2007), pp. 89–99.

[3] D. Karaboga. *An Idea Based on Honey Bee Swarm for Numerical Optimization.* Tech. rep. Erciyes University, 2005.

[4] D. Karaboga et al. "A Comprehensive Survey: Artificial Bee Colony (ABC) Algorithm and Applications". In: *Artificial Intelligence Review* (2012), pp. 1–37.

[5] V. Miranda and N. Fonseca. "EPSO - Evolutionary Particle Swarm Optimization, a New Algorithm with Applications in Power Systems". In: *Transmission and Distribution Conference and Exhibition 2002: Asia Pacific. IEEE/PES.* Vol. 2. IEEE Press, 2002, pp. 745–750.

[6] D. L. Souza et al. "A New Cooperative Evolutionary Multi-Swarm Optimizer Algorithm Based on CUDA Architecture Applied to Engineering Optimization". In: *Combinations of Intelligent Methods and Applications.* Ed. by I. Hatzilygeroudis and V. Palade. Vol. 23. Springer-Verlag, 2013, pp. 95–115.

[7] O. N. Teixeira et al. "Algoritmo Genético com Interação Social na Resolução de Problemas de Otimização Global com Restrições". In: 1st ed. Editora OMNIPAX, 2011. Chap. 10, pp. 197–223.

Evolved Transforms for Improved Reconstruction of Lossy-Compressed NASA Images

Frank W. Moore
University of Alaska Anchorage
3211 Providence Dr.
Anchorage, AK, USA 99508
1-907-786-4819
fwmoore@uaa.alaska.edu

Brendan J. Babb
University of Alaska Anchorage
3211 Providence Dr.
Anchorage, AK, USA 99508
1-907-786-4819
brendanbabb@gmail.com

ABSTRACT
This paper describes a methodology for evolving image reconstruction transforms consisting of an arbitrarily large, user-selected number of wavelet and scaling numbers. Given images previously subjected to lossy compression using NASA's wavelet-based ICER compressor, these novel transforms are capable of reconstructing those images with less error than ICER's own reconstruction scheme. This advance has the potential to enhance the science value of all images subjected to lossy compression.

Categories and Subject Descriptors
I.2.1 [ARTIFICIAL INTELLIGENCE] Applications and Expert Systems, I.4.5 [IMAGE PROCESSING AND COMPUTER VISION] Reconstruction – *transform methods*

General Terms
Performance.

Keywords
Image reconstruction, evolution strategies, wavelets.

1. INTRODUCTION
In 2004, we began a series of research efforts to use various forms of evolutionary computation to evolve wavelet and scaling numbers defining image compression and reconstruction transforms capable of outperforming wavelets for lossy image compression and reconstruction. These efforts were focused upon producing transforms having the same number of wavelet and scaling numbers as a particular wavelet, but different values for each of those numbers. We extended our approach to multiresolution analysis (MRA) transforms [1], evolving different sets of wavelet and scaling numbers at each multiresolution level. Our results successfully improved upon state-of-the-art techniques across a wide range of application areas, including digital photography, fingerprints, satellite imagery, and ultrasound.

GECCO '14, Jul 12-16 2014, Vancouver, BC, Canada
ACM 978-1-4503-2881-4/14/07.

In 2010, we began Alaska NASA EPSCoR-funded research into the task of using the CMA-ES evolution strategy [2] to optimize reconstruction transforms for images transmitted from Mars rover *Spirit* under conditions subject to quantization error [3]. For lossy compression, *Spirit* exclusively used an "integer 2/6" wavelet transform from the ICER compressor [4], which is defined as follows:

$$LoD = [-1/2, 1/2]$$
$$HiD = [-1/8, 1/8, 1, 1, 1/8, -1/8]$$
$$LoR = [-1/8, -1/8, 1, -1, 1/8, 1/8]$$
$$HiR = [1/2, 1/2]$$

Here, *LoD* and *HiD* represent the scaling and wavelet numbers for the integer 2/6's compression transform, respectively, while *LoR* and *HiR* are the corresponding values from the reconstruction transform. ICER uses uniform "dead zone" quantization to achieve much greater compression than lossless techniques; unfortunately, quantization also introduces permanent and irreversible data loss.

The research described in this paper had two primary goals:

1. First, we wanted to evolve a reconstruction transform that could reduce the mean squared error (MSE) in images previously compressed, quantized, encoded, decoded, and dequantized using ICER's integer 2/6 wavelet. This transform could be applied to more than 100,000 lossy-compressed images received from *Spirit*, potentially allowing NASA to improve the science value of these images. Our targeted MSE reduction was 5%.
2. Second, we wanted to evolve a reconstruction transform that could be applied to images subjected to greater compression by ICER software, without incurring additional error in comparison to that achieved by ICER's reconstruction transform. This transform would allow future missions to transmit images at lower bit rates without sacrificing the quality ICER achieved at higher bit rates. Our goal was to achieve the same image quality at 0.96 bits per pixel (bpp) as ICER could achieve at 1.00 bpp.

2. THE KEY BREAKTHROUGH
After months of work, it became clear that our previously successful approach – evolving transforms having the same number of wavelet and scaling numbers as the wavelet transform upon whose performance we were attempting to improve – was simply not producing the stellar results to which we had grown accustomed. We should not have been surprised: ICER's designers had carefully matched compression transform, quantizer, encoder, decoder, dequantizer, and reconstruction

transform and had employed sophisticated progressive compression and error containment techniques to get the best lossy-compressed images possible for transmission over the severely bandwidth-constrained deep space channel.

What ultimately allowed us to achieve (and even exceed) the targeted MSE and BPP reductions was the realization that the size and shape of the reconstruction transform need not be constrained in any way by the size of the corresponding compression transform. For example, instead of evolving an inverse transform with only eight wavelet and scaling numbers (i.e., having the same shape as the integer 2/6 wavelet), we were free to evolve arbitrarily complex transforms having such unusual shapes as 12/12 or 15/15.

3. RESULTS

To establish a baseline, we subjected a representative training set of 150 losslessly transmitted Mars images to a lossy image compression and reconstruction scheme commonly used by MERs: specifically, we applied the five-level MRA compression transform, quantization, encoding, decoding, dequantization, and five-level MRA reconstruction transform software used by ICER at 1.00 bpp, and measured the MSE in reconstructed images (relative to the original training set).

To accomplish goal 1 from above, we evolved several transforms having novel shape, culminating in a five-level 18/18 MRA reconstruction transform. Note that the evolved transform has a different number of scaling and wavelet numbers (i.e., a different shape) than the wavelet for which it has been evolved: in this example, instead of the wavelet inverse transform's 6 scaling numbers and 2 wavelet numbers, the evolved transform has 18 scaling numbers and 18 wavelet numbers (18/18), each of which is a floating-point value. Also note that unlike a wavelet transform, the evolved transform may have different wavelet and scaling numbers at each MRA level (e.g., a five-level 18/18 transform is defined by 180 different floating-point values). The evolved transform was trained on images previously compressed, quantized, encoded, decoded, and dequantized by ICER software at 1.00 bpp. Our best evolved transform was able to reduce the MSE in reconstructed images by an average of 7.76% in comparison to the baseline described above. This patent-pending technology [5] will allow NASA to go back through its entire library of images previously subjected to lossy compression and reconstruct them with less MSE, thus potentially improving the science value of these images.

To accomplish goal 2 from above, we repeated the experiment using ICER's compression transform, quantization, encoding, decoding, and dequantization software, but we subjected the images from the training set to a greater amount of compression; for example, instead of compressing the images at 1.00 bits-per-pixel (bpp), we compressed the images at a 0.936 bpp rate, thus reducing the compressed file sizes by 6.4%. Instead of using ICER's inverse wavelet transform to reconstruct these images, however, we evolved another 18/18 five-level MRA reconstruction transform (with different wavelet and scaling numbers than the transform evolved to accomplish goal 1). This evolved transform was capable of reconstructing images compressed at 0.936 bpp with 99.99% (ever so slightly less) MSE, averaged across the 150 test images, as ICER introduced to images compressed at 1.00 bpp. Our technology [5] will thus allow future missions to send a larger number of images over severely bandwidth-limited deep space communication channels without sacrificing image quality.

The specific results reported above were achieved using 1024x1024-pixel MER images with 4096 possible greyscale values (12 bpp). However, the methodology described in this paper is not limited to images of this size or resolution.

The primary advantage of the approach described in this paper is that it can be used with any existing wavelet-based lossy compression scheme. Signals may be compressed at lower bit rates without reducing the quality of the reconstructed signal, or may be compressed at the same bit rates with less error in the reconstructed signal.

Lossy signal compression is ubiquitous. MP3 audio signals, JPEG 2000 images, FBI fingerprint images, satellite images, medical images, multispectral images, and hyperspectral images are all routinely subjected to lossy compression. By reducing error in reconstructed signals (goal 1), our technology improves the quality of those signals without requiring additional bandwidth; by allowing signals to be compressed at lower bit rates without negatively impacting the quality of the corresponding reconstructed signals (goal 2), our technology significantly reduces signal storage and transmission costs. This technology thus has a diverse range of potential beneficiaries, including hospitals, clinics, and doctors; audio and video retailers; defense organizations and contractors; space organizations and contractors; law enforcement organizations; internet service providers; cell phone data, photos, and video; any organization with a large archive of lossy-compressed images; and any organization seeking to reduce its lossy image storage and transmission costs.

4. ACKNOWLEDGMENTS

The research described in this paper was funded by an Alaska NASA EPSCoR Cooperative Agreement Notice for Research. Additional support was provided by the University of Alaska Anchorage (UAA) INNOVATE program. Technical guidance was provided by scientists at NASA Jet Propulsion Laboratory (JPL). The authors are particularly grateful to Drs. Denise Thorsen (Alaska Space Grant Director), Aaron Kiely, (JPL), Matthew Klimesh (JPL), and Helena Wisniewski (UAA) for their support.

5. REFERENCES

[1] Mallat, S. 1998. *A Wavelet Tour of Signal Processing*, Academic Press.

[2] Hansen, N. 2006. The CMA Evolution Strategy: A Comparing Review. In *Towards a New Evolutionary Computation: Advances in Estimation of Distribution Algorithms*, 75-102, Springer.

[3] Gersho, A. and Gray, R. 1991. *Vector Quantization and Signal Compression*, Springer.

[4] Kiely, A. and Klimesh, M. 2003. The ICER Progressive Wavelet Image Compressor. In *IPN Progress Report 42-155*.

[5] Moore, F. and Babb, B. 2014. Evolved Transform for Processing Data, US Patent Application 61/944241 (pending), Feb. 25, 2014.

Adaptive Memetic Algorithm for the Vehicle Routing Problem with Time Windows

Jakub Nalepa
Institute of Informatics
Silesian University of Technology
Akademicka 16
44-100 Gliwice, Poland
jakub.nalepa@polsl.pl

ABSTRACT

This paper presents an adaptive memetic algorithm (AMA) to minimize the total travel distance in the NP-hard vehicle routing problem with time windows (VRPTW). Although memetic algorithms (MAs) have been proven to be very efficient in solving the VRPTW, their main drawback is an unclear tuning of their numerous parameters. Here, we introduce the AMA in which the selection scheme and the population size are adjusted during the search. We propose a new adaptive selection scheme to balance the exploration and exploitation of the search space. An extensive experimental study confirms that the AMA outperforms a standard MA in terms of the convergence capabilities.

Categories and Subject Descriptors

I.2.8 [**Artificial Intelligence**]: Problem Solving, Control Methods, and Search—*Heuristic methods*

Keywords

Memetic algorithm; self-adaptation; vehicle routing problem with time windows

1. INTRODUCTION

The vehicle routing problem with time windows (VRPTW) is a well-known NP-hard discrete optimization problem. Its applications are of wide range, thus, a number of exact [3] and approximate algorithms to solve the VRPTW emerged over the years. The latter include various improvement and construction heuristics [2], ant colony algorithms, simulated annealing, genetic and memetic algorithms, and more [5].

The VRPTW is defined on the graph G, where each customer v_i, $i \in \{1, 2, \ldots, C\}$ (and the depot v_0) is given as a vertex, and each edge is a travel connection with the cost $c_{i,j}$, $i, j \in \{0, 1, \ldots, C\}$, $i \neq j$. Customers define the demands d_i, $d_i \geq 0$, and service times s_i. The time windows $[e_i, l_i]$ are given for each v_i and the depot. Let K be a number of vehicles with a constant capacity Q in a solution σ. Then, σ is feasible if (i) Q is never exceeded, (ii) each v_i is served within $[e_i, l_i]$ in exactly one route, (iii) every vehicle starts and finishes at v_0 within $[e_0, l_0]$. The primary objective is to minimize K. Also, the total travel distance $T = \sum_{i=1}^{K} T_i$ is to be minimized, where T_i is the distance of the i-th route. σ_A is of a higher quality than σ_B if $(K(\sigma_A) < K(\sigma_B))$ or $(K(\sigma_A) = K(\sigma_B)$ and $T(\sigma_A) < T(\sigma_B))$.

The paper is organized as follows. The adaptive memetic algorithm is described in Section 2. The experimental study is reported in Section 3. Section 4 concludes the paper.

GECCO'14, July 12–16, 2014, Vancouver, BC, Canada.
ACM 978-1-4503-2881-4/14/07.
http://dx.doi.org/10.1145/2598394.2602273.

2. ADAPTIVE MEMETIC ALGORITHM

In the AMA, which extends our previous efforts [1, 6], a population of solutions evolves in time to decrease T. First, K is minimized by the guided ejection search [1], and a population of N_I feasible solutions (each containing K routes) is generated (Alg. 1, line 1). Then, according to a pre-selection scheme $\mathcal{S}$, N pairs (σ_A, σ_B) are determined (line 4) and crossed-over to generate N_c children σ_c for each pair using the edge assembly crossover (EAX) (line 8). If σ_c is infeasible then it is repaired, and it undergoes the education and mutation procedures based on applying local search moves (line 9). The best child σ_c^b is determined for each (σ_A, σ_B) (line 10). Finally, the next population is formed (line 13).

The AMA parameters are adjusted during the search. First, we propose to incrementally increase the population size N, starting from the initial size N_I (with step ΔN). Also, we combine the AB-selection scheme, which proved to have high exploration capabilities [4, 6], with the scheme locally exploiting best individuals (termed *Local Exploitation Selection*, LES). In LES, the population is sorted and divided into ϵ parts. Then, N/ϵ pairs of parents are drawn and crossed-over for each part. The children form the next population of size N. Here, the elitist strategy is applied.

In the AMA, s indicates the number of consecutive generations for which the best solution σ^B was not improved. $\mathcal{S}$ is switched to LES for better local exploitation once s exceeds S, i.e., the maximum steady state selection counter (line 19). If s surpasses P (the maximum steady state population counter), then $\mathcal{S}$ is set back to the AB-selection, and N increases to explore new regions of the search space (line 21). Finally, the best solution is returned (line 26).

3. EXPERIMENTAL RESULTS

The AMA was implemented in C++ and run on an Intel i7 2.3 GHz (16 GB RAM) computer. It was tested on the

Algorithm 1 Adaptive memetic algorithm (AMA).

```
Generate a population of N_I solutions with K routes;
done ← false; N ← N_I; s ← 0; T(σ_p^B) ← ∞; S ← AB;
while not done do
    Determine N pairs (σ_A, σ_B);
    for all (σ_A, σ_B) do
        σ_c^b ← σ_A;
        for i ← 1 to N_c do
            σ_c ← CrossoverAndRepair(σ_A, σ_B);
            σ_c ← Educate(σ_c); σ_c ← Mutate(σ_c);
            σ_c^b ← UpdateBestChild(σ_c^b, σ_c);
        end for
    end for
    Form the next population of size N and update σ^B;
    if T(σ^B) < T(σ_p^B) then
        s ← 0;
    else
        s ← s + 1;
        if (s > S and s < P) then
            S ← LES;
        else if s > P then
            S ← AB; N ← N + ΔN; s ← 0;
        end if
    end if
    σ_p^B ← σ^B; done ← CheckStoppingCondition();
end while
return best solution;
```

Gehring and Homberger's (GH) benchmark tests with 200 customers. GH tests are divided into six subclasses: C1, C2 (clustered customers), R1, R2 (random ones), RC1 and RC2 (both random and clustered). The subclasses C1, R1 and RC1 have smaller Q and shorter time windows than C2, R2 and RC2. There are 10 problem instances in each subclass.

Each test (out of 10) in each subclass was executed 5 times, and the best results (i.e., with the minimum T) were averaged for each subclass. The AMA parameters were set as follows: $N_I = \Delta N = 10$, $N_c = 20$, $\epsilon = 5$, $S = 20$, $P = S + 5$. For the MA we used the AB-Selection and $N = 20000/C = 100$, as suggested in [5]. The maximum execution time of the AMA was limited to $\tau = 5$ min.

The experimental results are given in Tab. 1. We compare the best travel distances obtained using the MA, the AMA without the selection scheme adaptation ($S = P$) and the AMA, in various time points τ_i (i stands for minutes). Also, we show the world's best known T averages (WB)[1]. In this study we obtained the world's best known K for each test.

It is easy to note that the initial best solutions (in τ_0) were of the highest quality in the MA, due to its large N – the probability of obtaining a well-fitted individual in the initial population was large. However, the MA, in which N is constant during the search, required much more time to converge to the better solutions compared with both versions of the AMA. They outperformed the MA in $\tau < \tau_1$. Here, the small populations were intensively exploited with LES and extended to include new individuals if necessary. The average populaton sizes N_1 and N_5 (in τ_1 and τ_5) prove that balancing the exploitation and exploration of the search space can be achieved by a smooth growth in N.

[1]See SINTEF website (ref.: March 18, 2014): `http://www.sintef.no/Projectweb/TOP/VRPTW/Homberger-benchmark`.

Table 1: The best results averaged for each subclass.

			C1	C2	R1	R2	RC1	RC2
MA	τ_0	T_0	**2853.57**	**1856.97**	**3988.23**	**3068.85**	**3790.70**	**2686.44**
MA	τ_1	T_1	2784.95	1848.77	3876.20	3043.86	3607.92	2657.72
MA	τ_5	T_5	2720.07	1837.44	3721.14	2969.83	3432.39	2575.97
AMA (S=P)	τ_0	T_0	2902.41	1870.89	4063.52	3102.48	3812.95	2705.66
AMA (S=P)	τ_1	T_1	**2720.06**	1834.78	3672.62	**2952.20**	3344.80	2566.55
AMA (S=P)	τ_1	N_1	24	14	12	10	11	10
AMA (S=P)	τ_5	T_5	2719.64	1832.59	3649.20	2937.43	3272.49	2546.71
AMA (S=P)	τ_5	N_5	60	34	30	18	29	19
AMA	τ_0	T_0	2880.22	1857.79	4043.66	3106.33	3842.79	2702.22
AMA	τ_1	T_1	2720.23	**1834.37**	**3671.78**	2957.36	**3334.32**	**2566.31**
AMA	τ_1	N_1	15	11	13	10	11	10
AMA	τ_5	T_5	**2718.87**	**1831.95**	**3647.68**	**2936.61**	**3270.71**	**2545.80**
AMA	τ_5	N_5	48	29	29	14	28	17
WB			2718.41	1831.59	3611.86	2929.41	3176.23	2535.88

4. CONCLUSIONS AND FUTURE WORK

We proposed an adaptive memetic algorithm for solving the VRPTW. The population size and the selection scheme are adjusted dynamically during the search in order to balance the exploitation and exploration of the search space. The experimental results proved its high convergence capabilities compared with the standard MA. Our ongoing research includes enhancing the AMA further, and incorporating it into our parallel algorithm.

5. ACKNOWLEDGMENTS

We thank the following computing centers where the computations were carried out: Academic Computer Centre in Gdańsk TASK, Academic Computer Centre CYFRONET AGH, Kraków, Interdisciplinary Centre for Mathematical and Computational Modeling, Warsaw University, Wrocław Centre for Networking and Supercomputing. This work was supported by BKM/515/RAu2/2013 grant from the Institute of Informatics, Silesian University of Technology.

6. REFERENCES

[1] M. Blocho, Z. J. Czech. A parallel memetic algorithm for the vehicle routing problem with time windows. Proc. IEEE 3PGCIC, 2013, pp. 144–151.

[2] O. Bräysy and M. Gendreau. Vehicle Routing Problem with Time Windows: Route Construction and Local Search Algorithms. Trans. Sc. **39**(1) (2005) 104–118.

[3] B. Kallehauge. Formulations and exact algorithms for the vehicle routing problem with time windows. Comput. Oper. Res. **35**(7) (2008) 2307–2330.

[4] M. Kawulok and J. Nalepa. Support vector machines training data selection using a genetic algorithm, Proc. S+SSPR 2012, ser. LNCS. Springer, 2012, vol. 7626, pp. 557–565.

[5] Y. Nagata, O. Bräysy, W. Dullaert. A penalty-based edge assembly memetic algorithm for the vehicle routing problem with time windows. Comput. Oper. Res. **37**(4) (2010) 724–737.

[6] J. Nalepa and Z. J. Czech. New selection schemes in a memetic algorithm for the vehicle routing problem with time windows. Proc. ICANNGA 2013, ser. LNCS, Springer, 2013, vol. 7824, pp. 396–405.

An Iterative Model Refinemen Approach for MOEA Computation Time Reduction

Mathias Ngo
Ecole Nationale des Travaux Publics de l'Etat
Rue Maurice Audin
69518 Vaulx-en-Velin Cedex France
mathias.ngo@entpe.fr

Raphaël Labayrade
Ecole Nationale des Travaux Publics de l'Etat
Rue Maurice Audin
69518 Vaulx-en-Velin Cedex France
raphael.labayrade@entpe.fr

Categories and Subject Descriptors

Computing Methodologies [**Artificial Intelligence**]: [Heuristic function construction, Randomized search]

General Terms

Algorithms

Keywords

Genetic algorithms, Multiobjective optimization, Pareto-optimal methods, Numerical experiments

1. INTRODUCTION

Optimization problems may present different solutions depending on the chosen model representing the system to optimize; in particular, from an initial coarse model, more refined ones can be derived with additional decision variables which may present better performances. However, in the context of generic algorithms, the computation time required to generate individuals and evaluate their fitnesses increases accordingly.

In this abstract, we present an Iterative Model Refinement Approach (IMRA) used to solve a Multi-Objective Optimization Problem (MOP) based on NSGA-II. It is aimed at decreasing the computation time and identifying the optimal number of decision variables to achieve the best performances.

This abstract will introduces a state of the art of related methods in Section 2. Section 3 presents the algorithm which is applied to a simple 2D geometric problem in Section 4.

2. STATE OF THE ART

The approach presented in this abstract builds upon prior works regarding design variables expansion [1] and model refinement in the field of Free-Form-Deformation [2]. Those works showed the benefits of an iterative model refinement in the case of monocriterion, non-evolutionary based optimization. More refined models presented better performances while the refinement strategy allowed a significant improvement in the computation time.

The proposed Iterative Model Refinement Approach (IMRA) extends such methods in the case of a Multi-Objective Evolutionary Algorithm (MOEA). The Hypervolume Estimator is therefore used to assess the global quality of a population regarding the MOP hence determining the need for further refinements of the model.

GECCO'14, July 12–16, 2014, Vancouver, BC, Canada.
ACM 978-1-4503-2881-4/14/07.
http://dx.doi.org/10.1145/2598394.2602284.

3. PROPOSED ALGORITHM

The IMRA can be used with any Genetic Algorithm (GA). The refinement consists in the introduction of new Decision Variables (DV) in the model, thus allowing better performances (assessed through hypervolume estimation).

It relies on a Trigger Operator ($\mathfrak{T}$) to identify a suitable moment for the refinement to happen, with regards to the computation time. $\mathfrak{T}$ operates on the basis of an Hypervolume Estimator (HVE) average slope and takes two parameters as inputs: an averaging window (w) and a threshold (t) under which the refinement is launched.

Algorithm 1: General algorithm

```
Data: MOP, initial_population
Result: Pareto Front Estimation, Optimized
        Population
P = initial_population
for i < MOP.num_gen do
    fast_non_dominated_search(P)
    P = make_new_pop(P)
    if T(P,w,t) then
        P = MOP.refine(P)
Return fast_non_dominated_search(P), P
```

The refinement function for P is problem dependant and is uniformely done over the entire population. In the case of a geometric problem, this refinement is most likely the addition of vertices in the model.

4. CASE STUDY

4.1 Description

The case study is an MOP that can be described as follows:

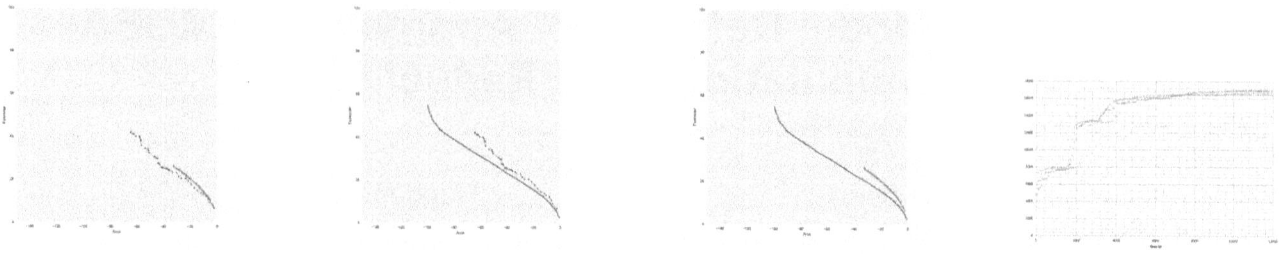

(a) 6 DV vs 12 DV (b) 12 DV vs 24 DV (c) 6 DV vs 24 DV (d) Threshold effect

Figure 1: Effect of the refinement on the Pareto-Front and the computation time

Algorithm 2: Trigger operator

Data: P, w, t

Result: Trigger decision: True if the model needs to be refined

```
HVE = compute HVE(P)
Append HVE to HVE_list
Average HVE = sum(HVE_list[:-w])/w
Append Average HVE to Average HVE List
if Average HVE < t * max(Average HVE List[:-w]) then
    Empty HVE List
    Empty Average HVE List
    Return True
Return False
```

$$\begin{array}{rl} \text{Maximize} & f_1(X) = Area(X) \\ \text{Minimize} & f_2(X) = Perimeter(X) \\ \text{Subject to} & \Omega = [-5;5] \times [-5;5] \\ & [(2,2);(3,3)]^T \in X \\ & [(0,0);(3,2);(4,4)]^T \notin X \end{array}$$

with X representing the polygon.

At first, X consists of three vertices (i.e. six DV). This MOP is solved with IMRA using NSGA-II, with the number of DV doubling with each refinement.

The computing times are compared to the one required by NSGA-II when optimizing directly the refined model (12 vertices i.e. 24 DV).

4.2 Optimization results

The optimization results of the IMRA are shown in Figure 1 After the first model performance stops improving it is refined, thus leading to a second step of performance enhancement. Those two optimization phase are compared in Figure 1a (with red being the coarse model). This behaviour continues upon reaching the Pareto-Front plotted in blue in Figure 1b and 1c.

4.3 Performances

Figure 2 shows the speedup provided by the IMRA with a suitable Trigger. The speedup happens in the second part of the optimization (Figure 2b), when the IMRA reaches its final model. The initial coarse model allows to explore a first part of the decision space while presenting a reduced computation time. The first part of the optimization gives

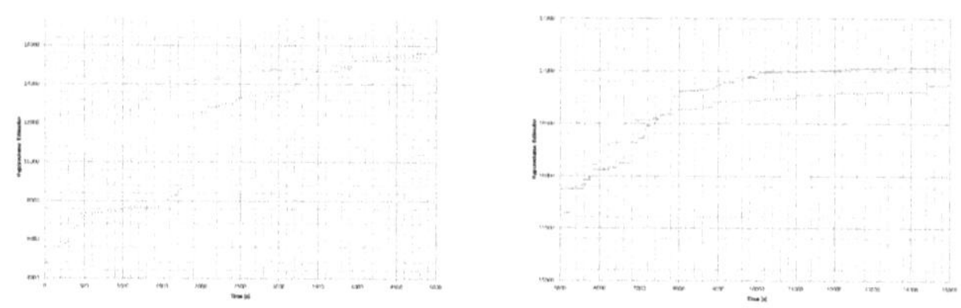

(a) First part: IMRA still not at its final model (b) Second part: IMRA and NSGA-II use the same 12 vertices model

Figure 2: Performance comparison: NSGA-II (blue dots) IMRA (red triangles)

the feeling of the IMRA being slower; however it is due to the fact that only a small portion of the objective space is reachable with a coarse model thus impacting the HVE.

The reachable space is being expanded with each refinement. In this case study, first triangles optimize low-area low-perimeter polygons. Then, the hexagons expands the decision space beyond the constraints points from already optimized triangles. Finally, the dodecagons complete the optimization while exploring high-area high-perimeter parts of the Pareto-Front from already optimized hexagons. Those phenomena explain the 3x speedup upon final convergence.

5. CONCLUSIONS AND FUTURE WORK

As can be seen in the different experimentations, the IMRA can yield satisfying results both in terms of computation speed and final estimation of the Pareto-Front. However, this algorithm seems to be very dependant of the Trigger operator, which takes two inputs: its sensibility and its averaging window. Future work will explore the possibility to handle 3D geometric problems, which is a class of real-world problems for which IMRA is likely to be suitable.

6. REFERENCES

[1] Cagan, J., and Agogino, A. M. Dimensional variable expansion : A formal approach to innovative desgin. *Research in Engineering Design* (1991).

[2] Han, X., and Zingg, D. W. An adaptive geometry parameterization for aerodynamic shape optimization. *Journal of Optimization and Engineering* (2013).

A Study on the Efficiency of Neutral Crossover Operators in Genetic Algorithms Applied to the Bin Packing Problem

Eneko Osaba
Deusto Institute of Technology
University of Deusto
Bilbao, Spain
e.osaba@deusto.es

Fernando Diaz
Telecommunications Dept.
University of Deusto
Bilbao, Spain
fernando.diaz@deusto.es

Roberto Carballedo
Deusto Institute of Technology
University of Deusto
Bilbao, Spain
roberto.carballedo@deusto.es

Idoia de la Iglesia
Deusto Institute of Technology
University of Deusto
Bilbao, Spain
delaiglesia@deusto.es

Enrique Onieva
Deusto Institute of Technology
University of Deusto
Bilbao, Spain
enrique.onieva@deusto.es

Asier Perallos
Deusto Institute of Technology
University of Deusto
Bilbao, Spain
perallos@deusto.es

ABSTRACT

This paper examines the influence of neutral crossover operators in a genetic algorithm (GA) applied to the one-dimensional bin packing problem. In the experimentation 16 benchmark instances have been used and the results obtained by three different GAs are compared with the ones obtained by an evolutionary algorithm (EA). The aim of this work is to determine whether an EA (with no crossover functions) can perform similarly to a GA.

Categories and Subject Descriptors

I.2.8 [**Artificial Intelligence**]: Problem solving, Control Methods and Search—*Heuristic methods*

Keywords

Genetic Algorithm; Crossover Operator; Bin Packing.

1. INTRODUCTION

Today, the genetic algorithm (GA) is one of the most used techniques to solve complex optimization problems. Since its formulation [3], the GA has been applied to a wide range of problems. Annualy, a lot of research studies use this kind of algorithms, either to solve a problem [8], to analyze some theoretical aspects of GAs, or to compare them with other techniques [6]. GAs are widely used in the industrial, transport and logistics fields. This is because in those contexts there are many problems with a simple definition, but complex to be solved. Such problems are known as combinatorial optimization problems. There are a lot of combinatorial optimization problems, being the one-dimensional bin packing (1d-BPP) one of the best known.

In this paper, a study on the efficiency of blind crossover operators in GAs applied to the 1d-BPP is carried out. The goal of this work is to determine if an evolutionary algorithm (EA) can perform as good as a classic GA for the 1d-BPP. Thereby, it can be concluded whether blind crossover functions are valuable for addressing this problem.

2. ONE-DIMENSIONAL BIN PACKING

The packing of items into boxes or bins is a daily task in distribution and production. Depending on the item characteristics, as well as the form and capacity of bins, a wide amount of different packing problems can be formulated. In [4] an introduction to bin-packing problems can be found. The 1d-BPP is the simplest one, and it has been used frequently as benchmarking problem [1]. The 1d-BPP consists of a set of items $I = \{i_1, i_2, \ldots, i_n\}$, each with an associated size s_i, and an unlimited supply of bins with the same capacity q. The objective of the 1d-BPP is to pack all the items into a minimum number of bins. In this way, the objective function is the number of bins, which has to be minimized.

In this study the solutions are encoded as a permutation of items. To count the number of bins needed in one solution, the item sizes are accumulated in a variable ($sumSize$). When $sumSize$ exceeds q, the number of bins is incremented in 1, and $sumSize$ is reset to 0. Thereby, supposing a simple instance of 10 items $I = \{i_1, i_2, \ldots, i_{10}\}$, each one with the same size (30), and q=120. One possible solution could be $X = (i_1, i_4, i_2, i_7, i_9, i_{10}, i_6, i_5, i_3, i_8)$, and its fitness would be 3 (the number of bins needed to hold all the items).

3. EXPERIMENTATION

In the experimentation conducted in this work the performance of four different algorithms are compared. The first technique is an EA based only on mutations. The remaining are three classic GAs. All meta-heuristics use the same parameters and functions, with the exception of the crossover operator. While the EA has no recombination phase, each GA has a different function. The neutral operators employed are the Order Crossover (OX) [2], Order Based Crossover (OBX) [9], and the Half Crossover (HX) [7].

GECCO'14, July 12–16, 2014, Vancouver, BC, Canada.
ACM 978-1-4503-2881-4/14/07.
http://dx.doi.org/10.1145/2598394.2602268.

Instance		EA			GA with OX			GA with OBX			GA with HX		
Name	Optima	Avg.	S. dev.	Time	Avg.	S. dev.	Time	Avg.	S. dev.	Time	Avg.	S. dev.	Time
N2C1W1_A	48	**53.0**	0.73	0.02	53.4	0.75	0.35	53.6	0.68	0.09	54.5	1.19	0.03
N2C1W1_B	49	**53.4**	0.50	0.02	54.0	0.79	0.21	53.9	0.79	0.09	54.7	0.86	0.03
N2C2W1_A	42	**45.9**	0.69	0.01	46.3	0.72	0.23	46.1	0.93	0.06	47.5	0.83	0.03
N2C2W1_B	50	54.0	1.28	0.02	**53.8**	0.70	0.24	54.3	0.81	0.06	55.6	0.94	0.03
N3C2W2_A	107	**120.4**	1.43	0.07	121.1	1.41	1.64	121.8	1.64	0.45	124.2	1.52	0.18
N3C2W2_B	105	117.0	1.00	0.07	**116.9**	1.57	1.92	117.7	2.00	0.37	118.8	1.40	0.18
N3C3W1_A	66	**73.0**	0.94	0.06	73.7	0.80	1.42	73.4	0.94	0.35	75.0	1.00	0.12
N3C3W1_B	71	**78.9**	0.89	0.06	80.1	0.94	1.33	79.7	1.42	0.37	81.1	0.91	0.13
N3C3W4_A	89	**99.9**	1.23	0.09	100.3	1.21	1.48	101.2	1.36	0.40	102.4	1.50	0.15
N3C3W4_B	88	**98.0**	1.10	0.06	98.8	1.51	1.44	98.7	1.38	0.40	100.3	1.50	1.76
N4C1W1_A	240	**272.9**	1.57	0.35	278.6	2.54	7.83	273.0	7.34	5.91	278.1	1.72	2.10
N4C1W1_B	262	**295.5**	2.16	0.43	300.5	3.02	7.75	298.5	1.57	6.52	301.0	2.25	2.15
N4C1W1_C	241	**273.4**	1.54	0.42	278.2	3.18	7.03	277.2	2.69	5.23	278.2	2.00	2.24
N4C2W1_A	210	**242.5**	1.82	0.46	246.0	2.45	7.90	244.5	2.16	5.40	247.9	2.35	2.24
N4C2W1_B	213	**246.5**	1.32	0.44	249.8	3.11	7.84	250.0	3.19	5.08	252.1	1.79	2.31
N4C2W1_C	213	**246.2**	1.77	0.49	250.2	3.02	7.69	248.3	2.74	5.96	252.0	2.51	2.10

Table 1: Results of the four techniques applied to the 1d-BBP

These functions are well-known, and they are widely used in the literature.

All the techniques have a population composed by 50 randomly created individuals. Each GA has a crossover probability (p_c) of 95%, and a mutation probability (p_m) of 5%. On the other hand, the EA has a p_c=0 and p_m=100%. Regarding the parents selection criteria of the GAs: first, each individual is selected with a probability equal to p_c. If one individual is selected for the recombination, the other participant is selected randomly. In relation to the survivor function, the 50% of the surviving population is selected by the elitist method. The remaining 50% is selected at random. About the ending criteria, the execution of each meta-heurstic ends when there are $n + \sum_{k=1}^{n} k$ generations without improvements in the best solution, where n is the size of the problem.

All the instances have been picked from the Scholl/Klein benchmark[1]. Each instance has been executed 30 times, and for each one, the results average, standard deviation and average runtime (in seconds) are shown (Table 1).

Looking at these results, it can be seen how the EA obtains better results for the 87.5% of the instances (14 out of 16). In the remaining two instances, GA with OX performs better. Additionally, in general (62.5% of the cases), the standard deviation of the EA is lower than the one of the other algorithms. This characteristic gives robutness to the EA, something important in real environments. Finally, regarding runtimes, the EA needs less execution time in the 100% of the instances.

The reason why the EA needs less execution time can be explained in the following way: the mutation operator consists of a simple modification in one chromosome, so it can be made in a short time. On the other hand, the crossover operates with two individuals, and its working way is more complex, needing more runtime. The reason why EA gets better results can also be explained. For the 1d-BPP, crossover helps to the exploration capacity of the technique, but it does not help to perform an exhaustive search. To perform a deeper search, a function that conducts small jumps in the space of solutions becomes necessary. For the 1d-BPP, the mutation function can handle this goal. These arguments are also based on a recent study on the traveling salesman problem [5].

[1] *http://www.wiwi.uni-jena.de/entscheidung/binpp/index.htm.*

4. CONCLUSIONS

In this paper a short study on the efficiency of the crossover phase in GAs applied to the 1d-BPP has been presented. Using the same parameters and funcions (except the crossover function), the performance of three different classic GAs has been compared with the one of an EA. According to the experimentation conducted, it can be concluded that the use of crossover functions does not lead to an improvement in results, or runtimes.

5. REFERENCES

[1] M. J. Brusco, H. F. Köhn, and D. Steinley. Exact and approximate methods for a one-dimensional minimax bin-packing problem. *Annals of Operations Research*, 206(1):611–626, 2013.

[2] L. Davis. Applying adaptive algorithms to epistatic domains. In *International joint conference on artificial intelligence*, volume 1, pages 161–163, 1985.

[3] J. H. Holland. *Adaptation in natural and artificial systems.* Michigan Press, 1975.

[4] S. Martello and P. Toth. *Knapsack problems. Algorithms and Computer Implementations.* John Wiley & Sons, 1990.

[5] E. Osaba, R. Carballedo, F. Diaz, and A. Perallos. Analysis of the suitability of using blind crossover operators in genetic algorithms for solving routing problems. In *Symposium on Applied Computational Intelligence and Informatics*, pages 17–22, 2013.

[6] E. Osaba, F. Diaz, and E. Onieva. Golden ball: a novel meta-heuristic to solve combinatorial optimization problems based on soccer concepts. *Applied Intelligence*, pages 1–22, 2014.

[7] E. Osaba, E. Onieva, R. Carballedo, F. Diaz, A. Perallos, and X. Zhang. A multi-crossover and adaptive island based population algorithm for solving routing problems. *Journal of Zhejiang University SCIENCE C*, 14(11):815–821, 2013.

[8] S. Swain and D. Mohapatra. Genetic algorithm-based approach for adequate test data generation. In *Intelligent Computing, Networking, and Informatics*, pages 453–462. Springer, 2014.

[9] G. Syswerda. Schedule optimization using genetic algorithms. *Handbook of genetic algorithms*, pages 332–349, 1991.

A Study on the Impact of Heuristic Initialization Functions in a Genetic Algorithm Solving the N-Queens Problem

Eneko Osaba
Deusto Institute of Technology
University of Deusto
Bilbao, Spain
e.osaba@deusto.es

Fernando Diaz
Telecommunications Dept.
University of Deusto
Bilbao, Spain
fernando.diaz@deusto.es

Roberto Carballedo
Deusto Institute of Technology
University of Deusto
Bilbao, Spain
roberto.carballedo@deusto.es

Enrique Onieva
Deusto Institute of Technology
University of Deusto
Bilbao, Spain
enrique.onieva@deusto.es

Pedro Lopez
Deusto Institute of Technology
University of Deusto
Bilbao, Spain
p.lopez@deusto.es

ABSTRACT

In this paper the influence of using heuristic functions to initialize the population of a classic genetic algorithm (GA) applied to the N-Queens Problem (NQP) is analyzed. The aim of this work is to evaluate the impact of the heuristic initialization phase on the results of the classic GA. In order to probe this, several experiments using two different initialization functions have been carried out. In this paper, the well-known NQP has been used as benchmark problem, but the objective of the authors is to contrast the findings of this study with other combinatorial optimization problems.

Categories and Subject Descriptors

I.2.8 [**Artificial Intelligence**]: Problem solving, Control Methods and Search—*Heuristic methods*

Keywords

Genetic Algorithm; Initialization; N-Queens Problem; Combinatorial Optimization.

1. INTRODUCTION

Thanks to its robustness and its capacity of adaptability to a wide variety of areas, genetic algorithms (GA) [2] are one of the most used meta-heuristics in the literature. Nowadays, a lot of research studies related to this kind of algorithm can be found. Something to keep in mind when developing genetic algorithms, is the way wherein the population is initialized. There are three ways to perform this process: randomly, by using initialization functions, or by a combination of both alternatives. When the GA is applied to solve a very complex problem, the first approach is the most used [6]. It is also the usual alternative when a GA is compared with other meta-heuristics [5]. On the other hand, heuristic initializaton functions are usually used when the goal is to obtain the best possible solution for a given problem [4].

In this paper, the influence of using heuristic functions to initialize the population of a classic GA is analyzed. For this purpose, the N-Queens Problem (NQP), and two heuristic functions has been used for the experimentation.

2. N-QUEENS PROBLEM

The NQP consists of placing N queens on a NxN chessboard, in order that they cannot attack each other. This is a classical configuration problem, but it can be also formulated as a combinatorial optimization problem [3]. In the experimentation presented in this paper, a solution is encoded as a N-tuple $(q_1, q_2, ..., q_n)$, which is a permutation of the set $(1, 2, ..., N)$. Each q_i depicts the row occupied by the queen positioned in the ith column. With this representation, horizontal and vertical collisions are avoided. Thereby, the objective function of the NQP is defined as the number of diagonal conflicts along the board. Notice that ith and jth queens collide diagonally if:

$$|i - q_i| = |j - q_j| \qquad \forall i, j : \{1, 2, ..., N\}; i \neq j \qquad (1)$$

Therefore, the objective of the NQP is to minimize the number of collisions, being 0 the optimum fitness. This same formulation is frequently used in the literature.

3. EXPERIMENTATION SETUP

For the experimentation two different heuristic initialization function has been used. Both of them are based on the Minimum Conflicts method [4]. The first one, called Order Minimum Conflicts (OMC), begins building a solution placing the first queen in a random row of the first column. Then, iteratively, it inserts the following queen in the next column, in that position which involves the smaller number of conflicts. If two or more position involves the same number of conflicts, the position is chosen randomly between them. The second function, called Random Minimum Conflicts (RMC), inserts the queens following the same

GECCO'14, July 12–16, 2014, Vancouver, BC, Canada.
ACM 978-1-4503-2881-4/14/07.
http://dx.doi.org/10.1145/2598394.2602269.

OMC	GA_0			GA_{10}			GA_{50}			GA_{100}		
Name	Avg.	S. dev.	Time	Avg.	S. dev.	Time	Avg.	S. dev.	Time	Avg.	S. dev.	Time
20-Queens	1.6	1.2	0.01	1.8	0.8	0.03	**1.4**	0.6	0.02	1.6	0.6	0.01
50-Queens	8.7	2.2	0.02	5.5	1.2	0.13	5.0	1.0	0.03	**4.3**	0.8	0.09
75-Queens	14.9	2.8	0.18	8.4	1.8	0.37	**7.4**	1.3	0.22	8.0	1.8	0.26
100-Queens	22.7	2.9	1.38	10.3	1.2	0.71	**8.8**	2.0	0.63	9.2	1.4	0.65
125-Queens	28.1	3.9	2.78	12.2	2.3	1.83	**10.0**	1.6	1.32	10.3	1.3	1.52
150-Queens	37.9	5.4	5.76	14.9	2.3	2.79	12.6	1.3	2.00	**12.0**	1.4	2.10
175-Queens	42.7	6.1	12.01	16.7	2.9	4.40	**12.4**	2.5	3.97	13.0	1.3	3.44
200-Queens	51.4	6.9	17.50	18.8	2.4	4.94	15.2	1.7	5.02	**14.6**	1.9	5.28
225-Queens	55.0	6.4	26.75	18.8	2.9	7.91	16.4	1.8	7.36	**15.8**	2.6	6.78
250-Queens	64.6	7.0	35.39	20.4	2.9	9.22	**16.0**	2.7	9.79	17.2	2.4	8.85
RMC	GA_0			GA_{10}			GA_{50}			GA_{100}		
20-Queens	1.6	1.2	0.01	1.5	1.2	0.02	**1.3**	0.5	0.02	1.6	0.8	0.02
50-Queens	8.7	2.2	0.02	5.4	1.1	0.15	**4.8**	1.5	0.04	5.1	1.3	0.08
75-Queens	14.9	2.8	0.18	8.9	2.1	0.31	7.9	1.7	0.28	**7.3**	1.5	0.31
100-Queens	22.7	2.9	1.38	10.1	1.4	0.65	**8.3**	2.4	0.75	8.8	1.2	0.71
125-Queens	28.1	3.9	2.78	11.9	2.8	1.72	9.8	2.1	1.41	**9.2**	1.7	1.48
150-Queens	37.9	5.4	5.76	15.2	2.9	3.10	12.9	1.9	2.11	**12.3**	2.1	2.11
175-Queens	42.7	6.1	12.01	16.5	2.7	4.33	**12.7**	2.9	4.04	13.5	1.4	3.28
200-Queens	51.4	6.9	17.50	18.9	2.5	4.78	15.1	1.8	7.66	**14.2**	2.2	5.30
225-Queens	55.0	6.4	26.75	19.2	3.5	8.12	**15.8**	2.1	7.49	16.3	2.6	6.82
250-Queens	64.6	7.0	35.39	20.5	3.0	9.05	**16.1**	3.2	9.80	16.9	2.5	8.71

Table 1: Results of the three techniques applied to the NQP

procedure as the OMC, but selecting at random the rows in which the queens are inserted.

Thereby, two experiments have been performed, each one with a different initialization function. For each experimentation, four different versions of the GA have been developed. These variants have been called GA_α, where α is the percentage of the population created using heuristic initialization functions. In this case, α takes four values: 0, 10, 50, 100. Every GA has a population composed by 50 individuals. In addition, the crossover probability has been set in 90%, and the mutation probability in 10%. Regarding the selection and survivor functions, a 50% elitist-random function has been used. About the ending criteria, the execution finishes when there are $n+\sum_{k=1}^{n} k$ generations without improvements in the overall fitness of the population, being n the size of the problem. Finally, the well-known order crossover [1] and the swapping function have been used as crossover and mutation operators, respectively.

4. RESULTS

For each experimentation ten different instances has been employed, and every instance has been executed 20 times. In Table 1 the average results, standard deviation and average runtime (in seconds) are shown. It is noteworthy that, in order to avoid redundant tests, the results depicted for GA_0 are the same in both experimentations.

First of all, it can be concluded that the use of initialization functions helps to reach a better solution. Regardless the proportion of the population initialized by heuristics, the results of GA_0 are the worst in all the instances. Anyway, this conclusion is logical, given that the individuals of the other versions of the GA go through an optimization process.

Secondly, it can be seen that GA_{50} obtains better results in the 60% of the cases (12 out of 20). This fact can be reasoned as follows: the overuse of heuristic initialization functions carries a decrease in the exploration capability of the technique and in the diversity of the population. On the other hand, maintaining a balance as the presented in the GA_{50}, the search can benefit from the previous optimization applied to the 50% of the individuals. Meanwhile, the diversity of the population is maintained by the remaining 50% randomly generated individuals.

5. CONCLUSIONS

In this work, the impact of the heuristic initialization phase on the results of the classic GA has been evaluated. For the tests, the well-known NQP has been used as benchmark problem. Anyway, the objetive of the authors is to extend this study to other combinatorial optimization problems. This extension has been planned as future work.

6. REFERENCES

[1] L. Davis. Applying adaptive algorithms to epistatic domains. In *International joint conference on artificial intelligence*, volume 1, pages 161–163, 1985.

[2] J. H. Holland. *Adaptation in natural and artificial systems*. Michigan Press, 1975.

[3] X. Hu, R. C. Eberhart, and Y. Shi. Swarm intelligence for permutation optimization: a case study of n-queens problem. In *Proceedings of the IEEE Swarm Intelligence Symposium*, pages 243–246, 2003.

[4] E. Masehian, H. Akbaripour, and N. Mohabbati-Kalejahi. Landscape analysis and efficient metaheuristics for solving the n-queens problem. *Computational Optimization and Applications*, 56(3):735–764, 2013.

[5] E. Osaba, F. Diaz, and E. Onieva. Golden ball: a novel meta-heuristic to solve combinatorial optimization problems based on soccer concepts. *Applied Intelligence*, pages 1–22, 2014.

[6] J. A. Ventura and S.-H. Yoon. A new genetic algorithm for lot-streaming flow shop scheduling with limited capacity buffers. *Journal of Intelligent Manufacturing*, 24(6):1185–1196, 2013.

Improving Reconstructed Images using Hybridization between *Local Search* and *Harmony Search* Meta-heuristics

Ahlem Ouaddah and Dalila Boughaci
University of Science and Technology Houari Boumediene USTHB
Electrical Engineering and Computer Science Department
El-Alia BP 32 Bab-Ezzouar
16111 Algiers, Algeria
aouaddah@usthb.dz,dboughaci@usthb.dz

ABSTRACT

Image reconstruction from projections in tomography is an ill-posed, inverse problem. This problem is always a challenge because there are no standard methods which give satisfactory results. In this paper we propose hybridization between Local Search (LS) and Harmony Search (HS) meta-heuristics to improve quality of reconstructed images. The proposed method is implemented, tested on some images and compared to LS and Filtered backprojection (FBP) methods. The preliminary results are promising and prove the efficiency of our method.

Categories and Subject Descriptors

G.1.6 [**Mathematics of Computing**]: Optimization—*Stochastic programming, Linear programming, Global optimization*; I.4.5 [**IMAGE PROCESSING AND COMPUTER VISION**]: Reconstruction—*Transform methods*

Keywords

image reconstruction in tomography; Harmony search meta-heuristic; Local search meta-heuristic ;

1. INTRODUCTION

Image reconstruction in tomography from projections is an inverse problem, ill posed: from a set of measures (projections), we have to find the object which produces these measures. It is also an ill-posed problem: the solution could exist or not and could be not unique. Several methods are proposed for tomographic reconstruction, the most used method in clinical routine is the FBP method [1]. Meta-heuristics have been used successfully in various optimization fields such as industry, scheduling and medical imaging. However in tomography reconstruction, there is only a few research dealing with meta-heuristics for tomographic images reconstruction as [3, 5]. In [4], we showed that a Local Search algorithm could be used for tomographic reconstruction in case of same concentration of physical parameter, the evaluation function was based only on a local distance of each point. In this paper, we propose an hybridization between Harmony Search (HS)[2] algorithm, which was never proposed for this problem and Local Search (LS) meta-heuristic [4] to improve more quality of reconstructed images. We demonstrate that hybridization between Harmony Search and Local Search meta-heuristics can be used to reconstruct and improve more the quality of images from its projections.

GECCO'14, July 12–16, 2014, Vancouver, BC, Canada.
ACM 978-1-4503-2881-4/14/07.
http://dx.doi.org/10.1145/2598394.2602283.

2. THE PROPOSED METHOD

2.1 Harmony Search algorithm (HS)

As following, the principles steps of HS method :

Step 1. Initialize the problem and algorithm parameters: After initialization of the problem, we specify the algorithm parameters as follows:

- **Harmony memory size (HMS)**: corresponds to the number of harmonies (solutions) in the harmony memory (HM).
- **Harmony Memory Considering Rate (HMCR)**: $HMCR \in [0, 1]$
- **Pitch Adjusting Rate (PAR)**:$PAR \in [0, 1]$
- **Number of improvisations (NI)**: corresponds to the stopping criterion.

Step 2. Initialize the Harmony Memory (HM): HM is a vector which contains all the solutions, the HM could be filled with randomly generated solutions.

Step 3. Improvise a new harmony from the HM: A new HM vector is estimated using three parameters: (1) memory consideration, (2) random selection and (3) pitch adjustment.

Step 4. Update the HM: The new harmony is added in the HM only if its evaluated as better than the worst solution of HM which will be removed and replace by the new harmony.

Step 5. Repeat Steps 3 and 4 until satisfaction of stopping criterion.

3. HS METHOD FOR THE PROBLEM

The problem consists to find the reconstructed image which has the minimum of distance between estimated and measured projections.

3.1 Initialization

3.1.1 *Initialize population called HM*

Initial solution corresponds to the reconstructed image by FBP method.

3.1.2 *Parameters Initialization*

1. **HMS**: $HMS \in [1, 4]$
2. **HMCR**: $HMCR \in [0, 1]$
3. **PAR**: $PAR \in [0, 1]$
4. **NI**: $NI = 300$

3.1.3 *New harmony*

For each iteration, we produce two new solutions:

1. If $rand < HMCR$ we produce a new solution from the HM, and choose randomly a value x_{k_t} from HM.
2. If $rand < PAR$, we produce from the current harmony, one new neighbors solution.

3.1.4 *Update HM*

Using the objective function for the two new solutions, we choose and add the best one which has the minimum value of distance in the HM and remove the historical solution which has the maximum value of distance.

3.1.5 *Objective function*

The Objective function corresponds to the distance between all measured projections (sinogram) and the estimated one. City block distance [7], is used because it's given a high quality of precision and it's a fast method.

We supposed that the projection is recorded into sinogram $H(s,\theta)$. We compute the sum of the distance (D) between each estimated projection of changed point that recorded into sinogram $H_c(s,\theta)$ and each measured projection for the same angle θ of the same point recorded into sinogram $H_m(s,\theta)$, such (1):

$$D = \sum_{s,\theta} |H_c(s,\theta) - H_m(s,\theta)| \qquad (1)$$

3.2 Hybridization between LS and HS

The basic principle is presented as follows:

1. Apply LS algorithm
2. compute rate of reconstructed image by step(1)
3. if $rate < value\ V$ Apply HS algorithm.

3.3 Results

To assess and validate our method in the simplest case, we have developed synthetic images. We compared our tested images with those of FBP method and the comparison as shown in Figure 1.

Also, we estimate the gap (the difference between the reconstructed image and the original one) and the NMP (number of misplaced pixels) for reconstructed image.
The values of reconstructed image are by: FBP method: $gap = 0.11$ and $NMP = 88.89\%$, LS algorithm: $gap = 0.2$ and $NMP = 2.77\%$ and HS algorithm: $gap = 0$ and $NMP = 0\%$. As we see HS improves quality of reconstruction comparing to FBP method.
However the gap of LS is $gap = 0.2$, the NMP proves that LS is better than FBP. After applying HS, the gap became $gap = 0$, therefore HS improves more the quality of reconstructed image.

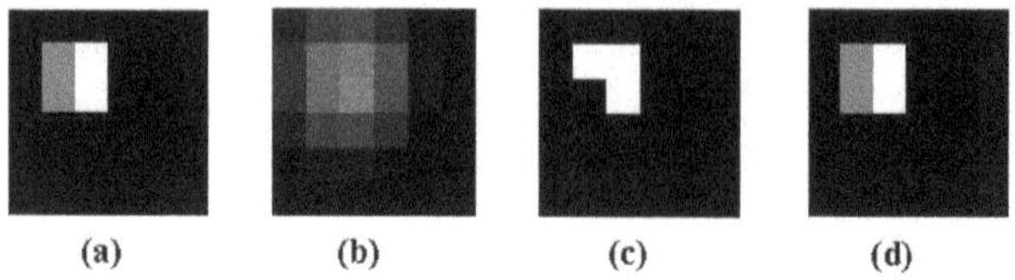

Figure 1: Reconstruction results for image (a). Reconstructed image: by FBP in (b), by LS method in (c), by HS method in (d)

4. CONCLUSION

In this paper we proposed hybridization between Local Search and Harmony Search algorithms for grayscale images reconstruction in tomography. We also compared our method with FBP and LS methods. The numerical results show the effectiveness of our method for grayscale images reconstruction in tomography. Further work will include parallel programming and a comparison with MLEM method.

5. REFERENCES

[1] Fessler,J.: Analytical Tomographic Image Reconstruction Methods., Chapter 3, November 19 (2009).

[2] Geem ZW., Kim, JH. and Loganathan, GV.: A new heuristic optimization algorithm: Harmony search. Simulation, 76:60-68.(2001).

[3] Mou,C., Pen,L.,Yao,D., Xiao,D.:Image Reconstruction Using a Genetic Algorithm for Electrical Capacitance Tomography, Tsinghua science and technology, ISSN 1007-0214 12/20, vol 10 No 5, 587-592 October (2005).

[4] Ouaddah,A. and Boughaci,D.: Local Search Method for Image Reconstruction with Same Concentration in Tomography, Advances in Intelligent and Soft Computing Springer Series, SIRS (2014).

[5] Qureshi,S. A., Mirza,S. M. and Arif, M.: A Hybrid Continuous Genetic Algorithm for Parallelray Transmission Tomography Image Reconstruction, Journal of Biomedical Informatics, in Process (2006).

[6] Radon J. On the determination of functions from their integrals along certain manifolds [in German]. Math Phys Klass.69:262-277 (1917).

[7] Vadivel, A., Majumdar, A.K. and Sural,S.: Performance Comparison of Distance Metrics in Content-based Image Retrieval Applications., International Conference on Information Technology (CIT), Bhubaneswar, India, 159-164 (2003).

First Results of Performance Comparisons on Many-core Processors in Solving QAP with ACO: Kepler GPU versus Xeon Phi

Mikiko Sato
Tokyo University of Agriculture and Technology,
Tokyo, 184-8588 Japan
mikiko@namikilab.tuat.ac.jp

Shigeyoshi Tsutsui
Hannan University
Osaka 580-8502, Japan
tsutsui@hannan-u.ac.jp

Noriyuki Fujimoto
Osaka Prefecture University
Osaka 599-8531, Japan
fujimoto@mi.s.osakafu-u.ac.jp

Yuji Sato
Hosei University
Tokyo 184-8584 Japan
yuji@hosei.ac.jp

Mitaro Namiki
Tokyo University of Agriculture and Technology
Tokyo, 184-8588 Japan
namiki@cc.tuat.ac.jp

ABSTRACT
This paper compares the performance of parallel computation on two types of many-core processors, Tesla K20c GPU and Xeon Phi 5110P, in solving the quadratic assignment problem (QAP) with ant colony optimization (ACO). The results show that the performance on Xeon Phi 5110P is not so promising compared to the Tesla K20c GPU on these problems. Further efficient implementation methods must be investigated for Xeon Phi.

Categories and Subject Descriptors
I.2.8 [Articial Intelligence]: Problem Solving, Control Methods, and Search–Heuristic Methods; D.1.3 [Programming Techniques]: Concurrent Programming–Distributed programming, Parallel programming

General Terms: Algorithms

Keywords
Parallel EA, GPU, Xeon Phi, ACO, QAP, Tabu search

1. INTRODUCTION
Applications of evolutionary algorithms (EAs) often take a long time to obtain acceptable solutions, or require a large amount of computational resources to obtain high-quality solutions in a given time. Thus, since the earliest studies, researchers have attempted parallel EAs in order to obtain high-speed execution of EAs.

Many of the traditional parallel EAs run on multi-core machines, massively parallel cluster machines, or grid computing environments. However, recent advances in General-Purpose computing on Graphics Processing Units (GPGPU) in scientific computing has made possible using Graphics Processing Units (GPUs) for parallel EAs. GPUs are low-cost, parallel, many-core processors and thousands of threads run in parallel in SIMD manner on a GPU. With the low-cost GPU found on ordinary PCs, it is becoming possible to use parallel EAs to solve optimization problems of all sizes [1].

In 2012, Intel® Xeon® Phi™ coprocessors, another type of many-core processor, became available. Xeon® Phi™ has 60 cores based on x86 architecture and can execute a maximum of 240 (60×4) threads in parallel in MIMD (multiple instruction, multiple data) manner [2]. This enables us to re-use existing programs which are written for parallel execution without a major re-coding.

In this paper, we compare performance of these two types of representative many-core units, NVIDIA® Tesla® k20c GPU (based on the Kepler architecture) and Intel® Xeon® Phi™ 5110P in solving the quadratic assignment problem (QAP) with ant colony optimization (ACO), a meta heuristics classified into EA.

2. ACO TO SOLVE QAP
The quadratic assignment problem (QAP) is the problem which assigns a set of facilities to a set of locations and can be stated as a problem to find a permutation ϕ which minimizes

$$f(\phi)=\sum_{i=1}^{n}\sum_{j=1}^{n}a_{ij}b_{\phi(i)\phi(j)}\,,$$

where $A = (a_{ij})$ and $B = (b_{ij})$ are two $n\times n$ matrices and ϕ is a permutation of $\{1, 2, 3..., n\}$. Matrix A is a flow matrix between facilities i and j, and B is the distance between locations i and j. The QAP is considered one of the hardest optimization problems. In this experiment, we use benchmark instances in QAPLIB [3].

ACO has been applied with great success to a large number of hard problems. Although the ACO is a powerful metaheuristic, in

GECCO'14, July 12–16, 2014, Vancouver, BC, Canada.
ACM 978-1-4503-2881-4/14/07.
http://dx.doi.org/10.1145/2598394.2602274

many applications of ACO in solving difficult problems, it is very common to combine it with a local search or metaheuristics. In this experiment, we combine ACO with the tabu search (TS) [5]. TS seeks the solution with the best evaluation among all the neighboring solutions in each TS iteration. If there are no improving moves, TS chooses one that least degrades the objective function. Thus, we need to calculate costs of all neighboring solutions efficiently. Let $N(\phi)$ be the set of neighbors of the current solution ϕ. Then a neighbor, $\phi' \in N(\phi)$, is obtained by exchanging a pair of elements (i, j) of ϕ. Then, we need to compute move costs $\Delta(\phi, i, j) = f(\phi') - f(\phi)$ for all the neighboring solutions. The neighborhood size of $N(\phi)$ ($|N(\phi)|$) is $n(n-1)/2$ where n is the problem size. Thus, the computation cost of $\Delta(\phi, i, j)$ is very costly.

3. IMPLEMENTATION OF ACO WITH TS ON TESLA® K20C AND XEON® PHI™ 5110P

Table 1 shows specifications of both Tesla® K20c and Xeon® Phi™ 5110P [4].

Table 1 Specifications of Tesla K20c and Xeon Phi 5110P

	Xeon Phi 5110P	Tesla K20c
Performance (Single precision)	2022 Gflops	3520 Gflops
Memory Bandwidth	320 GB/s (ECC off)	208 GB/s (ECC off)
Memory Size	8 GB	5 GB
Clock Speed	1.053 GHz	0.706 GHz
Number of Core	60	2496

Figure 1 shows the implementation of ACO described in Section 2 on Tesla® K20c. Here, all of the programs are executed on the GPU. Each calculation of $\Delta(\phi, i, j)$ in TS is assigned to the thread of the streaming multiprocessor of CUDA, and is executed in parallel (please refer to [5] for detail). Note here that all of the data of the algorithm are located in VRAM of GPU. They include ACO data (the population pools) the pheromone density matrix, TS data, and QAP data.

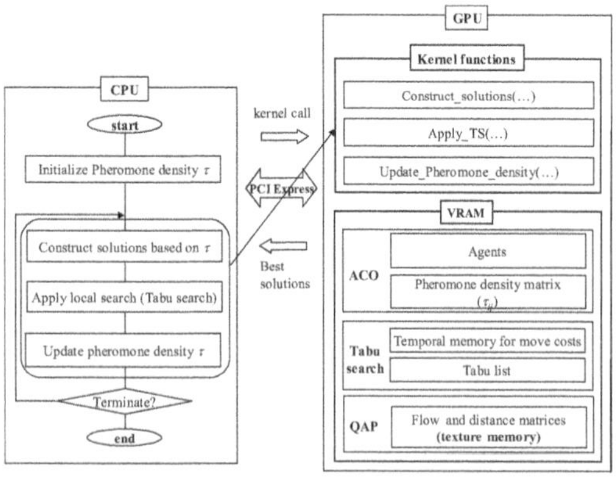

Figure 1 Implementation of ACO with TS on GPU

In the implementation using Intel Xeon® Phi™, almost all processing of ACO is offloaded to Xeon Phi, in a similar manner to the GPU method shown above. The program run on Xeon Phi and data transfer are specified by #pragma directive. First, the data which are needed for ACO processing, i.e., ACO data, the pheromone density matrix, TS data, and QAP data, are transferred to the memory on Xeon Phi. Then each individual of the population is assigned to a thread of Xeon Phi. This includes calculation of $\Delta(\phi, i, j)$. Note here that updating pheromone density is performed as a single thread. The host CPU functions only to receive solutions from the Xeon Phi cores for each generation and determines the termination.

4. RESULTS AND CONCLUDING REMARKS

We compared three types of runs, i.e., runs on Tesla® K20c with Intel Core i7 965 (3.2 GHz) CPU, runs on Xeon® Phi™ 5110P with Xeon X5690 (3.333GHz), and runs on Intel Core i7 965 (3.2 GHz) CPU with a single thread. For all three runs, population size was set to n (problem size). We run the algorithms until the optimal solutions are obtained. We measured the performance by the average run time T_{avg} over 25 runs. The results are summarized in Table 2.

The speedup ratios of Tesla GPU to CPU are in the range from x27.2 to 47.6, showing their average is x33.5. In contrast to these results on the GPU, the speedup ratios of Xeon Phi to CPU are in the range from x3.8 to 6.6, showing their average is 5.3. These speedup values of Xeon Phi are not so promising compared to Tesla K20c GPU on this application.

In this application, about 99% computation time is used by TS to find the best neighboring solution in each TS iteration [5]. On GPU, this computation was parallelized using the threads of CUDA. However, since the grain of the computation is very fine, the parallelization is difficult on Xeon Phi. Instead, using very wide (512-bit) SIMD units in Xeon Phi might be useful for an efficient parallelization. But this remains for future work.

Table 2 Summary of results

QAP instances	Run time in T_{avg} (sec)			Speedup in T_{avg}	
	Tesla K20c	Xeon Phi	CPU	CPU / Tesla K20c	CPU / Xeon Phi
tai50b	0.19	1.14	5.94	31.7	5.2
tai60b	0.39	2.75	12.77	32.8	4.6
tai80b	4.99	22.61	141.30	28.3	6.2
tai100b	6.22	57.35	296.28	47.6	5.2
tai150b	14.06	61.92	382.73	27.2	6.2
Average	-	-	-	**33.5**	**5.5**

5. REFERENCES

[1] S. Tsutsui and P. Collet (Ed). Massively parallel evolutionary computation on GPGPU, Natural Computing Series, Springer, 2013.

[2] Intel. http://blogs.intel.com/technology/2012/06/intel-xeon-phi-coprocessors-accelerate-discovery-and-innovation/

[3] QAPLIB - a quadratic assignment problem library, 2009. www.seas.upenn.edu/qaplib.

[4] T. Aoki. http://www.ocw.titech.ac.jp/index.php?module=General&action=T0300&GakubuCD=226&GakkaCD=226717&KougiCD=77065&Nendo=2013&Gakki=1&lang=JA&vid=05

[5] S. Tsutsui and N. Fujimoto. ACO with Tabu Search on a GPU for Solving QAPs using Move-Cost Adjusted Thread Assignment, Genetic and Evolutionary Computation Conference, pp. 1547-1554, ACM, 2011

Evaluation of Fitness Functions of GA Classification

Ming-Der Yang
Dept of Civil Engineering
National Chung Hsing University
250 Kuokuang Rd, Taichung, Taiwan
886-4-22854387
mdyang@nchu.edu.tw

Yeh-Feng Yang
Dept of Civil Engineering
National Chung Hsing University
250 Kuokuang Rd, Taichung, Taiwan
886-4-22854387
yf.yang@yahoo.com.tw

Yi-Ping Chen
Dept of Business Administration
DaYeh University
168, University Rd., Changhua, Taiwan
886-4-8511888
ypchen@mail.dyu.edu.tw

ABSTRACT
Genetic Algorithm (GA) classifier can automatically search a proper clustering number according to fitness evaluation instead of assignment by users. In this study, a GA classifier with various fitness functions is adopted to search the cluster centers and a suitable cluster number for digital images to overcome the disadvantages of the conventional unsupervised classifier. By employing a proper clustering index as fitness, a GA with length-variable chromosome can determine the most suitable number of clusters and the most proper cluster centers.

This paper evaluates three popular classification indexes, including DBI, FCMI, and PASI, as fitness functions in GA operation. The GA classifier is applied to SPOT-5 satellite image to verify its accuracy and robustness. The results show the GA classifier adopting FCMI having the best performance, followed by DBI and PASI, sequentially. Regarding to computation efficiency, the GA classification with DBI took much less computation time of the GA classifications with FCMI and PASI.

Categories and Subject Descriptors
I.5.2 **[Pattern Recognition]**: Design Methodology - *Classifier design and evaluation, Pattern analysis*

Keywords
Genetic Algorithm; Fitness function; Overall Accuracy; Unsupervised Classification.

1. INTRODUCTION
Genetic algorithm (GA) inspired by natural selection and survival of the fittest produces a serial processes simulating biological evolution to solve real-world problems. GA has been widely and successfully used in image processing, data interpretation, artificial intelligence, and many other areas. In particular, unsupervised image classification can be processed through GA operations, such as natural selection, cross-over, and mutation, to provide the optimal solutions. Multispectral SPOT imagery was adopted for overall affecting scoring by combining terrain factors through an aggregation function to produce a synthetic probability map of landslide reoccurrence for landslide reoccurrence in the Tsao-Ling area [1]. A GA-classifier was proven to be capable of performing automatically as well as a supervised classifier. Martini et al. employed multi-date images of Synthetic Aperture Radar to identify dry snow cover in Alps mountainous region in France [2]. DeAlwis et al. transformed Landsat 7 ETM+ satellite images into Normalized Difference Water Index (NDWI) that was processed through unsupervised classifier ISODATA for monitoring the storage capability of underground water [3]. A GA-classifier was adopted to search the cluster centers and a suitable cluster number for digital images to overcome the disadvantages of the conventional unsupervised classifier [4].

Clustering validity indices were developed to determine optimal clustering, such as separation index (SI), Daviers-Bouldin (DB) index, Xie-Beni (XB) index, Hubert's statistics, and Dunn's index (DI) in which DB index has both a statistical and geometric rational [5]. Regarding to fitness functions in GA classification, Bandyopadhyay and Maulik adopted DBI (Davies-Bouldin Index), DI (Dunn's index), FCMI (Fuzzy C-Means index), and CI (C-index) in GA classifiers for clustering problem solving [6]. Among those fitness functions, the GA classifier with DBI was found to perform best in satellite image classification. Also, Bandyopadhyay and Maulik integrated conventional unsupervised classifier, K-Means, and GA classifier to overcome the requirement of the initial cluster number in K-Means classification, and obtained better classification results than original individual classifiers [5]. PSI (Partition separation index) was proposed for clustering, and was compared with popular indexes, such as PCI (Partition Coefficient Index), PEI (Partition Entropy Index), FSVF (Fukuyama and Sugeno Validity Function), XBI (Xie and Beni Validity Function), and DBI (Davies and Bouldin validity function) for verifying its superiority [7].

2. METHODOLOGY
This paper adopts three popular classification indexes, including DBI (Davies-Bouldin Index), FCMI (Fuzzy c-Means Index), and PASI (Partition Separation Index, as fitness functions in GA operation for comparison in classification accuracy and computation time. The calculation of DBI, FCMI, and PASI can be checked in Yang's paper [9]. This paper experiments chromosome lengths of 6, 8, 12, and 20, and crossover rates of 0.2, 0.4, 0.6, and 0.8. Other GA operation setting includes real-number coding, population of 30, selection way of Roulette Wheel Selection, crossover way of two-points crossover, and mutation rate of 0.03. To verify the GA classifier, a SPOT 5 satellite image were processed under various condition setting.

3. RESULT ANALYSIS
Figure 1 shows the results varying with different chromosome lengths. The class numbers determined by PASI are inclined to beneath the number of landuse. DBI presents the unstable numbers increasingly with the increasing chromosome length. The clustering results by FCMI present the moderate number of landuse and the distributions of the related species. The overall accuracy and K-HAT of FCMI classification are the highest, followed by DBI and PASI. In the comparisons of computation

GECCO'14, July 12–16, 2014, Vancouver, BC, Canada.
ACM 978-1-4503-2662-9/14/07.

time between the three indices, DBI classification is the most computation-efficient, whereas PASI classification is the least. Figure 2 presents the classification images determined by the three indices varying with the different crossover rates, and shows no obvious impact of crossover rate on cluster numbers. Regarding to overall accuracy and K-HAT, high crossover rates can result in more accurate results for DBI and FCMI classification, whereas PASI classification shows an opposite relationship between crossover rate and overall accuracy and K-HAT. Furthermore, PASI and FCMI, which are based on the fuzzy logical modeling, spent more computation time than DBI and cost more as the increase of crossover rate. Furthermore, PASI and FCMI, which are based on the fuzzy logical modeling, spent more computation time than DBI and cost more as the increase of crossover rate.

4. CONCLUSION

According to the previous result analysis and discussion, the paper concludes the following points:

(1) Through various setting of chromosome and crossover rate, this paper shows the classifier with FCMI preformed the best, followed by DBI and PASI, sequentially.

(2) The GA classifications with DBI and FCMI have high accuracy as crossover rate increasing.

(3) Regarding to computation efficiency, the GA classification with DBI took much less computation time of the GA classifications with FCMI and PASI.

(4) The GA classification with DBI with the advantages of high accuracy and less computation is suitable for classification on large digital data, such as satellite images.

5. REFERENCES

[1] Yang, M.D., Yang, Y.F., and Hsu, S.C. 2004. Application of remotely sensed data to the assessment of terrain factors affecting the Tsao-Ling landslide. Canadian Journal of Remote Sensing. 30(4), 593-603.

[2] DeAlwis, D.A., Easton, Z.M., Dahlke, H.E., Philpot, W.D., and Steenhuis, T.S. 2007. Unsupervised classification of saturated areas using a time series of remotely sensed images. Hydrology and Earth System Sciences. Vol.11, 1609-1620.

[3] Martini, A., Ferro-Famil, L., Pottier, E., and Dedieu, J.P. 2005. Dry snow extent monitoring in strong topography conditions. Geoscience and Remote Sensing Symposium, IGARSS '05 Proceedings IEEE International. Vol.8, 5440-5443.

[4] Yang, M.D. 2007. A genetic algorithm (GA) based automated classifier for remote sensing imagery. Canadian Journal of Remote Sensing. 33(3), 593-603.

[5] Bandyopadhyay, S., and Maulik, U. 2002(a). An evolution technique based on K-Means algorithm for optimal clustering. Information Sciences. 146(2002), .221-237.

[6] Bandyopadhyay, S., and Maulik, U. 2002 (b). Genetic clustering for automatic evolution of clusters and application to image classification. IEEE pattern recognition. 35(2002), 1197-1208.

[7] Yang, M.S., and Wu, K.L. 2001. A new validity index for fuzzy clustering. IEEE International Fuzzy Systems Conference, 89-92.

[8] Sivanandam, S.N., and Deepa, S.N. 2008. Introduction to Genetic Algorithms, Springer. Berlin, 442p.

[9] Yang, M.D., Yang, Y.F., Su, T.C., and Huang, K.S. 2014. An efficient fitness function in genetic algorithm classifier for landuse recognition on satellite images, Scientific World Journal, doi:10.1155/2014/264512

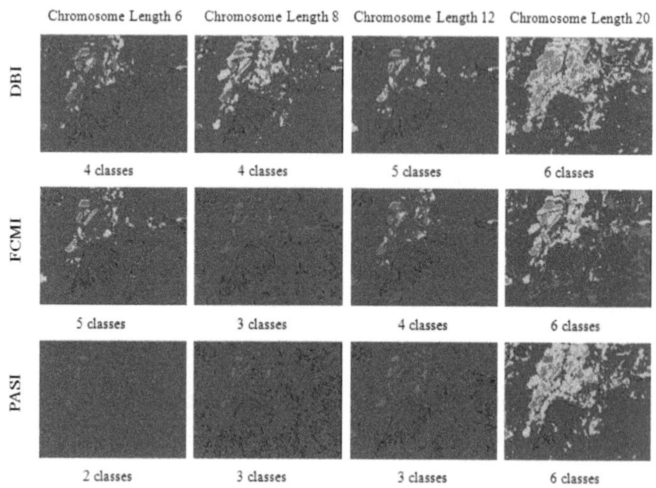

Figure 1. Classification varying with maximal centroid numbers

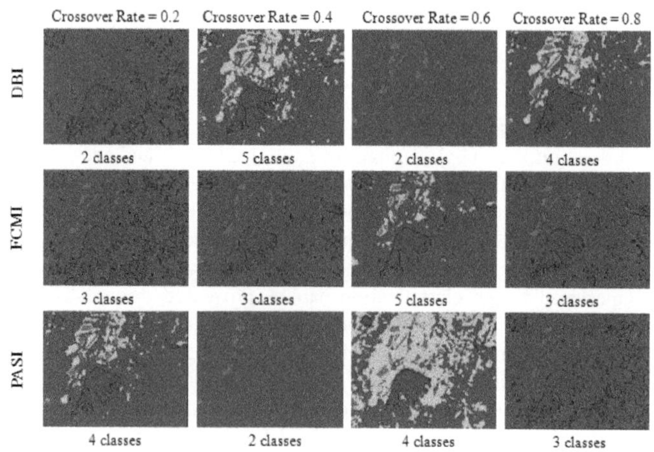

Figure 2. Classification determined by various populations

A Speed-Up and Speed-Down Strategy for Swarm Optimization

Haopeng Zhang
Department of Mechanical Engineering
Texas Tech University
Lubbock, TX 79409-1021
haopeng.zhang@ttu.edu

Fumin Zhang
School of Electrical and Computer Engineering
Georgia Institute of Technology
Atlanta, GA 30332-0250
fumin@gatech.edu

Qing Hui
Department of Mechanical Engineering
Texas Tech University
Lubbock, TX 79409-1021
qing.hui@ttu.edu

ABSTRACT

In this paper, inspired by speed-up and speed-down (SUSD) mechanism observed by the fish swarm avoiding light, an SUSD strategy is proposed to develop new swarm intelligence based optimization algorithms to enhance the accuracy and efficiency of swarm optimization algorithms. By comparing with the global best solution, each particle adaptively speeds up and speeds down towards the best solution. Specifically, a new directed speed term is added to the original particle swarm optimization (PSO) algorithm or other PSO variations. Due to the SUSD mechanism, the algorithm shows a great improvement of the accuracy and convergence rate compared with the original PSO and other PSO variations. The numerical evaluation is provided by solving recent benchmark functions in IEEE CEC 2013.

Categories and Subject Descriptors

G.1.6 [**Optimization**]: Unconstrained optimization

Keywords

Swarm intelligence

1. INTRODUCTION

Particle swarm optimization (PSO), firstly proposed in [1], has been widely used in various disciplines. As a swarm intelligence based optimization algorithm, a particle in PSO updates its velocity by comparing the difference between current position and local best position found by itself and the difference between current position and the global best position among all the particles, and then moves into the next position, after which the local best position and the global position will be updated simultaneously.

GECCO'14, July 12–16, 2014, Vancouver, BC, Canada.
ACM 978-1-4503-1964-5/14/07.
http://dx.doi.org/10.1145/2598394.2602285.

The update formulas for the PSO algorithm are shown in the following equation.

$$\begin{aligned} \mathbf{v}_{k+1}^{i,j} &= w\mathbf{v}_k^{i,j} + b_1 r_1(\mathbf{g}_{loc,i}^j - \mathbf{x}_k^{i,j}) + b_2 r_2(\mathbf{g}_k^j - \mathbf{x}_k^{i,j}) \\ \mathbf{x}_{k+1}^{i,j} &= \mathbf{x}_k^{i,j} + \mathbf{v}_{k+1}^{i,j}, \quad i = 1, \ldots, q, \quad j = 1, \ldots, n \quad (1) \end{aligned}$$

where $\mathbf{x}_k^{i,j}$ and $\mathbf{v}_k^{i,j}$ are the jth position and velocity element of particle i at iteration k, respectively, $\mathbf{g}_k^j$ is the jth element of the global best solution among all the particles and $\mathbf{g}_{loc,i}^j$ is the jth element of local best solution found by particle i, and w, b_1, b_2, r_1 and r_2 are positive constants.

Due to the great success of PSO, lots of research efforts have been conducted to improve the performance in both accuracy and efficiency. In this research, observed from the fish swarm behavior [3], a speed-up and speed-down (SUSD) mechanism is proposed for PSO as an extra force for the velocity towards both local and global best solutions. Moreover, this SUSD mechanism can be easily integrated into other PSO variants for performance enhancement. As an example, multiagent coordination optimization (MCO) [4] is introduced and illustrated by using the SUSD mechanism.

This work was supported by the Defense Threat Reduction Agency under Grants HDTRA1-10-1-0090 and HDTRA 1-13-1-0048.

2. SPEED-UP AND SPEED-DOWN MECHANISM

Based on the observation that a fish in a group speeds up when the light intensity at its current position is relatively high and slows down as the light intensity decreases [3], a SUSD mechanism is proposed as follows.

$$SUSD = \lambda_1(f_j(\mathbf{g}_k^j) - f_j(\mathbf{x}_k^{i,j}))\mathtt{sign}(\mathbf{g}_k^j - \mathbf{x}_k^{i,j})$$

where $f_j(z) = f(x_1, \ldots, x_n)|_{x_j=z}$, $i = 1, \ldots, q$, $j = 1, \ldots, n$, q is the number of particles, n is the dimension of the objective function $f : \mathbb{R}^n \to \mathbb{R}$, $\lambda_1 < 0$ is a constant, $\mathtt{sign}(x) = 1$ if $x > 0$, $\mathtt{sign}(x) = -1$ if $x < 0$, and $\mathtt{sign}(0) = 0$.

2.1 SUSD for the PSO algorithm

Now this SUSD mechanism is applied to the PSO algorithm, and the update formulas for position and velocity are proposed in Equations (2–3).

$$
\begin{aligned}
\mathbf{v}_{k+1}^{i,j} &= \mathbf{v}_k^{i,j} + b_1 r_1(\mathbf{g}_{loc,i}^j - \mathbf{x}_k^{i,j}) + b_2 r_2(\mathbf{g}_k^j - \mathbf{x}_k^{i,j}) \\
&\quad + \lambda_1 (f_j(\mathbf{g}_k^j) - f_j(\mathbf{x}_k^{i,j}))\mathtt{sign}(\mathbf{g}_k^j - \mathbf{x}_k^{i,j}) \qquad (2) \\
\mathbf{x}_{k+1}^{i,j} &= \mathbf{x}_k^{i,j} + \mathbf{v}_{k+1}^{i,j} \qquad (3)
\end{aligned}
$$

2.2 SUSD for the MCO algorithm

Multiagent coordination optimization (MCO) [4] is a novel swarm optimization algorithm by introducing the velocity consensus protocol and communication topology between particles into a PSO-like algorithm. The update formulas for position and velocity in MCO are shown in Equations (4–6).

$$
\begin{aligned}
\mathbf{v}_{k+1}^{i,l} &= w\mathbf{v}_k^{i,j} + \breve{\mu} \sum_{j \in \mathcal{N}_i} (\mathbf{x}_k^{j,l} - \mathbf{x}_k^{i,l}) + \breve{\eta} \sum_{j \in \mathcal{N}_i} + (\mathbf{v}_k^{j,l} - \mathbf{v}_k^{i,l}) \\
&\quad \breve{\kappa}(\mathbf{g}_k^l - \mathbf{x}_k^{i,l}) \qquad (4) \\
\mathbf{x}_{k+1}^i &= \mathbf{x}_k^i + \mathbf{v}_{k+1}^i \qquad (5) \\
\mathbf{g}_{k+1}^l &= \mathbf{g}_k^l + \breve{\kappa}(\mathbf{g}_{loc,i}^l - \mathbf{g}_k^l) \qquad (6)
\end{aligned}
$$

where $i = 1, \ldots, q$, $l = 1, \ldots, n$, $\breve{\eta} \sim U(0, 2\eta)$, $\breve{\mu} \sim (0, 2\mu)$, $\breve{\kappa} \sim (0, 2\kappa)$, $\eta, \mu, \kappa > 0$ are constants, $U(\cdot, \cdot)$ is the uniform distribution, $\mathcal{N}_i = \{j \in \mathcal{V} : \{i, j\} \in \mathcal{E}\}$ is the set of neighbors of node i and $\mathcal{E} \subseteq \mathcal{V} \times \mathcal{V}$ denotes the set of edges, which is the communication links between two particles, and the set of nodes $\mathcal{V} = \{1, \ldots, q\}$ denotes the index of the particles. Inspired by the SUSD mechanism, the SUSD-MCO algorithm is proposed in Equations (7-9).

$$
\begin{aligned}
\mathbf{v}_{k+1}^{i,l} &= w\mathbf{v}_k^{i,j} + \breve{\mu} \sum_{j \in \mathcal{N}_i} (\mathbf{v}_k^{j,l} - \mathbf{v}_k^{i,l}) \\
&\quad + \breve{\mu} \sum_{j \in \mathcal{N}_i} (\mathbf{x}_k^{j,l} - \mathbf{x}_k^{i,l}) + \breve{\kappa}(\mathbf{g}_k^l - \mathbf{x}_k^{i,l}) \\
&\quad + \lambda_1 (f_l(\mathbf{g}_k^l) - f_l(\mathbf{x}_k^{i,l}))\mathtt{sign}(\mathbf{g}_k^l - \mathbf{x}_k^{i,l}) \qquad (7) \\
\mathbf{x}_{k+1}^i &= \mathbf{x}_k^i + \mathbf{v}_{k+1}^i \qquad (8) \\
\mathbf{g}_{k+1}^l &= \mathbf{g}_k^l + \breve{\kappa}(\mathbf{g}_{loc,i}^l - \mathbf{g}_k^l) \qquad (9)
\end{aligned}
$$

where $l = 1, \cdots, n$ and $i = 1, \ldots, q$.

3. NUMERICAL EVALUATION

For numerical evaluation, 1000 particles are used to solve the 30-dimension benchmark functions in [2]. Specifically, we use the shifted sphere function, rotated Rosenbrock function, and rotated Griewank function to test the proposed SUSD mechanism. The shifted optimal solution is shown as X^*, where X^*=[98.7900 17.0400 25.7800 39.6800 7.4000 68.4100 40.2400 98.2800 40.2200 62.0700 15.4400 38.1300 16.1100 75.8100 87.1100 35.0800 68.5500 29.4100 53.0600 83.2400 59.7500 33.5300 29.9200 45.2600 42.2600 35.9600 55.8300 74.2500 42.4300 42.9400]. 20 executions of both PSO and SUSD-PSO algorithms solving the three benchmark functions have been conducted, and the results are shown in Table 1. It follows from the simulation results that the SUSD mechanism can largely improve the accuracy of PSO. Moveover, based on the results in Table 2 , the SUSD-MCO algorithm also improves the accuracy of MCO. Due to the page limitation, only the searching trajectories of PSO and SUSD-PSO algorithms solving the shifted sphere function is provided in Figure 1.

Table 1: Comparison between PSO and SUSD-PSO

Function	Min		Max	
	PSO	SUSD-PSO	PSO	SUSD-PSO
Sphere	1.64E-2	5.9263E-6	2.266	7.49E-2
Rosenbrock	2.10E-2	4.5727E-7	8.429E-1	3.1E-3
Griewank	2.0379E2	2.306E-1	2.3292E3	5.4249
Function	Median		Average	
	PSO	SUSD-PSO	PSO	SUSD-PSO
Sphere	2.135E-1	2.1E-3	4.543E-1	1.07E-2
Rosenbrock	1.0811E-1	1.7272E-4	1.597E-1	4.1827E-4
Griewank	8.5715E2	1.2871	1.0002E3	2.1007

Table 2: Comparison between MCO and SUSD-MCO

Function	Min		Max	
	MCO	SUSD-MCO	MCO	SUSD-MCO
Sphere	2.739E-1	8.6E-3	7.845E-1	2.56E-2
Rosenbrock	6.5E-3	4.0371E-4	7.32E-2	6.3E-3
Griewank	8.0663E3	9.2577E2	1.4405E4	1.0827E4
Function	Median		Average	
	MCO	SUSD-MCO	MCO	SUSD-MCO
Sphere	6.334E-1	1.55E-2	5.857E-1	1.45E-2
Rosenbrock	1.62E-2	2.3E-3	2.09E-2	2.8E-3
Griewank	1.0690E4	6.8156E3	1.1243E4	8.5082E3

4. REFERENCES

[1] J. Kennedy and R. Eberhart. Particle swarm optimization. In *Proc. IEEE Int. Conf. Neural Networks*, pages 1942–1946, 1995.

[2] J. Liang, B. Qu, P. Suganthan, and A. G. Hernández-Díaz. Problem definitions and evaluation criteria for the CEC 2013 special session on real-parameter optimization. *Comput. Intell. Lab., Zhengzhou Univ., China, and Nanyang Tech. Univ., Singapore, Technical Report*, 2012-12, 2013.

[3] W. Wu, I. D. Couzin, and F. Zhang. Bio-inspired source seeking with no explicit gradient estimation. In *Proc. IFAC Workshop on Distributed Estimation and Control in Networked Systems*, pages 240–245, 2012.

[4] H. Zhang and Q. Hui. Multiagent coordination optimization: A control-theoretic perspective of swarm intelligence algorithms. In *2013 IEEE Congr. Evolut. Comput.*, pages 3339–3346, Cancun, Mexico, 2013.

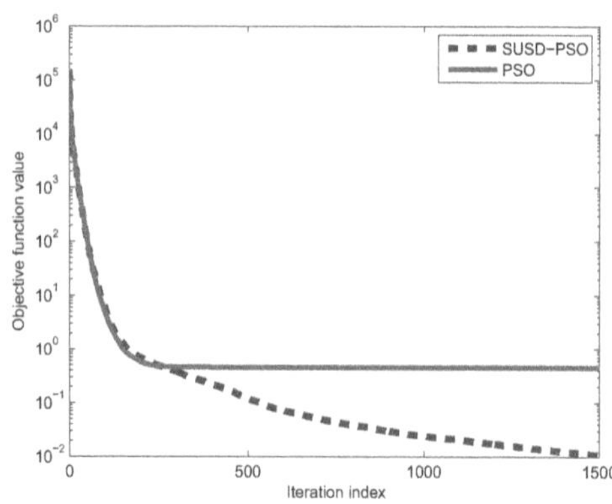

Figure 1: Test function: Shifted sphere function

A Novel Genetic Clustering Algorithm with Variable-length Chromosome Representation

Ming-an Zhang
Institute of Software, Chinese Academy of Sciences
4# South Fourth Street, Zhongguancun, Beijing 100190, PR.China
86 010 62661154
171166789@qq.com

Yong Deng*
Institute of Software, Chinese Academy of Sciences
4# South Fourth Street, Zhongguancun, Beijing 100190, PR.China
86 010 62661154
dengyong@iscas.ac.cn

Dong-xia Chang
Institute of Information Science, Beijing jiaotong University
No.3 Shang Yuan Cun,Hai Dian District Beijing 100040, PR.China
86 010 51684108
dxchang@bjtu.edu.cn

ABSTRACT
The paper proposed a new genetic clustering algorithm with variable-length chromosome representation(GCVCR), which can automatically evolve and find the optimal number of clusters as well as proper cluster centers of the data set. A new clustering criterion based on message passing between data points and the candidate centers described by the chromosome are presented to make the clustering problem more effective. The simulation results show the effectiveness of the proposed algorithm.

Categories and Subject Descriptors
I.4.6 Segmentation: pixel classification

General Terms: Algorithms

Keywords
Clustering; Genetic algorithm; Data segmentation

1. INTRODUCTION
People share their daily activities and opinions on social networking websites, opening the floodgates of information that can be analyzed by marketers as well as consumers. However, low barriers to publication and easy-to-use interactive interfaces have contributed to various information quality problems in the social media. Approaches such as data mining have begun to address these challenges[1]. Clustering techniques have been broadly employed in data mining. Clustering algorithms are essentially local search algorithms, using an iterative climbing technique to find the optimal solution[2]. And the algorithms are also apt to fall into a local optimum and the result is sensitive to initialization[3,4]. The paper proposes a clustering genetic algorithm with variable-length chromosome representation.

2. SIMILARITY MEASURE
We propose a similarity measure firstly. It uses two kinds of message, responsibility and availability, exchanged between data points and the candidate centers. Here, the responsibility and availability between the data set X={$x_1,\ldots,x_n$} and the candidate centers set C={$c_1,\ldots,c_n$} are defined. For the candidate center set C, an input preference that candidate centers with larger values of input preference are more likely to be chosen as a center. If a priori, the value can be set by the priori information.

$$IP(k)=-\frac{1}{n}\sum_{i=1}^{n}d^2(x_i,c_k)=-\frac{1}{n}\sum_{i=1}^{n}\|x_i-c_k\|^2,\quad k=1,2,\cdots K_i \tag{1}$$

This is the mean distance between a center and all the data point in the data set. This value will be optimized when c_k is the center. Note that the distance measure here is chosen with the Euclidean norm. $IP(k)$ represents the suitability of the candidate centers as the real one. The responsibility $r(i,k)$, sent from data point x_i to the candidate center c_k, reflects the evidence for how well-suited c_k is as the center for point x_i, taking into account other potential centers for point x_i. The availability $a(i,k)$, sent from candidate center c_k to point x_i, reflects the evidence for how appropriate it would be for point x_i to choose c_k as its center, taking into account the support from other points that c_k should be an center.

$$r(i,k)=d(i,k)-\max_{k's.t.k'\neq k}\{d(i,k')\}, i=1,2,\cdots,n; k=1,2,\cdots,K_i \tag{2}$$

Here, $d(i,k)$ denotes the distance between data point x_i and the candidate cluster center c_k. For each candidate cluster center, a self-attribution is defined as:

$$R(k)=IP(k)-\max_{k's.t.k'\neq k}\{d(c_k,c_{k'})\},\quad k=1,2,\cdots,K_i \tag{3}$$

Whereas the above responsibility update lets all candidate centers compete for ownership of a data point.

$$a(i,k)=\min\left\{0,R(k)+\sum_{i',s.t.i'\notin\{i\}}\max\{0,r(i',k)\}\right\}, i=1,2,\cdots,n; k=1,2,\cdots,K_i$$

(4)

This availability $a(i,k)$ reflects evidence that point c_k is a center. Then the similarity between the data point and the candidate center is defined by the sum of the responsibility r and the availability a. The similarities between data point x_i and the candidate centers C = {$c_1,\ldots,c_K$} are

$$s(i,k)=r(i,k)+a(i,k),\quad k=1,2,\cdots,K_i \tag{5}$$

then x_i will be assigned to the cluster with the maximum similarity.

3. GENETIC CLUSTERING ALGORITHM
3.1 Chromosome Representation and Population Initialization
A chromosome representation is needed to describe each individual in the population of interest. Extensive experiments

GECCO'14, July 12–16, 2014, Vancouver, BC, Canada.
ACM 978-1-4503-2881-4/14/07.

comparing real-valued and binary showed that the real-valued GA is more efficient in terms of CPU time. Here, a real-valued problem-specific chromosome representation is used. Each chromosome is described by a sequence of $M=N\times K_i$ real-valued numbers where N is the dimension of the feature space, K_i is the number of clusters described by the chromosome.

$$v = [v_{11}, v_{12}, \cdots, v_{1N}, v_{21}, v_{22}, \cdots, v_{2N}, \cdots, v_{K_i 1}, v_{K_i 2}, \cdots, v_{K_i N}] \quad (6)$$

Each of N values represents a cluster center. The K_i of individuals may take different values, and change in the course of evolution. Therefore, the representation is of variable-length. An initial population of size P can be randomly generated. For each population, K_i is generated randomly, districted by a lower and an upper bound. Then K_i points are chosen randomly from the data set but on the condition that there are no identical points to form a chromosome, presenting the K_i cluster centers. This process is repeated until P chromosomes are generated.

3.2 Fitness Function

The aim of the fitness function is to find a set of centers for which the within-cluster spread is small. The between-cluster spread is large in some sense, and the number of clusters is moderate. Considering the influence of the number of the centers on the clustering result, we define a penalized cost function as

$$J = \frac{1}{K^2} Tr\{S_W^{-1} S_B\} \quad (7)$$

where S_W is the within-cluster variation and S_B is the between-cluster variation, K is the number of cluster centers.

3.3 Crossover and Mutation

In the evolutionary process, we use crossover and mutation on the individuals to manipulate the centers to evolve chromosomes into possibly better ones. The crossover and mutation operators are selected by a probability. Simple crossover is used here. Note that although the crossover points can fall in different locations in the two individuals, they are districted to fall on the same location within each cluster description. There are 6 mutator operators: perturb, insert, delete, merge, split, and move.

3.4 Algorithm Procedure

(1)Initialize a group of cluster centers with size of P, only nontrivial clustering are considered. Each data point of the set is assigned to the cluster with the new similarity measure. (2)Evaluate each chromosome and copy the best chromosome say p_{best} of the initial population in a separate location. (3)If the termination condition is not reached, go to Step 4. Otherwise, select the best individual from the population as the best clustering result. (4)Select individuals from the population for crossover and mutation. (5)Apply crossover operator to the selected individuals based on the crossover probability. (6)Apply mutation operator to the selected individuals based on the mutation probability. (7)Evaluate the newly generated candidates. (8)Compare the worst chromosome in the new population with p_{best} in term of their fitness values. If the worst one is worse than p_{best}, then replace it by p_{best}. (9)Find the best chromosome in the new population and replace p_{best}. (10)Go back to Step 3.

4. SIMULATION

The performances of the GCVCR, GCUK[3] and K-means algorithms[4] are compared through the experiments. The artificial data set used is similar to those in Ref.3, consisting of 150 3D data points distributed over 3 clusters as shown in Fig. 1(a). Each cluster consists of 50 data points. Two of the clusters are overlapping. The population size is taken as 50. The crossover and mutation probabilities for GUCK are pc=0.8 and pm=0.001. For GCVCR, the mutation probability varies follow a inverse proportion function. We have started with a mutation probability value of pm = 0.5. The value is then varied as a step function of the number of iterations until it reaches a value of 0.001. The minimum value of the mutation probability is taken to be 0.001. The probabilities for the mutation operators are set to be equal to 1/6. The total number of generations is equal to 50. For the K-means algorithm, the actual number of clusters is known prior. All the experiments run for 20 independent times. AC is the true number of the clusters. From Tab.1 GCVCR obtains the exact K.

Table 1. The mean and variance of the adjusted rand index

AC	GUCK	GCVCR
3	2.05 ± 0.0500,1	2.09 ± 0.0947,18

Fig.1 provides the clustering results. It is clear that GCVCR is better than other algorithms. K-means results in a significant misclassification from Fig.1(b). GCUK only gets 2 clusters from Fig.1(c). The 2 aliasing clusters are classified to one. GCVCR obtains the correct number of clusters.

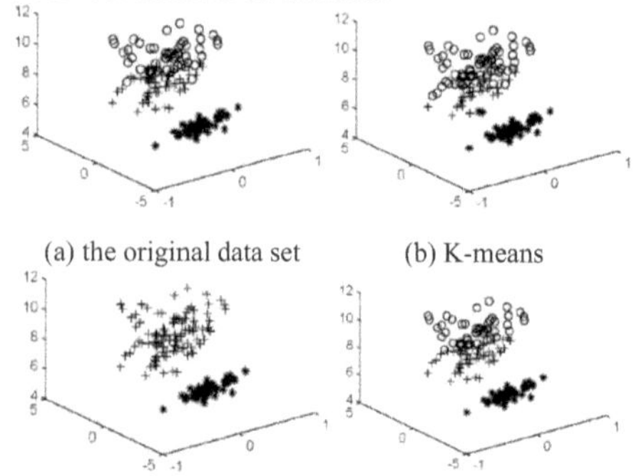

(a) the original data set (b) K-means

(C) GCUK (d) GCVCR

Figure 1. The original data set and the clustering results.

5. CONCLUSIONS

This paper presents a new genetic clustering algorithm, which can find automatically the optimal number of clusters as well as the cluster centers in the evolutionary process. Simulation results show that the algorithm proposed has better performance.

6. ACKNOWLEDGMENTS

This work was supported by Beijing Municipal Science Foundation No. 4133092 and 863 program (No.2012AA011206).

7. REFERENCES

[1] Agarwal Nitin, Yiliyasi Yusuf. Information quality challenges in social media. Proceedings of the 2010 International Conference on Information Quality, 2010.

[2] Chang D X, Zhang X D. A robust dynamic niching genetic algorithm with niche migration for automatic clustering problem. Pattern Recognition, 2010, 43(7): 1346-1360.

[3] Bandyopadhyay S, Maulik U, Genetic clustering for automatic evolution of clusters and application to image classification. Pattern Recognition, 2002, 35(6): 1197-1208.

[4] Kanungo T, Mount D, et al. An efficient K-means clustering algorithm: Analysis and implementation. IEEE Trans. Pattern Anal. Mach. Inteli., 2002, 24(7): 881-892.

A Novel Quantum Genetic Clustering Algorithm for Data Segmentation

Ming-an Zhang
Institute of Software, Chinese Academy of Sciences
4# South Fourth Street, Zhongguancun, Beijing 100190, PR.China
86 010 62661154
171166789@qq.com

Yong Deng*
Institute of Software, Chinese Academy of Sciences
4# South Fourth Street, Zhongguancun, Beijing 100190, PR.China
86 010 62661154
dengyong@iscas.ac.cn

Dong-xia Chang
Institute of Information Science, Beijing jiaotong University
No.3 Shang Yuan Cun,Hai Dian District Beijing 100040, PR.China
86 010 51684108
dxchang@bjtu.edu.cn

ABSTRACT
Based on the concept and principles of quantum computing, a novel genetic clustering algorithm is proposed, which can automatically clustering a data set into clusters, and evolve the optimal number of clusters as well as the cluster centers of a data set. A Q-gate with adaptive selection of the angle for every niche is introduced as a variation operator to drive individuals toward better solutions. Experiments show that the algorithm proposed is better than simple clustering algorithms.

Categories and Subject Descriptors
I.4.6 Segmentation: pixel classification

General Terms
Algorithms

Keywords
quantum genetic algorithm; quantum rotation; data segmentation

1. INTRODUCTION
Clustering algorithms have been extensively used to data segmentation[1]. But the traditional ones need to obtain the cluster number and the initial cluster centers in advance. Stochastic clustering algorithms based on simple genetic algorithm have been proposed to overcome these problems[2]. Some concepts[3] of quantum computing are adopted in the proposed algorithm (QGCA). A simpler representation with real-coded is adopted, whereby each individual represents a single cluster center.

2. QGCA DESCRIPTION
2.1 Quantum Concepts
In quantum computation, the smallest unit of information is called a quantum bit, or a qubit. A qubit is generally expressed as

$$|\varphi\rangle = \alpha\,|0\rangle + \beta\,|1\rangle \tag{1}$$

Where $|\alpha|^2 + |\beta|^2 = 1$, and complex α and β, known as the probability amplitude of the states, 0 and 1, respectively. The binary quantum coding method is commonly used, and a qubit can be represented by a plurality $[\alpha,\beta]^T$. The chromosome can be as follows:

$$v = \begin{bmatrix} \alpha_{11} & \cdots & \alpha_{1k} & \alpha_{21} & \cdots & \alpha_{2k} & \alpha_{m1} & \cdots & \alpha_{mk} \\ \beta_{11} & \cdots & \beta_{1k} & \beta_{21} & \cdots & \beta_{2k} & \beta_{m1} & \cdots & \beta_{mk} \end{bmatrix} \tag{2}$$

Here, m: the number of genes, k: the number of quantum bit in genes, and $|\alpha_{pq}|^2 + |\beta_{pq}|^2 = 1$,The traditional genetic algorithm keeps the population diversity with crossover, mutation operators, while quantum genetic algorithm with quantum probability amplitude method by quantum gates. The single qubit gate3 is used:

$$U(\theta) = \begin{pmatrix} \cos\theta & -\sin\theta \\ \sin\theta & \cos\theta \end{pmatrix} \tag{3}$$

Here, θ is the rotation angle of quantum rotation gate. There are many schemes of quantum rotation gate adjustment strategy4. Its core idea is: the current solution convergence to a higher fitness individual. If the *i*-th bit of the chromosome is 0, make $|\alpha|^2$ bigger. If *i*-th of the chromosome is 1, make $|\beta|^2$ bigger.

2.2 Algorithm Flow
1. Input the max generation, the probability of crossover and mutation. 2. Population initialization. 3. For each chromosome in the population, decoding the chromosome into real-valued; compute the fitness. 4. Dynamic niching[4]. 5. Quantum update by the quantum rotation gate. 6.If the generation is satisfied, output the niching masters, or continue the evolution process.

2.3 Chromosome Representation
The quantum chromosome can be represented as

$$|\varphi\rangle = \alpha\,|x^l\rangle + \beta\,|x^u\rangle \tag{4}$$

where the feature vector x^l and x^u are the lower and the upper bound of x, respectively. Obviously, a qubit may be in the x^l state, in the x^u state, or in any superposition of the two. Then the chromosome can be represented by qubit as follows:

$$q_k^t = \left[\begin{array}{cc|cc|cc|cc} \alpha_{k,11}^t & \alpha_{k,12}^t & \alpha_{k,21}^t & \alpha_{k,22}^t & \cdots & \cdots & \alpha_{k,N1}^t & \alpha_{k,N2}^t \\ \beta_{k,11}^t & \beta_{k,12}^t & \beta_{k,21}^t & \beta_{k,22}^t & \cdots & \cdots & \beta_{k,N1}^t & \beta_{k,N2}^t \end{array}\right] \tag{5}$$

The length of the quantum chromosome is 2N. We obtain a real-valued encoded mode. For any qubit $[\alpha_{i,k}^t, \beta_{i,k}^t]^T$, k=1,2, we generate a random number $r_{i,k} \in [0,1]$. If $r_{i,k} < |\alpha_{i,k}^t|^2$, the qubit will be in x^u state. Therefore, the qubit chromosome collapses into $[x^i, x^j]$, where $\{i,j\} \in \{l,u\}$. Any each dimension of the qubit chromosome will be in the 4 states: $[x^l, x^l]$, $[x^l, x^u]$, $[x^u, x^l]$, $[x^u, x^u]$. To decode

GECCO'14, July 12–16, 2014, Vancouver, BC, Canada.
ACM 978-1-4503-2881-4/14/07.

the chromosome into real value, a decoding criterion is introduced as Tab.1. Here $\Delta x_i=(x^u- x^l)/4$ and r is a random number between 0 and 1. If the chromosome is $[x^l, x^l]$, the x_i will take a small value inclining to the lower bound. If the chromosome is $[x^u, x^u]$, the x_i will take a small value inclining to the upper bound. So the chromosome can be transformed into a real-valued one.

Table 1. Encoded rules of the chromosome

Qubit	Encoded mode
$[x^l, x^l]$	$x_i = x^l + r\Delta x_i / 4$
$[x^l, x^u]$	$x_i = x^l + (1+r)\Delta x_i / 4$
$[x^u, x^l]$	$x_i = x^u - (1+r)\Delta x_i / 4$
$[x^u, x^u]$	$x_i = x^u - r\Delta x_i / 4$

The population size is P, and the initial population is generated randomly. $\alpha^0_{i,j}$ and $\beta^0_{i,j}$ are initialized to 1/2, i=1,…, P, j=1,2.

2.4 Fitness Function

The fitness function is defined as

$$f(\mathrm{c}) = \tilde{J}_s(\mathrm{c}) = \sum_{j=1}^{n}\left(\exp-\frac{\|\mathrm{x}_j\text{-}\mathrm{c}\|^2}{\beta}\right)^{\gamma}, j=1,\cdots,n \tag{6}$$

where, , j=1,…,n, are all points in the data set to be clustered.

2.5 Adaptive Quantum Rotation Strategy

We adopt a dynamic niching method[4] to divide the individuals in evolution into some small populations.

$$Pop = \bigcup_{i\in\{1,2,\cdots v(t)\}} S_t^i \cup S_t^* \tag{7}$$

After the population is divided into multiple sub ones, in order to make the qubit chromosomes effectively converge to the better states, we put forward an adaptive rotation angles computing method. For the real individuals, the rotation angle is as

$$\theta^{t,q}_{k,i} = sign\{\alpha^{t,q}_{k,i}\cdot\beta^{t,q}_{k,i}\cdot(f(c^t_l)-\bar{f}^q)\}\cdot\frac{f(M^{t,q}_i)-f(c^t_i)}{f(M^{t,q}_i-\bar{f}^q)}\times 0.05\pi \tag{8}$$

Where, $\mathrm{M}^{t,q}$ is the master of the q-th niche, c^t_l is the individual in the q-th niche, $f(\mathrm{M}^{t,q})$, $f(\mathrm{c}^t_l)$ and $\bar{f}^q$ are the fitness of $\mathrm{M}^{t,q}$, c^t_l and the average fitness of q-th sub population, sign(.) seen in Ref.6. When the performance is poor, the evolution of individual choice angle will increase. When good, we will choose small $\theta^{t,q}_{k,i}$ so as to avoid the better individual damaged. For the individuals in the isolated set S^*_t, which is not belong to any real one, the rotation angle is defined as:

$$\theta_{k,i} = \begin{cases} 0 & if \quad f(c_i) = f(c^t_{best}) \\ 0.02\pi & others \end{cases} \tag{9}$$

3. SIMULATION EXPERIMENTS

We use the UCI machine learning repository Iris, Breast Cancer and Wine data sets on GAC[1], KGAC[2], GAGR[5] and QGNC in the experiments. GAC, KGAC, GAGR algorithm can't automatically determine the number of clusters. We should set several different clusters. Then determine the appropriate clusters according to the clustering performance under the condition of different values. The initial populations are set to 50. The crossover probability and mutation probability of GAC, KGAC, GAGR are 0.8 and 0.001. QGNC can divide the population into different niche, and the number of niche is same as the one of clusters. Therefore, we first validate QGNC's performance of automatically determining clusters. We made experiments for each data independently 100 times. Results are in Tab.2.

Table 2. Mean, variance and correct estimate

Data set	Iris	Breast	wine
Actual	3	2	3
Obtained	2.86(0.4494),72	2(0.0408),98	3.0769(0.4130),65

Tab.2 shows QGNC algorithm can effectively determine the number of clusters. We will further analyze the algorithm efficiency of QGNC, GAC, KGAC and GAGR on Iris data set. We will run the algorithms independently 20 times. Tab.3 gives the running times (MATLAB R2009a, 2.33GHz Xeon (R) CPU). Tab.3 shows QGNC algorithm search the optimal solutions running better time than the other three algorithms. It spent shorter time to obtain the optimal solution.

Table 3.The average running times to four algorithms

Data set	GAC	KGAC	GAGR	QGNC
Iris	45.295	0.4494	0.3741	0.2040

4. CONCLUSIONS

In the paper, each chromosome is encoded a center of a cluster by a real-valued qubit. The dynamic niching is accomplished without assuming any a priori knowledge on the number of niches. An adaptive selection of the rotation angle used by the quantum rotation gate is introduced. The experiment results have shown that our algorithm is effective for data segmentation.

5. ACKNOWLEDGMENTS

This work was supported by Beijing Municipal Science Foundation No. 4133092 and 863 program (No.2012AA011206).

6. REFERENCES

[1] Murthy C A, Chowdhury N, In search of optimal clusters using genetic algorithms. Pattern Recognition Letters, 1996, 17: p 825-832.

[2] Bandyopdhyay S, Maulik U, An evolutionary technique based on K-Means algorithm for optimal clustering in RN. Information Sciences, 2002, 146: 221-237.

[3] Sha Lin-Xiu, He Yu-Yao. A novel self-adaptive quantum genetic algorithm[J]. International Conference on Natural Computation, 2012, p 618-621.

[4] B. L. Miller and M. Shaw. Genetic algorithms with dynamic niche sharing for multimodal function optimization, Proc. 1996 IEEE Trans. Evol. Comput., 786-791.

[5] Chang D X, Zhang X D, Zheng C W, A genetic algorithm with gene rearrangement for K-means clustering. Pattern Recogn, 2009, 42: p 1210-1222.

Women@GECCO 2014

Una-May O'Reilly
ALFA Group, CSAIL, MIT, USA
unamay@csail.mit.edu

Anna Esparcia
S2 Grupo, PLC, Spain
aesparcia@s2grupo.es

Anne Auger
TAO, INRIA, Fr.
anne.auger@inria.fr

Carola Doerr
CNRS, Paris VI, Fr.
Carola.Doerr@lip6.fr

Aniko Ekart
Aston University, UK
a.ekart@aston.ac.uk

Gabriela Ochoa
Stirling University, Scotland
gabriela.ochoa@cs.stir.ac.uk

Categories and Subject Descriptors

I.2.6 [**Artificial Intelligence**]: Miscellaneous

Keywords

evolutionary computation, under-represented minorities, women

1. WORKSHOP OVERVIEW

Women form an under-represented cohort in evolutionary computation, whether the cohort is examined in industry, academics or both. This situation is reflective of a larger scale demographic divide in computer science and STEM[1] in general. It prompts many pressing questions:

- How will industry's need for evolutionary technology expertise be filled without more equal representation?
- How can women be encouraged to enter the field of evolutionary computation?
- What will help women in evolutionary computation remain in the field long term?
- What different challenges along a career path affect persistence in the field?
- What strategies will help women navigate career and family responsibilities?
- What helpful changes can be adopted by women as a group, by our larger community with respect to our conferences and awards, or by our academic institutions with respect to positions and promotions?
- Is mentoring welcome and helpful?
- How can we promote evolutionary computation to women choosing graduate degrees?
- How can we efficiently disseminate evolutionary computation information to pre-college girls?
- Are there experiences and strategies that can be shared which allow senior women to support more junior ones or peers to support each other?
- Every women's experience is different and shaped by cultural, society, institutional and personal influences. Are there ways to support across these differences?
- Often, participation numbers are such that a woman can feel quite isolated. What can other women do to help?
- Would a network of women in evolutionary computation which promotes women's contributions to the field by means of a technical meeting be helpful?

The grand objective of this workshop is bring women attending GECCO together to share ways that will generate, encourage and support academic, professional and social opportunities for women in evolutionary computation.

2013 Recap

The first meeting of Women@GECCO took place in 2013 in Amsterdam. It was informally organized in very short time, only 6 weeks prior to the conference. Its "ring leaders" used the internet, email lists and manual labor to advertise the event and raise interest and participation. Prior to the meeting, these organizers reached out at the conference to advertise the event by word of mouth. Approximately 40 women attended the meeting and approximately a dozen more stated they would have liked to attend but were unable to attend GECCO or the meeting itself due to schedule conflicts. This is a very high percentage of the women at GECCO that day. We printed bright pink T-shirts with the GECCO logo and a humorous graphic and distributed them at the meeting. We shared extras with our children and GECCO organizers afterwards. We are grateful to the GECCO conference and SIGEVO for their support of this initial effort and funding for the t-shirts.

We prepared topics for the meeting's discussions beforehand. One particular focus driving the group's formation was the under-representation of women and what actions could remediate it. Options put forth included:

- high school outreach: Participants who had reached out reported that these events are very rewarding. It is fairly easy to explain EC and communicate why it is

[1]STEM is an (American) acronym that stands for Science, Technology, Engineering and Mathematics

GECCO'14, July 12–16, 2014, Vancouver, BC, Canada.
ACM 978-1-4503-2881-4/14/07.
http://dx.doi.org/10.1145/2598394.2611386.

compelling. Currently, if outreach occurs, it is driven from the bottom up, i.e. from individual relationships between an EC researcher and a local secondary school. This seems to be both practical and adequate. We recognized that there is an abundant of internet resources plus the resources prepared by individual, isolated efforts. The outstanding question is whether it is worthwhile to aggregate them and keep the compilation up to date. This would require something like a Women@GECCO website.

- addressing loss in participation after graduation and in later career: Loss often is due due to parenthood or "two body" constraints that limit options. In this context, the idea of a panel at GECCO in 2014 was put forward by Carola Doerr. She and Anne Auger offered to organize a panel on work life balance strategies in Vancouver. The panel will go forward in 2014 and include men and women at different points in the evolutionary computation careers. Efforts have been made to compose the panel to be diverse in multiple respects. Forum speakers will discuss the following questions:
  - What are tips to ease a good work and life balance?
  - (How) Is it possible to have a scientific career while working on a part-time basis?
  - How does having a family change the priorities between private life and research ambitions?
  - Is it more difficult for women to pursue a research career in EC? Or is it rather, independently of the gender, difficult per se to combine ambitious career plans (in academia or industry) with a satisfying private life?
  - What can the community do to support academics (and in particular young women) with families?

  Confirmed panel members are

  - Emma Hart, Director of Centre for Emergent Computing, Edinburgh Napier University, UK
  - Gabriela Ochoa, Lecturer at University of Stirling, UK
  - Una-May O'Reilly, Leader of the AnyScale Learning for All research group and Principal Research Scientist at the Computer Science and Artificial Intelligence Laboratory, MIT, USA
  - Katya Rodríguez, Investigadora Titular A, Universidad Nacional Autónoma de México
  - Marc Schoenauer, Scientific Head of Inria Saclay-Ile-de-France, France
  - Nur Zincir-Heywood, Professor, Dalhousie University, Canada
- providing mentorship: Mentorship appears to be needed in a variety of matters. These include life-work balance, grant writing and technical areas. It is useful during early developments stages ranging from graduate student to junior faculty. This became an outstanding action item.
- general fellowship: Forming a network was also recognized as important. Everyone enthusiastically embraced the meeting and felt it would help to hold it regularly. To that end, we decided to formalize the event as a workshop at GECCO and hold it annually, in some form, as long as the concept remains fresh, practical and welcome.
- intellectual fellowship: The Women in Machine Learning group runs an annual technical full day workshop co-located with the NIPS conference. They solicit abstracts of 500 words, hold poster and presentation sessions and feature distinguished guest speakers. They raise funds for travel grants to the workshop to enable attendance. We were inspired by this example and will consider how to work toward something similar. As a start, in 2014, this activity will fall into the purview of the Women@GECCO workshop.
- an organization dedicated to this cause: We decided to proceed under the umbrella of some sort of organization or society that would allow women in evolutionary computation who meet at GECCO to feel more united throughout the year. Thus, we elected officers: a chair, vice-chair and secretary - respectively Una-May O'Reilly (MIT, USA), Anna Esparcia (SU Grupo, Spain) and Gabriela Ochoa (Stirling U., Scotland).

2014 Preview

To further diversity, we composed the 2014 solicitation to attract students, academics at different career points, and professionals. Like 2013, in 2014 we are using the workshop to acquaint ourselves informally. No manuscript is required to attend. We have asked for proposals to introduce any relevant topic and lead a short group discussion. We hope this will support fair representation. We will be sharing general discussions, exchanging introductions and brainstorming. We will look at the (very quickly developed) goals set at the 2013 meeting and strategize how to advance them further, given their supporting activities since then. We will put forward the topics that were solicited from all participants ahead of time. After topics are introduced, we will run breakout discussions on them in which meeting participants will participate. The workshop's final activity will be the work-life balance panel.

Acknowledgments

The organizers thank the GECCO chair Dirk Arnold, the GECCO workshop chair Per Kristian Lehre and ACM SIGEVO. Dr. O'Reilly thanks her 3 daughters Glennie, Hannah and Leah for their help with the t-shirts.

Author Index

www.ingramcontent.com/pod-product-compliance
Ingram Content Group UK Ltd.
Pitfield, Milton Keynes, MK11 3LW, UK
UKHW051414290926
15471UKWH00009B/1600

9 781450 332699